HANDBOOK OF LATIN AMERICAN STUDIES: No. 44

A Selective and Annotated Guide to Recent Publications
in Art, Film, History, Language, Literature, Music,
and Philosophy

VOLUME 45 WILL BE DEVOTED TO THE SOCIAL SCIENCES:
ANTHROPOLOGY, ECONOMICS, EDUCATION, GEOGRAPHY, GOVERNMENT AND
POLITICS, INTERNATIONAL RELATIONS, AND SOCIOLOGY

EDITORIAL NOTE: Comments concerning the *Handbook of Latin American Studies* should be sent directly to the Editor, *Handbook of Latin American Studies*, Hispanic Division, Library of Congress, Washington, D.C. 20540.

HANDBOOK OF LATIN AMERICAN STUDIES: NO. 44

HUMANITIES

Prepared by a Number of Scholars
for the Hispanic Division of The Library of Congress

Edited by DOLORES MOYANO MARTIN

1982

UNIVERSITY OF TEXAS PRESS   *Austin*

International Standard Book Number 0-292-73023-3
International Standard Serial Number 0072-9833
Library of Congress Catalog Card Number 36-32633
Copyright © 1983 by the University of Texas Press
All rights reserved
Printed in the United States of America

Requests for permission to reproduce material from this work should be sent to
Permissions, University of Texas Press,
Box 7819, Austin, Texas 78712.

First Edition, 1983

CONTRIBUTING EDITORS

HUMANITIES

Earl M. Aldrich, Jr., *University of Wisconsin, Madison*, LITERATURE
Joyce Bailey, *Handbook of Latin American Art, New Haven, Conn.*, ART
Jean A. Barman, *University of British Columbia*, HISTORY
Roderick J. Barman, *University of British Columbia*, HISTORY
David Bushnell, *University of Florida*, HISTORY
Edward E. Calnek, *University of Rochester*, HISTORY
D. Lincoln Canfield, *Southern Illinois University at Carbondale*, LANGUAGES
Donald E. Chipman, *North Texas State University, Denton*, HISTORY
Don M. Coerver, *Texas Christian University*, HISTORY
Michael L. Conniff, *University of New Mexico, Albuquerque*, HISTORY
Edith B. Couturier, *National Endowment for the Humanities*, HISTORY
Ethel O. Davie, *West Virginia State College*, LITERATURE
Lisa E. Davis, *York College*, LITERATURE
Maria Angélica Guimarães Lopes Dean, *University of Wisconsin, Parkside*, LITERATURE
Ralph E. Dimmick, *Organization of American States*, LITERATURE
Roberto Etchepareborda, *Organization of American States*, HISTORY
Rubén A. Gamboa, *Mills College*, LITERATURE
Naomi M. Garrett, *West Virginia State College*, LITERATURE
Cedomil Goić, *The University of Michigan*, LITERATURE
Roberto González Echevarría, *Yale University*, LITERATURE
Richard E. Greenleaf, *Tulane University*, HISTORY
Oscar Hahn, *University of Iowa*, LITERATURE
Michael T. Hamerly, *Seattle, Washington*, HISTORY
John R. Hébert, *Library of Congress*, BIBLIOGRAPHY AND GENERAL WORKS
Carlos R. Hortas, *Yale University*, LITERATURE
Randal Johnson, *Rutgers University, Newark*, FILM
Djelal Kadir, *Purdue University*, LITERATURE
Franklin W. Knight, *Johns Hopkins University*, HISTORY
Pedro Lastra, *State University of New York at Stony Brook*, LITERATURE
Asunción Lavrin, *Howard University*, HISTORY
William Luis, *Dartmouth College*, LITERATURE
James B. Lynch, Jr., *University of Maryland, College Park*, ART
Murdo J. MacLeod, *University of Arizona*, HISTORY
Wilson Martins, *New York University*, LITERATURE
Carolyn Morrow, *University of Utah*, LITERATURE
Gerald M. Moser, *Pennsylvania State University*, LITERATURE
Robert J. Mullen, *University of Texas at San Antonio*, ART
John V. Murra, *Cornell University*, HISTORY
José Neistein, *Brazilian American Cultural Institute, Washington*, ART
Bruce Novoa, *Yale University*, LITERATURE
Betty T. Osiek, *Southern Illinois University at Edwardsville*, LITERATURE
José Miguel Oviedo, *University of California, Los Angeles*, LITERATURE
Margaret S. Peden, *University of Missouri*, LITERATURE

Vincent C. Peloso, *Howard University*, HISTORY
Humberto M. Rasi, *Inter-American Publications, Pacific Press*, LITERATURE
Daniel R. Reedy, *University of Kentucky*, LITERATURE
James D. Riley, *Catholic University of America*, HISTORY
Eliana Rivero, *The University of Arizona*, LITERATURE
Alexandrino E. Severino, *Vanderbilt University*, LITERATURE
Nicolas Shumway, *Yale University*, LITERATURE
Merle E. Simmons, *Indiana University*, FOLKLORE
Saúl Sosnowski, *University of Maryland, College Park*, LITERATURE
Robert Stevenson, *University of California, Los Angeles*, MUSIC
Juan Carlos Torchia-Estrada, *Organization of American States*, PHILOSOPHY
John Hoyt Williams, *Indiana State University*, HISTORY
Benjamin M. Woodbridge, Jr., *University of California, Berkeley*, LITERATURE
George Woodyard, *University of Kansas*, LITERATURE
Thomas C. Wright, *University of Nevada*, HISTORY
Winthrop R. Wright, *University of Maryland, College Park*, HISTORY

SOCIAL SCIENCES

Michael B. Anderson, *Inter-American Development Bank*, ECONOMICS
Patrick Brennan, *International Business Consulting, Kansas City*, SOCIOLOGY
Roderic Ai Camp, *Central College, Pella, Iowa*, GOVERNMENT AND POLITICS
Lyle Campbell, *State University of New York at Albany*, ANTHROPOLOGY
William L. Canak, *Brown University*, SOCIOLOGY
William E. Carter, *Library of Congress*, ANTHROPOLOGY
Manuel J. Carvajal, *Florida International University*, ECONOMICS
Donald V. Coes, *University of Illinois, Urbana*, ECONOMICS
Lambros Comitas, *Columbia University*, ANTHROPOLOGY
David W. Dent, *Towson State College*, GOVERNMENT AND POLITICS
Clinton R. Edwards, *University of Wisconsin, Milwaukee*, GEOGRAPHY
Everett Egginton, *University of Louisville*, EDUCATION
Robert C. Eidt, *University of Wisconsin, Milwaukee*, GEOGRAPHY
Gary S. Elbow, *Texas Tech University*, GEOGRAPHY
Yale H. Ferguson, *Rutgers University, Newark*, INTERNATIONAL RELATIONS
Michael J. Francis, *University of Notre Dame*, INTERNATIONAL RELATIONS
William R. Garner, *Southern Illinois University*, GOVERNMENT AND POLITICS
George W. Grayson, *College of William and Mary*, INTERNATIONAL RELATIONS
Norman Hammond, *Rutgers University, Newark*, ANTHROPOLOGY
Kevin Healy, *Inter-American Foundation*, SOCIOLOGY
John R. Hébert, *Library of Congress*, BIBLIOGRAPHY AND GENERAL WORKS
Mario Hiraoka, *Millersville State College*, GEOGRAPHY
John M. Hunter, *Michigan State University*, ECONOMICS
Thomas Hutcheson, *World Bank*, ECONOMICS
John M. Ingham, *University of Minnesota*, ANTHROPOLOGY
Quentin Jenkins, *Louisiana State University*, SOCIOLOGY
W. Jerald Kennedy, *Florida Atlantic University*, ANTHROPOLOGY
Waud H. Kracke, *University of Illinois at Chicago Circle*, ANTHROPOLOGY
Thomas LaBelle, *University of California, Los Angeles*, EDUCATION
Robert Malina, *University of Texas at Austin*, ANTHROPOLOGY
Markos Mamalakis, *University of Wisconsin, Milwaukee*, ECONOMICS
Tom L. Martinson, *Ball State University*, GEOGRAPHY
Betty J. Meggers, *Smithsonian Institution*, ANTHROPOLOGY
Ernesto Migliazza, *Hyattsville, Md.*, ANTHROPOLOGY

Andrew M. Modelski, *Library of Congress*, GEOGRAPHY
Lisandro Pérez, *Louisiana State University*, SOCIOLOGY
Jorge F. Pérez-López, *U.S. Department of Labor*, ECONOMICS
Sergio Roca, *Adelphi University*, ECONOMICS
Jorge Salazar-Carrillo, *Florida International University*, ECONOMICS
Margaret Sarles, *Agency for International Development*, GOVERNMENT AND POLITICS
John V. D. Saunders, *Mississippi State College*, SOCIOLOGY
Stephen M. Smith, *University of Idaho*, SOCIOLOGY
Barbara L. Stark, *Arizona State University*, ANTHROPOLOGY
Andrés Suárez, *University of Florida*, GOVERNMENT AND POLITICS
Francisco Thoumi, *Inter-American Development Bank*, ECONOMICS
Antonio Ugalde, *University of Texas at Austin*, SOCIOLOGY
Nelson P. Valdés, *University of New Mexico, Albuquerque*, SOCIOLOGY
Robert E. Verhine, *Universidade Federal da Bahia, Salvador, Brazil*, EDUCATION
Carlos H. Waisman, *University of California, San Diego*, SOCIOLOGY
Gary Wynia, *University of Minnesota*, GOVERNMENT AND POLITICS

Foreign Corresponding Editors

Marcello Carmagnani, *Università di Torino, Italy*, ITALIAN LANGUAGE
Krystian Complak, *Wrocław University, Wrocław, Poland*, POLISH SOCIAL SCIENCE MATERIAL
Lino Gómez-Canedo, *Franciscan Academy, Washington*, COLONIAL HISTORY
Wolf Grabendorff, *Lateinamerikareferat, Stiftung, Wissenschaft und Politik, Ebenhauser/Isar,*
    Federal Republic of Germany, GERMAN SOCIAL SCIENCE MATERIAL
Magnus Mörner, *Göteborgs Universitet, Sweden*, SCANDINAVIAN LANGUAGES
Wilhelm Stegmann, *Ibero-Amerikanisches Institut, Berlin-Lankwich, Federal Republic of*
    Germany, GERMAN LANGUAGE

Special Contributing Editors

Robert V. Allen, *Library of Congress*, RUSSIAN LANGUAGE
Georgette M. Dorn, *Library of Congress*, GERMAN AND HUNGARIAN LANGUAGES
George J. Kovtun, *Library of Congress*, CZECH LANGUAGE
Renata V. Shaw, *Library of Congress*, SCANDINAVIAN AND GERMAN LANGUAGES
Hasso von Winning, *Southwest Museum, Los Angeles*, GERMAN MATERIAL ON MESOAMERICAN
    ARCHAEOLOGY

CONTENTS

MUSIC

PHILOSOPHY

INDEXES

EDITOR'S NOTE

I. GENERAL AND REGIONAL TRENDS

Two countries where historical studies are flourishing are Mexico and Peru. The extraordinary increase in the quantity and quality of Mexican historical studies can be attributed to President López Portillo's interest in history as well as to the partial allocation of petroleum revenues to the study of the field. The result is evident in the proliferation of archival resources, documentary publication projects, the founding of new journals and the establishment of research institutes (p. 139). The Church and its secular and ecclesiastical institutions are leading themes for the colonial period (p. 140) as are Mexican labor and regional studies of the Revolution for the national period (p. 162).

As of *HLAS 38*, we began noting the remarkable improvement in the quality and quantity of publications issuing from Peru. The trend continues with one colonial historian observing that not only the most but the best work is being done on Peru which has taken the lead from Venezuela in colonial studies. A quantitative analysis of studies of the colonial period reveals that since the 1970s works on Peru have exceeded those on any other South American country (p. 233). The creation of the Sociedad Peruana de Etnohistoria has played a signficant part in stimulating interest in the nation's precolumbian past and the origins of its Andean population (p. 102). Studies of the national period also are thriving and the historian of this section uses the term "fecundity" to describe the new scholarship (p. 284). Equally plentiful is literature which, in contrast to history, must rely on private publishers, a dependence exemplified by the fact that of all Peruvian fiction works annotated in this volume (items **5430–5469**) not one was published by a commercial press (p. 454).

In contrast to the rising interest in the history of Mexico and Peru, interest in South America's independence period has declined, probably because Spanish Americans are "finally losing their obsession with the epic of independence." This *HLAS* section attained its peak in 1966–70 but has been shrinking steadily ever since. Although the approaching bicentennial of Bolívar's birth may stimulate a resurgence of interest, the decline seems to be an established trend (p. 261).

Another notable decrease is apparent in the HISTORY: GENERAL section of this volume which includes half the number of items annotated in *HLAS 42* (items **1753–1824**). The historian who prepares this section attributes the reduction to the increasing sophistication of social scientists interested in contemporary Latin America who have discarded the historical approach in favor of more contemporary methodologies, and to the extraordinary diversity of Latin American culture revealed by the new boom in regional and local history. The latter has made historians less prone to generalize about the hemisphere in the type of volume devoted to general themes that became so popular in the 1960s and 1970s (p. 220). Indeed, the preference for shedding light on specific issues rather than providing the panoramic view is evident in the paucity of works of synthesis and reference and the prevalence of articles and specialized studies, particularly in Mexican and Spanish South American colonial history.

Interest in historical demography, a field now being cultivated by anthropologists and geographers as well as historians has soared (p. 140), with works appearing on practically all former Spanish colonies of South America. There are exceptions, of course, such as the Argentine national period in which little demographic history has been written in the last biennium (p. 318). Interest in colonial Mexico's ethnic groups has also declined with most studies on Indians and blacks being confined to demographic works (p. 141).

The preeminence of women not only as subjects of scholarship and literary works but as authors of both, a trend noted in *HLAS 42* (p. xiii), continues in this volume. Women make up 20 percent of native-born and 25 percent of foreign historians of Argentina's national period (p. 316) and histories of Mexican women are on the rise both for the colonial and national periods (p. 141 and p. 162). The number of bibliographies and reference works devoted to women is further proof of the topic's ascendancy in all fields.

The impact of women on Brazilian letters is especially evident in the short story, a genre in which female authors have become the norm rather than the exception (p. 541), and in the novel, in which intimate relationships described from the female point of view provide an unprecedented perspective in Brazilian literature (p. 537).

In Chile, what was once a thriving publishing industry, among the liveliest in Latin America (see *HLAS 42*, p. xvi), continues to decline so dramatically that of the 600 bookstores that existed in the 1960s there were only 120 left by 1980 (p. 490).

Surprisingly, English translations of Latin American literature, supposedly in the vanguard of translations in the United States, lag well behind European literatures. In 1980, for example, there were only 40 translations from the Spanish (i.e., Spain and Spanish America) literature as compared to 62 from Italian, 106 from Russian, and 200 from both French and German literatures (p. 571).

The Cuban Revolution, a topic which has dominated past volumes, no "longer dwarfs the output on Cuba's 20th century" (p. 218). Likewise, the easing of Cuba's "ideological hold" (p. 404) on most sectors of the Latin American left can be partly attributed to the defection of six of Cuba's most important writers who left the island between 1979 and 1981 and who together with Guillermo Cabrera Infante and Severo Sarduy form a "powerful disidence abroad" (p. 444).

The interest once commanded by Cuba has shifted to Central America, a region where "political turbulence has affected the volume of books published as well as their subject matter" (p. 197). In Nicaragua, most works reflect the country's continuing obsession with the struggle against the Somoza dynasty and the lives of revolutionary heroes who defied it and the United States in the years of Manifest Destiny and Big Stick Diplomacy such as Domingo Zeledón and Augusto Sandino, or in the recent war that toppled the last of the Somozas (1976–79). The Sandinista leadership is determined to reeducate "its own population as well as audiences abroad by constructing its own pantheon of heroes" (p. 197). The Junta's emphasis on rediscovering or rather, recreating a new Nicaraguan national identity has led to a redefinition of the role of artists in a revolutionary society as "makers of culture . . . a force united with collective popular interests and the historical process of the nation" (p. 440).

In most Andean countries, the commanding theme in works of fiction is violence which ranges from the "sacralized" collective murder of the master of the genre Gabriel García Márquez (item **5439**)—winner of the 1982 Nobel Prize and citizen of a country where "violence is written with a definite article and a capital letter" (p. 454)—to the officially sanctioned mass murder depicted by the Peruvian writer Osvaldo Salazar (item **5456** and p. 454). In Brazilian fiction, however, violence is of a different order as in the case of João Ubaldo Rivera's latest novel (item **6007**) which portrays the mythic conflict between two opposing worlds: that of people who live off the land and that of invading technocrats who claim it (p. 537). Indeed, anthropologists have emphasized the tragic consequences which such claims or invasions by business prospectors (i.e., ranchers, road builders, oil and mining companies, etc.) are having on peasant communities as well as on tropical forest societies, usually dismissed by such invaders as "ignorant savages" (see *HLAS 43*, p. 142–143). It is ironic that the displacement of these societies is occurring just as anthropological studies begin to reveal the complexity and richness of their art, cosmology, social organization, ritual, and especially their deep understanding of the tropical forest's delicate ecological balance (see *HLAS 43*, p. 142–143). The impact of these anthropological revelations on Brazilian literature is most evident in the short story, as in Berthel Brasil's "marvelous Amazonian legends" (item **6013** and p. 542) and Raúl Longo's skillful portrayal of the poor Afro-Brazilians of Bahia (item **6030**).

As with anthropology and Brazilian literature, the increasing sophistication and influence of the social sciences in and about Latin America (see *HLAS 43*, p. xiii) is affecting other aspects of literature. One example is the decline of purely literary interpretations (p. 454) in favor of analysis that explores the social, political and historical context of a work of art in order to determine its extrinsic origins rather than its intrinsic meaning. Sociopolitical concerns such as those monopolizing the Latin American theatre, however, reflect less the influence of the social sciences than the endless struggle of Latin American societies against political and social systems whether of the right or the left that perpetuate repression, censorship, and injustice (p. 520).

A new development in this volume is the introduction of a subsection in ART, entitled ANCIENT, FOLK AND POPULAR ART. The art historian who prepared it notes that "The nomenclature of Ancient, Folk and Popular Art for the New World is inadequate because there are no European equivalents to these configurations— the works exist but not the phenomena, art historical theory being based on and biased by the European experience . . . The fascinating historical anomaly of Latin America is that the high official art of the ancient period became, in many cases, the folk art of the conquered peoples" (p. 34). The adoption of the term *ancient* instead of the more familiar *precolumbian* is due to the fact that, through use more than definition, *precolumbian* has bee applied almost exclusively, to the high cultures of Mesoamerica and the Andean region. Thus, to avoid terminological and geographical confusion, in *HLAS* the term *ancient* will refer to the art of *all* cultures of the Western Hemisphere that predate the arrival of Columbus in 1492 classified within contemporary boundaries (p. 33).

II. CHANGES IN VOLUME 44

Art

As noted above, the new subsection introduced in this volume, ANCIENT, POPULAR AND FOLK, was prepared by Joyce Bailey, Editor of the *Handbook of Latin American Art.*

Film

In *HLAS 42* (p. xvii) we explained the reasons for alternating Film and Folklore in the Humanities volume and noted that *HLAS 44* would carry the present film section entitled: "Brazilian Cinema: 1970–1980," prepared by Randal L. Johnson, Rutgers University, Newark, N.J. Since the next humanities volume, *HLAS 46* (1984), will feature Folklore, the next film section will not appear until 1986 in *HLAS 48*.

History

Thomas C. Wright of the University of Nevada, resumed his editorship of the history of Chile, national period. Roberto Etchepareborda, Director of Cultural Affairs for the Organization of American States, prepared the section on Argentina's national period.

Literature

William Luis of Darmouth College, annotated materials on Cuba and the Dominican Republic for the Hispanic Caribbean section. Ethel O. Davie, West Virginia State College, joined Naomi M. Garrett in preparing the section on the French and English West Indies.

Subject Index

The policy of the *HLAS* Subject Index is to use the Library of Congress Subject Headings as much as possible, but, when necessary, to adapt them to terms that predominate in the literature as familiar and useful ones to Latin Americanists.

In this volume, standard historic periods have been used under geographic areas at the suggestion of the contributing editors. For example,

> ARGENTINA
>> History
>>> Colonial Period
>>> Independence Period
>>> 19th Century
>>> 20th Century

Other Changes

Changes in the editorial staff of the *Handbook*, the administrative officers of the Library of Congress, and membership of the Advisory Board are reflected in the title page of the present volume.

Dolores Moyano Martin

Washington, D.C., December 1982

HANDBOOK OF
LATIN AMERICAN STUDIES:
No. 44

A Selective and Annotated Guide to Recent Publications
in Art, Film, History, Language, Literature, Music,
and Philosophy

BIBLIOGRAPHY AND GENERAL WORKS

JOHN R. HÉBERT, *Hispanic Division, Library of Congress*

DURING THE PAST YEAR, a large number of wide-ranging publications of interest to this section were reviewed. Among them were found national, subject, personal, and general bibliographies; guides to collections; key reference works; noteworthy contributions in the area of general studies on Latin America; useful new journals; and informative articles on library science developments in the region. Publications that encompass broad themes, facilitate the study of a segment of Latin American culture, or enhance areas of research are cited in this essay.

The problems of the absence of consistently published national bibliographies for the nations of Latin America persists, although, a few nations have produced such bibliographies. A few examples of such activities are the two volume bibliography from the Dominican Republic, *Bibliografía General de la Isla de Santo Domingo* (item **15**) which is a welcomed addition to these publications, as are the volumes recently issued of the national bibliography for Chile (i.e., 1976–79 and 1980). Among the other national works that have appeared are the Ecuadorean *Bibliografía Analítica* for 1979 (item **10**), the *Guyanese National Bibliography* for 1981 (item **11**), the *Anuario Bibliográfico Colombiano Rubén Pérez Ortíz, 1980* (item **12**), the *Jamaican National Bibliography* for 1980 (item **13**), the *National Bibliography of Barbados* for 1980 (item **14**), and the *Trinidad and Tobago National Bibliography* for 1981 (item **16**).

There are numerous bibliographies and research guides devoted to particular subjects (e.g., women in Latin America, literature, political leaders, religion, and immigration). A noteworthy example is Graciela Corvalán's *Latin American women writers in English translations* which provides references to works or criticism of 282 women writers. Additional reference aids on literature are: Janet Lynne Smith's annotated bibliography of and about Ernesto Cardenal (item **5812**); Jesús Cabel's *Bibliografía de la poesía peruana: 1905–1979* (item **5818**); Nilda González's *Bibliografía de teatro puertorriqueño: siglos XIX y XX* (item **5940**) and Arthur Natella's *Bibliography of the Peruvian theatre 1946–1970* (item **45**). Vol. 2 of *Dissertations in Hispanic languages and literatures: an index of dissertations compiled in the United States and Canada* (item **126**), by James R. Chatham in 1981, covers the period 1967–1977; vol. 1, appearing in 1972, listed dissertations completed between 1876 and 1966. Michael Hughes' *A companion to West Indian literature* (1979) introduces the reader to the best known West Indian writers and literary journals through brief biographical sketches; Perla Zayas de Lima's *Diccionario de autores teatrales argentinas, 1950–1980* (1981, item **173**) provides information on productions of Argentine authors inside and outside the country. Doris Dana compiled the *Index to Gabriela Mistral Papers on microfilm: 1912–1957* (item **101**) in 1982 to provide access to the microfilm reels of the papers in the Library of Congress' Manuscript Division. A new journal, *Studies in Latin American Popular Culture* (item **199**) published through the Department of Foreign Languages, New

Mexico State University at Las Cruces, appeared in 1982 and covered a wide range of topics (e.g., literature, art, cinema, and music) in this new field of study which still seeks an adequate definition.

Political figures were subjects of bibliographies and guides to collections. Among popular items or noteworthy works is the annotated listing of works on Augusto C. Sandino in the *Boletín de Referencias* (1982, item **58**) of the Instituto de Estudios del Sandinismo (Managua). A major bibliography, *Fuentes para el estudio de Rufino Blanco Fombona, 1874–1944* (item **64**) lists over 1700 works about the Venezuelan politician, diplomat, historian, author and editor and the Fundação Gertulio Vargas' Programa de História Oral published in 1981, *Catálogo de depoimentos* (item **149**) which serves as a guide to 102 oral history interviews conducted with leading Brazilian political figures of the past 50 years.

Another leading topic is religion exemplified by: Ernest Edwin Atkinson's *A selected bibliography of Hispanic Baptist history* (1981, item **20**); the Conferência Nacional dos Bispos do Brasil's *Bibliografia sobre religiosidade popular* (1981, item **24**) which provides a selected listing of works on popular religion, Protestantism, Afro-Brazilian cults, spiritism, and indigenous religions of Brazil; Jean Callender's selected bibliography, *The Church in the Caribbean* (1981, item **27**); Ana Lígia Silva Medeiros' and Maria Luiza de Andrade Queiroz's *Igreja e apostolado positivista do Brasil* (1981, item **42**); Alexandra Kennedy Troya's *Catálogo del Archivo General de la Orden Franciscana del Ecuador* (1980, item **109**) which describes various records of the order in Ecuador from the 16th to the 19th centuries; Virginia Mounce's *An archivists guide to the Catholic Church in Mexico* (1979, item **155**) provides information on the organization and functions of the Church in Mexico; and an entire issue of *American Jewish Archives* (item **176**) devoted to the theme of "New Perspectives on Latin American Jewry", which has enriched our knowledge of a neglected topic.

Themes of immigration and emigration were also subject to scrutiny in Raúl Rey Balmaceda's *Comunidades extranjeras en la Argentina: contribución a una bibliografía* (1978, item **49**) and in Marianne Kempeneers' and Raymond Massé's *Les migrations antillaises: bibliographie sélective et annotée* (1981, item **38**).

Women's study remains a lively topic for bibliographers and reference book publishers. For instance, Nelson Valdés' article *A bibliography of Cuban periodicals related to women* (1982, item **53**) lists nearly 60 serials on the theme published in Cuba since 1883; Fundação Carlos Chagas produced the two volume *Mulher brasileira: bibliografia anotada* (1979, item **35**) that covers the Brazilian woman in history, the family, ethnic groups, labor force, law, education, arts, and communications; and the Inter-American Center for Documentation and Agriculture Information (San José, Costa Rica) produced the *Bibliografía, participación de la mujer en el desarrollo rural de América Latina y el Caribe* (1980, item **37**). Two additional works are *Mujeres mexicanas, quién es quién, 1980–81* (1981, item **156**) which provides biographical sketches of 700 women and Lily Sosa de Newton's *Diccionario biográfico de mujeres argentinas* (1980, item **166**), an augmented and updated second edition which furnishes information mainly on contemporary women.

The book trade itself and aspects such as printing, and publishing have received much attention in a number of useful and interesting works: Vol. 5 of Pedro Sáinz y Rodríguez's *Biblioteca bibliográfica hispánica* (item **50**) which contains references to studies on the development of Spanish and Spanish American printing; María del Mar Meta García de Casasola's *Venezuela: el mercado del libros* (item **79**) which appeared in the Aug. 1981 issue of *El Libro Español*; Pierre Lagarde's thoughtful thesis *La politique de l'édition du livre en Argentine* (1981, item **74**) which provides an overview of the Argentine book industry and its ability to compete with foreign publishers; and Célia Maria Braid Ribeiro's and Maria Celeste Ferreira Cordeiro's *Editoras brasileiras e estrangeiras* (1979, item **84**) provides an extensive list of Brazilian publishers by state. Laurence Hallewell's *Books in Brazil: a history of the publishing trade* (1982, item **181**) covers the period from pre-printing to present and is supported with extensive statistical tables.

Norman Tutorow's *The Mexican American War: an annotated bibliography* (1981, item **43**) provides a wealth of information on the 1846–48 conflict. Guillermina Bringas and David Mascareño compiled a list of nearly 500 Mexican worker journals and newspapers appearing between 1871 and 1978, *Un siglo de publicaciones periódicas obreras en México* (1980, item **123**); the Archivo Nacional de Historia (Ecuador) produced the *Guía del Archivo Nacional de Historia* (1981, item **88**) which lists mainly colonial archives, although Supreme Court records to 1944 and notarial records for Quito to 1964 are included; *La hacienda agrícola en Mexico: guía de documentos localizados en la Biblioteca Nacional de Antropología e Historia* by Patricia Luna Marez (item **93**) includes information to records of Mexican colonial and national period haciendas; and Peter Gerhard's final volume of his three volume study of colonial New Spain has appeared, *The north frontier of New Spain* (1982, item **138**). A. Curtis Wilgus' final work, *Latin America, a guide to illustrations* (1981, item **172**) lists illustrations on Latin America appearing in selected 20th century English language publications. The fine contemporary collection at Stanford's Hoover Institution on War, Revolution, and Peace is described in the *Guide to the Hoover Institution Archives* (1980, item **167**), a collection which is strongly oriented to 20th-century Latin America, is especially interesting for the period 1954–64. The Real Academia de la Historia (Spain) published in 1981 the *Catálogo de la Colección Caballero de Rodas* (item **118**) compiled by Encarnación Rodríguez Vicente, which contains listings of documents related to the history of Cuba and its administration, 1868–81. *Catálogo histórico de publicaciones de la Coordinación General del Sistema Nacional de Información 1884–1977* (1978, item **113**) includes information on Mexican official statistics and the *Catalogue of OAS Technical Reports and Documents 1979–80: Supplement* (item **115**), published by the General Secretariat of the OAS, lists reports and studies not included in the OAS' Official Records series. A new journal, *Fuentes del Agrarismo* (item **194**), published by the Centro de Estudios Históricos del Agrarismo en Mexico, appeared in 1982; articles in it identify publications and library holdings in Mexico where research on the theme of agrarianism can be conducted.

Valuable reference aids and indexes designed to provide location and holdings of journals and other periodicals are exemplified by: *Catálogo de jornais catarinenses 1850–1980* (1981, item **136**) issued by the Fundação Catarinense de Cultura which lists newspapers found in the state library; the *Catálogo colectivo de publicaciones periódicas de la República Dominicana* (1981, item **125**) compiled by the Centro de Información Científica y Tecnología (Dominican Republic, 1981) reports holdings of science and technology journals found in 10 research libraries in that country; and Gerard McGowan's *Lista de fichas hemerográficas* (1981, item **153**) indicates holdings of official and privately-produced Mexican periodicals held in the Hemeroteca of the Mexican Archivo General de la Nación.

A number of indexes to publications have appeared which will be of interest to researchers. Among the more noteworthy are *Indice selectivo y temático: Barricada 1979* (item **121**) compiled by the Banco Central de Nicaragua in 1981, which indexes the first 155 issues of the Managuan newspaper (25 July–31 Dec. 1979); subsequent indexing of the newspaper is planned. The *Revista del Pensamiento Centroamericano* (Managua, item **162**) contains author, subject and general indexes to the first 161 issues (1960–78) of that popular Nicaraguan journal. Araceli García-Carranza has brought up to date the *Indice de la Revista de la Biblioteca Nacional José Martí 1976–1980* (1981, item **137**), a supplement to the author's compilation which provided access to the journal from 1901–75. Stanley R. Ross' edited *Guide to the Hispanic American Historical Review, 1956–1975* (1980, item **164**) is the third in a series of guides to the *HAHR*, with previous works providing coverage for 1918–45 and 1946–55 respectively. Cecilia Morales Navarro has compiled *Indices de Revista Montalbán* (1981, item **154**) which indexes 10 issues of the Caracas journal published between 1972–80 and Cándida Side Paniagua's *Indices bibliográficos de la Revista Antropología e Historia de Guatemala de 1949 a 1969* (item **147**) provides author and title access to the first 21 volumes of the publication. Finally, *Guía nacional de tesis 1960–1977* (1981, item **142**) compiled by the Bolivian Sistema y Fondo Nacional de Información para el Desarrollo (SYFNID), lists nearly 3600 theses presented at the nine universities of Bolivia.

A number of useful general subject works on individual countries have been published. Among those are William Setzekorn's revised *Formerly British Honduras: a profile of the new nation of Belize* (1981, item **190**); the third edition of Richard F. Nyrop's *Peru, a country study* (1981, item **187**), a Foreign Area Studies publication of American University; Herbert Klein's *Bolivia; the evolution of a multi-ethnic society* (1982, item **183**); the second edition of Faye Henderson's *Countries of the Caribbean Community: a regional profile* (1980, item **182**); *Bolivia, a country profile* (1978, item **179**) published by the Agency for International Development; and Richard Biesanz's *The Costa Ricans* (1982, item **178**). Woodman Franklin's *Guatemala* (item **34**) is a fine introductory bibliography of the nation published in 1981 in the world bibliographic series of ABC-Clio.

The Seminar for the Acquisition of Latin American Library Materials (SALALM) continues to discuss at its annual meetings topics pertinent to the development of Latin American research collections. The 24th SALALM in Pasadena, California, in June 1979, (item **82**), reviewed Caribbean studies teaching and research programs and described a number of Caribbean research libraries and special collections; the 25th SALALM in Albuquerque, New Mexico, in June 1980 (item **83**), considered the future of Latin American library resource growth in the 1980s in response to the recommendations of the Presidential Commission on Foreign Languages and International Studies and the impact of Hispanic American studies in the US.

Finally, it is evident from this introductory note that a wide variety of bibliographic and reference works have come to light in the past year. It is hoped that those annotated below will be of use for individual research and for library collection development.

GENERAL BIBLIOGRAPHIES

1   Berve, Nina. Latinamerika i norsk bibliografi/America Latina en la bibliografía noruega: 1976–1980. Stockholm: Latinamerika Institute, 1982. 54 p. (Latinoamericana; 9)

Lists books, journals and articles published in Norway in 1976–80. Items are presented in geographical order, by regions and countries. Within each section books appear first then journals, and articles. Works of a literary or literary-historical interest are in a separate chapter.

2   A Bibliography of Latin American bibliographies, 1975–1979: social sciences and humanities. Edited by Haydée Piedracueva. Metuchen, N.J.: The Scarecrow

Press, 1982. 313 p. (Supplement No. 3 to
Arthur E. Gropp's *A Bibliography of Latin
American bibliographies*)

There are 34 subject locations where
items appear in alphabetical order by author
or main entry. This third supplement complements previous ones and includes works
published before 1975, if not included in previous supplements. A new section is devoted
to the Spanish-speaking minority in the US.
Includes author and subject indexes.

3 *Bibliography of the English-Speaking
Caribbean: Books, Articles and Reviews in English from the Arts, Humanities
and Social Sciences.* Vol. 3, No. 2, 1981–.
Parkersburg, Iowa.

Lists works from the Caribbean, North
America and Europe primarily in English and
related to fields given and published in 1981.
Also lists North American dissertations
completed in 1981. Entries appear in alphabetical order within thematic sections. Includes geographic index. Edited by Robert J.
Neymeyer.

4 **Miller, E. Willard** and **Ruby M. Miller.**
Middle America and the Caribbean: a
bibliography on the Third World. Monticello,
Ill.: Vance Bibliographies, 1982. 98 p. (Public
administration series: bibliography, P-1063)

Lists 1151 references to works—general, political, economic, social and natural
resources—of the countries of Central America, the Caribbean, Mexico and Panama.
Contains primarily articles and monographs
in English published since 1976. Items are
not annotated.

5 ——— and ———. South America: a
bibliography on the Third World. Monticello, Ill.: Vance Bibliographies, 1972. 81 p.
(Public administration series: bibliography;
P-1064)

Lists nearly 1000 current articles and
monographs on the political, economic and
social conditions and natural resources of the
South American countries. Contains mainly
English language publications; entries are
not annotated.

6 **Nagelkerke, Gerard A.** Netherlands
Antilles, a bibliography, 17th century–1980. Leiden, Netherlands: Department of Caribbean Studies, Royal Institute of
Linguistics and Anthropology; The Hague:
Smits Drukkers-Uitgevers, 1982. 422 p.;
bibl.; indexes.

Revised edition of 1973 publication,
updated to 1980. Contains list of books and
periodical articles in alphabetical order according to author/title heading. Subject and
geographical indexes are included.

7 **Piedracueva, Haydée.** Annual report
on Latin American and Caribbean bibliographic activities 1982. Madison, Wis.:
SALALM Secretariat, 1972. 37 p. (XXVII
SALALM, working paper; A-2) (mimeo)

Lists over 340 recent bibliographies,
1980–82, on Latin American topics. Main
subdivisions are: National, Personal, General
and Subject Bibliographies, Indexes, and
Works in Progress. Includes subject and author indexes.

NATIONAL BIBLIOGRAPHIES

8 **Bibliografía chilena:** 1976–1979. Santiago, Chile: Ministerio de Educación
Pública, Biblioteca Nacional, 1981. 1 v.

This annual for 1976–79 lists books,
pamphlets, flyers, new newspapers and journals that appeared during the period. Items
also appear separately by year of publication.
Also includes official publications and works
submitted for copyright protection.

9 **Bibliografía chilena:** 1980. Santiago,
Chile: Ministerio de Educación Pública, Biblioteca Nacional, 1972. 216 p.

Contains citations to current publications (e.g., books, pamphlets, periodical publications and publications in series) arranged
by general themes (e.g., general, philosophy,
religion, social sciences, languages, pure sciences, technology, arts, literature, and history
and geography). Includes general index.

10 **Ecuador, Bibliografía Analítica.** Banco
Central del Ecuador. Centro de Inves-
tigación y Cultura. Vol. 2, No. 3, julio 1981–.
Cuenca, Ecuador.

Lists national and foreign publications
on Ecuador published in 1979. Includes separate sections for monographs and periodical
articles arranged in Dewey decimal classification. Includes personal names and subject
indexes.

11 **Guyanese National Bibliography.** National Library of Guyana. Jan./Dec.
1981–. Georgetown.

Consists of subject and alphabetical
lists of new books and non-book materials

published in Guyana during 1981. Bibliography is based on material deposited at the National Library. Acts, bills, legislation and parliamentary debates appear in appendix. Provides author, title, and series indexes and a list of Guyanese publishers. Also includes political party publications.

12 Instituto Caro y Cuervo. Departamento de Bibliografía. Anuario bibliografía colombiano Rubén Pérez Ortíz, 1980. Compilado por Francisco José Romero Rojas. Bogotá: Instituto Caro y Cuervo, Departamento de Bibliografía, 1982. 458 p.

Publications are listed according to subject and in alphabetical order within each. Also provides listing of new periodical titles and addresses for publishers and book dealers. Includes onomastic index.

13 Jamaican National Bibliography. National Library of Jamaica, Institute of Jamaica. Jan./Dec. 1980–. Kingston.

Lists all material published in Jamaica, works by Jamaicans published abroad, as well as works about Jamaica in 1980. Material is arranged by subject and there is an author, title and series index. Contains list of Jamaican publishers and selected list of Jamaican journal articles.

14 National Bibliography of Barbados. Public Library, Jan./Dec. 1980–. Bridgetown.

Lists new books published in Barbados and those works of Barbadian authorship published abroad. Works are presented in order by classification. Includes author/title index. Provides short title listing of statutory instruments, legislative bills and acts of 1980.

15 Pagán Perdomo, Dato. Bibliografía general de la Isla de Santo Domingo: contribución a su estudio. San Pedro de Macorís, R.D.: Universidad Central del Este, 1979. 2 v. (1167 p.) (Serie científica; 9)

Major bibliography on the island. Contains partially annotated entries divided into 15 chapters. Entries appear in alphabetical order by author. Includes author/title/subject index. Also provides separate chronological index to maps.

16 Trinidad and Tobago National Bibliography. Cumulated issue. Central Library of Trinidad and Tobago; University of

the West Indies Library. Vol. 7, No. 4, 1981–. St. Augustine, Trinidad.

Lists material published and printed in Trinidad and Tobago, classified according to the Dewey Decimal. Includes author, title and series index and list of Trinidad and Tobago publishers.

17 Universidad Nacional Autónoma de México. Instituto de Investigaciones Bibliográficas. Catalogación en Publicación. Anuario bibliográfico: 1964. México: 1980. 625 p.

Contains 4864 citations presented in alphabetical order in broad sections (e.g., general works, philosophy, religion, social sciences, exact and natural sciences, applied sciences, art, language and literature, geography, and history). An analytical index is included.

SUBJECT BIBLIOGRAPHIES

18 Aguilera M., María de los Angeles and **Federico Torres A.** Bibliografía sobre desarrollo regional y urbano de México. Azcapotzalco, México: Centro de Estudios del Medio Ambiente, Universidad Autónoma Metropolitana, UAM-Azcapotzalco, 1978. 446 p.; index (Casa abierta al tiempo)

Presents books and articles by theme (e.g., regional development, geography, land use, population, economic sectors). Both general and local (i.e., state related) publications are included. Author index appears.

19 Almonte C., Narciso and **Francisco Xavier Arnemann.** Bibliografía sobre recursos hidrobiológicos de la República Dominicana. Santo Domingo: Instituto Dominicano de Tecnología Industrial, 1979. 64 p. (Monografías/Instituto Dominicano de Tecnología Industrial; no. 1)

Lists citations on marine life affecting the Dominican Republic. Entries appear in alphabetical order by author. Provides subject index, abstracts of key articles, and library location of publications.

20 Atkinson, Ernest Edwin. A selected bibliography of Hispanic Baptist history. North Nashville, Tenn.: Historical Commission, SBC, 1981. 88 p.; index.

Identifies works on Baptists, especially Southern Baptists, in the Hispanic world (e.g., Spanish-speaking Latin America, Spain and the US). A personal names index appears.

21 Bibliografía agrícola de Honduras, 1977–1979. Secretaría de Recursos Naturales, Centro de Documentación e Información Agrícola. Tegucigalpa, Honduras: El Centro, 1980. 105 p.; indexes.

This is a recompilation of Honduran literature on agriculture produced by national and foreign authors during 1977–79. Materials are presented by subject arrangement. Also has key work, author, and institutional indexes.

22 Bibliografía económica de México: libros, 1979–1980. México: Banco de México, Subdirección de Investigación Económica, Biblioteca, 1981. 131 p.

Publications appear in alphabetical order in sections devoted to: General Economics, Developmental Economics, Quantitative Methods, Monetary and Fiscal Theory, International Economics, Administration, Labor, Industrial Organization, Agriculture, and Welfare Programs. Only publications appearing in 1979–80 are cited. Author index is included.

23 Bibliografía nacional comentada sobre desarrollo de la comunidad. Fundación para el Desarrollo de la Comunidad y Fomento Municipal, CEDISAM. Caracas: CESIDAM, 1981. 91 leaves.

This work contains nearly 200 annotated entries on the theme, with special emphasis on rural development, agrarian reform, urban marginality, and indigenismo. Includes author and subject indexes.

24 Bibliografia sobre religiosidade popular. São Paulo: Edições Paulinas, 1981. 101 p. (Coleção Estudos de CNBB; 27)

Sponsored by the national conference of Brazilian bishops, this bibliography contains citations to selected works on popular religion, popular Catholicism, Protestantism, Afro-Brazilian cults, Oriental religions as practiced in Brazil, spiritism, and other religions indigenous to the country.

25 Boletín Bibliográfico. Instituto de Capacitación Tributaria (INCAT), Departamento de Publicaciones, Centro de Documentación Fiscal. No. 5, enero/abril 1982–. Santo Domingo.

This bibliography (185 p.) is issued three times a year and contains citations of

works on fiscal matters. Items appear in three locations within the bibliography (i.e., by subject, geography, author). Entries are annotated.

Boschi, Caio César. Fontes primárias para a história de Minas Gerais em Portugal. See item **3504**.

Cabel, Jesús. Bibliografía de la poesía peruana: 1965/1979. See item **5818**.

26 Catálogo de publicaciones didácticas latinoamericanas de formación profesional: suplemento. Montevideo: CINTERFOR/OIT, 1981. 127 p.

This work is a supplement to a 1976 publication with the same title. Includes publications appearing between 1975–80. Contains works on education, training, and bibliographies on several related fields.

Cervo, Amado Luis. Fontes parlamentares brasileiras e os estudos históricos. See item **3562**.

Chile. Congreso. Biblioteca. Bibliografía chilena de filosofía: desde fines del siglo XVI hasta el presente. See item **7533**.

27 The Church in the Caribbean: a select bibliography. Compiled by Jean A. Callender. Cave Hill, Barbados: University of the West Indies, Main Library, 1981. 24 p.

Unannotated entries are divided by country and appear in alphabetical order.

28 Colombia. Cámara de Comercio de Barranquilla. Centro de Información y Documentación. Bibliografía sobre Barranquilla. Barranquilla, Colombia: 1982. 18 p.

Brief bibliography of mainly recent works on socioeconomic, historical, urban, industrial and commercial aspects of Barranquilla.

29 Cruz, María. Bibliografía: cana-de-açúcar; exportação e importação (IAA/BA, 99:4, abril 1982, p. 73–76, bibl.)

Selected bibliography of works related to sugarcane marketing and production.

30 Documentación paraguaya (CPES/RPS, 17:48, mayo/agosto 1980, p. 141–153)

Annotates 59 works on Paraguayan bibliography, literature, education, and the Church.

31 Documentación paraguaya (CPES/RPS, 17:49, set./dic. 1980, p. 165–178)

Annotated list of 41 recent works on Paraguay in anthropology, biography, cities, Guaraní, linguistics and population.

32 Documentos producidos por el Fondo Simón Bolívar. San José: IICA, Centro Interamericano de Documentación e Información Agrícola, 1980. 24 leaves; index (Documentación e información agrícola, 0301-438X; no. 84)

Contains 107 publications on rural development in Latin America and the Caribbean prepared since 1976. Includes author and subject index.

33 Foster, Stephanie. Economic development in the U.S.-Mexico border region: a review of the literature. Monticello, Ill.: Vance Bibliographies, 1981. 17 p. (Public administration series—bibliography, 0193-970X; P-692)

Summarizes and outlines trends in the literature on economic development of the border region, with emphasis on the balance of commercial trade, participation of Mexican nationals in US labor market and effects of Mexico's border industrialization program. This is a selected, annotated listing of recent publications, primarily US ones, with only one Mexican work.

34 Franklin, Woodman B. Guatemala. Oxford, England; Santa Barbara, Calif.: Clio Press, 1981. 109 p.; bibl.; index; map (World bibliographical series; v. 9)

Vol. 9 in the World Bibliographical Series is an annotated, selected bibliography of works (books and articles) on Guatemalan history, geography, economy, politics, religion, literature, and customs. Publication attempts to guide reader to an understanding of Guatemala's importance. Includes general index. Although intended for the nonspecialists, this is an excellent introductory work.

35 Fundação Carlos Chagas. Mulher brasileira: bibliografia anotada. v. 1, História, família, grupos étnicos, feminismo. v. 2, Trabalho, direito, educação, artes e meios de comunicação. São Paulo: Editora Brasiliense, 1979. 2 v.; index.

Excellent bibliographic source provides abstracts for each entry. Includes author index.

González, Nilda. Bibliografía de teatro puertorriqueño: siglos XIX y XX. See item **5940.**

36 Human rights in Latin America, 1964–1980: a selective annotated bibliography. Compiled and edited by the Hispanic Division. Washington: Library of Congress, 1983. 257 p.; index.

Provides annotated bibliographic entries divided into varied subjects: General Human Rights; Human Rights in Latin America; Human Rights in Various Countries; The Churches and Human Rights, the Organization of American States and the United Nations; US Policy Regarding Human Rights in Latin America. Includes author index and a list of human rights organizations.

37 Inter-American Center for Documentation and Agriculture Information. Bibliografía, participación de la mujer en el desarrollo rural de América Latina y el Caribe, enero 1980. San José: OEA, Instituto Interamericano de Ciencias Agrícolas, Centro Interamericano de Documentación e Información Agrícola, 1980. 103, 5 p.; bibl.; index (Serie Documentación e información agrícola; no. 78 0301-438X)

Lists nearly 2000 citations of books, pamphlets, articles, and conference papers on the subject. Also includes section on the general theme of women and rural development regardless of geographical location. Separate sections on economy-sociology, education, family, nutrition, health, home economics, and arts appear. Includes author index (for sociologist's comment, see *HLAS 43:8204*).

38 Kempeneers, Marianne and **Raymond Massé.** Les migrations antillaises: bibliographie sélective et annotée. Montréal: Centre de recherches caraïbes de l'Université de Montréal, 1981. 53 p.

Provides information on the immigration of Caribbeans, especially Haitians, Jamaicans, Barbadians and Trinidadians to Canada, US, and Europe and their adjustment in the new environment.

39 López Rosado, Diego G. Fuentes para el estudio de las clases sociales. México: Universidad Nacional Autónoma de México, 1980. 199 p. (Bibliografía de historia económica y social de México; 11) (Bibliografías/Universidad Nacional Autónoma de México; 8)

Vol. II in 11-volume bibliographic series on the economic and social history of Mexico. This selective work contains citations organized into five separate periods of

Mexican history (i.e., prehispanic; colonial; and three phases of the independence period: 1821–80, 1881–1910, and 1911–25). Includes general bibliography and brief subject index. Provides fine selection of introductory readings for the study of Mexican history to the end of the revolutionary period.

40   McDonald, Vincent. Annotated bibliography (in McDonald, Vincent R. The Caribbean issues of emergence: socioeconomic and political perspectives. Washington, D.C.: University Press of America, 1980, p. 333–344)

Annotated bibliography of 45 recent (e.g., 1961–74) publications on economic, political and social issues affecting the Caribbean, mainly the British Caribbean.

41   Marín, Gerardo. Four years of Latin American social psychology: an annotated bibliography for 1976–79. Los Angeles: University of California, Spanish-Speaking Mental Health Research Center, 1980. 47 p. (Occasional paper; 11)

Annotated work lists citations in alphabetical order within each topic. Only articles in Latin American journals published between 1976–79 appear. Annotations are in English. Includes sections on: Drugs and Health Psychology; Evaluation Research; Group Processes and Social Interaction; Personality; Racial and Ethnic Issues; Social Change and National Development; and Aggression.

42   Medeiros, Ana Lígia Silva and Maria Luiza de Andrade Queiroz. Igreja e apostolado positivista do Brasil: bibliografia anotada, versão preliminar. Rio de Janeiro: Fundação Getúlio Vargas, Instituto de Direito Público e Ciência Política, Centro de Pesquisa e Documentação de História Contemporânea do Brasil, 1981. 123 p.

This bibliography on positivism in Brazil presents material in alphabetical order by author. Most prominent are publications by R. Teixeira Mendes, C. Torres Gonçalves, Igreja e Apostolado Positivista do Brasil and Miguel Lemos. Brief annotations appear with each entry.

43   The Mexican-American War: an annotated bibliography. Compiled and edited by Norman E. Tutorow. Westport, Conn.: Greenwood Press, 1981. 427 p.

Annotated bibliography of works (i.e., reference aids, manuscript collections, government documents, books, theses, and miscellaneous materials) related to the war. Includes author index.

44   Myers, Robert A. Amerindians of the Lesser Antilles: a bibliography. New Haven, Conn.: Human Relations Area Files, 1981. 158 leaves; ill.; indexes (HRAFlex books; ST1-001. Bibliography series)

Some 1300 citations appear divided into five categories (i.e., archaeology and prehistory; archives, history, travel and description, and social science research; languages; biology, nutrition and medicine; and literature). First two categories contain bulk of material. Separate geographical and author indexes appear.

45   Natella, Arthur A., Jr. Bibliography of the Peruvian theatre 1946–1970 (Hispanic Journal [Indiana University of Pennsylvania, Department of Foreign Languages, Indiana, Pa.] 2:2, Spring 1981, p. 141–147)

Bibliography lists works of the Peruvian theatre produced since the formation of the National Repertory Company in 1946. Includes author, title and publication date (if given).

46   Parada Caicedo, Jorge Humberto. Bibliografía comentada sobre educación superior en Colombia, 1970–1979. Instituto Colombiano para el Fomento de la Educación Superior, División de Recursos Bibliográficos, Centro de Documentación. Bogotá: El Centro, 1981. 253 p.; indexes (Serie bibliográfica, 0120-0259; v. 6, no. 1)

Annotated bibliography of 678 entries covers all subjects related to higher education in Colombia. Separate subject and author indexes appear.

47   Peña, Devon Gerardo. Maquiladoras: a select annotated bibliography and critical commentary on the United States-Mexico border industry program. Austin: Center for the Study of Human Resources, University of Texas, 1981. 29, 121 p.; bibl.; index (CSHR bibliography series publication; 7–81)

Valuable introductory reflection on the origins, directions and political significance of border studies research. Lengthy annotations to selected bibliographic materials provides general description and outlines of major research findings and data used. Items are presented by type (i.e., general overviews; survey research studies; evaluation, impact, and policy studies; government reports and decrees; and socioeconomic and demographic profiles). Includes author index. Subjects of citations appear with each entry.

48 Ramírez, Axel. Bibliografía comentada de la medicina tradicional mexicana, 1900–1978. México: IMEPLAM, 1978 [i.e. 1979]. 147 p.; indexes (Monografías científicas-Instituto Mexicano para el Estudio de las Plantas Medicinales; 3)

Provides annotated listing of 500 works on the subject in alphabetical order by author. Includes author and subject indexes.

49 Rey Balmaceda, Raúl. Comunidades extranjeras en la Argentina: contribución a una bibliografía. Buenos Aires: Unidad de Investigación para el Urbanismo y la Regionalización, 1978 (1980 printing). 73 p. (Documento de referencia, ISSN 0325-4240; 1-02)

Recent reprinting of useful bibliography, with 1000 citations on immigration to Argentina. Excludes materials on Spanish colonial period immigration but includes those on Spanish immigrants after independence. Works are given a general section and in 41 individual ethnic/national groupings. Over 100 publications refer to Italians and nearly 200 works to Jewish immigrants. A general index is included.

50 Sáinz y Rodríguez, Pedro. Biblioteca bibliográfica hispánica. v. 5, Bibliografía sobre historia de la imprenta. Volumen preparado por Amancio Labandeira Fernández. Madrid: Fundación Universitaria Española, Seminario M. Pelayo, 1980. 1 v.; indexes (Publicaciones de la Fundación Universitaria Española: Monografías; 14)

Vol. 5 in the Biblioteca Bibliográfica Hispánica series contains nearly 500 studies on the development of Spanish and Spanish-American printing. In second part, work deals with typographic art in Latin America and lists specific works on various countries and cities. Includes onomastic and topographic indexes.

51 Servies, James A. The siege of Pensacola, 1781: a bibliography. Pensacola, Fla.: The John C. Pace Library, 1981. 42 p.

Consists of a bibliographic essay of key works on the siege of Pensacola during the US Revolutionary War. Its purpose is to give due credit to the achievements of Bernardo de Gálvez and the Spanish in the establishment of the US.

52 Solís, Miguel de J. Latin American independence: an historical and ideological view: a bibliography. Bloomington: Latin American Studies, Indiana University, 1980. 89 p. (Latin American studies working papers; 11)

Selected annotated bibliography of nearly 600 items on the subject found in the Mendel Collection, Lilly Library, Indiana University. Works are arranged in geographical sections, and within each section in alphabetical order. In addition to geographical sections, there are others on Enlightenment and Crisis, and Ideological Background to the Independence Movement. Publication's chronological framework extends from 1767 (expulsion of the Jesuits) to 1830 by which time most of Latin America had become independent. Excludes works on Cuba, Puerto Rico and the Dominican Republic.

Sousa, María Cecília Guerreiro de. Inventário de documentos históricos sobre o centro-oeste. See item **3541**.

53 Valdés, Nelson P. A bibliography of Cuban periodicals related to women (UP/CSEC, 12:2, July 1982, p. 73–80)

Lists 56 Cuban periodicals dealing specifically with women from 1883 to present. Holdings of these publications in the Biblioteca Nacional José Martí (Havana) are indicated.

54 Wagner, Erika and **Walter Coppens.** Cuarta bibliografía antropológica reciente sobre Venezuela. Quinta bibliografía antropológica reciente sobre Venezuela. Séptima bibliografía antropológica reciente sobre Venezuela (FSCN/A, 41, 1975, p. 35–45; 43, 1976, p. 53–64; 52, 1979, p. 109–124)

For previous installments of this serialized bibliography, see *HLAS 37:524–525*, *HLAS 39:270*, and *HLAS 43:1216*. As usual, the listing concerns anthropological works published as books or articles and including Ph.D. dissertations. "*Cuarta Bibliografía*" covers publications dated Nov. 1974–Dec. 1975, "*Quinta*" those appearing 1975–76, and "*Séptima*" those from Sept. 1978 to Dec. 1979.

55 Zapata, Francisco. Bibliografía sobre el sindicalismo en América Latina (CM/FI, 22:3, enero/marzo 1982, p. 320–336, bibl.)

Introductory bibliography to publications on the development of labor movements in Latin America in general and in each country in particular.

COLLECTIVE AND PERSONAL BIBLIOGRAPHIES

56   Agosin, Marjorie. Bibliografía de Violeta Parra (RIB, 32:2, 1982, p. 179–190)
Annotated listing of works by and about Violeta Parra, the Chilean poet. Includes fine introductory essay.

57   Bencomo de León, Guadalupe. Bibliografía de Carlos Augusto León y otras fuentes para el estudio de su obra. Caracas: Universidad Central de Venezuela, Ediciones del Rectorado, 1981. 189 p.
Lists separately poetry and prose of the Venezuelan author and references to him in dictionaries, histories, and other sources. Includes names index.

58   Boletín de Referencias. Instituto de Estudio del Sandinismo, Centro de Documentación. Vol. 1, No. 3, enero/marzo 1982– . Managua.
Contains an annotated listing of 115 items related to Augusto C. Sandino divided into 12 categories (e.g., documented works, biographies, interviews, Sandino's ideas, US imperialism in Nicaragua, Sandino's death, military and political recovery, art, and photography).

Coleção Alfredo Varela. v. 1/2. See item **3564.**

59   Constantine Morán, Carlota. Algunos datos sobre las actividades culturales de Agustín Velázquez Chávez. 2. ed. México: Editorial Libros de México, 1981. 122 p.; ill. (Páginas del siglo XX)
Biographical-bibliographical sketch of Agustín Velázquez Chávez, editor of *ARS* and *Nueva Voz.* Includes illustrations from most of the works in which he was involved as well as names index.

60   Corvalán, Graciela N.V. Latin American women writers in English translation: a bibliography. Los Angeles: California State University, Latin American Studies Center, 1980. 109 p. (Latin America bibliography series; 9)

Provides references to works of or criticism on 282 Latin American women writers available in English. Includes selected general bibliography on women writers, and a bibliography of bibliographies.

Fau, Margaret Eustella. Gabriel García Márquez: an annotated bibliography. See item **5387.**

61   Galbis, Ignacio R. M. Hugo Rodríguez-Alcalá: a bibliography, 1937–1981. Syracuse, N.Y.: Centro de Estudios Hispánicos, Syracuse University, 1982. 45 p. (Bibliotheca Hispana novissima; 6)
Provides listing of publications on and by the noted Paraguayan author.

62   Lozano, Stella. Selected bibliography of contemporary Spanish-American writers. Los Angeles: California State University, Latin American Studies Center, 1979. 149 p. (Latin America bibliography series; 8)
Intended for the undergraduate student, this selected bibliography contains critical books, essays, dissertations, interviews and book reviews of 47 Spanish American writers of the 20th century.

63   Rendón Hernández, José Angel. Alfonso Reyes, instrumentos para su estudio. Monterrey: Universidad Autónoma de Nuevo León, Biblioteca Central, 1980. 173 p.; ill. (Serie "Capilla Alfonsina;" no. 1)
Provides biographical and bibliographical publications by and about the noted Mexican writer including translations of his works.

64   Rivas Dugarte, Rafael Angel. Fuentes para el estudio de Rufino Blanco Fombona, 1874–1944. Caracas: Centro de Estudios Latinoamericanos Rómulo Gallegos, 1979. 244 p.; index (Colección Manuel Landaeta Rosales)
Lists 1722 works (i.e., books, pamphlets, essays in books, translations) by and about the noted Venezuelan historian, author, politician, editor and diplomat. Includes analytical index.

Smith, Janet Lynne. An annotated bibliography of and about Ernesto Cardenal. See item **5812.**

Vanden, Harry E. Mariátegui: marxismo, comunismo, and other bibliographic notes. See item **7621.**

LIBRARY SCIENCE AND SERVICES

65   Almada de Ascencio, Margarita. Relevance of UAP in a university library system in Mexico (UNESCO/JIS, 4 : 1, Jan./March 1982, p. 31–37)
Brief description of the library system at the National University of Mexico which covers pre-university, professional, and postgraduate studies and research. Describes the university's automated system for its libraries, begun in 1972 and refined by 1977.

66   Alpízar, Luis. La clasificación y catalogación en el Archivo Nacional (BNJM/R, 72[23] : 1, 3. época, enero/abril 1981, p. 35–44)
Brief historical sketch of the organization of archival materials in Cuba since the colonial period.

67   Becco, Horacio Jorge. La obra bibliotecológica de Carlos Víctor Penna. Tucumán, Argentina: Universidad Nacional de Tucumán, Biblioteca Central, 1981. 62 p.; 1 leaf of plates; port. (Ciencia de la documentación. Serie III, La Bibliografía; no. 2) (Publicación; no. 1296)
Biographical, bibliographical sketch of the noteworthy Argentine library specialist. Lists his published books, pamphlets, and articles on library development themes.

68   Bibliografía Bibliotecológica Argentina, 1976–1977: Documentación Bibliotecológica. Universidad Nacional del Sur. Centro de Documentación Bibliotecológica. No. 9, 1979– . Bahía Blanca, Argentina.
Lists 85 publications, books and articles, appearing in 1976–77 in Argentina on library science subjects. Compiled by Atilio Peralta.

69   Castro, Sergio. Afluencia de lectores: 1971 a 1980 (UBN/R, 20, 1980, p. 119–125, charts, graphs)
Provides statistical information on readership at the National Library (e.g., more than 86 percent of readers during period were students). Increasing number of professionals, however, are using the library.

70   Echevarría, Israel and **Siomara Sánchez.** Cronología histórica de la Biblioteca Nacional (BNJM/R, 72[23] : 2, 3. época, mayo/agosto 1981, p. 65–90)
Provides chronology of developments at the National Library, 1899–1958.

71   Ferreira, Lusimar Silva. Bibliotecas universitárias brasileiras: análise de estruturas centralizadas e descentralizadas. São Paulo: Livraria Pioneira Editora: Brasília: Instituto Nacional do Livro, Ministério da Educação e Cultura, 1980. 118 p.; bibl.; index (Pioneira, manuais de estudo)
Useful study of the organization of university libraries and debate over centralization or decentralization of Brazilian university libraries. Includes separate chapter on libraries and development.

72   Freudenthal, Juan. West Indies, Libraries in (in Encyclopedia of Library and Information Science. N.Y.: Marcel Dekker, 1982, v. 33, p. 38–92)
Provides overview of libraries and librarianship in the English-speaking West Indies, with emphasis on public libraries. Contains information on the region's historical, social and political development; the people and their literary traditions; library progress through 1978; national bibliographies; and library education. Includes selected annotated bibliography, list of acronyms and initials, and an historical, political, and library-related chronology.

73   Haro, Robert P. Developing library and information services for Americans of Hispanic origin. Metuchen, N.J.: Scarecrow Press, 1981. 286 p.; bibl.; index.
Chapters describe special library services available to Puerto Ricans, Cubans and other "Latinos" and Mexican Americans as separate groups. Also notes general library services of public, academic and research libraries devoted to Hispanics in the US.

74   Lagarde, Pierre. La politique de l'édition du livre en Argentine. Toulouse: Université de Toulouse-Le Mirail, 1981. 211 leaves; ill. (Travaux de l'Université de Toulouse-Le Mirail. Série A, ISSN 0204-2009; 15)
Provides interesting appraisal of Argentina's book industry. Contends that the nation has a book industry but no book policy, therefore, its position in Spanish American publishing continues to decline.

75   Library and information science education in the Americas, present and future: papers from a conference held in Austin, Texas, 14 February, 1980. Edited by William Vernon Jackson. State College, Pa.:

Association of American Library Schools, 1981. 85 p.; bibl.

Evaluates library education in the Americas with specific presentations on Mexico, US and Brazil. Participants in the meeting called for national and international level cooperation among regional library education programs.

76 Literary programmes and the public library service in Jamaica: prepared by the JAMAL Foundation (UNESCO/JIS, 3 : 4, Oct./Dec. 1981, p. 235–240)

Describes cooperation between the Jamaican Movement for the Advancement of Literary (JAMAL) and the Jamaica Library Service (JLS) in educational programs for Jamaica.

77 Lovera de Sola, Roberto J. Sobre la segunda parte de la *Historia* de Oviedo y Baños: informe sobre un viaje de investigaciones (VANH/B, 64 : 253, enero/marzo 1981, p. 165–202, facsim.)

Interesting description of a fruitless search to uncover the second part of José Oviedo y Baños' *Historia de la conquista y población de la provincia de Venezuela* (1723).

78 Martínez, Miriam. Balance crítico general de la aplicación de la nueva estructura en la Biblioteca Nacional (BNJM/R, 72[23]: 2, 3. época, mayo/agosto 1981, p. 15–27)

Outlines restructuring of National Library that occurred after 1976 in attempt to improve services and reduce duplication of effort.

79 Mata García de Casasola, María del Mar. Venezuela: el mercado del libro (El Libro Español [Instituto Nacional del Libro Español, Madrid] 284, agosto 1981, p. 379–392)

Up-to-date discussion of book trade and book publishers in Venezuela.

80 Melo, Aristeu Gonçalves de. O controle bibliográfico no Brasil: uma proposta. Colaboração, Maria Aparecida Silveira dos Santos. Brasília: Câmara dos Deputados, Centro de Documentação e informação, Coordenação de Publicações, 1981. 98 p.; ill.

Outlines program for bibliographic control of official publications in Brazil.

81 Sanz Briso-Montiano, María Teresa. Reorganización de la Biblioteca Nacional (EC/M, 28, 1980, p. 99–103)

Outline of planned reorganization of Chile's National Library.

82 Seminar on the Acquisition of Latin American Library Materials, *24th, University of California, Los Angeles, 1979.* Windward, leeward, and main: Caribbean studies and library resources: University of California, Los Angeles, California, June 17–22, 1979. Sonia Merubia, rapporteur general. Laurence Hallewell, editor, working papers. Coordinated by Suzanne Hodgman. Madison, Wis.: SALALM Secretariat, 1980. 354 p.; bibl. (Final report and working papers of the 24th Seminar on the Acquisition of Latin American Library Materials)

Contains papers that review Caribbean studies teaching and research programs in different areas, describes library and special collections developed to support Caribbean studies programs, examines state of bibliographic control in the area, and looks ahead to prospects for development of library services in region, utilizing modern technology through cooperation. Includes several lists and bibliographies, some of which were prepared by individual libraries within and outside the region, as aids to Caribbean researchers.

83 ———, *25th, University of New Mexico, 1980.* Library resources on Latin America: new perspectives for the 1980's: University of New Mexico, Albuquerque, New Mexico, June 1–5, 1980. Sharon Moynahan, rapporteur general. Dan C. Hazen, editor. Madison: University of Wisconsin; SALALM Secretariat, 1981. 318 p.; bibl.; index (Final report and working papers of the Seminar on the Acquisition of Latin American Library Materials; 25)

The SALALM meeting in Albuquerque, New Mexico, had as its theme the future of Latin American library resource growth in the 1980s. Major impact of Hispanic American studies in US was also discussed.

Sehlinger, Peter J. A select guide to Chilean libraries and archives. See item **3119.**

84 Simões, Célia Maria Braid Ribeiro and **Maria Celeste Ferreira Cordeiro.** Editoras brasileiras e estrangeiras. São Luís: Universidade Federal do Maranhão, Coordenadoria dos Orgãos Suplementares, 1978 [i.e. 1979]. 294 leaves.

Lists Brazilian publishers in alphabetical order by state. Includes selected number of foreign publishers. Does not indicate subject specialities of publishers (e.g., legal, scientific, general).

85 University of Puerto Rico (Río Piedras Campus). **Escuela Graduada de Bibliotecología. Biblioteca.** Bibliografía bibliotecológia puertorriqueña: fondos existentes en la Biblioteca de la Escuela Graduada de Bibliotecología. Compilado por Vilma Rivera de Bayrón. Río Piedras: Biblioteca, Escuela Graduada de Bibliotecología, Departamento de Bibliotecas Graduadas, Biblioteca José M. Lázaro, Universidad de Puerto Rico, 1980. 32 leaves.

Lists 376 works, books, articles, pamphlets, newspaper accounts on subjects related to Puerto Rican library science.

ACQUISITIONS, COLLECTIONS AND CATALOGS

86 Andrade, Ana Isabel de Souza Leão and **Carmen Lúcia de Souza Leão Rego.** Catálogo da correspondência de Joaquim Nabuco. v. 1, 1865–1884. v. 2, 1885–1889. Recife: Ministério da Educação e Cultura, Instituto Joaquim Nabuco de Pesquisas Sociais, 1978–1980. 2 v.; indexes (Série Documentos. Instituto Joaquim Nabuco de Pesquisas Sociais; 8, 13)

Correspondence is presented in chronological order; subject and onomastic indexes are included.

87 Archivo General de la Nación, *México.* Fondo Presidente Abelardo L. Rodríguez: índice de serie sindicatos. Elaborado por Enrique Arriola *et al.* México: Departamento de Publicaciones del Archivo General de la Nación, 1980. 173 leaves (Serie Guías y catálogos. Archivo General de la Nación; 33)

Guide offers useful information in Mexican archives on labor-manager relations, character and type of unions, and role of the state in the period 1932–34. Materials are presented in alphabetical order by state and organization. An onomastic index (with names of companies and unions) is included.

88 Archivo Nacional de Historia, *Ecuador.* Guía del Archivo Nacional de Historia. Quito: Editorial Casa de la Cultura Ecuatoriana, 1981. 219 p.; bibl.

Provides brief history of Quito's colonial and republican period archives as well as of presidential archives and more modern records. Includes indexes to the National Library; the collections of the Archivo Histórico Nacional; Quito's notarial records (1581–1964); the fondos of the Supreme Court (1593–1944) by type (e.g., alcabalas, residencias, oficios); and the archive of the presidency of Quito (1548–1904).

89 Argueta, Mario R. Documentos relativos a la historia colonial hondureña existentes en el Archivo General de Centroamérica, Guatemala (Boletín del Sistema Bibliotecario de la UNAH [Universidad Nacional Autónoma de Honduras, Tegucigalpa] 8 : 3, julio/sept. 1980, p. 29–33)

Lists documents on the processing of silver in Honduras from early 17th century to 1802. More than 80 documents are identified. Useful information on colonial mining.

90 Arquivo Odilon Braga: manifesto dos mineiros e a revolução de 1930. v. 1, José Eustáquio Romão, coordenador. Minas Gerais, Brazil: Universidade Federal de Juiz de Fora, Centro de Documentação Histórica, 1979. 100 p.; bibl.; facsims.

Useful guide to the papers of major Brazilian figure of first half of the 20th century.

91 Bahia, Brazil (state). **Universidade Federal. Centro de Estudos Baianos.** Catálogo da Biblioteca Frederico Edelweiss. v. 2. Organizado por Thereza de Sá Carvalho, com a colaboração de Maria Lucas Mattos e Margarida Querimurê Edelweiss Braga. Salvador: Universidade Federal da Bahia, Centro de Estudos Baianos, 1979. 211 p.; index.

Vol. 2 of catalog lists 1993 titles related mainly to the history of Brazil and Portugal, description and travel, and biographies (for vol. 1, see *HLAS 41 : 70*). Entries appear in alphabetical order by author within subject divisions. Author index included.

92 ――――. ――――. ――――. Catálogo das obras raras e valiosas Biblioteca Frederico Edelweiss. Organizado por Angela Braga. Salvador: Universidade Federal da Bahia, Centro de Estudos Baianos, 1981. 90 p.

Lists, in subject arrangement, 506 rare works in the library. Materials pertain to Latin America and Brazil, in particular. Includes general names index.

93 **Biblioteca Nacional de Antropología e Historia.** La hacienda agrícola en México: guía de documentos localizados en la Biblioteca Nacional de Antropología e Historia. Por Patricia Luna Marez, coord., Rubén Rodríguez, Kitula Libermann. México: Biblioteca Nacional de Antropología e Historia, I.N.A.H., 1978. 108 p. (Serie Bibliografía - Biblioteca Nacional de Antropología e Historia; no. 7)

Includes account books and other records of Mexican haciendas in colonial and national periods. No index appears.

94 **Brazil. Ministério da Justica. Biblioteca.** Obras raras na Biblioteca do Ministério da Justiça. Ministério da Justiça, Secretaria-Geral, Secretaria de Documentação e Informática, Biblioteca. Seleção, pesquisa e referências bibliográficas, Neuma Pinheiro Salomão Gonçalves, Maria Cristina Pedrinha de Lima. Brasília: A. Biblioteca, 1981. 147 p.; facsims.; ill. (Série Obras raras; 1)

Contains alphabetical listing of rare books (i.e., works by Brazilian and other authors published before 1860 or first editions, contained in the Ministry's collections). Lists a total of 1215 items.

95 **Catálogo colectivo de publicaciones periódicas existentes** en las bibliotecas universitarias del Uruguay: actualización 1969–1975: anexo. Universidad de la República, Escuela Universitaria de Bibliotecología y Ciencias Afines Ing. Federico E. Capurro. Montevideo: La Escuela, 1979. 24, 15 p.

Vol. 1 of union catalog of periodical holdings in university libraries in Uruguay, covers letters A-B and provides holdings from only two libraries (i.e., the Facultad de Derecho y Ciencias Sociales, Documentation Department; and from the Faculty of Agronomy, Experimental Station Library at Paysandú).

96 **Catálogo de documentos históricos de Bayamón.** v. 1/8. Edited by Ignacio Olazagasti. Bayamón, Puerto Rico: Instituto de Historia y Cultura de Bayamón, 1979/1982. 8 v.

Limited edition in eight volumes intended to identify materials in the general archives of Puerto Rico related to city of Bayamón. Among those identified are: Roberto L. Junghanns' collections of periodicals, phonorecords and books; files on public

works; and records of Puerto Rico's Spanish governors. Documents encompass 19th and 20th centuries. Some literary materials are reproduced in full. No indexes are provided. Vol. 8 is a selected listing of books, documents and periodicals which can serve to introduce the topic of Bayamón.

97 **Catálogo de publicaciones periódicas platenses:** informaciones. La Plata, Argentina: Biblioteca Pública de la Universidad Nacional de La Plata, 1982. 46 p.

Lists periodicals published in La Plata and notes library holdings of journals. Catalogue was published to commemorate the 100th anniversary of the city of La Plata (1882–1982).

98 **Centro de Documentación Antropológica** (Bolivia). Catálogo—materiales del Instituto Lingüístico de Verano sobre grupos étnicos de Bolivia, 1955–1980: microfichas existentes en el C.D.A. Editor responsable, Luis Oporto. La Paz: Instituto Boliviano de Cultura, Instituto Nacional de Antropología, Centro de Documentación Antropológica, 1981. 47 p.; indexes (Serie Bibliografía antropológica; 1)

Lists 183 reports, working papers, etc., on 517 microfiche (of some 20,267 p. of text) on Bolivian ethnic groups. These documents are part of the field notes series produced by the Institute. Includes ethnic group and author indexes.

99 **Contreras, Remedios.** Catálogo de la colección Manuscritos sobre América de la Real Academia de la Historia. Badajoz, Spain: Real Academia de la Historia, Institución Pedro Valencia, 1978. 101 p.; indexes.

Provides description of manuscript collection encompassing 18th to early 19th centuries. Materials related to New Spain and Peru predominate although works on the Río de la Plata appear. Collection contains nearly 500 items and includes documents on the general command of the Internal Provinces, on commerce and agriculture of Vera Cruz, medicine in Mexico, natural sciences, mining in Guatemala, tobacco in Peru, the boundary between Louisiana and Texas, and on California. Onomastic, geographic, and thematic indexes are included.

100 ———. Fondos americanistas de la Colección Salazar y Castro: catálogo. Madrid: Real Academia de la Historia, Institución Pedro de Valencia de la Diputación de Badajoz, 1979. 259 p.; bibl.; indexes.

Lists manuscripts in the Colección Salazar y Castro of the Real Academia de la Historia that contain material related to the New World. Most documents are from the 16th to beginning of the 18th centuries and cover areas of New Spain, New Granada, Peru, Chile and La Plata. Genealogies of viceroys, especially those for Peru and Mexico, and for other families in the 16th and 17th centuries appear. Also includes works on the Spanish fleet, audiencias, the house of trade, the Council of the Indies and the military orders. Luis de Salazar y Castro became chronicler of the Indies, among other duties, in 1698. His collection of 80,000 documents, of which the American segment is only part (some 1432 documents), is in the Royal Academy of History in Madrid. Provides subject, onomastic and geographic indexes.

101 Dana, Doris. Index to Gabriela Mistral papers on microfilm: 1912–1957. Washington: Department of Cultural Affairs, Organization of American States, 1982. 72 p.

Provides access to the Mistral papers on 43 reels of microfilm in the Library of Congress. Works include poetry, prose and correspondence of the Nobel Prize Chilean author. Papers related to her tenure in UNESCO and in the diplomatic corp of Chile also appear.

102 Echevarría, Israel *et al.* Bibliografía de la Biblioteca Nacional José Martí, 1901–1981 (BNJM/R, 72[23]: 2, 3. época, mayo/agosto 1981, p. 105–192)

Lists, by year of publication, the publications of the National Library. General index is included.

103 ———. Catálogo de libros del siglo XVI existentes en la Biblioteca Nacional José Martí (BNJM/R, 72[23]: 2, 3. época, mayo/agosto 1981, p. 28–56).

Lists 156 16th-century works (1504–99) in the National Library's collections. Provides full bibliographical listing, names of editors and printers, works by years of imprint, and number of books by place of imprint. No New World works appear (e.g., from Mexico or Peru) although one item from Manila is listed.

104 Federación Nacional de Cafeteros de Colombia. Centro de Documentación.
50 [i.e. Cincuenta] años de investigación en la Federación Nacional de Cafeteros de Colombia: bibliografía, 1929–1979. Federación Nacional de Cafeteros de Colombia, Secretaría General, Centro de Documentación. Bogotá: Impr. Banco Cafetero, 1980. 304 p.; indexes.

Lists works on coffee production published by Colombia's National Coffee Growers Federation. Includes key word, author and geographic indexes.

105 Feldman, Lawrence H. Colonial manuscripts of Chiquimula, El Progreso and Zacapa Departments, Guatemala. Columbia, Mo.: s.n., 1982. 597 p. (Informe; 3)

This is another publication in the OAS' series *Indice del pasado, guía para el futuro.* Author's first work on colonial manuscripts of Jalapa, Jutiapa and Santa Rosa Departments, Guatemala, appeared in 1981 (see *HLAS 43 : 100*). This volume contains brief listing and extensive indexes to manuscripts for the departments written prior to 1822 and found in the public archives of Central America and some archives in Spain. More than 3600 manuscripts are identified; a variety of subject indexes are appended.

106 García, Enildo A. Indice de los documentos y manuscriptos delmontinos en la Biblioteca Otto G. Richter de la Universidad de Miami, Coral Gables, Florida, U.S.A. Miami, Fla.: Ediciones Universal, 1979. 62 p.; facsims. (Colección Cuba y sus jueces)

Description of documents from the Domingo and Leonardo del Monte Collections at the University of Miami, Florida. Includes brief sketch of 19th-century Cuban Domingo del Monte.

107 González, Nelly S. Brazilian official serial publications: an acquisition strategy (The Serials Librarian [The Haworth Press, New York] 5 : 3, Spring 1981, p. 45–55, appendixes, bibl., tables)

Reviews problems in acquiring official publications from Brazil and summarizes various bibliographic tools available. Describes project to collect such materials at the University of Illinois.

108 Iconografía argentina, grabados y libros: exposición homenaje al cuarto centenario de la segunda fundación de Buenos Aires. Buenos Aires: Librería L'Amateur, 1980. 30 p.; ill. (Catálogo/Librería L'Amateur; no. 43)

Over 200 items (i.e., print albums, prints and illustrated books) which show Buenos Aires or Argentina are identified in this exhibit catalogue prepared in honor of the 400th anniversary of Buenos Aires' refounding.

109 Kennedy Troya, Alexandra. Catálogo del Archivo General de la Orden Franciscana del Ecuador (AGOFE). Quito: Banco Central del Ecuador: Instituto Nacional de Patrimonio Cultural, 1980. 330 p.; index (Colección Archivos y bibliotecas; 1)

This guide actually describes two collections in one (i.e., records of Franciscan convents and provincial administrative records for the Order, which encompassed the area of the Audiencia of Quito). Documents from the 16th to 19th centuries appear. This guide, truly a calendar to the materials, is divided into the archive's several series (e.g., cofradías, royal cédulas, convent accounts, land titles). Portion of documents described in the guide is available on microfilm at the Institute of American Franciscan History, Washington.

110 Koninklijk Instituut voor Taal-, Land- en Volkenkunde. Caraibische Afdeling. Handleiding/Manual Centrale Catalogus Caraibiana. Leiden: 1982 1 v. (Unpaged)

Cumulative catalog on microfiche gives survey of library holdings (books, and articles) at the Royal Institute of Linguistics and Anthropology, as well as a selection of books and articles available in other Netherlands' and Netherlands Antilles' libraries. Accompanying key provides library code, subject code, acronym list, and periodical list.

111 Larson, Everette E. A selective listing of monographs and government documents on the Falkland/Malvinas Islands in the Library of Congress. Washington: Library of Congress, 1982. 28 p. (Hispanic Focus; 1)

Lists 196 monographic publications and government documents currently available at the Library of Congress.

112 Merubia, Sonia M. The acquisition of serials at the Benson Latin American Collection (The Serials Librarian [The Haworth Press, New York] 5:2, Winter 1980, p. 41–48, bibl.)

Brief description of methods used by the collection to acquire serials from Latin America. Useful article for acquisitions specialists.

113 Mexico. Coordinación General del Sistema Nacional de Información. Catálogo histórico de publicaciones de la Coordinación General del Sistema Nacional de Información, 1884–1977. México: La Coordinación, 1978. 477, 30 p.; col. maps; index.

Listing of publications of the General Directorate of Statistics, the Design and Implementation of the National System of Information, the Studies of the National Territory, Systems and Electronic Processes, and the Unit of Information Integration. Includes brief overview of the entities of the General Directorate of Statistics. Lists monographs, serials and maps.

114 Nagel, Rolf. Archivistica brasiliae: zur Neuordnung des brasilianischen Archivwesens (IAA, 6:4, neue Folge, 1980, p. 373–376)

Discusses the existence or nonexistence of "arquivismo" in Brazil and the circumstances behind the law of July 1978 ordering the creation of a national archives system. [R. & J. Barman]

115 Organization of American States. General Secretariat. Catalog of OAS technical reports and documents 1979–1980. Supplement. Washington: 1982. 112 p. (OAS doc. no. SG/Ser. A/III.1/Supl. 1979–80)

Lists technical reports and studies which were not included in the Official Records (OAS) series nor offered for sale in the (OAS) *Catalog of publications.* Citations to documents in the following categories appear: technical reports resulting from direct or indirect services, studies and reports resulting from missions carried out under various programs; final reports of OAS sponsored seminars and workshops; papers presented by staff members at conferences; external surveys, and reports and theses prepared by OAS fellowship holders. Reports concern areas of cultural, economic and educational affairs, development cooperation, science and technology, women, statistics, legal and social affairs, regional development, and tourism. Includes separate English and Spanish subject, title and author lists and separate Portuguese and French title lists.

116 Pérez Gómez, Gonzalo. La Biblioteca Pública de Toluca. México: Biblioteca Enciclopédica del Estado de México, 1979. 103 p.; 1 folded leaf of plates; bibl.; facsims.; ill.; ports. (Biblioteca enciclopédica del Estado de México; 97)

Provides brief history of Toluca's public library from its establishment in 1830. Includes directory to other city libraries.

117 Petersen, Silvia Regina Ferraz.O movimento operário brasileiro: bibliografia (IFCH/R, 8, 1979/1980, p. 175–217, bibl.)

Lists books, articles, reviews and pamphlets on the history of the Brazilian worker movement. Items are presented in alphabetical order by author; no index or subject arrangement of materials is given.

118 Real Academia de la Historia (Spain). Catálogo de la Colección Caballero de Rodas. Por María Encarnación Rodríguez Vicente. Madrid: Real Academia de la Historia, 1981. 279 p.; 1 leaf of plates; bibl.; index; port.

Describes Colección Caballero de Rodas in the Real Academia de la Historia; documents in that collection pertain to history of Cuba and its administration (1868–81) and are highlighted by documents concerning the Ten Years War (1868–78), efforts of the Captains General of Cuba during that period, and the Peace of Zanjón that ended that conflict. There is a general index to the collection's 2676 documents.

Rosenbach Museum & Library. The Viceroyalty of New Spain and early independent Mexico: a guide to original manuscripts in the collection of the Rosenbach Museum & Library. See item **1852.**

119 Sohn, Jeanne and **Russ Davidson.** Out of the morass: acquiring Spanish-language materials from Latin America (Library Journal [Bowker, New York] 107:13, July 1982, p. 1290–1293)

Provides useful insights into methods for gathering library materials from Latin America.

REFERENCE WORKS AND RESEARCH

120 Argentine Republic. Archivo General. Indice temático general de unidades archivonómicas del período colonial-gobierno. Buenos Aires: El Archivo, 1978. 206 p. (Colección Auxiliares huerísticos: Serie Indices; 2)

This publication complements the 1961 Archive publication, *Indice del Archivo de Gobierno de Buenos Aires.* Date coverage of material and archival location are provided for materials arranged in alphabetical order by subject.

121 Banco Central de Nicaragua. Biblioteca y Servicios de Información. Indice selectivo y temático: *Barricada,* 1979. Managua: 1981. 71 p.

Consists of index to first 155 numbers of this Nicaraguan newspaper (July 25 to Dec. 31, 1979). Provides table of contents that identifies major articles appearing in each issue. Also includes subject index.

122 Bibliographie Latinoaméricaine d'Articles. Institut des hautes études de l'Amérique Latine. Centre de Documentation. No. 11, nov. 1981– . Paris.

Lists by country recent articles gleaned from nearly 200 journals. Within each country listing, citations are divided into themes.

123 Bringas, Guillermina and **David Mascareño.** Un siglo de publicaciones periódicas obreras en México (UNAM/RMS, 42:2, abril/junio 1980, p. 907–946)

Lists nearly 500 Mexican worker journals and newspapers appearing 1871–1978. Provides library or archival location of titles, from 20 Mexican and foreign libraries surveyed. Titles are mainly 20th-century publications.

124 Caribbean studies in The Netherlands (CEDLA/B, 27, dic. 1979, p. 97–100, bibl.)

Lists handful of recent publications in the social sciences by Antillean, Dutch and Surinamese authors. Titles appear in Dutch and/or English.

125 Catálogo colectivo de publicaciones periódicas de la República Dominicana. Compilado por Centro de Información Científica y Tecnología. Santo Domingo: INDOTEC, CENICIT, 1981. 252 p.

Lists, in alphabetical order by title and with holdings, journals mainly in the sciences and technology found in 100 Dominican research libraries. Titles are not limited to Dominican imprints.

126 Chatham, James R.; Carmen C. Mc-Clendon; Enrique Ruiz-Fornells; and **Sara Matthews Scales.** Dissertations in Hispanic languages and literatures: an index of dissertations completed in the United States and Canada. v. 2, 1967–1977. Lexicon: University Press of Kentucky, 1981. 162 p.

Lists 3527 dissertations for the period including works on literature, teaching of Catalan, Spanish and Portuguese, and bilingualism for Hispanic and Portuguese Americans. Separate subject indexes appear for dissertations on Catalan, Luso-Brazilian, and Spanish-American language and literature subjects. Vol. 1 covered dissertations for 1876–1966 (see *HLAS 34:3291*).

127 Diccionario manual de Venezuela:
geográfico, histórico y biográfico. Colaboradores: Alberto Amengual *et al.* Caracas: Editorial El Ateneo, 1982. 259 p.

Useful source of information of personages and Venezuelan toponimics also provides concise sketches on Venezuelan history, geography and biography. Identifications are presented in alphabetical order. Includes section on basic statistics for Venezuelan states.

128 Directorio de Servicios de Información y Documentación en el Uruguay. Centro Nacional de Documentación Científica, Técnica y Económica. Montevideo: Biblioteca Nacional, 1980. 128 p.

Identifies 196 facilities in Uruguay arranged in alphabetical order. Provides their addresses, research interests, size of collection, and facilities for research. Also includes indexes to institutions, subject interests and acronyms. Useful guide to sources for social science, science, technology and humanities studies in the country. Lists periodical publications issued by the facilities named.

129 Directorio de tesis universitarias.
Santo Domingo: INDOTEC-CENICIT, 1979. 288 p.; indexes.

Consists of theses since 1900 presented by the Universidad Autónoma de Santo Domingo, Universidad Católica Madre y Maestra and the Universidad Nacional Pedro Henríquez Ureña in the fields of business administration, agronomy, biology, accounting, cooperativism, economics, pharmacy, physics, civil and chemical engineering and chemistry. Includes subject and author indexes.

130 Directory of historians of Latin American art. Compiled by Ann Schlosser. Edited by Jacinto Quirarte. Rev. ed. San Antonio: Research Center for the Arts, the University of Texas, 1981. 47 p.

Revised edition updates information provided by Elizabeth Boone's 1979 edition

of this work. Each entry notes principal area of specialty, current research, publication, affiliation and addresses of individuals listed.

131 Durán A., René. Thesaurus de artesanías y artes populares. Versión provisional. Cuenca, Ecuador: Centro Interamericano de Artesanías y Artes Populares, 1980. 59 leaves.

Collection of terms related to artisans and popular art that seeks to develop a consensus in the use of terms in the field of popular culture. Useful for achieving consistent classification of research publications.

132 Encyclopedie van Nederlands West-Indië. Encyclopaedie van Nederlandsch West-Indië. Onder redactie van H. D. Benjamins en Joh. F. Snelleman. Amsterdam: Emmering, 1981. 782 p.; 3 folded col. maps; index.

Unrevised reprint of the 1914–17 ed. Contains information on peoples, flora and fauna, geographic locations and historical events in the Netherlands Antilles (i.e., Surinam, Curaçao, Aruba, Bonaire, St. Maarten).

133 Facultad Latinoamericana de Ciencias Sociales (FLACSO), *Santiago, Chile.* FLACSO en Chile: 1980–1982. Santiago: Facultad Latinoamericana de Ciencias Sociales, 1982. 27 p.

Describes three year activities of FLACSO in Chile (i.e., research in social movements, culture, education, political processes, and international and military relations; publications; seminars; and institutional developments).

134 Feldman, Lawrence. Indice de planos de tierras y pueblos del Oriente de Guatemala existentes en el Archivo General de Centroamérica: siglos 18 y 19 (IAHG/AHG, 2:3, 1981, p. 197–228, bibl.)

Lists plans from the colonial period, 18th and early 19th centuries, found in the Archive. Information is organized by department and within each department by municipio.

135 Fichas Analíticas de Artículos de Publicaciones Periódicas. Biblioteca del Poder Legislativo, Departamento de Selección y Registro de Material Bibliográfico. No. 1, julio 1981– . Montevideo.

Provides indexing of articles appearing in primarily Latin American news magazines. Initial issue contains information, arranged by subject, from 12 magazines. Issue no. 8 (Feb. 1982) contains information from 22 magazines. Dates of issues of magazines reviewed do not coincide with date of publication.

136 Fundação Catarinense de Cultura.
Catálogo de jornais catarinenses, 1850–1980. Florianópolis, Brazil: Estado de Santa Catarina, Secretaria de Cultura, Esporte e Turismo, Fundação Catarinense de Cultura, Unidade de Letras-Biblioteca Pública do Estado de Santa Catarina, 1980. 120 p.; ill.

Lists in alphabetical and chronological order (separately) titles of newspapers (1850–1980) found in Santa Catarina State Library. Among significant titles are: *Correiro do Povo* (1920–59), *O Estado* (1896–1980), *A Gazeta* (1933–80), *República* (1889–1937), and *Kolonia Zeitung* (1919–41).

137 García-Carranza, Araceli. Indice de la *Revista de la Biblioteca Nacional José Martí*: 1976–1980 (BNJM/R, 72[23]: 2, 3. época, mayo/agosto 1981, p. 193–228)

Index to the five years of the *Revista* (1976–80) updates the index to the publication since García-Carranza compiled his *Indice de la Revista de la Biblioteca Nacional José Martí: 1909–1969* in 1975 and the "Indice de la *Revista de la Biblioteca Nacional: 1970–1975*" in *Revista de la Biblioteca Nacional José Martí* (vol. 67, No. 2, 1976). Items appear in various subject categories. Analytical index is included.

138 Gerhard, Peter. The north frontier of New Spain. Princeton, N.J.: Princeton University Press, 1982. 454 p.; bibl.; index; map.

Vol. 3 in three-volume guide to Mexican colonial history, with earlier volumes related to central New Spain (see *HLAS 34:1526*) and southeastern frontier (see *HLAS 42:2038*). Areas of Nueva Galicia, Nueva Vizcaya, Sinaloa and Sonora, Baja California, Alta California, Nuevo México, Coahuila, Texas, Nuevo León, and Nuevo Santander are also included. Provides bibliography and general index.

139 Glade, William P. and Emily Baldwin.
Social studies: economics, international relations, and political science. Austin: Institute of Latin American Studies, University of Texas at Austin, 1981. 85 p.

(Latin American curriculum units for junior and community colleges; 4)

Includes sections entitled "Concepts and Themes for the Study of Latin American Economic Life: a Guide for Instructors" and "Problems of International Communication: The United States and Mexico" by William Glade and "The Rush Northward: Immigration and Underdevelopment" by Emily Baldwin. This publication is part of a package of seven instructural units developed to encourage more accurate teaching about Latin America in community colleges. Other publications deal separately with literature, Mexican women, Mexican-American literature, art and architecture in Mexico, and history.

140 Graham, Ann Hartness and Richard D. Woods. Latin America in English-language reference books: a selected, annotated bibliography. New York: Special Libraries Association, 1981. 49 p.

Basic collection of reference books incorporating all time periods, all geographic regions of Latin America, all subjects, and all reference formats, and in English. Contains 104 annotated citations. Author, title and subject indexes are included. A very useful tool.

141 Guía del Archivo Municipal de Cuauhtinchan, Puebla: años 1546–1900. Eustaquio Celestino *et al.* México: Centro de Investigaciones Superiores del INAH, 1979. 114 p. (Cuadernos de la casa chata: 27)

Lists contents of 82 packets of material found in the Archivo. Two packets relate to colonial materials, remainder cover 1820–1900.

142 Guía nacional de tesis, 1960–1977.
Ministerio de Planeamiento y Coordinación, Sistema y Fondo Nacional de Información para el Desarrollo (SYFNID), Centro International de Investigaciones para el Desarrollo (CIID-Canada). La Paz: SYFNID, 1981. 389 p.; indexes.

Lists 3596 theses presented at nine Bolivian universities. These appear at least three times: by university and discipline; by author; and by subject. Title is only indication of a thesis' content.

143 Hall, James Logan and Marjorie J. Brown. Online bibliographic databases: an international directory. 2. ed. London: Aslib; Detroit, Mich.: Gale Research Co., 1981. 213 p.; bibl.; ill.; index.

Provides inventory of 189 online databases readily available via standard telecommunication networks. Includes names of databases, suppliers, subject fields, description of database, charges for use, and documentation available. Has general index.

144 Hartog, Johannes. Geschiedenis van de Nederlandse Antillen. v. 1, Aruba, zoals het was, zoals het werd; van de tijd der Indianen tot op heden. v. 2, Bonaire, van Indianen tot toeristen. v. 3, Curaçao, van kolonie tot autonomie. v. 4, De Bovenwindse eilanden: Sint Maarten, Saba, Sint Eustatius; eens gouden rots, nu zilveren dollars. v. 5, Registerdeel en historische bibliographie bij de geschiedenis van de Nederlandse Antillen. Aruba: De Wit, 1953/1981. 5v.; bibl.; ill.; maps; ports.

Vol. 5, *Register en Historische Bibliografie* (1981) provides name and place indexes to four-volume historical study by Hartog on the Netherlands Antilles, completed between 1953–1964. Compact bibliography (63 p.) to the four volumes treats separately histories of Aruba, Bonaire, Curaçao and the Dutch Leeward islands.

145 Hughes, Michael. A companion to West Indian literature. London: Collins, 1979. 135 p.; bibl.

Introduces general reader to best known West Indian writers and literary journals through brief biographical/bibliographical sketches. Suggests additional sources of information.

146 Indice de Ciências Sociais. Instituto Universitario de Pesquisas do Rio de Janeiro. Vol. 1, Ano 3, março 1982– . Rio de Janiero.

Provides abstract of periodical articles appearing in 18 Brazilian journals, written by Brazilians, and related to Latin America and especially Brazil since 1930. Includes subject, author and key word title indexes.

147 Indices bibliográficos de la revista *Antropología e Historia de Guatemala* de 1949 a 1969: del volumen I al volumen XXI, primera época. Compiled by Cándida S. de Panigua (IAHG/AHG, 2:2, 1980, p. 261–325)

Indexed separately by author and title.

148 Institut für Iberoamerika-Kunde im Verbund der Stiftung Deutsches Ubersee-Institut Dokumentations-Leitstelle Lateinamerika. Handbuch der deutschen Lateinamerika-Forschung. Ergänzung 1981. Bearb. Wolfgang Brenz. Hamburg, Bonn: 1981. 128 p.

This is a supplement to the 1980 *Handbuch*. Provides information on German specialists, institutions and periodicals dedicated to Latin American research.

149 Instituto de Direito Público e Ciência Política (INDIPO), *Rio de Janeiro, Brasil*. Centro de Pesquisa e Documentação de História Oral (CPDOC). Programa de História Oral. Catálogo de depoimentos. Introdução e apresentação de Aspásia de Alcântara Camargo. Rio de Janeiro: 1981. 207 p.; ill.

Guide to 102 oral history interviews conducted with leading Brazilian political figures from 1930s to present. Provides information on subjects discussed in interviews and total length of interviews. Also includes subject index. For historian's comment, see item **3592**.

150 Instituto de Pesquisas Econômicas e Sociais. Programação de pesquisas 1981–82 e composição dos órgãos de apoio técnico. Estado de Maranhão, Sistema Estadual de Planejamento, Instituto de Pesquisas Econômicas e Sociais. São Luís: IPES, 1981. 79 p.

Contains listing of studies and research planned for 1981–82 by IPES, by center or subgroup. Provides brief descriptions of each project and the functions of the center or unit working on the project. Projects include cost of living studies for São Luís, economic and social studies for Northeast Brazil and various historical studies.

151 Latin America data catalog. Williamstown, Mass.: Roper Research Center, 1976. 268 p.

Provides access to Latin American data sets held at Roper Public Opinion Research Center, University of California (Berkeley) Survey Research Center, University of Florida Latin American Data Bank, and the University of Michigan Institute for Social Research, and by data sets held by individual researchers. Makes known Latin American data sets that are accessible in the US for purposes of secondary analysis. Citations are arranged by country and within each country by sample survey data held by major achives and census enumeration, other aggregate data, and miscellaneous data sets held by major archives and individual scholars in the US.

152 London. University Institute of Latin American Studies. Latin American studies in the universities of the United Kingdom, 1981. London: Institute of Latin American Studies, 1981. 47 p.

Lists teachers and guide to syllabuses for Latin American studies at UK universities.

153 McGowan, Gerald L. Lista de fichas hemerográficas. México: Archivo General de la Nación, 1981. 150 p. (Guías y catálogos; 63)

Lists titles and holdings of official and private Mexican periodicals. Divided into periodicals from Mexico City, states, and general journals. Listing is based strictly on holdings in the Hemeroteca of the Archivo General de la Nación.

154 Morales Navarro, Cecilia. Indices de *Revista Montalbán*: Nos. 1–10 (UCAB/M, 11, 1981, p. 893–905, bibl.)

Index to the 10 issues of *Montalbán* (Caracas) published between 1972–80. Content of each issue is given separately. Includes author and subject indexes.

155 Mounce, Virginia N. An archivists guide to the Catholic Church in Mexico. Palo Alto, Calif.: R&E Research Associates, 1979. 90 p.; bibl.

Publication is proposed as aid to archivists, historians and other researchers and will serve as guide to the organization and function of the Catholic Church in Mexico. Covers colonial period to present. Includes useful glossaries of religious terms.

156 Mujeres mexicanas, quién es quién, 1980–81. México: Antena, 1981. 536 p.

Briefly describes activites of prominent Mexican women (contemporary) in the fields of art, dance, music, theater and movies, science, communications, sports, business, letters, politics, education and health. Provides indexes by name and field of endeavor. Of 4000 women contacted, only 700 appear.

157 Organization of American States. General Secretariat. Business information

sources of Latin America and the Caribbean. Washington: 1982. 60 p. (Documentation and information series; 5. OEA/SG/o.1/IV/III.5)

Updated edition of 1977 publication, *Guide to Latin American business information sources.* Lists sources of information on economic and financial conditions. Citations appear in alphabetical order within each country's section.

158 ———. Secretaría de la Asamblea General. Reunión de Consulta. Consejo Permanente. Indice temático de las resoluciones de la Asamblea General. v. 1, 1970–1982. Washington: 1982. 33 p. (OEA/Ser. X/II.17.1 18 octubre 1982)

Provides subject access to resolutions adopted in the 11 ordinary and nine extraordinary sessions between 1970–82.

159 Pasquel, Leonardo. Biografías de veracruzanos porteños. México: Editorial Citlaltepetl, 1981. 418 p.; ill. (Colección Suma veracruzana. Serie Biografía)

Contains brief descriptions of nearly 200 individuals who were prominent in Vera Cruz from the 17th to 20th century.

160 Perl, Raphael. The Falkland Islands dispute in international law & politics: a documentary sourcebook. With an historic chronology & bibliography by Everette E. Larson. London: New York: Oceana Publications, 1983. 722 p.

Author presents introductory essay on geography and history of the Falklands/Malvinas which includes discussion of positions of Argentina and England over possession, analysis of sovereignty rights of each and recent historical precedents in Goa, Spanish Sahara, and East Timor. In addition, the sourcebook includes an historical chronology, bibliography and reproduction of 52 documents germane to ownership from Pope Alexander VI's Papal Bull (4 May 1493) to the question of the Falkland Islands UN Resolution (4 Nov. 1982). Useful source book of immediate interest.

161 Podestá, Bruno. Estudios latinoamericanos en Italia: el caso peruano, 1960–1979 (UP/A, 6:11, 1981, p. 70–91, bibl.)

Provides brief overview of Latin American studies in Italy with reference to the establishment of the Instituto Italo Latino Americano in 1965. Specific study is directed at research in Peru and includes list of books, articles and translations on the area in or by Italians.

162 **Revista del Pensamiento Centroamericano.** Centro de Investigaciones y Actividades Culturales. Vol. 34, Nos. 162/165, enero/dic. 1979– . Managua.

Contains author, subject and general indexes to nos. 1–161 of the Nicaraguan journal, which appeared between 1960–78. Journal was also known as the *Revista Conservadora del Pensamiento Centroamericano* (1960–72).

163 **Rodríguez Demorizi, Emilio.** Seudónimos dominicanos. 2. ed. Santo Domingo: Editora Taller, 1982. 280 p.; bibl.; index (Publicaciones/Fundación Rodríguez Demorizi; v. 14)

Reprint of original 1956 ed. Contains useful identifications to numerous Dominican nicknames and pseudonyms.

164 **Ross, Stanley Robert** and **Wilber A. Chaffee.** Guide to the *Hispanic American Historical Review*, 1956–1975. Edited with the assistance of Beecher C. Ellison, Donald E. Worcester and Walter A. Payne. Durham, N.C.: Duke University Press, 1980. 432 p.; index.

Vol. 3 in series of guides to the *Hispanic American Historical Review*, with previous works providing coverage for periods 1918–45 and 1946–55. Includes references to all articles, notes and comments appearing in the journal and divided according to historical period and geographical area. Each article, note and comment is abstracted. Includes listing of book reviews, obituaries, officers of the Conference on Latin American History, and editors of the *Review*. Provides index to contributors.

165 **Schroeder, Susan.** Cuba: a handbook of historical statistics. Boston, Mass.: G. K. Hall, 1982. 589 p.; bibl.; ill.; index (A Reference publication in international historical statistics)

Provides historical, economic, social and political development of Cuba in statistical terms from the 16th to 20th centuries. There are 22 separate chapters, each with a brief explanatory introduction, that provide information on: climate, population, demography, education, labor, agriculture, mining, energy, cultural activities, foreign trade, foreign aid, tourism and banking.

166 **Sosa de Newton, Lily.** Diccionario biográfico de mujeres argentinas: aumentado y actualizado. 2. ed. Buenos Aires: Plus Ultra, 1980. 533 p.; bibl.

Provides biographical information, often anecdotal accounts, of contemporary and famous women in Argentine history. Useful bibliography of pertinent sources appears.

167 **Stanford University. Hoover Institution on War, Revolution, and Peace.** Guide to the Hoover Institution archives. Charles G. Palm and Dale Reed. Stanford, Calif.: Hoover Institution Press, 1980. 418 p.; bibl.; index (Hoover bibliographical series; 59)

Describes archival and manuscript holdings covering fields of politics, economic, social and military history since the late 19th century for most geographical areas. Latin American holdings focus on boundary disputes, the Panama Canal, the Cuban Revolution and major political events from 1954–64. Entries are arranged in alphabetical order by main entry. Includes general index.

168 **A Study of the Latin American economies:** their structure and outlook into the 1980s. v. 1, Central America. v. 2, South America. London: Economist Intelligence Unit, 1979. 2 v.

Reference work designed for those interested in Latin American trade or investment. Details wide range of historic economic data, provides information on investment incentives and conditions in each country and includes outlook section which views future economic development and trade and investment potential. Each country report is prefaced by sections showing intraregional comparisons.

169 **Tauro, Alberto.** Diccionario enciclopédico del Perú ilustrado: apéndice. Lima: Editorial Mejía Baca, 1975. 338 p.; ill.

One volume appendix to the *Diccionario* that appeared in 1966–67. Contains information that did not appear in previous volumes and/or corrects information contained therein.

170 **TePaske, John Jay** and **Herbert S. Klein.** The royal treasuries of the Spanish Empire in America. v. 1, Peru. v. 2, Upper Peru (Bolivia). v. 3, Chile and the Río de la Plata. Vol. 1: With the collaboration of Kendall W. Brown. Durham, N.C.: Duke University Press, 1982. 3 v.; bibl.

Monumental product was part of larger project to compile and publish account summaries for five regions of the Spanish Empire in America: Mexico, Peru, Upper Peru (Bolivia), Chile and the Río de la Plata (Argentina, Uruguay and Paraguay). For Mexico, three volumes of account summaries for the 23 Cajas of Mexico were published by the Secretaría de Hacienda in Mexico City. Records reproduced cover period from second half of 16th century to independence (1820s).

171 Welch, Thomas L. The Organization of American States and its documentation dissemination (RIB, 32:2, 1982, p. 200–206)

Brief description of OAS' publishing program and its depository library system which ensure collections of OAS documents throughout the world. Defines what are information and technical publications, official records and technical reports series.

172 Wilgus, A. Curtis. Latin America, a guide to illustrations. Metuchen, N.J.: Scarecrow Press, 1981. 250 p.; bibl.; index.

Guide refers to illustrations on Latin America appearing in selected 20th-century English language publications. Sections on pre-colonial, discovery and conquest, colonial development, independence and national periods appear. Includes key to books indexed and persons index. Provides pictures of places, things, events, action pictures and personal portraits. Cartoons and caricatures have been excluded.

173 Zayas de Lima, Perla. Diccionario de autores teatrales argentinos, 1950–1980. Buenos Aires: Editorial R. Alonso, 1981. 188 p.

Provides information on productions of Argentine authors inside and outside the country. Individuals are presented in alphabetical order.

174 Zelaya de Villegas, Teresa. Catálogo de publicaciones periódicas de bibliotecas especializadas de La Paz, en ciencias de la tierra, minería y metalurgia. La Paz: Editorial CEDOMIN, 1981. 87 p.; bibl.

Lists locations and holdings of 293 scientific journals. Another list provides information on journals by country.

GENERAL WORKS

175 Alisky, Marvin. Latin American media: guidance and censorship. Ames: Iowa State University Press, 1981. 265 p.; bibl.; index.

Provides overview of Latin American media (i.e., newspaper, magazine, radio, television, and state controls on a country-by-country basis). Major portions are dedicated to the Mexican, Brazilian and Argentine media, although good descriptions of the Peruvian, Venezuela, Colombia and Cuban media also appear. Separates Latin American nations into: 1) those which provide guidance to the media (i.e., by controlling paper stock and/or other interests); 2) those which enjoy freedom of the press; and 3) those which exercise censorship. Includes good bibliographic information.

176 *American Jewish Archives.* Vol. 24, No. 2, Nov. 1982– . Cincinnati, Ohio.

Issue devoted to the theme of "New Perspectives on Latin American Jewry" is edited by Judith Laikin Elkin. Separate articles concern: historiographical problems in the study of the Inquisition and Mexican crypto-Jews of the 17th century; José Díaz Pimienta (a Cuban priest); Jews and gauchos and the search for identity in Argentine-Jewish literature; presentation of the Jewish white slave trade in Latin American writings; early Zionist activities among the Argentine Sephardim; intermarriage in São Paulo's Jewish community; demographic profile of Latin American Jewry; and a poem by Peruvian author Isaac Goldemberg.

177 *Anuario del Centro de Estudios Martianos.* Centro de Estudios Martianos. Vol. 1, 1978– . La Habana.

Contains articles and notes on the life and thoughts of José Martí.

178 Biesanz, Richard; Karen Zubris Biesanz; and Mavis Hiltunen Biesanz. The Costa Ricans. Englewood Cliffs, N.J.: Prentice-Hall, 1982. 246 p.; bibl.; ill.; index.

Good overview of Costa Rican society devotes specific chapters to: land and people; history; community; class and race; housing and everyday living; family; education; religions; arts; and politics. Sequel to earlier work, *Costa Rican life* (1944), which was written by authors' parents. Includes notes and general index.

179 Bolivia, a country profile. Prepared for the Office of U.S. Foreign Disaster Assistance, Bureau for Private and Development Cooperation, Agency for International Development, Department of State by Evaluation Technologies, Inc.; under contract AID/SOD/ PCD-C-0283. Washington: The Office, 1978. 94 p.; 2 leaves of plates; bibl.

Provides baseline country data in support of planning, analysis and relief operations of the Office of US Foreign Disaster Assistance. Includes key statistical data (e.g., population, health facilities, agricultural production and brief descriptions of the economy, geography, transportation networks, power and communications sources, governmental structure and disaster preparedness).

180 Favre, Henri. Las relaciones culturales entre América Latina y Europa: una perspectiva europea (UNAM/L, 14, 1981, p. 15–30)

Describes evolution of cultural relations between Europe and Latin America (e.g., diffusion of European culture in Latin America, academic exchanges, European study of Latin America). Author attributes serious downturn in interest in the study of Latin America in recent years to Europe's own economic problems.

181 Hallewell, Laurence. Books in Brazil: a history of the publishing trade. Metuchen, N.J.: Scarecrow Press, 1982. 485 p.; 25 p. of plates; bibl.; ill.; index.

History of publishing industry in Brazil from pre-printing stage to present with specific information on individuals who helped develop it. Contains extensive statistical tables related to Brazilian books and population. Final chapter deals with the trade's future (i.e., the book business in the 1980s).

182 Henderson, Faye. Countries of the Caribbean community: a regional profile. 2. ed. Washington: Office of Foreign Disaster Assistance, Agency for International Development, 1980. 338 p.; 1 leaf of plates; bibl.

Provides profiles of Antigua, Barbados, Belize, Dominicana, Grenada, Guyana, Jamaica, Montserrat, St. Kitts-Nevis-Anguilla, St. Lucia, St. Vincent, and Trinidad & Tobago (i.e., descriptions of the government, population, disaster preparedness, health, housing,

economy, agriculture, physical geography and land use, transportation, and power and communication). Designed to provide country and regional data in support of planning, analysis and relief operations of the US Office of Foreign Disaster Assistance. Data is current as of March 1980 except for political changes and US Mission staffing, updated in May 1981.

183 Klein, Herbert S. Bolivia: the evolution of a multi-ethnic society. New York: Oxford University Press, 1982. 318 p. (Latin American histories series)

Economic, social, cultural and political survey of Bolivia from prehistory to 1980s. Emphasizes changing role of Indian peasant and evolution of a multi-ethnic society. Includes a political chronology, excellent bibliographical essay, varied statistical tables and general index.

184 Mesa-Lago, Carmelo. Latin American studies in Japan (LARR, 17:3, 1982, p. 173–192)

Provides brief overview of post-war development of Latin American studies in Japan. Includes descriptions of about 20 institutions of importance to the field. Japanese have strong interest in the study of economics, history and political science of Latin American with primary interest in Brazil and Mexico. Author recommends further improvement in library collections, increase in the number of Latin Americanists trained in graduate programs, and more Japanese translations of important works on Latin America.

185 Noboa-Ríos, Abdín. An analysis of Hispanic doctoral recipients from U.S. universities, 1900–1973 with special emphasis on Puerto Rican doctorates (Metas [Aspira of America, New York] 2:2, Winter 1981/1982, p. 1–126)

Study involved national survey of Hispanic academic doctoral recipients from US universities during 1900–73. Survey was mailed to population of Spanish-surnamed Ph.D.s and analysis traces past and present trends in Hispanic doctoral attainment within and across ethnic groups while identifying socioeconomic, interpersonal and schooling backgrounds of Hispanic Ph.D.s.

186 Organization of American States. Inter-American Commission on Human Rights. Ten years of activities, 1971–

1981. Washington: 1982. 403 p.

Supplements the Commission's previous three-volume work that covered 1960–70, in series "The Organization of American States and Human Rights." Pt. 1 deals with historical background and normative aspects of the inter-American system and human rights; pt. 2 comprises summary of principal activities accomplished by the Commission during the decade. Also includes resolutions of the Commission, a bibliography, and resolutions of the General Assembly and other OAS organs relative to human rights.

187   Peru, a country study. Foreign Area Studies, the American University. Edited by Richard F. Nyrop. 3. ed. Washington: For sale by the Superintendent of Documents, U.S. Government Printing Office, 1981. 302 p.; bibl.; ill.; index (Area handbook series)

Revision of 1972 ed. contains information updated to 1979. Chapter authors are: Jack Child (history); Patricia Kluck (society and environment); Darrel Eglin (economics); James Rudolph (government); and Eugene Keefe (national security). Includes bibliography, tables, glossary and general index.

188   Ramos Galicia, Yolanda. Proyecto para la creación de museos locales en México. México: Instituto Nacional de Antropología e Historia, 1978. 3, 49, 12 p.; bibl.

Manual designed to assist the establishment of local museums in Mexico. Message is simply that local museums are important for the community and valuable sources of education because their appreciation does not require literacy.

189   Reinert, Harry. *Caveat Emptor*: the report of the President's commission (MLTA/MLK, 65:3, Autumn 1981, p. 248–253)

Article expresses concern over final report of the President's Commission on Foreign Language and International Studies, especially in the area of foreign language training in the US.

190   Setzekorn, William David. Formerly British Honduras: a profile of the new nation of Belize. Rev. ed. Chicago: Athens: Ohio University Press, 1981. 299 p.; bibl.; index; maps; port.

Provides overview of country, with geographical, cultural, social and economic features against a comprehensive historical

background from 1638 to present. Written for the non-Belizean reader.

NEW SERIAL TITLES

191   Amérique Latine. Centre de Recherche sur l'Amérique Latine et le Tiers Monde (CETRAL). No. 1, jan./mars 1980– . Paris.

Articles cover literature as well as current events, with emphasis on economic aspects. Includes book review section and bibliography of recent publications concerning Latin American studies.

192   Bibliotheca Americana. Vol. 1, No. 1, Sept. 1982– . Coral Gables, Fla.

First issue focuses on theme of regionalism in the Americas, with articles on: regional history; New France in a regional perspective; regionalism and rebellion in late colonial Peru; Michoacán in 1649; and sectionalism and authority in late 18th century North Carolina. Future issues will explore indigenous rebellions in the colonial Americas; social banditry in the independence movements; medicine in the colonial Americas; colonial family; women in colonial societies; and role of New Christians in American colonization. Journal will be issued five times a year and is available from Bibliotheca Americana, 301 Almería Avenue, Coral Gables, Florida 33134. Annual subscription is $30.00.

Boletín: Handbook of Latin American Art. Vol. 1, No. 1, Feb. 1981– . New Haven, Conn. See item **255**.

193   Cahiers du C.R.I.A.R. Centre de Recherches d'Etudes Ibériques et Ibéro-Américaines, Université de Rouen. No. 1, 1981– . Paris.

Replaces the Centre's first publication entitled *Etudes d'Histoire et de Littérature Ibero-Américaines.*

Cinejournal. Embrafilme. Vol. 1, No. 1, julho 1980– . Rio de Janiero. See item **993**.

194   Fuentes del Agrarismo. Centro de Estudios Históricos del Agrarismo en México (CEHAM). Año 1, No. 1, marzo/abril 1982– . México.

Through this journal, the center will selectively identify publications on the history of agrarianism in Mexico, indicating libraries in which each can be consulted.

Initial work identifies items, articles and monographs, and arranges them in groupings by general subject.

195 *Latin American Review.* Data Resources, Inc. Spring 1981– . Lexington, Mass.

This journal, published quarterly by Data Resources, Inc. (29 Hartwell Ave., Lexington, Mass. 02173) contains economic forecasting summaries for major countries of Latin America. Its contents also available online in the EPS Bank, LATAM/MODELBANK. The Spring 1982 issue contains articles on economic and financial matters in Argentina, Brazil, Colombia, Ecuador, Mexico and Venezuela. Issue also includes sample session for directions on how to load model work spaces or pull individual series from the modelbank.

Linden Lane Magazine. Vol. 1, No. 1, enero/marzo 1982– . Princeton, N.J. See item **5325**.

196 *Política.* Instituto de Ciencia Política, Universidad de Chile. No. 1, sept. 1982– . Santiago.

Contains articles on political theory in addition to country-specific studies. Copies of the publication are available for US $11.00 from the Institute (Calle Belgrado 10, Santiago, Chile). Frequency of journal is not given. No. 1 contains 167 p. with four articles, two notes and seven book reviews. Describes activities of the Instituto de Ciencia Política.

197 *Resúmenes Analíticos en Educación.* Instituto Nacional de Investigación y Desarrollo de la Educación. No. 1, dic. 1981– . Lima.

Initial issue contains abstracts of books and articles on education in Peru. Copies can be obtained from: Centro Nacional, Van de Velde 160, Urbanización San Borja, Lima, 34, Perú (Apartado Postal 1156).

198 *Revista de Estudios Políticos.* Editorial Jurídica Venezolana. No. 0, 1981– . Caracas.

Available for US $15.00 per year (quarterly) from Editorial Jurídica Venezolana (Apartado 17598, Parque Central, Caracas 1015-A, Venezuela). Provides articles and analytical reviews of national and international political issues prepared by political scientists and lawyers. Separate sections are devoted to reviews and abstracts of documents of national and international significance. First articles deal with Venezuelan boundary disputes with Colombia (Gulf of Venezuela) and Guyana.

Revista Tablas. Centro de Investigación y Desarrollo de las Artes Escénicas. No. 1, enero/mayo 1982– . La Habana. See item **5968**.

199 *Studies in Latin American Popular Culture.* Department of Foreign Languages, New Mexico State University. Vol. 1, 1982– . Las Cruces.

New journal attempts to define meaning of "popular culture," which editors perceive as aspect of culture that are accepted by or consumed by large numbers of people. It does not mean folk culture. Articles will concern findings of direct participation in popular culture, production and distribution of popular culture, new methodological approaches to its study, introduction into Latin America, and consumption therein of foreign popular culture, and how Latin American popular culture in itself fits an international perspective. Vol. 1 includes articles on the fotonovela, Mexican cinema, sports in Cuba and Nicaragua, stamps and myth-making in Argentina, cartoons, and music in Mexico. Frequency of the publication is not given. Available for US $15.00/year (individual) from Charles M. Tatum, Co-Editor, *Studies in Latin American Popular Culture* (Department of Foreign Languages, Box 3L, New Mexico State University, Las Cruces, New Mexico 88003).

200 *Tercer Mundo y Economía Mundial.* Centro de Estudios Económicos y Sociales del Tercer Mundo. Vol. 1, No. 1, sept./dic. 1981– . México.

Includes articles on the New International Economic Order and its effect on the Third World. Publication is available from Centro de Estudios Económicos y Sociales del Tercer Mundo (Coronel Porfirio Díaz 50, San Jerónimo, D. F. México).

JOURNAL ABBREVIATIONS BIBLIOGRAPHY AND GENERAL WORKS

ASB/PP Philologica Pragensia. Academia Scientiarum Bohemoslovenica. Praha.

BBAA B.B.A.A. Boletín Bibliográfico de Antropología Americana. Instituto Panamericano de Geografía e Historia, Comisión de Historia. México.

BNJM/R Revista de la Biblioteca Nacional José Martí. La Habana.

CEDLA/B Boletín de Estudios Latinoamericanos. Centro de Estudios y Documentación Latinoamericanos. Amsterdam.

CM/FI Foro International. El Colegio de México. México.

CM/HM Historia Mexicana. El Colegio de México. México.

CPES/RPS Revista Paraguaya de Sociología. Centro Paraguayo de Estudios Sociológicos. Asunción.

EC/M Mapocho. Biblioteca Nacional, Extensión Cultural. Santiago.

FSCN/A Antropológica. Fundación La Salle de Ciencias Naturales, Instituto Caribe de Antropología y Sociología. Caracas.

IAA Ibero-Amerikansiches Archiv. Ibero Amerikanisches Institut. Berlin, FRG.

IAA/BA Brasil Açucareiro. Instituto do Açucar e do Alcool. Rio de Janiero.

IAHG/AHG Antropología e Historia de Guatemala. Instituto de Antropología e Historia de Guatemala.

IAHG/AHG Antropología e Historia de Guatemala. Instituto de Antropología e Historia de Guatemala.

IFCH/R Revista do Instituto de Filosofia e Ciências Humanas. Univ. Federal do Rio Grande do Sul. Porto Alegre, Brazil.

IFH/C Conjonction. Institut Français d'Haïti. Port-au-Prince.

IJ/JJ Jamaica Journal. Institute of Jamaica. Kingston.

LARR Latin American Research Review. Univ. of North Carolina Press *for the* Latin American Studies Association. Chapel Hill.

MAGN/B Boletín del Archivo General de la Nación. Secretaría de Gobernación. México.

MLTA/MLJ Modern Language Journal. The National Federation of Modern Language Teachers Association. Univ. of Pittsburgh. Pittsburgh, Pa.

OAS/LE La Educación. Organization of American States, Dept. of Educational Affairs. Washington.

PCCLAS/P Proceedings of the Pacific Coast Council on Latin American Studies. Univ. of California. Los Angeles.

PEBN/B Boletín de la Biblioteca Nacional. Lima.

PUCP/CSH Cuadernos del Seminario de Historia. Pontificia Univ. Católica del Perú, Instituto Riva-Agüero. Lima.

RIB Revista Interamericana de Bibliografía [Inter-American Review of Bibliography]. Organization of American States. Washington.

UBN/R Revista de la Biblioteca Nacional. Ministerio de Educación y Cultura. Montevideo.

UCAB/M Montalbán. Univ. Católica Andrés Bello, Facultad de Humanidades y Educación, Institutos Humanísticos de Investigación. Caracas.

UMHN/RH Revista Histórica. Museo Histórico Nacional. Montevideo.

UNAM/L Latinoamérica. Anuario de estudios latinoamericanos. Univ. Nacional Autónoma de México, Facultad de Filosofía y Letras, Centro de Estudios Latinoamericanos. México.

UNAM/RMCPS Revista Mexicana de Ciencias Políticas y Sociales. Univ. Nacional Autónoma de México, Facultad de Ciencias Políticas y Sociales. México.

UNAM/RMS Revista Mexicana de Sociología. Univ. Nacional Autónoma de México, Instituto de Investigaciones Sociales. México.

UNESCO/CU Cultures. United Nations Educational, Scientific and Cultural Organization. Paris.

UNESCO/JIS Unesco Journal of Information Science, Librarianship and Archives Administration. United Nations Educational, Scientific and Cultural Organization. Paris.

UP/A Apuntes. Univ. del Pacífico, Centro de Investigación. Lima.

UP/CSEC Cuban Studies/Estudios Cubanos. Univ. of Pittsburgh, Univ. Center for International Studies, Center for Latin American Studies. Pittsburgh, Pa.

UTIEH/C   Caravelle. Cahiers du monde hispanique et luso-brésilien. Univ. de Toulouse, Institut d'Études Hispaniques, Hispano-Americaines et Luso Brésiliennes. Toulouse, France.

VANH/B   Boletín de la Academica Nacional de la Historia. Caracas.

ART

ANCIENT ART, FOLK ART AND POPULAR ART

JOYCE WADDELL BAILEY, *Director, Handbook of Latin American Art, New Haven, Connecticut*

ALTHOUGH WE ARE INAUGURATING a new section for ANCIENT, FOLK and POPULAR ART, the coverage of these areas in the *HLAS* is not new, only sporadic. In this first essay I will try to bring together the fragmentary information on the subjects in *HLAS 1* through *HLAS 42*, clarify the terminology and suggest some of the new trends and developments.

The ancient art of Brazil was the first to be treated as a separate section by Robert C. Smith in *HLAS 5* through *HLAS 8* (1940–43). This section, "Pre-Cabralian Art," was named after Pedro Alvares Cabral, who claimed Brazil for Portugal on April 25, 1500.

Precolumbian Art, named for Christopher Columbus, was introduced as a section in *HLAS 23* (1961), compiled by Ignacio Bernal and Doris Heyden. Through use but not definition (see item **255**), the term "precolumbian" has encompassed the high cultures of Mesoamerica and the Andean region. The *HLAS* bibliographic coverage began with titles from 1957–58 and continued, in three subsequent volumes, to 1963. The next volume, *HLAS 27*, was devoted to the social sciences but referred the user interested in ancient art to "Art Volumes and Catalogs" in the subject index. Precolumbian Art was continued in *HLAS 28* for the humanities; "Art Volumes and Exhibitions Catalogs" served as a guide to users again in *HLAS 29* for the social sciences. In the next humanities volume, *HLAS 30* (1968), it was announced that precolumbian materials would be included henceforth with Archaeology.

The ancient arts and culture of the Southwestern US, now called "Native American Art," were treated in *HLAS 5* (1940).

To avoid any terminological or geographical confusion in this section, the art of all cultures in the Western Hemisphere which pre-date the arrival of Columbus in 1492 will be referred to as "Ancient Art" and will be classified under contemporary (1980) political boundaries.

Folk Art and Popular Art have also been treated under a variety of rubrics. "Popular Arts" appeared in volumes *HLAS 2* throuth *HLAS 8* (1937–1943); "Dance and Theatre Arts," in *HLAS 4* through *HLAS 6*; "Primitive and Folk," in *HLAS 21* (1959); "Indian Art," in *HLAS 22* (1960); "Artes Populares," in *HLAS 34* (1972); and Folk Art was included in volumes *HLAS 36* through *HLAS 42* (1974–80). The publications grouped under the various headings included those with "folk art" or "popular art" in the titles, items dealing with the contemporary survivals of ancient artistic traditions and contemporary Indian art.

The preceding illustrates a basic confusion in the use of the terminology for Latin American art. In the art historical sense, Folk Art refers to content and Popular Art, to form. Any theme, from official art to folk art, may be treated in a popular style. A style which, by definition, strives to present images in such a way as to be generally comprehensible to any viewer. The more public or popular the art form, the more universal are the images in terms of viewer-recognition. For example, the ruler theme on stela sculpture at the ancient site of Tikal in Guatemala may be treated in an esoteric or elitist manner as in Stela 31, or in a popular, generally comprehensible manner as in Stela 7 and Stela 9. By the same token, José Guadalupe Posada is a popular artist because of his style. Even though he used folk themes for the content of many compositions, he is not a folk artist (item 397).

Folk Art, unlike Popular Art, designates special themes, techniques, conditions of production, and is not restricted to any particular style. In Latin America, these themes and techniques are largely, but not entirely, derived from ancient sources. Artists tend to work in rural settings, respecting local thematic and technical customs as opposed to academic standards. Innovation is generally less prized than tradition, which explains the anonymity of many of the artists. "Arte Indígena" will be subsumed under the heading of "Folk Art," whether the reference is to the survival of Indian Art of ancient or modern origin.

The nomenclature of Ancient, Folk and Popular Art in the New World is inadequate because there are no European equivalents to these configurations—the words exist but not the phenomena. Since art historical theory is based on and biased by the European experience, the study of these areas in Latin America will be enhanced by a more appropriate theoretical structure. Such a structure can only be developed from a more comprehensive bibliographic base than we presently have.

In addition to theoretical considerations, the next decade should be characterized by an increased number of studies that examine the genesis of Folk Art and its duration through the colonial and later periods (items **293** and **296**). The fascinating historical anomaly in Latin America is that the high or official art of the ancient period became, in many cases, the Folk Art of the conquered peoples. At the same time, the subjugated artists used their expert skills to execute monuments that would only reinforce the domination of their people.

As an extension of the genesis-type study, we should also see more research on the interrelations of Folk and Popular Art with other sectors of artistic expression (item **377**). One of the seminal works in this direction is *Posada's Mexico* (items **292, 381, 397** and **401**).

The limitations on entries for this volume of the *HLAS* will not permit us to update the bibliographies but several series of publications and serials will be helpful to scholars. The Dumbarton Oaks series, "Studies in Precolumbian Art and Archaeology," began publication in 1966 and now numbers 24 monographs (items **274–275, 277–278** and **281–282**). The proceedings of conferences, sponsored and published by the same institution and ably edited by Elizabeth P. Benson, are basic references for topical studies (items **258** and **261–262**).

The proceedings of the Palenque Round Table meetings, organized and edited by Merle Greene Robertson, include articles on many Maya sites and subjects in Central America and Mexico (item **266**). *Mexicon* (item **259**) is a new periodical published by the Internationale Gesellschaft für Mesoamerika-Forschung (IGM), which contains current information and bibliography on research on Mesoamerican topics. The *Boletín de Información del Centro Interamericano de Artesanías y Artes Populares* (item **252**) offers a forum for discussion of research, bibliography and exchange of information on Folk and Popular Art. Finally, the sale catalogs published by Sotheby Parke Bernet for their auctions of ancient, colonial, 19th and 20th-century art in Latin America should not be overlooked as important visual and documentary sources (items **264** and **265**).

GENERAL

251 Bailey, Joyce Waddell. Map of Texúpa, Oaxaca, 1579: a study of form and meaning. (The Art Bulletin [College Art Association of America, New York] 54:4, Dec. 1972, p. 452–472, 23 b/w ill.)

Article carefully examines the iconographic and stylistic transition of a Mixtec artist from ancient traditions to colonial. The medium for studying the transition is the colonial Mapa de Texúpa in conjunction with an earlier colonial map (Códice Sierra), 16th-century prints and an ancient manuscript, Codex Nuttall. The manuscript tradition did not continue in this particular town in Oaxaca but the study is a model for understanding of the transformation of ancient art into colonial and folk art.

252 *Boletín de Información del Centro Interamericano de Artesanías y Artes Populares.* Nos. 1/9, 1979/1981– Cuenca, Ecuador.

Publication of the Centro Interamericano de Artesanías y Artes Populares (CIDAP) focuses on the preservation and appreciation of popular culture in the Americas. CIDAP activities, programs, meetings are reported in the *Boletín* along with some notes on bibliography and short, informal articles.

253 *Documentos de Arquitectura Nacional y Americana.* Universidad Nacional del Nordeste, Departamento de Historia de la Arquitectura. Nos. 1/12, 1973/1981– . Resistencia, Argentina.

Directed by Ramón Gutiérrez and Ricardo Jesse Alexander, this serial is devoted primarily to architecture but frequently has articles on popular expressions in architecture and some on ancient excavations and sites.

254 Marín de Paalen, Isabel. Historia general del arte mexicano. v. 4, Etnoartesanías y arte popular. México: Editorial Hermes, 1974. 222 p.; bibl.; map; plates.

Vol. 4 of this series is a pictorial survey with some text. Despite some terminological inconsistencies, this is a useful reference for a regional review of Folk Art and Popular Art covering the ancient period, colonial period, and the 19th and 20th centuries.

ANCIENT ART
General

255 Bailey, Joyce Waddell. Planning of the Handbook 1973–1979 (Boletín: Handbook of Latin American Art [New Haven, Conn.] 1:1, Feb. 1981, p. 1–4)

Author outlines the planning, geographic extension, bibliographic content and philosophical considerations of the *Handbook of Latin American Art.* Includes a discussion of the terminology for Latin American art and the rationale for the use of the term "Ancient" art.

256 Boulton, Alfredo. El arte en la cerámica aborigen de Venezuela. Diseño gráfico, Néstor Maya. Fotografías, Alfredo Boulton, Oscar Ascanio. Caracas: Museo de Arte Contemporáneo de Caracas, 1979. 444 p.; ill.

Through expert photography, Boulton has created a small museum of ancient ceramics from Venezuela. In the text and captions author engenders the aesthetic experience of each object. A wonderful book!

257 Jerusalem. Israel Museum. The Maremont collection of pre-Columbian art: the human image: the Israel Museum, Jerusalem, Spring, 1979. Jerusalem: The Museum, 1979. 24, 22 p.; 21 leaves of plates; bibl.; ill. (Cat.—Israel Museum; no. 190)

Useful catalog of Maremont Collections at the Israel Museum, composed largely of preclassic figurines from Mexico and ceramic figures from Western Mexico.

258 Junius B. Bird Pre-Columbian Textile Conference, *Washington, D.C., 1973.* The Junius B. Bird Pre-Columbian Textile Conference, May 19th and 20th, 1973. Ann Pollard Rowe, Elizabeth P. Benson, Anne-Louise Schaffer, editors. Washington, D.C.: The Textile Museum & Dumbarton Oaks, Trustees for Harvard University, 1979. 278 p.; bibl.; ill.

These essays, in honor of Junius B. Bird, were presented as papers at a conference held jointly by the Textile Museum and Dumbarton Oaks 19–20 May 1973. Papers were then revised and skillfully edited for publication in this volume, a basic reference for the study of ancient textiles.

259 *Mexicon.* Aktuelle Informationen und Studien zu Mesoamerika. Internationale Gesellschaft für Mesoamerika-Forschung (IGM). Vol. 1, Nos. 1/6; Vol. 2, Nos. 1/6; Vol. 3, Nos. 1/4, 1979/1981– Berlin, FRG.

Mexicon is a new serial publishing useful information about current research, opinions, and events relating to Mesoamerica. The index to each volume is sent as a separate sheet to subscribers annually. Published bi-monthly.

260 Parsons, Lee Allen. Pre-Columbian art: the Morton D. May and the St. Louis Art Museum Collections. Photography by Jack Savage. Charts and drawings by Rnytha Johnson. New York: Harper & Row, 1980. 320 p.; 20 leaves of plates; bibl.; ill. (some col.) (Icon editions)

The Morton D. May Collection, supplemented by objects from the St. Louis Art Museum, certainly deserves Parson's excellent catalog. Combined, the May Collection and the Museum collection offer a balanced view of the artistic expressions of the ancient cultures in general and an in-depth view of preclassic objects from Mexico, Zapotec urns (Oaxaca, Mexico) and Western Mexican effigy pottery. The chronological charts for the Central Andes and the Intermediate Area were transposed but otherwise, the text and presentation is so clear that it could be used by the specialist and non-specialist. Exceptional color reproductions.

261 Pre-Columbian metallurgy of South America: a conference at Dumbarton Oaks, October 18th and 19th, 1975. Elizabeth P. Benson, editor. Washington, D.C.: Dumbarton Oaks Research Library and Collections, Trustees for Harvard University, 1979. 207 p.; bibl.; ill.

"Pre-Columbian Metallurgy of South America" was a timely theme for the Dumbarton Oaks conference in 1975. It was a topic ripe for discussion from the technical, anthropological and art historical perspectives. The report of Alberto Rex González on the metallurgy of Northwest Argentina is a new and important contribution to the field. Unfortunately several papers and the responses to the papers presented could not be published. For anthropologist's comment, see *HLAS 43:492.*

262 The Sea in the pre-Columbian world: a conference at Dumbarton Oaks, October 26th and 27th, 1974. Elizabeth P. Benson,

editor. Washington, D.C.: Dumbarton Oaks Research Library and Collections, Trustees for Harvard University, 1977. 188 p.; bibl.; ill.

Aside from the report of work at Tancah and Tulum, the proceedings of this conference are not as visually or intellectually stimulating as those of earlier conferences. Benson and Coe mention in the preface that several iconographic papers could not be published. As with other themes of Dumbarton Oaks conferences, the attention given a subject through the formal meetings will undoubtedly encourage more scholarly research on the topic.

263 Ségota Tomac, Dúrdica. Apuntes sobre algunos problemas de la investigación del arte prehispánico de Mesoamérica (IIE/A, 47, 1977, p. 23–30, bibl.)

Argues that the ancient art of Mesoamerica has many unappreciated qualities because of a European aesthetic bias among those who study it. Proposes that one understand the ancient culture completely through interdisciplinary cooperation before beginning studies of art.

264 Sotheby Parke Bernet Inc. The Bogousslavsky Collection of Precolumbian Art. New York: Sotheby Parke Bernet Inc., 1981. 1 v. (Unpaged); 107 ill. (some col.)

Catalogue for the sale of this collection (4747Y) which consists of many Mayan, Costa Rican, and Olmec carved stones.

265 ———. Important precolumbian art. New York: Sotheby Parke Bernet Inc., 1981. 1 v. (Unpaged)

Auction catalogue includes 300 objects from the ancient period, most of which are illustrated. Excellent color reproductions of Mayan painted vessels and ceramic figures from Veracruz.

266 Tercera Mesa Redonda de Palenque: proceedings of the Tercera Mesa Redonda de Palenque, June 11–18, 1978. Palenque: a conference on the art, hieroglyphics, and historic approaches of the late classic Maya. v. 1/2 Editors, Merle Greene Robertson and Donnan Call Jeffers. Palenque, Chiapas, Mexico: Pre-Columbian Art Research Center [and] Austin: University of Texas Press, 1978 or 1979/1980. 2 v. (232, 226 p.); 4 p. of plates; bibl.; ill. (some col.) (The Palenque Round Table series; v. 4/5. The Texas Pan American series)

These two volumes comprise the proceedings of the Tercera Mesa Redonda de Palenque held at the Pre-Columbian Art Research Center in Palenque, Chiapas, Mexico on June 11 through 18, 1978. Unlike the two earlier conferences that were devoted to the art, iconography, and dynastic history of Palenque (*HLAS 39:559, HLAS 37:813*), this meeting brought together papers dealing with approaches to the art, hieroglyphs and history of the late classic Maya. Thirty-four of the papers are published from the 3rd Round Table in volumes IV and V; the 4th Round Table (June 8–14, 1980) is described in the preface of the latter volume. All of the conferences are testimonies to the marvelous energy and creativity of Merle Green Robertson, who founded the Pre-Columbian Art Research Center at Palenque. The highlight of the 1978 meeting was an expedition to Bonampak, led by Giles G. Healy, the discoverer with José Pepe Chan Bor, of the murals at that site in 1946. Robertson describes this discovery and the photographs in her essay (p. 3–44). R. E. W. Adams and Robert C. Aldrich presented a reevaluation of the murals based on the paintings and texts (p. 45–59) and Peter Mathews published the first part of his notes on the dynastic sequence for the site in volume V. The improved quality of printing and graphic production is notable in the latest volume, which is now a continuing part of the Texas Pan American Series called "The Palenque Round Table Series."

ANCIENT ART
Mexico

267 Foncerrada de Molina, Marta. La pintura mural de Cacxtla, Tlaxcala (IIE/A, 46, 1976, p. 20, 13, 13 ill. [2 in color])

Preliminary report on murals discovered in 1975, archaeological zone of Cacaxtla. The murals are assigned an epiclassic date, making them contemporary with Teotihuacan. The style is a hybrid of types relating to Teotihuacan, Cholula, even Maya painting, and other areas. Author leaves final judgment of this and iconographic matters for a later, more comprehensive study.

268 Fuente, Beatriz de la. Pequeña obra maestra de la escultura olmeca (IIE/A, 47, 1977, p. 5–10, bibl., 10 b/w ill.)

Discusses the jadeite Figurilla de Las Choapas, now in the Museo de Antropología of the Universidad Veracruzana.

269 ———. Sobre una cabeza de piedra en el Museo de Antropología (IIE/A, 46, 1976, p. 21–23, 2 b/w fig.)

Note on a sculptured head which would have been included in author's *Escultura monumental olmeca* (1973, see *HLAS 37:713*) under "Monumentos Cuyas Características Hacen Dudosa su Plena Atribución a la Cultura Olmeca."

270 Furst, Jill Leslie and **Peter T. Furst.** Pre-Columbian art of Mexico. New York: Abbeville Press, 1980. 128 p.; bibl.; ill.

The generally excellent illustrations in this picture book are preceded by short summary on ancient cultures of Mexico. Each color plate is accompanied by a description of subject's significance.

271 Gutiérrez Solana, Nelly. Materiales utilizados en las imágenes mexicas: de acuerdo con Sahagún y sus informes (IIE/A, 47, 1977, p. 11–21, bibl., 1 b/w ill.)

Very interesting article that lists, in the form of a chart, all the materials used for making images and the types of images produced according to Sahagún's accounts.

272 ———. Xiuhcóatl tallada en piedra del Museum of Mankind, Londres (IIE/A, 48, 1978, p. 5–17, bibl., 19 b/w ill.)

Formal analysis of a Xiuhcóatl (serpent) sculpture temporarily in the British Museum.

273 Heyden, Doris. Pintura mural y mitología en Teotihuacán (IIE/A, 48, 1978, p. 19–33, bibl., 7 b/w ill.)

Summary of current research on the topic.

274 Milbrath, Susan. A study of Olmec sculptural chronology. Washington, D.C.: Dumbarton Oaks, Trustees for Harvard University, 1979. 75 p.; bibl.; ill. (Studies in Pre-Columbian art & archaeology; no. 23)

The use of stylistic analysis as a means of dating mutilated monuments is at best unsatisfactory. Milbrath seriates the sculpture into groups based on stylistic and scanty archaeological evidence and then tries to buttress or adjust these four groups by another type of inquiry—the stylistic relationship of sculptured motifs to those on dated ceramics and correlations with related monuments beyond the Olmec area. This is a good idea but author unwittingly exposes pitfalls of this approach in applying it to the first group. The dated ceramic motifs can be found on both Group I and Group II monuments (the relationships are tenuous to begin with), and the related sculptured monuments outside the Olmec area at Sin Cabezas are of no help. We know that the monuments were re-used by the ancient peoples but they may also have been re-carved, a consideration that might explain our difficulties with the various seriations.

275 Scott, John Frederik. The Danzantes of Monte Albán. pt. 1, Text. pt. 2, Catalogue. With an appendix by W. P. Hewitt. Washington, D.C.: Dumbarton Oaks, Trustees for Harvard University, 1979. 78 p.; bibl.; ill. (Studies in pre-Columbian art and archaeology; no. 20)

Scott's excellent study of the mysterious "danzantes" at Monte Albán brings all of the relevant research and visual materials together for the first time. Author's opinion is that the meaning of figures carved on the stone slabs ". . . more likely commemorates captives and conquest than ecstatic trances." (p. 30). All of the Danzantes were photographed for the catalog and each photograph is elucidated by a line drawing. Pt. 1, *Text* (79 p., bibl., 30 b/w figures) includes appendix by W. P. Hewitt. Pt. 2, *Catalogue* (unpaged) includes 200 b/w photographs and drawings.

276 ———. Los primeros "yugos" veracruzanos (IIE/A, 46, 1976, p. 25–48, 14 b/w ill.)

Discusses the funereal use of "yugos" from the sites of El Carrizal, Santa Luisa and El Zapotal in Veracruz.

277 Sharp, Rosemary. Chacs and chiefs: the iconology of mosaic stone sculpture in pre-conquest Yucatán, Mexico. Washington, D.C.: Dumbarton Oaks, Trustees for Harvard University, 1981. 48 p.; bibl.; ill. (Studies in pre-Columbian art and archaeology; no. 24)

The interpretive jump from formal complexes (masks, T-sequences, step-frets) to political and cultural changes is not convincing.

278 Townsend, Richard Fraser. State and cosmos in the art of Tenochtitlan. Washington, D.C.: Dumbarton Oaks, Trustees for Harvard University, 1979. 78 p.; bibl.; ill. (Studies in pre-Columbian art and archaeology; no. 20)

Townsend's highly intelligent study of Mexica art transcends disciplinary bias and establishes a standard for future research. This work, submitted as a doctoral dissertation at Harvard, presents outstanding examinations of the problem of continuity and disjunction, of the political ambition inherent in Mexica religion and of the commemorative monuments (Dedication Stone, Stone of Tizoc, Teocalli of Sacred War and Sun Stone). It constitutes as well, unintentionally so, a contribution to the dismantling of the scholar cults, which have done as much harm as good in this field of study.

ANCIENT ART
Peru

279 Arte precolombino: Museo Nacional de Antropología y Arqueología, Lima. v. 1, Arte textil y adornos. v. 2, Escultura y diseño. v. 3, Pintura. Texto de la introd., Luis G. Lumbreras. Asesoría artística, Sara de Lavalle. Fotografía, Werner Lang. Lima: Banco de Crédito del Perú, 1977. 3 v. (171, 177, 175 p.) bibl; chiefly col. ill. (Colección Arte y tesoros del Perú)

Lumbreras is probably the scholar most qualified to introduce a survey of such monumental scope of Peruvian art. Vol. 1, *Arte textil y adornos*, of the collection of the Museo Nacional de Antropología y Arqueología in Lima consists of a review of textile art, accompanied by excellent color plates. Vol. 2, *Escultura y diseño*, treats sculpture, carving and ceramics. Vol. 3, *Pintura*, is devoted to painting on cloth. The short essay at the end of vol. 3 by James Reid, "La Pintura Peruana Precolombiana Precursora del Arte Moderno," draws interesting parallels between these painted designs and the modern art of Lichtenstein, Mondrian, Torres-García, Warhol and others. Vols. 2/3 also include excellent color plates.

280 Bankes, George. Moche pottery from Peru. London: British Museum Publications, 1980. 55 p.; bibl.; ill.

Popular account of Moche culture and ceramics also includes contemporary potters.

Cordoy-Collins, Alana. The dual divinity concept in Chavín art. See *HLAS 43:758.*

281 Donnan, Christopher B. and **Donna McClelland.** The burial theme in Moche iconography. Washington, D.C.: Dumbarton Oaks, Trustees for Harvard University, 1979. 46 p.; bibl.; ill. (Studies in pre-Columbian art & archaeology; no. 21)

Seven examples of the burial theme from Phase V of the Moche style are illustrated and analyzed.

282 Florida. State University, Tallahassee. Art Gallery. Precolumbian exhibition, the John and Mary Carter Collection of Peruvian precolumbian artifacts and textiles. Organized by Bruce H. Dempsey. Text and catalogue by Diane Olsen. Tallahassee: Florida State University, 1979. 127 p.; ill.

Good catalogue of the Carter Collection at Florida State University. For Ina Van Stan's earlier article on the subject, see *HLAS 23:532.*

283 Kano, Chiaki. The origins of the Chavín culture. Washington, D.C.: Dumbarton Oaks, Trustees for Harvard University, 1979. 87 p.; bibl.; ill. (Studies in pre-Columbian art & archaeology; no. 22)

Kano traces the changes in the artistic style of the feline motif from the pre-Chavín period to Chavín. He then equates changes in the feline artistic system with developmental stages in the religious system, politics and society. Author is correct in stating ". . . the changes and developmental phases in the content of the religion and society were always extremely difficult to ascertain, and is probable that I have made some erroneous interpretations." (p. 39).

Saco, María Luisa. Fuentes para el estudio del arte peruano precolombino. See *HLAS 43:804.*

Velarde, Héctor. Arquitectura peruana. See item 357.

FOLK ART AND POPULAR ART
General

Alegría, Mela Pons. Taino Indian art. See *HLAS 43:408.*

284 Anderson, Marilyn. Guatemalan textiles today. New York: Watson-Guptill Publications, 1978. 200 p.; bibl.; ill.; index.

Depicts contemporary weaving techniques, hand and loom, and fabric structures through extensive photos of skilled weavers at work. Author, deeply impressed with values and varieties of weaving, does not believe the craft's demise is imminent. Quality b/w photos with color portfolio (8 p.). One of best works on subject. Includes drawings and glossary but no discussion of symbolism of motifs. [R.J. Mullen]

Boulton, Alfredo. El arte en la cerámica aborigen de Venezuela. See *HLAS 43:822.*

285 Díaz Castillo, Roberto. Artes y artesanías populares de Sacatepéquez. Fotos de Mauro Calanchina. Guatemala: Universidad de San Carlos de Guatemala, Centro de Estudios Folklóricos, 1976. 713 p.; bibl.; ill. (Colección breve—Centro de Estudios Folklóricos; v. 2)

Originally intended as a guide to the collection of the Museo de Artes y Artesanías Populares de Sacatepéquez, the book comprises an illustrated history of the folk arts of the Department of Sacatepéquez, of which Antigua Guatemala is the administrative center. The museum was damaged by earthquake and never opened.

286 Duarte, Carlos F. Pintura e iconografía popular de Venezuela. Caracas: E. Armitano, 1978. 267, 4 p.; ill. (some col.) (Serie Pintores venezolanos)

Hundreds of color reproductions of "folk art" paintings, many not made public heretofore. For each there is "catalogue" information plus a study of iconography and stylistic traits. A most thorough treatment and a unique contribution to our knowledge of the popular arts of Venezuela. Arranged by iconographic themes: "Life of Mary;" "Titles of Mary;" "Life of Christ;" "The Trinity and Purgatory;" "Angels and Archangels;" "The Saints;" and "Portraits and Scenes." Excellent photography. An enchanting and commendable work from this prolific scholar. [R.J. Mullen]

Henley, Paul and **Marie-Claude Mattéi-Müller.** Panare basketry: means of commercial exchange and artistic expression. See *HLAS 43:1124.*

287 Litto, Gertrude. South American folk pottery. Studio photography by Robert

Emerson Willis. Ill. by Frank Litto. New York: Watson-Guptill Publications, 1976. 223 p.; bibl.; ill. (some col.); index.

Litto has, through pioneering effort, prepared an excellent regional survey of this subject. The photographs of potters and techniques document these little-known traditions. The color plates show a great appreciation and sensitivity to the objects as works of art.

288   Macera dall'Orso, Pablo. Pintores populares andinos. Lima: Fondo del Libro del Banco de Los Andes, 1979. 221 p.; bibl.; col. ill.

Macera examines the various manifestations of popular painting from Andahuaylas, Ayacucho, Tacna, Cajamarca, Chachapoyas and Cuzco. He grapples with the various terms applied to these artists—primitives, rural artists, minor artists—and settles on "popular" because of the stylistic similarities. His discussion summarizes the background for the study of these neglected materials and ranges from the 16th century to the present. Of the 103 colored plates, some are of excellent quality.

289   Mitopoemas Yãnomam. Narradores e desenhistas, Koromani Waica, Mamokè Rorowè, e Kreptip Wakatautheri. Pesquisa e fotos, Cláudia Andujar. Tradução portuguesa, Carlos Zacquini, e Giovanni Battista Saffirio. Tradução italiana, P.M. Bardi. Tradução inglesa, Michael P. Potter. Rio de Janeiro?: Olivetti do Brasil, 1978. 72 p.; col. ill.

This luxurious volume of 49 color plates is based on interviews with three Yanomami Indians, who drew pictures on paper with felt pens of the myths they described. Myths are translated into Portuguese, Italian and English and, with the pictures, form a rich source for iconographical studies of this nomadic tribe from the Roraima Territory of Brazil. The five negatives interspersed in the text are apparently the work of photographer, Cláudia Andujar, who did a documentary survey of the Indians in 1974.

290   Oriol, Jacques. La alfarería haitiana: generalidades y particularidades. Traducción, France Claire Peynado de Taveras. Santo Domingo: Ediciones Fundación García-Arévalo, 1977. 78 p.; bibl.; ill. (Serie monográfica—Fundación García-Arévalo; no. 5)

Oriol has brought together information on an important and interesting subject but the study suffers from a lack of visual material. The five "fotos" are rough sketches of the objects and techniques.

291   Reina, Ruben E. and Robert M. Hill, II. The traditional pottery of Guatemala. Austin: University of Texas Press, 1978. 229 p.; bibl.; ill.; index (Texas Pan American series)

Authors have composed an excellent study of Guatemalan pottery from an anthropological point of view. The text gives—through maps, photographs and discussion—a detailed analysis of the pottery's geographical distribution, technical means of production and ethno-historic implications. However, study lacks any careful consideration of aesthetic or formal characteristics of the materials. For ethnologist's comment, see *HLAS 43:917.*

Zeballos Miranda, Luis. Mapa artesanal de Bolivia. See *HLAS 43:5575.*

FOLK ART AND POPULAR ART
Mexico

292   Bailey, Joyce Waddell. The penny press (in Posada's Mexico. Edited by Ronnie C. Tyler [see *HLAS 42:1362*] p. 84–121, 299–302, ill., map)

By exploring history of pictorial journalism, author places Posada in a more realistic art historical context. Shows that Posada was not the creator of a graphic tradition but its inheritor. Contemporary map of Mexico City indicates all major, popular print shops which are also keyed to periodicals and artists in the appendixes. Includes discussion of the term "popular" (p. 115–117).

293   Cordry, Donald Bush. Mexican masks. Austin: University of Texas Press, 1980. 280 p.; bibl.; ill. (some col.); index.

Posthumous publication of this volume is a tribute to author's life's work in the study of Mexican masks. The text, with its splendid photographs, is a delight to read; each page exudes the enthusiasm and dedication of the author and his wife, Dorothy. All of the major geographical regions of mask production in Mexico are covered and characterized by the author. The weakest part of the study is the justification of the mask as a work of art and the attempt to analyze the mask stylistically and iconographically according to standard art historical theory—it doesn't work. Rather, his functional analysis in Pt. 3 seems much more appropriate and promising. But he has left the task of methodology to other students, who will spend years savoring the great treasure that both Cordrys have willed to us.

294 **La Dicotomía entre arte culto y arte popular:** coloquio internacional de Zacatecas. México, D.F.: Universidad Nacional Autónoma de México, 1979. 283 p.; bibl.; ill.; 4 leaves of plates (Estudios de arte y estética; 14)

Essays from the Coloquio Internacional de Zacatecas, 1975, published in this book will long serve as the basic manual in discussing the terms "Arte Culto" and "Arte Popular." There are many thoughtful suggestions in the 11 essays, each of which is elucidated by commentaries of other specialists. My only general criticism of this impressive collection is that the title, "La Dicotomía entre Arte Culto y Arte Popular," precluded the consideration of certain aspects of the problem. Namely, that popular and fine art are not dichotomous terms. "Popular" generally refers to a style of presentation like Baroque Art or Impressionism. In this case, the posing of the question actually obscures part of the answer.

295 **Edson, Gary.** Mexican market pottery. New York: Watson-Guptill Publications, 1979. 168 p.; ill. (some col.); index.

General and regional survey from the point of view of a sensitive potter. Excellent photographs (some color) of objects and pottery markets in Mexico.

296 **Mompradé, Electra L.** and **Tonatiúh Gutiérrez.** Historia general del arte mexicano. v. 5, Indumentaria tradicional indígena. v. 6, Danzas y bailes populares. México: Editorial Hermes, 1976. 2 v. (251, 239 p.); bibl.; fold. plate; ill.; maps; plates.

Following the pattern for this series, vol. 5 is a study of Indian costume in its present manifestation preceded by a summary of ancient and colonial sources. Costume is classified first by tribe (e.g., Nahuas, Otomíes) then by pueblo. Even though the states in which the pueblos or towns are located are not noted, they are easy to find on the map (v. 5, p. 228–229). Vol. 6 of this series is a topical survey of the dance in Mexico. Most of the dances described are illustrated; the main body of the text is preceded by a summary of ancient and colonial antecedents.

297 **Moya Rubio, Víctor José.** Máscaras: la otra cara de México. México: Universidad Nacional Autónoma de México, Coordinación de Humanidades, 1978. 253 p.; bibl.; ill. (some col.)

Masks (clay, wooden, cloth, stone) have generally been treated in an ancillary manner by art historians. Many masks are stunning works of art and rich treasures of iconography, as Moya Rubio's study shows. Text consists of narrative description of 231 illustrated items (some in color), in which he points to ancient origins of the traditions and contemporary uses of masks.

298 **Vivienda campesina en México.** Coordinación general, Valeria Prieto. Colaboraron en la elaboración del texto y en la recopilación de material gráfico, Sonia Carrillo et al. México: Secretaría de Asentamientos Humanos y Obras Públicas, 1978. 224 p.; bibl; chiefly ill.; index.

Survey of rural housing in Mexico, documented largely by photographs of the houses and sketches of the technical means of construction.

SPANISH AMERICA: Colonial

ROBERT J. MULLEN, Associate Professor of Art History, The University of Texas at San Antonio

TWELVE COUNTRIES ARE REPRESENTED in the many works reviewed. Among the rare entries are articles on Cuba and Panama. A full account of the building programs of the two cathedrals in Panama is given in item **323**, while 16 excellent 18th-century retablos from several churches are described in item **322**. Among other rare works are an extensive study of the distinctive forms of sculpture and architecture produced among the Guarani of Paraguay (item **350**) and one of the few overall accounts of Argentina's architecture from colonial times to the present (item **300**).

There is a group of publications which warrants special mention for outstanding scholarship and superb bookmaking. Three books, published respectively in 1975, 1976 and 1977, by Banamex rank among the finest color reproductions to have come out of Mexico. Professional photographers produced new views of 16th-, 17th- and 18th-century Mexican architecture and sculpture with unmatched results (item **335**). A catalogue of the Museum of San Francisco in Chile (item **324**) is masterfully and beautifully represented. Also in the category of fine bookmaking is the scholarly monograph on the Colombian painter, Gregorio Vasquez (item **327**).

Bolivian scholar Teresa Gisbert has produced an extraordinary work (item **304**) which depicts the very rich but little known patrimony of the Lake Titicaca region in today's Peru and Bolivia. Especially startling are her examples of prehispanic values and symbols in colonial works. Gisbert's contribution is a breakthrough in scholarship and insights. Carlo Duarte follows up his earlier work on silversmiths of Venezuela by producing an erudite and very handsome book (item **362**) on one of that country's masters, Pedro Ignacio Ramos. The combined work of a number of scholars resulted in a monumental monograph on Mexico's Palacio Nacional (item **336**). Every aspect from the days of Moctezuma to Echeverría is carefully and exhaustively studied. It is filled with unique and superb illustrations, vintage photos and clarifying measured drawings. A smaller but just as delightful monograph (item **344**) vividly displays the glories and fantasies of Tonantzintla's tile and stucco work, while another (item **329**) examines anew its complex symbolism. One of Mexico's earliest industrial buildings, the cigar factory La Ciudadela, is imaginatively studied (item **346**) by applying a methodology heretofore "not used in the history of art of Mexico." Another significant contribution is a rarely seen general study of Peru's colonial art and architecture (item **353**), which fortunately encompasses more than urban (Spanish) centers.

There continues to be much interest in the study of coastal fortifications, as mentioned in *HLAS 42*, particularly as the result of the Congress held in Caracas in 1977 (item **365**). Annotated below are studies of forts in Venezuela (items **360** and **364**), Colombia (item **328**), Peru (item **354**), Cuba (item **315**), and those intended for the Straits of Magellan (item **359**).

GENERAL

299 La Dispersión del manierismo: documentos de un coloquio. México, D.F.: Universidad Nacional Autónoma de México, Instituto de Investigaciones Estéticas, 1980. 236 p.; 106 p. of plates; bibl.; ill. (Estudios de arte y estética; 15)

The diffusion of mannerism, especially into Latin America, is examined by seven scholars at a meeting in Oaxtepec, July 1976. Subjects include: "Cathedral of Mexico as a Manneristic Phenomenon;" Manneristic Traces in Sculpture of Guatemala;" "Mannerism or Counter-Mannerism in Latin American Painting." Illustrates again the difficulties of applying terminology applicable to European arts to those in the Hispanic world.

ARGENTINA

300 Arquitectura en la Argentina. v. 1, Noroeste. v. 2, Centro-Noroeste. v. 3, Litoral. Editor: María Angélica Correa. Buenos Aires: EUDEBA, 1982. 3 v.; ill.

Under this title 10 booklets cover Argentina's architecture from the 16th century to the present. Numbers one through five relate to the colonial period according to regions; number six through 10 concern 19th and 20th centuries. Well written by a number of architects. Reasonably good illustrations. A whole new group of colonial architecture with distinctive indigenous traces is revealed. A greatly needed overview.

301 Luque Colombres, Carlos. La Universidad Nacional de Córdoba: breve guía histórica (UNC/R, 2:1/5, 3. serie, marzo/dic. 1978, p. 7–50, ill.)

While mostly a history since its founding by the Jesuits in 1613, pictures (good quality) reveal various parts of the university.

302 Luqui Lagleyze, Julio A. Las iglesias de la Ciudad de la Trinidad y Puerto de Santa María de los Buenos Aires, 1536–1810. Buenos Aires: Municipalidad de la Ciudad de Buenos Aires, 1981. 166 p.; bibl.; ill. (Cuadernos de Buenos Aires; 57)

Significant documentary account of 20 churches established between 1580 and 1797 in Buenos Aires. However, lacks architectural details and the few illustrations are hopeless.

303 Núñez, Calixto José. Estudio histórico e historiográfico de la Estancia Santa Catalina: siglos XVII y XVIII. Córdoba, Argentina: Dirección de Historia, Letras y Ciencias, 1980. 199 p.; appendix; ill.

The Jesuits acquired the Estancia de Santa Catalina, near Córdoba, Argentina, before mid-17th century primarily for use as a novitiate. Extensive research supports careful description of church built in last half of century. Possible architects listed, many from Bavaria, Germany. Chapter on church is one of 10 exhaustive studies. A significant contribution marred only by (few) poor illustrations.

BOLIVIA

304 Gisbert, Teresa. Iconografía y mitos indígenas en el arte. La Paz, Bolivia: Gisbert, 1980. 250 p.; 144 p. of plates; bibl.; ill. (some col.); index.

Hundreds of iconographic instances convincingly depict the persistence of prehispanic cultural values into colonial times and even into the 19th century. This major undertaking is treated under five categories: 1) prehispanic myths in colonial art and ar-

chitecture; 2) indigenous representations modified in Christian setting: the Incas in paintings; 3) the descendants of the Incas; 4) the reconstitution of a "monarchy;" and 5) the indigenists in the conquest and in the rebellion. Includes copious notes, sources, indexes. Profusely illustrated with generally high quality reproductions. The most thorough analysis yet published on the persistence of native values in colonial sculpture, painting and architecture. An outstanding accomplishment. The work of a lifetime.

THE CARIBBEAN

305 Davila, Arturo. Valoración geográfica sobre la arquitectura religiosa en Puerto Rico (ICP/R, 17:63, abril/junio 1974, p. 34–38)

Reviews 20 years of preservation work of Puerto Rico's colonial religious architecture. Describes structures in: city of Puerto, San Germán, Hormigueros, Coamu valley, north coast. Briefly reviews certain neoclassic and neogothic buildings of the 19th century. Fine summary. Only three illustrations.

306 Dobal, Carlos. ¿Quienes construyeron la iglesia de Jacagua? (ADH/C, 49: 137, enero/dic. 1980, p. 46–51, bibl.)

Identifies those possibly involved in building the church in Jacagua, perhaps between 1509–12 which would make it the oldest in the Americas.

307 ———. El reloj de las Casas Reales (EME, 8:45, nov./dic. 1979, p. 109–113, bibl.)

Cites various sources to support claim that clock in Casas Reales in Santo Domingo, Dominican Republic, was in operation from 1537–1787.

308 García Santa, Alicia; Teresita Angel Bello; and Víctor Echenagusía. Pinturas murales de la Casa Ortiz (RYC, 65, enero 1978, p. 68–72, plates)

After brief account of murals in Trinidad, Cuba, those in Casa Ortiz are described in detail as typical of 19th-century work. Murals are not frescoes. Designs are floral, patterned, devoid of human figures.

309 Guadalupe Victoria, José. Una portada tequitqui desconocida (IIE/A, 12:48, 1978, p. 63–66, bibl., ill.)

Describes the "original" portal of the Dominican convento (16th century) in Tacubaya, now part of the parroquia.

310 Monte, Manuel del. Preservación del patrimonio cultural en la República Dominicana (*in* Cultural traditions and Caribbean identity: the question of patrimony. Edited by S. Jeffrey K. Wilkerson. Gainesville: Center for Latin American Studies, University of Florida, 1980, p. 85–106)

The Office of Cultural Patrimony was established in 1967 to foster the preservation of the colonial heritage of the Dominican Republic. The restoration of central Santo Domingo is described.

311 Monumentos coloniales de Santo Domingo. Santo Domingo: Círculo de Coleccionistas, Fundación Dominicana de Desarrollo, 1974. 23 p.; bibl.; ill.

History and description of six 16th-century structures in Santo Domingo: Cathedral, Alcázar de Colón, Torre del Homenaje, Casa de Enzombe, the Dominican and Franciscan conventos. Each is accompanied by a sketch and references.

312 Palace of the Royal Audiencia & Indias Chancery, Palace of Governors and Captains General: visitors guide. Text & coordination, Consuelo Sanz Pastor *et al.* English translation & correction, Nancy Lou Wilkes, Ana María Antoni, Altagracia Amelia Cabral. Photos., Onorio Montás. Santo Domingo: Museo de las Casas Reales, 1978. 78 p.; ill.

Casas Reales, now restored, in Santo Domingo were "first official institutions in America." Pocket-size guide displays two dozen rooms each devoted to differing aspects of colonial rule, civil and military. Set up as dioramas, these strive to depict "institutional personality." Text is English.

313 Pérez Montas, Eugenio. Biografía de un monumento/Biography of a monument. Prólogo, Frank Moya Pons; fotografía, Onorio Montás. Santo Domingo: Voluntariado de las Casas Reales, Comité Dominicano de ICOMOS, 1979. 127 p.; bibl.; ill. (some col.); indexes.

Full account, in English and Spanish, of research and restoration of Casas Reales, the first official institutions in America—two palaces and one chapel. Construction dates not known, but mentioned as early as

1520. Transformed into a museum based upon "exact knowledge regarding the functions of these buildings." Excellent drawings and photos (color) supplement a lively text which not only provides technical data but many facets of social and daily life as well of the colonial period.

314 Rubio, Vicente. Las casas moradas del secretario Diego Caballero. Dibujo portada, Dionisio Blanco. Santo Domingo: Fundación García-Arévalo, 1979. 60 p.; bibl.; ill. (Serie monográfica; Fundación García-Arévalo; no. 11)

Investigation of the earliest domestic architecture of Santo Domingo provides full account, mostly historical, of houses built in 1550 for the First Secretary of the Real Audiencia, Diego Caballero.

315 Sosa Montalvo, Gloria. El Castillo del Morro de San Pedro de la Roca. Cubierto, Deguis Fernández Tejeda. Fotos, Rafael González, Jerónimo Llauradó y Luis Rosaenz. Santiago de Cuba: Editorial Oriente, 1978. 98 p.; bibl.; ill.

Major dates from 16th to 19th century on this coastal fortification protecting Santiago de Cuba. Numerous photos (fair quality) include details of graffiti, some quite artistic. Restored 1962–64.

CENTRAL AMERICA

316 La Orden Miracle, Ernesto *padre.* El patrimonio artístico de Nicaragua (UCR/AEC, 1976, p. 231–290, bibl.)

General description of Nicaragua's cultural patrimony devoted to the colonial period (only two pages to the prehispanic period). After an overview of style, civil and religious architecture, major façades and retablos, the particulars of over 70 places are catalogued. An extraordinary work, perhaps unique.

317 Luján Muñoz, Jorge. Sebastiano Serlio, Martín de Andújar y Joseph de Porres, y las catedrales de Santiago de Guatemala y Ciudad Real de Chiapas (SGHG/A, 50:50, enero/dic. 1977, p. 35–60, plates)

Masterful analysis of Antigua's (Guatemala) third Cathedral of Santiago (1669–86), later repairs and modifications (earthquakes), and architects involved. Provides documentary sources. Convincingly traces conservative design of main portal to influence of Serlio's Book IV (1552) on architect Joseph de Porres. Main portal of Ciudad Real (now San Cristóbal las Casas, Chiapas, Mexico) is modeled upon Antigua's. Well illustrated. A significant contribution.

318   Luján Muñoz, Luis. La escultura ecuestre de Carlos III en la Plaza Mayor de la Nueva Guatemala (SGHG/A, 52:52, enero/dic. 1979, p. 267–278, ill.)

Traces history of equestrian statue of Charles III (1716–88) which once graced the fountain in the central plaza of Guatemala. It is the work of at least two sculptors. Describes materials and style.

319   ———. Fuentes de Antigua Guatemala. Guatemala: Editorial J. de Pineda Ibarra and Consejo Nacional para la Protección de la Antigua Guatemala, 1977. 71 p.; 1 fold. leaf of plates; bibl.; ill.

Fountains in and around Antigua are described at length according to setting: public, private, religious. Includes chronological tables, plans, elevations, sections, few photos. Unusual treatment of a neglected theme.

320   ———. El primer testimonio iconográfico de la Ciudad de Santiago de Guatemala (SGHG/A, 50:50, enero/dic. 1977, p. 157–166, ill.)

Plans of early Santiago, Guatemala, are scarce. A schematic plan/drawing of the city made about 1690 has been discovered. Most of its 53 notations are buildings.

321   Pereira, Octavio M. Las tejas de la catedral de Panamá (LNB/L, 98/99, enero/feb. 1981, p. 16–27, ill.)

Recollections of the city of Panama before its virtual destruction by fire in 1878.

322   Velarde B., Oscar A. Los retablos coloniales de Panamá (LNB/L, 291, junio 1981, p. 1–28, photos)

Sixteen retablos are illustrated (good quality) and described. Richly carved, all but one are of the 18th century. A fine contribution on a subject and an area about which little is known.

323   Vidal, Mercedes L. La nueva Panamá y la construcción de su nueva catedral (LNB/L, 98/99, enero/feb. 1981, p. 7–15)

Detailed history of the two cathedrals in Panama. The first one made of wood was begun in 1673 and destroyed by fire in 1737.

The second, of field stone (*mampostería*), was begun in 1677 but not consecrated until 1796. A telling and needed account based on archives.

CHILE

324   Cruz, Isabel. Museo Colonial de San Francisco. Santiago, Chile: Departamento de Extensión Cultural del Ministerio de Educación, 1978. 78 p.; ill. (Colección Museos chilenos. Serie El Patrimonio cultural chileno)

Beautifully illustrated catalogue (black/white and color) together with good text. Ranks among the better of its kind. Brief history of Convento, founded 1572 in Santiago, and full description of museum pieces (e.g., polychrome sculpture, wood furnishings, murals, oils) many of which show traces of Cuzco school.

325   González Echenique, Javier. Arte colonial en Chile. Santiago: Departamento de Extensión Cultural del Ministerio de Educación, 1978. 58 p.; ill. (some col.) (Colección Historia del arte chileno; libro 1. Serie El Patrimonio cultural chileno)

Survey of all colonial (17th and 18th centuries) arts intended only to familiarize. Good text and illustrations achieve this goal.

COLOMBIA

326   Bossa Herazo, Donaldo. El mueble colonial cartagenero del siglo XVIII. Cartagena de Indias: Gráficas "El Faro," 1975. 26 p.; ill.

Using examples from Cartagena, author discusses stylistic traits of furniture of the New World by contrasting rigid, heavy lines of Hapsburg era (16th, 17th centuries) with more ornate, flowing lines of Bourbon rule (18th century). Includes good illustrations (b/w) of 13 pieces.

327   Gil Tovar, Francisco. La obra de Gregorio Vásquez. Bogotá: Carlos Valencia Editores, Museo de Arte Moderno, 1980. 191 p.; ill. (some col.)

Combination of good scholarship and fine bookmaking have produced an excellent monograph on this painter who was born (1638), lived and died (1711) in Bogotá. More than 100 paintings are beautifully illustrated in either b/w or color and each is carefully described. Drawings are especially engaging. A delightful "discovery."

328 Zapatero, Juan Manuel. Historia de las fortificaciones de Cartagena de Indias. Madrid: Ediciones Cultura Hispánica del Centro Ibero-Americano de Cooperación y Dirección General de Relaciones Culturales del Ministerio de Asuntos Exteriores, 1979. 204 p.; bibl.; ill.

Cartagena's fortifications from the 16th through 19th centuries are carefully detailed. Includes crisply reproduced maps (78) and sketches, mostly derived from archival sources. Another 21 photos illustrate the fort as it is today and some of its previous military commanders. Excellent scholarship and bookmaking.

MEXICO

Boyer, Richard. La ciudad de México en 1628: la visión de Juan Gómez de Trasmonte. See item **1890**.

329 González Galván, Manuel. Tonantzin coronada en el Tlalocan (IIE/A, 12:48, 1978, p. 47–61, ill.)

Spirited and new interpretation of the rich symbolism in Tonantzintla's interior. Spatial (architectural) aspects are examined. Links Mary's location in the vault to the original name of pueblo which meant "the place of our little mother."

330 Iglesias y edificios antiguos de Guadalajara. Edición a cargo de Ramón Mata Torres. Dibujos, Guillermo de la Torre y Carlos Sandoval Linares. Guadalajara, México: Ayuntamiento de Guadalajara: Cámara Nacional de Comercio de Guadalajara, 1979. 384 p.; 29 leaves of plates; bibl.; ill.; plans (Los Cursos de información sobre Guadalajara; v. 5)

Includes reference material on 40 colonial structures in Guadalajara and vicinity (Tlaquepaque, Tonala, Atemajac, Zapopan). Authorship and scholarship varies. Limited illustrations, all line drawings. An unusual publication not easily assessed in one reading (vol. 5 in a series).

331 Luks, Ilmar. Tipología de la escultura decorativa hispánica en la arquitectura mexicana del siglo XVIII. Caracas: Universidad Central de Venezuela, Centro de Investigaciones Históricas y Estéticas, 1980. 259 p.

La obra consta de dos partes: 1) *Sociedad Barroca en la Nueva España*, con referencias a los motivos europeos y su trasmisión trasatlántica, trasmisión interna y trasmisión de motivos, participación del indígena y categorías estilísticas; 2) *Catálogo Razonado*, es decir explicación de las figuras decorativas que reduce a tres grupos: grutescos, humanos y de animales. Con profusas y muy buenas ilustraciones. [L.G. Canedo]

332 Mexico. Instituto Nacional de Antropología e Historia. Seminario de Historia Urbana. Ciudad de México, ensayo de construcción de una historia. Alejandra Moreno Toscano, coordinadora; Carlos Aguirre A. *et al.* México: SEP, Instituto Nacional de Antropología e Historia, Departamento de Investigaciones Históricas, 1978. 235 p.; 2 fold. leaves of plates; ill. (Colección científica—INAH; 61: Historia)

Essays study growth of city from colonial times. First of a series. This volume covers: production centers (artisans, bakeries, tobacco factory), properties, social classes, political and medical factors, expansion of city (transportation; suburbs; transformation of central zone, 1936–70).

333 Montejano y Aguiñaga, Rafael. Tres planos antiguos de la ciudad de San Luis Potosí. San Luis Potosí, México: Academia de Historia Potosina, 1976. 28 p.; 2 fold. leaves of plates; bibl.; maps (Biblioteca de historia potosina: Serie cuadernos; 41)

Territorial limits of this city in colonial times are portrayed as derived from legal documents, including reproduction of two maps.

334 Moyssén, Xavier. Una maqueta de Rafael Jimeno (IIE/A, 12:48, 1978, p. 67–70, ill.)

Murals by Jimeno in the Capilla del Señor de Santa Teresa, Mexico, were destroyed in the earthquake of 1845. Their subject matter is revealed in the model of the chapel made by Jimeno. Good scholarship.

335 El Paisaje religioso de México. [v. 1] Los conventos del siglo XVI. [v. 2] El paisaje barroco de México. [v. 3] El paisaje churrigueresco de México. México: Fomento Cultural Banamex, 1975/1977. 3 v. (150, 150, 144 p.); chiefly ill. (some col.)

These three "journeys" into the religious landscape of colonial Mexico contain the finest illustrations available: 1) concerns conventos established by the three religious orders (Franciscans, Dominicans, Augustinians) in the 16th century; 2) *Barroco* concentrates on religious architecture and its attendant sculpture of the 17th and early 18th centuries; and 3) *Churrigueresco* covers the last half of the 18th century, the age of exuberance. Each volume contains over 100 illustrations, almost all in color. The eye of the professional photographer (eight of them) has captured vistas and details with extraordinary perception and sensitivity. Many are close-ups not normally seen and must have been taken with special equipment. The quality of the reproductions is unmatched. Texts are brief but definitive. The books are a joy to behold. Fomento Cultural Banamex deserves a special commendation for excellence and for achieving their stated objective of contributing to the knowledge and diffusion of the visual heritage of Mexico.

336 Palacio Nacional. México: Secretaría de Obras Públicas, 1976. 564 p.; bibl.; ill. (some col.)

A few years ago Mexico produced a singular monograph on its famed Cathedral. This is another monumental work on a specific building in Mexico City: the Palacio Nacional. It is epoch making in its thoroughness, presentation, graphics and format. The folio volume measures 15" × 18", has 567 p. and weighs perhaps 20 lb. Covers history of the site from the days of Moctezuma to President Echeverría. Details every architectural event (e.g., pre-hispanic structures; the "casas viejas" of Cortés; the Casa Real; the Casa de Moneda; the Real Palacio; the old and new Palacio de los Virreyes; and, lastly, the Palacio Nacional with its 19th- and 20th century uses, abuses and modifications). Replete with superb illustrations, many hitherto unpublished. Includes plans, sections; glossary contains sketches. Architectural developments take up first 200 p.; then follows: 85 p. of documentation; 13 p. of architects, artists, artisans; 76 p. concerning its furnishings, including Rivera's murals (the best illustrations yet encountered); the last 150 p. detail changes and restorations since 1928. Decision to publish it all in a single volume led to the oversized format. The awkward size, however, is totally redeemed by what lies between covers. A remarkably smooth text assembles the results of dozens of researchers. An outstanding monograph.

337 Palm, Erwin Walter. La fachada de la Casa de los Muñecos en Puebla: un trabajo de Hércules en el Nuevo Mundo (IIE/A, 12:48, 1978, p. 35–46, ill.)

On this tile covered house are 16 Hercules figures. Themes are traced from 16th-century Spain to a set of mirrors in the house. Another fine piece of research.

338 ———. La fachada-retablo de azulejos en Puebla (FAIC/CPPT, 15, 1978, p. 99–102, plates)

Notes how tile façades of three Puebla churches (two illustrated) differ from Spanish antecedents (one illustrated). Former imitate retablos, latter paintings.

339 Pierce, Donna L. The Holy Trinity in the art of Rafael Aragón: an iconographical study (New Mexico Studies in the Fine Arts [The College of Fine Arts of the University of New Mexico, Albuquerque] 3, 1978, p. 29–33, ill.)

Our knowledge of the *santos* of New Mexico is considerably furthered. Aragón's sudden switch to an unusual iconographic treatment of The Holy Trinity is brilliantly presented. Well researched. Good illustrations.

340 ———. Identifications of the warriors in the frescoes of Ixmiquilpan (Research Center for the Arts Review [University of Texas, San Antonio] 4:4, Oct. 1981, p. 1–8, ill.)

These "unique" 16th-century frescoes have baffled scholars. Earlier interpretations are convincingly refuted and replaced. A fascinating version of prehispanic attitudes and pictorial methods is apparent in these early colonial paintings. The mystery of non-Christian symbols and themes being employed in a Christian church is solved by this enterprising young "detective."

341 Ramírez Aparicio, Manuel. Los conventos suprimidos en México: estudios biográficos, históricos y arqueológicos. 3. ed. México: Editorial Cosmos, 1975. 291 p.; 31 leaves of plates; bibl.; ill.

After the mid-19th-century secularization of many of Mexico's conventos, author wrote (1861) a series of articles on these "suppressed" conventos. Their historic value warrants this new edition of the assembled articles. Includes many contemporary illustrations, mostly lithographs, and some details from oil paintings. Covered are: Santo Domingo; La Encarnación; La Piedad; Santiago Tlaltelolco; Atzcapotzalco; Portacoeli; San Francisco; La Concepción; Santa Clara; and Santa Isabel. Text is mixture of history, biography, anecdote, description.

342 Reyes-Valerio, Constantino. Arte indocristiano: escultura del siglo XVI. México: Escuela Nacional de Conservación, Restauración y Museografía, SEP-INAH, 1978. 326 p.

Autor se propone descubrir la mano del indio en la escultura mexicana del siglo XVI. Primer libro sobre este tema específico. Contiene una enorme cantidad de datos, probablemente casi todo lo que es posible decir hasta el momento. Enriquecen la obra 262 ilustraciones. [L.G. Canedo]

343 Robb, James Willis. Caminos cruzados de Manuel Toussaint y Alfonso Reyes (CM/D, 16:3 [93] mayo/junio 1980, p. 4–9, ill.)

Encounters between Mexico's pioneer colonial art historian, Toussaint, and Mexico's famed author, Reyes, mainly in the 1920s.

Robinson, Willard B. Colonial ranch architecture in the Spanish-Mexican tradition. See item **1969**.

344 Rojas Rodríguez, Pedro Mario. Tonantzintla. Fotografías del autor. 2. ed. rectificada. México: Universidad Nacional Autónoma de México, 1978. 86 p.; 33 leaves of plates; bibl.; ill. (some col.) (Colección de arte; 2)

The colored tiles and intricate stucco work that literally cover Santa María Tonantzintla, a small church a few miles south of Puebla, are entirely the work of its inhabitants. Performed over several centuries, the work and its result are inimitable. A delightful and rigorous study of this jewel, the volume includes very good illustrations (13 color, 64 b/w) and fills a notable gap.

345 Romero Quiroz, Javier. El Convento Hospital de Nuestra Señora de Guadalupe y del Señor San José; Recolección de Nuestro Padre San Juan de Dios de Toluca; El Teatro de los Hospitalarios. Toluca: Gobierno del Estado de México, 1976. 100,

25 p.; 1 fold. leaf of plates; bibl.; ill. (Serie Chimalphain [i.e. Chimalpahin])

Founded around 1695 by the religious order of the Hospitalers of Saint John of God, the convento/hospital also housed a theater and was converted into the Palacio de Justicia in 1872. Includes description, reconstruction drawing, a few photos of remaining elements. Significant is fact that development of theater in Mexico is linked to religious orders.

346 Ruiz, Sonia L. de. La Ciudadela: ideología y estilo en la arquitectura del siglo XVIII. México: Universidad Nacional Autónoma de México, 1980. 94 p.; 15 leaves of plates; ill. (Instituto de Investigaciones Estéticas. Cuadernos de historia del arte; 10)

The Real Fábrica de Tabaco (La Ciudadela) was one of the first "industrial" plants constructed in Mexico (1776–1807). Study examines it architecturally (neoclassic), socially (urban context), and economically. Employs methodology heretofore "not used in the history of art in Mexico." Well illustrated.

347 Talavera poblana: Pinacoteca Marqués del Jaral de Berrio, Fomento Cultural Banamex, A.C., septiembre/octubre, 1979. Mexico City: Fomento Cultural Banamex, 1979. 68 p.; ill. (some col.)

Catalogue for exhibition of ceramics, known as "Talavera" of Puebla, and drawn from private collection. Describes brief history of businesses and processes and stylistic influences. Includes 121 pieces (17th, 18th and 19th centuries) beautifully illustrated. Another excellent contribution by Banamex.

348 Tovar de Teresa, Guillermo. Pintura y escultura del Renacimiento en México. Prólogo de Diego Angulo Iñiguez. México: Instituto Nacional de Antropología e Historia, 1979. 570 p.; bibl.; ill. (some col.); index.

Author, only 22, has assembled the most extensive work on painters and sculptors active in Mexico during the 16th century. After a puzzling introduction (85 p.) the next 150 p. (first half) provide many archival references as well as extensive illustrations of 15 painters. Some additional 20 p. are devoted to sculptors. The second half (200 p.) is devoted both to paintings still in place in retablos (10) and to many others from lost retablos; another 35 p. deal with associated sculpture. Includes archival sources, bibliography, tables. This fine work is marred by inferior quality b/w reproductions. Even the few color illustrations are of only fair quality.

349 Vargas Lugo, Elisa. Dos aclaraciones iconográficas: la Inmaculada y San Sebastián en la Parroquia de Santa Prisca de Taxco (IIE/A, 13:47, 1977, p. 31–35, ill.)

Immaculate Conception (anonymous) in Santa Prisca, Taxco, is one of few paintings in colonial Mexico to use symbol of ship (illustrated). Author associates symbol as one of Mary's many allegorical titles. Sculpted San Sebastián in main altar of Santa Prisca bears strong resemblance to 1656 painting by Juan Carreño de Miranda (illustrated).

PARAGUAY

350 Plá, Josefina. El barroco hispano guaraní. Asunción: Editorial del Centenario S.R.L., 1975. 274 p.; 10 leaves of plates; bibl.; ill.

Compendium of historical accounts of missionary effort by Jesuits among Guaraní. Focus is on cultural aspects which produced a unique form of baroque. Chapters cover: configuration of mission churches (30); indigenous impact upon symbols and architecture; books and prints; what remains of architecture, paintings and sculpture, especially objects of pilgrimage. Includes four appendixes and 20 quality photos. Impressive and needed work.

PERU

351 Bernales Ballesteros, Jorge. Esculturas de Roque de Balduque y su círculo en Andalucía y América (EEHA/AEA, 34, 1977, p. 349–371, ill.)

Primary works of this Flemish sculptor are in Spain, particularly in the Parroquia of Chiclone de la Frontera. Author identifies Balduque's stylistic traits in a group of Lima statues.

Gisbert, Teresa. Iconografía y mitos indígenas en el arte. See item **304**.

352 ———. Los incas en la pintura virreinal del siglo XVIII (III/AI, 39 [39]:4, oct./dic. 1979, p. 749–772, bibl.)

Various viceregal representations of Inca rulers are traced from an original version: a lost engraving by Alonso de la Cueva made between 1724–28. Most proximate copy is a lienzo in Ayacucho, Peru. Also discusses portraits of Inca rulers by native artists, other publications, legal controversies, last portrait publication in 1804. Another fascinating study by this prolific scholar.

353 Harth-Terré, Emilio. Perú, monumentos históricos y arqueológicos. México: Instituto Panamericano de Geografía e Historia, 1975. 252 p.; bibl.; ill. (Monumentos históricos y arqueológicos; 17. Publicación—Instituto Panamericano de Geografía e Historia; no. 338)

This complete account of Peru's colonial architecture is a rarity. Selections from documentary sources are woven into text in a very readable manner. Author, an architect, writes with understanding and thoroughness. Separate chapters are devoted to Lima, Cuzco, Arequipa, Puno, popular architecture, and works of native architects. Also investigates retablos of Lima, other works of colonial painters and sculptors. Includes 60 quality b/w photos that provide good coverage even if they are not directly linked to text. The contribution is significant chiefly because of its comprehensiveness.

354 Lohmann Villena, Guillermo. Murallas y fortificaciones en el Perú durante la época virreinal (in Congreso Venezolano de Historia, 3rd, Caracas, 1977. Memoria. [see item **1741**] t. 2, p. 171–188, maps)

History of 19th-century walls of Lima and its coastal fort as Callao is traced and superimposed upon plan of present city.

355 Samanez Argumedo, Roberto. Plan COPESCO: experiencias en la restauración de monumentos (III/AI, 39 [39]:4, oct./dic. 1979, p. 863–875)

Notes criteria (set down in Plan COPESCO and implemented by Instituto Nacional de Cultura) for restoring and determining values of prehispanic and colonial monuments of Cuzco-Puno, Peru, area. Analyzes preservation efforts since 1934.

356 Sarmiento, Ernesto. El arte virreinal en Lima. Lima, Perú: Editorial Arica, between 1971 and 1980. 78 p.; bibl.; col. ill.; index.

Detailed "guide," with good illustrations, of Lima's architecture (by century), sculpture and painting.

357 Velarde, Héctor. Arquitectura peruana. Carátula de Grimaldo Romero sobre un dibujo arquitectónico de Carlos Villalobos. Fotografías: Fondo de Cultura Económica, México, Instituto Nacional de Cultura, Miguel Cisneros Cox. 3. ed. Lima: Librería Studium Editores, 1978. 446 p.; bibl.; ill. (some col.)

Third edition of original classic (1946) on the architecture of Peru written by an architect. Text is precise, analytical, descriptive and as complete as possible in a compendium covering prehispanic to contemporary architecture. Richly illustrated with 247 photos, a few of which are color, and four drawings. Selections are exceptionally good, many unique. Particularly intriguing are the "neo-Inca" and "international style" buildings. Weaknesses are the poor-to-fair quality of reproductions; nonlinkage of photos to text; lack of dates.

358 ———. El barroco, arte de conquista: el neo-barroco en Lima. Fotografía, Adelaida Agüero Cruces, Carlos Castagnola Guerra. Lima: Universidad de Lima, 1980. 72 p.; ill.

Well illustrated (b/w) selection of colonial architecture/sculpture from 10 cities in Peru. Short text analyzes these according to surfaces, design details, mass and volume. Last dozen pages illustrate "neo-Baroque" structures built between 1925–55. Unusual format. The quality of detail is excellent and better than overall scenes.

359 Zapatero, Juan Manuel. El Castillo Real Felipe del Callao (EEHA/AEA, 34, 1977, p. 707–733, ill., maps)

Investigates Spanish fortifications in Pacific including the two forts intended for the Straits of Magellan. Detailed study of coastal fort in Callao (Lima) through three centuries. Documented. Insights into maritime traffic in Pacific during 16th century.

VENEZUELA

360 Bellard Pietri, Eugenio. Las fortificaciones coloniales de Caracas y La Guaira (in Congreso Venezolano de Historia, 3rd, Caracas, 1977. Memoria. [see item **1741**] t. 1, p. 173–201, bibl., ill., map)

Describes 24 installations that provide defense to colonial Caracas. The foremost one, the coastal fort La Guaira (levelled in 1886), is shown as having had three lines of defense. Includes few layout plans, based on ruins.

361 Duarte, Carlos F. Museo de Arte Colonial de Caracas, "Quinta de Anauco." Caracas: Ediciones de la Asociación Venezolana Amigos del Arte Colonial, 1979. 353 p.; ill. (some col.)

Complete account of this beautiful 18th-century "casa," which today is a museum in the center of Caracas. Includes sharp photos and extensive catalogue (250 p.) of hundreds of objects arranged in 25 categories.

362 ———. El orfebre Pedro Ignacio Ramos. Caracas: Equinoccio, Ediciones de la Universidad Simón Bolívar, 1974. 128 p.; ill.

This is a sequel to Duarte's Historia de la orfebrería en Venezuela (1970, see HLAS 36:251) and focuses on the life and works of one silversmith, Pedro Ignacio Ramos, active in Caracas in the second and third quarter of the 18th century. Documentary sources are quoted in an appendix. Each work is fully described in another appendix. Includes 39 excellent photos, several in color. In addition to real scholarship the book itself is a work of art.

363 Gasparini, Graziano. Caracas, la ciudad colonial y guzmancista. Caracas: E. Armitano, 1978. 351 p.; ill. (some col.)

Impressive study of urban growth of Caracas. Distinguishes between the "integral" aspects of colonial structures and the politically motivated "monumental" qualities of buildings created under Guzmán Blanco (1870–88). Includes extensive archival sources and some very early depictions of the city. Illustrates structures now demolished. Carefully details reconstructions and changes. Includes excellent reproductions, both b/w and color. A masterful study and exemplary bookmaking and layout.

364 ———. Las fortificaciones del Puerto de la Guaira durante el período colonial (in Congreso Venezolano de Historia, 3rd, Caracas, 1977. Memoria. [see item **1741**] t. 2, p. 9–98)

Includes exhaustive compilation and analysis of documents (1590–1793) as well as extensive technical data pertaining to this coastal fort that protected Caracas.

Misle, Carlos Eduardo. Plaza Mayor—Plaza Bolívar: corazón pulso y huella de Caracas. See *HLAS 43:5292.*

365 Zapatero, Juan Manuel. Sistemática y procedimiento en los reconocimientos técnico-históricos de las fortificaciones americanas (*in* Congreso Venezolano de Historia, 3rd, Caracas, 1977. Memoria. [see item **1741**] t. 3, p. 539–549, plan]

Sets forth objectives and methodology for examining the technical and historical aspects of Spanish coastal fortifications in the Americas. Model for this vast undertaking was research and restoration (1975) of Puerto Cabello.

19th and 20th Centuries

JAMES B. LYNCH, JR., *Professor of Art, University of Maryland*

IN THIS, OUR LAST CONTRIBUTION to *HLAS,* we should like to review our stewardship of 15 years, served under three editors.

Beginning with *HLAS 30,* ART: SPANISH AMERICA, 19TH AND 20TH CENTURIES became a separate section under the present writer. In that tome we noted a preponderance of material from Mexico and Argentina—a disproportion which, in this volume, is limited to Mexico. The Caribbean, in *HLAS 30,* was poorly represented with a single entry each for Cuba, Panama, and Puerto Rico. In *HLAS 40,* Cuba alone had eight entries, while Jamaica and Santo Domingo were represented for the first time.

In the last 14 years, as scholars in the US and England have turned their attention to Latin American art, the lack of valuable works in English on the subject, which we lamented in *HLAS 30,* is no longer the case.

By 1972, when *HLAS 34* was published, works from Mexico, Argentina, and Venezuela predominated. In *HLAS 32* we had already noted the growing volume and excellent scholarship of Venezuelan studies, a trend that continues to this day. In contrast, Central American works were characteristically few in *HLAS 34* and of the Caribbean islands, only Cuba was strongly represented.

By 1974, our introduction to this section in *HLAS 36* was tinged with melancholy as we deplored the decline in quantity and quality of most of the literature arriving at the Library of Congress, with the exception of Mexico and Venezuela. Undoubtedly escalating inflation in Latin America was a potent factor in this trend. In the case of Mexico and Venezuela, however, generous and powerful banks took up some of the slack by subsidizing very elegant and expensive editions. Incidentally, banks and other commercial enterprises—so often damned in Latin America as devils of exploitation and imperialism—are assuming larger roles as patrons and benefactors of art in country after country.

HLAS 38 (1976) included three rather important entries from US scholars: Elizabeth Wilder Weisman's *The history of art in Latin America* (*HLAS 38:266*), Shifra Goldman's *Siqueiros and three early murals in Los Angeles* (*HLAS 38:359*), and Lawrence Hurlburt's *The Siqueiros experimental workshop: New York 1936* (*HLAS 38:363*).

In *HLAS 40* (1978) we welcomed "the growing activity of conferences and panels devoted to Latin American art here in the US," above all, the formation of the Association of Latin American Art (ALAA). In this volume we salute the Museum of Modern Art at Oxford (England) and Mexico's Instituto Nacional de Bellas Artes (INBA) for their joint sponsorship of an Orozco retrospective in England in 1980 (item **394**). Our return to Guadalajara on sabbatical in the fall of 1981—after an absence of more than 30 years—reinforced our conviction that Orozco is one of the major artists of this century.

Before closing, we sadly bring to your attention the deaths of two outstanding figures in modern Mexican art: Inés Amor and Juan O'Gorman. In 1935, Carolina Amor opened the first gallery in Mexico devoted exclusively to modern art. Several years later her sister Inés took over the gallery, then located on Calle Abraham González and now nearby on Calle Milán. Among her early clients and protegés were Orozco, Siqueiros, Tamayo, Julio Castellanos, Roberto Montenegro, and many others. It was largely through her efforts that the great 1940 Surrealist Show was held in Mexico, with contributions by Ernst, Duchamp, Di Chirico, Giacometti, Kandinsky, Kahlo, Bellmer, Delvaux, Miró, and Klee. Above all this Mexican aristocrat was, for all those who knew her, a wonderful human being.

Juan O'Gorman, a noted architect and painter, died in late January 1982. He designed the library of the National University of Mexico as well as an exotic "Aztec" home—his own—in the Pedregal. Among his major works in Mexico City were murals at the National Museum of Anthropology, the airport, and the Museum of Natural History.

GENERAL

366 Bailey, Joyce Waddell. State of the bibliography for Latin American art: survey of coverage, *Handbook of Latin American Studies* (Boletín: Handbook of Latin American Art [New Haven, Conn.] 1 : 2, Sept. 1981, p. 1–3, charts)

Survey of bibliographic treatment in the *HLAS* (vols. 1–41) by country of art of the 19th and 20th centuries. [J. Bailey]

367 Bayón, Damian. Impressions of Latin American architecture (International Review [United States Department of Housing and Urban Development, Office of International Affairs, Washington, D.C.] 1 : 4, Oct. 1980, p. 72–85, photos)

Distinguished architectural historian surveys the scene from another tour of Latin America. He notes that the great impulse government agencies gave to building in the 1950s and 1960s has now been succeeded by private enterprise. Brazil disappoints him except for José Zanine and Vilanova Artigas; likewise Paraguay and even Venezuela. On the other hand, Bogotá was a pleasant surprise.

368 Edwards, Jay D. The evolution of vernacular architecture in the western Caribbean (*in* Cultural traditions and Caribbean identity: the question of patrimony. Edited by S. Jeffrey K. Wilkerson. Gainesville: Center for Latin American Studies, University of Florida, 1980, p. 291–339, bibl., ill., map, plates, tables)

Although obfuscated by jargon, this is an invaluable work of scholarship in a neglected area. Author distinguishes between "folk" architecture ("refers to architecture . . . designed and constructed primarily by the people who reside in it") and "vernacular architecture" ("houses . . . constructed under the direction of a master builder or carpenter who usually receives remuneration for his services"). Edwards emphasizes the vernacular architecture of San Andrés, Providencia, and Great Corn Island, tracing it from the early 17th century to the present.

369 García Canclini, Néstor. Arte popular y sociedad en América Latina: teorías estéticas y ensayos de transformación. México: Editorial Grijalbo, 1977. 287 p.; 12 leaves of plates; bibl.; ill. (Teoría y praxis; 38)

Although many books of this type are verbal jungles in which the unwary reader soon becomes lost, this is simply written, and the ideas, however theoretical, are lucidly expressed. Text divided into: 1) "Teoría del Arte y Ciencias Sociales;" 2) "De las Bellas Artes a la Crisis de las Vanguardias;" and 3) "Propuestos para un Arte Popular Contemporáneo." Author's central viewpoint is art as a social and communicational process.

370 International handbook of contemporary developments in architecture. Edited by Warren Sanderson. Westport, Conn.: Greenwood Press, 1981. 1 v.; bibl.; indexes.

This large, excellent volume includes chapters on Argentina (Elizabeth D. Harris); Bolivia (Gustavo Medeiros); Chile (Ramón Alfonso Méndez); Colombia (Jaime Salcedo Salcedo); Cuba (James B. Lynch, Jr.); and Mexico (Edith S. Sanderson and Warren Sanderson). Among introductory essays on "Worldwide Developments" there is one on "Urban and Regional Planning in South America" by José M.F. Pastor, well worth reading. Although this lengthy volume has numerous photographs they are rather small and b/w. Highly recommended.

371 Panorama Benson & Hedges de la nueva pintura latinoamericana: Museo Nacional de Bellas Artes, Capital Federal, del 10 abril al 8 de mayo. Buenos Aires: Massalin y Celasco, 1980. 120 p.; bibl.; ill.; ports.

The exhibition here memorialized was the third sponsored by Benson and Hedges, the others having occurred in 1977 and 1978. Evaluated by a distinguished council of Latin American jurors, the present exhibition is well worth study for its representative sampling of the latest tendencies. Reproductions (none in color) are barely adequate. Includes good bibliography as well as brief biographical data.

372 Segre, Roberto. Las estructuras ambientales de América Latina. Portada de Angelo Hernández. México: Siglo Veintiuno Editores, 1977. 377 p.; bibl. (Arquitectura y urbanismo)

A prolific writer on Latin American architecture, especially Cuban, Segre treats his subject from a specifically Marxist viewpoint. Castro's Cuba in general is the criterion by which he evaluates the social and economic character of Latin American urban and rural problems. Brasília, it goes without saying, is particularly vulnerable to such methodology.

373 Squirru, Rafael F. Arte de América: 25 años de crítica. Buenos Aires: Ediciones Gaglianone, 1979. 506 p.; ill. (some col.)

The mind of this distinguished critic skims, often brilliantly, over an incredible number of subjects ranging from Rufino Tamayo, Antonio Berni, Edward Hopper, to Dominican art, the so-called Washington

"school of Color" (Louis, Noland), etc. Although flawed by superficiality, the book is quite provocative.

374 Traba, Marta. Artes plásticas latinoamericanas: la tradición de lo nacional (HISP, 8:23/24, agosto/dic. 1979, p. 43–68, bibl.)

Traba analyzes the development of cultural and artistic nationalism in Mexico, Brazil, Colombia, and Peru. As can be expected, the Mexican mural movement comes off badly because, according to the author, political dogmatism blinded the muralists to the revolution in contemporary art. Her treatment of other areas in Latin America can be thus summarized: nationalism has many faces. This is not vintage Traba: the ideas are often fuzzy, and the prose is gassy and prolix.

MEXICO

375 Arenal, Angélica. Páginas sueltas con Siqueiros. México, D.F.: Editorial Grijalbo, 1980. 279 p.; 30 p. of plates; ports.

Much valuable information, biographical and otherwise, from the wife of the artist. She emphasizes the formative influence on Siqueiros of his father and grandfather. Many, if not most, of the photos are published for the first time, but are of poor quality.

376 Báez Macías, Eduardo. Guía del Archivo de la Antigua Academia de San Carlos: 1844–1867. v. 3. México: Universidad Nacional Autónoma de México (UNAM), Instituto de Investigaciones Estéticas, 1976. 438 p.; plates (Estudios y fuentes del arte en México; 35)

A work of inestimable scholarly worth for those researching 19th-century Mexican art. Period covered is of course crucial to the development of San Carlos in the 1800s.

377 Bailey, Joyce Waddell. José Clemente Orozco, 1883–1949: formative years in the narrative graphic tradition (LARR, 15:3, 1980, p. 73–93, bibl.; ill.)

This provocative article sends waves through Orozco scholarship. Bailey's thesis: Orozco's early graphics "show expressionistic qualities that relate, not to European influences, but more logically to the narrative tradition of graphics in Mexico." Bailey is the first to suggest, contrary to Charlot's and

Orozco's and others' information about his graphics, that Orozco cut his own prints long before the late 1920s (e.g., the political cartoons for *El Ahuizote*). Of two lithographs which she offers as evidence for her thesis, *The Hanged Men* surely owes little to 19th-century narrative graphics, while *The Franciscan* is Giottoesque in provenience.

378 Las Calaveras vivientes de Posada. Selección, prólogo y comentarios de Carlos Macazaga Ramírez de Arellano y César Macazaga Ordoño. 2. ed. México: Editorial Cosmos, 1977. 120 p.; bibl.; ill.

A work of high quality, both in the various texts and in the reproduction. By prefacing the calaveras of Posada with a selective representation of precolumbian "calaveras," the publisher has provided a sense of continuity that illuminates the creations of Mexico's greatest graphic artist.

379 Cárdenas de la Pesna, Enrique. Un paisajista mexicano en la América Istmica. México: Fértica, 1978. 145 p.; bibl.; col. ill.

The artist in question is Jaime Gómez del Payán. Most of the text in this exquisite edition is an effusive but sensitive essay on Mexican landscape painting of the 19th and 20th centuries. The plates (with explanatory texts) reproduce an extraordinarily beautiful series of oils of landmarks from Panama to Guatemala.

380 Cardiel Reyes, Raúl. La filosofía del arte en el Porfirismo: la obra de Manuel Sales Cepeda (IIE/A, 13:47, 1977, p. 59–74, ill.)

Although Alfonso Caso in our time is credited with having introduced aesthetics into Mexico, actually this discipline was born in the writings of Manuel Sales Cepeda (1896) and of Diego Baz (1905). According to the author, Sales Cepeda, in particular, expressed the intellectual ambience of the Díaz era. Still, one has to be very knowledgeable of that ambience in order to relate it to the abstractions of Sales Cepeda's doctrines.

381 Charlot, Jean. José Guadalupe Posada and his successors (*in* Posada's Mexico. Edited by Ronnie C. Tyler [see *HLAS 42:1362*] p. 28–57, 18 b/w ill.)

Charlot's essay, some of which appeared in an earlier article in *Print Review* (1977), writes with the authority of Posada's

discoverer and promoter. He discusses the artist's early life in Aguascalientes, his association with his publisher in Mexico City, his friends and foes in the city and finally his artistic legacy and influences on later generations. [J.W. Bailey]

382 Chávez Morado, José. Apuntes de mi libreta. Ensayo crítico y referencias biográficas de Raquel Tibol. Fotografía en color, José Luis Aguirre. Fotografía en blanco y negro, Fernando Dorantes, Jesús González. México: Ediciones de Cultura Popular, 1979. 293 p.; chiefly ill. (some col.) (Colección Arte y literatura)

Except for a brief introduction by Tibol and for biographical data, this work is devoted entirely to the graphic art of Chávez Morado, which, to one who knows only his paintings, is surprisingly varied. Aside from being numbered, the copious reproductions are otherwise unidentified and undated— annoying deficiencies.

383 Conde, Teresa del. Un pintor mexicano y su tiempo: Enrique Echeverría, 1923–1972. México, D.F.: Instituto de Investigaciones Estéticas, Universidad Nacional Autónoma de México, 1979. 164 p.; 36 leaves of plates; bibl.; ill. (some col.) (Cuadernos de historia del arte; 12)

On the one hand, this is the first monograph on an important rebel of the 1950s movement; on the other, it is the first work in book form to chronicle, document, and discuss "la polémica del arte mexicano al mediar el siglo." This is a most important book for the student of the contemporary movement in Mexican art.

384 Cuevas, José Luis. Cartas para una exposición. México, D.F.: Unidad Azcapotzalco, Universidad Autónoma Metropolitana, 1981. 240 p.; bibl.; ill. (Cuadernos temporales; 4)

This fascinating volume consists for the most part of illustrated letters from Cuevas to his dealer José María Tasende in the US. The illustrations are not mere doodles but rather works of art, some of which throw new light on his oeuvre. Unfortunately some of the drawings are reproduced on such a small scale that the text is difficult to decipher. The book also includes a few poems to Cuevas from his friends.

385 Debroise, Olivier. Diego de Montparnasse. México: Fondo de Cultura

Económica, 1979. 135 p.; 24 p. of plates; bibl.; ill.

A much needed study of Rivera's Paris years, when he played a not insignificant role in the development of Cubism. As the extensive bibliography reveals, the author has drawn on many sources to produce this definitive work. A thorough knowledge of Diego's cultural ambience abroad enhances this monograph.

386 Elitzik, Paul. Discovery in Detroit: the lost Rivera drawings (OAS/AM, 32:9, Sept. 1980, p. 22–27, plates)

A most important discovery which, surprisingly enough, received little publicity at the time, is ably reported and analyzed here, with good reproductions of the full-scale cartoons and frescoes. Elitzik accurately notes that the outcry and impact of the Detroit murals is over.

387 Fernández, Justino and **Diego de Mesa.** Juan Soriano. México: Universidad Nacional Autónoma de México, Dirección General de Publicaciones, 1976. 161 p.; chief ill. (some col.) (Colección de arte; 32)

In his preface Fernández deftly characterizes Soriano's art as "un mundo de recuerdos infantiles reconstruídos imaginativamente." Fernández concentrates on Soriano's career between 1935–51, although the artist lived on until the early 1970s. Some of his late abstract paintings and sculptures, well illustrated, are "eye openers."

388 Goldman, Shifra M. Contemporary Mexican painting in a time of change. Austin: University of Texas Press, 1981. 229 p.; bibl.; ill.; index (The Texas Pan American series)

If one can by-pass the heavy road blocks of Marxist ideology and jargon, one will be richly rewarded by a very thorough and scholarly analysis of "Nueva Presencia" and its position between "Social Realism" (Mexican mural painting) and Mexican abstraction. Author gives special attention to such members and/or associates of Nueva Presencia as Arnold Belkin, Francisco Icaza, and José Luis Cuevas. Many b/w illustrations, ranging from good to mediocre. Highly recommended: a milestone in its field.

389 Leonel Masiel: "el realismo mágico" en la pintura (URSS/AL, 5:29, 1980, p. 91–99, plates)

Masiel returns shrewdly articulate answers to such questions as how he got into painting: the influence of "los grandes," Gabriel García Márquez and Miguel Angel Asturias; Masiel's place in contemporary Mexican art; and his opinions of surrealist art; etc.

Mexico. Instituto Nacional de Antropología e Historia. Seminario de Historia Urbana. Ciudad de México, ensayo de construcción de una historia. See item **332.**

390 ———— (Federal District). Oficina de Conservación de Edificios Públicos y Monumentos. Catálogo de monumentos escultóricos y conmemorativos del Distrito Federal. México: La Oficina, 1976. 351 p.; bibl.; ill. (some col.)

Among the various categories listed are: Bibliotecas; Construcciones Olímpicas; Edificios del Gobierno; Playas, Parques y Jardines; etc. Monuments are indexed alphabetically and a map of locations is thoughtfully provided. This is an indispensable volume for students of 19th and 20th-century Mexican sculpture.

391 Moreno, Nicolás. Paisaje y naturaleza en la obra de Nicolás Moreno. Presentación de Salvador Elizondo. México: Coordinación de Humanidades, Universidad Nacional Autónoma de México, 1980. 93 p.; chiefly ill. (some col.)

Introduction consists of Elizondo's efforts to distinguish between "naturaleza" and "paisaje" and to sketch (which he does less successfully) the development of landscape from the Dutch abroad to Rugendas and Velasco in Mexico. Illustrations show works good enough to arouse interest in biographical information, but none—strangely enough—is forthcoming.

392 Moyssén, Xavier. El *Retrato de Detroit* por Diego Rivera (IIE/A, 13:47, 1977, p. 45–58, ill.)

Moyssén relates the Detroit murals to those which preceded them in San Francisco and those which followed them in New York. He believes that in Detroit Rivera fully realized his desire to forge a union between "industrial" North America and "artistic" Latin America. Full of imaginative insights such as the machine-like Coatlicue which Moyssén seems to discern on the south wall.

393 Naranjo, Rogelio. Elogio de la cordura: para un retrato de la clase gobernante. Prólogo de Carlos Monsiváis. México, D.F.: Ediciones Era, 1979. 223 p.; chiefly ill. (Biblioteca Era: Testimonio)

Rogelio Naranjo, Monsiváis points out in his introduction, may be a caricaturist, but his cartoons are not really caricatures; instead, they constitute portraits of the ruling class. Among his targets: Porfirio Díaz, the PRI, the CTM, bureaucrats, politicians, etc. Naranjo is very talented.

394 National Institute of Fine Arts (INBA) and Ministry of Foreign Affairs, Mexico. ¡Orozco!, 1883–1949: an exhibition. Foreword by Margarita Valladares de Orozco. Oxford: Museum of Modern Art, 1980. 128 p.; bibl.; ill.

Organized by INBA and assembled by Fernando Gambao, Director of the Museum of Modern Art in Mexico City, this exhibition held in Oxford, England is a "slightly smaller version of the larger retrospective exhibition of Orozco's work held in . . . Mexico City . . . in 1979." The catalog is a "must" for any scholar or researcher concerned with Orozco. It contains *inter alia* excellent essays on the major periods of his art, a comparative chronology, and an invaluable bibliography. Many good color and b/w reproductions—some rarely published—round out this commendable work.

395 El Niño mexicano en la pintura. Mexico: Fomento Cultural Banamex, 1979? 95 p.; chiefly ill. (some col.)

Catalogue of an exhibition held at the Palacio de Iturbide, May–June 1979. The theme is a charming idea, and the realization of it is implemented successfully, with a minimum of sentimentality and cuteness. The sampling includes portraits from both the 19th and 20th centuries, ranging from the popular "niños muertos" of the 1800s to first communion themes and portraits by Rivera, Siqueiros, Rafael Coronel, etc.

396 Ramírez, Fausto. Dos momentos del simbolismo en México: Julio Ruelas y Saturnino Herrán (CM/D, 17:1 [97], enero/feb. 1981, p. 14–20, ill.)

According to this persuasive study Ruelas, influenced by Rops and Böcklin, restructured subject matter and form in late 19th-century Mexican painting, much as did

writers of the period. Ramírez examines critically the domestic ambience which formed Ruelas and Mexican Modernism. Treatment of Herrán, however, is rather superficial.

397 Reuter, Jas. Popular traditions (*in* Posada's Mexico. Edited by Ronnie C. Tyler [see *HLAS 42:1362*] p. 58–83, 15 ill.)

Reuter examines Posada's figural types (human and skeletal) and themes from the standpoint of common Mexican traditions. He cites the Day of the Dead, popular holidays, typical diet, children's games, and local customs as sources for the artist's repertoire of subjects. [J.W. Bailey]

398 Rivera, Diego. Arte y política. Selección, prólogo, notas y datos biográficos por Raquel Tibol. México, D.F.: Editorial Grijalbo, 1979. 460 p.; 21 leaves of plates; bibl.; ill. (Teoría y praxis; 50)

First anthology of Rivera's writings (1921–57). This compilation, of great importance to students of this artist, consists of nearly 70 documents, including letters. Preceded by a penetrating analysis by Raquel Tibol, the text with its wide range of subjects almost covers Rivera's entire career.

399 ———. Diego Rivera. v. 1, Pintura de caballete y dibujos. México: Fondo Editorial de la Plástica, 1979– . 1 v.; bibl.; chiefly ill. (some col.)

Monumental and definitive work which greatly advances Rivera scholarship. Many works reproduced in color for the first time in our knowledge. The bibliography alone makes the book invaluable.

400 Salinas, Miguel. Sitios pintorescos de México. 2. ed. México, D.F.: Editorial Cosmos, 1979. 166 p.; ill.

Nostalgic throwback to the 19th century, although first published in 1929. Even the illustrations (by Catalina Ramírez de Arellano Gil) are evocative of the age of the "costumbristas."

401 Tyler, Ronnie C. Posada's Mexico (*in* Posada's Mexico. Edited by Ronnie C. Tyler [see *HLAS 42:1362*] p. 2–27, 21 ill.)

Tyler's article, bearing the same title as the book which serves also as an exhibition catalogue (see *HLAS 42:1362*) summarizes the main points of the other essays. His aim is to place the artist in his historical context not only through standard sources but through the use of contemporary photographs and newspaper accounts. This approach is immensely successful and enlightening as seen in the catalogue for the exhibition beginning on p. 141. Tyler juxtaposes, for example, photographs of the bullfighter Gaona and Posada's broadsides about this hero of the bullring. Tyler's interdisciplinary collection of essays will be the standard reference on Posada for some time to come. [J.W. Bailey]

Velarde, Héctor. Arquitectura peruana. See item **357.**

CENTRAL AMERICA

402 Gutiérrez, Samuel A. Arquitectura actual de Panamá, 1930–1980. Panamá: Gutiérrez S.A., 1980. 351 p.; bibl.; ill.

Serviceable text with many photographs, ground plans, elevations, etc. of adequate quality comprise this study. Author notes two transitions occurred in modern times: 1) from neo-classical and neo-colonial to "modern;" and 2) from "modern" to "contemporary." Examples illustrated reflect a blend of North American and Latin American techniques and styles.

403 Historia del arte guatemalteco. José A. Móbil, compilador. 3. ed. Guatemala: Serviprensa Centroamericana, 1977. 416 p.; bibl.; ill.

Ambitious but flawed attempt to compress the history of Guatemalan painting, sculpture, architecture, music, popular art, and even literature into a volume of about 400 p. Result is superficiality, but the wealth of data may be useful for some researchers.

404 Mariño Sánchez, César et al. Desarrollo de la escultura en El Salvador. San Salvador: Editorial Universitaria, 1974. 269 p.; bibl.; ill. (Publicaciones del Departamento de Letras)

Divided into three sections, the text is weighted heavily toward the modern era. On the whole, however, this is a comprehensive survey, although one can agree with the author that to speak of a specific or characteristic Salvadoran sculpture is inaccurate. Includes biographical information concerning artists of today but poor photos.

CARIBBEAN (except CUBA)

405 Bergés, Robert L. Preservación arquitectónica en la República Dominicana: métodos divergentes (*in* Cultural traditions and Caribbean identity: the question of patrimony. Edited by S. Jeffrey K. Wilkerson. Gainesville: Center for Latin American Studies, University of Florida, 1980, p. 63–84)

Bergés' thesis—paraphrased, incidentally, in English and French—begins with a questionable assumption: "More than any other place [in the Western Hemisphere, the Dominican Republic] . . . offers architectural monuments from all the historical periods beginning with the early part of the 16th century." His discussion of preservation methodology, however, is worth reading. He divides restorers into four groups: purists, romantics, scenographers, and eclectics. According to Bergés, restoration can preserve the architectural heritage and rescue it from the despoliations of the Trujillo regime.

406 Bowen, Pamela. Errol Lloyd: Jamaican painter in London (IJ/JJ, 45, 1981, p. 46–55, ill.)

Thoughtful and perceptive study of a Jamaican painter who, through his art, tries to analyze and clarify the contradictions of Anglo and Caribbean cultures in the British capital. Errol Lloyd does so largely through the medium of black children, examining their roots.

Edwards, Jay D. The evolution of vernacular architecture in the western Caribbean. See *HLAS 43:8191.*

407 García Cisneros, F. Santos de Puerto Rico y las Américas. Translated from the Spanish by Roberta West. Detroit: Blaine Ethridge, 1979. 122 p.; bibl.; ill.

Author's thesis: ". . . the longest and most fertile of the traditions of religious folk sculpture in Latin America belongs to Puerto Rico." García Cisneros records the history of Puerto Rican "santos," discusses technical stylistic peculiarities, and relates them to other forms of this genre outside the island. Poor lighting, however, flaws examples illustrated.

408 Gómez, Eneid Routté. The agony of Puerto Rican art (FIU/CR, 9:3, Summer 1980, p. 16–18, plates)

The rather lurid title is the only dubious element in an otherwise commendable essay on the tensions and conflicts within the Puerto Rican art scene: isolation, cloying traditionalism, and the fate of the Institute of Puerto Rican Culture as it faces a new rival: the newly founded Ministry of Culture.

409 Hoffman, León-François. Notes pour servir a l'histoire de la peinture haitienne au XIXe. siécle (IFH/C, 151, mai 1981, p. 43–70, bibl., ill.)

Long meandering essay packed with valuable information which fulfills exactly the needs neglected in item **413**. Highly recommended for the specialist in Haitian painting.

410 Lahens, Wébert. Table ronde sur la peinture haitienne avant 1930 (IFH/C, 151, mai 1981, p. 19–24, ill.)

This ought to be read in conjunction with items **409** and **413** on Haitian painting before the rise of the so-called "Primitives" of the 1940s. Participants in this conference seek primarily to demolish the "myth"—invented by white students of Haitian culture—that Haitian painting scarcely existed before the 1930s.

411 Miller, Jeannette. Gilberto Hernández Ortega: o, La trascendencia de un universo mágico y poética. Fotografía, Onorio Montás. Santo Domingo: Galería de Arte Moderno, 1978. 62 p.; bibl.; ill. (some col.)

This professes to be the first in a series of studies edited by the Gallery of Modern Art and published by Artes Plásticas of Santo Domingo; as such it is welcomed. Hernández Ortega is a powerful Expressionist, at times recalling Wilfredo Lam. His works are reproduced in good color and adequate b/w.

412 ———. Historia de la pintura dominicana. 2. ed. s.i.: Amigo del Hogar, 1979. 106, 6 p.; bibl.; ill. (some col.)

As author notes, Dominican painting and sculpture sprang fully born like Athena, for they had no traditions of worth in the colonial period. The seminal decades were those of the 1930s and 1940s, when many foreigners settled on the island and when the Escuela de Bellas Artes was founded. Tolerably good illustrations depict a cross-sampling of modern works, some of which are of high quality and great talent.

413 Monosiet, Pierre. L'art haitien avant 1930 (IFH/C, 151, mai 1981, p. 9–14, ill.)

This brief undocumented study indicates that patronage of foreign and native Haitian artists began under Henri Christophe and continued under subsequent regimes of the 19th and 20th centuries. Much more information on the long period before the emergence of the "Primitives" of World War II would have been highly desirable. Nevertheless, simply by focusing on the problem of the origins of Haitian modern art, this little article serves a modest purpose.

Museo de las Casas Reales. Plano monumental de Santo Domingo. See *HLAS* 43:5443.

414 Tolentino, Marianne de. Cándido Bidó: el artista y su obra. Prólogo, Arnulfo Soto. Fotografías, Onorio Montás. Barcelona: C. Bidó, 1980. 192 p.; ill. (some col.)

Interesting glimpse into the art of a Dominican painter of middle years, born into poverty, and of his struggle to become an artist. Perhaps this background accounts for the pervasive presence in his art of a symbolic and, at times, almost unbearable intense blue.

415 Volders, Jean Lonis. Bouwkunst in Suriname: driehondred jaren nationale architectur. Paramaribo, Surinam: C. Kerstein & Co., 1973. 152 p.; bibl.; ill.; maps; plates.

Fascinating book on the architecture of Surinam not previously annotated in *HLAS* because of lack of Dutch reviewer. Includes more than 280 pen drawings. Floor plans of buildings are reproduced on scale of 1:400. Although Surinam's architectural style is unique, it shares certain characteristics with Dutch and US colonial styles. Text is arranged according to: 1) topography (city, district); 2) ethnography (Indian, American Indian, Bush-Negro influences); 3) construction materials (wood, brick, etc.); 4) building's purpose/function (town house, plantation, fort, monument, etc.). Includes bibliography and English summary at the end of each chapter. [Joyce Darilek]

CUBA

416 Beltrán, Félix. Acerca del diseño gráfico antes y después de la Revolución (BNJM/R, 70 [21]:2, 3. época, mayo/agosto 1979, p. 52–72, ill.)

Before the Revolution, claims Beltrán,

the graphic arts were prostituted by the ruling bourgeois class; now they are at the service of the people. Moreover, in the bad old days, the Academy of San Alejandro excluded graphic artists: they had to teach themselves or learn through correspondence courses. These few lines reveal the general drift of Beltrán's essay.

417 Díaz Peláez, José Antonio. Actividades escultóricas en nuestro proceso actual (BNJM/R, 70 [21]:2, mayo/agosto 1979, p. 133–138)

Many Cuban sculptors teaching today recall years before the Revolution when they lived in poverty and could find no market for their works. In the mid-1970s collective projects began to proliferate, and as early as the late 1960s meetings and congresses—four in all—began to take place as described by author. Worth reading for its historical value.

418 Juan, Adelaida de. Pintura cubana: temas y variaciones. México, D.F.: Universidad Nacional Autónoma de México, 1980. 173 p.; 32 p. of plates; bibl.; ill. (some col.); index (Cuadernos de historia del arte/Instituto de Investigaciones Estéticas; 15)

This ambitious project consists of a series of essays on Cuban art from the end of the colonial period through Castro's Revolution. Not precisely a history it is rather a unified skein of studies based on "temas y variaciones." The result is a perceptive and highly informative text, well documented, but (surprisingly) without bibliography. The few illustrations are almost all b/w.

419 Museo Nacional de Cuba. Museo Nacional de Cuba, pintura: retratos de Fayum, pintura europea, pintura cubana. Edición, Ricardo González Jane, Liudmila Vedénskaia, Svetlana Khval. Redactor artístico, Serguey Diachenko, en colaboración con el Museo Nacional de Cuba. La Habana: Editorial Letras Cubanas [and] Leningrado: Editorial de Artes Aurora, 1978. 21, 248 p.; chiefly ill. (some col.)

Founded in 1913, the National Museum of Cuba is divided into three sections: Cuban, European, and Ancient. The European has some speculative attributions (e.g., Rubens, Memling, Carpaccio, Reynolds, Canaletto, etc.). Some Fayum portraits from Egypt grace the Ancient sector. Cuban art is represented by certain little known but fine landscapes of the 19th century as well as

such modern painters as Abela, Peláez, Portocarrero, and Lam.

420 Silva, Enrique. Ramón Haití: un paso firme en la escultura cubana (UEAC/GC, 167, mayo de 1978, p. 19, plates)

Brief but thoughtful essay on an artist who, although he came late to the craft of sculpture, attained quick mastery and maturity. Haití has opted for native Cuban woods in contrast to the more conventional materials of the modern sculptor.

421 Torriente, Loló de la. Exposición Sosa Bravo (UEAC/GC, 167, mayo 1978, p. 11–12, plates)

In the year of publication of this article La Galería Habana celebrated the prior three years of activity of Alfredo Sosa Bravo—painter, draftsman, printmaker, and ceramist. Author believes that the Cuban Revolution was a catalyst which transformed and enriched his art.

422 Veigas, José. El cartel cubano abierta la encuesta (RYC, 71, julio 1978, p. 76–80, plates)

Veigas poses, and others answer, these questions: Do differences exist between the posters of the 1960s and those of the present decade (1970s)? Have the latter maintained the quality of the period 1968–72? What ought the Cuban poster to be in the next few years? Important article for those investigating this specialized field.

423 ———. Mirta Cerra: prefirió la pintura (RYC, 91, marzo 1980, p. 58–61, plates)

Trained by Romanach, the father of modern Cuban painting, this member of the second generation of Cuban art has remained neglected—unaccountably so since Cerra's work is very talented. Her prints, executed in 1935–36 when Cerra was a student at the Art Students' League in New York, were virtually unknown until a recent exhibition in Havana.

SOUTH AMERICA
ARGENTINA

424 Alva Negri, Tomás. Miguel Angel Vidal, una versión clásica del arte geométrico. Traducción inglesa de I.E.N. Buenos Aires, Argentina: Ediciones de Arte Gaglianone, 1979. 101 p.; 11 leaves of plates; bibl.; col. ill.

Vidal is analyzed under the rubric of "arte generativo," a kind of synthesis of "op" and geometric art. Author succeeds in establishing European roots for the flowering of Vidal in a text which is unusually articulate and perceptive. Excellent color plates.

425 Arean, Carlos. La pintura de Miguel Angel Vidal y la tradición concretista argentina (CH, 348, junio 1979, p. 656–660, ill.)

Author believes that "arte generativo," one of the chief by-products of "arte concretista," owes far more to the tradition of the latter than to North American "hard edge" and op art. Indeed, so far as foreign influences are concerned, Vantongerloo, Rayonism, and Vasarely prevailed. Essential differences between Vidal and MacEntyre are perceptively analyzed in this well written essay.

426 Arte bajo la ciudad: murales cerámicos, cementos, relieves y esculturas de los Subterráneos de Buenos Aires = Art beneath the city: ceramic murals, cements, reliefs, and sculptures of the Buenos Aires Subway System. Obras, Fernando Alvarez Sotomayor *et al.* Textos y comentarios, Jorge Bossio *et al.* Fotografías, Hervé K. Cordón. Versión inglesa, Pamela Corey Archer. Buenos Aires: M. Zago, 1978. 275 p.; bibl.; ill. (some col.) (Colección Arte en Buenos Aires; 1)

Most of these Buenos Aires subway murals consist of ceramic tiles; others are of polychrome cement or of wooden, bronze or cement sculpture. They depict the following themes: Spanish Landscapes; America and Spain; Jesuit Missions; Argentine Myths and Legends; the Conquest of the Desert; etc. The ceramic murals are often hackneyed and tediously conventional; the polychrome cement ones, on the other hand, are more interesting.

427 Gaspar di Genaro: artífice y maestro; paisaje plástico puntano (Andén para la Cultura [Ediciones Candilejas, Córdoba, Argentina] 1 : 1, set./oct. 1979, p. 10–13, ill.)

About half of this article is a self-evaluation of Gaspar di Genaro; half is an appraisal of contemporary art in the province of San Luis, Argentina. As such, this latter section is a helpful addition to the growing studies of provincial Argentine art.

428 Magrini, César. José M. Moraña, 1973–1978 [i.e. mil novecientos setenta y tres hasta mil novecientos setenta y ocho]: estudio crítico-biográfico. Buenos Aires: Ediciones Dead Weight: distribuidas por Editorial Losada, 1979. 32 p.; 32 leaves of plates; ill. (some col.) (Colección La Barca gráfica: Arte)

The text is easily forgettable. The passably good illustrations, on the other hand, are worth study. They reveal an interesting and articulate addition to surrealism, Latin American style.

429 Nicolini, Alberto. La inmigración y sus consecuencias en la actividad arquitectónica: 1869–1914 (*in* La inmigración en la Argentina. San Miguel de Tucumán, Argentina: Universidad Nacional de Tucumán, Facultad de Filosofía y Letras, Centro de Historia y Pensamiento Argentino, 1979, p. 269–276 [Publicación—Universidad Nacional de Tucumán; 1255])

Thoughtful exposition of the theme that the enormous waves of foreigners between 1869 and 1914 transformed Argentina architecturally as well as sociologically. The relatively narrow Hispanic culture was enriched by technological and stylistic innovations from Europe and the US introduced by a "foreign" technical and professional element.

430 Payró, Julio E. 23 [i.e. Veintitrés] pintores de la Argentina, 1810–1900. 3. ed. Buenos Aires: Editorial Universitaria de Buenos Aires, 1978. 63 p.; ill. (some col.) (Biblioteca de divulgación: Colección Siglo y medio; E2)

The title is self-explanatory. After a thoughtful and informative introduction Payró has commendably inserted a chart with data regarding activities of Argentine and foreign artists. Concise helpful biographical information, along with at least one representative work by each artist, rounds out this study.

CHILE

431 Carvacho Herrera, Víctor. Veinte pintores contemporáneos de Chile. Santiago, Chile: Departamento de Extensión Cultural del Ministerio de Educación, 1979? 78 p.; ill. (some col.) (Colección Historia del arte chileno; libro 4. Serie El Patrimonio cultural chileno)

Highly recommended for the student of 20th-century Chilean painting. While not a history of this subject, the text manages to present a good cross section. Author, incidentally, is to be congratulated for his objective and indeed excellent study of Matta, an artist who is persona non grata in present-day Chile.

432 Helfant, Ana. Los pintores de medio siglo en Chile. Santiago, Chile: Departamento de Extensión Cultural del Ministerio de Educación, 1978. 66 p.; ill. (some col.) (Colección Historia del arte chileno; libro 3. Serie El Patrimonio cultural chileno)

Devoted to a number of painters active in the second half of the 19th century. While their works are provincial and sometimes naive compared to those of their European contemporaries, they are for the most part honest and truthful transcripts of life and nature.

433 Nagel, Victor F. Mireya Lafuente: escanfandrismo: color form and transparency. New York: Pilgrim Press, 1979. 36 p.; bibl.; ill. (some col.)

The poetic euphoria of the text is often mystical nonsense. On the other hand, the reproductions—especially those in color—reveal a novel and often impressive talent in the marriage of painting and astrophysics.

434 Núñez del Prado, Marina. Eternidad en los Andes: memorias de Marina Núñez del Prado. Fotografía, Carol Sioles, Antonio Eguino, Freddy Alborta Trigo. Dirección de arte, Mario Fonseca Velasco. Santiago, Chile: Editorial Lord Cochrane, 1973. 227 p.; 111 leaves of plates (5 fold.); ill.

Influences as disparate as prehispanic sculpture and the works of Archipenko and Arp can be seen in the art of Núñez del Prado. "Abstract eroticism" best characterizes this sculptor, who deserves wider recognition.

COLOMBIA

435 Carbonell, Galaor. Olga de Amaral, desarrollo del lenguaje. Bogotá: Litografía Arco, 1979. 136 p.; 1 leaf of plates; ill. (some col.)

According to author, Amaral is considered a "constructionist." The monograph traces Amaral's early training in Bogotá to her study at the Academy of Fine Arts in Cranbrook (US), where she studied textiles, and her return to Colombia. Excellent photographs, especially in color, reflect the sensitive play of color, texture and three-dimensional form of Amaral's works.

436 Cárdenas, Jorge and Tulia Ramírez de Cárdenas. Museo de Arte de Medellín Fco. Antonio Zea. Fotografías de Gabriel Carvajal. Cali, Colombia: Tall. Gráf. Banco Popular, 1977. 125 p.; ill. (some col.((Biblioteca Banco Popular)

Housed in a strikingly modern building, this collection has few masterpieces; nevertheless, there are a number of works of charm and quality, particularly of the late 19th and the 20th centuries. One finds here an impressive portrait by Francisco Antonio Cano, a fine picture of his son by Fernando Botero, and a striking portrait by Diego Rivera.

437 Mark, Edward Walhouse. Acuareles de Mark, 1843–1856: un testimonio pictórico de la Nueva Granada. Editor, Joaquín Piñeros Corpas. 2. ed. Bogotá: Banco de la República, Litografía Arco, 1963. 348 p.; 2 leaves of plates; col. ill.

The Banco de la República spared no expense in publishing this extraordinary volume. Edward Walhouse Mark was British Vice-Consul, beginning in 1843, at Santa Marta and then Bogotá. His water colors, handsomely reproduced, are those of a technically naif but discerning *costumbrista*.

438 Martínez Sanabria, Fernando. Trabajos de arquitectura. Diagramación, investigación y textos, Fernando Montenegro L., Jaime Barreto O., Carlos Niño M. Bogotá: Escala Fondo Editorial, 1979? 211 p.; ill. (Colección Arquitectura)

Modern Colombian architecture, dating so the author tells us from 1937, has been neglected by writers. This monograph serves to introduce a distinguished architect, beginning with his housing for the new town of Tumaco ("International Style" in design) through more expressive shapes of brick in the 1960s and 1970s. Houses such as the Casa Calderón, beautifully reproduced in color, reflect a powerful and original talent.

439 Serrano, Eduardo. Paisaje, 1900–1975 [i.e. mil novecientos–mil novecientos setenta y cinco]; exposición Museo de Arte Moderno, Bogotá, 1975. Bogotá: Salvat Editores Colombiana, 1975. ca. 150 p.; bibl.; 71 ill. (some col.)

Only by the widest stretch of the imagination could the reproductions of this book be subsumed under the rubric "landscapes." Nevertheless, it is good to have a monograph devoted to a genre which is not the most popular in Latin American art. The b/w illustrations do little to stimulate the reader's appreciation, the color plates are much more effective. The beginnings of Colombian landscape painting are inadequately presented.

440 Traba, Marta. Los grabados de Roda. Fotografías de Oscar Monsalve. Bogotá: Museo de Arte Moderno, 1977. 81 p.; ill.

Profound study of one of Latin America's most gifted printmakers. Traba traces Roda's stylistic and thematic development from the "Escorial" through the "Tumbas," self-portraits, "Retratos de un Desconocido," "Risa," and other series. Illustrations, however, are mediocre.

PERU

441 Szyszlo, Fernando de. Fernando de Szyszlo. Texto: Mario Vargas Llosa. Diseño fotografía: Werner Lang. Lima: LL Editores: Banco Popular del Perú, 1979. 117 p.; bibl.; ill. (some col.) (Colección Pintores peruanos)

Vargas Llosa rightfully singles out "elegance" as the major element of Szyszlo's art. Excellent reproductions in color reveal the strong influence of Mexico's Rufino Tamayo upon this artist's more recent paintings.

VENEZUELA

442 El Avila: Guaraira Repano. Caracas: Ediciones Armitano, 1978. 94 p.; ill. (some col.) (Serie Pintores venezolanos)

This originated in a 1977 retrospective honoring landscapists—old and modern—of the environs of Caracas. Included are Melbye and Pissarro, Baron Gros, and other *cos-*

tumbristas; Tovar y Tovar, Michelina, Boggio, Reverón, Monasterios, etc. Enchanting color reproductions and an excellent text.

443 Barrios, Armando. Armando Barrios. Textos por Juan Röhl. Fotos blanco y negro, Miguel Barrios. Caracas: E. Armitano, 1974. 160 p.; bibl.; ill. (some col.)

The text is unimpressive—the usual clichés about painting and music and about cubism—and can be passed over except by the beginner. On the other hand, the color reproductions, which are superb, are well worth the reader's viewing. A number of the latter appear to be published for the first time.

444 Calzadilla, Juan. Arturo Michelena. Fotografías, Georges de Stenheil. Caracas: E. Armitano, 1973. 234 p.; col. ill,

Valuable work divided into several parts including a chronological essay, a study of Michelena's time, and evaluation of his oeuvre and of his draftsmanship, etc. Good reproductions round out this definitive monograph.

445 ———. J. Arraga. Fotografías, Virgilio Azuaje. Caracas, Venezuela: Gráficas Armitano, 1972. 32 p.; bibl.; ill. (some col.)

Julio Arraga, whose career spanned the first half of our century, has rightfully been rescued from undeserved obscurity by Calzadilla. Besides an illuminating biography, this study contains a stylistic analysis of Arraga's art. Some of his views of Maracaibo are reproduced side by side with photographs for fruitful comparisons. A brief bibliography completes this worthwhile monograph.

446 ———. Movimientos y vanguardia en el arte contemporáneo en Venezuela. Sucre: Consejo Municipal del Distrito Sucre, 1978. 159 p.; ill. (some col.)

Covers virtually all movements in contemporary painting and sculpture, including "op art," abstract expressionism, surrealism, the integration of the arts in University City, Caracas, etc. Quite good reproductions but without titles and dates.

447 Elgar, Frank. Poleo. Edición a cargo de Graziano Gasparini. Caracas: Ediciones Armitano, 1980. 44 p.; 70 leaves of plates; bibl.; ill. (some col.)

In three texts—Spanish, French, and English—Elgar traces and adequately accounts for the abrupt stylistic changes in Poleo's art. Good plates; helpful biographical information.

Gasparini, Graziano. Caracas, la ciudad colonial y guzmancista. See item **363.**

448 Museo de Arte Contemporáneo de Caracas. Obras maestras de Armando Reverón. Caracas: Museo de Arte Contemporáneo de Caracas, 1979. 63 p.; ill. (some col.)

Two good essays, especially the one by Boulton, give a brief but cogent analysis of Reverón's genius. Difficult to photograph adequately, select works of his "white" and "sepia" periods are here reproduced with considerable accuracy.

449 Pineda, Rafael. Tres libros para Reverón (CONAC/RNC, 40:243, enero/marzo 1980, p. 90–100)

The three books (all of 1979) are: a new revised edition of Alfredo Boulton's monograph of 1969, including a most important autobiographical account by Reverón himself; a catalogue raisonnée by Juan Calzadilla; and a book of criticism, also by Calzadilla, comprised of opinions by 18 writers.

450 Ratto Ciarlo, José. Carlos Otero, su vida, su obra, su época. Caracas: Ediciones Armitano, 1978. 219 p.; bibl.; ill. (some col.) (Serie Pintores venezolanos)

Those who expect the highest quality in typography and photographic reproductions from the *taller* of Armitano will not be disappointed here. Although Otero never progressed beyond a vaguely Impressionist technique, he captured with charm and truth the Venezuelan landscape and the people, as these fine plates prove.

451 Reverón, 18 [i.e. dieciocho] testimonios. Gaston Diehl, et al. Compilación y selección, Juan Calzadilla y Wuilly Aranguren. Síntesis cronológica, Humberto Mata. Biblio-hemerografía y notas biográficas, Wuilly Aranguren. Fotos, Archivo Nacional de las Artes Plásticas, Galería de Arte Nacional y Archivo Fotográfico de Lagoven. Caracas: Lagoven, 1979. 100 p.; bibl.; ill.

A kind of *festschrift* for the greatest modern Venezuelan painter. Among the better known contributors: Alejo Carpentier, Alfredo Boulton, Marta Traba, Alejandro Otero. The texts originated in a plan to develop an exhaustive "biblio-hemerografía" for a catalogue raisonnée.

BRAZIL

JOSÉ NEISTEIN, *Director, Brazilian-American Cultural Institute, Washington, D.C.*

AMONG REFERENCE WORKS RECENTLY RELEASED, attention should be called to a history of silversmithing in Brazil (item **456**) and a richly illustrated overview of Brazilian art addressed to the general public (item **452**). Some polemical and theoretical works also deserve special mention, such as "Aspectos da Arte Brasileira" (item **463**), "O Moderno e o Contemporâneo" (item **457**), and two important works on Brazilian crafts (items **454** and **461**).

In colonial art, there is Fernando R. Cortez's essay, a novelty that is not solidly grounded (item **467**). A facsimile edition of Barlaeus's rare and basic work (item **465**), a great classic of 17th-century Brazilian studies, is most welcome as is the monograph of Eckhout (item **470**). The 19th-century is well represented by a book on Almeida Júnior (item **472**) and by an article entitled "Rugendas no Brasil" (item **474**).

Studies of 20th-century Brazilian art continue to command the most attention and to grow in volume and importance. Items **479, 486, 488–489** and **491** are worthy of special mention, for they deal with significant areas and offer overall views; item **487,** for its monographic interest.

In this volume, the subsection on "Indian Traditions" includes only one work but a very important one for it concerns three editions of the catalogue to an exhibit entitled "Arte Plumária no Brasil" (item 501), the most beautiful and comprehensive exhibition of Indian featherwork ever assembled.

There has been a remarkable increase in the quality and quantity of works on Brazilian photography, of particular interest being those that use photography as documentary, essay, or for aesthetic purposes (see especially items 503 and 507–510).

In the subsection on "Architecture and City Planning," items 514 and 516 are worthy of note, because of their sociohistorical implications.

In the subsection on "Cartoons," a stylistic study of comic strips and art-deco offers something new on the topic (item 519).

Finally, a catalogue entitled O *Design* no Brasil (item 522) constitutes an excellent source of information on Brazilian design and gathers a wealth of pictorial material on the subject.

REFERENCE AND THEORETICAL WORKS

452 Arte no Brasil. São Paulo: Abril S/A Cultural de Industrial, 1979. 2 v. (1080 p.); ill. (some col.); index.

Originally published in fascicles format for sale to the general public in newsstands all over Brazil, book was also bound in two volumes after all 50 fascicles appeared. An excellent vehicle for popular promotion, the volumes are written in straightforward language, contain basic information on the artists, trends and their historical contexts. Lavish reproductions are in color and portray the art of the native Indians of many tribes, Portuguese art brought across the Atlantic in the first centuries of the colonization, the gradual development of an aesthetic language uniquely Brazilian, architecture, decorative arts, the arts during the Dutch occupation of Pernambuco in the 17th century, naïve painters and folk traditions, etc. Although the work's comprehensiveness and breadth makes it somewhat superficial, the scholars, critics and photographers who worked on the project succeeded in making the volumes accessible, attractive, inexpensive and popular.

453 Arte transcendente: exposição de pintura. Introduction by Luiz Seraphico; essay and notes by Theon Spanudis. São Paulo: Museu de Arte Moderna de São Paulo, 1981. 40 p.; ill.

Subject of the show: art and religion, and their relationship both on the rational and irrational levels, especially the subtle non explicit religiosity of contemporary art. Artists included in the show were: Rubem Valentim, Niobe Xandó, Valdeir Maciel, Jandyra Waters, Milton Dacosta, José Antônio da Silva, Fernando Odriozola, Fang Cheen Kong, Eleonore Koch, Mira Schendel, Volpi, Arnaldo Ferrari, and Tomie Ohtake. Excellent illustrations in color.

454 Artesanato brasileiro. Equipe, Roberto Parreira *et al.* Pesquisa e legendas, Raul Giovanni da Motta Lody. Programação ao visual, Miriam Struchiner, Sara Grosseman. Colaboração do Rodolfo Capeto. Foto capa, Luís Antônio Duailibi. Texto introdução, Clarival do Prado Valladares. Textos capítulos, Vicente Juarimbu Salles. Participação de Luís Marcelo da Costa Camargo *et al.* Rio de Janeiro: Edição FUNARTE, 1978. 165 p.; bibl.; ill. (some col.)

Overall view of Brazilian handicraft and craftsmen covers ceramics, works on wood, fiber, weaving, lace, metal and other materials. Historical introductions underscore social milieus, demands and availability of specific materials in each environment, and resulting artifacts. Individual chapters deal with technical aspects of each medium, and resulting artistic end products. Many excellent photographs in color and b/w. Glossary and bibliography round up this commendable publication.

455 Azevedo, Paulo Ormindo D. de. Monumentos do Município do Salvador, Bahia. Executado por Paulo Ormindo D. de Azevedo. Coordenador, Vivian Lene R. Correia Lima. Auxiliares técnicos, Célia Maria Perdigão Coutinho *et al.* Salvador: Secretaria da Indústria e Comércio, Coordenação de Fomento ao Turismo, 1973. 323 p.; bibl.; ill. (Inventário de proteção do acervo cultural; v. 1)

Official inventory of architecture in city of Salvador, Bahia, Brazil, from 16th to 19th centuries arranged according to following categories: religious (52); military (8); public (18); private (46); industrial (1). Each building and site is extensively analyzed: history, dates, styles, renovations, materials, conditions, plans, photos (quality). Professional work. One of the most thorough inventories/catalogues yet encountered. Lengthy bibliography. [R. J. Mullen]

456 Bardi, Pietro Maria. Arte da prata no Brasil. São Paulo: Banco Sudameris Brasil, 1979. 135 p.; bibl.; col. ill. (Arte e cultura; 2)

Covers production of silver artifacts in Brazil from colonial days to late 19th century, chiefly in Bahia, Pernambuco, Minas Gerais and Rio de Janeiro. Storytelling journalistic text accurately describes historical aspects and artistic accomplishments, underscoring the relationship between the Portuguese and Spanish-speaking worlds. Great variety of excellent reproductions of religious and secular artifacts.

457 Brito, Ronaldo and Paulo Venâncio Filho. O moderno e o contemporâneo: o novo e o outro novo. Rio de Janeiro: FUNARTE, 1980. 48 p.; ill.

Vol. 1 of series on Brazilian contemporary art published by FUNARTE. Essays, some of them controversial, draw comparisons among Brazilian artists, discuss local and international influences, their concerns, anguish and critical approaches: Ronaldo Brito's "O Moderno e o Contemporâneo: o Novo e o Outro Novo;" Paulo Venâncio Filho's "Lugar Nenhum: o Meio de Arte no Brasil;" Hélio Oiticica's "Brasil Diarréia;" Cildo Meireles' "Cruzeiro do Sul;" and José Resende's and Ronaldo Brito's "Mamãe Belas Artes." Includes many illustrations b/w and color of works by European, American and Brazilian 20th-century artists.

458 Fekete, Joan. Dictionário universal de artistas plásticos. Prefácio e capa de Nelson Vainer. Rio de Janeiro: Editora Companhia Brasileira de Artes Gráficas, 1979. 377 p.; port.

Designed for quick consultation by the layman, dictionary contains only elementary information about artists (e.g., Brazilian painters, sculptors and printmakers). No illustrations.

459 Pintura e escultura II. Carlos Ott; Joaquim Cardoso; and Nair Batista. São Paulo: Ministério da Educação e Cultura; Instituto do Patrimônio Histórico Artístico Nacional: Universidade de São Paulo, Faculdade de Arquitetura e Urbanismo, 1978. 157 p.; bibl.; ill. (Textos escolhidos da Revista do Instituto do Patrimônio Histórico e Artístico Nacional; 8)

Consists of the following studies: Joaquim Cardoso's "Notas sobre a Antiga Pintura Religiosa em Pernambuco;" Nair Batista's "Pintores do Rio de Janeiro Colonial: Notas Bibliográficas;" Valentim da Fonseca e Silva's "Caetano da Costa Coelho e a Pintura da Ordem Terceira de São Fransico de Penitência;" and Carlos Ott's "José Joaquim da Rocha." These scholarly essays discuss their subjects with accuracy and detailed documentation. Volume includes b/w photographs and facsimiles of documents.

460 Rio antigo: roteiro turístico-cultural do centro da cidade. Rio de Janeiro: EMBRATUR; AGGS, 1979. 201 p.; ill.

Welcome new guide covers a fascinating aspect of Rio de Janeiro: its artistic and cultural heritage. Underscores the 18th and 19th centuries, their art, architecture, city planning, old streets, parks, and gardens. Rio is presented through its main centers and surrounding neighborhoods: Praça Quinze, Praça Mauá, Largo da Carioca, Largo de São Francisco, Passeio Público, Praça da República, Avenida Presidente Vargas, Gamboa, Saúde and Cais do Porto. Text provides essential information and many drawings complement the narrative.

461 Seminário Bases Culturais do Artesanato, Belo Horizonte, Brasil, 1978? Seminário Bases Culturais do Artesanato. Promoção e coordenação, Centro de Artesanato Mineiro. Patrocínio, FUNARTE, Coordenadoria de Cultura de Minas Gerais. Belo Horizonte: Impr. Oficial, 1978. 80 p.

In 1978 FUNARTE organized a seminar to study and sum up the realities of traditional handicrafts of Minas Gerais, including past and present, media and materials, the craftsman and his environment. Reproduces polemics on folk artist and/or versus craftsman. Compares with European traditions that were the basis for Minas Gerais. Unfortunately no illustrations and no bibliography.

462 Souza, Washington Peluso Albino de.
Aleijadinho: símbolo de cultura autô-
noma (UMG/RBEP, 48, jan. 1979, p. 7–46)
Speculative essay on Aleijadinho. Regards him not only as a symbol of Minas
Gerais' autonomous culture but as a symbol
of autonomous cultures in general. Attempts
to "read" Aleijadinho's plastic language in a
new way, in which reality and myth—or self-
generated myth as the case may be—are the
main coordinates. A debatable interpretation.

463 Souza, Wladimir Alves de *et al.* As-
pectos da arte brasileira. Introdução
de João Vicente Salgueiro. Rio de Janeiro:
FUNARTE, 1981. 133 p.
This anthology of texts edited by
Afonso Henriques Neto covers a number of
important chapters in the history of Brazilian
painting, architecture and printmaking:
"Frei Ricardo do Pilar and Manoel da Costa
Athayde;" "Taynay;" "Debret and Granjean
de Montigny;" "Vitor Meireles and Pedro
Américo;" "José Ferraz de Almeida Júnior
and Rodolfo Amoedo;" "The Group Grimm;"
"The Brothers Bernardelli;" "Eliseu Visconti and Art Criticism in Brazil;" "Carlos
Oswald;" "Raimundo Cela and Oswaldo
Goeldi;" "Anita;" "Di Cavalcanci;" "Tarsila:
the First Faces of Modernism;" and "Cândido
Portinari." Stimulating "mise-au-point." No
illustrations unfortunately for those who are
less familiar with the output of the artists
discussed.

COLONIAL PERIOD

464 Amaral, Aracy Abreu. A hispanidade
em São Paulo: da casa rural à Capela
de Santo Antônio. São Paulo: Nobel: Ed. da
Universidade de São Paulo, 1981. 1 v.; bibl.
Amaral discusses the influences of
Hispanic culture in Brazil, both in art and
architecture from the middle of the 16th century—in the Captaincy of São Vicente—to
the end of the 17th century, through trade
and family ties. Amaral continues questioning began by Mário de Andrade in the 1920s
and by Luís Saia in the 1940s and 1950s. Her
contribution underscores such influence particularly in the art produced in colonial São
Paulo. Some striking comparisons are drawn
among São Paulo, Paraguay, the River Plate
provinces, and Bolivia. Rich iconography,
documentation and bibliography cast new
light on this little studied subject.

465 Barlaeus, Gaspar. História dos feitos
recentemente praticados durante oito
anos no Brasil. Prefácio de José Antônio Gonçalves de Mello. Recife: Fundação de Cultura
Cidade do Recife, 1980. 1 v.
Gaspar van Baerle, alias Gaspar Barlaeus (1584–1648) was a humanist who accompanied Count Johann Mauritz von
Nassau-Siegen to Brazil in order to write the
history of his administration for the Dutch
Crown in Pernambuco (1637–44). The result
was this book, a major title in rare Brasiliana,
published in Latin (Amsterdam, 1647). The
printer and publisher, Johann Blaeu, included
55 prints after drawings by Frans Post in the
first edition. They covered many cities in
Northeastern Brazil other than Pernambuco,
but also important places in Portuguese Africa and Chile. This new edition includes a
portrait of the Count who later became a
Prince, the Portuguese translation of Barlaeus' text with many notes on and by European historians of the period who wrote
about Dutch Brazil, and reproductions of all
55 etchings printed in off-set from the 1647
original Dutch edition. This new one is so
well printed that it is destined to become a
rare book itself.

466 Bittencourt, José Bastos. Ouro Preto:
Aleijadinho, monumentos, outras
cidades. 2. ed. Belo Horizonte: Editora São
Vicente, 1977? 194 p.; 8 leaves of plates;
bibl.; ill.
Basically a visitor's guide, the book
underscores the strong presence of Aleijadinho in Ouro Preto. Author theorizes that
Aleijadinho projected his own spiritual life
into the Church as evident in the iconography of Saint Francis of Assisi in Ouro Preto.
Color reproductions and photographs of poor
quality.

467 Cortez, Fernando Russel. Vasco Fernandes, 1° pintor do Brasil (IHGB/R,
320, julho/set. 1978, p. 346–369)
Essay points out fact that Vasco Fernandes was probably the first artist to record
the appearance of the "new man" found by
Cabral in the New World: the aborigine of
Brazil. Uses panel of the Epiphany of Viseu
as an example. Discusses Vasco Fernandes'
role only in the context of Portuguese painters of the first half of the 16th century. Not
enough reference, comparison or analysis to
support essay's main point.

468   Museu de Arte Sacra da Bahia. Text by Antonio Jaime Soares. Photographs by Januário Garcia. Rio de Janeiro: FUNARTE/ Embratur, n.d. 28 p.; ill.

Chapters are devoted to the six Carmelites who founded in 1660 the Convent of Saint Thereza in Salvador which is now the Museu de Arte Sacra da Bahia; the location of the museum; the culmination of the Carmelites' mission in Bahia; the decline thereof; the museum and its collection of rare pieces. One of the best museums in Brazil, it was organized by Dom Clemente Maria da Silva Nigra and includes an extraordinary cross section of the best of Luso-Brazilian religious art from the 16th to the 19th centuries. The building itself is a masterpiece of colonial architecture. Excellent photographs and reproductions both in b/w and color.

469   Negro, Carlos del. Nova contribuição ao estudo da pintura mineira: norte de Minas: pintura dos tetos de igrejas. Rio de Janeiro: Ministério da Educação e Cultura, IPHAN, 1978. 431 p.; bibl.; ill.; index (Publicações do Instituto do Patrimônio Histórico e Artístico Nacional; 29)

Major study covers known and lesser known—but not less important for that matter—churches in Diamantina; Couto de Magalhães; Inhí; Conceição do Mato Dentro; Congonhas do Norte; Santo Antônio do Norte; Córregos; Costa Senna; Sêrro; Itapanhoacanga; São Gonçalo do Rio das Pedras; Alvorada de Minas; Santo Antônio do Itambé; Minas Novas; Berilo; Chapada do Norte; and Arcângelo. Includes 18th- and 19th-century paintings in churches and sacristies, many of which were not studied or photographically documented before. A standard work in its field.

470   Valladares, Clarival do Prado and **Luiz Emygdio de Mello Filho.** Albert Eckhout: pintor de Maurício de Nassau no Brasil, 1637–1644. Revisão crítica e atualidade por Clarival do Prado Valladares. Verbetes científicos por Luiz Emygdio de Mello Filho. Reproduções das obras do acervo da Seção Etnográfica do Museu Nacional de Copenhague-Dinamarca. Fotos, Claus Meyer. Rio de Janeiro/Recife: Livroarte, 1981. 148 p.; ill.; photos.

Dutch painter Albert Eckhout (b. Gröningen, 1610) was one of Prince Mauritz von Nassau-Siegen's group of artists and scholars who accompanied him to Brazil (1637–44) where he served as Governor of Pernambuco. Eckhout painted Brazil's fauna, flora and natives in minute detail and close-up, in contrast to his colleague Frans Post who painted the same subjects in panoramic views. For more than 300 years Eckhout's paintings have been in Denmark. This is a lavishly printed book whose excellent reproductions in color illustrate Luiz Emygdio de Mello Filho's explanations of the many plants, fruits, and animals depicted by Eckhout. Clarival do Prado Villadares' research identifies Eckhout as the most faithful among European artists to record the impact of experiences in Brazil. Moreover, the fact that 600 additional Eckhout drawings have been discovered in Krakow, Poland, as illustrations for "Theatrum Rerum Naturalium Brasiliae" augurs well for a thorough reevaluation of the artist's significance in Brazilian studies.

471   Verdier, Jeanine. Les tentures des Indes (OEIL, 297, avril 1980, p. 44–51, plates)

Discusses recent scholarly contributions to the study of the Gobelin tapestries made in the 17th and 18th centuries as depicted in the visual register of Maurice de Nassau's Dutch expedition to Brazil where he served as governor (1637–44). The so-called "Tentures" are perceived as based on Post's and Eckhout's drawings and paintings. Reality and imagination in the portrayal of Brazil's fauna and flora are the issue.

19TH CENTURY

472   Almeida, José Ferraz de. Almeida Júnior, vida e obra. Editor, Marcos Antônio Marcondes. Fotografias, Rômulo Fialdini Lula Rodrigues. São Paulo: Arte Editora, 1979. 58 p.; 54 leaves of plates; bibl.; ill. (some col.)

Born in Itu, São Paulo's interior, Alméida Júnior attended Rio's Academia Imperial de Belas Artes and later, under the patronage of Emperor Dom Pedro II, left to study in Paris arriving during Zola's hard-fought campaign for Cézanne's recognition. This episode together with his study of Delacroix, Corot and Millet exercised the greatest influence on his work. One of the most representative of Brazil's 19th-century painters, Almeida Júnior was nationalistic in his approach. He painted *caipiras*, Indians, mestiços, historical canvases, and portraits of some of the most representative personalities of São Paulo. This book draws together critical appraisals by his contemporaries, chronology of his life, and a basic bibliography. Reproductions, many in color, convey Almeida Júnior's best work to the contemporary reader.

473   Rio de Janeiro. Museu Nacional de Belas Artes. Aspectos da paisagem brasileira, 1816–1916: abril de 1977. Rio de Janeiro: MEC-DAD-FUNARTE-INAP-MNBA, 1977. 56 p.; ill.

Catalogue of an exhibition sponsored by FUNARTE and held at the Museu Nacional de Belas Artes, Rio de Janeiro. On display were some of the most representative national and foreign artists who painted the Brazilian landscape from 1816–1916. Information on the artists is sufficient for laymen but scanty for specialists and the introductory note is too general. Reproductions are b/w only.

474   Rugendas, Johann Moritz. Rugendas no Brasil. Textos y comentários por Newton Carneiro. Rio de Janeiro: Livraria Kosmos Editora, between 1976 and 1979. 225 p.; ill. (some col.)

Johann Moritz Rugendas (1802–58) was a fourth-generation member of a family of artists, Germans of Catalan origin. Especially important in the history of Brazilian iconography, Rugendas is regarded as one of the most expressive and comprehensive European artists who worked in Brazil in the 19th century. The talented and young (age 19) Rugendas was engaged by Russian Consul von Langsdorff to accompany him on a scientific expedition commissioned by the Imperial Academy of Sciences of St. Petersburg. The result was a remarkable collection of lithographs, drawings, watercolors, and paintings produced by Rugendas while in and after returning from Brazil. The great bulk of this collection remains to be published and is held in Leningrad collections. The chief merit of this book is the reproduction of drawings never published before, also held in private and public collections in Europe and Brazil. They include portraits, cityscapes, landscapes, farms, and aspects of life in Rio, São Paulo, Pernambuco and Minas Gerais as well as depictions of native tribes,

flora and fauna. Rarely reproduced lithographs and paintings never published before are also included. This valuable and limited edition is further enhanced by Newton Carneiro's scholarly text.

475   Tempski, Edwino Donato. Paulo Assumpção: o pintor e escultor de Curitiba (Boletim [Instituto Histórico, Geográfico e Etnográfico Paranaense, Curitiba, Brazil] 35, 1979, p. 219–237, plates)

With the help of family papers, newspapers collections and some bibliography, Tempski presents a short biography of Paulo Assumpção within the context of Curitiba's cultural life in the second half of the 19th century. Very little is said about Assumpção's art.

476   Valladares, Clarival do Prado. Tempo e lembrança de D. Pedro II: um estudo iconográfico de Clarival do Prado Valladares. Rio de Janeiro: Museu Nacional de Belas Artes, 1977. 64 p.; ill. (some col.)

Iconography gathered and studied by Valladares encompasses sculpture, painting, architecture and photographs, some of them lesser known, some rare. Author tries to establish the "style" of Brazil's Second Empire through a combination of history and visual arts. Many reproductions in b/w, some in color.

20TH CENTURY

477   Ayala, Walmir. O Brasil por seus artistas / Brazil through its artists. São Paulo: Círculo do Livro; Rio de Janeiro: Nórdica, 1980 or 1981. 211 p.; col. ill.

Consists of Brazil's landscape, life, symbols and nature as seen by 100 painters from the 18th and 19th centuries, but mostly from the 20th century. Each painting is reproduced both in its entirety and in close up. Text in Portuguese and English provides biographical information and short analysis of the artists selected. Deluxe edition. High quality of color reproductions.

478   Bento, Antônio. Macunaíma: ilustrações do mundo do herói sem nenhum caráter de Carybé. Rio de Janeiro: Livros Técnicos e Científicos Editora, 1979. 100 p.; ill.

Series of drawings illustrate principal scenes from *Macunaíma*, seminal book of

20th-century Brazilian literature by Mário de Andrade. The artist Carybé (pseudonym for Héctor Bernabó) was born in Argentina but spent his childhood in Italy after which he came to Rio. Returning to Buenos Aires for a few years, he eventually settled in Bahia as a Brazilian citizen. Carybé's illustrations, created in 1943 while in Argentina and enthusiastically received by Andrade himself, convey a visual synthesis of Macunaíma's life in a rhapsodic style reminiscent of the writer's own. Rich, exuberant, intricately detailed, the drawings exude biting humor and deep understanding of the "hero with no character," an interpretation of Brazilian psychology.

479 **Brecheret:** 60 anos de notícia. Sandra Brecheret Pellegrini, compiladora. s.l.: s.n., between 1976 and 1978. 172 p.; ill. (São Paulo: Companhia Melhoramentos de São Paulo)

This is a long overdue monograph on Brecheret (b. 1894, d. 1955, São Paulo), one of Brazil's greatest sculptors. Book gathers information covering 60 years, including decade following the artist's death. Biographical material is enriched with documentation and analysis of his output, from intimate little pieces to spectacular public monuments. Works in cemeteries deserve a special chapter. Rich iconography includes newspaper clippings, drawings, projects, actual reproductions, and aspects of the artist's private life. Opposite poles in his development, according to the book, were Brecheret's relationship to European art (1922–37), on the one hand and on the other, his fascination with native Brazilian Indian traditions. A superb "art deco" sculptor, Brecheret also knew how to channel his creativity by integrating the most genuine contributions of Brazil's past. The Brecheret Museum of São Paulo, his former residence, was the chief source for this book. Many statements by contemporaries and current artists and critics enhance this beautifully printed edition.

480 **Brentani, Gerda.** Gerda Brentani: edição realizada por ocasião da mostra retrospectiva realizada no Museu de Arte Moderna de São Paulo em setembro de 1977. São Paulo: MAM, 1977. 72 p.; chiefly ill. (some col.)

Well deserved recognition has been granted Gerda Brentani in recent years. This catalogue of her show (São Paulo, 1977) includes texts by João Leite, Luís Ernesto Kawall, and Paulo Vanzolini. Born in Trieste in 1908, she emigrated to Brazil in 1938, and was strongly influenced by some members of São Paulo's "Grupo Santa Helena." Good reproductions in color and b/w show many aspects of her creative imagination, but above all her love of animals and her sense of humor apparent in both paintings and drawings.

481 **Carlos Prado:** pintura, desenho, gravura. São Paulo: Museu de Arte Moderna de São Paulo, 1976. 1 v. (Unpaged); plates.

Catalogue of major show by unjustly neglected São Paulo artist active from the 1930s through 1970s, himself an indirect product of the Week of Modern Art of 1922. The show consisted of more than 120 works, among paintings, drawings and prints. Only seven are reproduced here but the introductory notes by Paulo Mendes Campos, who uses valuable contemporary remarks by Sérgio Millet, are good.

482 **Da grafia pura de Solange** e linguagem selvática de Miguel ao evocativo barroco de Maurino. Organização da exposição e coordenação de catálogo, Conceição Piló. Fotografias, Aderi Luiz da Costa. Belo Horizonte: Museu de Arte, Prefeitura de Belo Horizonte, Secretaria Municipal de Cultura, Turismo e Esportes, 1978. 95 p.; ill.

This reference work is reasonable as an iconography of this three-person show but a poor reference work insofar as their biographical, bibliographical and critical information is concerned.

483 **Grabadores brasileños contemporáneos.** Text by Emanuel von Lauenstein Massarani. México: Museo de Arte Carrillo Gil, 1980. 30 p.; ill.

Catalogue of an exhibition that included prints by: Aldemir Martins; Anna Letycia; Arthur Luiz Piza; Clarisse Gueller; Edith Behring; Fayga Ostrower; Gilvan Samico; Isabel Pons; Marcelo Grassmann; Maria Luisa Beer; Marília Rodrigues; Octávio Ferreira da Araújo; Thereza Miranda; Vera Bocayuva Mindlin; Walter Lewy; Bernardo Cid de Souza Pinto; Daro Bernardes; Darel Valença Lins; Eduardo Iglesias; Evandro Carlos Jardim; Guilherme de Faria; João Rossi; Maria Bonomi; Renina Katz; Saverio Castelano; Servulo Esmeraldo; and Ubirajara

Mota Lima Ribeiro. Includes excellent reproductions in color and information in Portuguese and Spanish.

484 Homenagem a Bonadei: junho/julho 1978. São Paulo: Museu de Arte Moderna de São Paulo, 1978? 1 v. (Unpaged); plates.

Neglected for a long time, Aldo Bonadei eventually attained recognition as one of Brazil's major painters of the last 30 years. His avant garde, abstract and figurative periods, his relationship to the immediate Brazilian tradition and to Cézanne's craft are underscored in the introductory essay by Mario Schenberg. Most of the 81 paintings included in the show are reproduced, many in color.

485 Leite, José Roberto Teixeira. Pintura moderna brasileira. Rio de Janeiro: Editora Record, 1978. 162 p.; bibl.; ill. (some col.); index.

In spite of the title's all-encompassing assumption, author discusses only 14 painters, all of whom are regarded as Brazil's major 20th-century artists, certainly among its most representative and seminal. Individual chapters, consisting of a biographical introduction and critical evaluation, are devoted to the following: Tarsila do Amaral; Lasar Segall; Alberto da Veiga Guignard; Alfredo Volpi; Emiliano Di Cavalcanti; Vicente do Rego Monteiro; Ismael Nery; José Pancetti; Cândido Portinari; Cícero Dias; Djanira da Motta e Silva; Iberê Camargo; Milton Dacosta; and Antonio Bandeira. Includes basic bibliography and excellent color reproductions.

486 Memória do Atelier Coletivo: 5/fevereiro/52 a outubro/57. José Cláudio, compilador. Recife: Artespaço; São Paulo: Renato Magalhães Gouvêa-Escritório de Arte, 1979. 88 p.; ill.

Art scholars have devoted much study to the brilliant and influential Week of Modern Art that took place in São Paulo in 1922. In contrast, younger scholars have concentrated on the emergence of other artists elsewhere in Brazil, a trend exemplified by this monograph on the Atelier Coletivo of Recife (1952–57). José Cláudio discusses the artistic role played by him as well as by Abelardo da Hora, Ionald Marius, and Samico. A well-documented study illustrated with many b/w photographs and reproductions.

487 Milton Dacosta. Texts by Luiz Antonio Seráphico de Assis Carvalho, Antônio Bento, Jacob Klintowitz, Olívio Tavares de Araujo, Olney Krüse, Jayme Maurício and Cesar Luís Pires de Mello. São Paulo: Museu de Arte Moderna, 1981. 174 p.; ill.

Catalogue for a major exhibition of Milton Dacosta's output (1936–81) constitutes the best reference work on the artist. Although partly influenced by concretism, it was in the 1950s, when constructivism held sway in Brazil, that Dacosta's career began. By the 1960s and 1970s he had become one of the most consistent Brazilian painters because of his sense of color, strong intuitions, a blend of humanism and geometry, and the sensuousness of his paintings. Short texts point out his principal traits. Catalogue also includes a resumé of the artist's life, his b/w portrait, individual descriptions of all 165 paintings displayed in the retrospective, many of which are admirably reproduced in color.

488 Morais, Frederido and **Barbosa Lima Sobrinho.** Cenas da vida brasileira 1930/1954: 10 pinturas e 100 litografias de João Câmara Filho. Recife: Prefeitura da Cidade do Recife, Fundação Roberto Marinho, Grupo Othon, 1980. 184 p.; ill.

Title of this book: *Scenes from Brazilian life: 1930–1954* is also the title of a series of 10 paintings and 100 lithographs by João Câmara Filho. In a critical manner, they depict episodes and characters in Brazilian public life during the time of Gétulio Vargas. Both the series and book deal with art as a social institution. Author Morais notes: "There is no surrealism in the *Scenes*. Everything in them is under rigid control and the scenes respond specifically to the plastic requirements of the series as a whole allowing paintings, in turn, to comment on each other." Book also includes essay on Getúlio Vargas by Barbosa Lima Sobrinho; an extensive interview with artist Câmara Filho by author Morais; many quotes from the catalogue published when the entire series was shown in Rio and São Paulo; a critical appreciation guide; some biographical and bibliographical information; and reproductions of 10 paintings, many in close up, as well as a whole set of lithographs. Unfortunately, book lacks information on the identity of many characters depicted in the series. The good quality of the printing makes this volume an important event in Brazilian art publishing.

489 Neistein, José. Feitura das artes. São Paulo: Editora Perspectiva; Washington: Brazilian-American Cultural Institute, 1981. 172 p.; ill.

Consists of 40 essays on Brazilian artists whose works have been exhibited at the Brazilian-American Cultural Institute's Gallery in Washington, D.C. Essays discuss over 100 artists who represent major techniques and aesthetic trends in Brazilian art since the 1970s. Book was written in the course of the past decade by BACI's director who organized exhibits of Brazilian art in the US. Prepared as introductions to the shows, the essays consist of critical analysis of painters, sculptors, draftsmen, as well as folk and Indian art. With rare exceptions, these artists are still alive and active. Major contemporary currents are also discussed and the book could serve as a reference on Brazilian art of the 1970s, presented from inside and outside Brazil. Written in Portuguese, the book is illustrated with dozens of b/w reproductions.

490 Panorama 81: Text by Luiz Seraphico. São Paulo: Museu de Arte Moderna, n.d. 52 p.; ill.

Catalogue of exhibition of 44 sculptors from all over Brazil who represent many different trends. Introductory essay discusses crisis and continuity in culture and how its results are reflected in contemporary Brazilian sculpture. The role played by the Museum of Modern Art is also examined. Excellent reproductions in b/w.

491 Um Século de escultura no Brasil/One century of sculpture in Brazil. Organized by Museu de Arte de São Paulo Assis Chateaubriand. Texts by P. M. Bardi and Jacob. Coordinated by Antonio Teixeira da Silva. Translated by Laura Viarengo. São Paulo: Raízes Artes Gráficas, 1982. 158 p.; ill.

The Art Museum of São Paulo organized a major retrospective show of Brazilian sculpture of the last 100 years with the cooperation of São Paulo's Skultura Gallery and private collectors from Brazil and abroad as well as the support of Philip Morris. P. M. Bardi served as curator of the show's figural sculptures and Jacob Klintowitz of the informal ones. Although incomplete and selective, the show was representative. The 123 b/w reproductions in this catalogue convey the development of sculpture in Brazil. They underscore the contributions of foreign artists who became lively participants of the Brazilian art scene, they note the native contribution as well as the symbiosis of both and the impact of international trends. The small and superficial texts are inappropriate for a show of this magnitude. They lack specific information on the artists exhibited and provide no analysis of their significance or aesthetic contribution.

492 20 [i.e. Veinte] pintores brasileños.

Catalogue of an exhibition organized for the Academy of Fine Artes in Santiago, Chile, on the occasion of the visit of President João Baptista Figueiredo, by the Art Museum of São Paulo Assis Chateaubriand. Text by P. M. Bardi. São Paulo: Raízes Gráficas, 1980. 44 p.; ill.

Catalogue of major exhibition of Brazilian painting held in Santiago, Chile, includes brief analysis of each artist, technical description of each work, and excellent color reproductions. Artists were: Eliseu Visconti, Lasar Segall, Anita Malfatti, Tarsila do Amaral, Alfredo Volpi, Alberto da Veiga Guignard, Emiliano Di Cavalcanti, Ismael Nery, Cândido Portinari, José Pancetti, José Antônio da Silva, Wesley Duke Lee, José Antônio van Acker, Evandro Carlos Jardim, Samuel Szpigel, Ermelindo Nardín, Maria Helena Chartuni, João Câmara Filho, Miguel Domingos dos Santos and Siron Franco.

493 Vergara, Carlos. Carlos Vergara. Texto de Hélio Oiticica. Rio de Janeiro: Edição FUNARTE, 1978. 46 p.; ill. (some col.) (Arte brasileira contemporânea)

Monograph discusses Vergara's participation in the Brazilian avant garde of the 1960s and 1970s, his ties to neo-concretism and events thereafter. Text is by Hélio Oiticica who was also a member of the avant garde and whose untimely death deprived Brazil of an important creative force. This fact lends special interest to the publication. Includes many excellent photographs and reproductions in color and b/w.

494 Volpi, as pequenas grandes obras: três décadas de pintura. Text by Olívio Tavares da Araújo. Curator: Ladi Biezus. São Paulo: Gallery A Ponte, 1980. 92 p.; ill.

According to the critical consensus, Volpi is the most important living Brazilian painter. In his 80s, he is still as creative as ever. Assembled from private collectors, this show consists only of small canvases produced over the past three decades, a small but representative selection. Text also emphasizes the last three decades of the artist's life and describes each one of the 65 canvases. Includes excellent quality color reproductions.

FOLK ART

495 Alvim, Fausto. A imaginária da Fausto Alvim. Pampulha, Belo Horizonte: Prefeitura de Belo Horizonte, Secretaria Municipal de Cultura, Informação, Turismo e Esportes, Museu de Arte Moderna, 1976? 37 p.; ill.

In her introductory essay to this folk sculptor, Lélia Coelho Frota points out Alvim's roots, the "language" of his carvings, his themes, and his relationship to nature. Also includes texts by Clarival Valladares, Fausto Alvim Júnior, Afonso Arinos de Mello Franco, Carlos Drummond de Andrade, Ciro dos Anjos, Henriqueta Lisboa, Alberto Deodato and Vivaldi Moreira. Good reproductions in b/w.

496 Corrêa, Carlos Humberto. Quatro artistas da cerâmica. Florianópolis, SC, Brazil: Universidade Federal de Santa Catarina, between 1978 and 1981. 103 p.; ill. (Arte e artesanato; 1. Cerâmica)

Santa Catarina's folk ceramics are less known but as fascinating and distinctive as the traditions of northern and northeastern Brazil. Published by the Federal University of Santa Catarina, the book examines the output of such individualized artists as Nézia, Ademar, Cascaes and Eli. Includes scholarly text by Carlos Humberto Corrêa and excellent b/w photographs.

497 Rodrigues, José Mário. A cultura do Nordeste expressa em Santo de Barro [Interior [Revista bimestral. Ministério do Interior, Brasília] 6:31, março/abril 1980, p. 4–7, plates)

Brief but clear essay in which Zé Caboclo, Benedito José da Silva, Severina de Tracunhaém and Maria Amélia de Tracunhaém are identified as the finest representatives of a living and vibrant folk art tradition in Brazil's Northeast.

498 Santos, Enéias Tavares dos. Album de xilogravuras. Alagoas: Universidade Federal de Alagoas, Museu Théo Brandão de Antropologia e Folclore, 1977. 1 portfolio; 15 leaves; 14 ill. (Coleção folclórica da UFAL; no. 50)

Original and interesting woodblock prints by printmaker and poet Enéias Tavares dos Santos depict various folk dances from Alagoas. Includes comparative iconographic material useful for the study of similar dances in neighboring states and of their medieval Portuguese roots.

499 Santos, Fernando Augusto Gonçalves. *Mamulengo:* o teatro de bonecos popular do Nordeste. Rio de Janeiro: FUNARTE, 1979. 204 p.; ill.

The most Brazilian form of puppet theatre is the genre known as *mamulengo*, common to Pernambuco, especially Recife. Of special interest to art and folk specialists is the chapter devoted to puppets both as sculptures and folk art. Includes many b/w illustrations.

500 Shaffer, Kay. O berimbau-de-barriga e seus toques. Rio de Janeiro: Ministério da Educação e Cultura, Secretaria de Assuntos Culturais, Fundação Nacional de Arte, Instituto Nacional do Folclore, 1977. 67 p.; ill.; music (Monografias folclóricas; 2)

A musical instrument closely linked to Bahia's Afro-Brazilian traditions, the *berimbau* appears often in Brazil's 19th-century iconography. Some are included in this monograph.

INDIAN TRADITIONS

501 Arte plumária do Brasil: catálogo. Texts by Aloísio Magalhães *et al.* Brasília: Fundação Nacional Pró-Memória, 1980/1981. 78 p.; ill.

Catalogue of major exhibition of Brazilian featherwork art, organized by Norberto Nicola, and first shown at São Paulo's Museum of Modern Art. Only a few dozen of the show's 350 pieces are reproduced here but they suffice to convey the splendor of the exhibit. Catalogue includes essays on diverse tribal traditions that gave rise to the artwork as well as accurate description of selected pieces. Three editions of this catalogue have appeared thus far: 1) São Paulo, Museum of

Modern Art, 1980, b/w reproductions; 2) Brasília, Itamaraty Palace, 1980–1981; and 3) Washington, D.C., Smithsonian Institution, 1982. They should contribute to the international recognition of this art form.

PHOTOGRAPHY

502 Amazonas, palavras e imagens de um rio entre ruínas. Fotografia, Isabel Gouvêa, João Luiz Musa, Sônia da Silva Lorenz. Poesia, Milton Hatoum. Capa, Carlos Bravo Villalba. São Paulo: Livraria Diadorim, 1979. ca. 100 p.; ill.

A recognized poet and three professional photographers traveled through the Brazilian Amazon area recording how both people and landscape resist radical change and destruction. The result is a beautiful and poignant book that intermingles words and images in order to make its point. Includes incisive introductions by Márcio de Souza and Milton Hatoum.

503 Andujar, Claudia and **George Love.** Amazônia. São Paulo: Editora Praxis, 1979? ca. 150 p.; all col. ill.

Consists of about 150 color photographs that show the environment and life of the Yanomami Indians, most of whom live in Roraima Territory. The photographs are masterpieces that transcend their basic documentary function of portraying man and nature by transmuting both into art.

504 Bethy and **Pedro.** Fotopoesia. Rio de Janeiro: Editora Gráfica Luna, 1979. 47 p.; ill.

Beth Pereira photographed nature, people, cities and objects with a poet's sensitivity. Pedro Castel interpreted these images verbally through poems. The photographs, especially the spontaneous ones that are not posed, are artistically valid *per se.*

505 Fotografias brasileiras raras da Biblioteca Oliveira Lima. Texts by Cunha Bueno, Boris Cossoy, Manoel Cardozo, and José Neistein. São Paulo: Secretaria de Estado da Cultura, 1981. 1 v.; ill.

Catalogue of an exhibition of 113 photographs belonging to the Oliveira Lima Library, The Catholic University of America, Washington, D.C. They covered the history of photography in Brazil, from its inception to 1920, with examples drawn from all over

the country, to illustrate aspects, styles and techniques of the art. The same selection was exhibited in 1977 at the Brazilian-American Cultural Institute, in Washington, D.C.

506 Guimaraens, Luiz Alphonsus de. Bares cariocas. Introdução de Eudoro Augusta Macieira. Rio de Janeiro: FUNARTE, 1980. 64 p.; facs.; ill.

At its most casual, the bar is one of the most important institutions in Brazilian daily life. The b/w photographs assembled for this booklet convey the social implications of Rio's bars while capitalizing on the artistic potential of their setting. The single color illustration is a photoengraving.

507 Kossoy, Boris. Origens e expansão da fotografia no Brasil: século XIX. Rio de Janeiro: FUNARTE, 1980. 128 p.; bibl.; ill.

Historical survey includes: the invention of photography in Brazil, independently from Europe and the US; the expansion of daguerreotype; the introduction of new photographic processes; the photographic record of Brazil in the second half of the 19th century; photography in the 20th century; and the first illustrated publications. Very well-documented both verbally and visually, the book also includes a comprehensive list of photographers active in Brazil in the 19th century and a bibliography.

508 Malta, A. Fotografias do Rio de ontem. Rio de Janeiro: Prefeitura da Cidade do Rio de Janeiro, 1979. ca. 500 p.; chiefly ill. (Coleção Memória do Rio; 7)

Consists of valuable reproductions of 2,500 glass negatives taken by Augusto Cesar Malta de Campos which were recently found and restored. He photographed Rio de Janeiro's landscape, cityscape and people at the turn of the century with detachment and sensitivity. Some photographs have artistic merit, most are interesting as records of Rio from early 1900s to late 1930s. The book, well printed on excellent paper, was designed as an homage of Rio's City Hall to its most important photographer.

509 I [i.e. Primeiro] **Trienal de Fotografia do Museu de Arte Moderna de São Paulo.** Text by Moracy R. de Oliveira. São Paulo: Museu de Arte Moderna, 1980. 154 p.; ill.

One of the most ambitious exhibitions of contemporary photography in Brazil, the

1st Triennial displayed the work of 71 artists from all over the country. Representing many styles and approaches to a great variety of subjects, the show included several works by each photographer. However, only one photograph per artist is reproduced in the catalogue. An excellent reference source, nevertheless.

510 Verger, Pierre. Retratos da Bahia, 1946 a 1952. Edição de textos e tradução, Aparecida Nóbrega. Salvador, Bahia: Corrupio, 1980. ca. 200 p.; chiefly ill.

Ethnologist and photographer Pierre Verger (b. France 1902) left Paris in 1932 and, for 15 years, traveled in and photographed countries as varied as the US, China, Ecuador, Benin, Mexico, and Nigeria. After settling for good in Bahia in 1946, he became one of the most authoritative scholars in African and Afro-Brazilian studies. His love for and identification with Bahia are reflected not only in his scholarly works, some of which are regarded as standards in the field, but also in thousands of negatives recently rediscovered by Arlette Soares and Maria Aparecida de Nóbrega. They selected the 250 b/w shots reproduced in this book that portray the architecture, streets, people, traditions, magic and poetry of Bahia. An autobiographical text by Verger and introductions by Carybé and Jorge Amado enhance this excellent book.

CITY PLANNING AND ARCHITECTURE

511 Barro, Máximo and Roney Bacelli. Ipiranga. Sáo Paulo: Departamento do Patrimônio Histórico, Divisão do Arquivo Histórico, 1979. 130 p.; bibl.; ill. (História dos bairros de São Paulo; v. 14)

Monograph is part of series on São Paulo neighborhoods (their history, architecture, traditions). This one is devoted to Ipiranga, where Dom Pedro I declared Brazil's independence in 1822. Includes much visual material from the 19th and 20th centuries drawn from the press and historical sources (e.g., reproductions of paintings, photographs, plans, aerial views, aspects of industry, leisure habits, etc.).

512 Bruno, Ernani Silva. O equipamento da Casa Bandeirista segundo os antigos inventários e testamentos. São Paulo: Prefeitura do Município de São Paulo, Secretaria Municipal de Cultura, Departamento do Patrimônio Histórico, Divisão de Iconografia e Museus, 1977. 102 p. (Registros—Departamento do Patrimônio Histórico; 1)

Not merely of historical interest, the housing occupied by *bandeirantes* is worthy of study as a unique architectural manifestation. This monograph discusses the economic and social context that gave rise to *bandeirante* society and their rural and urban dwellings, the nature of which is also reflected in their art, handicraft, and other accouterments (e.g., fabrics, clothes, arms, ammunitions, musical instruments, books, etc.). For another study of the subject, see item **514.**

Delson, Roberta Marx. New towns for colonial Brazil: spatial and social planning of the eighteenth century. See *HLAS 43:5337.*

513 Dutra de Moraes, Geraldo. A primitiva Capela do Amparo (IHGSP/R, 74, 1978, p. 97–105, plate)

The original chapel in the state of São Paulo was demolished in 1850 and in its place is now the main Church of Amparo. Through documents and old iconography, Dutra de Moraes attempts to show what the chapel looked like.

Empresa Metropolitana de Planejamento da Grande São Paulo. O desafio metropolitano. See *HLAS 43:5339.*

Freyre, Gilberto. Oh de casa!: em torno da casa brasileira e de sua projeção sobre um tipo nacional de homem. See *HLAS 43:8365.*

Joffily, Geraldo Irenêo. Brasília e sua ideologia. See *HLAS 43:5358.*

514 Katinsky, Julio Roberto. Casas bandeiristas: nascimento e reconhecimento da arte em São Paulo. São Paulo: Universidade de São Paulo, Instituto de Geografia, 1976. 183 p.; bibl.; ill. (Série Teses e monografias—IGEOG-USP; no. 26)

Monograph discusses 12 houses built on the outskirts of São Paulo in the 17th and 18th centuries, some of which have been restored down to the last detail. That neither the design nor the apportionment of space have any European counterpart, lead the author to hypothesize that the *casa bandei-*

rante was the unique creation of a strikingly original society that flourished in the São Paulo highlands during the first two centuries of Portuguese colonization. Well illustrated book that addresses technical and aesthetic questions. For another study of the topic, see item **512.**

515 Macedo, Francisco Riopardense de. O solar do almirante: história pela arquitetura. Porto Alegre: Universidade Federal do Rio Grande do Sul: Instituto Estadual do Livro, Departamento de Cultura, Secretaria de Cultura, Desporto e Turismo, 1980. 126 p.; ill.

Monograph about a colonial upperclass house in Rio Pardo, Rio Grande do Sul, that discusses its historical context, architectural features and technical skills required to build it as well as conditions set by the family that commissioned it (e.g., needs, style, urban landscape, etc.). Provides additional information on the museum housed therein today. Includes many plans, drawings, photographs. A work of historical and artistic interest.

516 Marx, Murilo. Cidade brasileira. São Paulo: Melhoramentos: Ed. da Universidade de São Paulo, 1980. 1 v.; bibl.

Urban attitudes and Brazil's urban development are the subjects of this book. Author first discusses towns and villages in order to explain the general and special aspects of cities: built-up areas, street layout, design of parks and squares, so-called empty spaces, all types of buildings (public, private, military, religious), everything that we see and don't see, from the best to the worst that cities offer. He considers social, political and historical factors in the development of cities and provides many good quality reproductions and a basic bibliography. Many quotations on urban life drawn from Brazilian literature enhance this dynamic and fascinating work.

Moreira Pinto, Alfredo. A cidade de São Paulo em 1900. See *HLAS 43:5382.*

517 Passaglia, Luiz Alberto do Prado. Mercado velho de Santo Amaro. São Paulo: Prefeitura do Município de São Paulo, Secretaria Municipal de Cultura, Departamento do Patrimônio Histórico, Divisão de Preservação, 1978. 67 p.; ill. (Série registros; 2)

Santo Amaro was an independent county with its own history, traditions and architecture before becoming part of Greater São Paulo. Despite being engulfed by the megalopolis, Santo Amaro preserves major features and monuments. One of them is the recently restored old market, now a cultural center for the community. This excellent monograph examines the old market from a historical and technical perspective and includes many b/w drawings and photographs.

CARTOONS AND COMIC STRIPS

518 Fernandes, Anchieta. Desenhistas potiguares: caricatura e quadrinhos. Natal: SMEC, 1973. 14 p.; ill. (Informação—SMEC; 1)

Attempt to redefine the nature and function of comic strips in Brazil, especially in Rio Grande do Norte. Author regards João da Escóssia as a forerunner, but also discusses Erasmo, Balãozinho, and GRUPEHO. Unfortunately, the work is too short (14 p.) for an adequate study of the subject.

519 Luyten, Sonia Maria Bibe. Elementos art-déco em histórias em quadrinhos: um exemplo brasileiro (Comunicações e Artes [Universidade de São Paulo, Escola de Comunicações e Artes, São Paulo] 8, 1979, p. 17–35, bibl., ill., plates)

By means of a fascinating stylistic approach, article analyzes art déco influences on 1920s comic strips in Brazil, the Americas and France (e.g., Alain Saint-Ogan, George MacManus, J. Carlos). Author discusses issues from both aesthetic and social perspectives. Includes appropriate illustrations and succinct bibliography.

520 Zokner, Cecília Teixeira de Oliveira. Do humor gráfico brasileiro: "Rango," um exorcismo latino-americano (COLOQ, 60, março 1981, p. 23–30, bibl., ill.)

A character in a comic strip, Rango is the "synthetic outsider," devoid of human features and having only a brain and a voice. Created in 1970 by Edgar Vasques at the School of Architecture in Porto Alegre, Rango represents the underworld of the big city whose role is to criticize. Zokner's essay emphasizes how Rango performs this function.

MISCELLANEOUS

521   Arte no Palácio dos Bandeirantes. São
        Paulo: Governo do Estado de São
Paulo, 1979. 159 p.; col. ill.

The Palácio dos Bandeirantes in São
Paulo serves three purposes: 1) as seat of the
Executive Power of São Paulo State; 2) as
quarters for its administration; and 3) as the
Governor's residence. Built in 1965 by the
Francisco Matarazzo Foundation, the palace
was later purchased by the Government of
São Paulo. In addition, the palace now houses
a large art collection from Brazil (16th to
20th centuries) and from countries such as
Portugal, Italy, France and the Netherlands. A
good introduction and guide to this collection, this lavishly printed book includes texts
in Portuguese and English and descriptions of
many pieces (e.g., sculptures, paintings, furnishings, silver, china, textiles, etc.).

522   O *Design* **no Brasil,** história e reali-
        dade: exposição inaugural do Centro
de Lazer—SESC, Fábrica Pompéia, Museu de
Arte de São Paulo Assis Chateaubriand. Text
by P. M. Bardi. São Paulo: Raízes Artes
Gráficas, 1982. 118 p.

SESC (Social Service for Commerce
Employees) established "Centro de Lazer," a
unique leisure/recreation center rebuilt from
an abandoned São Paulo factory with a design
by Lina Bó Bardi. After its opening, "Centro
de Lazer" became an instant success and one
of the most interesting cultural spaces in São
Paulo. This catalogue of its inaugural exhibition emphasizes the variety of design in Brazil which ranges from such practical pieces
as rural tools of colonial times to the most
sophisticated of urban designs. Text discusses the significance of beauty in everyday
objects for the development of modern aesthetics. Includes excellent b/w photographs
and reproductions.

523   Fundação Museu Carlos Costa Pinto:
        catalogue of the Museum Carlos Costa
Pinto, Salvador, Bahia, 1979. Text by Mer-
cedes Rosa; lay-out and photography by
Bruno Furer; English version by John Treacy.
São Paulo: Gráficos Brunner, 1979. 43 p.; ill.

Collection encompasses European,
Oriental and Brazilian art, from the 16th to
the 20th centuries. Of particular interest for
this section are gold and silver religious and
secular artifacts, furniture built in Bahia in
the 17th and 18th centuries, and canvasses
by Bahia painters of the 19th and 20th centuries. Includes many b/w and color reproductions and extensive text which discusses
the collection from historical, aesthetical
and technical perspectives.

524   Jordão, Vera Pacheco. A imagem da
        criança na pintura brasileira. Rio de
Janeiro, Brasil: Salamandra, 1979. 92 p.; 1 leaf
of plates; col. ill.

Consists of over 40 paintings of children, some by the same artists (e.g., Portinari, four; Tarsila, Guignard, and Pancetti,
two each) most of them from the 20th century but including some 18th- and 19th-cen-
tury portraits. Author provides individual
analysis of each painting, biographical note
for each artist, and excellent color reproductions. Vera Pacheco Jordão (d. 1981), teacher,
art critic, and author, was raised in São Paulo
and traveled widely, including the foreign
service.

525   Klintowitz, Jacob. Pedro Luiz Correia
        de Araújo. São Paulo: André Galeria de
Arte, 1981. 62 p.; ill.

Correia de Araújo (b. Paris 1874, d.
Brazil 1961) came from a Pernambucan family and lived in Paris where, strongly influenced by Cézanne and Gauguin, he became
a close friend of Picasso, Gris, Léger, Diego
Rivera, and Matisse. After moving to Brazil
in 1929, he befriended Portinari, Guignard,
Di Cavalcanti, Lucio Costa, Cícero Dias and
Ismael Nery. Correia de Araújo's chief subjects were the female body in all of its Brazilian manifestations, white, mulatto and
black, as well as the landscapes of Rio de
Janeiro. Chapters discuss: "Natureza da Pintura;" "Do Intimismo;" "Do Método e
Saber;" and "Esta Cor Irreal." Includes short
biography of the artist and excellent b/w and
color reproductions of his drawings, studies
of his paintings, and canvases. Book was published on the occasion of a major show of
Correia de Araújo's work (São Paulo Museum
of Art, 1981).

526   Octavio Ignacio. Os cavalos de Oc-
        tavio Ignacio. Fotografias de Humberto
Franceschi. Rio de Janeiro: Sociedade Amigos
do Museu de Imagens do Inconsciente, 1978.
61 p.; ill.

Book reproduces a series of schizo-
phrenic horse drawings and related commentary by Octavio Ignacio. Statements on the

psychological and symbolic implications of the man/horse relationship by Freud and Jung are included together with observations on the cultural and artistic consequences of such a relationship, by Alain Gheerbrant, Jorge de Lima, and Marino Marini.

JOURNAL ABBREVIATIONS
ART

A Abside. Revista de cultura mexicana. México.

ADH/C Clio. Académia Dominicana de la Historia. Santo Domingo.

BBAA B.B.A.A. Boletín Bibliográfico de Antropología Americana. Instituto Panamericano de Geografía e Historia, Comisión de Historia. México.

BNBD Boletín Nicaragüense de Bibliografía y Documentación. Banco Central de Nicaragua, Biblioteca. Managua.

BNJM/R Revista de la Biblioteca Nacional José Martí. La Habana.

CA Critica d'Arte. Studio Italiano di Storia dell'Arte. Vallecchi Editore. Firenze, Italy.

CDLA Casa de las Américas. Instituto Cubano del Libro. La Habana.

CFC/RBC Revista Brasileira de Cultura. Ministério da Educação e Cultura, Conselho Federal de Cultura. Rio de Janeiro.

CH Cuadernos Hispanoamericanos. Instituto de Cultura Hispánica. Madrid.

CM/D Diálogos. Artes/Letras/Ciencias humanas. El Colegio de México. México.

COLOQ Colóquio. Revista de artes e letras. Propriedade: Fundação Calouste Gulbenkian. Lisbon.

CONAC/RNC Revista Nacional de Cultura. Consejo Nacional de Cultura. Caracas.

EEHA/AEA Anuario de Estudios Americanos. Consejo Superior de Investigaciones Científicas [and] Univ. de Sevilla, Escuela de Estudios Hispano-Americanos. Sevilla.

EME Revista Eme-Eme. Estudios dominicanos. Univ. Católica Madre y Maestra. Santiago de los Caballeros, Dominican Republic.

FAIC/CPPT Comunicaciones Proyecto Puebla-Tlaxcala. Fundación Alemana para la Investigación Científica. Puebla, México.

FIU/CR Caribbean Review. Florida International Univ., Office of Academic Affairs. Miami.

FJB/BH Boletín Histórico. Fundación John Boulton. Caracas.

HISP Hispanófila. Univ. of North Carolina. Chapel Hill.

HUMB Humboldt. Revista para o mundo ibérico. Ubersee-Verlag. Hamburg, FRG.

IAI/I Indiana. Beiträge zur Volker-und Sprachenkunde, Archäologie und Anthropologie des Indianischen Amerika. Ibero-Amerikanisches Institut. Berlin, FRG.

ICP/R Revista del Instituto de Cultura Puertorriqueña. San Juan.

IFH/C Conjonction. Institut Français d'Haïti. Port-au-Prince.

IGFO/RI Revista de Indias. Instituto Gonzalo Fernández de Oviedo [and] Consejo Superior de Investigaciones Científicas. Madrid.

IHGB/R Revista do Instituto Histórico e Geográfico Brasileiro. Rio.

IHGGB/R Revista do Instituto Histórico e Geográfico Guarujá/Bertioga. São Paulo.

IHGSP/R Revista do Instituto Histórico e Geográfico de São Paulo. São Paulo.

IIE/A Anales del Instituto de Investigaciones Estéticas. Univ. Nacional Autónoma de México. México.

III/AI América Indígena. Instituto Indigenista Interamericano. México.

IJ/JJ Jamaica Journal. Instituto of Jamaica. Kingston.

INAH/A Anales del Instituto Nacional de Antropología e Historia. Secretaría de Educación Pública. México.

LAP Latin American Perspectives. Univ. of California. Riverside.

LARR Latin American Research Review. Univ. of North Carolina Press *for the* Latin American Studies Association. Chapel Hill.

LNB/L Lotería. Lotería Nacional de Beneficencia. Panamá.

MEC/C Cultura. Ministério da Educação e Cultura, Diretoria de Documentação e Divulgação. Brasília.

MNDJG/A Anales del Museo Nacional David J. Guzmán. San Salvador.

OAS/AM Américas. Organization of American States. Washington.

OEIL L'Oeil. Revue d'art mensuelle. Nouvelle Sedo. Lausanne, Switzerland.

PMNH/HC Historia y Cultura. Museo Nacional de Historia. Lima.

REVIEW Review. Center for Inter-American Relations. New York.

RYC Revolución y Cultura. Publicación mensual. Ministerio de Cultura. La Habana.

SCHG/R Revista Chilena de Historia y Geografía. Sociedad Chilena de Historia y Geografía. Santiago.

SGHG/A Anales de la Sociedad de Geografía e Historia de Guatemala. Guatemala.

UCLV/I Islas. Univ. Central de las Villas. Santa Clara, Cuba.

UCR/AEC Anuario de Estudios Centroamericanos. Univ. de Costa Rica. Ciudad Universitaria "Rodrigo Facio." San José.

UEAC/GC Gaceta de Cuba. Unión de Escritores y Artistas de Cuba. La Habana.

UMG/RBEP Revista Brasileira de Estudos Políticos. Univ. de Minas Gerais. Belo Horizonte, Brazil.

UNC/R Revista de la Universidad Nacional de Córdoba. Dirección General de Publicaciones. Córdoba, Argentina.

URSS/AL América Latina. Academia de Ciencias de la URSS (Unión de Repúblicas Soviéticas Socialistas). Moscú.

USP/RH Revista de História. Univ. de São Paulo, Faculdade de Filosofia, Ciências e Letras, Depto. de História [and] Sociedade de Estudos Históricos. São Paulo.

UY/R Revista de la Universidad de Yucatán. Mérida, Mex.

VOZES Vozes. Revista de cultura. Editora Vozes. Petrópolis, Brazil.

FILM

Brazilian Cinema: 1970–1980

RANDAL JOHNSON, *Assistant Professor of Spanish and Portuguese, Rutgers University*

THIS IS THE FOURTH *HLAS* SECTION on Latin American cinema (for previous ones, see *HLAS 38, HLAS 39* and *HLAS 40*) and the first one to focus on the Brazilian cinema. It covers publications issued between 1970 and 1981 but also includes some background materials which are essential for serious research in the discipline. It emphasizes publications in English, Portuguese, and Spanish, with additional entries in French and Italian. I have avoided duplicating items included in previous general bibliographies (see *HLAS 38* and *HLAS 40*) except in the cases of new editions of long out-of-print monographs (item **988**) and Portuguese-language translation of works published in other countries (item **1024**). I have also avoided duplicating the 20 items on Brazilian cinema in Julianne Burton's *The New Latin American Cinema: an annotated bibliography of English-language sources* (published by *Cineaste*, 419 Park Avenue South, New York, N.Y. 10016).

Newspapers such as *O Estado de São Paulo* and *Jornal do Brasil* are major sources of information concerning many different aspects of cinema in Brazil, but have not been included in the present bibliography. Deserving mention, however, is Carlos Roberto Rodrigues de Souza's panorama of Brazilian film history, "A Fascinante Aventura do Cinema Brasileiro," published in two parts in *O Estado de São Paulo*'s "Suplemento do Centenário," 25 Oct. and 2 Nov. 1975.

Filmmakers associated with Cinema Novo continue to dominate Brazilian cinema and consequently dominate this bibliography as well. Due to the untimely death of Glauber Rocha in Aug. 1981, I have included a number of his writings and interviews published in the 1960s which are crucial for understanding the theoretical development of Cinema Novo as well as the films of Brazil's greatest director. Rocha's *Revolução do Cinema Novo* (1981, see item **1071**) is perhaps the single most important item in the bibliography.

This section attempts, at the same time, to include items on a wide array of topics relating to many different aspects of Brazilian cinema: the country's film pioneers (items **963, 975, 1017, 1026** and **1085**); conservation and preservation of the Brazilian cinematic memory (items **974** and **1087**); modes and techniques of production (items **971, 1001** and **1079**); the production and distribution of cultural films (item **976**); film industry statistics (items **972, 993** and **1027**); legislation (items **1043** and **1064**); film industry congresses and professional organizations (items **1036, 1051** and **1063**); plus numerous items on individual filmmakers or genres.

The definitive history of Brazilian cinema has yet to be written. Histories that do exist are based, for reasons beyond the control of their authors, on faulty or incomplete data. A great portion of early national film production has been destroyed due to negligence or to fires in the few, underfunded *cinematecas* existing in the country. Therefore, the inventory of Brazilian cinema has become a priority among a number of Brazilian critics, who have engaged in painstaking research to determine the true dimensions of national production (see items **966** and **1061**). São Paulo's Fundação Cinemateca Brasileira is currently undertaking the ambitious project of compiling a filmography including all Brazilian feature and documentary production in 35mm, 16mm, and even 8mm.

Before his death in 1977, University of São Paulo professor Paulo Emílio Salles Gomes (see items **969–970, 1022** and **1056**), encouraged historical research concerning Brazilian cinema. The direct and indirect results of his encouragement can be seen in Ismail Xavier's discussion of the theory underlying early cinematic activity in the country (item **1097**), Maria Rita Galvão's study of the Vera Cruz Studios (item **1019**), as well as in numerous theses, dissertations, and research projects at the University of São Paulo and other institutions throughout the country.

The publication of film scripts has increased over the past five years (see items **962, 1004, 1028, 1076** and **1094**) and even one novel (item **1075**) has been written based on a screenplay. Monographs on Brazilian cinema continue to be published in Europe (items **964** and **996**), and the first book on the subject in English appeared in 1982 (item **1033**).

Film periodicals have appeared sporadically in Brazil throughout the 1970s and into the 1980s, but are usually short-lived. *Cinema BR* (São Paulo) ran for two issues in 1977; *Cine Olho* (São Paulo) began in 1977 and has appeared irregularly since then, most recently devoting its space to avant-garde cinema. The Fundação Cinemateca Brasileira's *Cinema* (São Paulo) also appears with great irregularity. The most important development in Brazilian film periodicals has been the transformation of *Filme Cultura* from a superficial publication to a high-quality,, serious film magazine. *Filme Cultura* began in 1965 as a joint publication of the Instituto Nacional do Cinema Educativo (founded 1937) and the Grupo Executivo da Indústria Cinematográfica (GEICINE, established 1961), the former subject to the Ministry of Education and Culture and the latter to the Ministry of Industry and Commerce. In 1966 the magazine was transferred to the newly-founded Instituto Nacional do Cinema, where it remained until 1975 when the Instituto was absorbed by Embrafilme (Empresa Brasileira de Filmes, created in 1969). After a lapse of three years the magazine was revitalized under the editorship of Leandro Tocantins. *Filme Cultura* entered its current and most fruitful phase in 1980 when its editorial board consisted of critics such as Ismail Xavier, Jean-Claude Bernardet, and José Carlos Avellar. Today the magazine is obligatory reading for anyone seriously interested in studying Brazilian cinema. This bibliography provides the first selective index to *Filme Cultura* in the period 1970–81.

With the US success of films such as *Dona Flor and her two husbands, Bye Bye Brasil, Gaijin,* and *Pixote,* coverage of Brazilian cinema has increased considerably in journals in this country. Periodicals such as *Cineaste* and *Millenium* have devoted space to Brazilian film, but to this date only *Jump Cut: A Review of Contemporary Cinema* has provided a consistent forum for new material. In 1979 and 1980 it published two special sections on recent production in Brazil (Nos. 21 and 22). It is hoped that such works will open doors for other scholars interested in research in the discipline.

951 **Alencar, Miriam.** O cinema em festivais e os caminhos do curtametragem no Brasil. Apresentação de Heloisa Buarque de Hollanda. Prefácio de Leandro Tocantins. Rio de Janeiro: Editora Artenova *em convênio com a* Empresa Brasileira de

Filmes, 1978. 142 p.; 4 leaves of plates; bibl.; ill. (Cinebiblioteca Embrafilme)

As the title suggests, this is a study of film festivals and the production of short documentaries in Brazil. Lacks organization and a unified focus.

952   **Andrade, Rudá de.** Cronologia da cultura cinematográfica no Brasil. São Paulo: Fundação Cinemateca Brasileira, 1962. 40 p. (Cadernos da Cinemateca; 1)

Chronological panorama of the development of Brazilian cinematic culture (film societies, journals, *cinematecas*, publications, festivals, etc.).

953   **Anos 70:** 4—cinema. Rio de Janeiro: Europa Empresa Gráfica e Editora, 1979/1980. 130 p.; plates.

Collection of articles on Brazilian cinema in the 1970s. Includes Jean-Claude Bernardet on documentary, the image of the working class, and historical films; José Carlos Avellar on the *pornochanchada*; and Ronald F. Monteiro on notions of popular cinema and on avant-garde cinema. Good panorama of the decade.

954   **Anselmo 4 e ½** (MEC/FC, 14, abril/ maio 1970, p. 6–19)

Collection of articles and interviews outlining the career of Anselmo Duarte (*O pagador de promessas*, 1962). Includes filmographies as director and actor.

955   **Arlorio, Piero** and **Michel Ciment.** Entretien avec Glauber Rocha (*Positif* [Paris] 91, jan. 1968, p. 19–35)

Rocha discusses his work through *Terra em transe* (1967).

956   **Arnaldo Jabor e** *Tudo bem* (MEC/FC, 30, agôsto 1978, p. 2–11)

In this interview director Jabor discusses the genesis and production of his award-winning 1978 film, *Tudo bem*. Includes director's filmography.

957   **Assaf, Alice Gonzaga** and **Ernesto Saboya.** Moacyr Fenelon e a Chanchada (MEC/FC, 13:34, jan./março 1980, p. 12–16)

Overview of the career of producer-director Fenelon (1903–52) describes his relationship to studios such as Cinédia and Atlântida (which he helped found). Includes his complete filmography.

958   **Aumont, Jacques** *et al.* Entretien avec Carlos Diegues (Cahiers du Cinéma

[Paris] 225, nov./déc. 1970, p. 44–55)

In this extensive interview Diegues discusses political cinema in Europe and Latin America, provides a view of the evolution and significance of Cinema Novo, and looks at his own work.

959   **Avellar, José Carlos.** O Velho e o Novo (MEC/FC, 32, fev. 1979, p. 4–19)

Jornal do Brasil critic Avellar analyzes Geraldo Sarno's *Coronel Delmiro Gouveia* (1978) in terms of (possible) spectator response to cinematic language used. Although perceptive, his analysis becomes forced by excessive detail. Followed by Sarno's complete filmography.

960   —— *et al.* Pra começo de conversa (MEC/FC, 13:34, jan./março 1980, p. 4–11)

Avellar, Jean-Claude Bernardet, David Neves, Luiz Rosemberg, Sérgio Santeiro, Zulmira Tavares, Andrea Tonacci, Teresa Trautman, and Ismail Xavier discuss the current situation of Brazilian cinema, including documentary production as well as experimental films. Richly illustrated with frame enlargements from recent films.

961   **Azeredo, Ely** and **Carlos Fonseca.** Roberto Farias em ritmo de artindústria (MEC/FC, 3:15, julho/agôsto 1970, p. 6–17)

A look at the career of one of Brazilian cinema's most active producers and directors (and director of Embrafilme 1974–79). Includes filmography.

962   **Back, Sílvio.** *Aleluia, Gretchen.* Porto Alegre, Brazil: Editora Movimento, 1978. 80 p.; plates.

The screenplay of Back's 1976 film. Includes introductions by Deonísio da Silva and Inácio Araújo.

963   **Barros, Luiz de.** Minhas memórias de cineasta. Prefácio de Leandro Tocantins; apresentação de Modesto de Abreu; pesquisa, organização e revisão de texto, Maria Helena Saldanha, Alex Viany. Rio de Janeiro: Editora Artenova *em convênio com a* Empresa Brasileira de Filmes S.A. EMBRAFILME, 1978. 266 p.; 4 leaves of plates; filmography; ill. (Cinebiblioteca Embrafilme)

Anecdotal memoirs of Brazil's most prolific filmmaker, whose career stretches 1914–77. Includes his complete filmography.

964   **Bellumori, Cinzia di.** Rocha: Glauber Rocha. Firenze: La Nuova Italia, 1975.

127 p.; bibl.; filmography (Il Castoro cinema; 13)

After brief interview with Rocha, author provides short history of Cinema Novo before discussing Rocha's work in general and analyzing each of his films (through *História do Brasil*).

965 Bernardet, Jean-Claude. Cinema brasileiro: propostas para uma história. Rio de Janeiro: Paz e Terra, 1979. 103 p.; bibl.; filmography (Coleção Cinema; v. 7)

Notes for a history of Brazilian cinema indicates areas for future research. Discusses massive presence of imported films in the domestic market and its effect on viewers, evolution of ideas concerning the film industry, role of the state, and relationship between Brazilian and foreign cinemas. Useful, though sources of quotes and information not always provided.

966 ———. Filmografia do cinema brasileiro, 1900–1935: jornal *Estado de São Paulo*. São Paulo: Secretaria da Cultura, Comissão de Cultura, 1979. 1 v. (Unpaged); ill.

A filmography of Brazilian films exhibited in São Paulo in period indicated based on research in the *Estado de São Paulo*. Includes published description, dates and places of exhibition. Produces advertising and photographs from the newspaper. An important first step in establishing the corpus of Brazilian cinema.

967 ———. O que é cinema? São Paulo: Brasiliense, 1980. 118 p.; plates (Coleção Primeiros passos)

Introduction to the cinema for high school students.

968 ———. Trajetória crítica. São Paulo: Livraria Editora Polis, 1978. 264 p.; ill.

Collection of journalistic texts written between 1960–74 by one of Brazil's top critics. Includes author's self-criticism after each article or series of articles. Excellent.

969 ——— and **Antônio Cândido de Mello e Souza.** Paulo Emílio (Ensaios de Opinião [Rio de Janeiro] 6, 1978, p. 6–37)

Collections of essays and letters published as posthumous homage to Paulo Emílio Salles Gomes. Includes texts by Gomes himself, Raquel Gerber, Victor de Azevedo, David Neves, Ligia Moraes Leite, and Maurício Segall.

970 ——— *et al.* Cinema: trajetória no subdesenvolvimento (MEC/FC, 13: 35/36, julho/set. 1980, p. 2–20)

Transcription of a round-table discussion held in São Paulo in 1977 to debate Paulo Emílio Salles Gomes' seminal article "Cinema: Trajetória no Subdesenvolvimento." Participants include Bernardet, Maria Rita Galvão, Maurício Segall, Antônio Cândido de Mello e Souza, and Zulmira Tavares. An excellent and fascinating exploration of Gomes' polemical article.

971 ——— *et al.* O som do Cinema Brasileiro (MEC/FC, 14: 37, jan./março 1981, p. 2–34)

Wide-ranging discussion of sound production in Brazilian cinema. Includes contributions by directors, technicians, and composers. Useful for understanding modes of production of cinema in Brazil.

972 *Boletim Informativo SIP: Anuário.* Instituto Nacional do Cinema. Ano 3, Anuário de 1973 [and] Ano 4, Anuário de 1974– . Rio de Janeiro.

Consists of the *Boletim*'s yearly publication: *Anuário de 1973* (published 1974, 46 p.) and the *Anuário de 1974* (published 1975, 50 p.). They provide Brazilian film industry statistics in charts and tables.

973 Brandão, Vera. Alice Gonzaga: o futuro da Cinédia (MEC/FC, 29, maio 1978, p. 38–44)

In this interview Alice Gonzaga Assaf, daughter of Cinédia founder Adhemar Gonzaga, discusses history and future of Cinédia Studios (founded 1930).

974 ———. Importância e urgência da conservação de filmes (MEC/FC, 31, nov. 1978, p. 65–77)

Alex Viany, Jurandyr Noronha, Cosme Alves Neto and Carlos Augusto Calil discuss the problems involved in preserving the Brazilian cinematic memory through the conservation and restoration of films.

975 ———. Pedro Lima em "flash-back:" uma odisséia no tempo (MEC/FC, 8: 26, set. 1974, p. 6–20)

An interview with one of Brazil's cinematic pioneers.

976 ———. Produção e difusão do filme cultural (MEC/FC, 30, agôsto 1978, p. 112–120)

Brief history of the production and distribution of cultural films by official organizations such as the Instituto Nacional do Cinema Educativo (founded 1937), the Instituto Nacional do Cinema (1966), and Embrafilme (starting in 1975).

977 *Brasile: "Cinema Novo" e Dopo.* Quaderni della Mostra Internazionale del Nuovo Cinema. Nuovocinema/Pesaro No. 9 (34), 1981– . Venezia.

Collection of a wide variety of translated articles on Brazilian cinema (by Brazilians) published to accompany an exhibition of recent production. Articles cover topics ranging from the *pornochanchada* to state intervention in the film industry, from militant documentary to Rocha's *A idade da terra.* Together they constitute a good overview of developments in Brazilian cinema since 1970.

978 **Brazilian cinema.** Edited by Randal Johnson and Robert Stam. Rutherford, N.J.: Fairleigh Dickinson University Press; London: Associated University Presses, 1982. 373 p.; bibl.; ill.; index.

First book on the subject to be published in English. Composed of four sections: 1) "The Shape of Brazilian Film History;" 2) "The Theory of Brazilian Cinema: The Filmmakers Speak;" 3) "Cinema Novo and Beyond: The Films;" and 4) "Special Topics and Polemics."

979 **Bruce, Graham.** Music in Glauber Rocha's films (Jump Cut [A review of contemporary cinema, Berkeley, Calif.] 22, May 1980, p. 15–18)

Excellent analysis of the structural role of music in Rocha's first four features.

980 **Bruce, Ian.** Cinema censorship (INDEX, 8:4, July/Aug. 1979, p. 36–42)

An overview of film censorship by the military government. Includes short list of filmmakers who were arrested or exiled by the regime. The full history of film censorship in Brazil has yet to be written.

981 **Bueno, Wilson** and **Ricardo Dias.** Joaquim Pedro o *O homem do pau Brasil* (MEC/FC, 14:37, jan./março 1981, p. 50–55)

A look at the production of Andrade's 1982 film, *O homem do pau Brasil*, which is based on the life and work of Oswald de Andrade.

982 **Canongia, Ligia.** Quase cinema: cinema de artista no Brasil, 1970/80. Rio de Janeiro: Edição FUNARTE, 1981. 52 p.; plates (Arte brasileira contemporânea, caderno de textos; 2)

A panorama of avant-garde film production by plastic artists and filmmakers such as Hélio Oiticica, Raymundo Colares, Lygia Pape, and Artur Omar. Richly illustrated.

983 **Capriles, René** and **Federico de Cárdenas.** Glauber: el "transe" de América Latina (Hablemos de Cine [Lima] 47, mayo/junio 1969, p. 34–48)

Wide-ranging interview on Latin American and world cinemas, art and politics, and especially Rocha's *Terra em transe* (1967).

984 **Cárdenas, Federico de.** Glauber Rocha (Hablemos de Cine [Lima] 35, mayo/junio 1967, p. 10–15)

Rocha speaks of Cinema Novo and his career through *Terra em transe* (1967).

985 ———. Joaquim Pedro de Andrade (Hablemos de Cine [Lima] 49, sept./oct. 1969, p. 11–16)

Director Andrade discusses his career, *Macunaíma* (1969), and the political problems faced by Cinema Novo.

986 **Carlos Oscar Reichenbach Filho** (MEC/FC, 28, fev. 1978, p. 73–83)

São Paulo director Reichenbach talks of his filmmaking career.

987 **Catani, Afrânio Mendes.** Vinícius de Moraes: crítico de cinema (MEC/FC, 14:38/39, agôsto/nov. 1981, p. 42–52)

Traces little-known aspect of the career of the late poet/composer/singer Vinícius de Moraes, his work as a film critic starting in 1941 (with the journal *Clima*). In Alex Viany's words, Vinicius' film criticism is composed of "pequenas jóias de exercício poético do espírito crítico."

988 **Cavalcânti, Alberto.** Filme e realidade. Rio de Janeiro: Artenova/Embrafilme, 1977. 276 p.; filmography; plates.

Reprint of 1951 collection of Cavalcânti's writings. Includes brief panorama of Brazilian cinema.

989 **César, Ana Cristina.** Literatura não é documento. Rio de Janeiro: Edição FUNARTE, 1980. 122 p.; bibl.; plates.

Study of short documentaries on important Brazilian literary figures and the relationship of these films to the state. Includes interviews with filmmakers David Neves, Márcio Souza, Sérgio Santeiro, Heloísa Buarque de Hollanda, Raymundo Amado, Ana Carolina, and João Carlos Horta, as well as two film scripts. Informed by a simplistic leftist ideology that irritates more than enlightens.

990 Cicco, Cláudio de. Hollywood na cultura brasileira: o cinema americano na mudança da cultura brasileira na década de 40. São Paulo: Convívio, 1979. 130 p.; plates.

Study of the ideological influence of Hollywood on Brazilian culture in the 1940s. Author's Master's thesis.

991 Ciclo de Debates do Teatro Casa Grande. Rio de Janeiro: Editora Inúbia, 1976. 238 p.; ill.

In 1975 Rio de Janeiro's Teatro Casa Grande held a series of public debates on problems confronting various areas of Brazilian culture. Critics José Carlos Avellar and Alex Viany joined with filmmaker Leon Hirszman for a discussion of the cinema. Good introduction to problems faced by the film industry at that time.

992 Ciment, Michel and Jacques Demeure. Entretien avec Ruy Guerra (Positif [Paris] 123, jan. 1971, p. 3–9)

Guerra speaks of Os deuses e os mortos (1970) and Sweet hunters (1967).

993 *Cinejournal.* Embrafilme. Vol. 1, No. 1, julho 1980– . Rio de Janeiro.

Statistics concerning the dimensions of the Brazilian film market followed by a speech delivered by the Director-General of Embrafilme, Celso L. N. Amorim, to the Federal Chamber of Deputies on 30 May 1979. Useful publication (44 p.).

994 Cinema brasileiro: 8 estudos. Rio de Janeiro: Embrafilme/FUNARTE, 1980. 234 p.; plates.

Consists of prize-winning essays in 1977 contest held by Embrafilme. Includes studies of the film Pátria redimida (João Batista Groff, 1930) and of early pioneers such as Eduardo Abelim, Annibal Requião, and Paulo Benedetti. Also includes articles on the country and the city in Brazilian cinema (by Jean-Claude Bernardet), the image of the Indian, and the Brazilian cinema's representation of the national pastime, soccer.

995 Cinema de rua: entrevista com João Batista de Andrade (Cinema [Fundação Cinemateca Brasileira, São Paulo] 4, 1974, p. 13–28)

Director Andrade talks of his work making documentaries for television, combining video reporting with the language and techniques of the cinema. A good introduction to the work of one of Brazil's most important documentarists.

996 Le Cinema Novo brésilien: 2—Glauber Rocha. Michel Estève, editor. Paris: Minard, 1973. 1 v.; bibl.; filmography; plates (Lettres modernes)

Collection of articles on Brazil's most important filmmaker, including Barthélemy Amengual's excellent "Glauber Rocha ou les chemins de la liberté."

997 Correa, José Celso Martinez et al. Cinemação. São Paulo: Cine Olho Revista de Cinema/ 5° Tempo/ Te-Ato Oficina, 1980. 170 p.; plates.

In the mid-1960s José Celso Martinez Correa was the force behind São Paulo's Teatro Oficina. He is now active in cinema. In this book he, Noilton Nunes, Celso Luca, and Alvaro Nascimento discuss the making of the film "25" in Mozambique, ideological differences with that country's Instituto Nacional do Cinema, and a project for the creation of a new "revolutionary" cinema in Brazil based on "transversal" distribution circuits. Claims that his film O rei da vela will be the spark to ignite this new movement, whose poetic manifesto is included in text. A hodge-podge.

998 Dahl, Gustavo. Uirá (Cinema [Fundação Cinemateca Brasileira, São Paulo] 3, jan. 1974, p. 5–11)

Dahl discusses the genesis and production of his 1973 film, Uirá: um índio à procura de Deus, based on the book by anthropologist Darcy Ribeiro.

999 Dassin, Joan R. Tent of miracles: myth of racial democracy (Jump Cut [A review of contemporary cinema, Berkeley, Calif.] 21, Nov. 1979, p. 20–22)

This perceptive article analyzes Nelson Pereira dos Santos' Tenda dos milagres (1977) as a critique of the myth of racial democracy, but also shows that the film contains certain elements which render the critique ambiguous.

1000 Delahaye, Michel; Pierre Kast; and **Jean Narboni.** Entretien avec Glauber Rocha (Cahiers du Cinéma [Paris] 214, juillet/août 1969, p. 23–40)
Rocha discusses his work within the political and industrial context of Brazilian cinema.

1001 16 (Dezesseis) **mm** (MEC/FC, 28, fev. 1978, p. 24–48)
Discusses use of 16mm equipment in Brazilian film production. Includes interviews with filmmakers Jom Tob Azulay, Orlando Senna, Zelito Vianna, Jorge Bodansky as well as with representatives of major laboratories.

1002 Dias, José Umberto. Nordeste, cinema e gente (MEC/FC, 13 : 35/36, julho/set. 1980, p. 21–25)
Panorama of film production in Brazil's Northeast.

1003 Diegues, Carlos. Brésil: 39 degrés, ou le cinema novo será toujours nouveau (Positif [Paris] 116, maio 1970, p. 43–52)
In a manifesto style recalling the writings of Glauber Rocha, Diegues discusses his career, Cinema Novo (which he describes as "théorie en action"), and especially *Os herdeiros* (1969).

1004 ———. *Chuvas de verão.* Rio de Janeiro: Editora Civilização Brasileira, 1977. 108 p.; plates.
Screenplay of Diegues' 1977 film preceded by director's introductory note.

1005 ———. A crítica esperava um *That night in Maceió*: eu fiz *Joana Francesa* (Status [São Paulo] 2, set. 1974, p. 105–108)
Diegues discusses his *Joana Francesca* (1974) and the "cultural crisis" facing Brazilian society.

1006 Dossiê crítico: *Ajuricaba: o rebelde da Amazônia* (MEC/FC, 30, agôsto 1978, p. 106–111)
Collection of reviews of Oswaldo Caldeira's *Ajuricaba: rebelde da Amazônia* (1977).

1007 Dossiê crítico: *Aleluia, Gretchen* (MEC/FC, 30, agôsto 1978, p. 91–97)
Collection of reviews of Sílvio Back's *Aleluia, Gretchen* (1976).

1008 Dossiê crítico: *Barra pesada* (MEC/FC, 32, fev. 1979, p. 107–113)
Collection of reviews of Reginaldo Farias' *Barra pesada* (1977).

1009 Dossiê crítico: *Lição de amor* (MEC/FC, 29, maio 1978, p. 94–105)
Collection of reviews of Eduardo Escorel's *Lição de amor* (1975), which is based on Mário de Andrade's novel, *Amar: verbo intransitivo.*

1010 Dossiê crítico: *Mar de rosas* (MEC/FC, 32, fev. 1979, p. 114–128)
Collection of reviews of Ana Carolina Teixeira Soares' *Mar de rosas* (1977).

1011 Dossiê crítico: *Tenda dos milagres* (MEC/FC, 30, agôsto 1978, p. 98–105)
Collection of reviews of Nelson Pereira dos Santos' *Tenda dos milagres* (1977).

1012 Dossiê crítico: *Xica da Silva* (MEC/FC, 29, maio 1978, p. 81–93)
Collection of reviews of Carlos Diegues' *Xica da Silva* (1976).

1013 Enquête: perspectivas do cinema brasileiro (MEC/FC, 29, maio 1978, p. 2–14, plates)
What are the perspectives for Brazilian cinema? What tendencies now exist? What paths should be taken? These questions and others are asked of filmmakers Eduardo Escorel; Luiz de Miranda Correia; Carlos Diegues; Nelson Pereira dos Santos; Roberto Santos; Arnaldo Jabor; Walter Lima, Jr.; David Neves; Oswaldo Caldeira; and Ana Carolina.

1014 Espírito-Santo, Michel do. Escritores brasileiros: filmografia (MEC/FC, 6 : 20, maio/junho 1972, p. 42–44)
Filmography of Brazilian literary works adapted to the screen.

1015 ———. O futebol no cinema brasileiro (MEC/FC, 8 : 26, set. 1974, p. 56–60)
Annotated filmography of works dealing with the national pastime.

1016 Um Filme em questão: *A idade da terra* (MEC/FC, 14 : 38/39, agôsto/nov. 1981, p. 58–75)
Texts by Jean-Claude Bernardet, Paulo César Saraceni, José Carlos Avellar, Eduardo Mascarenhas, Ismail Xavier, and Raquel Gerber on Glauber Rocha's controversial last film. In the words of Saraceni, the film "con-

vida os críticos a se libertarem de seus pre-
conceitos de subdesenvolvidos e aceitarem
seu subdesenvolvimento para entender
as palavras do Papa João Paulo II, quando
afirmou que o Brasil, sem renegar sua cultura, poderá ser a grande opção para salvar o
mundo." As a whole the texts provide a kaleidoscopic view of a difficult yet extremely
important film.

1017 Fonseca, Carlos. Luis de Barros: 60
anos de cinema (MEC/FC, 7:24, 1973,
p. 16–25)

A look at Brazil's most prolific filmmaker, whose career in the cinema dates
from 1914. Includes interview with Barros
and his filmography up to 1962.

1018 Frenais, Jacques. Brésil: 'le cinema
novo: une histoire vielle de dix ans'
(Cinéma [Paris] 214, oct. 1976, p. 70–74)

Director Nelson Pereira dos Santos
discusses his own work within the broader
context of Cinema Novo and Brazilian cinema as a whole.

1019 Galvão, Maria Rita. Cinema e burguesia: o caso Vera Cruz. Rio de Janeiro: Civilização Brasileira/Embrafilme,
1981. 282 p.; plates.

In 1949 the Vera Cruz Studios were
created in São Paulo with capital from the
Matarazzo group. Modelled on the MGM studios in Hollywood, Vera Cruz attempted to
create a "quality" cinema reflecting the values of São Paulo's industrial bourgeoisie. The
studios went bankrupt in 1954 after producing 18 feature films. Galvão's book traces
the rise and fall of Vera Cruz, its relationship
to the bourgeoisie, and its cinematic production. An important addition to the bibliography on the history of Brazilian cinema.

1020 ———. O desenvolvimento das idéias
sobre cinema independente (Cinema
BR [São Paulo] 1, set. 1977, p. 15–19; 2, dec.
1977, p. 15–19)

Study of the evolution of concepts of
independent cinema in the 1950s, coinciding
with the rise and fall of the São Paulo attempt at concentrated industrialization with
the Vera Cruz Studios. Cites a number of theses presented at film industry congresses in
1951 and 1952, including Nelson Pereira dos
Santos' O problema do contéudo no cinema
brasileiro. An important source for understanding the rise of Cinema Novo at the end
of the decade.

1021 Gardies, René. Structural analysis of
a textual system: presentation of a
method (Screen [London] 15:1, Spring 1974,
p. 11–31)

English translation of abbreviated version of Gardies' excellent structural analysis
of the films of Glauber Rocha. For original
monograph, see HLAS 38:990; for original
abbreviated version, HLAS 38:989; and for
Portuguese-language version, HLAS 40:990.

1022 Gomes, Paulo Emílio Salles. Cinema:
trajetória no subdesenvolvimento. Rio
de Janeiro: Paz e Terra/Embrafilme, 1980.
88 p.; ill.

This volume brings together three of
the author's major short texts: "Pequeno
Cinema Antigo," published originally in
1969; "Panorama do Cinema Brasileiro:
1896/1966," published in 1966 under the
joint authorship of Gomes and Adhemar
Gonzaga; and the seminal "Cinema: Trajetória no Subdesenvolvimento," which first
appeared in Argumento in 1973. An important introduction to the work of one of
Brazil's most important film professors, historians, and critics.

1023 Hector Babenco (Cinema BR [São
Paulo] 2, déc. 1977, p. 25–30)

Director Babenco discusses his Lúcio
Flávio: o passageiro da agonia (1977) and
problems of cinematic production in Brazil.

1024 Hennebelle, Guy. Os cinemas na-
cionais contra Hollywood. Translators:
Paulo Vidal and Julieta Viriato de Medeiros.
Rio de Janeiro: Paz e Terra, 1978. 246 p.;
plates (Coleção Cinema; 6)

Portuguese-language version of
Quinze ans de cinéma mondial, 1960–
1975 (see HLAS 40:960).

1025 Hollanda, Heloísa Buarque de. Macunaíma: da literatura ao cinema. Rio de
Janeiro: Livraria José Olympio Editora/Em-
brafilme, 1978. 127 p.; plates.

Book divided into three parts: 1) Mário
de Andrade's writings on the novel Macunaíma; 2) brief analysis of the adaptation; 3)
Joaquim Pedro de Andrade's statements on
his film version. Original sources unfortunately not provided. Richly illustrated.

1026 Humberto Mauro: sua vida, sua arte,
sua trajetória no cinema: depoimentos
sobre a riqueza da filmografia maureana e sua
importância na moderna cultura brasileira.

Prefácio de Leandro Tocantins. Rio de Janeiro: Editora Artenova *em convênio com a Empresa Brasileira de Filmes S.A.*, EMBRAFILME, 1978. 360 p.; 16 leaves of plates; ill. (Cinebiblioteca Embrafilme; v. 3)

Collection of short, personal articles by friends of Mauro, followed by a selection of the director's writings, speeches, and interviews. Includes his complete filmography as well as documentaries made for the Instituto Nacional de Cinema Educativo. Important source of information for the study of this Brazilian cinematic pioneer.

1027 *Informações sobre a Indústria Cinematográfica Brasileira.* Embrafilme. Anuário de 1975– . Rio de Janeiro.

Brazilian film industry statistics in charts, plates, and tables (62 p.).

1028 Jabor, Arnaldo and **Leopoldo Serran.** Tudo bem: um filme de Arnaldo Jabor. Rio de Janeiro: Editora Civilização Brasileira, 1978. 100 p.; plates.

Screenplay of Jabor's 1978 film includes comments by Jabor and Serran.

1029 Johnson, Randal. Brazilian cinema today (Film Quarterly [University of California, Berkeley] 31 : 4, Summer 1978, p. 42–45)

Brief view of the situation of Brazilian cinema at the time, focusing primarily on its relationship to the state.

1030 ———. *Macunaíma* as Brazilian hero: filmic adaptation as ideological radicalization (LALR, 7 : 13, Fall/Winter 1978, p. 39–44)

Analysis of Joaquim Pedro de Andrade's 1969 adaptation of Mário de Andrade's 1928 novel, *Macunaíma*.

1031 ———. Sex, politics, and culture in *Xica da Silva* (Jump Cut [A review of contemporary cinema, Berkeley, Calif.] 22, May 1980, p. 18–20)

Discussion of Carlos Diegues' 1976 film.

1032 ———. Toward a popular cinema: an interview with Nelson Pereira dos Santos (Studies in Latin American Popular Culture [New Mexico State University, Department of Foreign Languages, Las Cruces] 1, 1982, p. 225–236)

Dos Santos discusses his "Manifesto for a Popular Cinema" and his films *O amu-*

leto de Ogúm (1974) and *Tenda dos milagres* (1977).

1033 ——— and **Robert Stam.** Brazilian Renaissance: beyond Cinema Novo (Jump Cut [A review of contemporary cinema, Berkeley, Calif.] 21, Nov. 1979, p. 13–18)

Introduction to Brazilian cinema from the beginnings until 1979.

1034 Jorge, Thereza. Um fotógrafo: Dib Lufti (MEC/FC, 31, nov. 1978, p. 30–41)

Brazil's leading cinematographer discusses his career. Includes complete filmography.

1035 ———. Um montador: Mair Tavares (MEC/FC, 31, nov. 1978, p. 24–29)

One of Brazilian cinema's top editors (*Xica da Silva*, *Chuvas de verão*, among others), discusses his work. Includes complete filmography.

1036 Lima, Antônio. Uma cooperativa do cinema (MEC/FC, 32, fev. 1979, p. 39–48)

Nelson Pereira dos Santos, Marcos Faria, and the president of INCRA, Lourenço Vieira da Silva, provide an introduction to the activities and importance of the Cooperativa Brasileira de Cinema, founded in 1978 to provide its members with technical assistance in the production of films.

1037 ——— and **José Haroldo Pereira.** Um diretor: Alex Viany (MEC/FC, 32, fev. 1979, p. 20–38)

Critic/director Viany discusses *A noiva da cidade* (1979), his cinematic homage to Humberto Mauro. Followed by biographical chronology.

1038 Mahieu, Augustín. Brasil: una cinematografía em expansión (CH, 349, julio 1979, p. 152–163)

Panorama of the historical development of Brazilian cinema from the beginnings until 1979. Includes brief but perceptive discussion of the relationship between Cinema Novo and the state film enterprise (Embrafilme).

1039 Mahieu, José Agustín. La literatura en el cine brasileño (CH, 369, marzo 1981, p. 579–587)

Brief but well-informed discussion of the historical relationship between Brazilian cinema and the classics of national literature, especially with regards to cinema's search for national identity.

1040 Os mais importantes filmes brasileiros (VOZES, 74:6, agôsto 1980, p. 47–60)

A survey of 49 filmmakers, critics, professors, and film enthusiasts to determine the most important films in the history of Brazilian cinema. Top three are Rocha's *Deus e o diablo na terra do sol*, dos Santos' *Vidas secas*, and Rocha's *Terra em transe*. Includes interesting comparison with similar 1968 survey, when top three were Barreto's *O cangaceiro*, Khoury's *Noite vazia*, and Mauro's *Ganga bruta*. Current survey totally dominated by Cinema Novo.

1041 Mascarenhas, Eduardo. Sófocles não está morto: Viva Nelson Rodrigues! (MEC/FC, 13:35/36, julho/set. 1980, p. 80–92)

One of Brazil's leading psychoanalysts discusses Neville d'Almeida's 1980 adaptation of Nelson Rodrigues' play *Os sete gatinhos* as an Oedipal drama. Important article in the ongoing revision of the late Rodrigues' work.

1042 Meerapfel, Jeanine. Entretien avec Ruy Guerra (Positif [Paris] 207, June 1978, p. 58–60)

Guerra discusses his and Nelson Xavier's award-winning *A queda* (1977) and the "institutionalization" of Brazilian cinema.

1043 Mello, Alcino Teixeira de. Legislação do cinema brasileiro. 2 v. Rio de Janeiro: Embrafilme, 1978. 2 v. (634 p.)

Collection of the most important federal legislation concerning the film industry in Brazil, including resolutions of the Instituto Nacional do Cinema (1966–75) and the Conselho Nacional do Cinema (1976–78). Essential source for anyone seriously interested in studying the film industry in Brazil.

1044 Mello, Saulo Pereira de. *Límite*: filme de Mário Peixoto. Rio de Janeiro: Edição Funarte, 1979. 210 p.; ill.; plates.

Meticulous and lavish reconstruction or "map" of Peixoto's 1930 classic through extensive frame reproduction and indication of punctuation devices. Preceded by description of method used. The film is better.

1045 Menezes, Cláudia. Cinema encontra realidade na vida simples do índio (Revista de Atualidade Indígena [Minas Gráfica Editora, Brasília] 1:5, julho/agôsto 1977, p. 36–43, plates)

Critical evaluation of film production concerning Brazil's indigenous population. Derides most official and commercial documentaries while praising Darcy Ribeiro's collaboration with Heinz Foerthmann (1950–53) as the best anthropological films yet made in the country. Author also discusses fictional treatments of Indians and points to Gustavo Dahl's *Uirá: um índio à procura de Deus*, based on Ribeiro, as providing the first indigenous hero of Brazilian cinema. Useful.

1046 Mesquita, Fernando. Júlio Bressane: a solidão lunar (Cine Olho [São Paulo] 5/6, junho/agôsto 1979, p. 62–74)

Analyzes the work of avant-garde filmmaker Bressane using *O anjo nasceu* as a starting point. Discusses the director's use of "radical criminality" as a focal point of his political and esthetic critique of society.

1047 Monteiro, José Carlos. Nelson Pereira dos Santos: o realismo sem fronteiras (MEC/FC, 3:16, set./oct. 1970, p. 6–15, bibl., filmography)

Overview of the work of the "conscience" of Cinema Novo.

1048 Mosier, John. The importance of popular cinema in Latin America (Studies in Latin American Popular Culture [New Mexico State University, Department of Foreign Languages, Las Cruces] 1, 1982, p. 179–186)

Attempts to trace the development in Brazil of a "genuinely popular cinema" which "speaks both to the people at large and for them." Ill-informed about the history and modes of production of Brazilian cinema, author erroneously sees this "popular cinema" as growing at least partially out of the *pornochanchada* genre.

1049 Naves, Sylvia Bahiense *et al.* Hector Babenco (Cinema [Fundação Cinemateca Brasileira, São Paulo] 5, Spring 1980, p. 9–22)

In this interview Babenco discusses his filmmaking career (1969–80). Focus on *Lúcio Flávio* (1977), *Pixote* (1980), and the relationship between Brazilian cinema and the state film enterprise, Embrafilme.

1050 Neves, David E. Um filme esquecido: *Rio Zona Norte* (MEC/FC, 28, fev. 1978, p. 90–107)

Critic/director Neves looks back at the impact of Nelson Pereira dos Santos' second film, *Rio Zona Norte* (1957). Richly illustrated, article includes excerpts from screenplay.

1051 Newlands, Lilian. CORCINA: a cooperativa do Curta (MEC/FC, 13:34, jan./março 1980, p. 21–23)

Introduction to the work of the Cooperativa de Realizadores Cinematográficos Autônomos Ltda., a cooperative designed to promote the production of short films.

1052 Nobre, F. Silva. O livro de cinema no Brasil. Fortaleza, Ceará: Gráfica Editorial Cearense, 1976. 286 p.

Extensively annotated bibliography of all film books published in Brazil. Includes a list of film journals. Useful.

1053 ———. A margem do cinema brasileiro. Rio de Janeiro: Pongetti, 1963. 158 p.

Superficial history of Brazilian cinema.

1054 Nogueira, Rui and **Nicoletta Zalaffi.** Table Ronde: les deux vagues du Cinema Novo (Cinéma [Paris] 150, nov. 1970, p. 60–74)

Origins, evolution, and present situation of Cinema Novo are discussed by Glauber Rocha, Zelito Viana, and three representatives of Cinema Novo's "second wave:" Neville d'Almeida, Júlio Bressane, and Maurício Gomes Leite.

1055 Ortiz, Carlos. Romance do gato preto. Rio de Janeiro: Editora da Casa do Estudante do Brasil, n.d. 198 p.; plates.

Summary of the lectures given by the author during São Paulo film seminars between 1949–52. While most of the volume concerns international cinemas, the final chapter is an overview of the development of Brazilian cinema.

1056 Paulo Emílio Salles Gomes (MEC/FC, 28, fev. 1978, p. 2–23)

Special section in honor of the late Paulo Emílio Salles Gomes. Includes poems, letters, excerpts from Gomes' work, and statements by Leandro Tocantins, Alex Viany, Jean-Claude Bernardet, Carlos Augusto Calil and others.

1057 Pereira, Carlos Alberto M. and **Heloísa Buarque de Hollanda.** Patrulhas ideológicas marca reg.: arte e engajamento em debate. Capa, Otávio Roth, Felipe Doctors; revisão, Valéria C. Salles. São Paulo: Brasiliense, 1980. 269 p.; ill.

In a 1976 interview with the *Estado de São Paulo*, Carlos Diegues denounced what he called "ideological patrols," which demand that artists follow narrow and orthodox political formulas. This volume brings together opinions on the subject, including interviews with filmmakers Diegues, Glauber Rocha, Antônio Calmon, and Ana Carolina, among others. Useful as an overview of the vast polemic Diegues provoked, but questions asked are predictable and lacking in originality.

1058 Pereira, José Haroldo. Alberto Shatovsky: o problema da exibição (MEC/FC, 31, nov. 1978, p. 4–14)

Experienced critic and exhibitor Shatovsky discusses his activity in the exhibition sector and analyzes the place of Brazilian cinema within its own market. Enlightening.

1059 ———. Walter Lima Júnior: o tempo como uma ficção (MEC/FC, 29, maio 1978, p. 67–71, plates)

In this interview Walter Lima, Jr., discusses genesis and production of his 1978 film *A lira do delírio*, the last film of his wife, the late Anecy Rocha.

1060 ——— and **Sérvulo Siqueira.** Um roteirista: Leopoldo Serran (MEC/FC, 32, fev. 1979, p. 96–106)

One of Brazil's top screenwriters (*Dona Flor e seus dois maridos*, *Bye bye Brasil*, among others), discusses his work. Includes complete filmography.

1061 Pereira Júnior, Araken Campos. Cinema brasileiro, 1908–1978: longa metragem. Santos: Editora Casa do Cinema, 1979. 2 v. (791 p.)

Compilation of Brazilian feature film production in 1908–78. Although it is the first work of its kind, it contains *many* errors and should be consulted with extreme caution.

1062 Pifer, Rudolf. Filmusical brasileiro e chanchada. 2. ed. São Paulo: Global Editora, 1977. 142 p.; bibl.; plates.

Superficial overview of the Brazilian musical comedy and *chanchada*.

1063 I (Primeiro) **Congresso da Indústria Cinematográfica Brasileira** (MEC/FC, 6:22, nov./déc. 1972, p. 6–23)
Report on important industry conference held Oct. 1972. Summarizes viewpoints of all sectors of the industry.

1064 **A Resolução dos 98 Dias:** alguns depoimentos (MEC/FC, 4:18, jan./fev. 1971, p. 10–23)
The screen quota for Brazilian cinema debated by leading directors and producers. Important for setting out some of the issues involved in compulsory exhibition legislation.

1065 **Rocha, Glauber.** Cela s'appelle l'aurore (Cahiers du Cinéma [Paris] 195, nov. 1967, p. 39–41)
Rocha sets forth this theory of the Tricontinental filmmaker and "guerrilla" cinema. For English translation, see item **978** (p. 76–80).

1066 ———. Cinema Novo, o delírio de um gol por cima da carne seca (Status [São Paulo] 26, set. 1976, p. 123–129)
A defense of Cinema Novo through a panorama of the work of Carlos Diegues. Written in a highly elliptical yet sometimes brilliant style, Rocha says that *Joana Francesa* (1974), for example, reveals in "Joana/DeGaulle montada em Ganga Zumba/Lubumba a verdadeira Hestória da colonização . . ."

1067 ———. Cinema Novo y la aventura de la creación (Hablemos de Cine [Lima] 47, mayo/junio 1969, p. 21–33)
One of the best outlines of the theoretical and practical concerns of Cinema Novo. Essential.

1068 ———. De la sécheresse aux palmiers (Positif [Paris] 114, mars 1970, p. 42–47)
In an elliptically allegorical language, Rocha reports to Europe on the state of Brazilian cinema. At the same time, he radicalizes his esthetic concerns, rejecting "the commercial-popular esthetics of Hollywood, the populist-demagogic esthetics of Moscow, and the bourgeois-artistic esthetics of Europe" in favor of a new, revolutionary esthetic deriving from the violent reality of the Third World. For English translation, see item **978** (p. 86–89).

1069 ———. Uma estética da fome (RCB, 1:3, julho 1965, p. 165–170)
Key manifesto of the Cinema Novo movement. For English translation, see item **978** (p. 68–71).

1070 ———. Lucha y destino de un cine personal (Hablemos de Cine [Lima] 47, mayo/junio 1969, p. 17–19)
Director's introduction to his ideas on cinema and politics in Brazil.

1071 ———. Revolução do Cinema Novo. Rio de Janeiro: Alhambra/Embrafilme, 1981. 476 p.
This volume combines an anthology of some of Rocha's most important writings and interviews with "memoirs" of the development of Cinema Novo and the author's relationships with its personalities. A seminal work by Brazil's greatest and most controversial filmmaker, published shortly before his death in 1981.

1072 **Rodrigues, João Carlos.** Tizuka Yamasaki (MEC/FC, 14:37, jan./março 1981, p 45–49)
Director Yamasaki discusses her filmmaking activity and especially her first feature, *Gaijin* (1980).

1073 **Sant'Anna, João** and **Elias Farjado da Fonseca.** Ruy Guerra (Ele, Ela [Rio de Janeiro] 9:102, oct. 1977, p. 75–83)
Guerra talks about his films and his often tumultuous relationship with Brazilian cinema. A lucid analysis of the conflicts within the once-unified Cinema Novo.

1074 **Santeiro, Sérgio.** Conceito de dramaturgia natural (MEC/FC, 30, agôsto 1978, p. 80–85)
Discusses the critical and self-reflexive usage of direct sound and other direct cinema techniques in the Brazilian documentary. "Natural dramaturgy" is that of the person filmed within his or her social context.

1075 **Santos, João Felício dos.** *Xica da Silva.* Rio de Janeiro: Civilização Brasileira, 1976. 202 p.
A novel based on the script of Carlos Diegues' 1976 film of the same name. Includes an introductory note by Diegues.

1076 Sarno, Geraldo and **Orlando Senna.** *Coronel Delmiro Gouveia.* Rio de Janeiro: Editora Codecri, 1979. 142 p.; plates (Coleção Edições Pasquim; v. 53)

The screenplay of Sarno's 1978 film. Includes articles by Sarno (on the script), Senna (on the assassination of Gouveia), José Carlos Avellar (on the film), and Robert Gréllier (on Sarno's work). Appendix includes several items on the life and death of Delmiro Gouveia.

1077 Silva, Alberto. A face desigual: notas sobre o filme policial brasileiro (MEC/FC, 4:19, março/abril 1971, p. 22–27)

Brief history of the Brazilian police drama. Includes a filmography compiled by Michel do Espírito-Santo.

1078 Simões, Inimá Ferreira. O imaginário da boca. São Paulo: Secretaria Municipal de Cultura, Departamento de Informação e Documentação Artística, Centro de Documentação e Informação sobre Arte Brasileira Contemporânea, 1981. 74 p.; plates (Cadernos; 6)

Lucid discussion of films and modes of production of São Paulo's *Boca do lixo,* home of the *pornochanchada.* Includes excerpts of interviews with directors, producers, and actresses. Useful for understanding cinematic production independent of the state's tutelage.

1079 Siqueira, Sérvulo *et al.* Fotografia de cinema no Brasil, hoje (MEC/FC, 14:38/39, agôsto/nov. 1981, p. 2–41)

Highly useful special section on problems of photography in Brazilian cinema. Divided into several parts ("Os Fotógrafos," "Ampliar a Ampliação," "Os Técnicos," "Projeção: Imagem Indefinida, Som Distorcido"), the section includes interviews with the country's leading cinematographers and with laboratory technicians. A glossary explains technical terms, and charts reveal the skyrocketing costs of film stock and processing.

1080 Sisson, Rachel. Cenografia e vida em *Fogo morto.* Rio de Janeiro: Artenova/Embrafilme, 1976. 78 p.; ill.; plates.

Description of the construction of sets for Marcos Farias' adaptation of José Lins do Rego's *Fogo morto* (1976).

1081 Stam, Robert. Brazilian avant-garde cinema: from *Límite* to the *Red light bandit* (Millenium Film Journal [New York] 4/5, Summer/Fall 1979, p. 33–42, plates)

Traces development of Brazilian avant-garde from 1930 (date of Mário Peixoto's classic *Límite*) until 1968 (date of Rogério Sganzerla's *Red light bandit*). The best treatment of the subject to date.

1082 ———. O espetáculo interrompido: literatura e cinema de desmistificação. Rio de Janeiro: Paz e Terra, 1981. 200 p.; ill.; plates (Coleção Cinema; v. 11)

Lucid analysis of novels and films that foreground their process of composition. Focuses primarily on Godard, but includes cogent analyses of Andrade's *Macunaíma,* Rocha's *Terra em transe,* Guerra and Xavier's *A queda,* and Jabor's *Tudo bem.* Excellent.

1083 ———. Formal innovation and radical critique in *The fall* (Jump Cut [A review of contemporary cinema, Berkeley, Calif.] 22, May 1980, p. 20–21)

Cogent analysis of Ruy Guerra and Nelson Xavier's award-winning *A queda* (1977), a film which "combines energy and authenticity with searing political consciousness and dazzlingly original techniques."

1084 ——— and **Ismail Xavier.** Brazilian avant-garde: metacinema in the *Tristes tropiques* (Millenium Film Journal [New York] 6, Winter/Spring 1980, p. 82–89, plates)

Second part of author's exploration of avant-garde cinema, this time focusing primarily on the work of Júlio Bressane, Andrea Tonacci, and Artur Omar. Excellent.

1085 Sternheim, Alfredo. O jovem José Medina (MEC/FC, 7:24, 1973, p. 27–31)

In this interview film pioneer Medina (*Exemplo regenerador,* 1919) looks back at his career.

1086 Tavares, Zulmira Ribeiro. Conselho Superior de Censura (MEC/FC, 13:35/36, julho/set. 1980, p. 26–31)

Informative look at the Conselho Superior de Censura, which was set up in 1968 to oversee the censorial actions taken by the Federal Police.

1087 Thompson, Cecília. Cinemateca Brasileira e seus problemas. São Paulo: Fundação Cinemateca Brasileira, 1964. 164 p.

A history of the long struggle of the

Fundação Cinemateca Brasileira to preserve the national cinematic memory.

1088 Tocantins, Leandro. O processo de transposição de linguagem (MEC/FC, 30, agôsto 1978, p. 35–43)

Looks at the relationship between literature and cinema, especially adaptations of works by José Américo de Almeida (*Soledade*, by Paulo Thiago, based on *A bagaceira*) and José Lins do Rego (*Fogo morto*, by Marcos Farias).

1089 Torres, Miguel. Entrevista con el director brasileño Carlos Diegues, realizador del film *Los herederos* (Cine Cubano [La Habana] 60/62, 1969, p. 84–88)

Diegues discusses *Os herdeiros* within the general context of Cinema Novo.

1090 ———. Entrevista con Glauber Rocha sobre su película *Antônio das Mortes* (Cine Cubano [La Habana] 60/62, 1969, p. 68–77)

Extensive interview focusing primarily on Rocha's *O dragão da maldade contra o santo guerreiro* (*Antônio das Mortes*, 1969).

1091 Tournès, Andrée. Nelson Pereira: "Une lutte de chaque jour" (Jeune Cinéma [Paris] 112, juillet/août, 1978, p. 6–8)

In this interview Nelson Pereira dos Santos speaks of the organization of Brazilian cinema, its relationship to the state, and of his film *Tenda dos milagre* (1977).

1092 30 (Trinta) **anos de cinema paulista.** São Paulo: Fundação Cinemateca Brasileira, 1980. 88 p.; plates (Cadernos da cinemateca; 4)

Consists of Maria Rita Galvão's article, "O Desenvolvimento das Idéias sobre Cinema Independente," followed by interviews with São Paulo filmmakers Primo Carbonari, Walter Hugo Khouri, João Batista de Andrade, Hermanno Penna, Aloysio Raulino, and Ozualdo Candeias and with critic Jean-Claude Bernardet. As a whole the volume constitutes a good introduction to filmmaking in São Paulo (especially documentary production), but the absence of representatives of the *pornochanchada* is glaring.

1093 Van Wert, William F. Ideology in the Third World cinema: a study of Sembene Ousmane and Glauber Rocha (Quarterly Review of Film Studies [Redgrave Publishing Co., Pleasantville, N.Y.] 4:3, Spring 1979, p. 207–226)

Perceptive comparison of Sembene's *Emitai* (1970) and Rocha's *Barravento* (1962) focusing on the directors' complex character typage and on "distanciation" techniques which "forcefully provoke action, not complacency, in the spectator." Despite minor inaccuracies (saying, for example, that the personage Leda dies in Guerra's *Os cafajestes*—she doesn't), a thoughtful and well-considered analysis.

1094 Viana, Zelito. *Terra dos índios*: um filme de Zelito Viana. Rio de Janeiro: Embrafilme/DPP/DONAC, 1979. 118 p.; plates.

The complete text of Viana's 1979 documentary. Fascinating and highly useful to students of Brazilian cinema and of the country's indigenous populations.

1095 Viany, Alex. Introdução ao cinema brasileiro. Rio de Janeiro: Ministério de Educação e Cultura/Instituto Nacional do Livro, 1959. 250 p.; filmography; plates.

Despite numerous research flaws, this book remains a seminal work on the history of cinema in Brazil. Includes texts of selected film legislation.

1096 Xavier, Ismail. O mal estar na incivilização (Cine Olho [São Paulo] 5/6, junho/agôsto 1979, p. 54–62)

Excellent analysis of "inconclusion" as a structuring device in the work of avant-garde filmmaker Júlio Bressane. As the author says, "Subvertida a noção clássica de fim, abre-se o espaço para diferentes formas de exercícios desta inconclusão, numa terra-de-ninguém que abriga as personages e situações dos filmes de Bressane . . ."

1097 ———. Sétima arte, um culto moderno: o idealismo estético e o cinema. São Paulo: Editora Perspectiva, 1978. 275 p.; bibl.; ill. (Coleção Debates; 142: Cinema)

Pt. 1 of this book by Brazil's leading film theorist discusses the formation of film theories in France in the period between World War I and the advent of sound and the idealistic ideology behind then. Pt. 2 examines the repercussion of such theories in Brazil, with chapters on Brazilian literary modernism and the cinema, the magazine

Cinearte, and Rio de Janeiro's Chaplin Club. Excellent.

JOURNAL ABBREVIATIONS
FILM

CH Cuadernos Hispanoamericanos. Instituto de Cultura Hispánica. Madrid.

INDEX Index on Censorship. Writers & Scholars International. London.

LALR Latin American Literary Review. Carnegie-Mellon Univ., Dept. of Modern Languages. Pittsburgh, Pa.

MEC/FC Filme Cultura. Ministério de Educação Cultural, Embrafilme (Empresa Brasileira de Filmes). Rio de Janeiro.

RCB Revista Civilização Brasileira. Editora Civilização Brasileira. Rio de Janeiro.

VOZES Vozes. Revista de cultura. Editora Vozes. Petrópolis, Brazil.

HISTORY

ETHNOHISTORY: Mesoamerica

EDWARD E. CALNEK, *Associate Professor of Anthropology, The University of Rochester*

ANY LIST OF OUTSTANDING works published during the current review period must surely include Carmack's meticulously detailed study of the Quiche Maya (item **1506**), Davies' comprehensive review of post-Toltec documentation in Central Mexico (item **1515**), and the impressive theoretical contributions of Mercedes Olivera's study of the agricultural economy in Tecali and adjoining regions (item **1548**).

Otherwise, recent trends display increasingly interesting and sophisticated interpretations of Mesoamerican religious ideologies, with particularly intriguing results drawn from the recently revived field of archaeoastronomy.

Since this is to be my final contribution to the "Mesoamerican Ethnohistory" section of this vitally important *Handbook,* I conclude by expressing my personal gratification at the remarkable promise and growth of the field, stimulated by a new generation of exceptionally imaginative and well trained young scholars in a discipline which only a decade ago was staffed by a mere half dozen or so of committed specialists.

1501 Alvarado Tezozomoc, Fernando. Crónica mexicana. Anotada por Manuel Orozco y Berra, y precedida del Códice Ramírez, manuscrito del siglo XIV intitulado Relación del origen de los indios que habitan esta Nueva España según sus historias, y de un examen de ambas obras, al cual va anexo un estudio de cronologia mexicana por el mismo Orozco y Berra. 2. ed. México: Editorial Porrúa, 1975. 712 p.; 12 leaves of plates; bibl.; ill. (Biblioteca Porrúa; 61)

Facsimile reissue of Orozco y Berra's now classic edition of two of the most important extant sources dealing with historical development of Mexica of Tenochtitlan.

1502 Aveni, Anthony F.; Horst Hartung; and **J. Charles Kelley.** Alta Vista, Chalchihuites: astronomical implications of a Mesoamerican ceremonial outpost at the Tropic of Cancer (SAA/AA, 47:2, 1982, p. 316–335, bibl.; tables)

Principally concerned with archaeological data, but involves skillful use of ethnohistorical materials to describe instruments used for astronomical observation in preconquest Mesoamerica.

1503 Berdan, Frances. The Aztecs of Central Mexico: an imperial society. New York: Holt, Rinehart & Winston, 1982. 195 p.; bibl.; ill. (Case studies in cultural anthropology)

Excellent survey and discussion of Mexica (Aztec) history, religion, economy, social organization, and art, with brief concluding review of early post-conquest social change.

1504 Bittman Simons, Bente. El Mapa de Coatlinchán: pictografía de Acolhuacan. Glosas del mapa de Coatlinchán, Ismael Díaz C. México: Biblioteca Nacional de Antropología e Historia, INAH, 1978. 77, 22 p.; bibl. (Serie Investigación-Biblioteca Nacional de Antropoligía e Historia; no. 3)

Includes general review of ethnohistorical documentation available for the once powerful Acolhua city-state, together with valuable commentary on the informational content of the 16th century map itself.

1505 Brand, Donald D. The persistent myth in the ethnohistory of western Mexico (UNAM/T, 8, 1980, p. 419–436, bibl.)

Wide-ranging investigation of documentary evidence supporting Brand's conclusion "that the Mexicans held a few towns on the Costa Grande for a few years, and that Zacatula town and area proper . . . was within the sphere of Tarascan influence." If correct, maps of the Aztec imperial frontiers in Guerrero region must be significantly redrawn.

1506 Carmack, Robert M. The Quiché Mayas of Utatlan: the evolution of a highland Guatemala kingdom. Norman: University of Oklahoma Press, 1981. 435 p.; bibl.; ill.; maps; tables.

Long awaited study which reviews virtually every aspect of archaeological and documentary record relating to the Quiché Maya, a major politico-military power in late prehispanic Highland Guatemala. Also includes detailed examination of post-conquest development in same region. See also item **1562**.

1507 ———. La verdadera identificación de Mixco Viejo (SGHG/A, 48 : 1/4, enero/dic. 1975, p. 124–147, bibl., map)

Carefully documented and convincing identification of archaeological site mistakenly called Mixco Viejo by the Guatemalan chronicler, Fuentes y Guzmán, as Jilotepeque Viejo, located within the territories of a larger principality known as San Martin Jilitepeque in colonial and modern times. Mixco itself is identified with archaeological remains now called Chinautla Viejo described in land title dated 1565.

1508 ——— and **John M. Weeks.** The archaeology and ethnohistory of Utatlan: a conjunctive approach (SAA/AA, 46 : 2, 1981, p. 323—341, bibl., ill.)

Insightful attempt at close coordination of archaeological and ethnohistorical data, which do not always agree, to reconstruct social organization at Quiche Maya capital at Utatlan.

1509 Carrasco, David. City as symbol in Aztec thought: the clues from the Codex Mendoza (UC/HR, 20 : 3, Feb. 1981, p. 199–223)

Applies Paul Wheatley's view that a "cosmo-magical consciousness" was heavily involved in spatial organization of traditional cities to quadripartite layout of the Aztec capital, Tenochtitlan, which was symbolically represented in the *Codex Mendoza* frontispiece, and in complex architectural design of the Templo Mayor and ceremonial precinct as known from recent archaeological and ethnohistorical investigations.

1510 ———. Quetzalcoatl's revenge: primordium and application in Aztec religion (UC/HR, 19 : 4, May 1980, p. 296–320)

Intriguing discussion of ideological ambivalence surrounding figure of the famed Toltec priest-king-god, Topiltzin Quetzalcoatl, whose worship first legitimated and then finally undermined the Aztec's quest for imperial power.

1511 Carrasco Pizana, Pedro. Comment on Offner (SAA/AA, 46 : 1, 1981, p. 43–61, bibl.)

Maintains that Offner's dismissal of Marxist concept of "Asiatic Mode of Production" as not pertinent in late prehispanic Central Mexico (see item **1545**) is based on serious misrepresentation of primary ethnohistorical and archaeological documentation (see item **1546**).

1512 ———. Los Otomíes: cultura e historia prehispánica de los pueblos mesoamericanos de habla otomiana. México: Biblioteca Enciclopédica del Estado de México, 1979. 255 [i.e. 355] p.; ill. (Biblioteca Enciclopédica del Estado de México; 69)

Very welcome facsimile reedition of classic study of prehispanic history and culture of Otomí speaking peoples of Mesoamerica, long out of print and all but unavailable.

1513 Caso, Alfonso. Reyes y reinos de La Mixteca. v. 2, Diccionario biográfico de los señores mixtecos. México: Fondo de Cultura Económica, 1977–1978. 1 v.; bibl.; ill. (Sección de obras de antropología)

Last major study of historical content of Mixtec codices completed by Caso shortly before his death in 1970. Final editing with minor corrections by Bernal.

1514 Códice Aubin: manuscrito azteca de la Biblioteca Real de Berlín, anales en mexicano y jeroglíficos desde la salida de las tribus de Aztlan hasta la muerte de Cuauhtemoc. Enriquecida con un suplemento de Alfredo Chavero. México: Editorial Innovación, 1979. 99 p.; ill.

Facsimile reproduction of 1902 publication. Includes printed transcription of original Nahuatl text as well as b/w reproduction of pictorial material.

1515 Davies, Nigel. The Toltec heritage: from the fall to the rise of Tenochtitlán. Norman: University of Oklahoma Press, 1980. 401 p.; bibl.; ill.; index (The Civilization of the American Indian series, v. 153)

Valuable and meticulously documented outline of historical texts relating events in late prehispanic Central Mexico, with emphasis on period between collapse of Toltec capital, Tollan, and rise of Aztec capital, Tenochtitlan.

1516 Durán, Diego. Ritos y fiestas de los antiguos mexicanos. Introducción y vocabulario por César Macazaga Ordoño. México: Editorial Cosmos, 1980. p. 69–246, 14 p.; 11 leaves of plates; ill. (El Arte y la historia de México en libros)

Facsimile reproduction of 1880 edition of this exceptionally important text, with 11 pictorial illustrations from the originally separate *Atlas* intercalated with the text, and useful list of 203 Nahuatl terms with Spanish translations in *Vocabulario náhuatl de Durán* prepared by César Macazaga Ordoño.

1517 Edmonson, Munro S. Los Popol Vuh (CEM/ECM, 11, 1978, p. 249–266, bibl., tables)

Notes and evaluates stylistic similarities present in *Popol Vuh* of Quiche Maya and the *Libro de Chilam Balam de Tizimín* as preliminary step toward reconsideration of real historical significance of Yucatec works of this type.

1518 ———. Some postclassic questions about the classic Maya (CEM/ECM, 12, 1979, p. 157–178, bibl., map, tables)

Outlines and discusses 20 questions relating to authenticity and utility of kinship, calendric, and literary evidence from *Books of Chilam Balam* to understanding of classic Maya, based on author's conclusion that all extant versions postdate end of classic period by 500–1000 years.

1519 Evans, Susan T. Spatial analysis of Basin of Mexico settlement: problems with the use of the central place model (SAA/AA, 45:4, 1980, p. 866–875, ill., tables)

Criticizes appropriateness of central place market model used by M.E. Smith to account for settlement distribution in Valley of Mexico in late preconquest era. Argues that in fact this pattern is "more likely to have been shaped by political interactions and by the variable productive potential over a highly distorted landscape" (see item **1560**).

1520 Freeze, Ray. A petición of 1619 in K'ekchi' Maya (UNAM/T, 8, 1980, p. 111–129, table)

Apart from general linguistic interest, this text in K'ekchi' Maya deals in part with individuals mentioned by the ecclesiastical historians, Remesal and Ximenez, who figure prominently among current available sources of information relating to late prehispanic and early colonial period Guatemala and Highland Chiapas.

1521 Garza, Mercedes de la. Quetzalcoatl: Dios entre los mayas (CEM/ECM, 11, 1978, p. 199–213, bibl.)

Argues that Kukulcán-Gucumatz as described and represented in Maya sources of the post-classic era, cannot be identified with the primitive plumed serpent deity found at Izapa and other early Mayan archaeological sites, but rather a kind of "assimilated" version of Ce Acatl Topiltzin Quetzalcoatl best known in Central Mexico as the *founder* of the Toltec capital at Tula, Hidalgo.

1522 Gossen, Gary H. Cuatro mundos del hombre: tiempo e historia entre los chamulas (CEM/ECM, 12, 1979, p. 179–190)

Deals with historical sense of contemporary Chamula Indians of highland Chiapas, but conveys sense of how non-written tradition—including much revised preconquest material—was modified to accord with postconquest community experience.

1523 ———. The Popol-Vuh revisited: a comparison with modern Chamula narrative tradition (CEM/ECM, 11, 1978, p. 267–283, bibl.)

Fascinating study of close similarities of style and content linking contemporary oral literature of the Chamula, a Maya-speaking people of Highland Chiapas, with the ancient traditions expressed in the Popol Vuh.

1524 Graulich, Michel. The metaphor of the day in ancient Mexican myth and ritual (UC/CA, 22:1, Feb. 1981, p. unavailable, bibl., ill., tables)

Stimulating and controversial attempt to show that, in general, main themes of Mesoamerican myths were closely modeled on *the day*, as understood within the framework of "the 18 20-day 'months' which, along with 5 additional 'inauspicious' days, constitute the solar year in Mesoamerica." Graulich's views are critically discussed by several specialists, with a final summary and response by the author.

1525 Guzmán M., Virginia and **Yolanda Mercader M.** Bibliografía de códices, mapas y lienzos del México prehispánico y colonial. México: SEP, Instituto Nacional de Antropología e Historia, 1979. 2 v. (470 p.; 8 p. of plates); ill. (Colección científica. Fuentes para la historia; 79)

Comprehensive listing of pictorial manuscripts dealing with Mesoamerica in European and North American collections, with useful bibliographic references. Includes list of microfilmed texts available in library of Museo Nacional de Antropología, Mexico City.

1526 Hassig, Ross. Periodic markets in pre-columbian Mesoamerica (SAA/AA, 47:2, 1982, 346–355, bibl., ill.)

Relates ritual-calendrical considerations to practical exigencies which in fact dictated frequency of actual holding of market-days in large and small population centers.

Helms, Mary W. Ancient Panama: chiefs in search of power. See item **2333**.

1527 Heyden, Doris. La comunicación no verbal en el ritual prehispánico. México: Departmento de Etnología y Antropología Social, Instituto Nacional de Antropología e Historia, 1979. 52 p.; bibl. (Cuadernos de trabajo. Departamento de Etnología y Antropología Social, Instituto Nacional de Antropología e Historia; 25)

Stimulating essay concerns role of non-verbal sounds and odors in preconquest religious ceremonies.

1528 Horcasitas, Fernando. The Aztecs then and now. Drawings by Alberto Beltrán. México: Editorial Minutiae Mexicana, 1979. 168 p.; bibl.; ill. (Indian peoples of México series)

Thoughtfully written popular account with greater emphasis on ethnographic content of historical sources than is common in ethnohistorical works prepared for a general readership.

1529 Izquierdo, Ana Luisa. El derecho penal entre los antiguos mayas (CEM/ECM, 11, 1978, p. 215–247, bibl.)

Summarizes principal historical sources available for partial reconstruction of legal norms, among preconquest Maya societies, conceived from anthropological rather than strictly legalistic standpoint.

1530 Jones, Grant D.; Don S. Rice; and **Prudence M. Rice.** The location of Tayasal: a reconsideration in light of Peten Maya ethnohistory and archaeology (SAA/AA, 46:3, 1981, p. 530–547, bibl., ill.)

Detailed review of archaeological and ethnohistorical data which, in author's view, support conclusion that the Peten Itza capital of Tayasal was in fact located in Lake Peten, rather than at site of Topoxté, as previously suggested by Chase (see *HLAS 38:1975*).

1531 León, Nicolás. Los tarascos: notas históricas, étnicas y antropológicas, colegidas de escritores antiguos y modernos, documentos inéditos y observaciones personales: historia primitiva, descubrimento y conquista. México: Editorial Innovación, 1979. 157 p.; 8 leaves of plates; bibl.; ill.

Outdated in many respects, but still a useful introduction to material dealing with Tarascan ethnohistory some 80 years after first publication.

1532 León-Portilla, Miguel. Carta de los indígenas de Iguala a Don Luis de Velasco, circa 1593 (UNAM/T, 8, 1980, p. 13–19)

Transcription and translation of brief Nahuatl text, introduced by León-Portilla. Interesting primarily as an example of local dialect as written down in late 16th century.

1533 ———. Los olmecas en Chalco-Amaquemecan: un testimonio de Sahagún aprovechado por Chimalpahin. Amecameca, Estado de México: Centro de Estudios Bernardino de Sahagún, 1980. 41 p.; bibl.

Documents manner in which Chimalpahin utilized and readapted information from Chap. 29 of Book 10 of Sahagún's *Historia general* when describing early history of Chalco Amecameca. Includes transcriptions and translations of pertinent Nahuatl texts and valuable commentary by León-Portilla.

1534 Lockhart, James. Y la Ana lloró: cesión de un sitio para casa: San Miguel Tocuilan, 1583 (UNAM/T, 8, 1980, p. 21–33)

Especially valuable introduction by

Lockhart outlines idiosyncracies of speech and outlook to be considered when evaluating Nahuatl texts (or Spanish translations of Nahuatl texts) of the early colonial period. Well exemplified with text and translation of document concerned with grant of house site in San Miguel Tocuilan on east shore of Lake Texcoco in Valley of Mexico.

1535 Luckenbach, Alvin H. and Richard S. Levy. The implications of Nahua Aztecan lexical diversity for Mesoamerican culture-history (SAA/AA, 45 : 3, July 1980, p. 455–461, maps, table)

Argues that historical-linguistic investigations described provide strong "support for the theoretical validity of glottochronology." If supported by future research, glottochronological techniques may prove more useful for ethnohistorical research than supposed in recent years.

1536 Macazaga Ordoño, César. Los ritos de la fertilidad. México: Editorial Innovación, 1981. 72 p.; ill.; index.

Brief non-technical review of religious concepts, ceremonies, and gods associated with agriculture and fertility based mainly on the works of Sahagún. Notes possible links with offerings and other finds made during recent archaeological research at site of Templo Mayor of Tenochtitlan.

1537 Macías, Pablo G. Los chichimecas, apuntes para escribir la historia prehispánica de Michoacán: precedidos de un breve estudio sobre el origen del hombre y los primeros habitantes de América. Morelia: Gobierno del Estado de Michoacán, 1979. 272 p.; 21 leaves of plates; bibl.; ill.

Detailed reconstruction of Tarascan history based primarily on the well-known *Relación . . . de Michoacán*, with sometimes useful comments derived from author's examination of modern commentary by Kirchoff, and other colonial and modern sources.

1538 Martínez Girón, Eric Jorge. Los chorotegas de Mesoamérica meridional (YAXKIN, 3 : 1, junio 1979, p. 1–225, bibl., maps, plates)

Judiciously balanced review of unfortunately limited archaeological, linguistic, and ethnohistorical data dealing with southern frontier zone of preconquest Mesoamerica.

1539 Monjarás-Ruiz, Jesús. Sobre el testamento y la fundación de una capella-nía por parte de Don Alonso de Axayacatl, Cacique de Ixtapalapa (UNAM/T, 8, 1980, p. 289–321)

Published text of Don Alonso's *testamento* and related documents contain invaluable data concerning barrio organization, land-holding system, and early colonial organization at Ixtapalapa, with exceptionally useful analytic introduction by Monjarás-Ruiz.

1540 Münch, Guido. La población del obispado de Oaxaca en 1570 (UNAM/AA, 15, 1978, p. 67–82, maps, tables)

Critically reviews documentary evidence for late 16th century demographic trends based on both published and unpublished archival sources.

Myers, Robert A. Amerindians of the Lesser Antilles: a bibliography. See item **44**.

1541 Native Mesoamerican spirituality: ancient myths, discourses, stories, doctrines, hymns, poems from the Aztec, Yucatec, Quiche-Maya and other sacred traditions. Edited with a foreword, introd., and notes by Miguel León-Portilla. Translations by Miguel León-Portilla *et al.* Pref. by Fernando Horcasitas. New York: Paulist Press, 1980. 300 p.; bibl.; indexes (The Classics of Western spirituality)

Excellent selection of religiously inspired myths, hymns and poetic texts includes general introduction to Mesoamerican literature and civilization by León-Portilla. Most items reflect specifically Central Mexican literary production, with relatively brief samples from *Popul Vuh*, representing the Quiche of Highland Guatemala, and from sacred books of Yucatan.

1542 Ochoa, Lorenzo and Ernesto Vargas. El colapso maya, los chontales y Xicalango (CEM/ECM, 12, 1979, p. 61–91, bibl., ill., maps, plates, tables)

Skillfully organized discussion of archaeological as well as ethnohistorical sources for understanding possible or probable role of Chontal-Maya "invasion," which authors view as relatively abrupt rather than as gradual intermixing of ethnically distinct populations, in collapse of the classic Maya.

1543 Offner, Jerome A. Archival reports of poor crop yields in the early postconquest Texcocan heartland and their implications for studies of Aztez period population

(SAA/AA, 45:4, 1980, p. 847–856, bibl., ill., tables)

Analyzes quantitative data relating to crop yields from tribute fields in several towns in east and north parts of Valley of Mexico. Suggests that estimates of preconquest maize productivity by modern archaeologists and historians may be too high.

1544 ————. Aztec political numerology and human sacrifice: the ideological ramifications of the number six (UCLA/JLAL, 6:2, 1980, p. 205–215, bibl., ill.)

Argues that a sixfold division, "intimately connected with human sacrifice" and other important features of religious organization, was particularly salient at Tenochtitlan and Texcoco.

1545 ————. On Carrasco's use of theoretical "first principles" (SAA/AA, 46:1, 1981, p. 43–61, bibl.)

Brief response to critique of article by Carrasco (see item **1511**). Despite polemical tone, provides useful summary of points to be considered by scholars interested in this long-standing but still unresolved theoretical dispute.

1546 ————. On the inapplicability of "oriental despotism and the "Asiatic mode of production" to the Aztecs of Texcoco (SAA/AA, 46:1, 1981, p. 43–61, bibl., tables)

Argues that Texcocan state did not in fact dominate economic system to extent required by theoretical formulations cited in title, but was, as shown by both archaeological and ethnohistorical evidence, "neither a monolith capable of absolute power of enforcement, nor an internally unified entity" (see items **1511** and **1545**).

1547 ————. A reassessment of the extent and structuring of the empire of Techotlalatzin, fourteenth century ruler of Texcoco (ASE/E, 26:3, Summer 1979, p. 231–241, bibl., ill., tables)

Valuable for analysis of probable errors in Torquemada's reading of pictorial text of Codex Xolotl, as well as for judicious reconstruction of salient events during Techotlalatzin's reign.

1548 Olivera, Mercedes. Pillis y macehuales: las formaciones sociales y los modos de producción de Tecali del siglo XII al XVI. México: Centro de Investigaciones Superiores del INAH, 1978. 246 p.; bibl.; ill. (Ediciones de la Casa Chata; 6)

Brilliantly developed study of relatively small Chichimec state founded in 12th century AD. Emphasizes changing internal social formations under changing types of superordinate political rule during late preconquest and early colonial eras.

1549 Ortiz de Montellano, Bernard. The rational causes of illnesses among the Aztecs (UNC/K, 10:2, June 1977, p. 23–43, tables)

Carefully documented survey of early post-conquest literature to show that "the Aztecs were accurate observers of the physiological effects produced by plants." However, actual treatments used were derived more likely from beliefs about etiology than from actual medicinal properties of specific plants.

1550 Pérez Bolde, Alfredo. Interpretación del Códice Boturini. Guanajuato, México: Universidad de Guanajuato, Centro de Investigaciones Humanísticas, Escuela de Filosofía y Letras, 1980. 45 leaves; ill.

Straightforward if not always exact interpretation of glyphs and figures shown on each of the manuscript's 21 pictorial segments.

1551 Piña Chán, Román. Campeche durante el período colonial. México: Instituto Nacional de Antropología e Historia, 1977. 156 p.; ill.

Informative essay in regional history based on archival records together with small group of carefully selected published sources.

1552 Pohl, Mary. Ritual continuity and transformation in Mesoamerica: reconstructing the ancient Maya *cuch* ritual (SAA/AA, 46:3, 1981, p. 513–529, bibl., ill.)

Uses both ethnohistoric and ethnographic data to link modern ritual bullfights linked with cargo transfer ceremony throughout much of modern Maya region with deer sacrifice of *cuch* ritual as depicted in prehispanic art.

1553 Polo Sifontes, Francis. Título de Alotenango. Introd., epílogo y notas por Francis Polo Sifontes. Guatemala: Editorial José de Pineda Ibarra, 1979. 61 p.; bibl.; ill.

First publication of 1565 text concerning preconquest and early colonial history, land claims, and related documentation for the Cakchiquel town of San Juan Alotenango, with some information dealing with nearby Pipil Indians of Escuintla.

1554 Quezada, Noemí. Hernando Ruiz de Alarcón y su persecusión de idolatrías (UNAM/T, 8, 1980, p. 323–354)

Interesting series of previously unpublished texts from the Ramo Inquisición of the Archivo General de la Nación in Mexico City dealing with religiously motivated inquiries and activities of author of the *Tratado de las supersticiones y costumbres gentílicas,* an early 17th-century text dealing primarily with non-Christian rites of Central Mexico, many apparently derived from pre-Christian religious ideologies.

1555 Reyes García, Luis. Documentos manuscritos y pictóricos de Ichcateopan, Guerrero. México: Universidad Nacional Autónoma de México, 1979]i.e. 1980]. 217 p.; 25 p.; plates; bibl.; facsims.; ill. (Dictámenes Ichcateopan / Instituto de Investigaciones Históricas; 5)

Masterly study of alleged 16th-through 18th-century documents which claimed that Mexica emperor, Cuauhtemoc, was actually buried in Ichcateopan, Guerrero, after execution by Cortés in Tabasco. Reyes García shows still once again that the so-called "secret of Ichcateopan" arose in a context of regionally based historical nationalism, expressed through work of not very skilled forgers.

1556 ———. Documentos sobre tierras y señorío en Cuauhtinchan. México: Instituto Nacional de Antropología e Historia, Centro de Investigaciones Superiores, 1978. 220 p.; bibl.; indexes (Colección científica—Instituto Nacional de Antropología e Historia; 57: Fuentes [historia social])

Important series of 47 documents, most here published for the first time, dealing with political organization and land-holding arrangements in Cuauhtinchan, Tepeaca, and other nearby towns important in late prehispanic and colonial times.

1557 Romero Quiroz, Javier. Relación del pueblo de Ocuila a la parte del mediodía, por el prior fray Andrés de Aguirre, teólogo, confesor y predicador de españoles y lengua mexicana: fragmentos de la historia de Ocuila: el Monasterio de Ocuila. México: Gobierno del Estado de México, Oficialía Mayor, 1979. 145 p.; bibl.; ill. (Colección Historia)

Publishes one-page facsimile text and transcription of the actual *Relación,* followed by useful compilation of historical and archaeological information relating to Ocuillan in preconquest and colonial times.

1558 ———. La tierra del maíz, Nepintahihui. Metepec: Comisión Coordinadora para el Desarrollo Agrícola y Ganadero del Estado de México, 1979. 2 v.; bibl.; ill. (Colección Historia)

Simply written regional history provides helpful introduction to main sources dealing with Matlatzinca-speaking areas. Of particular interest to Mesoamericanists are late 16th-century map and litigation record sheding light on political geography in late preconquest and early colonial times.

1559 Sahagún, Bernardino de. General history of the things of New Spain. pt. 3, book 2, The ceremonies. Translated from the Aztec into English, with notes and illus., by Arthur J.O. Anderson and Charles E. Dibble. 2d ed., rev. Santa Fe, N.M.: School of American Research, 1981? 1 v.; bibl.; ill. (Monographs of the School of American Research; no. 14, pt. 3)

Substantially revised and greatly improved translation of Nahuatl text (Chaps. 20–38 and Appendix) of this fundamentally important source dealing with Aztec deities and ceremonialism. Translators' notes are updated to reflect progress in linguistic and ethnohistorical research since publication of first edition in 1951.

1560 Smith, Michael E. The role of the marketing system in Aztec society and economy: reply to Evans (SAA/AA, 45:4, 1980, p. 876–883, bibl.)

Response to critique by S. T. Evans (see item **1519**) of use of central place theory to explain settlement distribution in late prehispanic Central Mexico. Emphasizes problems inherent in any use of ethnohistorical data to explain Aztec-period socioeconomic system, and heuristic value of central place studies as contribution to "our emerging understanding of that system."

1561 Strecker, Matthias and Gloria Lara Pinto. Die *Relación Geográfica de Quinacama o Moxopipe* von Pedro de Santillana und Gaspar Antonio Chi (1851) (DGV/ZE, 104:1, 1979, p. 64–78, bibl., facsim.)

Transcription and German translation

of text now in Archivo General de Indias, Seville, Spain.

1562 Szecsy, Janos de. Utatlan (BBAA, 41 : 50, 1979, p. 149–175, map)

Posthumously published study completed in 1954 provides general description of site of Utatlan, reviews pertinent ethnohistorical documentation, and outlines program for future investigation. Recent survey of actual results of intensive investigations by Carmack (see item **1506**) and his associates can be usefully read in conjunction with this highly stimulating early work.

1563 Terga, Ricardo and **Emilio Vásquez Robles.** Tactic "el corazón del mundo," re ru cux c'cal: un estudio histórico etnológico de un pueblo Pokomchi de Alta Verapaz (GIIN/GI, 12 : 3/4, julio/dic. 1977, p. 67–126)

Well organized review of archaeological, ethnohistorical, and ethnographic data relating to Pokomchi in general as well as town cited in title.

1564 Troike, Nancy P. The identification of individuals in the Codex Colombino-Becker (UNAM/T, 8, 1980, p. 397–418, bibl.)

Insightful study of animal-head headdresses that provide pictorial clues to identity of extensively and intentionally damaged animal heads in codex, which "might typically be expected to appear in year and day dates, calendar and personal names, place signs, and the headdresses of individual figures."

1565 Williams, Barbara J. Pictorial representation of soils in the valley of Mexico: evidence from the Codex Vergara (in Historical geography of Latin America: papers in honor of Robert C. West. Editors, William V. Davidson and James J. Parsons. Baton Rouge: School of Geoscience, Louisiana State University, 1980, p. 51–62, bibl., ill.; tables [Geoscience and man; 21])

Brief description of informational content of the Codex Vergara, recently identified with barrio of La Asunción Tepetlaoztoc in eastern Valley of Mexico by author and H. R. Harvey. Valuable analysis of glyphs identifying soil types reflecting "a complex classification system that incorporated a number of different criteria," in this case applied to individual landholdings within area of approximately two km^2.

ETHNOHISTORY: South America

JOHN V. MURRA, *Professor of Anthropology, Cornell University and Institute of Andean Research*

LOOKING BACK TO 1967, when this contributor began recording in HLAS advances made in South American ethnohistory, it is evident that although the volume of research has increased greatly, the location of sources is as difficult as ever. Our request noted in 1967 (HLAS 29, p. 201) asking colleagues to bring to our attention ethnohistoric publications that were missed, especially outside the Andean area, went unanswered.

Two recent activities deserve special attention: the Instituto Otavaleño de Antropología continued to publish its journal Sarance (see HLAS 40 : 2165) and inaugurated a new monographic series, Colección Pendoneros, consisting of 100 volumes more than a score of which have been published, including reprints of original monographs. Many concern ethnohistory such as vol. 10, Frank Salomon's Los señores étnicos de Quito en la época de los incas (item **1673**), a translation of the author's dissertation at Cornell and awarded the 1981 Lewis Hanke Prize in ethnohistory by the Latin American Conference of the American Historical Association. This is the second time within recent years that the prize was awarded for Andean research (see HLAS 42, p. 136).

The establishment of the Sociedad Peruana de Etnohistoria and its sponsorship of several meetings in recent years has created an awareness of many topics in the nation's history which deal with the Andean population. The third gathering which met in Lima in May 1981 was devoted to "mitos, símbolos y rituales andinos." One session dealt with origin myths, another with communal rituals and the last with priesthood and shamanism. A special feature of the proceedings was the participation of Polish scholars of the Andes—one of whose contributions was noted in *HLAS 38:2153*. The proceedings of the second conference, devoted to the *ayllu*, are now published and annotated below.

A major new effort was the publication of an issue of the *Bulletin* of the Institut Français d'Etudes Andines (vol. 10, nos. 34) edited by France-Marie Renard-Casevitz. Its articles covered the Eastern lowlands from about the latitude of Quito to Cochabamba and combined ethnographic field work with serious study of the historical record. Most of these papers emerged from a seminar conducted in Paris by Simone Dreyfus-Gamelon and were at a later date the object of comparative discussion. This issue of *Bulletin* provides a superb introduction to the study of the *selva alta* and its past inhabitants. Moreover, the maps supplied by each author in addition to the four special ones prepared by the editor and the Institut Français make this the most important contribution to the study of lowland ethnohistory since Alfred Métraux's *Handbook of South American Indians*, published 40 years ago.

The Fundación La Salle of Caracas has undertaken a new monographic series entitled *Los aborígenes de Venezuela*, edited by Walter Coppens. Vol. 1, dedicated to *Etnología antigua* came out in 1980, on excellent paper, well illustrated and indexed. Planned as far back as 1970, this series intends to make available in Spanish a ready reference to the country's Amerindian groups. In every case the group's own name for itself will be the one used rather than more familiar ones (e.g., the Guajiro will be the Wayú).

Another new series hospitable to South American ethnohistory was inaugurated at Syracuse University and will be edited by Rolena Adorno. Its first publication, *From oral to written expression: native Andean chronicles of the early colonial period* (item **1602**) consists of several articles most of which are annotated below.

The location of new sources stimulated the growing interest in the insurrections of the late 18th century in Cusco, Puna and Charcas about which new interpretations are offered. A thesis on Thupa Amaru's revolt was defended by Jan Szeminski at the Academy of History in Warsaw. Its translation into Spanish is being circulated in typescript and one hopes that it will soon find a publisher.

In addition to their well known contributions to Andean archaeology, scholars at the University of Tokyo have initiated ethnological and historical research as well. There is available now, in both Japanese and Spanish, an account of relations between the populations of Lake Titicaca's altiplano region and the coast.

Rómulo Cúneo Vidal's papers have been the subject of much interest for a long time. He lived in Tacna when its fate was to be decided by plebiscite and collected materials throughout the region to strengthen Peru's position. Published partially during his lifetime, the papers were issued recently by the family as collected works and include materials of ethnohistoric interest.

Most of the journals annotated below continue to publish, if irregularly. A new one, *Historia Boliviana*, issued in Cochabamba by Josep Barnadas, published two issues in 1981. This journal encourages contributions from ethnohistorians as well as scholars concerned with the colonial and republican periods.

1566 Adorno, Rolena. El arte de la persuasión: el Padre de las Casas y Fray Luis de Granada en la obra de Waman Puma de Ayala (UCV/E, 4:8, julio/dic. 1979, p. 167–189, facsims.)

Among European writers used by Waman Puma (see *HLAS 42:1581*), some of those most interesting are those he shared with Garcilaso de la Vega, the Inca. Both Andean writers engaged in quite different dialogues with same interlocutors. Waman Puma thought highest of European writers who composed grammars and dictionaries; next came those who defended the humanity of the American population; chronicles were marginal to the text and even if used, not quoted. In his use of biblical material, his model was Fray Luis de Granada. "Waman Puma eligió la retórica del sermón como método discursivo . . . es el estilo por excelencia de la persuasión."

1567 Agurto, Santiago. Cusco: la traza urbana de la cuidad incaica. Cuzco, Peru: UNESCO, 1980. 158 p.; charts; ill.; maps (UNESCO project PER; 39)

Detailed exploration of Inka capital's archaeological and architectural remains. Written sources are used sporadically to check assertions but clearly primary records were not consulted to determine survey priorities. This internationally financed project was not committed to search for new documents.

1568 Alès, Catherine. Les tribus indiennes de l'Ucayali su XVIème siècle (IFEA/B, 10:3/4, 1981, p. 87–97, bibl., chart, map)

Ucayali was traced somewhat later than more northern rivers flowing east of the Andes. Study centers on Juan de Salinas Loyola's 1557 expedition. Size of villages described depended on size of households: if these people lived in communal houses like those found elsewhere in the region, towns may have had as many as 5,000 inhabitants.

1569 Almeida, Ileana. Códigos culturales y movilidad semántica en el Kechua (III/AI, 39:4, 1979, p. 721–731, bibl.)

Operating with a 19th-century evolutionary scheme about place of "totemism" in human history, author attempts to trace transformation of falcon cult to Inca sun worship. Finds evidence in phonetic shift from *indi* (a bird) to *inti* (the Sun). However, author is aware that "dichos universales se refieren a procesos bastante generales, pues, cada lengua expresa correlaciones internas propias a su sistema y ésto impone ciertas limitaciones para fijar universales lingüísticos . . .".

1570 Antolínez, Gilberto. Sobre biografías e iconografías de indígenas notables de Venezuela (VMJ/BIV, 18:15, enero/junio 1979, p. 155–192, bibl.)

Alphabetic compilation of native leaders from various periods and several places on Venezuelan territory, based on published sources.

1571 Ascher, Marcia and **Robert Ascher.** Code of quipu databook. Ann Arbor: University of Michigan Press, 1978. 1 v.; microfiche.

Provides uniform system for describing and analyzing the *khipu*, based on detailed examination of 191 specimens in many repositories.

1572 —— and ——. Code of the quipu: a study in media, mathematics and culture. Ann Arbor: University of Michigan, 1981. 166 p.; charts; ill.

On the basis of hundreds of *khipu* in museums and private collections, the Aschers consider many functions postulated by regularities of knot distribution. Some of their information is drawn from 16th-century written sources. Significant contribution to the search for Andean sources about the Andean past.

Barthel, Thomas S. The eighth land: the Polynesian discovery and settlement of Easter Island. See *HLAS 43:602*.

1573 Blancpain, Jean-Pierre. Le Chili républicain et la fin de la frontière araucane (PUF/RH, 531, juillet/sept. 1979, p. 79–116, map)

Araucanians came to Chile from across the Andes. Their resistance to European conquest gave a special tone to colonial rule south of the Bíobío. Article based on secondary sources stresses 19th-century image of Araucanian territory as an "intolerable anachronism." After 1870, efforts to integrate Araucanians into the national processes were more successful: railroad crossed the territory and new settlers were encouraged to settle on Indian lands.

1574 Caillavet, Chantal. Etnohistoria ecuatoriana: nuevos datos sobre el Otavalo prehispánico (BCE/C, 11, 1981, p. 109–127, bibl., charts, map)

Confusion exists as to the names of ethnic groups, their lords, and later colonial towns. These are frequently interchangeable and with time the geographic identification has prevailed over ethnic names. Author uses the case of Otavalo to show factors one must take into account. Sophisticated and methodologically ingenious article.

1575 ———. Tribut téxtil et caciques dans le nord de l'Audiencia de Quito (Mélanges de la Casa de Velásquez [E. de Boccard, Paris] 16, 1980, p. 179–201, bibl., ill., map)

Use of textiles as tribute was probably an Inka imposition in the northern Andes; their role greatly expanded in colonial times. Caillavet attempts to separate earlier from later exactions, and examines role played by ethnic lords in mobilizing energies and distributing the product. Marginal continuities can be detected today.

1576 Cajías de la Vega, Fernando. La población indígena de Paria en 1785 (*in* Estudios bolivianos en Homenaje a Gunnar Mendoza [see *HLAS 42:2638*] p. 41–100, bibl., chart, map)

A major administrative center in pre-European times, Paria—on the main north-south Inka highway—was also a major redistribution center for state maize. Before independence, when the figures here discussed were compiled, Paria was a rather insignificant, provincial backwater, consisting of seven subdivisions from which *mitayos* were sent to Potosí—a few thousand peasants. As late as 1785, highlanders still hung on to small lowland territories and to pastures elsewhere. Census papers used here were found in Buenos Aires' National Archives.

1577 Cardich, Augusto. Dos divinidades relevantes del antiguo panteón centroandino: Yana Raman o Libiac Cancharco y Rayguana. La Plata, Argentina: Universidad de La Plata, 1981. 36 p.; bibl.; map (Cátedra de Arqueología Americana. Serie monográfica; 1)

At the sources of the Marañón one can still find a high-altitude population of herders and cultivators who worship pre-European deities. Cardich connects contemporary practices with rites described and condemned by the "extirpadores de idolatrías" in the

17th century. Archaeological connections with the "Yaro empire" (see *HLAS 40:2048*) are suggestive but require excavation for fuller verification.

1578 Carrera Colín, Juan. Apuntes para una investigación etnohistórica de los cacicazgos del corregimiento de Latacunga: siglos XVI y XVII (BCE/C, 11, 1981, p. 129–179, bibl., tables)

Litigation over lands and records of purchases by Indians over a century allow us to trace changes in status and wealth of several Andean ethnic groups. There was considerable geographic mobility in central Ecuador in the 17th century and a weakening of ethnic ties, particularly those related to Inka social structure.

1579 Celestino, Olinda and Albert Meyers. La dinámica socioeconómica del patrimonio cofradial en el Perú colonial: Jauja en el siglo XVII (UM/REAA, 11, 1981, p. 183—206, bibl., charts, map)

Of the many European religious institutions imposed in the Andes, the *cofradía* was remarkably successful. It established a continuum with prehispanic practices while furthering adaptation to a new colonial world. Authors survey in detail how this transition was implemented at Jauja; the *cofradías* acquired land, sponsored rituals, and served as meeting places for both Indians and mestizos.

1580 Chang-Rodríguez, Raquel. Writing as resistance: Peruvian history and the *Relación* of Titu Cusi Yupanqui (*in* From oral to written expression: native Andean chronicles of the early colonial period [see item **1602**] p. 41–62, bibl., ill.)

Attempt to magnify the importance of a short text, dictated by the Inka prince, a refugee in the Eastern forest, to a European missionary. Seeks to make intelligible the Andean point of view and sense of grievance in the new terminology.

1581 Chaumeil, Jean-Pierre and Josette Fraysse-Chaumeil. "La canela y el Dorado:" les indigènes du Napo et du Haut-Amazone au XVIème siècle (IFEA/B, 10:3/4, 1981, p. 55–86, bibl., ill., map)

In order to prepare an ethnohistoric atlas of the Eastern lowlands of the Andes, authors have restudied records of incursions by Orellana (1541) and Ursúa (1561). While very different, both expeditions were all concerned with finding El Dorado. After a thorough study of the bibliography, authors begin here with Inka penetration of the East, which will be followed by Alonso de Alvarado and others referred to as "los amazonautas."

Chávez Velásquez, Nancy A. La materia médica en el Incanato. See *HLAS 43 : 1488.*

1582 Choque-Canqui, Roberto. Cacicazgos aymara: siglos XVI–XVII (Historia [Boletín de la Carrera de Historia, Universidad de San Andrés, La Paz] 3 : 13, 1979?, p. 1–19)

"El estudio del cacicazgo es una de las tareas primordiales de la historiografía boliviana, para así poder comprender las relaciones socio-económicas qui vinculaban el mundo andino con la sociedad colonial." Stresses documenting how Aymara lords were forced to participate in colonial exactions. Their sources of wealth are described.

1583 ———. Las haciendas de los caciques guarachi en el Alto Perú: 1673–1734 (III/AI, 39:4, 1979, p. 733–748, bibl.)

Of several Aymara lords, active in colonial times, the richest documentation concerns the Guarachi (see *HLAS 40:2107*). Their preeminence in the historiography is due to their claim to high status in Inka times, their skills in accumulating wealth in both Andean and colonial economies and their literacy. Most interesting part of their claims concerns lands first administered by the Guarachi as lords of the Pacaje, but which in time were claimed as personal property. Some of these lands were in the Eastern lowlands, though apparently they did not harvest coca-leaf.

1584 Choy, Emilio. Antropología e historia. Lima: UNMSM, 1979. 437 p.; bibl.; ill.

Reproduces 10 articles by Choy in diverse publications (1945–76). While all have some ethnohistorical content, the one most frequently used is "Sistema Social Incaico," published in *Idea, artes y letras* (1960) where he argues that a "slave mode of production" was characteristic of the Inka state.

1585 Civrieux, Marc de. Los cumanogoto y sus vecinos (in Los aborígenes de Venezuela. v. 1, Etnología antigua. Edited by Audrey Butt Colson. Caracas: Fundación La Salle de Ciencias Naturales, Instituto Caribe de Antropología y Sociología, 1980, v. 1, p. 29–239, bibl., ill., indexes, maps)

Detailed survey of early records of coastal dwellers whose descendants are alive today. In addition to their frequent mention in earliest sources, author documents their presence throughout colonial period, on the basis of detail provided by missionaries. Given author's familiarity with ethnology of other forest groups, he is able to interpret information provided by historical accounts. Includes few pages on present-day Cumanogoto.

1586 Cock Carrasco, Guillermo. El ayllu en la sociedad andina: alcances y perspectivas (in Ethnohistoria y antropología andina. Edited by Amalia Castelli, Marcia Koth de Paredes and Mariana Mould de Pease. Lima: n.p., 1981, p. 231–253, bibl.)

While it is difficult to define what an *ayllu* was in Andean social organization, it is easier to discern what it was not. It was somehow related to the "cosmovisión," the perception of the heavens and man's fate in relation to them. *Ayllus* fit within the tripartite and dual divisions of society; also, they may have served tribute and land-holding functions.

1587 ——— and Mary Eileen Doyle. Del culto solar a la clandestinidad de Into y Punchao (PMNH/C, 12, 1979, p. 1–23, bibl.)

Assumption that the solar cult disappeared upon Inka state's destruction is commonplace in Andean studies. While this may be true of the state cult, there is no reason to assume it vanished at local and regional levels. One trace of its persistence is apparent in the Taki Onqoy cult of 1560s whereby the defeated Sun is recalled; more significantly the 17th-century "extirpation of idolatries" campaign provides ample evidence that belief in the sun as procreator, guarantor of the crops and destination of the souls was fully functional.

1588 Colson, Audrey Butt. Introducción (in Los aborígenes de Venezuela. v. 1, Etnología antigua. Edited by Audrey Butt Colson. Caracas: Fundación La Salle de Ciencias Naturales, Instituto Caribe de Antropología y Sociología, 1980, v. 1, p. 15–25, bibl.)

Discusses background of series dedicated to ethnology of groups, most of whom have disappeared. Rejects label of "ethnohistory" for these studies; this term "se deja para describir el estudio de la propia visión histórica y de los procesos sociales en general que ha recorrido a través del tiempo determinada sociedad." Otherwise, author welcomes routine use of historical records by ethnologists in South America.

1589 Curatola, Marco. Posesión y chamanismo en el culto de crisis del Taqui Ongo (*in* Congreso Peruano del Hombre y la Cultura Andina, *3d, Lima, 1977*. El hombre y la cultura andina [see *HLAS 43:253*] v. 3, p. 43–64)

Combines ethnohistoric materials drawn from 17th-century "extirpations of idolatries" records in an attempt to clarify meaning of a messianic cult which arose in 1560s. Latter is defined as "una religión de carácter chamánico, en cuanto están presentes en él . . . todos los elementos clásicos del chamanismo clásico."

1590 Deustua, José. Derroteros de la etnohistoria del Perú (IPA/A, 15, 1980, p. 173–178)

Inquiry into specifics of Andean ethnohistory, provoked by Pablo Macera's musing of future of Peruvian history in his *Historia en el Perú: ciencia e ideología*. Deustua shows there are several kinds of ethnohistory: one based on reinterpretations of the "chronicles;" other more recent ones which use administrative and litigation records; but particularly María Rostworowski's work.

1591 Diez de Medina, Francisco Tadeo. Diario del Cerco de La Paz, 1781. La Paz: s.n., 1981. 275 p.; bibl.; ill.; index; maps.

Existence of this diary kept by oidor of Audiencia of Chile who survived Andean rebels' siege of La Paz has been noted before but this is the first edition of the full text. Diez de Medina made frequent notes during siege, commenting on persons, policies, individual actors. Although he was not familiar with the Andes and many of his comments are either naive or of second and even third hand, he was inquisitive and tried to understand what he saw. "Si bien el oidor no trasmitió su propio juicio, fue portavoz, en cambio, de un grupo de hombres que vio, sufrió y produjo un hecho histórico [sic]." Edited by María Eugenia del Valle de Siles; introduction by Gunnar Mendoza.

1592 Dillehay, Tom. Relaciones prehispánicas costa-sierra en el valle del río Chillón (*in* Congreso Peruano del Hombre y la Cultura Andina, *3d, Lima,*

1977. El hombre y la cultura andina [see *HLAS 43:253*] v. 3, p. 120–140, bibl., map)

Relations existing between coastal and highland ethnic groups continue to elicit interest. While the two life patterns seemed very different, regions' inhabitants were familiar with one another. Highland penetration of coastal valleys like Chillón, so well documented in historical sources, is confirmed by archaeological study. Given their small size, "highland colonies" provide unsatisfactory explanation, a better one would be commerce, subordination and struggles, "interaction spheres," and temporary migrations. Coastal groups had to defend not only their upriver installations but also their shore settlements against other maritime peoples.

1593 Duviols, Pierre. Algunas reflexiones acerca de las tesis de la estructura dual del poder incaico (PUCP/H, 4:2, 1980, p. 183–196, bibl.)

Possibility that the Inka king list transmitted by 16th-century European observers was expanded deliberately by separating the two monarchs ruling simultaneously, has been mentioned before (see *HLAS 42:1618*). Duviols returns to subject and suggests that list's extension took place in Cusco in order to make Inka system more understandable to European administration and to increase numbers of those eligible for "noble" status.

1594 ———. La Capacocha: mecanismo y función del sacrificio humano, su proyección geométrica, su papel en la política integracionista y en la economía redistributiva del Tawantinsuyu (PIA/A, 9, 1976, p. 11–57, bibl., charts)

Human sacrifices offered in Cusco provided blood and other ritual benefits to many shrines located along *zeque* lines, radiating from the center. Other sacrifices were made at the periphery and eventually reached the center. Beyond their ritual ends, such sacrifices bound together the capital with incorporated polities. Various meanings of such sacrifices are considered; Duviols thinks the real spelling should be *Capac ucha*, the main expiatory or purifying rite.

1595 ———. Periodización y política: la historia prehispánica del Perú según Guaman Poma de Ayala (IFEA/B, 9:3/4, 1980, p. 1–18, bibl., ill.)

Compares periods in ancient history utilized by Waman Puma to record Andean and Biblical traditions. Waman Puma attempted to fit both traditions into one original common creation scheme for all men. An exception to the latter were the Inka whose rule was illegitimate and lacked the "spark" connecting them to mankind's common original creator. Duviols suggests such perception forces Waman Puma into an anti-Las Casas position, favoring paradoxically, Viceroy de Toledo, who also claimed the Inka were illegitimate rulers.

1596 Earls, John and **Irene Silverblatt.** Sobre la instrumentación de la cosmología Inca en el sitio arqueológico de Moray (*in* Runakunap Kawsayninkupaq Rurasqankunaqa: la tecnología en el mundo andino. Heather Lechtman and Ana María Soldi, editors. México: UNAM, 1981, p. 444–473, bibl., charts, ill., maps)

In contrast to European science, reference points in the perception of the universe are not absolute in the Andes but culturally defined and changeable depending on the immediate context. Neither does Andean science separate time from space in ways familiar to Westerners (see *HLAS 42:1626–1627*). Cosmologies are not only systems for ordering the universe but also classifications designed to fit tasks assigned by society. The "Amphitheater" at Moray, Cuzco region, is now perceived as an agricultural monument, a "greenhouse." Its tier measurements confirm levels' wide range of temperatures and climates. Fieldwork confirms oral tradition that astronomical observations could be made at the monument. Postulates a biospheric system for Andean science which produces hierarchical organization necessary to give man a productive causality. System results from dialectic transformation of male solar cycle and female ecologic-climatologic cycle.

1597 Ellefsen, Bernardo. Las concubinas de los Sapa incas difuntos (IFEA/B, 11:1/2, 1982, p. 11–18, bibl.)

Dead Inka kings kept their revenues including services of women from their harems and of a "double," who spoke in the name of the deceased. Mummy itself became a shrine, not unlike the Sun. The latter, however, was present in many state installations, while the king's mummy remained in the Cusco region.

Espinoza Soriano, Waldemar. Los chachapoyas y cañares de Chiara, Huamananga, aliados de España. See item **2674.**

1598 ———. El curaca de los cayambé y su sometimiento al imperio español, siglos XV y XVI (IFEA/B, 9:1/2, 1980, p. 89–119, bibl.)

Inhabitants of northern Tawantinsuyu provinces resisted Inka conquest as is well documented in Cusco-centric sources. Here Espinoza attempts to trace such claims by concentrating on the genealogy of several 16th-century ethnic lords.

1599 ———. 1780 [i.e. Mil setecientos ochenta]: movimientos antifiscales en la sierra norte de la Audiencia de Lima y repercusiones tupamarista en la misma zona: nuevas perspectivas (IPA/A, 17/18, 1981, p. 169–201, bibl.)

Places 1780 Tupamaro movement within wider context of resistance and insurrection. In northern Peru, movement was directed against increased taxes and forced distribution of commercial goods. Once these exactions were extended to non-Indian population, resistance grew. Espinoza surveys modes of resistance in northern region and manner in which it was defeated, largely under the leadership of Bishop Martínez Compañón. *Cabildos de naturales* lost many of their rights as consequence.

1600 ———. El Reino de los Chono, al este de Guayaquil, siglos XV–XVII: el testimonio de la arqueología y la etnohistoria (PMNH/HC, 13/14, 1981, p. 7–60, bibl., maps)

Uses 1599–1603 description from Sevillan Archives to assert existence and importance of a polity located in Daule and Guayas basins. Inhabitants were apparently of eastern, Amazonian derivation. Espinoza suggests they could be identified with Milagro archaeological remains. Includes only a few texts of ones quoted.

1601 Esquivel y Navia, Diego de. Notas cronológicas de la gran ciudad del Cuzco. Edited by Féliz Denegri Luna. v. 1/2. Lima: Biblioteca de Cultura Peruana, 1980. 2 v (310, 472 p.)

Written in 18th century, these *noticias* offer direct connection to much earlier chronicles, while also reflecting contemporaneous debates about Peru's future and possibility of an Andean solution. It seems that like Gregorio García (see item **1650**), Esquivel had access, if almost two centuries later, to sources like pt. 2 of Betanzos (1551) which reproduces interviews with surviving members of royal lineages in Cusco.

Fernández Esquivel, Franco. Procedencia de los esclavos negors, analizada a través del complejo de distribución, desarrollado desde Cartagena. See item **2586**.

1602 From oral to written expressions: native Andean chronicles of the early colonial period. Edited by Roleno Adorno. Syracuse, N.Y.: Maxwell School of Citizenship and Public Affairs, Syracuse University, 1982. 181 p.; bibl., facsims. (Foreign and comparative studies. Latin American series; no. 4)

Collection of essays prefaced by editor, focusing "on those first ethnic Americans who took up the pen . . . to recall the oral tradition out of which they drew their sources."

1603 Fuenzalida V., Fernando. El Cristo pagano de los Andes: una cuestión de identidad y otra sobre las eras solares (PUCP/DA, 4, 1979, p. 1–10, bibl.)

Ethnographic accounts of religion in the Andes frequently mention population's identification of God, Christ and other European deities with Andean Sun who, in turn, may be thought inseparable from Inka kings such as Wayna Qhapaq. Inkarri also may be listed along with figures in Christian pantheon; even the Trinity is believed to have Andean counterparts.

1604 Gisbert, Teresa. Iconografía y mitos indígenas en el arte. La Paz, Bolivia: Gisbert, 1980. 250 p.; 144 p. of plates; bibl.; ill. (some col.); indexes.

Andean component in colonial art is more pervasive than has been admitted. Even when overt theme is Christian, Andean deities and ideas are present (e.g., Pachamama, the mountain peaks, the Sun and the Pleiades, the Incas, native facial features). With chronology in mind, author shows who and when "mestizo" traits emerge in painting and architecture. For art historian's comment, see item **304**.

1605 ———. Los Incas en la pintura virreinal del siglo XVIII (III/AI, 39:4, 1979, p. 749–772, bibl.)

In early 18th century, limeño artist, Alonso de la Cueva, produced an engraving of Inka kings. His models are unknown but it is established that other portraits and statues were produced during colonial years. Gisbert analyzes colonial context of engravings, including hand-lettered texts stressing continuity between Inka and European royalty. It is not clear where engraving is today—it was studied by Imbelloni in the 1940s. Author traces various copies and alterations of this model. As Thupa Amaru II's rebellion threatened European rule, reproductions were censored. Article reproduces decision to suppress them, a few years before Independence.

1606 ———. Toynbee y la civilización andina (Illimani [Revista del Instituto de Investigaciones Históricos y Culturales de la H. Municipalidad de La Paz] 10, 1978, p. 11–27)

". . . pero su error principal estriba en considerar extinta la Civilización Andina . . . Toynbee desconoce el caracter 'mestizo' de esta parte de América . . . La Civilización Andina es una civilización sumergida pero no extinta . . ."

1607 González, Alberto Rex. La Cuidad de Chicoana: su importancia histórica y arqueológica (Síntomas [Buenos Aires] 3, 1981, p. 15–21, bibl., ill., maps)

Although Chicoana was major "city" in southern Andes, through which passed all early invaders of what today are Argentina and Chile, its location is still a matter of debate. González thinks that by combining archaeological evidence with historical descriptions the urban center can be located. In valleys known today as Calchaquí, only La Paya qualifies as a "city"; it was a populated place even before the Inka. González and P. P. Díaz excavated it and are certain that architecture and storehouses are Inka in date.

1608 ———. Patrones de asentamiento incaicos en una provincia marginal del imperio: implicancias socioculturales (in Prehistoric settlement pattern studies: retrospect and prospect. New York: s.n., 1980, p. 1–32, bibl. [Burg Wartenstein Symposium; no. 861])

Main attraction of Northwest Argentina for Inka was mineral wealth. Although Inka road is visible, administrative centers, palatial architecture and other signs of intensive occupation are few. González surveys terraces, fortresses, high altitude offerings, both those built from scratch and above preexisting installations. Inka settlements south of Lake Titicaca should be compared to other peripheral areas, particularly in the north.

1609 Gow, David D. Símbolo y protesta: movimientos redentores en Chiapas y en los Andes peruanos (III/AI, 39 : 1, 1979, p. 47–80, bibl.)

An Andean protest movement against European rule and worship of European deities emerged in 1560s (see *HLAS 29:2174*). Labeled Taqui Onqoy, it urged followers to "dance" away the opressors ritually. Gow compares it to three other messianic movements, two of them in Chiapas. Andean rebels wanted not the return of historic Inka rulers whose defeat was evident but that of an earlier and broader class of Andean power wielders. Examines role of the Virgin and of Santiago as mediators between both religious systems.

1610 Guachalla, Luis Fernando. El imperio de los cuatro suyus: breve exposición político-social del incario. La Paz: s.n., 1981, 189 p.; ill.

1611 Guillén Guillén, Edmundo. Titu Cusi Yupanqui y su tiempo: el estado imperial inka y su trágico fin (PMNH/HC, 13/14, 1981, p. 61–991, bibl.)

Stresses Inka resistance to European rule and attempts chronology of first 40 years, ending with Thupa Amaru's 1572 execution. Describes resistance as "guerra de españoles contra el Perú." Pizarro's Nov. 1533 entry into Cusco was at invitation of new Inka king who later rose against his European allies because of their atrocities. Guillén considers rising a war of reconquest against Spain, not just a local rebellion. Describes penultimate king in some detail and analyzes his 1570 memorandum. Author suggests it offers a reliable "Peruvian perspective."

1612 Harrison, Regina. Modes of discourse: the *Relación de antigüedades deste Reino del Perú* by Juan de Santacruz Pachacuti Yamqui Salcamaygua (*in* From oral to written expression: native Andean chronicles of the early colonial period [see item **1602**] p. 65–99, bibl.)

Pachacuti Yamqui was aware of difficult task undertaken: to send a message about his own culture in the victors' code. Analyzes series of Quechua verbs dealing with oral reporting, their use in mythic contexts. Reviews principles of Quechua poetics. Cognitive processes not readily translatable

into Spanish but Salcamaygua lists those he struggled with. A much neglected text is thus made accessible.

1613 Hartmann, Roswith and **Olaf Holm.** La "romana" en tiempos prehispánicos y su uso actual en la costa del Ecuador (Miscelánea Antropológica Ecuatoriana [Boletín de los museos del Banco Central del Ecuador, Museo Antropológico y Pinacoteca del Banco Central del Ecuador, Guayaquil] 1, 1981, p. 155–178, bibl., ill.; tables)

Andean weights and measures are of interest to students of the Andes but progress in this field has been slow (see *HLAS 29:2187*). One approach consists of measuring existing prehistoric buildings; another concentrates on enduring ethnographic artifacts. Authors review sketchy information in early written sources and survey state of the art. Major contribution is a study of existing balances on the Manabi coast, comparable to the *wipi*, further south, in the highlands.

1614 ——— and Udo Oberem. Quito: un centro de educación de indígenas en el siglo XVI (*in* Contribuições à antropologia em homenagem ao professor Egon Schaden. São Paulo: Universidade de São Paulo, 1981, p. 105–127 [Coleção Paulista. Serie ensaios; 4])

Early existence of schools for sons of ethnic lords is well documented. In Quito such schools appear very early; one was run by Greek, but most teachers were Franciscan monks. One purpose was conversion, but recruitment of interpreters is also mentioned in reports. Since many Andean dwellers did not know "lengua general de ynga," Quechua was taught along with Spanish. Some students eventually became prominent members of native administrative corps (see item **1672**), like Pedro de Zámbiza. By 17th century such educational activities were curtailed and eventually abandoned. By the 18th, pre-Inka languages began to disappear.

1615 Hidalgo Lehuedé, Jorge. Culturas y etnías protohistóricas: área andina meridional (Chungara [Universidad del Norte, Arica, Chile] 8, 1981, p. 209–253, bibl., maps)

Attempts to classify Andean polities in contemporary territories of Chile and Argentina as nuclear groups in altiplano and peripheral ones to east and south. Correlates information from 16th-century sources with recent archaeology. Notable improvement over information on this region in *Handbook of South American Indians.*

1616 ———. Fases de la rebelión indígena en 1781 en el Corregimiento de Atacama y esquema de la inestabilidad política que la precede, 1749–81 (Chungara [Universidad del Norte, Arica, Chile] 9, 1982, p. 192–246, bibl., maps)

Continuing his studies of echoes of Tupa Amaru and Tupa Catari rebellions in what today is northern Chile (see *HLAS* 42:1650–1651), Hidalgo uses Archivo de Indias' unpublished sources to document reasons why desert dwellers joined in the revolt. Paniri, leader of the movement "tenía el estatus de indio noble . . . cacique y alcalde; de gran movilidad . . . hubiera podido estar vinculado a la arriería; hablaba varias lenguas . . . ; su nombre . . . 'el que viene' pudo tener un sentido mesiánico . . ." Before he was captured and killed, Paniri ordered "la revaloración del traje indígena y la negación de la potencia de las divinidades cristianas . . ."

1617 Hurtado de Mendoza S., W. Wiraqocha. Carátula, César Gavancho, Jorge Grados. Illus., César Gavancho. Lima?: Editorial Nueva Epoca, 1980. 187 p.; 21 leaves of plates; ill. (Mitos prehispánicos)

Bilingual version, rewritten for the layman.

1618 Jérez, Francisco de. La conquête du Pérou, 1534. Introduction by Pierre Duviols. Paris: s.n., 1982. 142 p.; appendixes; bibl.; ill.; map.

Republished 19th-century French translation by Henri Ternaux Compans of official report by Pizarro's secretary about invasion of the Andes. Pierre Duviols' introduction places report in wider historical context. He also supplies five short appendixes.

1619 Julien, Catherine J. Koli: a language spoken on the Peruvian coast (Andean Perspective Newsletter [The University of Texas, Austin] 3, 1979, p. 5–11, bibl., maps)

As late as 1790, Koli was spoken in Moquegua valley, along with better known Andean languages. Moreover, highland Aymara polities had "settlements" on the coast. What were the relations between Koli and Aymara, remains to be determined.

1620 Knapp, Gregory. El nicho ecológico llanura húmeda en la economía prehistórica de los Andes de altura: evidencias etnohistóricas, geográficas y arqueológicas (Sarance [Instituto Otavaleño de Antropología, Otavalo, Ecuador] 9, 1981, p. 83–95, bibl., charts)

Discussions of complementarity among several tiers lack specificity about geography: they do not distinguish sufficiently between level surfaces and terraces. Northern Ecuador survey, where some archaeological evidence has been collected, shows frequent remains of ridged fields. Cultural ecology of high altitude Andes is still to be refined.

1621 Kuz'mishchev, Vladimir Aleksandrovich. U istokov obschchestvennoĭ mysli Peru: Garsilaso i ego istoriia inkov. Moskva: Nauka, 1979. 383 p.; bibl.

Places Garcilaso in lascasian and utopian tradition and compares him with Campanella and similar writers in the West. Historical approach to Garcilaso is not enough; ethnographic evaluation is also necessary. Older bibliography is readily used. Welcome addition to Andean field by Soviet scholar.

1622 Larraín Barros, Horacio. Cronistas de raigambre indígena. Otavalo, Ecuador: Instituto Otavaleño de Antropología, 1980. 2 v. (376, 351 p.); bibl.; charts; ill. (Serie Etnohistoria. Colección Pendoneros; nos. 13/14)

Anthology based on published sources.

1623 ———. Demografía y asentamientos indígenas en la Sierra Norte del Ecuador en el siglo XVI. Otavalo, Ecuador: Instituto Otavaleño de Antropología, 1980. 2 v. (230, 223 p.); bibl.; charts (Serie Etnohistoria. Colección Pendoneros; nos. 11/12)

Based on secondary sources.

1624 ———. Identidad cultural e indicadores eco-culturales del grupo étnico chango (UCC/NG, 6, 1978/1979, p. 63–76, bibl.)

As early as 1640, coastal fishermen and mollusk gatherers of what today is northern Chilean coast were known as *changos.* Their habitat is referred to by ecologists as "perennial drought, year 'round.'" This explains their exclusive adaptation to the sea, with occasional hunting inland. Larraín notes that earlier descriptions of coastal populations include such fishermen but do not use the term *chango*.

1625 López-Baralt, Mercedes. La persistencia de las estructuras simbólicas andinas en los dibujos de Guamán Poma de Ayala (UCLA/JLAL, 5 : 1, Summer 1979, p. 83–116, bibl., plates)

Symbolic perception of space in Inka times is hard to ascertain through European sources. While Waman Puma did follow western models (see *HLAS 42:1662*), there is a major Andean component in his work: bipartition, tripartition and division into four. Author's very name relates falcon, associated with upper realm, with puma, land-related beast. Author's handling of left and right suggests he did not merely reflect prevailing pairing but actively tried to influence reader.

1626 Luxton, Richard N. The Inca quipus and Guaman Poma de Ayala's *First new chronicle and good government* (IAA, 5 : 4, 1979, p. 315–341, bibl., facsims.)

Assumes that Waman Puma's historical materials derive from oral tradition recorded on khipu. Suggests comparisons with similar materials in Mesoamerica.

1627 Martínez, Gabriel. Espacio Lupaqa: algunas hipótesis de trabajo (Etnohistoria y Antropología Andina [Museo Nacional de Historia, Lima] 1981, p. 263–280, bibl., chart, maps)

Using published sources from 16th and 17th century, Martínez tried to locate various "towns," moieties, ayllus and individual land parcels on a map. There is no territorial set to moieties: "upper" and "lower" moieties have lands in several tiers. Each could share acreage. Since work is based on data provided by maps (fieldwork still in planning stage) it is particularly difficult to identify what pastures correspond to what layers in the social organization. What seems clear is that dispersion over the ethnic territory also applies to the nucleus of the ethnic group, although a certain longitudinal pattern within the central region can be detected.

1628 Marzal, Manuel. Funciones religiosas del mito en el mundo andino cuzqueño (PUCP/DA, 4, 1979, p. 11–22, bibl.)

Analyzes four contemporary myths from the Cusco region. All show close similarities of motifs to texts collected centuries ago, some of them of prehispanic pedigree.

1629 Masferrer Kan, Elio. Aproximación a un modelo de las relaciones hombre-naturaleza en la religión andina colonial: el punto de vista del ritual (*in* Congreso Peruano del Hombre y la Cultura Andina, 3d, Lima, 1977. El hombre y la cultura andina [see *HLAS 43:253*] v. 3, p. 27–42, bibl.)

Several written sources on punishable ritual practices, dating from different centuries and various parts of Andes, have in common certain sacrifices and offerings. These are common in situations of rapid social change or in threatening ones. "Los rituales que 'restablecen' el equilibrio con la naturaleza son considerados también operativos para incidir sobre la dinámica de las relaciones sociales y humanas."

1630 Maxwell, Thomas J. The Inca priesthood and animism (UNV/ED, 3 : 1, April 1978, p. 62–75, bibl., ill.)

Defines shamans as religious practioners who "practiced" spirit possession concluding there were no shamans in Inca religion. Surveys some chroniclers and secondary sources but appears unfamiliar with studies of Andean religion by students from the Andean republics.

1631 Millones, Luis. Los cazadores del antiguo Perú: economía y ritual de la cinegética precolombiana (PUCP/DA, 4, feb. 1979, p. 43–50, bibl.)

Survey of dispersed primary sources mentioning Andean hunting. Most refer to the systematic hunting of birds for their feathers, used in textiles with military and religious connotations.

1632 ———. Los dioses de Santa Cruz. Lima: s.n., n.d. 47 p. (mimeo)

Commentary on Andean writer Juan de Santa Cruz also known as Pachakuti Yamqui and as Salcamaygua. Urges new reading of this early 17th-century source seen as "un tratado de moral."

1633 ———. Etnohistoriadores y etnohistoria andina: una tarea difícil, una disciplina heterodoxa (Historia Boliviana [Cochambamba, Bolivia] 1, 1981, p. 83–105, bibl.)

Review article, considers several recent publications by María Rostworowski and J. V. Murra. Ethnohistory is not just a rereading of 16th-century chronicles; it implies an anthropological approach to such sources. Its chronological span is brief: some decades before the European invasion to some 40 years after 1532. For English version of this article, see item **1634**.

1634 ———. Ethnohistorians and Andean ethnohistory: a difficult task, a heterodox discipline (LARR, 17:1, 1982, p. 200–216)

English version of item **1633**.

1635 ——— and **Richard P. Shaedel**. Plumas para el Sol: comentarios a un documento sobre caza y cotos de caza en el antiguo Perú (IFEA/B, 9:1/2, 1980, p. 59–88, bibl.)

Litigation records from 1685 concerning two altiplano villages provides additional evidence for existence of specialized hunters before 1532. Primary pay of such hunters were feathers, used in high status textiles. Also camelids, deer, and many kinds of birds were hunted; one of the litigants, from Mañazo, gave their name to professional butchers at Potosí.

1635a Los Modos de producción en el imperio de los incas. Compilación de Waldemar Espinoza Soriano. Lima: Editorial Mantaro, 1978. 390 p.: bibl.

Editor assembles 16 articles including three of his own which shed light on possible definition of economic and social relations prevailing before 1532. Virtually none of the authors agree among themselves. Seven modes of production have their sponsors: some see a slave society (i.e., Núñez Anavitarte, Choy); others a socialist one (i.e., Baudin, Valcárcel); there are also partisans of primitive communism, social imperialism, Asiatic, Early Feudalism, and, of course, the Incaic mode. Some authors discuss institutions but take no position on a particular designation or label. Editor's position has been discussed earlier (see *HLAS 42:1632*).

1636 Moreno Yánez, Segundo and **Udo Oberem**. Contribución a la etnohistoria ecuatoriana. Otavalo, Ecuador: Instituto Otavaleño de Antropología, 1981. 406 p.; bibl. (Serie Etnohistoria) (Colección Pendoneros; no. 20)

Series of articles (some published earlier, often in other languages) consider role of ethnohistory in the Andes, highland political economy or earlier decades of European rule. Extremely useful collection.

1637 Morey, Nancy C. Ethnohistorical evidence for cultural complexity in the western llanos of Venezuela and the eastern llanos of Colombia (FSCN/A, 45, 1979, p. 41–69, map, table)

Brings together primary sources indicating considerable "cultural complexity" for a region previously missed or underestimated. Proposes kind of research "necessary to further knowledge."

1638 ——— and **Robert V. Morey**. Los saliva (*in* Los aborígenes de Venezuela. v. 1, Etnología antigua. Edited by Audrey Butt Colson. Caracas: Fundación La Salle de Ciencias Naturales, Instituto Caribe de Antropología y Sociología, 1980, v. 1, p. 241–306, bibl., ill., index, maps)

Mentioned in early missionary accounts of savanna dwellers in the Orinoco, the Saliva still survive in Colombian territory. Urgent need to study them stressed by Colombian scholars, who have access to ca. 2,000 Saliva.

1639 Morris, Craig. Huánuco Pampa: nuevas evidencias sobre el urbanismo inca (PEMN/R, 44, 1978/1980, p. 139–152, bibl., map)

Inka urbanism included network of provincial administrative centers imposed on landscape by the state. Their rapid build-up, as part of Inka expansion, implied access to large and rotating labor force drawn from region's population. In effort to understand distribution of buildings, storehouses, state edifices, Huanuco Pampa was carefully mapped. Excavations tested various hypotheses as to function. Some 3,000 buildings were used as residences. Production and administrative buildings also were identified. Large part of city was used for cooking and feeding troops along Inka highway.

1640 Mott, Luiz R. B. Etno-história dos índios do Piauí colonial (MAN, 12:7, 1981, p. 16–32, bibl.)

Assigned to provide historical background to French team studying Piauí, Mott was allowed only 15 days in archives. But having surveyed region's aboriginal population in Lisbon archives, he was familiar with Portuguese colonial system's administrative materials. Earliest paper was from 1697: Piaui's American population only 13.5 percent of total but Mott identifies 36 separate ethnic groups. In 1713, Indian rebellion; in 1764, campaign designed to exterminate Gueguês; in 1811, Piauí man complained to authorities about dangers to his people's lands.

1641 ———. Relação nominal dos índios de
Sergipe del Rey, 1825 (MAN, 11 : 10,
1981, p. 3–14, photos, tables)

Brazilian Northeast includes few
Amerindians. In 16th century: ca.
20,000; by 1825, census reported ca.
1200 in Sergipe. Their activities are tabulated by age, sex and
ethnic affiliation.

1642 Nardi, Ricardo L.J. Etnohistoria bonaerense (IPGH/FA, 27, junio 1979,
p. 53–73, bibl.)

Ethnic map of Buenos Aires province
not easy to draw since traditional labels
cover variety of polities: also, province cannot be separated from pampas in general, and
partakes of their ethnology. Some groups
were hunters and gatherers. Emergence of
"horse complex" is mentioned briefly; it did
not lead always to abandonment of agriculture. Few pages discuss araucanization of
pampas in colonial times.

1643 Oberem, Udo. Los Quijos, historia de
la transculturación de un grupo indígena en el Oriente Ecuatoriano. Otavalo,
Ecuador: Instituto Otavaleño de Antropología, 1980. 394 p.; ill. (Serie Etnohistoria) (Colección Pendoneros; 16)

Reproduction of Oberem's 1971 book
published Madrid (see *HLAS 36 : 1423*).

1644 Ortega, Julio. Historia y ficción: una
modelo de relato (Andean Perspective
Newsletter [The University of Texas, Austin]
3, 1979, p. 17–21)

Waman Puma's *Nueua coronica y
buen gouierno* "sobre todo es un archivo de
la escritura americana: el documento de su
discurso naciente . . . La historia y la ficción
que . . . se elaboran son también un modelo
textual: el discurso produce un radical sentido crítico y utópico al sostenerse sobre la
desconstrucción del saber discursivo de su
tiempo."

1645 Ortiz Rescaniere, Alejandro. El dua-
lismo religioso en el antiguo Perú (*in*
Historia del Perú antiguo. Lima: Editora
Mejía Baca, 1981, v. 3, p. 11–72, charts)

Compares mythology at state level as
recorded by Garcilaso, Calancha and Huarochiri's oral tradition. "Las nuevas formas religiosas son paralelas a cambios a nivel de
significado." Dualism of title is minor concern of article.

1646 ———. Huarochirí, cuatrocientos años
después. Lima: Departamento de Cien-

cias Sociales, Pontificia Universidad Católica
del Perú, 1980. 140 p.; bibl.; ill.

Publication of Huarochiri's oral tradition in Spanish (see *HLAS 29 : 2137b*) generated attempts to compare it with contemporary lore and motifs in region and elsewhere.
Concludes that mythological material allows
us to perceive Andean culture as it endured
through centuries or since Avila collected his
materials.

1647 Ossio, Juan M. La estructura social de
las comunidades (*in* Historia del Perú
antiguo. Lima: Editora Mejía Baca, 1981, v. 3,
p. 203–377, bibl., ill.)

While account is chiefly concerned
with contemporary village life, when kinship
and R.T. Zuidema's studies are mentioned,
ethnohistoric works creep in.

1648 Parejas, Alcides. Dos noticias sobre levantamientos indígenas en Potosí,
siglo XVI (Historia y Cultura [Sociedad Boliviana de Historia, La Paz] 4, 1981, p. 33–35,
bibl.)

During first century of colonial rule
rumors spread through alien community in
Potosí's mining center that Francis Drake
maintained contacts with Andean lords in
preparation for rebellion. No evidence is ad-
duced nor possibility considered that such
rumors were planted.

1649 Pease G.Y., Franklin. Continuidad y
resistencia de lo andino (IPA/A, 17/18,
1981, p. 105–118, bibl.)

In 18th century, when a "república de
indios" becomes perceptible, there was an
identification shift from particular precolombian polity to pan-Andean awareness that resulted in 1780–81 revolts. Connecting such
identifications with modern movements, in
which "lo andino" is not always clearly identifiable, is more difficult.

1650 ———. Estudio preliminar to Gregorio
García's *Origen de los indios del
Nuevo Mundo.* México: Biblioteca Ameri-
cana, 1981. 1 v., bibl. (mimeo)

New, photostated edition of 1607 work
stresses European interest in origins of
American population. Possibility of descent
from Israel's lost tribes and precolumbian
presence of some apostles in Americas preoccupied public opinion. García, who spent
nine years in Perú, was familiar with literature on subject, even with unpublished
works (e.g., Garcilaso's). He collected materi-

als, both written and observational. Among manuscripts he consulted were some since lost (e.g., Betanzos, 1551).

1651 ———. Felipe Guaman Poma de Ayala: mitos andinos e historia occidental (PMNH/HC, 13/14, 1981, p. 155—170, bibl.)

Intellectual context of eyewitness accounts needs more careful study. It is indispensable for evaluating data they collected and analyzed. When writer himself is of Andean origins, quality of information requires additional scrutiny. Guaman Poma's early and protracted familiarity with European priests must be evaluated—Pease finds him a better source about his own time than about prehispanic periods, which he shoe-horns into biblical concordances.

1652 ———. Historia andina: hacia una historia del Perú (PEIH/RH, 32, 1979/1980, p. 197–212.

Author's speech on being inducted into Academia de Historia of Perú. Stresses continuities between pre- and post-European events and institutions. Does not think it sufficient to write a "version of the vanquished," but that country must become aware of Andean population and their role yesterday and today.

1653 ———. Los Incas (in Historia del Perú antiguo. v. 2. Lima: Editora Mejía Baca, 1981, p. 197–293, bibl., ill.)

Displays excellent knowledge of primary sources, extending to administrative papers, beyond chronicles. Devotes special attention to formation of Inka state, ayllu, common people and the *yana*.

1654 ———. Prólogo (in Poma de Ayala, Felipe Huamán. Nueva corónica y buen gobierno. Caracas: Biblioteca Ayacucho, 1980, p. lx–xcii, chronology, notes)

Another transcription of handwritten text with Mexico's Siglo XXI (see *HLAS 42:1708*). Pease's prólogo is a careful review of biographical material about Waman Puma; his perception of Andean history and light it shed on archaeology and future historical writing; map he had drawn in order to accommodate new European geography with Andean view of physical world; doubts about legitimacy of Inka when compared with earlier ethnic lords; his use of European literary and ecclesiastic sources; his evaluation of Europeans who undertook invasion; disaster

for Andean wealth and reproduction of *reducciones* policy. Along with bibliography and notes, this is the best existing introduction to Waman Puma's *Letter to the King.*

1655 ———. Las relaciones entre las tierras altas y la costa del sur del Perú: fuentes documentales (in Estudios etnográficos del Perú meridional. Edited by Shozo Masuda. Tokyo: University of Tokyo, 1981, p. 193–221, bibl.)

Survey of archival materials in Arequipa, Tacna and Moquegua dealing with interregional complementarity and other Andean topics. Reproduces in full Don Diego Caqui's last will and testament (1588) showing evidence of his trading operations between coast and Potosí.

1656 ———. Unidades étnicas y noción de identidad en el Perú colonial (Cielo Abierto [Lima] 6:17, 1981, p. 39–48, bibl.)

While more information has become accessible concerning Andean ethnic groups that precede and survived Inka, questions posed are also more searching now. New map, drawn according to Andean circumstances, is needed as also are a reevaluation of ayllu and its territorial implications; and spread of messianic anti-European movements that culminates in 1780–81 insurrections.

1657 Platt, Tristan. Mapas coloniales de la provincia de Chayanta: dos visiones conflictivas de un solo paisaje (in Estudios bolivianos en homenaje a Gunnar Mendoza [see *HLAS 42:2638*] p. 101–118, bibl., ill., maps)

Analyzes litigation of Aymara of Pocoata against one Carvajal in 1651. Both sides filed maps of their claims; those of Pocoata claimed lowlands far from their puna domicile, which they "always" had controlled but which were threatened by Carvajal's plans to build an *ingenio*. Each side uses familiar facts from two quite different views of the universe. Both maps are reproduced.

Prien, Hans Jürgen. Indianerpolitik und katolische Mission in Brasilien im 19. und 20. Jahrundert. See *HLAS 43:1176.*

1658 Ramírez-Horton, Susan E. La organización económica de la costa norte: un análisis preliminar del período prehispánico tardío (Etnohistoria y Antropología Andina [Lima] 1981, p. 281–297, bibl., charts)

Neglected by ethnohistorians, the coast is more difficult to study than the highlands, partly because ethnic unit is not always clear. Even term *valle* is not always well defined. Systematic work on archival coast materials may permit identifying settlements with ethnic subdivisions. Artisan groups cut across by maintaining complementary relations within a given "valley" but identifying with similar craftsmen elsewhere. Much interaction in both directions was mediated by lords.

1659 Randall, Robert. Qoyllur Rit'i, an Inca fiesta of the Pleiades: reflections on time and space in the Andean world (IFEA/B, 10:1/2, 1982, p. 37–81, bibl., charts, maps)
Contemporary festival that attracts thousands and is reenacted annually, at appearance and disappearance of Pleiades in southern sky, leads author to trace continuities in belief and world-view hoping that "analysis of contemporary mythology can throw light on Inca thought . . ."

1660 Ravines, Rogger. Chanchan, metrópoli chimú *in* Ravines, Rogger. Chanchán, metrópoli chimú. Colaboradores, Anthony Andrews *et al.* Lima: Instituto de Estudios Peruanos: Instituto de Investigación Tecnológica Industrial y de Normas Técnicas, 1980, p. 21–129 [Fuentes e investigaciones para la historia del Perú; 51])
Thinks that as late as 15th century, Chimú was "confederación de curacazgos." Mostly devoted to "inter-cambio," northwards. Uses Calancha as primary source.

1661 ———. Reinos y señoríos locales de los Andes centrales, 800–1476 ADC (*in* Historia del Perú antiguo. v. 2. Lima: Editora Mejía Baca, 1981, v. 2, p. 93–184, bibl., ill.)
Ambitious attempt to combine archaeological and ethnohistoric evidence. Useful even if 1981 is too early in our knowledge of the Andes for such a synthesis. Most interesting is author's handling of Chimú evidence for which there is virtually no written source. Coastal people "fueron todo menos agricultores," although "poder burocrático chimú para movilizar y dirigir masas," is not discussed in irrigation context. "La cerámica no responde a una producción de tipo clasista." Of written sources, considers Calancha, who enjoys new vogue.

1662 Renard de Casevitz, France-Marie. Las fronteras de las conquistas en el siglo XVI en la montaña meridional del Perú (IFEA/B, 10:3/4, 1981, p. 113–140, bibl., map)
Despite frequent mentions of lowland ethnic groups "paying" tribute to Inka, evidence for such intimate contacts is vague and insubstantial. Author reverses usual view of forest from Andes by attempting to document view of highlands from banks of Amazon basin, North and Northwest Cusco. One commodity of considerable interest to highlands was coca leaf whose distribution and cultivation is traced by author showing how marginal was highland control.

1663 Rivera Cusicanqui, Silvia. De la *ayma* a la hacienda: cambios en la estructura social de Caquiaviri (*in* Estudios bolivanos en homenaje a Gunnar Mendoza [see *HLAS 42:2638*] p. 249–264, bibl.)
Organized very early in lowlands, haciendas utilized established outliers of altiplano Pacaje Indians. Estates eventually emerged in highlands as well, particularly near Lake Titicaca. Among owners were traditional lords, who claimed Andean rights to land (*haymatha*) in order to gain title according to European procedures. Such attempts led to litigation with both "el común" and Europeans.

1664 Rostworowski de Diez Canseco, María. Guarco y Lunaguana: dos señoríos prehispánicos de la costa sur central del Perú (PEMN/R, 44, 1978/1979, p. 153–214, bibl., ill., maps)
Cañete valley connects coast with Yauyu highland country but lower reaches were part of local, coastal polities. Effort is made to delimit these and describe relation to Inka, since at least one, Guarco, resisted Cusco conquest. Special section studies presence in valley of Incahuasi, allegedly copies from early model of Cusco. "A nuestro parecer fue un magnífico capricho y un derroche de poderío de un Inca."

1665 ———. Mediciones y cómputos en el antiguo Perú (Cuadernos Prehispánicos [Seminario Americanista de la Universidad, Valladolid] 6, 1978, p. 21–48)
Updates her 1962 publication dealing with weights and measures. In addition to late 16th-century dictionaries, author uses

administrative and litigation records from early decades of European rule. She does not neglect observations of 19th-century geographers who travelled through Andes, frequently providing evidence of continuity. Also surveys measurement of time, both in life-cycle and historic contexts. Best work of its kind.

1666 ———. Recursos naturales renovables y pesca, siglos XVI y XVII. Lima: Instituto de Estudios Peruanos, 1981. 180 p.; bibl.; ill.

Continuing her studies of coastal ethnic groups and activities (see *HLAS 40:2110* and *HLAS 42:1720*), concentrates on secondary resources: artificial lagoons, occasional vegetation of *lomas*, riverbottom timber and salt. Pays special attention to fishing and specialized population, endogamous but connected to inland ethnic groups through traditional exchange patterns.

1667 Saignes, Thierry. Historia de Cumbay: derrotero de un líder chiriguano (*in* Estudios bolivianos en homenaja a Gunnar Mendoza [see *HLAS 42:2638*] p. 125–129)

By fortunate coincidence, Cumbay's career appears often in archival record. At one time he sided with Europeans; early in 19th century he is recorded as their enemy, only to reappear in wars of independence as patriot in Gen. Belgrano's entourage. Saignes explores what could have been his private, Chiriguano reasons for changing sides.

1668 ———. Les Lupacas dans les vallées orientales des Andes: trajets spatiaux et repères démographiques: XVI–XVII siècles (Mélanges de la Casa de Vélasquez [E. de Boccard, Paris] 17, 1981, p. 147–182, bibl., charts, map)

While highlanders from Lake Titicaca area always had outlying populations in Eastern woodlands (see *HLAS 42:1727*), further documentation from Archivo de Indias indicates that such settlements grew in colonial times. Some consisted of runaways from the mita to Potosí or of others attracted by *hacendados* growing food for miners. Original ethnic lords tried but usually failed to have migrants returned to ethnic group which enumerated them.

1669 ———. El piedmonte amazónico de los Andes meridionales: estado de la cuestión y problemas relativos a su ocupación en los siglos XVI y XVII (IFEA/B, 10:3/4, 1981, p. 141–176, bibl., charts, maps)

Detailed examination of sparse sources about *entradas* to lowlands, south of Cuzco. Saignes makes major effort to cover entire literature in chronological order following particular rumors through (e.g., El Dorado, Inka refuge in forest). Concludes that European invasion arrested Inka expansion eastward, well advanced via the Carabaya and Larecaja towards the Beni. Invasion did not halt considerable highland to lowland cultural exchange; in fact, as region became refuge zone, penetration of highland ideas and people are documented in colonial times.

1670 ———. Una provincia andina a comienzos del siglo XVII: Pacajes según una relación inédita (EEHA/HBA, 24, 1980, p. 3–21, bibl.)

Relaciones Geográficas of 1586 are well known and were republished in Madrid in 1965. Only 20 years later, new survey was ordered of many of same places but answers are mostly unavailable. National Archives in Sucre tried to locate them and one is reproduced and commented on here. One tenth of Pacajes' population, on southern shores of Lake Titicaca, had disappeared. There is less ethnographic detail and more stress on tribute collection.

1671 Salomon, Frank. Chronicles of the impossible: notes on three Peruvian indigenous historians (*in* From oral to written expression: native Andean chronicles of the early colonial period [see item **1602**] p. 9–39)

Surveys the "uncomfortable [if not impossible] common ground" among four Andean writers who tried to reconcile two drastically different viewpoints about how to deal with the past. European historiography treats events as a chain of unique steps; Andean sense of history demands a pattern, a cycle of repeated ages, punctuated by cataclysm: Andean "sources of diachronic knowledge were completely different and had never been organized on the principles of absolute chronology . . .". Methodological problems that follow are insoluble. All three Andean writers, Titu Cusi, Pachakuti Yamqui and anonymous collector of Huarochiri's oral tradition strived to reclaim in the new language way—writing—sense of order built over millenia. Yet they cannot make themselves heard: "they necessarily speak partly through ideas and myths not their own, and partly through those that are too much their own to be readily conveyed in a foreign vehicle . . . Only defeated writers make insolubility their home ground."

1672 ———. Don Pedro de Zambiza, un *varayuj* del siglo XVI (CCE/CHA, 42, 1975 [1980] p. 285–315, bibl.)

During three colonial centuries, indigenous leadership in Quito region was exercised in recognizably Andean ways; traces of some of these can still be distinguished. Outlines Tupiça's notable career (b. ca. 1550), long-time *alcalde ordinario de naturales*, known as Pedro de Zambiza. His leadership role drew on North Andean traditions, on Inka institutions and on Spanish expectations, even though he was first non-Inka to attain alcalde's post in 1576. Documents how Quito lords, as did Wanka further south, welcomed European invasion, hoping to end Inka rule.

1673 ———. Los señores étnicos de Quito en la época de los incas. Otavalo, Ecuador: Instituto Otavaleño de Antropología, 1980. 370 p.; ill.; tables (Serie Etnohistoria. Colección Pendoneros; no. 10)

Translation of author's dissertation. Stresses natural and cultural differences between northern and central Andes in attempt to define characteristics of ethnic groups beyond areas where *puna* prevail. Alien impact from south which brought Cusco armies and political economy is analyzed separately. Considers possibility that redistribution met a commercial tradition in the north and, in that light, examines *mindala*'s role (see *HLAS 42:1732*). Book won 1979–80 Ethnohistory Prize in honor of Howard F. Cline awarded by American Historical Association.

1674 **Scazzocchio, Françoise.** La conquête des Motilones du Huallaga Central aux XVII et XVIII siècles (IFEA/B, 10:3/4, 1981, p. 99–111, bibl., map)

Jesuits reported in 1762 that a century earlier population was five times as large. Author stresses formation of Lamista Quechua group from fragments of ethnic groups "reduced" by the missionaries. Such ethnogenesis, author believes, was common in forest area. General name used for such forest dwellers was and frequently still is, Motilones. Legend that these people derived from highland Chanca escaping Inka rule in highlands is unfounded.

1675 **Schjellerup, Inge.** Documents on paper and in stone: a preliminary report on the Inca ruins in Cochabamba, province of Chachapoyas, Peru (DEF/F, 21/22, 1979/1980, p. 299–311, bibl., map)

Cochabamba, in northeastern Peru, was Inka installation in territory of the Chachapoya. They were old enemies of the Inka, who repeatedly had to "reconquer" them, after revolts against Cusco rule. Located on main north-south route, Cochabamba's study should help understand late Andean rule on Eastern slope.

1676 **Segarra Iñiguez, Guillermo.** Probanza de don Juan Bistancela cacique de Toctén: 1594. Quito: s.n., 1976. 38 p. (mimeo)

Cañari's role as standing army in last years of Inka rule and their later support of Europeans against Atahualpa have been noted (see *HLAS 40:2089* and *HLAS 42: 1690*). Pamphlet includes photostatic reproduction of original and transcription of primary source claiming Cañari supported European invasion from earliest days, in Túmbez.

1677 **Silva Galdames, Osvaldo.** Rentas estatales y rentas reales en el imperio inca (Cuadernos de Historia [Santiago] 1, 1981, p. 31–64, bibl.)

Traditional sources confused Inka state and royal revenues, since both were collected in labor, not as tribute. They should be regarded as separate revenues. Suggests that even within state revenues, ordinary should be distinguished from special assessments. However, Inka ideology encouraged confusion of several prestations: "el Inca aparece, entonces, como la *persona* que crea, mantiene y fomenta los nexos entre . . . la jerarquía burocrática con el Estado. Entabla vínculos a título personal . . ."

1677a **Stern, Steve J.** Peru's Indian peoples and the challenge of Spanish Conquest: Huamanga to 1640. Madison: University of Wisconsin Press, 1982. 295 p.: bibl.; ill.; indexes; maps.

Concerns pre-Columbian background and early resistance of ethnic lords in Huamanga area. Interesting chapter deals with crisis in Andean societies expressed in the *taki onqoy* messianic movement of 1560s, balanced by contemporary attempts at reform by the colonial society. Later, dependency created by mines and weakening of ethnic leadership, wrought profound changes in Andean life. Successful members of the Andean elite used sham ethnic ties and privileges to invest in the new system. "Nativist" claims, tied to enduring Andean religious practices surfaced in the early 17th century; resistance to mita, the sending of forced labor to mercury mines; to gradual impoverishment, affected the elite as well as province's people.

1678 ———. The rise and fall of Indian-white alliances: a regional view of "conquest" history (HAHR, 61:3, 1981, p. 461–491, bibl., map)

Huamanga region, north of Cusco, provided Europeans with numerous allies against the Inka. Some encomenderos understood that more rewarding than cruelty in the long run was cultivating Andean-like relations with native lords. Later, European entrepreneurs and Andean lords became partners in diverse mining and commercial activities; this "dramatizes the dependence of Europeans upon indigenous communities, governed by Andean-style labor relations." By end of 16th century such dependencies were undermined by new settlers, new demands, depopulation. Eventually "alliance" would collapse as lords' authority eroded.

1679 Sternberg, Hilgard O'Reilly. Frontières contemporaines en Amazonie brésilienne: quelques consequences sur l'environment. Paris: Institut des hautes études de l'Amérique latine, 1979. 178 p.; bibl.; charts; maps (Travaux e mémoires de l'Institut des hautes études de l'Amérique latine; 34)

Considers "les phenomènes des frontières dans les pays tropicaux." While most of the discussion centers on contemporary changes, some of the text deals with Amazonian population in the past.

1680 Taylor, Anne-Christine and **Philippe Descola.** El conjunto jívaro en los comienzos de la conquista española del Alto Amazonas (IFEA/B, 10:3/4, 1981, p. 7–54, bibl., maps)

Effort to delimit Jívaro's distribution and composition at time of European invasion. Good utilization of recently published primary sources from Quito's National Archives. Makes serious effort to identify various ethnic groups, their size and approximate location. Final section looks into highland penetration of ethnic groups related to Jívaro.

Total population surveyed may have reached 60,000.

1681 Torres Luna, Alfonso. Puno histórico. Naña, Lima: Tall. Gráf. del Colegio Unión, 1968. 321 p.; 2 folded leaves of plates; bibl.; ill.

Reproduces secondary sources.

1682 Urbano, Henrique-Osvaldo. Del sexo, incesto y los ancestros de Inkarrí: mito, utopía e historia en las sociedades andinas (IPA/A, 17/18, 1981, p. 77–103, bibl., charts)

While present-day myths show some continuity with pre-European versions, one should not overlook many changes and profound transformations undergone during intervening centuries. Two mythical cycles prevailed before 1532: Viracocha's and another, Ayar's. Both were rebels, at least potentially. Contemporary myth of Inkarri is seen as their continuation, hidden underground, awaiting better times.

1683 Urioste, George L. The editing of oral tradition in the Huarochirí manuscript (in From oral to written expression: native Andean chronicles of the early colonial period [see item **1602**] p. 101–108)

Considers Francisco de Avila as original editor and initiator of collection. Current editor, however, concentrated on grammar rather than on organizing manuscript whose various themes appear and reappear many pages later. Urioste distinguishes 33 basic texts, in which writer refers to events as reported by others, while in two unnumbered fragments we hear author's voice. Applies similar techniques to use of Spanish words in various contexts. Urioste is convinced editor was cleric, who did not necessarily report literally what informants told him.

1684 Urioste de Aguirre, Marta. Los caciques guaraches (in Estudios bolivianos en homenaje a Gunnar Mendoza [see HLAS 42:2638] p. 131–140)

Part of continuing studies of Andean lordship in Lake Titicaca's altiplano (see HLAS 42:1604a). Bundle of papers on which study is based appeared rather suddenly and covers several centuries. Aymara kinship system is made to fit European genealogical norms; Guarachis claim to have ruled since before the Inka and give considerable detail about their treaties with Cusco and exchange of daughters and gifts of cloth. For last will

and testament of one of them, see *HLAS*
40:2107.

1685 Urton, Gary. Astronomy and calendrics on the coast of Peru (*in* Ethnoastronomy and archaeoastronomy in the
American tropics. Edited by Anthony F.
Aveni and Gary Urton. New York: New York
Academy of Sciences, 1982, p. 231–247,
bibl.; charts)

Ethnoastronomy in the past concentrated on Cusco as capital and on wider region around it. As expected, desert coast
calendars were different, and given centuries
long extinction of original population, they
are harder to reconstruct ethnographically.
Urton inquired about calendar at fishing village on North Coast, Huanchaco, and compared information with Huarochiri's data.
Several periodicities—lomas vegetation, sierra waters flowing down, Pleiades' movements—were all important ingredients.

1686 ———. At the crossroads of the earth
and the sky: an Andean cosmology.
Austin: University of Texas Press, 1981.
248 p.; bibl.; ill.; index (Latin American
monographs)

While 16th-century sources leave only
partial description of heavens and their role
in human life, ethnographically it is still possible to elicit a statement about what is visible on the night sky according to oral tradition. Urton did his field work in Cusco
region (see *HLAS 40:2119*), where 40 different stars and constellations can be identified by peasant inhabitants. Divisions of time
are directly related to divisions of space, and
both to cosmology. When correlated to 16th-
century records about Inka astronomy, Urton
finds that their system "was as complex and
sophisticated as any that existed at that time
anywhere in the world."

1687 Valcárcel, Luis E. Memorias. Lima:
Instituto de Estudios Peruanos, 1981.
478 p.; bibl.; ill.; index.

Dictated memoirs mostly concern author's stormy public career as Director of
Museo de la Cultura Peruana and creator and
editor of *Revista del Museo Nacional.* However, his experiences as first Minister of Education to make use of Quechua language
official and as Dean of San Marcos University who was first to teach a course called
ethnohistory, provide enough material to include this welcome volume here. Memoirs

were first recorded by Ana María Soldi and
revised by José Matos Mar, José Deustua and
J.L. Renique. Instituto de Estudios Peruanos
has produced a fine edition of one founder's
memoirs.

1688 ———. La religión inca (*in* Historia del
Perú antiguo. v. 3. Lima: Editorial Juan
Mejía Baca, 1981, p. 75–202, bibl., ill.)

Stresses syncretism in Andean religion, utilizing materials from standard
chronicles but refers as well to local *waka,*
calendars, clergy.

1689 Valle de Siles, María Eugenia del. Testimonios del cerco de La Paz: el campo
contra la ciudad, 1781. 2. ed. La Paz, Bolivia:
Ultima Hora, 1980. 197 p.; 20 leaves of plates
(1 folded); bibl.; ill. (Biblioteca popular boliviana de Ultima hora)

Siege of La Paz was last stage in 1780–
81 Andean insurrection. Author uses five diaries kept by Europeans trapped in besieged
city to reconstruct events. Examines reasons
why siege failed, such as rivalries among
Aymara leaders and Quechua allies.

1690 Vega, Juan José. La segunda Batalla de
Jauja y la del Yacusmayo (*in* Congreso
Peruano del Hombre y la Cultura Andina, *3d,*
Lima, 1977. El hombre y la cultura andina
[see *HLAS 43:253*] v. 5, p. 1032–1043, bibl.)

Confronting administrative sources
such as Wanka litigation (see *HLAS 36:1397*)
with traditional European sources sheds new
light on events of earliest part of invasion.
Such correlations confirm extreme dependence of Europeans on their Andean allies
and latter's ability to mobilize large numbers
of soldiers and additional resources. Also
uses military records from Archivo de Indias.

1691 Wolf, Freda Yancy. Parentesco aymara
en el siglo XVI (*in* Parentesco y mat-
rimonio en los Andes. Edited by Enrique
Mayer and Ralph Bolton. Lima: s.n., 1980,
p. 115–135, bibl., charts, glossary)

Parallel study to R.T. Zuidema's (see
HLAS 41:1329), in which 16th-century dictionaries are used to gather kinship terms
(see *HLAS 42:1665*). Aymara system turns
out to be quite different from Inka's, lacking
parallel descent, and manifesting many
"Omaha" features. A pioneer work.

1692 Yaranga Valderrama, Abdon. La di-
vinidad Illapa en la región andina (III/
AI, 39:4, 1979, p. 697–720)

In colonial regime's early years, most European observers noted importance of deity sometimes identified as Lightning. Identified later with Santiago, Illapa was concerned with rain, crops, serpents. Twins were his offspring. Beautiful Quechua hymn to Illapa collected by Blas Valera is reproduced in author's Spanish translation. Yaranga thinks he was third most important deity in Andean pantheon, after Wirakocha, the Maker, and Inti, the Sun. Offers much evidence concerning Illapa's importance in colonial times. That he is still active today is documented by author who has collected literary material on his presence in Ayacucho. Author's knowledge of Quechua helps clarify allusions and symbolic references.

1693 Zapater Equioiz, Horacio. Los Incas y la conquista de Chile (UCCIH/H, 16, 1982, p. 29–68, bibl.)

Restudies early sources published by J. Toribio Medina. Suggests two periods in resistance to European occupation: 1) 1536–43, when Marco II was still capable to lead "al mantenerse la infrastructura del imperio; and 2) 1543–49 when "la reación indígena . . . se centró en los propios grupos sin enlace" elsewhere.

1694 Zuidema, R. T. Catachillay: the role of the Pleiades and of the Southern Cross and Centauri in the calendar of the Incas (*in* Ethnoastronomy and archaeoastronomy in the American tropics. Edited by Anthony Aveni and Gary Urton. New York: New York Academy of Sciences, 1982, p. 203–229, bibl., charts, ill., maps)

In recent years there has been major progress in understanding the Inca calendar through the collaboration of astronomers and anthropologists, particularly Zuidema and his students. Southern skies were mapped; equinoxes and solstices, highest and lowest points for astral bodies were observed. Observation points in and around Cuzco were located with help of ceque list found in Bernabé Cobo's book. Result is an elaborate calendar, which could not have been derived from historic sources alone. Special role is played by Pleiades constellation, stars seen as female and related to water, springs.

1695 ——— and Deborah Poole. Los límites de los cuatro suyus incaicos en el Cuzco (IFEA/B, 11 : 1/2, 1982, p. 83–89, bibl., charts, maps)

Using list of towns assigned in 1577 to four *suyu* of Cusco and of the Inka state, Zuidema and Poole locate them on present-day maps. These are said to correspond to *suyu* that emerge from authors' field study of *ceque* lines. Center was Coricaucha, temple of the Sun. In passing, authors refute opinions attributed to Zuidema by Waldemar Espinoza (see *HLAS 40:2047*).

1696 ——— and Gary Urton. La Constelación de La Llama en los Andes peruanos (IPA/A, 9, 1976, p. 59–119, bibl., ill., map)

In both ancient and modern times, average farmer could explain map of heavens. Comparing information from chronicles, older dictionaries and contemporary explanations, we find remarkable continuities. Llama and its calf are visible in sky. Authors list various times per year when llama became significant object of worship.

HISTORY: GENERAL

DONALD E. CHIPMAN, *Professor of History, North Texas State University*
JAMES D. RILEY, *Professor of History, The Catholic University of America*

IT DOES NOT REQUIRE the services of a statistician to note the drastic decline in the number of items in the HISTORY: GENERAL section. In the past three volumes (*HLAS 38, HLAS 40* and *HLAS 42*), the number of entries was halved in each volume while the totals in the subsection HISTORY: GENERAL: 20TH CENTURY dropped precipitously between *HLAS 42* and this volume.

Among the possible reasons that would explain this phenomenon are: 1) the increasing sophistication of economists and political scientists interested in Latin

America may have led to the discarding of historically-oriented approaches in favor of more contemporary methodologies such as model building; and 2) the sudden and almost complete disappearance of those familiar volumes of essays devoted to general themes; and 3) a new and salutary reluctance on the part of historians to generalize at a time when so many regional and local studies are illustrating the diversity of experiences.

The quantitative decline notwithstanding a number of works of quality are annotated below and merit special notice: two provocative interpretations by Véliz (item 1725) and Weaver (item 1726) should be consulted by thoughtful readers; Mörner (item 1772) has produced a first-rate summary of the literature on slave supply; the Hardoy-Langdon piece (item 1710) contains much useful demographic data; and the García Calderón reprint (item 1706), though dated, reads well and gives considerable insight into the intellectual climate of a much earlier period. In the Colonial subsection, Georges Baudot (item 1735) presents a panoramic view of Spanish American language, race and society in the reign of Philip II. Martínez Reyes (item 1768) has produced an exhaustive and probably definitive study of diocesan finance in colonial Spanish America. Hanke's ongoing work on viceregal administration under the Hapsburgs has resulted in an indispensable guide to Spanish American manuscript materials (item 1757).

There are several distinguished contributions on the late colonial and independence periods that deserve careful attention by scholars. Noteworthy on politics, finance and commerce are Walker's on the Carrera de Indias (item 1799), Fisher's on Imperial "Free Trade" (item 1749), Malamud's on the rise and decline of a commercial firm in Cádiz (item 1766), Esteban's on colonial trade prior to and during the wars of independence (item 1747), Barbier's on financial crises of the Spanish central government (item 1731), and Costeloe's on free trade controversy (item 1742). Of similar quality are Walker's excellent analysis of the British slave trade (item 1799), Stein's study of Bourbon bureaucracy and business (item 1791), and Barbier's suggestion for revised interpretations of early Bourbon reforms (item 1732). Also worthy of mention is a colloquium (1978) and resultant papers on Latin American independence (item 1803).

The best work on the 19th century is Burn's study of Latin American poverty (item 1802). Soto Cárdenas' work (item 1816) on the diffusion of North American political thought in Latin America is useful.

In the 20th-century group, the outstanding book, without question, is Johnson's study of caricature (item 1828). Cultural and diplomatic historians searching for material for classrooms will find it invaluable. Readers interested in other types of visual propaganda will also want to consult the Woll volume (item 1837). An interesting work which offsets prevailing political studies written from a North American perspective is the collected general text by Latin American political scientists, compiled by González Casanova (item 1819).

Chipman wishes to acknowledge the continuing support of the Faculty Research Committee at North Texas State University, and the capable assistance of students Olga Paradis, Julie Mays and Beth Broyles.

GENERAL

1697 **Acedo, Clemy M. de.** El análisis sociológico y la historia (in Encuentro de Historiadores Latinoamericanos y del Caribe, 2d, Caracas, 1977. Los estudios históricos en América Latina: ponencias, acuerdos y resoluciones: Caracas, 20–26 de marzo de 1977. Caracas: Universidad Central de Venezuela, Facultad de Humanidades y Educación, Escuela de Historia, 1979, v. 1, t. 1, p. 263–282, bibl.)

Decries the separation in Latin American schools of sociology of theory and method. Believes that more attention should be paid to the strides being made in the field of social history and calls for more training in historical methodologies for students in sociology.

1698 Arconada Merino, Luis. El peso de las categorías del materialismo histórico en la interpretación de la historia (*in* Encuentro de Historiadores Latinoamericanos y del Caribe, 2d, Caracas, 1977. Los estudios históricos en América Latina: ponencias, acuerdos y resoluciones: Caracas, 20–26 de marzo de 1977. Caracas: Universidad Central de Venezuela, Facultad de Humanidades y Educación, Escuela de Historia, 1979, v. 1, t. 1, p. 126–141)

Essay attacking Marxist historians' view that all history is economic history.

1699 Arencibia-Huidobro, Yolanda. The modern concept of Latin America (UNESCO/CU, 5:3, 1978, p. 147–177)

Selected bibliography compiled in 1977 by UNESCO's Regional Office for Culture in Latin America and the Caribbean. Includes extracts presenting a variety of opinions and definitions for the historical amalgamation that is Latin America.

1700 Aspects of the history of medicine in Latin America: report of a Conference. Edited by John Z. Bowers and Elizabeth F. Purcell. New York: Josiah Macy, Jr., Foundation, 1979. 196 p.: bibl.; ill.; index.

Collection of nine papers presented at 1971 conference. Most are devoted to prehispanic and colonial medicine and cover both medical education and medical practices. Geographical coverage extends to Brazil, Colombia, Mexico, Venezuela and Peru. Only one contribution (Charles Boxer's) is by a professional historian.

1701 Bergquist, Charles W. Latin America: a dissenting view of Latin American history in world perspective (*in* International handbook of historical studies: contemporary research and theory. Edited by George G. Iggers and Harold T. Parker. Westport, Conn.: Greenwood, Press, 1979, p. 371–386, bibl.)

Takes Woodrow Borah to task for asserting pessimistically that there is no hope for mainstream historiography in Latin America. Bergquist sees room for innovation in historiography that emerged in last quarter century as critique of liberal historiography. Dominated by structuralists and neo-Marxists, historiographical debate focuses on a distinction between undeveloped and underdeveloped societies. Ends with attention to the promises of this new paradigm of underdevelopment, and suggests that its significance lies in its potential impact on policy. Essay is part of significant collection on other regions and countries which offer broadening perspectives and encouraging fresh approaches. Volume suggests outlines of the "leading edge" of historical studies. [V.C. Peloso]

1702 Cardoso, Ciro Flamarión S. La brecha campesina en el sistema esclavista (*in* Encuentro de Historiadores Latinoamericanos y del Caribe, 2n, Caracas, 1977. Los estudios históricos en América Latina: ponencias, acuerdos y resoluciones: Caracas, 20–26 de marzo de 1977. Caracas: Universidad Central de Venezuela, Facultad de Humanidades y Educación, Escuela de Historia, 1979, v. 1, t. 2, p. 424–433)

Comparative overview, in no way profound, of the place of the subsistence farmer, or "peasant," in the different slave economies of the New World. [R. Barman]

1703 Carrera Damas, Germán. Sobre algunos de los factores estructurales de continuidad y de cambio en el nivel teórico-ideológico de las sociedades implantadas latinoamericanas (*in* Encuentro de Historiadores Latinoamericanos y del Caribe, 2d, Caracas, 1977. Los estudios históricos en América Latina: ponencias, acuerdos y resoluciones: Caracas, 20–26 de marzo de 1977. Caracas: Universidad Central de Venezuela, Facultad de Humanidades y Educación, Escuela de Historia, 1979, v. 1, t. 2, p. 808–814)

Brief paper identifying historical forces for conservatism and change in Latin America. Includes in former category a passivity toward nature, a stagnant society, the Indian base and a monarchical culture. Forces for change are all linked to Latin America's involvement in the "world capitalist system" after 1830. Treatment is superficial.

1704 Castellanos, Jorge and **Miguel Martínez.** El dictador hispanoamericano como personaje literario (LARR, 16:2, 1981, p. 79–105)

Examines treatment of the dictator personality in the Latin American novel. Notes that prior to 1970s, despite large number of novels devoted to dictatorship, the dictator himself was always a secondary character. Concludes that, until recently, most novelists were fighting against tyranny and were not interested in psychological portraits of the personalities involved.

Contreras, Remedios. Catálogo de la colección Manuscritos sobre América de la Real Academia de la Historia. See item **99.**

————. Fondos americanistas de la Colección Salazar y Castro: catálogo. See item **100.**

1705 Favre, Henri. L'état et la paysannerie en Mesóamerique et dans les Andes (Etudes Rurales [Ecole des hautes études en sciences sociales, Paris] 81/82, jan./juin 1981, p. 25–56)

Interpretive essay which compares impact of emergence of nation state on Indian cultivators in Mexico, Bolivia and Peru between 1860–early 1970s.

1706 García Calderón, Francisco. Las democracias latinas de América: la creación de un continente. Prólogo, Luis Alberto Sánchez. Cronología, Angel Rama y Marlena Polo. Caracas: Biblioteca Ayacucho, 1979. 468 p.; bibl. (Biblioteca Ayacucho; 44)

Reprint of political history of Latin America by noted Peruvian intellectual originally published in 1913.

1707 Gibson, Charles. Latin America and the Americas (*in* The Past before us: contemporary historical writing in the United States. Edited for the American Historical Association by Michael Kammen. Ithaca, N.Y.: Cornell University Press, 1980. p. 187–202, bibl.; ill.; index)

Masterful survey of Latin American historiography in the US, especially of post-World War II developments. Important because Gibson not only reviews accomplishments but previews all that remains to be done. [M.T. Hamerly]

1708 Godio, Julio. Historia del movimiento obrero latinoamericano. v. 1, Anarquistas y socialistas, 1850–1918. Caracas: Nueva Sociedad; Mexico: Editorial Nueva Imagen, 1980. 1 v.; bibl.

First of projected three volumes examines from Marxist perspective, development of urban proletariats and labor movements in Latin America. Gives general overview of development of urban working classes and theories behind labor organizing, and provides

three case studies: Argentina, Chile and Mexico.

1709 Goldwert, Marvin. History as neurosis: paternalism and machismo in Spanish America. Lanham, Md.: University Press of America, 1980. 75 p.

Interprets Latin American history and ian categories. Applies to history concept that societies like individuals go through stages of neurotic development—early trauma, defense, latency, outbreak of the neurosis, and full blown repression. First stage is represented by king's overthrow at independence and last by modern military dictatorships. Also interprets machismo in relation to Freud's formulation of Eros and Thanatos.

1710 Hardoy, Jorge Enrique and **María Elena Langdon.** Desigualdades regionales en Hispanoamérica: 1850–1930 (IGFO/RI, 38:151/152, enero/junio, 1978, p. 11–133, tables)

Book-length article which argues that Latin America was marked by social, economic and spacial homogeneity in 1850. Development thereafter brought heterogeneity by confirming process of urbanization and primacy of single city in each country. Authors provide three unrelated case studies of this process based on an analysis of census data for changes in occupational structure and residential patterns.

Ianni, Octávio. Escravidão e racismo. See *HLAS 43:8028.*

1711 Lafaye, Jacques. Unity and diaspora: the Hispanic cultural equation (UNESCO/CU, 7:1, 1980, p. 11–28)

Interesting interpretive essay which considers difficulties in defining characteristics of the "Hispanic culture area" arising from the remarkable diversity created by contacts with so many different culture areas. In particular, author analyzes difference in attitudes toward the state and the Anglo-Saxon world.

1712 Lapa, José Romero do Amaral. Historiografía latinoamericana contemporánea: problemática de sus tendencias (*in* Encuentro de Historiadores Latinoamericanos y del Caribe, *2d, Caracas, 1977.* Los estudios históricos en América Latina: ponencias, acuerdos y resoluciones: Caracas, 20–26 de marzo de 1977. Caracas: Universidad Central de Venezuela, Facultad de Humanidades y Educación, Escuela de Historia, 1979, v. 1, t. 1, p. 147–158)

Progress report on project in which a number of historians are participating, designed to ascertain state of Latin American historiography. Explains project's goals and conceptual framework.

1713 Le Riverend, Julio. Función histórico de los elementos ibéricos en el desarrollo de las culturas latinoamericanas. La Habana: UNESCO, Oficina Regional de Cultura para América Latina y el Caribe, Centro de Documentación, 1980. 12 p. (La cultura en América Latina. Monografías; 9)

Traces development of Hispanic cultures in the Americas and suggests priorities for future research. [F. Knight]

Magdoff, Harry. Imperialism: from the colonial age to the present; essays. See *HLAS 43:7080.*

1714 Mazet, Claude. Utilización de los libros parroquiales para la investigación demográfica, con alicación al caso de las fuentes hispanoamericanas (EEHA/HBA, 23, 1979, p. 35–84, bibl., tables)

Précis on how to exploit Latin American parish registers for demographic purpose, using aggregative analysis or family reconstruction techniques as developed by French historical demographers, especially Louis Henry. Examples are drawn from Mazet's parish register work on colonial Lima (see item **2687**). [M.T. Hamerly]

1715 Minguet, Charles. Le noir dans la sensibilité et l'idéologie deš créoles americains a l'époque de l'indépéndance: 1780–1816 (Centre de Recherches Latino-Américaines [Université Paris X-Nanterre, France] 11, mars 1976, p. 1–15)

Occasional paper that cites treatment of blacks in *Mercurio Peruano*, a report of Antonio Narváez of New Granada, and José J. Fernández de Lizardi's *Periquillo sarmiento* to document apparent shift toward greater understanding. Author attributes change to impression made by blacks' struggles for liberation in Haiti and elsewhere. Hardly comprehensive analysis, but suggestive. [D. Bushnell]

Morales Crespo, Eddle and **Asdrúbal Aguiar Aranguren.** De la integración colonial a la desintegración republicana. See *HLAS 43:2880.*

1717 Morón, Guillermo. Historia contemporánea de América Latina. Caracas: Equinoccio, 1975. 225 p.; bibl. (Colección Parámetros)

Series of brief and quite superficial essays on various aspects of Latin American politics and society from colonial to modern times.

1718 Morse, Richard M. Urban development in Latin America: introduction (ISA/CUR, 8:1, 1980, p. 5–13, bibl.)

Introduction to a volume containing six papers delivered at a 1976 symposium on Latin American urbanization. Provides brief overview of role of cities in Latin America, trends in their research, and synopsis of following six papers.

1719 Oszlak, Oscar. The historical formation of the state in Latin America: some theoretical and methodological guidelines for its study (LARR, 16:2, 1981, pp. 3–32)

Synthetic article probes applicability of general theoretical literature on development of the state to its specific appearance in Latin America. In particular author analyzes relationships between formation of nationality, market structures and class systems, and the emergence of the national state.

1720 Pérez, Joseph. The Hispanic element in Latin America (UNESCO/CU, 7:1, 1980, p. 45–61)

Highly derivative and superficial account of role of conquest culture in general development of Spanish American culture.

1721 Pérez Brignoli, Héctor. Crisis agrarias y economías de exportación en América Latina: siglos XIX y XX (*in* Encuentro de Historiadores Latinoamericanos y del Caribe, 2d, Caracas, 1977. Los estudios históricos en América Latina: ponencias, acuerdos y resoluciones: Caracas, 20–26 de marzo de 1977. Caracas: Universidad Central de Venezuela, Facultad de Humanidades y Educación, Escuela de Historia, 1979, v. 1, t. 2, p. 492–501, tables)

Brief consideration of themes presented in author's previous article (see *HLAS 42:1937*), subsequently published in English in *Latin American Research Review* (15:2, 1980, p. 3–33).

1722 Sanz, Víctor. En torno a una historia de la historiografía latinoamericana

(*in* Encuentro de Historiadores Latinoamericanos y del Caribe, *2d, Caracas, 1977.* Los estudios históricos en América Latina: ponencias, acuerdos y resoluciones: Caracas, 20–26 de marzo de 1977. Caracas: Universidad Central de Venezuela, Facultad de Humanidades y Educación, Escuela de Historia, 1979, v. 1, t. 1, p. 309–316)

Analyzes reasons why so little has been done with the history of history in Latin America, examines continuing obstacles to the development of a hemispheric work on the subject, and offers a plan for the organization of a project that would generate such a work.

1723 Simposio sobre Santander y el Nuevo Mundo, *Santander, Spain, 1977.* Santander y el Nuevo Mundo: segundo ciclo de estudios históricos de la provincia de Santander octubre 1977. Santander: Institución Cultural de Cantabria, Diputación Provincial [and] Centro de Estudios Montañeses, 1977. 661 p.; bibl.; ill.

Collection of 38 papers presented in 1977 on Spain's Santander province and the New World. Topics include commercial relations, biographical and genealogical treatment of prominent emigrants, and a who's who of native sons who made significant contributions, in politics, arts, and literature.

TePaske, John Jay and **Herbert S. Klein.** The royal treasuries of the Spanish Empire in America. See item **170.**

1724 Tigner, James. Japanese immigration into Latin America: a survey (JIAS, 23:4, Nov. 1981, p. 457–482)

Presents brief study of causes, characteristics and impact of Japanese immigration to Latin America. Entirely based on secondary literature.

1725 Véliz, Claudio. The centralist tradition of Latin America. Princeton, N.J.: Princeton University Press, 1980. 355 p.; bibl.; index.

Interesting interpretation of Latin American political and social culture. Argues that the constant tendency in Iberian culture toward centralization and authoritarian modes of social and political organization can be attributed to the lack of any truly pluralistic or egalitarian institutions or experiences. For sociologist's comment, see *HLAS 43:8068.*

1726 Weaver, Frederick Stirton. Class, state, and industrial structure: the historical process of South American industrial growth. Westport, Conn.: Greenwood Press, 1980. 247 p.; bibl.; ill.; index (Contributions in economics and economic history; no. 32 0084–9235)

Interesting but somewhat superficial study which argues for including more historical analysis in the formulation of theories and models concerning problems of underdevelopment. Illustrates argument by examining theories developed to explain US and European industrial development and comparing the latter with historical evidence of industrial development in Latin America.

Wilgus, A. Curtis. Latin America, a guide to illustrations. See item **172.**

1727 Witker, Alejandro. Historia, conciencia nacional y el proyecto de una sociedad: apuntes preliminares (*in* Encuentro de Historiadores Latinoamericanos y del Caribe *2d, Caracas, 1977.* Los estudios históricos en América Latina: ponencias, acuerdos y resoluciones: Caracas, 20–26 de marzo de 1977. Caracas: Universidad Central de Venezuela, Facultad de Humanidades y Educación, Escuela de Historia, 1979, v. 1, t. 2, p. 700–706)

Polemic argument in favor of historians becoming "relevant" by devoting themselves to a single task: understanding the reasons for lack of development in Latin America today.

COLONIAL

1728 Alvado, Alejandro Filqueira. Capacidad intelectual y actitud del indio ante el castellano (IGFO/RI, 155/158, enero/dic. 1979, p. 163–185)

In addressing the problem of Castilianization of the Indian, author examines areas such as economics, religion, politics, and philology. Recounts opinions regarding Indian's rational capacity as well as his attitude toward Spaniards.

1729 Apología: de Juan Ginés de Sepúlveda contra Fray Bartolomé de las Casas y de Fray Bartolomé de las Casas contra Juan Ginés de Sepúlveda. Traducción castellana de los textos originales latinos. Introducción, notas e índices por Angel Losada. Madrid:

Editora Nacional, 1975. 413, 43 p., 253 leaves.

English translation of Las Casas' *Apologia*, drawn from Latin text in Bibliothèque Nationale, Paris, published by Stafford Poole, C.M. in 1974 (see *HLAS 38:2262a*). In publications honoring the quincentennial of Las Casas' birth, Angel Losada gave notice of his completed but unpublished Spanish translation of the *Apologia* of both Sepúlveda and Las Casas. This volume fills that gap and contains facsimile reproductions of the Latin texts.

1730 Arciniegas, Germán. El revés de la historia. Bogotá: Plaza & Janés Editores-Colombia, 1980. 350 p.; bibl.; ill. (Ensayos históricos) (Narrativa colombiana)

As title implies, this book is something of a curiosity. Arciniegas apparently plumbed recesses of his vast knowledge and experience in constructing a mixed collection of 15 essays. Topics generally concern the colonial era, but one essay that transcends the time frame treats Giuseppe and Anita Garibaldi's role in Uruguayan independence.

1731 Barbier, Jacques A. Peninsular finance and colonial trade: the dilemma of Charles IV's Spain (JLAS, 12:1, May 1980, p. 21–37, tables)

Presents additional evidence that central government's financial crises during struggle with UK produced negative political impact. Interests of peripheral provinces of the peninsula were sacrificed by officially sanctioned neutral trade with the colonies, which in effect constituted tacit admission that the colonies no longer figured importantly in the economic development of Spain.

1732 ———. Towards a new chronology for Bourbon colonialism: the *Depositaría de Indias* of Cádiz; 1722–1789 (IAA, 6:4, 1980, p. 335–353, tables)

Persuasive argument backed by statistical data suggests that earlier Bourbon Reforms were not of retrograde dimensions when compared to the era of Charles III. Barbier especially urges need for closer examination of Ferdinand VI's reign as the key to "a more nuanced view" of Bourbon colonialism.

1733 Barragán Barragán, José. Temas del liberalismo gaditano. México: Universidad Nacional Autónoma de México, Coordinación de Humanidades, 1978. 251 p.; bibl.

Author carefully examines central issues deliberated by Cortes of Cádiz: freedom of press; concept of legislative sovereignty; incarceration and individual freedom; social and political posture of the Americans; etc. Useful analysis of *gaditano* influences on 1812 Constitution.

1734 Batllori, Miguel. Del descubrimiento a la independencia: estudios sobre Iberoamérica y Filipinas. Prólogo de Pedro Grases. Caracas: Universidad Católica Andrés Bello, 1979. 363 p.; bibl.; index (Colección Manoa; 20)

Collection of 17 essays all of which have been published previously or presented as papers to learned societies. Majority of pieces deal with Latin American topics, but Spanish and Portuguese presence in Far East also receives attention. Thematic topics include discovery and conquest, evangelization, and emancipation.

1735 Baudot, Georges. La vie quotidienne dans l'Amérique espagnole de Philippe II, XVIe siècle. Paris: Hachette, 1981. 302 p.; bibl.; maps.

Part of Hachette's extensive series *Daily life . . .* , Georges Baudot's volume recounts social life and customs of Spanish America in the reign of Philip II. Includes his panoramic views on language, race, culture, religious life, rural life, urbanization, etc. Useful synthesis of a wide range of literature.

1736 Betancourt Infante, Luis Antonio. La defensa en el período hispánico (*in* Congreso Venezolano de Historia, *3rd, Caracas, 1977.* Memoria [see item **1741**] v. 3, p. 191–231)

Broad overview of Spanish defense posture in the colonial era, especially as it applies to Venezuela and the Caribbean. While well organized and systematically presented, the approach is generally recapitulative.

1737 Cantu, Francesca. Italia: documentos lascasianos (EEHA/HBA, 19:20, 1975/1976, p. 127–155)

Lists and summarizes 16th-century Lascasian materials housed in Italian archives according to four categories of documentation: 1) episcopal appointment; 2) Las Casas as a Dominican; 3) copies of Bishop's works and writings; and 4) biographical data.

1738 Comas, Juan. Fray Bartolomé, la esclavitud y el racismo (EEHA/HBA, 19/20, 1975/1976, p. 1–9)

Brief defense of Las Casas as vanguard opponent of slavery and racial discrimination.

1739 Compañy, Francisco Domínguez. Contenido urbanístico de las actas de fundación (PAIGH/H, 91, enero/junio 1981, p. 9–27, map, table)

Examines Crown policy with regard to founding of New World cities before 1573 Ordenanzas de Población. Since conversion of Indians was their main objective, author discusses founding acts in relation to site selection requirements, and more importantly to village's or city's arrangement.

1740 Conde Jahn, Franz; Carlos R. Travieso; and **Ceferino Alegría.** La salud en adelantados, capitanes descubridores y pobladores durante el período hispánico (*in* Congreso Venezolano de Historia, 3rd, Caracas, 1977. Memoria [see item **1741**] v. 3, p. 233–250)

Documents presence and importance of physicians, surgeons, and apothecaries in earliest voyages of exploration, discovery, and conquest. Also includes selected list of medical specialists assigned to colonial military garrisons.

1741 Congreso Venezolano de Historia, 3rd, *Caracas, 1977.* Memoria del tercer Congreso Venezolano de Historia del 26 de septiembre al 1 de octubre de 1977. Caracas: Academia Nacional de la Historia, 1979. 3 v.; bibl., ill.

Proceedings of third Venezuelan Congress of History, held in Caracas, Sept. 26– Oct. 1, 1977. Devoted to military history of Spanish and Portuguese colonies, especially Captaincy General of Venezuela. Useful compendium, many of the topics considered have been better dealt with by participants and other scholars elsewhere. For individual contributions of significance, see items **364, 1736, 1740, 1752, 1795, 1800, 2599, 2603, 2606, 2609, 2611, 2616, 2633, 2650, 2732, 2741** and **2743.** [M.T. Hamerly]

1742 Costeloe, Michael P. Spain and the wars of independence: the Comisión de Reemplazos, 1811–1820 (JLAS, 13:2, Nov. 1981, p. 223–237)

Describes activities of small group of Cádiz merchants and their participation in military expeditions sent to América to support independence movements. Author advances thesis that the Comisión exercised more influence than any other single group in determining policy concerning rebellion in America.

1743 Crawford, Leslie. Las Casas, hombre de los siglos: contemporaneidad de sus ideas antropológicas: la verosimilitud de la denuncia y su incidencia en la legislación para sociedades en proceso de aculturación. Washington: Secretaría General, Organización de los Estados Americanos, 1978. 205 p.; bibl.; maps.

Addressing the theme that Las Casas was a man for all centuries, Crawford divides his treatment into four major segments: 1) destruction and reconstruction of the Indies; 2) institutional; and 3) legislative responses to Las Casas's entreaties; and 4) contemporaneousness of Bishop's anthropological ideas.

1744 Domínguez Ortíz, Antonio. Los caminos de la plata americana (VANH/B, 62:248, oct./dic. 1979, p. 811–825)

Brief paper presented to Venezuelan Academy of History in which author summarizes hazards of trans-Atlantic bullion shipments, especially those resulting from shipwreck and fraud. Also includes references to precious gems.

1745 Dussel, Enrique D. El Episcopado Latinoamericano y la liberación de los pobres, 1504–1620. México: Centro de Reflexión Teológica, 1979. 442 p.; bibl.; index (Serie Historia latinoamericana; 6)

Dussel sees Latin American Episcopacy as protectors of Indians, champions of the poor, and defenders of the oppressed. Vitality of faith in early Church is also seen as crucial to social and political development. Short biographical sketches of 11 representative bishops are included.

Duviols, Jean-Paul. Voyageurs français en Amérique: colonies espagnoles et portugaises. See *HLAS 42:40.*

1746 Escudero, José Antonio. Los cambios ministeriales a fines del antiguo regimen. Sevilla: Publicaciones de la Universidad, 1975. 155 p.; bibl. (Anales de la Universidad Hispalense. Serie Derecho; no. 22)

Extensively footnoted and documented guide to ministerial changes in Spanish government between last year of Charles III's reign and Constitution of Cádiz. Appendix contains documentation dated as late as 1850.

1747 Esteban, Javier Cuenca. Statistics of Spain's colonial trade, 1792–1820: consular duties, cargo inventories, and balances of trade (HAHR, 61 : 3, Aug. 1981, p. 381–428, tables)

Exhaustive research in Spanish national and provincial archives yielded most complete and impressive statistical data now available on Spain's colonial trade prior to and during wars of independence. Quantitative analysis underscores disastrous impact on colonial trade of two naval wars with England and charts balance of trade in second decade of 1800s.

1748 Ezcurra Semblat, Isabel. La conquista española en Indias: realidad y valor. Montevideo: 1979. 94 p.; bibl.

Brief treatment of Spanish conquest with emphasis on multiplicity of factors insuring its success. Triumph of conquistadors over Indians is attributed in large measure to psychic and religious motivations.

1749 Fisher, John. Imperial "free trade" and the Hispanic economy, 1778–1796 (JLAS, 13 : 1, May 1981, p. 21–56, graphs, tables)

Excellent analysis of imperial "free trade" between Spain and her American colonies in last quarter of 18th century. Fisher concentrates on breakdown between Spanish and foreign goods and distribution of exports to American ports. Statistical data, painstakingly compiled from archival sources, are impressive and convincingly revisionistic.

1750 Franklin, Wayne. Discoverers, explorers, settlers: the diligent writers of early America. Chicago: University of Chicago Press, 1979. 252 p.; 30 leaves of plates; bibl.; ill.; index.

Traces "Diligent Writers of Early America" through discovery, exploration, and settlement stages of the New World. Each stage, as presented through eyes and influence of early writers, shaped the mood of America and created "a world from words." Contains 30 plates depicting early Americana scenes.

1751 García-Baquero González, Antonio. Cádiz y el Atlántico, 1717–1778: el comercio colonial español bajo el mono-

polio gaditano. Sevilla: Escuela de Estudios Hispano-Americanos, C.S.I.C.: Excelentísima Diputación Provincial de Cádiz, 1976. 2 v.: bibl.; ill. (Publicaciones de la Escuela de Estudios Hispano-Americanos de Sevilla; 237)

Impressively researched and superbly organized study of structure and dynamics of Spanish colonial commerce during years 1717–78. During those years which marked the height of Bourbon reforms, Cádiz was the hub of Spanish imperial trade. Read as a complimentary work to that of the Chaunu's on Seville and the Atlantic, scholars have available for the first time a panoramic view of the Carrera de Indias. Vol. 2 is statistical appendix to vol. 1.

1752 García-Gallo, Alfonso. La Capitanía General como institución de gobierno político en España e Indias en el siglo XVIII (in Congreso Venezolano de Historia, 3rd, Caracas, 1977. Memoria [see item **1741**] v. 1, p. 535–582)

Places detailed examination of political and military responsibilities of captain general within context of colonial administration. Analyzes post's supposed autonomy as well as creation of three new captaincy generals in 18th-century Spain.

1753 Genovese, Eugene D. From rebellion to revolution: Afro-American slave revolts in the making of the modern world. Baton Rouge: Louisiana State University Press, 1979. 173 p.; bibl.; index (The Walter Lynwood Fleming lectures in southern history, Louisiana State University)

Examines two major problems: 1) phasing of slave revolts and guerrilla warfare, and 2) relationship of slave revolts to their time's international political movement. Discusses difficulties of rebellion in context of standard query (e.g., why slaves rebelled so little) and offers response that, given circumstances, it was extraordinary that they did at all. Evaluates Maroon revolts and lastly, analyzes relationship among 18th-century bourgeois-democratic revolutions. Far-ranging, thought-provoking essays accompanied by very helpful, introductory bibliographic essay on all the Americas. [V.C. Peloso]

1754 Gerbi, Antonello. La naturaleza de las Indias Nuevas: de Cristóbal Colón a Gonzalo Fernández de Oviedo. Traducción de Antonio Alatorre. Mexico: Fondo de Cultura

Económica, 1978. 562 p.; bibl.; index.
Spanish translation of *La natura delle Indie nove* (1975).

1755 Góngora, Mario. Estudios de historia de las ideas y de historia social. Valparaíso: Ediciones Universitarias de Valparaíso, Universidad Católica de Valparaíso, 1980. 392 p.; bibl. (Colección jurídica. Serie mayor) (Publicaciones de la Escuela de Derecho)

Welcome anthology of not readily accessible essays on history of ideas and social history of Spain, colonial Spanish America and Chile, originally published between 1959–75, some of which Góngora has revised. Pt. 1: eight essays on history of ideas in Spain, colonial Spanish America, and Chile; pt. 2: four essays on social history of colonial Chile. Except for the first essay, does not replicate Góngora's *Studies in the colonial history of Spanish America* (see *HLAS 38:2276*). [M.T. Hamerly]

1756 Greenleaf, Richard E. comp. The Roman Catholic Church in colonial Latin America. Edited with an introduction by Richard E. Greenleaf. Tempe, Arizona: Center for Latin American Studies, Arizona State University, 1977. 272 p.; bibl.

Reprint of 1971 Brozoi Book on Latin America (see *HLAS 34:1341*).

1757 Hanke, Lewis. Guía de las fuentes en Hispanoamérica para el estudio de la administración virreinal española en México y en el Perú, 1535–1700. Preparada por Lewis Hanke y Gunnar Mendoza, con la colaboración de Celso Rodríguez. Contribuciones de Manuel Burga Díaz et al. Washington, D.C.: Secretaría General, Organización de los Estados Americanos, 1980. 523 p.; bibl.; index.

Valuable guide to Spanish American manuscript sources and guides relating to viceregal administration under the Hapsburgs. Includes names of archives and current directors, addresses of archives, telephone numbers, and hours of admission. Ecclesiastical and notarial archives are excluded because of problems of accessibility and lack of inventories. For many scholars, however, this volume will be an indispensable aid.

1758 Hera, Alberto de la. El patronato indiano en la historiografía eclesiástica (Hispania Sacra [Madrid] 65/66, 1980, p. 229–264)

Analiza en particular el método empleado por el jesuíta Mariano Cuevas en su *Historia de la Iglesia en México*, comparándolo ligeramente con el enfoque del peruano Rubén Vargas Ugarte y del argentino Cayetano Bruno. [L.G. Canedo]

1759 Heredia Herrera, Antonio M. La carta como tipo diplomático indiano (EEHA/AEA, 34, 1977, p. 65–95, facsims.)

Systematic and analytical study of correspondence originating from secular and religious officials in the Indies during 16th, 17th, and 18th centuries. Discusses general characteristics and paleographic similarities of each century. Includes facsimile reproductions.

1760 Junguera, Mercedes. In quest of Columbus (OAS/AM, 32:10, Oct. 1980, p. 49–53, plates)

Biographical article on Columbian research accomplished by the indefatigable and legendary archival sleuth, Alice Bache Gould (1868–1953). Nicely summarizes her four decades of travel and search for documents in Spain that resulted in the most detailed register of Columbus' crewmen.

1761 Klein, Herbert S. The middle passage: comparative studies in the Atlantic slave trade. Princeton, N.J.: Princeton University Press, 1978. 282 p.; bibl.; index.

Demographically probes known aspects of slave trade, concentrating on 18th and early 19th centuries, including material on 19th-century Brazilian internal trade. Studies quantitative characteristics of the trade in Virginia, Jamaica, Cuba, Haiti and Brazil and draws comparisons from information sifted through in European and Brazilian archives. Includes ca. 80 tables and graphs on movement, age, sex, survival and mortality of slaves, activities of slave ships, etc. Concludes that slave trade was fairly standardized business, that mid-passage deaths (not counting those caused by assaults or force) seem more related to disease than to overcrowding. Raises questions about impact of African immigrants upon demographic growth in the Americas. [V.C. Peloso]

1762 Liehr, Reinhard. Staatsverschuldung und Privatkredit: Die "Consolidación de Vales Reales" in Hispanoamérica (IAA, 6:2, 1980, p. 149–185)

A base de fuentes impresas disponibles, de los mejores estudios sobre la materia y de nueva documentación de archivo, expone lo que fué y significó aquella operación hacendística, utilizada por la España de fines del siglo XVIII y principios del XIX para detener la crisis financiera a que había llegado. Cifras sobre las cantidades recaudadas y alusiones a las consecuencias políticas de la medida en Hispanoamérica. [L.G. Canedo]

1763 Lockwood, Daniel. Indian homosexuality and the Spanish conquest of America. Utica: State University of New York, College of Technology, 1979. 14 p.

Advances thesis that Biblical injunctions against homosexuality as well as the conquistador's personal revulsion of the practice of sodomy justified the extermination of many New World natives.

1764 Lombardi, John V. Population reporting systems: an eighteenth-century paradigm of Spanish imperial organization (*in* Studies in Spanish American population history [see item **1792**] p. 11–23)

Highlights and comments on economic and social as well as demographic utility of 18th-century population sources, especially ecclesiastical *matrículas* or registers of households. [M.T. Hamerly]

1765 McLynn, Francis James. France and Spanish America during the War of Austrian Succession (JGSWGL, 17, 1980, p. 187–198)

Curious reference to the Spanish dual convoys (*flotas* and *galeones*), implying that they were Bourbon creations. Of interest are the delicate diplomatic efforts of France, while allied with Spain, directed toward the rupture of mercantilistic ties between Spain and her colonies.

1766 Malamud, Carlos D. El fin del comercio colonial (IGFO/RI, 38:151/152, enero/junio 1978, p. 287–347, tables)

Using unplumbed documentation in Archivo del Conde de Guaqui (Madrid) and impressive array of statistical data, Malamud presents excellent analysis of rise and decline of a commerical firm in Cádiz, Sobrinos de Aguerrevere y Lostra. His insights into the decline of colonial commerce during 1792–1827 lends broader significance to the study.

1767 Mantilla Ruiz, Luis Carlos. Un franciscano colombiano, Obispo en México (AGH/BHA, 65:722, julio/sept. 1978, p. 357–408, bibl., map, tables)

Well researched biography of heretofore virtually unknown Mateo de Zamora y Penagos (1968–1744), first Franciscan born in what is now Colombia to take office as a Bishop. Rector of the Colegio de San Buenaventura in Bogotá (1729–33), Zamora held other important ecclesiastical posts prior to becoming Bishop of Yucatán (1743–44). [M.T. Hamerly]

1768 Martínez Reyes, Gabriel. Finanzas de las 44 diócesis de Indias, 1515–1816. Bogotá: Ediciones Tercer Mundo, 1980. 492 p.; bibl.; ill.; index.

Utilizing archival sources, especially in Sevilla, Madrid, and Simancas, Martínez Reyes researched and compiled an exhaustive study of the finances of 44 dioceses in colonial Spanish America. Formulates useful picture of monetary resources commanded by colonial Church. A definitive work on ecclesiastical finance.

1769 Martinière, Guy. Frontiéres coloniales en Amérique du Sud: entre tierra firme et Maranhão, 1500–1800 (CDAL, 18:2, 1978, p. 147–182)

Carefully analyzes territorial evolution of colonial Brazil, especially as affected by treaties between Spain and Portugal and by designs of other European powers for establishing colonies on the north coast.

1770 ———. Les stratégies frontalières du Brésil colonial et l'Amérique Espagnole (CDAL, 18:2, 1978, p. 45–68, maps)

Analyzes from geo-historical perspective strategies affecting frontiers of colonial Brazil during three centuries of Spanish and Portuguese competition. Examines bilateral treaties which partitioned the South American continent between two nations, especially the 1750 Treaty of Madrid. Contains eight useful maps.

1771 Martiré, Eduardo. Guión sobre el proceso recopilador de las leyes de las Indias. Buenos Aires: Editorial Perrot, 1978. 53 p. (Lecciones de historia jurídica; 5)

Brief guide to those who directed their efforts toward compiling, summarizing, and systematizing the diversity and multiplicity of Spanish laws drafted for the Indies. Features familiar names such as Puga, Zorita, and León Pinelo as well as others not so familiar.

1772 Mörner, Magnus. "Comprar o criar:" fuentes alternativas de suministro de esclavos en las sociedades plantacionistas del Nuevo Mundo (PAIGH/H, 91, enero/junio 1981, p. 37–81, bibl., tables)

Important study of practice and economics of slave importation versus reproduction. Mörner notes that slave labor systems varied from country to country. Generally, reproduction sustained the slave population in North America, while importation was more important in Brazil and the Caribbean. Tables include interesting data on male-female ratios among imported slaves.

1773 Molina de Lines, María and **Josefina Piana de Cuestas.** Gonzalo Fernández de Oviedo, representante de una filosofía política española para la dominación de las Indias (*in* Centenario de Gonzalo Fernández de Oviedo, 5th, Nicoya, Costa Rica, 1978. Memoria del Congreso sobre el Mundo Centroamericano de su Tiempo, 24–25–26 y 27 de agosto 1978. Nicoya, Costa Rica: Comisión Nacional Organizadora, 1978, p. 77–87, bibl.)

Brief tribute to Gonzalo Fernández de Oviedo as loyal and staunch defender of the Spanish right to empire in the Americas.

1774 Mora Mérida, José Luis. La Visita Eclesiástica como institución en Indias (JGSWGL, 17, 1980, p. 59–67)

Traces fusion of religious and civil legislation regarding Indians of the New World, especially in the reign of Philip II. Coexistence of both influences helped shape a more complete and accurate picture of Indian culture.

1775 Olaechea Labayen, Juan B. Categoría socio-política y profesional de los mestizos hispano-indianos (CSIC/RIS, 32:7/8, julio/dic. 1973, p. 55–82)

While admitting that legal barriers impeded social advancement of many mestizos, author cites examples of mixed bloods who entered Spanish peerage, attained membership in military orders, and achieved high office. Also discusses status of mestizos in several colonies with regard to tribute obligations and rights of encomienda possession.

1776 Palmer, Colin A. Human cargoes: the British slave trade to Spanish America 1700–1739. Urbana: University of Illinois Press, 1981. 183 p.; 2 maps; bibl.; index (Blacks in the New World)

Well written, researched, and organized monograph on the nature and dimensions of the British slave trade to Spanish America. Emphasizes organization and structure of asiento trade. Concludes that the British contract unquestionably established that nation's supremacy in human traffic.

1777 Peralta, Germán. Rutas negreras. Lima: Universidad Nacional Federico Villarreal, Dirección Universitaria de Investigación, 1979, 1980. 43 p.; bibl. (Publicación/Universidad Nacional Federico Villarreal, Centro de Investigaciones Históricas Sociales; [nov. 1979] no. 4)

Brief but well researched treatment of major and minor commercial routes plied in the African slave trade during 1595–1640. Examines considerations which influenced establishment of fixed routes such as port facilities and localized economies.

1778 Pérez, Joseph. El humanismo español frente a América (CH, 375, sept. 981, p. 477–489)

Brief examination of two works by 16th-century Spanish humanist, Hernán Pérez de Oliva. Author sees in him a universality which encompassed the view that good and evil did not reside exclusively in either Spaniard or Indian and the belief that all humanity is one.

1779 Prutschi, Manuel. The strange and wonderful case of Juan Rodríguez Mejía, chaplain in the Spanish Royal Navy, 1780–1783: some preliminary thoughts on the Jewish question in Spanish territories (PAIGH/H, 88, julio/dic. 1979, p. 11–31)

Interesting account of a naive, overzealous chaplain in the Spanish Royal Navy who feigned commitment to Judaism in order to entrap suspected crypto-Jews on his vessel. Author sees incident as evidence of the repressive nature of 18th-century Spanish state and of its use of Judaism long after circumstances justified it.

1780 Ramos, Demetrio. Audacia, negocios y política en los viajes españoles de "descubrimiento y rescate." Valladolid, Spain: Seminario Americanista de la Universidad de Valladolid, 1981. 626 p.

Vol. 1 de la colección "Tierra Nueva y Cielo Nuevo," que se orienta hacia la conmemoración del medio milenario del descubrimiento de América. Analiza los descubrimientos como resultado de una política global en que la Corona dirige y apoya, mientras los descubridores asumen los riesgos.

Método implantado en 1495, que—con breves interrupciones y titubeos—perduró tanto como la misma actividad descubridora. Obra minuciosa y rigurosamente documentada, de la que saca conclusiones novedosas, dignas de ser muy tenidas en cuenta. Libro indispensable en la biblioteca de todo americanista. [L.G. Canedo]

1781 ———. Un paralelo seglar del Padre Las Casas: Juan de Ampiés (EEHA/AEA, 34, 1977, p. 149–171)

Traces character and career of Juan de Ampiés whose concern and sympathy for the Indians somewhat paralleled Las Casas' humanitarian commitments.

1782 Rech, Bruno. Las Casas und die Kirchenväter (JGSWGL, 17, 1980, p. 1–47)

Author discusses whether Las Casas should be regarded as a theologian or political propagandist. Sees lack of conflict in both concepts, and challenges, by tracing spiritual influences of Church Fathers on Las Casas, Menéndez Pidal's contention that the Bishop of Chiapas professed an anti-Christian and anti-Biblical ideology.

1783 Robles, Gregorio. América a fines del siglo XVII: noticia de los lugares Anzoategui. Valladolid, Spain: Seminario Americanista de la Universidad de Valladolid, 1980. 102 p.

Edición del manuscrito que, bajo el título de *Declaración y noticias*, contiene el relato que un Gregorio Robles hizo ante un miembro del Consejo de Indias sobre sus extraordinarias andanzas por casi toda América durante los primeros años del siglo XVII y primeros del XVIII. Es una rica mina de informes. [L.G. Canedo]

1784 Rodríguez Vicente, María Encarnación. Los Cargadores a Indias y su contribución a los gastos de la monarquía, 1555–1750 (EEHA/AEA, 34, 1977, p. 211–232, appendix)

Documents activities of Consulado of Cádiz which acted as intermediary between Crown and merchants. Merchants, hoping to preserve commercial monopolies, contributed substantial loans and donations to help defray royal expenses. Contains statistical data.

1785 Ruiz de Lira, Rafael. Colón, el Caribe y las Antillas. Madrid: Hernando, 1978? 249 p.; bibl.; ill.; indexes (Historia de América Latina; 3)

Vol. 3 of projected 18-volume series on history of Latin America. Succinctly outlines background of Columbian voyages, Columbus' four voyages, governorships of Nicolás de Ovando, Diego Columbus, and the Jeronymite friars.

1786 Ruiz Povedano, José. Algunas precisiones eruditas sobre uno de los homónimos-coetáneos de Francisco de Bobadilla (EEHA/AEA, 34, 1977, p. 233–240)

Brief tribute to quality of scholarship in Francisco de Bobadilla's biography published 1964 by Incháustegui Cabral. Cabral documented existence of three, possibly four, men with identical names who have been confused with Española's governor.

1787 Sanz, Eufemio Lorenzo. La requisición de las remesas de oro y plata de mercaderes y particulares por la Corona en el siglo XVI (EEHA/AEA, 34, 1977, p. 271–293, tables)

Discusses disposition of individual consignments of wealth sent to Spain in 16th century. Financially strapped Crown followed inconsistent policies which at times included outright confiscation without compensation. Such actions made business enterprises hazardous for colonial merchants.

1788 Sanz López, Carlos. La ciencia moderna fué realmente una consecuencia normal y necesaria del descubrimiento de América (EEHA/AEA, 34, 1977, p. 295–328)

Theorizes that modern sciences was not the result of human inspiration or creative genius, but rather the necessary and logical consequence of geographic discoveries in the New World. Latter influenced the development of Copernican concepts of a heliocentric and global system and by extension, modern science.

1789 Serrera, Ramón María. Un uso marginal de la riqueza minera indiana: la acumulación suntuaria de metales preciosos (EEHA/AEA, 34, 1977, p. 487–515)

Discusses uses of gold and silver which prevented their entry in the monetary system. Elaborate ornamentation in churches, displays of wealth by religious houses, and accumulation of precious metals as indicators of social status significantly reduced the supply of specie.

1790 Steckly, George F. The wine economy of Tenerife in the seventeenth century: Anglo-Spanish partnership in a luxury trade

(The Economic History Review [Popperand Co., Ltd., Hertfordshire, U.K.] 33 : 3, Aug. 1980, p. 335–350, maps, tables)

By 1650s Tenerife was almost totally dependent on England as a market for its native wines. Gradual changes in wine taste in second half of 17th century followed by dissolution of Anglo-Spanish partnerships due to War of Spanish Succession created chaotic economic problems for Tenerife businessmen.

1791 Stein, Stanley J. Bureaucracy and business in the Spanish empire, 1759–1804: failure of a Bourbon reform in Mexico and Perú (HAHR, 61 : 1, Feb. 1981, p. 2–28)

Discusses failure of reform in Bourbon intendancy system, especially with regard to the corregimiento in Peru and the alcaldía mayor in New Spain. Of interest are conflicts between colonial bureaucrats and merchants in the exploitation of Indians. Examines social and economic pressures within imperial imperatives.

1792 Studies in Spanish American population history. Edited by David J. Robinson. Boulder, Colo.: Westview Press, 1981. 274 p.; bibl.; ill.; index (Dellplain Latin American studies; no. 8)

Interdisciplinary approach to population studies offering new insights on changing size, structure, and distribution of Spanish American population during colonial era. Contributors (11) are historians, anthropologists, and geographers who address demographic topics in Andean South America, Central America, and Mexico.

1793 Tanzi, Héctor José. El derecho militar indiano: importancia, contenido de la materia y estado actual de la investigación (in Congreso Venezolano de Historia, 3rd, Caracas, 1977. Memoria [see item 1741] v. 3, p. 251–288)

Broad summary of literature pertaining to development of Spanish military law in colonial era. Includes ordinances and statutes emanating from Spain and New World agencies as well as published works on subject. Author appeals for additional research and synthesis to understand totality of process and its influence on contemporary military organizations.

1794 Tardieu, Jean-Pierre. Les principales structures administratives espagnoles de la traite des noirs vers les Indes Occidentales (UTIEH/C, 37, 1981, p. 51–84)

Revisionist interpretation of administrative structure of slave *asientos* granted by Spanish government. Based on licenses in AGI's Contratación section, explores similarities and differences in contracts.

1795 Troconis de Veracoechea, Ermila. Cárceles coloniales (in Congreso Venezolano de Historia, 3rd, Caracas, 1977. Memoria [see item 1741] t. 3, p. 477–515)

Descriptive and informative account of prisons in colonial Venezuela. Includes kinds of prisons, principal offenses leading to incarceration, work obligations of prisoners, and modes of punishment for offenders.

1796 Uribe, Angel. Colegio y colegiales de San Pedro y San Pablo de Alcalá: Siglos XVI–XVIII. Madrid: Editorial Cisneros, 1981. 524 p.

Trabajo publicado antes en la revista *Archivo Ibero-Americano* (Madrid), 1976–80. El Colegio era un centro universitario para estudiantes franciscanos. Varios de los colegiales estuvieron en América o relacionados con ella. La obra está escrupulosamente documentada y constituye una buena fuente de consulta. [L.G. Canedo]

1797 Verlinden, Charles. L'Etat et l'administration des communautés indigènes dans l'Empire Espagnol d'Amérique: quelques réflexions (EEHA/AEA, 34, 1977, p. 695–705)

Brief assessment of protagonists who influenced Indian policy in early colonial period—Crown, clergy and colonist. Concludes that reality of local conditions in the Indies often dictated administrative decisions.

1798 Vives Azancot, Pedro A. El espacio americano español en el siglo XVIII (IGFO/RI, 38 : 151/152, enero/junio 1978, p. 135–175)

Traces regional influences such as population, geography, climate, natural resources, urban development, etc. which shaped direction and adaptation of imperial policy. Author sees these variables as important considerations in shaping the course and aftermath of Spanish American independence.

1799 Walker, Geoffrey J. Spanish politics and imperial trade, 1705–1789. Bloomington: Indiana University Press, 1979.

297 p.; 4 leaves of plates; bibl.; ill.; index.

Well written and thoroughly researched treatment of political undercurrents of 18th-century Spanish imperial trade. Also under discussion are trade fairs, *flotas* and *galeones*, individual register ships, *avisos*, *azogues*, and contraband associated with the *Asiento de Negros*. A major work on the Carrera de Indias under Spanish Bourbons.

1800 Zorraquin Becú, Ricardo. El Adelantado Indiano: título honorífico (*in* Congreso Venezolano de Historia, *3rd, Caracas, 1977.* Memoria [see item **1741**] t. 3, p. 551–578)

Good summary of considerable powers enjoyed by Adelantados in Spain from the era of Alfonso X to the Reconquest's conclusion. In contrast, use of title in Spanish America was honorific and especially conferred on those leading expeditions to little known outposts of empire.

INDEPENDENCE AND 19TH CENTURY

1801 Armellada, Cesáreo de. La causa indígena americana en las Cortes de Cádiz (UCAB/M, 1979, p. 497–564)

Highly useful study that both itemizes all discussion of American questions at Cortes of Cádiz and relates in more detail handling of those directly concerning Indians. Documentary appendix of Cortes measures. [D. Bushnell]

1802 Burns, E. Bradford. The poverty of progress: Latin America in the nineteenth century. Berkeley: University of California Press, 1980. 183 p.; 4 leaves of plates; bibl.; ill.; index.

Introduces new interpretation of Latin American development in 19th century and resultant poverty today. Contends that progress, Western style, as inflicted on Latin America contributed to poverty, conflict, and dependency, not modernization and progress. Raises question: Were there alternative lifestyles more conducive to genuine advancement of the masses?

1803 Coloquio Ilustración Española e Independencia de América, *Bellaterra, Spain, 1978.* Homenaje a Nöel Salomon: ilustración española e independencia de América. Edición preparada por Alberto Gil No-

vales. Barcelona: Universidad Autónoma de Barcelona, 1979. 440 p.; bibl.; ill.; index.

Homenaje volume issued in remembrance of Noël Salomon, noted French Hispanist (d. 1977). Consists of 32 papers, addressing broad theme of Latin American independence, presented at 1978 colloquium in Salomon's honor. Topics range from influence of Decembrists in Russia to Francisco de Miranda's travels in Toledo province (1788) with accompanying maps.

1804 Costeloe, Michael P. Spain and the Latin American wars of independence: the free trade controversy, 1810–1820 (HAHR, 61:2, May 1981, p. 209–234)

Among proposals for pacifying America and effecting its reunification with Spain was the granting of international free trade to colonies. Costeloe traces unsuccessful efforts of free trade advocates to overcome opposition from vested economic interests in Spain, from military hawks, and from political factions at court who used issue solely to discredit their enemies. Excellent research, writing, and analysis.

1805 ———. Spain and the Spanish American wars of independence: the *Comisión de Reemplazos,* 1811–1820 (JLAS, 12:2, Nov. 1981, p. 223–237)

Good short article, crammed with facts, concerning agency created and managed primarily by Cádiz merchants. Besides lobbying against trade liberalization and for military solution to the American rebellion, it succeeded in assembling and dispatching, against great odds, a substantial quantity of men and equipment. [D. Bushnell]

1806 Grases, Pedro. La peripecia bibliográfica de Simón Rodríguez. Caracas: Universidad Nacional Experimental Simón Rodríguez, 1979. 47 p.; bibl.

Bibliographic glosses on work of Bolívar's famous tutor and visionary educator, with special attention to his translation of Chateaubriand's *Atala.* [D. Bushnell]

1807 Hunt, Shane J. La economía de las haciendas y plantaciones en América Latina (PMNH/HC, 9, 1975, p. 7–65, bibl., tables)

Translation of study that originally appeared in English in Oct. 1972 published by Woodrow Wilson School, Research Program in Economic Development, Princeton University, Discussion Paper No. 29. [V.C. Peloso]

1808 Lucena Samoral, Manuel. El comercio de los Estados Unidos con España e Hispanoamérica e comienzos de la presidencia de Madison: 1809 (*in* Congreso de Historia de los Estados Unidos, Universidad de la Rábida, 1976. Actas. Madrid: Servicio de Publicaciones del Ministerio de Educación y Ciencia, 1978?, p. 171–241, maps, tables)

Using Spanish archives as well as published sources, detailed reconstruction and analysis of US commercial relations with Spain and colonies as of beginning of independence period. [D. Bushnell]

1809 Nineteenth-century Latin Americans in the United States. Carlos E. Cortés, editor. New York: Arno Press, 1980. 169 p. in various pagings; bibl.; port.

Focuses on major figures of the Latin American-US connection in 19th century. Four of six essays in this anthology are reprints.

1810 Novales, Alberto Gil. La independencia de América en la concienca española, 1820–1823 (IGFO/RI, 155/158, enero/dic. 1979, p. 235–265)

Spanish attitudes toward Latin American independence, ranging from favorable to opposed, are examined in detail. Novales makes clear distinctions between public and governmental opinion.

1811 Pérez, Joaquín. El comercio francés en la época de la Restauración y el proceso de la independencia americana (ANH/IE, 26, enero/junio 1979, p. 259–269)

Brief note, using French press and archives, on conflict of viewpoints with respect to Spanish America in France in 1820s. [D. Bushnell]

1812 Platt, D.C.M. Dependency in the 19th century: an historian objects (LARR, 15 : 1, 1980, p. 113–130)

Argues that dependency analysis with its assertion that all stimuli for development were exogenous, is unsustainable. Also criticizes view that there was a smooth transition between the colonial and neo-colonial economic systems in 19th century. Believes that Latin American economies were shaped more by local circumstances than by the planned needs of metropolitan economies.

1813 ———. Objeciones de un historiador a la teoría de la dependencia en América Latina en el siglo XIX. Traducción: Nora Titiunik. Revisión técnica: Alejandro Titiunik (IDES/DE, 19 : 76, enero/marzo 1980, p. 435–451)

Translation of item preceding.

1814 Ramos Pérez, Demetrio. Posibles planes realistas de *supervivencia* en torno a 1810 (Revista del Instituto de Historia Argentina y Americana Doctor Emilio Ravignani [Universidad de Buenos Aires, Buenos Aires] 26, 1980, p. 393–414)

Reviews several schemes hatched in Spain or by royal officials in colonies, from possible transfer of Junta Central to America to establishment of peninsular-controlled provisional government in America. [D. Bushnell]

1815 Rodríguez, Simón. Ideario de Simón Rodriguez. Compilado por Alfonso Rumazo González. Caracas: Ediciones Centauro, 1980. 384 p.

Collection of quotations from writings of Simón Rodríguez, grouped under broad topical headings. Preceded by lengthy introduction in which compiler justly acclaims Rodríguez as one of most original Spanish American thinkers of independence period and first half of 19th century. [D. Bushnell]

Solís, Miguel de J. Latin American independence: an historical and ideological view, a bibliography. See item **52**.

1816 Soto Cárdenas, Alejandro. Influencia de la independencia de los Estados Unidos en la constitución de las naciones latinoamericanas. Washington, D.C.: Secretaría General, Organización de los Estados Americanos, 1979. 202 p.

Well researched and well written account of ideological diffusion of North American political thought and value systems in Latin America. While focusing primarily on constitutional influences in early national charters, also discusses more gradual and continuing shadings of American experience as reflected in historical evolution of the Hispanic republics.

1817 Tanzi, Héctor José. Orígenes ideológicos del movimiento emancipador americano. Caracas: Instituto Panamericano de Geografía e Historia, Comisión de Historia, Comité Orígenes de la Emancipación,

1979. 119 p.; bibl. (Publicación—Instituto Panamericano de Geografía e Historia, Comisión de Historia, Comité Orígenes de la Emancipación; no. 23)

Brings together separate studies on ideological antecedents of independence, generally in line with conservative Hispanist perspective of author's *El poder político y la independencia argentina* (see *HLAS* 40:2378). [D. Bushnell]

1818 Vila Vilar, Enriqueta. La esclavitud americana en la política española del siglo XIX (EEHA/AEA, 34, 1977, p. 563–588)

Discusses internal and external political problems associated with the institution of slavery in America. Author uses information found in records of Spanish cortes which reflect attitudes toward slavery in Spain and repercussions thereof in the colonies.

20TH CENTURY

1819 América Latina: historia de medio siglo. Coordinación, Pablo González Casanova. México: Siglo Veintiuno Editores, 1977– . 2 v.; bibl. (Historia)

Two volumes of essays by Latin American social scientists on political and social history of individual countries from mid-1920s to present. Vol. 1 covers South American nations; vol. 2) Central American and Caribbean area.

1820 L'Amérique latine au XXe [i.e. vingtième] siècle. Joseph-Henri Denécheau *et al.* Paris; New York: Masson, 1979. 119 p.; maps (Dossier d'histoire Pierre Goubert 0070-7147)

Brief textbook treatment of 20th-century history of Latin America.

Baily, Samuel L. The United States and the development of South America, 1947–1975. See *HLAS* 43:7362.

1821 Burns, E. Bradford and **Thomas E. Skidmore.** Elites, masses, and modernization in Latin America, 1850–1930. Introd. by Richard Graham. Edited by Virginia Bernhard. Austin: University of Texas Press, 1979. 156 p.; bibl. (The Texas Pan American series)

Consists of two major essays: one on historic conflicts between elite and folk cultures (Burns), another on growing confrontation between armies and labor movements

(Skidmore). Graham's excellent introduction compares and evaluates both noting absence of analysis of economic interests. All three provide valuable insights. Useful classroom tool. [V.C. Peloso]

1822 Caldera, Rafael. Simón Bolívar (OAS/AM, 33:4, April 1981, p. 44–48, plates)

Article is adapted from speech by former Venezuelan President Caldera delivered Dec. 1980, Washington, D.C., to commemorate 150th anniversary of Bolivar's death. Focus is on the Liberator's philosophy of Latin American unity as the criteria for survival and success.

1823 Child, John. Unequal alliance: the inter-American military system, 1938–1979. Boulder, Colo.: Westview Press, 1980. 253 p.; bibl.; map (A Westview replica edition)

Analysis from US perspective of functioning of hemispheric military system. Concludes that creation of joint strategy and cooperative military efforts has ebbed and flowed since World War II in response to shifting American foreign policy priorities. Describes four phases of such cooperation: 1) period of growth during World War II; 2) divergence and decline during early Cold War; 3) rebirth of cooperation in formulation of 1960s anti-guerilla strategies; and finally, contemporary situation marked by fragmentation and dysfunction.

1824 Conniff, Michael L. Introduction: toward a comparative definition of populism [*in* Latin American populism in comparative perspective. [see item **1830**] p. 3–30, bibl.)

Interesting interpretive essay on origins, characteristics and historiography of populism in Latin America. Views main tenet of populism as "the desire for social integration of the masses." Considers this a reaction to destruction of independent holistic and organic urban societies of colonial period by authoritarian and capitalistic character of urban reform during the late 19th century, based on European models.

1825 Gellman, Irwin F. Good neighbor diplomacy: United States policies in Latin America, 1933–1945. Baltimore: Johns Hopkins University Press, 1979. 296 p.; bibl.; index (The Johns Hopkins University Studies in historical and political science; 97th ser., 2).

Moderate descriptive analysis of Good Neighbor policy arranged chronologically and topically. Emphasizes interaction of principal actors—Roosevelt, Hull and Welles—and how clash of personalities and goals affected formulation of economic policy during Depression, attempts to limit German influence and the creation of a unified front among American states after World War II started. Concludes that policy was not simplistic mishmash but sophisticated set of economic, political and military policies generated by Roosevelt's administration. For political scientist's comment, see *HLAS 43:7040.*

1826 Halperin Donghi, Tulio. La cuantificación histórica: trayectoria y problemas (*in* Encuentro de Historiadores Latinoamericanos y del Caribe, 2d, Caracas, 1977. Los estudios históricos en América Latina: ponencias, acuerdos y resoluciones: Caracas, 20–26 de marzo de 1977. Caracas: Universidad Central de Venezuela, Facultad de Humanidades y Educación, Escuela de Historia, 1979, v. 1, t. 2, p. 434–447)

Erudite analysis of impact of important figures of *Annales* school and new US economic historians on methodologies of history in recent past.

1827 Hanke, Lewis. The early development of Latin American studies in the United States, 1930–49 (*in* Studying Latin America: essays in honor of Preston E. James [see item **1834**] p. 103–120)

Author's personal reminiscences regarding important personalities and institutions involved in field, 1930–40, with particular emphasis on his own role.

1828 Johnson, John J. Latin America in caricature. Austin: University of Texas Press, 1980. 330 p.; bibl.; ill.; index (The Texas Pan American series)

Very interesting approach to reconstructing cultural values. Examines US attitudes toward Latin America and its problems as conveyed by newspapers and journals in editorial cartooning. Examines period 1898–1930 and analyzes intent of cartoons stereotyping Latin America as monolithic, female, infantile or black. Last two chapters discuss treatments of militarism and social reform, and use of non-black males in cartooning. For political scientist's comment, see *HLAS 43:7054.*

1829 Knothe, Tomasz. Los estados de América Latina en la Conferencia de Paris de 1919 (PAN/ES, 3, 1976, p. 111–128)

Examines how Latin American participants at Paris Peace Conference were selected, role they played and reasons behind inclusion of Monroe Doctrine in treaty creating the League of Nations. Concludes that because of US involvement in selection process, Latin American interests were poorly represented. Based on published sources.

1830 Latin American populism in comparative perspective. Edited by Michael L. Conniff. Albuquerque: University of New Mexico Press, 1981. 1 v.; bibl.; index.

Ten brief essays by experts analyze nature and practice of populist politics. Six contributions deal with Latin America: two compare Latin American experience with late Tzarist Russia and US. Michael Conniff provides introductory general essay (item **1824**) and Paul Drake a retrospective conclusion.

1831 Pike, Frederick. Latin America (*in* Spain in the twentieth-century world: essays on Spanish diplomacy, 1898–1978. Edited by James W. Cortada. Westport, Conn.: Greenwood Press, 1980, p. 181–212)

Essay on directions and themes of Spanish foreign policy toward Latin America during 20th century. Concludes that Spanish have never been able to take advantage of "Hispanism"—the feeling of cultural linkage and shared heritage. Attributes this to lack of political compatibility and shared economic interests plus effect of "black legend" propagated by political exiles and economic emigrants (see item **1833**).

1832 Robinson, David J. On Preston E. James and Latin America: a biographical sketch (*in* Studying Latin America: essays in honor of Preston E. James [see item **1834**] p. 1–101)

Lengthy portrait of the career of noted geographer based on unedited materials from National Archives, and subject's personal papers at the University of Michigan and Syracuse University. For geographer's comment, see *HLAS 43:5024.*

Rosenberg, Emily S. The exercise of emergency controls over foreign commerce: economic pressure on Latin America. See *HLAS 43:2925.*

1833 Rubio, Javier. El desarraigo en las emigraciones políticas: el caso del exilio de la Guerra Civil española de 1936–1939 (CSIC/RIS, 35:21, enero/marzo 1977, 2. época, 113–138)

Examines the attitudes of political exiles toward things Spanish, and their degree of acceptance of their adopted country. Concludes that political exiles have a more difficult time than economic emigrants in accepting the permanence of their situation and in being absorbed into their country of refuge. Based on writings of exiles and secondary works about them.

Schiff, Warren. German-Latin American relations: the first half of the twentieth century. See *HLAS 43:7125.*

1834 Studying Latin America: essays in honor of Preston E. James. Edited by David J. Robinson. Ann Arbor, Mich.: Published for Dept. of Geography, Syracuse University by University Microfilms International, 1980. 237 p.; ill.; index (Dellplain Latin American studies; 4) (Monograph publishing: Sponsor series)

For articles by Hanke and Robinson see items **1827** and **1832**. For education specialist's comment, see *HLAS 43:4358.*

1835 Tobler, Hans Werner and **Peter Waldmann.** German colonies in South America: a new Germany in the Cono Sur? (UM/JIAS, 22:2, May 1980, p. 227–245)

Reviews recent works on German immigration to and colonization in Argentina, Brazil, and Chile, and examines consequences of German settlement, especially on economic development of host countries. [M.T. Hamerly]

Torshin, Mijaíl. Relaciones internacionales de los trabajadores de la URSS y de América Latina. See *HLAS 43:7147.*

1837 Woll, Allen L. The Latin image in American film. Los Angeles: UCLA Latin American Center Publications, University of California, 1980. 128 p.; 12 p. of plates; ill. (UCLA Latin American studies; v. 50)

Well-done monograph examines image of Latin American presented by film industry from its inception to early 1970s. Concludes that there has been little effort to portray Latin Americans honestly on screen. Most films have stereotyped them, most often as either buffoons or bandits.

MEXICO: General and Colonial Period

ASUNCION LAVRIN, *Associate Professor of History, Howard University*
EDITH B. COUTURIER, *National Endowment for the Humanities*

THE FLOURISHING OF HISTORICAL STUDIES in Mexico in the past several years can be attributed to President Lopez Portillo's interest in history as well as to the oil-generated economic boom. The result has been a proliferation of archival resources and documentary publication projects, the establishment of research institutes and of new historical journals. For additional publications that exemplify the importance Mexico now attaches to historical research, the reader should also consult the *HLAS* section entitled BIBLIOGRAPHY AND GENERAL WORKS (items **1–200**).

The listing of *Guías y Catálogos* (item **1847**) published by the National Archives of the Nation has increased from 28 to 63 during this biennium thanks to the continuing task of reorganization and improvement of local and national archives (for initial volumes in this series, see *HLAS 42:1965*). These guides have been produced by the collaborative effort of students, researchers of various nationalities, and archival personnel. They have made many sections of the national archives infinitely more accessible for research and opened up others hitherto uncatalogued or unknown. Copies of these volumes are available at the Hispanic Division of the Library of Congress, courtesy of the Embassy of Mexico.

The Colegio de Michoacán, an institute for graduate research in history and anthropology, launched a trimester publication, *Relaciones: Estudios de Historia y Sociedad* (item **1851a**). The Centro de Estudios Históricos "Fray Antonio Tello," in Guadalajara, renewed publication of *Estudios Históricos*, now in its third epoch (item **1900**). These journals constitute a welcome addition to already existing publications on regional and state history, now a thoroughly established field of Mexican historiography. Thus, it is not surprising that regional history was the dominant theme of some of the most important works appearing in the last two years. Herman Konrad's Bolton Prize winner, *A Jesuit hacienda in colonial Mexico: Santa Lucía, 1576–1767* is an excellent source for the history of the region north of Mexico City, seen through the prism of the Society of Jesus' management of land and labor (item **1910a**). Eric Van Young's *Hacienda and market in eighteenth-century Mexico* (item **1941**) analyzes the relationship of the city of Guadalajara and its surrounding region. In his study of the Archbishopric of Michoacán in the 18th century, *Michoacán en la Nueva España del siglo XVIII* (item **1920**), Claude Morin integrates the history of that region with the economy and demography of other areas of central New Spain. The Puebla-Tlaxcala area continues to be the subject of a major inter-disciplinary project of various scholars from the German Federal Republic (items **1924, 1938–1940**). Another important study of the Puebla region, based on Inquisition materials, and one of the few works dealing with the 17th century during this biennium, is that of Solange Behocaray Alberro (item **1888**).

Interest in demographic studies, which declined in the 1978–79 biennium, has soared. A major collective work, edited by David Robinson, *Studies in Spanish American Population History* (item **1792**) includes three important contributions on colonial Mexico: Robinson's own "La migración regional yucateca en la época colonial" (item **1926**), John K. Chance's "The Ecology of Race and Class on Late Colonial Oaxaca" (item **1895**), and Linda L. Greenow's "Marriage Patterns and Regional Interaction in Late Colonial Nueva Galicia" (item **1905**). Rudolph Zambardino (item **1944**) raises new questions on the Cook-Borah precolumbian population estimate but from a methodological viewpoint rather than on the basis of documentary evidence. Other noteworthy contributions are those of Elsa Malvido (item **1915**), Georges Baudot (item **1887**), and Claude Morin (item **1920**).

In the field of ethnohistory, Inga Clendinnen's perceptive articles provide new interpretations of Indian-Spanish relations in 16th-century Yucatán (items **1897** and **1898**). Also focusing on Yucatán's indigenous communities, Nancy Farris's study of confraternity ownership among the Maya, blends ethnohistory with economic history in an elegant rendition (item **1901**). Yucatecan economic development is examined by Mario Humberto Ruz in a study of the indigo industry in the 16th and 17th centuries (item **1930**). Like demographic history, studies of economic development also command much scholarly attention.

Hacienda studies continue to decline in numbers, although the regional studies by Konrad and Van Young mentioned above represent not only superb scholarship but contain extensive materials on hacienda organization and history. Noteworthy for this biennium are Cheryl Martin's study of landownership by the Bethlemite order (item **1916**), and the extensive study of San Antonio Xala by Juan F. Leal and Mariano Huacuja Rountree (item **1849**).

Research on Church history has tapped new sources, and points to an increasing interest in the secular Church and local ecclesiastical institutions such as *cofradías*. One should also note the following studies, J. Frederick Schwaller's of the Cathedral Chapter of Mexico City (item **1934**); Stafford Poole's of Church law (item **1870**); and Asunción Lavrin's (item **1911**). We look forward to the publication of Tulane University 1982 Conference's proceedings on the Church and Society in Latin America as well as to that of other ongoing research projects, that will contribute much to the enrichment of the field.

Institutional history, which used to be the backbone of historical research in the colonial period is represented by a small number of titles. Cristina Sarabia Viejo's study of the salt monopoly (item **1932**) and James Lewis' on the gunpowder monopoly (item **1913**) can be added to Luis Navarro Garcia's work on the royal accounting office (item **1868**) as principal contributions to the topic. All address issues extending beyond the mere institutional and economic boundaries and provide useful data within limited time frames.

The small number of works on women that have appeared during the period confirm the tentative nature of research in this field. Lavrin and Couturier's testimonial work on potential sources for women's history is one of the few on lay women (item **1864**). A work on the foundation of the first teaching religious order for women in New Spain, by Pilar Foz y Foz (item **1902**) focuses more on this institution's educational role than on women *per se*, although it provides useful data on the educational role of nuns. Two family studies by J.F. Schwaller and Paul Ganster, respectively, *Tres familias mexicanas del siglo XVI* (item **1875**) and *La familia Gómez de Cervantes* (item **1860**) offer new data on this important subject. Other forms of social and intellectual history, such as works on education by D. Tanck de Estrada (item **1877**) and on Mexico City's foundling home by Pilar Gonzalbo Aizpuru (item **1904**) suggest an ebb in the scholarly production of these fields.

Biographies published during this period fall into the categories of scholarly and popular works. Among them are Stafford Poole's study of the *oidor* Farfán (item **1925**) and Rodríguez García's on an audiencia *fiscal* (item **1873**). Based on sound research and offering glimpses into the lives of lesser known members of society, is Richard Boyer's study of a muleteer bigamist (item **1891**), an interesting example of history from the bottom up.

Studies of Indian and blacks have been relatively scarce. Ethnic groups have been treated largely in demographic works. Two contributions on indigenous groups should be noted. One by Elinore Barrett concerns Indian hospitals (item **1884**), and another by Robert Wasserstrom, the 1712 Tzetzal rebellion (item **1942**). Mining and pulque are two leading themes in economic history works. Representing these trends are E. Barrett's study of a copper mine (item **1885**). Studies of the pulque trade combine economic and social history with expertise. John Kicsa explores the socioeconomic elite's participation in the pulque trade (item **1910**) while Michael Scardaville documents pulque's social effects (item **1933**).

Concern with ecological and meteorological phenomena has led to new areas of investigation exemplified by Guadalupe Castorena (item **1894**), Enrique Florescano (item **1859**), and Susan Swan (item **1876**).

A work that represents a unique category is John Super's study of nutrition (item **1935**).

The period of the wars of independence is discussed in the scholarly works of Christon Archer who carries his study of the late colonial army into the 1820s (item **1882**), and Brian Hamnett who focuses on the local and class bases of the war (item **1907**).

In northern borderland studies, some writers continue to emphasize the secular aspects of colonization, rather than the military or missionary angles of that area's history. Readers should note Oakah L. Jones' work on settlers (item **1958**), and the studies by Piñera Ramírez (item **1965**), Stuart F. Voss (item **1980**), and María del

Carmen Velázquez (item **1975**). A particularly interesting study combining ethnohistory and institutional history is Evelyn Hu-DeHart's work on the Yaquis (item **1956**) which focuses on the interrelations of Jesuits, Indians and the civilians to account for the Yaquis' survival. A Spanish scholar, G. Porras Muñoz, supplies one of the few works on the 17th century (item **1966**).

In the last few years, the contributing editors to this section have observed a paucity of major works of synthesis. Scholars have turned to writing articles and monographs rather than book-length manuscripts. This trend may be attributed partly to economic constraints on the publication of long and expensive works, but also may be the result of a tendency to raise new questions in traditional fields, and to use new methodologies in recently developed areas.

GENERAL

1838 Archivo General del Estado de México. Catálogo y síntesis de documentos manuscritos relativos a pueblos del Estado de México, 1542–1823 por José Luis Alanís Boyso, Leopoldo Sarmiento Rea, Rodolfo Alanís Boyso. México: Archivo General del Estado de México, 1978. 163 p.; 36 p. of plates; facsims.; indexes.

Summary of 191 documents selected from Mexican state archives, largely from late colonial period and early 19th century, which deal with villages. Includes censuses, bandos, disputes, mortgages, among other materials. Supplements extensive lists of documents, collected by Mario Colín, from a number of ramos in the AGNM, which relate to villages in State of Mexico. Includes indexes and transcriptions. [EBC]

1839 Arnaud, Pascal. La evolución económica de México: de la colonia a 1850 (PCE/TE, 47[3]: 187, julio/sept. 1980, p. 651–677)

Interpretive essay based on secondary sources. Attempts to define economy's major components, their dynamic relationship with sociopolitical structures and main changes from 16th through mid-19th century. Interesting overview even if its use to historians will depend on their willingness to accept its theoretical premises. [AL]

1840 Artís Espriu, Gloria and **Virginia García Acosta.** Empresarios de la industria harinera y panificadora en México en los siglos XVIII y XIX (*in* Simposio sobre empresarios en México. Gloria Artís *et al.* México: Centro de Investigaciones Superiores del INAH, 1979. v. 1, p. 5–51 [Cuadernos de la casa chata: 21])

Two papers delivered at 1978 conference on ethnic entrepreneurs. Although research is in preliminary stages, data indicates that mayorázgo families and their allies dominated wheat and bread trade through their control of flour mills. Authors suggest interesting explanations for continued Spanish control of bakeries. Also trace temporal changes in monopolistic control of wheat supply, credit and sales. [EBC]

1841 Bibliografía general del desarrollo económico de México, 1500–1976. v. 1/2. Jorge Ceballos *et al.* Enrique Florescano, coordinador. México: Departamento de Investigaciones Históricas, Antropología e Historia (INAH), 1980. 2 v. (1177 p.); index (Colección científica: bibliografías; 76)

Extensive annotated bibliography of works on Mexican history, which contain economic data. Especially valuable for 19th-century materials, including extensive summaries of periodicals. For bibliographer's comment, see *HLAS 43 : 20*. [EBC]

Biblioteca Nacional de Antropología e Historia. La hacienda agrícola en México: guía de documentos localizados en la Biblioteca Nacional de Antropología e Historia. See item **93**.

1842 *Boletín del Archivo General del Estado de México.* No. 1, enero/abril 1979– . Toluca, México.

Beginning in 1979, Archives of the State of Mexico have published a trimester bulletin containing brief articles based on materials in collection, indexes, surveys, municipal archives, maps, and illustrations. Archive's holdings are primarily from 19th and 20th centuries. [EBC]

1843 Cabrera Ypiña, Octaviano and **Matilde Cabrera Ypiña.** San Francisco Javier de La Parada. San Luis Potosí, México: Editorial

Universitaria Potosina, 1978. 127 p.; 4 leaves of plates; ill.

Family and local history written in the old style by descendants of some of the actors. [EBC]

1844 La Clase obrera en la historia de México. v. 1–17. Coordinador, Pablo González Casanova. México: Siglo Veintiuno Editores: Instituto de Investigaciones Sociales de la UNAM, 1980/1981. 5 v.; bibl.; ill.

Study consisting of 17 vols. of which only five have been published and are annotated in this *HLAS*: v. 1 (item **1845**); v. 2 (item **2059**); v. 3 (item **2012**); v. 6 (item **2189**); v. 9 (item **2167**); v. 15 (item **2154**). [EBC]

1845 La Clase obrera en la historia de México. v. 1, De la colonia al imperio. Por Enrique Florescano *et al.* México: Siglo XXI Editores: Instituto de Investigaciones Sociales de la UNAM, 1980. 350 p.; bibl.; ill.; tables.

Series of interesting interpretive essays, produced by INAH, one of Mexico's research institutes. Summarizes and analyzes published sources of work in progress on theme of the role of labor systems in Mexico's economic development. Long article by Enrique Florescano summarizing information on labor systems from conquest of 1750, is followed by three articles on rural, mining and industrial workers. Last article contains materials on the 19th century. [EBC]

1846 Florescano, Enrique. El poder y la lucha por el poder en la historiografía mexicana (Nova Americana [Giulio Einaudi Editore, Torino, Italy] 3, 1980, p. 199–238)

Reviews historiography of Mexico since precolumbian times through end of 19th century, concluding that most works of history written during this period served to legitimate authority of ruling classes. The use of the past, in this struggle for power among different groups, has contributed to a classist, not a national, historical conscience. [AL]

Gómez-Jara, Francisco A. Bonapartismo y lucha compesina en la Costa Grande de Guerrero. See *HLAS 43:8093.*

Guía del Archivo Municipal de Cuauhtinchan, Puebla: años 1546–1900. See item **141.**

1847 Guías y Catálogos. Archivo General de la Nación. No. 1, 1977– . México.

Listed below are guides and catalogues, part of Archivo General de la Nación's continuing publication effort (for annotations of previous ramos, see *HLAS 42:1965*):

No. 28, *Ramo: Historia* (1981, 6 v., 726 p.): revised version of prior catalogue. Vols. 1/6 cover only 220 vols. out of total 591. Extensively described by Bolton, this ramo contains materials about borderlands, missions, censuses, correspondence, and wars of Independence. Largely material from latter part of 18th century. Catalogue still incomplete, lacks indexes.

No. 29, *Ramo: Correspondencia de Diversas Autoridades* (1978, 6 v., 1024 p.): guide to 70 vols. of correspondence between Viceroy of New Spain and governors and military authorities of Veracruz, Havana and Yucatán. Also includes materials on New Orleans, Florida, Campeche and Caribbean ports. Some correspondence deals with cities in interior New Spain. Vols. 63/70 cover period 1823–55 and include correspondence between Executive Power and Tribunal of Accounts and other ministries.

No. 30, *Catálogo del Ramo Bienes Nacionalizados* (1979, 36 p.): two manuscript vols. produced 1856–75 on procedures for nationalization of ecclesiastical properties. Includes materials on capellanías, cofradías and other obras pías. Much economic data.

No. 31, *Fondo Presidente Abelardo L. Rodríguez: Serie Conflictos Electorales* (1979, 2 v., 198 p., unpaged index): includes names' index. Largely materials from 1930s local elections.

No. 32, *Fondo Presidente Abelardo L. Rodríguez: Serie Conflictos Obreros y Huelgas* (1979, 1 v., 109 p.; 21 p., index): materials from 1932–34, arranged by locality, by union of organization, and by industry.

No. 33, *Fondo Presidente Abelardo L. Rodríguez: Serie Sindicatos* (1980, 173 p.; index): materials from 1933–34, organized by states and referring to specific unions at points of conflict (see *Guides* Nos. 39 and 50 for this *Fondo*).

No. 34, *Fondo Presidente Alvaro Obregón-Plutarco Elías Calles, 1920–1928: Catálogo de la Serie Armas* (1980, 1 v., 153 p., index): armed rebellions and various efforts to suppress them in correspondence of private secretaries of Northern Dynasty Presidents.

No. 35, *Ramo Pasaportes* (1980, 196 p. +30): a guide to first 23 volumes (from total 58) covering 1821–30. Includes documentary appendix. Consists of applications for Mexican visas requested 1821–30.

No. 36, *Archivo Genovevo de la O* (1980, 149 p.): beginning with activities of Zapatista army in western Morelos, this archive contains papers through 1958—14 boxes of materials about Revolutionary years, and 114 boxes of post-1920 sources.

No. 37, *Ramo Cárceles* (see *HLAS 42:1965*).

No. 38, *Archivo de Francisco Bulnes* (1979, 182 p., no index): 27 boxes of publications and other documents on Bulnes' ideas and career, organized thematically. Lacks personal correspondence.

No. 39, *Fondo Presidente Abelardo L. Rodríguez: Serie Atropellos de autoridades* (no date, 92 p. +16): of particular interest for sources of Lazaro Cárdenas' election.

No. 40, *Fondo Departamento del Trabajo, 1915–1917* (1979, 80 p. +xi +14, index): consists of Labor Department archive from date of independent organization. Information is arranged by states and volume includes detailed index.

No. 41, *Ramo Bulas y Santa Cruzada* (see *HLAS 42:1965*).

No. 42, *Ramo Inquisición* (for v. 1, see *HLAS 42:1965*; v. 2, 1980, 106 p.): vol. 2 of Inquisition guide includes vol. 76/90, and contains cases occurring between 1573–1646, as well as list of *familiares*.

No. 43, *Ramo de Congregaciones* (1980, 63 p.): record of early 17th-century congregation and grouping of Indian villages.

No. 44, *Códices Mexicanos de la Biblioteca Nacional de París* (1981, 132 p., index): annotated separately under editor's name, Joaquín Galarza, as it does not consist of AGN materials.

No. 45, *Archivo Alfredo Robles Domínguez* (2 v., 1981, 316 p., no index): 18 vols. of materials 1909–16, including Revolution and Federal District government.

No. 46, *Bienes de Comunidad* (see *HLAS 42:1965*).

No. 47, *Ramo del Real Junta* (1980, 153 p. + 4): information and inventories collected from time of Jesuits' expulsion, but including histories of early Jesuit establishments.

No. 48, *Archivo de Buscas* (v. 1, 1981, 240 p., index): catalogue of first 42 vols. of materials requested by municipalities and individuals in order to prove their titles, dates 1869–89. Index to places, but not to people.

No. 49, *Documentos sobre el Noroeste de México* (2 v., 1980, 703 p.): vols. are result of search in eight AGN *ramos* and in 2800 vols. for sources on history of Sonora, Sinaloa, and the Californias. One of more valuable tools produced in this series as it has three different indexes. Largely 18th-century materials.

No. 50, *Fondo Presidente Abelardo L. Rodríguez: Confederaciones, uniones y organizaciones* (1980, 199 p. +23): sources on trade unions, with good indexes.

No. 51, *Concursos de Calvo, Cotilla y Peñaloza* (1980, 67 p.): description of materials from three backrupcty cases; two from 17th century, one from 18th century. Information on prices, legal procedures and debt collection.

No. 52, *Directorio de Burócratas en la Ciudad de México: 1761–1832* (1980, 301 p., bibl.): alphabetical listing of officials. Annotated separately under compiler's name, Linda Arnold, as data is not from AGN.

No. 53, *Indice del Ramo Alcaldes Mayores* (7 v., 1980/1981, 827 p., indexes): 12 vols. of Viceregal orders to Alcaldes mayores, 1759–84. Treats of matters as different as sealed paper and secularization of parishes.

No. 54, *Ríos, Acequias, Mercados, Abastos y Panaderías* (1980, 102 p., indexes): guides to various small branches of AGN. *Ramo Ríos y Acequias* consists of five vols. including information on drainage, canals and potable water: Ramo Mercados (6 v.) largely deals with meat supply to cities in late 19th and early 20th centuries. *Ramo Abastos y Panaderías* has material on bakeries as well as on meat supply. While bulk of documentation on supplying food to urban areas is located in municipal archives, these AGN ramos supplement local data.

No. 55, *Ramo Escribanos* (24 v., 1980, 168 p., indexes): important source for study of bureaucracy and colonial political institutions, consists of 24 vols. collected from 1600–1841, deals with auctioning of office of escribano, permission to appoint others to serve, various aspects of licensing for lawyers, etc.

No. 56, *Ramo Correspondencia de Virreyes: Marqués de Croix* (1980/1981, 6 v., v. 1, 86 p.; v. 2, 108 p.; v. 3, 95 p.; v. 4, 142 p.; v. 5, 88 p.; v. 6, 326 p.): catalogue of copies of correspondence sent to Spain 1766–71. Based on v. 4 17 bis of this *ramo*. Researchers should note that only small selection of copies remain, and that AGI originals in Seville are much more extensive.

No. 57, *Ramo Obras Pías, Derechos Parroquiales, Cultos Religiosos e Iglesias* (1980, 41 p.): guide to three small *ramos* of the archives. Includes guide to six vols. of obras pías, which are copies of testaments establishing obras pías, two vols. of protests of villages against excessive parroquial charges, and two vols. on construction of particular church.

No. 58, *Ramo Oficio de Soria y Oficio de Hurtado* (1980, 84 folios, no index): largely 18th and 19th-century materials from offices of two official notaries. Total 15 vols. of miscellaneous materials, including information on mining, presidios, tax collections.

No. 59, *Ramo Templos y Conventos* (1980, 200 fol.): consists of 161 vols. or legajos, concerning economic aspects of religious organizations.

No. 60, *Ramo Aguardiente de Caña* (1981, 151 fol., index): 14 vols. of documents on illegal distilleries, and licenses to produce intoxicating beverages.

No. 61, *Guía Documental del Archivo Histórico de Hacienda* (1980, v. 1, *Documents*, 218 fol.; v. 2, 118 fol., index): consists of materials not included in 1940 publication. Subjects range from 17th-century Jesuit professions, *fianzas* for alcaldes mayores, ship movements and muleteers activities.

No. 62, *Guía del Archivo Histórico de la Compañía de Minas de Real del Monte y Pachuca* (1981, 173 fol.): is annotated separately under principal compiler's name, Eduardo Flores Clair *et al.*, as it is not part of AGN.

No. 63, *Lista de Fichas Hemerográficas* (1981, 150 fol.): lists Mexican periodicals and serial publications and date at which publication began. [EBC]

1848 Kessell, John L. Sources for the history of a New Mexico community: Abiquiú (UNM/NMHR, 54:4, Oct. 1979, p. 249–286)

In an imaginative literature search, author leads us from works of Hubert Howe Bancroft to computer generated data. In between, includes secondary sources, manuscript collections, both original and photocopied, analyzes materials and suggests topics still to be researched. [EBC]

1849 Leal, Juan Felipe and **Mario Huacuja Rountree.** San Antonio Xala: contrapunteo del funcionamiento económico de una hacienda pulquera en la segunda mitad del siglo XVIII y en el último tercio del siglo XIX (UNAM/RMCPS, 24:91, enero/marzo 1978, p. 59–119, map, plan, tables)

Excellent study of pulque hacienda northeast of Mexico City. Authors study production, labor and crop distribution in two different periods. Main thesis is that notwithstanding passage of time, hacienda operated as pre-capitalist enterprise. Based on archival sources, study offers a wealth of interesting information. [AL]

López Rosado, Diego G. Fuentes para el estudio de las clases sociales. See item **39.**

1850 Malo Camacho, Gustavo. Historia de las cárceles en México: etapa precolonial hasta el México moderno. México: Instituto Nacional de Ciencias Penales, 1979. 135 p. (Cuadernos del Instituto Nacional de Ciencias Penales; 5)

Based on statutes and secondary sources, this history of penal law notes that purposes of early prisons was to prevent flight of accused, and not to inflict punishment. Contains list of different colonial jails. Lacks analysis. [EBC]

Mirafuentes Galván, José Luis and **Arturo Soberón Mora.** Mapas y planos antiguos de Colima y del occidente de México, 1521–1904. See *HLAS 43:5530.*

Mounce, Virginia N. An archivists guide to the Catholic Church in Mexico. See item **155.**

1851 Navarrete, Nicolás P. Historia de la Provincia Agustiniana de San Nicolás de Tolentino de Michoacán. México: Editorial Porrúa, 1978. 2 v.; bibl. (Biblioteca Porrúa; 68–69)

Thorough survey of history of Augustinian Order in Mexico from foundation to 20th century. Based on contemporary printed sources and material from Order's own archives. Includes much information on lives and deeds of order's provincials and considerable number of its notable members. Information is compartmentalized and lacks integration but it should be useful for those interested in Augustinian Order. [AL]

Pasquel, Leonardo. Biografías de veracruzanos porteños. See item **159.**

1851a *Relaciones: Estudios de Historia y Sociedad.* El Colegio de Michoacán. Vol. 1, invierno 1980– . Michoacán, México.

Format of this new review consists of two major articles, publication of an annotated document, essays and notes and book reviews. Material covers both colonial and national periods. [EBC].

1852 Rosenbach Museum & Library. The Viceroyalty of New Spain and early independent Mexico: a guide to original manuscripts in the collections of the Rosenbach Museum & Library. Compiled by David M. Szewczyk. Edited by Catherine A. Barnes and David M. Szewczyk. Philadelphia: The Museum & Library, 1980. 139 p., a-j p. of plates; ill.

Valuable collection of manuscripts is abstracted and indexed. Historians can find material about social and political history, economic enterprise, Cortes family, the Church, women and ethnic groups, etc. [EBC]

1853 Semana de la Historia de Yucatán, *1st, Mérida, México, 1978.* Memorias de la primera Semana de la Historia de Yucatán, 25 de febrero de 1978–3 de marzo de 1978. Mérida, México: Ediciones de la Universidad de Yucatán, 1978. 2 v.; ill.; port.

Collection of 28 papers read in 1978 conference, covering history of Yucatan from 16th through 20th centuries. Topics range from encomienda and colonial market to Lebanese migration and labor unions. [AL]

1854 Tibón, Gutierre. Historia del nombre y de la fundación de México. Prólogo de Jacques Soustelle. 2. ed. México: Fondo de Cultura Económica, 1980. 883 p.; bibl.; ill.; index (Sección de obras de historia)

Multi-disciplinary work on origin and development of name México-Tenochtitlán utilizing archaeological, ethnographic, mythic, linguistic, etymological, and symbolic as well as historical sources. Exceptional amount of information about all aspects of toponomy of Mexico City. [EBC]

COLONIAL PERIOD: GENERAL

1855 Avonto, Luigi. Mercurino Arborio di Gattinara e l'America: documenti inediti per la storia delle Indie Nuove nell'Archivio del Gran Cancelliere di Carlo V. Vercelli, Italy: n.p., 1981, 203 p.

Nueva redacción del estudio presentado al Convegno di Studi Storici de 1980 y publicado en *Atti.* En apéndice publica tres importantes documentos del Archivo Gattinara, que ilustran los sucesos de México en 1523, 1525 y 1926. [L.G. Canedo]

1856 Chevalier, François. La formación de los latifundios en México: tierra y sociedad en los siglos XVI y XVII. Traducción de Antonio Alatorre. 2. ed., aumentada. México: Fondo de Cultura Económica, 1976. 510 p.; 32 p. of plates; bibl.; ill. (Sección de economía)

Second Spanish edition of classic history of haciendas in central and northern Mexico published in French in 1952. Spanish translation (1956) included additional bibliography. This 2d. edition includes new introduction noting few of more important works which appeared before 1974. Scholars are advised to use this edition rather than English translation. [EBC]

1858 Crovetto, Pier Luigi. Dispositivi e agenti di una aggressione combinata: conquistadores, storiografi, "missionari" in Nueva España (Nova Americana [Giulio Einaudi Editore, Torino, Italy] 3, 1980, p. 239–270)

Interpretive essay on meaning of conquest as evinced in its major historians. [AL]

1859 Florescano, Enrique. Las sequías en las economías preindustriales: el caso de Nueva España, 1521–1821 (*in* Análisis histórico de las sequías en México. Coordinated by Enrique Florescano. México: Comisión del Plan Nacional Hidráulico, Secretaría de Agricultura y Recursos Hidráulicos, 1980, p. 21–39, tables)

Synthesis of data on droughts in colonial Mexico. Analyzes extension, intensity and demographic consequences of droughts, explaining policies adopted to countereffect their consequences. Useful and informative. [AL]

1860 Ganster, Paul. La familia Gómez de Cervantes: linaje y sociedad en el

México colonial (CM/HM, 31:2, oct./dic. 1981, p. 197–232, tables)

Detailed study of leading colonial family from 16th through late 18th centuries. Underscores mechanisms used by family members to maintain their power and status, arguing that they were typical not only of colonial Mexico, but of all Spanish America. [AL]

1861 Garrido Aranda, Antonio. Moriscos e indios: precedentes hispánicos de la evangelización en México. México: Universidad Nacional Autónoma de México, 1980. 181 p.; bibl.; ill.; index (Serie antropológica / Instituto de Investigaciones Antropológicas; 32. Etnología)

Comparative study of methodology of conversion of moriscos in Granada and of Indians in New Spain. Timely and useful study puts evangelization task in broader political and religious context. [AL]

1862 Hassig, Ross. Conquest or commerce: the Caballo Ordinance of 1526 (UNM/NMHR, 55:4, Oct. 1980, p. 331–333)

Using 1526 legislation which required parity in ownership of mules and horses, author explains complicated steps necessary to produce mules needed for commerce. Interesting addenda to history of livestock raising in New Spain. [EBC]

1863 Ixtlilxóchitl, Fernando de Alva. Obras históricas: incluyen en texto completo de las llamadas *Relaciones e Historia de la Nación chichimeca* en una nueva versión establecida con el cotejo de los manuscritos más antiguos que se conocen. v. 2, Historia de la nación chichimeca. Estudio introductorio y un apéndice documental por Edmundo O'Gorman. 3. ed. México: Universidad Nacional Autónoma de México, Instituto de Investigaciones Históricas, 1975/1977. 2 v. (516, 539 p.); bibl.; index (Serie de historiadores y cronistas de Indias; 4)

New edition of this work. See *HLAS 40:1987.* [AL]

1864 Lavrin, Asunción and Edith Couturier. Las mujeres tienen la palabra: otras voces en la historia colonial de México (CM/HM, 31:2, oct./dic. 1981, p. 278–313)

Authors explore potential sources and themes in colonial women's history, using illustrative archival documentation. [AL]

1865 MacLachlan, Colin M. and Jaime E. Rodríguez. The forging of the cosmic race: a reinterpretation of colonial Mexico. Berkeley: University of California Press, 1980. 362 p.; 6 leaves of plates; bibl.; ill.; index.

Survey of Mexico's colonial history, including precolumbian civilizations. Extensive treatment of socioeconomic issues makes volume readable and informative. [AL]

1866 México, un pueblo en la historia. v. 1, México prehispánico por Enrique Nalda. México colonial por Enrique Semo. Las reformas borbónicas por Masae Sugawara. Enrique Semo, coordinador. Puebla: Universidad Autónoma de Puebla; México: Editorial Nueva Imagen, 1981. 265 p.; 48 p.; bibl.; graphs, ill.; maps; plates.

In vol. 1 of well-illustrated university text, three noted historians analyze Mexico's colonial history from Marxist viewpoint. Utilizes most recent research. [EBC]

1867 Motolinía, Toribio. Relación de los ritos antiguos, idolatrías y sacrificios de los indios de la Nueva España, y de la maravillosa conversión que Dios en ellos ha obrado: Manuscrito de la Ciudad de México. Introd., transcripción paleográfica y notas de colación con los manuscritos de la Biblioteca del Monasterio de San Lorenzo, El Real de El Escorial y de The Hispanic Society of América de la Ciudad de Nueva York por Javier O. Aragón. México: J. Cortina Portilla, 1979. 131 p.; 126 leaves of plates; ill.

Existing three versions of Motolinía's work are in : 1) Mexico City; 2) El Escorial's library; and 3) Hispanic Society of America, New York. Oldest one is in Mexico, followed by those in Spain and New York. Aragón has completed paleographic version of manuscript in Mexico City, collating it with other two for accuracy. This facsimile edition of original is carefully edited and commented, with modernized spelling and punctuation to facilitate reading and interpretation. Excellent paleographic work in deluxe edition. [AL]

1868 Navarro García, Luis. El Real Tribunal de Cuentas de México a principios del siglo XVIII (EEHA/AEA, 34, 1977, p. 517–535)

Institutional study of New Spain's Royal Accounting Office during Bourbon dynasty's early years. Surveys office's membership, activities, reforms of its government and modes of operation, and its relations with Viceroy. Useful, due to scarcity of publications on this governmental agency. [AL]

1869 Olaechea Labayen, Juan B. Promoción indígena en el siglo dieciocho mexicano (CSIC/RIS, 36:25, 2. época, enero/ marzo 1978, p. 52–89)

Deals with education of Indians in Central America and Mexico and efforts to establish one special school for them in Mexico. Started by Indian priest in 1754, project eventually took shape after Jesuits' expulsion made College of San Gregorio available as educational center for Indian boys. Informative and uncomplicated narrative. Makes no reference to female education. [AL]

1870 Poole, Stafford, C.M. Church law on the ordination of Indians and *castas* in New Spain (HAHR, 61:4, Nov. 1981, p. 637–560)

Carefully analyzes thorny issue of ordination to priesthood of Indians and *castas.* Establishes existence of two different policies: 1) royal, against ordination; and 2) papal, more flexible, allowing potential incorporation of Indians and others into Church ranks. Defines well theoretical bases of this policy issue. [AL]

1871 Reyes G., Cayetano. Expósitos e hidalgos, la polarización social de la Nueva España: *Los expósitos; Los hijodalgos* (MAGN/B, 5:2, abril/junio 1981, p. 3–43)

Correspondence from *Ramo de Tributos* dealing with orphans and exposed children reveals ways in which late 18th-century officials viewed them. Sheds light on issues of ethnicity, race, child-rearing and attitudes toward poor. Also includes proposed regulations for an orphanage. Second series of documents, from *Ramo de Bandos*, regularizes rights of noble title holders, and spells out military's special position. Includes illustrations and informative introduction. [EBC]

1872 Rheenen, Gerlof B. van. The term *casados* in 16th-century sources and the discussion around the historical demography of New Spain, Mexico (CEDLA/B, 30, junio 1981, p. 125–135, tables)

Tries to correct previous estimates of 16th century Mexico's indigenous population through linguistic clarification of term *casa-*

dos (married persons). Corrected estimate led author to conclude that extended family was indigenuous community's dominant living unit. [AL]

1873 Rodríguez García, Vicente. El Fiscal Posada: índice para una biografía (EEHA/AEA, 34, 1977, p. 187–210)

Biographical outline of hard-working career bureaucrat who served the Crown for over 40 years in various capacities in Spain, Guatemala, Lima and Mexico. Brief but useful. [AL]

1874 Rublúo Islas, Luis. La décima musa: historia de su fama; pt. 1, Presencia de Sor Juana en la época virreinal, 1695–1819 (Boletín del Archivo General del Estado de México [Toluca] 5, mayo/agosto 1980, p. 3–21, ill.)

Discusses degree of recognition accorded Sor Juana after her death as poet and writer both in Mexico and Europe. Uses commentaries and critical judgments issued by writers of period under survey. [AL]

1875 Schwaller, John Frederick. Tres familias mexicanas del siglo XVI (CM/HM, 31:2, oct./dic. 1981, p. 171–196, tables)

General survey of history, through first generations, of three leading 16th-century conquistador families of the vice royalty. Demonstrates that endogamous connections established shortly after conquest enhanced and preserved members' social and economic status. Based on archival sources. [AL]

1876 Swan, Susan L. Mexico in the Little Ice Age (JIH, 11:4, Spring 1981, p. 633–647, graphs)

Correlates weather patterns and agricultural production in late 18th-century New Spain (end of Little Ice Age in European climatology). Obtained data from Regla family papers and focuses on Molino de Flores hacienda. Interesting but tentative results indicate need to conduct more research on weather and agriculture. [AL]

1877 Tanck de Estrada, Dorothy. Tensión en la torre de marfil: la educación en la segunda mitad del siglo XVIII mexicano (*in* Ensayos sobre la historia de la educación en México. Coordinated by Josefina Vázquez. México: El Colegio de México, 1981, p. 23–113)

Broad survey of New Spain's educational centers and policies in 18th century's last three decades. Work covers broad range of issues (e.g., secularization of doctrines, of Jesuits' expulsion, *ayuntamiento*'s role as sponsor of public education, intellectual nationalism). Partial use of archives, but mostly based on printed sources. [AL]

1878 Theimer-Sachse, Ursula. Kenntnisse in Deutschland über Mexiko und seine indianischen Kulturen von der Eroberung bis zum Entstehen eines wissenschaftlichen Mexiko-Bildes im 19. Jahrhundert (EAZ, 20:2, 1979, p. 315–344, bibl.)

German artisans, merchants and missionaries in colonial Mexico failed to transmit information about precolumbian civilizations, but limited themselves to collecting artifacts. [EBC]

1879 Viqueira, Juan Pedro. El sentimiento de la muerte en el México ilustrado del siglo XVIII a través de dos textos de la época (CM/RE, 2:5, invierno 1981, p. 27–62)

Mentalité study of concept of death in 18th-century Mexico based on analysis of two texts, one satirical, one religious. Suggestive but limited in scope, study draws much from Philippe Ariès' work on death. [AL]

1880 Zambrano, Francisco. Diccionario bio-bibliográfico de la Compañía de Jesús en México. v. 15. México: Editorial Jus, 1977. 839 p.; indexes.

Part of monumental work on Mexican Jesuits, volume includes biographies of 18th-century individuals surnamed A through K. As in previous volumes, inclusion of documentation relevant to individuals in some biographies make this work more than mere catalogue of names. [AL]

CENTRAL AND SOUTH

1881 Alanis Boyso, Rodolfo. Fundación y establecimiento del Beaterío del Carmen en la ciudad de Toluca (Boletín del Archivo General del Estado de México [Toluca] 2, mayo/agosto 1979, p. 3–7, photos)

Provides brief, mostly descriptive account of involved process of founding a provincial retreat house for lay women based on archival sources. [AL]

1882 Archer, Christon I. The Army of New Spain and the wars of independence, 1790–1821 (HAHR, 61:4, Nov. 1981, p. 705–714)

Describes Spanish Army's general lack of striking capability in Mexico in 1810, and Gen. Calleja's efforts to reinvigorate this body through increased autonomy. However, growing disenchantment of Creole officers and lack of commitment to Spain helped to bring about the eventual collapse of Spanish political control. [AL]

1883 ———. The Royalist Army in New Spain: civil-military relationships, 1810–1821 (JLAS, 13:1, May 1981, p. 57–82)

Provides narrative of military operations summoned and political issues raised by 1810 popular insurrection. Author's thesis: Revolt gave army leadership, under civilian constitutional control until 1810, opportunity to make significantt gains at civil regime's. [AL]

1884 Barrett, Elinore M. Indian community hospitals in colonial Michoacan (*in* Historical geography of Latin America: papers in honor of Robert C. West. Editors for the volume, William V. Davidson and James J. Parsons. Baton Rouge: Louisiana State University, School of Geoscience, 1980, p. 83–96, bibl., maps, tables [Geoscience and man; 21])

Follows foundation and development of Indian hospitals in Michoacán from 16th through 18th century in three main archival sources. Economic organization of hospitals and parent institutions, confraternities, are especially highlighted in this informative study. [AL]

1885 ———. The King's copper mine: Inguarán in New Spain (AAFH/TAM, 38:1, July 1981, p. 1–29, map, tables)

Contribution to relatively unknown aspect of mining industry, article traces colonial history of Michoacán copper mine from encomienda, congregación, royal ownership, and to mine's 1787 sale to private entrepreneur. Based on extensive research in primary materials. [EBC]

1886 Basurto, J. Trinidad. El Arzobispado de México: jurisdicción relativa al Estado de México. Preparada por Mario Colín con adiciones y notas. México: Biblioteca Enciclopédica del Estado de México, 1977. 388 p.; ill. (Biblioteca enciclopédica del Estado de México; 60)

Originally published 1901, this edition contains only description of parishes of present state of Mexico (not whole archbishopric). To complement information, editor adds excerpts from description 1572 of Mexico by Fray Agustín de Vetancurt, J.A. Villaseñor y Sánchez, and other sources. Useful. [AL]

1887 Baudot, Georges. La population des villes du Mexique en 1595 selon une enquête de l'Inquisition (UTIEH/C, 37, 1981, p. 5–18)

Presents partial 1595 census of main cities of New Spain carried out by Inquisition which at time was interested in promoting royal appointment of "familials" or lay custodians to the Holy Office. Census did not include Indians and Baudot considers it of limited value in helping to establish reliable population figures. [AL]

1888 Behocaray Alberro, Solange. Inquisition et société: rivalités de pouvoirs à Tepeaca, 1656–1660 (AESC, 36:5, sept./oct. 1981, p. 758–784, table)

Using mid 17th-century inquisitorial record, author dissects colonial provincial society, revealing power struggles for political posts, personal, ethnic, and sexual antagonisms, and similar engaging details of daily colonial life. Demonstrates potential wealth of data for social history of inquisitorial records. [AL]

1889 Boyer, Richard. Absolutism versus corporatism in New Spain: the administration of the Marquis of Gelves, 1621–1624 (The International History Review [Vancouver, Canada] 4:4, Nov. 1982, p. 475–503)

Explains Gelves' character and that of his administration in terms of new austere values established by Philip IV and his Minister Olivares. Gelves clashed with corrupt and patronage-ridden local establishment in New Spain. Thesis is that local nexus fought central authority, and that Spain's success as colonial power was due to its ability to avoid confrontations with local establishments. [AL]

1890 ———. La ciudad de México en 1628: la visión de Juan Gómez de Trasmonte (CM/HM, 24:3, enero/marzo 1980, p. 447–471, bibl., map)

Scenic map of Mexico City drawn by architect Juan Gómez de Trasmonte is used as basis for furnishing information on author's career, city's physical setting and people in early 17th century. [AL]

1891 ———. Juan Vázquez: muleteer of seventeenth-century Mexico (AAFH/TAM, 37:4, April 1981, p. 421–443)

Popularly written account contains didactic information on life of a man accused of bigamy by Inquisition. Indicates wealth of material to be found in these investigations for biographies of lives of ordinary people. [EBC]

1892 Brading, David A. El clero mexicano y el movimiento insurgente de 1810 (CM/RE, 2:5, invierno 1981, p. 5–26)

Surveys Michoacán clergy's socioeconomic status in colonial period's last decades. Wide economic gap between upper and lower clergy, increasing secularizing and antagonistic royal policy toward Church, prepared lower clergy to accept idea of independence. [AL]

1893 Cárdenas, José Eduardo. Memoria a favor de la Provincia de Tabasco. México: Consejo Editorial del Gobierno del Estado de Tabasco, 1979. 90 p. (Serie Historia; 6)

Rarely read work by distinguished member of provincial clergy and Tabasco representative in Royal Cortes of 1811. Contains valuable information on socioeconomic conditions of one of New Spain's poorest and undeveloped areas, ca. 1811. Useful facsimile edition. [AL]

1894 Castorena, Guadalupe. Las sequías en el México antiguo (in Analísis histórico de las sequías en México. Coordinated by Enrique Florescano. México: Comisión del Plan Nacional Hidráulico, Secretaría de Agricultura y Recursos Hidráulicos, 1980, p. 15–21)

Survey of available data on precolumbian droughts in Central Valley and Maya area, and measures taken in both regions to prevent them and remedy their effects. [AL]

1895 Chance, John K. The ecology of race and class in late colonial Oaxaca (in Studies in Spanish American population history [see item 1792] p. 93–117, maps, table)

Study of residential distribution of several ethnic groups in Antequera City, Oaxaca, based on 1792 census data. Author found that there were no all-white areas and that all neighborhoods were racially mixed, inferring that by this period "there was no longer a viable system of racially defined estates in Antequera." Worthwhile application of quantitative methodology to social history. [AL]

1896 Chardon, Roland. The elusive Spanish league: a problem of measurement in sixteenth-century New Spain (HAHR, 60:2, May 1980, p. 294–302, map)

Identifies and differentiates between two different leagues used in colonial measurements: 1) statute and legal league used to measure land grants; and 2) common league used by travelers. Demonstrates modern equivalents of these measurements with reference to Yucatan. [EBC]

La Ciudad de México, 1520. See *HLAS 43:5508.*

1897 Clendinnen, Inga. Landscape and world view: the survival of Yucatec Maya culture under Spanish conquest (CSSH, 22:3, July 1980, p. 374–393)

Explains survival of Maya culture, despite many attempts to hispanize or mexicanize it in colonial and independence periods, as result of Maya perception of time, space and recurrence of historical events, convictions that deeply permeated their religious beliefs. Suggestive and sensitive work, combining ethnohistory and mentalité methodologies. [AL]

1898 ———. Reading the inquisitorial record in Yucatán: fact or fantasy? (AAFH/TAM, 38:3, Jan. 1982, p. 327–345)

Beautifully written study reconstructs and revised previous accounts of political context of events surrounding 1562 idolatry trials. Author analyzes evidence for persistence of human sacrifice after conquest and conversion, noting wealth of information and interpretation still to be gleaned from Inquisition records. [EBC]

1899 Documentos para la historia de Tabasco. Ser. 1, t. 1–2, Siglos XVI y XVII. Ser. 1, t. 3, Siglo XVIII. Ser. 1, t. 4, Siglo XIX. Ser. 2, t. 1, Siglos XVII y XVIII. Ser. 2, t. 2, Siglos XVIII y XIX. Ser 2, t. 4, Siglos XVIII y XIX. Recopilados y ordenados por Manuel González Calzada. México: Consejo Editorial del Gobierno del Estado de Tabasco, 1979/[1980]. 4 t. in 9 v. (Serie Historia; 1/2, 9, 11/15)

Documents on Tabasco's history

culled from several sections of National Archives. Topics comprise broad spectrum of social and institutional activities (e.g., municipalities, Indian labor, militia, encomiendas, etc.). Chronologically arranged without subject guide. [AL]

1900 *Estudios Históricos.* Revista trimestral. Centro de Estudios Históricos Fray Antonio Tello. No. 1, 3. época, marzo 1977– . Guadalajara, México.

First published 1943–46, this journal has been revived by its former editor, Luis Medina Ascencio, S.J. Another sign of current interest in local history. Journal will concentrate on Jalisco's history. So far it has published short articles, book reviews and documents from Jalisco's archives. [AL]

1901 Farriss, Nancy M. Propiedades territoriales en Yucatán en la época colonial: algunas observaciones acerca de la pobreza española y la autonomía indígena (CM/HM, 30:2, oct./dic. 1980, p. 153–209, tables)

Excellent article on indigenous confraternities of colonial Yucatán. Supplies information on development of cattle ranches as source of income and protection against famine. Argues that area's indigenous groups succeeded in maintaining their properties until late 18th century, when large number of properties were forcefully sold by Bishop Piña y Mazo. Based on archival sources. [AL]

1902 Foz y Foz, Pilar. La revolución pedagógica en Nueva España: 1754–1820. Madrid: Instituto Gonzalo Fernández de Oviedo, 1981. 2 v. (507, 271 p.); architectural plans, graphs, index; plates.

Exhaustive and definitive study of foundation of La Enseñanza Convents, of the Teaching Order of Mary in New Spain, relevant to social, women's and ecclesiastical history. In addition to order's institutional history, there is much information on founder, María Ignacia Azlor y Echeverz, and her family, Counts of San Miguel de Aguayo. Vol. 2 is extensive documentary appendix with large number of previously unpublished sources. [AL]

1903 Garner, Richard L. Silver production and entrepreneurial structure in 18th-century Mexico (JGSWGL, 17, 1980, p. 157–185, tables)

Considers capital formation, technology, government policy and individual miners' work in order to explain two 18th-century booms in Zacatecas mines. Concludes that entrepreneurial skill was essential element in increased silver production in both Guanajuato and Zacatecas. [EBC]

1904 Gonzalbo Aizpuru, Pilar. La Casa de Niños Expósitos de la ciudad de México: una fundación del siglo XVIII (CM/HM, 31:3, enero/marzo 1982, p. 409–430)

Discusses idea behind establishment of foundling home, reception of children, their education and treatment, and institution's patrons and administration. Useful information culled from archival sources. [AL]

1905 Greenow, Linda L. Marriage patterns and regional interaction in late colonial Nueva Galicia (in Studies in Spanish American population history [see item **1792**] p. 119–147, maps, tables [Dellplain Latin American Studies; no. 8])

Study of inter-marriage and inter-parish marriages in selected parishes of New Galicia, including peripheral as well as central locations, but excluding Guadalajara City itself. Although general patterns are difficult to establish, results point to greater ratio of endogamy among Indian and Spanish populations than among mixed ones, but a certain tendency to a greater degree of exogamy than assumed. [AL]

1906 Hamill, Hugh M., Jr. Royalist propaganda and *La Porción Humilde del Pueblo* during Mexican independence (AAFH/TAM, 36:4, April 1980, p. 423–444)

Discusses variety of royalist pamphlets written for consumption of Mexican lower classes, 1810–11, as part of psychological warfare against Hidalgo revolt. [AL]

1907 Hamnett, Brian R. The economic and social dimension of the revolution of independence in Mexico: 1800–1824 (IAA, 6:1, 1980, p. 1–27, tables)

Author argues for regional study of social and economic origins of Mexican independence movement. Distinct economic conditions produced different political reactions, as illustrated by Bajío and central valleys areas. Advances theory that lower class unrest could not have led to revolution prior to 1810 and that Creole bourgeoisie changed movement's political character. Useful synthesis of data, although paper's two sections do not correlate as closely as they should. [AL]

Horstman, Connie and **Donald V. Kurtz.** Compadrazgo and adaptation in sixteenth-century central Mexico. See *HLAS 43:877.*

1908 Izard, Miguel. Metropolitanos, criollos y reformistas: la Nueva España de Revillagigedo, 1789–1794 (UB/BA, 22:30, 1980, p. 181–222, map, tables)

Work focuses on administration of second Court of Revillagigedo (1789–94).

After considering expansion of manufacturing and trade, and beneficiaries of wealth generated during this period, author switches to paper's main thrust: analysis of Spanish policies on political issues, and ideological effects of French Revolution on these policies. Claims that transformation of enlightened reformers into conservatives—caused by fear of revolution within the viceroyalty—had deep implications as preface for independence. Interesting thesis. [AL]

1909 Kicza, John E. La mujer y la vida comercial en la ciudad de México a finales de la colonia (Revista de Ciencias Sociales y Humanidades [Universidad Autónoma Metropolitana, Azcapotzalco] 2:4, sept./dic. 1981, p. 39–59, ill.)

Informative description of many commercial activities in which women of all social classes and ethnic groups were involved during 1785–1820. Based on notarial records and other archival sources. [AL]

1910 ———. The pulque trade of late colonial Mexico City (AAFH/TAM, 37:2, Oct. 1980, p. 193–221, tables)

Based on a 1784 royal report supplemented by extensive research in Mexico City notarial archives, this lucid account of pulque trade describes methods of distribution from hacienda to retail outlets. Kicza identifies ways in which nobility cornered both production and sales for this beverage. [EBC]

1910a Konrad, Herman. A Jesuit hacienda in colonial Mexico: Santa Lucía, 1567–1767. Stanford, Calif.: Stanford University Press, 1980. 455 p.: bibl.; ill.; index; maps; tables.

A seminal contribution to colonial Mexican hacienda studies, this history and analysis of the functioning of a complex of haciendas, which extended north from Mexico City to the Zacatecas region, explores a variety of issues related to the agrarian system. Questions of profitability of haciendas in general, and Jesuit enterprises in particular are examined with an abundance of data, ably drawn from many sources. The skills of the anthropologist as well as those of the historian inform this study. Of great value are his treatment of questions on hacienda administration, hacienda life and an imaginative chapter on slavery. With this book, Mexican hacienda studies have reached a new level of maturity. Available archival wealth, in the hands of a virtuoso craftsman, can describe and explain changes in colonial society at all levels. [EBC]

1911 Lavrin, Asunción. La Congregación de San Pedro: una cofradía urbana del México colonial, 1640–1730 (CM/HM, 29:4, abril/junio 1980, p. 562–601, bibl., chart)

Part of author's continuing investigation of cofradías, this study of one founded 1577 for clerics, includes materials on membership (included wealthy men and women as well as priests), investments and philanthropic activities. This cofradía founded and supported hospital for clergy as one of its chief missions. Cofradía activities touched number of aspects of colonial social life, and this essay demonstrates variety of information which can be gleaned from official archives. [EBC]

1912 Lemoine Villicaña, Ernesto. Morelos y la revolución de 1810. Morelia: Gobierno del Estado de Michoacán, 1979. 458 p.; bibl.; ill.

Chatty life-and-times hero-worshipping biography of Morelos attempts to resolve number of disputed aspects of his life, but fails to deal adequately with political motivations and ideas. [EBC]

1913 Lewis, James A. The royal gunpowder monopoly in New Spain: 1766–1783; a case study of management, technology, and reform under Charles III (IAA, 6:4, neue Folge, 1980, p. 355–372, table)

Using royal monopoly on gunpowder, author illustrates problems encountered by Bourbon administrative and economic reforms. [AL]

1914 Licate, Jack A. Creation of a Mexican landscape: territorial organization and settlement in the eastern Puebla basin, 1520–1605. Chicago: University of Chicago, Dept. of Geography, 1981. 143 p.; bibl.; maps (Research paper / The University of Chicago, Department of Geography; no. 201)

Geographer's view of historical sources for villages in Tecamachalco-Quecholac area, east of Tepeaca. Deals with linguistic, territorial, architectural continuities and changes. Largely based on published primary sources and secondary materials, but author surveyed local and national archives. [EBC]

1915 Malvido, Elsa. El abandono de los hijos: una forma de control del tamaño de la familia y del trabajo indígena; Tula, 1683–1830 (CM/HM, 34:4, abril/junio 1980, p. 521–561)

Indicates ways in which computer generated data can inform us about familiar reactions to economic crisis and differing reactions of urban and rural families to social mores. Imaginative use of parish registers' information on *padrinos* reveals that wealthier families adopted abandoned children for domestic service and estancia and obraje labor. [EBC]

1916 Martin, Cheryl E. Crucible of Zapatismo: hacienda hospital in the seventeenth century (AAFH/TAM, 38:2, July 1981, p. 31–44)

Detailed study of administration of rural estates of Order of Saint Hipólito in 17th-century central New Spain. Order's severe economic problems and poor administration of its properties belie stereotype of wealthy ecclesiastical rural landlords. Based on solid archival data. [AL]

1917 Méndez Martínez, Enrique. Indice de documentos relativos a los pueblos del Estado de Puebla: ramo tierras del Archivo General de la Nación. México: SEP, Instituto Nacional de Antropología e Historia, 1979. 150 p.; index (Colección científica; 70. Fuentes [Etnohistoria])

Archival listings taken from *Ramos de Tierras*, National Archives, with limited subject index, but complete list of each village in Puebla. [AL]

1918 Menes Llaguno, Juan Manuel. Fuentes para la historia de la tenencia de la tierra en el Estado de Hidalgo: indice de documentos del ramo de tierras del A.G.N. Pachuca: Centro Hidalguense de Investigaciones Históricas, 1976. 242 p.; 1 leaf of plates; indexes; map (Colección Ortega-Falkowaska; no. 1)

Index to law suits in *Ramos de Tierras* dealing with Hidalgo state. Organized by place, with dates and names of principal litigants. Index includes only place names. [EBC]

1919 Moreno García, Heriberto. Zamora en 1789 (CM/RE, 1:1, invierno 1980, p. 91–127)

Reprint of description of Zamora ordered shortly after 1789 adoption of system of *intendencia* in New Spain. Originally, this document was printed in *Boletín del Archivo General de la Nación* (1944) Useful. [AL]

1920 Morin, Claude. Michoacán en la Nueva España del siglo XVIII: crecimiento y desigualdad en una economía colonial. México: Fondo de Cultura Económica, 1979. 328 p.; bibl.; graphs; maps; tables (Colección Tierra firme)

Significant contribution of *Annales* School to Mexican economic and social history, this study of 18th-century in Bishopric of Michoacán is based on research in local, state, national and Spanish archives and libraries. Author subjects tithe records to accuracy tests and compares them to other price series, analyzes merchants inventories and varous types of hacienda documents, and compares figures for metal exports in order to analyze structural problems generated by growing economy based on silver exports. Also examines population figures using censuses, and compares them with various kinds of parrochial records. A model regional economic study. [EBC]

1921 Muñoz, Diego. Descripción de la Provincia de San Pedro y San Pablo de Michoacán cuando formaba una con Xalisco. Escrita por Fray Diego Muñoz, años de 1585. Guadalajara: Instituto Jalisciense de Antropología e Historia, 1965. 135 p. (Serie de historia / Instituto Jalisciense de Antropología e Historia; 8)

Reissue of long out of print 16th-century description of Franciscan province of Santiago, which covered New Galicia (Jalisco). Contains information on indigenous groups and order's most notable members. Documentary appendix includes description of New Galicia and several letters. [AL]

1922 Parker, Angelika Ertinger. San Mateo Huiscolotepec a Piedras Negras: historia de una hacienda tlaxcalteca 1580–1979. Traducido del inglés por Mario G. Menocal. México: Costa Amic Editores, 1979. 163 p.; ill.

Demonstrates importance of strategic location of this hacienda along principal Mexico City-Veracruz route. In 18th century, Bethlemite Order operated a posada on hacienda which produced profit; from latter part of 19th century until present, its production of bulls sustained and preserved the hacienda. Based on AGN *Tierras* materials and limited 19th-century materials private archive. [EBC]

1923 Peña, Francisco. Estudio histórico sobre San Luis Potosí. Introd., transcripción, notas e índice de Rafael Montejano y Aguiñaga. San Luis Potosí: Academia de Historia Potosina, 1979. 299 p.; 25 leaves of plates (1 fold.); bibl.; ill.; index (Biblioteca de historia potosina: Serie Estudios; 17)

New edition of classic 1894 chronicle of San Luis Potosí with extensive explanatory notes and illustrations. [EBC]

1924 Pohl, Hans; Jutta Haenisch; and Wolfgang Loske. Aspectos sociales del desarrollo de los obrajes textiles en Puebla colonial (FAIC/CPPT, 15, 1978, p. 41–45

Brief survey of social composition and working conditions of obraje labor. [AL]

1925 Poole, Stafford C.M. Institutionalized corruption in the letrado bureaucracy: the case of Pedro Farfán, 1568–1588 (AAFH/TAM, 38–2, Oct. 1981, p. 149–172)

Follows career of Oidor in Audiencia of Mexico, as illustrative case of government corruption, which Crown could not control. Well researched and argued work. [AL]

1926 Robinson, David J. and Carolyn G. McGovern. La migración regional yucateca en la época colonial: el caso de San Francisco de Umán (CM/HM, 30:1, julio/ sept. 1980, p. 99–125, bibl., maps, tables)

Study of demographic trends and population mobility in Yucatan, based on records of ecclesiastical jurisdiction of Uman, southwest of Mérida. Authors indicate high degree of internal regional migration among indigenous groups and suggest that notion of closed and narrowly-bounded communities is not applicable to this area. Good research. [AL]

1927 Romero, María de los Angeles. Los intereses españoles en la Mixteca: siglo XVII (CM/HM, 29–2, oct./dic. 1979, p. 241–251)

Using local archives of Teposcopula,

author describes growth of cattle industry and trading activities of Mixteca's hispanic community. [AL]

1928 Romero L., María Eugenia. Funcionamiento interno de la hacienda San José Acolman y Anexas, Estado de México: fines del siglo XVIII principios del siglo XIX (*in* Encuentro de Historiadores Latinoamericanos y del Caribe, 2d, Caracas, 1977. Los estudios históricos en América Latina: ponencias, acuerdos y resoluciones: Caracas, 20–26 de marzo de 1977. Caracas: Universidad Central de Venezuela, Facultad de Humanidades y Educación, Escuela de Historia, 1979, v. 1, t. 2, p. 602–610)

Brief analysis of production and labor structure of this hacienda. Samples years 1733–1849. Skimpy on data, author concentrates on defining general characteristics of hacienda structure. Lacks conclusions. [AL]

1929 Romero Quiroz, Javier. La tierra del maíz, Nepintahihui. Metepec, México: Comisión Coordinadora para el Desarrollo Agrícola y Ganadero del Estado de México, 1979. 2 v.; bibl.; ill. (Colección Historia)

Consists largely of documents related to Toluca area haciendas, with stress on Cortes family properties. Includes useful maps, lists of all haciendas and owners, and handsome photographs. Lacks in-depth study of land ownership or hacienda administration. [AL]

1930 Ruz, Mario Humberto. El añil en el Yucatán del siglo XVI (CEM/ECM, 12, 1979, p. 111–156)

Study of development of indigo production in Yucatán since mid-sixteenth century through early decades of 17th. Furnished data on other dyeing products. Based on archival and printed sources, includes information on indigenous labor used in the industry. [AL]

1931 Ruz Menéndez, Rodolfo. Los yaquis en las haciendas henequeneras de Yucatán (UY/R, 22:127, enero/feb. 1980, p. 58–72, bibl.)

Presents several new documents such as labor contracts and newspaper articles dealing with Yaquis in Yucatán. Suggests that John Kenneth Turner might have exaggerated abuse of laboring Indians, but does not deny system's basic injustice thus imparting slightly ambivalent tone to article. [AL]

1932 Sarabia Viejo, María Justina. El estanco de la sal en Yucatán: 1591–1610 (EEHA/AEA, 35, 1979, [i.e. 1981], p. 379–405, maps, tables)

Thorough study of royal monopoly on salt production in Yucatán. Includes data on labor, technology or production, administration, sales, etc., during 20 years that monopoly was enforced. [AL]

1933 Scardaville, Michael C. Alcohol abuse and tavern reform in late colonial Mexico City (HAHR, 60:4, Nov. 1980, p. 643–671)

Contribution to unknown aspect of Bourbon reforms, study analyzes efforts of authorities to stem epidemic dimension of alcoholism by limiting the number of taverns, enlarging police force and other ameliorative measures. [EBC]

1934 Schwaller, John Frederick. The Cathedral Chapter of Mexico in the sixteenth century (HAHR, 61:4, Nov. 1981, p. 651–674)

Careful explanation of internal organization and social composition of Cathedral Chapter of Mexico City, and political meaning of confrontation with Archbishop. Traces institutional changes within Cabildo throughout century, and argues that internal tensions and squabbles served to define members' power and prestige. Well researched and convincing work. [AL]

1935 Super, John C. Pan, alimentación y política en Querétaro en la última década del siglo XVIII (CM/HM, 30:2, oct./dic. 1980, p. 247–271)

Study of role of bread as food and as marketable product in urban areas of late colonial Mexico, with specific focus on Querétaro. Explores several issues in bread's production and consumption. Part of author's broader concern with history of nutrition in Mexico and Spanish America. [AL]

1936 Torre Villar, Ernesto de la. La política americanista de Fray Servando y de Tadeo Ortiz (UNL/H, 20, 1979, p. 317–337)

Comparative study of major political and economic ideas of two gifted Mexican patriots. Biographical profile of relatively unknown Tadeo Ortiz, who is treated in greater depth than Mier, is very useful. [AL]

1937 Trabulse, Elías. Aspectos de la tecnología minera en Nueva España a finales del siglo XVIII (CM/HM, 30:3, enero/marzo 1981, p. 311–357, ill., tables)

Study of attempts to reform silver refinement technique in late colonial Mexico. Describes mostly suggestions of José Gil Barragán and reasons why industry failed to adopt any innovations. [AL]

1938 Trautmann, Wolfgang. El cambio económico y social de los pueblos de Tlaxcala en la época colonial (FAIC/CPPT, 15, 1978, p. 93–97)

Report of result of one of several ongoing studies of Tlaxcala by German scholars. Stresses changes in rural landownership patterns and role played in process by several factors: interplay in Indian upper-class and Hispanic settlers; mestizaje; and lack of enforcement of legislation protecting Indian lands. Also dwells on demographic changes experienced in area throughout colonial period. Brief but useful report based on serious archival research. [AL]

1939 ———. Ergebnisse der wüstungsforschung in Tlaxcala (Mexiko) (UBGI/E, 28:2, 1974, p. 115–124, bibl., maps, plates, tables)

History of Tlaxcalan settlements from time of conquest to present, based on place names, documents and archaeology concludes there are 40 percent fewer settlements now than in late 16th century. Confirms previous hypothesis that bulk of towns and villages disappeared between latter half of 16th century and first quarter of 17th. [EBC]

1940 ———. Examen del proceso de despoblamiento en Tlaxcala durante la época colonial (FAIC/CPPT, 7, 1983, p. 101–103)

Report on larger research project. Using tribute lists, parochial records and notarial deeds, author studies process of depopulation. Between 1557–1623 nearly 70 percent of Tlaxcalan indigenous towns disappeared, mostly due to disease and congregation policies. Hacienda expansion, cattle raising and lack of water sources, are other factors contributing to depopulation throughout the colonial period. Useful abstract, keeps reader informed of larger project. [AL]

1941 Van Young, Eric. Hacienda and market in eighteenth-century Mexico: the rural economy of the Guadalajara region, 1675–1820. Berkeley: University of California Press, 1981. 1 v.; bibl.; index.

Profiting from abundant and well-ordered archival resources of Guadalajara, book analyzes regional transformation from economy based on livestock and commerce to intensively exploited agricultural area with rapid growing population. Utilizing data on markets, production, family history, labor and legal conflicts, author contributes to growing body of material on debt peonage, Indian villages, hacienda ownership, credit and modernization. [EBC]

1942 Vázquez, Josefina Z. El pensamiento renacentista español y los orígenes de la educación novohispana (in Ensayos sobre historia de la educación en México. México: El Colegio de México, 1981, p. 3–22)

Survey of main educational ideas prevailing in Spain at time of conquest and how they influenced development of educational policies for Indians of New Spain. [AL]

1943 Wasserstrom, Robert. Ethnic violence and indigenous protest: the Tzeltal (Maya) Rebellion of 1712 (JLAS, 12:1, May 1980, p. 1–19)

Author's thesis is that 1712 rebellion was due to continuous exploitation of indigenous groups by civil and ecclesiastical authorities. In this class struggle, Mayas rejected acculturation and rebelled to maintain their own culture and ethnicity. [AL]

1944 Zambardino, Rudolph A. Mexico's population in the sixteenth century: demographic anomaly or mathematical illusion? (JIH, 11:1, Summer 1980, p. 1–27)

Subjects Borah and Cook's precolumbian population estimates to further analysis and concludes that part of their methodology is unreliable, casting serious doubts on their 25 million inhabitants estimate. After re-evaluation of data, author concludes that five–10 million inhabitants is better estimate. [AL]

NORTH AND BORDERLANDS

1945 Alessio Robles, Vito. Francisco de Urdiñola y el norte de la Nueva España. 2. ed. México: Editorial Porrúa, 1981. 333 p.; 8 leaves of plates (3 folded); bibl.; ill. (some col.); index (Biblioteca Porrúa; 76)

Reprint of 1931 biography. [EBC]

1946 Aragón, Janie T. Santa Fe de Nuevo México (PCCLAS/P, 7, 1980/1981, p. 29–36)

Brief review of Santa Fe's social characteristics based on random mining of microfilmed censuses. [EBC]

1947 Bargatzky, Thomas. Aspects of aboriginal trade and communication between northeast Mexico and southwest Texas in the 16th century (AI/A, 75:3/4, 1980, p. 447–464, bibl., ill., map)

Reviews and analyzes 16th-century accounts of Cabeza de Vaca and Oviedo for evidence of precolumbian trade routes and culture traits in Texas borderlands. Utilized variety of secondary sources and compares different editions and translations. Model example of textual analysis combined with evidence of material culture and trade patterns. [EBC]

1948 Cabrera Ypiña, Octaviano. El cerro de San Pedro (UNL/H, 20, 1979, p. 339–355)

Brief history of mines which formed basis for foundation and development of San Luis Potosí. Also includes transcription of documents containing testimonies of mines' discovery (1594–96). [AL]

1949 Cavazos Garza, Israel. Controversias sobre jurisdicción espiritual entre Saltillo y Monterrey, 1580–1652 (Revista Coahuilense de Historia [Colegio Coahuilense de Investigaciones Históricas, Saltillo, México] 4, nov./dic. 1978, p. 5–21)

Interesting biographical data, based on primary sources dealing with friars and priests serving in two northern jurisdictions. Details ecclesiastical as well as personal conflicts. Based on Nuevo León archival materials. [EBC]

1950 ———. La Misión de San Pablo de los Labradores, hoy Ciudad de Galeana, Nuevo León (UNL/H, 20, 1979, p. 303–316)

Using Monterrey's Municipal Archives and Galeana's parochial archive, author describes foundation of this Indian town (1678), adjudication of land and establishment of its church. [AL]

1951 Diario del Padre Fray José Gaspar de Solís en su visita a los misiones de Texas, 1768. Edited by Rafael Cervantes. Guadalajara: Editorial Font, 1981. 90 p. (Documentación histórica mexicana; 7)

El *Diario* es un testimonio muy valioso sobre los indios de Texas y el estado de las misiones que los franciscanos mantenían

entre ellos. El texto ha sido muy bien editado, quien lo anotó copiosamente por el Padre Cervantes, de quien es también la erudita introducción (p. 7–34). [L.G. Canedo]

1952 Documentary sources for the wreck of the New Spain fleet of 1554. Prepared by David McDonald, translator and J. Barto Arnold, III. Austin: Texas Antiquities Committee, 1979. 330 p.; bibl.; ill. (Publication—Texas Antiquities Committee; no. 8)

Documents contain surprising amount of interesting information on navigation, commerce, politics, material culture and biography. Indicates important material which can be found in ship registers. [EBC]

Gerhard, Peter. The north frontier of New Spain. See item **138.**

1953 Gómez Canedo, Lino. El reformismo misional en Nuevo México, 1760–1768: ilusiones secularizadoras del Obispo Tamatón. Guadalajara: Universidad Autónoma, Dirección de Bibliotecas, 1981. 60 p.

Nuevos documentos sobre el intento de secularización de las misiones de Santa Fe, Albuquerque, Santa Cruz de la Cañada y El Paso: entre ellos el paracer del Comisario General Franciscano (México, 3 oct. 1766). En la introducción explica el problema de las relaciones entre los cleros regular y secular respecto a la evangelización de América. [L.G. Canedo]

1954 Griffen, William B. Indian assimilation in the Franciscan area of Nueva Vizcaya. Tuscon: University of Arizona Press, 1979. 122 p.; bibl.; ill. (Anthropological papers of the University of Arizona; no. 33)

Study of complex ethnography of New Vizcayan region. Compendium of enormous amount of information based on extensive use of many local and national archival materials. Lacks interpretation. [EBC]

1955 Hanna, Warren Leonard. Lost Harbor: the controversy over Drake's California anchorage. Berkeley: University of California Press, 1979. 459 p.; bibl.; ill.; index.

Further data on history of California's discovery. [EBC]

1956 Hu-DeHart, Evelyn. Missionaries, miners, and Indians: Spanish contact with the Yaqui nation of Northwestern New Spain, 1533–1820. Tucson: University of Arizona Press, 1981. 152 p.; bibl.; ill.; index; maps.

Clearly written and thorough explanation for Yaquis' survival. Combining work in mines with permanent residence in villages and missions and independent policy toward Jesuits, enabled Yaquis to satisfy both needs of settlers and to assure their own survival. [EBC]

1957 Iborra, Vicente Ribes. Texas en las postrimerías del tiempo hispánico, 1800–1820 (IGFO/RI, 38 : 151/152, enero/junio 1978, p. 12–199)

Describes activities of US nationals Philip Nolan, Aaron Burr, and James Long in Texas in first decades of 19th century, as reflected in words and policies of Spanish officials. Concludes that both US incursions into Texas and its eventual fate as North American territory, originated in years before Mexican independence. [EBC]

1958 Jones, Oakah L. Spanish settlers of the northern borderlands: origins and occupations (PCCLAS/P, 7, 1980/1981, p. 11–28)

Emphasizing importance of *pueblo* (as opposed to the mission and presidio) in the settlement of northern borderlands, provides information on aspects of settlement and population of region's towns. For more thorough review of population figures, see *HLAS 36:1972* and *HLAS 42:2160*. [EBC]

1959 Kessell, John L. Kiva, cross, and Crown: the Pecos Indians and New Mexico, 1540–1840. Washington: National Park Service, U.S. Dept. of the Interior, 1979. 587 p.; bibl.; ill.; index.

Abundantly illustrated and popularly written, but thoroughly researched account of Pecos area. Containing long quotes from original sources, this study of frontier community between plains and mountains is essentially a narrative one. Includes much detail on Franciscans and valuable information on architecture and its anecdote. [EBC]

1960 ———. The missions of New Mexico since 1776. Aubuquerque: Published for the Cultural Properties Review Committee by University of New Mexico Press, 1980. 276 p.; 6 leaves of plates; bibl.; ill.; index.

Review of history of New Mexico's missions from foundation to present. Particularly valuable are abundant 19th-century doc-

umentation and complete bibliography of sources. [EBC]

1961 Kinnaird, Lawrence and **Lucia Kinnaird.** Nogales: strategic post on the Spanish frontier (MHS/J, 42 : 1, Feb. 1980, p. 1–16)

Description of origins of Fort Nogales, later city of Vicksburg, in 1790s. Viewed by Spain as key to control of Mississippi, article examines activities of Indians, Spaniards, French and North Americans in this crucial period when boundaries and settlements were still fluid. [EBC]

1962 León-Portilla, Miguel. Baja California: algunas perspectivas en términos de historia universal (Meyibó [UNAM, México] 1 : 2, sept. 1979, p. 7–19)

Inquiry into meaning of Baja California's history from prehistoric times to present. [AL]

1963 Navarro García, Luis. La conquista de Nuevo México. Madrid: Ediciones de Cultura Hispánica del Centro Iberoamericano de Cooperación, 1978. 125 p.

Popular written account, based on author's extensive knowledge of borderlands. Emphasizes conquest's adventurous aspects. [EBC]

1964 Nentvig, Juan. El rudo ensayo: descripción geográfica, natural y curiosa de la Provincia de Sonora, 1764. Introd., apéndice, notas e índice por Margarita Nolasco Armas, Teresa Martínez Peñaloza y América Flores. México: SEP, INAH, 1977. 202 p.; 2 fold. leaves of plates; bibl.; ill. (Colección científica—Instituto Nacional de Antropología e Historia; 58: Etnología)

Sixth publication of valuable description of Sonora and Arizona includes maps, critical indexes and annotations. Account contains botanical, historical, ethnographical, geographical materials. [EBC]

1965 Piñera Ramírez, David. Inicios de la colonización civil en Baja California (Meyibó [UNAM, México] 1 : 2, sept. 1979, p. 47–56, tables)

Traces process of village and town formation during and after Gálvez's Visita. Describes social background of first land-grant recipients and ties between mission and pueblo. [EBC]

1966 Porras Muñoz, Guillermo. La frontera con los indios en Nueva Vizcaya en el siglo XVII. México: Fomento Cultural Banamex, 1980. 457 p.; bibl.; map.

Major work on 16th and 17th-century history of greater Chihuahua region, filled with military and political details. Traces relations between Spaniard and Indian, estimating political and economic costs of conquest and colonization. Based on both Spanish and Mexican archives, includes extensive quotes from contemporary documents. [EBC]

1967 La Provincia de Coahuila o Nueva Extremadura. Informe del Gobernador Don Antonio Cordero y Bustamante, 1804. Edited by Israel Cavazos Garza. Monterrey: Universidad Autónoma de Nuevo León, 1980. 11 p. (Actas; 14)

Relaciones editadas según manuscritos del Archivo Municipal de Monterrey (vol. 84) y del British Museum (Add. 17,557). [L.G. Canedo]

1968 Robinson, David J. Population patterns in a northern Mexican mining region: Parral in the late eighteenth century (*in* Historical geography of Latin America: papers in honor of Robert C. West. Editors for the volume, William V. Davidson and James J. Parsons. Baton Rouge: Louisiana State University, School of Geoscience, 1980, p. 83–96, bibl., graphs, maps, tables [Geoscience and man; 2])

Demographic history of Parral (1760–1805) provides data on ethnic groups, household and family structure, marriage patterns and general trends of population decline and growth. Author indicates high degree of social openness in this area. Excellent, well-grounded study. [AL]

1969 Robinson, Willard B. Colonial ranch architecture in the Spanish-Mexican tradition (TSHA/SHQ, 83:2, Oct. 1979, p. 123–150, map, plates)

Well illustrated description of rural architecture along Río Grande. Author used on-site surveys and interviews to reconstruct construction techniques and style of first *jacales*, which were wattle and daub huts. Buildings constructed for owners, studied at greater length, followed Andalusian methods and outlines, utilizing large stone blocks and building high ceilings and flat roofs. Interesting study of interaction of architecture, local needs and imported traditions. [EBC]

1970 Ruiz, Antonio. Relación de Antonio Ruiz: la conquista en el Noroeste. Introducción y notas por Antonio Nakayama. México: Instituto Nacional de Antropología e Historia, SEP, Centro Regional del Noroeste, 1974. 85 p.; bibl.; ill.; maps; plates (Colección Científica, historia regional; 18)

Annotated edition of late 16th-century account of conquest and early settlement of Sinaloa. Transcription of AGN manuscript provided unique viewpoint of frontier soldier, many years earlier than most of our eyewitness sources. [EBC]

1971 Sánchez García, José Hermenegildo. Crónica del Nuevo Santander. Prólogo de Candelario Reyes Flores. Ciudad Victoria, Tamaulipas: Universidad Autónoma de Tamaulipas, Instituto de Investigaciones Históricas, 1977. 229 p.; 5 leaves of plates (1 fold.); ill.

Publication of early 19th-century didactic chronicle of Tamaulipas' history, based on oral sources and personal experience from 1760–ca. 1800. Contributes significantly to our knowledge of frontier, military and social life in this region. [EBC]

1972 Simmons, Marc. Governor Cuervo and the beginnings of Albuquerque: another look (UNM/NMHR, 55:3, July 1980, p. 188–207)

Contribution to urban history of New Mexico which indicates that Governor falsified his 1706 account of Albuquerque's foundation. Evidence indicates that throughout most of 18th century, settlers lived scattered on their farms. [EBC]

1973 Swann, Michael M. The demographic impact of disease and famine in late colonial northern Mexico (*in* Historical geography of Latin America: papers in honor of Robert C. West. Editors for the volume, William V. Davidson and James J. Parsons. Baton Rouge: Louisiana State University, School of Geoscience, 1980, p. 97–109, bibl., graphs, maps, tables [Geoscience and man; 21])

Excellent study of impact of disease, famine and drought on Durango's population in 18th century's last decade. Impact on Indian and poorer elements of population indicate correlation of status, lack of medical attention and population changes. Author stresses importance of interrelating epidemiological and demographic research. [AL]

1974 **Tapia Méndez, Aureliano.** La creación del primitivo Obispado de Linares (UNL/H, 20, 1979, p. 283–301)

Traces history of foundation of Bishopric of present day Nuevo León in 1779 Monterrey City, stressing second Bishop Fray José Verger's role in establishing site in Monterrey instead of Saltillo. [AL]

1975 **Velázquez, María del Carmen.** De los presidios internos coloniales a las colonias militares republicanas (*in* Congreso Venezolano de Historia, *3rd, Caracas, 1977.* Memoria [see item **1741**] t. 3, p. 393–412)

Narrative essay based on information obtained from 1724–28 Visitas, 1729 Reglamento, 1766–68 Visita, and the 1772 Reglamento. Finds territorial relationship between 1768 presidios and 1848 military colonies. [EBC]

1976 ———. Don Matías de la Mota Padilla y su política de poblamiento (UNAM/EHN, 7, 1981, p. 79–98)

Analysis of history of Mota Padilla completed in 1742 which concludes that he advocated policy of settling the frontier with Spanish settlers rather than with presidios and missions. [EBC]

1977 **Vigil, Ralph E.** Bartolomé de las Casas, Judge Alonso de Zorita, and the Franciscans: a collaborative effort for the spiritual conquest of the borderlands (AAFH/TAM, 38:2, July 1981, p. 45–57)

Describes Alonso de Zorita's plan for occupation of borderlands by Franciscan missionaries. Gives additional biographical material on Zoria. [EBC]

1978 **Villarreal Lozano, Javier.** Fray Juan Larios (Revista Coahuilense de Historia [Colegio Coahuilense de Investigaciones Históricas, Saltillo, México] 3:13, mayo/junio 1980, p. 66–72)

Biographical sketch of Fray Juan Larios (1633–75) Franciscan missionary in present-day Coahuila, ardent defender of Indians against powerful Agustín Echever y Subisa, first Marquis of San Miguel de Aguayo. Too brief and without footnotes to be of much use for the scholar. [AL]

1979 **Visita general del Nuevo Reino de León** por el Gobernador Don Pedro de Barrio Junco y Espriella en 1754. Edited by Israel Cavazos Garza. Monterrey: Universidad de Nuevo León, 1979. 16 p. (Actas; 10)

Relaciones editadas según manuscritos del Archivo Municipal de Monterrey (vol. 84) y del British Museum, (Add. 17,577). [L.G. Canedo]

1980 **Voss, Stuart F.** Societal competition in northwest New Spain (AAFH/TAM, 38:2, Oct. 1981, p. 185–203)

Interpretive study based on published materials. Sheds light on conflict between Jesuits, Governor Huidobro, settlers and Indians. Suggests that Franciscans failed to supplant Jesuits, whose expulsion facilitated growth of urban, secular society. [EBC]

MEXICO: 19th Century, Revolution and Post-Revolution

RICHARD E. GREENLEAF, *Director, Center for Latin American Studies, Tulane University*
DON M. COERVER, *Chairman, Department of History, Texas Christian University*

THE LAST BIENNIUM PRODUCED outstanding regional studies of the Mexican Revolution. Douglas Richmond reviews some of the literature in "Regional Aspects of the Mexican Revolution" (item **2249**), while Barry Carr discusses the value of such studies in "Recent Regional Studies of the Mexican Revolution" (item **2159**). Among the best were Douglas Richmond's "Factional Political Strife in Coahuila, 1910–1920" (item **3348**), Mark Wasserman's "The Social Origins of the 1910 Revolution in Chihuahua" (item **2284a**), Gilbert M. Joseph's "Mexico's 'Popular Revolution:' Mobilization and Myth in Yucatán, 1910–1940" (item **2206**), Romana Falcón's "¿Los Orígenes Populares de la Revolución de 1910?: El Caso de San Luis Potosí" (item **2179**), Alicia Hernández Chávez's "La Defensa de los Finqueros en

Chiapas, 1914–1920" (item **2196**), Thomas Benjamin's "Revolución Interrumpida: Chiapas y el Interreinato Presidencial, 1911" (item **2149**), and David G. LaFrance's "Madero, Serdán y los Albores del Movimiento Revolucionario en Puebla" (item **2111a**). Other valuable works on the Revolution: Peter Henderson's *Felix Díaz, the Porfirians, and the Mexican Revolution* (item **2195**) and David Brading's *Caudillo and peasant in the Mexican Revolution* (item **2161**).

Important for the post-revolutionary period was the much needed political biography of Obregón written by Linda Hall, *Alvaro Obregón: power and revolution in Mexico, 1911–1920* (item **2192**). The political struggle between Obregón and Calles is addressed by Rafael Loyola Díaz in *La crisis Obregón-Calles y el estado mexicano* (item **2223**). Research on local political consolidation appears in Gilbert M. Joseph's "The Fragile Revolution: Cacique Politics and Revolutionary Process in Yucatan" (item **2205**), and Romana Falcón's "Veracruz: Los Límites del Radicalismo en el Campo, 1920–1934" (item **2180**).

Important research on the fall of the royalist government and counterinsurgency was carried by Timothy Anna's *The fall of the royalist government in Mexico City* (item **1985**), Hugh Hamill, Jr.'s "Royalist Propaganda and 'La Porción Humilde del Pueblo' during Mexican Independence" (item **1906**), and Brian Hamnett "Royalist Counterinsurgency and the Continuity of Rebellion: Guanajuato and Michoacán, 1813–1820" (item **2049**) and "Mexico's Royalist Coalition: the Response to the Revolution, 1808–1821" (item **2048**).

Well-researched studies of the 19th century continue to appear. Carmen Blázquez presented a political biography, *Miguel Lerdo de Tejada: un liberal veracruzano en la política nacional* (item **2003**). The Díaz era is seen as a logical extension of the Reform era in Charles R. Berry's *The Reform in Oaxaca, 1856–76: a microhistory of the liberal revolution* and Richard N. Sinkin's *The Mexican Reform 1855–1876: a study in Liberal nation-building* (item **2113**). These two works dealing with the Reform period showed the value of a subnational approach to history and of the application of quantitative methodology. Charles Berry's profile of the Reform movement in the key state of Oaxaca demonstrated the possibilities inherent in extending the "microhistorical "approach to other areas of Mexico during the crucial decades involved. Richard Sinkin's analysis of the Liberals as a nation-building elite not only helps to illuminate the Reform period but also provides a valuable background for developments during the Restored Republic and the Porfiriato.

The Porfiriato continues to attract scholarly attention. Many worthy studies address 19th-century agrarian labor and economics: Leticia Reina's *Las Rebeliones campesinas en Mexico, 1819–1906* (item **2095**) and Roberto Melville's *Crecimiento y rebellión: el desarrollo económico de las haciendas azucareras en Morelos 1880–1910* (item **2072**) analyze peasant uprisings. Harry Cross' "Debt Peonage Reconsidered: a Cast Study of Nineteenth Century Zacatecas, Mexico" (item **2020**), Frans Schryer's "A Ranchero Economy in Northwestern Hidalgo: 1889–1920" (item **2109**), and Hans Günther Mertens' "La Situación Económica de Peones de Campo en una Hacienda del Valle de Atlixco a Fines del Porfiriato" (item **2076**), continue revisionism of rural working conditions. A broad view of agrarian politics with emphasis on Díaz is presented by Miguel Mejía Fernández's *Política agraria en México en el siglo XIX* (item **2071**).

Additional information analyses of the Porfiriato include Enrique Cortes' *Relaciones entre México y Japón durante el Porfiriato* (item **2018**), Paul Vanderwood's "Mexico's Rurales: Image of a Society in Transition" (item **2126**), and David Walker's "Porfirian Labor Politics: Working Class Organizations in Mexico City and Porfirio Díaz, 1876–1902" (item **2128**).

Robert Matson surveys the historiography on Church wealth in "Church Wealth in the Nineteenth Century Mexico: a Review of Literature" (item **2070**). Various aspects of the Church-State struggle are addressed by James H. Lee's "Bishop Clemente Munguía and the Clerical Resistance to the Mexican Reform, 1855–1857," "Clerical Education in Nineteenth Century Mexico: The Conciliar Seminaries of Mexico City and Guadalajara, 1821–1910" (items **2064** and **2065**), and Milada Bazant de Saldaña's *La Desamortización de los bienes de la Iglesia en Toluca durante la Reforma: 1856–1875* (item **1994**).

Education continues to be a popular subject. *Historia Mexicana* devoted its julio–sept. 1979 issue to the history of Mexican education (see items **2022**, **2114**, **2119**, and **2239**). An entire volume of the *Historia de la Revolución Mexicana* series was given over to an excellent study of the efforts of the Cárdenas administration to introduce socialist education (item **2220**). There was further examination of the educational policies of José Vasconcelos (item **2222**) as well as a commemorative work on the granting of autonomy to the National University (item **2171**).

The historiography of Mexican labor has grown. Two more volumes appeared in the projected 17-volume series, *La clase obrera en la historia de México* (items **2012** and **2189**). These two works analyzed the working class during the Porfiriato and the early revolutionary period and were particularly valuable when used in conjunction with Walker's study of Porfirian labor politics. Roman's analysis of the problems and politics involved in the transfer of the railorads to workers' administration under the Cárdenas regime rounds out another excellent biennium for labor studies.

Study of agrarian labor also focused on the 20th century. Noteworthy were Dana Markiewicz's *Ejido organization in Mexico, 1934–1976* (item **2229**) and Marc Edleman's "Agricultural Modernization in Smallholding Areas of Mexico: a Case Study of the Sierra Norte de Puebla."

A number of fine works on US-Mexico relations have been produced. Study of Villa's raid on Columbus, the German conspiracy and border security are examined by Michael C. Meyer's "Villa, Sommerfeld, Columbus y los Alemanes" (item **2238**), James A. Sandos' "Pancho Villa and American Security: Woodrow Wilson's Mexican Diplomacy Reconsidered" (item **2259**), and W. Dirk Raat's *Revoltosos: Mexico's rebels in the United States, 1903–1923* (item **2245**). Cardoso's basic work on the immigration issue, Coerver's and Hall's on federal-state conflict over border policy and Sandos' examination of the prostitution and drug problems experienced by the Pershing Expedition deserve special mention (items **2158**, **2166** and **2260**).

Studies of the role of women in Mexican history are increasing. Their role in the Revolution is examined by Anna Macías' "Women and the Mexican Revolution, 1910–1920" (item **2225**), and by Shirlene Ann Soto's *The Mexican woman: a study of her participation in the Revolution, 1910–1940* (item **2272**).

Interesting studies of the borderlands were produced: Robert J. Rosenbaum's *Mexican resistance in the Southwest* (item **2104**) and David J. Weber's "American Westward Expansion and the Breakdown of Relations between Pobladores and 'Indios Bárbaros' on Mexico's Northern Frontier, 1821–1846" (item **2131**) described American expansion. Weber also examined the Church in "Failure of a Frontier Institution: the Secular Church in the Borderlands under Independent Mexico" (item **2032**). Economic aspects were addressed by Sergio Ortega Noriega's "Los Intercambios Económicos entre el Noroeste Mexicano y los Estados Unidos a Fines del Siglo XIX: el Caso de Topolobampo" (item **2087**).

Several extensive and multi-volume works appeared during the last biennium: *La República Federal Mexicana: gestación y nacimiento* (8 vols.; item **2096**) studies the early history of the federal republic; the series *La Clase obrera en la historia de México* (6 vols.; item **1844**); Gustavo Casasola's *Seis siglos de historia gráfica de México, 1325–1925* (5 vols.; item **2160**); and the six-volume illustrated *Historia del Estado de Querétaro:* (item **2021a**). *El Ejército mexicano* is a high quality work on the history of the Mexican Army (item **2024**).

Major works also appeared which described the background, organization and development of the official party during the 20th century. Alejandra Lajous treated the origins of the party, explaining how the personalistic centralism of the Porfiriato became the presidentialistic government of the revolutionary period (item **2212**). The crucial role played by Alvaro Obregón in the formation of the party was examined in two articles and a major book by Linda Hall (items **2192–2193**). The recruitment of the party elite during the institutional phase of the Revolution was the subject of an excellent quantitative study by Roderic Camp (item **2155**). These works, in conjunction with the new installments in the *Historia de la Revolución Mexicana* series (see items **2220** *and* **2234**), tell us a great deal about how the one-party system in Mexico developed and still operates.

The editors wish to recognize the major contribution to this section of David R. Lessard who searched, read and extracted the literature.

19TH CENTURY

1981 Alanis Boyso, Rodolfo. La conspiración de Montaño: un intento de implantar el centralismo en México (Boletín del Archivo General de Estado de México [Toluca] 4, enero/abril 1980, p. 3–15, ill.)

Discusses revolt planned by José Manuel Montaño and led by Vice-President Nicolás Bravo in 1827 to impose centralist government in Mexico. Revolt failed, marked fall of the Scottish Rite Masons, and contributed to the security of the federal system in Mexico.

1982 ———. Establecimiento del milicia cívica en Toluca (Boletín del Archivo General del Estado de México [Toluca] 1, enero/abril 1979, p. 8–12, ill.)

Discusses formation of civilian militia during Iturbide era. Creation was due in part to need to keep order in cities and towns and in part to pursue and arrest deserters from the liberation army.

1983 ———. Instalación del Primer Ayuntamiento en el Municipio de Capulhuac (Boletín del Archivo del Estado de México [Toluca] 6, sept./dic. 1980, p. 25–29)

Presents jurídical basis for creating ayuntamientos (1824–27) and installation of the first Ayuntamiento in Capulhuac (1827).

Creation of Ayuntamiento started formal territorial integration of the state of Mexico.

1984 Andrade, Rolando. Juárez-Díaz: the breaking of friendship (*in* Hispanic-American essays in honor of Max Leon Moorhead [see *HLAS 42:1787*] p. 157–186, maps, plates)

Break between Juárez and Díaz occurred during Empire's last days and first two months of the Restored Republic. Author examines in detail the political, military, economic, and personal friction that developed between them.

1985 Anna, Timothy E. The fall of Royal Government in Mexico City. Lincoln: University of Nebraska Press, 1978. 289 p.; bibl.; index.

Anna shows that Spanish viceregal government defeated all insurgents despite great odds such as social and economic crises, epidemics, natural disasters, and radical reforms from Spain. While the viceroys won, Spain lost authority to govern. Thesis: independence was not achieved through counter-revolution; rather it was the culmination of upper and middle classes quest for home rule which began in 1808. Independence was largely result of political errors by Spanish liberals and Fernando VII, and from compromise between Mexican elite and rebels, but such compromise could not endure.

1986 Antuñano, Estevan de. Obras: documentos para la historia de la industrialización en México, 1833–1846. México: Secretaría de Hacienda y Crédito Público, 1979. 2 v.; bibl.; ill.

Collection of letters, articles and essays of the author (1792–1847) on the growth of industrialization and the political economy of Mexico.

Archives and manuscripts in the Nettie Lee Benson Latin American Collection: a checklist. See *HLAS 42:91.*

Archivo General de la Nación (México). Fondo Presidente Abelardo L. Rodríquez, índice de serie sindicatos. See item **87.**

1987 Arreola Cortés, Raúl. Epitacio Huerta, soldado y estadista liberal. México: Impr. Madero, 1979. 253 p.; bibl.; ill.

Favorable and sympathetic political biography of 19th-century liberal politician and soldier. One-half book contains Huerta's documents and memoirs.

1989 Barragán Barragán, José. Introducción al federalismo: la formación de los poderes en 1824. México: Universidad Nacional Autónoma de México, Coordinación de Humanidades, 1978. 372 p.; bibl.

Analysis of executive, legislative, and judicial functions of Mexican federalism. Discusses in detail 1824 Constitution. Includes extensive bibliography.

1990 ———. El juicio de responsabilidad en la Constitución de 1824. Antecedente inmediato del amparo. México: UNAM, 1978. 197 p.

Contrary to the most legal-historical opinion, author argues that the *amparo* derives directly from the *residencia.* Demonstrates similarities of intent and of procedure.

1991 Baum, Dale. Retórica y realidad en el México decimonónico: ensayo de interpretación de su historia política (CH/MH, 27:1, julio/sept. 1977, p. 79–102, bibl.)

Argues that historiography of 19th-century Mexico must begin with social analysis rather than on an examination of the conflict of ideas between liberals and conservatives. Presents good case for examining social and political realities and goals of those who struggled for power in order to understand the history of 19th-century Mexico and its subsequent development.

1992 Bazant, Jan. La escuela primaria de la hacienda de San Bartolomé Tepetates: alumnos, maestros, equipo (CM/HM, 29:1, julio/sept. 1979, p. 163–179, tables)

Statistical study of school on hacienda belonging to Protasio Tagle, prominent figure in early years of Porfiriato. Data covers period 1892–1903.

1993 ———. Joseph Ivés Limantour, 1812–1885 y su aventura californiana: pt. 2 (CM/HM, 29:2, enero/marzo 1980, p. 353–374)

Continuation of *HLAS 42:2172* in which author deals with Limantour's legal problems with his California land-holdings. Concludes that Limantour's documentation to defend his land titles was authentic but that his claims were null and void because he had not complied with Mexican land law.

1994 Bazant de Saldaña, Milada. La desamortización de los bienes de la Iglesia en Toluca durante la Reforma, 1856–1875. México: Biblioteca Enciclopédica del Estado de México, 1979. 114 p.; bibl.; ill. (Biblioteca enciclopédica del Estado de México; 67)

Liberal reform brought economic progress but also contributed to inequality in land tenure. Liberalism favored creation of small property holdings but did not favor equality or social reform. Based on substantial archival research. Includes bibliography and statistics on Church wealth.

1995 Bellingeri, Marco. Del peonage al salario: el caso de San Antonio Tochatlaco de 1880 a 1920 (UNAM/RMCPS, 24:91, enero/marzo 1978, p. 121–136, tables)

Analysis of transition from debt peonage to salaried work on one hacienda during the Porfiriato. Examines effects of such changes on various types of workers.

1996 ——— and **Isabel Gil.** Elementos para el estudio de la estructura agraria de México en el siglo XIX (UNAM/RMCPS, 24:91, enero/marzo 1978, p. 9–45)

Historiography of 19th-century Mexican agrarian history has been limited by lack of theoretical and methodological frameworks resulting in general descriptive monographs. Authors propose more rigorous and scientific method be used, and to that end, offer series of hypotheses about function of haciendas and modes of production.

1997 Beneski, Charles de. Una narración de los últimos momentos de la vida de

Don Agustín de Iturbide, ex-imperador de México. Traducida del inglés por el profesor Quintín González Gómez. Victoria: Universidad Autónoma de Tamaulipas, Instituto de Investigaciones Históricas, 1977. 65 p.; 2 leaves of plates; bibl.; ill.

Author accompanied Iturbide during last days of his life. Book contains author's few memoirs; most of the work contains letters of Iturbide and other documents.

1998 Benoit, Joachim. Contribución a la historia de las formaciones sociales en América Latina: Puebla en el México de los siglos XIX–XX (*in* Encuentro de Historiadores Latinoamericanos y del Caribe, *2d, Caracas, 1977.* Los estudios históricos en América Latina: ponencias, acuerdos y resoluciones: Caracas, 20–26 de marzo de 1977. Caracas: Universidad Central de Venezuela, Facultad de Humanidades y Educación, Escuela de Historia, 1979, v. 1, t. 1, p. 326–349)

Presents a detailed plan for writing social history of Puebla. Investigation would include examination of demography, geography, geopolitical and geoeconomic structures, class relationships, and social movements. Study is only concerned with examining social history within two finite periods: 1810–20, 1910–17.

1999 Berbusse, Edward J. General Rosecran's forthright diplomacy with Juárez's Mexico, 1868–1869 (AAFH/TAM, 36:4, April 1980, p. 499–514)

Describes blunt, direct diplomacy of William S. Rosecrans, US Minister to Juarez's government (Dec. 1868–June 1869), who saw Juarez government as weak, and opposed to the introduction of US commerce, industry and investment—all of which he believed would cure Mexico's economic ills. Concludes that much of what Rosecrans argued for would be delivered by Díaz improving trade and political relations between both countries. Article seems largely a treatment of history through the study of personality. For political scientist's comment, see *HLAS 43:7169.*

2000 Black, Shirley J. Napoleon III and European colonization in Mexico: the substance of an imperial dream (*in* Hispanic-American essays in honor of Max Leon Moorhead [see *HLAS 42:1787*] p. 133–155, plates)

Napoleon's "plans for Mexico were logical, well-conceived, and humanitarian for the 1860's." Napoleon wanted silver and cotton from Mexico and hoped European colonization would produce political and economic stability and develop Mexican infrastructure. Maximilian failed to comprehend the plans. He was slow in producing a colonization program and faced opposition from republicans and monarchists in Mexico.

2001 Blanquel Morán, Mario. Notas sobre la vida de los alumnos del Instituto Literario en Toluca, 1832 (Boletín del Archivo General del Estado de México [Toluca] 2, mayo/augosto 1979, p. 15–22)

Discusses social and political conflicts of emerging country as reflected in one institute. Analyzes disruption caused by a few students who were accused of stealing and fraternizing with staff-member's family. Author feels that prejudice and lack of understanding on the part of school authorities led to unreasonable punishments.

2002 ———. Los trabajadores del gobierno del Estado de México ante la lucha por el poder en 1832 (Boletín del Archivo General del Estado de México [Toluca] 6, sept./dic. 1980, p. 30–44)

Sympathetic portrayal of plight of government workers caught between liberals and conservatives in their struggle for political power.

2003 Blazquez, Carmen. Miguel Lerdo de Tejada: un liberal veracruzano en la política nacional. México: El Colegio de México, 1978. 201 p.; 4 leaves of plates; bibl.; ill.; index (Nueva serie. Centro de Estudios Históricas; 27)

Short biography presents portrait of Lerdo as advocate of annexation to US and as champion of development of Mexican infrastructure designed to benefit an emerging commercial bourgeoisie in Veracruz and Mexico City to which he belonged. Lerdo and his followers shifted their allegiance from conservative dictatorship to liberal republic after recognizing the economic possibilities in the reforms. Shift secured eventual victory of liberalism.

2004 Bornemann, Margarita Menegus. Ocoyoacac, una comunidad agraria en el siglo XIX (CM/HM, 30:1, julio/sept. 1980, p. 33–78, maps, tables)

Author examines Ocoyoacac municipio in Toluca Valley and impact that laws of disamortization had on inhabitants. Study includes Church property, municipal lands, ejidos, and vacant lands. Emphasis is on Porfirian period.

2005 Bringas Colín, Martha Idalia. La compañía "Tranvías de Toluca:" un ejemplo de monopolia porfirista (Boletín del Archivo General del Estado de México [Toluca] 5, mayo/agosto 1980, p. 30–34, ill.)

Discussion of dispute between brewery and railroad over rights to construct and operate an additional line during late 19th century.

2006 ———. Los lavaderos públicos de Toluca "Carmen Romero Rubio de Díaz" (Boletín del Archivo General del Estado de México [Toluca] 4, enero/abril 1980, p. 16–21, ill.)

Description of construction and operation of public laundries in Toluca during Díaz period. Such shops were built to benefit those who did not have facilities for laundry or lacked plumbing.

2007 Buisson, Inge. Gewalt und Gegengewalt im "guerra de castas" in Yukatan, 1847–1853 (JGSWGL, 15, 1978, p. 7–28, map)

Explains factors that characterized origins of Caste War. Rebellion was motivated above all by political, economic, and fiscal changes: appropriation of land and its commercialization, growth of sugar plantations, and fiscal and ecclesiastical taxes.

Cárdenas, Héctor. Las relaciones mexicano-soviéticas: antecedentes y primeros contactos diplomáticos, 1789–1927. See *HLAS 43:7172.*

2008 Castaneda Batres, Oscar. Verdad y mito de Prim: la actuación del General Juan Prim en México (CAM, 234:1, enero/feb. 1981, p. 113–143)

Attempts to unravel myth of leader of Spanish expedition to Mexico in 1862 as a hero. Concludes that he was not.

2009 Castelot, André. Maximilien et Charlotte du Mexique: la tragedie de l'ambition. Paris: Librairie Academique Perrin, 1977. 647 p.; ill.; maps.

While many Mexican specialists may question the need for yet another book on Maximilian's doomed empire, this one has some new sources (the correspondence of a member of the French legation in Mexico and that of a Foreign Legion captain) and some new insights, particularly of a personal nature (e.g., menus for imperial meals).

2010 Chávez Orozco, Luis. El sitio de Puebla, 1863. México: Comisión Nacional Editorial, 1976. 94 p.; bibl.; ill.

Descriptive history of the fortifications around Puebla following the battle of 5 May 1862.

2011 Chávez Peralta, Saúl. Codallos, un gran hombre, dos naciones: México-Venezuela. Michoacán: FONAPAS, 1980. 91 p.; bibl.

Brief biography of relatively unknown Venezuelan general who fought and died for independence and federalism in Mexico.

2012 La Clase obrera en la historia de México. v. 3, De la dictadura porfirista a los tiempos libertarios. Ciro F.S. Cardoso *et al.* México: Siglo Veintiuno Editores: Instituto de Investigaciones Sociales de la UNAM, 1980. 248 p.; bibl.; charts.

Third installment in projected 17-volume series *La clase obrera en la historia de México.* Work is divided into two parts: 1) rise of industrial capitalism and its interrelationship with politics, social structure, and working class; and 2) Partido Liberal Mexicano and its role in strikes at Cananea and Rio Blanco and invasion of Baja California in 1911.

2013 Coatsworth, John H. Growth against development: the economic impact of railroads in Porfirian Mexico. DeKalb: Northern Illinois University Press, 1981. 249 p.; ill.; maps; tables.

Translation and revision of author's *El impacto económico de los ferrocarriles en el Porfiriato: crecimiento y desarrollo* (see *HLAS 40:2604*). In terms of problem posed by title, author concludes that railroad expansion during Porfiriato did much to stimulate growth but also created new obstacles to long-term development.

2014 ———. Indispensable railroads in a backward economy: the case of Mexico (EHA/J, 39:4, Dec. 1979, p. 939–960, tables)

Freight savings and indirect benefits of railroads accounted for increased productivity of the economy prior to 1910. Yet, railroads also created underdevelopment. Benefits went to export sector to detriment of Mexican industry and economy. For economist's comment, see *HLAS 43:2988*.

2015 Colín, Mario. Guía de documentos impresos del Estado de México. t. 3, 1861–1911. México: Biblioteca Enciclopédica del Estado de México, 1977. 1 v.; facsims.; indexes (Biblioteca enciclopédica del Estado de México; 58)

Annotated bibliography of state documents, proclamations, and decrees.

2016 Congreso Obrero, *México, 1876.* Congreso Obrero de 1876. México: Centro de Estudios Históricos del Movimiento Obrero Mexicano, 1980. 248 p.

Collection of conference proceedings.

2017 Cordero Martínez, Javier. Consideraciones relativas a la constitución política del estado libre y soberano de Nuevo León y Coahuila (Revista Coahuilense de Historia [Colegio Coahuilense de Investigaciones Históricas, Saltillo, México] 3:13, mayo/junio 1980, p. 73–86)

Brief account of Santiago Vidaurri's work to create state of Nuevo León and Coahuila in 1856; his disagreements with Juárez led latter to nullify annexation of both states in 1864. Vidaurri later supported Maximilian's regime and was executed. Summarized constitution which Vidaurri and others created for the state in 1857.

2018 Cortés, Enrique. Relaciones entre México y Japón durante el Porfiriato. México: Secretaría de Relaciones Exteriores, 1980. 133 p. (Archivo Histórico Diplomático Mexicano; cuarta época; no. 1)

Examination of factors which led to establishment of diplomatic relations between Mexico and Japan and events that flowed from this relationship. Author believes Japanese emigration to Mexico was most important development of relations. Based on archival sources in Mexico, Japan, and US.

2019 Covián Martínez, Vidal. Cuatro estudios históricos. Ciudad Victoria, Tamaulipas: Universidad Autónoma de Tamaulipas, Instituto de Investigaciones Históricas, 1977. 59 p.; 2 leaves of plates (1 fold.); ill.

Contains four regional studies of Tamaulipas: "Ciudadela Huaxteca;" "El Gran Teatro Juárez;" "José Nicolás Balli;" and "Rosa María Hinojosa de Balli." Based on state and local archival research.

2020 Cross, Harry E. Debt peonage reconsidered: a case study in nineteenth-century Zacatecas, Mexico (HU/BHR, 53:4, Winter 1979, p. 473–495, tables)

Revision of notion that 19th-century Mexico was replete with peonage. Records of Zacatecas hacienda show that laborers did not suffer pervasive debts. Records span 60 years from 1821. Most debts were small and were within the ability of workers to repay them.

2021 Cuéllar Valdés, Pablo M. Historia del Estado de Coahuila. Saltillo, Coahuila, México: Universidad Autónoma de Coahuila, 1979. 419 p.; bibl.; ill. (some col.); index (Biblioteca de la Universidad Autónoma de Coahuila; v. no. 1)

History of Coahuila dating largely from the Conquest. Includes brief account of pre-conquest history; extensive sections of maps; social and demographic statistics; geographical data; and governmental divisions.

2021a Díaz Ramírez, Fernando. Historia del Estado de Querétaro. t. 1, 1821–1836. t. 2, 1837–1851. t. 3, 1851–1867. t. 4, 1867–1900. t. 5, 1901–1931. t. 6, 1931–1979. Querétaro, México: Ediciones del Gobierno del Estado, 1979. 6 v.; ill.

Well-illustrated narrative, chronological history of the state of Querétaro with reproductions and facsimiles of documents.

2022 Díaz Zermeño, Héctor. La escuela nacional primaria en la ciudad de México, 1876–1910 (CM/HM, 29:1, julio/sept. 1979, p. 59–90, tables)

Detailed description of primary education in Mexico City during Porfiriato describes systems of education, educational methodology, programs, funding, absenteeism, examination policy, and even juvenile alcoholism.

2023 Documentos para el estudio de la industrialización en México: 1837–1845. Edited by Horacio Labastida. México: Secretaría de Hacienda y Crédito Público, 1977. 452 p.

Collection of documents relating to Mexico's early economic development, mostly provided by Lucas Alamán, the well-known Conservative politician, and Robert

Wyllie, who made lengthy report to English bondholders of the Mexican national debt.

2024 El Ejército mexicano. Jesús de León Toral *et al.* México: Secretaría de la Defensa Nacional. 1979. 647 p.; bibl.; ill.

Beautifully illustrated history of Mexican Army. Includes brief bibliography.

2025 Encuentro sobre Historia del Movimiento Obrero, *Universidad Autónoma de Puebla, 1978.* Memorias del Encuentro sobre Historia del Movimiento Obrero. v. 1 and 3. Puebla: Universidad Autónoma de Puebla, 1980– . 2 v.; bibl.; ill. (Colección Fuentes para el estudio de la historia del movimiento obrero y sinidical)

Series of well-documented studies of workers' movement in Mexico within various industries. Includes selections on methodology and historiography of studying the subject matter.

2026 La Estrella polar: polémica federalista. Guadalajara: Poderes de Jalisco, 1977. 207 p.; 40 leaves of plates; facsims. (Los Libros del federalismo; 9) (Serie conmemorativa del CL [i.e. sexagésimo] aniversario del federalismo en México)

Transcription and facsimile of radical liberal document, *La Estrella polar*, published in 1822.

2027 Estudios de historia moderna y contemporánea de México. México: Universidad Nacional Autónoma de México, 1980. 252 p.; 1 folded leaf of plates; map (Universidad Nacional Autónoma de México, Instituto de Investigaciones Históricas; v. 8)

Series of articles and book reviews covering politics, economics, and history of 19th and 20th-century Mexico.

2028 Figueroa, José. Manifesto to the Mexican Republic, which Brigadier General José Figueroa, Commandant and political chief of Upper California, presents on his conduct and on that of José María de Hijar and José María Padrés as directors of colonization in 1834 and 1835. Translated, with an introd. and notes by C. Alan Hutchinson. Berkeley: University of California Press, 1978. 156 p.; bibl.; index.

Hutchinson challenges Figueroa's justification for disbanding group of colonizers who came to California from Mexico. Argues that colonizers were not traitors and conspirators out to make their own fortunes as

Figueroa asserted in 1835. Includes facsimile of original Spanish version.

2029 Florescano, Enrique. La influencia del Estado en la historiografía (*in* Encuentro de Historiadores Latinoamericanos y del Caribe, 2d, Caracas, 1977. Los estudios históricos en América Latina: ponencias, acuerdos y resoluciones: Caracas, 20–26 de marzo de 1977. Caracas: Universidad Central de Venezuela, Facultad de Humanidades y Educación, Escuela de Historia, 1979, v. 1, t. 1, p. 350–373)

Examines role of powerful centralized states in Mexico and their effects on the development of historiography. Devotes small portion to role of the state in prehispanic and colonial times, and concentrates on post-independence and modern eras. Concludes in general that historiography has been a powerful instrument to create a national identity when entrusted to the dominant classes. It has legitimized the power of the state and defended its interests against opposition.

2030 Formación y desarrollo de la burguesía en México, siglo XIX. Coordinación y presentación de Ciro F.S. Cardoso, Margarita Urías *et al.* México: Siglo Vientiuno Editores, 1978. 286 p.; 1 leaf of plates; ill. (Sociología y política)

Shows how six entrepreneurs in Mexico City and some in Nuevo León managed to use the "dislocating" Mexican political scene for their own advancement and profit. After 1830 they became indispensable to the national governments by providing road maintenance, toll collection, etc.

2031 Frías Olvera, Manuel. Historia de la Revolución Mexicana en el Estado de Puebla: 1555–1910. México: Instituto Nacional de Estudios Históricos de la Revolución Mexicana, 1980. 222 p.; bibl. (Biblioteca del Instituto Nacional de Estudios Históricos de la Revolución Mexicana; 84)

Attempts to demonstrate that struggle for liberty and freedom has been constant in Puebla's history and was factor in the Revolution. Title is misplaced; author deals with colonial period in four short chapters. Based on limited and deficient bibliography.

2032 Fuentes Mares, José. Miramón, el hombre. 3. ed. México: J. Mortiz, 1978. 262 p.; 10 leaves of plates; ill. (Contrapuntos)

History of the political and military life of Miguel Miramón. States that book is based on primary sources but does not cite them nor include bibliography. Attempts to sort out his activities as president, as conservative leader during War of the Reform, and during Maximilian's reign.

2033 García Cantú, Gastón. Utopías mexicanas. México: Fondo de Cultura Económica, 1978. 222 p.; 2 leaves of plates; ill. (Sección de obras de historia)

Collection of author's essays on social, political and economic themes that span Mexican history since independence. Not monographs for researchers nor an historical synthesis, but rather a collection of enlightened essays about Mexico.

2034 García-Luna Ortega, Margarita. La construcción del mercado "16 de septiembre" en la Ciudad de Toluca, 1900–1910 (Boletín del Archivo General del Estado de México [Toluca] 5, mayo/agosto 1980, p. 28–29, graph, ill.)

General account of construction of Toluca market at height of economic prosperity. Architectural style imitated European forms and demonstrated growth of bourgeois society.

2035 ———. El ferrocarril Toluca-Tenango, 1891–1910 (Boletín del Archivo General del Estado de México [Toluca] 1, enero/abril 1979, p. 3–7, ill., tables)

Discusses construction of Toluca-Tenango railroad as example of how internal commerce and trade were increased.

2036 García Quintana, Josefina. Cuauhtémoc en el siglo XIX. México: UNAM, 1977 [i.e. 1978]. 135 p.; bibl.; facsims. [Dictámenes Ichcateopan; 1]

Analysis of historiography and official publications of 19th-century Cuauhtemoc. Consists mostly of lists of sources consulted, archival documents.

2037 Gastélum, Bernardo J. Semblanza de Maximiliano Ruiz Castañeda. Toluca: Patrimonio Cultural y Artístico del Estado de México, 1978. 75 p.; port. (Serie José Antonio Alzate y Ramírez; 14)

Short biography of scientist and doctor who made advances in health care in Mexico.

2038 González, José María. Del artesanado al socialismo: selección de artículos.

Prólogo de Luis Chávez Orozco. México: Secretaría de Educación Pública, 1974. 180 p. (SepSetentas; 163)

Series of short essays written by anarchist leader in late 19th century. Essays revolve around attempts of artisans to defend themselves against capitalism's growth by forming mutual organizations and developing alliances with workers. Movement culminated with strikes of Río Blanco and Canaea.

2039 González Loscertales, Vicente. La resistencia de un imperio a la disgregación (IGFO/RI, 38:151/152, enero/junio 1978, p. 201–217)

Good research note, based especially on Mexican archives, demonstrates New Spain's assistance to loyalist forces in Venezuela; Cuban role was mainly intermediary. Briefly discusses also abortive pleas for help from officials assigned to New Granada. [D. Bushnell]

2040 González Navarro, Moisés. Las guerras de castas (UI/R, 21:125, sept./oct. 1979, p. 25–53, bibl.)

Discussion of effects of 1848 revolution in France on Mexico's dominant classes who feared socialist repercussions in their country. Eruption of Caste Wars, in which Indians fought to retain their land, struck fear in dominant classes. These revolts were traced to middle of 18th century. Author reviews theory and practices of Mexican leaders to subdue uprising. Special attention is devoted to its manifestations in Yucatan and Sierra Gorda.

2041 ———. El primer salario mínimo (CM/HM, 28:3, enero/marzo 1979, p. 370–400)

History of political and philosophical struggles over minimum wage principle during Porfiriato and Revolution's early years, culminating in 1912 passage of first minimum wage law for textile workers.

2042 ———. El trabajo forzoso en México: 1821–1917 (in Encuentro de Historiadores Latinoamericanos y del Caribe, 2d, Caracas, 1977. Los estudios históricos en América Latina: ponencias, acuerdos y resoluciones: Caracas, 20–26 de marzo de 1977. Caracas: Universidad Central de Venezuela, Facultad de Humanidades y Educación, Escuela de Historia, 1979, v. 1, t. 2, p. 408–423)

Neither abolition of slavery nor tribute, following independence, affected basic structure of rural society—peonage. Author traces development of laws and reforms that failed to eliminate debt peonage until Constitution of 1917 was promulgated.

2043 González Polo, Ignacio. Polotitlán de la Ilustración: una villa mexicana del siglo XIX (Boletín del Archivo General del Estado de México [Toluca] 7, enero/abril 1981, p. 3–6, facsim., ill.)

Brief description of town's growth from 19th century to present.

2044 Graebner, Norman A. The Mexican War: a study in causation (UC/PHR, 49:3, Aug. 1980, p. 405–426)

President Polk adopted policies on dual assumption that Mexico was weak and that acquisition of certain territories would satisfy long-range American interests. Polk could have avoided war and could have ignored Mexico. Animosity between countries did not cause the war; rather, claims boundaries and future of Texas led to conflict.

2045 Gurría Urgell Z., Isidoro. La rebelión de los mestizos: ensayos analítico de la Revolución Mexicana. México: M.A. Porrúa, 1980. 80 p.

Popular history of War of Independence and Revolution, their causes and participants.

2046 Gutiérrez de Velasco, Manuel. Historia de las constituciones mexicanas. Guadalajara: Instituto de Estudios Sociales, Universidad de Guadalajara, 1978. 78 p. (Colección Monografías—Instituto de Estudios Sociales, Universidad de Guadalajara)

Series of lectures focus mainly on Constitutions of 1824, 1857, 1917 as a continual progress in the constitutional evolution of Mexico.

2048 Hamnett, Brian R. Mexico's Royalist coalition: the response to the Revolution, 1808–1821 (JLAS, 12:1, May 1980, p. 55–86)

Shows evolution of Royalist opposition to Mexican independence, leaders, and achievements. Consensus operated until Liberal regime's policies dismantled it after 1820. Nevertheless, many counter-revolutionary ideas would survive and contribute to formation of conservative opposition to liberal reform during later decades of 19th century.

2049 ———. Royalist counterinsurgency and the continuity of rebellion: Guanajuato and Michoacán, 1813–20 (HAHR, 62:1, Feb. 1982, p. 19–48)

Studies struggle for control of intendency of Guanajuato and Michoacán, the original basis of the insurgency following Morelos' defeat. Royalist government launched counterinsurgent movements to subdue autonomous rebel bands to control population and restore social stability. Government's emphasis on regionalized counterinsurgency movements contribute to creation of military satrapies in provinces.

2050 Hernández Montemayor, Laura. Catálogo de fuentes para el estudio de la historia de Tamaulipas: introducción, ordenamiento, selección y traducción de datos y notas de documentos y manuscritos en lo concerniente a la historia de Tamaulipas, en los catálogos de los archivos de Juan E. Hernández y Dávalos et al. Victoria, Tamaulipas: Universidad Autónoma de Tamaulipas, Instituto de Investigaciones Históricas, 1979. 284 leaves.

Catalogue of the original documents found in the following archives: Juan E. Hernández y Dávalos, The Mariano Riva Palacio Archives, and Valentín Gómez Farías.

2051 Herrejón Peredo, Carlos. Problemas limítrofes entre México y Michoacán (Boletín del Archivo General del Estado de México [Toluca] 1, enero/abril 1979, p. 13–16, map)

General listing of boundary disputes between Mexico and Michoacán states. Traces reasons for disputes from pre-conquest through colonial to modern periods.

2052 Hitchcock, Ethan Allen. México ante los ojos del ejército invasor de 1847: diario del coronel Ethan Allen Hitchcok [sic]. George Baker, editor. México: Universidad Nacional Autónoma de México, 1978. 150 p.; bibl.

Diary of US military leader during Mexican War. Describes siege of Veracruz, various battles (including Chapultepec), Treaty of Guadalupe, and final evacuation of US troops. Although he completed his military obligations, the colonel displayed a feeling of disgust for the war and its effects on Mexico. Hitchcock was highest ranking American official who left a diary of the Mexican War.

2053 Iracheta Cenecorta, María del Pilar. La alameda toluqueña (Boletín del Archivo General del Estado de México [Toluca] 4, enero/abril 1980, p. 22–27, ill.)

General description of construction and finance of central park in Toluca, 1831–42.

2054 ———. El cobro del peage en el camino de Acapulco: defensa de un estado federado ante el poder central (Boletín del Archivo General del Estado de México [Toluca] 2, mayo/agosto 1979, p. 10–14, photos)

General account of friction between Mexico state and central government over autonomy and right of various states to run their affairs. At issue are provisions of Constitution of 1824 and federal decree of 1834 which attacked the autonomy of the state.

2055 ———. La colonia sericicultora de Tanancingo, 1886–1910: un fracaso de la política colonizadora del Porfiriato (Boletín del Archivo General del Estado de México [Toluca] 7, enero/abril 1981, p. 15–24, ill.)

Discusses Díaz regime's efforts to form agricultural and textile colonies. Among problems associated with program were construction of railroad lines for communication and transportation, irrigation, and unwillingness of latifundistas to sell tracts of their land. Article focuses on one such colony.

2056 ———. Guerrillas durante la invasión norteamericana, 1846–1848. (Boletín del Archivo General del Estado de México [Toluca] 3, sept./dic. 1979, p. 22–33, ill.)

Presents activities of guerrilla bands formed in several states to assist debilitated federal army in opposing American invasion of Mexico. Concludes that efforts were destined to be insufficient against superior American forces.

2057 Lamar, Curt. Genesis of Mexican-United States diplomacy: a critical analysis of the Alaman-Poinsett confrontation, 1825 (AAFH/TAM, 38:1, July 1981, p. 87–110)

Confrontation of both men started pattern of strained relations between Mexico and US that lasted until third decade of 20th century. Poinsett came to Mexico with intent of encouraging Mexico to implement a democratic system and to discuss acquisition of territory. His counterpart, Alamán, represented minority social class which hoped to achieve centralist government. Alamán admired constitutional monarchy of Great Britain, and Poinsett was aggravated when Mexico discussed commercial treaty with British. Poinsett was doomed to failure as diplomat because he represented to Alamán antithesis of type of government he wanted for Mexico. Poinsett accomplished nothing of significance for US during his tenure in Mexico City.

2058 Lander, Ernest McPherson, Jr. Reluctant imperialists: Calhoun, the South Carolinians, and the Mexican War. Baton Rouge: Louisiana State University Press, 1980. 189 p.; 3 leaves of plates; bibl.; ill.; index.

Prominent southern officials opposed the Mexican War. Led by John C. Calhoun, South Carolina leaders were critical of America's involvement in a protracted guerrilla war that would be costly, that would increase authority of federal government, and would cause problems with abolitionists. Good presentation of war's opponent's side.

2059 Leal, Juan Felipe and **José Woldenberg.** La clase obrera en la historia de México. v. 2, Del estado liberal a los inicios de la dictadura porfirista. México: Siglo Veintiuno Editores: Instituto de Investigaciones Sociales de la UNAM, 1980. 301 p.; maps; tables.

Studies role of urban proletariat in formation of liberal oligarchy and consolidation of Díaz government to 1884. Argues that rise of worker class took place between 1867–80. Afterward, fall of movement took place as country experienced growth of foreign capital.

2060 ———; **Mario Huacuja Rountree;** and **Mario Bellingeri Martini.** La compañía expendedora de pulques y la monopolización del mercado urbano: 1909–1914 (UNAM/RMCPS, 24:91, enero/marzo 1978, p. 177–241, tables)

Extensive study of effects of urban markets on cultivation of maguey and commercialization of pulque. Examines growth of regional economy, construction of railroads and their impact on production and prices of pulque, general characteristics of pulque haciendas during Porfiriato and transformations they underwent around 1900, and monopolization of pulque market and its position during Revolution's early years.

2061 Lecompte, Janet. The independent women of hispanic New Mexico: 1821–1846 (WHQ, 12:1, Jan. 1981, p. 17–35)

Using traveler's accounts and court records, author describes social and legal position of women during Mexican period of New Mexico's history. Independence enjoyed by women during this period was in stark contrast to their Anglo counterparts, but this independent position quickly eroded after introduction of American control.

2062 ———. Manuel Armijo and the Americans (JW, 19:3, July 1980, p. 51–63, ill., maps)

Brief, mildly-revisionist biography of leading political and military figure of the Mexican period of the history of New Mexico. Emphasis on Armijo's land grants (see item **2116**).

2063 Ledesma Uribe, José de Jesús. Las comunidades rurales en México durante el siglo XIX (UNAM/RFD, 28:110, mayo/agosto 1978, p. 415–440, bibl.)

Review of agrarian law and legislation during 19th century. Argues that laws of previous century ignored rights and protection of Indian which sowed seeds for revolution.

2064 Lee, James H. Bishop Clemente Munguía and clerical resistance to the Mexican reform, 1855–1857 (ACHA/CHR, 66:3, July 1980, p. 374–391)

Author presents ecclesiastical defenses of Bishop Munguía whose combative nature, legal training, and historical context of times conditioned his reaction to Church's liberal reforms. Used theory of divided authority (Church/State) to counter liberal attacks on Church. Conflict between Church and State was a struggle for power; both institutions advanced distinct theories to maintain their autonomy. Liberals did not seek to absorb the Church; Munguía did not assert ecclesiastical sovereignty over society.

2065 ———. Clerical education in nineteenth century Mexico: the conciliar seminaries of Mexico City and Guadalajara, 1821–1910 (AAFH/TAM, 36:4, April 1980, p. 465–477)

Explores educational role seminaries played in training men for priesthood in early 19th century before they lost status to liberal changes. Seminaries enrolled lay students who sought careers outside the Church; yet

many rejected regimen and discipline demanded of them. Conflict did not create strong partisans of the Church.

2066 León, Gerardo de. Implicaciones de la historia de la restauración de la República, en la estructura geopolítica del noreste de México (Revista Coahuilense de Historia [Colegio Coahuilense de Investigaciones Históricas, Saltillo, México] 2:12, marzo/abril 1980, p. 91–114, bibl.)

Brief sketches of historiography of Northeast Mexico cover wide range of topics.

2067 Maciel, David R. Ideología y praxis: Ignacio Ramírez y el Congreso Constituyente, 1856–1857 (CAM, 221:6, nov./dic. 1978, p. 119–129)

Presentation of Ramírez's liberal, anticlerical, federalist views which were substantially modified in final form of 1857 Constitution.

2068 ———. Ignacio Ramírez: ideólogo del liberalismo social en México. México: UNAM, 1980. 220 p.

Political biography of one of Mexico's leading Liberal thinkers and politicians. Ramírez was especially concerned with questions of political legitimacy, economic development, and education.

2069 Macune, Charles W., Jr. El Estado de México y la Federación mexicana, 1823–1835. México: Fondo de Cultura Económica, 1978. 276 p.; appendices, maps.

Well-researched analysis of federal-state relations during first republic, using state of Mexico as case study. Identifies four major areas of contention: creation of the Federal District; competition for tax revenue; conflict over ecclesiastical patronage; and broader Liberal-Conservative dispute. Financial problems ultimately proved the most important.

2070 Matson, Robert W. Church wealth in nineteenth-century Mexico: a review of literature (ACHA/CHR, 65:4, Oct. 1979, p. 600–609)

Largely reviews work of Michael P. Costeloe, Jan Bazant, Asunción Lavrin, and Robert J. Knowlton who have tackled subject of extent of Church's wealth and effectiveness of liberal reforms. All are willing to criticize liberals and to accept some of the clergy's claims that it used its position wisely. Extensive use of Church records in

Mexico permits more informed view of Church's operation.

2071 Mejía Fernández, Miguel. Política agraria en México en el siglo XIX. Portada de Anhelo Hernández. México: Siglo Veintiuno Editores, 1979. 285 p. (Historia)

Studies evolution of agrarian policy 1810–1910. Discusses economy and agrarian problems of Hidalgo and Morelos. Records locations and dates of principal rebellious, agrarian problems, Church-state battle over property, colonization program and Díaz's legislation. Author believes Díaz's land tenure policies against indigenous villages led to the landless peasantry of late 19th century.

2072 Melville, Roberto. Crecimiento y rebelión: el desarrollo económico de las haciendas azucareras en Morelos, 1880–1910. Portada, Kurtycz. México: Centro de Investigaciones del Desarrollo Rural, 1979. 113 p.; bibl.; map.

Short, valuable analysis of agroindustrial development and management of sugar haciendas during the Porfiriato. Economic growth of haciendas was characterized by increased production, technological innovations in transportation and expanding internal market. Evolution of other social and economic institutions was conditioned by sugar haciendas. Also studies relations between workers and management and causes for rebellion. Includes extensive statistics on production.

2073 Mendizábal, Miguel Othón de. La minería y la metalurgia en México. 2. ed. México: Centro de Estudios Históricos del Movimiento Obrero Mexicano, 1980. 113 p. (Cuadernos obreros; 24)

Short essay on Mexican mining industry emphasizes colonial period. Original edition was not completed at time of author's death in 1945.

2074 Menéndez, Iván. La historia regional: aproximación a la historia de Yucatán (CAM, 229:2, marzo/abril 1980, p. 99–116, bibl.)

Brief sketch of history of Yucatán from conquest to early 20th century. Includes bibliography.

2075 Mentz, Brígida von. México en el siglo XIX visto por los alemanes. México: Universidad Nacional Autónoma de México, 1980. 481 p.; 40 p. of plates; bibl.; ill. (Historia moderna y contemporánea; 11)

Based on Ph.D. dissertation, book sketches German view of Mexico in 19th century through letters, stories, newspapers, novels, and travels of von Humboldt. Author focuses on following questions: Did Germans have a vision of Mexico in 19th century? Was Mexico an attractive location for German emigrants? What was attitude of Germans in Mexico? Not only did Germans fail to integrate into Mexican society but they also maintained superior and imperialist attitudes about Mexico.

2076 Mertens, Hans-Günther. La situación económica de peones de campo en una hacienda del Valle de Atlixco a fines del Porfiriato (FAIC/CPPT, 15, 1978, p. 85–91, tables)

Statistical analysis of amount of money an hacienda worker needed to cover basic necessities. Argues that life for hacienda laborer and family was not as severe as for majority of agrarian population. This may explain workers' relatively passive attitude during Revolution.

2077 México en el siglo XIX, 1821–1910: historia económica y de la estructura social. Ciro Cardoso, coordinador. José Antonio Bátiz Vázquez *et al.* México: Editorial Nueva Imagen, 1980. 525 p.; ill.; maps (Serie Historia)

Series of essays analyze formation of state, economic policies, changes in agriculture, mining, industry, transportation, commerce, and social structures in Mexico (1821–1910). Essays reflect two hypotheses: that history of 19th-century Mexico reflects transition toward peripheral capitalism and that such transition constitutes process of national capital accumulation.

2078 Meyer, Jean. Los franceses en México durante el siglo XIX (CM/RE, 1–2, primavera 1980, p. 5–54, bibl., tables)

Study of socioeconomic and demographic characteristics of French immigrants to Mexico during 19th century.

2079 La Minería en México: estudios sobre su desarrollo histórico. Miguel León-Portilla *et al.* México: Universidad Nacional Autónoma de México, 1978. 183 p.; 14 leaves of plates; bibl.; ill.

Series of four short papers on mining history from pre-conquest to modern times. Concentrates mostly on colonial period.

2080 Montalvo Ortega, Enrique. La hacienda henequenera, la transición al capitalismo y la penetración imperialista en Yucatán: 1850–1914 (UNAM/RMCPS, 24–91, enero/marzo 1978, p. 137–175, diagram, table)

Investigation of traits of social formation of Yucatan that can explain the development of henequen haciendas and their role in the economic and political development of Yucatan. Studies modes of production, finances, industrialization and the transitions of the henequen economy from pre-capitalist to capitalist and imperialist stages.

2081 Morelia en la historia y en el recuerdo: sesquicentenario del cambio de nombre de Valladolid a Morelia, 1828–1978. Coordinadores, Leopoldo Herrera Morales, Enrique Areguín Vélez. Morelia, México: Gobierno del Estado de Michoacán, 1978. 174 p.; ill.

Social, cultural, and popular history of Morelia.

2082 Müller, Wolfgang. El financiamiento de la industrialización: el caso de la industria textil poblana, 1830–1910 (FAIC/CPPT, 15, 1978, p. 35–40)

Study of methods and forms of financing industrialization of textile industry and sources of investment capital. Discusses roles of the state, Church, private and foreign capital. Based on archival research in Puebla, Tlaxcala, and Mexico City.

2083 Nakayama A., Antonio. Sinaloa, el drama y sus actores. México: Instituto Nacional de Antropología e Historia, Centro Regional del Noroeste, 1975. 296 p.; bibl.; ill. (Colección científica—Instituto Nacional de Antopología e Historia 20: Historia regional)

Brief biographical sketches and bibliographical references on major figures in Sinaloa's history from colonial to modern times.

2084 Nava Rodríguez, Luis. Historia de Huamantla. Portada, D.H. Xochitiotzin, representa el escudo de Huamantla. Tlaxcala: s.n., 1974. 348 p.; bibl.; ill.

Political, social, cultural, economic, popular, and biographical history from colonial times to present.

2085 Navarro de Anda, Ramiro. Apuntes para una cronología de la Revolución Mexicana. México: Biblioteca del Instituto Nacional de Estudios Históricos de la Revolución Mexicana, 1980. 163 p.; bibl. (Biblioteca del Instituto Nacional de Estudios Históricos de la Revolución Mexicana; 83)

Compilation of facts and events relating to the Revolution, 1861–1920. Includes bibliography of some major items on Revolution, but contains many notable deletions.

2086 Orígen y progreso de la Revolución de Sierra Gorda, 1847–1849. Edición e introd. de Rafael Montejano y Aguiñaga. San Luis Potosí: Academia de Historia Potosina, 1977. 18 p. (Série Cuadernos—Biblioteca de Historia Potosina; 53)

Contains anonymous essay published in 1849 that reflects public opinion of the revolt of Sierra Gorda.

2087 Ortega Noriega, Sergio. Los intercambios económicos entre el noroeste mexicano y los Estados Unidos a fines del siglo XIX: el caso de Topolobampo (UAEM/H, 1, sept./dic. 1979, p. 13–24, ill., map, tables)

Economic relations between northwestern Mexican states and southwestern US accelerated in late 19th century. Following aggressive policy of territorial expansion, embarked on different policy of peaceful penetration in Mexico (e.g., railroad construction, trade, raw materials, direct investment). Such activities in Topolobampo developed local economy, created basic infrastructure, imported technology, and opened area to national and foreign markets. Post-revolutionary economic changes did not alter capitalist structure nor area's economic dependence on US.

2088 Ortiz de Ayala, Tadeo. De la inviolabilidad de las instituciones políticas y leyes fundamentales. México: Centro de Documentación Política, 1977. 23 p. (Cuadernos de causa; 5)

Short essay by the liberal philosopher (1788–1833) in defense of federalism.

2089 Otero, Mariano. La cuestión social y política en la República Mexicana. México: Centro de Documentación Política, 1979. 131 p.; bibl. (Cuadernos de causa; 15)

Reprint of 1842 essay in which Otero analyzes political and social questions in terms of organization and ownership of property. Includes bibliography of Otero's writings and works written about him.

2090 Paulsen, George E. The legal battle for the Candelaria Mine in Durango, Mexico: 1890–1917 (UA/AW, 23:3, Autumn 1981, p. 243–266, ill., maps)

Chronicle of business activities of and lengthy legal battle over Candelaria Mine in Durango. After quarter of a century of litigation, winners refused to take possession of mine because of problems with Article 27 of 1917 Constitution. Subsequent claim was never adjudicated, and matter was still pending as late as 1937.

2091 Peniche Vallado, Leopoldo. Los "Comentarios sobre una bibliografía selecta de la guerra de castas" de Howard E. Cline (CAM, 222:1, enero/feb. 1979, p. 163–174)

Discussion of Cline's study on historiography of the Caste War in which he distinguishes cause and results of war by using views of various writers.

2092 Percheron, Nicole. Formations des petites et moyennes propriétés paysannes au XIX siècle, dans les villages mexicains de l'Ajusco (CDLA, 19, 1979, p. 215–234)

Study of development of small and medium sized estates in Ajusco. Rural communities resisted efforts to impose reform laws, but in the end appearance of new middle class and effects of Porfiriato split up the communities.

2093 Periodismo insurgente. v. 1, *El Despertador Americano. Ilustrador Nacional. Ilustrador Americano. Seminario Patriótico Americano. Gaceta del Gobierno Americano. Clamores Contra la Opresión.* v. 2., *Correo Americano del Sur.* México: PRI, 1976–   . 2 v.; ill.

Collection of facsimiles of insurgent periodicals that appeared during the independence movement.

2094 Razo Zaragoza, José Luis. La Barca que viera Hidalgo y su ejército insurgente. Guadalajara: Instituto Jalisciense de Antropología e Historia, 1980. 37, 15 p.; bibl.; ill.; facsims. (Serie de historia / Instituto Jalisciense de Antropología e Historia; 18)

Description of a town occupied by Hidalgo in late 1810.

2095 Reina, Leticia. Las rebeliones campesinas en Mexico, 1819–1906. Mexico: Siglo Vientiuno Editores, 1980. 437 p.; maps; notes.

Essentially a military view of 19th-century peasant rebellions that relies heavily upon Archivo Histórico de la Defensa Nacional. Includes extensive run of documents from Defensa archives.

2096 La República Federal Mexicana: gestación y nacimiento: obra conmemorativa de la fundación de la República Federal y de la creación del Distrito Federal en 1824. v. 1/2, M. Calvillo, La consumación de la independencia y la instauración de la República Federal, 1820–1824. v. 3/4, E. Lemoine, La revolución de independencia, 1808–1821. v. 5/6, T. García Díaz, La prensa insurgente. v. 7, A. Lira, La creación del Distrito Federal. v. 8, S. Novo, La vida en la ciudad de México en 1824. Director general, Octavio A. Hernández. Autores, Manuel Calvillo et al. México: Organización Editorial Novaro, 1974. 8 v.; bibl.; ill.

Encyclopedia of early history of the Federal Republic of Mexico.

2097 Reunión Día de la Fraternidad del Estado de México, *11th, Cruces Mountain, México, 1979.* 11a. Reunión Día de la Fraternidad del Estado de México, Monte de las Cruces, octubre 30 de 1979. Toluca: Gobierno del Estado de México, 1979. 210 p.; bibl.; ill.

Proceedings of conference whose theme was battle of Monte de la Cruces, important event in Hidalgo's insurrection. Includes brief analyses of historiography, battle events, and bibliography.

2098 Reyes, Candelario. De como y por quien cuenta Tamaulipas con henequenales. Ciudad Victoria, Tamaulipas: Universidad Autonoma de Tamaulipas, Instituto de Investigaciones Históricas, 1980. 51 p.; 3 leaves of plates; ill.

Largely a descriptive rather than interpretive essay about how and by whom henequen was introduced in Tamaulipas.

2099 Riese, Berthold. Kulturelle Aspekte indianischer Gewalt in Kastenkrieg in Yukatan (JGSWGL, 15, 1978, p. 29–40, tables)

Explains Caste War's cultural aspects. Indians created messianic movement based on traditional culture and values. One group separated totally from the national movement.

2100 Rivera Ruiz, Roberto Javier. Recopilación hemerográfica: José María González y González, 1840–1912 (CEHSMO, 5:19, mayo 1980, 2. época, p. 30–40)

Reproduces six articles written by an exponent of workers' rights and problems during late 19th century. González looked for harmony among all classes and never opposed private property. Article includes brief analysis of his ideas.

2101 Rivière, Henri Laurent. La marina francesa en México. Traducida directamente del francés por Renato Gutiérrez Zamora. Preliminar de Leonardo Pasquel. México: Editorial Citaltepetl, 1967. 259 p.; 39 leaves of plates; ill. (Colección Suma veracruzana: Serie Traducciones)

Translation of *La marine française au Mexique.* History (first published 1881) of French Navy during the intervention in Mexico. Author was Navy officer during French invasion.

2102 Rock, Michael J. Antón Chico and its patent (JW, 19:3, July 1980, p. 86–91, ill., map)

Author traces history of Antón Chico land grant in New Mexico from the 1820s to its final legal disposition almost a century later (see items **2062** and **2116**).

2103 Rosado, José María. "A refugee of the War of the Castes makes Belize his home": the memoirs of J.M. Rosado by Richard Buhler. Belize City: Belize Institute for Social Research and Action, 1970? 19 p.; ill. (Occasional publications—BISRA; no. 2)

Memoirs of a witness to the Caste War. Describes role played by war refugees in forming Belize.

2104 Rosenbaum, Robert J. Mexicano resistance in the Southwest: "the sacred right of self-preservation." Austin: University of Texas Press, 1981. 241 p.; bibl.; ill.; index. (The Dan Danciger publication series)

Describes resistance of Mexican US residents to American encroachments in Texas, New Mexico, and California, 1848–1916. Sympathetic portrayal of issue from Mexican point of view. Based on extensive use of archival materials, folklore, and newspapers.

2105 Ruibal Corella, Juan Antonio. Perfiles de un patriota: la huella del general Ignacio Pesqueira García en el noroeste de México. Prólogo de Héctor Aguilar Camín. México: Editorial Porrúa, 1979. 251 p.; 1 leaf of plates; bibl.; ill.

Biography of military and political leader who fought for liberal cause and against French intervention and filibusters. Concludes that, on the whole, Pesqueira left favorable legacy as progressive, charismatic leader whose major fault was desire to remain in power. Based on substantial primary and secondary sources.

2106 Ruiz, Ramón Eduardo and **Mario T. García.** Conquest and annexation (UCSD/NS, 7:1/2, 1978 [i.e. 1979] p. 237–254, bibl.)

Discusses effects of conquest on Indian population, colonization of Mexico during Mexican War, and effects of American expansion overseas in Puerto Rico, Philippines, and Guam in late 19th century. Includes bibliography.

2107 Schoonover, Thomas. Anteproyecto de Thomas Corwin para un tratado comercial en 1861 (CM/HM, 38:4, abril/junio 1979, p. 596–609)

Discussion of diplomatic background of US Ambassador Thomas Corwin's proposed commercial treaty with Mexico. Reflects shift in US policy from territorial expansion to economic penetration. Includes complete text of proposed treaty.

2108 ———. Misconstrued mission: expansionism and black colonization in Mexico and Central America during the Civil War (UC/PHR, 49:4, Nov. 1980, p. 607–620)

Examination of project by US government during Civil War to establish colonies of freed slaves in Mexico and Central America. Project eventually failed due primarily to fears of American expansionism. Primary emphasis is on Central America.

2109 Schryer, Frans J. A ranchero economy in northwestern Hidalgo: 1889–1920 (HAHR, 59:3, Aug. 1979, p. 418–443)

Analyzes social and economic structure of rural region in Hidalgo inhabited by ranchero, landowning farmers. Concludes that many rancheros were not poor family farmers relying on their own and their families' labor. Many employed wage laborers and rented out land to sharecroppers and could exercise effective political and economic power in their areas. Pre-revolutionary Mexico was more than a dichotomy between hacendados and landless peasants.

2110 Shur, Leonid A. Kyrill Khelbnikov's diaries of his travels in Spanish California, 1820–1831: a new source material on the history and ethnology of Mexico (IAA, 5:4, 1979, p. 343–352, bibl.)

Travel notes by Russian adventurer written for the Russian-American Company. Notes reveal his conservatism, monarchism and lack of sympathy for Mexico's independence. They include useful records of conversations and correspondence with merchants, resident foreigners, clergy, and California political figures, as well as data on social life, cultural make-up, geography and California demography.

2111 Sierra, Carlos J. Los indios de la frontera México-Estados Unidos. México: Ediciones de la Muralla, 1980. 113 p.; 2 folded leaves of plates; bibl.; ill.

Studies northern border conflict between fierce Indians and Mexican towns during 19th century (1821–85). Argues that northern tribes were more valuable in defense of North American agression than history leads one to believe.

2112 Silva Herzog, Jesús. De la historia de México, 1810–1938: documentos fundamentales, ensayos y opiniones. México: Siglo Veintiuno Editores, 1980. 300 p.; bibl. (Historia)

Collection of major historical documents of modern Mexico: Iturbide's proclamation of independence, Treaty of Guadalupe, and Cárdenas decree on oil expropriation. Historical background accompanies some of documents. Includes brief bibliography.

2113 Sinkin, Richard N. The Mexican reform, 1855–1876: a study in liberal nation-building. Austin: Institute of Latin American Studies, University of Texas at Austin, 1979. 263 p.; bibl.; index (Latin American monographs; no. 49)

Well-researched study of Mexican Liberals as nation-building elite. Liberal leadership is depicted as young, upwardly-mobile, and anti-Church. Author demonstrates that Liberal leadership was neither "populist" nor "popular" in its outlook and was concerned with questions of power and legitimacy. Liberal policy helped to promote nationalism but also played major role in Mexico's economic dependency on the US.

2114 Staples, Anne. Alfabeto y catecismo, salvación del nuevo país (CM/HM, 29:1, julio/sept. 1979, p. 35–58, bibl.)

Amid economic and political disruptions in Mexico following independence, only education made any notable advances. Secondary and higher education were considered more important than primary education; however, this did not mean that primary education was ignored. Nation's leaders wanted to extend primary education but were often restrained by economic crises.

2115 Sten, María. Brasseur de Bourbourg y el Emperador Maximiliano (CH/MH, 27:1, julio/sept. 1977, p. 141–148)

Brief biographical sketch of this ethnographer and writer of prehispanic history. Article reproduces Brasseur's lengthy letter about encounters with Maximilian and Carlota. At issue is why the governor of Yucatán refused to allow him to do excavations in the area. Article lacks interpretations and conclusions.

2116 Stoller, Marianne L. Grants of desperation, lands of speculation: Mexican period land grants in Colorado (JW, 19:3, July 1980, p. 22–39, ill., maps)

Author examines efforts of Mexican government to secure its boundary in north through large land grants. Concludes that grants may not have always been in strict conformity with law but that they did conform to Hispanic and Mexican land-grant practice.

2117 Suárez, Eusebio. Toluca en 1866: descripción de la ciudad, historia y noticias estadísticas (Boletín del Archivo General del Estado de México [Toluca] 3, sept./dic. 1979, p. 3–17, facsims., ill.)

General description of Toluca and events of the time as recorded in 1866 by town's mayor Eusebio Suárez. Notes and introduction by Rodolfo Alanis Boyzo.

2118 Suárez y Navarro, Juan. Informe sobre las causas y carácter de los frecuentes cambios políticos . . . Yucatán ante la creación del Estado de Campeche. México: Ediciones de la Muralla, 1979. 101 p.

Reprint of original published 1861 about political differences between Yucatán and Campeche and formation of Campeche state.

2119 Tabasco, México (state). Governor, 1887–1894. Memoria sobre el estado de la administración pública de Tabasco. Presentada a la H. Legislatura por el gobernador constitucional C. Simón Sarlat, diciembre 8 de 1890. 2. ed. facsimilar. México: Consejo Editorial del Gobierno del Estado de Tabasco, 1979. 215 p. (Serie Historia; 5)

Reprint of original document issued 1890 by state governor Sarlat (1887–94).

2120 Terradas, Ignasi. Orden social y economía política: un replanteamiento a partir de la historia industrial mexicana (CM/RE, 1:2, primavera 1980, p. 55–131, bibl.)

Lengthy monograph studies tensions between mercantilist political economy and nationalist political economy in 19th-century Mexico within context of industrialization. Includes valuable bibliography.

2121 Timmons, W.H. The El Paso area in the Mexican period, 1821–1848 (TSHA/SHQ, 84:1, July 1980, p. 1–28)

Descriptive, chronological study of area under Mexican government.

2122 Torre, León Alejo. Apuntes históricos de Tabasco: o sea ojeada sobre el primer período constitucional de la administración de Dn. Victorio V. Dueñas. 2. ed. México: Consejo Editorial del Gobierno del Estado de Tabasco, 1979. 110 p. (Serie Historia; 10)

Analysis of administration of Victorio N. Dueñas, governor of Tabasco (1857–60), first published 1862.

2123 Tyler, Daniel. Mexican Indian policy in New Mexico (UNM/NMHR, 55:2, April 1980, p. 101–120)

Study focuses on efforts to develop and implement a policy in regard to nomadic Indians of northern Mexican frontier. While policy formulation and execution was often left in local hands, author concludes that frontier Indian policy often continued Spanish policy of late colonial period with its emphasis on gift giving, trade, Indian allies, and peace treaties.

2124 Valadés, José C. Breve historia de la guerra con los Estados Unidos. 2. ed.

México: Editorial Diana, 1980. 220 p.

Sympathetic history of Mexican War commends valor and sacrifices of Mexican soldiers against superior American forces.

2125 Vanderwood, Paul J. Disorder and progress: bandits, police, and Mexican development. Lincoln: University of Nebraska Press, 1981. 1 v.; bibl.; index.

Examination of interrelationship of order, disorder, and development in Mexico from colonial period to early 20th century. Emphasizes period 1857–1911, especially activities of rurales under Díaz (see also item **2126** and *HLAS 40:2668–2669*).

2126 ———. Mexico's rurales: image of a society in transition (HAHR, 61:1, Feb. 1981, p. 52–83)

Uses personnel records to study nation's massive and unsettled lower classes, given that all guards recruited during Porfiriato were common people from central part of country (e.g., recruitment, dropout rates, desertions, drinking, discharges, punishments, occupational backgrounds, etc.). Rurales' inability to retain personnel reflected nature of Porfiriato and Mexican society's instability. Both society and rurales became less stable as Díaz government wore on. But when the Revolution broke out, rurales proved steadfast in defense of the government, not surprisingly since "war tends to firm up units that had been desultory in peacetime."

2127 Villoro, Luis. La independencia mexicana y la norteamericana: paralelos y divergencias (Meyibó [UNAM, Mexico] 1:2, sept. 1979, p. 57–72)

Discussion of comparable and contrasting features of US and Mexican independence. Concludes that situations of dependency and ideas of liberty and democracy were different for both countries. Both revolutions retained previous groups in power and preserved the former social structures.

2128 Walker, David. Porfirian labor politics: working class organizations in Mexico City and Porfirio Díaz, 1876–1902 (AAFH/TAM, 37:3, Jan. 1981, p. 257–289)

Author challenges traditional interpretations of Porfirian labor policy which classified Díaz regime as either repressive or neutral in its labor relations. Such interpretations were based on over emphasis of labor radicalism in Porfiriato's last decade. Author concludes that there were "few fundamental differences" in pre-revolutionary and post-revolutionary labor policy.

2129 Walker, Samuel Hamilton. Samuel H. Walker's account of the Mier expedition. Edited with an introd. by Marilyn McAdams Sibley. Austin: Texas State Historical Association, 1978. 110 p.; bibl.; ill.; index.

Well-edited presentation of Walker's diary and personal accounts dealing with the Mier expedition that resulted in his capture, his march to Mexico City, and his later escape from Mexico.

2131 Weber, David J. American westward expansion and the breakdown of relations between pobladores and "indios bárbaros" on Mexico's northern frontier: 1821–1846 (UNM/NMHR, 56:3, July 1981, p. 221–238)

Although a continuation of 18th-century Indian policies lost their effectiveness in controlling northern border, American expansion westward made those policies impossible.

2132 ———. Failure of a frontier institution: the secular church in the borderlands under independent Mexico: 1821–1846 (WHQ, 12:2, April 1981, p. 125–143)

Well-organized and written account of failure of secularization on northern Mexican frontier. Author attributes failure to weak leadership, decline in number of secular clergy, Church's fiscal problems, and decline in morale and morality on the part of frontier secular clergy. Winner of 1980 Bolton Award in Spanish Borderlands History.

2133 Wells, Allen. Actuación de los Molina y los Peón en el Yucatán porfiriano (UY/R, 22:128, marzo/abril 1980, p. 41–61)

Analyzes and amplifies idea that henequen plantation owners constantly fought a paradox: how to assure income during economic instability. Studies two families and their ability to adapt to economic change and diversify their enterprises. Ability to adapt to change may explain why revolution arrived late in Yucatán.

2134 Werne, Joseph Richard. Esteban Cantú y la soberanía mexicana en Baja California (CM/HM, 30:1, julio/sept. 1980, p. 1–32, bibl.)

Discusses Mexican fears to lose sov-

ereignty and control of Baja California in early part of 20th century. Recounts efforts of Cantú to preserve area's territorial rights from threats by US and political pressure from Mexico City.

2135 Zaragoza, Ignacio. Ignacio Zaragoza, correspondencia y documentos. Selección, introd. y notas de Jorge L. Tamayo. México: Centro de Investigación Científica Jorge L. Tamayo, Consejo Editorial del Gobierno del Estado de Puebla, 1979. 374 p.; 4 leaves of plates; bibl.; ill.

Collection of diverse writings of Zaragoza during his military campaigns against the French.

2136 Zavala, Silvio. Apuntes sobre relaciones culturales entre Francia y México (CAM, 224:3, mayo/junio 1979, p. 168–176)

Contrasts current official relations between Mexico and France with those of the 19th century which resulted from spontaneous forces to infuse French education, culture and art models in Mexico.

REVOLUTION AND POST-REVOLUTION

2137 Abad de Santillán, Diego. Ricardo Flores Magón, el apóstol de la revolución social mexicana. México: Centro de Estudios Históricos del Movimiento Obrero Mexicano, 1978. 121 p. (Cuadernos obreros; 18)

Brief, sympathetic account of personality and political career of Flores Magón. Contains lengthy citations of his documents and letters.

2138 Aguilar Camín, Héctor. Nociones presidenciales de cultura nacional: de Alvaro Obregón a Gustavo Díaz Ordaz, 1920–1968 (*in* Seminario de Historia de la Cultura Nacional, Instituto Nacional de Antropología e Historia, 1976. En torno a la cultura nacional. Héctor Aguilar Camín *et al.* México: Instituto Nacional Indigenista, Secretaría de Educación, Pública, 1976, p. 95–133 [Colección SEP-INI; 51])

Interesting review of presidential ideas on roles of education, the Revolution, and intellectuals in 20th-century Mexican culture.

2139 Aguirre Benavides, Adrián. Errores de Madero. México: Editorial Jus, 1980.

178 p. (Documentos históricos de la Revolución Mexicana)

Praises activities and ideas of Madero who initiated the Revolution. Nevertheless, points out his errors, specifically: 1) ingratitude toward those who helped him launch the Revolution; 2) the Treaty of Ciudad Juárez; 3) the De la Barra interim presidency; 4) expenses of the Revolution; 5) Limantour's influence on Madero; 6) use of laywers in revolutionary forces; 7) imposition of Pino Suárez as vice-president; 8) formation of his cabinet; 9) nepotism; 10) imposition of his choices for certain governorships; 11) incapacity to govern. Includes Madero documents. Lacks bibliography.

2140 Alanís, José Luz. ¡Los marrazos no hacen ruido!: vida y hazañas del general Lázaros S. Alanís, cuyo artero asesinato en Ixmiquilpan, Hgo., constituye una de las manchas más negras en la historia de la Revolución Mexicana y que mina el prestigio de muchos que se ostentaron como triunfadores en el movimiento. México: Litográfica Limón, 1979. 64 p.; ill.

Author recounts deeds and activities of his father during the Revolution.

2141 Alanís Boyso, Rodolfo. Notas sobre la Revolución de 1910 en Toluca (Boletín del Archivo General del Estado de México [Toluca] 7, enero/abril 1981, p. 7–14, ill.)

Describes political, economic, and social situation of Toluca in 1910 and narrates principal events in area from 1910–20. Author notes that Revolution disrupted social, political, and economic progress of the area only to be recovered during the 1940s.

Angelier, Jean-Pierre. Le secteur de l'énergie au Mexique. See *HLAS 43:2980.*

Archives and manuscripts on microfilm in the Nettie Lee Benson Latin American Collection: a checklist. See *HLAS 42:91.*

2142 Arias, Patricia and **Lucía Bazán.** Demandas y conflicto: el poder político en un pueblo de Morelos. Portada, Marcos Kurtycz. México: Centro de Investigaciones Superiores del Instituto Nacional de Antropología e Historia: Editorial Nueva Imagen, 1979. 180 p.; bibl.; ill.

Discussion of change in political power from ayuntamiento elected by town meeting to one chosen by small local elite. Covers period dating from 1935, when the

town, Tetela del Volcan, became a *municipio libre*. Political change was made possible by competition between two families and their relatives, friends and clients.

2143 Arreola, Antonio. Francisco Villa, biografía ilustrada. Portada, pirografía en madera Villa campesino, de Fernando Mijares Calderón. 2. ed. s.l.: s.n., 1979 or 1980. 174 p.; bibl.; ill.

Chronological, factural history of Villa with interesting photographs.

2144 Ashby, Joe C. La organización obrera y la Revolución Mexicana bajo el régimen de Lázaro Cárdenas (CEHSMO, 5 : 19, mayo 1980, 2. época, p. 17–29)

Elaborates on theories, philosophy, and leadership of workers' movement during Cárdenas era. Concludes that socioeconomic theory of Cárdenas regime followed middle course between socialism and capitalism. Intention was to follow soviet model while allowing Mexico to maintain good relations with US.

2145 Baird, Peter and **Ed McCaughan.** Beyond the border: Mexico & the U.S. today. With investment profile by Marc Herold. Index by Zoia Horn. Designed by Rini Templeton. Assisted by Tessa Martínez and Elizabeth Patelke. New York: North American Congress on Latin America, 1979. 205 p.; bibl.; ill.; index.

Decidedly leftist portrayal of workers' struggle in both countries.

2146 Barkin, David and **Gustavo Esteva.** Inflación y democracia: el caso de México. México: Siglo XXI Editores, 1979. 167 p.; bibl. (Economía y demografía)

Authors argue that inflation, as in this case study, is a reflection of interaction among social groups. Solution to Mexico's inflation is to increase political participation among rural and urban workers, though authors admit it might be an unrealistic solution.

2147 Batallas de la Revolución y sus corridos. Edited by Daniel Moreno. Mexico: Editorial Porrua, 1978. 169 p.; ill.; maps.

Sketches of 15 battles of the Revolution (1911–16). Presentation is pro-Villa and anti-Carranza.

2148 Benítez, Fernando. Lázaro Cárdenas y la Revolución Mexicana. v. 1, El por-

firismo. v. 2, El caudillismo. v. 3, El cardenismo. México: Fondo de Cultura Económica, 1977/1978. 3 v.; bibl. (Sección de obras
de historia)

History of Cárdenas from infancy
and youth to military years of Revolution
through administrations of Carranza, Obregón, and Calles. Ends prior to 1934 election.
Based on secondary sources.

2149 Benjamín, Thomas. Revolución interrumpida: Chiapas y el interreinato
presidencial, 1911 (CM/HM, 30:1, julio/sept.
1980, p. 79–98)

Excellent study of confused situation
that existed in Chiapas during interim presidency of Francisco León de la Barra. Focus is
on struggle over governorship which produced four governors in four months as well
as two revolts. Net result of confusion at
both state and federal levels was placement
of a porfirista in the governorship.

2150 Blanquel, Eduardo. El anarco-mago-
nismo (Meyibó [UNAM, México] 1:2,
sept. 1979, p. 89–118)

Review of materialist, political, economic, and revolutionary thinking of Ricardo
Flores Magón.

2151 Boils Morales, Guillermo. El movimiento de los trabajadores en Yucatán
durante la gubernatura de Salvador Alvarado,
1915–1917 (UNAM/RMS, 41[41]:3, julio/
sept. 1979, p. 621–649)

Government of Yucatán created sym-
biotic relationship with workers. It created
positive climate for growth of labor organizations in order to guarantee itself a base of
support. Both fought, common enemy: regional oligarchy of landowners. Alvarado's
administration helped to form Yucatán's
proletariat.

2152 Buve, Raymond. Peasant mobilization
and reform intermediaries during the
1930s: the development of a peasant clientele
around the issues of land and labor in a central Mexican highland municipio; Huamantla, Tlaxcala (JGSWGL, 17, 1980, p.
355–393, maps)

Studies peasant mobilization by local
politicians in 1930s. Considers possibility
that such mobilization led to riots in 19th
century. Examines problems of maintaining
peasant clientele which became, in late
1930s, focus of competition for mobilization

by state and federal interests. Author presents compelling study of local control and
personal power during height of agrarian
reform.

2153 Calles, Plutarco Elías. Declaraciones y
discursos políticos. México: Ediciones
del Centro de Documentación Política, 1979.
195 p.; bibl. (Cuadernos de causa; 12)

Collection of Calles' speeches, interviews, and proclamations. Introduction
states that selections show Calles was not
merely reacting to his times but that his
thinking was based on a definite philosophy.

2154 Camacho, Manuel. La clase obrera en
la historia de México. v. 15, El futuro
inmediato. México: Siglo XXI, 1980. 167 p.;
tables.

Discusses options available for future
relations of the working class in Mexico.
Concludes that strategies of center are most
viable options in face of constant threat of
dictatorship. Author calls upon the workers
to continue to work within their alliances
and organizations.

2155 Camp, Roderic Ai. Mexico's leaders:
their education and recruitment.
Tuscon: University of Arizona Press, 1980.
259 p.; bibl.; index.

Using interviews and extensive background and career data on political and educational elites (1935–75) author traces importance of university degree for political
recruitment, growing centrality of UNAM as
career pool for national government, and extensive personal networks. Educational networks and socialization experiences help
overcome discontinuity in government.
Shows that experience in PRI is no longer
prerequisite for achieving political office.
While elites have mastered art of advancement through small groups and networks
they may be unable in future to appeal to
large groups or acquire broad based support.
For political scientist's comment, see *HLAS
43:6104.*

2156 Campa S., Valentín. Mi testimonio:
experiencias de un comunista mexicana. México: Ediciones de Cultura Popular,
1978. 360 p.; ill.

Wide ranging but personal and slanted
account of author's career as labor leader
(1920–60). Contains factual errors regarding
1959 railroad strike and CIA operations during it.

2157 Cardiel Reyes, Raúl. La democracia social (CAM, 226:5, sept./oct. 1979, p. 55–74)

Well-written essay discusses formulation of Mexico's social democracy following Revolution in terms of property, culture, and politics. Ties development of modern Mexico to liberal ideas of 19th century and to socialist ideas of the 20th.

2158 Cardoso, Lawrence A. Mexican emigration to the United States, 1897–1931. Tucson: University of Arizona Press, 1980. 192 p.; bibl.; maps; tables.

Examination of emigration process from a basically Mexican point of view. Author demonstrates that system of emigration was already well established by outbreak of 1910 Revolution and that efforts by Mexican government to reduce number of emigrants were essentially unsuccessful. Basic work for study of immigration question.

2158a ———. Protestant missionaries and the Mexican: an environmentalist image of cultural differences. See *HLAS 43:8080.*

2159 Carr, Barry. Recent regional studies of the Mexican Revolution (LARR, 15:1, 1980, p. 3–14)

Succinct exposition of value of regional studies which links local aspects of Revolution to the whole. Article's merit is to show how regional studies can fit into complete framework for studying the Revolution. Readers should not expect to find detailed analysis of works, though many are cited in footnotes.

2160 Casasola, Gustavo. Seis siglos de historia gráfica de México, 1325–1925. v. 6/8, 10/11. Recopilación y fotografía del "archivo Casasola." 4. ed. México: s.n., 1968– . 5 v.; coats of arms; facsims.; ill.; maps; ports.

Multivolume political, social, economic, military, cultural, athletic history of Mexico in photographs during 20th century. Includes text.

2161 Caudillo and peasant in the Mexican Revolution. Edited by D.A. Brading. Cambridge, Eng.; New York: Cambridge University Press, 1980. 311 p.; bibl.; index; map (Cambridge Latin American studies; 38)

Covers peasant uprisings in various regions (e.g., Sonora, Guerrero, San Luis Potosí); areas where no significant uprisings occurred are also examined (e.g., Yucatán, Veracruz, Tlaxcala, Michoacán). Essays show that what took place was mass mobilization under the control of caudillos who helped to institutionalize the Revolution and to consolidate the modern Mexican state.

2162 Cerutti, Mario. La formación de capitales en Monterrey en las décadas anteriores a su industrialización, 1850–1890 (Revista Coahuilense de Historia [Colegio Coahuilense de Investigaciones Históricas, Saltillo, México] 2:12, marzo/abril 1980, p. 134–166, appendices)

Capitalist formation in Monterrey was based on appropriation and exploitation of land, commerce, speculation, loans, and emergence of manufacturing. Discusses effects of national and international instability on area and major families involved in industrialization process.

2163 Ching Vega, Oscar W. La última cabalgata de Pancho Villa. Chihuahua, México: Centro Librero La Prensa, 1977. 180 p.; ill.

Journalist writes about exhumation and transportation of Villa's remains from Chihuahua to Mexico City.

2164 Cleaves, Peter S. Mexican politics: an end to the crisis? (LARR, 16:2, 1981, p. 191–202)

Review essay about the following works which address the crisis of Mexican economy and politics between 1965–81: Judith Adler Hellman's *Mexico in crisis* (New York: Holmes and Meier, 1978); Kenneth F. Johnson's *Mexican democracy: a critical view* (New York: Praeger, 1978); Yoram Shapira's *Mexican foreign policy under Echeverría* (London: Sage Publications, 1978); Peter H. Smith's *Labyrinths of power: political recruitment in twentieth century Mexico* (Princeton: Princeton University Press, 1979); John Walton's *Elites and economic development: comparative studies on the political economy of Latin American cities* (Austin: Institute of Latin American Studies, University of Texas, 1977); and Pablo González Casanova's and Enrique Florescano's *Mexico, hoy* (Mexico: Siglo XXI, 1979).

2165 Coalson, George O. The development of the migratory farm labor system in Texas: 1900–1954. San Francisco: R and E Research Associates, 1977. 132 p.; bibl.; maps.

Primary focus is on the institutional structure of migratory labor rather than on the interaction between workers and employers, or on social circumstances of Mexican workers. Concentrates more on the American side than on the Mexican.

2166 Coerver, Don M. and Linda B. Hall. Revolution on the Rio Grande: Governor Colquitt of Texas and the Mexican Revolution, 1911–1915. San Antonio: Trinity University Press, 1981. 92 p. (Border research series; 5)

Examination of Texas-Mexican border during early years of Revolution. Particular emphasis is devoted to problem of coordinating federal and state activities in face of more activist and sometimes belligerent policy pursued by state officials. Based on state and federal archives.

2167 Córdova, Arnaldo. La clase obrera en la historia de México. v. 9, En una época de crisis: 1928–1934. México: Siglo XXI Editores, 1980. 240 p.

Discussion of problems of working class during tumultuous years 1928–34 in which Mexico suffered political and economic crises. Workers regained stature in Mexico's development through efforts of Vicente Lombardo Toledano and Lázaro Cárdenas who believed that the working class was the strength of state.

2168 Corral viuda de Villa, Luz. Pancho Villa en la intimidad. Prólogo a la 1. ed. por José Vasconcelos. Prólogo a la 2. ed. por Alfonso Escárcega C. 4. ed. Chihuahua, México: Centro Librero la Prensa, 1977. 273 p.; ill.

Memoirs of Villa's last wife. Tries to diminish criticism that he robbed, murdered and inflicted violence upon Mexico during the Revolution. States that all wars and revolutions suffer from such events and persons. Presents positive and negative sides of Villa in a sympathetic style.

2169 La CROM, de Luis N. Morones a Antonio J. Hernández. Favio Barbosa Cano, comp. Puebla, México: ICUAP, Editorial Universidad Autónoma de Puebla, 1980. 476 p.; bibl. (Biblioteca Francisco Javier Clavijero. Serie mayor. Colección Fuentes para el estudio de la historia del movimiento obrero y sindical en México)

Brief historical description of leadership and activities of CROM from its origins

(1918–46). Majority of book contains reprints of documents and proclamations.

2170 DeWalt, Billie R. Modernization in a Mexican ejido: a study in economic adaptation. New York: Cambridge University Press, 1979. 303 p. (Cambridge Latin American studies; 33)

Studies on ejido in northwestern Mexico. Studies difference in wealth, leadership in the community, the operation of the religious cargo system, and abuse of alcohol.

2171 Dromundo, Baltasar. Crónica de la autonomía universitaria de México. México: Editorial Jus, 1978. 218 p.; ill.

Commemorative work on 50th anniversary of granting of autonomy to National University in 1929. As student activist at the time, author displays distinct bias toward student movement, characterizing concession of autonomy as response to student demands.

2172 Ehrlich, Paul R.; Loy Bilderbach; and Anne H. Ehrlich. The golden door: international migration, Mexico and the United States. New York: Ballantine, 1979. 402 p.

History and analysis of Mexican immigration, border industry, agrarian problems, and demography. Book suffers from numerous factual errors. Authors argue for humane immigration policy but recognize complexity of problem.

2173 Emiliano Zapata y el movimiento zapatista. México: Instituto Nacional de Antropología e Historia, 1980. 381 p.; bibl.

Series of articles on Zapatismo discuss activities of local leaders, movements' origins, Zapata historiography, and Marxist interpretations of movement. Each selection includes bibliography.

2174 Entrevistas con un solo tema: Lázaro Cárdenas por Fernando Benítez. México: Facultad de Ciencias Políticas y Sociales, Universidad Nacional Autónoma de México, 1979. 124 p. (Serie Estudios; 61)

Collection of memoirs of various individuals who had contact with Cárdenas. Different points of view are presented.

2175 Esteves, José. Historia oral: entrevista con Dionisio Encinas (CEHSMO, 5 : 19, mayo 1980, 2. época, p. 6–14)

Memoirs of a miner who witnessed Revolution's military years as young boy in

Zacatecas. Contains lengthy account of Villa's activities. His family supported the Revolution.

2176 Estrada Hernández, Elisa. Pensamiento y acción del campesino del centro-sur de México durante la Revolución (Boletín del Archivo General del Estado de México [Toluca] 2, mayo/agosto 1979, p. 8–9, facsim.)

Summary of activities of Zapata and peasant movement in Morelos and state of Mexico. Article maintains that Plan de Ayala and return of communal lands justified revolutionary activity. Actioñs and thought of peasants and Zapata were not only product of revolutionary era but stemmed from policies of Díaz era.

2177 Fabela, Isidro. La política interior y exterior de Carranza. Editado por la Comisión de Investigaciones Históricas de la Revolución Mexicana. México: Editorial Jus, 1979. 269 p.; bibl. (Documentos históricos de la Revolución Mexicana)

Analyses of Carranza's rise to power in Mexico and his dealings with US in terms of occupation of Veracruz, Pershing Expedition and Zimmermann Telegram. Also includes analysis of Carranza's rejection of Monroe Doctrine.

2178 ———. La victoria de Carranza. México: Editorial Jus, 1978. 327 p.

Principal architect of Carrancismo hails Carranza as leader of the "social revolution of 1913," one who translated revolutionary principles into the Constitution of 1917 in spite of opposition from Villa, Zapata, and other assorted undesirable elements.

2179 Falcón, Romana. ¿Los orígenes populares de la Revolución de 1910?: el caso de San Luis Potosí (CM/HM, 29:2, oct./dic. 1979, p. 197–240)

Detailed examination of political situation in key Mexican state in late Porfiriato and early Revolution. While evaluating Revolution's popular origins, author presents complicated picture of political and military interaction involving "ambivalent elite," middle class elements, urban workers, and peasants. Concludes that early leaders of Revolution were united on one point: restricting political participation by the masses.

2180 ———. Veracruz: los límites del radicalismo en el campo, 1920–1934

(UNAM/RMS, 41[41]:3, julio/sept. 1979, p. 671–698)

Discusses rise of agrarian radicalism in Veracruz under leadership of Adalberto Tejada and subsequent events that led to centralization of agrarian reform in national government.

2181 Flores Magón, Ricardo. Artículos políticos: 1910–1911. México: Ediciones Antorcha, 1980. 2 v. (142, 21 p.)

Collection of articles and editorials from *Regeneración* as well as selections from his private correspondence.

2182 ———. Discursos. 2. ed. México: Ediciones Antorcha, 1979. 103 p.

Reproduction of revolutionary leader's various speeches.

2183 ———. Epistolario revolucionario e íntimo. 2. ed. México: Ediciones Antorcha, 1978. 243 p.

Letters translated from their original English, with the exception of those addressed to Nicolás T. Bernal, Mexico. Collection of his letters and documents.

2184 Friedlander, Judith. The secularization of the cargo system: an example from postrevolutionary central Mexico (LARR, 16:2, 1981, p. 132–143, bibl.)

Suggests that a new cargo system has been emerging in Central Mexico to meet 20th-century needs. Native school teachers, trained by federal government, have taken over original Hispanic Catholic cargo system. Government continues colonial tradition of taking patches of indigenous customs and transforming them into nationalistic system of postrevolutionary Mexico.

2185 Gámiz, Everardo. La Revolución en el Estado de Durango. Durango, México: s.n., 1978. 72 p.; ill.

Brief, general history of revolutionary events in Durango.

2186 García, Genaro. Leona Vicario, heroína insurgente. México: Editorial Innovación, 1979. 210 p.; 21 p. of plates; bibl.; ill.

Reprint of 1910 edition of biography of woman who helped insurgent cause during independence.

2187 Garza Sáenz, Ernesto. Rurales de Camargo fusilaron al General Eugenio Aguirre Benavides (Revista Coahuilense de Historia [Colegio Coahuilense de Investigaciones Históricas, Saltillo, México] 3 : 13, mayo/junio 1980, p. 58–65)

Account of capture and shooting of Benavides and 12 other soldiers in June 1915, based on recollections of two Camargo natives who participated in event. Author feels killing was deplorable action.

2188 González, Luis. El match Cárdenas-Calles o la afirmación del presidencialismo mexicano (CM/RE, 1 : 1, invierno 1980, p. 5–33, bibl.)

Presents in detail struggle for power between Calles and Cárdenas that led to stronger presidency and enabled Cárdenas to begin major land reform. Based largely on secondary sources with minimal interpretation and strong support for Cárdenas.

2189 González Casanova, Pablo. La clase obrera en la historia de México. v. 6, En el primer gobierno constitucional, 1917–1920. México: Siglo XXI, 1980. 227 p.

Analysis of role of working class in formation of Mexican state (1917–20). In particular, book discusses relations among labor leadership, socialist and communist parties, and government. Promulgation of Constitution of 1917 created diverse ways for workers to deal with government.

2190 González y González, Luis. Los artífices del cardenismo. México: Colegio de México, 1979. 273 p.; bibl.; ill.; index (Historia de la Revolución Mexicana; 14: Período 1934–1940)

Popular narration of political, social, economic, and cultural basis of the Cárdenas years. Includes extensive bibliography.

2191 Guerrero, Práxedis G. Artículos de combate. México: Ediciones Antorcha, 1977. 203 p.

Reproduces various journalistic articles and pronouncements of this revolutionary leader.

2192 Hall, Linda B. Alvaro Obregón: power and revolution in Mexico, 1911–1920. College Station: Texas A&M University Press, 1981. 290 p.; ill.; map.

Major work on Obregón before his assumption of the presidency. Author emphasizes Obregón's role in building various revolutionary coalitions into a political organization which foreshadowed official party established by Calles in late 1920s. Obregón succeeded in identifying the govern-

ment with the Revolution and the Revolution with the masses. Extensive use of archival sources and of interviews with revolutionary participants.

2193 ———. Alvaro Obregón and the politics of Mexican land reform, 1920–1924 (HAHR, 60 : 2, May 1980, p. 213–238, tables)

Fascinating study of Obregón's use of agrarian reform to build political support while operating within larger framework of national economic reconstruction. Author demonstrates that Obregón enjoyed considerable success in using land redistribution to undercut political opposition and to centralize economic and political control in the presidency. Extensive use of archival sources.

2194 Harris, Charles H., III and **Louis R. Sadler.** The 1911 Reyes Conspiracy: the Texas side (TSHA/SHQ, 83 : 4, April 1980, p. 325–48)

Uses sources from FBI to study effects of activities of Bernardo Reyes on Texas. Although Reyes was an inept conspirator, his plans would not have advanced without help from two Texan politicians and the tacit approval of Governor Colquitt. Authors show close collaboration among Texas politicians and provide insight into border history.

2195 Henderson, Peter V.N. Félix Díaz, the Porfirians, and the Mexican Revolution. Lincoln: University of Nebraska Press, 1981. 239 p.; bibl.; index; port.

Félix Díaz demonstrates willingness to reform in early years of Revolution. Although he advocated a return to Porfirian policies that encouraged stability and economic growth, he also knew reforms of the old system were needed. Lack of political acumen, the legacy of the Porfirian Cause, and his name contributed to his failure to hold a prominent place in politics.

2196 Hernández Chávez, Alicia. La defensa de los finqueros en Chiapas: 1914–1920 (CM/HM, 28 : 3, enero/marzo 1979, p. 335–369, tables)

Excellent study of social, political, and economic developments in Chiapas during Porfiriato which led to *finqueros'* dominant position (medium-size landholders). Finqueros retained control during early years of Revolution, resisted "northern invasion" of carrancistas between 1914–20, and emerged victorious in 1920 when Obregón recognized their position.

2197 ———. La mecánica. México: Colegio de México, 1979 [i.e. 1980]. 236 p.; bibl.; ill.; index (Historia de la revolución mexicana; 16: Período 1934–1940)

Analysis of Cárdenas' government and main events and actors: role of workers and peasants, political conflict with Calles, control of military, labor and agrarian reforms, and national party. Author ignores oil expropriation.

2198 Herrera-Sobek, María. The bracero experience: elitelore versus folklore. With an introd. by James W. Wilkie. Los Angeles: UCLA Latin American Center Publications, University of California, 1979. 142 p.; bibl.; discography; index (UCLA Latin American studies; v. 43) (A Book on lore)

Refutes assumptions that *bracero* was subjected to exploitation, fraud and shattered dreams. Studies bracero from two perspectives: as seen by novelists and intellectuals and as perceived by the bracero himself. Contrast is between elitelore and folklore. Literature portrays their experience as negative; bracero describes pleasant experiences, fairminded employers and an awakened awareness of new horizons. Mostly valuable for cultural and literary history.

2199 Hoernel, David. Las grandes corporaciones y la política del gran garrote en Cuba y en México (CM/HM, 30:2, oct./dic. 1980, p. 209–246, table)

Author deals with problem of interaction between government and business policy in the face of inconsistency in foreign policy and major divisions among the US interest groups involved. Employing a "new trust" versus "old trust" division of business interests, work focuses on Mexico, particularly Revolution's early years.

2200 Homick, Stephen J. Soledad y comunión: Octavio Paz y el desarrollo de la idea mexicana de la historia (CAM, 228:1, enero/feb. 1980, p. 99–113)

Discussion of ties among Caso, Ramos, Vasconcelos and Paz in their development of Mexican history. Concludes that Paz is able to weave history, myth, and poetry to develop the Mexican idea of man and culture which also has universal value. Includes bibliography.

2201 Hoyo, Eugenio del. Historiografía mexicana en el siglo XX (UNL/H, 20, 1979, p. 231–241)

Text of author's lecture states that a discussion of 20th-century historiography must contain references to 19th-century works. Both *México a través de los siglos* and *México: su evolución social* are culmination of 19th-century liberalism whose influences persisted into early part of 20th. Latter century topics and themes have dealt with mass participation in revolution, socialism, anarchism, and anticlericalism. Resurrection of indigenous past was countered by a movement in praise of Spanish traditions. Author ends with list of notable writers of philosophy, biography, diplomatic history, institutions, and historiography.

2202 Ianni, Octavio. El estado capitalista en la época de Cárdenas. México: Ediciones Era, 1977. 146 p.; notes; tables.

Well-known Brazilian sociologist analyzes Cárdenas administration and its reform program. Author recognizes political and economic limitations that confronted the program as Cárdenas pursued policies that had capitalistic as well as revolutionary characteristics.

2203 Immigrants and immigrants: perspective on Mexican labor migration to the United States. Edited by Arthur F. Corwin. Westport, Conn.: Greenwood Press, 1978. 378 p.; 6 leaves of plates; bibl.; ill.; index (Contributions in economics and economic history; no. 17)

Series of 13 essays (seven by Corwin), mostly written by historians with contributions by two economists. Corwin's conservative position on Mexicans is noticeable, but his piece on President Carter's immigration policy and dilemma of human rights is necessary to follow development of future US policies. Also valuable are Abraham Hoffman on repatriation during Depression years and Paul Taylor's essays on future of Mexican immigration.

2204 Interpretaciones de la Revolución Mexicana. México: Editorial Nueva Imagen, 1979. 150 p.

Collection of five essays of uneven quality providing various Marxist interpretations of the Mexican Revolution.

2205 Joseph, Gilbert M. The fragile revolution: cacique politics and revolutionary process in Yucatán (LARR, 15:1, 1980, p. 39–64)

Examines rise and fall of revolutionary governor of Yucatán, Felipe Carrillo Puerto, and his attempts to unite local caciques and popular allies in social reform program which he carried out during growing consolidation and centralization of Mexican state Obregón-Calles period. Includes useful discussion of role of caciques and caudillos in Mexican history and their myths in Mexican politics.

2206 ———. Mexico's "popular revolución": mobilization and myth in Yucatán, 1910–1940 (LAP, 6[22]: 3, Summer 1979, p. 46–65, bibl.)

Presents concise summary of revisionist writers who argue that Revolution constituted an aggression from above, from northern, petty-bourgeois who fought to legitimize their authority rather than articulate interests of peasants and workers. Goes on to show that events in Yucatán fit this pattern. Includes bibliography.

2207 Juárez, Antonio. Las corporaciones transnacionales y los trabajadores mexicanos. México: Siglo XXI Editores, 1979. 292 p.; notes; tables.

Polemical examination of growth of multinational corporations and their relationship to automobile industry, government, and trade unions in Mexico. Author believes that combination of unemployment and underemployment has led to unusual degree of control over Mexican workers.

2208 Kane, N. Stephen. The United States and the development of the Mexican petroleum industry, 1945–1950: a lost opportunity (IAMEA, 35:1, Summer 1981, p. 45–72)

Examination of unsuccessful efforts by US and Mexico to "realign their petroleum relations" after World War II. While US worked to gain reentry for American companies into Mexican oil, Mexican government was pushing for a government-to-government loan to expand PEMEX activities. Neither position was ever fully realized.

2209 Katz, Friedrich. Innen- und aussenpolitische Ursachen des mexikanischen Revolutionsverlaufs (JGSWGL, 15, 1978, p. 95–101)

Northern revolutionary movement and its insignificant social-reform activity depended largely on external political factors, such as relations with US during 1910–20. Later success of Cárdenas reforms and failure of conservative revolt are explained by exterior factor of World War II and fact that old oligarchy had been destroyed along with federal military.

2210 Krauze, Enrique. Daniel Cosío Villegas: una biografía intelectual. México: J. Moritz, 1980. 318 p., 16 leaves of plates, bibl., ill., index (Confrontaciones: Los Críticos)

Book reviews Cosío Villegas' theories on social, political, and cultural life of Mexico and Latin America. Discusses his life and major enterprises he created: Fondo de Cultura Económica, El Colegio de México, and *Historia Moderna de México*.

2211 ———. La reconstrucción económica. Con la colaboración de Jean Meyer y Cayetano Reyes. México: Colegio de México, 1977. 323 p., bibl., ill., index (Historia de la Revolución Méxicana; 10: Período 1924–1928)

Vol. 10 of this series on history of Mexican Revolution traces origins, execution and impact of various planks of official policy. Book is organized around themes such as fiscal and administrative reform, banking system, foreign debt, state investment in agriculture, and international trade. Administrative program is viewed as attempt to win sympathy and support of international capitalism for recovery in foreign investment and refinancing the foreign debt.

2211a LaFrance, David G. Madero, Serdán y los albores del movimiento revolucionario en Puebla (CM/HM, 29:3, enero/marzo 1980, p. 472–512)

Well-researched examination of internal factionalism and external repression which accompanied rise of the revolutionary movement in Puebla. Serdán—"radical, intransigent, and authoritarian"—played important role in linking lower class supporters of Mexican Liberal Party with middle-class membership of anti-reelectionist group, but eventually his radicalism alienated more moderate elements.

2212 Lajous, Alejandra. Los orígenes del partido único en México. Mexico: UNAM, 1979. 258 p.: appendices.

Author believes that origins of revolutionary party lay in political views and organizational patterns that existed before 1910. "Personalistic centralism" of Porfirio Díaz ultimately became "presidentialistic government" of later revolutionary regimes.

2213 ———. El Partido Nacional Revolucionario y el congreso de la unión (UNAM/RMS, 41[41]: 3, julio/sept. 1979, p. 651–669)

Demonstrates that PNR transformed diverse political forces into a centralized institution which led to end of personal politics.

2214 Langle Ramírez, Arturo. El militarismo de Victoriano Huerta. México: UNAM, Instituto de Investigaciones Históricas, 1976. 165 p., 5 leaves of plates, bibl., ill. (Cuadernos: Serie histórica, Instituto de Investigaciones Históricas, 17)

Huerta's militarism derived both from the Díaz regime and his youth at Escuela Nacional Preparatoria. Though Huerta may have been the solution to problems facing Mexico at the time, his methods condemned him from the start.

2215 ———. Los primeros cien años de Pancho Villa. México: Costa-Amic, 1980. 165 p., 8 p. of plates: bibl.; discography; ill.

Popular history of Villa. Includes corridos, brief biographical sketch, and bibliography of Villa in fiction, cinema, records, and newspapers.

2216 Leñero Otero, Luis. Sociocultura y población en México: realidad y perspectivas de política. México: Editorial Edicol, 1977. 143 p.

Analyzes sociocultural, economic, and political realities associated with population increase. Less commonly identified variables which have contributed to population growth are revolutionary ideology that equates development with population growth, and stance of Mexican socialists who press for population growth in reaction to American propaganda for small families. Also discusses more common factors contributing to population growth: Catholicism, lack of education, values about large families, machismo, etc. Pessimistic about Mexico's future development.

2217 León Portilla, Miguel. Los manifiestos en náhuatl de Emiliano Zapata. México: Universidad Nacional Autónoma de México, Instituto de Investigaciones Histo-

ricas, 1978. 112 p.; bibl.; ill. (Serie Monografías de cultura náhuatl; 20)

Sociolinguistic study of Zapata pronouncements in Nahuatl. Includes brief discussion of Zapata's attitude toward indigenous groups.

2218 Lerner, Victoria. Los fundamentos socioeconómicos del cacicazgo en el México postrevolucionario: el caso de Saturnino Cedillo (CM/HM, 24: 3, enero/marzo 1980, p. 375–446, bibl., tables)

Analysis of development of agrarian cacique leader. Follows Cedillo's rise (1925–35) from local into national leader, includes details on economy of San Luis Potosí and family background (1910–20). Rise occurred in period when agrarian leaders could rely on peasant support while becoming moderating force in consolidation of political power. His fall occurred between 1935–38 as political power was concentrated in a civilian president. Article contains basis for future research.

2219 ———. Historia de la reforma educativa: 1933–1945 (CM/HM, 28: 1, julio/sept. 1979, p. 91–132)

Excellent discussion of social and political factors that led to introduction of socialist education of groups which supported and opposed it, and of its trajectory during 1934–45. Author clearly demonstrates that educational reform has been more a function of "political-ideological" factors than of educational concerns.

2220 ———. Historia de la Revolución Mexicana, período 1934–1940: la educación socialista. México: El Colegio de México, 1979. 199 p.; ill.; notes; tables.

Latest installment in multivolume *Historia de la Revolución Mexicana* under a Luis González's editorship. Author focuses on politics of Mexican education during its most controversial period, maintaining that controversy surrounding socialist education often obscured importance of reforms being applied and their relationship to overall Cardenas' program.

2221 Lipp, Solomon. Leopoldo Zea: from Mexicanidad to a philosophy of history. Waterloo, Ont.: Wilfrid Laurier University Press, 1980. 146 p.; bibl.; index.

Examines psychoanalytical and sociological approaches to Mexicanidad: Francisco González Pineda, Jorge Carrión, Jorge Segura Millán, Santiago Ramírez, Octavio Paz, Manuel Gamio, Erich Fromm, Maria Elvira Bermúdez, Oscar Lewis, César Garizurieta. For Zea, the heritage of Mexicanidad is point of departure to move from particular Mexican circumstance to universal awareness and a philosophy that will provide an understanding of Western man's alienation. Author observes that Zea is not doing philosophy proper but philosophizing from and about history in order to solve social and political problems. For philosopher's comment, see item **7550**.

2222 Llinás Alvarez, Edgar. Revolución, educación y mexicanidad: la búsqueda de la identidad nacional en el pensamiento educativo mexicano. México: UNAM, 1979, 277 p.

Study of the background, formation, and program of the Ministry of Education under José Vasconcelos. Author sees Vasconcelos as a reconciler of different educational views who was able to use the Ministry of Education to promote national identity.

2223 Loyola Díaz, Rafael. La crisis Obregón-Calles y el estado mexicano. México: Siglo Veintiuno Editores, 1980. 169 p.; bibl. (Sociología y política)

Obregón-Calles' alliance was fortified after victory over Adolfo de la Huerta, but victory did not resolve problem of centralized power. Author studies background of political crisis that culminated in Obregón's attempt to assume the presidency in 1928 and political changes that followed his assassination. Obregón's use of personal power and influence and Calles' use of state institutional machinery were two different methods of governing, but their logical conclusion was to fortify the state's authority and position.

2224 McCain, Johnny M. Texas and the Mexican labor question, 1924–1947 (TSHA/SHQ, 85 : 1, July 1981, p. 45–64)

Presents conflict between Texas farmers and Mexican government concerning laws protecting Mexican workers. Government failed to guarantee such protection while Texas farmers succeeded in nullifying it.

2225 Macias, Anna. Women and the Mexican Revolution: 1910–1920 (AAFH/TAM, 37 : 1, July 1980, p. 53–81)

Discussion of intellectual contributions of three women during Revolution: journalist, school teacher, and Carranza's private secretary, who became supporters of social and anticlerical reforms. Their activities are contrasted with those of conservative women who opposed Constitution's anticlerical provisions. Also includes praise for *soldaderas'* work.

2227 Magdaleno, Mauricio. Escritores extranjeros en la Revolución. México: Patronato del Instituto Nacional de Estudios Históricos de la Revolución Mexicana, 1979. 216 p. (Biblioteca del Instituto Nacional de Estudios Históricos de la Revolución Méxicana; 77)

Brief bibliographical sketches and selections of writings about the Revolution by North Americans, South Americans and Europeans.

2228 Malagón, Javier. El exiliado político español en México: 1939–1977 (ARBOR, 409, enero 1980, p. 26–36, tables)

Brief, positive account of the contributions and activities of political exiles from the Spanish Civil War in Mexico. Praises government's decision to admit them.

2229 Markiewicz, Dana. Ejido organization in Mexico, 1934–1976. Los Angeles: UCLA Latin American Center Publications, 1980. 84 p.; bibl.; index (Special studies—UCLA Latin American Center Publications; v. 1)

Studies development of ejidos from Cárdenas era through Echeverría's administration. Concentrates on collectivization of ejidos under Cárdenas and related difficulties. Problems inherited from Cárdenas years and neglect of ejidos during 1940s and 1950s caused additional difficulties for Echeverría. Studies ejido organization from national level.

2230 Martínez Assad, Carlos R. El laboratorio de la Revolución: el Tabasco garridista. Portada de Anhelo Hernández. México: Siglo Veintiuno Editores, 1979. 309 p., 6 leaves of plates; bibl.; ill. (Historia)

Leftist interpretation of efforts of Mexican leaders to create stability while developing capitalist economy. Studies effects of caudillos and Revolution's institucionalization. Focuses on events in Tabasco and its leader Tomás Garrido Canabal. Includes extensive bibliography.

2231 ———. La rebelión cedillista o el ocaso del poder tradicional (UNAM/RMS, 41[41]: 3, julio/sept. 1979, p. 709–728)

Discusses elements that motivated Cedillo to revolt against Cárdenas in 1938, his position relative to political forces, his ideas concerning the country's political and economic development, and his position on national problems. Cedillo's defeat represented end of caudillismo and solidified government's strength.

2232 Martínez de la Vega, Francisco. Mito y realidades del petróleo en México (CAM, 224: 3, mayo/junio 1979, p. 7–14)

Brief discussion of events leading to 1938 oil expropriation. Author argues that México's resources are not only sources of wealth but a symbol of victory for nationality. Continues this theme in discussing current events about petroleum issue in Mexico.

2233 Matute, Alvaro. Una concesión impugnada: Bahía de Magdalena, 1921 (Meyibó [UNAM, Mexico] 1:2, sept. 1979, p. 73–87)

Text of letter criticizing land grant to US Senator. Letter addressed to Obregón was written by Gen. Amado Aguirre, former official in Carranza administration. Article includes brief introduction and presents summary of relations between US and Mexico at the time.

2234 Medina, Luis. Del Cardenismo al Avilacamachismo. México: Colegio de México, 1978. 410 p. (Historia de la Revolución Mexicana; 18. Período 1940–1952)

Focuses on years 1940–46, mostly domestic politics and social problems, with no foreign affairs. Avila Camacho is portrayed as conciliator between differing political factions and ideological extremes. One section examines three fundamental problems for him: agrarian policy, labor unions, and education. Newspapers constitute the principal sources; US State Department files outweigh Mexican sources.

The Mexican-American War: an annotated bibliography. See item **43**.

2235 Mexican workers in the United States: historical and political perspectives. Edited by George C. Kiser and Martha Woody Kiser. Albuquerque: University of New Mexico Press, 1979. 295 p.; bibl.; index.

Collection of essays that provide historical and political perspectives of Mexican workers in the US. The collection does not include literature that focuses on economic factors involved in Mexican labor migration.

2236 Meyer, Eugenia. La historia oral y la historiografía contemporánea: condiciones metodológicas en América Latina (in Encuentro de Historiadores Latinoamericanos y del Caribe, 2d, Caracas, 1977. Los estudios históricos en América Latina: ponencias, acuerdos y resoluciones: Caracas, 20–26 de marzo de 1977. Caracas: Universidad Central de Venezuela, Facultad de Humanidades y Educación, Escuela de Historia, 1979, v. 1, t. 1, p. 240–248)

Justification for using oral history to study and write history, especially 20th-century Mexico. Describes services on Archivo de la Palabra, Instituto Nacional de Antropología e Historia, which has as its functions the collection and preservation of interviews and oral testimony.

2237 Meyer, Jean A. Estado y sociedad con Calles. Con la colaboración de Enrique Krauze y Cayetano Reyes. Mexico: El Colegio de México, 1977. 371 p.; bibl.; ill.; index (Historia de la Revolución Mexicana; 11: Período 1924–1928)

Characterizes new social order as democratic despotism. Deals extensively with Church-state conflict, foreign affairs, political parties, CROM, and the peasantry. Lumps discussion of peasantry and working class to treatment of CROM *agraristas* and Cristeros. Pays little attention to dominant classes, and has only three pages on middle class.

2238 Meyer, Michael C. Villa, Sommerfeld, Columbus y los alemanes (CM/HM, 28: 4, abril/junio 1979, p. 546–566)

Discussion of persistent questions of why Villa attacked Columbus, New Mexico in March 1916. Meyers discusses Germans' role in inciting Villa's raid to involve the US in war with Mexico. In particular, examines role of German agent Felix Sommerfeld. Though evidence may be strong to support German activities, it is still inconclusive.

2239 Mora Forero, Jorge. Los maestros y la práctica de la educación socialista (CM/HM, 29:1, julio/sept. 1979, p. 133–162)

Discusses some of the difficulties in creating socialist education in various parts of Mexico: parental opposition, Church's attitude, lack of understanding of new doctrine. In addition, teachers were faced with political struggles within labor organizations, and a few were killed in the struggles. Concludes that educational reform was largely a political matter. Includes bibliography.

2240 O'Brien, Dennis J. Petroleo e intervención: relaciones entre los Estados Unidos y México (CH/MH, 27:1, julio/sept. 1977, p. 103–140, bibl., tables)

Examination of Wilson's policy and attitude of US oil companies in the face of Mexican Revolution and need for a continuous flow of oil from Mexico to US. Wilson had to balance oil companies demands for intervention to protect Mexican oil possessions and oil resources need for war in Europe. Concise examination of options presented to Wilson.

2241 Palacios, Guillermo. México en los años treinta (*in* América Latina en los años treinta. Luis Antezana E. *et al.* Coordinador, Pablo González Casanova. Mexico, Instituto de Investigaciones Sociales, UNAM, 1977, p. 515–555)

Mexico suffered social, political, and economic crises between 1929–32 which were resolved by Cárdenas through populist and consolidating social reforms. Cárdenas' measures institutionalized Revolution and assisted development of national bourgeoisie.

Paz, Octavio. Mexico and the United States. See *HLAS 43:7198.*

2242 Perkins, Clifford Alan. Border Patrol: with the U.S. Immigration Service on the Mexican boundary, 1910–1954. El Paso: Texas Western Press, 1978. 126 p., ill.

First hand account of life on the border between 1911–28 by officer who served at Tucson, El Paso, Douglas, Del Rio, Laredo, and San Antonio. The 1954 date comes from rapid switch to author's retirement party at Tijuana in 1954. Good fun and informative.

2243 Posada's Mexico. Edited by Ron Tyler. Washington, D.C., Library of Congress, 1979. 315 p., appendices, ill., notes.

Lavishly-illustrated collection of essays dealing with life and times of person often referred to as "first artist of the Revolution." Posada was best known for his *calaveras*, or skeleton figures, which were used in a wide variety of publications in the late Porfiriato and early revolutionary period. For art historian's comment, see *HLAS 42:1362.*

2244 El Primer jefe por Isidro Fabela. Editado por la Comisión de Investigaciones Históricas de la Revolución Mexicana. 2. ed. México: Editorial Jus, 1980. 200 p. (Documentos históricos de la Revolución Mexicana)

Collection of essays on Carranza and three of his speeches. Popular and sympathetic portrayal of the First Chief.

2245 Raat, W. Dirk. Revoltosos: Mexico's rebels in the United States, 1903–1923. College Station: Texas A&M University Press, 1981. 344 p., 4 leaves of plates; bibl.; ill.; index.

Studies Mexico's rebels in US between Immigration Act of 1903 and end of the Red Scare era in early 1920s. While *revoltosos* were from left and right factions who sought refuge in the US and were generally not in violation of American laws, US government favored moderates rather than radicals or reactionaries. Author devotes most attention to magonistas and maderistas. Includes valuable bibliographical essay.

2246 Revueltas, José. Mexico 68 [i.e. sesenta y ocho]: juventud y revolución. Prólogo de Roberto Escudero. Recopilación y notas de Andrés Revueltas y Philippe Cheron. México: Ediciones Era, 1978. 347 p. (His Obras completas; 15)

Collection of essays, letters, and diary entries on analysis of student movement, theory and practice of self-learning and how it was reflected during student movement. Revueltas shows that student movement took up proletariat banner after 1959 railroad strike was crushed by government. University became refuge and center for resistance to PRI hegemony.

2247 Reyes Heroles, Jesús. La historia y la acción: la Revolución y el desarrollo político de México. México: Ediciones Oasis, 1978. 301 p.

Collection of author's four essays and nine lectures. Believes that only intellectuals have the openness of mind to recognize new needs and values and that only politicians have the power to do something with this knowledge. Praises early Liberals and supports ideas of federalism and capitalism. States that revolutionaries (Madero) launched political revolution that reflected Porfiriato's economic and social problems. They became politicians before social reformers, economists or bureaucrats.

2248 Richmond, Douglas W. Factional political strife in Coahuila, 1910–1920 (HAHR, 60:1, Feb. 1980, p. 49–68)

Well researched examination of state political programs as implemented by succession of administrations, going from Porfirian to carrancista to huertista to villista and back to carrancista. Author attributes ultimate success of carrancistas to their decisiveness, organization, and introduction of popular reforms.

2249 ———. Regional aspects of the Mexican Revolution (UCSD/NS, 7:1/2, 1978 [i.e. 1979], p. 297–304)

Reviews briefly regional studies of Revolution (e.g., Friedrich Katz, John Womack, William Beezley, Michael C. Meyer, all major contributions to the field). Concentrates on Héctor Aguilar Camín, *La frontera nómada: Sonora y la Revolución Mexicana*, who discusses elites role in opposing *científicos'* plans to wipe out the Indians and bring in foreign developers. Professionals and landowners opposed this policy which would endanger labor supply. Also discusses conflicts between political factions. Shows how regional history affected Revolution's outcome.

2250 Rivera, Librado. ¡Viva tierra y libertad! México: Ediciones Antorcha, 1980. 228 p.

Correspondence of one of the leading figures in the Partido Liberal Mexicano (see item **2183**).

2251 Rodríguez Araujo, Octavio. La reforma política y los partidos en México. México: Siglo XXI, 1979. 267 p.; bibl.

Rodríguez Araujo presents a Marxist perspective on the development of parties since 1910, linking this history to interests of a domestic dominant class that has been closely allied with foreign imperialists. Political reforms are designed to coopt dissidents. Says that workers can take advantage of reforms to move regime closer to an authentic redistribution of power.

2252 Rodríguez Aviñoá, Pastora. La prensa nacional frente a la intervención de México en la Segunda Guerra Mundial (CM/HM, 29:2, oct./dic. 1979, p. 252–300)

Examination of attitudinal changes in Mexican press as Mexico evolved from position of strict neutrality to one of belligerence. Viewpoint is primarily from Mexico City, and focus is on Germany. Author skillfully traces parallel developments in international affairs, domestic politics, and shifting press coverage with emphasis on influence of ideology and editorial position.

2253 Roman, Richard. Railroad nationalization and the formation of Administración Obrera in Mexico, 1937–1938 (IAMEA, 35:3, 1981, p. 3–22)

Detailed analysis of one of the Cárdenas regime's more radical decisions: the transfer of railroads to workers' administration. Workers viewed transfer as a way of avoiding federalization while Cárdenas administration saw change as opportunity to introduce needed efficiencies without being subjected to criticism by workers.

2254 Ruiz, Ramón Eduardo. The great rebellion: Mexico, 1905–1924. New York: Norton, 1980. 530 p.; bibl.; index.

Argues that the events of 1905–24 constituted a "cataclysmic rebellion but not a social 'Revolution.'" Book discusses causes of revolution, key figures in period and their activities, and obstacles that prevented creation of social revolution. Well documented and researched, author shows convincingly that there was no social revolution by 1924, but perhaps larger question to be addressed is whether there was a social revolution afterward.

2255 Salamini, Heather Fowler. Agrarian radicalism in Veracruz, 1920–38. Lincoln: University of Nebraska Press, 1978. 239 p.; bibl.; index; maps.

Uses regional study to understand Mexican political history and sociology. Describes use of Tejada's ideology and military power to create a radical agrarian reform program (1929–32). Such reform partly failed because of force of Calles' central government.

2256 Sánchez, Andrea. Tres socialistas en la historiografía mexicana contemporánea (*in* Encuentro de Historiadores Latinoamericanos y del Caribe, 2d, Caracas 1977. Los estudios históricos en América Latina: ponencias, acuerdos y resoluciones: Caracas, 20–26 de marzo de 1977. Caracas: Universidad Central de Venezuela, Facultad de Humanidades y Educación, Escuela de Historia, 1979, v. 1, t. 1, p. 222–231, bibl.)

Analysis of three Marxist historians' interpretations of Mexican Revolution: José Mancisidor, Rafael Ramos Pedrueza, Alfonso

Teja Zabre. Author agrees with theory of writing history with scientific criteria and with categories used by these three historians of recent Mexican history: class struggle, modes of production, imperialism, proletariat revolution. Concludes that study of historiography is essential and that all three were pioneers in studying Mexican history as a social science.

2257 Sánchez Lamego, Miguel A. Generales de la Revolución: biografías. México: Patronato del Instituto Nacional de Estudios Históricos de la Revolución Mexicana, 1979. 1 v. (Biblioteca del Instituto Nacional de Estudios Históricos de la Revolución Mexicana; 81)

Brief biographical sketches of 18 important generals of the Revolution.

2258 Sandos, James A. International water control in the lower Rio Grande basin, 1900–1920 (AHS/AH, 54:4, Oct. 1980, p. 490–501, map, table)

Analysis of inequitable distribution of water between Texas and Tamaulipas in which about 70 percent of water originated in Mexico but was used in Texas. Attributes this inequitable distribution to failure of International Boundary Commission to manage water-taking practices, especially after outbreak of Revolution in 1910.

2259 ———. Pancho Villa and American security: Woodrow Wilson's Mexican diplomacy reconsidered (JLAS, 13:2, Nov. 1981, p. 293–311)

Revisionist interpretation ranging over a variety of topics dealing with border policy in 1915–16. Among author's conclusions: Villa was not only present at Columbus but was also wounded; Carranza tried actively to suppress Plan of San Diego; the Pershing expedition was a military success but much more expensive than generally believed. Excellent addition to growing border literature.

2260 ———. Prostitution and drugs: the United States Army on the Mexican-American border, 1916–1917 (UC/PHR, 49:4, 1980, p. 621–645)

Evaluation of US Army's efforts—particularly Pershing's—to deal with problems of prostitution, alcoholism, and drug usage on the border. Drawing upon experience in the Philippines, Pershing was generally successful in regulating prostitution but pursued a policy of prohibition rather than regulation in regard to alcohol and drugs.

2261 Santamaría, Francisco Javier. El periodismo en Tabasco. Viñetas de Luis Aguirre. 2. ed. México: Consejo Editorial del Gobierno del Estado de Tabasco, 1979. 314 p.; index (Serie Historia; 10)

Annotated bibliography of newspapers and journals published in Tabasco (1825–1935).

2262 ———. La tragedia de Cuernavaca en 1927 y mi escapatoria célebre. Villahermosa, México: Editorial Independencia, 1979. 151 p. (Colección de estudios históricos; v. 1)

Author's memoirs justify his escape from capture and death.

2263 Schmidt, Henry C. The Mexican intellectual as political pundit, 1968–1976: the case of Daniel Cosío Villegas (UM/JIAS, 24:1, Feb. 1982, p. 81–103)

Fine review of Cosío's ideas of Mexican history and his role in Mexican politics and intellectual debates 1968–76. Includes bibliography of his works written before his death in 1976 and secondary sources on his life and publications.

2264 Schryer, Frans J. The rancheros of Pisaflores: the history of a peasant bourgeoisie in twentieth-century Mexico. Toronto: University of Toronto Press, 1980. 210 p.; 2 leaves of plates; bibl.; ill.; index.

Analyzes peasant bourgeoisie as social group in Mexican revolutionary politics. During Porfiriato ranchero class transformed a subsistence agricultural economy into commercial one which increased from 12 to 21 percent of population, constituting local upper class in Pisaflores. After losing economic position in 1930s, ranchero class reacted as rival faction rather than as class. Schryer attempts to apply conclusions to all Mexico (e.g., main concern of official party to control rural politics through manipulation of peasant bourgeoisie rather than poor peasantry).

2265 Seis aspectos del México Real por Enrique Semo et al. México: Biblioteca Universidad Veracruzana, 1979. 243 p.; bibl. (Política, economía y administración)

Collection of six Marxist essays covering periodization of modern Mexican history (e.g., role of monopolies in Mexican economy, public education, health care problems, role of intellectuals since 1917).

2266 Semo, Enrique. Historia mexicana: economía y lucha de clases. México: Ediciones Era, 1978. 338 p.; bibl. (Serie popular Era; 66)

Series of essays with Marxist slant on Mexican history. Discusses way in which modes of production have succeeded each other and critical moments affecting class struggle since arrival of Spanish. Based primarily on secondary sources, few of which are written from a Marxist perspective.

2267 Serrón, Luis A. Scarcity, exploitation, and poverty: Malthus and Marx in Mexico. With foreword by Irving M. Zeitlin. Norman: University of Oklahoma Press, 1980. 279 p.; bibl.; index.

Assembles data to test whether Malthus or Marx was right about reasons for poverty and scarcity in Mexico. Slant suggests Marx is the winner. Interesting thesis but there are serious problems: no data presented after 1970; illegal aliens are discussed in terms of braceros; no mention of Echeverría's presidency, little mention of US-Mexico trade patterns.

2268 Silva-Herzog Flores, Jesús. Durante la presidencia del General Plutarco Elías Calles: sucesos que es menester recordar (CAM, 225:4, julio/agosto 1979, p. 123–148)

Amid Cristero War's turmoil and difficult relations with US, Calles established economic and social bases of Mexico in terms of roads, schools, and financial infrastructure. Article includes lengthy proclamation by Francisco Serrano, anti-reelectionist candidate in 1928 and Calles' final speech to Congress 1 Sept. 1928 in which Calles called for the end of rule by caudillos in Mexico.

2269 Smith, Peter. Labyrinths of power: political recruitment in twentieth-century Mexico. Princeton, N.J.: Princeton University Press, 1979. 384 p.; bibl.; ill.; index.

Shows that official party has been an open one. Whereas under Díaz percentage of officeholders with prior elite officeholding experience ranged from 60 to 61 percent, Madero reduced it to about 33, norm for all subsequent presidential periods. Upward mobility has existed and Smith suggests that neoporfirismo has not. Argues that middle class became dominant in political process,

because they realized need for higher education and professional training for access to elite.

2270 La Sombra de Serrano: de la matanza de Huitzilac a la expulsión de Calles por Cárdenas. Recopilación de Federico Campbell. Presentación de Francisco y Federico Serrano Díaz. Textos de Luis Alamillo Flores et al.; y el Manifiesto a la Nación (1927) del General Francisco R. Serrano. México: Proceso, 1980. 120 p.; ills.; ports.

Compilation (essays, interviews, documents) assembled by *Proceso* to investigate reasons behind Francisco Serrano's death in 1927, anti-reelectionist candidate for president. Analyzes roles of Calles, Obregon, and power struggle between Cárdenas and Calles. Open conclusions.

2271 Sotelo Inclán, Jesús. Raíz y razón de Zapata. 3. ed., corr. México: Comisión para la Conmemoración del Centenario del Natalicio del General Emiliano Zapata, 1979. 192 p.; bibl.; ill.

Author was compelled to find truth between Zapata, the bandit and Zapata, the apostle. Traces origins of Zapata and his activities to pre-conquest era and continues to examine land struggles during colonial era through independence to Revolution. Concludes Zapata was merely one of many who defended local lands throughout history.

2272 Soto, Shirlene Ann. The Mexican woman: a study of her participation in the Revolution, 1910–1940. Palo Alto, Calif.: R and E Research Associates, 1979. 118 p.; bibl.

Shows that women made many contributions to society in education, health, journalism, but these went unnoticed until 1940 because of machismo and fear that enfranchised women, under Church influences, would vote for reactionary candidates.

2273 Taracena, Alfonso. La vida en México bajo Miguel Alemán. México: Editorial Jus, 1979. 355 p.

Narration of major events and actors during Alemán's presidency presented in a refined literary style.

2274 Téllez Vargas, Eduardo. El asesinato de Trotsky (Comunidad CONACYT [Consejo Nacional de Ciencia y Tecnología, México] 7:121/122, enero/feb. 1981, p. 118–132, photos)

Account of how Trotsky entered Mexico, and political in-fighting between Cárdenas and Lombardo Toledano. Cárdenas supported his entry; Lombardo Toledano did not. Author knew Trotsky and reports events that led to his assassination.

2275 Thompson, John K. Inflation, financial markets, and economic development: the experience of Mexico. Foreword by Raúl Martínez Ostos. Greenwich, Conn.: JAI Press, 1979. 239 p.; bibl.; graphs (Contemporary studies in economic and financial analysis; v. 16)

Examines characteristics of economic growth under inflationary and stable conditions. Identifies three periods of inflation: 1) 1935–40; 2) 1940–46; and 3) past 1947. Period prior to early 1950s was one of economic growth with relative price stability. Shows how internal funds and external borrowing were used to achieve rapid growth without inflation.

2276 Tobler, Hans Werner. Einige Aspekte der Gewalt in der mexikanischen Revolution (JGSWGL, 15, 1978 p. 83–94)

Deals with conditions, manifestations, and function of violence during Revolution, (1910–17). Points out differences between north and south. Shows how southeast was not affected by revolutionary events until 1915. Violent course of events between 1913–14 provoked radicalization in Revolution. Such action destroyed old politico-administrative regimes of Díaz and Huerta, which, at the same time, represented conditions for the success of Cárdenas' later social reforms.

2277 Torres Gaytán, Ricardo. Un siglo de devaluaciones del peso mexicano. México: Siglo XXI Editores, 1980. 431 p.; figures, tables.

History factors surrounding peso's six devaluations in relation to dollar from 1867 (a one-to-one exchange rate) to 1977 (a 22 to one ratio). Author chronicles successive failures of various monetary systems employed and offers his own program for future growth.

2278 Torres Ramírez, Blanca. México en la Segunda Guerra Mundial. México: Colegio de México, 1979. 380 p.; bibl.; ill.; index (Historia de la Revolución Mexicana; 19: Período 1940–1952)

Discusses consequences of World War II for Mexico's economy and international relations. War gave Mexico new possibilities for improving its industry and its status with US. Largely concentrates on period's economics and politics. Includes extensive economic statistics.

2279 Toussaint Aragón, Eugenio. Quién y cómo fué Pancho Villa. México: Editorial Universo, 1979. 159 p.: bibl.

Studies Villa's motives and actions during Revolution's military years. Analyzes why Villa has been so popular in Mexico and dispels many myths about his life. Author presents serious psychological analysis of Villa.

2280 van Oss, Adriaan C. La Iglesia en Hidalgo hacia 1930 (CM/HM, 29:2, oct./dic. 1979, p. 301–324, bibl.)

Based on statistical and historical data from Hidalgo state author contends that effects of government pressure on Church and suspension of religious services between 1926–29 had minimal effect. Includes bibliography.

2281 Vasconcelos Aguilar, Mariano. José Vasconcelos: maestro de América. México: Editorial Jus, 1978. 171 p.

Book's theme is Vasconcelos as hemispheric teacher and cultural hero. Serves as introduction to his philosophy and opinions on variety of subjects. Author takes selected passages from Vasconcelos' works and casts them into interview form.

2282 Vasilkova, I. El diario mexicano de Alexandra Kollotai (URSS/AL, 26:2, 1980, p. 105–118, plates)

Brief, positive account of career of Russian woman who served as ambassador to Mexico (1926–27). Includes numerous entries from her diary.

2283 Vellinga, Menno. Industrialización, burguesía y clase obrera en México: el caso de Monterrey. México: Siglo XXI, 1979. 275 p.

Studies mechanisms of control that maintain Mexican system. Monterrey's development shows instance of successful autonomous industrialization in which the working class subject to a system of cooptation and control, is incapable of expressing its demands.

2284 Vida política contemporánea: cartas de Marte R. Gómez. Edited by Antonio Carrillo Flores. México: Fondo de Cultura Económica, 1978. 2 v. (1191, 1118 p.) ills.

Correspondence of agrarian technocrat and revolutionary politician whose career extended 1915–73. A politician who hated politics, Gómez served as director of the National School of Agriculture, governor of Tamaulipas, minister of agriculture, and minister of finance. Disillusioned with bureaucratization of Revolution, he retired to private life and became a successful businessman.

Villaseñor, Guillermo. Estado e Iglesia: el caso de la educación. See *HLAS 43:4523.*

2284a Wasserman, Mark. The social origins of the 1910 revolution in Chihuahua (LARR, 15:1, 1980, p. 15–38)

In addition to standard explanations of causes of revolt in Chihuahua (economic exploitation by Terrazas-Creel family), other factors must be examined: consequences of 1907 depression, weather conditions that caused drought and frost 1907–09, and encroachment on communal and municipal lands following passage of Municipal Land Law of 1905. Though such conditions occurred earlier during Díaz period they intensified by 1910.

2285 Weinstein, Michael A. The polarity of Mexican thought: instrumentalism and finalism. University Park: Penn State University Press, 1976. 128 p.: bibl.; index.

Discusses Caso, Vasconcelos, Ramos, Paz, Zea, and Augustín Basave Fernández del Valle who rejecting positivism, have accepted elements of vitalism and existentialism. Weinstein organizes his views around notion of "finalism"; that human beings should act to realize intrinsic values. Attempts to show that these philosophers seek a new humanism, even though they hold different positions and perspectives. Finalists tend to accept *Zozobra* and try to coordinate opposing forces in life.

2286 Werne, Joseph Richard. Esteban Cantú y la soberanía mexicana en Baja California (CM/HM, 30:1, julio/sept. 1980, p. 1–32)

Fascinating character study of political-military figure that dominated Baja California between 1914–20. Cantú was political opportunist of first order passing as huertista, carrancista, convencionista, and villista. Cantú also played a leading role in Baja's economy, including promotion of prostitution and drug trade. Despite such activities, concludes that Cantú did help keep Baja under Mexican control by maintaining political stability.

2287 Wolff, Thomas. Mexican-Guatemalan imbroglio: fishery rights and national honor (AAFH/TAM, 38:2, oct. 1981, p. 235–248)

Description of confrontation between Mexico and Guatemala over fishing rights which led to air attack on Mexican ships and break in diplomatic relations. Illustrative of longstanding inter-American dispute over law of the seas.

2288 Zapata: selección de textos. Por José Angel Aguilar. México: Patronato del Instituto Nacional de Estudios Históricos de la Revolución Mexicana, 1980. 217 p. (Biblioteca del Instituto Nacional de Estudios Históricos de la Revolución Mexicana; 79)

Collection of essays on Zapata by outstanding historians.

CENTRAL AMERICA

MURDO J. MACLEOD, *Professor of History, University of Arizona*

ONCE AGAIN, DURING THE LAST TWO YEARS, the nations of Central America continue to be the most distracted region of the hemisphere. Guatemala and El Salvador were in the midst of civil wars that pitted guerrilla coalitions against central governments allied to military establishments. Belize, completely independent at last, looked over its shoulder at Guatemala, which had not recognized it. The embattled revolutionary government of Nicaragua, facing hostility from within and without, felt that its very existence was threatened. Meanwhile, the Sandinista government reeducated its own population as well as audiences abroad by constructing its own pantheon of heroes through a barrage of writing. Costa Rica suffered from its worst economic depression since the 1930s, and observers warned of possible social unrest and political upheaval. Panama, the quietest of all, also suffered from the world recession and from the accidental death of Gen. Omar Torrijos, a popular figure who negotiated the Panama Canal Treaty.

It is evident that such turbulence has affected both the volume of books published as well as their subject matter. The notable interest in the historical roots of El Salvador's present war has resulted in several excellent analyses of the nation's 20th-century economic, ecclesiastical and political processes. Works by Rodolfo Cardenal (items **2387** and **2388**), Rafael Guidos Véjar (item **2419**), and Francisco Morán (item **2437**), were especially thoughtful. Works from Nicaragua reflect its scholars' continuing involvement with the struggle against Somoza and the lives of revolutionary heroes such as Augusto C. Sandino and Benjamín E. Zeledón. Costa Rica continued to provide outstanding contributions to social science topics such as the evolution of the nation's social structure, class relations and coffee boom. Of importance were studies by Rodolfo Cerdas Cruz (item **2292**), José Abdulio Cordero (item **2399**), Carlos Luis Fallas Monge (item **2409**), Marco A. Gandásegui *et al.* (item **2429**), Carolyn Hall (item **2420**), Mario Samper Kutchbach (item **2424**) and Manuel Solís A. (item **2464**).

Several new and interesting trends are becoming apparent despite the habitual flow of eulogies to hoary heroes of the independence movements, and adulatory biographies of obscure 19th-century presidents. There is now a solid, well based corpus on the history of the working class, early strikes, and first trade unions exemplified by the notable contributions of Andrés Achong (item **2365**), Vladimir de la Cruz (items **2400** and **2401**) and Víctor Meza (item **2434**).

The colonial period continues to be well served with interesting new research by established scholars such as Lowell Gudmundson (items **2331** and **2332**), Jorge Luján Muñoz (items **2336** and **2337**), Manuel Rubio Sánchez (item **2353**), Carmelo Sáenz de Santamaría (items **2354** and **2355**) and Francisco Solano (items **2358** and **2359**). Less notable were studies of both the colonial and national periods with the exception of two fine contributions, Agustín Estrada Monroy's (item **2295**) and Miles L. Wortman's (item **2314**). Worthy of note as well is the volume on Guatemalan historical demography edited by Carmack, Early and Lutz (item **2297**).

It is impossible to predict research trends in Central America given the region's political and economic crises. Nevertheless, one must register admiration for the region's historians who, doggedly and often courageously, ply their trade in the face of enormous difficulties.

GENERAL

2289 *Anuario de Estudios Centroamerica-*
nos. Universidad de Costa Rica, Instituto de Estudios Centroamericanos. Vol. 2, 1975– . San José.

Vol. 2 of outstanding Costa Rican publication contains articles by Augusto Cazali Avila on Costa Rica's coffee and labor in 1870s, Mario Flores Macal on University of El Salvador's history, and J. Jesús Martínez on Panama's contemporary theater.

2290 Argueta, Mario and **Edgardo Quiñónez.** Historia de Honduras. 2. ed. Tegucigalpa: Escuela Superior del Profesorado "Francisco Morazán," 1979 [i.e. 1980]. 251, 4 p.; 2 folded leaves of plates; bibl.; ill.

Second edition of well-known traditional history. Some useful documents from 19th and 20th century are reprinted in appendix.

Bolland, O. Nigel. Labour control in post-abolition Belize. See *HLAS 43:957.*

2291 Bosch, Juan. Una interpretación de la historia costarricense. 2. ed. San José: Editorial Juricentro, 1980. 51 p. (Colección Mundo de ayer)

Provocative short essay on basic nature of Costa Rican history and on its decisive crises, by radical ex-president of the Dominican Republic.

2292 Cerdas Cruz, Rodolfo. Formación del estado en Costa Rica. 2. ed. Ciudad Universitaria Rodrigo Facio, San José: Editorial Universidad de Costa Rica, 1978. 203 p.; bibl.

Second edition of 1967 work by political scientist and congressman. Discusses various competing theories of the state ending with class struggle model. Studies evolution of Costa Rican state from independence period with brief discussion of colonial period for state's basic underpinnings to early 19th-century wars and presidencies, ending with Braulio Carrillo's dictatorship when, according to author, new central power consolidated its hold, materially and psychologically, over area and inhabitants.

2293 Conte Porras, J. Panameños. s. l.: Litho Impresora, 1978. 215 p.; bibl.; ill.

Brief biographies ranging from precolombian chieftains, through conquistadors, colonial officials, heroes of independence, and modern journalists and politicians.

2294 Crawley, Eduardo D. Dictators never die: a portrait of Nicaragua and the Somoza dynasty. New York: St. Martin's Press, 1979. 180 p.; bibl.; maps.

Well written account by social democrat of Nicaraguan history and especially of Somoza dynasty.

2295 Datos para la historia de la Iglesia en Guatemala. Escrita por Agustín Estrada Monroy, compilador. Prólogo, Jorge Rodríguez. Guatemala: Sociedad de Geografía e Historia de Guatemala, 1973. 1 v.; bibl.; ill. (Biblioteca Goathemala; v. 26)

Extremely valuable reference volumes containing many original documents and discussions of lives and activities of Guatemala's bishops and archbishops up to Fran-

cisco de Paula García Pelaez. Wealth of raw material for historian.

2296 Díaz, Victor Miguel. Narraciones. Guatemala: Editorial "José de Pineda Ibarra," 1980. 307 p. (Biblioteca de cultura popular "20 de octubre"; 6. ser., v. 58)

Impressionistic essays, many of them historical, on: colonial earthquakes, Bishop Cortés y Larraz, Presidents Matías de Gálvez and Justo Rufino Barrios, etc.

Feldman, Lawrence. Indice de planos de tierras y pueblos del Oriente de Guatemala existentes en el Archivo General de Centroamérica: siglos 18 y 19. See item **134.**

2297 The Historical demography of highland Guatemala. Robert M. Carmack, John Early, and Christopher Lutz, editors. Albany: Institute for Mesoamerican Studies, State University of New York at Albany, 1982. 202 p.; bibl.; ill. (Publication / Institute for Mesoamerican Studies, State University of New York at Albany; no. 6)

Collection of 16 essays, most printed for first time, which sum up state of art of demographic history of Guatemala, and to lesser extent, Central America. Consists of preface, introductory essay and three parts: 1) five essays on prehispanic period; 2) five essays on colonial period; and 3) five essays on modern Guatemala. Stimulating, controversial findings represent great advance, given scattered and uncoordinated nature of Central American demographic history.

2298 Jaén Suárez, Omar. Cinco siglos de poblamiento en el Istmo de Panamá (LNB/L, 291, junio 1981, p. 75–94, maps, tables)

Study of the evolution of frontiers, population and land use in Panama since colonial period. Well argued but poorly documented.

2299 Martínez Zelada, Eliseo. Antes que criollos el pueblo forjó la independencia. Guatemala: Impr. Galindo, 1979, 48 p.; bibl.

Severo Martínez Peláez and others have depicted struggle for independence in Central America as struggle of Creole elites vs. Spanish empire, thus lack of social change. The center now accuses the left of elitism, and claims that people of every class participated in fight. Thin, poorly substantiated polemic.

2300 Mata Gavidia, José. Independencia religiosa en la emancipación del Reino de Guatemala (SGHG/A, 52 : 53, enero/dic. 1979, p. 57–73)

Ecclesiastical independence which came with end of colonial Patronato, according to clerical author, improved Church's quality and gave it more freedom to follow its true interests.

2301 Meléndez Chaverri, Carlos. Historia de Costa Rica. San José: Editorial Universidad Estatal a Distancia, 1979. 175 p.

Uninspired but useful brief outline, apparently designed for undergraduate audience. Bibliographical and illustrative material is poor, and it is doubtful if such an outline will entice students toward further reading and study of the subject.

2302 Monterrey, Francisco J. Historia del El Salvador: anotaciones cronológicas. Recopiladas por Francisco J. Monterrey. Carátula por Alfredo González A. 2. ed. San Salvador: Editorial Universitaria, 1977–1978. 2 v.; indexes (Colección eterna)

New two-volume edition of valuable reference work: vol. 1 : 1810–42; vol. 2, 1843–71.

2303 Pardo Gallardo, José Joaquín. Miscelánea histórica: Guatemala, siglos 16 a 19, vida, costumbres, sociedad. Guatemala: Universidad de San Carlos de Guatemala, 1978. 228 p.; port. (Colección "Realidad nuestra"; v. 6)

Collection of Pardo's minor newspaper writings (1933–44), some important to colonialists. Discusses Indian tributes and *cofradías*, workings of *real hacienda*, convents, festivities, independence, and President Gálvez's fall.

2304 Parker, Franklin Dallas. The Central American republics. Westport, Conn.: Greenwood Press, 1981. 348 p.; 2 fold. maps; bibl.; index.

Reprint of unrevised 1971 edition, first published 1964.

2305 Pérez Valle, Eduardo. Larreynaga, su tiempo y su obra. Managua: Fondo de Promoción Cultural, Banco de América, 1978. 57 p.; bibl. (Colección Cultural Banco de América. Serie Biografías; no. 1)

Short but interesting biography of Nicaraguan historian, educator, scientist and independence leader (1771–1847). Larreynaga

is best known to historians of Central America as compiler of *Prontuario de todas las Reales Cédulas.*

2306 Rodríguez Vega, Eugenio. Biografía de Costa Rica. San José: Editorial Costa Rica, 1980. 190 p.; bibl.

Fairly straightforward, unassuming, but bland history of nation pays brief attention to precolumbian Indians and colonial period and emphasizes late 19th and 20th centuries.

2307 Rubio Sánchez, Manuel. Don Gabino Gainza y Fernández Medrano (SGHG/A, 46 : 1/4, enero/dic. 1973, p. 22–52)

Biographical survey of life of Spanish colonial official who joined independence movement in Guatemala, governed area for Iturbide, and became one of his generals in Mexico. In general, author takes favorable view of Gainza.

2308 ———. Historia del comercio del café en Guatemala: siglos XVIII y XIX (SGHG/A, 50 : 50, enero/dic. 1977, p. 167–193, ill., tables)

Economic historian who specializes in agricultural production, trade routes and ports, examines late 18th and 19th-century coffee boom in Guatemala. Useful, well documented material.

2309 Sáenz de Santa María, Carmelo. El proceso ideológico-institucional desde la Capitanía General de Guatemala hasta las Provincias Unidas del Centro de América (IGFO/RI, 38 : 151/152, enero/junio, 1978, p. 219–285)

Experienced historian of colonial Central America turns his attention to years 1809–23 and to first constitution of United Provinces. It becomes clear that local cabildos and *diputaciones provinciales* played key roles in decisions made, and that their decisiveness may be related to area's later fragmentation.

2310 Sibaja Chacón, Luis Fernando and Chester Zelaya. La anexión de Nicoya. 2. ed. San José: Editorial Universidad Estatal a Distancia, 1980. 185 p.; 4 p. of plates; bibl.; facsims.; index.

Story of how Nicoya became part of Costa Rica in 1824. Basing their history heavily on archival sources authors go back to province's discovery, colonial centuries, and diplomatic negotiations with Nicaragua which led to its incorporation into Costa Rica. Includes large documentary appendix and bibliography.

2311 Sosa, Juan Bautista and Enrique J. Arce. Compendio de historia de Panamá: edición facsímil de la de 1911 con un estudio preliminar de Carlos Manuel Gasteazoro. Panamá: Editorial Universitaria, 1977. 322 p.; bibl.; ill. (Editorial universitaria: Sección Historia: Serie Información general)

Facsimile of rare 1911 ed. Expanded versions were published in 1934 (vol. 1) and 1940 (vol. 2 which did not circulate). All are standard, solid accounts.

2312 Walker, Thomas W. Nicaragua, the land of Sandino. Boulder, Colo.: Westview Press, 1981. 137 p.; 1 leaf of plates; bibl.; ill.; index, map (Nations of contemporary Latin America)

General history of Nicaragua emphasizes period since independence, especially years since Somoza family came to power. Author is enthusiastic supporter of Sandinistas and of 1979 revolution.

2313 Williams, Max Harrison. Gateway through Central America: a history of the San Juan River—Lake Nicaragua Waterway, 1502–1921. La Paz: Empresa Editora Urquizo, 1976. 156, 54 p.; bibl.; ill.; index.

History of San Juan River and adjacent lakes in Nicaragua, and of their use as transisthmian route. Discusses region's early Indian inhabitants; Spanish plans to use these waterways as route to Peru; pirates; "forty-niners" in Nicaragua; William Walker; and US-British rivalry over proposed canal. Includes large and useful bibliography.

2314 Wortman, Miles L. Government and society in Central America, 1680–1840. New York: Columbia University Press, 1982. 1 v.; bibl.; index.

Major contribution to region's history emphasizes government's role and its impact upon region and its different peoples. Takes reader from waning days of Hapsburg *ancien régime* through Bourbon Reforms, wider involvement in world market, economic and governmental decline of empire's last years, and centrifugal impact of independence and immediately after.

COLONIAL

2315 Amador Zúñiga, Victoria E. Influencia del comercio colonial en el financiamiento económico de la provincia de Costa Rica (UNCR/R, 4:7, julio/dic. 1981, p. 27–36, bibl.; graphs, tables)

Costa Rica's royal *cajas* were in deficit throughout 17th century and León, Nicaragua, had to make up the difference.

2316 Arellano, Jorge Eduardo. Oviedo y la provincia de Nicaragua (*in* Centenario de Gonzalo Fernández de Oviedo, *5th, Nicoya, Costa Rica, 1978.* Memoria del Congreso sobre el Mundo Centroamericano de su Tiempo, 24–25–26 y 27 de agosto 1978. San José: Comisión Nacional Organizadora, 1978, p. 99–104)

Very brief, sketchy analysis of what Oviedo did in Nicaragua and had to say about it.

Argueta, Mario R. Documentos relativos a la historia colonial hondureña existentes en el Archivo General de Centroamérica, Guatemala. See item **89.**

2317 Becerra, Longino. La comunidad primitiva en Honduras. Tegucigalpa: Universidad Nacional Autónoma de Honduras, Editorial Universitaria, 1981. 51 p.; bibl. (Colección Cuadernos universitarios; no. 4)

Simplistic brief description and analysis of indigenous society and culture of Honduras immediately before the Spanish conquest.

2318 Bozzoli de Wille, María E. Continuidad del simbolismo del cacao, del siglo XVI al siglo XX (*in* Centenario de Gonzalo Fernández de Oviedo, *5th, Nicoya, Costa Rica, 1978.* Memoria del Congreso sobre el Mundo Centroamericano de su Tiempo, 24–25–26 y 27 de agosto de 1978. San José: Comisión Nacional Organizadora, 1978, p. 229–240, bibl.)

Cacao, a crop of mystical as well as economic importance to Central America's indigenous peoples, has enjoyed special place in their cultures since before conquest. Discusses some Costa Rican Indian beliefs about cacao.

2319 Cabella Carro, María Paz. Evaluación demográfica de los huetares, talamancas y borucas, Costa Rica, en el momento de la conquista (*in* Centenario de Gonzalo Fernández de Oviedo, *5th, Nicoya, Costa Rica, 1978*. Memoria del Congreso sobre el Mundo Centroamericano de su Tiempo, 24–25–26 y 27 de agosto de 1978. San José: Comisión Nacional Organizadora, 1978, p. 225–228, bibl.)

Attempt to estimate contact population of certain Indian groups in Costa Rica on basis of interpretation of passing references in documents of time.

2320 Cabezas, Horacio. Creación de la Universidad de San Carlos de Guatemala y consolidación de los sistemas de explotación colonial (PAIGH/H, 88, julio/dic. 1979, p. 155–165, bibl.)

Links the rise of university in Guatemala to exploitation of agricultural sector and its peoples. Much emphasis is placed on what author perceives as double role of Bishop Marroquín.

2321 Carías, Marcos. La memoria y sus consecuencias. Tegucigalpa: Editorial Nuevo Continente, 1973. 222 p.

Curious and entertaining series of whimsical essays, most of them on various aspects of early 16th-century Honduran history.

2322 ————. La tiranía de los conquistadores en Honduras (*in* Centenario de Gonzalo Fernández de Oviedo, *5th, Nicoya, Costa Rica, 1978.* Memoria del Congreso sobre el Mundo Centroamericano de su Tiempo, 24–25–26 y 27 de agosto de 1978. San José: Comisión Nacional Organizadora, 1978, p. 311–321, bibl.)

Prolonged and violent conquest of Honduras left its mark, but a silver mining province emerged in spite of it. Very brief statement of the theme.

2323 Castillero Calvo, Alfredo. Economía terciaria y sociedad de Panamá en los siglos XVI y XVII (*in* Centenario de Gonzalo Fernández de Oviedo, *5th, Nicoya, Costa Rica, 1978.* Memoria del Congreso sobre el Mundo Centroamericano de su Tiempo, 24–25–26 y 27 de agosto 1978. San José: Comisión Nacional Organizadora, 1978, p. 331–386, diagrams, tables)

Panama's economy depended on its geographical position in 16th and 17th centuries just as much as today. Discusses services to travelers, trade fairs, customs dues, transportation, population and its relative wealth. Solid article includes wealth of statistics and documentation.

2324 ————. Estructuras funcionales del sistema defensivo del Istmo de Panamá durante el período colonial (*in* Congreso Venezolano de Historia, *3rd, Caracas, 1977* Memoria [see item **1741**] t. 1, p. 349–384, tables)

History of colonial efforts to put together adequate defenses for Isthmus of Panama. Describes expenses of such undertaking, how they were met, organization of local militias, and distribution of regular troops.

2325 Centroamérica en los cronistas de Indias. With introd. and notes by Eduardo Pérez Valle. Managua: Banco de América, 1977. 2 v.; bibl.; ill.; index (Serie Cronistas; nos. 4/5) Colección Cultural Banco de América)

Excerpts from Oviedo's *Historia general y natural de las Indias*. Eduardo Pérez Valle's introduction contains chronicler's biography and brief discussion of his written work.

2326 Cuesta Domingo, Mariano. La Baja Centroamericana en Alonso de Chaves: actitud crítica de Fernández de Oviedo (*in* Centenario de Gonzalo Fernández de Oviedo, *5th, Nicoya, Costa Rica, 1978.* Memoria del Congreso sobre el Mundo Centroamericano de su Tiempo, 24–25–26 y 27 de agosto 1978. San José: Comisión Nacional Organizadora, 1978, p. 105–112)

Geographical quarrels between cosmographer Alonso de Chaves and Fernández de Oviedo over characteristics of lower Central America, still only partly explored at the time.

2327 Dary R., Mario. Tomás Gage, su época y las referencias ictiológicas de su obra (SGHG/A, 47:1/4, enero/dic. 1974, p. 44–86, bibl.)

General survey, sprinkled with long quotations, of Gage's beliefs and observations. Barrage of quotes apparently selected to show that this *pícaro* friar was preoccupied with fish!

Documentos atinentes a la historia colonial hondureña existentes en el Archivo General de Centroamérica en Guatemala: comercio lícito e ilícito. See *HLAS 42:99.*

Feldman, Lawrence H. Colonial manuscripts of Chiquimula, El Progreso and Zacapa Departments, Guatemala. See item **105.**

2328 Fiehrer, Thomas. Slaves and freedmen in colonial Central America: rediscovering of forgotten black past (ASNLH/J, 64:1, Winter 1979, p. 39–57)

Review article, based mostly on secondary sources, of what we know about black slaves and freedmen in colonial period. Useful background reading for those beginning to study blacks in Central America.

2329 Franco, Juan. Breve noticia o apuntes de los usos y costumbres de los habitantes del Istmo de Panamá y sus producciones, 1792. Introd. por Omar Jaén Suárez. Panamá: Instituto Nacional de Cultura, Dirección Nacional del Patrimonio Histórico, Museo de Historia de Panamá, 1978. 60 p.; 3 leaves of plates; bibl.; ill.

Juan Franco's prolix, detailed report on isthmus of Panama (1792), drawn up for Malaspina expedition. Tone is that of 18th-century scientific enlightenment. Discusses people, towns, cattle industry, agriculture, snail dye, pearl fisheries, Indian anthropology and linguistics, and flora and fauna. Original manuscript in Bancroft Library, University of California, Berkeley.

2330 González Cicero, Stella María. Dos cartas del Oidor Tomás López Medel. Guadalajara, México: s.n. 1980. 124 p. (Documentación histórica mexicana; 8)

Son dos cartas escritas desde Guatemala: 1) 9 julio 1550 ya publicada pero cuya edición se mejora; y 2) 25 marzo 1551. El autor llega a Guatemala julio 1550, su experiencia personal es escasa, habla por informes de otros. Toca problemas generales y es de los que encuentran poco bueno; pero sus propuestas—muchas de sentido común, demasiado generales y no probadas en situación alguna particular—son interesantes, como soluciones ideales. [L.G. Canedo]

2331 Gudmundson, Lowell. La expropiación de los bienes de las obras pías en Costa Rica, 1805–1860: un capítulo en la consolidación económica de una élite nacional (UNCR/R, 4:7, julio/dic. 1978, p. 37–92, maps, tables)

Expropriation of various kinds of Church funds and their transfer to private, mostly cattle ranching individuals, helped to consolidate national elite in Costa Rica before beginnings of coffee boom. Impressive, well argued and documented study.

2332 ———. Mecanismos de movilidad social para la población de procedencia africana en Costa Rica colonial: manumisión y mestizaje (UNCR/R, 2:3, julio/dic. 1976, p. 131–182, bibl.; graphs, tables)

Manumission brought on by erratic and unstable economy, and mestizaje involving black women and males of other castes, helped some children achieve social mobility. Author does not wish to give impression of racial democracy, but social mobility promoted integration and weakened discrimination on Atlantic coast.

2333 Helms, Mary W. Ancient Panama: chiefs in search of power. Austin: University of Texas Press, 1979. 228 p.; bibl.; ill.; index (The Texas Pan American series)

Account of tribal elites ruling Panama who met first Spanish invaders. Draws much evidence from early Spanish chroniclers, later visitors such as Lionel Wafer, and ethnographic data. Result is blend of little known history and theoretical propositions on nature of culture contacts and chiefdoms as a form of government.

2334 Jiménez, Alfredo. Pensamiento y comportamiento políticos de los primeros españoles en Centroamérica (in Centenario de Gonzalo Fernández de Oviedo, 5th, Nicoya, Costa Rica, 1978. Memoria del Congreso sobre el Mundo Centroamericano de su Tiempo, 24–25–26 y 27 de agosto 1978. San José: Comisión Nacional Organizadora, 1978, p. 271–280)

What kind of people were first Spaniards in Central America, and what cultural background did they bring with them? Impressionistic article provides few answers.

2335 Lemistre Pujol, Annie. Gonzalo Fernández de Oviedo y los conquistadores de Nicaragua, Costa Rica, y Perú (in Centenario de Gonzalo Fernández de Oviedo, 5th, Nicoya, Costa Rica, 1978. Memoria del Congreso sobre el Mundo Centroamericano de su Tiempo, 24–25–26 y 27 de agosto 1978. San José: Comisión Nacional Organizadora, 1978, p. 291–302, bibl.)

What we can discover about people who conquered Nicaragua, Costa Rica and Peru from reading Oviedo.

2336 Luján Muñoz, Jorge. Los escribanos en las Indias Occidentales: y en particular en el Reino de Guatemala. 2. ed. Guatemala: Instituto Guatemalteco de Derecho Notarial, 1977. 224 p., bibl., fold. ill., ill.

Careful study of office of *escribano*, or scribe, in colonial Spanish America. In three final chapters, describes various kinds of escribanos, and requirements, prices and functions of these posts as well as jobs they performed and formulas and styles in their writings. Includes lengthy documentary appendix, full bibliography, and list of archival sources in Guatemala City, Seville, and Mexico City.

2337 ———. San Miguel Petapa, Guatemala, en la segunda mitad del siglo XVI (*in* Centenario de Gonzalo Fernández de Oviedo, 5th, Nicoya, Costa Rica, 1978. Memoria del Congreso sobre el Mundo Centroamericano de su Tiempo, 24–25–26 y 27 de agosto 1978. San José: Comisión Nacional Organizadora, 1978, p. 241–256, appendixes)

Part of Luján Muñoz' continuing study of this village, which begins before conquest and reaches to present. Example of microhistory school, Luján's history shows prosperous town which was not suffering from demographic loss, and was increasingly surrounded by Spanish haciendas and *trapiches*.

2338 MacLeod, Murdo J. Historia socio-económica de la América Central española, 1520–1720. Traducción al español de Irene Piedra Santa. Guatemala: Editorial Piedra Santa, 1980. 521 p.; appendix; bibl.; maps; tables (Biblioteca centroamericana de las ciencias sociales)

Spanish translation of *HLAS 36:2186.*

2339 Martínez Castillo, Mario Felipe. Comayagua durante la centuria de Fernández de Oviedo (*in* Centenario de Gonzalo Fernández de Oviedo, 5th Nicoya, Costa Rica, 1978. Memoria del Congreso sobre el Mundo Centroamericano de su Tiempo, 24–25–26 y 27 de agosto 1978. San José: Comisión Nacional Organizadora, 1978, p. 387–401)

Sketch of history of colonial Comayagua, Honduras, which rose and fell in importance depending on state of nearby silver mines.

2340 Martínez Peláez, Severo and Alberto Baeza Flores. Las raíces de la sociedad guatemalteca, el indio y la revolución (NSO, enero/feb. 1974, p. 68–75)

Consists of conversation with author of *La patria criolla* in which he gives his views of economic structure and place of Indian during Guatemalan colonial period. Short "think piece."

2341 Matarrita Ruíz, Bach Mario. Elementos para una interpretación de la dominación española en Nicoya (*in* Centenario de Gonzalo Fernández Oviedo, 5th, Nicoya, Costa Rica, 1978. Memoria del Congreso sobre el Mundo Centroamericano de su Tiempo, 24–25–26 y 27 de agosto 1978. San José, Costa Rica: Comisión Nacional Organizadora, 1978, p. 323–330, bibl.)

Conquest and colonization of Nicoya, very briefly and impressionistically done.

2342 Meléndez Ch., Carlos. Acerca del trabajo indígena en Costa Rica durante el siglo XVII (UTIEH/C, 37, 1981, p. 37–50)

Very general, impressionistic and poorly documented essay on Indian labor in 17th-century Costa Rica.

2343 Mencos Franco, Agustín. Crónicas de la Antigua Guatemala. 7. ed. Guatemala: Piedra Santa: IDAEH, 1980. 113 p.; ill. (Biblioteca centroamericana de las ciencias sociales) (Colección historia)

Latest edition of some deservedly famous historical mood pieces about colonial capital of Audiencia of Guatemala.

2344 Miranda Flamenco, Jaime. El añil en El Salvador: ensayo económico-social (Anales [Administración del Patrimonio Cultural, San Salvador] 50, 1977, p. 43–62, bibl., tables)

Another work on the much studied indigo industry of El Salvador, using familiar sources.

2345 Molina de Lines, María and Josefina Piana de Cuestas. El indígena costarricense a través de la historia general de Gonzalo Fernández de Oviedo (*in* Centenario de Gonzalo Fernández de Oviedo, 5th, Nicoya, Costa Rica, 1978. Memoria del Congreso sobre el Mundo Centroamericano de su Tiempo, 24–25–26 y 27 de agosto 1978. San José: Comisión Nacional Organizadora, 1978, p. 195–207, bibl.)

Authors plead for use of Oviedo's texts as source for study of Costa Rica's precolumbian Indians. These brief references are not convincing evidence.

2346 Moziño Suárez de Figueroa, José Mariano. Tratado del xiquilite y añil de Guatemala. San Salvador: Ministerio de Educación, Dirección de Publicaciones, 1976. 63 p. (Colección Antropología e historia; no. 5)

Reprint of rare 1799 ed. Moziño was member of Spanish scientific expedition (1792–94) and conducted various scientific inquiries from Chiapas to Nicaragua. This manual is great improvement on better known *Puntero* . . . , and in it Moziño deplores conservative, unproductive approach of Central American indigo growers, and suggests ways of improving productivity, health, and quality.

2347 Osorio O., Alberto. Judaismo e Inquisición en Panamá colonial. Panamá: Ediciones Instituto Cultural Panamá-Israel, 1980. 245 p.; bibl.; ill.

Chapters on origins of Iberian Jews, their expulsion, and clandestine presence in post-conquest America, lead to study of the Inquisition in Panama. Explains prosecutions of lutheranism, sorcery, blasphemy and sexual irregularities. Only second half is devoted to persecution of small Jewish community. Work is strange mixture of sweeping, vague generalizations and well documented specific cases. Includes useful documentary appendix and good bibliography.

2348 Oviedo y Valdéz, Gonzalo Fernández de. Costa Rica vista por Fernández de Oviedo. Introd. de Carlos Melendez Ch. San José: Ministerio de Cultura, Juventud y Deportes, Departamento de Publicaciones, 1978. 100 p.; ill. (Serie Nos ven; no. 7)

Excerpts from Spanish chronicler and conquistador which describe Costa Rica.

2349 Pérez Estrada, Francisco. Historia precolonial de Nicaragua. Managua: Editorial Nueva Nicaragua: Ministerio de Cultura, 1980. 41 leaves, 2 leaves of plates; maps.

Little more than sketch, pamphlet contains some glaring errors. Who was Olaf, son of "the Icelander Erick the Red," who reached Canada about 1000 AD? Sources used are Oviedo, León Portilla and other well-known authors. Pamphlet seems part of Nicaraguan government's literacy campaign.

2350 Polo Sifontes, Francis. Título de Alotenango. Introd. epílogo y notas por Francis Polo Sifontes. Guatemala: Editorial José de Pineda Ibarra, 1979. 61 p.; bibl.; ill.

Previously unknown Indian land title from 1565, presented in defense of 1667 land claim, this Cakchiquel document from Alotenango, Sacatepéquez, is of considerable importance. Should be compared with other titles in small Guatemalan corpus, and confirms information in them. Title adds information on neighboring Pipiles of Escuintla, Alotenango's rivals for land 1565, and on the first Cakchiquel revolt against invading Spaniards ending in 1530.

2351 Reina, Rubén E. et al. Guía de la colección de Documentos del Archivo General de Indias correspondiente a la Audiencia de Guatemala (SGHG/A, 52:52, enero/dic. 1979, p. 151–217)

Guide to archival material from AGI in Seville microfilmed by Guatemala project in Philadelphia, supported by American Philosophical Society.

2352 Romero Vargas, Germán. Fuentes, métodos y problemas de la historia demográfica del Antiguo Reino de Guatemala, 1524–1821 (*in* Encuentro de Historiadores Latinoamericanos y del Caribe, *2d, Caracas, 1977.* Los estudios históricos en América Latina: ponencias, acuerdos y resoluciones Caracas, 20–26 de marzo de 1977. Caracas: Universidad Central de Venezuela, Facultad de Humanidades y Educación, Escuela de Historia, 1979, v. 1, t. 1, p. 374–380)

General impressionistic survey of state of demographic history on colonial Central America.

2353 Rubio Sánchez, Manuel. Alcaldes Mayores: historia de los Alcaldes Mayores, Justicias Mayores, Gobernadores Intendentes, Intendentes Corregidores, y Jefes Políticos, de la Provincia de San Salvador, San Miguel y San Vicente. San Salvador: Ministerio de Educación, Dirección de Publicaciones, 1979. 2 v.; bibl.; ill.

One of the most prolific of Central American historians writes about colonial governors of El Salvador: Vol. 1, biographies of *alcaldes mayores* of San Salvador, San Miguel, La Choluteca, and San Vicente. Vol. 2 introduces *intendentes* and *gobernadores intendentes*. Includes large appendix of interesting documents and full scholarly documentation to text.

2354 Saénz de Santamaría, Carmelo. Algunos rasgos históricos de Don Juan Martínez de Landecho, primer Presidente-Gobernador de la Audiencia de Guatemala (SGHG/A, 48 : 1/4, enero/dic. 1975, p. 30–46)

Saénz de Santamaría has devoted considerable attention to Landecho, enigmatic, 16th-century Governor of Audiencia de Guatemala. Finds that Landecho was efficient President and has been much maligned by his enemies of the time.

2355 ———. Costa Rica se implanta en Centro América (in Centenario de Gonzalo Fernández de Oviedo, 5th, Nicoya, Costa Rica, 1978. Memoria del Congreso sobre el Mundo Centroamericano de su Tiempo, 24–25–26 y 27 de agosto 1978. San José: Comisión Nacional Organizadora, 1978, p. 281–289)

Carefully traces and examines slow integration of Costa Rica into Audiencia of Guatemala in 16th century. Schemes of President Landecho receive particular attention.

2356 Saint-Lu, André. Los Dominicos de Chiapas y Guatemala frente al Confesionario Lascasiano (IAHG/AHG, 2 : 1, 1979, p. 88–102)

French scholar of Verapaz missions and of Guatemalan colonial history of ideas turns his attention to aged Las Casas' accusations against Dominicans of Chiapas, formerly under his tutelage. Saint-Lu finds that Las Casas exaggerated and was out of touch with real conditions in province. These Dominicans were not guilty of errors as alleged.

2357 Samoya Guevara, Héctor Humberto. El bochinche estudiantil del 12 de noviembre de 1821 (SGHG/A, 46 : 1/4, enero/ dic. 1973, p. 11–21)

Students impeded start of classes in 1821 because of disagreements with state and university authorities, and rioted intermittently for two days. Possible main cause of this confused protest was dislike of newly elected, pro-Spanish university Rector.

2358 Solano y Pérez Lila, Francisco de. Análisis de la poblacion indígena en la Audiencia de Guatemala en 1572 (IAHG/AHG, 2 : 1, 1979, p. 73–87, bibl., tables)

Analysis of 1572 document in University of Texas Library leads Solano to decide that Indian population of Guatemala, El Salvador, and Tuxtla-Soconusco was less than 200,000 in that year.

2359 ———. El fenómeno urbano centroamericano en tiempos de Fernández de Oviedo (in Centenario de Gonzalo Fernández de Oviedo, 5th, Nicoya, Costa Rica, 1978. Memoria del Congreso sobre el Mundo Centroamericano de su Tiempo, 24–25–26 y 27 de agosto 1978. San José: Comisión Nacional Organizadora, 1978, p. 303–310)

Study of processes of settlement and abandonment of early Central American Spanish cities.

2360 ———. Tierra y sociedad en el Reino de Guatemala. Guatemala: Editorial Universitaria, 1977. 462 p.; bibl. (Colección Realidad nuestra; v. 4)

Detailed analysis of agrarian structures, agriculture, and agricultural products in 18th-century Central America, is followed by large and important archival section on land and land legislation, ranging from earliest days of colonial period to 1772. Documents are for most part, *Reales Cédulas*, Instructions to Viceroys and Governors, and *Ordenanzas* about agriculture.

2361 Valdés Oliva, Arturo. Fueron determinantes para la independencia los movimientos de tipo político en el Reino de Guatemala a principios del siglo XIX (SGHG/ A, 46 : 1/4, enero/dic. 1973, p. 76–90, bibl., table)

Former director of National Archives claims historical record shows that Guatemalan independence would have been impossible without political uprisings preceding it, revolts dismissed by some as minor and inconclusive.

2362 Vázquez de Coronado, Juan. 1562 [i.e. Mil quinientos sesenta y dos]: primera Carta de Relación sobre la Conquista de Costa Rica enviada a S. M. el Rey de España D. Felipe II. San José: Comisión Nacional de Conmemoraciones Históricas, 1977. 11 p.; facsims. (Colección de Documentos—Comisión Nacional de Conmemoraciones Históricas; no. 1, ser. 2, pt. 2a)

Yet another edition of Vázquez de Coronado's first *relación* contains photo reproduction of original document and modern transcription.

2363 Volio, Marina. Costa Rica en las cortes de Cádiz. Prólogo de Mario Hernández Sánchez-Barba. San José: Editorial Juricentro, 1980. 206 p. (Colección Mundo de ayer)

Doctoral dissertation from Complutense in Madrid, based on original archival documentation, and very complete account of Costa Rica's role in Cortes (1810–12). Bibliography is exceptional.

NATIONAL

2364 Acevedo, Antonio. Sandino y sandinismo: pt. 2 (BNBD, 32/33, nov. 1979/feb. 1980, p. 140–177, facsim., plates)

Good bibliography on movement and its hero followed by important selection of writings by Carlos Fonseca Amador, Emigdio E. Maraboto, Augusto C. Sandino, and bibliographical note by René Rodríguez Masís.

2365 Achong, Andrés. Orígenes del movimiento obrero panameño. Panamá: Centro de Estudios Latinoamericanos Justo Arosemena, 1980. 24 p., bibl., ill., tables (Cuadernos populares; 10)

Working class movement in Panama and the uprising of 1885 are closely linked to railroad construction and subsequent history. Brief but pointed essay.

2366 Administración del general Francisco Malespín. A cargo de María Leistenschneider y Freddy Leistenschneider. San Salvador: Ministerio del Interior, 1980. 1 v.; port.

President of El Salvador for two brief periods in 1844, Malespín founded the University of El Salvador, repelled a Guatemalan invasion, invaded Nicaragua, and was killed in 1846 while attempting to regain the presidency via invasion from Honduras.

2367 Aguilar Bulgarelli, Oscar R. Costa Rica y sus hechos políticos de 1948: problemática de una década. 2. ed. Ciudad Universitaria Rodrigo Facio, San José: Editorial Universitaria Centroamericana, 1974. 568 p.; bibl. (Colección Rueda del tiempo)

Third edition of important work (see *HLAS 40:2849*).

2368 Araúz, Celestino Andrés. La independencia de Panamá en 1821: antecedentes, balance y proyecciones. Prólogo de Carlos Manuel Gasteazoro. Panamá: Academia Panameña de la Historia, 1980. 251 p.; apéndices; bibl.; ports., facsims.

Solid account of Panama's role in 1821 independence movement which led to establishment of Gran Colombia. Extensive footnotes, documentary appendixes, and full bibliography add to book's value.

2369 Arellano, Jorge Eduardo. El padre-indio Tomás Ruíz, prócer de Centroamérica. Managua: Ediciones Nacionales, 1979. 72 p.; bibl.

Amplification of previous work (see *HLAS 40:2813*) with excellent documentation and bibliography.

2370 Arévalo, Juan José. Memorias de aldea. 2. ed. Guatemala: Editorial Académica Centroamericana, 1980. 322 p.

Guatemalan reformist ex-president describes his country childhood and youth in evocative, nostalgic essays.

2371 Arosemena, Justo. Justo Arosemena, patria y federación. Compilación y prólogo de Nils Castro. La Habana: Casa de las Américas, 1977. 485 p.; bibl. (Colección Pensamiento de nuestra América)

Long analytical introduction precedes text by Panamanian savant and politician whose ideas appear in five major works: 1) disquisition on moral and political science; 2) speech against US expansionism; and 3/5) federalist ideas for creating a greater and more unified Latin America. Arosemena emerges as significant 19th-century Latin American thinker, too long ignored.

2372 Arosemena, Mariano. Historia y nacionalidad: testimonios éditos e inéditos. Edición y estudio preliminar de Argelia Tello de Ugarte. Panamá: Editorial Universitaria, 1971. 245 p.; bibl.; ill. (Monumenta histórica panameña: Serie Testimonios del siglo XIX)

Essay (74 p.) on early 19th-century Panamanian journalist, politician and historian, by Argelia Tello, is followed by ca. 200 p. of letters and writings by and about Arosemena. Valuable book for those interested in Columbian era of Panamanian history. history.

2373 Aycinena, Juan José de. El toro amarillo. Guatemala: Editorial José de Pineda Ibarra, 1980. 167 p. (Biblioteca de cultura popular 20 de octubre; v. 54. Sexta serie)

From US exile, Aycinena reflects on Central America's distraught condition (1831–32), and suggests conservative, anti-federalist, anti-Morazón reform movement for various Central American nations. This was first serious intellectual attack on Union of Central America.

2374 Baeza Flores, Alberto. Daniel Oduber, una vida y cien imágenes. San José: Editorial Eloy Morúa Carrillo, 1976. 302 p.; ill.

Favorable biography of Costa Rican diplomat, politician and ex-President Daniel Oduber (1974–78).

2375 Barahona Portocarrero, Amaru. Estudio sobre la historia contemporánea de Nicaragua. San Pedro de Montes de Oca, San José, Costa Rica: Instituto de Investigaciones Sociales, Facultad de Ciencias Sociales, Universidad de Costa Rica, 1977. 62 p.; bibl. (Avances de investigación, 0378-0473; no. 24)

Thoughtful study of US intervention, Somoza's rise, cotton industry's growth, and events up to 1976 in Nicaragua. Well documented from a bibliography of printed sources.

2376 Bardini, Roberto. Belice, historia de una nación en movimiento. Tegucigalpa: Editorial Universitaria, 1978. 207 p.; bibl.; ill.

Restatement from left perspective of Belize's right to self-determination by Argentinian journalist. His thesis is that Guatemalan threats, not British colonialism, delayed independence for the tiny nation.

2377 La Batalla de Nicaragua. Ernesto Cardenal *et al.* Mexico: Bruguera Mexicana de Ediciones, 1980. 451 p.; bibl.

Leading writers and intellectuals of Sandinista Revolution and distinguished outsiders (e.g., García Márquez) discuss various aspects of anti-Somoza struggle. Most of essays date from period just before Sandinista victory, but Gregorio Selser provides summing up after Somoza's fall.

2378 Beltranena Sinibaldi, Luis. La tragedia de Chalchuapa (SGHG/A, 52:53, enero/dic. 1979, p. 21–43)

Speech to Sociedad de Geografía e Historia de Guatemala which outlines events leading up to President Justo Rufino Barrios' death, and promises more complete study of subject.

2379 Biografía del héroe, Sandino. Mexico: Publicaciones Cruz O., 1979. 31 p.

Brief, restrained, but favorable biography of Nicaraguan hero.

2380 Blandón, Jesús Miguel. Entre Sandino y Fonseca Amador. s.l.; s.n.; 1979 or 1980. 224 p.; ill.

Chatty history of Sandinista guerrilla movement, 1937–79. Carlos Fonseca Amador emerges as hero, a second Sandino to author.

2381 Bonilla, Harold H. Los presidentes. San José: Editorial Universidad Estatal a Distancia: Editorial Costa Rica, 1979. 2 v. (865 p.); bibl.; ill.; index.

Reissue of work published 1942 entitled *Nuestros presidentes.*

2382 Bovallius, Carl Erik Alexander. Viaje por Centroamérica, 1881–1883. Traducido del sueco por Camilo Vijil Tardón. Managua: Fondo de Promoción Cultural, Banco de América, 1977. 315 p.; ill.; indexes (Colección cultural Banco de América)

Translation of Resa i Central-Amerika, 1881–1883. First complete Spanish translation of Swedish scientist's account of travel through Panama, Costa Rica and Nicaragua. Spanish translation of Nicaraguan section was published in *Revista Conservadora del Pensamiento Centroamericano* (Managua, 1963).

2383 Bowdler, George A. The downfall of Somoza (SECOLAS/SELA, 25:3, Dec. 1981, p. 1–10)

Finds that sanctuary in neighboring countries and outside material and political support were crucial factors in overthrow of Somoza regime. Ends with plea for more US understanding of Nicaraguan revolutionary process.

2384 Cáceres Lara, Víctor. Gobernantes de Honduras en el siglo 19. Tegucigalpa: Banco Central de Honduras, 1978 or 1979. 390 p.; bibl.

Brief biographies of Honduras' 19th-century presidents which, when taken together, constitute an interesting and useful political history of the nation. Final chapter sums up century neatly and clearly. Should be useful as introduction to subject and as reference tool.

2385 Cacua Prada, Antonio. Pedro Molina, patricio centroamericano. Guatemala:

Editorial José de Pineda Ibarra, 1978. 193 p.; 6 leaves of plates; ports.

Another biography of famous Guatemalan independence leader, chief of state, and educator, based on printed sources. Includes interesting material on Molina's residence in Colombia.

2386 Calvo Gamboa, Carlos. Rafael Yglesias Castro. Presentado por Carlos Calvo Gamboa. San José: Ministerio de Cultura, Juventud y Deportes, Dirección de Publicaciones, 1980. 234 p.; bibl.; graphs (Serie Quién fué y qué hizo?; no. 27)

More than biography of Costa Rican President (1894–1902), this well documented little book discusses coffee boom years and era's political and social life.

2387 Cardenal, Rodolfo. Acontecimientos sobresalientes de la Iglesia de Honduras, 1900–1962: primeros pasos para la elaboración de una historia de la Iglesia hondureña. Tegucigalpa: Instituto Socio-Religioso Juan XXIII, between 1974 and 1979. 74 leaves.

Outline of 20th-century Honduran Church history emphasizes setting up of new bishoprics, entry of foreign clergy and money, and Church's loss of influence in Honduran society.

2388 ———. El poder eclesiástico en El Salvador, 1871–1931. San Salvador: UCA Editores, 1980. 336 p.; bibl.; ill. (Colección Teología latinoamericana. Serie Historia de la Iglesia; v. 1.)

Balanced history of Church-state relations in El Salvador, 1870s–1930s. Judicious study fully discusses liberal anti-clericalism in 1870s secularization of state in following decade, emergence of coffee elite and its alliance with Church, and adoption of official rather than popular religion in 1930s.

2389 Castillero R., Ernesto J. Raíces de la Independencia de Panamá. Edición de la Academia Panameña de la Historia en conmemoración de las bodas de diamante de la República de Panamá. Panamá: Academia Panameña de la Historia, 1978. 233 p.; apéndice; bibl.; ill., ports.

Examines separation from Spain, incorporation into Colombia, Panamanian separatist movements (1830, 1831, and 1840) and final independence. Useful documentary appendix.

2390 Cerutti, Franco. Medio siglo de historia centroamericana en la obra de Barrios Dávila (IGFO/RI, 38:151/152, enero/junio 1978, p. 403–427)

Praise for Liberal Nicaraguan historian, journalist and statesman Modesto Barrios (1849–1926).

2391 Charles, Rubén Darío. La historia de Panamá y su canal. s.l.; s.n.; 1980 or 1981. 95 p.; ill.

Prolific author gives brief journalistic account, mostly excerpted from newspapers, of country's and its canal's recent history (1950s–present).

2392 Chávez Alfaro, Lizandro. Identidad y resistencia del "criollo" en Nicaragua (UTIEH/C, 36, 1981, p. 87–97)

Except for El Salvador, Central American nations face both ways, towards Caribbean where they have been threatened by British intrusion and must accommodate to remnants of foreign colonial peoples, and towards a more Latin Pacific. Nicaragua's revolutionary state has found this a grave problem and, says author, must tackle it before situation is used by others.

2393 50 [i.e. Cincuenta] años de la guerra civil libero-conservadora, 1926–1976. León? Nicaragua: El Centroamericano, 1977. 208 p.; ill.

Heavily illustrated excerpts from El Centroamericano, on Nicaragua's Liberal-Conservative Civil War (1926–27). Useful for day-to-day details and personalities, but contains little on general trends. Includes long account by Gen. Sandino of 1926–27 Liberal Constitutionalist campaign.

2394 Clegern, Wayne M. Transition from conservatism to liberalism in Guatemala, 1865–1871 (in Hispanic-American essays in honor of Max Leon Moorhead [see HLAS 42:1787] p. 98–110)

Brief but well documented account of events leading to 1871 Liberal Revolution. Argues that little divided both Guatemalan parties before 1869, and that Liberal resort to force came when members realized that Conservative institutions could not be removed otherwise, and were permanent obstacles to progress.

2395 Clemente Marroquín Rojas, un hombre de América: obituario a su memoria. Finca Las Charcas, Guatemala: Editorial José de Pineda Ibarra, 1980. 558 p.; ill.

Collection of obituaries to late iconoclastic Guatemalan journalist and vice-president.

2396 Colindres, Eduardo. Fundamentos económicos de la burguesía salvadoreña. San Salvador: UCA Editores, 1977. 434 p.; bibl.; ill. (Colección Estructuras y procesos; v. 2)

Excellent economic history of El Salvador based on extensive, carefully collected data. Land tenure, ownership, use, agricultural technology and credit, all received detailed attention. Author examines process of industrialization, business organizations, foreign trade and balance of payments, banking, and tax structure. All this adds up to an emerging bourgeois system guaranteed by the armed forces. Anexos (150 p.) provide extensive documentation for this important book.

2397 Conte Porras, J. Comentarios sobre el grupo coclesano en la historia nacional (LBN/L, 293/294, agosto/sept. 1980, p. 1–14)

Role played by people from Coclé in Panama's history, at times a mere listing rather than an analysis.

2398 ———. Enrique A. Jiménez, 1888–1970. Panama: Talleres de Litho-Impresora Panamá, 1976. 214 p.; ill.

Sympathetic biography of late journalist, President of Panama (1945–48) and UN representative.

2399 Cordero, José Abdulio. El ser de la nacionalidad costarricense. 2 ed. San José: Universidad Estatal a Distancia (UNED), 1980. 129 p., bibl.

History of emergence of nationalism and of nation state in Costa Rica. Finds roots of nationalism in relative isolation and autonomy of colonial period, in movement for independence, in development of national educational system, and in decisions made in 1848, especially crucial year of 1856, when infant state was threatened from outside.

2400 Cruz, Vladimir de la. Apuntes para la historia del movimiento obrero centroamericano. Tegucigalpa, Honduras: Colegio de Profesores de Educación Media de Honduras, 1980. 28 p.

Brief outline of origins of trade union movement in Central America. Nicaragua,

Honduras and Costa Rica receive most attention. Essay is useful as introduction to subject, but recent research on labor movements in region have gone far beyond this level.

2401 ———. Las luchas sociales en Costa Rica, 1870–1930. San José: Editorial Costa Rica: Editorial Universidad de Costa Rica, 1980. 304 p.

History of emergence of working class movement in Costa Rica, beginning with construction of Atlantic railroad, fight against Tinoco regime, and first strikes in 1920–21, and continuing to organization of first general trade union and founding of Communist Party of Central America.

2402 Darío, Rubén. Textos socio-políticos. Presentación de Francisco Valle. Selección y notas de Jorge Eduardo Arellano. Managua: Ediciones de la Biblioteca Nacional, 1980. 77 p.; bibl.

Collection of social and political writings of famous Nicaraguan poet.

2403 Doctor y general Benjamín F. Zeledón. Managua: Ediciones Ministerio de Educación, 1980. 46 p.; port.

Gen. Zeledón, killed 1912 by invading US troops, has become a hero and precursor of Sandinista Revolution. Includes useful documentary appendix about Zeledón with some of his writings.

2404 El Salvador de 1840 [i.e. mil ochocientos cuarenta] **a 1935** [i.e. mil novecientos treinta y cinco]. Estudiado y analizado por los extranjeros John Baily et al. Selección, traducción, prólogo y notas de Rafael Menjívar y Rafael Guidos Véjar. San Salvador: UCA Editores, 1978. 269 p.; bibl.; ill (Colección Estructuras y procesos; v.4)

Foreigners look at El Salvador and its history. Spanish translations of essays by John Baily, J. Fred Rippy, Percy F. Martin, Maurice de Perigny, Dana G. Munro, Everett A. Wilson, and Kenneth J. Grieb.

2405 Escobar Morales, César. Sandino en el panorama nacional. Managua, Nicaragua: s.n., 1979. 149 p.; bibl.; ill.

Solid, advanced high school text introduces Sandino to Nicaraguan youth.

2406 Escobar Pérez, José Benito. Ideario sandinista. La Habana: Comisión Exterior de la Representación en Cuba, del Frente Sandinista de Liberación Nacional, 1979. 19 p.; ill.

Frente Sandinista's representatives in Havana present ideas of their eponymous hero to Cuban audience. Brief chapters discuss Sandino's ideas on government, imperialism, class struggle, Central America, and nationalism.

2407 Eugarrios, Manuel. Dos . . . uno . . . Cero, comandante. San José: Lehmann, 1979. 128 p.; ill.

Account of seizure (Aug. 1978) by elements of the Sandinista Front led by guerrilla Comandante Cero of Somoza's Chamber of Deputies. Event secured release of 59 political prisoners and severely damaged prestige of Somoza dictatorship.

2408 Fairweather, Donald Norman Albert. A short history of the volunteer forces of British Honduras (now Belize). s. l.; s.n.; 197– . 43 p.; 1 leaf of plates; ill.

Dry, terse history by former commandant (1947–63) of Volunteer Guard. To some extent this history mirrors military and diplomatic history of the country.

2409 Fallas Monge, Carlos Luis. Apuntes para una historia del movimiento obrero en Costa Rica: siglo XIX (UNCR/R, 4:7, julio/dic. 1978, p. 93–122, bibl.)

Brief history of early 19th-century beginnings of Costa Rican working class movement, from artisans guilds and societies to first small strikes.

2410 Figueroa Navarro, Alfredo. Visión de Panamá durante la época del canal francés (LNB/L, 292, julio 1980, p. 17–25, table)

French scandals and failure brought relative prosperity to some Panamanians. It also brought Jamaicans, Barbadians, Saint Lucians and Martinicans to the country, and many stayed. Federalist versus Centralist disputes in Columbia and independence movements in Panama further complicated these years.

2411 Flores Andino, Francisco A. Doscientos años de un sabio: José Cecilio del Valle (YAXKIN, 2:2, dic. 1977, p. 77–84, bibl.)

Brief and unoriginal survey on much studied Central American savant and statesman.

2412 Galich, Manuel. Del pánico al ataque. 2. ed. Guatemala: Editorial Universitaria, 1977. 388 p. (Colección Realidad nuestra)

Series of anecdotal articles, first published in *El Libertador* (1946), and gathered into first edition anthology in 1949. In it Galich gives his anti Ubico account of events at time of dictator's overthrow. New epilogue gives explanation of failures of Arévalo and Arbenz governments, and of 1954 counter-revolution in Guatemala. Galich has since become a Marxist and would no longer agree with some early opinions expressed in this book.

2413 Gálvez Estrada, Héctor. Conozca a Estrada Cabrera. Guatemala: Editorial Prensa Libre, 1976. 266 p.: ill.

Adulatory biography of important Guatemalan president. Includes many interesting documents and appendix, but level of narrative and analysis is such that serious historian must turn elsewhere for information.

2414 García Laguardia, Jorge Mario. Plan de realización del supremo sueño de Bolivar: un documento inédito de Augusto César Sandino (Alero [Univ. de San Carlos, Guatemala] 1, 4. época, mayo/junio 1979, p. 91–94, plate)

Previously unknown document, reprinted in full takes up most of this article. Shows Sandino to have been a pan-Latin Americanist, in favor of federation of 21 states.

2415 ———. El significado de la reforma liberal en Guatemala (SGHG/A, 46:1/4, enero/dic. 1973, p. 91–114, tables)

Basically same as introductory essay in author's anthology (see item **2414**).

2416 García Salgado, Andrés. Yo estuve con Sandino. s. l.; Bloque Obrero General Heriberto Jara, 1979 or 1980. 123 p.; ports.

Communist's memoirs of his campaigns with Augusto César Sandino until his death in 1934. Includes historical introduction to Sandino years in Nicaragua, and useful documentary appendix.

2417 Goytía, Victor Florencio. Episodios del siglo XX en Panamá. v. 1. Rumbos equivocados. v. 2 Las décades formativas de la República. Panamá: Editorial Linosa: Inter-American Pub. Co., distribuidores exclusivos, 1975. 2 v.; ill.

History, largely diplomatic and political in emphasis, of Panama since 1900. Question of future of canal and canal zone looms large throughout. Tone is at once combative and impressionistic.

2418 Grieb, Kenneth J. Guatemalan caudillo, the regime of Jorge Ubico: Guatemala 1931–1944. Athens: Ohio University Press, 1979. 384 p.; bibl.; index; maps.

Author deplores fact that writing about Ubico has been so partisan, and says that his will be a scholarly study which will not satisfy supporters or opponents of Guatemalan dictator. After exhaustive study of regime's programs and activities, both in Guatemala and abroad, concludes that Ubico regime provided some measure of progress during first eight years, but decayed and became increasingly repressive during last five. Whether such limited progress can justify so many years of repression is not addressed.

2419 Guidos Véjar, Rafael. El ascenso del militarismo en El Salvador. San Salvador: UCA Editores, 1980. 156 p.; bibl. (Colección Estructuras y procesos; v. 8)

Account of growing role of the Salvadoran military in political life after the world crisis of 1929. Formation and decay of Liberal oligarchy (1871–1927), failure of more open politics (1927–32), and restoration of oligarchy with military backing (1932–35), are main subjects discussed.

2420 Hall, Carolyn. Formación de una hacienda cafetalera, 1889–1911. San José: Editorial Universidad de Costa Rica, 1978. 49 p.; bibl.; ill.

Expert on historical geography of Costa Rican coffee industry here turns her attention to one coffee hacienda, thanks to discovery of Cóncavas estate's records. We thus have a complete account of one state's purchase, growth, climate and business affairs. Careful and most useful short essay.

2421 Homenaje a la memoria del gran francés en el 150 aniversario de su natalicio (LNB/L, 292, julio 1980, p. 80–124, facsims., photos)

A collection of speeches, pictures, and studies about and in honor of De Lesseps and his work in Panama.

2422 Jiménez Oreamuno, Ricardo. Ricardo Jiménez Oreamuno, "su pensa-

miento." Prólogo, selección y bibliografía, Eugenio Rodríguez. San José: Editorial Costa Rica, 1980. 459, 6 p. (Biblioteca patria; 17)

Selections from the writings of the Costa Rican Liberal and President. His importance for understanding of Costa Rican politics and government from 1910–40 is considerable. His minor writings on education and literature are also of some interest.

2423 Karnes, Thomas L. Tropical enterprise: the Standard Fruit and Steamship Company in Latin America. Baton Rouge: Louisiana State University Press, 1978. 332 p.; 5 leaves of plates; bibl.; ill.; index.

Rather favorable account, based on extensive company and state department documentation of Standard Fruit's activities in Central America, Haiti, and Hawaii. In 1968 Standard became a subsidiary of Dole.

2424 Kutchbach, Mario Samper. Los productores directos en el siglo del café (UNCR/R, 4:7, julio/dic, 1978, p. 123–217, bibl., tables)

Pt. 2 of thesis on evolution of sociooccupational structure in Costa Rica. Long, dense article, based on deep knowledge of documentary material takes story from postindependence period of economic transition and smallholders, through beginnings of economic dependence with sugar and tobacco, to coffee age. Carefully discusses class struggles, occupational structures, Liberal economic policies, and transient economic crises.

2425 Lainfiesta, Francisco. Apuntamientos para la historia de Guatemala: período de 20 años, corridos del 14 de abril de 1865 al 6 de abril de 1885. Guatemala: Editorial J. de Pineda Ibarra, 1975. 487 p. (Publicación especial—Sociedad de Geografía e Historia de Guatemala; no. 18)

Written from Honduran exile, this account of 1865–85 period in Guatemala by poet, congressman, and Cabinet Minister who was later unsuccessful presidential candidate, is somewhat of a Liberal unionist manifesto and explanation of events, and an expression of disillusionment at failure to find workable constitution for Guatemala. President Barrios is work's central figure.

2426 Leistenschneider, María and Freddy Leistenschneider. Gobernantes de El

Salvador: biografías. San Salvador: Publicaciones del Ministerio del Interior, 1980. 279 p.; 86 leaves of plates; ports.

Biographies and legislation of presidents and other rulers of El Salvador since 1821, presented in dry catalog format. Of use as reference work.

2427 Leiva Vivas, Rafeal. Presencia de Máximo Gómez en Honduras. Santo Domingo: Ediciones Fundación García-Arévalo, 1977. 34 p.; bibl.; ill. (Serie monográfica Fundación García-Arévalo; no. 6)

Gómez (b. Dominican Republic) was leader in Cuban independence struggle. This slim volume is an account of his periods of exile in Honduras.

2428 ———. Vigencia del sabio Valle. Ciudad Universitaria Rodrigo Facio, Costa Rica: Editorial Universitaria Centroamericana, 1980. 442 p. (Colección Rueda del tiempo)

Yet another account of life and times of Honduran and Central American *pensador* and statesman. Effusive praise for Valle is blended with historical analysis. Research and documentation appear to be unusually thorough.

2429 Las Luchas obreras en Panamá, 1850–1978. Marco A. Gandásegui, hijo *et al.* Panamá: Centro de Estudios Latinoamericanos, "Justo Arosemena," 1980. 216 p.; bibl.; ill.

Pt. 1 begins with construction of railroad and work on "French canal," both crucial events in history of Panamanian working class. Building of American canal, setting up of its enclaves, demographic growth, rural to urban migration, and growth in manufacturing sector are all studied as contributors to emergence of proletariat. Pt. 2 is concerned with events, and major strikes and workers organizations. Pt. 3 studies demographic structure of modern Panama, occupation categories, wages, public and private employment, migration again, unions, and much else. Volume is serious, pioneering work based on extensive data and surveys.

2430 Luján, Enrique Robert. Genealogía de Pablo de Alvarado: precursor y prócer de la independencia de Costa Rica. San José: Impr. Nacional, 1976 [i.e. 1979]. p. 27–121: 1 geneal. table; bibl.

Pablo de Alvarado was leading figure in independence movement in Costa Rica, and was descended from conquistadors Jorge de Alvarado and Angel Villafañe.

Marcoleta, José de. Documentos diplomáticos de José de Marcoleta, Ministro de Nicaragua en los Estados Unidos, 1854. See *HLAS 43:7256.*

2431 Marroquín, Alejandro D. Estudio sobre la crísis de los años treinta en El Salvador (*in* América Latina en los años treinta. Luis Antezana E. *et al.* Coordinador, Pablo González Casanova. México: Instituto de Investigaciones Sociales, Universidad Nacional Autónoma de México, 1977, p. 113–190, tables)

Crash of 1930 caused catastrophic decline in Salvadoran coffee exports, and brought many forms of hardship to the people. Convincing statistical graphs on matters as diverse as consumption of beef and juvenile delinquency vividly illustrate these statements.

2432 Martínez Peláez, Severo. Centroamérica en los años de la independencia: el país y sus habitantes (SGHG/A, 47:1/4, enero/dic. 1974, p. 12–43, bibl.)

Economic and class configuration of Central America at time of independence will serve as introduction to book on period. Basically background material, but presented with fresh, Marxist interpretation.

2433 Méndez Pereira, Alberto. Ferdinand de Lesseps y los canales (LNB/L, 289, abril 1980, p. 18–29)

Familiar tale of De Lesseps' failure to build a canal in Panamá. Brief and standard fare.

2434 Meza, Víctor. Historia del movimiento obrero hondureño. Tegucigalpa: Editorial Guaymuras, 1980. 170 p.; bibl. (Colección Códices)

Brief survey takes reader from first Honduran Federation of workers (1921), their first strikes in banana plantations, first ideological schisms, and reorganization in years following World War II, to great banana strike of 1954, emergence of Honduran Workers Confederation (1963–65), and recent problems with "reformist" military governments. Excellent introduction to the subject.

2435 Millett, Richard. Guardianes de la dinastía: historia de la Guardia Nacional de Nicaragua, creada por Estados Unidos, y de la familia Somoza. Traducción al español de Mario Samper K. San José: Editorial Universitaria Centroamericana, 1979. 344 p.; bibl.; ill. (Colección Seis)

Spanish translation of *Guardians of the dynasty* (see *HLAS 40:2901*).

2436 Montiel Argüello, Alejandro. Artículos históricos. Managua, Nicaragua: Editorial Unión, 1978. 238 p.; bibl. (Serie Historia; 1) (Colección Biblioteca Banco Central de Nicaragua)

Potpourri of historical articles about Nicaragua in particular, Central America in general. Noteworthy is long section on Frederick Chatfield and Nicaragua, and sycophantic evaluation of Anastasio Somoza's role in recent Nicaraguan history.

2437 Morán, Francisco. Las jornadas cívicas de abril y mayo de 1944. San Salvador: Editorial Universitaria, 1979. 150 p. (Colección Eterna)

Concise detailed account of events of Salvadoran revolution of 1944 which led to overthrow of dictator Gen. Hernández Martínez, ruler for 13 years. Argues effectively that this political change marked end of era of traditional dictators and unleashed constitutional, political, and even social crisis which is still unresolved in El Salvador.

2438 Núñez M., Francisco María. Periódicos y periodistas. San José: Editorial Costa Rica, 1980. 113 p.; bibl.

Biographies of journalists and newspaper owners, which, when combined, give fair idea of history of profession in Costa Rica.

2439 Obando Sánchez, Antonio. Memorias, la historia del movimiento obrero en Guatemala en este siglo. Carátula, Mauro Calanchina. Guatemala: Editorial Universitaria, 1978. 161 p.; ill. (Colección popular Mario López Larrave)

Personal account by a union organizer and Marxist of anti-Ubico struggle in Guatemala, and of imprisonment and execution of working class leaders during that era.

2240 Oconitrillo García, Eduardo. Alfredo González Flores, estadista incomprendido. San José: Editorial Universidad Estatal a Distancia, 1980. 359 p.; bibl.; ports. (Serie Estudios socio-políticos; no. 6)

Period 1910–17 saw rapid changes in social and economic life of Costa Rica and, according to author, country was fortunate in having as deputy and president a man of flexibility and imagination such as González Flores who believed in the interventionist reformist state. His premature overthrow prevented many of his projects from developing.

2441 ———. Los Tinoco, 1917–1919. San José: Editorial Costa Rica, 1980. 240 p.; 8 p. of plates; bibl.; ports.

History of coup d'etat carried out by Tinoco brothers and their followers in 1917, which overthrew constitutional president of Costa Rica, Alfredo González Flores. Author outlines sweeping reformist program started by González, and explains growing alarm which this caused among certain groups. Federico Tinoco governed dictatorially until 1919, reversing many of reforms, and much of social legislation passed by his predecessor. Growing rivalry and armed conflict forced his resignation.

2442 Ortega Arancibia, Francisco. Cuarenta años: 1838–1878 [i.e. mil ochocientos treinta y ocho-mil ochocientos setenta y ocho] de historia de Nicaragua. 3. ed. Managua: Fondo de Promoción Cultural, Banco de América, 1975. 510 p.; 8 leaves of plates; index; ports. (Serie histórica; no. 6) (Colección cultural Banco de América)

New edition of 1911 account of these years by 19th-century liberal participant. Rhetorical, emotional, personal history, with much on 1854 revolution, William Walker, Costa Rica's role, and Nicaraguan personalistic politics.

2443 Ortega Saavedra, Humberto. Cincuenta años de lucha sandinista. Portada de Efraín Herrera. México: Editorial Diógenes, 1979. 139 p.; 8 leaves of plates; bibl.; ill.

A *Comandante* of Sandinista guerrilla army writes intricate theoretical account of 50 years of anti-Somoza struggle. Essay is marred by jargon and sloganeering.

2444 El Pensamiento liberal de Guatemala: antología. Compilada por García Laguardia. San José: Editorial Universitaria Centroamericana, 1977. 362 p.; bibl. (Colección Rueda del tiempo)

Long satisfactory introduction discusses liberal reform in Guatemala. Traces Liberalism from independence period through first failure and Conservative governments era to 1871 Liberal triumph. Includes documentary anthology containing writings and speeches by Miguel García Granados, Justo Rufino Barrios and others. Important material for late 19th-century Guatemalan history.

2445 Pérez, Jerónimo. Obras históricas completas del Licenciado Jerónimo Pérez. Impresas bajo la dirección y con notas del doctor Pedro Joaquín Chamorro Zelaya. Managua: Fondo de Promoción Cultural, Banco de América, 1975. 875 p.; 16 leaves of plates; index; ports. (Serie histórica; no. 5) (Colección cultural)

Reissue of 1928 edition, work describes Nicaraguan 1854 Revolution, William Walker's invasion, and national campaign against him (1856–57). There is valuable documentary appendix and several biographies of leading participants in events.

2446 Pinaud, José María. *comp.* La epopeya del civismo costarricense. San José: Ministerio de Cultura, Juventud y Deportes, Dirección de Publicaciones, 1979. 162 p.; ill. (Serie del rescate; no. 5)

Reprint of 1942 study of 1889 constitutional crisis. Attempt was made to bypass elected candidate for President, José Joaquín Rodríguez, the Constitutional or Conservative candidate. Eventually, under pressure, Liberals in power handed power to him. Some scholars believe these events helped to institutionalize political participation and constitutional elections in Costa Rica.

Poitevin, René. El proceso de industrialización en Guatemala. See *HLAS 43:3105.*

2447 Polo Sifontes, Francis. Mariano Gálvez, éxitos y fracaso de su gobierno. Diseño de portada, Oscar Barrientos. Guatemala: Instituto de Antropología e Historia, Ministerio de Educación, 1979. 42 p.; bibl.; port. (Colección Historia: Serie Historia republicana) (Publicación especial—Instituto de Antropología e Historia; no. 11)

Brief essay decides that Gálvez failed because he imposed alien laws and concepts by force, granted too many concessions to foreigners, and introduced too many innovations too quickly. Careful, reasoned essay based on period's printed sources.

2448 Ramírez, Sergio. Biografía de Sandino. Managua: Ediciones Ministerio de Educación, 1979. 76 p.; port.

Brief biography of guerrilla hero of Nicaraguan revolution by member of present government.

2449 Ramírez Morales, José. José de Marcoleta: padre de la diplomacia nicaragüense. v. 1/2. Páginas de nuestra historia. Managua: Talleres de la Imprenta Nacional, 1975–1977. 2 v.; bibl.

Spaniard with experience in European diplomacy, Marcoleta was awarded Nicaraguan citizenship in 1846. Thereafter he helped his new country to negotiate peace treaty with Spain, participated in negotiations over Mosquito Coast, was involved in various questions raised by possibility of Nicaraguan canal and by William Walker's invasions. Died in Paris while serving as Nicaraguan Minister Plenipotentiary to the Vatican. Vol. 2 is curious in that it contains several essays on Nicaraguan history in which Marcoleta's role is not always clear.

2450 Reina Valenzuela, José. Hondureños en la independencia de Centroamérica. Tegucigalpa: EDISOFF, 1978. 173 p.; bibl.; ill.

Well documented discussion of Honduras at time of independence, emphasizing population, economics, regional rivalries, and leaders of independence movement. Superior to usual hagiographies about this period.

2451 ——— and Mario Argueta. Marco Aurelio Soto: reforma liberal de 1876. Tegucigalpa: Banco Central de Honduras, 1978. 250 p.; bibl.; ill. (Publicaciones culturales)

Political life of Marco Aurelio Soto, a leader of 1871 Liberal Revolution in Guatemala. Served in Miguel García Granados' cabinet, became Honduras' president, and tried to reform its agriculture, mining, education, public health, etc., but his program did not have enough time to develop and results were inconclusive.

2452 Sáenz, Adela de. Crónicas de un tiempo. Adela Ferreto. Dibujos de José Manuel Lépiz L. Diseño de la portada, Osvaldo Salas. San José: Editorial Costa Rica, 1978. 314 p.; ill.

Nostalgic evocations by skilled essayist of city of Heredia and of Costa Rican countryside at beginning of century. Excellent, unadorned "belles lettres."

2453 Salazar Mora, Jorge Mario. Calderón Guardia. Presentado por Jorge Mario Salazar Mora. San José: Ministerio de

Cultura, Juventud y Deportes, Dirección de Publicaciones, 1980. 240 p.; bibl. (Serie Quién fué y qué hizo?)

Part of revisionist literature which rehabilitated controversial Costa Rican president and caudillo who, in the 1940s, led radical reformist coalition which lost 1948 civil war to José Figueres Ferrer's supporters. Subsequently Calderón and his followers twice invaded Costa Rica from Nicaragua, then settled down to political opposition to Liberación Nacional Party.

2454 Sandino, Augusto César. Augusto César Sandino. Prólogo, selección y notas de Sergio Ramírez. San José: Ministerio de Cultura, Juventud y Deportes, 1978. 408 p.; 11 leaves of plates; ports. (Serie Pensamiento de América; no. 11)

One of better commentaries and selections of Sandino's work, this is an expanded version of Ramírez' *Biografía* (see item **2448**). Essential reading and fine source for those interested in Sandino and modern Nicaragua.

2455 ———. Escritos literarios y documentos desconocidos. Presentación, recopilación, notas y bibliografía fundamental de Jorge Eduardo Arellano. Managua: Ministerio de Cultura, 1980. 98 p.; bibl.

Selection of Sandino's literary writings (poetry, pamphlets, short essays, tales and fables), and of some previously unpublished documents by him from his guerrilla years. Useful bibliography concludes this slim volume.

2456 ———. Ideario político del general Augusto César Sandino. Recopilado por Carlos Fonseca. Managua: Secretaría Nacional de Propaganda y Educación Política, F.S.L.N., 1980. 37 p.

Founder of Frente Sandinista de Liberación Nacional selects collection of Sandino's political and ideological writings.

2457 ———. Ideario político del General Augusto César Sandino. s.l.: Comisión de Información, de la Representación en Cuba, del Frente Sandinista de Liberación Nacional, between 1976 and 1979. 54 p., 3 leaves of plates; ports.

Pamphlet obviously designed to introduce the Nicaraguan guerrilla hero to the Cuban people, much of it consisting of quotations from Sandino's speeches and writings.

2458 Sandino, el rebelde de América: antología bibliográfica. 2. ed. Managua? Nicaragua: Ediciones Monimbo, 1979. 208 p.

Yet another collection about the life of Sandino, his political and social ideas, and his writings.

2459 Santacruz Noriega, José. Gobierno del capitán general D. Miguel García Granados. Guatemala: Delgado, 1979. 522 p.; bibl.; ill.; index (Colección Gobiernos de Guatemala; 1)

Lengthy, detailed account of life, campaigns, politics, and legislation of Miguel García Granados until he left the Guatemalan presidency in 1873. Views García sympathetically but not uncritically. Book is based largely on published sources.

Seligson, Mitchell A. Peasants of Costa Rica and the development of agrarian capitalism. See *HLAS 43:3109.*

2460 Selser, Gregorio. El pequeño ejército loco: Sandino y la operación México-Nicaragua. México: Bruguera Mexicana de Ediciones, 1980. 414 p.; bibl.

Famous account of Sandino guerrillas and of Somoza's rise to power. Essential reading for understanding of history and passions of that era in Nicaragua.

2461 Senior, Olive. Corollary: the Chinese who came from Panama (IJ/JJ, 44, 1980, p. 78–79)

Some of Jamaica's Chinese citizens came to island via Panamá because railroad company "swapped" them for Jamaican laborers. Chinese in Panama suffered heavily from tropical diseases, and many committed suicide in despair. Company was pleased to trade away small remnant which survived.

2462 ———. The Panama Railway (IJ/JJ, 44, 1980, p. 66–77, ill., map)

Jamaican writer evokes time of building of Panamanian railroad from point of view of Jamaican immigrant laborer. Working environment and living conditions were very poor, and questions of color, class and language provoked sporadic violence. Nevertheless, many stayed on.

2463 Soler, Ricaurte. Formas ideológicas de la nación panameña; Panamá y el problema nacional hispanoamericano. Con ilus. de la Folletería Histórica Panameña. 5. ed. San José: Editorial Universitaria Centroamericana, 1977. 147 p.; 6 leaves of plates; bibl.; ill.; index (Colección Seis)

Third edition of well-known study of factors involved in formation of Panamanian nationhood.

2464 Solís A., Manuel. Notas sobre la agroindustria capitalista en el período 1900–1930: los ingenios y otras agroindustrias. San José: Instituto de Investigaciones Sociales, Facultad de Ciencias Sociales, Universidad de Costa Rica, 1980. 64 p.; bibl.; tables (Avances de investigación; 40)

Purpose of study is to show that agrobusiness in Costa Rica is older than usually supposed. Although coffee now dominates nation's capitalist agriculture, first steps in development of such agriculture were intensification and rationalization of sugar production for making alcohol. Period 1900–25 saw large imports of foreign machinery, considerable foreign ownership of various aspects of sugar business, and growth in all phases of industry.

2465 Tjark, Germán; Flora María Fernández; Julio César Espinoza; and Edwin González. La epidemia del cólera de 1856 en el Valle Central; análisis y consecuencias demográficas (UNCR/R, 2:3, julio/dic. 1976, p. 81–129, bibl., graphs, tables)

Dramatic increase in deaths and fall in fertility were only two results of this devastating epidemic. Authors examined appropriate statistics by parish, thus adding a new and more exact dimension to previous general discussion of this episode.

2466 Tobar Cruz, Pedro. Crónica de la conspiración de Antonio Kopesky, 1877, y el gobierno liberal de J. Rufino Barrios (IAHG/AHG, 2:1, 1979, p. 127–137, bibl.)

Account of cruel and brutal suppression of minor revolt against Barrios regime in 1877. Executions had profound effect upon citizens of Guatamala City.

2467 Torres, Edelberto. Influencia de la crísis del 29 en Nicaragua (in América Latina en los años treinta. Luis Antezana E. et al. Coordinador Pablo González Casanova. México: Instituto de Investigaciones Sociales, Universidad Nacional Autonóma de México, 1977, p. 89–112, tables)

Global economic crash of 1929 left as part of its legacy Nicaragua's Somoza dynasty. Author's solution to Central America's

many problems is a socialist, federal republic consisting of all the region's countries.

2468 Townsend Ezcurra, Andrés. Las Provincias Unidas de Centroamérica: fundación de la República. San José: Editorial Costa Rica, 1973. 488 p.; bibl.; index.

New edition of constitutional history of setting up of the United Provinces of Central America. Published in 1958 under title: Fundación de la República.

2469 Valle, José Cecilio del. Antología. Introducción, selección y notas, R. Oquelí. Tegucigalpa: Editorial Universitaria, 1981. 599 p.; bibl.; ill. (Colección Letras hondureñas; no. 6)

Confusing collection of Valle's writings, organized alphabetically by subject. Difficult to use unless one seeks Valle's views on specific topic. For a much better compilation, see item **2470**.

2470 ———. Escritos de José Cecilio del Valle: una selección. Certidumbres y vacilaciones de un provinciano por Ramón Oquelí. En torno al pensamiento de Valle, selección de textos y bibliografía por Carlos Meléndez Ch. Washington, D.C.: Secretaría General, Organización de Estados Americanos, 1981. 255 p.; bibl.

Useful compendium of major writings by Central American savant, liberal, independence leader and statesman, in honor of 200th anniversary of his birth. Much more useful to scholar and general reader than the Antología (see item **2469**).

2471 Valle, Pompeyo del. El hondureño, hombre mítico. Ilus., Juan Ramón Laínez. Tegucigalpa: Departamento de Producción Intelectual, Secretaría de Cultura, Turismo e Información, 1977. 163 p.; bibl.; ill.; index.

In an attempt to establish set of national characteristics, author puts together potpourri of folklore, tales, supersititions, local crafts, and history. Essays vary widely in quality and interest. Of doubtful use to working historian.

2472 Vega Carballo, José Luis. Estado y dominación social en Costa Rica: antecedentes coloniales y formación del estado nacional. San José: Instituto de Investigaciones Sociales, Facultad de Ciencias Sociales, Universidad de Costa Rica, 1980. 61 p.; bibl. (Avance de investigación, Instituto de Investigaciones Sociales, Facultad de Ciencias Sociales, Universidad de Costa Rica, 0378-0473; no. 35)

Little more than historical outline of what obviously will be a much larger study of period 1820–1930. Consists of two parts: 1) colonial period which author considers one of backwardness and marginality; and 2) early republican period, defined as era of patriarchal state. Too short to serve more than as brief outline but contains arguments and concepts of interest.

―――. Etapas y procesos de la evolución sociopolítica de Costa Rica. See HLAS 43:8162.

2473 Wheeler, John Hill. Diario de John Hill Wheeler, Ministro de los Estados Unidos en Nicaragua, 1854–1857. Managua: Fondo de Promoción Cultural, Banco de América, 1974. 171 p.; index (Serie Fuentes históricas; 1) (Colección cultural Banco de América)

US Minister of Nicaragua Wheeler negotiated two treaties on trade and navigation between both countries in 1835. His mission was overtaken by William Walker's invasion.

His recognition of Walker's presidency led to his recall by President Pierce, who accepted his resignation 2 March 1857. Wheeler's diary recounts most of these events in bland, uninformative manner.

2474 Wheelock, Jaime. Frente Sandinista, diciembre victorioso. Managua?: Secretaría Nacional de Propaganda y Educación Política, F.S.L.N., 1979 or 1980. 92 p.; bibl.

Leader of the Sandinistas recounts events of 27 Dec. 1974, in which hostages were taken to obtain release of political prisoners. Interspersed are attacks on Somoza regime, and defenses of Sandinista policy and actions.

2475 Yglesias Hogan, Rubén. Un recuerdo histórico: la Revolución de 1830 en Francia y su comentario por un centroamericano (CRAN/R, 40/43: 1/2, enero 1976/dic. 1979, p. 50–54)

Costa Rican observer, Gen. Francisco Ignacio de Rascón, applauds overthrow of Charles X of France who, he points out, had given protection to odious Fernando VII of Spain. Thus, he warns his compatriots, will end all Central American despotism too.

THE CARIBBEAN AND THE GUIANAS

FRANKLIN W. KNIGHT, *Professor of History, The Johns Hopkins University*

AS INTEREST IN THE CARIBBEAN INCREASES in both political and academic circles, the historiography of the region grows in quantity and quality at an accelerated rate. Books of higher caliber reflecting great sophistication in various disciplines and encompassing diverse geographic areas have appeared. The pronounced recognition of peripheral areas is exemplified by collections such as Roberta Marx Delson's *Readings in Caribbean history and economics* (item **2496**), original works such as Virginia Radcliffe's popular overview, *The Caribbean heritage* (item **2494**), and Jack Watson's *The West Indian heritage* (item **2499**), designed for high school readers. In a general category the most notable books are: David Nicholl's *From Dessalines to Duvalier* (item **2491**); Cornelius Goslinga's *A short history of the Netherlands Antilles and Surinam* (item **2485**); and Ian Bell's *The Dominican Republic* (item **2477**). Specialists should take note of the reissue of Elsa Goveia's analytical classic, *A Study on the historiography of the British West Indies to the end of the nineteenth century* (item **2486**) which delivers far more than the title indicates, and of the final report of the 24th meeting of SALALM (item **2498**). In addition to resource acquisitions and deposits, this report contains several assessments of the state of Caribbean studies at the university level.

The increasing interest in the early colonial period is producing some truly outstanding works. Isabelo Macías Domínguez's *Cuba en la primera mitad del siglo*

XVII (item **2505**), examines the social and economic condition of the colony between 1598 and 1660 and reveals there was far more dynamism than had been assumed previously. He includes a wealth of statistical tables and charts that will be of great benefit to scholars. Michael Devèze's *Antilles, Guyanes, la Mer des Caraïbes de 1492–1789* (item **2502**) looks at the Caribbean from the unusual perspective of the periphery, but manages to portray the fluctuating fortunes and emerging problems of the entire region. Paul Hoffman's *The Spanish Crown and the defense of the Caribbean, 1535–1585* (item **2504**) is the type of book which makes an author and his publisher proud. It is solidly researched, persuasively argued, clearly written, and manages to challenge or demolish a wide range of hallowed, generally accepted propositions on the history of the early Caribbean. It will force a complete reassessment of this period as symptomatic of Spanish naval weakness or Spanish economic decline.

The 1976 bicentennial celebrations of US independence stimulated much interest in the Spanish borderlands exemplified at its best by Pablo Tornero Tinajero's *Relaciones de dependencia entre Florida y Estados Unidos: 1783–1820* (item **2520**), a masterful examination of economic, demographic and political interrelationships. Joseph Starr's *Tories, dons, and rebels: the American Revolution in British West Florida* (item **2519**), on the other hand, demonstrates that a regional focus can provide a sobering qualification.

The theme of slavery dominates late colonial period through 19th century works with slave revolts attracting much attention. The first issue of *Cimarróns* (item **2511**) published in Guadeloupe concerns this topic, as does Michael Craton's fine article "Proto-Peasant Revolts? the Late Slave Rebellions in the West Indies, 1816–1832" (item **2525**).

Another leading theme examined by Aida R. Caro Costas is *El Cabildo o régimen municipal puertorriqueño en el siglo XVIII* (item **2509**) which reminds us of the cardinal importance of this vital Spanish colonial institution. David Geggus' "The British Government and the Saint Domingue Slave Revolt, 1791–1793" (item **2512**) looks at the imperial impact of the decision to reconquer the French colony. Monica Schuler's *Alas, Alas Kongo: a social history of indentured African immigration into Jamaica, 1841–1865* (item **2545**) concerns the cultural impact of free African immigrants. The emergence of the working class is the focus of the following works: Fernando Picó's *Libertad y servidumbre en el Puerto Rico del siglo XIX* (item **2537**) and *Registro general de jornaleros, Utuado* (item **2540**), Walter Rodney's *A History of the Guyanese working people, 1881–1905* (item **2542**), and W.K. Marshall's *Metayage in the sugar industry of the British Windward Islands* (item **2533**). Other excellent contributions on the period are Pierre Pluchon's *Toussaint Louverture* (item **2538**), Liliane Chauleau's *La Vie quotidienne aux Antilles françaises* (item **2524**), and Fé Iglesias' "Algunos Aspectos de la Distribución de la Tierra en 1899" (item **2530**).

The literature on the Cuban Revolution no longer dwarfs the output on the 20th century, but Mario Mencía's *La prisión fecunda* (item **2564**) and John Dorschner's and Roberto Fabricio's *The Winds of December* (item **2552**) are good, useful journalistic contributions. Race and class continue to command much attention from John Dumoulin's *Azucar y lucha de clases* (item **2553**), Carlos Doré y Cabral's *Reforma agraria y luchas sociales en la República Dominicana* (item **2551**), Anthony Layne's "Race, Class and Development in Barbados" (item **2560**) and Joel Figarola's *Cuba: 1900–1928* (item **2555**). Two studies of Puerto Rico which should not be overlooked are Idsa Alegría Ortega's *La Comisión del Status de Puerto Rico* (item **2547**), and Juan Flores's *The Insular vision: Pedreira's interpretation of Puerto Rican culture* (item **2556**). Similarly, no one interested in migration should miss the excellent collection of articles included in *La República neocolonial* (item **2571**). The Caribbean continues to attract scholars whose approach transcends conventional disciplinary boundaries and whose methodologies are the most innovative of all disciplines.

GENERAL

2476 Antonin, Arnold. La larga y desconocida lucha del pueblo de Haití. Prólogo, Luis Beltran Prieto. Presentación, Orlando Araujo. Traducción, Argenis Martínez y Arnold Antonin. Diseño portada, Jorge Pizzani. Caracas: Editorial Ateneo de Caracas, 1979. 126 p.; bibl.; ill. (Colección Testimonios)

Synoptical history with emphasis on chronology.

2477 Bell, Ian. The Dominican Republic. Boulder, Colo.: Westview Press; London: Ernest Benn, 1981. 392 p.; bibl.; ill.; index (Nations of the modern world)

Solidly researched, thoughtful, and reliable general history of Dominican Republic, admirably balanced with emphasis on 20th century. Author had long diplomatic career and was Ambassador from UK to the Dominican Republic.

Catálogo de documentos históricos de Bayamón. v. 1–8. See item **96**.

2478 Chez Checo, José and **Rafael Peralta Brito.** Azúcar, encomiendas y otros ensayos históricos. Portada de Leonardo Alvarado. Santo Domingo: Ediciones Fundación García-Arévalo, 1979. 218 p.; bibl.; ill. (Serie Investigaciones; no. 10)

Good survey based on extensive secondary material, and handsomely illustrated.

2479 Conference of Caribbean Historians, *5th, St. Augustine, Trinidad, 1973.* Political protest and political organisation in the Caribbean from the late nineteenth century: papers presented at the Fifth Conference of Caribbean Historians, April 9th–13th, U.W.I., St. Augustine, Trinidad. s.l.: Association of Caribbean Historians, 1976. 2 v.; bibl.

Some papers given at the 5th Annual Conference of Caribbean Historians. Uneven in quality, some are of great interest, especially Fitzroy Baptiste's "The Seizure of the

Dutch Authorities in Curaçao by Venezuelan Political Exiles in June 1929, Viewed in Relation to the Anglo-French Landings in Aruba and Curaçao in May 1940"; Bridget Brereton's "The Reform Movement in Trinidad in the Later 19th Century"; and Assad Shoman's "The Birth of the Nationalist Movement in Belize, 1950–1954."

2480 Corvington, Georges, Jr. Port-au-Prince au cours des ans. v. 1, La ville coloniale, 1743–1789. v. 2, Sous les assauts de la Révolution, 1789–1804. v. 3, La métropole haïtienne du XIXe siècle, 1804–1888. v. 4, La métropole haïtienne du XIXe siècle, 1888–1915. 2. ed. Port-au-Prince: Impr. H. Deschamps, 1974? 4 v. (213, 247, 318, 326 p.); bibl.; ill.

Four-volume work is interesting, beautifully illustrated, and often remarkable for its recapture of more than a century in the life of a city and a state. Limited edition reprint.

2481 Deive, Carlos Esteban. La esclavitud del negro en Santo Domingo: 1492–1844. Santo Domingo: Museo del Hombre Dominicano, 1980. 2 v. (374, 433 p.)

Most thorough, and up-to-date history of slavery in the Dominican Republic. Far supersedes all previous works. Based on extensive archival research in the country as well as in Europe. Deals with all aspects of society and economy. Bibliography reasonably up-to-date.

2482 Doucet, Louis. Voux avez dit Guyane! Paris: Denoïl, 1981. 251 p.; map.

Basically a descriptive work spiced with history and humor.

2483 Fergus, Howard A. History of Alliouagana: a short history of Montserrat. Plymouth?, Montserrat: University Centre, 1975. 66 p.; bibl.; map.

Local history by local historian.

Galvin, Miles. The organized labor movement in Puerto Rico. See *HLAS 43:3259*.

2484 Gastmann, Albert L. Historical dictionary of the French and Netherlands Antilles. Metuchen, N.J.: Scarecrow Press, 1978. 162 p.; bibl. (Latin American historical dictionaries; no. 18)

Contains basic citations, list of French colonial governors and fairly good bibliography.

2485 Goslinga, Cornelis Christiaan. A short history of the Netherlands Antilles and Surinam. The Hague; Boston: M. Nijhoff, 1979, 198 p.; bibl.; index; map.

Welcome addition to region's historiography, this book fills very large void in field of Caribbean history. Covering more than 300 years, work is readable, and provides excellent introduction. Bibliographical essay is very good.

2486 Goveia, Elsa V. A study on the historiography of the British West Indies to the end of the nineteenth century. Washington, D.C.: Howard University Press, 1980. 181 p.; 1 fold. leaf of plates; bibl.; map.

Reprint of Elsa Goveia's celebrated 1956 study of Caribbean historiography will provide a great service to all who have an interest in the area. There is nothing quite like it in the field.

2487 Hartog, Johannes. History of Saba. Translation by Frank Hassell. Saba, Netherlands Antilles: Van Guilder, 1975. 140 p.; ill.

Interesting account with excellent illustrations of the broad sweep of Saba history, from pre-European societies to present. Good statistics on small population.

2488 Hirst, George S.S. Notes on the history of the Cayman Islands. Grand Cayman, B.W.I.: Caribbean Colour, 1967. 5 v. in 3 (412 p.); ill.

Reprinting of original 1910 version of most thorough, informative account of Cayman Islands at turn of century, complete with the then current advertisements. These, along with the pictures of houses and businesses no longer in existence are fascinating.

2489 Levine, Barry B. Miguel Barnet on the testimonial (FIU/CR, 9:4, Fall 1980, p. 32–35, ill.)

Valuable as background for understanding and evaluating *Biografía de un cimarrón* (see *HLAS 32:1944*) which Barnet collected and edited.

Lizardo Barinas, Fradique. Cultura africana en Santo Domingo. See *HLAS 43:8212.*

Manyoni, Joseph R. Extra-marital mating patterns in Caribbean family studies: a methodological excursus. See *HLAS 43:1022.*

2490 Miller, Joseph C. Mortality in the Atlantic slave trade: statistical evidence on causality (JIH, 11:3, Winter 1981, p. 385–423, graphs, tables)

Miller carefully examines literature on mortality during period of slave trade and tries to calculate varying patterns of mortality, bearing in mind various circumstances. His argument supports rational conduct on slavers' part, and great self-interest in operation of trade.

2491 Nicholls, David. From Dessalines to Duvalier: race, colour, and national independence in Haiti. Cambridge, UK; New York: Cambridge University Press, 1979. 357 p.; bibl.; index; map (Cambridge Latin American studies; no. 34)

Probably best book written about Haitian history after its independence, a thorough, thoughtful, extremely well-researched work which sees color and race—carefully defined and differentiated by author—as most salient variables in continuing problems of political instability. Even more than a history, Nicholls reviews writers and writings which have probed Haitian personality and presence in international politics. Valuable book not merely for Haiti but for the Caribbean as a whole.

Ohiorhenuan, John F. Dependence and noncapitalist development in the Caribbean: historical necessity and degrees of freedom. See *HLAS 43:3058.*

2492 Peguero, Luis Joseph. Historia de la Conquista, de la Isla Española de Santo Domingo trasumptada el año de 1762: traducida de la *Historia general de las Indias* escrita por Antonio de Herrera, Coronista mayor de Su Magestad, y de las Indias, y de Castilla, y de otros autores que han escrito sobre el particular. Edición, estudio preliminar y notas de Pedro J. Santiago. Santo Domingo: Museo de las Casas Reales, 1975. 2 v.; ill. (Publicaciones del Museo de las Casas Reales)

Peguero was one of the earliest American historians to write about Santo Domingo's early history from mid-18th century perspective. Manuscript has been in Madrid's Biblioteca Nacional for years. Illustrated with plants and animals of American origin, it relies heavily on Antonio de Herrera's earlier work.

2493 Puerto Rico, cien años de lucha política. t. 1, Programas, y manifestos, 1869–1952. t. 2, Documentos varios, 1869–1936. t. 3, Documentos varios, 1937–1950. t. 4, Documentos varios, 1951–1975. Compilador, Reece B. Bothwell González. Río Piedras: Editorial Universitaria, Universidad de Puerto Rico, 1979. 4 v. in 5.

Documents drawn from newspapers trace political party manifestoes from middle of 19th century, and indicate that party platforms have certain consistency throughout. Vol. 1 has very useful introduction. Especially valuable for studies of Albizu Campos and Muñoz Marín.

2494 Radcliffe, Virginia. The Caribbean heritage. New York: Walker, 1976. 271 p.; 2 leaves of plates; bibl.; ill. (some col.); index.

Delightfully readable and handsomely illustrated, this interesting book is for the intelligent reader. Covers all Caribbean islands. Good bibliography.

2495 Readings in Belizean history. Edited by John Maher. Belize City, Belize: BISRA, 1978. 1 v.; bibl.; ill.

Articles originally published in *Journal of Belizean Affairs* contribute to still small historiography of the country.

2496 Readings in Caribbean history and economics: an introduction to the region. Edited by Roberta Marx Delson. New York: Gordon and Breach Science Publishers, 1981. 1 v.; bibl.; index (Caribbean studies, 0275–5793; v. 1)

Interesting selection encompasses variety of disciplines and spans early 16th century to present. And even if, title notwithstanding, there is very little on French or Danish Caribbean, coverage is broader than most. Authors excerpted include: Sidney Mintz; Shirley Gorenstein; Robert Tomson; Jenaro Artiles; Bartolomé de las Casas; Richard Hakluyt; Matthew Edel; Richard Sheridan; George Beckford; Franklin W. Knight; Harry Hoetink; Silvia de Groot; Jerome Handler; Jill Shephard; Gwendolyn

Hall; Daniel Mannix; Michael Craton; Woodville Marshall; Richard Lobdell; Ken Boodhoo; Thomas Ott; John Fagg; Manuel Maldonado-Denis; José Martí; John Blassingame; Robert Smith; Jaap van Soest; Michael Manley; and Louise Bennett.

2497 Santiago, Pedro Julio. Estudios sobre comercio marítimo, naufragios y rescates submarinos en la República Dominicana. Santo Domingo: Museo de las Casas Reales, 1980. 128 p.; bibl.; ill (Publicaciones del Museo de las Casas Reales: Monografías y ensayos; 1)

Contains some fascinating tidbits on maritime commerce throughout the ages (e.g., sailing information, currency, shipwrecks, ship sizes).

Schroeder, Susan. Cuba: a handbook of historical statistics. See item **165.**

2498 Seminar on Acquisition of Latin American Library Materials, *24th, University of California, Los Angeles, 1979.* Windward, Leeward, and Main: Caribbean studies and library resources: final report and working papers of the twenty-fourth Seminar on the Acquisition of Latin American Library Materials, University of California, Los Angeles, California, June 17–22, 1979. Sonia Merubia, rapporteur general. Laurence Hallewell, editor. Coordinated by Suzanne Hodgman. Madison, Wis.: SALALM Secretariat, 1980. 354 p.

Following practice last carried out 20 years ago, this meeting of SALALM focused on Caribbean and surrounding Latin American states. Though somewhat deficient for non-English speaking territories, the reports cover not only resource base for archival and library materials, but also ways in which Caribbean in researched and taught (or neglected) both locally and abroad.

2499 Watson, Jack Brierley. The West Indian heritage: a history of the West Indies. London: J. Murray, 1979. 210 p.; facsim.; ill.; index; maps; plans; ports.

This highly readable book, designed for high school readers, includes some dated and/or questionable terms and interpretations. Covers entire Caribbean, although focus is on English Antilles. Impressive illustrations.

EARLY COLONIAL

2500 Arranz Márquez, Luis. Emigración española a Indias: poblamiento y despoblación antillanos. Santo Domingo: Ediciones Fundación García-Arévalo, 1979. 39 p.; bibl. (Serie monográfica—Fundación García Arévalo; no. 13)

Author asserts that population figures of approximately one million indigenous inhabitants for Antilles could not have been far off the mark. Based on archival and secondary sources.

2501 Breton, Raymond. Relations de l'Ile de La Guadeloupe. Basse-Terre: Société d'histoire de la Guadeloupe, 1978. 214 p.; bibl. (Bibliothèque d'histoire antillaise; 3)

Examines early development of Guadeloupe society, against background of fauna and flora, indigenous Carib groups, and contest with rival Europeans in commerce and war.

2502 Devèze, Michel. Antilles, Guyanes, la mer des Caraïbes, de 1492 à 1789. Paris: SEDES, 1977. 382 p.; bibl.; ill. (Regards sur l'histoire; 29: II, Histoire générale)

Good basic survey of region devotes much attention to pre-hispanic population as well as circum-Caribbean region. Narrative's bibliographic base is impressive.

2503 Du Tertre, Jean Baptiste. Histoire générale des Antilles habitées par les Français. De l'ordre des F. Prêcheurs. Paris: Edition et diffusion de la culture antillaise, 1978. 4 v. (551, 526, 380, 379 p.); ill.

Most welcome reissue in handsome volumes of Du Tertre's history, certainly one of the most consulted by serious scholars. This French Dominican priest traveled widely while closely observing English, French and Dutch early colonists.

2504 Hoffman, Paul E. The Spanish Crown and the defense of the Caribbean, 1535–1585: precedent, patrimonialism, and royal parsimony. Baton Rouge: Louisiana State University Press, 1980. 312 p.; bibl.; ill.; index.

Absolutely essential reading for early colonial era challenges all previous work on the period. Based on archival material and expert analysis of treasury records for 1535–85 gleaned from Casa de Contratación and nearly a score of treasuries, 17 from the Caribbean.

Hulse, F.S. Migration et selection de groupe: le cas de Cuba. See *HLAS 43:8203.*

2505 Macías Domínguez, Isabelo. Cuba en la primera mitad del siglo XVII. Prólogo de Francisco Morales Padrón. Sevilla: Escuela de Estudios Hispano-Americanos, 1978. 654 p.; 10 leaves of plates; bibl.; ill.; index (Publicaciones de la Escuela de Estudios HispanoAmericanos de Sevilla; 251 [no. general])

Includes outstanding and varied quantitative data on crops, property ownership, shipping and commerce, salaries and wages, and local income (including the *situado*) and expenditure. Volume certainly makes significant contribution to rather undeveloped and unexamined area of Spanish colonial and Cuban history.

2506 Rodríguez Demorizi, Emilio. El pleito Ovando-Tapia: comienzos de la vida urbana en América. Santo Domingo: Editora del Caribe, 1978. 326 p.; bibl.; index (Publicaciones—Fundación Rodríguez Demorizi; v. 10)

Details construction of Santo Domingo City and establishment of early colonial organizations by Nicolás de Ovando. Based on primary and secondary material.

Vega, Bernardo. Los cacicazgos de La Hispaniola. See *HLAS 43:5433.*

2507 Wood, Peter and the **Editors of Time-Life Books.** The Spanish Main. Alexandria, Va.: Time-Life Books, 1979. 176 p.; bibl.; ill.; index (The Seafarers)

Popular work, beautifully illustrated—indeed, visual aids are far better than the text.

LATE COLONIAL

2508 Barreau, Jean. Les guerres en Guadeloupe au XVIIIe siècle, 1703, 1759 et 1794. Nerac, France: J. Owen, 1976. 128 p.; maps.

Besides detailed descriptions of battles with appropriate illustrations, book also has 1790 breakdown of population, crops, cane growers, and sugar factories, for Guadeloupe, Marie Galante, Les Saintes and Desirade.

2509 Caro Costas, Aída R. El cabildo o régimen municipal puertorriqueño en el siglo XVIII. San Juan: Instituto de Cultura

Puertorriqueña, 1974. 2 v.; bibl.

Spanish town councils were vitally important to the development of Spanish society and culture in the Americas. Study examines several aspects of this body in Puerto Rico: legislative and judicial functions, economic regulation, sources of income as well as expenditure and various ceremonial functions of town council. Based on extensive Spanish and Puerto Rican archival sources.

Debien, Gabriel. Les esclaves des plantations Mauger à Saint-Dominique: 1763–1802. See *HLAS 43:973.*

2510 García del Pino, César and **Alicia Melis Cappa.** Catálogo parcial de los fondos de la Sección XI, Cuba, del Archivo General de Indias. La Habana: Editorial ORBE, 1978. 215 p.; indexes.

Documents cover period 1729–1866, and were part of old Archivo General de la Isla de Cuba sent to Spain in 1888.

2511 Gaspar, David Barry. A dangerous spirit of liberty: slave rebellion in the West Indies during the 1730s (Cimarrons [Institut Caraibe de recherches historiques, Guadeloupe] 1, 1981, p. 79–92)

Examines wave of slave unrest not only in West Indies but also in North America during period and opines that this challenged system of slavery, and increased masters' feelings of insecurity.

———. Runaways in seventeenth-century Antigua, West Indies. See *HLAS 43:983.*

2512 Geggus, David. The British government and the Saint Domingue slave revolt, 1791–1793 (EHR, 96:379, April 1981, p. 285–305)

Geggus, most prolific writer on French Revolutionary period in Saint-Domingue, argues that decision to send 15,000 English soldiers to their deaths in Saint Domingue, and to spend nearly 10 million pounds in attempt to conquer Haiti, ranks "among the greatest disasters in British imperial history." Examines English reasons for expedition. Concludes no single persuasive one can be found for such a war against France and that English motivations changed as the war dragged on. Excellent research.

Handler, Jerome S. and **Frederick W. Lange.** Plantation slavery on Barbados, West Indies. See *HLAS 43:429.*

2513 Hart, Richard. Slaves who abolished slavery. Kingston, Jamaica: Institute of Social and Economic Research, University of the West Indies, 1980. 1 v.; ill.

Interesting not only for variety of slave conditions described but also for author's importance. A labor of love as well as of political and national conviction. Good primary and secondary research.

2514 Hartog, Johannes. The Courthouse of St. Maarten: life and work of Dr. Willem Hendrik Rink, Commander and Governor of the island, 1790–1806. Translation by E.D. Fowler. Cover design, Nigel Matthew. Aruba: De Wit Stores, 1974. 49 p.; ill.

Interesting insights into problems of administration of small island, an outpost of empire. Readable but lacking in broader historical context.

2515 Lara, Oruno D. Le procès de résistance des nègres de Guadeloupe: guerilla et conspirations des nègres cimarrons, 1736–1738 (Cimarrons [Institut Caraibe de recherches historiques, Guadeloupe] 1, 1981, p. 13–78)

Mainly a long list of documents dealing with the conspiracy.

Marrero y Artiles, Leví. Cuba: economía y sociedad. v. 6/7, Del monopolio hacia la libertad comercial: 1701–1763, pts. 1/2. See *HLAS 43:3222.*

Price, Richard. Kwasimukamba's gambit. See *HLAS 43:1042.*

SPANISH BORDERLANDS OF FLORIDA AND LOUISIANA

2516 Cubeñas, José A. Presencia española e hispánica en la Florida desde el descubrimiento hasta el bicentenario. Madrid: Ediciones Cultura Hispánica, 1978. 69, 8 p.; bibl.

Short summary of Florida's settlement under Adelantado Pedro Menéndez de Aviles also deals with problems of converting Indians. Pt. 2 traces Florida history to present. Author tries to show that Spanish never adopted policy of exterminating Indians, nor of expelling them from land, but rather of trying to harmonize their interests with well-being of indigenous inhabitants.

2517 Cummins, Light T. Spanish administration in the eastern Borderlands (PCCLAS/P, 1980/1981, p. 1–9)
Study of transformation of institution of captaincy general after the seven years war which centralized administration of Eastern Borderlands. [E.B. Couturier]

2518 Montero de Pedro, José. Españoles en Nueva Orleans y Luisiana. Madrid: Ediciones Cultura Hispánica del Centro Iberoamericano de Cooperación, 1979. 225 p.
Interesting and varied look at impact of Spain and Spaniards on New Orleans and Louisiana. Covers wide cross-section of individuals, from governor to artists. Mainly for general reader.

Servies, James A. The siege of Pensacola, 1781: a bibliography. See item **51**.

2519 Starr, Joseph Barton. Tories, dons, and rebels: the American Revolution in British West Florida. Sponsored by the American Revolution Bicentennial Commission of Florida. Gainesville: University Presses of Florida, 1976. 278 p.; bibl.; index; map (on lining paper)
Delightfully readable history which virtually supports assertion that West Florida's importance during American Revolutionary period was its insignificance.

2520 Tornero Tinajero, Pablo. Relaciones de dependencia entre Florida y Estados Unidos, 1783–1820. Madrid: Ministerio de Asuntos Exteriores, Dirección General de Relaciones Culturales, 1979. 205 p.; 3 leaves of plates; bibl.; ill. (Trabajos monográficos sobre la independencia de Norteamérica; 4)
Excellent analysis of economic, political and demographic development of Florida during period. Tables, maps and graphs convey variety of information, and analyze it with considerable skill. Includes impressive bibliography and work should have wide appeal.

19TH CENTURY

2521 Aguilera, Francisco Vicente. Epistolario. Recopilación documental preparada por Marta Cruz, con la colaboración de Olimpia López Laurel. La Habana: Editorial de Ciencias Sociales, Instituto Cubano del Libro, 1974. 268 p.; index (Pensamiento cubano)

Contains letters of Aguilera and others of the period.

The Amerindians in Guyana, 1803–73: a documentary history. See *HLAS 43:945*.

2522 Boin, Jacqueline and **José Serulle Ramia.** El proceso de desarrollo del capitalismo en la República Dominicana, 1844–1930. t. 1, El proceso de transformación de la economía dominicana, 1844 a 1875. t. 2, El desarrollo del capitalismo en la agricultura, 1875–1930. Santo Domingo: Gramil, 1979. 2 v.; bibl.; ill.
Rich economic data on development of Dominican economy during period when sugar was dominant, with valuable statistics on trade, production, commerce, and wages, as well as areas under cultivation. Authors claim that Dominican economy's being "precapitalist," or "semi-feudal" is partly responsible for political frustrations. Marxist slant, but very good research.

Cabrera, Lydia. Reglas de Congo: Palo Monte Mayombé. See *HLAS 43:8178*.

2523 Céspedes y del Castillo, Carlos de. Diario, julio de 1872 [i.e. mil ochocientos setenta y dos] a enero de 1873. Ed., Mayra Díaz Arango. La Habana: Editorial de Ciencias Sociales, 1978. 94 p. (Ediciones políticas)
Small part of diary preserved in National Archives demonstrates internal torment which Cuban Republic's first president endured as he carried on frustrating war against Spain, and constant struggle with his fellow insurrectionists.

2524 Chauleau, Liliane. La vie quotidienne aux Antilles françaises au temps de Victor Schoelcher: XIXe siècle. Paris: Hachette littérature, 1979. 379 p.; bibl.
Chauleau writes with great charm of 19th-century people, politics, economy, culture, festivities, flora and fauna, of Martinique and Guadeloupe. Book useful in several disciplines.

2525 Craton, Michael. Proto-peasant revolts?: the late slave rebellions in the British West Indies, 1816–1832 (PP, 85, Nov. 1979, p. 99–125, maps)
Examination of causes and consequences of slave revolts in three quite different English slave colonies at time when British Parliament pursued policy of general amelioration in slave treatment.

2526 Documents d'histoire antillaise et guyanaise, 1814–1914. Recueillis par Jacques Adélaïde-Merlande. Noyon, Oise: Finet, 1979. 323 p.; ill., maps

Variety of documents (many incomplete) include social, economic, demographic and agricultural data on territories, relations with Trinidad, enfranchisement certificates for non-whites immigration, civil unrest, and political affairs. Useful.

2527 Forslag til ordning af vestindiske forfatningsforhold angaaende negerne med mere = A proposal for regulating the situation of Negroes in the West Indies, etc. Anon. 1826. Translated with an introd. and notes by N.A.T. Hall. Charlotte Amalie: Bureau of Libraries, Museums & Archaeological Services, Department of Conservation & Cultural Affairs, Government of the Virgin Islands, 1979. 24 p.; bibl.; ill. (Occasional paper—Bureau of Libraries, Museums & Archaeological Services, Government of the Virgin Islands; no. 5)

Introductory essay is especially impressive, and author places situation of Danish Virgin Islands in broader Atlantic perspective. Useful for comparative purposes.

Guyanese sugar plantations in the late nineteenth century: a contemporary description from the *Argosy.* See *HLAS 43:990.*

2528 Helly, Denise. Idéologie et ethnicité: les Chinois Macao á Cuba, 1847–1886. Montréal: Presses de l'Université de Montréal, 1979. 345 p.; bibl.; ill. (Collection Recherches caraïbes)

Based on research in Spain and Cuba, this is major contribution to understanding role of Asian, especially Chinese migrants in the 19th-century sugarcane plantation socioeconomic complex. Apart from details of the work regime, Helly examines racial, religious and juridical aspects of Chinese in Cuba. For ethnologist's comment, see *HLAS 41:1036.*

Higman, Barry W. Growth in Afro-Caribbean slave populations. See *HLAS 43:1675.*

2529 Hoetink, Harry. The Dominican people, 1850–1900: notes for a historical sociology. Translated by Stephen K. Ault. Baltimore: The Johns Hopkins University Press, 1982. 246 p.

Excellent translation of outstanding work which has been rather hard to find. Still a major contribution to Caribbean historiography.

2530 Iglesias, Fé. Algunos aspectos de la distribución de la tierra en 1899 (Santiago [Revista de la Universidad de Oriente, Santiago de Cuba] 40, dic. 1980, p. 119–178, bibl.; tables)

Remarkable article provides statistics which refute widely held concepts about land use and exploitation between 1860–1931. Among author's findings: acreage under sugarcane cultivation did not fall substantially during Ten Years War and all major products except coffee held their own; also shows progressive alienation after 1899 of non-white land users in island's eastern part. Main hypothesis is that landownership was not held in large parcels by 1899.

2531 Levy, Claude. Emancipation, sugar, and federalism: Barbados and the West Indies, 1833–1876. Gainesville: University Presses of Florida, 1980. 206 p.; bibl.; ill.; index (Latin American monographs; 2d ser., 25)

Treats most important period of Barbados history or when island was prosperous but faced with number of crises: emancipation of slaves; preferential duties for its sugar abolished by British government; and government's failure. Through all this Barbados managed to maintain its prosperity, and rejected attempts to form federation with neighbors. But after 1876, increase in beet sugar production began economy's slow decline, and political and labor troubles which would continue into 20th century.

2532 Lewis, Lancelot S. The West Indian in Panama: black labor in Panama, 1850–1914. Washington: University Press of America, 1980. 271 p.; bibl.; ill.

Unreconstructed doctoral dissertation (includes much interesting information without analysis about West Indians in Panama). Extensive quotations of documents are great value for study of migrants and conditions in Panama during the canal's construction.

Manzano, Juan Francisco. The life and poems of a Cuban slave. See item **6293.**

2533 Marshall, W.K. Metayage in the sugar industry of the British Windward Islands, 1838–1865: social and economic problems in the Windward Islands, 1838–1865. Mona, Jamaica: University of the West Indies, Department of History, 1980? 45, 43 p.; bibl.

Solidly researched article dealing with transition from slave to wage labor in Windward Islands and problems which continued to plague a system in which majority were divorced from active political participation in local affairs.

2534 Martí, José. El Partido Revolucionario Cubano y la guerra. Ed., Pedro Alvarez Tabío. La Habana: Editorial de Ciencias Sociales, 1978. 306 p. (Ediciones políticas)

Selected letters (1891–95) from Martí to various Cubans (e.g., Antonio Maceo, Máximo Gómez, Serafín Sánchez, Marcos Morales, Enrique Collazo, Eduardo Gato) establishing and coordinating Revolutionary Party against Spain.

2535 Pando, Magdalena. Cuba's freedom fighter, Antonio Maceo, 1845–1896. Gainesville, Fla.: Felicity Press, 1980. 144 p.; 1 leaf of plates; bibl.; index; map.

Delightfully readable biography which not only outlines military career of one of Cuba's heroes, but conveys dismal reality of nationalists cause against Spain in war of independence.

Peralta Brito, Rafael and **José Chez Checo.** Religión, filosofía y política en Fernando A. de Meriño, 1857–1906: contribución a la historia de las ideas en la República Dominicana. See item **7606.**

Pérez, Louis A., Jr. Cubans in Tampa: from exiles to immigrants, 1892–1901. See *HLAS 43:8227.*

2536 Pérez Guzmán, Francisco. La batalla de Las Guásimas. La Habana: Editorial de Ciencias Sociales, 1975. 231 p.; 2 fold. leaves of plates; ill.

Battle of Las Guásimas is considered as decisive an engagement in the Ten Years War as that of March 1874 when insurgents failed to invade the West and take the battle to the Spanish. Although plan stalled, the Spanish took more than 100 casualties in five days of fighting. Includes much detail and illustrations of battle positions.

2537 Picó, Fernando. Libertad y servidumbre en el Puerto Rico del siglo XIX: los jornaleros utuadeños en vísperas del augue del café. Río Piedras, P.R.: Ediciones Huracán, 1979. 173 p.; bibl.

Interesting investigation of impact of coffee culture on small rural Puerto Rican community during 19th century, focuses on working classes, their daily life and Church's role.

2538 Pluchon, Pierre. Toussaint Louverture: de l'esclavage au pouvoir. Paris: L'Ecole, 1979. 399 p.; bibl.

More than a biography of Toussaint, work examines St. Domingue's broader politics, society and economy during final years of French colonial rule. Contains much statistical information indicating how coffee was challenging sugar's hegemony.

2539 Price-Mars, Jean. Antenor Firmin. Port-au-Prince?: Imp. Séminaire, 1964? 423 p.; bibl.; ports.

More than biography of Haiti's Ambassador to Paris for short time after 1900, this is also an investigation of Haitian politics during tumultous period.

Real Academia de la Historia (Spain). Catálogo de la Colección Caballero de Rodas. See item **118.**

2540 Registro general de jornaleros, Utuado, Puerto Rico, 1948–50. Fernando Picó, Editor. Santa Rita, Río Piedras, P.R.: Ediciones Huracán, 1976. 190 p.; bibl. (Colección Este)

Includes 856 descriptions of famous *libreta* system used in Puerto Rico to control labor during 19th century. Registers often indicated kin in addition to physical characteristics of coffee municipality workers.

2541 Revista de la Biblioteca Nacional José Martí. Año 71, 3. época, Vol. 22, sept./dic. 1980– . La Habana.

Issue devoted to centenary of abolition of slavery in Cuba: José Luciano Franco's "Los Cimarrones en el Caribe"; Hortensia Pichardo's "Las Ordenanzas Antiguas para los Indios: las Leyes de Burgos, 1512"; Julio Le Riverend's "El Esclavismo en Cuba: Perspectivas del Tema"; María del Carmen Barcia's "Algunas Cuestiones Teóricas Necesarias para el Análisis del Surgimiento y la Crisis de la Plantación Esclavista"; Fé Iglesias' "Características de la Población Cubana en 1862"; Norma Peraza's "Esclavos Gallegos en Cuba"; Juan Losada's and Jorge Mayor's "Esclavitud y Psicología: una Investigación Interdisciplinaria"; Orestes García García's "Una Obra Inédita de José Antonio Saco?"; Rafael López Valdés' "Problemas del Estudio de los Componentes Africanos en la Historia Etnica de Cuba"; Salvador García Aguero's "El Negro en Nuestra Cultura."

2542 Rodney, Walter. A history of the Guyanese working people, 1881–1905.

Foreword by George Lamming. Baltimore: Johns Hopkins University Press, 1981. 256 p.; ill.

Posthumously published work by Guyanese historian makes major contribution to 19th-century historiography, especially with regard to problems of developing groups in a difficult environment such as Guyana's. Socioeconomic in orientation, Rodney's "working people" encompasses all of the territory's different groups.

2543 Sánchez Bermúdez, Juan A. Las pretensiones anexionistas de los Estados Unidos en Cuba colonial (UCLV/I, 64, set./ dic. 1979, p. 43–63)

Discusses Cuban-US relations in light of Manifest Destiny, "mature fruit" principle, and Monroe Doctrine.

2544 Schoelcher, Victor. Colonies étrangères et Haïti. t. 1, Colonies anglaises. Iles espagnoles. Quelques mots sur la traite et sur son origine. t. 2, Colonies danoise. Haïti. Du droit de visite. Coup-d'oeil sur l'état de la question d'affranchissement. Paris: Désormeaux, 1973. 2 v.; bibl. (Collection Histoire de l'esclavage aux Antilles)

By reprinting this contemporary classic, editors have done great service to Caribbean historiography. Schoelcher's account is filled with economic, political and demographic data useful to both scholar and general reader. Vol. 1 deals with English islands Dominica, Jamaica, Antigua and Spanish islands Cuba and Puerto Rico; vol. 2 with Danish islands and Haiti. Vol. 1 includes perceptive comments on impact of abolition.

2545 Schuler, Monica. "Alas, alas, Kongo:" a social history of indentured African immigration into Jamaica, 1841–1865. Baltimore, Md.: Johns Hopkins University Press, 1980. 186 p.; bibl.; index (Johns Hopkins studies in Atlantic history and culture)

Based on archival research in Jamaica and Africa as well as interviews with number of descendants of these interesting free African immigrants, Schuler's book appeals to wide variety of disciplines. She shows how some Central Africans and some Yoruba, though small in numbers, could maintain viable community and exert their influence far beyond their own group. Important for any study of the process of Creolization and adaptation.

————. Myalism and the African religious tradition in Jamaica. See *HLAS 43:1047.*

2546 Vassady, Bela, Jr. Transplanting prejudices: the failure of the Baptist experiment using Jamaican "native agents" in Fernando Po and Cameroons, 1841–1850 (UWI/ CQ, 25:1/2, March/June 1979, p. 15–39)

Attributes failure of attempt to use Jamaicans to spread the gospel in West Africa not only to ignorance but to West Indians' behavior being distinct from their English compatriots and to their susceptibility of epidemics as were other recent immigrants.

Verna, Paul. Petión y Bolívar: una etapa decisiva en la emancipación de Hispanoamérica, 1790–1830. See item **2815.**

Wessman, James W. The demographic structure of slavery in Puerto Rico: some aspects of agrarian capitalism in the late nineteenth century. See *HLAS 43:1061.*

20TH CENTURY

2547 Alegría Ortega, Idsa E. La Comisión del Status de Puerto Rico: su historia y significación. Río Piedras: Universidad de Puerto Rico, 1982. 214 p.; bibl.

Relevant history of Puerto Rico's status until 1979 includes very useful bibliography, and wide selection of documents on which analysis is based.

2548 Baptiste, Fitz A. The United States and the West Indian unrest, 1918–1939. Mona, Jamaica: Institute of Social and Economic Research, University of the West Indies, 1978. 1 v. (Working paper; 18)

By using British and American archival material, Baptiste shows that the US' growing interest in the Caribbean derived from a combination of strategic concerns among which were local political and economic unrest plus attacks by the region's black intellectuals on British colonialism. US identified security with local stability.

Bonniol, Jean-Luc. Terre-de-Haut des Saintes: contraintes insulaires et particularisme ethnique dans La Caraïbe. See *HLAS 43:968.*

Brizan, George I. The Grenadian peasantry and social revolution, 1930–51. See *HLAS 43:8175.*

Casal, Lourdes. Race relations in contemporary Cuba. See *HLAS 43:8180.*

2549 Cruz Peralta, Rafael. Santo Domingo, la guerra de 1965. Caracas: s.l., 1979. 150 p.; bibl.

Participant's view of 1965 American invasion also includes broad sweep of Dominican 20th-century history.

2550 De La Demajagua a Playa Girón: "un encuentro de pueblo con su propia historia." Compilador, Juan José Soto Valdespino. Diseño, Rolando Zerquera Falcato. La Habana: Editorial de Ciencias Sociales, 1978. 464 p.

Speeches (1968–76) by Fidel Castro, Armando Hart Dávalos, Ernesto Guevara, Sergio Valle, Raúl Castro, Ramiro Valdés Menéndez and Pedro Miret.

Díaz Barreiro, Francisco. El Dr. Nicolás I. Vavílov y las primeras relaciones científicas soviéticas con Cuba. See *HLAS 43:7298.*

2550a Dore y Cabral, Carlos. Problemas de la estructura agraria dominicana. Santo Domingo: Ediciones Taller, 1979. 122 p.

Seven essays discuss development of minifundism and latifundism in Dominican Republic with rich statistical data (p. 101–120). Includes bibliography on local agrarian problems.

2551 ———. Reforma agraria y luchas sociales en la República Dominicana, 1966–1978. Prólogo de Wilfredo Lozano. Santo Domingo: Editora Taller, 1981. 105 p.

Author views period as one in which local oligarchies gave way to new incipient bourgeoisie allied to North American capitalist interests. Nevertheless, as economy developed, small farming groups became more politically active. As title suggests, these events are perceived with a strong sense of class struggle.

2552 Dorschner, John and **Roberto Fabricio.** The winds of December. New York: Coward, McCann & Geoghegan, 1980. 552 p.; 8 leaves of plates; bibl.; ill.; index

Two *Miami Herald* reporters provide close-up and personal history of the Cuban Revolution during final weeks of 1958.

2553 Dumoulin, John. Azúcar y lucha de clases, 1917. La Habana: Editorial de Ciencias Sociales, 1980. 288 p.

Pt. 1 of this history examines first major Cuban sugar industry strike in 1917, which author interprets as reflecting a crisis in the industry's capitalist structure. Pt. 2 contains various documents which put this local event in wider context.

Elkins, W.F. The black princess of Jamaica. See *HLAS 43:979.*

2554 Ferrán, Fernando I. Tabaco y sociedad: la organización del poder en el ecomercado de tabaco dominicano. Santo Domingo: Fondo para el Avance de las Ciencias Sociales, Centro de Investigación y Acción Social, 1976. 209 p.; bibl.

Anthropological work includes significant data on social, economic and political organization at local level. Also uses tobacco industry as window on nation's economic organization. Methodologically more rigorous than Fernando Ortiz's celebrated study of Cuba but lacking in its lyricism.

2555 Figarola, Joel James. Cuba, 1900–1928 [i.e. mil novecientos-mil novecientos veintiocho]: la República dividida contra sí misma. La Habana: Instituto Cubano del Libro, Editorial Arte y Literatura, 1976. 339 p.; 1 fold. leaf of plates; bibl.; ill.

Excellent analysis of elite's political fragmentation during period, and complex relationship which existed both in terms of class and kin. Important for the background conditions which promoted rise of José Antonio Mella and Communist Party.

2556 Flores, Juan. The insular vision: Pedreira's interpretation of Puerto Rican culture. New York: C.U.N.Y., Centro de Estudios Puertorriqueños, 1978. 104 leaves; bibl. (Centro working papers; 1)

Critical study of one of Puerto Rico's foremost *pensadores* often considered "the father of modern Puerto Rican letters." Important because it tries to come to grips with the psychology of the Puerto Rican.

2557 Gavrikov, IUriĭ Pavlovich. Kuba: stranitsy isotorii. Moskva: Nauka, 1979. 165 p.; bibl., ill. (Seriia Strany i norody)

Soviet history designed for readers wishing to go further into the topic. Provides footnotes and bibliography. Emphasizes American imperialism and contrast between pre and post-1959. [R.V. Allen]

2558 González del Valle Ríos, Antolín. Fulgencio Batista, trayectoria nacionalista. Wilmington, N.C.: Ediciones Patria, 1980. 126 p.; bibl.

Apologia for Batista's regime in Cuba.

2559 Hablan sobre Albizu Campos. Luis Muñoz Marín *et al.* Recopilación, introd. y notas por J. Benjamín Torres. Oleo cubierta, Fran Cervoni. Fotografía, Jorge Santana. San Juan: Editorial Jelofe, 1979. 128 p.; 2 leaves of plates; bibl.; ports.

Testimonials to Pedro Albizu Campos drawn from a veritable who's who in Latin America and the Caribbean (e.g., José Vasconcelos, Gabriela Mistral, Ernesto Che Guevara, Luis Muñoz Marín, Juan Mari Bras, Juan Marinello).

Langley, Lester D. The United States and the Caribbean, 1900–1970. See *HLAS 43:7327*.

2560 Layne, Anthony. Race, class and development in Barbados (UNWI/CQ, 25: 1/2, March/June 1979, p. 40–51, tables)

Concludes that political independence has not made much difference to reality of race, class and occupation in Barbados, and that high expectations of early 1960s have not been fulfilled.

2561 López Segrera, Francisco. Raíces históricas de la Revolución cubana, 1868–1959: introducción al estudio de las clases sociales en Cuba en sus relaciones con la política y la economía. La Habana: Unión de Escritores y Artistas de Cuba, 1980. 526 p.; bibl.

López sees continuity in period outlined and attributes Martí's failure to implement democratic revolution to establishment of "puppet republic." Highly marxist in orientation.

2562 Luque de Sánchez, María Dolores. La ocupación norteamericana y la Ley Foraker: la opinión pública puertorriqueña, 1898–1904. Río Piedras: Editorial Universitaria, Universidad de Puerto Rico, 1977. 197 p.; 12 leaves of plates; bibl.; ill.

Based on extensive research into primary and secondary material, author demonstrates that Puerto Rico's incorporation into US corresponded with latter's economic interest, and that after few months of euphoria, Puerto Ricans began to have second thoughts about their newly-acquired metropolis. Problems of early period have continued to plague the island.

Manley, Robert H. Guyana emergent: the post-independence struggle for nondependent development. See *HLAS 43:1021*.

2563 Melis, Antonio. Il percorso di Fernando Ortiz nella definizione della cultura cubana (Nova Americana [Giulio Einaudi Editore, Torino, Italy] 3, 1980, p. 13–39)

Traces intellectual growth of Fernando Ortiz via his writings, and concludes that although Ortiz began as classical thinker, the reality of Cuba's cultural situation led him into an independent exposition of its national thought.

2564 Mencia, Mario. La prisión fecunda. La Habana: Editora Política, 1980. 292 p.; facsims.; ill.; plates.

Based on series of journalistic articles published in *Bohemia* to commemorate 25th anniversary of Castro's and the Moncada group's release from prison. Includes additional selections of rare documents. Important for any examination of Revolution's early phase, especially various contacts and ways in which 26th of July Movement operated.

2565 Miller, Kethly. Les paysans haïtiens et l'occupation américaine d'Haïti, 1915–1930. La Salle, Québec: Collectif Paroles, 1978. 157 p.; bibl.; maps

Uninspiring account of peasant response to US occupation includes good map of regional cultivation and guerrilla activity during period.

New York (city). City University of New York. Center for Puerto Rican Studies. History Task Force. Labor migration under capitalism: the Puerto Rican experience. See *HLAS 43:8225*.

2566 Nicholls, David. Casta, clase y color en Haiti (EME, 8:43, julio/agosto 1979, p. 35–52, bibl.)

Argues that despite some reservations, contemporary Haiti still uses status and family considerations which correlate with color and class in social and political affairs.

2567 Pérez Betancourt, Rolando. Sucedió hace veinte años. La Habana: Editorial de Ciencias Sociales, 1978. 2 v.; ill. (Testimonio)

Journalist's 1976 reconstruction of

1956 events when Fidel Castro returned from Mexico to launch final phase of Cuban Revolution, offering the people freedom or martyrdom. Published as series of articles in *Granma*, 1976.

2568 Pierre-Charles, Gérard. Haití, las crisis ininterrumpida, 1930–1975. La Habana: Casa de las Américas, 1978 [i.e. 1979]. 84 p.; bibl. (Cuadernos Casa; 19)

Divides time after US occupation of Haiti into four periods during which country's continued political and economic deterioration has been masked by informal US support. Sees little difference between Duvalier and regimes preceding him.

Post, Ken. Arise ye starvelings: the Jamaican labour rebellion of 1938 and its aftermath. See *HLAS 43:1039*.

2569 Puerto Rico. Governor, 1949–1965. Muñoz Marín. Mensajes al pueblo puertorriqueño no pronunciados ante las cámaras legislativas, 1949–64. Pref. por Antonio J. Colorado. San Juan: Universidad Interamericana de Puerto Rico, 1980. 358 p.; index

Consists of 16 speeches by Luis Muñoz Marín on: economy, industrial development, agriculture, commerce, education, labor conditions, health and public services, land use, and housing. They represent annual assessment of Puerto Rican achievement under stewardship of its first elected local governor.

2570 Quevedo Pérez, José. La batalla del Jigüe. Cubierta, Rusky Gamboa. La Habana: Editorial Letras Cubanas, 1979. 158 p.

Participant account of battle against Batista's forces in 1958. For battle buffs.

Quintero-Rivera, A.G. Notes on Puerto Rican national development: class & nation in a colonial context. See *HLAS 43:6320*.

2571 La República neocolonial. Juan Pérez de la Riva *et al*. La Habana: Instituto Cubano del Libro, Editorial de Ciencias Sociales, 1979. 2 v. (475 p.); bibl.; ill.; tables (Anuario de estudios cubanos; 1/2) (Nuestra historia)

Excellent collection of articles on intra-Caribbean migration, labor organization, sugar industry's operation, and nature of military expenditure for 1907–33.

St. Pierre, Maurice. The 1938 Jamaica disturbances: a portrait of mass reaction against colonialism. See *HLAS 43:1045*.

2572 Santamaría, Haydée. Moncada, memories of the attack that launched the Cuban Revolution. Afterword by Roberto Fernández Retamar. Secaucus, N.J.: L. Stuart, 1980. 118 p.

Santamaría's recollections of Revolution's important early phase, as told to youthful audience at University of Havana. Her adoration of Fidel and devotion to the Revolution are evident.

Wessman, James W. Division of labour, capital accumulation and commodity exchange on a Puerto Rican sugar-cane hacienda. See *HLAS 43:1062*.

SPANISH SOUTH AMERICA: General

MICHAEL T. HAMERLY, *Seattle, Washington*
JOHN HOYT WILLIAMS, *Professor of History, Indiana State University, Terre Haute*

2573 Golte, Jürgen. Determinanten des Entstehens und des Verlaufs bäuerlicher Rebellion in den Anden vom 18. zum 20. Jahrhundert (JGSWGL, 15, 1978, p. 41–74, maps)

Two part study: 1) summarizes Golte's recent book on economic aspects of Indian rebellions in 18th-century Peru and Bolivia (see item **2677**); 2) compares and contrasts economic aspects of Indian rebellions

in Peru from 18th century through early 20th in attempt to establish casual similarities. [MTH]

2574 Historia general de la Iglesia en América Latina. v. 7, Colombia y Venezuela. Salamanca, Spain: CEHILA (Comisión de Estudios de Historia de la Iglesia en América Latina) [and] Ediciones Sígueme, 1981. 689 p.; bibl.; ill.; maps (El Peso de los días; 17)

Vol. 7 and first to appear in projected 11 volume history of Catholic Church and to lesser extent of Protestantism in Latin America from discovery through Medellín's Episcopal Conference. Analyzes and interprets history of Christianity in Colombia and Venezuela from perspective of Vatican II and Medellín. Although tendentious, it is scholarly and incorporates existing literature and reflects new research. Thematic coverage of colonial period (i.e., missionary activities, Church organization, life among religious and faithful); chronological coverage of national period, with chapters on Protestantism for both. Complemented by excellent maps, especially of Colombia, and bibliography. Indexed. [MTH]

2575 Minería y espacio económico en los Andes, siglos XVI–XX. Carlos Sempat Assadourian et al. Lima: Instituto de Estudios Peruanos, 1980. 103 p.; bibl. (Colección mínima; 10)

Preliminary study of mining in Peru and Bolivia from colonial times through present. Partly synthesis, partly original work inasmuch as authors (Carlos Sempat Assadourian, Heraclio Bonilla, Antonio Mitre, and Tristan Platt) are concerned with impact of mining on internal development. [MTH]

2576 Oviedo Cavada, Carlos. Los Obispos de Chile, 1561–1978. Santiago, Chile: Editorial Salesiana, 1979. 271 p.; bibl; index.

Well done, very useful biographical dictionary of all colonial and national period bishops of Chile. Enhanced by valuable supplements (e.g., chronology of dioceses, and of synods and councils) and solid bibliography. [MTH]

2577 Research guide to Andean history: Bolivia, Chile, Ecuador, and Peru. Contributing editors, Judith R. Bakewell et al. Coordinating editor, John J. TePaske. Durham, N.C.: Duke University Press, 1981. 346 p.; bibl.; index.

Useful but dated guide to major and minor archival holdings of Bolivia, Chile, Ecuador, and Peru at national, regional and local levels (most contributions ca. 10 years old). Sections Bolivia and Ecuador (edited by Judith R. and Peter J. Bakewell, Jaime E. Rodríguez O.) consist of descriptions of repositories; Chile and Peru (edited by William F. Sater, Leon G. Campbell) include essays on countries' historiographies. Only Campbell updated his introduction. Nonetheless, indispensable for beginning researchers. [MTH]

SPANISH SOUTH AMERICA: Colonial Period

MICHAEL T. HAMERLY, Seattle, Washington
JOHN HOYT WILLIAMS, Professor of History, Indiana State University, Terre Haute

FOR THE MOST PART WHAT WAS SAID regarding the two previous bienniums (1976–77 and 1978–79) in the introduction to this section in *HLAS 42*, holds true for this one (1980–81). Fewer studies of importance were published or came to our attention in 1980–81 than in 1976–77 or 1978–79. This can be partly attributed to 1981 being the bicentennial of the Comunero, Tupac Amaru, and Tupac Katari rebellions in Colombia, Peru, and Bolivia, most publications on them consisting of rehashes at best and mythifying at worst. The decline in the number of studies is also due to North American and European cuts in funding for research on Latin American topics.

It is a pleasure, on the other hand, to welcome several fledgling Latin Americanists, who are to be commended for the quality of their work and for persevering despite adverse circumstances, such as part time or temporary appointments. The new North American colonialists are: Robert J. Ferry, Kathy Waldron (Venezuela); Jane M. Loy (Colombia); Frank Salomon (Ecuador), the 1981 recipient of the Cline Ethnohistory Memorial Prize for *Los señores étnicos de Quito en la época de los Incas* (Otavalo: Instituto Otavaleño de Antropología, 1980); Kenneth J. Adrien, Paul

B. Ganster, Ann M. Wightman (Peru); and David Block, Brian M. Evans, and Brooke Larson (Bolivia).

At least one other significant change also occurred. For some time I have maintained that much of the best work is being done on colonial Peru. Now it seems that more work is being done on Peru as well. Quantitative analysis of the number of annotations on the former Spanish South American colonies in the past five Humanities volumes of the *Handbook* (*HLAS 34, HLAS 36, HLAS 38, HLAS 40* and *HLAS 42*) reveals that works on Peru have exceeded those on any single other former colony since the mid 1970s. Annotations on Peru proper averaged 22.5 percent of all "Spanish South America, Colonial Period" items in *HLAS 38, HLAS 40* and *HLAS 42* with a standard deviation of 0.7 percent vis-à-vis an average of 17 percent in *HLAS 34* and *HLAS 36*. Surely this is not fortuitous but reflects more as well as better work by Peruvian scholars and Peruvianists abroad. Nor can there be any doubt that Venezuela, which used to be in first place, now occupies second. The average weight of items on colonial Venezuela in *HLAS 38, HLAS 40* and *HLAS 42* was 14.9 percent as against an average of 20.9 percent in *HLAS 34* and *HLAS 36*.

GENERAL WORKS: Only one major general work in the thematic as well as chronological sense came to our attention during the 1980–81 biennium, the 12-vol. "Historia del Perú" series, published by Mejía Baca, of which vols. 4/5 treat the colonial period (item **2679**). Consisting of monographic essays by leading specialists, these two volumes synthesize and articulate the considerable data compiled and fresh interpretations advanced in recent years, especially during the last two decades, on the demographic, economic, ethnic, and social history of Peru from the Spanish conquest through the eve of independence. Among the contributors is Waldemar Espinoza Soriano who has finally given us a digest of his own numerous specialized findings as well as those of others on "La Sociedad Andina Colonial" (v. 4, p. 129–337). Also praiseworthy is Javier Tord Nicolini's and Carlos Lazo Garcia's magisterial model of "Economía y Sociedad en el Perú Colonial" (v. 4, p. 339–571; v. 5, p. 9–328).

Several thematically specialized but chronologically or geographically general works appeared on the other hand. Especially noteworthy are: 1) the inaugural volume of the CEHILA *Historia general de la Iglesia en América Latina*, vol. 7, *Colombia y Venezuela*, a scholarly compendium of the history of the Catholic Church and the Protestant faith from colonial times through the present in both countries (item **2574**); 2) Silvio Zavala's digest of and guide to sources, archival and published, on forced and voluntary Indian labor in the Viceroyalty of Peru (item **2593**); and 3) Gabriel Guarda's *Historia urbana del Reino de Chile*, a veritable vademecum, complete with an exceptionally comprehensive list of sources (item **2733**).

BIBLIOGRAPHY, HISTORIOGRAPHY, AND OTHER RESEARCH AIDS: Only a few reference works appeared. With one exception, all were specialized. The exception is the long awaited *Research guide to Andean history* (item **2577**). Although neither as complete nor up-to-date as it might have been, beginning researchers on Ecuador, Peru, Bolivia, and Chile will find the *Research guide to Andean history* helpful. In addition to Zavala (item **2593**) and Guarda (item **2733**), the specialized items of importance, including several older ones late in reaching *HLAS*, are: 1) a catalogue of AGI holdings on Barinas (item **2607**); 2) Francisco de Solano's guide to late colonial *descripciones de la tierra* and maps of the Caribbean littoral of Colombia and Venezuela in the Servicio Histórico Militar and the Servicio Geográfico Militar of Madrid (item **2633**); 3) the guide to colonial and national period holdings of the Archivo Nacional de Historia of Quito (item **2635**); 4) Antonio Heredia Herrera's schematic introduction to and description of AGI, Audiencia of Quito holdings (item **2648**); 5) Heraclio Bonilla's review of recent Peruvian historiography (item **2663**); and 6) Franklin Pease's introduction to *visitas de indios* as ethnohistorical sources (item **2694**). Also important is Alexandre Kennedy Troya, *Catálogo del Archivo General de la Orden Franciscana en el Ecuador* (Quito: Banco Central del Ecuador, 1980), which I have not seen.

CONQUEST AND EARLY COLONIAL PERIOD: Only one item of more than passing interest on the conquest came to our attention, Edmundo Guillén Guillén's "La Conquista del Perú de los Incas (1531–1572)" in the "Historia del Perú" series (v. 4, p. 9–127). Guillén's contentions that the Spanish conquest did not end at Cajamarca (1532) but with the taking of Vilcabamba 40 years later or that Tahuantinsuyo fell largely because of internal dissension are not new but his approach is. Guillén attempts to interpret the conquest from the Indian or "Peruvian" perspective.

An appreciable number of significant publications appeared on the early colonial period or the Hapsburg era. Those which strike me as especially important dealt primarily with historical demography, discussed separately below, or economic and/ or social history. To some extent this may reflect a personal bias, but it seems that in the colonial period, much of the best work is in these areas. Beginning with economic history and the northern tier (Venezuela, Nueva Granada, and Quito), Enrique Otte has produced a superb account of the pearl industry of Cubagua (item **2608**); Robert J. Ferry, an excellent analysis of the emergence of cacao in the 17th century as the economic motor of the Province of Caracas (item **2601**); and Julián B. Ruiz Rivera, an almost complete time series for the 17th century of the remission of bullion from Nueva Granada to the mother country (item **2632**). Finally, Christiana Borchart de Moreno has begun to delineate the emergence of haciendas in highland Ecuador (items **2638–2640**).

Turning to Lower and Upper Peru, in first place is Tord Nicolini's and Lazo García's already mentioned "Economía y Sociedad en el Perú Colonial." A close second is Nicholas P. Cushner's *Lords of the land: sugar, wine, and Jesuit estates of coastal Peru* (item **2672**), which takes in the late colonial periods as well and illuminates many aspects of the agrarian history of colonial Peru. Worthy of note also is Kenneth J. Andrien's pithy analysis of royal efforts to raise badly needed funds in the Viceroyalty of Peru through the sale of *juros* or annuities (item **2578**), and Brooke Larson's fine outline of the agrarian history of Cochabamba through 1800 (item **2717**). Only two especially noteworthy items on the southern cone (Chile and the Río de la Plata) came to our attention. Both reflect painstaking research and pioneer period or place: Armando de Ramón's sophisticated analysis of trade between Chile, Lower and Upper Peru, and the Río de la Plata as of the late 17th century and of the Chilean merchants involved (item **2591**); and Carlos A. Luque Colombres' detailed reconstruction of the history of *solares* and their holders in 16th and 17th-century Córdoba (item **2770**). In Spanish South American historiography, Luque Colombres' work is comparable only to Ramón's socioeconomic study of real estate in Santiago de Chile between 1650 and 1700 (see *HLAS 40: 3254* and *HLAS 42:2821*).

As for social history *per se*, Fred Bronner examines the emergence as well as composition of elites in 17th-century Peru (item **2664**). Brooke Larson probes continuity and change in the class structure of Indian communities of highland Bolivia throughout the entire colonial period (item **2716**). And Bernard Lavalle offers two case studies of the struggle for supremacy between peninsular and local-born friars in Quito (item **2649**) and Lima (item **2681**), in which strife he sees a larger force at play, *criollismo.*

LATE COLONIAL PERIOD: As usual many new studies of importance appeared on the late colonial period or Bourbon era. Almost all of these treat demographic, economic and/or social themes. Moreover, those few concerned with political developments or individuals are influenced by the social sciences: 1) Jane M. Loy's very good "Forgotten Comuneros: the 1781 Revolt in the Llanos of Casanare" (item **2628**); 2) the collection of essays on the Ecuadorian *pensador* Eugenio Espejo (item **2646**); 3) Mark A. Burkholder's elegant analysis of José Baquijano's ultimately successful efforts to obtain an appointment to the Audiencia of Lima (item **2667**); 4) Leon G. Campbell's paper on the "Social Structure of the Tupac Amaru Army in Cuzco," the badly needed beginnings of a long overdue reassessment of that rebellion (item **2668**); and 5) Timothy E. Anna's novel but somewhat disappointing *The Fall of the royal government in Peru* (item **2662**).

Returning to economic history, the most important of the new works are: 1) German Colmenares' *Popayán, una sociedad esclavista* (item **2623**), nominally vol. 2 of his *Historia económica y social de Colombia* (see *HLAS 38:3049*), but in fact one in a series of superior monographs by him on the demographic, economic, and social history of the component regions of Nueva Granada; 2) Jurgen Golte's detailed book on the economic background and aspects of the Tupac Amaru and Tupac Katari rebellions (item **2677**); and 3) Sergio Villalobos' solid economic history of colonial, especially 18th-century Tarapacá.

The most significant studies of social or socioeconomic developments are all articles, but no less important on that account. Those which contributed the most new data and ideas are: 1) Kathy Waldron's piece on the impact of late 18th-century distribution of municipal land in Caracas on its urban growth and social mobility (item **2619**); 2) Herbert S. Klein's quantitative study of the hacendado class in the Intendency of La Paz (item **2715**); 3) Brooke Larson's fascinating analysis of relationships between crises and grain production in Cochabamba, a first in Andean historiography (item **2719**); 4) Susan Migden Socolow's equally fascinating case study of women and crime in Buenos Aires (item **2781**); and 5) Pedro A. Vives Azancot's essay on urban/rural dichotomies in late 18th-century Asunción (item **2784**).

HISTORICAL DEMOGRAPHY: Historical demographic studies appeared on every former colony except for Venezuela and Quito. Most of the works in question are of the late colonial period. The exceptions are: 1) Juan and Judith Villamarin's analysis of major sources for the recontruction of the postconquest population history of the Chibcha of the Sabana de Bogotá (item **2634**); 2) Noble David Cook's *Demographic collapse: Indian Peru, 1520–1620* (Cambridge: Cambridge University Press, 1981), which reached me too late for inclusion in this *Handbook*, the data base for which appeared separately as "Population Data for Indian Peru: Sixteenth and Seventeenth Centuries," in *Hispanic American Historical Review* (vol. 62, No. 1, Feb. 1982, p. 73–120); and 3) Claude Mazet's parish register study of

16th and 17th-century San Sebastian (Lima, item **2687**). See also Mazet's cursillo on exploitation of Latin American parish registers (item **1714**).

Almost all of the items on the late colonial period are important. David L. Chandler enlightens us on the demographics and structure of slave families in 18th-century Colombia (item **2621**). Linda L. Greenow analyzes raw returns of the 1777 census of Cartagena (item **2627**). Cook has done another parish register study, this time of Yanque of the Collaguas (item **2671**). Fernando Ponce and Alejandro Reyes Flores analyze the state and select characteristics of the population of a highland community (urban and suburban Arequipa) and a lowland community (Miraflores) respectively (items **2696** and **2698**). Juan Rial Roade discusses sources for the reconstruction of the demography of 18th and 19th-century Uruguay (item **2776**). Susan Socolow analyzes fertility patterns among 18th-century merchants of Buenos Aires (item **2782**), and Pedro A. Vives Azancot re-examines population growth in late 18th-century Paraguay (item **2785**).

With one exception the above mentioned authors are anthropologists, geographers or historians who cultivate historical demography as *genre*, not as a discipline. The exception is Cook. The three related monographs by Carmen Arretx, Rolando Mellafe, and Jorge L. Somoza on estimates of mortality in 18th and 19th-century Chile are doubly novel in their use of hypothetical models and incomplete data (items **2726**, **3064**, and **3065**). Not only are the promising methodologies employed unusual but Arretx and Somoza are demographers. Unfortunately, whoever was responsible for the drafting of these case studies, fails to make clear how the research team reached its findings.

SOURCES: Once again many primary sources were published, some for the first time, others in new, more scholarly editions. Proceeding from north to south and in chronological order, the most significant are: 1) the anthology of royal decrees on treatment of Indians in colonial Venezuela (item **2614**) and its companion, a compendium of locally issued *repartimientos de encomiendas* and *ordenanzas* (item **2617**); 2) what are apparently the first account books of the Caja Real of Coro and therefore the oldest treasury records of Spanish South America (item **2618**); 3) a monumental compendium of inventories of individual and institutional libraries in 17th and 18th-century Venezuela (item **2602**); 4) the 1561 *relación* of privately held *encomiendas* and Crown *repartimientos de indios* in the Viceroyalty of Peru (item **2587**); 5) a coeval summary of the only known portion of the 1559 *visita* of Indian pueblos of Quito (item **2656**); 6) the 1621 *ordenanzas de obrajes* of Quito (item **2655**); 7) a 1607–09 *expediente* in which the Indians of San Damián denounce their pastor, Francisco de Avila, for abuses, the date of which suggests that Avila's subsequent accusations that his parishioners were guilty of idolatry were a smokescreen for his own transgressions (item **2660**); 8) the novel and extremely valuable anthology of documents on the irrigation system of Cuzco and the distribution of water (item **2704**); 9) a new, scholarly edition of Esquivel y Navia's chronicle of Cuzco (item **2675**); 10) the first volume of a true facsimile edition of the Martínez Compañón commissioned illustrations of Trujillo, of which more below (item **2702**); 11) a heretofore all but unknown early 17th-century chronicle and description of Sucre (item **2722**); and 12) a new transcription of Bibar's chronicle of the conquest of Chile (item **2728**), not necessarily more faithful than Irving A. Leonard's (see *HLAS 34:2299*), but welcome anyway as Leonard's appeared in a very limited edition.

The most remarkable source was the inaugural volume of the facsimile edition of the pen and ink, water color illustrations, of which altogether there are 1,411, commissioned by Bishop Baltasar Jaime Martínez Compañón of places and people, flora and fauna, archaeological and religious monuments of the Diocesis of Trujillo, then comprehensive of the whole of northwestern Peru, during and immediately after his all encompassing *visita* thereof (1782–85). Hopefully the publisher, the Centro Iberoamericano de Cooperación, will not be long in publishing the remaining eight volumes of this extraordinary graphic set. [MTH]

GENERAL

2578 Andrien, Kenneth J. The sale of juros and the politics of reform in the Viceroyalty of Peru, 1608–1695 (JLAS, 13, pt. 1, May 1981, p. 1–19, tables)

In desperate need of funds, Crown imposed new taxes throughout Viceroyalty of Peru in 17th century. Union of arms levies failed but sale of *juros* or state supported annuities succeeded (1608–41). Attributes failure of former and success of latter to attitudes of local citizenry toward taxation (i.e., opposed as not in their interest and vice versa). [MTH]

2579 Arias Divito, Juan Carlos. Expedición científica de los hermanos Heuland: 1795–1800. Madrid: Edic. Cultura Hispánica del Centro Iberoamericano de Cooperación, 1978. 150 p.; 3 leaves

Anthology of sources in whole (e.g., Christian Heuland's travel diary) or abstract whose originals are in Real Jardín Botánico and Museo de Ciencias Naturales in Madrid, on late 18th-century explorations by brothers Christian and Konrad Heuland, German geologists in employ of Spanish Crown, to Argentina, Chile, Peru, and Bolivia. One of lesser known Bourbon sponsored scientific expeditions to the colonies. Lacks index and adequate introduction. [MTH]

2580 Birckel, Maurice. Inquisición, libertades y mestizaje: el caso del Capitán Francisco de Aguirre (PMNH/HC, 12, 1979, p. 28–50, bibl.)

Francisco de Aguirre (1500?–81), active in conquest of Chile, was Valdivia's *lugarteniente* in La Serena and Barco (1551–57) and twice governor of Tucumán (1563–66, 1569–70). In this controversial figure who was removed from office and charged by Inquisition, Birckel finds seeds of American nationalism (e.g., separatist leanings, feudal attitudes, pro-mestizo actions and statements). [MTH]

2581 Castañeda, Paulino and **Juan Marchena.** Las órdenes religiosas en América: propiedades, diezmos, exenciones y privilegios (EEHA/AEA, 35, 1978, p. 125–158, tables)

Preliminary comparative study of properties, tithes, exemptions and privileges of Dominicans, Franciscans, Augustinians, Mercedarians, and Jesuits throughout early 17th-century Viceroyalty of Peru. Correctly stresses need for additional work. [MTH]

2582 Díaz Rementería, Carlos J. El cacique en el Virreinato del Perú: estudio histórico-jurídico. Sevilla: Universidad de Sevilla, Departamento de Antropología y Etnología de América, 1977. 260 p.; bibl.; ill. (Serie Publicaciones del Seminario de Antropología Americana; v. 15) (Publicaciones de la Universidad de Sevilla)

Juridical study of *cacicazgos* as Spanish institution in Viceroyalty of Peru. Based primarily on archival research. Interesting, but a comparison of Indian and Spanish perceptions of *cacicazgos* would be more enlightening. [MTH]

2583 Escobedo Mansilla, Ronald. La alcabala en el Perú bajo los Austrias (EEHA/AEA, 33, 1976 [i.e. 1979] p. 257–271, table)

Useful overview of imposition and initial collection of *alcabalas* (sales tax) in Viceroyalty of Peru. Includes city-by-city review of *encabezonamiento* (municipal collection of fixed alcabalas) through 1631. [MTH]

2584 ———. Bienes y cajas de comunidad en el Virreinato Peruano (CSIC/RIS, 32:37, 2. época, oct./dic. 1979, p. 465–492)

Institutional study of Indian *cajas de comunidad* (communal treasuries) and *cajas de census* ("mortgage banks") in Viceroyalty of Peru: origins, sources of funds, nominal uses, functions, administration, and misuse by Spanish Crown administrators. Informative. We need more case studies such as item 2686). [MTH]

2585 ———. El tributo indígena en el Perú: siglos XVI y XVII. Pamplona: Ediciones Universidad de Navarra and Oficina de Educación Iberoamericana, 1979. 354 p.; bibl.; index.

Doctoral dissertation on Indian tribute in Viceroyalty of Peru from conquest through Montesclaros' 1611 reforms. Contains some new data. Supplemented by documentary appendix. [MTH]

2586 Fernández Esquivel, Franco. Procedencia de los esclavos negros, analizada a través del complejo de distribución, desarrollado desde Cartagena (UNCR/R, 2:3, julio/dic. 1976, p. 43–80, bibl., maps)

Attempts to establish tribal origins of slaves imported into South America via Cartagena de Indias in 16th and 17th centuries. Reflects considerable archival research, especially in Inquisition records (Madrid's Archivo Histórico Nacional) but failure to quantify limits usefulness. [MTH]

2587 Hampe M., Teodoro. Relación de los encomenderos y repartimientos del Perú en 1561 (PMNH/HC, 12, 1979, p. 75–117, tables)

First publication of three-part 1561 relación of encomiendas in Viceroyalty of Peru: 1) summary of total Indian population, tributaries, tribute per Spanish township—only part of this critical source previously known; 2) "Relación de los vecinos encomenderos" lists encomiendas, rent, grantor, grantee, and Indian pueblo(s) held per Spanish township; and 3) "Relación de los repartimientos . . . en la corona real." [MTH]

2588 Hernández Palomo, José Jesús. El "Estado general de la Real Hacienda" del Perú, Chile, y Río de la Plata de Alfonso Rodríguez Ovalle (EEHA, 22, 1978, p. 3–58, tables)

Publishes with good introduction "General State of the Royal Fisc of the Kingdom of Peru . . ." (ca. 1775). Knowledgeable official about whom little is known, Rodríguez Ovalle details revenues and expenditures (1774) of six Royal Fiscs (Reales Cajas) of Upper Peru and 13 of Lower Peru; then analyzes viceroyalty's economic state and proposes reforms. Remarkable and valuable source. [MTH]

2589 Lavalle, Bernard. Del "espíritu colonial" a la reivindicación criolla o los albores del criollismo peruano (PUCP/H, 2:1, julio 1978, p. 39–61, bibl.)

Cogent review of 16th-century origins of criollismo or belief in criollo's primacy right as well as supremacy in Viceroyalty of Peru. [MTH]

2590 Lohmann Villena, Guillermo. La memorable crisis monetaria de mediados del siglo XVII y sus repercusiones en el Virreinato del Perú (EEHA/AEA, 33, 1976 [i.e. 1979] p. 579–639, ill.)

Original study of coin debasement and falsification in mid-17th century, repercussions and viceregal efforts to cope with problem. Although not as quantitative as desirable, author provides much new data on Viceroyalty's monetary crisis. [MTH]

2591 Ramón, Armando de. Mercaderes en Lima, Santiago de Chile y Buenos Aires, 1681–1695 (in Historia, problema y promesa: homenaje a Jorge Basadre. Edición a cargo de Francisco Miró Quesada C., Franklin Pease García Yrigoyen y David Sobrevilla A. Lima: Pontificia Universidad Católica del Perú, 1978, v. 1, p. 141–176, bibl., maps, tables)

Sophisticated analysis of trade between Santiago and other towns in Chile, Peru, Upper Peru and Río de la Plata. Examines commercial elites, products, markets, concentration of sales and capital, prices, and investment of profits in rural estates, especially through loans. Novel—for period, late 17th century—and highly significant study. [MTH]

2592 Los Virreyes españoles en América durante el gobierno de la Casa de Austria: Peru. v. 6/7. Edición de Lewis Hanke con la colaboración de Celso Rodríguez. Madrid: Ediciones Atlas, 1980. 2 v. (318, 246 p.); bibl.; indexes (Biblioteca de autores españoles; 285/286)

Final two volumes in monumental set of sources for study of Peru's Hapsburg Viceroys, their administration, and Spanish South America during 16th and 17th centuries. Vol. 6 covers Melchor de Navarra y Rocafull, Duque de la Palata (concluded in vol. 7); vol. 7, Melchor Portocarrero Lasso de la Vega, Conde de la Monclova. Vol. 7 contains indexes and bibliography for whole set, which belongs in every research collection (for vols. 1/5, see HLAS 42:2675). [MTH]

2593 Zavala, Silvio. El servicio personal de los indios en el Perú. México: El Colegio de México, 1978/1980. 3 v. (360, 299, 251 p.); bibl.; indexes; tables.

Detailed digest of archival and published sources on compulsory and voluntary Indian labor throughout Viceroyalty of Peru during colonial period. Result of many years of research, this vademecum belongs in all major and specialized collections. Organized chronologically; vol. 1 covers 16th century; vol. 2, 17th; and vol. 3, 18th. Includes documentary and audiencia specific appendixes. Exceptionally well indexed. [MTH]

VENEZUELA

2594 Amézaga Aresti, Vicente de. El elemento vasco en el siglo XVIII venezolano. Bilbao: Editorial La Gran Enciclopedia Vasca, 1979. 372 p.; bibl. (Obras completas de Vicente de Amézaga Aresti; v. 3) (Biblioteca de La Gran Enciclopedia Vasca)

Catalogue of numerous Basque who sailed to or settled in Venezuela at one time or another in 18th century. Skeletal but utilitarian entries include references, mostly archival. [MTH]

2595 Barbier, Jacques A. Venezuelan "libranzas," 1788–1807: from economic nostrum to fiscal imperative (AAFH/TAM, 37:4, April 1981, p. 457–478, tables)

Pithy quantitative study of *libranzas* or bills of exchange, initially device for bolstering flagging trade between Venezuela and mother country, but after 1800, used primarily to raise badly needed funds for Crown. [MTH]

2596 Campo del Pozo, Fernando. Los agustinos en la evangelización de Venezuela. Caracas: Universidad Católica Andrés Bello, 1979. 301 p.; bibl. (Colección Manoa; 18)

Well documented but tendentious study of early colonial missionary activities, methods, and mentality of Augustinians. Chapter on *doctrinas* or Indian parishes assigned to them, is highly informative. [MTH]

2597 Castillo Lara, Lucas Guillermo. Las acciones militares del Gobernador Ruy Fernández de Fuenmayor: 1637–1644. Caracas: Academia Nacional de la Historia, 1978. 342 p.; bibl.; fold. ill.; ill.; maps (Biblio-

teca de la Academia Nacional de la Historia; 134) (Fuentes para la historia colonial de Venezuela)

Detailed, thoroughly researched monograph on subject's military activities as Venezuela's governor and captain general (1637–44) when he coped with English invasion and Dutch threat. Unsuccessful in ousting Dutch from Curaçao, Fernández de Fuenmayor succeeded in defending La Guaira and Maracaibo from English attacks (1642, 1643). [MTH]

2598 ———. Nuestra Señora de la Copacabana de las Guarenas: apuntes para una historia colonial (VANH/B, 113:250, abril/junio 1980, p. 351–421, tables)

Documented notes on origins and early history of Guarenas (east of Caracas in Central Coastal Range) provides useful sources and informed analysis of their data. [MTH]

2599 Cortés, Santos Rodulfo. Las milicias de pardos de Venezuela durante el período hispánico (*in* Congreso Venezolano de Historia, 3rd, Caracas, 1977. Memoria. [see item **1741**] v. 3, p. 9–85, charts)

Preliminary, somewhat static study of black militias. Draws bleak but unsubstantiated picture of their raison d'être, prejudices and restrictions to which they were subject. [MTH]

2600 ———. El régimen de "las gracias al sacar" en Venezuela durante el período hispánico. Caracas: Academia Nacional de la Historia, 1978. 2 v. (163, 296 p.); bibl.; maps; tables (Biblioteca de la Academia Nacional de la Historia; 135/136) (Fuentes para la historia colonial de Venezuela)

Competent but stilted Ph.D dissertation on *gracias de sacar* or patents of unblemished European ancestry sold to free coloreds during late colonial period. Worth wading through for wealth of data and source appendix (v. 2, *Documentos anexos*). [MTH]

2601 Ferry, Robert J. Encomienda, African slavery, and agriculture in seventeenth-century Caracas (HAHR, 61:4, Nov. 1981, p. 609–635, map, tables)

Excellent quantitative analysis and interpretation of transformation of Caracas Province's economy in 17th century—from relatively small scale, somewhat diversified farming, relying on Indian labor, to major scale cacao production, predicated on slave labor—and of forces at play (e.g., decline in Central American production and Mexican demand). [MTH]

Gasparini, Graziano. Las fortificaciones del Puerto de La Guaira durante el Período colonial. See item **364**.

2602 Leal, Ildefonso. Libros y bibliotecas en Venezuela colonial, 1633–1767. Caracas: Academia Nacional de la Historia, 1978. 2 v. (410, 517 p.); bibl.; ill.; indexes; ports. (Biblioteca de la Academia Nacional de la Historia; 132/133. Fuentes para la historia colonial de Venezuela)

Monumental compendium of inventories of libraries from first listing through Jesuits' expulsion. Vol. 3 will cover 1768–1821. Result of eight years of painstaking research. Solid preliminary study by Leal on kinds of literature read and preferred titles. Basic source collection for cultural and intellectual history. [MTH]

2603 Lucena Salmoral, Manuel. El sistema de Caudrillas de Ronda para la seguridad de los Llanos a fines del período colonial: los antecedentes de las *Ordenanzas de Llanos* de 1811 (*in* Congreso Venezolano de Historia, 3d, Caracas, 1977. Memoria. [see item **1741**] v. 2, p. 189–225)

Well known 1811 *Ordenanzas de Llanos* had origins in late colonial legislation, and as author demonstrates, their chief intent was not so much maintaining law and order as preserving status quo (i.e., domination by region's cattle barons). [MTH]

2604 Manzo Núñez, Torcuato. Montalbán: hijo de la pugna racial, capítulo del libro inédito *Pasado histórico de Montalbán* (VANH/B, 62:247, julio/sept. 1979, p. 621–639)

Argues that Montalbán was offshoot of rivalry between Spanish and free black settlers in western Central Coastal Range, latter of whom concentrated in Nirgua, which gained city status first and opposed granting it to Montalbán. Includes documentary appendix on Nirgua's origins. [MTH]

2606 Mijones Pérez, Lucio. La organización de las milicias venezolanas en la segunda mitad del siglo XVIII (*in* Congreso Venezolano de Historia, 3d, Caracas, 1977. Memoria. [see item **1741**] v. 2, p. 359–382)

Brief but well documented account of

establishment and initial organization of milicias in 1760s and 1770s. [MTH]

2607 Nectario María, Brother. Barinas: fundación, provincia autónoma, gobernadores, documentos, mapas, y planos. Caracas: Universidad Católica Andrés Bello, 1977. 250 p.; index (Colección Manoa; 6)

Catalogue of sources in Archivo General de Indias on city and province of Barinas in Portuguesa Llanos. Lists 1040 documents and 12 maps. [MTH]

2608 Otte, Enrique. Las perlas del Caribe: Nueva Cádiz de Cubagua. Caracas: Fundación John Boulton, 1977. 620 p.; 25 leaves of plates; appendices; bibl.; ill.; index.

Exhaustively researched, highly detailed and definitive history of pearl industry in early 16th century, center of which was Cubagua, off eastern Caribbean coast. Also reconstructs history of city and society of Cubagua. [MTH]

2609 Ponce de Behreno, Marianela. Los capitanes pobladores y la política poblacional de los Welser en la Provincia de Venezuela (*in* Congreso Venezolano de Historia, 3d, Caracas, 1977. Memoria. [see item **1741**] v. 2, p. 491–526)

Demonstrates that the Welsers' interest and actions were not only not compatible with but detrimental to Crown's settlement policies. During Welser governorship (1528–45), no new towns were founded; Coro lost settlers; and Maracaibo ceased to exist. Based on recently published *Juicios de residencia* . . . , v. 1, *Los Welser* (see *HLAS 42:2741*). [MTH]

2610 Ramos Pérez, Demetrio. La fundación de Venezuela: Ampiés y Coro, una singularidad histórica. Valladolid: D. Ramos, 1978. 401 p.; 4 leaves of plates; bibl.; ill.; indexes (Bernal, serie americanista; v. 12)

Amply researched account of 1528 foundation of Coro, first Spanish settlement in mainland Venezuela and an epicenter of its conquest, and of its founder Juan de Ampiés. Somewhat "white-legendish," however. Founded to combat Spanish slave raids on coastal Indians, Coro did not remain a "city of peace" for very long. [MTH]

2611 ———. Los maestros mayores de reales obras de fortificación y los sobrestantes: conocimientos exigidos, funciones, sueldos y aspiraciones sociales (*in* Congreso de Historia, 3d, Caracas, 1977. Memoria. [see item **1741**] v. 2, p. 527–552)

Tantalizing exploratory essay on head masters and overseers of fortifications. Examines and exemplifies their qualifications, duties, wages, privileges, and social aspirations. [MTH]

2612 Rey Fajardo, José del. El archivo y biblioteca del Colegio Jesuítico de Maracaibo, inventariados en la expulsión de 1767 (VANH/B, 62:247, julio/sept. 1979, p. 573–606)

Publishes but does not analyze inventory of archive and library of Maracaibo's Jesuit Colegio, compiled at time of expulsion. Not included in Leal (see item **2602**). Introduction delineates confiscation of Jesuit properties and their expulsion from Maracaibo. [MTH]

2613 ———. El patrimonio económico del Colegio Jesuítico del Maracaibo hispánico (VANH/B, 63:249, enero/marzo 1980, p. 73–112)

Publishes and analyzes inventory of Jesuit properties held by Colegio of Mérida at time of expulsion. [MTH]

2614 Spain. Sovereigns, etc. Cedulario indígena venezolano (1501–1812). Compilación y prólogo, Carmela Bentivenga de Napolitano. Caracas: Universidad Católica Andrés Bello, Instituto de Investigaciones Históricas, 1977. 333 p.; bibl.; index.

Useful anthology of royal *cédulas* issued 1501–1812, relating to conversion, evangelization, treatment and education of Indians, mostly but not exclusively of Venezuela, and to labor regimes and tribute schedules to which they were subject. Chronologically and thematically, but not geographically indexed. See also item **2617**. [MTH]

2615 Suárez, Santiago Gerardo. Las fuerzas armadas venezolanas en la colonia. Caracas: Academia Nacional de la Historia, 1979. 461 p.; bibl.; plates (Fuentes para la historia colonial de Venezuela) (Biblioteca de la Academia Nacional de la Historia; 137)

Chronologically organized compendium of 196 heretofore unpublished sources on armed forces of colonial period, originals of which are mostly in Archivo General de la Nación, Caracas, and Archivo General de Indias. Compendium spans 1557–1809, all but 39 documents are from second half of 18th

century. Preliminary study is of military service in Spain and Indies, from Roman times through 17th century. [MTH]

2616 Troconis de Veracoechea, Ermila. Cárceles coloniales (*in* Congreso Venezolano de Historia, 3d, Caracas, 1977. Memoria. [see item **1741**] v. 3, p. 477–515)

Excellent working paper on history of prisons in city and province of Caracas. Treats several types of prisons (ecclesiastical, royal, correctional, for women, Indian), custodianship of prisoners, labor to which they were subject, their maintenance, daily life, etc. Notable contribution on neglected subject. [MTH]

2617 Venezuela. Comisión Indigenista. Fuero indígena venezolano. pt. 1, Período de la colonia, 1552/1783 por J. Gabaldón Márquez. Caracas: Universidad Católica Andrés Bello, Instituto de Investigaciones Históricas, 1977. 233 p.; bibl.

Useful compendium of colonial legislation relating to Indians. Publishes 1552 *Repartimiento hecho de los principales y naturales de la Nueva Ciudad de Segovia* (i.e. Barquisimeto), coeval *ordenanzas* regulating said encomiendas, local Cabildo's protest thereof; 1605 *ordenanzas* of Mérida; and six other similar basic sources of demographic, ethnohistorical and socioeconomic as well as institutional or juridical importance. Not indexed. Comparable anthology of republican period legislation, compiled by Cesareo de Armellada, will be published separately (see also item **2614**). [MTH]

2618 Venezuela (province). **Real Hacienda.** El Primer libro de la Hacienda Pública Colonial de Venezuela 1529–1538. Eduardo Arcila Farías, compilador y director del proyecto. Caracas: Instituto de Investigaciones Históricas, Facultad de Humanidades y Educación, Universidad Central de Venezuela, 1979. 442 p.; bibl.; ill.; indexes; tables (Serie Proyecto de la Hacienda Pública Colonial Venezolana; v. 1)

Publishes oldest, probably first Treasury account books of Venezuela, generated by Real Caja of Coro, first mainland settlement, originals of which are in AGI: 1) *Libro común*, 1529–38, transcribed by María del Nogal; 2) *Libro de toma de cuentas*, 1529–38, transcribed by Eduardo Arcila Farías; and 3/4) *Libro(s) de cuentas de bienes de difuntos*, 1532–34 and 1534–38, transcribed by

Carlos Molina Argüello. Onomastic indexes, tables, notes and Arcila Farías' solid introductory study enhance utility of sources for reconstructing area's economic and social history. [MTH]

Vila, Marco Aurelio. La geoeconomía de la Venezuela del siglo XVI: notas. See *HLAS 43:5303.*

2619 Waldron, Kathy. Public land policy and use in colonial Caracas (HAHR, 61:2, May 1981, p. 258–277, table)

Careful study of partition of *ejido* or public lands in Caracas (1770–1809) and of its socioeconomic consequences. As city grew in number of inhabitants, urban poor benefitted as more than 90 percent of 900 plus *solares* were granted to "pardo *jornaleros,* widows, orphans, and old or incapacitated people who claimed poverty." [MTH]

NUEVA GRANADA

2620 Ariza S., Alberto E. El Colegio-Universidad de Santo Tomás de Aquino de Santa Fe de Bogotá, 1580, 13 de junio, 1980. Bogotá: Editorial Kelly, 1980. 148 p.; 2 leaves of plates; bibl.; ill.

Well documented chronicle of four-century old Dominican University of Bogotá, especially strong on colonial period. [MTH]

2621 Chandler, David L. Family bonds and the bondsman: the slave family in colonial Colombia (LARR, 16:2, 1981, p. 107–131, tables)

Pioneering demographic and socioeconomic study of slave families in late colonial New Granada. Based on numerous inventories of haciendas, mines and former Jesuit estates. Chandler demonstrates not only that family flourished as institution among slaves but that it was encouraged by Colombian society, and once again argues that slavery was less harsh in New Granada than in many other areas in the Americas (see also *HLAS 36:3046*). [MTH]

2622 Chenu, Jeanne. Problemática del espacio neo-granadino en vísperas de la independencia: Nueva Granada, ¿entidad y/o realidad? (*in* Coloquio Ilustración Española e Independencia de América, Bellaterra, Spain, 1978. Homenaje a Nöel Salomon: ilustración española e independencia de América. Edición preparada por Alberto Gil Novales. Barcelona: Universidad Autónoma de Barcelona, 1979, p. 207–216)

Analyzes attitudes of literate criollos, particularly those influenced by Enlightenment, towards New Granada as entity. Followed by interesting exchange between author, Manuel Lucena Salmoral, and Manfred Kossok. [MTH]

2623 Colmenares, Germán. Historia económica y social de Colombia. t. 2, Popayán: una sociedad esclavista, 1680–1800. Bogotá: La Carreta, 1973? 1 v.; bibl.; indexes.

Another monograph on colonial Colombia's demographic, economic and social history by one of its best historians (for vol. 1, see *HLAS 38:3049*; and for his other monographs, *HLAS 34:2221, HLAS 36:2533, HLAS 38:3048,* and *HLAS 40:3131*). Treats slavery, mining, farming, ranching, society, politics in late 17th and 18th-century Popayán. Based on considerable research in local, regional, national and Spanish repositories, and appropriate secondary literature. Highly detailed and heavily quantitative yet interpretative as well as analytical in keeping with *Annales* school in which Colmenares was trained. [MTH]

2624 Coughlin, Edward V. and **John F. Wilhite.** Some notes on the independence movement at the Colegio del Rosario (*in* Coloquio Ilustración Española e Independencia de América, Bellaterra, Spain, 1978. Homenaje a Noël Salomon: ilustración española e independencia de América. Edición preparada por Alberto Gil Novales. Barcelona: Universidad Autónoma de Barcelona, 1979, p. 357–366)

Archival notes on impact of French Revolution on faculty and students of Dominican University of Bogotá. Includes documentary appendix. [MTH]

2625 González Luna, María Dolores. Características de las gobernaciones de Santa María y Cartagena en relación al tema de los resguardos indígenas (UB/BA, 29, 1979, p. 65–82, col. plates)

Introduction to unpublished Ph.D. dissertation on *resguardos* (Indian reserves) in Caribbean coast governorships. Rest of this promising work will be published in future issues of *Boletín Americanista.* [MTH]

2626 Graff, Gary W. Archives in Pamplona, Norte de Santander, Colombia (AFH/TAM, 37:2, Oct. 1980, p. 223–225)

Brief guide to colonial and national period holdings of notarial, parish and episcopal archives of Pamplona. [MTH]

2627 Greenow, Linda L. Family, household, and home: a micro-geographic analysis of Cartagena, New Granada, in 1777. Editorial committee, David J. Robinson, editor, *et al.* Syracuse, N.Y.: Department of Geography, Syracuse University, 1976. 51 p.; bibl.; ill. (Discussion paper series—Department of Geography, Syracuse University; no. 18)

Exemplifies extent to which raw returns of late colonial censuses permit reconstruction of social as well as demographic infrastructure, in this case family and household structure, size, composition and spatial distribution in three Cartagena *barrios*: Santo Toribio, San Sebastián, and Gethsemani. Joint Oxford-Syracuse Population Project contribution. [MTH]

2628 Loy, Jane M. Forgotten comuneros: the 1781 revolt in the Llanos of Casanare (HAHR, 61:2, May 1981, p. 235–257, map, table)

Well researched, original, integral study of all but forgotten participation of eastern lowland Casanare Province in 1781 Comunero Rebellion. Includes analysis of uprising's local background and its consequences. [MTH]

2629 Mantilla Ruiz, Luis Carlos. Actividad misionera de los franciscanos en Colombia durante los siglos XVII y XVIII: fuentes documentales. Bogotá: Editorial Kelly, 1980. 167 p.; 5 leaves of plates; appendices; bibl.

As subtitle implies, not a history but collection of sources on Franciscan missionary activities in 17th and 18th-century Colombia. Sources published include 18th-century chronicle of said missions. [MTH]

2630 Mesa, Carlos E. Primeras diócesis novogranadinas y sus prelados: pt. 4, El obispado de Cartagena de Indias durante el periódo hispánico, 1534–1650 (ISTM/MH, 34:100/102, enero/dic. 1977, p. 305–332, bibl.)

Useful digest of what is known about early colonial bishops of Cartagena (for pts. 1/3 of this article, see *Missionalia Hispánica*,

vol. 33, Nos. 97/99, enero/dic. 1976, p. 93–164, covering bishops of other early dioceses). [MTH]

2631 Restrepo de García, Inés. El ataque a Cartagena de 1741: una lucha de mercados (CH/BHA, 64:719, oct./dic. 1977, p. 597–637, bibl.)

Examines commercial motives underlying British 1741 attempt to take Cartagena. Includes some new data on port's defense. [MTH]

2632 Ruiz Rivera, Julián B. Remesas de caudales del Nuevo Reino de Granada en el XVII (EEHA/AEA, 34, 1977, p. 241–271, graphs, tables)

Quantifies remission of bullion, especially gold, from New Granada to Spain during 17th century. Ruiz Rivera has found more or less complete sources for all years except three. Resultant time series demonstrates overall decline in remissions, especially toward century's end. [MTH]

2633 Solano, Francisco de. Las relaciones geográficas y descripciones topográficas realizadas por el Ejercito Expedicionario de la Costa Firme, 1815–1816 (*in* Congreso Venezolano de Historia, 3d, Caracas, 1977. Memoria. [see item **1741**] v. 3, p. 99–124)

Lists 130 geographic descriptions and maps of Colombia's and Venezuela's Caribbean coast prepared by members of Spanish Expeditionary Army of 1815–16. Most sources are in Servicio Geográfico del Ejército, Madrid. [MTH]

2634 Villamarín, Juan and **Judith Villamarín.** Colonial census and tributary lists of the Sabana de Bogotá Chibcha: sources and issues (*in* Studies in Spanish American population history [see item **1792**] p. 45–93, maps, tables)

Solid analysis of major sources, particularly censuses of 1592–95, 1636–40, and 1758–59, and tribute lists of 1804–06, for reconstruction of state and movement of Chibcha population of Bogota's Sabana. [MTH]

QUITO

2635 Archivo Nacional de Historia (Ecuador). Guía del Archivo Nacional de

Historia. Quito: Edit. Casa de la Cultura Ecuatoriana, 1981. 219 p.; bibl.

First complete chronological guide to Archive's organized *fondos* comprising: 1) holdings of six historic and one modern notary of Quito; 2) "Archivo de la Presidencia de Quito," divided into "Colonia, Gran Colombia, República" and "incorporación de Abogados"; and 3) Archivo de la Corte Suprema de Justicia, organized into 47 series. Not organized or inventoried are: Archivo(s) de la Corte Superior de Justicia de Quito and del Ministerio de Gobierno (formerly del Interior) *fondos*. Neither appear in guide. Supplements but does not supersede Juan Freile Granizo's detailed guide to colonial holdings of Quito's National Archive (see *HLAS 38: 3089*). [MTH]

2636 Beerman, Eric. Bosquejo biográfico y genealógico de Francisco Requena y su *Descripción de la Provincia de Guayaquil hecha en 1774* (AHG/R, 7:14, dic. 1978, p. 3–23, map, table)

Data on life and career of Francisco Requena (1743–1824), peninsular military engineer and bureaucrat, assigned to Guayaquil 1770–75, who prepared detailed description of relación geográfica of Guayaquil published with accompanying map. At least one version without map was published in Requena's lifetime in *El viagero universal* . . . (vols. 22/23, Madrid, 1799, p. 324–378, 5–29). [MTH]

2637 Bernal Ruiz, María del Pilar. La toma del puerto de Guayaquil en 1687. Prólogo del Dr. D. Luis Navarro García. Sevilla: Escuela de Estudios Hispano-Americanos, 1979. 116 p.; 2 leaves of plates; bibl.; index; maps (Publicaciones de la Escuela de Estudios Hispano-Americanos de Sevilla; 257 [no. general])

Senior thesis marking incursion of students from Escuela de Estudios Hispano-Americanos into history of Guayaquil and its province. Important for AGI data on first taking of port city by pirates—second and last occurred 1710—but marred by careless mistakes. [MTH]

2638 Borchart de Moreno, Christiana. Composiciones de tierras en la Audiencia de Quito: el valle de Tumbaco a finales del siglo XVII (JGSWGL, 17, 1980, p. 121–155, map, tables)

Delineates extent, types and origins of Spanish landholdings in Valley of Tumbaco, north of Quito, as of end of 17th century. Well researched. [MTH]

2639 ———. Landbesitz im Machachi—Tal am Ende des 17. Jahrhunderte (IAA, 5:3, Neue folge, 1979, p. 243–266, bibl., map, table)

Analyzes origins of Spanish landholdings in Valley of Machachi, to south of Quito, as of late 17th century. Based on 1692 *visita de tierras*. Companion piece to item **2638**. [MTH]

2640 ———. La transferencia de la propiedad agraria indígena en el Corregimiento de Quito hasta finales del siglo XVII (UTIEH/C, 34, 1980, p. 5–19, bibl., tables)

Original study of land acquisition by Spaniards at Indians' expense in northern highland during 16th and 17th centuries. In this and items **2638** and **2639**, Borchart adds appreciably to knowledge of colonial Ecuador's agrarian history. [MTH]

2641 Bravo Guerreira, María Concepción. ¿Fue Francisco de Xérez el autor de la *Relación Sámano*?: anotaciones al viaje de descubrimiento del Perú (EEHA/AEA, 33, 1976, [i.e. 1979] p. 33–55)

Argues that Francisco de Xérez was not author of the *Relación Sámano* as maintained by Porras Barrenechea, but unidentified master sailor who accompanied Bartolomé Ruiz. Also attempts to clarify chronology of Ruiz's exploratory voyage of 1526. Not as informed nor as informative as Szaszdi's riposte study (see item **2657**). [MTH]

2642 Bromley, Rosemary D.F. Change in the ethnic composition of the population of central highland Ecuador (UC/CA, 21:3, June 1980, p. 412–414, bibl., table)

Succinct quantitative analysis of changes in "racial" composition of populations of Latacunga and Ambato districts during late colonial and early national periods. [MTH]

2643 Castro y Velázquez, Juan. El *Libro Primero de Matrimonios* de la Iglesia de Santa Catalina de Colonche (CCE/CHA, 25:42, 1975 [i.e. 1980] p. 317–377, bibl., tables)

Publishs first extant and at least second, if not first, compiled marriage register of Colonche, an Indian pueblo on Santa Elena peninsula. Covers years 1763–1808 and includes three *padrones,* apparently from 1778. Ethnohistorical as well as historical demographic source. Colonche also has baptism and burial registers from 1710 and 1789 respectively. [MTH]

2644 Clayton, Lawrence A. Caulkers and carpenters in a new world: the shipyards of colonial Guayaquil. Athens: Ohio University, Center for International Studies, 1980. 189 p.; bibl. (Papers in international studies: Latin American series; no. 8)

Somewhat revised English version of *HLAS 42:2788.* Lacks supplementary materials which appear in Spanish original. [MTH]

2645 Documentos para la historia militar.
v. 3, Documentos para la historia de la República del Ecuador. Por la Dirección de Historia y Geografía Militar del E.M.C. de las FF. AA. Quito: Edit. Casa de la Cultura Ecuatoriana, 1977. 642 p. (Boletín del Departamento de Historia)

Compendium of 119 sources on 16th and 17th-century Ecuador, originals in AGI. Transcriptions from Vacas Galindo Collection in Quito's Dominican Archives. Lacks indexes, selection of sources reflect no criteria, but of interest, nevertheless. Vol. 3's title *Documentos para la historia de la República del Ecuador* is appropriate given their eclectic nature (for vols. 1/2, see *HLAS 40:3169*). [MTH]

2646 Eugenio Espejo: conciencia crítica de su época. Quito: Centro de Publicaciones, Pontificia Universidad Católica del Ecuador, 1978. 369 p.; bibl.

Luminous, well researched and written essays which add to knowledge and understanding of Espejo and his times: Freile Granizo is noteworthy on cultural, economic and social conditions in second half of 18th century (p. 1–48); Guerra Bravo reviews literature on Espejo (p. 49–76) and ably delineates his intellectual development as philosopher (p. 239–349); Peña Novoa summarizes Espejo's life (p. 77–132); and Paladines carefully examines economic, political, and social thought (p. 133–238). [MTH]

Freile Granizo, Carlos E. Un milenarista ecuatoriano del siglo XVIII: José de Valdivieso, introducción a su estudio. See item **7590.**

2647 Hamerly, Michael T. Archives of Cuenca (AAFH/TAM, 37:3, Jan. 1981, p. 379–392)

Detailed guide to colonial period and 19th-century holdings of historical, administrative, and ecclesiastical archives of Cuenca. Supersedes author's "Archives and Libraries of Cuenca" in *Research guide to Andean history* (see item **2577**, p. 175–181). [Ed.]

2648 Heredia Herrera, Antonio. Organización y descripción de los fondos de la Audiencia de Quito del Archivo General de Indias (EEHA/HBA, 21, 1977, p. 139–165)

Excellent introduction to and description of Audiencia of Quito *subsección* (record group) AGI holdings. Records span 1537–1836, and consist of those dispatched from Quito and those generated in Spain, each of which is divided into four subgroups, corresponding to the branches of colonial government (i.e., administration, finances, army and navy, and ecclesiastical). A model guide. [MTH]

2649 Lavallé, Bernard. Créolisme et alternance: les Augustins de Quito au XVIIe siècle (UB/BH, 81:3/4, juillet/déc. 1979, p. 223–264)

Well documented case study of struggle for supremacy between peninsular born and native born Augustinians in 17th-century Quito and of Crown's not altogether successful attempt to minimize friction and disruptive consequences by imposing alternation rule in provincialship (see also items **2587** and **2681**). [MTH]

2650 León Borja de Szaszdi, Dora. Guayaquil y la Real Armada del Mar del Sur, 1579–1624 (*in* Congreso Venezolana de Historia, 3rd, Caracas, 1977. Memoria. [see item **1741**] v. 1, p. 239–298)

Contributes some new archival data on construction of vessels for Armada del Mar del Sur at Guayaquil and Puna in early colonial period, but covers much same ground as Bradley (*HLAS 40:3191–3192, HLAS 42:2659* and *HLAS 42:2678*) and Clayton (see *HLAS 42:2788*). [MTH]

2651 Moreno Egas, Jorge. Resúmen alfabético del *Primer Libro de Matrimonios de Españoles* en la Parroquia de El Sagrario de Quito, 1723–1764 (AHG/R, 7:14 dic. 1978, p. 81–182)

Not altogether satisfactory alphabetical abstract of first known, possibly first extant register of "Spaniards" resident and/or married in Quito's Cathedral Parish (1723–64). Useful social historical source. Demographers will prefer original. [MTH]

2652 Moreno Yáñez, Segundo E. Una rebelión indígena anticolonial: Chambo, 1797 (UTIEH/C, 34, 1980, p. 21–32)

Solid study of yet another heretofore ignored Indian rebellion of late colonial period in Ecuador's central highlands (see also Moreno Yáñez's *Sublevaciones indígenas en la Audiencia de Quito* noted in *HLAS* 40:3718). [MTH]

2653 ———. Traspaso de la propiedad agrícola indígena a la hacienda colonial: el caso de Saquisilí (JGSWGL, 17, 1980, p. 97–119, tables)

Detailed case study of formation and expansion of former Jesuit estate of Saquisilí, west of Latacunga, at expense and to detriment of local Indians who formerly owned properties making up estate. [MTH]

2654 Oberem, Udo. Ein Beispiel für die soziale Selbsteinschätzung des indianischen Hochadels im kolonialzeitlichen Quito (IAA, 5:3, 1979, p. 215–225)

Publishes and comments on five letters of petition to Crown (1610–13) from Doña Bárbara Atahualpa Inca, descendant of Atahualpa. Petitions are significant because Doña Bárbara, an orphan, does not plead with King but defends her rights and those of her ancestors, especially her great great grandfather, the Inca. [MTH]

2655 Ortiz de la Tabla Ducasse, Javier. Las ordenanzas de obrajes de Matías de Peralta para la Audiencia de Quito, 1621 (EEHA/AEA, 33, 1976, p. 875–931)

Publishes and analyzes local ordinances of 1621 for *obrajes* (textile sweat shops) of Quito, which remained in effect at least through 1725 (see *HLAS* 42:2789). [MTH]

Salomon, Frank. Don Pedro de Zambiza, un *varauuj* del siglo XVI. See item **1672.**

2656 ———. Seis comunidades indígenas en las cercanías de Quito, 1559: la visita de Gaspar de San Martín y Juan Mosquera (EANH/B, 59:127/128, enero/dic. 1976, p. 139–190, bibl., tables)

Detailed summary of only known portion of 1559 visita of Quito's Indian pueblos (Puembo, Pingolqui, El Inca, Urin Chillo, Anan Chillo, and Uyumbicho). Earliest known source for reconstruction of ethnohistory and historical demography of northern highlands, of which Salomon's "Introductory Essay" is excellent preliminary analysis. See also author's prize-winning *Los señores étnicos de Quito en la época de los Incas* (item **1673**). [MTH]

2657 Szaszdi, Adam. En torno a la balsa de Salango, Ecuador, que capturó Bartolomé Ruiz (EEHA/AEA, 35, 1978, p. 453–554, map, plates)

Somewhat redundant monograph argues: 1) that *Relación Samanó* was written not by Francisco de Xérez but by Fernández de Oviedo; and 2) that balsa captured 1 Oct. 1526, by Bartolomé Ruiz and crew were not Peruvian but Ecuadorian. First conclusion unverified, second no longer in dispute; still, work provides more complete, precise chronology of Ruiz's 1526 exploratory voyage and identifies pueblos mentioned in *Relación Samanó* and other voyage accounts (see item **2641**). [MTH]

2658 ——— and Dora León Borja. Reconstrucción tentativa de la hidrografía de la Provincia de Guayaquil en el siglo XVIII (EEHA/AEA, 32, 1975, p. 447–483, ill., maps)

Fascinating attempt to reconstruct river course changes in Guayaquil Province during colonial period in order to locate sites of Spanish towns (e.g., Guayaquil) and Indian pueblos (e.g., Pimocha). Important contribution to coast's barely known historical geography. [MTH]

2659 Velasco, Juan de. Historia del Reino de Quito en la América meridional. t. 1, Historia natural. t. 2, Historia antigua. t. 3, Historia moderna. Quito: Edit. Casa de la Cultura Ecuatoriana, 1977/1979. 3 v. (510, 453, 532 p.); bibl.; indexes; map.

Ninth edition of standard late 18th-century natural history and history of prehispanic and colonial Quito. This is first edition based on both manuscript originals, in Madrid's Royal Academy of History and Cotocollao's Jesuit Library. Edition includes useful index and scientific terminology for flora and fauna described by Velasco (v. 1, p. 439–473). [MTH]

PERU

2660 Acosta Rodríguez, Antonio. El pleito de los indios de San Damián, Huarochiri, contra Francisco de Avila, 1607 (EEHA/BHA, 23, 1979, p. 3–33)

Based on rediscovered 1607–09 expendiente, in Lima's Archdiocesan Archives in which San Damián's Indian parishioners (Huarochiri Province) denounced their pastor for extortion, sexual and other abuses. Author argues that Francisco de Avila, first to be appointed *Juez Visitador de las Idolatrías,* initiated 1610 campaign against vestiges of Andean religious practices in revenge. Use of "idolatries" campaign by *doctrineros* as control mechanism needs to be examined in depth. [MTH]

2661 Adorno, Rolena. Las otras fuentes de Guamán Poma: sus lecturas castellanas (PUCP/H, 2:2, dic. 1978, p. 137–158, bibl., ill.)

Analyzes Spanish works published in Europe and America which influenced Poma de Ayala's style and thought (see also *HLAS 42:1581*). [MTH]

Andrien, Kenneth J. The sale of juros and the politics of reform in the Viceroyalty of Peru, 1608–1695. See item **2578.**

2662 Anna, Timothy E. The fall of the royal government in Peru. Lincoln: University of Nebraska Press, 1979. 291 p.; bibl.; tables.

Major reassessment of final years of Spanish rule in Peru, especially of Abascal's lengthy viceregency (1806–16). Based on considerable archival research in Peru and Spain. Argues that independence—"separation" would be better word—from Spain was gained through default, and that economic problems are key for understanding Peruvian apathy towards independence. Work's value lies in new data on period rather than in Anna's thesis which somehow confuses Lima with Peru. Written for specialists. [MTH]

2663 Bonilla, Heraclio. The new profile of Peruvian history (LARR, 16:3, 1981, p. 210–224)

Assesses recent accomplishments in Peruvian historiography. Reviews writings on colonial period thematically, and those on national period chronologically. Provocative as well as insightful analysis of state of the art. [MTH]

2664 Bronner, Fred. Elite formation in seventeenth-century Peru (CEDLA/B, 24, 1978, p. 3–26)

Thought provoking analysis not only of composition of elites in 17th-century Peru, but of social mobility. Includes critique of Mörner's *sociedad de castas* model. Mandatory reading for all colonialists. [MTH]

2665 ———. Hernando de Valencia: tax promoter (*in* Stuggle and survival in colonial America. Berkeley: University of California Press, 1981, p. 311–330)

Well told tale of trials and tribulations of tax-collector sent by Madrid to Lima in 1631 to ensure payment of *arbitrios* or Olivares' union of the arms imposts. Illuminates social behavior and mentality of times as upstart Valencia clashed with Viceroy and other local officials. [MTH]

2666 ———. El tesoro del perulero: Martín de Ysasi y la armadilla de 1632 (*in* Historia, problema y promesa: homenaje a Jorge Basadre. Edición a cargo de Francisco Miró Quesada C., Franklin Pease García Yrigoyen y David Sobrevilla A. Lima: Pontificia Universidad Católica del Perú, 1978, v. 1, p. 15–32, bibl., tables)

Begins to answer question of role played by commercial agents in intraimperial trade. Use coeval *protocolos* to determine how much specie and bullion were entrusted to Ysasi and by whom in the sailing of 1632. [MTH]

2667 Burkholder, Mark A. Politics of a colonial career: José Baquíjano and the Audiencia of Lima. Albuquerque: University of New Mexico Press, 1980. 184 p.; 4 leaves of plates; bibl.; index.

Not biography but model study of efforts, ultimately successful, of member of late colonial Creole elite to obtain status as well as sinecure of audiencia appointment. Illuminates aspirations as well as mentality of well-born native sons. Elegantly written. [MTH]

2668 Campbell, Leon G. Social structure of the Tupac Amaru Army in Cuzco, 1780–81 (HAHR, 63:4, Nov. 1981, p. 675–693, table)

Demonstrates that 1780–81 rebellion was neither uprising of exploited Indians or peasants against oppressors nor resurgence of Inca nationalism by examining ethnic and occupational makeup "of command and staff group assembled by Tupac Amaru II in Cuzco in 1780." Far fewer local ethnic lords and *indios forasteros* followed Condorcanqui than Creoles and mestizos. Rebellion was "regional expression of discontent" but in order to know what else it was, further research is needed. [MTH]

2669 ——. Teaching the history of colonial Peru (The History Teacher [University of Notre Dame, Notre Dame, Indiana] 14:3, May 1981, p. 349–359)

Outlines major themes in colonial Peruvian history and comments on basic literature in English. Useful for undergraduates and nonspecialists. [MTH]

2670 Castañeda Delgado, Paulino. Don Bartolomé Lobo Guerrero, tercer Arzobispo de Lima (EEHA/AEA, 33, 1976 [i.e. 1979] p. 57–103)

Well documented but apologetic review of subject's prelacy (1609–22). Secular priest author maintains Lobo Guerrero was reform prelate (true); replaced friars as *doctrineros* with diocesan clergy because latter were more disinterested (doubtful); and combatted idolatry with charity, Christian zeal, and morally upright *visitadores* such as Avila (for more correct interpretation, see item **2660**). Pt. 4 on state of diocesis, based on detailed 1619 description, somewhat redeems study. [MTH]

2671 Cook, Noble David. Eighteenth-century population change in Andean Peru: the Parish of Yanque (*in* Studies in Spanish American population history [see item **1792**] p. 243–270, maps, tables)

Pioneering study of demography of rural, primarily Indian, highland parish, Yanque of the Collaguas in middle Colca Valley. Based on aggregate analysis of parish registers. This work, Cook's "La Población de la Parroquia de Yanahuara" (see *HLAS 40: 2038*), and Mazet's "Population et Société à Lima" (see item **2687**) are only published studies of historical demography of Peru based on aggregative analysis of parish registers. [MTH]

2672 Cushner, Nicholas P. Lords of the land: sugar, wine, and Jesuit estates of coastal Peru, 1600–1767. Albany: State University of New York Press, 1980. 225 p.; bibl.; index; tables

First major study in any language of Jesuit sugar and wine estates on Peru's coast. Examines input, operation, output (i.e., acquisition of land, estates management, free and slave labor, production and profit, finances, and Jesuit trade network within Peru and between Lower and Upper Peru, Quito, and Río de la Plata). Illuminates many aspects of economic, especially agrarian history of Peru. Exceptionally well researched and written, *Lords of the land* is vol. 1 of three on Jesuit estates in Spanish South America. [MTH]

2673 Durán Montero, María Antonia. Fundación de ciudades en el Perú durante el siglo XVI: estudio urbanístico. Sevilla: Escuela de Estudios Hispano-Americanos de Sevilla, 1978. 210 p.; 19 leaves of plates (3 fold.); bibl.; ill.; index (Publicaciones de la Escuela de Estudios Hispano-Americanos de Sevilla; 247)

Exceptionally well researched licentiate thesis on foundation of Spanish cities and refoundation of Indian towns as Spanish cities in 16th-century Peru. Draws together much of and adds to what was known regarding early colonial Piura, Jauja, Trujillo, Lima, Callao, Chachapoyas, Ayacucho, Huanuco, Arequipa, Cuzco and other new and hybrid towns. [MTH]

Durán Pombo, Jaime. Los Alcedos. See *HLAS 43:5011.*

2674 Espinoza Soriano, Waldemar. Los chachapoyas y cañares de Chiara, Huamanga, aliados de España (*in* Historia, problema y promesa: homenaje a Jorge Basadre. Edición a cargo de Francisco Miró Quesada C., Franklin Pease García Yrigoyen y David Sobrevilla A. Lima: Pontificia Universidad Católica del Perú, 1978, v. 1, p. 231–253, bibl.)

Reconstructs more or less successful attempts by Chachas and Cañares who settled in Chiara—a postconquest *aldea*, not a *reducción*—to south of Huamanga, to obtain and retain privileges throughout colonial period as descendants of allies of Spanish conquistadores. [MTH]

2675 Esquivel y Navia, Diego de. Noticias cronológicas de la gran ciudad del Cuzco. Ed., prólogo y notas de Félix Denegri

Luna, con la colaboración de Horacio Villanueva Urteaga y César Gutiérrez Muñoz. Lima: Fundación Augusto N. Wiese: Banco Wiese, 1980. 2 v.; bibl.; ill.; indexes (Biblioteca peruana de cultura)

Critical, first scholarly acceptable edition of basic 18th-century chronology of Cuzco from alleged 1043 foundation by Incas through 1749. Well annotated and indexed, edition was prepared from original manuscript and all known coeval copies. Esquivel (1700?–79), *cuzqueño* and priest, drew on oral tradition and local archival sources. Introductory essays by Denegri Luna, Villanueva Urteaga, and Gutiérrez Muñoz on chronicle, author, and his sources are first rate. [MTH]

2676 Ganster, Paul B. Cristóbal Bequer: wayward prebend (*in* Struggle and survival in colonial America. Edited by David G. Sweet and Gary B. Nash. Berkeley: University of California Press, 1981, p. 189–207)

Sketches life and career of rogue Bequer (1693–1753), who although murderer and thief, obtained holy orders and even minor cathedral post, *media ración* appointment. As Ganster notes, Bequer could have led debauched cleric's life, but he made mistake of insulting viceroy, and would have been jailed or exiled had he not died first. [MTH]

Golte, Jürgen. Determinanten des Entstehens und des Verlaufs bäuerlicher Rebellion in den Anden vom 18. zum 20. Jahrhundert. See item **2573**.

2677 ———. Repartos y rebeliones: Túpac Amaru y las contradicciones de la economía colonial. Traducciones de Carlos Degregori Caso. Lima: Instituto de Estudios Peruanos, 1980. 256 p.; bibl.; maps (Serie Estudios históricos; 6)

First detailed study of economic background and aspects of Tupac Amaru (1780–81) and Tupac Katari rebellions (1781). Reconstructs forced distribution of goods (*repartimientos*) among Indians by corregidores and their agents, and local protests and uprisings that preceded 1780–83 rebellions. Important work which details and illuminates economic and social history of 18th-century Peru and Bolivia. [MTH]

2678 Gutiérrez, Ramón. Notas sobre organización artesanal en el Cusco durante

la colonia (PUCP/H, 3 : 1, julio 1979, p. 1–15, bibl., table)

Research notes on heretofore unstudied Cuzco guilds. Reflects considerable archival research. Author is professor of history in Argentina. [MTH]

2679 Historia del Perú. v. 4/5. Lima: Editorial Juan Mejía Baca, 1980. 2 v. (576, 504 p.); bibl.; maps; plates; tables

Neither general nor integral, volumes represent new approach to history of colonial Peru (i.e., monographic essays by leading specialists): Edmundo Guillén Guillén's "La Conquista del Perú de los Incas, 1531–1572"; Waldemar Espinosa Soriano's "La Sociedad en el Perú Colonial"; Javier Tord Nicolini's and Carlos Lazo García's "Economía y Sociedad en el Perú Colonial;" Luis Alberto Sánchez, "La Literatura en el Virreinato"; and Luis Millones' "La Religión Indígena en la Colonia." Essays constitute remarkable distillation of ongoing research on basic themes and praiseworthy attempt to produce articulated account of demographic, economic, ethnohistorical, and social history of colonial Peru. Part of 12-volume history of Peru from pre-Inca times through present. [MTH]

2680 Holguín Callo, Oswaldo. Los actividades lucrativas del Dr. Diego de Salinas, letrado de Lima: 1558–1595 (IGFO/RI, 38 : 154, julio/dic. 1978, p. 618–651)

Well researched study of one of first but short-lived Creole lawyers of Lima. Chiefly concerned with licit and illicit attempts to enrich himself. [MTH]

2681 Lavalle, Bernard. La crise mercedaire au Peru, 1690–1703: ou les chemins difficiles du creolisme conventuel (CDAL, 20, 2. semestre, 1979, p. 131–144)

Sophisticated case study of struggle for local supremacy between peninsular and Creole friars. [MTH]

2682 Lazo García, Carlos and **Javier Tord Nicolini.** Del negro señorial al negro bandolero: cimarronaje a palenques en Lima, siglo XVIII. Lima: Biblioteca Peruana de Historia, Economía y Sociedad, 1977. 111 p.; 1 fold. leaf of plates; bibl.; map (Colección Colonia; v. 6)

Research paper on virtually forgotten aspect of Peruvian history, *palenques* or fortified communities of refugee slaves (*ci-*

marrones). Authors document and analyze four palenques in Lima's vicinity: Huachipa (1713) apparently the first; Carabayllo and Zambrano (1761); and Vicentelo (1796). [MTH]

2683 —— and ——. El tumulto esclavo en la Hacienda San José de Nepeña, 1779: apuntes metodológicos para una historia social. Lima: Biblioteca Peruana de Historia, Economía y Sociedad, 1978. 58 p.; bibl. (Colección Colonia; v. 7)

Careful analysis of 1779 slave uprisings on former Jesuit estate. Also abstracts text of primary source on which study is based, trial transcript of rebellious slaves. [MTH]

2684 **López Serrano, Matilde.** Trujillo del Perú en el siglo XVIII. Madrid: Editorial Patrimonio Nacional, 1976. 74 p.; 19 col. ill.; bibl. (Colección Selecta; 9)

Excellent introduction to what is known regarding Baltasar Jaime Martínez Compañón, Bishop of Trujillo (1779–91) and Archbishop of Santa Fe de Bogotá (1791–97), and remarkable nine volume set of color illustrations of people and places, flora and fauna of the Diocesis of Trujillo commissioned by him (see item 2702). [MTH]

2685 **Málaga Medina, Alejandro.** Aspecto urbano de las reducciones toledanas (PAIGH/H, 88, julio/dic. 1979, p. 167–183)

Examines urban aspects of *reducciones*, especially their socioeconomic functions and physical layout. Although there were several kinds of reducciones, Málaga Medina treats only two, rural and suburban. [MTH]

2686 **Martín Rubio, Carmen.** La Caja de Censos de Indios en Cuzco (IGFO/RI, 39:155/158, enero/dic. 1979, p. 187–208)

Pioneering study of Cuzco's Caja de Censos de Indios (1587–1824) and how its funds were siphoned off by Spanish administrators for public as well as private purposes. Only occasionally benefitted Indians as intended. Sufficient documentation exists for full scale study of this intriguing institution. [MTH]

2687 **Mazet, Claude.** Population et societé a Lima aux XVIe et XVIIe siècles: la Paroisse San Sebastian, 1562–1689 (CDAL, 13/14, 1. semestre, 1976, p. 51–100, map, tables)

Microstudy of population movement in San Sebastián, second oldest Lima parish but one of five before 17th century's end. Uses aggregative analysis methodology. Extent to which San Sebastián's demographic experience reflects Lima's not broached (see also item **1714**). [MTH]

2688 **Mörner, Magnus.** Proyecto: sobre historia agraria en el Cuzco (PUCP/H, 2:1, julio 1978, p. 93–97)

Interim report on ongoing research on agrarian history of Cuzco district. [MTH]

2689 —— and **Francisco Martínez.** Medidas con precio y como instrumentos para la explotación: uno expediente cuzqueño del siglo XVIII (IPA/A, 15, 1980, p. 133–150, charts)

Publishes and analyzes 1785 *Expediente relativo a . . . las medidas que hay en sus partidos del Cuzco de granos, legumbres, y como se da a los indios la ropa de la tierra.* Major social as well as economic source which raises as many questions as it answers about relation between measures and prices in southern highlands during late colonial period. [MTH]

2690 **Moreyra Paz-Soldán, Manuel.** El remate público en la Lima del siglo XVIII (*in* Historia, problema y promesa: homenaje a Jorge Basadre. Edición a cargo de Francisco Miró Quesada C., Franklin Pease García Yrigoyen y David Sobrevilla A. Lima: Pontificia Universidad Católica del Perú, 1978, v. 1, p. 367–388)

Illuminating case study of 1757 auction of *fielatura* of Mint of Lima. Preceded by explication of auctions of colonial offices and services, and of the *fielatura*. [MTH]

2691 **O'Phelan Godoy, Scarlett.** Cuzco 1778: el movimiento de Maras, Urubamba (*in* Congreso Peruana: El Hombre y el Cultura Andina, 3d, Lima, 1977. El hombre y la cultura andina: actas y trabajos [see *HLAS 43:253*] v. 3, p. 424–437, tables)

Solid outline and analysis of 1778 uprising of Indians, Creoles and mestizos of Maras pueblo, Urubamba Valley against local corregidor, his tax collector, caciques or ethnic lords, and even Cuzco's bishop, there on *visita*—he was stoned. Apparently, true peasant as well as regional rebellion. [MTH]

2692 ——. El Norte y las revueltas anticlericales del siglo XVIII (PMNH/HC, 12, 1979, p. 119–135)

After breaking new ground on local tax riots in northwestern Peru (see *HLAS* 42:2710), O'Phelan does same for coeval protests against clerical abuses in same region. Finds such protests increased in number and intensity towards end of 18th century, because local clergy took advantage of suspension of *repartimiento* to systematize imposition and collection of fees and tithes. [MTH]

2693 ———. El sur andino a fines del siglo XVIII: cacique o corregidor (IPA/A, 11/12, 1978, p. 17–32)

Demonstrates that Intendancy system was even more exploitative of altiplano Indian peasantry than former corregimiento. Indians had to contend with abuses of *subdelegados* (many former corregidores), more exacting ethnic lords (e.g., interim caciques) who took advantage of temporary power vacuum and disappearance of cacional lineages to enrich themselves. [MTH]

2694 Pease G.Y., Franklin. Las visitas como testimonio andino (*in* Historia, problema y promesa: homenaje a Jorge Basadre. Edición a cargo de Francisco Miró Quesada C., Franklin Pease García Yrigoyen y David Sobrevilla A. Lima: Pontificia Universidad Católica del Perú, 1978, v. 1, p. 437–453, bibl.)

Useful introduction to *visitas* as ethnohistorical sources. Includes bibliography of those published as of 1975. [MTH]

2695 Pinto Vallejos, Sonia. Aportes extraordinarios a La Real Hacienda Española en el Virreinato Peruano: la región de Cuzco, 1575–1600 (JGSWGL, 17, 1980, p. 69–95, tables)

Solid quantitative study of extraordinary donations, including so-called *préstamos*, made by Cuzco's vecinos and Indians to Crown between 1575–1600. Includes comparative tables of amounts "lent" by inhabitants of other Spanish towns in Viceroyalty of Peru. [MTH]

2696 Ponce, Fernando. Población y familia en una zona rural en Arequipa prerepublicana (*in* Historia, problema y promesa: homenaje a Jorge Basadre. Edición a cargo de Francisco Miró Quesada C., Franklin Pease García Yrigoyen y David Sobrevilla A. Lima: Pontificia Universidad Católica del Perú, 1978, v. 1, p. 473–489, tables)

Microstudy of differences in demography and family structure of rural (Bellavista) and urban (Santa Marta) Arequipa parishes as of early 19th century. Valuable contribution to neglected themes. [MTH]

2697 Reyes Flores, Alejandro. Contradicciones en el Perú colonial: región central, 1650–1810. Lima: Universidad Nacional Mayor de San Marcos, Dirección de Programas Académicos de Ciencia Social, 1979. 203 p.; bibl.

Focuses on free peasantry, especially communal Indians, of central Peru, coastal as well as highland. Analyzes and exemplifies their exploitation by clergy and hacendados, and their resistance to usurpation of land holdings and water rights. Well researched. [MTH]

2698 ———. Contradicciones y demografía en Miraflores (*in* Congreso Peruano: el Hombre y la Cultura Andina, 3d, Lima, 1977. El hombre y la cultura andina: actos y trabajos [see *HLAS* 43:253] v. 4, p. 595–613, tables)

Detailed demographic and economic study of former Miraflores pueblo—nowadays integral part of Lima—in second half of 18th century. Based on local censuses of 1759, 1777, 1791 and 1813. [MTH]

2699 Rivera Serna, Raúl. El trigo: comercio y panificación en las áreas de Lima y Huamanga, siglo XVI (*in* Historia, problema y promesa: homenaje a Jorge Basadre. Edición a cargo de Francisco Miró Quesada C., Franklin Pease García Yrigoyen y David Sobrevilla A. Lima: Pontificia Universidad Católica del Peru, 1978. v. 1, p. 533–545)

Primarily concerned with grinding of wheat and baking of bread, and their municipal regulation in early colonial Lima and Huamanga. [MTH]

2700 Serrera Contreras, Ramón M. El trabajo indígena como soporte económico de la fundación del Colegio de la Merced de Lima, siglo XVII (Gades [Colegio Universitario de Filosofía y Letras de Cádiz, Spain] 1, 1978, p. 55–86, photographs, table)

More or less a history of foundation of Mercedarian Colegio de San Pedro Nolasco in Lima (now Jésus Desamparado), building of which Serrera Contreras demonstrates was largely financed by profits from Mercedarian held *obrajes* (textile sweat shops). [MTH]

2701 Stern, Steve J. Algunas consideraciones sobre la personalidad histórica
de Don Felipe Guamán Poma de Ayala
(PUCP/H, 2:2, dic. 1978, p. 225–228)

On basis of recently rediscovered *expediente: La poseción de Chilca por los indios
Chachapoyas*, published by Juan Zorilla
Aramburu in *Wari* (Ayacucho, 1, 1977, p.
49–64), Stern argues that enigmatic Poma
de Ayala was lesser and hence frustrated
member of colonial bureaucracy and that he
is better interpreted as marginal man than
as outraged spokesman for the conquered.
[MTH]

2702 Trujillo del Perú. (Commissioned by)
Baltasar Jaime Martínez Compañón.
Prólogo de Su Majestad de Rey Don Juan Carlos I. Nota Editorial. Carta de Raúl Porras
Barrenechea a Aurelio Miró Quesada a propósito de la obra del Obispo Martínez Compañón sobre Trujillo del Perú en el siglo
XVIII. Informe de Raúl Porras Barrenechea
respecto a la obra del Obispo Martínez Compañón sobre Trujillo de Perú en el siglo XVIII.
Madrid: Ediciones Cultural Hispánica del
Centro Iberoamericano de Cooperación,
1978. Fac. ed. v. 1. 34 p.; 126 col. leaves
(some fold.); 14 blank leaves.

In Madrid's Royal Palace Library are
nine, late 18th-century volumes containing
1,411 pen, ink, water color illustrations, labeled *Trujillo del Perú* and commissioned to
unknown artist by Baltasar Jaime Martínez
Compañón (1735–97), Bishop of Trujillo
(1779–91) during his diocesis inspection
(1782–85). This complete facsimile edition
provides full color, faithful illustrations. Vol.
1: 37 maps of diocesis, provinces, cities,
towns; six statistical tables; 11 floor plans of
religious buildings; façade of *Cacique de las
Siete Guarangas'* Cajamarca house; and 71
portraits of religious and local officials. Vols.
2/9 to be published will be as interesting
(e.g., illustrations of classes and castes, their
occupations and distractions, flora and fauna,
including marine, and region's antiquities).
This monumental set of realistic, sometimes
humorous drawings constitutes extraordinary graphic source for students of archaeology, ethnography, geography, history, botany,
zoology, etc. [MTH]

2703 Varón Gabai, Rafael. Curacas y encomenderos: acomodamiento nativo en
Huaraz, siglos XVI y XVII. Lima: P.L. Villa-

nueva, 1980. 103, 2 p.; 8 leaves of plates (1
folded); bibl.; ill.; maps.

Revised version of original MA thesis
(Univ. of Texas, Austin). Delineates transformation of Huaraz from Indian pueblo into
colonial settlement. Especially concerned
with role played by ethnic lords in "accom-
modating" Indian to Spanish system. Based
primarily on *visitas*. [MTH]

2704 Villanueva Urteaga, Horacio and
Jeanette Sherbondy. Cuzco: aguas y
poder. Carátula, diseño de Teresa Gianella.
Estudio preliminar por Jeanette Sherbondy.
Cuzco: Centro de Estudios Rurales Andinos
Bartolomé de Las Casas, 1979 or 1980. 2, 153
p.; bibl.; map (Archivos de historia rural an-
dina; 1)

Valuable, well edited, unique collection of mostly unknown basic sources on
control and distribution of water in Cuzco.
Covers colonial and early national periods.
Reproduces 1659 *Repartición de las aguas
desta ciudad* which shows preconquest
irrigation system through delineation of
postconquest changes. Excellent preliminary
study by Sherbondy. Fine collaborative effort
of historian and historical geographer. [MTH]

2705 Wightman, Ann M. Diego Vasicuio:
native priest (*in* Struggle and survival
in colonial America. Edited by David G.
Sweet and Gary B. Nash. Berkeley: University of California Press, 1981, p. 38–48)

Popular account of how 17th-century
native priest and worshippers of Sorimana—
possibly corn goddess Saramama—in San
Francisco de los Chichas near Arequipa,
hoodwinked their *doctrinero* into believing
they saw error of their ways and continued
worshipping native deities in private. [MTH]

2706 Zapatero, Juan Manuel. El Castillo
Real Felipe del Callao (EEHA/AEA, 34,
1977, p. 707–733, plates)

Detailed, well illustrated history of
construction and embellishment (1747–
1776) of Real Felipe of Callao. Supplements
Lohmann Villena's *Las defensas militares
de Lima y Callao hasta 1746* (see *HLAS
28:912*). [MTH]

2707 Zevallos Quiñones, Jorge. Consideraciones sobre la fiesta del Corpus en
Cajamarca el año 1684 (*in* Historia, problema
y promesa: homenaje a Jorge Basadre. Edición
a cargo de Francisco Miro Quesada C., Frank-

lin Pease García Yrigoyen y David Sobrevilla A. Lima: Pontificia Universidad Católica de Perú, 1978, v. 1, p. 621–635, map)

Chatty account of life and times in late 17th-century Cajamarca by *hijo de la ciudad.* Includes tantalizing description of Indian preparations for celebration of Corpus Christi. [MTH]

2708 Zudaire Huarte, Eulogio. Análisis de la rebelión de Tupac Amaru en su bicentenario, 1780–1980 (IGFO/RI, 40:159/162, enero/dic. 1980, p. 13–79)

Thematic/chronological review of 1780–81 Tupac Amaru rebellion which incorporates useful new archival data but reaches no major new conclusions. Tends to support Campbell's analysis (see item **2668**). [MTH]

ALTO PERU

2709 Arze Aguirre, René. El cacicazgo en las postrimerías coloniales (AVA, 1 feb. 1978, p. 47–50)

Brief but detailed, documented review, from Indian as well as Spanish point of view, of ways in which *kurakas* (ethnic lords) of late colonial period abused their authority. [MTH]

2710 Block, David. Links to the frontier: Jesuit supply of its Moxos missions, 1683–1767 (AAFH/TAM, 37:2, Oct. 1980, p. 161–178, tables)

Entirely original study of Jesuit financing and supply of Moxos missions. Its dependence on subsidies from other Jesuit enterprises (e.g., Lower Peru) contradicts isolated outpost notion. Also examines economic relations between Franciscan and Jesuit frontier missions, placing findings in comparative context. [MTH]

Choque Canqui, Roberto. Las haciendas de los caciques guarachi en el Alto Perú: 1673–1734. See item **1583**.

2711 ——. Pedro Chipana: cacique comerciante de Calamarca (AVA, 1, feb. 1978, p. 28–32, bibl.)

Thin essay on commercial activities of late 17th-century ethnic lord, Calamarca *kuraka*, Sicasica province. [MTH]

2712 Cobb, Gwendolyn Ballantine. Potosí y Huancavelica, bases económicas del Perú, 1545–1640. Traducción del inglés por Jorge Muñoz Reyes. La Paz: Academia Boliviana de la Historia: Banco Minero de Bolivia, 1977. 204 p.; bibl. (Biblioteca "BAMIN")

Spanish edition of Cobb's never before published but still standard 1947 Berkeley dissertation on early colonial silver and mercury mining at Potosí and Huancavélica respectively, and interrelationships between two. [MTH]

2713 Díaz de Guzmán, Ruy. Relación de la entrada a los chiriguanos. Edición crítica de los manuscritos existentes en la Biblioteca Nacional de Paris. Includes a prelim. Study and notes by Ch. de Crozefon, translated from the French by Roger de Barneville, and a pref. and additional notes by Hernando Sanabria Fernández. Santa Cruz de la Sierra, Bolivia: Fundación Cultural Ramón Darío Gutiérrez, 1979. 173 p.; bibl.; facsims.

Díaz de Guzmán's 1617–18 original accounts of conquest of Chiriguanos are in Paris' National Library. They also narrate "origins" of Spanish *entradas* into Chiriguano territory. Includes numerous notes by Crozefon and Sanabria Fernández. [MTH]

2714 Evans, Brian M. Census in late seventeenth-century Alto Perú: the *numeración general* of 1683–1684 (*in* Studies in Spanish American population history [see item **1792**] p. 25–44, map, tables)

Solid introduction to 1683–84 general census, ordered by Viceroy Duque de la Palata in Ecuador, Peru, Bolivia, and northwestern Argentina. Returns found (only for Alto Peru provinces) were initially used by Sánchez-Albornoz (see *HLAS 38:3164* and *HLAS 42:2841*). Evans discusses reason for census, its organization, realization, and utility, and suggests additional research. [MTH]

Golte, Jürgen. Repartos y rebeliones: Túpac Amaru y las contradicciones de la economía colonial. See item **2677**.

2715 Klein, Herbert S. The structure of the hacendado class in late eighteenth-century Alto Perú: the Intendencia de La Paz (HAHR, 60:2, May 1980, p. 191–212, map, tables)

Well written, researched and organized quantitative study "of the size, distribution, relative wealth, and composition of the Spanish landed elite" in La Paz Province. Findings support increasingly sharp, revisionist portait of Spanish American haciendas. Not only were they market and profit oriented, but their features were determined by "standard" economic forces. [MTH]

2716 Larson, Brooke. Caciques, class structure and the colonial state in Bolivia (Nova Americana [Giulio Einaudi Editora, Torino, Italy] 2, 1979, p. 197–235, tables)

Exploratory essay on continuity and change in class structure of altiplano Indian communities from initial 1549 Crown intervention through Viedma's Bourbon reforms. Advances discussion considerably beyond current literature's static portrait of haves (*naturales*) and have nots (*forasteros*). [MTH]

2717 ———. Cambio agrario en una economía colonial: el caso de Cochabamba, 1580–1800 (CLACSO/ERL, 3 : 1, enero/abril 1980, p. 111–132, bibl., map)

Solid outline of agrarian history of colonial Cochabamba. Especially noteworthy is Larson's analysis of changes in modes of production and in market demands, and their significance. [MTH]

2718 ———. Ritmos rurales y conflictos de clases durante el siglo XVIII en Cochabamba (IDES/DE, 20 : 78, julio/sept., 1980, p. 183–214, map, tables)

More extensive version of item **2719**. Should be consulted for appendix "Diezmos Aportados a la Iglesia por las Parroquias de Cochabamba, 1765–1810." [MTH]

2719 ———. Rural rhythms of class conflict in eighteenth-century Cochabamba (HAHR, 60 : 3, Aug. 1980, p. 407–430, map, tables)

Fascinating case study of cycles, especially crisis, in grain production and marketing, and their impact on relationships between hacendados and peasants in late colonial Cochabamba. A first in Andean historiography. Among Larson's important findings is that hacendados used tithe in their capacity as rentiers to accumulate capital and to control market-oriented peasant/tenants. [MTH]

2720 Lewinski, Liliana. Archivos históricos de Oruro (LARR, 15 : 3, 1980, p. 195–198, tables)

Most up-to-date and complete introduction to historical archives of Oruro and

Poopo. Complements Peter J. Bakewell's "Los Archivos de Oruro" in *Research guide to Andean history* (item **2577**, p. 28–29) and Juan Siles Guevara's "Dos Archivos Históricos Bolivianos poco Conocidos: Oruro y Cochabamba in *Anuario de Estudios Americanos* (Seville, no. 26, 1969, p. 35–39) and republished in inaugural issue of *Boletín del Archivo de la Paz* (vol. 1, no. 1, 1976, p. 3–6). [MTH]

2721 Parejas Moreno, Alcides. Don Lázaro de Ribera, gobernador de la provincia de Moxos, 1784–1792 (EEHA/AEA, 33, 1976 [i.e. 1979] p. 949–962)

Brief but insightful essay on efforts of first governor of Moxos to impose state control and of his policies' disastrous consequences, especially for the formerly Jesuit-protected Indians. [MTH]

2722 Ramírez del Aguila, Pedro. Noticias políticas de Indias y relación descriptiba de la Ciudad de La Plata, metrópoli de las provincias de los Charcas y nuebo Reyno de Toledo en las occidentales del gran Imperio del Perú . . . : Dirigidas al illmo. Sor. don fray Franco. de Borja Arpo de ella del Consejo de su Maj. y su predicador en La Plata primero de henero de 1639. Transcripción de Jaime Urioste Arana. Sucre, Bolivia: División de Extensión Universitaria, 1978. 186 p.; 13 leaves of plates; ill.; index; facsims.

First edition of little known 1639 chronicle and description of La Plata (La Paz) and Audiencia of Charcas, original of which is in Lilly Library. Major historical geographical source on early colonial Bolivia. [MTH]

2723 Tandeter, Enrique. Forced and free labour in late colonial Potosí (PP, 93, Nov. 1981, p. 98–136, tables)

Revisionist and quantitative study of free and forced labor in Potosí's silver mines during 18th century's second half. Finds forced labor still more important than free in late colonial period, and argues that former was not only crucial for well being but essential for survival of mining by enabling entrepreneurs to shift majority of indirect as well as direct labor costs to Indian communities of Peruvian-Bolivian altiplano. [MTH]

2724 Valle de Siles, María Eugenia del. Testimonios del cerco de La Paz: el campo contra la ciudad, 1781. 2. ed. La Paz: Ultima

Hora, 1980. 197 p.; 20 leaves of plates (1 folded); bibl.; ill. (Biblioteca popular boliviana de Ultima hora)

Revised edition of well researched, written and illustrated study of 1781 Tupac Katari led seige of La Paz (for first edition particulars, see *HLAS 38:3167*). [MTH]

2725 ———. Tupac Katari y la rebelión de 1781: radiografía de su caudillo aymara (EEHA/AEA, 34, 1977, p. 633–664)

Psychohistorical analysis of Julian Apaza or Tupac Katari, messianic leader of 1780–81 rebellion. Noteworthy approach which includes new data on him (far less known than Tupac Amaru). [MTH]

CHILE

2726 **Arretx, Carmen; Rolando Mellafe;** and **Jorge L. Somoza.** Adult mortality estimate based on information on age structure of deaths: an application to data for San Felipe around 1787. Santiago: Centro Latinoamericano de Demografía, 1977. 24 p.; tables (Serie A.; no. 153)

Third in monographic series designed to test applicability of extraregional, mostly European, methodology to Latin American data. Examines method of estimating cohort-specific life expectancy from ages 10 and above from burial registers and coeval censuses, neither of which permit determination of M_0 and hence q_0. Uses promising methodology but fails to explain statistics employed. [MTH]

2727 **Barbier, Jacques A.** Reform and politics in Bourbon Chile, 1755–1796. Ottawa, Canada: University Ottawa Press, 1980. 218 p.; bibl. (Cahiers d'histoire; no. 10)

Detailed, well researched study of Bourbon reforms in Chile, especially in Santiago, its local administration and elites. Reaffirms and develops earlier thesis (see *HLAS 36:2602*) that royal officials continued to be coopted by local elite in 18th-century's second half, largely through intermarriage, thwarting Crown's reform efforts. Praiseworthy contribution to knowledge of area and period. [MTH]

2728 **Bibar, Gerónimo de.** Crónica y relación copiosa y verdadera de los Reinos de Chile, 1558. Ed. de Leopoldo Saez-Godoy. Berlin: Colloquium-Verlag, 1979. 343 p.;

bibl.; ill. (Biblioteca Ibero-Americana; Bd. 27)

New literal transcription of this basic chronicle on Chile's conquest, allegedly more faithful than Leonard's (see *HLAS 34: 2299*). Copiously annotated. [MTH]

2729 **Böhm, Günter.** Simon de Caseres y su plan de conquista de Chile: antecedentes históricos (IAA, 6:2, 1980, p. 117–147)

Caseres (Cáceres) era un judío de origen español que vivía en Londres a mediados del siglo XVII. El y otros miembros de la comunidad judía trataron de ganar el apoyo de Cromwell para lograr la legalización de su "nación" en Inglaterra y con este fin apoyaron sus planes contra las posesiones españolas. A propósito de estos proyectos, que no tuvieron éxito, el autor da a conocer una gran cantidad de datos sobre tales intrigas. [L.G. Canedo]

2730 **Concha, Manuel.** Crónica de La Serena desde su fundación hasta nuestros días, 1549–1870: escrita según los datos arrojados por los archivos de la municipalidad, intendencia y otros papeles particulares. Ed. crítica moderada de Mario Ferreccio Podestá. La Serena: Universidad de Chile, 1979. 551 p.; 6 leaves of plates; bibl.; ill.; port. (Biblioteca chilena regional; 1)

Reprint of 1870 chronicle of colonial and early national period Serena, capital of Coquimbo Province, with explanatory notes by Ferreccio Podestá. Useful because Concha (1834–91) knew his city, history and archives better than anyone at anytime. [MTH]

2731 **Flusche, Della M.** Chilean councilmen and export policies, 1600–1699 (AAFH/TAM, 36:4, April 1980, p. 479–497)

Delineates and analyzes policies of Santiago's Cabildo concerning intercolonial trade, particularly with Peru, and responses to commercial developments in 17th century. Not surprisingly, finds that Cabildo, whose members were of the propertied elite, mostly saw to their own interest but did not neglect those of merchants. [MTH]

2732 **Gímenez de Arcondo, Floraligia.** La defensa militar del sur de Chile: un fuerte de aopyo, La Reina Luisa de Osorno (*in* Congreso Venezolano de Historia, 3d, Caracas, 1977. Memoria. [see item **1741**] v. 2, p. 99–123)

Reconstructs history of no longer existent and all but forgotten Fort of Reina Luisa, established 1794, on ruins of 16th-century Osorno, and which gave birth to modern Osorno. [MTH]

Góngora, Mario. Estudios de historia de las ideas y de historia social. See item **1755.**

2733 Guarda, Gabriel. Historia urbana del Reino de Chile. Santiago: Editorial Andrés Bello, 1978. 509 p.; bibl.; ill.

Exceptionally well researched, extraordinarily detailed, splendidly illustrated history of cities and towns of colonial Chile. Includes chapters on economic life, public works, urban environment, thought, daily life and origins, chronology of cities and towns by period and type. Includes many maps, plans and 444 illustrations mostly coeval. Serves also as research guide by thematically listing 4,648 studies and sources, mostly archival. Monumental reference work which belongs in all Latin American collections. [MTH]

2734 ———. La sociedad en Chile austral antes de la colonización alemana, 1645–1850. Santiago: Editorial Andrés Bello, 1979. 566 p.; bibl.; ill.; index.

Who-was-who of southern Chile, especially Valdivia and Osorno, consists of biographies and genealogies of 1,935 area bureaucrats, military personnel, and ecclesiastics (1645–1850). Result of 30 years of careful research, includes solid introduction on origins of settlers and social structure and change during colonial and early national periods. Complemented by excellent bibliography and index. [MTH]

2735 Gunckel Lüer, Hugo. Bibliografía moliniana. Santiago: Fondo Andrés Bello, 1980. 166 p.

Descriptive bibliography of literature on or relating to Juan Ignacio Molina, 18th-century Jesuit expatriate author of *Compendio della storia geografica, naturale, e civile del Regno del Chili* (Bologna: 1776). [MTH]

2736 Larraín Melo, José Manuel. Movimiento de precios en Santiago de Chile, 1749–1808: una interpretación metodológica (JGSWGL, 17, 1980, p. 199–259, tables)

Methodologically sophisticated, data extensive study of food, housing and clothing prices in Santiago during late colonial period. [MTH]

2737 Lorenzo Sch., Santiago and **Rodolfo Urbina B.** La política de poblaciones en Chile durante el siglo XVIII. Quillota, Chile: Editorial El Observador, 1978. 90 p.; bibl.

Pithy, well researched essay on Junta de Poblaciones' role (established 1717) in foundation and organization of new 18th-century towns. [MTH]

2738 Ronan, Charles E. and **Walter Hanisch.** Epistolario de Juan Ignacio Molina, S.J. Chicago, Ill.: Loyola University Press; Santiago: Editorial Universitaria, 1979. 257 p.

Collection of letters by and to Molina, many appearing for first time and each one introduced and explained. Of interest to specialists (see also item **2735**). [MTH]

2739 Sater, William F. History of Chile from the conquest to Arturo Alessandri (The History Teacher [University of Notre Dame, Notre Dame, Illinois] 14:3, May 1981, p. 327–339)

Outlines history of Chile from precolonial times through 1920, and lists basic studies, mostly in English. Useful for undergraduates and non-specialists (e.g., junior college and high school teachers, see also *HLAS 42:3264*). [MTH]

2740 Soriano, Ramón L. Perfil político de Pedro de Valdivia (EEHA/AEA, 34, 1977, p. 415–464)

Good, reasonably objective summary of what is known about Valdivia as conqueror of Chile, especially his ideology and his politics. Somewhat revisionist in that Soriano paints more somber and realistic Valdivia than most biographers. [MTH]

2741 Torres Sánchez, Jaime. La Real Hacienda del Reino de Chile y los gastos militares: 1770–1780 (*in* Congreso Venezolano de Historia, 3d, Caracas, 1977. Memoria. [see item **1741**] 1979, v. 3, p. 289–313, tables)

Quantitative analysis of military expenditures (1770–80). Military outlays comprised an average of 59 percent of all expenditures made by Royal Treasury during 11 years in question. Study marred by faulty or poorly explained statistics, especially in summary table. [MTH]

2742 Villalobos R., Sergio. La economía de un desierto: Tarapacá durante la Colonia. Diseño, portado y diagramación, Jessie

Cintolesi, Lucia Wormald. Ilustraciones, Andrés Jullián. Santiago: Ediciones Nueva Universidad, 1979. 278 p.; bibl.; ill.; maps.

Solid economic history of colonial Tarapacá. Especially strong on 18th century, for which sources are more abundant. Includes chapters on encomiendas, exploitation of sea, land, and mineral resources, commerce and manufacturing, and labor systems. Major contribution to regional as well as economic history of colonial Chile. [MTH]

2743 ———. Tipos fronterizos en el Ejército de Arauco (in Congreso Venezolano de Historia, 3d, Caracas, 1977. Memoria. [see item 1741] v. 3, p. 517–537, chart)

Fascinating social historical study of specialized functionaries who emerged during prolonged war with Araucanians in South: interpreters; commissioners (comisarios de naciones); and Indian agents (capitanes de amigos), and of role they played in acculturation/assimilation as well as pacification. [MTH]

RIO DE LA PLATA

2744 Abadie-Aicardi, Aníbal. La idea del equilibrio y el contexto geopolítico fundacional del Virreinato Rioplatense (JGSWGL, 17, 1980, p. 261–295)

Centers around Pedro Cevallos' 1776 expedition. Deals with 18th-century Río de la Plata affairs concerning Spain vis-a-vis Portugal/Britain. Britain sustained Portugal's claims but would not take final step of guaranteeing its ally's claim to Uruguay in 1776. Footnotes constitute massive historiographical exercise. [JHW]

2745 Al'Perovich, M.S. New World Arcadia: unknown materials on Paraguay in the 1820s (in Soviet historians on Latin America [see HLAS 42:1817] p. 158–176)

Interesting pieces of detective work track down origins and author of detailed work on Dr. Francia and his Paraguay published in Russia in 1825. Author, who realistically explains problems of doing research on periodicals within Soviet Union, finds most probable source of information to have been Francia himself, who secretly sent emissaries and information to Europe in 1824. [JHW]

Argentine Republic. Archivo General. Indice temático general de unidades archivonómicas del período colonial-gobierno. See item 120.

2746 Arias Divito, Juan Carlos. Dificultades para establecer la renta de tabaco en Paraguay (EEHA/AEA, 33, 1976 [i.e. 1979] p. 1–17)

Unsurprisingly, finds that Asunción Cabildo spent much of 1779 arguing against imposition of tax on tobacco and playing cards. In contrast to other provinces, Paraguayan tobacco was produced by very poor rural militiamen for whom renta constituted one more burden. [JHW]

2747 Catholic Church. Diocese of Tucumán, Argentine Republic. Sínodo. Los sínodos del antiguo Tucumán celebrados por fray Fernando de Trejo y Sanabria, 1597, 1606, 1706. Ed. crítica, con introd. y notas, preparada por José M. Arancibia y Nelson C. Dellaferrera. Buenos Aires: Facultad de Teología de la U.C.A.: Editora Patria Grande, 1979. 334 p.; bibl.; indexes (Teología; 3)

Very useful critical edition of texts of three synods of Tucumán's Bishop Fray Fernando de Trejo y Sanabria (1597, 1606, 1607). Often overlooked as source of data on colonial Latin America, synods reflect Church's concerns and its self-image at the time. Complemented by excellent historical introduction and documental appendix. Thoroughly professional job. [JHW]

2748 Cooney, Jerry W. Paraguayan astilleros and the Platine Merchant Marine: 1796–1806 (PAT/TH, 43:1, Nov. 1980, p. 55–74, tables)

Excellent piece shows creation of shipyard complex in Paraguay following Spanish loosening of commercial restrictions (e.g., astilleros built 20 ships including six frigates in four years). Paraguay provided industry's needs: fabulous woods, cables, cotton and surplus labor. Industry declined when Spain opened its ports to neutral vessels and permitted purchase of foreign ships. [JHW]

2749 Destéfani, Laurio H. La defensa militar del Río de la Plata en la época hispana (in Congreso Venezolano de Historia, 3d, Caracas, 1977. Memoria. [see item 1741] t. 1, p. 463–533, bibl., ill., maps)

Military historian (himself rear admiral), Destéfani stresses physical aspects of viceregal defense; mostly fortifications.

While Montevideo's fort was true citadel, Buenos Aires' was so poorly designed its cannon did not reach ships in estuary. Lacks notes but has adequate bibliography. [JHW]

2750 ———. Las Malvinas en la época hispana, 1600–1811. Buenos Aires: Corregidor, 1981. 424 p.; bibl.; documents; facsims.; ill.; indexes; maps; ports (Série mayor; 1279)

That the Malvinas (Falkland Islands) were *Spanish* possessions during 1600–1811 will not be forgotten by readers of this volume. Destéfani presents detailed, conventional history of islands during Spanish years, rarely digressing into anti-British polemic. Well-documented, with excellent indices, strong documental appendix and good bibliography. Focuses on late 18th century. [JHW]

2751 Díaz de Guzmán, Ruy. Anales del descubrimiento, población y conquista del Río de la Plata. Asunción, Paraguay: Ediciones Cumeros, 1980. 305 p.; 1 folded leaf of plates; 1 map; bibl.; indexes.

Grandson of Domingo Martínez de Irala, Díaz de Guzmán (b. 1560) was famous leader of expeditions, founder of cities and first true historian of Río de la Plata who wrote this work in 1612 both as glorification of conquest and sympathetic defense of Guaraní and other regional Indians. Volume includes useful, introductory *"estudios"* which place man and his work in perspective. [JHW]

2752 Doucet, Gastón Gabriel. Los autos del Visitador Don Antonio Martínez Luján de Vargas (Revista de Historia del Derecho [Buenos Aires] 8, 1980, p. 123–154)

Analiza los dos autos de la visita publicados en item **2754**. [L.G. Canedo]

2753 ———. Comisiones para un visitador: El Marqués de Montesclaros y la visita de Don Francisco de Alfaro a las Gobernaciones de Tucumán y Paraguay (EEHA/AEA, 34, 1977, p. 17–47)

Famous and very productive Alfaro *visita* (1611–12) was brainchild of Viceroy Marqués de Montesclaro, a man with much interest in Paraguay and Tucumán. Although Alfaro brought with him cédulas reales and other Crown documents, his visita was a general one, mandated from Madrid. Information and recommendations he brought back to Lima led to reforms. [JHW]

2754 ———. Introducción al estudio de la visita del Oidor Don Antonio Martínez Luján de Vargas a las encomiendas de indios del Tucumán (IHADER/B, 26, 1980, p. 205–246)

Estudia antecedentes, itinerario del visitador y resultados de la visita. En apéndice, lista las encomiendas en el Tucumán (1693) y texto de dos autos de reforma provistos por el visitador. [L.G. Canedo]

2755 Duviols, Jean-Paul. The cultural consequences for the expulsion of the Jesuits from the Río de la Plata (UNESCO/CU, 7:1, 1980, p. 73–84, bibl.)

Brief article, partly based on shaky population figures, is neither pro-Jesuit ("Golden Legend") nor anti-Jesuit ("Black Legend"). Finds that decline of mission population after 1767 was largely due to fact that for first time, Indians *could* migrate elsewhere. Many went to Brazil. [JHW]

2756 Gadelha, Regina Maria A.F. As missões jesuíticas do Itatim: um estudo das estruturas sócio-econômicas coloniais do Paraguai, séculos XVI e XVII. Capa, Mario Roberto Corrêa da Silva. Rio de Janeiro: Paz e Terra, 1980. 324 p.; bibl.; maps (Coleção Estudos latino-americanos; v. 15)

Very worthwhile examination of neglected topic, Itatin missions established after 1610 by Jesuits in today's Mato Grosso. Properous missions, free from Indian tribute, produced variety of crops, much cotton, were finally destroyed by *bandeirantes* in 1640s. Includes superb bibliography. [JHW]

2757 Galileano, Ana María. Las reducciones guaraníticas. Buenos Aires: Ministerio de Cultura y Educación, Secretaría de Estado de Cultura, Ediciones Culturales Argentinas, 1979. 100 p.; 16 p. of plates; bibl.; ill.

Galileano, who considers Jesuits "un ejército de héroes," presents nicely illustrated, but very brief, superficial outline of Jesuit activities in Río de la Plata. [JHW]

2758 Gandía, Enrique de. Los enigmas del descubrimiento del Río de la Plata (IHGB/R, 321, out./dez. 1978, p. 237–241)

"Enigma" concerns actual discoverer of estuary (e.g., Vespucci, Solís, etc.). Gandía picks Portuguese-born Esteban Froes and Rodrigo Alvarez, who apparently blundered into area in 1512, but did not penetrate inland. Solís gathered from them that estuary might be passage to Orient. [JHW]

2759 García Heras, Raúl. Aspectos económicos y sociales del Virreynato del Río de la Plata en 1776. Buenos Aires: Fundación para el Estudio de los Problemas Argentinos, 1978. 19 p.; bibl. (Documento de trabajo; no. 1)

Short overview of Viceroyalty in year of its creation, with traditional fixation on "la dualidad Interior y Litoral." [JHW]

2760 Gutiérrez, Ramón. Los pueblos jesuíticos del Paraguay: reflexiones sobre su decadencia (UCNSA/SA, 14:1/2, dic. 1979, p. 179–199, ill.)

In attempt to defend Jesuit "experiment," shows how seven Paraguayan mission towns, in excellent condition at time of Jesuits' expulsion and suffering moderate decline thereafter, were almost destroyed economically and socially by Carlos Antonio López's 1848 decree. It ended "pueblos de indios'" special status and made inhabitants Paraguayan citizens transferring all lands and properties to the state. Indians were left with "libertad sin justicia." [JHW]

2761 Heredia, Edmundo A. Algunos aspectos de la reconquista del Río de la Plata durante el régimen constitucional español (EEHA/AEA, 1977, p. 49–63)

Heredia deals persuasively with actions (both in Spain and Río de la Plata) of what may be termed a "Spanish" party dedicated to resuming royal rule in 1821. Also shows that transition in Spain from absolute to constitutional, "liberal" monarchy did nothing to dampen Spanish desire to reclaim—by force, if necessary—its Platine colonies. [JHW]

2762 Johnson, Lyman L. The entrepreneurial reorganization of an artisan trade: the bakers of Buenos Aires, 1770–1820 (AAFH/TAM, 37:2, Oct. 1980, p. 139–160)

Intriguing essay about bakery business, largely dominated by *peninsulares* and other Europeans. Finds that bakers were successful economically but that "extraordinary contributions" and taxes eliminated smaller ones in favor of big entrepreneurs by 1820s. Correctly argues that more work needed on Spanish artisans in American cities. [JHW] ies. [JHW]

2763 ———. Francisco Baquero: shoemaker and organizer (*in* Struggle and survival in colonial America. Edited by David G.

Sweet and Gary B. Nash. Berkeley: University of California Press, 1981, p. 86–101)

Excellent, well documented piece on dark-skinned mestizo master shoemaker who fought long and hard to prevent racial discrimination within shoemaker's guild he established in Buenos Aires (1779–91). Spokesman for *casta* makers, Baquero even went to Spain in 1793 on their behalf, obtaining favorable decision from Council of the Indies in 1794. Still plagued by racial restrictions, Baquero unsuccessfully attempted to form guild of Negro and mulatto shoemakers, but at least had satisfaction of seeing white-dominated guild dissolved in 1799, restoring some freedom to all involved. [JHW]

2764 Kirbus, Federico B. La primera de las tres Buenos Aires. Arte, Jorge Petray, Luis Juárez. Buenos Aires: Kirbus, 1980. 128 p.; bibl.; ill. (Documenta rerum Argentinorum) (Investigación)

Not very exciting, month-by-month, meter-by-meter examination of exact site of 1536 or first foundation of Buenos Aires by Pedro de Mendoza. Not likely to change anyone's interpretation. [JHW]

2765 Krüger, Hildegard Thomas de. Asunción y su área de influencia en la época colonial (UNCSA/EP, 6:2, dic., 1978, p. 33–42)

Examines Asunción's decline, in political power and geographic jurisdiction. Despite late 16th-century foundings of Corrientes, Santa Fe and other cities, Asunción claimed jurisdictional radius of 100 leagues. By 1800, however, legal and actual radius had shrunk to 40 leagues and Asunción's status in Río de la Plata dwindled. [JHW]

2766 ———. Der Cabildo von Asunción: Stadtverwaltung u. städt. Oberschicht in d. 1. Hälfte d. 18. Jh., 1690–1730. Frankfurt am Main; Bern [and] Cirencester, U.K.: Lang, 1979. 222 p.; bibl. (Europäische Hochschulschriften: Reihe 3, Geschichte und ihre Hilfswissenschaften; Bd. 126)

Set in unappealing typescript, this is a history of Asunción Cabildo and its many jurisdictional squabbles from foundation until 1730s, despite title's dates. Of interest is story of conflict between Cabildo and Church. Includes solid documentation, mostly from Archivo Nacional. [JHW]

2767 Lafuente Machain, Ricardo de. Buenos Aires en el siglo XVII. Buenos Aires: Municipalidad de la Ciudad de Buenos Aires, Secretaría de Cultura, 1980. 240 p.; bibl.; ill. (Colección IV centenario)

Excellent addition to valuable collection, this well written and illustrated history covers all basic aspects of 17th-century city, especially public health and housing. Includes 1664 *Padrón de Vecinos* with biographical data on 211 of city's leaders. Unfortunately, lacks even rudimentary footnotes. [JHW]

2768 ——. Buenos Aires en el siglo XVIII. Buenos Aires: Municipalidad de la Ciudad de Buenos Aires, Secretaría de Cultura, 1980. 288 p.; bibl.; ill. (Colección IV centenario)

What author did for 17th century (see item **2767**), he does even better for the next 100 years. Lively and informative social history of the "port," has vivid descriptions of daily life (e.g., cock fights, funeral ceremonies, cafés, social welfare institutions, culture). Includes good bibliography but, as in item **2767**, no footnotes. Highly recommended. [JHW]

2769 Lugones, Leopoldo. El imperio jesuítico. Introducción y edición de Roy Bartholomew. Buenos Aires: Editorial de Belgrano, 1981. 247 p.; bibl.; ill. (Colección Clásicos argentinos)

First published in 1904, Lugones' description of Jesuits' "perfect theocracy" in Río de la Plata still makes good reading. Theocracy notion so coincided with Hapsburg ideas and medieval aspirations that Spanish Monarchy strongly encouraged it. However, the arrival of the Bourbons and 18th-century ideals dimmed the appeal of the Mission Empire. It had outlived its times. [JHW]

2770 Luque Colombres, Carlos A. Orígenes históricos de la propiedad urbana de Córdoba: siglos XVI y XVII. Córdoba, Argentina: Universidad Nacional de Córdoba, Facultad de Filosofía y Humanidades, Instituto de Estudios Americanistas Doctor Enrique Martínez Paz, Dirección General de Publicaciones, 1980. 437 p.; 2 folded leaves of plates; bibl.; ill.; 1 facsim.; plans (Serie histórico; no. 17)

Uses materials from Córdoba's archives to describe first urban plan (and allocation of *solares*) promulgated 1577 by Córdoba's Cabildo. Presents biographical data on who occupied the lots (*manzana por manzana*) in 1600, 1625, 1650, 1675 and 1700. Useful approach permits scholar to trace permanence (or its lack) in urban settlement for century and a quarter. Useful volume for specialists. [JHW]

2771 Masini Calderón, José Luis. Aspectos económicos y sociales de la acción de los Agustinos en Cuyo, siglos XVII, XVIII y XIX (UNC/RHAA, 9:17/18, 1972/1979, p. 69–98)

Encyclopedic examination of (economic) activities of Augustinians in Mendoza, from monastery's 1657 establishment to its 1825 closure by liberals. Includes particularly interesting data on large number of slaves owned by order before 1800 and their part in the ceramic industry and vineyards. Solid piece of work. [JHW]

2773 Murga, Ventura. La emigración española a América en la época de la conquista y de la colonia: la formación regional del NOA [i.e. Noroeste Argentino], migraciones, clases sociales (*in* La inmigración en la Argentina. San Miguel de Tucumán, Argentina: Universidad Nacional de Tucumán, Facultad de Filosofía y Letras, Centro de Historia y Pensamiento Argentinos, 1979, p. 13–23 [Publicación. Universidad Nacional de Tucumán; 1255])

Slow-moving article concerning migration from Spain to Argentine Northwest through three centuries. Author's slim documentation and belief that in 1600–1700 Spain's population declined from 12 to eight million (!) because of emigration should give the reader pause. [JHW]

2775 Pistilli S., Vicente. La cronología de Ulrich Schmidel. Asunción: Instituto Paraguayo de Ciencia del Hombre, 1980. 64 p.; bibl.; ill.

According to author, Schmidel was only true cronista of Buenos Aires' first founding and Paraguay's conquest. His writings should not be dismissed by historians doubtful of (his) chronological accuracy. Includes rudimentary chronology for 1535–1555. [JHW]

2776 Rial Roade, Juan. Sources for studies of historical demography in Uruguay, 1728–1860 (LARR, 15:2, 1980, p. 180–200, bibl., maps, tables)

Valuable survey of historical demographic sources, especially of returns and results of population counts and cadastral surveys in Archivo General de la Nación, Montevideo and of their 18th and 19th-century data. Also lists published sources and limited historical demographic literature on Uruguay. [MTH]

2777 Saeger, James A. Survival and abolition: the eighteenth-century Paraguayan encomienda (AAFH/TAM, 38:1, July 1981, p. 59–85, tables)

Excellent study of encomienda in Paraguay during Bourbon era, continuing existence and importance of which in 18th century had not heretofore been treated in depth. Heavily quantitative. [MTH]

2778 Salas, Alberto Mario. Diario de Buenos Aires, 1806–1807. Buenos Aires: Editorial Sudamericana, 1981. 680 p.; 1 folded leaf of plates; bibl.; map.

Very valuable, actually the best history of British invasions of Río de la Plata. Written in diary form, work is heavily documented for "chronicler registers events, he does not invent them." Salas portrays with feeling the city and people at time of great crisis and enthusiasm. [JHW]

2779 Serra y Canals, Francisco de. El celo del español y el indiano instruido. Estudio preliminar por Jorge Comadrán Ruíz. Cubierta de Rafael de Armas. Buenos Aires: Facultad de Filosofía y Letras de la Universidad de Buenos Aires, Centro de Estudios Interdisciplinarios de Hispanoamérica Colonial: Librería Editorial Platero, 1979. 129 p. (Documentos—Facultad de Filosofía y Letras de la Universidad de Buenos Aires, Centro de Estudios Interdisciplinarios de Hispanoamérica Colonial; 2)

Spanish-mining engineer in Río de la Plata wrote this slightly irreverent book in 1800, hoping to prod local authorities. In series of six dialogues between *europeo* and *indio*, concerning their different perceptions of colonial society and its problems, author makes sharp references to treatment of Indians, inefficiency of bureaucracy and other traits. [JHW]

2780 Siles Guevara, Juan. Ricardo Jaimes Freyre, historiador del Tucumán (EEHA/AEA, 34, 1977, p. 323–348)

Revindication of Jaimes Freyre, early 20th-century author of several books on Tucuman's colonial history and of its role in Argentine independence. According to Siles Guevara, Jaimes Freyre was not only modern in methodology—he cited his sources—but first to have more or less complete access to local sources. [MTH]

2781 Socolow, Susan Migden. Marriage, birth, and inheritance: the merchants of eighteenth-century Buenos Aires (HAHR, 60:3, Aug. 1980, p. 387–406, tables)

Study of fertility patterns of 178 wholesale merchants in late 18th-century Buenos Aires concludes that high fertility encountered reflects success of this rather small, but influential social group. Includes many excellent charts and piece is superbly documented and very clearly drawn out. One hopes similar studies will be undertaken for other epochs. [JHW]

2782 ———. Women and crime: Buenos Aires, 1757–97 (JLAS, 12:1, May 1980, p. 39–54)

Author notes lack of study of crime in colonial Latin American cities, especially of women as victims and perpetrators. Despite very small sample (70 criminal cases), finds women most often were victims of sexual offenses (e.g., rape, most common in *rural* areas, kidnappings, hair-cutting). Women found scant support or justice in the courts when reporting these crimes or wife-beating. Author emphasizes interpersonal violence as characteristics of Buenos Aires' lower-class life so that kidnapping and rape were often regarded as part of courtship. [JHW]

2783 Velázquez, Rafael Eladio. Organización militar de la Gobernación y Capitanía General del Paraguay (*in* Congreso Venezolana de Historia, 3d, Caracas, 1977. Memoria. [see item **1741**] v. 3, p. 413–475)

Well written, well documented article covers 1530s to independence and provides wealth of information on Paraguayan militia through reforms and transformations (e.g., weapons required, wages, composition of officer corps). Under threat of attack from Brazil and hostile Indian tribes, colonial Paraguay was heavily militarized. Of particular interest is long section on 17th century. [JHW]

2784 Vives Azancot, Pedro A. Asunción, 1775–1800: persistencias rurales en la revitalización de su estructura urbana (IGFO/RI, 39:155/158, enero/dic. 1979, p. 209–234, maps)

Novel study on how Asunción was as much rural village as urban center in final quarter of 18th century. Vives Azancot (Universidad Complutense, Madrid) rightly considers his analysis preliminary as he only consulted Spanish repositories. [MTH]

2785 ———. Demografía paraguaya, 1782–1800: bases históricas y primera aproximación para su análisis, sobre datos aportados por Félix de Azara (IGFO/RI, 40:159/162, enero/dic. 1980, p. 159–217, maps, tables)

Very important study of neglected Paraguayan demography. Uses censal materials (mostly printed) of Aguirre (1781, 1792); Azara (1785); Malaspina (1781); Melo de Portugal (1783, 1785); Alos (1788); and Soria (1801–02), and is impressed by small variation among sources. Presents lengthy demo-graphic background covering early colonial era. Very professional study which also covers Misiones. Calculates that crude growth rate of period's population was 1.12 percent. [JHW]

2786 Zabala, Rómulo and Enrique de Gandía. Historia de la ciudad de Buenos Aires. Buenos Aires: Municipalidad de la Ciudad de Buenos Aires, Secretaría de Cultura, 1980. 2 v.; ill. (Colección IV centenario)

Originally written in 1936 to commemorate 400th anniversary of Buenos Aires' first founding, this well written, documented and illustrated work is very strong on economic growth and relies heavily on census documents from archives. Vol. 1 spans 1536–1718, and vol. 2, 1719–1800, provides richer coverage for 18th century. Large portion of vol. 2 deals with Buenos Aires and vexing question of Banda Oriental. [JHW]

Independence Period

DAVID BUSHNELL, *Professor of History, University of Florida*

THE SECTION THAT FOLLOWS is one of the slimmest to have appeared since *HLAS 23* (1961), when the Independence period was cut loose from the *HLAS* section on Spanish South America: 19th and 20th Centuries, to stand by itself, and it is definitely the shortest since the Humanities volume became a biennial rather than annual offering. The decision to make this a separate section was taken in the first place not so much because of the intrinsic validity of such a periodization scheme, or even because the roster of contributing editors happened to include a specialist in Spanish South American independence, but because in the historical literature of the countries in question independence studies constituted such a large, distinct genre. The new section attained its peak size during 1966–70, when it was flooded with various sorts of sesquicentennial publications among other things, but since then it has been shrinking, albeit in a somewhat irregular pattern. The approaching bicentennial of Bolívar's birth will presumably bring another spurt against the trend, but that trend seems well enough fixed to raise doubt as to the long-term viability of a separate section. To some extent, the trend itself may reflect only the fact that when a single contributing editor has been reviewing material in a given field for 25 years—as this one has—there is less and less that he does not quickly recognize as something he has encountered in one form or another countless times already and has pushed aside. However, that is almost certainly not the whole story. It is hard to avoid the conclusion that Spanish South Americans are finally losing their obsession with the epic of political independence. Such a conclusion could no doubt be proved quantitatively, if necessary; and it is obviously of more than merely historiographical importance.

This is not to say that there is nothing left worth doing in the field, but neither can it be said that the items listed in this *Handbook* have made great progress toward either filling the remaining gaps or advancing needed new interpretations. Several of the most important are in fact reeditions, though not the kind of reeditions that seemingly appear (especially in Venezuela) only because there is extra paper and ink lying around to be used. A welcome reissue of a primary source is that of the memoirs of Francisco Burdett O'Connor (item **2796**). Even more welcome are new and revised editions of Paul Verna's work on Pétion and Bolívar (item **2815**); Heraclio Bonilla's compilation of studies relating to the reluctant independence of Peru, to which he has added a new essay of his own (item **2820**); and the notable study of Artigas as agrarian reformer by Lucía Sala de Touron *et al.* (item **2839**). Of works that are entirely new, the most significant, though not the best from a purely scholarly standpoint, is probably the Marxist interpretation of Bolívar by Miguel Acosta Saignés (item **2787**). The freshness of its approach, among the recent crop of leftist treatments of the Liberator, is readily apparent by comparison with the somewhat more conventional populism of J. R. Núñez Tenorio (item **2795**). Both of these works naturally emphasize the social and economic dimensions of the independence process, particular aspects of which provide subject matter for some good scholarly articles. Among the latter are those by Michael Costeloe on Spanish trade policy (item **1805**) and Carlos S. A. Segreti on that of the *porteño* revolutionaries (item **2841**); those by Armellada (item **1801**) and Hünefeldt (item **2819**) on the Spanish liberal interlude and the Indians; and Francisco de Solano's interesting review of Spanish reports concerning the state of Venezuela (item **2813**). John Fisher's article on Peru (item **2817**) gives a look at ethnic as well as regional rivalries, generally in line with what he has written before but still offering some new observations.

The period covered by this *Handbook* brings two interesting items by Jerry W. Cooney on the ecclesiastical history of independence in Paraguay (items **2831** and **2832**), and also a certain resurgence of studies on intellectual background and climate. Alfonso Rumazo González has prepared an anthology of the thought of Simón Rodríguez (item **1815**), who receives additional attention in a set of skillful bibliographic essays by Pedro Grases (item **1806**). Several more examples of the justifiable reedition of previous publications are to be found in the field of intellectual history, including two volumes of the collected works of Grases that are inevitably miscellaneous in content but have a good bit to say about the thought and writings of the period (item **2792**); Manuel Pérez Vila's excellent work on the intellectual formation of Bolívar (item **2799**) and separate studies of the journalism of the period (item **2812**); and Ella Dunbar Temple's introductory study on the University of San Marcos (item **2822**). Beatriz Martínez has further contributed an article on the intellectual formation of San Martín (item **2794**); and there is some intellectual and cultural history in the useful *Conferencias O'Higgins* (item **2825**). The latter, indeed, offers a little of almost everything. And so does the selection of titles that follows—despite the shrinking size of the section.

GENERAL

2787 Acosta Saignés, Miguel. Acción y utopía del hombre de las dificultades. La Habana: Casa de las Américas, 1977. 520 p.; bibl.

Coherent Marxist perspective on Bolívar, which sees him as always seeking objectives of his class, however much he also espoused, as secondary aim, greater justice for slaves and oppressed. Occasionally inaccurate, uneven in coverage—with greatest emphasis on colonial Venezuelan economy as background, nature of revolutionary armies, Panama Congress—but possibly most successful of recent leftist interpretations.

2788 Astesano, Eduardo. Juan Bautista de América: el Rey Inca de Manuel Belgrano. Buenos Aires: Castañeda, 1979. 205 p.; bibl.; ill. (Colección Tiempo de América; 1) Biography of Juan Bautista Túpac Amaru, younger brother of leader of 1780 uprising, who was deported for almost 40 years to North Africa and died eventually in Buenos Aires. A figure best known for fact that Manuel Belgrano had him in mind as ruler of restored Inca empire, to be based in Río de la Plata. Though incorporating original research on Juan Bautista, much of this work deals with phenomenon of *indigenismo* (rhetorical or otherwise) of Platine patriots and subsequent treatments of the same topic in Argentine historiography.

2789 Colombres Mármol, Eduardo L. San Martín y Bolívar en la entrevista de Guayaquil, a la luz de documentos definitivos. Prólogo del Dr. Rómulo D. Carbia. 3. ed. Buenos Aires: Plus Ultra, 1979. 356 p.; bibl. (Colección Política e historia)
New printing of what is definitive statement of traditional Argentine version—whether or not documents referred to are truly "definitive"—of Guayaquil Interview. Reproduces second edition which had incorporated some of the reactions to first one of 1940 (see *HLAS 6:3097*).

2790 Documentos inéditos del Gran Mariscal de Ayacucho Antonio José de Sucre (VANH/B, 63:250, abril/junio 1980, p. 287–307)
Not all literally *inéditos*, and somewhat miscellaneous. Most important are decrees issued by Sucre for Bolivia, Jan.–Oct. 1826.

2791 Genio y apoteosis de Bolívar en la campaña del Perú. Introducción, notas histórico-bibliográficas y recopilación por el doctor Leonardo Altuve Carrillo. Presentación por el señor Ministro de la Defensa. Barcelona: Herder, 1979. 598 p.; ill.
Consists mostly of facsimile reproductions of pamphlets concerning war of independence in Peru in its Bolivarian phase. Also a few other items (e.g., posthumous tributes). Each comes with "explicación histórico-bibliográfica."

2792 Grases, Pedro. Obras. v. 3, Preindependencia y emancipación: protagonistas y testimonios. v. 4, Estudios bolivarianos. Barcelona: Seix Barral, 1981. 2 v. (608, 628 p.); ill.
These two volumes of his *Obras* bring together numerous writings on background of independence, on independence movement itself and concretely on Bolívar; there is some relative emphasis on bibliographic ramifications. They are all of high scholarly standards and had been published before in many different places.

2792a Instituto Nacional Sanmartiniano. Campañas del Libertador Don José de San Martín en el bicentenario de su nacimiento. Buenos Aires: Talleres Gráficos del Instituto Geográfico Militar, 1978. 100 p., maps (Homenaje del Banco de la Ciudad de Buenos Aires)
Overview of all San Martín's military campaigns briefly presented with corresponding cartographic aids. [R. Etchepareborda]

2793 Mariluz Urquijo, José María. El fidelismo como elemento descentralizador: un catecismo político y seis proclamas fidelistas de Pedro Vicente Cañete (UBA/RIHD, 24, 1978 [i.e. 1979] p. 179–203)
Examines record of Pedro Vicente Cañete as Royalist spokesman in Platine region and especially Alto Perú, underscoring the appeal he made to anti-Buenos Aires sentiment. As appendix, includes his *Catecismo real patriótico.*

2794 Martínez, Beatriz. Los temas preferidos de San Martín a través del examen de su biblioteca (CH, 369, marzo 1981, p. 533–550)
Little has survived of the library San Martín carried to Lima and donated to Peru, nor do we know precisely which books he read. This analysis of his own inventory of his books does reveal preeminence of such categories as French literature and contemporary history, and at very least gives further insight into intellectual climate.

2795 Núñez Tenorio, J. R. Bolívar y la guerra revolucionaria: reencarnar el espíritu de Bolívar. 2 ed. Caracas: Ediciones de la Biblioteca, Universidad Central de Venezuela, 1977. 276 p.; bibl. (His En defensa de la revolución libro 1) (Colección Avance; 46)
Interpretation of Bolívar as anti-

imperialist social reformer, with many contemporary allusions. Of value as expression of particular viewpoint more than as history in strict sense.

2796 O'Connor, Francisco Burdett. Un irlandés con Bolívar: recuerdos de la independencia de América del Sur en Venezuela, Colombia, Bolivia, Perú y la Argentina, por un Jefe de la Legión Británica de Bolívar. Caracas: El Cid Editor, 1977. 320 p.

Memoirs of Irish volunteer who fought at Ayacucho, eventually settled in Bolivia, and died there 1871. Important source both on independence movement and on early national history of Bolivia, last published 1915.

2797 Pérez, Joaquín. Guido: un cronista inédito de la Expedición Libertadora del Perú (UNLP/TC, 23, 1978, p. 127–147)

With introductory comments, presents interesting set of letters written by San Martín's friend and confidant Tomás Guido to his wife, Aug. 1820–Aug. 1821.

2798 Pérez Amuchástegui, Antonio Jorge. San Martín y la emancipación sudamericana (Boletín del Instituto de Historia Argentina y Americana Doctor Emilio Ravignani [Universidad de Buenos Aires] 26, 1980, p. 17–44)

Good restatement, in lecture form but with ample reference notes, of what author has said often before concerning "American" or "continental" vocation of San Martín.

2799 Pérez Vila, Manuel. La formación intelectual del Libertador. 2. ed. Caracas: Ediciones de la Presidencia de la República, 1979. 255 p.; appendix; bibl.; ill.; index; ports (Colección Contorno bolivariano; 4)

This is "edición revisada y ampliada" of a sound study of Bolívar's intellectual roots and influences that appeared in the introductory volume of *Escritos del Libertador* (see *HLAS 28:952a*).

2800 ———. Para acercarnos a Bolívar: vida, bibliografía, escritos. Prólogo de Carlos Felice Cardot. Portada, Mariano Díaz Bravo. Caracas: Equinoccio, 1980. 305 p.; bibl.; index (Colección Proceso)

Collection of widely different items, ostensibly aimed at a broad public but by highly qualified specialist: some general essays (e.g., "La Sensibilidad Social del Libertador"), a useful annotated "Bibliografía Básica," textual analysis of certain Bolivarian documents.

2801 Pi Sunyer, Carlos. Patriotas americanos en Londres: Miranda, Bello y otras figuras. Ed. y prólogo por Pedro Grases. Caracas: Monte Avila Editores, 1978. 364 p.

Soundly researched and well written studies on Miranda, Andrés Bello, Luis López Méndez and certain other topics, all somehow relating to the British connection in origins and course of independence movement.

2802 Seminario Internacional Sanmartiniano, *1st, Madrid, 1980.* Actas. San Martín en España. Madrid: Instituto Español Sanmartiniano, 1981. 582 p.; folding charts; plates.

These published proceedings, of conference held in Spain, reflect some relative emphasis on Spain-related topics (from Spanish roots of San Martín to his image in Spanish historiography). But there is a little of everything, in quality as well as subject matter. One of best works has virtually nothing to do with San Martín (see item **2817**).

2803 Sucre, Antonio José de. Cartas y otros escritos. Caracas: Monte Avila Editores, 1980. 251 p.; port. (Colección Eldorado)

Good selection of letters and other documents, 1820–30. Nothing new, but convenient.

GRAN COLOMBIA

2804 Bencomo Barrios, Héctor. Campaña de Bomboná. Caracas: Imprenta del Congreso de la República, 1974. 109 p.; appendixes; bibl.; map; plates.

Succinct and sober analysis of 1822 campaign and battle in which Bolívar's leadership has often been criticized. This account naturally pays him tribute, but without rhetorical excesses.

2805 Boza, Guillermo. Estructura y cambio en Venezuela republicana: el período independentista. Portada, Carlos Tosco. Caracas: Equinoccio Editorial de la Universidad Simón Bolívar, 1979. 163 p.; bibl. (Colección Parámetros)

Stresses increase in relative importance of military-political determinants of status as key to understanding tensions and changes of independence period. A little too much social science jargon, no original research, but does offer some suggestive observations.

2806 Colección de disposiciones del gobierno sobre manumisión desde 1821 hasta 1835 (VAGN/B, 69:236/237, enero/dic. 1979, p. 66–113)

Useful compilation, which includes Gran Colombian measures of general applicability but also contains orders specifically referring to Venezuela and some subsequent measures of independent Venezuela.

2807 Diez documentos sobre la participación del clero en la independencia de la Real Audiencia de Quito (EANH/B, 62, enero/dic. 1979, p. 211–224)

From archiepiscopal archives, these are documents of some interest on the attitude and conduct of clergy in immediate aftermath of Pichincha.

2808 Duarte French, Jaime. Poder y política: Colombia, 1810–1827. Diseño de la portada, Ligia Córdoba. Bogotá: C. Valencia Editores, 1980. 542 p.; bibl.

Examines "the process of consolidation of power" with much interesting data on internal history of Gran Colombia but no table of contents, index, or even chapter divisions; hence rather difficult to use. Good for browsing. Author's viewpoint is highly idiosyncratic but in longer perspective is close to that of Bolívar's traditional conservative admirers.

2809 Farré, Joseph. La ilustración en precursores y próceres de la independencia del Virreinato de Nueva Granada: algunos apuntes y una bibliografía (in Coloquio Ilustración Española e Independencia de América, Bellaterra, Spain, 1978. Homenaje a Noël Salomon: ilustración española e independencia de América. Edición preparada por Alberto Gil Novales. Barcelona: Universidad Autónoma de Barcelona, 1979, p. 125–148, bibl.)

With main focus on Venezuela, and an interesting comparison between Declaration of Rights of Man and select Venezuelan bills of rights of independence period, argues that Enlightenment concepts were used by bourgeois elements seeking power for themselves. This same *Homenaje* contains a number of other papers relating to Spanish American independence, of generally lesser interest.

González Loscertales, Vicente. La resistencia de un imperio a la disgregación. See item **2039**.

2810 Ha muerto el Libertador: homenaje de la Universidad Central de Venezuela en el sesquicentenario de su muerte. Compilación de documentos, estudios e introducción, Ildefonso Leal. Fotos, Joaquín Torres, Luciano Pérez y José A. Becerra C. Caracas: Rectorado de la UCV, 1980. 572 p.; bibl.; facsims.; ill.; ports.

This compilation is of greater importance for history of Bolívar cult than for study of his life and times; but it is also a convenient reference, especially on his final days and repercussions of his death.

2811 Linares, Julio E. Bolívar, el Congreso Antifictiónico y la soberanía sobre el Canal de Panamá (UNL/H, 20, 1979, p. 535–555)

Passes in review Bolívar's thoughts concerning Panama, with some special emphasis on its canal potential and on refuting idea that he ever really meant to give the Isthmus to Great Britain.

2812 Pérez Villa, Manuel. Para la historia de la comunicación social: ensayos. Caracas: Academia Nacional de la Historia, 1979. 139 p. (El Libro menor; 6)

Good collection of articles, mostly published before but widely scattered, and mostly on Venezuelan press of independence period (including reflection of Venezuelan events in foreign press). Also one essay on Andrés Bello as journalist in Chile, two on political press in era of Antonio Guzmán Blanco.

2813 Solano, Francisco de. La imagen de Venezuela vista por el militar profesional, 1815/1820 (PAN/ES, 6, 2. pt., 1980, p. 241–278)

Article that serves two very different but equally valuable purposes: 1) to describe and list reports (now in Spanish archives) drawn up by royalist military on geographic, social, and economic conditions in Venezuela; and 2) to present (with supporting tables) some highlights of that mass of information.

2814 Tisnés Jiménez, Roberto María. Don Juan del Corral: libertador de los esclavos. Cali, Colombia: Banco Popular, 1980. 463 p.; appendixes; bibl. (Biblioteca Banco Popular; 83)

Study of dictator of Antioquia during *Patria Boba*—under whose auspices first free-birth law was issued—is written in traditional style and with many digressions but incorporates substantial research.

2815 Verna, Paul. Petión y Bolívar: una etapa decisiva en la emancipación de Hispanoamérica, 1790–1830. 3. ed. rev. y aum. Caracas: Ediciones de la Presidencia de la República, 1980. 564 p.; bibl.; ill. (some col.); indexes (Colección Bicentenario; no. 1)

Another "edición revisada y aumentada," of a major scholarly study of the relationship between Haiti and Bolívar (see also *HLAS 32 : 1328*).

PERU

Anna, Timothy E. The fall of the royal government in Peru. See item **2662**.

2816 *Colección Documental de la Independencia del Perú.* Comisión Nacional del Sesquicentenario de la Independencia. Tomo 1 [through] tomo 27, 1971–   . Lima.

In this important series (for previously published tomos and volumes, see *HLAS 42 : 2925*), the following additional volumes have been published or have finally come to light: t. 1, *Los ideólogos* (consisting of v. 3, *José Baquíjano y Carrillo*, v. 6, *Cartas araucanas*, v. 8, *Hipólito Unánue*, and v. 10, *José Faustino Sánchez Carrión*); t. 3, *Conspiraciones y rebeliones en el siglo XIX* (consisting of v. 7, *La revolución de Cuzco de 1814*); t. 14, *Obra gubernativa y epistolario de Bolívar* (consisting of v. 1, *Legislación 1823–1825*, v. 2, *Legislación de 1826*, and v. 3, *Libro de decretos 1824*); t. 15, *Primeros congresos constituyentes* (consisting of v. 3 of same title); t. 16, *Archivo Riva Agüero* (consisting of one v. of same title); and t. 19, *La Universidad* (consisting of v. 1, *Libros de posesiones de cátedras y actos académicos, 1780–1826. Grados de bachilleres en cánones y leyes. Grados de abogados*—which is not to be confused with t. 19 of same title but differently subtitled in *HLAS 36 : 2721*).

2817 Fisher, John. Antecedentes de la llegada de San Martín en el Perú: alianzas raciales y regionales (*in* San Martín en España [see item **2802**] p. 367–378)

These "antecedents" go back to Túpac Amaru and early independence period, and in Fisher's suggestive treatment they reflect the existence of an uneasy and discontinuous "alliance" of Creoles and Indians in *sierra* vs.

whatever party held Lima. He notes that San Martín, after all, was just one more of the latter.

2818 Historia del Perú. v. 6, Perú republicano. Lima: Editorial Juan Mejía Baca, 1980. 1 v.; bibl.; ill. (some col.)

Most of this volume is devoted to Virgilio Roel Pineda's "Conatos, Levantamientos, Campañas e Ideología de la Independencia," which starts before Túpac Amaru, goes to Ayacucho, and further sketches in continental developments; it is fast-moving but somewhat superficial, despite intermittent efforts at socioeconomic explication of military-political events. Heraclio Bonilla's "Entre la Independencia y la Guerra con Chile" fills less than 100 p. at end, with an overview of Peruvian society and economy (to 1870s) which is more analytical and buttressed by tables and citations of recent research but hardly does justice to such a broad title.

2819 Hünefeldt, Christine. Los indios y la Constitución de 1812 (IPA/A, 11/12, 1978, p. 33–57)

Well researched, highly suggestive article. Notes often contradictory nature of Indians' reaction to reforms ostensibly enacted for their benefit (e.g., abolition of tribute) and more basic contradiction between Indian aspirations and those of Creole patriots.

2820 La Independencia en el Perú. Heraclio Bonilla *et al.* 2. ed. Lima: Instituto de Estudios Peruanos, 1981. 240 p.; bibl.; graph; table (Perú problema; 7)

Reissue of significant and controversial volume that first appeared in 1972 (see *HLAS 36 : 1639*), with addition of one new essay by Bonilla himself, in which he takes note of more recent research while trying to suggest why Peruvians proved incapable of gaining "independence" by their own efforts.

2821 Miscelánea documental de la emancipación peruana (PEAGN/R, 29, 1971, p. 115–229)

Contains mostly *hojas de servicios* and lists of more of same—but, as title suggests, that is not all. Indeed the same title really could be given to this entire issue, which came to hand regrettably late but should still be annotated. In particular, it offers as well: Alberto Rosas Siles' "Miguel

Tadeo y Manuel José Fernández de Córdova: Ignorados Personajes de la Independencia del Perú" (p. 19–55) which concerns civil functionary who became member of Corte Superior and cleric named Bishop of Ayacucho, with documentary appendix on both; and "Correspondencia entre Abascal y Goyeneche, 1812," (p. 57–114) which includes documents on relationship between Viceroy José de Abascal and Creole royalist José Manuel de Goyeneche, pacifier of Alto Peru.

2822 Temple, Ella Dunbar. La Universidad de San Marcos en el proceso de la emancipación peruana. Lima: Universidad Nacional Mayor de San Marcos, 1974. 1 v.; bibl. (Colección Documental de la Independencia del Perú; t. 19, La Universidad)

Solid scholarly contribution first published as prologue to vol. 1 of tomo 19, *La Universidad: libros de posesiones de cátedras y actos académicos, 1780–1826. Grados de bachilleres en cánones y leyes. Grados de abogados,* in *Colección documental de la independencia del Perú* (see item **2816**).

Villanueva Urteaga, Horacio. Gamarra y la iniciación republicana en el Cuzco. See item **2999**.

2823 Yaranga Valderrama, Abdón. El papel de las comunidades indígenas en la guerra de la independencia del Perú (*in* Coloquio Ilustración Española e Independencia de América, Bellaterra, Spain, 1978. Homenaje a Noël Salomon: ilustración española e independencia de América. Edición preparada por Alberto Gil Novales. Barcelona: Universidad Autónoma de Barcelona, 1979, p. 217–240, bibl., ill., map)

With various appendixes, a tribute to participation of Indian *montoneras* in struggle for independence.

ALTO PERU

2824 Portugal Ortiz, Maz. Documentos para la historia del período emancipatorio: Archivo Histórico Municipal (Illimani [Revista del Instituto de Investigaciones Históricas y Culturales de la Municipalidad de La Paz] 10, 1978, p. 67–97)

Proclamations, bandos, miscellaneous documents relating to the struggle 1810–13, from Archivo General de Indias.

2824a Bidondo, Emilio A. La guerra de la independencia en el Alto Perú. Buenos Aires: Círculo Militar, 1979. 284 p. (Biblioteca del Oficial; 700)

Excellent systematic study by distinguished military historian of what was chiefly a guerrilla war described by Mitre as "guerra de las republiquetas." Very useful coverage of period preceding the "Guerra Gaucha" fought by Güemes and his Montoneros. [R. Etchepareborda]

CHILE

2825 Las Conferencias O'Higgins, *Instituto de Chile, 1978.* Las conferencias O'Higgins. Santiago: Editorial Universitaria, 1979. 201 p.; 1 leaf of plates; bibl.; col. port.; ill.; index.

On bicentennial of O'Higgins' birth, lectures on his life and times by qualified specialists for larger audience. Authors include: Luis Valencia Avaria on military aspects; Julio Heise González on O'Higgins as organizer of republic; others on his political ideas, literary image, and public health, art, etc. of his epoch.

2826 Cox Balmaceda, Ricardo. Carrera, O'Higgins y San Martín. Santiago: Corporación de Estudios Contemporáneos, 1979. 320 p.

Ostensibly an analysis of relationships among José Miguel Carrera, O'Higgins, and San Martín, but can also be read as narrative political-military history of Chilean independence. In a traditional vein, well researched; unpolemical despite clear preference for O'Higgins.

2827 Kilapán, Lonko. O'Higgins es araucano: 17 pruebas tomadas de la historia secreta de la Araucanía. Santiago: Editorial Universitaria, 1978. 61 p.; ill.; maps.

Historiographical curiosity, full of Araucanian lore and language (latter fortunately translated in footnotes). Seeks to prove identification of O'Higgins, via his mother's family, with Araucanian Indians, whose origins are in turn traced back to Sparta.

2828 Valencia Avaria, Luis. Bernardo O'Higgins, el "buen genio" de América. Santiago: Editorial Universitaria, 1980. 487 p.; bibl.; ill.

This will clearly stand as one of the better biographies of O'Higgins: comprehensive, favorable to its subject but no mere panegyric, by a conscientious and capable historian of traditional school.

RIO DE LA PLATA

2828a *Boletín del Instituto de Historia Argentina y Americana Emilio Ravignani.* Facultad de Filosofía y Letras, Universidad Nacional de Buenos Aires. Año 16, Vol. 16, No. 26, 2 época, 1980– . Buenos Aires.

Special issue devoted to the bicentennial of Gen. San Martín's birth also memorializes two distinguished Argentine historians, Ricardo R. Caillet-Bois and Julio César González. Includes several important contributions on the post-independence period: Olga M. García de D'Agostino's "Aspectos de las Relaciones Argentinas con Chile, Bolivia y Perú: 1874–1879" (p. 247–268); Graciela Lapido's and Beatriz Spota de Lapieza Elli's "Algunas Propuestas y Realidades de la Política de Fomento de la Inmigración en la Argentina: 1862–1873" (p. 269–286); Susana Irene Rato de Sambucetti's "El Fraude Electoral en 1886" (p. 415–482); Elena Rebok's "Informes del Ministro Residente Alemán acerca de la Presidencia de Sarmiento" (p. 483–500). [R. Etchepareborda]

2829 Cabral, Salvador. Andresito Artigas en la emancipación americana. Buenos Aires: Ediciones Castañeda, 1980. 225 p. (Colección Tiempo de América; 2)

Study of obscure but noteworthy figure, a Misiones Indian who became Artigas' adoptive son and his collaborator against *porteños*, Portuguese and other foes, and who for a time served as Governor of Corrientes. In interpretation generally similar to item **2830**, but offers documentary appendix and some admixture of original research.

2830 ———. Artigas y la Patria Grande. Buenos Aires: Castañeda, 1978. 162 p.; bibl. (Colección Perspectiva nacional; 5)

Following same left-revisionist line as his *Artigas como caudillo argentino* (see *HLAS 40:3399*), Cabral here studies Artigas' relations with Dr. Francia and with Corrientes, and the Congreso de Oriente held by the *artiguista* Liga de los Pueblos Libres in 1815. Emphasizes Artigas' populism and commit-

ment to larger unity of Platine area, in opposition to self-centered *porteño* bourgeoisie. Nothing that has not been said before, but a readable and documented presentation.

2831 Cooney, Jerry W. The destruction of the religious orders in Paraguay, 1810–1824 (AAFH/TAM, 36:2, Oct. 1979, p. 177–198)

Fills out, through original research, details of orders' initial adjustment to independence and then liquidation at hands of Dr. Francia.

2832 ———. Independence, dictatorship, and Fray Pedro García de Panés, O.F.M.: last bishop of colonial Paraguay, 1838 (AFH, 68:3/4, July/Dec. 1975, p. 421–449)

Focusing on Paraguay's ill-fated bishop, suggests some of the impact on Church of both independence *per se* and Dr. Francia's idiosyncratic anti-clericalism. Good brief article that anticipates some of author's later ones on religious orders (see item **2831**).

2832a Cruz, Josefina de Caprile. Saavedra: el hombre de mayo. Buenos Aires: Ediciones Culturales Argentinas, Secretaría de Estado de Cultura, 1980. 520 p.

Very readable text written by a well known *literata*. [R. Etchepareborda]

2833 Fernández, Ariosto. Francisco Ramírez y las milicias entrerrianas defensoras de España en Montevideo, 1811–1814. Montevideo: Arbol Impresores, 1977. 26 p.; facsim.

Pamphlet full of documentary excerpts and citations, whose title is adequately explanatory. Minor but enlightening, on royalist forces that included later caudillo of Entre Ríos, Francisco Ramírez.

2833a Güemes documentado. Edited by Luis Güemes. Buenos Aires: Plus Ultra, 1979. 4v. (511, 509, 508, 473 p.); bibl.

Impressive collection of primary sources traces Güemes' activities (1795–1818) and is intended to refute distortions of traditional historiography. Unfortunately, it makes reading difficult due largely to editor's lengthy interpolations not clearly separated from the primary sources. [R. Etchepareborda]

2834 Gutiérrez de Lafuente, Antonio. El *Diario* y documentos de la Misión

Sanmartiniana de Gutiérrez de la Fuente, 1822. t. 1, Diario del Comandante Antonio Gutiérrez de la Fuente que trata de la comisión encomendada por el general San Martín, para promover el envío de fuerzas que apoyasen al Ejército Libertador en el Perú. t. 2, Selección documental. Estudio y selección documental de los académicos de número, Ricardo R. Caillet-Bois y Julio César González. Presentación del presidente, Enrique M. Barba. Prólogo del académico de número, Carlos S. A. Segreti. Buenos Aires: Academia Nacional de la Historia, 1978. 2 v.; bibl.

Detailed and lengthy preliminary study by Caillet-Bois and González introduces journal of Antonio Gutiérrez de la Fuente, commissioned by San Martín to enlist aid of Argentine provinces for attack on Alto Peru; it is followed by selection of illustrative documents. Much has been published on this affair. Nevertheless, a net contribution to knowledge, and one which should satisfy needs of scholars for some time to come.

2834a Heredia, Edmundo A. Algunos aspectos de la reconquista del Río de la Plata durante el régimen constitucional español (EEHA/AEA, 1977, p. 49–63)

Heredia deals persuasively with actions (both in Spain and Río de la Plata) of what may be termed a "Spanish" party dedicated to restoring royal rule in 1821. Also shows that transition in Spain from absolute to constitutional, "liberal" monarchy did nothing to dampen Spanish desire to reclaim—by force, if necessary—its Platine colonies. [JHW]

2835 ———. El "Carlotismo," los ingleses y el comercio exterior (CEHA/NH, 10:20, 1977, p. 80–100)

Detailed look at relationship between movement in favor of rights of Infanta Carlota and demand for greater freedom of trade. *Porteño* liberals who favored Carlota hoped that she, for tactical reasons, would support opening of port to English and others; when viceroy himself opened port, they tended to lose interest in her.

2836 Pérez de Arévalo, Lilia Fanny. El fuero gaucho (Revista de Historia del Derecho [Instituto de Investigaciones de Historia del Derecho, Buenos Aires] 6, 1978, p. 109–134)

Discusses exemption from rent pay-

ments given to gaucho militia of Salta by Martín Güemes during independence struggle, its application, and resulting controversies. Unpretentiously descriptive, with extensive documentary excerpts, but a definite contribution to social history of period.

2837 Petra de Popoff, Mirta L. La misión de Diego Saavedra y Juan Pedro Aguirre a los Estados Unidos en 1811–12 (Boletín del Instituto de Historia Argentina y Americana Doctor Emilio Ravignani [Buenos Aires] 26, 1980, p. 321–359)

Extended research note on little-studied early mission sent by Buenos Aires revolutionary authorities; it was not especially successful, gave rise to recriminations, and on both counts was perhaps fairly representative.

2838 Representación de D. Carlos María de Alvear dirigida al ministro español en Rio de Janeiro, 1819; otras calumnias refutadas, 1819; noticia preliminar de Santos Fernández Arlaud (Historiografía Rioplatense [Buenos Aires] 1, 1978, p. 181–216, facsims.)

Reproduces two examples of pamphlet war carried on between Supreme Director Juan Martín de Pueyrredón and his political rivals, with solid introductory note.

2839 Sala de Touron, Lucía; Nelson de la Torre; and Julio C. Rodríguez. Artigas y su revolución agraria, 1811–1820. Portada de Anhelo Hernández. México: Siglo Veintiuno, 1978. 322 p.; bibl.; ill. (Colección América nuestra; 12)

Reedition of "substantial part" of same authors' *La revolución agraria artiguista* (see *HLAS 34:2478*), a landmark in Platine independence historiography and social reinterpretation of Artigas. Incorporates new and extended introduction aimed especially at non-Platinists.

2840 Saravi, Mario G. Cuyo y el artiguismo 1816–1817 (Historiografía Rioplatense [Buenos Aires] 1, 1978, p. 106–124)

Reviews struggle between Buenos Aires Directorate and followers of Artigas, with special consideration to repercussions in Cuyo region. Solid research, full documentation, no new insights.

2841 Segreti, Carlos S. A. La política económica porteña en la primera década revolucionaria (ANH/IE, 25, julio/dic. 1978, p. 31–74)

With side glances at taxation and monetary policy, chiefly examines handling of tariff and of foreign merchants' participation in internal transactions. Well researched; emphasizes fundamentally "liberal" trends even during illusory protectionist reactions.

2842 Tonda, Américo A. Itinerario y forja intelectual del Deán Funes (ANH/IE, 25, julio/dic. 1978, p. 303–339)

Examines formal education of key ecclesiastical-political figure Gregorio Funes, in Argentina and Spain, and who were the authors of books owned by Funes or cited in his works. More descriptive than analytical, but a serious contribution to intellectual background of independence.

2843 Uruguay. Comisión Nacional Archivo Artigas. Archivo Artigas, v. 15/17. Advertencia de Juan E. Pivel Devoto. Montevideo: Impresores A. Monteverde y Cía, 1976/1980. 3 v. (442, 425, 674 p.); folded tables; tables.

Documents of 1814–15, edited with usual high standards of this series (see HLAS 42:2966 for previous volumes). Pivel Devoto's "Advertencia" in t. 15 gives rather extensive introduction to topics covered in it and next volume which are "La Ocupación Militar de Montevideo y la Provincia Oriental por los Ejércitos del Directorio," "La Reacción Artiguista y el Tratado del 9 de julio de 1814," and "Gobierno y Administración de los Representantes del Directorio." With only somewhat cursory "Introducción," t. 17 covers "Campaña Militar contra la Dominación Porteña; la Batalla de Guayabos," and "La Desocupación del Territorio de la Provincia Oriental por el Ejército del Directorio."

2844 Wiederspahn, Henrique Oscar. Bento Gonçalves e as guerras de Artigas: achegas para uma biografia de acordo com uma reformulação histórica, políticomilitar e global, abrangendo desde a campanha de D. Diogo de Sousa até as antevésperas da rebelião dos 33 orientais, em 1825. Capa, Clarice C. J. Dorneles. Caxias do Sul, Brazil: Universidade de Caxias do Sul, 1979. 218 p.; bibl.; ill. (Coleção Temas gaúchos; 12)

Treats early phase in career of later leader of Rio Grande do Sul's Farroupilha uprising, when he was fighting for Luso-Brazilian cause in Uruguay. Extensive bibliography, numerous maps. Useful particularly for telling story from standpoint of someone on other side.

19th and 20th Centuries
Colombia, Venezuela and Ecuador

WINTHROP R. WRIGHT, *Associate Professor of History, University of Maryland, College Park*

VENEZUELA: THE TREND IN THE NATION'S HISTORIOGRAPHY that began in the early 1970s has continued. The eras of Juan Vicente Gómez and his ultimate successor Rómulo Betancourt have received the lion's share of attention from historians of modern Venezuela. The period from 1935 through 1948 has become a favorite one for those who deal with political topics. Without doubt, political history prevails in Venezuela, with new interest in the Medina regime and the *trienio*. Political parties, their formation and development, also provide focus of major interest, especially among foreign scholars. All together, Venezuelans have published an unusually large number of books on 20th-century subjects. The increased amount of historical literature in part reflects the nation's affluence, as individuals turn to vanity presses to publish unpolished works, most of which do not merit inclusion in this bibliography. But taken together, the increased volume of publication demonstrates a growing interest in contemporary history among Venezuelans, a fact that should please those members of the Academia Nacional de la Historia who have called for an effort to study the nation's recent past.

Interest in the Gómez era seems to have waned somewhat. Yet memoirs from that period, such as those of Emilio Arévalo Cedeño (item **2868**) and Rafael Arévalo González (item **2869**), still appear on the scene. They, along with the very important documents from the Gómez administration published in the *Boletín del Archivo de Miraflores* (items **2871–2873**), continue to shed light on the political developments of the Gómez years. To date, few historians seem inclined to tackle questions related to the social or economic dimensions of Venezuela during the same period.

Interest in the political history of the immediate post-Gómez period has increased. Several North American scholars have dealt with related aspects of this era. In several articles and a book-length manuscript, Steven Ellner (items **2878–2881**) has dealt with the evolution of Romulo Betancourt as a pragmatic populist who sought a less radical solution to Venezuela's problems than did the Communist Party. Ellner has also touched upon the struggle between Acción Democrática and the Communist Party to gain control over the nation's labor movement (item **2878**). A series of articles written by Betancourt in 1945 (item **2870**) complements the Ellner studies, especially in understanding the modernizing tendencies of the Medina administration and the fact that Betancourt counted on the armed forces for support of a civilian president in 1945. Luis Cordero Velásquez has also presented a detailed and well thought out monograph on the crisis of 1945, somewhat less complementary of Betancourt (item **2877**). The same holds true for Juan B. Fuenmayor's treatment of events between 1942 and 1945 (item **2883**). Fuenmayor, a founding member of the Communist Party, presents a highly critical analysis of Betancourt's participation in the 1945 coup, which he argues moved Venezuela away from socialism. Finally, a collection of three essays by Ramón Velasquez, J. F. Sucre Figarella, and Blas Bruni Celli (item **2896**) deals sympathetically with Betancourt as a national political figure on a par with Lazaro Cárdenas of Mexico, and treats the Venezuelan as a humanist who organized Venezuelans into political parties.

A number of manuscripts deal with the Betancourt era in less personal terms. Donald L. Herman has written the first major history of the Christian Democrats in Venezuela (item **2886**). In his analysis of the party from 1936 to the 1970s, he linked COPEI's success to its cooperation with Acción Democrática. Four works touch upon the overthrow of Marcos Pérez Jiménez. Fania Petzoldt and Jacinta Bevilacqua, trained as sociologists, used interviews with 32 women who took part in the resistance against Pérez Jiménez in order to describe the feminine role in politics (item **2891**). Another series of interviews, selected by Agustín Blanco Muñoz from some 500 focuses upon the violence that followed Pérez Jiménez's overthrow (item **2894**). North American historian Judith Ewell has treated Betancourt and Pérez Jiménez as two contrasting types of modernizers (item **2882**). She follows their struggle through the extradition and trial of the latter for crimes he committed as dictator. In vol. 1 of a projected four-volume work, Carlos Ramírez Faría gives an account of the military involvement in the Jan. 23 coup and the subsequent rise to power of Betancourt (item **2893**).

Oil, economic dependency, and diplomatic relations provide topics for other noteworthy studies of modern Venezuela. Stephen Rabe has written a well documented chronology of the diplomatic relations between Venezuela and the US that resulted from oil negotiations between the two nations from the Gómez regime through the founding of OPEC (item **2892**). An equally interesting and well documented study of Venezuelan relations with Great Britain during the 19th century can be found in George E. Carl's able study (item **2876**). A more polemical diplomatic history, written solely from the Venezuelan sources, appears in Nicolas Pe-rrazo's history of relations between Venezuela and Colombia (item **2890**). Two other works worth noting include Julio Godio's (item **2884**) attempts to write a history of Venezuelan labor, in which he tries to establish the presence of early class consciousness during the 19th century, and a documentary collection related to slavery and abolition edited by Antonieta Camacho (item **2875**).

COLOMBIA: Though not as prolific, students of modern Colombian history have published a number of significant studies in the past year or so. Many have chosen political themes, probably because of the access to archival materials, but several paid attention to social and economic problems. In general, historians working in Colombia have made better use of the archival collections than their Venezuelan counterparts. Even though political history continues to dominate, there has been a refreshing and important diversity in the works that have appeared in recent years.

Although no clear trends seem to hold the attention of scholars in Colombia, two North Americans have touched upon questions related to 19th-century liberalism and conservatism. One, Helen Delpar (item **2850**), has pointed out that following their defeat, liberals did not evolve a set of consistent ideological positions. She also goes on to challenge Charles Bergquist's interpretations of the causes of the outbreak of the War of a Thousand Days. Robert C. Means (item **2858**) has also dealt with 19th-century elites, and has argued that they lacked the technical legal capacity required for rational borrowing from abroad. Means contends that the Colombians wrote codes that proved irrelevant to the Colombian condition.

In other areas, several Colombian scholars demonstrated sound use of archival materials in their work. José Antonio Ocampo has added to the debate concerning Colombia's economic development in a careful statistical study of 19th century trade figures (item **2861**). In treating the local aspects of the abolition movement in southern Colombia, Jorge Castellanos has shown how abolition became a part of the formation of the Liberal/Conservative split in the Popayán region (item **2848**). In two short essays, Jorge Villegas has combined with Fernando Botero and Antonio Restrepo to show the need for research into social and economic topics. In one, the authors demonstrate how various administrations have used *tierras baldías* to foment immigration for labor and to service foreign debts (item **2867**). In the second essay, they give a graphic description of abuses inflicted on Indians by rubber companies in the Caquetá and Amazonas regions during the late 19th and 20th centuries (item **2867**). Two other studies round out the important Colombian works. One, by German scholar Heinrich Krumwiede (item **2854**) notes that the Church has contributed to the limiting of the left until Vatican II, at which time the Church itself turned to the left, which may foster social change which the traditional parties have resisted. The second, selected works by Jorge Eliécer Gaitán, demonstrates the longevity of Gaitán as a figure of historical importance (item **2851**).

ECUADOR: The nation's prosperity has led to an increase in the publication of works dealing with modern historical topics. Although many of these leave much to be desired, a small group of professional historians have begun to publish well researched manuscripts. One, the Spanish translation of Lois Crawford Roberts' Ph.D. dissertation on Ecuador during the cacao epoch (item **2904**), shows the inter-est that Ecuadorians have in knowing more about the economic history of their nation at the turn of the century. In an equally impressive and more important work, Oswaldo Hurtado (item **2900**) has analyzed the unchallenged control of the ruling elite from colonial times until the mid-20th century, at which time modern capitalists, technocrats, and intellectuals began to use the powers of the state to introduce reforms that helped the otherwise immobilized and weak masses. In a work that complements the two just cited, Andrés Guerrero (item **2899**) has provided a Marxist analysis of the formation of the cacao oligarchy of coastal Ecuador in which he suggests that cacao production did not lead to the formation of a rural proletariat of campesinos. Rather, it made the campesinos more dependent upon the landowners, who in turn formed ties with the world capitalist system through bankers and merchants in Guayaquil, who gave the cacao interest their national character.

COLOMBIA

2845 Alzate Avendaño, Gilberto. Obras selectas. Jorge Mario Eastman, presentación y compilación. Bogotá: Cámara de Representantes, 1979. 619 p. (Colección Pensadores políticos colombianos; t. 7)

Essays and article by mid-20th century political thinker.

Ariza S., Alberto E. El Colegio-Universidad de Santo Tomás de Aquino de Santa Fe de Bogotá, 1580, 13 de junio, 1980. See item **2620**.

2846 Arizmendi Posada, Ignacio. Gobernantes colombianos, 1819–1980. Medellín, Colombia: Interprint Editores, 1980. 263 p.; ports.

Popular history, aimed at broad public. Short sketches of all Colombian presidents since Bolívar. Readable, and useful for chronological information concerning national leaders.

2847 Caro, Miguel Antonio. Discursos y otras intervenciones en el Senado de la República, 1903–1904. Edición, introducción y Carlos Valderrama Andrade. Bogotá: Instituto Caro y Cuervo, 1979. 909 p.; ill. (Obras completas de Miguel Antonio Caro; t. 1) (Biblioteca colombiana; 19)

Collection of speeches by Senator from Antioquia. Introductory essay by Carlos Valderrama Andrade gives outline of the important issues addressed by Miguel Antonio Caro during 1903–04 sessions.

2848 Castellanos, Jorge. La abolición de la esclavitud en Popayán, 1832–1852. Cali, Colombia: Departamento de Publicaciones, Universidad del Valle, 1980. 132 p.; bibl.; map.

Treats local aspects of abolition movement in southern Colombia. Findings much like those of John Lombardi's in Venezuela, show that Juntas de Manumisión represented rich who intimidated majority of slaves and practiced gradualism following 1821 Cúcuta Law. Shows how abolition led to Liberal/Conservative split in Popayán region with two positions prevailing: Tomás Cipriano de Mosquera's, who sought alternative economic solutions and flexibility; and Julio Arboleda's, who did not want alternatives and remained inflexible and opposed to abolition. For their part, the Conservative argument against abolition was apocalyptic rather than truly political.

2849 Castrillón Arboleda, Diego. Tomás Cipriano de Mosquera. Bogotá: Litografía Arco, 1979. 327 p.; 31 leaves of plates; bibl.; ill. (Publicación del Banco del Estado)

Beautifully illustrated tribute to Mosquera. Basically anecdotal history, with little new information.

2850 Delpar, Helen. Red against blue: the Liberal Party in Colombian politics, 1863–1899. University: University of Alabama Press, 1981. 262 p.; bibl.; index.

Narrates Liberals' defeat and efforts to regain power after 1885. Regional, race, and family differences made Liberals a diverse lot. Mostly from eastern provinces and heterogeneous in racial makeup, their elite was less likely to descend from colonial elites than Conservatives. Delpar points out that Liberals had no ideological consistencies, and were not doctrinaire on laissez-faire economic policies. Challenges Bergquist on causes of outbreak of War of a Thousand Days. Characterizes Liberal outlook toward human society as secular and individualistic, but expression of these values differed from leader to leader.

2851 Gaitán, Jorge Eliécer. Obras selectas. Jorge Mario Eastman, compilación y presentación. Bogotá: Impr. Nacional, 1979. 2 v.; bibl. (Colección Pensadores políticos colombianos; t. 5/6)

Collection of writings, speeches, lectures, youthful articles, and debates, including 1929 debate on Las Bananeras in which Gaitán discussed human rights abuses by government forces. Gives lasting impression of forcefulness of Gaitán's rhetoric.

González, Fernán E. Educación y estado en la historia de Colombia. See *HLAS 43:4430*.

Graff, Gary W. Archives in Pamplona, Norte de Santander, Colombia. See item **2626**.

2852 Gutiérrez Azopardo, Ildefonso. Historia del negro en Colombia: sumisión o rebeldía? Bogotá: Editorial Nueva América, 1980. 113 p.; bibl.; ill. (Contestación; 5)

Brief study of slavery and racism from colonial times. Focus is mostly on slave period. Points out growth of a Negritud movement during 1970s.

2853 Jaramillo Ocampo, Hernán. 1946–1950 [i.e. Mil novecientos cuarenta seis–mil novecientos cincuenta], de la unidad nacional a la hegemonía conservadora. Bogotá: Editorial Pluma, 1980. 410 p.

Personal account by author who served in Mariano Ospina Pérez's government. Treats Gaitán period in considerable detail and shows his impact upon Colombian Liberals and Conservatives during 1946–50.

2854 Krumwiede, Heinrich-W. Politik und katholische Kirche im gesellschaftlichen Modernisierungsprozess: Tradition und Entwicklung in Kolumbien. Hamburg: Hoffman und Campe, 1980. 308 p. (Historische Perspektiven, ISSN 0173-217X; 16)

Author notes that social revolutionary parties have had only sporadic success in Colombia. Attributes this to fact that 19th-century parties have survived and to religious splits that hindered formation of left-wing parties. Both Liberals and Conservatives have elicited new loyalties from middle-class, and workers. Furthermore, Catholic Church contributed to limiting growth of left. Last part of study analyzes changes after Vatican II in Church and its leftward turn which may foster social change.

2855 Liévano Aguirre, Indalecio. Rafael Núñez. 3. ed. Bogotá: Instituto Colombiano de Cultura, Subdirección de Comunicaciones Culturales, División de Publicaciones, 1977. 521 p.; bibl. (Colección Historia viva; 2) (Biblioteca colombiana de cultura)

Reprint of biography. Mostly anecdotal.

2856 Lleras Restrepo, Carlos. Los días y los años: prosas de lucha, de estudio, de servicio, 1941–1979. Portada, Jorge Valencia Z. Medellín: Editorial Letras, 1979. 639 p. (Colección Biblioteca Pública Piloto; v. 3)

Collection of writings, newspaper articles, and speeches by ex-President, covering political career, 1941–79. Many appeared in *El Tiempo*. Useful for gaining insights into Colombian political mentality.

2857 McGreevey, William Paul. Reinterpreting Colombian economic history (SAGE/JIAS, 23:3, Aug. 1981, p. 352–363)

Critical review of recent works by Bergquist, Palacios, Brew and Arango. Suggests that more analysis by historians and economists is needed to correct flaws in books under discussion.

2858 Means, Robert Charles. Underdevelopment and the development of law: corporations and corporation law in nineteenth-century Colombia. Chapel Hill: University of North Carolina Press, 1980. 327 p.; bibl.; index (Studies in legal history)

Defines legal underdevelopment as a legal system that cannot perform "tasks assigned to it within a modern political system," (p. ix). Argues that 19th-century Colombian elites lacked technical legal capacity required for rational legal borrowing from abroad. Colombians could not adapt commercial law, especially since they lacked a full time legal faculty, their legal curriculum lacked instruction in civil and commercial law, and they had no published works in such fields. Colombian codes were irrelevant to the Colombian condition.

2859 Medina, Medófilo. Historia del Partido Comunista de Colombia. Bogotá: Centro de Estudios e Investigaciones Sociales, 1980– . 1 v.; bibl.; index.

Fairly detailed study by Soviet trained historian in celebration of 50th anniversary of founding of the Colombian Communist Party. Volume takes account from the party's antecedents through 1949. Not too polemical.

2860 Murillo Toro, Manuel. Obras selectas. Jorge Mario Eastman, compilación y presentación. Bogotá: Cámara de Representantes, 1979. 387 p.; bibl. (Colección Pensadores políticos colombianos; t. 3)

Selected articles and reports by 19th-century paladin of radicalism.

2861 Ocampo, José Antonio. Las exportaciones colombianas en el siglo XIX (CEDE/DS, 4, julio 1980, p. 165–226, tables)

Careful statistical study of 19th-century trade figures which provides sound estimates of foreign trade.

2862 Ocampo T., José Fernando. Colombia siglo XX [i.e. veinte]: estudio histórico y antología política. v. 1, 1886–1934. Carátula de Luciano Jaramillo. Bogotá: Ediciones Tercer Mundo, 1980– . 1 v., bibl.

Essentially a political history of the Liberal party between 1886–1934, a period which author depicts as having been under control of US capital. Basically polemical in nature. Last third of book consists of documents author considered pertinent to his analysis.

2863 Rojas Garrido, José María. Obras selectas. Jorge Mario Eastman, compilador. Bogotá: Impr. Nacional, 1979. 519 p.; bibl. (Colección Pensadores políticos colombianos; t. 4)

Collection of speeches and addresses, especially useful for understanding some aspects of Church-State relationships during mid-19th century.

2864 Salazar, Diego Renato. Historia constitucional de Colombia. Bogotá: Librería Jurídicas Wilches, 1980. 386 p.; bibl.

Useful but extremely limited compilation of evolution of laws touching major social and economic issues from colonial times to present. Gives interesting insights into changing values of societies over the centuries.

Taussig, Michael. Black religion & resistance in Colombia: three centuries of social struggle in the Cauca Valley. See *HLAS 43:6368.*

2865 Twinam, Ann. From Jew to Basque: ethnic myths and antioqueño entrepreneurship (UM/JIAS, 22:1, Feb. 1980, p. 81–107, bibl.)

Debates "myth" of Jewish origins of the antioqueñas from 19th and 20th-century sources. Shows that arguments can be made for Basque origins of New Breed of Colombians, too. Anti-semitism played role in antioqueño reaction to myth as well as added to tensions between antioqueños and bogotanos. Author discards both origins, and attributes them to anti-antioqueño sources.

2866 Uribe Uribe, Rafael. Obras selectas. Jorge Mario Eastman, compilación y presentación. Bogotá: Cámara de Representantes, 1979. 2 v. (393, 463 p.); bibl. (Colección Pensadores políticos colombianos; t. 1/2)

Well chosen collection of selected works on liberalism, local powers, and related themes by leading late 19th-century political figure. Touches questions such as "thieves and savages" as well as more mundane topics of political importance.

Vázquez Carrizosa, Alfredo. El poder presidencial en Colombia: la crisis permanente del derecho constitucional. See *HLAS 43:6371.*

2867 Villegas A., Jorge and **Antonio Restrepo.** Baldíos, 1820–1936. Putumayo, indígenas, caucho y sangre por Jorge Villegas y Fernando Botero. Medellín: Centro de Investigaciones Económicas, Universidad de Antioquia, 1978. 78, 30 p.; bibl.

These short essays show need for more research on these topics: 1) demonstrates how various administrations used *tierras baldías* or *baldios* to foment immigration for labor and to service foreign debts and how laws came to favor landowners rather than colonists. Excellent for quick summation of data on topic; 2) deals with exploration for rubber in the Caquetá and Amazons regions by Colombian and Peruvian companies, where the Winchester was the only law. Dwells on 1909–10 accounts of torture and killing of Indians by representatives of rubber companies. Suggests that revelations of these horrors were suppressed by British owners because it would have ruined area's rubber trade had such information become widely known. Far Eastern plantations and synthetic rubber led to eventual decline in natural rubber.

VENEZUELA

2868 Arévalo Cedeño, Emilio. Viva Arévalo Cedeño!: *El libro de mis luchas*: autobiografía de E. Arévalo Cedeño. Portada, Régulo Pérez. Caracas: Publicaciones Seleven, 1979. 409 p.; ports.

First completed in 1936 under title *El libro de mis luchas*. This edition has introduction by J. A. de Armas Chitty. Book is autobiography by man who raided Venezuela seven times in 21 years during Gómez regime. Arévalo Cedeño, one of Gómez's most persistent opponents, appears as honest man who fought for Venezuelan people. Text's appearance reflects growing Venezuelan interest in Gómez era.

2869 Arévalo González, Rafael. Memorias. Prólogo de Luis Villalba-Villalba. Caracas: s.n., 1977. 291 p.; 3 leaves of plates; ill.

Autobiography was written by one of Castro's and Gómez's many foes and victims. Author edited leading paper, *El Pregonero*. Long introduction by Luis Villalba-Villalba gives interesting background on era.

Banco Central de Venezuela, *Caracas.* La economía venezolana en los últimos treinta y cinco años. See *HLAS 43:3375.*

2870 Betancourt, Rómulo. El 18 [i.e. dieciocho] de octubre de 1945: génesis y realizaciones de una revolución democrática. Introducción de Simón Alberto Consalvi. Prólogo y notas de Diógenes de la Rosa. 2. ed. Barcelona: Seix Barral, 1979. 412 p.; 6 leaves of plates; ill. (His Obras selectas; 4)

Collection of articles written by Betancourt for *El País* before 1945 coup in which he advocated Venezuela First and Third World positions. He counted on Venezuelan armed forces to support a civilian president. He saw both López Contreras and Medina as representatives of the old oligarchy, as reactionaries.

2871 Boletín del Archivo Histórico de Miraflores. Año 20, Nos. 101/106, enero/dic. 1978 [through] enero/marzo 1979– . Caracas.

Includes text of book *El peligro de la intervención en Venezuela*, published by Pedro José Jugo Delgado in 1930; documents touching upon *Falke* incident; and 1915 political documents from states of Apure, Trujillo, and Táchira.

2872 ———. Año 21, Nos. 107/108, abril/dic. 1979– . Caracas.

Large segment deals with 1918 outbreak of epidemic of "Spanish grippe" that led to anti-Gómez demonstrations. Also includes documents on World War I's end, activities of Cornelio Filpo and Cipriano Castro, and 1918 roadbuilding and governors' reports.

2873 ———. Año 22, No. especial 111, nov./dic. 1980– . Caracas.

Mostly concerns arbitration with Colombia between 1902–16, including reports by José Gil Fortoul and Gil Borges. Other documents deal with Gen. Juan Pablo Peñaloza's extradition.

Brito Figueroa, Federico. Historia económica y social de Venezuela: una estructura para su estudio. See *HLAS 43:3379.*

2874 Cabrera Sifontes, Horacio. Guayana y El Mocho Hernández: breve semblanza de los generales Anselmo Zapata y Domingo Sifontes. Caracas: Ediciones Centauro/80, 1980. 240 p.; 9 p. of plates; appendix; facsims.; ill.

Anecdotal history, based especially on material found in Hernández Collection at Academia de la Historia. Very much in favor of José Manuel Hernández, "El Mocho."

2875 Camacho, Antonieta. Materiales para el estudio de la cuestión agraria en Venezuela, 1810–1865: mano de obra, legislación y administración; estudio preliminar. Caracas: Universidad Central de Venezuela, Facultad de Humanidades, 1979. 1 v.; bibl.; indexes (Ediciones de la Facultad de Humanidades y Educación; 4)

Collection of documents from period 1810–65. Most deal with questions of slaves, their participation in independence struggle, and abolition. Includes laws, debates and letters. Documents reveal drift in abolition movement and problems government had making payments to former slave owners.

2876 Carl, George E. First among equals: Great Britain and Venezuela, 1810–1910. Ann Arbor, Mich.: Department of Geography, Syracuse Univerity, University Microfilms International, 1980. 171 p.; bibl.; index; maps (Dellplain Latin American studies; 5) (Sponsor series) (Monograph publishing: Sponsor series)

Treats British-Venezuelan relations in terms of a British "informal empire." Refutes D. C. M. Platt's claim that British established patron/client relationship. Venezuelan concern over colonial status, imposed by

British diplomacy, led to resentment over such unequal partnership with anti-British feelings reaching peak in 1887 when relations were severed. Yet, it is unlikely that Venezuela could have established clearly advantageous arrangement with any other industrial nation during 19th century. Based on British PRO/Foreign Office records, Robert Ker Porter's correspondence, and records of banking and business houses. Very objective.

2877 Cordero Velásquez, Luis. Betancourt y la conjura militar del 45. Caracas: s.n., 1978. 307 p.; bibl.; ill.

Many crises (military, national political, international, petroleum, agrarian) combined to cause Medina's downfall. Supports Medina's position that 1945 coup broke constitutional thread that made gradual and peaceful liberalization possible. Coup aroused personal ambitions of military. Officers resented Betancourt's insistence upon an Acción Democrática majority in new government. Narrative history, tight and well written for popular audience. Based largely on newspaper accounts, detailed and anecdotal. Sympathetic to Medina. Points out that his land reform was regarded as dangerous step towards Marxism in Washington, D.C. Like others, Cordero Velásquez notes Betancourt's rapprochement with Rockefeller.

2878 Ellner, Steven. Los partidos políticos y su disputa por el control del movimiento sindical en Venezuela, 1936–1948. Caracas: Universidad Católica Andrés Bello, 1980. 181 p.; bibl.

Focus on inter-party and intra-party rivalry between 1935–48, especially concerning relationship between Acción Democrática and Venezuelan Communist Party (PCV). Emphasizes attitudes of each party towards labor. In 1936, unity of left characterized dealings between AD and PCV; during 1937–45, the left split into communist and noncommunist factions; and 1945–48, AD's years in power, saw it consolidate its control over labor.

2879 ———. Political party dynamics in Venezuela and the outbreak of guerrilla warfare (IAMEA, 34:2, Autumn 1980, p. 3–24)

Reviews efforts of PCV and MIR against Rómulo Betancourt in 1962. Venezuelan left tried to wage war and form alliance with moderates, a policy that failed.

Left could not successfully emulate Cuba's July 26th Movement, especially since it could not get public support against Betancourt and his party.

2880 ———. Populism in Venezuela, 1935– 48: Betancourt and the Acción Democrática (in Latin American populism in comparative perspective [see item **1830**] p. 135–149)

Treats Betancourt as Venezuelan populist who saw democracy as essential feature of initial bourgeois stage of development. Betancourt preferred strong multiclass party to weak workers' party. Sees Betancourt's avoidance of socialism as pragmatic. As leader, he displayed three characteristics that were trademarks of Latin American populism: nationalism, advocacy of middle class party, and commitment to electoral expansion. Pragmatism led Betancourt to reject Marxism in favor of populism before 1948.

2881 ———. The Venezuelan left in the era of the Popular Front, 1936–45 (JLAS, 11, pt. 1, 1979, p. 169–184)

Traces Communist and AD policies in wartime era. PCV's break from AD is explained in considerable detail. Medina's progressive policies drove wedge between two populist left parties. AD posed main leftist alternative to orthodox Marxism.

2882 Ewell, Judith. The indictment of a dictator: the extradition and trial of Marcos Pérez Jiménez. College Station: Texas A&M Press, 1981. 203 p.; appendixes; bibl.

Treats extradition and trial of Pérez Jiménez within context of his struggle with Betancourt as leaders who represented different approaches to modernizing Venezuela. Based on Venezuelan court records, interviews, and extensive research in Venezuelan and US archives. Effort to hold Pérez Jiménez responsible for his crimes helped legitimize Betancourt's new government. Pérez Jiménez's return to politics was due to his skill and abilities as politician.

Fondo de Inversiones de Venezuela. Evolución de la deuda pública de Venezuela. See *HLAS 43:3389.*

2883 Fuenmayor, Juan Bautista. Historia de la Venezuela política contemporánea, 1899–1969. v. 4/5. Caracas: s.n., 1975, 2 v. (437, 450 p.); bibl.

Vol. 4 treats 1942–44, Medina regime

period; vol. 5 concerns 1945, year of Medina's rule. Latter volume is especially polemical, as Fuenmayor continues his multivolume account of modern Venezuelan political history. Written by founding member of Partido Comunista, these volumes are based on personal recollections and archives as well as public documentation, especially newspapers. Highly critical of Betancourt, whom Fuenmayor attacks. Argues that 1945 golpe moved Venezuela away from socialism.

2884 Godio, Julio. El movimiento obrero venezolano, 1850–1944. Caracas: Editorial Ateneo de Caracas: ILDIS, 1980. 193 p.; bibl. (Colección M.O.L.A.C. Serie Movimiento obrero)

Despite title, mostly about recent movement. Tries to establish emergence of early class consciousness in workers movement during 19th century. Much of book devoted to founding of Communist Party and its aid to organization of labor after 1936.

2885 Grases, Pedro and Manuel Pérez Vila. Política y políticos del siglo XIX venezolano. Prólogo por Ramón J. Velásquez. Caracas: Colegio Universitario Francisco de Miranda, 1978. 195 p.; bibl.; index.

Reprints of Grases' and Pérez Vila's lectures at Universidad Central de Venezuela during early 1960s. Traces Venezuelan political thinkers from Lander and A. L. Guzmán through Liberalism and positivism. Useful but not important work by two leading historiographers.

2886 Herman, Donald L. Christian Democracy in Venezuela. Chapel Hill: University of North Carolina Press, 1980. 289 p.; bibl.; index.

Traces evolution of COPEI from 1936–58 to present. Notes move from its right wing 1936 generation to 1958 left-of-center party. Links COPEI's existence as party to its cooperation with Acción Democrática. Since 1948, both parties have come to realize that their mutual success depends upon compromise and cooperation which guarantee democracy and social reform. Gives in-depth analysis of COPEI and its internal relationships, with special emphasis upon Caldera's administration, which undertook major shifts in Venezuela's foreign policy after 1968. In internal policies, COPEI followed AD by advocating moderate,

middle-of-the-road democracy. But regional foreign policy led to conflicts with Brazil, Colombia and US.

2887 Herrera de Weishaar, María Luisa. Parroquia La Pastora: estudio microhistórico. Caracas: Consejo Municipal del Distrito Federal, 1979. 370 p.; bibl.; ill.

Original licenciate thesis on history of La Pastora, urban Caracas parish since 1908 which originated in 16th-century encomiendas of Torrequemada and Puricane. Especially strong in demographic, economic and social data. [M.T. Hamerly]

2888 ——; María Leonor Ferreira Ferreira; and Carlos Néstor Alvarez Cabrera. Parroquia La Vega: estudio micro-histórico. Caracas: Consejo Municipal del Distrito Federal, 1977. 176, 50 p.; 3 leaves of plates; bibl.; ill.

Traces La Vega neighborhood of Caracas from founding as agricultural sector through recent migration that turned it into housing region, both marginal and modern. Shows that factories located therein do not employ local population. Concludes that "La Vega is a conglomerate in conflict."

Historia de las finanzas públicas en Venezuela. v. 20, t. 9A, 1871–1874. See *HLAS 43:3393.*

2889 Kozhevnikov, Emil. Estudios soviéticos sobre Venezuela (URSS/AL, 12, 1980, p. 114–125)

Survey of Russian historiography on Venezuela since 1933. Since 1950s, number of Soviet works on Venezuelan topics has increased notably, and includes a wide range of topics from Miranda to 20th-century politics.

Lovera, José Rafael. La conciencia del papel del conocimiento científico y de la tecnología en el desarrollo de la sociedad: el caso de Venezuela en la segunda mitad del siglo XIX. See item **7595.**

Martínez, Aníbal R.. El camino de Petrolia. See *HLAS 43:3400.*

Maza Zavala, D. F. Venezuela: coexistencia de la abundancia y la escasez, la difícil acumulación del excedente petrolero. See *HLAS 43:3404.*

Nehru Tennassee, Paul. Venezuela, los obreros petroleros y la lucha por la democracia. See *HLAS 43:6405.*

2890 Perazzo, Nicolás. Historia de las relaciones diplomáticas entre Venezuela y Colombia. Caracas: Presidencia de la República, 1981. 618 p.; bibl.

Written entirely from Venezuelan sources, mostly secondary, with some reference to treaties between both countries. Contains texts of several treaties. Not pathfinding.

Perdereau-Blanchet, Liliane. L'évolution des investissements français au Venezuela, 1830–1970. See *HLAS 43:3409.*

2891 Petzoldt, Fania and **Jacinta Bevilacqua.** Nosotras también nos jugamos la vida. Caracas: Editorial Ateneo de Caracas, 1979. 446 p.; ill. (Colección F)

Based on interviews with 32 women, mostly middle class members of Acción Democrática, COPEI, or Partido Comunista who took part in resistance to Pérez Jiménez. Authors used interviews to show important roles played by Venezuelan women in political history of their nation.

2892 Rabe, Stephen G. The road to OPEC: United States relations with Venezuela, 1919–1976. Austin: University of Texas Press, 1982. 262 p.; bibl.; index (Texas Pan American series)

Careful analysis of diplomatic relations between US and Venezuela concerning oil, from the Gómez era until shortly after OPEC's establishment. Based extensively on US diplomatic archives. Placed in context of Good Neighbor, Alliance for Progress and aftermath.

2893 Ramírez Faría, Carlos. La democracia petrolera. Caracas: El Cid Editor, 1978. 359 p. (His De Rómulo Betancourt a Carlos Andrés Pérez; 1)

Vol. 1 of projected history of Venezuela, that will cover 1958–78 or from Betancourt to Pérez. Vol. 1 (1958–59), gives account of military involvement in overthrow of Pérez Jiménez and Betancourt's rise to power. Criticizes latter for having contributed to subdevelopment in 1959. Polemical but provocative treatment of Venezuelan politics, 1958–59.

Santander Laya, Gustavo and **Rafael Santander Garrido.** Los italianos: forjadores de la nacionalidad y del desarrollo económico de Venezuela. See *HLAS 43:8259.*

Silva, Carlos Rafael. Bosquejo histórico del desenvolvimento de la economía venezolana en el siglo XX. See *HLAS 43:3423.*

2894 El 23 [i.e. veintitrés] **de enero**: habla la conspiración. Agustín Blanco Muñoz, editor. Jovito Villalba *et al.,* contribuidores. Caracas: FACES-UCV: Ateneo, 1980. 421 p.; index; ports. (Testimonios violentos; 1)

Selected from over 500 taped interviews with leaders of political factions, military men, guerrillas, members of Unidades Tácticas de Combate, and others who participated in 23 Jan. 1958 movement that overthrew Pérez Jiménez. Gives focus to 1960s violence. Includes testimonies by Jovito Villalba, Martín Parda, José Vicente Azopardo, Hugo Trejo, Oscar Centeno, Wolfgang Larrazábal, Edgar Sanabria, Manuel Azuaje, Juan de Dios Moncada Vidal, Carlos Savelli Maldonado, and Diógenes Caballero.

2895 Velásquez, Ramón J. Aspectos de la evolución política de Venezuela en el último medio siglo (*in* Venezuela moderna, medio siglo de historia, 1926–1976. Ramón J. Velásquez *et al.* 2. ed. Caracas: Fundación Eugenio Mendoza: Editorial Ariel, 1979, p. 13–433 [Horas de Venezuela; 3])

Anecdotal, but well written essay on period from last 10 years of Gómez regime to Carlos Andres Pérez. Short synopses of each administration serve as introductions to each. Brief, mostly political comments on each period. Liberal in outlook, selects highlights and major issues faced by each government.

2896 ———; J. F. Sucre Figarella; and **Blas Bruni Celli.** Betancourt en la historia de Venezuela del siglo XX. Caracas: Ediciones Centauro, 1980. 381 p.; 92 p. of plates; bibl.; facsims.; ill.; ports.

Velásquez traces Betancourt's metamorphosis from Plan of Barranquilla to middle class leadership. Sympathetic survey of Betancourt's career and his role in Acción Democrática organization. Compares Betancourt to Cárdenas of Mexico as *máximo* leader of national movement. Betancourt's major contribution seen as organizing Venezuelan people into political parties. In separate essay, Sucre Figarella places Betancourt above Fidel Castro as important Latin American political thinker and reformer on grounds that Cuba has become more dependent than ever whereas Venezuela has become less. Blas Bruni Celli sees Betancourt as humanist who above all opposed corruption in government.

ECUADOR

Bromley, Rosemary D. F. Change in the ethnic composition of populations of central highland Ecuador. See item **2642.**

2897 ———. The role of commerce in the growth of towns in central highland Ecuador, 1750–1920 (in International Congress of Americanists, 43d, Vancouver, Canada, 1979. Proceedings. Section 7. Urbanization in the Americas: the background in comparative perspective; the process of urbanization. Edited by Woodrow Borah, Jorge Hardoy and Gilbert A. Stelter. Ottawa: History Division, National Museum of Man, 1980, p. 25–34, maps, tables)

Excellent quantitative analysis of role played by commerce in differential urban development of Latacunga, Ambato and Riobamba in Ecuadorian sierra during late colonial and national periods. Especially concerned with reasons why Ambato displaced Riobamba as most important of three cities [M. T. Hamerly]

Federico González Suárez y la polémica sobre el Estado laico. See item **7588.**

2898 Goncharov, Valerian. Ecuador, tierra y hombres. Guayaquil: Casa del la Cultura Ecuatoriana, Núcleo del Guayas, 1979. 144 p. (Colección Nuestramérica)

Essays by Russian historian, who has researched Eloy Alfaro period. Treats role of Indians in Liberal Revolution and Alfaro's position on Cuban Independence, among other more general topics.

2899 Guerrero, Andrés. Los oligarcas del cacao: ensayo sobre la acumulación originaria en el Ecuador: hacendados cacaoteros, banqueros, exportadores y comerciantes en Guayaquil (1890). Quito: Editorial El Conejo, 1980. 101 p.; bibl.; map.

Marxist analysis of 1890–1910 formation of cacao oligarchy on coastal Ecuador. Argues that production of cacao did not create rural proletariat of campesinos nor clear-cut bourgeoisie, rather it made campesinos dependent upon landowners, who in turn developed ties with world capitalist system through Guayaquil bankers and merchants. Latter two gave cacao interests their national character.

Hamerly, Michael T. Archives of Cuenca. See item **2647.**

2900 Hurtado, Oswaldo. El poder político en el Ecuador. 4. ed., actualizada. Barcelona: Ariel, 1981. 356 p.; bibl. (Nuestro siglo por dentro)

Shows how ruling class' hacienda-based control remained unchallenged until 1950s. But even though export sector determined course of nation's economy, Hurtado rejects dependency as major cause of underdevelopment. Points out that masses have remained unmobilized and weak, and that reforms adopted since 1930s have been work of intellectuals and technocrats who used state powers to push reforms behind backs of entrenched elites. First published in 1979, this is one of best studies of country available in English: *Political power in Ecuador* (Albuquerque: University of New Mexico, 1980).

2901 Moncayo, Pedro. El Ecuador de 1825 y 1875, sus hombres, sus instituciones y sus leyes. Quito: Editorial Casa de la Cultura Ecuatoriana, 1979. 2 v.; ill.

Written by 19th-century intellectual shortly before his death in 1888 and following destruction of his archives and library by fire and at time when he could no longer see. Consists of eyewitness account of Ecuador's 19th-century growth by one who fled to Chile from 1860–75 escaping García Moreno.

2902 Moreno Yánez, Segundo E. *El Formulario de las ordenanzas de indios*: una regulación de las relaciones laborales del Quito colonial y republicano (IAA, 5 : 3, 1979, p. 228–241, bibl.)

Published 1851 *Formulario de las ordenanzas de indios* or schedule of salaries to be paid different kinds of Indian laborers in *obrajes* (textile sweatshops). Said *ordenanzas* were virtual restatement of those by Juan de Luja y Bedia, Fiscal of Quito Audiencia and Protector General de Naturales, in 1730s. If so, these wage regulations replace Matias de Peralta's of 1621 (see item **2655**). [M. T. Hamerly]

2903 Pareja y Díez Canseco, Alfredo. Ecuador, la república de 1830 a nuestros días. 6. ed. corr. y aumentada. Quito: Editorial Universitaria, 1979. 557 [i.e. 549] p.; bibl.; index.

Organizes 19th century into four periods, each dominated by a great figure: Flores, Rocafuerte, García Moreno, and Alfaro. Highlights 20th-century political history, politicians, and major national issues. Also includes short review of cultural developments and constitutional evolution. Useful for general information.

2904 Roberts, Lois Crawford de. El Ecuador en la época cacaotera: repuestas locales al auge y colapso en el ciclo monoexportador. Translated by Erika Silva and Rafael Quintero. Quito: Editorial Universitaria, 1980. 276 p.; appendixes; bibl.; tables.

Translation of author's Ph.D. dissertation. Traces rise and fall of cacao production between 1890–1925 on Ecuadorian coast, and subsequent impact upon Ecuador's entry into world economy. Deals with cultural as well as economic and political consequences of cacao economy.

2905 Rosero Ravelo, Luis Alberto. Memorias de un veterano de la Guerra del

41. Quito: Editorial Casa de la Cultura Ecuatoriana, 1978. 117 p.

Memories of veteran of 1941 war with Peru. Defends glory of his cavalry group. Paints Peru as aggressor and Ecuador as seeker of arbitration. Most fighting consisted of air attacks and skirmishes. Ecuadorians were outnumbered 10 to one, but held on well. Argues that Ecuadorian troops did well in defending the patria from invasion.

2906 Vasco de Escudero, Grecia. Directorio ecuatoriano de archivos. Quito: Instituto Panamericano de Geografía e Historia, Sección Nacional del Ecuador, 1979. 163 p.; ill. (Biblioteca Ecuador)

Directory of episcopal and some parish, provincial, municipal, colegial, other administrative, and historical archives, and some private collections in the provinces. Includes useful information on physical volume, longevity and nature of holdings, but not altogether accurate as based on responses to questionnaire (see also *HLAS 40:3189*). [M. T. Hamerly]

Peru

VINCENT C. PELOSO, *Associate Professor of History, Howard University*

DURING THE PAST DECADE these introductory essays have recorded a notable surge in the publication of Peruvian history. The works reviewed were largely the result of research by enthusiastic, well trained scholars, and they have ranged over a wide variety of topics. National and regional politics and economics, Peruvian relations with the US, with world capitalism, and with neighboring republics, agrarian reform and rural society, provincial elites and the ruling class, the military, the Church, 19th and 20th centuries, and biography, each subject in its turn has warranted attention as a focal point of professional interest among specialists.

In the search for outstanding accomplishments and significant trends in this flood of literature, some themes overshadow others and their dominance has resulted in a mainstream of Peruvian historiography very different from the one that was identifiable only a dozen years ago. Meanwhile, the intellectual struggle that was a feature of the new mainstream resulted in a corpus of studies that sustains a high level of consistency and professional value. This literature required unwavering scholarly commitment and institutionalization of the training process for historians, grants, contacts with Peruvianists elsewhere and similar activities. The founding of new journals like *Allpanchis, Análisis,* and *Histórica,* complemented the established historical periodicals and testified to the altered scope of historical interests. Only *Histórica* could be considered strictly historical among the three periodicals and even at that its scope reflects the widest dimensions of the field.

Another source of institutional support for historical research in Peru is a product of faculty interest in the major universities of Lima, particularly the Universidad Mayor de San Marcos, the Universidad Pontificia Católica, the Universidad del Pacífico, and the Universidad Agraria La Molina, to cite the best known, who along with their counterparts in Andean centers of learning conduct periodic workshops on general problems in the field. Led by the highly respected Instituto de Estudios Peruanos and the interdisciplinary faculties in the capital, workshops arose from the ashes of civilian political struggles in the 1960s and the subsequent "decenio," as Luis Pásara called it. In this thoughtful characterization of the dozen-year military regime, Pásara joined other well known Peruvian scholars in a wide-ranging 12-volume *Historia del Perú* (item **2949**) to provide rich evidence of the current "state of the art" in the heartland of the Andes.

The scholars who organized these seedbeds circulate the results in mimeograph form. These reports often consist of chapters of theses or independent projects. Many of them land eventually in the Library of Congress. Were it not for the workshops, scholars outside Peru could monitor trends only through dense communication networks or through close ties with the institutions that nurture historical scholarship. Further institutional support comes from libraries, archives and the example set by previous generations. The respective staffs of the Biblioteca Nacional and the Archivo General de la Nación which served as models for that of the Archivo del Fuero Agrario. Once thought to be stillborn, the new archive is now, thanks to pressures from the scholarly community and a bit of government support, leading a precarious life. In recent years other archives, ministerial and provincial, have opened their doors with fruitful results. Finally, the enthusiasm and determination of a number of publishers, despite critical shortages of basic technical and cash support, facilitate the dissemination of historical works. Together these institutions deserve a share of the credit for the attention Peruvian historiography receives far beyond the limits of this specialty.

Publications reviewed for this biennium amply reinforce the developments of the past decade. Between institutions and publishers on the one hand, and scholarly drive on the other, more studies were received at the Library of Congress in the last two years than ever before, and more of them contribute to the advancement of Peruvian historiography than was ever the case, developments that necessitated a corresponding tightening of priorities. On the whole, a work is annotated below if it exploits new archives or old archives in new ways; if it refreshes a tired theme or shifts the focus of ideas on a predictable subject; if it introduces to specialists a new scholar in the field; or if it signals new work by a veteran historian.

The research preoccupations of new mainstream historians stimulate these categories. From debates on social and economic problems has arisen a preoccupation with the cultural history of Peru, no mean step in the formation of national self-consciousness. This change promises some difficult and yet dimly perceived problems ahead. It can, for example, lead to sharper definition and greater consciousness of the sources of tension within Peruvian culture. In the past decade, some of its dimensions have crystallized.

The War of the Pacific (1879–83) offers an excellent example of the outlines of self-consciousness in Peru. Far from fading away as a subject for historians, its centennial reawakened old antagonisms that sent academics scurrying for the archives. On the one hand, the immediacy of the war is reflected in the exploitative centenary reprinting of old standards, exemplified by the reissue of Mariano Felipe

Paz Soldán's *Narración histórica de la guerra de Chile contra Perú y Bolivia* (item **2969**), one of several of this type; and after many years lying in the dust, the sudden appearance of Pardo y Barreda (item **2968**) on the open character of the so-called "secret" treaty between Peru and Bolivia. Centennial reflections predictably occasioned a restatement of the military view that equates civilian rule with national disaster, citing Nicolás de Piérola's hastily organized defense of Lima in 1880 as the glaring instance. To protest this view, defenders of the civilian caudillo, such as Lopez Martínez (item **2956**), sharpen not their tongues as in the old days but their search for contrary evidence.

The coastwise war also recalls the debate over the competency of Peru's 19th-century leadership and awakens this issue as part of the mainstream restructuring process. New biographies expose the weaknesses of leadership as well as the special qualities of leaders far earlier in the republican era, as demonstrated in the detailed study of Agustín Gamarra by Horacio Villanueva Urteaga (item **2999**), and in a brief but provocative essay by Jeffrey Kaliber (item **2952**), whose insights into the tortuous path trod by independence era priests to keep the Church both whole and Peruvian is a model of clarity and insight. Journalist Guillermo Thorndike contributed immeasurably to the new image of society by presenting old photos as a collective self-portrait with palpable results (item **2993**).

Examination of the culture of Peru signifies that a special moment has arrived: Peruvianists are avidly picking apart the brains of the past, from the broadbrush efforts by Flores Galindo and Burga (item **2920**) to probe the economic and ideological crises managed by the new bourgeoisie at the turn of the 20th century, to Basadre's testing of the same group's sources of electoral control (item **2911**). But far and away the most exciting sign of the emergence of intellectual history is the growing attention devoted to José Carlos Mariátegui, Peru's autodidactic culture interpreter and ideologist whose premature death at age 30 foreshortened the reach of his ideas. Or so it seemed. Although a frequent object of study since his death, Mariátegui is now looked at from every angle in a horde of articles and books. Moreover, he has influenced Peruvian historiography in a number of ways. A trio of outstanding works by Julio Cotler's *Clases, estado y nación* (item **2931**), Steven Stein's *Populism in Peru* (items **2988** and **2989**), and José A. Tamayo Herrera's *Historia del indigenismo cuzqueño* (item **2991**), all reflect Mariátegui's influence.

Though very dissimilar in approach and style, together these works represent the best recent efforts in the field for the manner in which they portray the contours of the new mainstream of Peruvian historical scholarship. Each in its way contributes to the debate over Peruvian culture and to an understanding of its 20th-century development, and each is influenced to some extent by ideas Mariátegui formulated. Cotler, the historical sociologist, probes the rising political tensions between the oligarchy, peasants and workers in the context of imperialism, searching for the sources of anti-imperialist ideology in Mariátegui's Communist Party of Peru, APRA, and their epigones. In his monograph, Stein sifted through interviews, a half dozen archives and contemporary periodicals to learn what glue kept the two social poles, oligarchy and masses, from flying apart in the critical years 1930–33. He concludes that a paternalistic tradition manifested itself in the major political movements, Aprismo and Sanchezcerrismo, after Mariátegui's death. Tamayo Herrera, the least willing of the three analysts to focus on class antagonisms, depicts a far more firmly rooted intellectual tradition connecting *indigenismo* (nativism) and a recent phenomenon he labels *neoindigenismo*, than heretofore has been portrayed. Interestingly, he demonstrates that this tradition is formed in large part by protest against domination by the European-oriented, ruling class culture, and thereby he opens the door to greater understanding of the role of intellectuals in the relationship between culture and class leadership in Peru.

Add to these the appearance of a work that forms a welcome point of departure for study of the role of women in the formation of Peruvian culture by Prieto de Zegarra (item **2972**) and an astringent analysis of the military regime by Henry Pease García (item **2970**) that incisively scrutinizes its contribution to the formation of the Peruvian state, and there can be no other conclusion but that in this installment fecundity hardly seems an adequate word to describe the new mainstream of historical scholarship on Peru.

Agricultura en el Perú, a XX [i.e. siglo veinte]: documentos. See *HLAS 43:3499*.

2907 Arroyo Posadas, Moisés. La correspondencia de José Carlos Mariátegui a Jauja (IPA/A, 14:16, 1980, p. 61–74)

Acting as informant, author, a Jauja intellectual active in cultural movements early in this century, summarizes experiences that led him toward important correspondence with Mariátegui. Reprints 1929 exchange of letters that shows how strongly Mariátegui maintained his ties with Andean movements and intellectuals of that era.

2908 Balbi, Carmen Rosa. El Partido Comunista y el APRA en la crisis revolucionaria de los años treinta. Lima: G. Herrera, 1980. 154 p.; bibl.; ill.

Explores why APRA became mass political party and Communist Party did not. Uses government statistics, periodical literature, broadsides, pamphlets, theoretical works and recent studies. Examines economic conditions under Leguía, ties with UK and US, growth of popular discontent in 1920s, workers confederation, discontent of petit-bourgeoisie and peasant movement, 1930s activities of the three mass parties, concluding that fault lay with tactics of Communist Party leaders, especially its relations with Comintern.

2909 —— and **Laura Madalengoitia.** Parlamento y lucha política, Perú, 1932. Lima: Centro de Estudios y Promoción del Desarrollo, 1980. 199 p.

Employs congressional debates for 1931, established newspapers and scarce periodicals issued by political parties, and recent studies to set conditions in Peru that made constituent congress of 1932 so important. Studies actions of constituent body that led to political confrontation resulting in expulsion of Aprista delegates. Rather than fade away, APRA became more belligerent as oligarchy's power was preserved in Constitution. Parliament became "resonator" of political struggle, Sánchez Cerro's assassination brought further disaster and oligarchy consolidated dominion when Trujillo uprising was smashed. Only at this point could congress discuss individual guarantees and other such concerns.

2910 Ballón Lozada, Héctor. Arequipa y la guerra con Chile, 1879. Arequipa: s.n., 1979. 73 p.; bibl.; maps.

Brief, not well documented, descriptive essay on official reaction to Chileans in important regional center. Unfortunately, it makes only casual use of local newspapers and reflects no archival digging.

2911 Basadre, Jorge. Elecciones y centralismo en el Perú: apuntes para un esquema histórico. Lima: Centro de Investigación de la Universidad del Pacífico, 1980. 172 p.; bibl.; appendix.

With typical breadth of vision, author finds that democratization of the vote during the "república aristocrática," was acceeded to by the oligarchy while they cheapened its meaning and removed its effectiveness by institutional means. Electoral decentralization resulted in greater power for local landlords down to 1929. Appendix includes annotated bibliography on history of vote in Peru and discussion of value of congressional debates.

2912 ——. La multitud, la ciudad y el campo en la historia del Perú: con un colofón sobre el país profundo. 3. ed. Lima: Ediciones Treintaitrés & Mosca Azul Editores, 1980. 257 p.; bibl.

Work (first ed. 1929) sets out late author's initial ideas. Marked him as imaginative cultural historian and prefigured breadth of his later interests. Volume also retains original notes and 1941 postscript.

2913 ———. La vida y la historia: ensayos sobre personas, lugares y problemas. 2. ed. rev. y aum. Lima: Industrial Gráfica, 1981. 726 p.; bibl.; port.

Edition expanded beyond that of 1975 (see *HLAS 40:3488*) by addition of materials in major sections. Otherwise, its chief advantage is its relatively inexpensive, soft-cover format in contrast with earlier version.

2914 Benoit de Velazco, Beatriz. El ideario anarquista y su penetración en el área rural: informe de investigación. La Molina, Peru: Universidad Nacional Agraria, Departamento de Ciencias Humanas, Taller de Estudios Andinos, 1980. 76 p.; bibl. (Serie Movimientos sociales; no. 6)

Studies turn-of-the-century rise of anarchist ideology among workers on central coast plantations. Pinpoints stages of growing sophistication through period journals. Concludes that anarchists were among first to organize workers, paving way for later socialist efforts.

Bernales B., Enrique. Origen y evolución de la universidad en el Perú. See *HLAS 43:4534*.

2915 Blanchard, Peter. The recruitment of workers in the Peruvian sierra at the turn of the century: the *enganche* system (IAMEA, 33:3, Winter 1979, p. 63–83, appendix)

Attacks assumption that *enganche* was harmful and exploitative by suggesting that its endurance was based on self interest among all parties—state, landlords, and peasants. Uses AFA materials, Peruvian Corporation papers, Biblioteca Nacional documents, and especially newspaper accounts of early 20th-century to cite advantages of wage labor under *enganche* for Indians. Asserts that wages and short-term employment were attractive and that fights and strikes diminished after World War I reforms. Concludes *enganche* slowed Peruvian development but also channeled Indians into modern economy.

Bonilla, Heraclio. The new profile of Peruvian history. See item **2663**.

2916 ———. Un siglo a la deriva: ensayos sobre el Perú, Bolivia y la guerra. Lima: Instituto de Estudios Peruanos, 1980.

236 p.; bibl. (Serie Estudios históricos; 7)

Brings together essays published 1968–79, developing context for understanding relations between Peruvian state and the forces that shaped War of the Pacific. Essay on Bolivia summarizes literature that demonstrates rise of its export-oriented economy. Extensive statistical data throughout.

2917 ——— and **Alejandro Rabanal**. La hacienda San Nicolás, Supe, y la Primera Guerra Mundial (PUCP/E, 2:3, junio 1979, p. 3–47, tables)

Notes quick enslavement of Peruvian economy under foreign pressure between War of the Pacific and World War I, and sees it as erratic process. Wild swings of fortune and destitution were created by World War I demand. War's inflation hurt rural wage workers. Studies production of coast sugar hacienda to understand relations between market and productive structure of export plantation economy. Examines Chancay valley plantation: account books, labor force, capital, technology, investment procedures before World War I. Finds that despite low rises in production, profit margins rose dramatically.

2918 Breve antología del pensamiento anarquista en el Perú. Compilador, Manuel Torres. La Molina: Taller de Estudios Andinos, Departamento de Ciencias Humanas, Universidad Nacional Agraria, 1979. 171 p.; bibl. (Serie Movimientos sociales; no. 3) (Informe de investigación - TEA, Universidad Nacional Agraria)

Anthology drawn from contemporary periodicals of apogee period of anarcho-syndicalist thought in Peru (1890–1930). Questions view that migrants to cities from countryside were proletarianized. Illustrates point with effective extracts from reviews and periodicals. Helpful point of departure.

2919 Burga, Manuel. La hacienda en el Perú, 1850–1930: evidencias y métodos (Tierra y Sociedad [Revista del Archivo del Fuero Agraria, Lima] 1:1, abril 1978, p. 9–38, tables)

Uses Pablo Macera's *Las plantaciones azucareras en el Perú, 1821–1875* (1975, see *HLAS 38:3483*) to raise questions about social relations of production in African slavery on Peruvian plantations and various forms of controlled labor that followed it on export sugar and cotton properties. Ends with effort to formulate an economic theory of the Peruvian hacienda (1850–1930). Extended, thoughtful review essay.

2920 ——— and **Alberto Flores Galindo.**
Apogeo y crisis de la República Aristocrática: oligarquía, aprismo y comunismo en el Peru, 1895–1932. 2. ed. Lima: Ediciones Rikchay Perú, 1981. 235 p.; bibliographical essays; graphs (Ediciones Rikchay Perú; no. 8)

Extensive readings provide ideas for assessing conditions under which oligarchy attempted to achieve political domination by consensus, effort that failed when workers movement led by intellectuals came to life to oppose an oligarchic consensus until 1930s crisis led to 1932 electoral confrontation. Pt. 1 contains discussion of economic changes that spurred agricultural export modernization; pt. 2 concentrates on oligarchy's ideology and Andean mass uprising of 1919–22, and Leguiista "new fatherland" ideology that opposed combination of *gamonalismo* with export capitalism; pt. 3 notes spread of mass movement. A bold interpretation.

2921 ——— and **Wilson Reátegui.** Lanas y capital mercantil en el sur: la casa Ricketts, 1895–1935. Lima: Instituto de Estudios Peruanos, 1981. 215 p.; appendixes; bibl.; tables (Serie Estudios históricos; 9)

Use of records of major British wool merchandising house in Arequipa make study a classic testing ground of dependency theory. Divided into three parts: 1) examines relationship between world market and growth of Ricketts House; 2) discusses social structure of marketing; and 3) analyzes national Peruvian market and slow turnover of capital in the wool marketing business. Major, challenging study of modernization of traditional, pastoral industry in Peru. Distinct emphasis on history of capital rather than history of labor.

2922 Caivano, Tomaso. Historia de la guerra de América entre Chile, Perú y Bolivia. v. 1, Causas aparentes y verdaderas de la guerra. v. 2, Campañas naval y terrestre. La dictadura de De Pierola. Rendición de Lima. v. 3, Bolivia. El Perú después de las batallas de San Juan y Miraflores. Lima: Lima S.A., 1979. 3 v.

Reprint of Spanish translation of 1881 work by Italian consul in Lima. Translation

of *Stória della guerra d'America fra il Chili, il Perú e la Bolivia.* Constitutes one of small group of narratives on Tripartite War by uncommitted foreign observers sympathetic to region and its problems (others were Clement Markham and Jacinto López), and is considered rather reliable for that reason. Takes action through Battles of San Juan and Miraflores and truce between Chile and Bolivia.

2923 Caravedo Molinari, Baltazar. Desarrollo desigual, movilización popular y conducción burguesa (*in* Congreso Peruano del Hombre y la Cultura Andina, 3d, Lima, 1977. El hombre y la cultura andina [see *HLAS 43:253*] v. 4, p. 559–574)

Unequal capitalist development made possible emergence of Arequipa bourgeois faction with capacity to propose ideological program different from that of other bourgeois sectors. Leadership of 1950 popular movement in Arequipa was captured by regional bourgeoisie, after which ensuing civil war resulting in 200 deaths. Uses periodicals, censuses, official publications and interviews with participants. Finds capitalism weaker than elsewhere in Peru, paternalism stronger, and political alliances among opposing parties more easily formed. Cautions against hasty generalization about regional-national relationships in Peru.

2924 ———. Estado, pesca y burguesía, 1939–1973: teoría y realidad. Lima: Centro de Proyección Cristiana, 1979. 196 p.; bibl.; tables.

In continuing effort to understand social dimensions and behavior of the Peruvian bourgeoisie, author studies rise of fishing industry (1939–59). Export value of the industry increased after 1960 and monopoly of capital set in as consequences of periodic crisis. "Fishing" means commercial anchovies and locale is Chancay valley coast. Sources: public ministry materials, periodicals, official reports, etc.

2925 Cárdenas Sánchez, Inés L. Biografía y campañas del Gran Mariscal del Perú Andrés A. Cáceres en el centenario de la Guerra del Pacífico, 1879–1883. Lima: Editora Lima, S.A., 1979. 97 p.; ill.; map.

Dutifully and eulogistically recounts each major episode in the life of the most successful Peruvian general of the War of the Pacific for the benefit of the young. Cites standard sources. Definitely not definitive.

2926 Carlessi, Carolina. Primeras luchas del proletariado rural en el Norte: valles de Huaura-Sayán, 1916–1917 (in Congreso Peruano del Hombre y la Cultura Andina, 3d, Lima, 1977. El hombre y la cultura andina [see *HLAS 43:253*] v. 3, p. 401–412)

Contends that day laborers' efforts to organize around wage issues, prompted by jumps in basic prices during World War I, constituted first attempts to organize rural proletariat on coast into labor unions. Heavy reprisals were followed by wage raises when workers' protests against murder and other abuses subsided. Intellectuals of *El Tiempo* supported workers throughout. Described as major source of anarcho-syndicalist thought in Peru, periodical's editor at time was José Carlos Mariátegui.

2927 Carmelino Seijas, Ernesto. Batalla del Zarumilla: 1er. Escuadrón del Regimiento de Caballería No. 5, objetivo Chacras, día 24–julio–1941. Lima: s.n., 1977. 113 p.; 2 leaves of plates; maps.

Documents submitted to sustain Peruvian argument concerning 1941 attack and takeover of village on Río Zarumilla. Claims that attack was made in civilized and orderly fashion and that author was under orders designed to counter view that action was impulsive and unprovoked. Documents consist largely of testimonial letters from author's peers. Of limited value.

2928 Carrillo Rodríguez, Alberto. Luis Pardo, El Gran Bandido. 2 ed. Lima: Imprenta y Encuadernación Yaraví 394, 1976. 252 p.; ill.

Impassioned plea for a turn-of-the-century rebel active in Chiquián region, Ancashs Dept. cattle raising region with strong ties to coastal plantations. Wrongly accused of murder and banditry, Pardo was considered Inca by local peasants, and according to legend played Robin Hood role until trapped and killed by government troops. Work lacks framework to place folkloric quality of the subject in useful context. Author insists Pardo had no ideology and was accused of being an anarchist.

2929 Castro Pozo, Hildebrando. Nuestra comunidad indígena. Prólogo a la segunda edición de Rodrigo Montoya. 2. ed. Lima: Perugraph Editores, S.A., 1979. 344 p.

Republication of classic study by outstanding Peruvian self-proclaimed lawyer-cum-ethnographer, writer, and 20th-century socialist politician. Includes prologue by Rodrigo Montoya who reminds readers that Castro Pozo was leading proponent of protective laws for sharecroppers during World War II. Indispensable for study of ideology of the Indian community and of indigenista movement.

2930 Chirinos Lizares, Guido and Enrique Chirinos Soto. El septenato, 1968– 1975. 2. ed. Lima: Editorial Alfa, 1977. 560 p.; bibl.; ill.; index.

Skimpy documentation accompanies angrily-written text dedicated to proposition that Velasco *golpe* of 3 Oct. 1968, and ensuing regime undermined Peruvian tradition so adequately represented by Fernando Belaúnde Terry's government. Surveys each of major political crises of the Velasco era. Handy rogue's gallery of photos composed of principal figures of Velasco years makes this handy reference work for author's particular point of view.

2931 Cotler, Julio. Clases, Estado y Nación en el Perú. Lima: Instituto de Estudios Peruano, 1978. 407 p.; bibl.; graphs (Perú problema; 17)

Wide-ranging essay in historical sociology applies Haya's and Mariátegui's analyses of Peruvian society in order to judge the validity of the 1968–78 military government. Concludes that the political process inaugurated by it was facilitated by a prolongation of colonialism in economic and social relations. This combination prevented social cohesion and resolution of antagonisms. A disciplined, thoughtful survey of central features of historic Peruvian underdevelopment. Overly schematic, but a formidable point of departure for future historical study of state and society in republican Peru.

2932 Davies, Thomas M., Jr. A teaching guide to the history of republican Peru, 1826–1980 (The History Teacher [Society for History Education, California State University, Long Beach] 14:3, May 1981, p. 361–386)

Provides outline of course along with basic resources for course in history of Peru, emphasizing theme of Peruvian cultural clash and amalgamation. Unfortunately, title was misprinted, conveying impression that subject ends in 1890 instead of 1980. Thoughtful outline and accompanying bibliography carry major theme through election of 1980 and Haya's death. Lists Spanish and English sources that are accessible in major university libraries. Very useful.

2933 Degregori, Carlos Iván; Mariano Valderrama; Augusta Alfajume; and Marfil Franck Ballve. Indigenismo, clases sociales y problema nacional: la discusión sobre el "problema indígena" en el Perú. Lima: Ediciones CELATS, 1978. 251 p.

Four authors write five provocative, ambitious essays of historical topics: 1) exploration of class conflict and national cohesion; 2) discussion of turn-of-the-century agrarian question and so-called Indian problem; 3) study of right wing thinkers in early 20th-century; 4) Cuzco indigenista movement; and dialogue between Mariátegui and Haya on indigenista and national questions: and 5) restatement of indigenista question after 1930. Last is called neoindigenismo.

2934 Documentos para la historia del campesinado peruano, siglo XX. Wilson Reátegui Chávez, editor. Lima: Universidad Nacional Mayor de San Marcos, Departamento Académico de Ciencias Histórico-Sociales, 1978. 140 p.; bibl. (Ediciones Kallpa; no. 1)

Volume of documents reflects interest of young historians from "Centro de Investigaciones Historicas-Kallpa" in historic struggles of peasants at regional and national levels, largely in Andean south. Includes contemporary studies, eyewitness and newspaper accounts and official reports from variety of sources, archival, public and private for 1904–32, covering Puno, Cuzco, and Huancavelica areas. Useful point of departure.

Falcón, Jorge. Amauta, polémica y acción de Mariátegui. See item **7586.**

2935 Flores Galindo, Alberto. La agonía de Mariátegui: la polémica con la Komintern. Lima: DESCO, 1980. 134 p.; bibl.

Puzzled by articulation of Marxism and nationalism, upon his return from Europe in 1923 until his death in 1930, Mariátegui plunged into the debate raging between the Comintern Latin American intellectuals on this question. He lived the issue but wrote no known definite essay. Agony refers to his struggle to accomplish this task. Makes use of new notes and letters from his

papers and many sources (archives, interviews, etc.) including good essay on them.

2936 ——; Orlando Plaza; and Teresa Oré. Notas sobre oligarquía y capitalismo en Arequipa, 1870–1940 (in Congreso Peruano del Hombre y la Cultura Andina, 3d, Lima, 1977. El hombre y la cultura andina [see HLAS 43:253] v. 4, p. 523–537)

Report of research project examines character of Peru's 20th-century ruling class. Uses southern highlands case to illustrate appearance of fissures among merchants, landlords and other identifiable socioeconomic interests. Concludes that Arequipa's oligarchy is "class in transition." Based on Arequipa's notarial materials and municipal library though references are not specific (see also Flores Galindo's Arequipa y el sur andino, HLAS 40:3515).

2937 ——; and ——. Oligarquía y capital comercial en el sur peruano, 1870–1930: informe preliminar. Lima: Departamento de Ciencias Sociales, P.U.C., 1977. 60 p.; bibl.

Proposes to reopen debate on character of dominant class in contemporary Peru by examining Andean south where single ruling class has been dominant since end of 19th-century. Authors contrast this wool merchant oligarchy with that of north coast sugar plantations and find that wool merchants' search for labor was easy by comparison. They could not improve technology, cultivate pasturage or force wages onto peasants until third decade of 20th century. Power of southern oligarchy was based on complicated network of alliances, a fragile structure which kept area backward despite—or rather because of—its links with world market.

2938 Flores Marín, José A. Lucha de clases en la explotación del caucho (in Congreso Peruano del Hombre y la Cultura Andina, 3d, Lima, 1977. El hombre y la cultura andina [see HLAS 43:253] v. 3, p. 413–423, table)

Report of research on local officials and labor during rubber boom era dominated by foreign-owned Tambopata Rubber Syndicate and problems encountered (e.g., resistance, flight, strikes, attacks upon gathering gangs by primitive tribes, etc.) which led to company's abandonment of region. Based on company's papers located in Archivo del

Fuero Agrario. Despite title, class struggle depicted seems inchoate.

2939 Flores Ochoa, Jorge A. and **Abraham Valencia E.** Rebeliones indígenas, quechuas y aymaras: homenaje al bicentenario de la rebelión campesina de Thupa Amaro, 1780–1980. Cuzco: Centro de Estudios Andinos Cuzco, 1980. 154 p.; bibl.

Studies of peasant uprisings (1900–30) in southern Andean Peru demonstrate that Tupac Amaru's spirit is vibrant. Magnus Mörner's essay on Tupac Amaru rebellion suggests that loss of life in rebellion was not as great as assumed. Flores Ochoa's essay and Palacio Ríos' on Chichillapa refer to 1901 shepherd's rebellion; Valencia Espinoza's describes 1921 movement in Canas; and Orlove's analyzes 1931 Espinar province uprising. Basic documentation for 20th-century studies is oral testimony.

2940 Franco, Carlos. El nacionalismo andino (IPA/A, 14:16, 1980, p. 19–44)

Studies Luis Valcárcel, activist-anthropologist, author of *Tempestad en los Andes* (1927), articles in *Amauta* (1926–30), and later studies, reflecting his preoccupation with Andean pre-Conquest ideology. Examines his turn to theme of title and growing relationship with Mariátegui. Unfortunately, original documentation was left out when article was published.

2941 García Salvatecci, Hugo. El anarquismo frente al marxismo y el Perú. Lima: Mosca Azul Editores, 1972. 126 p.; bibl.

Having published one study of Manuel González Prada and another of his anarchism (winner of national prize), author of this slim volume surveys here major philosophical clashes of both schools of thought. Makes use of traditional anarchist literature and some of Gonzalez Prada's published writings. Of introductory value.

2942 ———. Haya de la Torre o el marxismo indoamericano. Lima: Editora María Ramírez V., 1980. 264 p.; bibl.; notes.

Links Haya to anarcho-syndicalist tradition, including ideological precursor such as Manuel González Prada. Examines relations of APRA and Marxism, and relations between Haya and Mariátegui. Concludes with examination of Aprista program. Study of theory. For philosopher's comment, see item **7591**.

2943 ———. Sorel y Mariátegui. Lima: Enrique Delgado Editor, 1979. 276 p.; bibl.; notes.

Argues that Mariátegui's theoretical master was not Marx but Georges Sorel. Examines break between Mariátegui and Haya and asserts that former's views were influenced less by Antonio Gramsci's than by Trotsky's (e.g., validity of general strike as purifying agent of society and unifying agent of working class). No mention of Peruvian thinkers who influenced Mariátegui.

2944 Gardiner, C. Harvey. Pawns in a triangle of hate: the Peruvian Japanese and the United States. Seattle: University of Washington Press, 1981. 222 p.; bibl.; index.

Sequel to author's earlier work (see *HLAS 38:3472*) studies World War II deportation and internment program of Peru's Japanese community in cooperation with parallel actions in US. Finds that many Peruvian Japanese who were deported from Peru never returned after war; either they stayed in US or went to Japan. Based largely on US National Archives records (RG 59), INS files and interviews. Monograph weaves cultural prejudices and diplomatic history. Little examination of problem's economic aspects.

2945 Gonzales, Michael J. Capitalist agriculture and labour contracting in northern Peru, 1880–1905 (JLAS, 12:2, Nov. 1980, p. 291–315, appendix, maps)

Argues that labor contracting system on north coast combined coercion and wage incentives by focusing on one plantation in Lambayeque dept. Suggests poverty and social chaos were reasons highlanders migrated to coastal valley. Describes coercion to keep them in the plantations by means such as wages, physical force, vigilantism. Concludes by noting importance of market incentives in labor system, and asserts that *enganche* reflected marketplace demands. Makes extensive and effective use of AFA plantation records.

2946 La Guerra con Chile en sus documentos. Compilador, Fernando Lecaros Villavisencio. Diseño de la carátula, Jesús Ruíz Durand. 2. ed., ampliada. Lima: Ediciones Rikchay Perú, 1979. 216 p.; ill. (Rikchay Perú; no. 6)

Includes documents on 1833 statement by Chilean Diego Portales on Chile's need to dominate South Pacific chronology of important treaties and diplomatic events prior to 1879 Chilean declaration of war. Other documents concern naval campaigns, peace negotiations, etc. Portrays conflict's impact on Peru's common foot soldier and citizen. The War of the Pacific documented as social history.

2947 Haya de la Torre, Víctor Raúl. Obras completas. Diseño gráfico, José Bracamonte. Lima: Librería-Editorial J. Mejía Baca, 1976/1977. 7 v.; bibl.; port.

Vol. 1 of several brings together Haya's essays, speeches, letters, newspaper articles and other works (e.g., *Por la emancipación de América Latina,* 1927; *Ideario y acción Aprista,* 1931; and *Teoría y táctica del Aprismo,* 1931). Includes compilers' succinct biographical essay, and explanatory notes and footnotes describing circumstances under which a particular item was written. Nothing new or surprising except compilers are all longtime associates of Haya and cofounders of APRA.

2948 Heysen, Luis E. Temas y obras del Perú a la verdad por los hechos. 2. ed. Lima: E. Bracamonte Vera, 1975. 434 p.; bibl.; ill.

Selections from author's essays (1931–69) on APRA's history involving this key leader and covering topics such as: "continuing" Aprista revolution, agrarian reform and law, democratization of Peruvian law, etc. Important because of materials for APRA history and as introduction to a leading Aprista's mind.

2949 Historia del Perú. t. 6/7, Perú republicano. t. 8, Perú republicano y procesos e instituciones. t. 9/12, Procesos e instituciones. Lima: Editorial J. Mejía Baca, 1980. 12 v.; bibl.; ill. (some col.)

Multi-authored, topical history of republican Peru displays continuing interests of traditionally-trained Peruvian scholars as well as those of historians who more recently entered the field. Vol. 7: Jorge Basadre, Percy Cayo and Ernesto Yepes del Castillo on war with Chile and early 20th-century economy; v. 8: synthesis of literature of republican era and interpretive piece by Baltazar Caravedo Molinari on production, labor and 20th-century economy; v. 10: Enrique González Carré and Virgilio Galdo Gutiérrez on history of education, Fernando Cabreses on science and technology from pre-Incaic to

present, and Raúl Rivera Serna in outstanding study of history of historical writing since 16th century; v. 11: Manuel Burga and Flores Galindo survey Andean feudalism and social movements over 100 years (1866–1965), Daniel Sobrevilla views contemporary ideas and their impact for understanding Peruvian culture, Armando Nieto Vélez summarizes Church activities from colonial era to "menace" of Protestantism in contemporary Peru; v. 12: Fernando Silva Santisteban introduces mágico-religious thought and Wilfredo Kapsoli Escudero elucidates popular movements throughout republican era, Alfredo Chirif and Carlos Mora plot Amazonian events from perspective of riverine cultures from time of resistance to Incas until 1970s, Luís Pásara surveys military regime (1968–80) and search for national identity. Volumes constitute highly useful, stimulating look at "state of the art" in Peru. Highly recommended for university libraries.

2950 Kápsoli Escudero, Wilfredo. El APRA y los movimientos campesinos (*in* Congreso Peruano del Hombre y la Cultura Andina, 3d, Lima, 1977. El hombre y la cultura andina [see *HLAS 43:253*] v. 3, p. 282–288)

Brief report on number of theses being tested to find gap between APRA's programmatic promises to peasants and its performance. Cites case of 1950s Aprista leader in Andahuaylas who politicized peasants but was unprepared for consequences when they established a cooperative.

2951 ———. Mariátegui y los congresos obreros. Lima: Biblioteca Amauta, 1980. 164 p.; bibl.; ill. (Serie Conmemorative 50.0 aniversario de la muerte de J.C.M.)

Lima's textile workers led Workers' Congresses that met periodically after 1921 to strengthen organization. They were influenced by intellectuals and especially by Mariátegui's writings. Brief essay emphasizes their revolutionary impact on labor and the organizing movement. Based on interviews and periodical literature.

2952 Klaiber, Jeffrey L. La escasez de sacerdotes en el Perú: una interpretación histórica (PUCP/H, 5:1, julio 1981, p. 1–19, bibl.)

Attributes clerical scarcity to: Rome's central control; undermining of Church's economic power by liberal reforms; and lack of pastoral and intellectual authority during republican era that could have developed local clergy adapted to popular needs. Number of clergy decreased as did Peruvians among it. Decline was aggravated by 1859 suppression of *diezmos* and later laws which signified loss of Church properties. Uses effectively clerical reports, contemporary studies, and materials from Lima's Archivo Arzobispal.

2953 ———. Independencia, Iglesia, y clases populares. Cubierta, Cèsare Salinari. Lima: Centro de Investigación de la Universidad del Pacífico, 1980. 66 p.; bibl.

Critically examines Church's role in independence movement. Notes its ambiguous position: both elitist and popular, serving as social unifier and defender of colonial social hierarchy. Traces ambiguity to Tupac Amaru rebellion and clerical precursors of Emancipation ideology. Clergy fought on both sides during independence, some of its advocates favoring freedom of religion in 1822–23 Constituent Assembly. Concludes that Church was challenged by independence to overcome internal divisions, and had it not, it might have remained a colonial institution. Succinct exposition of important ideas.

2954 Laite, Julian. Miners and national politics in Peru, 1900–1974 (JLAS, 12, pt. 2, Nov. 1980, p. 317–340)

Traces relationship of local to national factors in rise of miners to central position in Peru's labor movement. In early 20th-century, Cerro de Pasco Company workers organized country's largest industrial trade unions. Relations between miners and the state consist of dilemma: how to reconcile foreign investors' attitudes with miners' political aspirations. State's favoring investors resulted in a confrontation/compromise cycle.

2955 López, Jacinto. Historia de la guerra del guano y el salitre. v. 1, Causas y orígenes de la guerra. La guerra naval. v. 2, La guerra naval. Fotografías, E. Courret *et al.* Ed., ilus. y epígrafes, Carlos Milla Batres. Lima: Editorial Milla Batres, 1979. 2 v.; bibl.; ill.; indexes (Biblioteca histórica de la Guerra del Pacífico)

Diplomatic history in which origins and causes of war are attributed to diplomatic disputes over border delimitation problems. Excellent period photographs of cities, ports, battlefields and personalities were added for this edition.

2956 López Martínez, Héctor. Piérola y la defensa de Lima con testimonios sobre las jornadas del 13 y 15 de enero de 1881. Lima: Editorial Ausonio Talleres Gráficos, 1981. 202 p.

Examine Piérola's political decisions in early stages of War of Pacific as background for Lima's defense in battles of San Juan and Miraflores, Jan. 1881. Attributes "black legend" about Piérola's inadequate military defense to military writers' implicating a civilian in order to exculpate their institution. Relies upon periodicals and Archivo Piérola, in Lima's Biblioteca Nacional. Refreshing volume irritatingly vague on sources.

2957 Lynch, Nicolás. Mariátegui y la cuestión nacional (TAREA [Centro de Publicaciones Educativas Tarea, Lima] 1, junio 1980, p. 8–13)

Argues that Mariátegui held orthodox Marxist views, accepted Peruvian Communist Party membership in Third International, and was not a social democrat. Sketchy review of early 20th-century intellectual debates that shaped Mariátegui's decisions on "national question" and "indigenous community" deemed so applicable today by author.

2958 ———. El pensamiento social sobre la comunidad indígena en el Perú a principios del siglo XX. Diseño carátula, Teresa Gianella. Cuzco: Centro de Estudios Rurales Andinos Bartolomé de las Casas, 1979. 115 p.; bibl. (Debates rurales)

Brief introductory essay outlines well known 1930s liberal to "revolutionary" perspectives on place of indigenous community in Peruvian society. Includes relevant congressional debates, speeches and essays on subject by outstanding intellectuals (e.g., Tudela, Encinas, Mayer de Zulen, Belaunde, Haya, Mariátegui).

2959 Marcera dall'Orso, Pablo. Conversaciones con Basadre. 2. ed. aumentada con un epílogo y notas de Jorge Basadre. Lima: Mosca Azul Editores, 1979. 171 p.

Second edition enhanced by extended introductory historiographical essay by Pablo Macera. Consists of interviews in which Basadre expresses trenchant views on historian's responsibility, Marxism and history, Peruvian historians, political action, etc.

2960 Mallon, Florencia E. Minería y agricultura en la Sierra Central: formación y trayectoria de una clase dirigente regional, 1830–1910 (*in* Congreso Peruano del Hombre y la Cultura Andina, 3d, Lima, 1977. El hombre y la cultura andina [see *HLAS 43:253*] v. 4, p. 543–558)

Hypothesizes that new ruling class emerged in central highlands after independence combining mining investment with agrarian land. After 1850, clan gained control of local power structure yet did not solidify hold because of various crises (e.g., War of the Pacific, competing foreigners, etc.). Concludes that Cerro de Pasco and Mantaro Valley families were squeezed by peasant resistance and lack of resources. Based on documentation from Archivo del Fuero Agrario, AGN, Lima, Biblioteca Nacional, US and British consular records and local informants. Partial synthesis of Ph.D. research.

2961 Manrique, Nelson. La Guerra del Pacífico y la crisis de la fracción terrateniente de la Sierra Central del Perú, 1879–1888. La Molina: Taller de Estudios Andinos, Universidad Nacional Agraria, Departamento de Ciencias Humanas, 1980. 38 p.; bibl. (Serie Andes centrales; no. 8)

Preliminary research report analyzes internal market of central highlands, 1830–80, and posits silver mining as basis of capital formed and invested in cattle. Old landholding class lost their lands to usurers and new landlords concentrated land and converted Junín cattle-raising into era's most advanced industry. Describes effect of Chilean invasion, peasant seizures of collaborators' lands, and landlords' vicissitudes. Another fascinating, well-written study by young, ambitious historian. Based on his earlier studies, plus prefectural and Junín records in Lima's AGN.

2962 ———. San Juan y Miraflores: los días oscuros (DESCO/Q, 8, nov./dic. 1980, p. 64–73, ill.)

Based on contemporary accounts and memoirs, presents brief summary of social impact of 1881 Chilean invasion on Lima. Attributes disastrous results of battles and ensuing consequences (e.g., inter-racial conflict among populace) to civilian Piérola's poor leadership.

Mariátegui, José Carlos. 7 [i.e. Siete] ensayos de interpretación de la realidad peruana. See item **7599**.

2963 Marzal, Manuel. La comunidad indígena y su transformación según Castro Pozo (IPA/A, 14:16, 1980, p. 75–86)

Study that does not go beyond analysis of writings of another Peruvian intellectual who influenced 1920s social movements and whose works became classics. Like Mariátegui, Castro Pozo sought to resurrect ancient Peruvian culture but unlike the journalist he was an anthropologist formally trained in law who also served as deputy and senator.

2964 Maude, Henry Evans. Slavers in paradise: the Peruvian slave trade in Polynesia, 1862–1864. Stanford, Calif.: Stanford University Press, 1981. 244 p.; bibl.; ill.; index.

Unique study of 1862–63 invasion of Polynesian islands by Peruvians in search of labor during break in Chinese indenture trade. Discusses trade's origins; numbers kidnapped per island; ships; working conditions in Peru; responses of Great Britain, France, US; abolition; etc. Based on public and private records in US, Great Britain, Hawaii, France, Tasmania, Chile, Peru, Tahiti. Beautifully wrought narrative that will not be superseded.

2965 Mercado J., Edgardo. Política y estrategia en la guerra de Chile. Prólogo del Dr. Emilio Castañon Pasquel. Lima: s.n., 1979. 179 p.; bibl.; ill.

Essentially summary of Peru's military strategy in War of Pacific (1879–83) by Minister of Foreign Relations, Prime Minister, Minister of War, and Commandant General of Armed Forces during 1968–80 military governments. Standard exculpation of the military preparedness.

2966 Morales Bermúdez Cerrutti, Francisco. La Revolución Peruana. v. 3. Lima: Oficina Central de Información, 1977? 1 v. (various pagings)

Speeches and writings by last military president reveal his attitudes toward peasants, workers, agrarian reform, irrigation, national economy, etc. No unifying theme.

2967 Ochoa Flores, Jorge A. and Félix Palacios Ríos. La protesta de 1901: un movimiento de pastores de la puna alta a comienzos del siglo XX (*in* Congreso Peruano del Hombre y la Cultura Andina, 3d, Lima, 1977. El hombre y la cultura andina [see *HLAS 43:253*] v. 3, p. 375–389, bibl.)

In context of sources of peasant protest movements, studies ecology of pastoralism in Chucuito province, Puno. Finds brutal treatment of shepherds as typical instrument of domination, with shepherds losing power and pasturage after losing control of villages. Sources are turn-of-the-century Comisión de Indígenas Investigación and Chucuito province Subprefecture documents. Impressive ethnohistory.

Palmer, David Scott. Peru: the authoritarian tradition. See *HLAS 43:6468.*

2968 Pardo y Barreda, José. Historia del Tratado "Secreto" de Alianza Defensiva entre el Perú y Bolivia. Ed., ilus., y epigrafes, Carlos Milla Batres. Lima: Editorial Milla Batres, 1979. 86 p.; 8 leaves of plates; ill.

Originally offered as rebuttal to Chilean thesis that Peru/Bolivia alliance triggered War of Pacific, essay remained unpublished 1933–79. Written by former president of Peru, work absolves his grandfather, Manuel Prado, who was president when 1873 alliance was signed. Claims Chileans knew of pact as early as 1873 through Argentine sources and references in *El Mercurio.*

2969 Paz Soldán, Mariano Felipe. Narración histórica de la guerra de Chile contra el Perú y Bolivia. t. 1, Antecedentes y declaración de guerra; la campaña marítima. t. 2, La campaña del Sur. t. 3, Campaña sobre Lima. Fotografías, Archivo Eugene Courret. Ed. y epigrafías, Carlos Milla Batres. Lima: Editorial Milla Batres, 1979. 3 v.; bibl.; ill.; indexes.

Commemorative reprint of edition published 1884, Buenos Aires, includes modernized orthography, documents and spectacular photos from Eugene Courret's archive, Jorge and Antonio Rengifo Fowler's repository, Felix Denegri Luna's and Rubén Vargas Ugarte's libraries, etc. Good biographical sketches of leading wartime figures.

2970 Pease García, Henry. El ocaso del poder oligárquico: lucha política en la escena oficial, 1968–1975. Lima: Desco, 1977. 313 p.; bibl.

Examines conflict and cohesion of class interests and social structures during 1968–80 military government in context of oligarchic state and its few, weak nuclei of political activity. Explains character of military regime through 1975 overthrow of Velasco, highlighting most significant events

of populist general's regime. Emphasizes conjunction of national and international forces that made period an unprecedented one in Peruvian history. Ends with massive, exhaustive bibliography of published and unpublished sources, along with government documents, periodicals, etc.

Pezo del Pino, César; Eduardo Ballón Echegaray; and Luis Peirano Falconi. El magisterio y sus luchas, 1885–1978. See *HLAS 43:4542.*

2971 La Polémica del indigenismo: José Carlos Mariátegui, Luis Alberto Sánchez. Textos y documentos recopilados por Manuel Aquézolo Castro. Prólogo y notas de Luis Alberto Sánchez. Lima: Mosca Azul Editores, 1976. 172 p.

Brings together documents that outline debate between Mariátegui and Luis Alberto Sánchez in 1927. Over next three years other Peruvian intellectuals entered heated discussion, and their exchanges, along with occasional commentary written specifically by Sánchez for this publication, make up this slim volume. Helpful for students of Peru's intellectual and social history.

2972 Prieto de Zegarra, Judith. Mujer, poder y desarrollo en el Perú. Callao: Editorial DORHCA Representaciones, 1980. 2 v.; bibl.; ill.

Survey of women's activities in Peru. Vol. 1 from pre-history to end of 18th century; vol. 2 through end of 19th century. Vol. 1 shows women's participation in Peruvian history as companion-warrior or hand servant of males. Vol. 2 examines women's roles in culture through formal education, in labor movement and in community leadership. Uses materials from Lima's AGN, Seville, Latin American archives, newspapers, Indiana University collection, Lima's Biblioteca Nacional, and periodicals. Handy reference and effective contribution to social history.

2973 Quiroz Paz-Soldán, Eusebio. El espíritu del Tratado de Ancón (PUCP/H, 4:2, dic. 1980, p. 221–228, bibl.)

Attempts to clarify sentiments that resulted in final clauses of treaty ending War of Pacific, ratified 1884 Peru. Focuses on intentions of both parties in agreeing to Article Three, ceding possession of Tacna and Arica to Chile for 10 years followed by plebiscite. Concludes that given inflexibility of conditions in 1883, Peru secured most honorable terms possible from treaty.

2974 Reátegui Chávez, Wilson. Movilización campesina en Huancané, Puno (*in* Congreso de Hombre y de la Cultura Andina, 3d, Lima, 1977. El hombre y la cultura andina [see *HLAS 43:253*] v. 3, p. 289–310)

Landlord-community conflict over land claims in 1920s covered southern Andes. Explains that careful lodging of complaints by peasants received no response, leading to bloody confrontations over the years. By 1927, commission formed to investigate causes of extended uprising secured truce and found landlord irregularities and abuse of peasants. Findings heightened class conflict and landlords' role as source or problem. Based on congressional debates, archives of Ministerio de Trabajo y Comunidades, which houses papers of Patronato de la Raza Indígena.

2975 —— *et al.* La Guerra del Pacífico. v. 1. Lima: Universidad Nacional Mayor de San Marcos, 1980. 264 p.; bibl.; ill.; tables.

San Marcos University historians and sociologists collaborate in commemorative volume providing fresh view of War of Pacific in their essays (e.g., war's social and economic processes, consequences of Chilean land invasion, conditions of national treasury, peasant participation in war of Cajamarca and Junín, black rebellion in south coast plantations, etc.). Essays confirm that study of social and economic dimensions of Peru's most consequential war has barely begun.

2976 Rénique, Gerardo. Tendencias y características en el desarrollo de una empresa ganadera en los Andes centrales: el caso de la Sociedad Ganadera del Centro, 1910–1960 (Tierra y Sociedad [Revista del Archivo del Fuero Agrario, Lima] 1:1, abril 1978, p. 39–59, tables)

Uses company records in AFA and other sources to demonstrate that appearance and persistence of large cattle haciendas in central sierra in 20th century was unique socioeconomic phenomenon. Cerro de Pasco Corporation led to formation of Sociedad Ganadera del Centro which concentrated large land holdings into one corporation until modernization of production began in 1930 lasting until 1960. Process involved moving away from shepherding toward wage labor.

2977 Rénique C., José Luis. El Centro Científico del Cusco, 1897–1907 (PUCP/H, 4:1, julio 1980, p. 41–52, bibl.)

Draws attention to provincial sources of Peruvian nationalist thought in 1920s, principally Cuzco and Arequipa. Describes structure of Cuzco intellectual life as supported by Centro Científico, founded 1897, and attributes Centro's success to intellectuals' efforts to unearth links between Cuzco and Peru's lowland cultures. Another aspect of sources of indigenismo and national culture.

2978 Rodríguez Pastor, Humberto. La rebelión de los rostros pintados. Huancayo, Perú: Instituto de Estudios Andinos, 1979. 145 p.; 1 leaf of plates; bibl. map.

Concerns Chinese field-workers uprising (Pativilca Valley, 1870) whose leaders painted their faces harlequin style, red and blue for identification in angry reprisal against plantation owners. Brutal government repression followed it. Author notes similarities of landowner responses in other valleys. Based on several archives including Lima's AFA.

2979 Rodríguez-Peralta, Phyllis. González Prada's social and political thought (RIB, 30:2, 1980, p. 148–156)

Survey of his major ideas placing them in context of other contemporary Latin American radical thinkers and ascribes them to positivism's influence. For philosopher's comment, see item **7608.**

Roel Pineda, Virgilio. La República de las frustraciones: 1827–1878. See *HLAS 43:3544.*

2980 Samamé Boggio, Mario. El Perú minero. v. 1, Historia. v. 2, Letras y artes. Lima: INCITEMI, 1979. 2 v.; ill.

Largely legal and administrative history of mining in Peru, pre-Incaic through 1978, with emphasis on republican period. Notes production, spread of mines, types of minerals, etc. Ignores problems of ownership, capital concentration, industry's social and economic impact, etc. Ends with handy listing of military government's mining laws (1968–78). No bibliography.

2981 Sánchez, Luis Alberto. Apuntes para una biografía del APRA. v. 1, Los primeros pasos, 1923–1931. v. 2, Una larga guerra civil, 1931–1934. Lima: Mosca Azul Editores, 1978/1979. 2v. (248, 201 p.)

Vol. 1: movement's founding in 1923 to 1931 electoral campaign. Vol. 2: 1931 Sánchez Cerro government to 1934 APRA's outlawing by Benavides government. Contains author's view of Trujillo uprising and repression in 1932, and his estimate of body count (5000 Apristas vs. less than 100 government forces). Based on official records and author's own letters (Penn State University). Fascinating reading.

2982 ———. Haya de la Torre y el APRA. 2. ed. Lima: Editorial Universo, 1980. 410 p.; bibl. (Serie Biografías/Editorial Universo)

Unchanged second ed. (first 1954, see *HLAS 19:2934*), based on interviews with Haya, his associates, unrevealed documents, memoirs, private notes and pre-1954 studies. Discusses Haya/Mariátegui rift, 1932 uprising, denies APRA's complicity in Oct. 1948 military uprising, ends with Haya's exile (Montevideo 1954). Author has expanded theme into book on APRA (two vols. so far, see item **2981**).

2983 ———. Historia de una industria peruana: Cervecería Backus y Johnston S.A. Lima: Cervecería Backus y Johnston, 1978. 300 p.; 41 leaves of plates (1 fold.); bibl.; ill.

Commissioned by Cerveza Cristal makers, narrative contains some nuggets. Relates circumstances of firm's sale to all-Peruvian ownership in 1950s. Connects its history to country's politics, reviews legislation affecting breweries and relations between company's Peruvian and British investors. Not business history but laudatory remembrance filled with gossipy items. Apparently, author lacked access to company's financial records.

2984 Seeger, Martin L. The Ten Cent War: naval phase (AN/AN, 39:4, Oct. 1979, p. 271–288)

Recounts how Peruvian naval tactics and encounters that led to Grau's defeat and Huascar's capture in 1880, effectively ended Peru's naval capabilities in War of Pacific and exposing Peru's coast to Chilean attack. Exceptional summary of well-known sources.

2985 Silva Santisteban, José. Breves reflexiones sobre los sucesos ocurridos en Lima y el Callao, con motivo de la importación de artefactos. Lima: Centro Peruano de Historia Económica, 1979. 63 p.

Reports on 19th-century riots by artisans who objected to competitive impact of European artifacts. Author disagrees arguing that imports stimulate competition improving quality. Early expression of continuing debate in economic history.

2986 Solar, Francisco José del. El militarismo en el Perú. Prólogo, Mario Castro Arenas. Caracas: Solartre Libros, 1976. 134 p.; bibl.; ill.; ports.

General essay on civil military relations in republican Peru up to 1895 revolution. Uses few well-known studies and ignores vast bibliography on subject. Epilogue surveys civilian governments of early 20th century and includes sketches of repeated military golpes.

2987 Sotomayor Roggero, Carmela and **Ramón Aranda de los Ríos.** Sublevación de campesinos negros en Chincha, 1879. Lima: Universiad Nacional Mayor de San Marcos, 1979. 67 p.; ill.

Describes economic and social conditions in 19th-century Chincha province haciendas, and explains reasons for Afro-Peruvians' rebellion on three: San José, Hoja Redonda, and Larán. Plantation workers took advantage of Chilean invasion to seize properties of oppressive landlords. Sources: Lima's AGN, Biblioteca Nacional's Hermeroteca, provincial libraries, oral testimony.

2988 Stein, Steve. Populism in Peru: APRA, the formative years (*in* Latin American populism in comparative perspective [see item **1830**] p. 113–134)

Emphasizes most recent findings on APRA's role in Peruvian politics: instrument for social betterment of masses rather than vanguard of class struggle. Though APRA's ideology was little understood by loyal masses, its claim to be "new religion" was one key to its resilience. Sees APRA as example of political clientelism dominated by charismatic leadership.

2989 ———. Populism in Peru: the emergence of the masses and the politics of social control. Madison: University of Wisconsin Press, 1980. 1 v.; bibl.; index.

Author employs wide range of personal and public archival materials in penetrating study of emergence of urban mass political activity in early 20th-century Peru. Offers perceptive characterization of populism, especially relationship between leader and followers. Assesses socioeconomic conditions in which populism emerged setting off oligarchy's disintegration. Study skillfully gauges success of popular movements within patron-clientelist framework and finds their very similar. Sheds much light on Peru's political culture.

Stepan, Alfred C. The state and society: Peru in comparative perspective. See *HLAS 43:6480.*

2990 Tamayo Herrera, José. Artesanos, burgueses by proletariado textil en los Andes cuzqueños: siglos XIX y XX (*in* Congreso Peruano del Hombre y la Cultura Andina, 3d, Lima, 1977. El hombre y la cultura andina [see *HLAS 43:253*] v. 5, p. 1044–1047)

Overview of social relations in Cuzco's textile industry during 19th–20th centuries. Points out that when artisan crafts were replaced by British goods, a local proletariat was created. Summary of author's work on Cuzco's social history.

2991 ———. Historia del indigenismo cuzqueño, siglos xvi–xx. Prólogo de Luis E. Valcárcel. Lima: Instituto Nacional de Cultura, 1980. 394 p.; bibl.; ill.; ports.

Views Cuzco nativism not simply as regionalist strain but as root and bastion of Andean nativist ideas developed to resist overbearing self-consciousness of European and criollo notions. Surveys 19th-century thinkers (e.g., Clorinda Matto de Turner), traces 20th-century movement through leading intellectuals (e.g., Luis E. Valcárcel, Mariátegui) and their influence on Cuzco's intelligentsia, identifies "neoindigenismo" with current social scientists, etc. A breathtaking survey of existing literature which places it within provocative framework. Challenges Peruvian historiography at new level.

2992 ———. Mariátegui y la *inteligentsia* del sur andino (IPA/A, 14:16, 1980, p. 45–60)

Non-Marxist Mariátegui admirer explores persistence of myth that never became false legend and attributes it to his ability to capture Andean spirit so deeply and write about Andean experience so effectively, having neither visited the Andes nor attended a university. Insightful essay.

2993 Thorndike, Guillermo. Autorretrato, Perú 1850–1900. Lima: Promoinvest

Compañía de Inversiones, 1979. 164 p.; chiefly ill.

Volume includes magnificent series of 1850s–1890s photographs of all levels of society in Peru and materials on other topics (e.g., war with Spain; War of Pacific; 1895 civil war; women; men; sierra, selva, but mostly Lima; etc.). Very valuable collection.

2994 Tibesar, Antonine. Raphael María Taurel, Papal Consul General in Lima, Peru, in 1853: *Report on conditions in Peru* (RIB, 31:1, 1981, p. 36–69, tables)

Silk merchant Taurel had himself appointed Vatican's representative to Peru but died before assuming post. His report on Peru, however, appeared serially in *El Comercio* thereafter. Written from French Conservative Catholic perspective, it sparked internal political debate between Peruvian Church factions of 1850s.

2995 300 [i.e. Trescientos] **documentos para la historia del APRA:** conspiraciones apristas de 1935 a 1939. Thomas M. Davies, Jr., Víctor Villanueva, compiladores. Lima: Editorial Horizonte, 1978. 468 p.; bibl.

Fascinating collection of archival materials from: 1) Col. César E. Pardo, Aprista officer located in Santiago, Chile, charged with coordinating APRA exile activities; 2) Marshall Oscar Benavides, President of Peru (1933–39); 3) declassified documents from US State and Defense Departments. Mostly concerned with clandestine efforts of APRA to overthrow Benavides government. What emerged is picture of "popular" party whose vision (and perhaps success) was limited by willingness of its leaders to sacrifice party principles to personal ambition, even to the extent of allying themselves with antidemocratic military elements. Introductory essay places documents in historical context.

2996 Vargas Hurtado, Gerardo. La batalla de Arica. Lima: Comisión Nacional del Centenario de la Guerra del Pacífico, 1980. 556 p.; 44 leaves of plates; appendices; bibl.; ill.; indexes; ports. (Colección documental; t. 3. Serie A, Obras de historia; t. 3)

Facsimile edition of 1921 work on Arica's 1880 assault and capture by Chileans. Event's anniversary stimulated republication of this work of national exculpation sponsored by military commission. Of interest to military historians.

2997 Vega, Juan José. Inmigración china en el Perú: un modelo de antipluralismo

(*in* Coloquio Latinoamericano sobre Pluralismo Cultural, 2d, Buenos Aires, 1978. Pluralismo cultural: segundo Coloquio Latinoamericano. Organizado por el Congreso Judío Latinoamericano, rama del Congreso Judío Mundial Centro Cultural General San Martín de la Municipalidad de la Ciudad de Buenos Aires, 4, 5 y 6 de diciembre de 1978. Buenos Aires: Congreso Judío Latinoamericano, 1978?, p. 180–193)

Finds evidence of Peruvian antipluralism in disappearance of all aspects of Chinese culture among Peruvian Chinese—save for food habits so thoroughly integrated into *criollo* life that their distinctively Chinese quality has been obliterated. Antipluralism is poorly defined and carelessly examined.

2998 Vigil, Juan D. La rebelión del caudillo andino Eleodoro Benel Zuloeta. Trujillo: Litografía Offset Color, 197? 178 p.; ill.

Concerns 1920s Cajamarca *gamonal* somewhat like Pancho Villa, who terrorized countryside and was executed 1927 by government troops. Author notes Benel's political plots, feuds and alliances (e.g., anti-Leguía, pro Benavides, etc.). Based on family records, newspapers, interviews, but no sources are cited.

2999 Villanueva Urteaga, Horacio. Gamarra y la iniciación republicana en el Cuzco. Lima: Fondo del Libro del Banco de los Andes, 1981. 310 p.; bibl.; notes; plates.

Biography of early republican regional leader, details problems of war debt reduction, administration of Cuzco, relations with Bolívar and the Church, militia, education, welfare and justice issues. Somewhat lacking in analysis but illustrates early republican leadership formation.

3000 Werlich, David P. Peru: the Lame-Duck "Revolution" (CUH, 76:444, Feb. 1979, p. 62–65, 85–87, table)

Recounts military government's 1979 problems (e.g., popular unrest, military factionalism, dismantling of programs for worker management, newspapers' return to private ownership, failure to satisfy country's creditors, etc.). For political scientist comment, see *HLAS 43:6484.*

3001 Wilson, Fiona. The generation of commodity production in an Andean province during the nineteenth century. Copenhagen: Centre for Development Research, 1981. 36 p.; bibl.; maps (CDR project papers; A.81.4)

Study of Tarma's 19th-century provincial oligarchy, especially its exploitation of labor. Silver and *aguardiente* were produced in haciendas owned by nine Euro-Peruvian families who dominated local mestizos and Indians while feuding among themselves. Chief labor source was local peasants but indentured Chinese were also used. Labor needs and capital accumulation led to struggles for regional control between *aguardiente* growers in *montaña* and Tarma merchants. Effective use of local archives.

3002 ———. Propiedad e ideología: estudio de una oligarquía en los Andes centrales, siglo XIX (Análisis [Cuadernos de Investigación, Lima] 8/9, mayo/dic. 1979, p. 36–54)

Studies formation of landlord ideology and regional division of Tarma area into two distinct zones, each dominated by faction of new regional oligarchy of European immigrants who fought over control of *aguardiente* production. Valuable study of 19th-century regional kinship, land and class relations in historical perspective.

3003 Yepes del Castillo, Ernesto. Burguesía y gamonalismo en el Perú (Análisis [Cuadernos de Investigación, Lima] 7, enero/abril 1979, p. 31–66)

Towards end of 19th century, export agricultural modernization did not proletarianize but perpetuated a servile peasantry and maintained landlord dominance. Author analyzes reasons for this (e.g., unequal development of industry and agriculture, urban and rural proletarians, nature of oligarchic state, etc.). Synthesis based on author's previous research.

3004 Zanutelli Rosas, Manuel. El Capitán de Navío, Leopoldo Sánchez Calderón. Lima: s.n., 1979. 39 p.; bibl.

Brief tracing of subject's naval career (e.g., 1866 war against Spain, engineering adviser for central railway project, second to Admiral Grau on *Huascar*, naval adviser to Pierola administration, etc.). Uses some archival sources.

3005 Zimmermann Zavala, Augusto. Los últimos días del General Velasco: ¿quién recoge la bandera? Lima: Talleres Gráficos de la Empresa Editora Humboldt, 1978. 174 p.; ill.

Memoir by Velasco's former press secretary offers anecdotal information on last two months of his life and recalls significant events of his presidency. Much on his deteriorating health and how he held up. Ghoulish reading.

3006 Zolezzi Velásquez, Silvia M. and Luis M. Salgado Ortiz. Demografía y antecedentes socio-económicos de Arica entre los años 1824 y 1879 (UCC/NG, 6, 1978/1979, p. 46–61, bibl., tables)
Studies sources of demographic evolu-

tion in Peruvian port city turned Chilean after War of Pacific. Also analyzes health conditions, death rates, demographic structure and distribution. Uses early 19th-century travel accounts, Peruvian censuses and contemporary periodicals. Helpful for understanding pre-Chilean war conditions on south coast.

Bolivia and Chile

THOMAS C. WRIGHT, *Associate Professor of History, University of Nevada, Las Vegas*

BOLIVIA: THE PAST TWO YEARS have witnessed substantial progress in publication on Bolivian history since 1825. While the old themes of war, politics, and biography have continued to receive much attention, the overall quality of scholarship in these areas is improving. Several good works have also appeared on social, economic, and intellectual history. The most consistent domestic source of scholarly books on history continues to be Editorial Los Amigos del Libro; and among several new historical journals struggling to survive, the most promising is the semi-annual *Historia Boliviana*, published in Cochabamba by Josep Barnadas (address: Casilla 2946, Cochabamba).

The centennial of the War of the Pacific has stimulated considerable research and publication in Bolivia. Some of these studies follow the old prescription of finding scapegoats for Bolivia's misfortune, although President Daza, the standard culprit, has found his defenders. Roberto Querejazu's thoroughly-researched and even-handed *Guano, salitre, sangre* (item **3051**) is the best new history of the war, and the collection of 19th-century pamphlets on the war compiled by Costa de la Torre is also noteworthy (item **3023**). The Chaco War continues to intrigue Bolivians, and Antezana Villagrán's book (item **3013**) is a major contribution to that field. Encompassing the two major wars and the whole history of Bolivia's foreign relations is an excellent two volume study by Abecia Baldivieso (item **3008**).

Another major theme of recent research is 19th century rural history, a rich but heretofore largely fallow field of investigation. Two articles by Rivera Cusicanqui, one by Grieshaber and another by Rodríguez O. (see items **3052–3053, 3029** and **3056** respectively) have examined change and continuity in Indian communal landholding and in peasant movements. "Fuentes de Historia Social Americana" (item **3043**), a major collection of documents edited under the general direction of Pablo Macera, has published four volumes on the "contribución indígena," demography, agricultural production, and other data for rural history. Other volumes in this very useful series deal with mining, public health, the Church, and urban life, all primarily in the 19th century.

Herbert Klein has made two outstanding contributions to the historical literature: his history of Bolivia in the Oxford series (item **3059**) and, with Jonathan Kelley, a new interpretation of the Bolivian Revolution of 1952 based on a model of the resurgence of inequality following revolutions (item **3058**). The 19th-century historian and bibliographer Gabriel René Moreno is the subject of two fine studies (items **3007** and **3060**), and the impact of social Darwinism is examined in an interesting article by Demelas (item **3021**). Other noteworthy contributions include a collection of letters by Alcides Arguedas, a study of Bolivian nationalism by Demelas, the fourth volume of Lora's history of the Bolivian labor movement, and a survey of the politics of the contemporary Bolivian church (see items **3014, 3022, 3042** and **3034**).

CHILE: Recent historical scholarship on Chile also earns high marks, on the whole. The launching of a new journal of Chilean history, *Nueva Historia*, is a particularly bright note. *Nueva Historia* is published by the Asociación de Historiadores Chilenos (UK), a group of young Chileans working in Britain. The editorial board of Leonardo León, Luis Ortega and Gabriel Salazar is ably advised by British colleagues Harold Blakemore, John Lynch, Simon Collier, and Andrew Barnard. Each of the first four numbers (1981) contained a single lengthy article, but beginning with No. 5 (1982) the format features two articles. (Address: c/o Institute of Latin American Studies, 31 Tavistock Square, London WC1H 9HA.)

The major disappointment in recent work is the low quality of writing on the War of the Pacific, a theme that has received much more attention in Chile than in Bolivia. As the victors, Chileans have felt little need to ask hard questions about the causes, conduct, or consequences of the war; instead, they have followed the easier and more patriotic course of glorifying Chilean arms and worshipping military heroes. Several classic accounts of the war have been republished, while most of the new research has yielded gratuitous additional detail on heroic men and acts. Only a few publications, such as the diaries edited by Ruz Trujillo, Pinochet de la Barra's study of pre-war diplomacy, a collection of diplomatic correspondence, and Mayo's articles on the Antofagasta Company have added substantively to the historiography of the war (items **3083, 3087, 3108** and **3096–3097**).

Two other 19th-century themes have been addressed more successfully. Economic history has been well served by Ortega's articles on coal mining and the beginnings of industrialization (items **3102–3103**) and Oppenheimer's studies of railroads (items **3100–3101**). Nineteenth-century intellectual history is the subject of extensive research and publication: Woll's book on the writing and uses of history (item **3129**) and Yeager's study of Barros Arana (item **3132**) shed new light on important themes, and the articles by Martínez Baeza, Pereira Larraín, Spindler, and Vidal Muñoz are also useful contributions (items **3093, 3105, 3122** and **3127**).

Twentieth-century political history has been approached in several ways. Emphasizing different periods and themes, Carrière and Wright have examined the role of landowners and the Sociedad Nacional de Agricultura in Chilean politics (items **3073** and **3130**). Sater offers a detailed account of the 1931 naval mutiny (item **3116**). The Roddick and Zemelman articles (items **3113** and **3133**) provide interesting interpretations of the labor movement and left parties through the 1930s. Barnard examines US involvement in Chilean politics in the 1940s (item **3067**). A major collaborative effort adds substantively to the literature on Arturo Alessandri (item **3120**). Bravo Lira's analysis of government and parties since the 1920s (item **3069**) is a right-wing interpretation of what was wrong with the political system prior to 1973.

Several other noteworthy publications fall outside the preceding categories. The first volume of Gonzalo Vial's multi-volume history of Chile from 1891 to 1973 (item **3125**) is a solid and comprehensive social history of the 1891–1920 period. Vol. 5 of Luis Vitale's fine Marxist analysis of Chilean history (item **3128**) brings the story to 1970. The two volumes of historical statistics compiled by Mamalakis (item **3092**) are an unusually valuable resource for researchers on modern Chilean history. Mayo's article on British-Chilean relations (item **3096**) is useful, and Blancpain and León have shed new light on the Araucanian question in the 19th century (items **1573** and **3091**). Ann Johnson offers new material on the evolution of the family (item **3089**), and Santa Cruz *et al* contribute an excellent survey of women and their roles throughout Chilean history (item **3123**). Finally, the Chilean section by Sater (item **3117**), in the *Research guide to Andean history* edited by TePaske, is a manual on historiography as well as a practical research guide, while Sehlinger's more general guide to archives and libraries will also be useful (item **3119**).

BOLIVIA

3007 Abecia Baldivieso, Valentín. El historiador Gabriel René Moreno (PAIGH/H, 88, julio/dic. 1979, p. 123–153)

Serious, well-documented study of life, times and works of outstanding historian and bibliographer. Moreno is portrayed as a solitary figure whose ambiguous role in the War of the Pacific earned him the unjustified label of traitor to Bolivia. Scrutinizes Moreno's methodology and values, dunning him for positivism and racism but confirming lasting value of his works.

3008 ———. Las relaciones internacionales en la historia de Bolivia. La Paz: Editorial Los Amigos del Libro: Academia Nacional de Ciencias de Bolivia, 1979. 2 v. (839, 901 p.); bibl.; index; maps.

Monumental, well-researched and heavily documented history of Bolivia's international relations since independence, with 250 p. on colonial background of Bolivia's national identity and boundaries. Author rises above common tendency to find scapegoats for Bolivia's repeated diplomatic and military defeats, treating all parties with equanimity. Based on close and dispassionate analysis of documents and secondary literature, volumes also have notes, bibliography and index. Major step for Bolivian historiography.

3009 Aguirre Achá, José. De los Andes al Amazonas: recuerdos de la campaña del Acre. 3. ed. La Paz?: La Familia del autor, 1980. 406 p.; ill.

New edition (first: 1902) of interesting account by participant of 1900–01 military expedition that temporarily pacified Acre. Also noteworthy are author's geographical and anthropological observations on lower Beni. Includes photographs and postscript to original edition tracing subsequent loss of Acre to Brazil.

Albarracín Millán, Juan. La sociedad opresora: la transición del positivismo al materialismo histórico. See item **7578**.

3010 Alcázar, Moisés. Drama y comedia en el Congreso. 3. ed., rev. La Paz: Librería Editorial Juventud, 1980. 243 p.

Third edition (first: 1947) of collection of essays and vignettes on Bolivian parliamentary life between independence and 1940s, by former long-time chief official of Chamber of Deputies. Describes important speeches, votes of confidence, duels, assassinations and other colorful episodes that capture spirit of sterile drama that is Bolivia's political history.

3011 Alvarado, Roberto. Apuntes para una visión dialéctica de Bolivia. Dibujo de la tapa, Rosa Mónica Salinas. La Paz: Ed. Roalva, 1979. 124 p.; bibl.

Collection of previously published essays by well-known sociologist, writer and communist leader who died a political prisoner in 1972. Offers a Marxist overview of Bolivia's history and sociology focusing on ideology of dominant groups and class relations since 1825.

3012 Antezana E., Luis. Proceso y sentencia a la reforma agraria en Bolivia. La Paz: Ediciones Puerta del Sol, 1979. 171 p.; bibl.; ill. (Luces y sombras)

Agrarian economist's critical analysis of Bolivia's rural economy since independence, emphasizes period since 1952 revolution. Focuses on constant conflict between campesinos' struggle for agrarian democracy based on preservation of their communities and "Melgarejismo" of elite wishing to retain "feudalism." Calls for new democratic agrarian reform to undo results of 1953 MNR agrarian reform.

3013 Antezana Villagrán, Jorge. La Guerra del Chaco: análisis y crítica sobre la conducción militar. La Paz: Distribuidores exclusivos, Librería Los Amigos del Libro, 1979. 799 p.; bibl.; ill.

Detailed, highly technical military history of Chaco War through battle of Campo Vía (Dec. 1933). After blaming Salamanca for Bolivia's lack of preparedness, analyzes planning and execution of both Bolivian and Paraguayan military operations during war's first year and a half. Use of wide variety of official and private documents and histories from both sides gives book a perspective and balance rarely found in the literature. Without superseding Zook's book (see *HLAS 24:4321*), this is more detailed and an important contribution to Chaco War historiography.

3014 Arguedas, Alcides. Cartas a los presidentes de Bolivia. Selección, prólogo, y notas de Mariano Baptista Gumucio. La Paz: Ultima Hora, 1979. 223 p.; ill. (Biblioteca popular boliviana de Ultima Hora)

Author's private and public letters (1908–44) to seven Bolivian presidents. Unsolicited, frank, sometimes bold, they offer advice on matters ranging from general principles of government to specific policy issues. Includes a few presidents' answers. Interesting in themselves, letters are helpful for understanding this controversial Bolivian intellectual. For political scientist's comment, see *HLAS 43:6491*.

3015 Arze, José Antonio. Bosquejo sociodialéctico de la historia de Bolivia. Preparación y prólogo, José Roberto Arze. La Paz: Ediciones Camarlinghi, 1978. 181 p.; bibl.; port. (Colección popular; ser. 21, v. 58)

Collection of historical and sociological writings by important Marxist politician and sociologist (d. 1955). Includes author's biographical sketch and bibliography.

3016 Baptista Gumucio, Mariano. Historia contemporánea de Bolivia, 1930–1978. 2. ed., corr. y aumentada. La Paz: Gisbert, 1978. 399 p.; bibl.

Second, updated edition (first: 1976) published as second half of *Nueva historia de Bolivia*, co-authored by E. Finot (see *HLAS 40:3587*).

3017 Barrero, Francisco. Conducción político-diplomática de la guerra con Paraguay. La Paz: Editorial El Siglo, 1979. 433 p.; 11 leaves of plates; bibl.; ill.

History of war focusing on political and diplomatic aspects. Contains numerous documents, sources unidentified. Blames President Salamanca for launching war when Bolivia was diplomatically isolated, militarily unprepared, and socially and politically fragmented.

3018 Boccolini, Rosa. Medicina social en Bolivia, 1776–1869: documentos. Lima: s.n., 1978. 101 p. (Fuentes de historia social americana; 3) (Biblioteca andina)

Vol. 3 of "Fuentes de Historia Social Americana" (see item **3043**) consists of 32 interesting documents on virtually unexplored topic of medicine and public health that address questions such as rations for beggars, regulation of medical practice, hospitals, potable water, epidemics. Emphasizes 1825–50 period.

3019 ——— and Rosario Jiménez. Estadísticas de contribución indígena en Bolivia, 1770–1902. Lima: Biblioteca Andina, 1979. 2 v. (255 p.); bibl. (Fuentes de historia social americana; 8) (Biblioteca andina)

Two tomes constitute vol. 8 of "Fuentes de Historia Social Americana" (see item **3043**) and offer valuable sources on 19th-century Bolivian social history and land tenure. Data are scattered in time and space and varied as to detail, including some tables on *yanaconaje*, geographic mobility, and land ownership among tributaries. Important source.

Bonilla, Heraclio. Un siglo a la deriva: ensayos sobre el Perú, Bolivia y la guerra. See item **2916**.

Caivano, Tomaso. Historia de la guerra de América entre Chile, Perú y Bolivia. See item **2922**.

3020 Choque Canqui, Roberto. Sublevación y masacre de los comuneros de Jesús de Machaca (Antropología [Instituto Nacional de Antropología, La Paz] 1:1, 1. semestre 1979, p. 1–31)

Study of causes and repercussions of one of most important 20th-century altiplano Indian uprisings, 1921 revolt of Jesús de Machaca's comuneros. Includes notes, bibliography and graphs.

3021 Demelas, Danièle. Darwinismo a la criolla: el darwinismo social en Bolivia, 1800–1910 (Historia Boliviana [Amauta Books, Cochabamba] 1/2, 1981, p. 55–82, plate)

Interesting examination of social Darwinism in Bolivia, based on inventories of personal libraries, bookstore catalogues, proceedings of famous 1901 trial of Indian followers of "El Temible" Willka, and European and Bolivian secondary literature. Concludes that Bolivian elites profited from social Darwinism by shedding religious for scientific views that justified but did not cause increased racism and oppression of Indians. Worthwhile contribution.

3022 ———. Nationalisme sans nation? : la Bolivie aux XIXe–XXe siècles. Paris: Editions du C.N.R.S., 1980. 227 p.; bibl.; ill.

Interesting, thoughtful study of Bolivia (1880–1920) replete with graphs, tables, maps. Thesis is that Bolivian nationalism began out of humiliation of War of Pacific as sentiment for recovering littoral, but that underpopulation, economic dependency, and rule by "pigmentocracy" denied Bolivia essentials for nationhood during period. Fruitful approach to problem of Bolivia's existence as a nation.

3023 Diarios y memorias de la Guerra del Pacífico. Recopilación de Arturo Costa de la Torre. Introducción de Edgar Oblitas Fernández. La Paz: Biblioteca Paceña, Honorable Municipalidad, 1980. 2 v. (Biblioteca Paceña. Nueva serie)

Reproduces 16 rare memoirs and diaries published as pamphlets during and after War of Pacific (1880s–90s). Claims they were suppressed after publication for contradicting ruling elite's version of war (i.e., that President Daza rather than they sold Bolivia out). Useful sources on key battles and important War personalities.

3024 Díaz Arguedas, Julio. Síntesis histórica de la ciudad: La Paz, 1548–1958. 2. ed. La Paz: Casa Municipal de la Cultura Franz Tamayo, 1978. 484 p.; bibl.; ill.

History of La Paz's first four centuries divided into chronological (330 p.) and topical (121 p.) sections. Deals primarily with events, personalities, and matters of antiquarian interest, providing little social or economic analysis and no documentation. Useful reference for basic information on La Paz history.

3025 Dunkerley, James. Reevaluación del caudillismo en Bolivia (Historia Boliviana [Amauta Books, Cochabamba] 1/2, 1981, p. 59–77, table)

Interpretive article grapples with Bolivia's 19th-century pattern of political instability and caudillismo. Downplaying importance of free trade-protectionist conflict and of regional struggles, author focuses on control of state apparatus, and thus of silver, as main motivating factor in endless rebellions and turnovers in office.

3026 Goicochea, Alvaro. Documentos sobre el sector urbano en Bolivia, 1756–1877. Lima: s.n., 1979. 99 p. (Fuentes de historia social americana; 6) (Biblioteca andina)

Collection of 30 documents, vol. 6 of "Fuentes de Historia Social Americana" (see item **3043**), deals with 19th-century Bolivian urban social, economic and political life. Documents are diverse topically and geographically and should be useful for 19th-century urban history.

3027 Gómez de Aranda, Blanca. Casimiro Olañeta, diplomático, 1824–1839. La Paz: Instituto Boliviano de Cultura, 1978. 121 p.; bibl.

Analysis of controversial Olañeta's diplomatic career through 1839 collapse of Peru-Bolivian Confederacy. Provides useful detail on republican Bolivia's early foreign relations and sheds new light on Olañeta's central role in period. Includes notes and bibliography.

3028 González Quintanilla, Luis. La cuestión del petróleo en Bolivia: de las primeras concesiones a la nacionalización de la Standard Oil Co. of Bolivia. Stockholm: Institute of Latin American Studies, 1977. 42 p. (Research paper series; 5)

Overview of petroleum politics and policy (1910s–42) focuses on developments surrounding 1937 nationalization of Standard Oil. Acknowledges role of Standard-Shell rivalry in causing Chaco War but denies that Standard aided Bolivia's war effort.

3029 Grieshaber, Erwin P. Survival of Indian communities in nineteenth-century Bolivia: a regional comparison (JLAS, 12, pt. 2, Nov. 1980, p. 223–269, map, tables)

Thoroughly documented study of survival of Indian communities in Bolivia during 1830s–70s, based on tribute censuses. Demonstrates that communities held their own in most areas, and that decline was not due to hacienda pressure but to demographic and ecological conditions. Includes valuable and detailed demographic data on tributaries.

Important contribution to 19th-century Bolivian social history.

3030 Guachalla, Luis Fernando. Jayacubás: comentarios y crónicas de la Guerra del Chaco. La Paz: Editorial Los Amigos del Libro, 1978. 454 p.

Second edition (first: 1957, not annotated in *HLAS*). First half is Chaco War history; more useful second half, is chronicle of author's participation.

3031 Gutiérrez Gutiérrez, Mario R. De la vida de colegio a la política: referencias probatorias de una vocación patriótica. t. 2, Libro de separatas: correspondiente a la obra de la vida de colegio a la política. New York: s.n., 1977. 196 p.

Collection of diverse writings by and about Gutiérrez, leader of Falange Socialista Boliviana, from colegio days to 1970s. Useful for his biography or study of the party.

3032 Guzmán, Augusto. Proceso histórico y cultural de Cochabamba. La Paz: Librería Editorial Juventud, 1979. 97 p.

Brief narrative history of Cochabamba, emphasizing personalities, events, architecture and letters. Useful general introduction.

Hermosa Virreira, Wálter. Breve historia de la minería en Bolivia. See *HLAS 43:3571*.

3033 Historia gráfica de la Guerra del Pacífico. Bajo la dirección de Mariano Baptista Gumucio. La Paz: Ultima Hora, 1978. 119 p.; 44 leaves of plates; ill. (Colección Litoral boliviano) (Biblioteca popular boliviana de Ultima Hora)

Interesting collection of photos, drawings, maps and documents from War of Pacific.

3034 La Iglesia de Bolivia, ¿compromiso o traición?: de Medellín a Puebla: ensayo de análisis histórico. La Paz: s.n., 1978. 153 p.; bibl.

Serious, well-documented study of Bolivian Church between Vatican Council II (1962–65) and 1978 by sociologist, journalist, historian and priest who support Church's new social activism. Illuminates activists' approaches to revitalizing Church and records successes and failures in struggle against conservative hierarchy and repressive governments. Important analytical piece on recent Bolivian political history and new Latin American Church.

3035 Iturri Núñez del Prado, Julio. La Paz, ayer, hoy y mañana: historia viviente. La Paz: Ultima Hora, 1980. 299 p.; ill. (Biblioteca popular boliviana de Ultima Hora)

Reminiscences of patrician paceño about city's material development and this century's leading personalities. Useful for antiquarian aspects of urban history.

3036 Jiménez, Rosario. Curatos en Bolivia, 1800–1923: documentos. Lima: s.n., 1978. 153 p. (Fuentes de historia social americana; 4) (Biblioteca andina)

Vol. 4 of "Fuentes de Historia Social Americana" (see item **3043**) is collection of very interesting documents on parish boundaries, parish income, religious fiestas and miscellaneous information on Church and religion. Emphasis on 1800–44.

3037 ——— and Honorio Pinto. Minería en Bolivia, 1826–1848: documentos. Lima: Biblioteca Andina, 1979. 130 p. (Fuentes de historia social americana; 7) (Biblioteca andina)

Well-selected collection of documents on technology, capital, government policy and labor in mining sector of early 19th-century Bolivia is vol. 7 of "Fuentes de Historia Social Americana" (see item **3043**).

3038 Kelley, Jonathan and Herbert S. Klein. Revolution and the rebirth of inequality: a theory applied to the national revolution in Bolivia. Berkeley: University of California Press, 1981. 279 p.; bibl.; ill.; index.

Ground-breaking study based on sophisticated social science methodology develops model of revolution's effects on inequality and inherited privilege in predominantly rural, preindustrial societies, and applies theory to 1952 Bolivian Revolution. Drawing heavily on quantitative and attitudinal data from survey conducted in six representative rural areas by Research Institute for the Study of Man, authors perform battery of computer analyses to conclude that Bolivia fits general pattern of initially reduced inequality and inherited privilege, followed by reappearance of these societal characteristics with some new beneficiaries. Important contribution to theory as well as to understanding Bolivian Revolution and its consequences.

3039 Klein, Herbert S. Bolivia, the evolution of a multi-ethnic society. New

York: Oxford University Press, 1982. 318 p.; bibliographical essay; index; maps (Latin American histories)

Excellent, very readable synthesis of Bolivian history from pre-Inca civilizations to present. Offers incisive socioeconomic and political analysis and considerable information on culture within interpretive framework set forth in book's sub-title. Includes extensive bibliographical essay. Klein's work will serve scholars' needs while providing English-language history of Bolivia for course adoption.

3040 Lema Peláez, Raúl. Con las banderas del Movimiento Nacionalista Revolucionario: el sexenio, 1946–1952. La Paz: Editorial Los Amigos del Libro, 1979. 441 p.; ill.

Memoir of leading MNR figure sheds valuable light on six years preceding 1952 Revolution. Expanded edition of 1951 original (not annotated in *HLAS*), very much worth republishing.

3041 Lora, Guillermo. Agar Peñaranda, la revolucionaria ejemplar. La Paz: Ediciones Isla, 1979. 63 p.

Eulogistic biographical sketch of first and most influential woman militant of Trotskyist Partido Obrero Revolucionario (d. 1977) by party's prolific historian. Includes useful information on party's history.

———. Contribución a la historia política de Bolivia. See item **6501**.

3042 ———. Historia del movimiento obrero boliviano. v. 4, 1933–1952. La Paz: Editorial Los Amigos del Libro, 1980. 1 v.; bibl.; ill.; ports (Enciclopedia boliviana)

Vol. 4 of Lora's extensive work on Bolivian labor movement, whose publication has been delayed since 1971 by political circumstances (for vol. 1, see *HLAS 32:2653*, and for its English abridgement, see *HLAS 42:3162*). Examines labor's role (1933–52), focusing on changing forms of organization, big massacres, and background to 1952 Revolution. Story is told from personalist and Trotskyist viewpoint by Partido Obrero Revolucionario's long-time leader.

3043 Macera dall'Orso, Pablo. Bolivia, tierra y población, 1825–1936. Lima: s.n., 1978. 125 p.; tables (Fuentes de historia social americana; 1) (Biblioteca andina)

Vol. 1 inaugurates "Fuentes de Historia Social Americana," series of 10 projected volumes of documents and rare materials from Sucre's Archivo Nacional on 19th-century Bolivia. Series directed by Macera, volumes edited by participants in Lima's Seminario de Historia Andina. Vol. 1 reproduces documents and rare materials on demography, political geography and Indian tribute. For vols. 2–8, see items **3018–3019, 3026, 3036–3037, 3049** and **3050**. Vol. 9 will concern series' sources, vol. 10 will be Macera's socioeconomic history of republican Bolivia. Series should be boon to researchers on 19th-century Bolivia.

3044 Mansilla, H. C. F. La Revolución de 1952 en Bolivia: un intento reformista de modernización (FH, 18:215, dic. 1980, p. 751–761)

Well written but unoriginal interpretation of 1952 Revolution as essentially modernizing and reformist movement, ends by condemning MNR for alleged repressiveness.

3045 Montenegro, Carlos. Montenegro el desconocido. Selección, prólogo y notas de Mariano Baptista Gumucio. La Paz: Ultima Hora, 1979. 380 p.; ill. (Colección Clásicos bolivianos contemporáneos) (Biblioteca popular boliviana de Ultima Hora: Colección Ensayos)

Collection of previously published writings by Montenegro (1903–53), man of letters, politician and MNR founding member. Includes political tracts, character sketches, reviews, historical pieces, prose and poetry.

3046 Oblitas Fernández, Edgar. Historia secreta de la Guerra del Pacífico. Buenos Aires: A. Peña Lillo Editor, 1978. 316 p.; bibl. (Biblioteca de estudios americanos; 12)

War history preceded by chapter reiterating Bolivia's historic claim to littoral. Untold truths revealed by author include number of conspiracies with Chileans and British as protagonists and, as primary *vendepatria*, Aniceto Arze rather than President Daza. Author's serious intentions, reflected in notes and historiographical references, are invalidated by his xenophobia.

O'Connor, Francisco Burdett. Un irelandés con Bolívar: recuerdos de la independencia de América del Sur en Venezuela, Colombia, Bolivia, Perú y la Argentina, por un Jefe de la Legión Británica de Bolívar. See item **2796**.

Pardo y Barreda, José. Historia del Tratado "Secreto" de Alianza Defensiva entre el Perú y Bolivia. See item **2968.**

3047 Paredes, Manuel Rigoberto. Don Daniel Salamanca. La Paz: Ediciones ISLA, 1979. 79 p.

Brief chronicle of early political career of Salamanca, President during the Chaco War, carries story through 1925.

3048 Parrenin, Georges. Genèse des mouvements indiens-paysans en Bolivie, 1900–1952 (FDD/NED [Problèmes d'Amérique Latine, 62] 4649/4650, 28 déc. 1981, p. 31–53)

Overview of background and emergence of Bolivia's "modern" Indian movement, focusing on peasant sindicatos. Useful summary based on secondary sources.

Paz Soldán, Mariano Felipe. Narración histórica de la guerra de Chile contra el Perú y Bolivia. See item **2969.**

3049 Pinto Herrera, Honorio. Bolivia, tierra y población, 1844–1939. Lima: s.n., 1978. 164 p.; tables (Fuentes de historia social americana; 2) (Biblioteca andina)

Vol. 2 of "Fuentes de Historia Social America" (see item **3043**) is a continuation of vol. 1. Contains statistical data on economic activities, especially agriculture, from early census and unpublished sources.

3050 ———. Contribución indígena en Bolivia, 1829–1911: documentos. Lima: Universidad Nacional Mayor de San Marcos, Dirección de Proyección Social, 1979. 125 p.; bibl. (Fuentes de historia social americana; 5) (Biblioteca andina)

Collection of 30 documents comprises vol. 5 of "Fuentes de Historia Social Americana" (see item **3043**) and complements vol. 8 of series (item **3019**). These are well selected to illuminate key institution of 19th-century Bolivia.

3051 Querejazu Calvo, Roberto. Guano, salitre, sangre: historia de la Guerra del Pacífico. La Paz: Editorial Los Amigos del Libro, 1979. 825 p.; bibl.; ill.

Based on extensive bibliography of primary and secondary works, this is the best new Bolivian study of War of Pacific and most authoritative one produced in Bolivia. Without denying his Bolivian nationalism, author avoids facile judgments and typical characterizations of Chileans and English, offering even-handed, thoughtful history of causes, conduct, and results of war. By one of Bolivia's most respected historians, book is required reading for those interested in Bolivian perspective.

3052 Rivera Cusicanqui, Silvia. La expansión del latifundio en el altiplano boliviano (IPA/A, 12/13, 1979, p. 189–218)

Well-argued, detailed study of Indian community-land purchase in Pacajes province, La Paz dept. (1860s–1920). Explores how land purchases led to emergence of new power structure linking landless Indian masses to national elites, with local merchants as intermediaries. Dynamics of tin export economy worked against modernization of capitalist agricultural sector. Interesting revisionist contribution.

3053 ———. Rebelión e ideología: luchas del campesinado aymara del altiplano boliviano, 1910–1920 (Historia Boliviana [Amauta Books, Cochabamba] 1:2, 1981, p. 83–99)

Rejecting current "archaic" vs. "modern" typologies of peasant movements and rebellions, article offers alternate analytical scheme derived from analysis of Bolivian altiplano (1910s–20s). Finds that archaic and modern elements were fused in Aymara rebellions of period, and suggests campesino ideologies must be understood in their own terms. Potentially useful contribution to study of historical peasant movements.

3054 Roberts Barragán, Hugo. Gran traición en la Guerra del Pacífico: dolorosa versión histórica y relación verídica de los hechos. La Paz: Roberts Barragán, 1979. 426 p.; bibl.; ports.

Interpretation of war follows new trend of exonerating President Daza, the traditional scapegoat. Author blames Bolivia's defeat on two conspiracies: the "Mafia" and the Masons, who gave away littoral before war began, overthrew Daza and governed until turn of century, disseminating self-serving interpretation of Bolivia's loss. Few documents are cited.

3055 Roca, José Luis. Fisonomía del regionalismo boliviano. La Paz: Editorial Los Amigos del Libro, 1980. 419 p.; bibl.; index.

Collection of new and previously published essays on role of regionalism in

Bolivia's history. Defines Bolivian history as history of regional struggles. Nonetheless, this geopolitical analysis underscores critical theme in Bolivian development: absence of true nationhood.

3056 Rodríguez O., Gustavo. Original accumulation, capitalism, and precapitalistic agriculture in Bolivia: 1870–1885 (LAP, 8[4]: 27, Fall 1980, p. 50–66, tables)

Focuses on concentrated assault on Indian cummunal land, examining different forms of production and accumulation. Explains why gestation of modern capitalism in Bolivia did not destroy, but reinforced "feudal" agricultural structure. Interesting and potentially useful hypotheses.

3057 Rodríguez Rivas, Julio. Don Julio: retrato en los años cruciales de la turbulenta Bolivia, 1843–1926. Cochabamba: Los Amigos del Libro, 1978. 380 p.; 14 leaves of plates; bibl.; ill.

Biography of author's grandfather, Julio Rodríguez (1843–1926), Cochabamba medical doctor and politician. Provides potentially useful information on social and medical history of Cochabamba as well as perspective on national affairs.

3058 Russe, Jean. La obra de Gabriel René Moreno. Potosí: Universidad Boliviana Mayor Tomás Frías, División de Extensión Universitaria, 1978. 58 p. (Cultura potosina: Serie H, Ensayo y crítica; v. 1)

Brief study lists and summarizes Moreno's bibliographical and historical works. Useful as introduction to the topic.

Sanabria Fernández, Hernando. Miguel Suárez Arana y la Empresa Nacional de Bolivia. See HLAS 43:3584.

3059 Sarmiento, Emilio. Memorias de un soldado de la Guerra del Chaco. Caracas: El Cid Editor, 1978. 251 p.; 16 leaves of plates; ports (Colección Historia americana)

Memoirs of author's youthful participation in Chaco War. Lacking trappings of political or military analysis, this kind of memoir is useful as straightforward narrative of one soldier's experience.

3060 Siles Guevara, Juan. Gabriel René Moreno, historiador boliviano. La Paz: Editorial Los Amigos del Libro, 1979. 119 p.; bibl.; facsims.

Thoroughly documented critical study of Moreno's ideas, methodology, writings, legacy and his place in Bolivian and American historiography. Siles dares to take Moreno off pedestal and subject him to thorough analysis before pronouncing him equal of any 19th-century American historian. Excellent treatment of much-worked subject.

3061 Tabera R., Félix. Apuntes para la historia de la Guerra del Chaco: Picuiba. 2. ed. La Paz: s.n., 1979. 629 p.; 1 leaf of plates; ill.

Second edition (first: 1960, see HLAS 25:3684) of still valuable source on Chaco War.

3062 Terán Erquicia, Vicente. La muerte del tirano: asesinato del General Melgarejo en Lima. La Paz: Producciones CIMA, 1980. 264 p.; bibl.; ill.; ports.

Over half deals with Melgarejo and varied interpretations of his career and exploits. Second, more original part, examines Melgarejo's assassination based on archival record of trial of his alleged killer.

3063 Trigo, Bernardo. Tarija y sus valores humanos. Tarija: Universidad Boliviana Juan Misael Saracho, 1978. 2 v. (705 p.); bibl.

Biographical dictionary of Tarija's "Hijos ilustres," primarily born 18th and 19th centuries, by member of prominent local family. Despite hagiographic tone and vague selection criteria, work provides useful, basic information on provincial elite.

CHILE

3064 Arretx, Carmen; Rolando Mellafe; and Jorge L. Somoza. Estimaciones de mortalidad: religiosos de Chile en los siglos XVIII y XIX. Santiago: Centro Latinoamericano de Demografía, 1976. 44 p.; tables (Serie A; no. 135)

Utilizes friar and nun records to obtain adults' life tables in 18th and 19th centuries. Resultant e_{25} for males in first half of 19th century is 33 years, and for females, 35.7 years. First in series of monographs by team of demographers (Arretx and Somoza) and historian (Mellafe) designed to test methods for reconstruction of historical demography. See also item 2726. [M. T. Hamerly]

3065 ——; ——; and ——. Mortality estimates in a parish of Santiago from orphanhood information: Ñuñoa, 1866–

1871. Santiago: Centro Latinoamericano de Demografía, 1976. 20 p.; tables (Serie A; no. 145)

Tests applicability of methods of Louis Henry, and of William Brass and Ken Hill for estimating adult mortality rates and life expectancies from indirect information. Second in series of model monographs. [M. T. Hamerly]

3066 Avila Martel, Alamiro de. Reseña histórica de la Universidad de Chile, 1622–1979. Presentación por Hernán García Vidal. Santiago: Ediciones de la Universidad de Chile, 1979. 79 p.; ill.; ports.

Slim tract designed to correct common understanding that University of Chile was founded in 1843. Emphasizes university's Hispanic and religious (rather than national and secular) roots and adds two centuries of tradition, arguing without documentary support that university operated without interruption under different names and organizational forms since 1622.

El Banco Central de Chile: reseña de su historia, funciones y organización. See *HLAS 43:3439.*

3067 Barnard, Andrew. Chilean Communists, Radical presidents and Chilean relations with the United States, 1940–1947 (JLAS, 13:2, Nov. 1981, p. 347–374)

Well researched article examines US State Department's involvement in Chilean politics by isolating three cases in which Radical presidents broke off their party's alliance with Communists, which began with 1936 Popular Front coalition. Despite Communist allegations that US manipulated Aguirre Cerda (1940), Ríos (1946) and González Videla (1947), concludes that domestic political factors outweighed foreign pressures, and that only last instance indicates evidence of US pressure. However, suggests that Chile's growing economic dependence on US constituted major restriction on Communists' influence.

Blancpain, Jean-Pierre. Le Chili républicain et la fin de la frontière araucane. See item **1573**.

3068 Braun Menéndez, Armando. Mis memorias del año veinte. Santiago: Editorial Antártica, 1979. 155 p.; 20 leaves of plates; ill.; index.

Officer's reminiscences of episode known as "la guerra de don Ladislao," 1920 mobilization of Chilean army and reserves to counter alleged Peru-Bolivian move to recover lost territories. Offers useful insights into attitudes and activities of upper class youth during this brief, almost festive interruption of their normal lives. Insists on authenticity of foreign threat, rejecting view that mobilization was contrived diversion from Chile's internal strife in crucial 1920 election year.

3069 Bravo Lira, Bernardino. Régimen de gobierno y partidos políticos en Chile, 1924–1973. Santiago: Editorial Jurídica de Chile, 1978. 320 p.; bibl.; graphs.

Political and legal analysis of Chilean government institutions and parties serves to justify post-1973 government and emerging institutional order. Distinguishing between fundamental institutions and form of government, author finds entire 19th and 20th century Liberal parliamentary and party system suspiciously un-Chilean but feels that junta is compatible with more fundamental and enduring political traditions. Despite obvious political purpose, or because of it, an interesting analysis that reflects current official views. For political scientist's comment, see *HLAS 43:6520.*

3070 Bulnes, Gonzalo. Guerra del Pacífico. 4. ed. Santiago: Editorial del Pacífico, 1979. 3 v.; ill.; indexes.

New edition of 1911–19 original, testimonial to enduring popularity of this version of the war.

Caivano, Tomaso. Historia de la guerra de América entre Chile, Perú y Bolivia. See item **2922**.

3071 Campos Harriet, Fernando. Historia de Concepción, 1550–1970. 2. ed. corr. y aum. Santiago: Editorial Universitaria, 1980. 382 p.; bibl.; ill.

Nicely illustrated and bound second edition (first, 1979) of general urban and regional history of Concepción. Blends personalities and heroic events with some social, economic, cultural and political analysis. Given ambitious scope and relative brevity, more useful to layman than to historian. Contains extensive appendixes of civil, military, and religious officials.

3072 ———. Jornadas de la historia de Chile. Santiago: Academia Superior de Ciencias Pedagógicas de Santiago, 1981. 191 p.; bibl.

Collection of essays, some previously published, on various aspects of Chilean culture and history from colonial to contemporary period. Useful as introduction to thought and writings of prolific and influential historian.

3073 Carrière, Jean. Landowners and politics in Chile: a study of the Sociedad Nacional de Agricultura, 1932–1970. Amsterdam: Centrum voor Studie en Documentatie van Latijns-Amerika, 1981. 245 p. (CEDLA incidentele publicaties; 18)

Questions widely held view that limited capitalist outlook on part of landowners explains Chile's underdevelopment. Employs Society's files to examine organization within theoretical framework formed by debate over class cohesion, ends by talking about uneasy coalition of unequal partners, landowners and industrialists. Also examines republican agricultural problems to 1930, formation of landowner network that served as SNA's base of power, 1930s rural labor organization, etc. Final essay is on 1960s Christian Democratic agrarian and labor reforms. Useful diagrams illustrate SNA activities and power, but presentation is weak on examination of ideological sources of interest group behavior and thus SNA seems lifeless. Emphasizes period since 1930. [V. C. Peloso]

3074 Chile. Congreso. Biblioteca. Bibliografía de la Guerra del Pacífico. Santiago: Biblioteca del Congreso Nacional, 1979. 57 p. (Bibliografía-Biblioteca del Congreso Nacional; no. 80)

Unannotated catalogue of National Congress Library's holdings on War of the Pacific, divided into two: 1) ca. 320 books and pamphlets; and 2) 90 journal articles. Includes foreign publications.

3075 Collier, Simon. Allende's Chile: contemporary history and the counterfactual; review article (JLAS, 12, pt. 2, Nov. 1980, p. 445–452)

Reviews 12 books published 1974–79 on Allende's Chile, ranging from Trotskyite to "democratic left." Finds that besides problems of partisanship and passion, greatest difficulty in dealing with UP experience is continuing fascination with the "counterfactual" or what might have been if only . . . Attracted by same magnet, Collier focuses on differing answers to central question of what Allende and UP could or should have done differently to avoid 1973 denouement.

3076 Cunill Grau, Pedro. La geografía social histórica en el empobrecimiento paisajístico chileno (in Encuentro de Historiadores Lationoamericanos y del Caribe, 2d, Caracas, 1977. Los estudios históricos en América Latina: ponencias, acuerdos y resoluciones: Caracas, 20–26 de marzo de 1977. Caracas: Universidad Central de Venezuela, Facultad de Humanidades y Educación, Escuela de Historia, 1979, v. 1, t. 2, p. 392–407, maps)

Sketches impact of various patterns of exploitation and settlement on Chile's landscape, flora and fauna from colonial beginnings through 19th century. Focuses on mining as major element in deforestation, depletion of water resources and reduction or extinction of plants and animals in north, and considers also effect of population growth, cultivation of marginal soils and whaling in other parts of country. Preliminary study of important topic.

3077 Donoso Vergara, Guillermo. La prensa talquina en el primer semestre de 1879 (SCHG/R, 147, 1979, p. 98–124)

Uses Talca press to analyze impact of early stages of War of the Pacific at local level. Torn by political struggles into early 1879, Talquinos quickly forgot their differences and rallied 'round the flag, demonstrating war's unifying effect.

3078 Edwards Bello, Joaquín. La deschilenización de Chile. Selección y ordenación de Alfonso Calderón. Prólogo de Guillermo Blanco. Santiago: Ediciones Aconcagua, 1977. 212 p. (Colección Mistral)

Collection of essays, one of which provides book's title, by well known man of letters and author of El roto. Originally published in La Nación, they offer insights into the man and his times.

3079 Eyzaguirre, Jaime. Hispanoamérica del dolor y otros estudios. Madrid: Ediciones de Cultura Hispánica del Centro Iberoamericano de Cooperación, 1979. 436 p.; bibl.

Handsomely presented collection of essays from several of late historian's works, including all of Fisonomía histórica de Chile, divided into section of general essays and another on Chilean history. Usefulness to historians limited because original sources of selections are not identified.

3080 Fernández, Manuel A. El enclave salitrero y la economía chilena, 1880–

1914 (Nueva Historia [University of London, Institute of Latin American Studies] 1 : 3, 1981, p. 2–42)

Overview of nitrate industry's impact on Chile reaches three conclusions: 1) nitrate sector provided modest stimulus to agricultural production and only indirect stimulus to national industry; 2) export duties on nitrates basically replaced ordinary revenue sources, creating richer state but not contributing to development; and 3) there was no significant transfer of technology from nitrate sector to native enterprise. Author asserts conclusions fully justify application of enclave concept to Chile's nitrate sector.

3081 Fernández Larraín, Sergio. Santa Cruz y Torreblanca: dos Héroes de las campañas de Tarapacá y Tacna. Santiago: Editorial Mar del Sur, Fundación Pacífico, 1979. 226 p.; 16 leaves of plates; bibl.; ill.; index.

Well written, thoroughly documented, illustrated but uncritical history of two Chilean martyrs of the War of the Pacific. Based largely on protagonists' letters and diary, book provides interesting personal perspectives on war.

3082 Fuenzalida Bade, Rodrigo. El Contralmirante Francisco 2.° Sánchez Alvaradejo (SCHG/R, 147, 1979, p. 28–52, ill.)

Story of unsung hero of battle of Iquique, *Esmeralda*'s highest-ranking officer to survive. Written by a retired naval officer, article is more useful as commentary on 1979 Chile than as a contribution to literature on War of the Pacific.

La Guerra con Chile en sus documentos. See item **2946.**

3083 Guerra del Pacífico. Recopilador, Fernando Ruz Trujillo. Ilus. de portada, Andrés Jullián. Santiago: Editorial Andrés Bello, 1979. 135 p.; bibl.

Publishes intact for first time two useful and interesting personal accounts of the war. Vergara, a reserve officer, criticizes professional military. Duble Almeida's campaign diary is both descriptive and critical of some aspects of war effort.

3084 Historia ilustrada de la Guerra del Pacífico, 1879–1884. Santiago: Editorial Universitaria, 1979. 329 p.; ill.; index.

Handsome, nicely illustrated coffee table book, ideal for military history buffs and Chilean patriots.

3085 Huerta de Pacheco, María Antonieta. Reforma agraria chilena 1938–1978: evolución histórica (PUJ/UH, 11, dic. 1979, p. 159–188, bibl.)

Overview of politics, programs, and results of agrarian reform since 1962 Alessandri law, based on secondary sources, with minimal treatment of Popular Front's efforts. Useful as introduction to 1962–78 period and for lengthy bibliography.

3086 Humberstone, J. T. Huída de Agua Santa en 1879. Santiago: Editorial Andrés Bello, 1980. 73 p.; map.

Autobiographical account of nitrate engineer Humberstone's flight from Agua Santa (Tarapacá) to Tacna to escape early combat in War of Pacific. As useful for geographic descriptions as for information on war.

3087 Informes inéditos de diplomáticos extranjeros durante la guerra del Pacífico: Alemania, Estados Unidos de Norteamérica, Francia, Gran Bretaña. Santiago: Editorial Andrés Bello, 1980. 437 p.

Previously unpublished material by ministers of US, Britain, France and Germany stationed in Chile during War of the Pacific concerning Chilean domestic developments, war and related diplomacy, protection of ministers' nationals, and most importantly four powers' mediation efforts. Useful addition to literature on war, documents were gathered and edited by Chilean historians.

3088 Izquierdo Araya, Guillermo. Eduardo Llanos y Nava, el generoso español vinculado a la gesta naval de Iquique (SCHG/R, 147, 1979, p. 5–27)

Story of Spaniard who rescued cadavers of Arturo Prat and Ignacio Serrano from burial in common grave with bodies of ordinary Chilean sailors following battle of Iquique.

3089 Johnson, Ann Hagerman. Migration, the individual, and the family in Latin America: a historical perspective (*in* World Conference on Records and Genealogical Seminar, Salt Lake City, 1980. Preserving our heritage. Salt Lake City, Utah: Genealogical Society of the Church of Jesus Christ of Latter-Day Saints, 1980?, p. 1–21 [Series; 703])

Analytical paper deals with historical patterns of internal migration in Chile and their changing impacts on family's composition and functioning. Drawing on census data and range of other sources, concludes that new "social family" based on communal living and support networks among unrelated people replaced nuclear family among rural-to-urban migrants by turn of 20th century.

Kay, Cristóbal. El sistema señorial europeo y la hacienda latinoamericana. See *HLAS 43:3469.*

3090 Lagos Carmona, Guillermo. Historia de las fronteras de Chile: los tratados de límites con Argentina. 2. ed. aum. y actualizada. Santiago: Editorial Andrés Bello, 1980. 398 p.; 5 folded leaves of plates; bibl.; maps (some col.)

Revised and updated history of Chilean-Argentine boundaries (for 1966 ed., see *HLAS 31:5472*) by former Director of Boundaries in Chilean Ministry of Foreign Relations. Partisan but very useful summary of main border questions between both countries also portrays Chilean view of current problems, which author sees as stemming from Argentina's "new geopolitical ambitions."

El Laudo Arbitral del Canal Beagle. See *HLAS 43:7374.*

3091 León Solís, Leonardo. Alianzas militares entre los indios araucanos y los grupos indios de las pampas: la rebelión araucana de 1867–1872 en Argentina y Chile (Nueva Historia [University of London, Institute of Latin American Studies] 1:1, 1981, p. 3–49)

Lengthy, heavily documented article, based on author's Master's thesis, focuses on relatively neglected study of Araucanian resistance: trans-Andean political and military ties uniting Argentine and Chilean Indians in 19th century. After tracing patterns of Araucanian migration into Argentine territory, León examines 1867–72 "rebellion" to demonstrate that a politically independent, cohesive and culturally homogeneous Indian territory developed in area beyond effective national control on both sides of the Andes. Important contribution for understanding Indian resistance.

Loveman, Brian. Political participation and rural labor in Chile. See *HLAS 43:6557.*

3092 Mamalakis, Markos. Historical statistics of Chile. v. 1, National accounts. v. 2, Demography and labor force. Westport, Conn.: Greenwood Press, 1978/1980. 2 v. (262, 420 p.); bibl.; tables.

Vol. 1 (1978) provides extensive methodological critique of official statistics since 1940 and offers tables on all aspects of national income and expenditure (1940–74). Vol. 2 (1980) includes introduction and 176 tables on population, migration, urbanization, education, employment, wages and salaries, etc., primarily post-1940 period but with considerable data from late 19th century and population figures from early colonial period. Both volumes are invaluable resources for researchers on modern Chilean history. For economist's comment, see *HLAS 43:3473.*

3093 Martínez Baeza, Sergio. Cuatro historiadores: Vicuña Mackenna, Barros Arana, Mitre y Medina (UC/AT, 441, 1980, 1. semestre, p. 79–92)

Account of personal and intellectual relationships among the Argentine Mitre and three leading 19th-century Chilean historians, based on letters, articles, books and memorabilia. Documentation mostly found in Buenos Aires' Museo Mitre. Interesting for history of Chilean and Argentine historiography.

3094 Martinic Beros, Mateo. Los alemanes en Magallanes. Punta Arenas, Magallanes, Chile: Instituto de la Patagonia, 1978. 32 p.; bibl. (Serie Monografías. Instituto de la Patagonia; no. 10)

Another of Martinic's competent mini-studies of Magallanes, this one deals with individual Germans and the collective German contribution to Chile's extreme south.

3095 Matte Varas, J. Joaquín. Presencia de los capellanes castrenses en la Guerra del Pacífico (UCCIH/H, 15, 1980, p. 179–236)

Account of names, numbers and roles of military chaplains accompanying Chilean forces in War of the Pacific. Includes biographical sketches and several documents.

3096 Mayo, John. Britain and Chile, 1851–1886: anatomy of a relationship (SAGE/JIAS, 23:1, Feb. 1981, p. 95–120, tables)

Case study of Chilean "dependency" vis-á-vis Britain prior to nitrate age challenges some common interpretations. Mayo describes the Chilean political and economic climate, British community and its investment patterns, and mechanisms of British commercial dominance, especially the commission house. Ascribes establishment and continuance of "informal empire" to individual British merchants rather than to British government policies, and to Chilean conditions and attitudes. Interesting perspective on important topic.

3097 ———. La Compañía de Salitres de Antofagasta y la Guerra del Pacífico (UCCIH/H, 14, 1979, p. 71–102)

Thoroughly researched, detailed analysis of long and intensely-debated role of Anglo-Chilean nitrate company in bringing about the war. Based largely on company records, study finds that while Bolivia's treaty violations in taxing the company's exports motivated Chile's military action, the company itself desired only to have its status under the 1874 treaty respected by Bolivian authorities. Despite new evidence, this will not end the debate. For abbreviated Spanish translation, see *Boletín de Estudios Latinoamericanos* (Amsterdam, No. 28, 1980, p. 3–11)

3098 Miquel, Janine. Proceso de gestación y desarrollo histórico del movimiento laboral chileno. Stockholm: Institute of Latin American Studies, 1979. 43 p.; bibl. (Research paper series; 16)

Superficial overview of history of Chilean labor movement, useful as introduction to topic.

3099 Nunn, Frederick M. El Chile antiguo y el nuevo: la política de transición, 1973–79. Santiago: Pontificia Universidad Católica de Chile, Instituto de Ciencia Política, 1979. 48 leaves (Cuadernos del Instituto de Ciencia Política; no. 28)

Nunn's reflections on Chilean experience under Allende draw attention to some earlier developments and the junta. Argues that Chile's fragile democracy was more form than substance and could not withstand determination of minority Marxist government to destroy it. Analyzes transition toward new institutional order under a junta that is less autocratic, Nunn claims, than foreign press admits. Concludes that nothing has dissuaded the military from its mission of institutionalizing a new Chilean political order.

Oppenheimer, Robert. Chile. See *HLAS* 43:6569.

3100 ———. Chile's Central Valley railroads and economic development in the nineteenth century (PCCLAS/P, 6, 1977/1979, p. 73–86)

Thoughtful statement of the problématique of role of Central Valley railroads in Chilean economic history. After describing railroad growth pattern, article examines contribution of railroads to Chile's economic development and lays out problems requiring further research.

3101 ———. National capital and national development: financing Chile's Central Valley railroads (Business History Review [Harvard University, Cambridge, Mass.] 56:1, Spring 1982, p. 54–75)

Demonstrates central role of native entrepreneurs in constructing Central Valley's first two rail lines. Chilean capitalists also persuaded government to support and coordinate their efforts. Detailed socioeconomic profile of stockholders places railroad investors within context of national economic elite. Important contribution.

3102 Ortega, Luis. Acerca de los orígenes de la industrialización chilena, 1860–1879 (Nueva Historia [University of London, Institute of Latin American Studies] 1:2, 1981, p. 3–54)

Important revisionist article, based on author's University of London dissertation, joins longstanding debate as to when Chilean industrialization really began. After reviewing appropriate literature, argues that industrialization process began in 1860s and accelerated in 1870s. Examines industries by sector, concluding that although modern factories were few in number, their total production was important and they provided basis for more sustained industrialization after War of the Pacific.

3103 ———. The first four decades of the Chilean coal mining industry, 1840–1879 (JLAS, 14:1, May 1982, p. 1–32)

Thoroughly researched, well argued article describes development of Chilean coal industry from its inception to War of the Pacific. Responding to demand generated by new activities (e.g., steam navigation, railways, manufacturing and especially copper smelting) coal mining grew into sophisticated capitalist enterprise with expanding impact on national economy. This case study of native capitalism, set within a dependency theory framework, offers important insights into ties between export-oriented economies and domestic economic development.

3104 Oviedo Cavada, Carlos. La Iglesia en la revolución de 1891 (UCCIH/H, 14, 1979, p. 275–314)

Step-by-step narrative of Church's role in 1891 civil war, focusing on Archbishop of Santiago, Mariano Casanova, and the Vatican. Based primarily on formal Church pronouncements, concludes that despite ties with Conservatives and partisan attitudes of some clerics, hierarchy and Vatican remained neutral and worked solely for restoration of peace, a course which author finds to be "one of the noblest tasks of the Catholic Church."

Pardo y Barreda, José. Historia del Tratado "Secreto" de Alianza Defensiva entre el Perú y Bolivia. See item **2968**.

Paz Soldán, Mariano Felipe. Narración histórica de la guerra de Chile contra el Perú y Bolivia. See item **2969**.

3105 Pereira Larraín, Teresa. El pensamiento de una generación de historiadores hispanoamericanos: Alberto Edwards, Ernesto Quesada y Laureano Vallenilla (UCCIH/H, 15, 1980, p. 237–337)

Analyzes ideas and approaches common to these Chilean, Argentine and Venezuelan historians who wrote in late 19th and early 20th centuries. Rejecting 19th-century Liberal historiography with its emphasis on forms of government and political programs, these men embraced relativism and "antidogmatism" and searched for reality in their countries' cultures, psyches, social structures, and geographic and racial characteristics, lending support to conservative interpretations. Well researched and interesting article, useful for comparative study of Latin American historiography.

3106 Pérez Ovalle, Javier. La encomienda de Catapilco. Santiago: Editorial Andrés Bello, 1979. 231 p.; ports.

Part memoir, part anecdotal history deals with hacienda of Catapilco near Zapallar, and its owners, the Ovalle Vicuña family. *Apuntes* by family member, finished in 1939 but not published until now, offer nostalgic, romanticized picture of untroubled past from vantage point (1930s) of impending change.

3107 Perry, Richard O. Argentina and Chile: the struggle for Patagonia, 1843–1881 (AAFH/TAM, 36:3, Jan. 1980, p. 347–363)

Informative and timely analysis of conflict over Patagonia from beginnings of steam navigation through Straits of Magellan to 1881 treaty that served as basis of 1902 arbitration settlement. Drawing on sources from both sides, Perry argues that despite more ambitious claims and continuing recriminations of Chilean nationalists, Chile in 19th century neither aspired nor possessed the power to occupy all of Patagonia, and was satisfied to settle for Straits of Magellan area. For political scientist's comment, see *HLAS* 43:7387.

3108 Pinochet de la Barra, Oscar. Misión en Bolivia de C. Walker Martínez y R. Sotomayor Valdés. Santiago: Editorial del Pacífico, 1980? 216 p.; 8 p. of plates; bibl.; ill.; ports.

Based on public and private archives as well as secondary sources, book deals with Chilean diplomatic missions from 1866 to 1874 boundary treaty with Bolivia. Author sets stage, then selects appropriate memoirs and letters through which both diplomats describe their impressions of Bolivia, dealings with Melgarejo, and general process of altiplano diplomacy. Result is entertaining as well as interesting and informative.

3109 Pregger Román, Charles G. Economic interest groups within the Chilean government, 1851 to 1891: continuity and discontinuity in economic and political evolution (SS, 43:2, Summer 1979, p. 202–233)

Argues that intermittent political instability afflicting Chile during this period resulted from temporary political displacement of economically dynamic sectors of the oligarchy. Based on an unwieldly categorization of main economic sectors and unsupported by relevant documentation, effort contributes little to understanding of economic basis of 19th-century political power.

3110 Raveau Viancos, Estanislao. Los tripulantes de la *Esmeralda* y la *Covadonga* el día 21 de mayo de 1879 (SCHG/R, 147, 1979, p. 84–97)

Exercise in patriotism rescues from oblivion names of 16 martyred crewmen of Chilean ships *Esmeralda* and *Covadonga*, victims of naval Battle of Iquique. Names were inscribed on Valparaíso monument in 1979.

3111 Revista Chilena de Historia y Geografía. Sociedad Chilena de Historia y Geografía. No. 146, 1978– . Santiago.

Issue devoted to Bernardo O'Higgins' bicentennial includes articles of interest for post-independence period: "La Población del Fuerte San Diego de Alcalá: Tucapel del Laja;" "La Hacienda Las Canteras y el Gran Cono de Lajas;" "Identidad Geohistórica de la Integración Andina: Legado Común y Fragmentación Microrregional;" "Después del Laudo del Beagle;" and "Justo Abel Rosales: su Labor Histórica y Literaria." For articles concerning independence period, see *HLAS* 42:2942.

3112 Reyno Gutiérrez, Manuel. El mando militar y la injerencia del gobierno en la Guerra de 1879 (SCHG/R, 147, 1979, p. 53–83, bibl., ill.)

Colonel author argues that 1839 ordinances that established civilian command over the military, while bringing 40 years of relative internal peace and stability, were responsible for politicizing war effort and delaying Chile's victory in War of the Pacific. Example of history at the service of the official present.

3113 Roddick, Jackie. The failure of populism in Chile: labour movement and politics before World War II (CEDLA/B, 31, dic. 1981, p. 61–89, bibl., tables)

Provocative analytical survey history of Chilean labor movement seeks explanation for its resistance to populist politics that diverted others (e.g., Argentine, Brazilian) from leftist revolutionary path. Finds that conditions favored development of movement's close alliance with parties and, equally important, that competition among labor-based parties offered working class chances to obtain benefits from state without being co-opted by it. This pattern saved Chilean labor from lure of populism but created insurmountable problems of UP government. Very worthwhile contribution.

3114 Ruz Trujillo, Fernando. Rafael Sotomayor, el organizador de la victoria. Santiago: Editorial Andrés Bello, 1980. 232 p.; bibl.; ill.

Biography of public figure focuses on his crucial role in War of Pacific as civilian coordinator of Chilean military efforts in the field. Based on extensive documentary sources as well as secondary literature. Study of the "Minister of War in campaign" exemplifies high-level hero worship.

3115 Salinas Fuenzalida, Augusto. Un pastor santo: el Eminentísimo Señor Cardenal Don José María Caro Rodríguez, 1866–1958. Santiago: Editorial Andrés Bello, 1981. 399 p.; 20 p. of plates; ill.

Biography of man who became Chile's first cardinal and who, as Archbishop of Santiago (1939–58) was instrumental in identifying the Chilean Church with social activism. Laudatory but very useful biography by close friend is informative about the cardinal's life, religious vocation and politics.

3116 Sater, William F. The abortive Kronstadt: the Chilean naval mutiny of 1931 (HAHR, 60:2, May 1980, p. 239–268)

Detailed examination of little-known 1931 naval uprising, based on US and British diplomatic documents as well as Chilean sources. Reveals strong radical sentiment among naval lower ranks and their supporters, and sheds valuable light on national political crisis between fall of Ibáñez and advent of Socialist Republic.

3117 ———. Chile (*in* Research guide to Andean history: Bolivia, Chile, Ecuador and Peru. [see item **2577**] p. 53–58)

Chilean section of *Research guide to Andean history* contains introduction, two essays on colonial sources and eight essays on national period covering various aspects of political, economic and labor history, all by knowledgeable scholars. Going beyond description of primary sources, most essays discuss state of historiography, delineate research problems, critique reliability and value of sources, and offer practical advice. Valuable for both neophyte and experienced researchers in Chilean history.

3118 Seeger, Martin L. The Ten Cent War: naval phase (The American Neptune [Quarterly journal of maritime history, Peabody Museum of Salem, East Indian Marine Hall, Salem, Mass.] 39:4, Oct. 1979, p. 271–288)

Analysis of Peruvian and Chilean naval strengths, strategies and battles in War of the Pacific. Based heavily on secondary sources, useful as introduction to topic.

3119 Sehlinger, Peter J. A select guide to Chilean libraries and archives. Bloomington: Latin American Studies Program, Indiana University, 1979. 35 p. (Latin American studies working papers; 9)

Very useful practical guide to Chilean collections for researchers in humanities and social sciences. Lists and describes government, university, international organization, foundation and private libraries and archives in Santiago and a few in provinces. Recommends more detailed published guides to major collections.

3120 7 [i.e. Siete] **ensayos** sobre Arturo Alessandri Palma. Claudio Orrego V. *et al.* Santiago: Instituto Chileno de Estudios Humanísticos, 1979. 464 p.; bibl.; ill.

Collection of well researched essays by young historians who collaborated in similar works on Alberto Edwards (see *HLAS 40: 3607*), Horacio Walker (see *HLAS 40:3655*) and Jaime Eyzaguirre (see *HLAS 42:3222*). Alessandri's pivotal role in Chilean history is examined in seven essays on the man and his times, early political career, 1920 campaign, and the social question, church and state, the military, and political parties during his presidencies. Competent, indepth essays shed new light on his impact on Chile.

3121 Societá feudale e imperialismo en America Latina: i caso del Cile. A cura di Eugenia Scarzanella e Salvatore Sechi. Bologna: Zanichelli, 1977. 224 p.; bibl. (Letture storiche; 16)

Collection of essays, generally left in orientation, taken from published works of an international group of scholars and organized chronologically to provide selective interpretive history of Chile. Useful addition to literature in Italian.

3122 Spindler, Frank MacDonald. Francisco Bilbao: Chilean disciple of Lamennais (JHI, 41 : 3, July/Sept. 1980, p. 487–496)

Brief but thoroughly researched and incisive essay examines great influence of Lamennais on intellectual formation of Chilean political thinker Francisco Bilbao (1823–65). Tracing relationship from Bilbao's literary acquaintance with Lamennais in Santiago's Instituto Nacional through four years of personal discipleship in Paris, Spindler focuses on Bilbao's 1856 essay "Lamennais as Representative of the Dualism of Modern Civilization," written in homage to departed master.

Tobler, Hans Werner and **Peter Waldmann**. German colonies in South America: a new Germany in the Cono Sur? See item **1835**.

3123 Tres ensayos sobre la mujer chilena: siglos XVIII–XIX–XX. Lucía Santa Cruz *et al.* Santiago: Editorial Universitaria, 1978. 328 p.; bibl.; ill.

Three excellent essays on women through Chilean history. Santa Cruz, covering colonial period through chronicles and travelers' accounts, deals at length with Araucanian women; Teresa Pereira develops a sociology of 19th-century women; and Isabel Zegers and Valeria Maino cover demography and changing women's roles in 20th century. All use sources with imagination and skill to produce best single historical study of Chilean women.

3124 Valladares Campos, Jorge. La hacienda Longaví: 1639–1959 (UCCIH/H, 14, 1979, p. 103–205)

Based on notarial and private archives, monograph traces in detail the hacienda Longaví from Jesuit origins through numerous changes of ownership and subdivisions to 1959. Does not address questions of labor, forms of production, or sources of capital, but is useful in laying out precise evolution of property ownership of important Jesuit hacienda.

3125 Vial Correa, Gonzalo. Historia de Chile, 1891–1973. v. 1, La sociedad chilena en el cambio de siglo, 1891–1920. Santiago: Editorial Santillana del Pacífico, 1981. 2 v. in 1 (1004 p.); bibl.

Massive vol. 1 (1004 p. in two tomes) of Gonzalo Vial's projected 11-volume history of Chile from 1891 civil war to 1973 coup is a very promising beginning. Analyzes factors that broke down "social consensus" between 1891–1920, principally new intellectual currents, economic problems, "social question," ineffectual politics, and attitudes and actions of directing, middle and popular classes. Includes notes and extensive bibliography. Most comprehensive, balanced and up-to-date social history of Parliamentary Republic. One hopes succeeding volumes measure up to this one.

3126 Vicuña MacKenna, Benjamín. El album de la gloria de Chile. Portada, J. A. C. Arthur. Ed. facsimilar. Santiago: Editorial Vaitea, 1977. 622 p.; 27 leaves of plates; ill. (Colección Historia de Chile)

Facsimile reproduction of 1883 original glorifying Chile's victorious war and its martyrs.

3127 Vidal Muñoz, Santiago. El pensamiento científico de Claudio Gay (UC/AT, 439, 1979, p. 35–58)

Analysis of scientific training and thought of Claudio Gay, 19th-century French naturalist who spent many years in Chile and left volumes of incisive observations on society as well as nature. Based on Gay's works and secondary sources, essay is useful as summary of Gay's ideas and role in Chilean intellectual history.

Villalobos R., Sergio. El Beagle, historia de una controversia. See *HLAS 43:7394.*

3128 Vitale, Luis. Interpretación marxista de la historia de Chile: de semicolonia inglesa a semicolonia norteamericana. Barcelona: Fontamara, 1980. 219 p. (Ensayo contemporáneo)

Vol. 5 (vol. 1/4, 1967–75) carries Vitale's ambitious history through the Frei years (see also *HLAS 32:2692; HLAS 34:2866a; HLAS 36:3013;* vol. 4 not reviewed). Major themes are: labor movement, class basis of politics and penetration of foreign capital. A thoroughly researched, thoughtful and very readable analysis of Chilean history from a Marxist viewpoint.

3129 Woll, Allen. A functional past: the uses of history in nineteenth-century Chile. Baton Rouge: Louisiana State University Press, 1982. 211 p.; bibl.; index; notes.

Interesting, incisive study of the writing of history in 19th-century Chile. Thesis is that despite insistent claims to the contrary, this period's historiography was a highly political exercise in which historians used their works to disseminate philosophical views and argue partisan issues. Woll deals first with early republican historians and their controversies over methodology and meaning in history, then analyzes several historiographical themes to reveal political content of ostensibly objective writings. Valuable contribution to Chilean intellectual history and to the interpretive literature on Latin American historiography.

3130 Wright, Thomas C. Landowners and reform in Chile: the Sociedad Nacional de Agricultura, 1919–1940. Urbana: University of Illinois Press, 1982. 249 p.; bibl.; ill.; index.

Study of organized landowners' responses to threats against their hegemony focuses on Sociedad Nacional de Agricultura of Chile, founded 1869, as it sought to become a sophisticated pressure group against mass politics. Finds that provincial and central interests were combined with difficulty into class objectives to pressure for shallow modernization or delay in agrarian reform. Epilogue brings story of landowner maneuvers down to 1979 and subsequent reinstatement of their privileges. Documentation from several government ministries, congressional debates, Chilean periodicals, SNA archival records and published works is supplemented by wide reading in extensive secondary literature. Indispensable study of politics of manipulation by a Latin American ruling class. [V. C. Peloso]

3131 ———. The politics of agrarian reform in Chile: 1919–1940 (PCCLAS/P, 6, 1977/1979, p. 59–71)

Highlights legislative struggles for agrarian reform in Chile. Focuses on treatment of agrarian reform bills in Chilean legislature, pressures applied to them by interests groups (especially National Agrarian Society) to dilute them, and congressional battles which resulted in token or poorly applied laws in 1928 and 1935. Popular Front government preserved unity at cost of effective agrarian reform. Explains that landowners failed to seize opportunities for gradual reform earlier, thereby preparing their own demise in 1960s and 1970s. Based on SNA documentation and contemporary newspaper accounts. [V. C. Peloso]

3132 Yeager, Gertrude Matyoka. Barros Arana's *Historia jeneral de Chile*: politics, history and national identity. Fort Worth: Texas Christian University Press, 1981. 187 p.; bibl.; notes.

Premise is notion that 19th-century Latin American historians were "intellectual agents of nation-building who plied their craft in ways designed to direct national development." Thoughtful book offers intellectual biography of this historian as well as analysis of his works and influence. In multiple roles, Barros Arana molded minds of the nation's elite to fit his own eclectic vision of Chile's past and future (e.g., endowing colonial elites with Liberal virtues, etc.). Valuable as study of Latin American historiography as well as Chilean history.

3133 Zemelman M., Hugo. El movimiento popular chileno y el sistema de alianzas en la década de los treinta (*in* América Latina en los años treinta. Luis Antezana E. *et al.* Coordinador, Pablo González Casanova. México: Instituto de Investigaciones Sociales, Universidad Nacional Autónoma de México, 1977, p. 378–450, bibl., map)

Thorough analysis of 1930s politics, set in historical perspective, focuses on emerging left challenge to traditional governing groups. Sees 1930s as decade of frustration for "popular movement," co-opted by petit bourgeois leadership and system of political alliances culminating in Popular Front that tied the working class to the system. Although not new, this is cogent analysis and good synthesis. For economist's comment, see *HLAS 43:3498.*

Argentina, Paraguay and Uruguay

ROBERTO ETCHEPAREBORDA, *Director, Department of Cultural Affairs, Organization of American States*

ARGENTINA: An examination of recent publications reveals a satisfactory level of achievement in the field. Indicators such as areas investigated, topics of research, and selection of chronological periods corroborate this impression.

With regard to authorship, of a total 278 works annotated in this section, 229 were written by Argentines and 49 by foreigners. The total consists of an almost equal number of books, 149; and articles, 129. Of 37 foreign works, a majority, as can be expected, were written by American historians. An interesting development is the growing number of contributions by women which make up 20 percent of Argentine authors and 25 percent of foreigners, a notable advance over previous years.

With regard to chronology, of the three periods examined (i.e., 19th century; 20th century to 1930; and 20th century post-1930) foreign authors clearly prefer the latter. On the other hand, Argentine works are divided along more traditional lines with 140 for the 19th century, 28 and 30 for the other two periods, respectively.

Insofar as topics are concerned, traditional fields are represented by a total of 139 entries; or 56.3 percent, divided as follows: political history (75); military (16); religious (7); international relations (25); biographies (14); documentary works (2). Less traditional fields consist of 104 items or 42.1 percent and are divided as follows: economic history (44), social history (36), cultural and scientific history (20) and geohistory (4), with only four contributions on miscellaneous topics.

Foreign authors, by subject, are reflected in the following figures: political history (28) and international relations (7) accounting for 69 percent of the total; and social history (8), economic history (7), and scientific history (1), making up the remainder 31 percent.

Familiar subjects such as Rosas (17) and peronism (30) continue to dominate the literature and represent 25 percent of foreign publications. To this figure one can add works pertaining to military (8) and labor matters (8). The growing interest in provincial history is reflected in 54 publications annotated below which make up 22 percent of the total. For reasons of space this section does not include more than 400 papers on political, economic and social aspects of provincial history that were presented at national meetings organized by the National Academy of History, and other institutions.

Of the works annotated below, several deserve special mention. Of primary importance is the collection of writings by the late José Luis Romero, especially his reflections on the last 50 years (item **3360**). Tulio Halperin Donghi's well researched *Guerra y finanzas* (item **3269**), reveals information unknown until now. Another leading work of investigation is that of I. Oved on the origins and struggles of labor organizations (item **3326**).

The first complete analysis of Rosas and his time by a non-Argentine author is John Lynch's (item **3300**), a very solid study that opens new perspectives and which undoubtedly will stimulate further analysis and research. Bartolomé Mitre's biography by José S. Campobassi (item **3172**) provides a valuable and clear picture of his time, in a manner similar to the author's *Sarmiento* (see *HLAS 40:3712*).

The success of Robert A. Potash's scholarly publication on the armed forces and politics (item **3338**) attests its high qualities as well as its influence on the field. Also worthy of attention is the revised reprint of Horacio Gilberti's *Historia económica de la ganadería* (item **3251**). Gary W. Wynia skillfully describes the influence of economics on politics (item **3412**) while Mario Rapoport delineates a revealing picture of the impact of World War II on Argentine politics and foreign relations (item **3347**).

A scholarly examination of peronism's first years can be found in Peter Waldman's study (item **3408**). Cayetano Bruno completes a vast undertaking on the history of the Church, with a final volume that carries his narrative to the beginning of the 20th century (item **3164**). Miguel Angel de Marco's excellent study of the Spanish squadron in the River Plate presents a panoramic view of more than a half a century of the national period (item **3196**). A powerful evocation of old Buenos Aires and its traditional families is Manuel Mujica Láinez's contribution to the city's fourth centennial, a work which combines historical facts with literary excellence (item **3321**).

Among new general histories two are important, one by Julio Irazusta, his *Breve historia argentina* (item **3279**), posthumous reflections on the national past, and an abridged reprint of *Historia general* published by Centro Editor (item **3274**). Although histories of the provinces have grown in quantity, their quality is still somewhat uneven. Worth mentioning are Armando R. Bazán's works on La Rioja (item **3154**), Emilio A. Bidondo's on Jujuy (item **3156**), and among local historians, José C. Busaniche's *Hombres y hechos de Santa Fe* (item **3169**), a vivid portrayal of life in the Littoral.

One of the most worthwhile biographies is Nicholas Fraser's and Marysa Navarro's history of Eva Perón (item **3240**). Other biographical and autobiographical works are studies of the Alvear family (item **3223**); Josefina Cruz de Caprile's work on Saavedra (item **2832a**); a brief portrait of Federalist leader Juan B. Bustos (item **3317**); a study of Rodolfo Irazusta's political and historical contributions (item **3357**); and Francisco P. Moreno's *Reminiscencias* (item **3319**) which presents a clear picture of Patagonia at the turn of the century.

The Rosas period continues to command the usual interest but without the customary polemics. In addition to the above mentioned interpretation by Lynch, the crucial period of Anglo-French intervention is objectively analyzed by Néstor S. Colli (item **3180**). José M. Ramallo (item **3343**) examines the economy of the Rosas period in a concise study, and Silvestre Peña y Lillo (item **3330**) traces Facundo Quiroga's presence in the Cuyo region in a posthumous but recently published work.

The post-Caseros era is depicted in an excellent compilation prepared by Halperin Donghi (item **3340**). Solid studies that cover years of representative government are: Horacio Sanguinetti's (item **3368**) of Socialist Party divisions in the 1920s, and Ann L. Potter's (item **3339**) on how the 1930 crisis can be attributed to the disruption of political participation.

The political phenomenon of peronism continues to command growing interest as exemplified by the following: Peter Ranis' careful research on Perón's early ideas and how they shaped his political movement (item **3345**), Waldman's above mentioned study on Perón's two first presidencies, and Fraser's and Navarro's cited biography of Eva Perón. Also worth mentioning are Julie M. Taylor's outstanding sociological analysis (item **3393**), and Walter Little's study of the reactions of the working class (item **3291**). Likewise, M. Mora y Araujo's and Ignacio Llorente's compilation on electoral demography (item **3406**) opens new perspectives and sheds light on a number of controversial issues. As is to be expected, the 1973 peronist comeback is the subject of valuable study in Julio Godio's leftist peronist interpretation (item **3256**), Carlos J. Moneta's monograph on foreign policy (item **3318**), and Guido Di Tella's work on the economic policies of a labor-based government (item **3200**).

A number of anniversaries were celebrated in this biennium such as the fourth centennial of Buenos Aires' foundation and the anniversary of its federalization, the centennial of the "Campaña del Desierto," and of the so-called Generation of 1880s. The first event is commemorated in a well presented summary of narratives from travelers who visited Buenos Aires in 1870–1910. The consolidation of the nation's territory achieved through the "Campaña del Desierto" is recalled by Serres Güiraldes in his *Estrategia del general Roca* (item **3376**), a work which sharply delineates the nation's domestic and international situation at the time. Missionary work in the southern region is portrayed in a joint and informative study (item **3219**), while new developments in the area are analyzed in *Geopolítica, ciencia y técnica* (item **3378**). Ezequiel Gallo and Gustavo Ferrari (item **3145**) are the editors of a history of the 1880s which, despite some uneven contributions, provides an excellent picture of the period until 1910. A scholarly and thorough look at the economic and social circumstances of the 1880s is offered by Roberto Cortés Conde who does away with several familiar clichés about this period (item **3187**).

Among the few works of military history worth mentioning are Emilio A. Bidondo's (item **2824a**) on the war of independence; and Fernando A. de Baldrich's article on the national character of the Confederate forces (item **3152**), which is interesting because of its revisionist stand. The above mentioned book by Potash (item **3338**) has much to say about the military presence in the country's political life as do the translation of Alain Rouquié's work (item **3363**), the first part of which leads up to 1930, and the late Miguel A. Scenna's last contribution, *Los militares* (item **3373**).

International relations of the 19th and 20th centuries are subject to much scrutiny in an outstanding monograph by I. Ruiz Moreno (item **3365**), articles by Luis S. Sanz (items **3369–3370**) which reveal a novel and interesting approach; and one by Nora L. S. de Gentile (item **3377**) includes important source material.

World War II, an important period in international relations, is illuminated by Gary Frank (item **3239**) and Randall B. Woods (item **3411**). Together with Rapoport's above mentioned book, they enrich our knowledge of this period.

An area that has been little explored is demographic history. Ernesto J. Maeder's article (item **3308**) proves there is a definite correlation between declining population and civil strife; and Lyman Johnson's demographic study of Buenos Aires (item **3283**) marshalls important new data that supersedes previous estimates.

Historiographical studies, usually scarce, are well represented in this *HLAS* by valuable contributions such as Julio Irazusta's revisionist analysis of Ramos Mejía's *Rosas y su tiempo* (item **3280**); Pérez Amuchástegui's censure of politicized history and defense of objective scholarship (item **3333**); and *La geografía y la historia* *en la identidad nacional* (item **3250**) a series of contributions that update both disciplines.

Although no major work of economic history was published in this biennium, numerous aspects of the topic have been researched. For example, there is Jorge A. Mitre's excellent history of the Banco de la Provincia de Buenos Aires which traces the role of this institution as an agent of *porteño* dominance (item **3313**). The economic and social history of Entre Ríos in the first half of the 19th century is the subject of Urquiza Almandoz's study (item **3402**). Finally, Santa Fe's economic history has been skillfully explored by Oscar L. Ensinck (items **3206–3210** and **3212**), and Córdoba's by Norma Riquelme de Lobos and María C. Flachs (items **3352–3353**).

Important developments in social history are evident, first of all, in Mark D. Szuchman's *Mobility and integration in urban Argentina: Córdoba in the Liberal era* (item **3390**), a work that challenges many assumptions and common beliefs regarding social mobility. Another pioneer effort is Donna J. Guy's study of female labor (item **3268**). María Sáenz Quesada examines the role of a very influential sector of society in *Los estancieros* (item **3367**) while Richard W. Slatta analyzes, from a revisionist viewpoint, another significant element of rural Argentina, the gaucho and his environment (item **3380–3382**).

One welcomes the publication of two collections of primary sources: Güemes documents (item **2833a**), a major undertaking, and *La correspondencia Mitre-Urquiza* (item **3186**).

Among new journals appearing in this period are: *Historia* (item **3215**), a periodical in book form; the *Revista Nacional de Cultura* (item **3146**) with a greater share of historical contributions; *Res Gesta* of Rosario (item **3241**); and *Folia Histórica del Nordeste* of Resistencia (item **3308**). Publishers that continue to promote historical works are Editorial Sudamericana, La Bastilla and Plus Ultra, and more recently, Editorial de Belgrano. One should also acknowledge the long-standing commitment of the Academia Nacional de la Historia to the publication of historical research.

Topics not properly explored at present are the following: the 1880–1910 period, and in particular, monographic studies of its industrial sector, press, and educational and cultural developments; the 1930s in studies that are scholarly, in-depth, and non-partisan; and peronist figures other than the leader himself, as well as of members of the opposition, studies of whom are especially lacking.

In conclusion, one can state that, overall, most works annotated below are objective, scholarly, and free of lingering polemics between classic-liberal and revisionist schools.

PARAGUAY: Unfortunately, upward trends noted in past volumes of *HLAS* have declined into fewer contributions and a narrowing of focus. Among the few valuable titles published are: vol. 11 of the series initiated by the late Efraím Cardozo *Hace cien años* (item **3420**), and a reprint of his monumental *Historiografía* (item **3421**); a cultural history by Luis G. Benítez, *Historia de la educación* (item **3418**) to which we can add the *Breve historia de la imprenta* (item **3441**), and a helpful *Bibliografía* (item **3427**) by David Lewis Jones.

Always of interest and therefore important are works related to Francia such as Raúl de Andrada e Silva's valuable and challenging research on this figure (item **3438**), and the Russian historian Al'perovic's interesting perception of the *Supremo's* policies (item **3414**). Paraguayan authors also examine additional aspects of Francia's life and thoughts (items **3414, 3433, 3436** and **3442**).

Church and State relations are thoroughly documented in a study by Carlos A. Heyn Schupp (item **3426**), and the noted historian Sánchez Quell deals with the little-known field of Paraguay's bilateral relations with France (item **3426**). On the country's two great wars, there are no noteworthy contributions excepting E. Nicholas Tate's refutation of alleged British participation in the destruction of López's incipient empire (item **3439**).

URUGUAY: Historiographical production has been scarce and not above the ordinary, a trend noted in previous volumes of *HLAS*. Some valuable reprints, such as Alberto de Herrera's *Orígenes de la Guerra Grande* (item **3455**) have appeared as have some classics by Acuña de Figueroa (item **3455**) have appeared as have some classics by Acuña de Figueroa (item **3446**), Javier de Viana (item **3470**) and Ponce de León (item **3458**). Worthy of mention is Fernando O. Assunção's *El gaucho: estudio socio-cultural* (item **3447**), a significant intellectual effort of regional scope that will be difficult to surpass. José C. Williman's strongly revisionist biography of President Santos (item **3472**) is excellent. An important historiographical work by José C. Barran examines Batlle and his times (item **3448**), while Dante Turcatti studies his foreign policy (item **3467**) and Milton I. Vangar (item **3469**) presents a balanced analysis of his life (as pt. 2 of a biography in press).

Juan E. Pivel Devoto's exploration of the origins and main collaborators of the celebrated *Revista Histórica* (item **3457**) enhances our knowledge of Uruguay's cultural history.

Emigration from the Canary Islands to Uruguay, so relevant to the nation's history, is thoroughly researched by Nelson Martínez Díaz (item **3456**). An incursion into the neglected field of the history of journalism opens new perspectives on the country's origins (item **3471**). Finally, a good synthesis of mid-century Uruguay has been written by Isaac Ganón (item **3454**) while Martin H. J. Finch (item **3453**) raises many questions and reveals many paradoxes in his overall view of the nation's economic history.

ARGENTINA

3134 Acevedo, Edberto Oscar. Las elecciones mendocinas de 1823: ecos de una polémica (ANH/IE, 22, enero/junio 1977, p. 191–231)

Examines five case-studies to determine different responses of diverse sectors of the community towards the electoral process and their differing social and political attitudes.

3135 ——. Ideario político-religioso de un sacerdote mendocino hacia la cuarta década del siglo XIX (UNC/RHAA, 9:17/18, 1972/1979, p. 9–27)

Preliminary results of research into the ideology of relevant personalities of the interior. Argues that principal differences can be found in their attitude towards religious-cultural traditions inherited from Spain.

3136 ——. Investigaciones sobre el comercio cuyano, 1810–1830. Buenos Aires: Academia Nacional de la Historia, 1981 [i.e. 1982]. 201 p.; bibl. (Colección de historia económica y social; v. 5)

New contribution from a provincial perspective. Analyzes both economic and practical thinking of men of the interior concerning the effects of free trade. In 24 related chapters, examines development of the region's economy.

3137 Aguirre Cámara, José. Aportes para una biografía del General Juan Bautista Bustos. Córdoba: Junta Provincial de Historia de Córdoba, 1980. 91 p. (Cuadernos de historia; 2)

Another contribution about the Arequito rebellion leader and spokesman for Federalism.

3138 Alippi, Juan Arturo. Notas para la historia de la ingeniería de Córdoba: los estudios, las obras, el medio (JPHC/R, 7, 1978, p. 35–54)

Summary of more than a century's activities in engineering (e.g., dams, utilities, etc.)

3139 Allende, Andrés R. La candidatura presidencial de Dardo Rocha en 1886. La Plata: Ministerio de Educación, Subsecretaría de Cultura, 1978. 20 p.

Brief sketch of election process stresses fact that being a "porteño" handicapped Rocha's possibilities.

3140 ———. La cuestión de límites entre Córdoba y San Luis, 1863–1881: un fallo del Presidente Roca. Buenos Aires: The Author, 1981. 74 p.; maps.

Researched exposé of the complicated process of defining these limits. Concludes by approving the equity of Roca's decision favoring Córdoba.

3141 Alonso Piñeiro, Armando. Juan José Viamonte: historia de un patricio. Buenos Aires: The Jockey Club, 1980. 24 p.

Brief summary of his military and political life, written by his best biographer.

3142 Alzola de Cvitanovic, Nilsa M. Imagen tradicional y participación real de la mujer en la sociedad argentina, 1810–1920 (UNS/CS, 12, julio/dic. 1979, p. 97–110)

Explores social and legal limitations to which women have been submitted. Based on detailed use of primary data.

3143 ———. Imagen tradicional y realidad de la mujer en el ámbito político argentino, 1810–1920 (RIB, 31:2, 1981, p. 246–257)

Explores principal political events in which women participated.

3144 Arenas Luque, Fermín Vicente. Cómo era Buenos Aires. Buenos Aires: Plus Ultra, 1979. 266 p. (Colección Esquemas históricos; 29)

Highly readable chronicle commemorates city's fifth centennial.

3145 La Argentina del ochenta al centenario. Gustavo Ferrari and Ezequiel Gallo, eds. Buenos Aires: Editorial Sudamericana, 1980. 927 p.

Exhaustive attempt to describe and understand a period of outstanding development. Argentine and foreign historians submit 45 contributions under four main

subdivisions: political history, socioeconomic aspects, international relations and cultural development. Also includes short biographical vignettes of outstanding personalities. A major contribution despite some unevenness.

3146 Arze, María Estela. Comercio exterior del Río de la Plata, 1816–1880 (Revista Nacional de Cultura [Ministerio de Cultura y Educación, Secretaría de Estado de Cultura, Buenos Aires] 10, 1981, p. 65–104)

Well informed article summarizes important information drawn from foreign travelers' books and reports. Describes following topics: Buenos Aires port, foreign trade, maritime traffic, and principal commercial institutions.

3147 Así vieron a Rosas los ingleses. Andrew Graham-Yooll, editor. Buenos Aires: Editorial R. Alonso, 1980. 111 p.

Useful selection of diplomatic documents and newspaper excerpts offer interesting glimpses of the British perception of Rosas during his dictatorship.

3148 Auza, Néstor, Tomás. Correo del Domingo: 1864–1868, 1879–1880. Buenos Aires: s.n., 1980. 72 p.; ill.

New contribution by noted bibliographer on the two epochs of the illustrated journal founded by José María Cantilo. Although mostly literary, shows general ideological currents of the times. Also published in Revista Histórica (Instituto Histórico de la Organización Nacional, Buenos Aires, No. 5, 1980, p. 133–203).

3149 ———. El crecimiento de la conciencia territorial argentina (Revista Nacional de Cultura [Ministerio de Cultura y Educación, Secretaría de Estado de Cultura, Buenos Aires] 2:5, 1980, p. 11–33)

Informative outline argues that concern for territorial integrity began in the aftermath of the Paraguayan War. Sketches relevant protagonists and main institutions involved in the movement.

3150 ——— and Juan Mario Raone. Iconografía de Patagones. Buenos Aires: Ediciones Marymar, 1979. 94 p.; ill.; index (Colección Patagonia)

Describes 200 years in the life of Patagonia's first city founded by the Spanish through an excellent selection of illustrations.

3151 Baigorria, Manuel. Memorias del Coronel Manuel Baigorria. 2. ed. Buenos Aires: Editorial Universitaria de Buenos Aires, 1977. 127 p.; 4 leaves of plates; ill.; (Lucha de fronteras con ed indio)

New edition with introductory study by Baigorria's grandson adds new elements for a better appraisal and understanding of life in "tierra adentro" (for another version, see *HLAS 40:3692*).

3152 Baldrich, Fernando Amadeo de. ¿Fueron nacionales las Fuerzas Armadas entre 1828 y 1852? (IAEERI/E, 64/65, mayo/junio [through] julio/agosto 1980, p. 110–120)

Rejects claims of "liberal" classical historiographical school that during Rosas period there were no national armed forces. Mentions different campaigns (e.g., against Indians in 1833, "Guerra Grande," Anglo-French interventions) that were fought under the Confederation's flag.

3153 Bayer, Osvaldo. La Patagonia rebelde. México: Editorial Nueva Imagen, 1980. 429 p.; 16 p. of plates; ill.; ports (Serie Testimonios / Editorial Nueva Imagen)

Complete and final version of outstanding chronicle of the anarcho-syndicalist struggle in Argentina's far south during the 1920s. Thoroughly documented.

3154 Bazán, Armando Raúl. Historia de La Rioja. Buenos Aires: Plus Ultra, 1979. 607 p.; bibls. (Colección Historia de nuestras provincias; 6)

Excellent contribution by noted local historian stresses continuous struggle against *proteño* hegemony. Descriptions of Peñaloza's and Varela's uprisings (Chap. 19) are especially worthwhile. Underscores social and economic aspects of political development. Short final chapter summarizes last half century.

3155 Bernardo A. Houssay: su vida y su obra. Buenos Aires: Academia Nacional de Ciencias Exactas, Físicas, y Naturales, 1981. 261 p.

Compilation of several essays on life and deeds of eminent Nobel Prize scientist. Also includes some of his writings on science policies.

3156 Bidondo, Emilio A. Historia de Jujuy, 1535–1950. Buenos Aires: Plus Ultra, 1980. 482 p.; 4 leaves of plates; bibl.; maps (Colección Historia de nuestras provincias; 9)

Provincial history, from precolumbian times to 1943, by distinguished military historian is based on solid archival and bibliographical research.

3157 ———. La preparación de las tropas de Jujuy para la guerra contra el Mariscal Santa Cruz (ANH/IE, 26, enero/junio 1979 [i.e. 1980] p. 367–387)

Short study examines northern provincial army preparedness. Approximately 10 percent of the population was drafted for the campaign.

3158 Blasi, Hebe J. Evolución de la población patagónica entre los censos de 1895 y 1914 (UNLP/TC, 23, 1978, p. 29–40)

Summarizes and compares relevant data concerning immigration to the region, particularly female/male and rural/urban population ratios.

3159 Bohdziewicz, Jorge C. Bibliografía de bibliografías individuales: historia y antropología (Historiografía Ríoplatense [Instituto Bibliográfico Antonio Zinny, Buenos Aires] 1, 1978, p. 127–178)

Useful compilation of 206 entries of bibliographies that include references to 32,000 titles.

3160 ———. Impresos relativos a la guerra franco-argentina, 1837–1841: contribución bibliográfica y crítica (Historiografía Ríoplatense [Instituto Bibliográfico Antonio Zinny, Buenos Aires] 2, 1982, p. 182–253)

Highly useful list of printed materials, broadsides, etc., published in Argentina, Uruguay and France. Each entry is carefully catalogued, annotated and evaluated. Rich source of hemerographic and archival data.

3161 Bosch, Beatriz. Urquiza y su tiempo. 2. ed. Buenos Aires: Editorial Universitaria de Buenos Aires, 1980. 796 p.; 32 p. of plates; bibl.; ill.; index. (Temas)

New revised edition of solid and well documented biography as well as history of the times.

3162 Brailovsky, Antonio Elío. Política ambiental de la Generación del Ochenta (*in* Siegrist de Gentile, Nora L.; Noemí Girbal de Blacha; and Antonio Elío Brailovsky. Tres estudios argentinos. Buenos Aires: Editorial Sudamericana, 1982, p. 287–364)

Original essay concerns intentions to reduce the adverse impact of man on nature. Exemplifies good use of ecology as an auxiliary science of history but shows the lack of positive response to such awareness during the 1880–1930 period.

3163 Bruno, Cayetano. El Canónigo Mastei, futuro Pío IX, en la Argentina (ANH/IE, 24, enero/junio 1978, p. 187–213)

Summarizes, for first time, contents of future Pope's diaries and travel notes during his River Plate stay in 1824.

3164 ———. Historia de la Iglesia en la Argentina. Buenos Aires: Editorial Don Bosco, 1982. 593 p.

Final volume of ambitious effort initiated in 1966. Covers period 1881–1900. Makes full use of recently opened Archivi Vaticani. Throws new light on Church-State confrontation and describes Franciscan and Salesian Missions to Chaco and Patagonia.

3165 ———. León XIII y el conflicto argentino-chileno en 1896 (ANH/IE, 26, enero/junio 1979 [i.e. 1980] p. 491–516)

Uses primary-sources in order to describe important antecedents to present papal border conflict mediation. Based on recently declassified documentation of Vicente G. Quesada's 1896 mission to the Vatican.

3166 ———. El Presidente Julio A. Roca y Monseñor Juan Cagliero, Vicario Apostólico de la Patagonia (ANH/IE, 22, enero/julio 1977 [i.e. 1979] p. 233–281)

Documented study of missionary work in country's southern region during tense confrontation between Church and State.

3167 ———. Los Salesianos y las Hijas de María Auxiliadora en la Argentina. v. 1. Buenos Aires: Instituto Salesiano de Artes Gráficas, 1981. 52 p.; ill.

Historian of religious matters describes Don Bosco missionaries' endeavor in Patagonia during 1875–94.

3168 Buchrucker, Cristian. La visión de la historia contemporánea en cuatro nacionalistas de los años 30: Ibarguren, Meinvielle, Doll y Osés (CRIT, 52 : 1829/1830, 28 de feb. de 1980, p. 60–76)

Reviews performance and intellectual contributions of four leading personalities of the Argentine right or of what can be called "nacionalismo doctrinario." Provides balanced summary of their influence in creating a nationalistic ideology and in rejecting the liberal tradition. Also elaborates on how their thinking was permeated by world-wide conspiracy theories (e.g., Socialism, international finance, Judaism, etc.).

Buenos Aires (province *Argentina*. **Dirección de Geodesia. División Cartografía.** Provincia de Buenos Aires, referencias cartográficas de la Conquista del Desierto. See *HLAS 43 : 5552*.

3169 Busaniche, José Carmelo. Hombres y hechos de Santa Fé. Prólogo de Gastón Gori. Santa Fé, Argentina: Edición Cuadernos de ARCIEN, 1979. 217 p. (Serie Cuadernos ARCIEN; 4)

Local history at its best depicts day-by-day life in its social dimensions.

3170 Bushnell, David. Postal images of Argentine *próceres*: selective myth-making (Studies in Latin American Popular Culture [New Mexico State University, Department of Foreign Languages, Las Cruces] 1, 1982, p. 91–105, ill.)

Very perceptive analysis of popular culture as reflected in the use of postage stamps. Compares dominant ideological and cultural trends of each period and shows gradual deterioration of liberal historical interpretation of the nation's past.

3171 La Campaña de la integridad nacional. Benjamín Victoria con estudio preliminar de Isidoro J. Ruiz Moreno y Néstor Tomás Auza. Buenos Aires: Instituto Histórico de la Organización Nacional, 1979. 229 p.; bibl.; port. (Documentos-Instituto Histórico de la Organización Nacional; no. 1)

Reprints part of the War Ministry's annual report to Congress in 1860 which includes a wealth of documentation on Cepedas's campaign and peace negotiations with Francisco Solano López. Two solid introductory studies by Isidoro J. Ruiz Moreno and Néstor Tomás Auza provide biographical data on Victorica.

3172 Campobassi, José Salvador. Mitre y su época. Buenos Aires: Editorial Universitaria de Buenos Aires, 1980. 532 p.; bibl. (Colección Argentina)

Very worthwhile life-and-times biography. Companion volume to author's *Sarmiento y su época* (1975, see *HLAS 40 : 3712*). Chap. 8 provides concise appraisal of Mitre's intellectual contribution. In general, offers a coherent picture of the subject's personality.

3173 Canclini, Arnoldo. Allen F. Gardiner: marino, misionero y mártir. Waite H. Stirling: el centinela de Dios en Ushuaia. Tomás Bridges: pionero en Ushuaia. Buenos Aires: Editorial Marymar, 1980. 3 v. (135, 82, 118 p.)

Three monographs on the lives and deeds of several pioneering missionaries in Tierra del Fuego.

3174 Cárdenas, Eduardo J. and Carlos Manuel Payá. El primer nacionalismo argentino en Manuel Gálvez y Ricardo Rojas. Buenos Aires: A. Peña Lillo, 1978. 150 p.; bibl.

Balanced analysis of the writings of Ricardo Rojas and Manuel Gálvez. Regards these two scions of provincial oligarchic families as initiators of the nativist reaction against cosmopolitanism and materialism.

3175 Carranza, María Inés; Inés María Viñuales; and Luis A. Ferrari. Notas sobre fuerzas políticas en el período 1930–1943. Buenos Aires: Fundación para el Estudio de los Problemas Argentinos, between 1977 and 1981. 28, 2 p.; bibl. (Documento de trabajo / Fundación para el Estudio de los Problemas Argentinos; no. 12)

Positive attempt to determine principal manifestations of the political process after the 1930 breakdown of democracy. Includes thorough examination of different issues at stake, Uriburu's political proposals as well as the inside story and attitudes of both Radicals and Nationalists.

3176 Casas, David Jorge, hijo. Historia de las comunicaciones en Jujuy. San Salvador de Jujuy, Argentina: s.n., 1980. 31 p. (notas de la Junta de Estudios Arqueológicos de Jujuy; t. 1, no. 1)

Succinct and original examination of the topic from prehistoric times to the advent of the railroad.

Cavarozzi, Marcelo. Sindicatos y políticas en Argentina, 1955–1958. See *HLAS 43:6601.*

3177 ——. Unions and politics, 1955–1962. Washington: The Woodrow Wilson International Center for Scholars, Smithsonian Institution, 1980. 19 p. (Latin American program working papers; no. 63)

Argues that the new role of unions after Perón's downfall is one of the most important features of the new Argentine political order.

3178 Chernenko, Anatoli and Alexei Shliajov. Participantes de la primera revolución rusa en Argentina (URSS/AL, 1/2:37/38, 1981, p. 276–282)

Refers to the revolutionary activities of participants in the *Potemkin* uprising and other Russian rebellions who settled in the privinces of Tucumán and Buenos Aires where they pursued their political cause.

3179 Cignetti, Ana María. La diplomacia norteamericana y los Tratados de 1853 con la Confederación Argentina (UNS/CS, 12, julio/dic. 1979, p. 111–118)

Brief account based on US diplomatic sources.

3180 Colli, Néstor S. Rosas y el bloqueo anglo-francés. Diseño de la portada, Luis A. Sarlinga. Buenos Aires: Editora Patria Grande, 1978. 351 p.; bibl. (Amanece; 9)

Excellent, carefully researched, well balanced but mildly revisionist contribution covers Guerra Grande period (1841–50). Follow-up to author's earlier work *La política francesa en el Río de la Plata: Rosas y el bloqueo Francés de 1838–1840* (Buenos Aires: s.n., 1963, 396 p.).

3181 Comadrán Ruiz, Jorge. Notas sobre la creación y evolución de la Legislatura de Mendoza, 1820–1854 (UNC/RHAA, 9:17/18, 1972/1979, p. 29–67)

Summary of institutional history contains wealth of detail. Describes requirements for membership, numbers, elections and internal organization of the Legislature.

3182 Conferencia Internacional sobre el Desarrollo de las Areas Nuevas: Argentina y Australia, *1st, Buenos Aires, 1977.* Argentina y Australia. John Fogarty, Ezequiel Gallo, Héctor Diéguez. Traducciones, Frances Lutman. Revisión técnica de las traducciones, Alejandro Titiunik. Buenos Aires: Instituto Torcuato Di Tella, 1979. 246 p.; bibl. (Serie verde, Jornadas) (Cuaderno- Instituto Torcuato Di Tella; no. 201)

Held in 1977 and organized by the Di Tella Institute, the conference's goal was to determine a more realistic and solid base for further research. Excellent introduction by Ezequiel Gallo, "El Método Comparativo en Historia," is followed by two valuable contributions: John Fogarty's "Australia y Argentina de 1914–1943" and Guido Di Tella's "Controversias Económicas en la Argentina y

Australia, 1930–1970." For economist's comment, see *HLAS 43:3640*.

3183 Congreso de Historia Argentina y Regional, *3rd, Santa Fe, Argentina and Paraná, Argentina, 1975.* Tercer Congreso de Historia Argentina y Regional: celebrado en Santa Fe y Paraná, del 10 al 12 de julio de 1975. Introducción pro Laurio H. Destefani. Buenos Aires: Academia Nacional de la Historia, 1977/1980. 4 v. (540, 526, 526, 510 p.)

Meeting devoted to two principal themes: 1) country's situation during the Avellaneda administration; and 2) Littoral land settlement and colonization from colonial times to present. Vols. 1/2 on first topic consist of 78 contributions broken into the following aspects of the period: 22 economic, 18 political, 10 military, and 28 on social and cultural matters. Vols. 3/4 deal with the second topic and include 70 contributions. First two volumes effectively update period 1874–80 and those on second topic are highly original and ground-breaking.

3184 Congreso Nacional de Historia sobre la Conquista del Desierto, *Buenos Aires, 1979.* Congreso Nacional de historia sobre la Conquista del Desierto. Buenos Aires: Academia Nacional de la Historia, 1982. 4 v. (513, 509, 636, 625 p.)

Congress held in commemoration of the centennial of the Argentine army's occupation of the Southern region (1879). Includes 164 papers of which 60 are on political and military history, 47 on socioeconomic history, 33 on cultural and scientific history, and seven on international relations.

3185 Congreso Nacional y Regional de Historia Argentina, *4th, Mendoza, Argentina, 1979.* Cuarto Congreso Nacional y Regional de Historia Argentina. Buenos Aires: Academia Nacional de la Historia, 1982. 540 p.

Vol. 1 of meeting that took place in Mendoza and San Juan on San Martín's birth bicentennial. Consists of papers dealing with economic history, 19 concerning Cuyo and 16 on the northern provinces.

3186 Correspondencia Mitre-Urquiza, 1860–1868. Prefacio de Jorge Carlos Mitre. Buenos Aires: Museo Mitre [and] Fundación Banco de la Provincia de Buenos Aires, 1980. 170 p.; plates.

Selected letters cover crucial period between Cepeda's aftermath (1859) and presidential election (1868). Also includes descriptive listing of the remainder of their correspondence.

3187 Cortés Conde, Roberto. El progreso argentino, 1880–1914. Buenos Aires: Editorial Sudamericana, 1979. 291 p.; appendix; charts (Colección Historia y sociedad)

Outstanding quantitative history challenges assumptions about land tenure and labor's living standards (for economist's comment, see *HLAS 43:3649*).

3188 Corvalán Lima, Héctor. Rosas y la formación constitucional argentina. Mendoza, Argentina: Editorial Idearium, 1979. 149 p.; bibl. (Colección Ensayos; 1)

On the basis of bibliographical information, revisionist author argues that the Dictator favored the institutionalization of the country. Appendix examines period's cultural developments rejecting usual cliché notion about its backwardness.

3189 Crespo, Alfonso. Eva Perón, viva o muerta. Lima: Librerías-Editorial Stidium, 1978. 444 p.; 4 p. of plates; bibl.; index; ports.

Popular but generally informative biography written in a novelistic vein. In accordance with recent trendy interpretations, enhances her role while diminishing Perón's.

3190 Cuccorese, Horacio Juan. Carlos Pellegrini el artífice de la segunda candidatura presidencial de Julio A. Roca (ANH/IE, 23, julio/dic. 1977 [i.e. 1979] p. 275–294)

Interesting account of how the clever king-maker's artful political moves in this instance were motivated by foreign policy issues and the need for a strong leader.

3191 ———. Carlos Pellegrini impone un gobernador mitrista en 1894 y un gobernador radical en 1898: momentos claves en la historia política de la Provincia de Buenos Aires (ANH/IE, 24, enero/junio 1978 [i.e. 1980] p. 215–270)

Shows Pellegrini's outstanding role during period known as "La República Conservadora."

3192 ———. La elección de Gobernador en la Provincia de Buenos Aires, 1897–1898, y sus trascendentales consecuencias jurídicas (Revista de Historia del Derecho [Buenos Aires] 6, 1978, p. 9–44)

Offers additional sidelights on Pellegrini's shrewd participation.

3193 ———. El estanco de alcohol como recurso financiero: la practicidad económica de Carlos Pellegrini (UNLP/TC, 23, 1978, p. 41–60)

Focuses on controversial debate in which a Pellegrini-backed tax proposal was rejected. Contends that military expenses provoked by confrontation with Chile in 1890s justified such a proposal.

3194 ———. ¡Ha caído el más fuerte!: revivificación del pensamiento de Carlos Pellegrini (Revista Nacional de Cultura [Ministerio de Cultura y Educación, Secretaría de Estado de Cultura, Buenos Aires] 1:2, 1979, p. 43–59)

Leading Pellegrini historian analyzes his contribution to the attainment of national objectives and presents a contemporary appraisal of his personality. Describes in detail his outlook on the border confrontation with Chile.

3195 ———. La justicia penal y la política nacional: un histórico proceso contra el Gobernador de la Provincia de Buenos Aires, Don Marcelino Ugarte, por infracción a la Ley Electoral (ANH/IE, 26, enero/julio 1979 [i.e. 1980] p. 285–326)

Deals with political confrontations among factions of ruling Conservative Party. Praises Pellegrini's reformist outlook.

3196 De Marco, Miguel Angel. La Armada espáñola en el Plata: 1845–1900. Rosario: Facultad de Derecho y Ciencias Sociales, Pontificia Universidad Católica Argentina, 1981. 485 p.; bibl.; ill.; index.

Detailed examination, based on a wealth of primary sources, yields first-rate informative compendium of period's principal conflicts and crisis, especially the 1880 and 1890 rebellions.

3197 ———. Notas sobre la política santafesina: de Cepeda a Pavón. Rosario: Instituto de Historia, Facultad de Derecho y Ciencias Sociales, Pontificia Universidad Católica Argentina, 1982. 75 p. (Monografías y ensayos; no. 20)

Well documented accounts of effects of the national political situation at the local level, particularly the results of the battle of Pavón.

3198 ———. Notas sobre la política santafesina: 1856–1858. Rosario: Instituto de Historia, Facultad de Derecho y Ciencias Sociales, Pontificia Universidad Católica Argentina, 1980. 53 p. (Monografías y ensayos; no. 55)

Political account of the governorship of Juan Pablo López "Mascarilla."

3199 Deheza, José A. ¿Quienés derrocaron a Isabel Perón? Buenos Aires: Ediciones Cuenca del Plata, 1981. 292 p.

Former Cabinet member of last Peronist government—also son-in-law of Gen. Lonardi who overthrew Perón in 1955—denies allegations of corruption against deposed President Isabel Perón and describes political intrigues that undermined her administration from inside the Justicialista Movement, the opposition and the military. Very passionate but full of facts.

3200 De Tella, Guido. The economic policies of Argentina's labor based government, 1973–1976. Washington: The Woodrow Wilson International Center for Scholars, Smithsonian Institution, 1979. 67 p. (Latin American program working papers; no. 47)

Monographic essay about economic problems and policies carried out by four successive peronist administrations. Asserts viability of moderate, reformist regimes.

3201 Di Tella, Torcuato S. Working-class organization and politics in Argentina (LARR, 12:2, 1981, p. 33–56)

Solid theoretical reassessment of the labor movement in both the pre-Perón era and during the populist periods of mass organizations. Concludes that internal dynamics and massive influx of new members produced fundamental changes, mainly at the second level of leadership, which destroyed the old structure opposed to Perón.

3202 Díaz, Violeta; Milna C. Marini de Díaz Zorita; and **Norma Benítez.** Gobernadores de La Pampa: Ayala, Pico, Luro, Luque. Santa Rosa: Facultad de Ciencias Humanas, Universidad Nacional de La Pampa, 1981. 91 p.; bibl.; maps.

Pioneer work about the first local administrations of the then national territory of La Pampa covers period 1885–1902.

3203 Dodson, Michael. Catholic radicalism and political change in Argentina (in

Religion in Latin America: life and literature. Lyle G. Brown and William F. Cooper, eds. Waco: Markham Press Foundation, 1980, p. 317–330)

Outlines rapid rise of "Tercermundistas" priests movement during Onganía's regime showing how the Church's hierarchy was open to new currents during that crucial period.

3204 Dugini de de Cándido, María Inés. Aspectos de la política exterior de Rosas: 1831–1839 (UNC/BCPS, 26, 1980, p. 79–106)

After examining background of the conflict between the Peruvian-Bolivian Confederation and Argentina and Chile, analyzes internal and external situation of each country as well as Argentine participation in the war.

3205 Endrek, Emiliano S. La Conquista del Desierto durante el segundo gobierno de Rosas (Historia [Revista-libro trimestral, Buenos Aires] 1 : 4, dic. 1981/enero 1982, p. 44–57)

Presents main developments arguing that the Rosas political syndrome affects the study of other unrelated aspects of the period.

3206 Ensinck, Oscar Luis. La ganadería en la Provincia de Santa Fe durante el siglo XIX (Historia [Revista-libro trimestral, Buenos Aires] 1, marzo/mayo 1981, p. 152–176, ill.)

Describes developments until 1914.

3207 ———. Historia de la inmigración y la colonización en la Provincia de Santa Fe. Buenos Aires: Fundación para la Educación, la Ciencia y la Cultura, 1979. 359 p.; bibl.

Competent and insightful study, rich in data, analyzes impact of immigration on local institutions.

3208 ———. Historia de los ferrocarriles en la Provincia de Santa Fe. Rosario: Facultad de Derecho y Ciencias Sociales de la Pontificia Universidad Católica Argentina, 1980. 103 p.; bibl. (Monografías y ensayos; no. 14)

Traces accurate picture of developments following the 1890s expansion of railways in the province.

3209 ———. Industria saladeril en Santa Fe: el frigorífico (Res Gesta [Boletín del

Instituto de Historia de la Facultad de Derecho y Ciencias Sociales de la Pontificia Universidad Católica Argentina, Rosario] 2 : 8, julio/dic. 1980, p. 21–29)

Well documented essay covers 1889–1924 expansion period.

3210 ———. Proceso histórico de la agricultura en la Provincia de Santa Fe (ANH/IE, 27, julio/dic. 1979 [i.e. 1981] p. 229–290)

Very complete and informative contribution thoroughly examines land settlement, crops and corresponding legislation.

3211 ———. El puerto de la ciudad de Rosario: su proceso histórico. Rosario, Argentina: Editorial de Textos Universitarios, Universidad Nacional de Rosario, 1980. 72 p.

Useful contribution, part of major work: *Historia de las comunicaciones y medios de transporte en la Provincia de Santa Fe*, by this able provincial historian.

3212 ———. Tropas de carros y diligencias en la Provincia de Santa Fe: proceso histórico (ANH/IE, 22, enero/junio 1977 [i.e. 1979] p. 345–379)

Another useful monograph by a prolific economic historian.

3213 Epopeya del desierto en el sur argentino. Buenos Aires: Círculo Militar, 1979. 298 p.; maps; plates (Biblioteca del oficial; no. 698)

Essays concerning principal aspects of this military campaign by five renowned military historians: José T. Goyret, Isaías J. García Enciso, Luis A. Leoni Houssay, Emilio A. Bidondo, and Rosa Meli.

3214 Estrada, Marcos de. El negro en las invasiones inglesas (Revista Nacional de Cultura [Ministerio de Cultura y Educación, Secretaría de Estado de Cultura, Buenos Aires] 9, 1981, p. 41–62)

Well written and informed synthesis about the participation of blacks in the 1806–07 events.

3215 Etchepareborda, Roberto. Estanislao S. Zeballos y los debates secretos de 1914 en la Cámara de Diputados (Historia [Revista-libro trimestral, Buenos Aires] 1 : 3, sept./nov. 1981, p. 25–44, ill., tables)

Leading historian of Argentine foreign relations analyzes Zeballos' lengthy speeches in secret parliamentary debates over foreign policy in 1914. President of the Chamber of

Deputies' Foreign Relations Committee and three-time foreign minister, Zeballos was leading exponent of what author has called Argentina's "Manifest Destiny." His speeches in secret debates provide interesting hard liner's perspective on 1914 situation and on evolution of Argentine foreign policy from mid-19th century (for the definitive study, see item **3218**). [T. C. Wright]

3216 ———. Lucio Mansilla: testigo de su tiempo (*in* Essays on Lucio Victorio Mansilla, 1831–1913. Riverside: University of California, Latin American Studies Program, 1981, p. 43–65 [Commemorative series; 5])

Thoughtful and carefully researched essay focuses on neglected but interesting aspect of the works of Mansilla, a man of letters, journalist, politician, and soldier whose career kept him at the center of Argentine public life for over half a century. Through careful analysis of his voluminous writings, author extracts revealing observations of the Argentine scene from Rosas' time to turn of century that shed new light on important events and personalities. Also examines Mansilla's approaches to the writing of history. [T. C. Wright]

3217 ———. Política de poder en el Cono Sur: revelaciones históricas (Historia [Revista-libro trimestral, Buenos Aires] 1 : 4, enero/feb. 1982, p. 19–43, ill.)

Describes how Zeballos revealed several unknown facets of Argentina's Southern Cone relations as those with Chile, Brazil and Uruguay since 1880s were secretly debated. For the definitive work on the subject of Zeballos and Argentine foreign policy, see item **3218**. [T. C. Wright]

3218 ———. Zeballos y la política exterior Argentina. Buenos Aires: Editorial Pleamar, 1982. 121 p.; appendix; table.

Thoroughly-researched study offers biographical sketch of Zeballos, critical assessment and bibliography of his historical writings, and summary of scholarship on him. Focuses on rivalry between Zeballos and his Brazilian counterpart, Río Branco, and on the 1914 secret debates. With this book and two current articles (see items **3215** and **3217**), Etchepareborda has significantly advanced knowledge of Argentine foreign policy and one of its major architects. [T. C. Wright]

3219 La Expedición al Desierto y los Salesianos, 1879. Juan Esteban Belza *et al.* Buenos Aires: Ediciones Don Bosco-Argentina, 1979. 240 p.; 32 p. of plates; bibl.; ill.; ports (some col.)

Collected works by four Salesian priests examine both pastoral activities in Patagonia and Church participation in the expedition: Juan Esteban Belza's "La Expedición al Desierto y el Amanecer de las Misiones Salesianas Patagónicas" (p. 9–32); Raúl A. Entraigas's "Los Capellanes de la Expedición al Desierto" (p. 33–110); Cayetano Bruno's "El Presidente Julio A. Roca y Monseñor Juan Cagliero, Vicario Apostólico de la Patagonia" (p. 113–175); Pascual R. Paesa's "Los Indígenas Patagónicos hacia 1879 y la Acción Misionera Salesiana" (p. 177–240)

3220 Falcoff, Mark. Original sin and Argentine reality: peronist history and myth of the traitors (PCCLAS/P, 6, 1977/1979, p. 217–230)

Thorough study of film script written by leftist peronist, this provocative essay depicts confrontation between Patria Socialista and Justicialism. Ably reconstructs 1970s atmosphere in its crudest dimensions.

3221 Faure, Raúl. La soledad de los precursores: ensayos de historia política. Córdoba, Argentina: Editorial Imagen, 1979. 133 p.; ill.; ports.

Collection of short newspaper articles, concerning Córdoba's political history, describes relevant episodes of the 1870–1940 period involving Juárez Celman and Ramón J. Cárcano.

3222 La Federalización de Buenos Aires: debates y documentos. Isidoro J. Ruiz Moreno, compilador. Buenos Aires: Emecé Editores, 1980. 337 p.; bibl.

Collection of selected documents and parliamentary debates concerning the federalization of the city of Buenos Aires. Includes scholarly contribution by Isidoro J. Ruiz Moreno in the form of an introduction designed to clarify issues involved.

3223 Fernández Lalanne, Pedro E. Los Alvear. Buenos Aires: Emecé Editores, 1980. 505 p.; 48 p. of plates; bibl.; ill.; index.

Biographical chronicle about the lives and deeds of members of this patrician family. Despite the old-fashioned overall tone, some biographical entries are useful (e.g., Diego de Alvear, 1749–1830, naval officer and geographer; Carlos de Alvear, 1789–1852, military, politician and diplomat; Torcuato de Alvear, 1822–90, politician and mayor of Buenos Aires; Marcelo T. de Alvear, 1868–1942, politician, diplomat and President).

3224 Ferrari, Gustavo. El Canciller Saavedra Lamas (CRIT, 52 : 108, 22 marzo 1979, p. 123–126)

Discusses his principal diplomatic achievements, highlighting their overall consistency.

3225 ———. Estanislao S. Zeballos o la pasión por el interés nacional (Revista de la Escuela de Comando de la Fuerza Aérea Argentina [Buenos Aires] 99, junio 1979, p. 113–127)

Concise outline of the life and deeds of the outstanding and passionate representative of Argentina's own "Manifest Destiny."

3226 ———. Las ilusiones del ochenta (CRIT, 53 : 1831, 13 marzo 1980, p. 84–98)

Well written essay rejects unfounded yet prevalent notion that there existed a "planned" National Project in 1880s. On the contrary, shows that personalities such as Alberdi and Roca became true nation-builders through their actions and motivations. In brief survey of following decades, attributes responsibility for successive military interventions to politicians' mistakes emphasizing they also failed to develop a viable program or achieve effective results.

3227 ———. La política exterior argentina a través de la bibliografía general (RIB, 30 : 2, 1980, p. 133–147)

Bibliographical survey of principal contributions to the 20th-century history of Argentine foreign policy.

3228 ———. La política exterior argentina entre 1930 y 1940 (Revista de la Escuela Superior de Guerra Aérea de la Fuerza Aérea Argentina [Buenos Aires] 112, agosto 1980, p. 90–111)

Brief sketch of main developments from Yrigoyen's isolationism to the Havana's Foreign Ministers Consultation Meeting.

3229 ———. El primer embajador argentino (Revista Nacional de Cultura [Ministerio de Cultura y Educación, Secretaría de Estado de Cultura, Buenos Aires] 7, 1980, p. 131–145)

Short biography of Rómulo S. Naón, first ambassador to US. Underscores his efforts to establish a working relationship between both countries.

3230 Ferrero, Roberto A. La colonización agraria en Córdoba. Córdoba: Junta Provincial de Historia de Córdoba, 1978. 229 p.; bibl. (Libros de la Junta Provincial de Historia de Córdoba; 5)

Solid study of characteristics and developments of Córdoba's rural economy examines its different stages (e.g., state-sponsored development, landownership, tenancy).

3231 Ferretti, Martha B. Primo de Rivera: prisionero de Alvear, al servicio de España (EEHA/AEA, 33, 1976 [i.e. 1979] p. 309–342, facs.)

New study confirms that Supreme Director Alvear sought a conciliatory agreement between patriots and royalists in 1815.

3232 Fitte, Ernesto J. Reclamaciones inglesas satisfechas por Rosas a raíz de la Guerra del Brasil (ANH/IE, 22, enero/junio 1977 [i.e. 1979] p. 101–115)

Short assessment contends that by acting as he did, Rosas safeguarded national honor without partisanship.

3233 ———. Ultraje inferido a la Confederación Argentina por la fragata norteamericana *Congress* (ANH/IE, 24, enero/junio 1978 [i.e. 1980] p. 137–156)

Describes incident during Montevideo's naval blockade in 1844 during the Guerra Grande.

3234 Florit, Carlos. El roquismo. Buenos Aires: Hachette, 1979. 187 p.

Perceptive interpretative essay examines this political movement, describing its ideology, strategies and fundamental policies. Strongly vindicatory effort that sheds much light on international and foreign policy issues.

3235 Follari, Rodolfo S. San Luis, 1874–1880: panorama político y cultural (ANH/IE, 27, julio/dic. 1978 [i.e. 1981] p. 291–322)

Careful analysis of province's overall situation after 1874 agitations when there began a period of stability and institutional development.

3236 Fontana, Esteban. Una etapa crítica del comercio mendocino, 1873–1883

(JEHM/R, 1:9, 1979, p. 29–52, tables)

Depicts harsh conditions of subsistence economy before arrival of the railway that would connect Mendoza to the Littoral.

3237 Francis, Michael J. The limits of hegemony: United States relations with Argentina and Chile during World War II. Notre Dame, Indiana: University of Notre Dame Press, 1977. 292 p. (International studies of the Committee on International Relations)

Solid research reveals how negative impact of US pressures provoked increased nationalistic reactions and led to final political failure (for political scientist's comment, see *HLAS 41:8805*).

3238 Frank, Gary. Juan Perón vs. Spruille Braden: the story behind the *Blue book*. Lanham, Md.: University Press of America Inc., 1980. 172 p.

On the basis of new primary sources, presents well known confrontation in great detail.

3239 ———. Struggle for hegemony: Argentina, Brazil and the United States during the Second World War. Coral Gables, Fla.: Center for Advanced International Studies, University of Miami, 1979. 1 v.; bibl.; index (Foreign affairs monograph)

Informative monograph based on rich primary documentation drawn mainly from Brazilian sources. Ably describes regional power rivalry and argues that US aid to Brazil altered the regional balance of power assuring Brazil's eventual dominance.

3240 Fraser, Nicholas and **Marysa Navarro.** Eva Perón. New York: W. W. Norton, 1981. 192 p.; bibl.; index; plates.

Best biography written to date is scholarly and very readable. Demythifies many aspects of her life.

Frigerio, Rogelio. Síntesis de la historia crítica de la economía argentina: desde la conquista hasta nuestros días. See *HLAS 43:3664*.

3241 Furlong, Guillermo. La *Matrona Comentadora* y su índole pedagógica (Res Gesta [Facultad de Derecho y Ciencias Sociales, Instituto de Historia, Pontificia Universidad Católica Argentina, Buenos Aires] 6, 2. época, julio/dic. 1979, p. 1–7)

Posthumous article written by distinguished Jesuit historian describes contents of one of many journals that Fray Francisco de Paula Castañeda published under awkward titles such as, in this case, *Matrona Comentadora de los Cuatro Periodistas*, which appeared 1820–22.

3242 Gallardo, José María. Los naturalistas y la afirmación de la soberanía argentina en la Patagonia (Revista Nacional de Cultura [Ministerio de Cultura y Educación, Secretaría de Estado de Cultura, Buenos Aires] 2:8, 1980, p. 31–58, ill.)

Summary account of more relevant explorations of Patagonia, notes contributions of many scientists to its better knowledge.

Gallo, Ezequiel. Lo evitable y lo accidental en la historia. See item **7754**.

3243 ———. Paul Groussac: reflexiones sobre el método histórico (Historia [Revista-libro trimestral, Buenos Aires] 3, set./nov. 1981, p. 19–23)

Short essay summarizes eminent historian's historical approach and methodology.

3244 Gandía, Enrique de. Las ideas políticas de Juan Facundo Quiroga. Mendoza, Argentina: s.n., 1981. 47 p.

Very partisan, traditional liberal interpretation, introduces Silvestre Peña y Lillo's book about the Caudillo de los Llanos.

3245 ———. La polémica López-Mitre en 1881 y 1882 (ANH/IE, 24, enero/junio 1978 [i.e. 1980] p. 15–63)

Informative account of well known debate finds that it originated in previous political confrontations.

3246 ———. Sarmiento y la reacción de 1856 y 1857 (JEHM/R, 1:9, 1979, p. 9–27, photograph)

Informative description of power politics in the River Plate and *porteño* political struggles concerning a possible resurgence of rosismo.

3247 García Basolo, J. Carlos. Historia de la penitenciaría de Buenos Aires, 1869–1980. Buenos Aires: Talleres de la Penitenciaría Nacional, 1980. 300 p.

Satisfactory study of this institution weaves in a wealth of generally scarce information. Elaborates on first experiences in prison work programs and occupational therapy.

3248 García Enciso, Isaías J. Tolderías, fuertes y fortines. Buenos Aires: Emecé, 1980. 225 p.

Ably documented and vivid description of Argentine frontier life.

3249 Gariazzo, Alicia. Orígenes ideológicos de los obreros chilenos y argentinos (CPES/RPS, 18:51, junio/sept. 1981, p. 59–96)

Valuable comparative study shows principal differences between both groups of workers and attributes them to the countries' different economic structures. Thus, according to author, Agentina's labor movement was always better off but more violent.

3250 La Geografía y la historia en la identidad nacional. Patricio Randle, editor. Buenos Aires: OIKOS, Asociación para la Promoción de los Estudios Territoriales y Ambientales, 1981. 2 v. (302, 283 p.); ill.; maps.

Compilation resulting from a symposium on the importance of both history and geography as disciplines that can help define what constitutes "el Ser Nacional." Consists of 30 papers of a definitely nationalistic and revisionist bent. Vol. 1 deals with teaching and research, others chiefly concern their relationship to the formulation of territorial and foreign policies. Most important are: vol. 1, Mario Guillermo Saraví's "La Enseñanza de la Historia Económica Argentina;" vol. 2, Néstor Tomás Auza's "La Investigación Histórica en el Marco Cultural de la Sociedad Argentina;" Jorge Bohdzievicz's "La Investigación Histórica en la Argentina: Dificultades Prácticas;" Jorge Comadrán Ruiz's "El Sentido de las Fronteras en la Historia Nacional;" Ernesto J. Maeder's "El Caso Misiones: su Proceso Histórico y su Posterior Distribución Territorial;" Pedro Santos Martínez's "La Diplomacia en los Archivos Europeos;" and Julio Irazusta's "Influencia de la Diplomacia en la Historia."

3251 Giberti, Horacio C. E. Historia económica de la ganadería argentina. Buenos Aires: Ediciones Solar, 1981. 275 p. (Biblioteca dimensión argentina)

New edition of pioneering economic history has been revised and updated and includes two new sections covering the present century in all its diversity.

3252 Girbal de Blacha, Noemí M. Los Centros Agrícolas en la Provincia de Buenos Aires: análisis histórico de economía regional en la década del 80 hasta sus últimas consecuencias. Buenos Aires: Fundación para la Educación, La Ciencia y la Cultura, 1980. 184 p.; facsim.; map.

Uses the Centros' establishment in 1887 as a case study to analyze and document regional history in last decades of 19th century.

3253 ———. Historia de la agricultura argentina a fines del siglo XIX. Buenos Aires: Fundación para la Educación, la Ciencia y la Cultura (FECIC), 1982. 295 p.; bibl.; charts; ill.; index; maps.

Another contribution to a better knowledge of Argentine economic history by an able researcher. Wealth of data represents major effort.

3254 ———. La producción agrícola argentina y sus principales competidores en el mercado internacional: 1900–1914 (in Siegrist de Gentile, Nora L.; Noemí Girbal de Blacha; and Antonio Elio Brailovsky. Tres estudios argentinos. Buenos Aires: Editorial Sudamericana, 1982, p. 231–286)

Valuable study of trade competition among US, Russian and Argentina during the latter's great economic expansion.

3255 ———. Saladeros y frigoríficos: intereses y mercados (Historiografía Rioplatense [Instituto Bibliográfico Antonio Zinny, Buenos Aires] 1, 1978, p. 57–74)

Explores beef industry's changing patterns at the time when differences emerged between "criadores" and "invernadores."

3256 Godio, Julio. El último año de Perón. Bogotá: Universidad Simón Bolívar, 1981. 272 p.; bibl. (Colección Universidad y pueblo)

Highly politicized left peronist interpretation of Perón's last administration (1971–75). Severely critical of peronist orthodox leadership as represented by López Rega and trade union bosses, book is designed to rescue the old leader's progressive image, particularly in author's analysis of Perón's last speech (June 1974).

3257 Gomariz Moraga, Enrique. Sobre las causas del fenómeno peronista (IEP/RPI, 163, 1979, p. 127–138)

Overview of different interpretations of this political phenomenon includes appraisal of period's social development and interaction of economic and political factors.

3258 Gómez Ríos de Boffo, Virginia. Noticia sobre el comercio interprovincial durante la presidencia de Mitre, 1862–1868 (UNLP/TC, 23, 1978, p. 107–118)

Challenging article about a neglected topic: the reactivation of inter-provincial commerce in the Interior.

3259 González Lonziéme, Enrique. La Armada en la Conquista de Desierto. Ilus. de Emilio Biggeri. 2. ed. Buenos Aires: Editorial Universitaria de Buenos Aires, 1977. 165 p.; bibl.; ill. (Lucha de fronteras con el indio) (Colección Argentina)

Highly readable inventory of naval events and general overview of the Navy's presence in the southern region from colonial times until century's end.

3260 Goodwin, Paul B., Jr. Anglo-Argentina commercial relations: a private sector view: 1922–43 (HAHR, 61: 1, Feb. 1981, p. 29–51)

Argues against dependency theory contending that British Chamber of Commerce records show a very different picture: "the Argentine Government was master in its own house."

3261 Graham Yooll, Andrew. The press in Argentina, 1973–1978. London: Writer and Scholars Educational Trust, 1979. 171 p.

Walter Little's introduction describes how political confrontation, civil strife and hyperinflation disrupted Argentine society. Attempts to show how censorship and particularly self-censorship also contributed to social disorder. A day-by-day chronology accompanies each chapter.

3262 Groussac, Paul. Paul Groussac. Edición de Martín Alberto Noel. Buenos Aires: Ediciones Culturales Argentinas, 1979. 237 p. (Ediciones de la Secretaría de Estado de Cultura)

Consists of historical selections of writings by the distinguished Franco-Argentine historian and man of letters. Editor's introduction provides general overview of his life and works.

3263 Guenaga de Silva, Rosario. Algunas aspectos de la Patagonia austral en la década del 80 (Cuaderno del Centro de Estudios Interdisciplinarios de Fronteras Argentinas [Consejo Nacional de Investigaciones Científicas y Técnicas, Universidad Nacional de Cuyo, Mendoza, Argentina] 4, mayo 1980, p. 7–18)

Short overview of how initial population settlements in National Territory of Santa Cruz can be largely attributed to cheaper land grants and sheep raising.

3264 Guglialmelli, Juan E. El General Savio: industrias básicas, poder militar y poder nacional (IAEERI/E, 60, sept./oct. 1979, p. 5–36)

Brief and precise biographical portrait of founder of Argentina's iron and steel industry. Sketches main developments of 1930s military's intensive industralization policy. Final part criticizes present stages as disruption of economic development caused by liberal policies.

3265 Gutiérrez, Leandro H. Vida material y experiencia de los sectores populares: Buenos Aires, 1880–1914. Buenos Aires: Centro de Investigaciones sobre el Estado y la Administración, Programa de Estudios de Historia Económica y Social Americana (PEHESA), 1981. 1 v.

Excellent informative contribution. Proposes that only by conducting research into the particular problems of groups engaged in a specific trade or profession can one effectively grasp the reality of the past.

3266 Gutiérrez, Ramón. La búsqueda de lo nacional en la arquitectura, 1915–1920 (Revista Nacional de Cultura [Ministerio de Cultura y Educación, Secretaría de Estado de Cultura, Buenos Aires] 1:4, 1979, p. 35–46)

Outlines beginning of movement which challenged traditional Euro-centric vision.

3267 Guy, Donna J. Política azucarera argentina: Tucumán y la generación del 80. Tucumán, Argentina: Ediciones Banco Comercial del Norte, 1981. 166 p.; bibl.

Spanish translation of HLAS 42:3360.

3268 ———. Women, peonage and industrialization: Argentina, 1810–1914 (LARR, 16:3, 1981, p. 65–89, tables)

Careful research opens new perspectives on the impact of modernization on female labor in non-industrialized societies. Continual state of warfare in inland provinces resulted in preponderance of women in the working force. After 1870s, and as a result of economic development, number of working females fell sharply in provinces in contrast to coastal regions where participation of immigrant women increased by end of century. Demonstrates how the mechanism of peonage served as regulator of scarce labor supply in critical areas of the economy.

3269 Halperin Donghi, Tulio. Guerra y finanzas en los orígenes del estado argentino, 1791–1850. Buenos Aires: Editorial de Belgrano, 1982. 284 p.; charts.

Outstanding work, superbly researched, shows from fiscal perspective and as of end of Spanish period to Rosas' fall, process of formation and development of an Argentine state centered in Buenos Aires. Answers some relevant questions: From what sources did the emerging state draw its income? How was it transferred and apportioned? Study also shows that threat of war loomed throughout period (1791–1850).

3270 Heaps-Nelson, George. La aprobación de la Ley Sáenz Peña (UNCR/R, 4:7, julio/dic. 1978, p. 9–26, bibl.)

Perceptive account of parliamentary debate, shows legislators attitudes and regional voting profiles. Ratifies, once again, Conservatives' appraisal of minority status of opposition Radical party.

3271 Heredia, Edmundo A. La diplomacia brasileña ante la cuestión de La Banda Oriental (Historia [Revista-libro trimestral, Buenos Aires] 2:6, junio/set. 1982, p. 19–31)

Short presentation of topic with good diplomatic source materials.

3272 Hernández, Pablo José. Conversaciones con José María Rosa. Buenos Aires: Colihué, 1978. 245 p.; 5 leaves of plates; ill. (Colección Diálogos polémicos)

Prominent nationalist and revisionist historian speaks about his political life and historical works with a wealth of detail. Controversial and passionate, but highly informative account, particularly in regard to revolutions of 1930, 1943, and peronism's last phase.

Hilton, Stanley E. Brazil and the post-Versailles world: elite images and foreign policy strategy, 1919–1929. See item **3587.**

3273 Historia de Mendoza. Pedro Santos Martínez, editor. Buenos Aires: Plus Ultra, 1979. 358 p.; bibl.; ill. (Colección Historia de nuestras provincias; 7)

Another contribution to regional history includes much factual information as well as more general data on cultural, educational, economic and labor matters.

3274 Historia integral argentina. Buenos Aires: Centro Editor de América Latina, 1980. 3 v. (314, 286, 286 p.)

Partial reprint of previous edition presents interesting monographic studies by Enrique M. Barba, Beatriz Bosch, Gregorio Weinberg, Sergio Bagú, Julio Irazusta.

3275 Informe Worthington; condiciones y perspectivas del comercio británico en algunos países sudamericanos; tercer informe: la República Argentina, 1898 (IDES/DE, 19:76, enero/marzo 1980, p. 539–572, tables)

Useful primary source consists of official British economic report. Offers perceptive overview of country's general economic conditions as it recovered from hazards of 1890 crisis. Generated by concern over decline of British exports, the report contains wealth of data on imported goods and principal Argentine industrial products, especially textiles.

3276 Informes sobre el comercio exterior de Buenos Aries durante el gobierno de Martín Rodríguez: edición de homenaje al Libertador General Don José de San Martín en el bicentenario de su nacimiento. Estudio preliminar de Enrique M. Barba. Buenos Aires: Academia Nacional de la Historia, 1978. 88 p. (Colección de historia económica y social; 3)

Translation of highly informative British report dated 1824, first published by R. A. Humphreys. Concerns regional trade opportunities and shows level of progress and prosperity achieved by Rodríguez-Rivadavia administration. Also includes another report from Lezica's trading firm with much information on commerce with Chile, Bolivia and Peru.

3277 Iñigo Carrera, Héctor. La experiencia radical, 1916–1922. Buenos Aires: Ediciones La Bastilla, 1980. 2 v. (316, 320 p.); bibl. (Memorial de la patria)

Rather elementary and jumbled chronicle of President Yrigoyen's first administration is nevertheless useful because of a wealth of data.

3278 La Inmigración en la Argentina. Tucumán, Argentina: Universidad Nacional de Tucumán, Facultad de Filosofía y Letras, Centro de Historia y Pensamiento Argentinos, 1979. 320 p.; bibl. (Publicación no. 1255)

Multidisciplinary papers presented at two symposia held in 1976–77. Different contributions come together to reveal panoramic vista of topic. Especially valuable are: Irene García de Sator's "Antecedentes de la Política Migratoria: Bernardino Rivadavia;" Orlando Lázaro's "Alberdi, Avellaneda y la Inmigración;" F. Rubén González's "Iglesia e Inmigración en la Argentina, 1810–1914;" Orlando Lázaro's "Inmigración y Sociedad;" Estela Barbieri de Santamarina's "La Inmigración y sus Consecuencias en la Organización del Territorio Argentino." Two contributions concern Tucumán: Carlos Paéz de la Torre's "Los Franceses en Tucumán" and Israel Blumenfeld's "Los Judíos en Tucumán."

3279 Irazusta, Julio. Breve historia de la Argentina. Buenos Aires: Ediciones Independencia, 1982. 270 p.

Argentina's past is projected in a general framework of world events. Ten chapters examine, from a foreign relations perspective, country's development since discovery to Lonardi's government in 1955.

3280 ———. José María Ramos Mejía y el *Rosas y su tiempo*: pts. 1/2 (Historiografía Rioplatense [Instituto Bibliográfico Antonio Zinny, Buenos Aires] 1, 1978, p. 75–104; 2, 1982, p. 43–72)

Excellent historiographical essay, strongly critical of a classic written against Rosas.

3281 Jassén, Raúl. Argentina: de Bolívar a la Trilateral. Buenos Aires: Ediciones Integridad Americana, 1979. 200 p.; bibl.; map.

Rambling exposition of Argentina's territorial fragmentation from the Viceroyalty's breakdown to the Beagle question. Based on a conspiratorial nationalistic interpretation.

3282 Jaumendreu, Paco. Evita fuera del balcón. Buenos Aires: Ediciones del Libro Abierto, 1981. 1 v.; ill.

Consists of intimate, apolitical notes, written by her dressmaker and designer. Provides fresh sketches of Eva Perón's daily life, before and after her triumph.

3283 Johnson, Lyman L. Estimaciones de la población de Buenos Aires en 1744, 1778 y 1810 (IDES/DE, 19:73, abril/junio 1979, p. 107–119)

Solid study, based on new data, mainly birth and burial registers, reveals a population greater than estimated so far. Author's figures, particularly for 1810, are more accurate. Also argues that an important segment of the population, the black freedmen, were omitted from counts because of their poverty.

3284 Jones, Charles. "Business imperialism" and Argentina, 1875–1900: a theoretical note (JLAS, 12, pt. 2, Nov. 1980, p. 437–444)

Analyzes character of capitalism through a study of Argentina in period under scrutiny. Considers spread of competitive capitalism as fundamental cause of imperialism: "to be regarded as a condition affecting the world economy as a whole and characterized by the development of strong but costly States and firms with strategies designed to delay or halt the disruptive effects of cost-cutting capitalist revolution." Shows that the neo-mercantilist transformation of the Argentine state was the result of British business pressure.

3285 Kopp, Thomas. Walgadeutschen Siedeln im argentinischen Zwischenstromland. Marburg, FRG: s.n., 1979. 287 p.; maps (Schriftenreihe der Kommission für Ostdeutsche Volkskunde in der Deutschen Gesellschaft für Volkskunde; Bd. 21)

Reviews "Russian German" settlements in Entre Ríos through brief historical overview and through analysis of this immigrant German society. Originally welcomed into Russia by Catherine the Great, Russian Germans found it difficult to integrate into Slavic society, many of them emigrating to Siberia, Eastern Europe and the Americas by end of 19th century. Entre Ríos' Volga Germans date back to 1870s. Kopps's scholarly work updates and expands Jakob Riffel's *Die Russlanddeutschen insbesondere die Wolgadeutschen am La Plata* (1928). [G. M. Dorn]

3286 Larra, Raúl. Desafío a los Andes. Tapa de Sigfredo Pastor. Dibujos a pluma de Bartolomé Mirabelli. Buenos Aires: Ediciones Anfora, 1978. 157 p.; ill.

Short biographical sketches of Argentine pioneer aviators describe their efforts to conquer Andean peaks.

3287 Lascano, Luis C. Alén. Causa y alternativas del estancamiento en el Noroeste argentino (FEPA/EI, 1:1, abril 1979, p. 25–29)

Severe criticism of economic and social consequences of *porteño* liberal policies as exemplified by the effect of railway lines and excessive timber exploitation on the Northeast.

3288 Lattes, Alfredo E. La dinámica de la población rural en la Argentina entre 1870 y 1970. Buenos Aires: Centro de Estudios de Población, 1979. 42 p.; bibl.; ill. (Cuadernos del CENEP: no. 9)

Provides important demographic data consisting of two parts: 1) chronologically or before and after 1930; and 2) topically or within wider perspective of Argentine economic and social development. Also examines urban demographic evolution.

3289 Leonard, Virginia W. Education and the Church-state clash in Argentina: 1954–1955 (ACHA/CHR, 45:1, Jan. 1980, p. 34–52)

Chronological study of main events. Suggests that conflict originated with peronism's purposeful interference with the Church's capability to educate youth (for political scientist's comment, see *HLAS* 43:6608).

3290 Lewis, Paul H. Was Perón a fascist? an inquiry into the nature of fascism (SPSA/JP, 42, 1980, p. 242–256)

Important contribution on the true nature of peronism. Compares methods for mobilization and control of the masses in both fascism and peronism.

3291 Little, Walter. La organización obrera y el estado peronista, 1943–1955 (IDES/DE, 19:75, oct./dic. 1979, p. 331–376, tables)

Examines evolution of peronist regimes' relationship with trade unions through different periods, before and after 1946. After experiencing a variety of responses from labor that ranged from defined opposition to blind loyalty, the relationship, fragile in the beginning, grew consolidating into a final monolithic association. Denies that the "Partido Laborista" represented a viable possibility for the creation of a reformist and democratic system (for political scientist's comment, see *HLAS* 43:6609).

3292 Llanes, Ricardo M. Biografía de la Avenida Santa Fe. Buenos Aires: Municipalidad de la Ciudad de Buenos Aires, 1978. 122 p.; ill. (Cuadernos de Buenos Aires; no. 50)

Vivid chronicle of one of the principal city streets highlights social aspects.

3293 Lobos, Héctor R. La frontera sur de Córdoba, 1810–1820. Córdoba, Argentina: Junta Provincial de Historia de Córdoba, 1979. 122 p. (Junta Provincial de historia de Córdoba; 6)

Well researched account of region's military and political conditions. Part of more ambitious project designed to examine the economic and social impacts of the war of independence.

3294 Lonardi, Marta. Mi padre y la Revolución del 55. Buenos Aires: Ediciones Cuenca de Plata, 1980. 306 p.; ill.

Polemical, strongly apologetic account of Gen. Lonardi's participation in the rebellion against Perón and of his short administration. Mainly based on author's brother's previous contribution, *Dios es justo*. Does not add much to existing knowledge.

3295 López Piacentini, Carlos P. Historia de la Provincia del Chaco. t. 1, El Chaco primigenio. t. 2, Los fundadores. t. 3, La conquista del Desierto Verde. t. 4, Los pioneros. t. 5, Chaco territorio y Chaco Provincia. Ilus. de tapa, Humberto Horianski. Resistencia, Argentina: Editorial Región, 1979. 5 v.; bibl.; ill.

Vast but unfortunately chaotic chronicle, from colonial times to present. Contains useful information, nevertheless.

3296 Lorini, José Víctor. Misiones aeronáuticas extranjeras, 1919–1924. Buenos Aires: Instituto Argentino de Historia Aeronáutica, 1981. 239 p.

Good research of first years of Argentine aviation, records main foreign participants and principal events.

3297 Loudet, Osvaldo. Vocación y vida. Buenos Aires: Emecé Editores, 1979. 222 p. (Escritores argentinos)

Collection of essays covers different topics but shares common link: individual vocation. Examines different personalities in that light (e.g., San Martín, Alberdi, J. M. Gutiérrez, etc.).

3298 Luna, Félix. Conflictos y armonías en la historia argentina. Buenos Aires: Editorial de Belgrano, 1980. 513 p. (Colección Figuras contemporáneas)

Well written collection of essays whose

verve and ingenuity do not make up a lack of interest for historians.

3299 Luque Colombres, Carlos A. Apuntes para una crónica histórica de los orígenes de Luque. Córdoba, Argentina: Junta Provincial de Historia de Córdoba, 1979. 52 p.; 9 leaves of plates; ill. (Cuadernos de historia; 1)

Engaging narrative about the origins and development of small urban center describes a typical transformation from railroad station into small community.

3300 Lynch, John. Argentine dictator: Juan Manuel De Rosas, 1829–1852. Oxford; Clarendon; New York: Oxford University Press, 1981. 414 p.; bibl.; index.; map; port.

First-class contribution, best thought out and researched book published in English on this controversial topic. Argues that, being the product of circumstances, Rosas "represented the rise to power of a new economic interest, a new social group: The Estanciero." Considers that his regime was the result of environment and idiosyncrasy. Chapters that examine the structure of society (Ch. 3) and the process of terror (Ch. 6) are outstanding. Makes good use of bibliographical materials.

3301 Macchi, Manuel E. El breve gobierno de Urquiza en Buenos Aires (ANH/IE, 26, enero/junio 1979 [i.e. 1980] p. 389–438)

Descriptive summary of this administration's manifold activities (Feb.–Aug. 1852).

3302 ———. La primera Presidencia constitutional argentina. Concepción del Uruguay: Museo Justo J. de Urquiza, 1980. 282 p.

Highly informative study of Urquiza's efforts to institutionalize national government during his administration (1854–60).

3303 MacDonald, C. A. The politics of intervention: the United States and Argentina, 1941–1946 (JLAS, 12:2, Nov. 1980, p. 365–396)

Documented study of Argentine-US confrontation during World War II. Characterizes US attitude as one of interference in Argentina's internal affairs without knowledge of its real developments, in full contrast to Britain's realistic perceptions. Argues that both Castillo's and ensuing military regimes were predominantly nationalistic and acted

defensively. According to author, despite differences, US decision-makers shared identical goals: establishing an open-door economic order in which US interests would be dominant, paralleling US leadership in the inter-American system.

3304 McGee, Sandra F. The Liga Patriótica Argentina and the defense of order (Latinamericanist [Center for Latin American Studies, University of Florida, Gainesville] 13:2, 1 March 1978, p. 1–4)

Brief outline of Liga's origin, principal features and main activities during 1920s.

3305 McLynn, F. J. The frontier problem in nineteenth-century Argentina (History Today [Longman Group Ltd., Periodicals and Directories Division, London] 30, Jan. 1980, p. 28–32, map, plates)

Concise overview of prolonged warfare with Pampa Indians. Finds striking similarities with US frontier wars, but regards Argentine situations as much more threatening. Argues that in both countries, expansionist Manifest Destiny favoured land speculators.

3306 ———. The Montonero risings in Argentina during the eighteen-sixties (Canadian Journal of History/Annales Canadiennes d'Histoire [Journal of History Co. Ltd., Saskatoon, Canada] 15:1, April 1980, p. 49–66)

Evaluates significance of rebellions within context of a violent decade. Both El Chacho's and Varela's revolts are partly attributed to the Paraguayan War which is regarded as principal cause of most uprisings. Author explains them as resistance to *porteño* centralization, as reaction to perceived threat to a traditional way of life, and rejects other ideological causes.

3307 ———. Political instability in Córdoba province during the eighteen-sixties (IAA, 6:3, 1980, p. 251–269, bibl.)

Excellent study of political scenario that made Córdoba unique during Mitre's administration. Attributes provincial turmoil (bloody radicalized factionalism, montonero rebellions, inter-party confrontation, etc.) to several factors: central province's own geopolitical situation, impact of Paraguayan War, increasing military intervention and, finally, shock of structural economic change resulting from integration into national economy. Sarmiento's presidency and building of railroads would close cycle.

3308 Maeder, Ernesto J. A. Guerra civil y crisis demográfica en Corrientes: el censo provincial de 1841 (Folia Histórica del Nordeste [Instituto de Historia, Facultad de Humanidades, Universidad Nacional del Nordeste, Instituto de Investigaciones Geohistóricas, CONICET, Resistencia, Argentina] 4, 1980, p. 55–90)

Notable contribution by celebrated historical demographer who, by comparing two local censuses, shows negative effects of continual warfare on the population.

3309 Marini de Díaz Zorita, Milna C. El avance de la frontera: vías de circulación; las rastrilladas. Santa Rosa, Argentina: Facultad de Ciencias Humanas, Universidad Nacional de La Pampa, 1979. 37 p.; bibl.; maps.

New conditions of Pampas environment are seen as resulting from the advance and consolidation of the frontier. Effective contribution to geohistory.

3310 Martín de Codoni, Elvira. La política sanitaria en el primer medio siglo: Mendoza, 1810–1960 (UNC/RHAA, 19/20, 1979/1980, p. 37–52)

Informative and well documented survey traces in detail main regulations and characteristics of this neglected aspect of social history.

3311 Martínez Zuviría, Gustavo. La Conquista del Desierto y sus consecuencias (SRA/A, 18:8/9, agosto/sept. 1979, p. 64–74, bibl.)

Concise survey of background and final consequences of this campaign.

3312 Massini Ezcurra, José M. Ezequiel N. Paz y el agente fiscal que acusó a Rosas: crónica de La Pampa. Buenos Aires: The Author, 1981. 143 p.; facsim.

Mild revisionist attempt consists of several short narratives that share a common link: to vindicate Rosas and condemn his enemies.

3313 Matijevich, Nicolás. Bibliografía sobre el Canal de Beagle. 2. ed. Bahía Blanca, Argentina: Centro de Estudios Patagónicos, Departamento de Ciencias Sociales, Universidad Nacional del Sur, 1979. 40 p.

Very complete, updated bibliography includes 612 entries.

3314 Mitre, Jorge A. Buenos Aires y su banco. Buenos Aires: Banco de la Provincia de Buenos Aires, 1981. 732 p.

Exhaustive account of Buenos Aires' first banking institution includes wealth of primary sources and statistics. Traces roots of this province's hegemony over the others.

3315 Molinari, Ricardo Luis. Buenos Aires, 4 siglos. Fotos, Carlos Alberto Guastavino. Buenos Aires: Tip. Editora Argentina, 1980. 416 p.; ill. (some col.)

Concise account of city's past includes outstanding illustration of value to historians.

3316 Moliné de Berardoni, Enriqueta E. Historia de Marcos Paz: desde sus orígenes hasta la creación del Partido, 1636–1880. La Plata: Archivo Histórica de la Provincia de Buenos Aires Ricardo Levene, 1978. 184 p.; bibl.; ill. (Contribución a la historia de los pueblos de la Provincia de Buenos Aires; 43)

Well researched monograph examines city's evolution until 1880.

3317 Monacci, Gustavo A. La colectividad británica en Bahía Blanca. Bahía Blanca: Universidad Nacional de Sur, 1979. 107 p.; 17 leaves of plates; bibl.; ill.

Useful account of British community's impact on the city's economic and cultural development.

3318 Moneta, Carlos Juan. La política exterior del peronismo, 1973–1976 (CM/FI, 20:2, 1979, p. 220–276)

Knowledgeable if partly biased survey favors Perón's pragmatic policy of nonalignment but criticizes Isabel Perón's foreign policy.

3319 Moreno, Francisco P. Reminiscencias de Francisco P. Moreno. Versión propia documentada, recopilada por Eduardo V. Moreno. Buenos Aires: Eudeba, 1980. 230 p.

Useful compilation concerns author's Patagonia explorations and consists of family letters, recollections, travel journals and other accounts written 1906–19. Includes important observations on Mapuche culture of use to anthropologists.

3320 Most, Benjamin A. Authoritarianism and the growth of the state in Latin America: an assessment of their impacts on Argentine public policy (CPS, 13:2, July 1980, p. 173–203)

Explores how changing forms of authoritarian rule and the development of a bureaucratic state have affected Argentina. Pin-points factors that have obstructed development of a policy making process: expansion of the public sector, limitations in the ability to press demands, hegemonic crisis, and scarcity of resources.

3321 Mujica Láinez, Manuel. Los porteños. Buenos Aires: Ediciones Librería La Ciudad, 1979. 182 p.; bibl.; ill.

Consists of author's numerous essays and other materials related to Buenos Aires and its inhabitants, written over 40 years. Essential for cultural history, book offers kaleidoscopic view of the city's development.

Musso Ambrosi, Luis Alberto. Anotaciones de bibliografía uruguaya sobre historia argentina en el período, 1831–1852. See *HLAS* 42:56.

Nardi, Ricardo L. J. Ethnohistoria bonaerense. See item **1642.**

3322 Navarro, Marysa. Evita and the crisis of 17 October 1945: a case study of peronist and anti-peronist mythology (JLAS, 12:1, May 1980, p. 127–138)

Thorough analysis of this incident. Concludes that Evita's minimal role was deliberately magnified by the opposition to minimize Perón's.

3323 ———. Evita charismatic leadership (*in* Latin American populism in comparative perspective. Michael L. Conniff, editor. [see item **1830**] p. 47–66)

Successful attempt to capture Evita Perón's character and influence. Includes a particularly interesting examination of her rhetoric. Finds that her participation in a dual leadership began in 1948.

3324 Newton, Ronald C. The German Argentines between Nazism and nationalism: the Patagonian plot of 1939 (The International History Review [University of Toronto Press, Canada] 3:1, Jan. 1981, p. 76–114)

Well researched article reaches provisional conclusion that the affair was fabricated by opponents of the Naza regime. Second half presents an accurate picture of Argentina's German community under the spell of Hitlerism.

3325 Núñez, Urbano J. Historia de San Luis. 2. ed. Buenos Aires: Plus Ultra, 1980. 617 p.; bibl. (Colección Historia de nuestras provincias; 8)

Satisfactory but somewhat parochial

contribution on local history tainted with *anti-porteño* bias.

3326 Oved, Iaácov. El anarquismo y el movimiento obrero en Argentina. México: Siglo Veintiuno, 1978. 459 p.; bibl.; index (Colección América nuestra; 14: Caminos de liberación)

Outstanding research presents accurate and objective picture of a period dominated by the anarchist movement (1897–1905). Makes full use of notable documentation deposited in Amsterdam's International Institute of Social History. A real contribution to Argentine history.

3327 Parchappe, Narciso. Expedición fundadora del Fuerte 25 de Mayo en Cruz de Guerra, año 1828. 2. ed. Buenos Aires: Editorial universitaria de Buenos Aires, 1977. 108 p.; 6 leaves of plates; bibl.; ill.

Second edition of diary by former French military engineer, involved in building new forts along the Indian frontier. Thoroughly documented, it includes numerous descriptions of people, customs and garments.

3328 Pavón Pereyra, Enrique. Los últimos días de Perón. Buenos Aires: Ediciones La Campaña, 1981. 237 p.; bibl.

Account of Perón's last term in office by his noted biographer. Highly critical of how negligent close associates were about his health. Describes López Rega's influence.

3329 Pellettieri, Osvaldo *et al.* La década del 10. Buenos Aires: Editorial de Belgrano, 1980. 351 p. (Colección Conflictos y armonías en la historia argentina)

Successfully recreates year 1910, centennial of Argentine independence, via process of historical collage (e.g., news clippings, biographical materials, memoirs, private papers, public documents).

3330 Peña y Lillo, Silvestre. Juan Facundo Quiroga en Cuyo. Prólogo de Edmundo Correas. Mendoza, Argentina: The Author, 1981. 350 p.

Written in 1936, study still provides a balanced appraisal of the life and deeds of the *Caudillo de los Llanos*, that goes beyond local history. The picture presented differs considerably from Sarmiento's classic portrayal. Book includes wealth of primary sources consisting of 240 bibliographic entries. Correas' introduction offers an objective examination of leading historiographical contributions on the topic.

3331 Peralta Ramos, Mónica. Acumulación de capital y crisis política en Argentina, 1930–1974. México: Siglo Veintiuno Editores, 1978. 453 p.; bibl. (Sociología y política)

Scholarly but ideologically loaded attempt to portray characteristics of the Argentine political process, especially peronism (1970–74), through an analysis of class alliances and their responses to capitalism.

3332 Pereira Larraín, Teresa. Doña Emilia Herrera de Toro (JEHM/R, 1:9, 1979, p. 195–250 photographs)

Brief life-and-times biography of relevant Chilean matron mostly concerns Chilean history but also includes correspondence with Argentine citizens during boundary confrontation period.

3333 Pérez Amuchástegui, Antonio J. ¿Metodología o doctrinosofía?: nacionalismo, liberalismo y marxismo en la historiografía argentina (in Encuentro de Historiadores Latinoamericanos y del Caribe, 2d, Caracas, 1977. Los estudios históricos en América Latina: ponencias, acuerdos y resoluciones: Caracas, 20–26 de marzo de 1977. Caracas: Universidad Central de Venezuela, Facultad de Humanidades y Educación, Escuela de Historia, 1979, v. 1, t. 1, p. 142–146)

Severe critique of the effect of ideology on historical studies. Blames not only classic-liberal and nationalist-revisionist schools, but Marxist tendencies for the politicization of Argentine history. Favors an undogmatic approach.

3334 Perina, Rubén. Raíces históricas de la participación política de los militares argentinos (MN, 3:7/8, enero/junio 1981, p. 35–67)

Well thought out paper tries to demonstrate that the political role of Argentina's armed forces has deep historical roots. According to author, political scientists have not taken this fact into account. Identifies and categorizes different kinds of military participation since independence.

Perry, Richard O. Argentina and Chile: the struggle for Patagonia, 1843–1881. See HLAS 43:7387.

3335 Pirovano de Isleño, Martha. Aporte documental para una historia de la irrigación del sur mendocino (UNC/RHAA, 19/20, 1979/1980, p. 61–84)

Worthwhile, documented outline de-

scribes different policies implemented concerning use of waters of Río Atuel, during 1824–1914.

3336 Pisano, Natalio J. La política agraria de Sarmiento: la lucha contra el latifundio. Buenos Aires: Ediciones Depalma, 1980. 449 p.; bibl.

Innovative contribution on neglected topic: the struggle against the large landed estate. After careful research and scrutiny of Sarmiento's writings, author clarifies many aspects of an issue vigorously debated during second half of 19th century (e.g., immigration, colonization, public land distribution, rural education).

3337 Poissek Prebisch, Lucía. Juan B. Terán: una de la historia (Revista de Cultura [Ministerio de Cultura y Educación, Secretaría de Estado de Cultura, Buenos Aires] 2:8, 1980, p. 69–83, ill.)

Perceptive, updated discussion of the distinguished historian's ideas about his field reveals the influence of Nietzsche and Bergson.

3338 Potash, Robert A. The army & politics in Argentina. v. 2, 1945–1962: Perón to Frondizi. Stanford, Calif.: Stanford University Press, 1980. 480 p.; bibl.; index; plates.

Continuation of author's previous provocative work (for vol. 1, 1928–1945: Yrigoyen to Perón, see HLAS 32:2599a). Outstanding study, thoroughly researched and based on an impressive number of first-rate primary sources and a wealth of oral history accounts. Emphasizes events and issues in which the military participated. Provides invaluable outline of recent political developments (for political scientist's comment, see HLAS 43:6625).

3339 Potter, Anne L. The failure of democracy in Argentina, 1916–1930: an institutional perspective (JLAS, 13:1, May 1981, p. 83–109)

Valid intent to determine, through a study of the Argentine case, the causes for the disruption of an institutional system. After an intelligent analysis of standard explanations for the Revolution of 1930, author finds its root causes in Conservative opposition. These forces feared losing their political turf and the spoils of office as well as their own extinction.

3340 Proyecto y construcción de una nación: Argentina, 1846–1880. Selección, prólogo y cronología, Tulio Halperin

Donghi. Caracas: Biblioteca Ayacucho, 1980.
599 p.

Compilation of representative texts by leading personalities of this controversial and complex period (e.g., Sarmiento, Alberdi, Mitre, Roca, Echeverría, José Hernández). Brillant prologue by Halperin Donghi puts principal issues in true perspective.

3341 Puiggrós, Rodolfo. La Argentina en la década de los treinta (*in* América Latina en los años treinta. Luis Antezana E. *et al.* Coordinator, Pablo González Casanova. México: Instituto de Investigaciones Sociales, Universidad Nacional Autónoma de México, 1977, p. 305–325)

Highly critical and involved chronicle of the period, written by deceased Marxist historian. Contradictions notwithstanding, useful because of wealth of detail.

Quinterno, Carlos Alberto. Militares y populismo: la crisis argentina desde 1966 hasta 1976. See *HLAS 43:8327.*

3342 Raicovich de Tellez, Cristina E. Rosario, 1879: las fuerzas políticas locales y las elecciones de 1880, a través de la prensa (Res Gesta [Facultad de Derecho y Ciencias Sociales, Instituto de Historia, Pontificia Universidad Católica Argentina, Rosario] 7, 2. época, enero/junio 1980, p. 38–46)

Brief account of how press opinion reflected party alignment during presidential campaign. Emphasizes confrontation between *La Capital*, which supported Carlos Tejedor, the Liberals and local candidate Nicasio Oroño, vs. *El Independiente*, which backed Roca, the Autonomistas and Simón Iriondo's political machine.

3343 Ramallo, José María. Algunos aspectos de la economía de la época de Rosas. Buenos Aires: s.n., 1980. 31 p.

Good account includes basic data on important trade aspects (e.g., hides, "saladeros," cattle raising, market places, ports).

3344 Ramos, Jorge Abelardo. La era del peronismo, 1943–1976. 8 ed. Buenos Aires: Ediciones del Mar Dulce, 1981. 294 p.

Eighth edition of a part of book originally entitled *Revolución y contrarrevolución en la Argentina* has many significant additions and new concluding chapter covering 1973–76 period. Includes strong criticism of "terrorist adventurism."

3345 Ranis, Peter. Early peronism and the post-liberal Argentine state (UM/JIAS, 21:3, Aug. 1979, p. 313–338)

Scholarly study of how Perón's early thinking shaped socioeconomic policies in post-World War II Argentina.

3346 Rapoport, Mario. Gran Bretaña, Estados Unidos y las clases dirigentes argentinas, 1940–1945. Buenos Aires: Editorial de Belgrano, 1980. 313 p.; bibl. (Colección Conflictos y armonías en la historia argentina)

Major study of triangular relationship. Based on British primary sources and US edited materials, presents, according to author: "la interpretación más amplia que procure clarificar la problemática que se presentaba a la clase dirigente de la época."

3347 ———. Las relaciones anglo-argentinas: aspectos políticos y económicos; la experiencia del gobierno militar, 1943–1945. Buenos Aires: Fundación para el Estudio de los Problemas Argentinos, 1979. 32 p. (Documento de trabajo; 20)

Describes how Britain's attitude towards Argentine neutrality (1943–45) was, in general, not negative. Also discusses policies of the military government (for political scientist's comment, see *HLAS 43:7407*).

3348 Ratzer, José. El movimiento socialista en Argentina. Buenos Aires: Ediciones Agora, 1981. 190 p.; bibl.

Ambitious attempt to describe the socialist movement as a whole and through its different manifestations and factions, particularly in their writings. Highly critical of reformist social-democrats. Author's death prevented book's completion.

3349 La Regeneración argentina: reproducción y comentario de la obra de Justo Maeso Publicada en 1880. Buenos Aires: Academia Nacional de la Historia, 1980. 18, 96 p.

Facsimile but incomplete edition of rare 1870 pamphlet. Reproduces important documents of 1851–52 period.

3350 Relación entre Argentina y Estados Unidos: la década de 1930. Paraná: Asociación Argentina de Estudios Americanos, 1977. 195 p.

Pt. 1 deals with literary topics; pt. 2, includes five papers on 1930s: María Inés Soulés' "Argentina y Estados Unidos Frente al Conflicto Paraguayo-Boliviano y la Declaración del 3 de Agosto de 1932;" Norma Dolores Riquelme de Lobos' and María Cristiana Vera de Flachs' "Un Conflicto entre Argentina y Estados Unidos por el Mercado Harinero del Brasil;" Fernando Miguel's "Aportes para el Estudio de la Neutralidad en la Conferencia de Consolidación de la Paz;" Jorge Antonio Lobos' "Protocolo de No-Intervención en la Conferencia de Consolidación de la Paz;" Adriana B. Martino's and Mary Theda Develgado's "Influencias del 'New Deal' en el gobierno de Luciano Molinas: Concreción Legislativa en Cuatro Aspectos Fundamentales, 1933–1935." Three other papers cover relations between Argentina and US: María Inés Soulés' "Las Relaciones Comerciales entre Argentina y los Estados Unidos durante la Década de 1890;" Hernán A. Silva's "La Producción Triguera Argentina en la Transición hacia el Siglo XX y la Competencia de Estados Unidos;" and Néstor Tomás Auza's "Estados Unidos Visto y Juzgado por Paul Groussac."

3351 Rey, María Abelia; Delia I. Errazu de Mendiburu; and Norma B. de Abraham. Historia de la industria en Bahía Blanca, 1828–1930. Bahía Blanca, Argentina: Departamento de Ciencias Sociales, Universidad Nacional del Sur, 1981. 174 p.; appendix.

Sound research first examines principal factors in production (e.g., capital, labor force, primary products) and then studies leading business enterprises responsible for city's industrial expansion.

3352 Riquelme de Lobos, Norma Dolores and María Cristine Vera de Flachs. Cincuenta años de industria molinera en Córdoba: su repercusión en la actividad nacional (ANH/IE, 24, enero/junio 1978, p. 445–478)

Sequel to authors' previous works on this central province's economic development. Here they scrutinize its exports to Brazil and how they competed with those from the US.

3353 ——— and ———. La sal de Córdoba: historia de una industria decadente, 1860–1914 (JPHC/R, 7, 1978, p. 93–108)

Another aspect of this provincial economy is examined in a well informed monographic study.

3354 Rivera, Alberto A. Una descripción inédita de Manuel F. Mantilla sobre la Ciudad de Corrientes (Folia Histórica del Nordeste [Universidad Nacional del Nordeste, Facultad de Humanidades, Instituto de Historia, Instituto de Investigaciones Geohistóricas, CONICET, Resistencia, Argentina] 4, 1980, p. 185–204)

Reproduces long-lost manuscript that should have been published in *Second National Census* of 1895. Includes vivid description of city and its social development.

3355 Robinson, Karla. The merchants of post-independence Buenos Aires (*in* Hispanic-American essays in honor of Max Leon Moorhead. Edited by William S. Coker. Maps by Jerome F. Coling. Index by Polly Coker. Pensacola, Fla.: Perdido Bay Press, 1979, p. 111–132, tables)

Fine research attempts to settle controversial topic: what was the real impact of the British trading community on Buenos Aires Creole society? Notes that the number of British residents has been grossly exaggerated, and that the city's economic and financial community invested its resources in land rather than business. Concludes that there was no urban vs. rural confrontation in this period.

3356 Rock, David. Repression and revolt in Argentina (UCSD/NS, 7 : 1/2, 1978 [i.e. 1979] p. 105–120)

Short account of political and social unrest during last quarter of this century. Emphasizes 33 months of populist governments in 1970s.

3357 Rodolfo Irazusta, 1897–1967: testimonios. Buenos Aires: Librería Huemul, 1980. 170 p.; 12 leaves of plates; bibl.; ill.

Commemorative essays written by friends and admirers of the distinguished writer and politician, of which the best are: Enrique Zuleta Alvárez's "Rodolfo Irazusta y la Idea de una Política Nacional" (p. 17–36) which concerns his ideology; and Félix S. Fares' "Rodolfo Irazusta: Testimonio Personal," a short biographical sketch (p. 115–161).

3358 Rodríguez Sánchez, Margarita. Gravitación política de Perón, 1955–1973. México. Extemporáneos, 1979 [i.e. 1980]. 148, 12 p.; bibl. (Colección Latinoamérica. Serie Ensayo; 10)

Brief, informative but somewhat naive monographic study. Useful as general overview.

3359 Roig, Arturo Andrés. Deodoro Roca y el *Manifiesto de la Reforma* de 1918 (UUAL/U, 20:79, 3. serie, enero/marzo 1980, p. 88–115)

Incisive analysis of 1918 *Manifiesto's* author, his ideological background and evolution of his thinking. Sheds much light on a seminal document that exemplified a generation (for philosopher's comment, see item **7610**).

3360 Romero, José Luis. La experiencia argentina y otros ensayos. Compilados por Luis Alberto Romero. Diseño de tapa, Pablo Barragán. Buenos Aires: Editorial de Belgrano, 1980. 522 p.; bibl.

Collection of historical and political writings by an eminent Argentine historian which constitute the best synthesis of Argentina's past. Several essays are published for the first time. Book is divided into four sections: 1) History; 2) Men; 3) The University; and 4) History and Politics.

3361 Rosas, Juan Manuel José Domingo Ortiz de. Cartas inéditas de Rosas, Roxas y Patrón. v. 1, 1852–1862, monarquía republicana. A cargo de José Raed. Buenos Aires: Platero, 1980. 1 v.; facsim.; index (Serie Reestructuración histórica. El General Rosas tiene la palabra)

Consists of documentary sources that contribute significantly to a better understanding of the times and mind of Rosas. Vol. 1 includes 34 letters (1852–62) covering a wide variety of topics.

3362 Rouquié, Alain. Groupes de pression et Forces Armées en Argentine: la logique de l'État Prétorien (Revue Française d'Histoire d'Outre-mer [Société de l'Histoire des Colonies Françaises, Société Française d'Histoire d'Outre-mer, Paris] 66:244/245, 1979, p. 377–383)

Applies theories of Huntington and Perlmutter to the Argentine case in order to show how the army has remained in control of the decision-making process by exchanging roles with the political parties.

3363 ———. Poder militar y sociedad política en la Argentina. Buenos Aires: Emecé Editores, 1982. 345 p.; index.

This cross-disciplinary two-volume work of history, military sociology and comparative politics constitutes an outstanding addition to the literature. Vol. 1 describes emergence of the military establishment until 1943. Vol. 2, *Poder militar y sociedad política en la Argentina, 1943–1973*, will include general bibliography and source information. By exploring the significance of military intervention, author identifies its more notable and permanent features. Argues that military interventions are not the cause but rather the glaring manifestation of chronic political instability (for sociologist's comment of French original, see *HLAS 43:8328*).

3364 Roth, Roberto. Los años de Onganía: relatos de un testigo. 3. ed. Buenos Aires: Ediciones La Campaña, 1981. 410 p.

Provocative and revisionist assessment of this administration by former high government official. Presents concise and interesting account of in-fighting between government's liberal and nationalist factions.

3365 Ruiz Moreno, Isidoro J. Relaciones hispano-argentinas: de la guerra a los tratados. Buenos Aires: The Author, 1981. 364 p.; appendix; bibl.; index.

First systematic attempt to deal with this topic. Thoroughly describes 1852–62 period, especially how Alberdi's mission was misunderstood. Also concerns Spanish citizens who lived in Argentina at the time.

3366 Sábato, Hilda; Juan Carlos Korel; and Ricardo González. Los trabajadores y el mercado de trabajo en Buenos Aires, cuidad y campaña, 1850–1880. Buenos Aires: Centro de Investigaciones sobre el Estado y la Administración, Programa de Estudios de Historia Económica y Social Americana (PEHESA), 1981. 1 v.

Reports preliminary results of ongoing research. Useful contribution to topic of labor potential and eventual transformation of the occupational structure during this transitional period.

3367 Sáenz Quesada, María. Los estancieros. Buenos Aires: Editorial de Belgrano, 1980. 340 p.; bibl. (Colección Conflictos y armonías en la historia argentina)

Good narrative provides a panoramic view of this crucial group from its origin to 1914. Stresses its political participation and dominance.

3368 Sanguinetti, Horacio. Los socialistas independientes. Buenos Aires: Editorial Sudamericana, 1981. 422 p.

Well written narrative about Socialist Party faction is based on careful research, primary sources and numerous oral reports. By examining how two leading personalities of this group, Antonio De Tomaso and Federico Pinedo, participated as ministers in Gen. Justo's administration, sheds much light on the latter.

3369 Sanz, Luis Santiago. Consideración parlamentaria del Tratado de 1881: pts. 2/3 (ANH/IE, 26, enero/junio 1979 [i.e. 1980] p. 327–366; 27, julio/dic. 1979 [i.e. 1981] p. 179–228)

Documented chronological narrative follows debates on the 1881 Boundary Treaty in Argentine and Chilean congresses.

3370 ———. El poder naval y la Junta de Notables de 1906 (IAEERI/E, 46/47, 1977, p. 47–95)

Documented study of conflict with Uruguay concerning jurisdiction over the River Plate's waters and ensuing tensions with Brazil.

3371 Saraví, Mario Guillermo. Cuyo y el artiguismo, 1816–1817 (Historiografía Rioplatense [Instituto Bibliográfico Antonio Zinny, Buenos Aires] 1978, p. 105–126)

Describes how the Interior (inner provinces) reacted to the Portuguese invasion of the Banda Oriental and to porteño attitudes.

3372 ———. Una misión unitaria a Chile, 1830–1831 (UNC/BCPS, 25, 1979, p. 167–195)

Studies relations between Chile and Unitarian leader José María Paz concerning his request for arms and economic help to confront the Littoral's Federal League.

3373 Scenna, Miguel Angel. Los militares. Buenos Aires: Editorial de Belgrano, 1980. 363 p. (Colección Conflictos y armonías de la historia argentina)

Very well written and informative survey of the military as a social group covers 1806–1976. Brings together all available bibliographical information and covers the 1880–1932 period best.

3374 Segreti, Carlos S. A. La economía del Interior en la primera mitad del siglo XIX: correlación documental. v. 1, Cuyo.

Buenos Aires: Academia Nacional de la Historia, 1981 [i.e. 1982]. 224 p. (Colección de historia economíca y social; V, IV)

Vol. 1 of projected four on ambitious study of different regional economies of Argentina. Ably uses 35 relevant documents (1810–52) and comments on each.

3375 Senkman, Leonardo. La inmigración judía en América Latina: integración e identidad (in Coloquio Latinoamericano sobre Pluralismo Cultural, 2d, Buenos Aires, 1978. Pluralismo cultural: segundo Coloquio Latinoamericano. Organizado por el Congreso Judío Latinoamericano, rama del Congreso Judío Mundial Centro Cultural Gral. San Martín de la Municipalidad de la Ciudad de Bs.As., 4, 5 y 6 de diciembre de 1978. Buenos Aires?: Congreso Judío Latinoamericano, 1978?, p. 159–179)

Excellent paper places successful development of Argentina's Jewish community in larger Latin American perspective. Notes group's principal features such as its being urban, quick to seek modernization and entry into the middle class as well as its general adaptability and political participation.

Serres Güiraldes, Alfredo Marcelo. De cómo la República Argentina perdió su salida al Océano Pacífico. See *HLAS 43:7411.*

3376 ———. La estrategia del General Roca. Cartografía original del autor. Diseño de la tapa, Juan Carlos Martínez. Buenos Aires: Editorial Pleamar, 1979. 387 p.; bibl.; maps (Testimonios nacionales)

Wide-ranging account of Argentina's boundary question with Chile concerning Patagonia. Also describes Araucanian Indians' predatory invasions of the pampas and 1880 final occupation of this hinterland. Includes well researched examination of Argentina's diplomatic involvement in the War of the Pacific.

3377 Siegrist de Gentile, Nora L. Política exterior argentina durante la presidencia de Figueroa Alcorta, 1906–1910 y el *memorandum secreto* del Doctor Estanislao S. Zeballos (in Siegrist de Gentile, Nora L.; Noemí Girbal de Blacha; and Antonio Elío Brailovsky. Tres estudios argentinos. Buenos Aires: Editorial Sudamericana, 1982, p. 7–229)

Relevant study of Argentine aims during regional power struggle. Notes that Foreign Minister Zeballos' plans consisted of an alliance with Chile to counterbalance what he regarded as threats from Brazil. Reproduces his memorandum in full for the first time.

3378 ——— and **María Haydée Martín.** Geopolítica, ciencia y técnica a través de la Campaña del Desierto. Buenos Aires: Editorial Universitaria de Buenos Aires, 1981. 228 p. (Colección Lucha de Fronteras con el indio)

Innovative study examines how final occupation of national territory contributed to geography, science and technology (e.g., advances in cartography, exploration, accomplishments in diplomacy, national defense, etc.). Makes good use of new archival sources, especially Gen. Roca's archive.

3379 **Sigwald Carioli, Susana Beatriz.** Historia de barbas y caftanes. Carlos Casares, Argentina: Centro Cultural José Ingenieros [and] Archivo Histórico Antonio Maya, 1976. 17 l.; bibl.; plates (Serie Pueblo maya; 4)

Sensitive study of Jewish immigration. Recaptures the success of settlements inspired by Baron Hirsch and compares this achievement with other experiences.

3380 **Slatta, Richard W.** Gaucho and *gaúcho*: comparative socio-economic demographic change in Rio Grande do Sul and Buenos Aires Province, 1869–1920 (Estudos Ibero-Americanos [Pontificia Universidad Católica do Rio Grande do Sul, Instituto de Filosofía y Ciencias Humanas, Departamento de Humanidades, Porto Alegre] 6:2, dez. 1980, p. 191–202)

Applies theory of demographic transition arguing that both areas experienced similar economic and socio-demographic development.

3381 ———. Pulperías and contraband capitalism in nineteenth-century Buenos Aires province (AAFH/TAM, 38:3, Jan. 1982, p. 347–362)

Harshly critical appraisal of the negative and repressive social impact on the gaucho's survival of pulperías and smuggling.

3382 ———. Rural criminality and social conflict in nineteenth-century Buenos Aires Province (HAHR, 60:3, Aug. 1980, p. 450–472)

By using a "conflict perspective" and a wealth of sources, author illuminates sociopolitical aspects of life in the pampas. Drastic living conditions imposed on gaucho population were caused by dominant economic interests and process of social change.

3383 **Slodky, Javier.** El movimiento obrero argentino durante el peronismo: período 1943–1955. Lima: Taller de Estudios Urbano Industriales, Progama Académico de Ciencias Sociales, Pontifica Universidad Católica, 1980. 31, 2 p.

Lecture notes present general picture of peronist era. Contends that peronism is popular nationalism, product of an alliance of reciprocal interests.

3384 **Sofer, Eugene F.** Immigrants, entrepreneurship and political participation in Buenos Aires, 1890–1927: the Jewish case (PCCLAS/P, 6, 1977/1979, p. 87–106)

Perceptive case study offers alternative view to widely accepted assumption that democracy and stability are linked to middle-sector expansion, a conclusion that author's own data does not entirely substantiate.

3385 **Solc, Václav.** Sága jihu. Il. Miroslav Váša. Praha: Čs. spis., 1980. 189 p.; bibl.; ill. (Edice Spirála)

General Czech survey of Patagonia, its history and culture, by ethnographer. Includes many references to early Czech contacts and Slavic groups in Patagonia. [G. J. Kovtun]

3386 **Speranza, Sergio.** Economía contra política in Argentina [Affari Esteri [Asociazione Italiana per gli Studi di Politica Estera, Roma] 42, 1979, p. 256–260)

Examines 1976 liberal inspired process and its economic policies.

Stemplowski, Ryszard. Zale zność i wyzwanie: Argentyna wobec rywalizacji mocarstw anglosaskich i III Rzeszy. See *HLAS 43:7413.*

3387 **Stoetzer, O. Carlos.** Two studies on contemporary Argentine history: on the eve of the 1976 crisis and a review of current U.S.-Argentine relations. New York: Argentina Independent Review, 1980. 86 p.; bibl.

Journalistic attempt to explain the background of the 1976 military takeover. Also outlines US-Argentine relations but discusses more thoroughly confrontations regarding human rights violations.

3388 Strauss, Norman S. Brazil after the Paraguayan War: six years of conflict (JLAS, 10:1, May 1978, p. 21–35)

Describes conflict that arose between Argentina and Brazil concerning Paraguay's new boundaries during the victors' peacemaking and settlement process. Chiefly based on US diplomatic reports, does not reflect recently published research and lacks balanced view of the topic (see also *HLAS 42:3758*).

3389 Suárez Urtubey, Pola. La aurora de la musicografía argentina (Revista Nacional de Cultura [Ministerio de Cultura y Educación, Secretaría de Estado de Cultura, Buenos Aires] 1:2, 1979, p. 61–90)

Examination of members of the generation of 1837 reveals that Alberdi was the leading music pioneer.

3390 Szuchman, Mark D. Mobility and integration in urban Argentina: Córdoba in the Liberal era. Austin: University of Texas Press, 1980. 236 p.; bibl.; ill.; index (Latin American monographs; no. 52)

Pioneer exploratory work concerns social change at the local level. Stresses need to reexamine traditional interpretations of urban expansion during liberal era. Wealth of statistical data refutes accepted view of Argentina's successful social mobility. "The Argentine middle-class that is said to have begun developing toward the end of the century was, to a large degree, a fiction."

3391 Tamarin, David. Yrigoyen and Perón: the limits of Argentine populism (*in* Latin American populism in comparative perspective. Michael L. Conniff, ed. [see item **1830**] p. 31–46)

Hasty review of period. Argues that if both popular movements "made great strides in the direction of democratization," they finally failed "to transcend basic class antagonisms." Suggests that 1973–76 events represent demise of populism.

3392 Tanzi, Héctor José. Historiografía argentina contemporánea. Caracas: Instituto Panamericano de Geografía e Historia, 1976. 167 p.; index (Historiografías; no. 9)

Careful and intelligent presentation of historical literature of last 30 years includes excellent study of revisionist currents and politization of Argentine culture. Follows previous historiographical efforts of Rómulo S. Carbia and Raúl Molina.

3393 Taylor, Julie M. Eva Perón, the myths of a woman. Chicago: University of Chicago Press, 1979. 175 p.; 4 leaves of plates; bibl.; ill.; index.

Detailed, essentially anthropological study of the origins and peculiar developments of three relevant interpretations of Eva Duarte's life and deeds: 1) the peronist "Lady of Hope;" 2) the anti-peronist evil image; and 3) the left's "revolutionary leader." Argues that all three myths are directly related to basic splits within Argentine society. One chapter consists of her biography.

3394 Tedesco, Juan Carlos. La crisis de la hegemonía oligárquica y el sistema educativo argentino, 1930–1945 (UPN/RCE, 4, 2. semestre 1979, p. 53–84, tables)

Studies effects of sociopolitical process on education, from Marxist perspective. Shows how traditional rejection of technological curricula negatively affected the educational system (for education specialist's comment, see *HLAS 43:4385*).

3395 Teichman, Judith. Interest conflict and entrepreneurial support for Perón (LARR, 1, 1981, p. 144–155)

Significant analysis of two labor groups, "metalúrgicos" and "textiles," which make up nearly half of all industrial workers. Confirms that they are anti-status-quo and share similar interests with the rest of labor movement (e.g., improving living standards, protectionist policies, etc.).

3396 Tesler, Mario. Aportes de Diego Luis Molinari a la cultura hispanoamericana: pt. 1, Ensayo biblio-hemerográfico (Historia [Revista-libro trimestral, Buenos Aires] 2:6, junio/sept. 1982, p. 122–159)

Pt. 1 of study of the distinguished and controversial historian and politician. Thoroughly covers his historical works.

3397 Tissera, Ramón. Calendario histórico del Chaco: desde 1526 a 1976. Dibujo de tapa, Rubén Ocampo. Resistencia: Editorial Cultural Nordeste, 1977. 156 p.

Lists relevant events in this province's history. Records 450 years in chronological order.

Tobler, Hans Werner and **Peter Waldmann.** German colonies in South America: a new Germany in the Cono Sur? See item **1835**.

3398 Todo es Historia. Revista mensual de divulgación histórica. Honnegger, S.A.

No. 162, Nov. 1980 [through] No. 174, Nov. 1981– . Buenos Aires.

Popular magazine devoted to Argentine history includes several issues of interest to historians: No. 162 (Nov. 1980) dedicated to the Argentine black has essays by Ricardo Rodríguez Molas, Narciso Binayán Carmona and Néstor Ortiz Oderigo; No. 163 (Dec. 1980) discusses the 1880s with Natalio Botana and Ezequiel Gallo noting that much remains to be done historically on this period; No. 167 (April 1981) includes useful article by Rodolfo Audi and Oscar R. Cardozo, "Hace Veinte Años: la CGT a sus Dueños;" No. 171 (agosto 1981) examines Argentines who went to California during the Gold Rush and the anti-Rosas campaign of "El Chacho" Peñaloza; No. 174 (Nov. 1981) includes informative account by Mariano R. Monteverde "Balbín Preso."

3399 Tonda, América A. El Doctor Gregorio Funes y el fallecimiento de Pío VII. Rosario: Instituto de Historia, Facultad de Derecho y Ciencias Sociales, Pontificia Universidad Católica Argentina, 1980. 22 p.

Heated journalistic debate that occurred in Rivadavia's anticlerical times.

3400 Ugarte, Manuel. La nación latinoamericana. Compilación, prólogo, notas y cronología, Norberto Galasso. Caracas: Biblioteca Ayacucho, 1978. 447 p.; bibl. (Biblioteca Ayacucho; 45)

Selection of writings by outstanding spokesman for the Patria Grande. Texts are arranged chronologically and according to many topics (e.g., anti-imperialism, unification of Spanish America). Galasso's introduction is somewhat biased.

3401 Unamuno, Miguel. La muerte de Ramírez y las olvidadas memorias del General Anacleto Medina. Buenos Aires: A. Peña Lillo, 1980. 111 p.

Reprint of document, first published 1895, contradicts romanticized version of the Federalist caudillo's death.

3402 Urquiza Almandoz, Oscar R. Historia económica y social de Entre Ríos: 1600–1854. Rosario, Argentina: Banco Unido del Littoral, 1980. 574 p.

Important contribution on local history devotes separate chapters to specific topics of which the most useful are: Chap. 1 on population and land settlement; Chap. 3 on agriculture; Chaps. 5/6 on commerce; Chap. 11 on communications.

Vázquez-Presedo, Vicente. Crisis y retraso: Argentina y la economía internacional entre las dos guerras. See *HLAS 43:3697.*

3403 Vera de Flachs, María Cristina. El desarrollo socio-económico del sud de la Provincia de Córdoba (JPHC/R, 7, 1978, p. 109–124)

2Succinct but well informed survey of a decade of outstanding progress based on excellent tables.

3404 ———. El Ferrocarril Andino: de Villa María a Villa Mercedes (JPHC/R, 7, 1978, p. 17–33)

Chronological description of the building of a strategically important railway.

3405 Villarino, María de. Memoria de Buenos Aires: narración de la ciudad desde el nacimiento hasta el siglo XX. Buenos Aires: Editorial Sudamericana, 1979. 287 p.; bibl. (Colección El Espejo)

Very readable account of how the city developed includes final section on cultural life.

3406 El Voto peronista: ensayos de sociología electoral argentina. Manuel Mora y Araujo and Ignacio Llorente, eds. Buenos Aires: Editorial Sudamericana, 1980. 526 p; maps; tables.

Important compilation of recently published studies on the character and social basis of peronism. Llorente's and González Estévez's essay on how the conservative vote contributed to peronism's success in the 1946 elections, is a ground-breaking historical contribution, aspects of which are yet to be fully explored.

Wachowicz, Ruy Christovam. O "Uti possidetis" brasileiro na questão de palmas. See item **3641.**

3407 Wahnish, José A. and **Carlos R. French.** Creación de la Fuerza Aérea Argentina y síntesis de la evolución del poder aéreo nacionl: pts. 1/2 (IAEERI/E, 59, julio/agosto 1979, p. 107–112; 60, sept./oct. 1979, p. 105–125)

Records development of military aviation (1912–79). Notes Perón's positive influence on behalf of its modernization in 1940s.

3408 Waldmann, Peter. El peronismo, 1943–1955. Buenos Aires: Editorial Sudamericana, 1981. 257 p.; bibl.

Skillfully analyzes Perón's ideology, political style and strategies. Examines relations of his regime with principal pressure groups. Unfortunately, fails to take some factors into consideration such as opposition political parties. Based on bibliographical sources.

3409 Walter, Richard J. The socialist press in turn-of-the-century Argentina (AAFH/TAM, 37:1, July 1980, p. 1–24)

Surveys principal newspapers, *La Vanguardia, El Obrero* and *La Montaña,* and notes how they parallel the period's growing social unrest.

3410 Weinberg, Félix. El pensamiento de la Generación del Ochenta (UNS/CS, 13, enero/dic. 1980, p. 17–38)

Interpretative essay describes principal ideological positions of this generation's leading personalities. Includes sensitive presentation of President Juárez Celman's thoughts on political parties.

3411 Woods, Randall Bennett. The Roosevelt foreign-policy establishment and the Good Neighbor: the United States and Argentina, 1941–1945. Lawrence: Regents Press of Kansas, 1979. 277 p.; bibl.; index.

Interesting approach to better understanding of the issue. Applies one of Graham Allison's paradigms by examining attitudes of American decision-makers involved in the US-Argentine confrontation. Underscores fact that Argentina's stand was the consequence of its geography, culture, economy, politics and diplomatic traditions. Examines how contradictions implicit in the Wilsonian tradition affect US foreign policy which tends to oscillate between acceptance of the self-determination of nations and a tendency towards missionary crusades.

3412 Wynia, Gary W. Argentina and the postwar era: politics and economic policy making in a divided society. Albuquerque: University of New Mexico Press, 1978. 289 p.; bibl.; index.

Excellent account of policy-making in a confrontational society with a low level of political participation and lacking a national consensus. Describes diverse economic policies implemented, from Perón's coming to power in 1940s to 1973–76, by both civilian and military regimes. Concludes that if participation is ignored and social unrest on the rise, a government's structure and its economic policies become largely irrelevant (for economist's comment, see *HLAS 43:3699*).

PARAGUAY

3413 Aguirre, Andrés. Acosta Ñú, epopeya de los siglos. Prólogo del ministro de defensa nacional Gral. de Div. Marcial Samaniego. Eusebio Ayala, Paraguay: Municipalidad de Eusebio Ayala, 1979. 309 p.; bibl.; ill.

Recreates tragic resistance against superior forces of the Triple Alliance, especially battle of Aug. 1869 in which 3500 youths, the *niños soldados,* went to their deaths.

3414 Al'peróvič, Moisei Samuilovič. La dictadura del Dr. Francia en Paraguay y la opinión pública rusa del siglo XIX (PAN/ES, 6:2, 1980, p. 11–17)

Brief survey of Russian materials on Paraguay, mostly translations. Although negative perceptions of Francia predominate, some radical writers extoll his democratic character and popular support. Author argues these perceptions reflect local political attitudes.

3415 Anécdotas de la Guerra del Chaco. Asunción: Editora Hoy, 1980. 300 p.; ill. (some col.)

Lavish account brings together anonymous or lesser known episodes. Includes excellent photographs.

3416 Aragaña, Luis María. Historia de las ideas políticas en el Paraguay. Asunción: Instituto Colorado de Cultura, 1979. 304 p.; bibl. (Biblioteca Colorados contemporáneos; 5)

Very partisan interpretation of how ideological thinking and political parties have evolved in Paraguay, written by Colorado Party member. Definitely not history but interesting as example of party's thinking.

3417 Bejarano, Ramón César. Perfil y trayectoria de un militar. Asunción: Editorial Toledo, 1978. 135 p.; 1 fold. leaf of plates; bibl.; ill.

Short biographical sketch written by Bejarano's son, covers 1900–30.

3418 Benítez, Luis G. Historia de la educación paraguaya. Asunción: Industrial Gráfica Comuneros, 1981. 282 p.; bibl.

Worthy attempt to summarize history of Paraguayan education provides overview of different periods from colonial times to present.

3419 Cabrera, Gaspar Natalicio. Historia sintética de la ciudad de Caazapá (Kaásāpa). Asunción: Impr. Zamphirópolos, 1980. 68 p.

Brief local history.

3420 Cardozo, Efraím. Hace cien años: crónicas de la guerra de 1864–1870 publicadas en *La Tribuna* de Asunción en el centenario de la epopeya nacional. t. 11, 10 de enero de 1869 a 30 de abril de 1869. Mapas de Roberto Thompson. Asunción: Ediciones EMASA, 1980. 366 p.; maps.

Continuation of series (for previous volumes, see *HLAS 42:3450*).

3421 ———. Historiografía paraguaya. v. 1, Paraguay indígena, español y jesuita. 2. ed. México: Instituto Panamericano de Geografía e Historia, 1979. 610 p.; bibl.; indexes (IPGH; 5)

Overdue reprint of indispensable historiographical masterpiece (first ed. 1959).

3422 Cazal, José María. Batalla de Ingavi, junio de 1935. Asunción: s.n., 1979. 387 p.; 12 leaves of plates (5 fold.); bibl.; ill.

Strong and colorful narrative of military operations during Chaco War's last phase based on wealth of military sources and written by Paraguayan commanding officer in that decisive battle.

3423 Duarte Barrios, Miguel Angel. Jirones históricos, por los senderos del heroísmo y de la gloria. Asunción: Editorial Don Bosco, 1979. 251 p.; bibl.; ill.

Publishes radio talks concerning important historical episodes. Those on the Chaco War should be of interest to historians.

3424 Franco, Víctor I. Un hispano y un italiano en la Guerra contra la Triple Alianza. Asunción: Academia Paraguaya de la Historia, 1979. 72 p.; bibl.; ill.

Biographical accounts of two foreigners who fought with Paraguayan forces: Col. Dionisio Lirio, a Spaniard, and Major Sebastian Bullo, Italian.

3425 La Generación paraguaya, 1928–1932: temas de América Latina. Editor, Ruperto D. Resquín. Buenos Aires: Editorial Paraguay en América, 1978. 257 p.; 8 leaves of plates (2 fold.); ill.

Reminiscences by Paraguay's Colegio Nacional Alumni who participated in the Chaco War.

Reminiscences by Paraguay's Colegio Nacional Alumni who participated in the Chaco War.

3425a Gutiérrez, Ramón. Los pueblos jesuíticos del Paraguay: reflexiones sobre su decadencia (UCNSA/SA, 14:1/2, dic. 1979, p. 179–199, ill.)

In attempt to defend Jesuit "experiment," shows how seven Paraguayan mission towns, in excellent condition at time of Jesuits' expulsion and suffering moderate decline thereafter, were almost destroyed economically and socially by Carlos Antonio López's 1848 decree. It ended "pueblos de indios'" special status and made inhabitants Paraguayan citizens transferring all lands and properties to the state. Indians were left with "libertad sin justicia." [JHW]

3426 Heyn Schupp, Carlos Antonio. Iglesia y estado en el Paraguay durante el gobierno de Carlos Antonio López, 1841–1862 (UCNSA/EP, 9:2, dic. 1981, p. 135–349)

Pt. 2 of useful essay, especially strong on religious and legal topics. Also includes chronology and list of primary sources.

3427 Jones, David Lewis. Paraguay: a bibliography. New York: Garland Publishing Inc., 1979. 500 p.; index (Colección social sciences)

Excellent reference tool includes 4500 entries published in Paraguay mostly until 1977, some 1979. Also provides impressive list of serial titles and subheadings for regional and urban histories and migrations.

3428 Lewis, Paul H. Paraguay under Stroessner. Chapel Hill: University of North Carolina Press, 1980. 256 p.; bibl.; index.

Solid research provides balanced picture of political history in recent decades.

3429 Pastore, Carlos. Entrevistas con el Mariscal Estigarribia: proclamación de la candidatura a la Presidencia de la República del . . . (UCNSA/EP, 9:2, dic. 1981, p. 105–134)

Sketches designed to offer a more accurate portrayal of the personality and thoughts of this Paraguayan statesman. Author, distinguished Liberal politician, was close friend and collaborator of Estigarribia during his administration and the Chaco War.

3430 Pesoa, Manuel. Biografía de Don Antonio Taboada: fundador principal y jefe del Partido Liberal Paraguayo, 1848–

1913. Asunción: s.n., 1979. 93 p.; ports.
Concise life-and-deeds account of leading politican who instituted prolonged Liberal Party rule (1904–40s).

3431 ———. José Segundo Decoud, estadista del Partido Colorado. Asunción: s.n., 1979. 101 p.; ill.
Valuable contribution to better knowledge of traditional parties. Explores significance of Decoud, outstanding personality who was politically influential from Paraguayan War's aftermath until 1904, an era dominated by Colorado Party.

3432 **Plá, Josefina.** Whytehead: ser o no ser (UCNSA/EP, 6:2, dic. 1978, p. 9–32)
Three essays by noted specialist on: 1) life and deeds of English associate of Francisco Solano López; 2) study of role played by foreign community in outstanding development that took place during López's rule; and 3) brief account of how Madame Lynch positively influenced the nation's modernization.

3433 **Ramos, R. Antonio.** Los restos del dictador Francia (Anuario [Instituto de Investigaciones Históricas Dr. José Gaspar Rodríguez de Francia, Asunción] 3:3, sept. 1981, p. 37–48)
Noted historian speculates on an unsolved mystery, the location of Francia's remains.

3434 **Samaniego, Marcial.** Las FF.AA. de la Nación en el decenio de la preguerra del Chaco hasta la victoria de Boquerón. Asunción: Dirección de Publicaciones de las FF.AA.NN., Impr. Militar, 1979. 146 p.; 8 leaves of plates; ill.
Well documented account concerns military background of Chaco War. Emphasizes how army was reorganized and what weapons were purchased in prewar period.

3435 **Sánchez Quell, Hipólito.** Arquitectura, vestimenta y costumbres asunceñas e través del tiempo (APH/HP, 17, 1980, p. 37–55)
Short colorful vignettes convey accurate picture of Asunción throughout its history.

3436 ———. Historia de las relaciones entre Francia y Paraguay: de Napoleón III y Solano López a De Gaulle y Stroessner. Asunción: Casa América, 1980. 204 p.; bibl.; ill.

Distinguished historian combines personal recollections of diplomatic activities with general interview of bilateral relations in a useful but somewhat disorganized account.

3437 **Seiferheld, Alfredo M.** Los judíos en el Paraguay (UCNSA/EP, 9:2, dic. 1981, p. 9–104)
Narrative account provides interesting information of which pt. 3 covers Jewish immigration from 19th century through 1920s.

3438 **Silva, Raul de Andrada e.** Ensaio sobre a ditadura do Paraguai, 1814–1840. São Paulo: Universidade de São Paulo, Fundo de Pesquisas do Museu Paulista, 1978. 267 p.; bibl.; ill. (Série Ensaios - Fundo de Pesquisas do Museu Paulista; v. 3) (Coleção Museu Paulista)
Solid scholarly study shows how sequence of historical events in the River Plate pushed Paraguay towards a separatist policy and contributed to cementing a dictatorship that was conditioned by social factors. Argues that Francia's system worked because social and economic conditions inherited from the colonial past made it possible. Maintains that Paraguay's alleged isolation was not as total as is generally assumed.

3439 **Tate, E. Nicholas.** Britain and Latin America in the nineteenth century: the case of Paraguay, 1811–1870 (IAA, 5:1, 1979, p. 39–70, bibl.)
Perceptive examination of unexplored topic. Demonstrates Britain's lack of interest in trading with Paraguay until 1870. Rejects revisionist thesis of British accountability for disrupting the López regime as explanation for Britain's favoring the Triple Alliance. Study also includes general assessment of Britain's relations with Latin America and features of 19th-century British diplomacy in the region.

3440 **Vargas Peña, Luis.** El Paraguay, la guerra y el Chaco. Asunción: s.n., 1978. 266 p.; 8 leaves of plates; bibl.; ill.
Another Chaco War book consists of actual reminiscences, not history.

3441 **Villamayor Sánchez de Díaz, Celia J.** Breve historia de la Imprenta Nacional y bibliografía de sus publicaciones desde sus orígenes hasta la Guerra del Chaco. Asunción: Universidad Nacional de Asunción, Escuela de Bibliotecología, 1979. 118 leaves; bibl.

Brief monograph on the history of this press. Pt. 1 covers Jesuit period until present and includes interesting data, especially on periodicals of the period. Pt. 2 lists 314 bibliographic entries.

3442 Viola, Alfredo. Moneda y control de cambio durante el gobierno del Dr. Francia (Anuario del Instituto de Investigaciones Históricas Dr. José Gaspar de Francia [Asunción] 3 : 3, 1980, p. 11–21)

Interesting study of Francia's monetary policies designed to prevent bullion exports but disregarded when importing armaments.

3443 ———. Reseña del desarrollo cultural del Paraguay. Asunción: Ediciones Comuneros, 1979. 194 p.; bibl.

Examines Paraguay's cultural development from colonial period to present, offering a more complete portrayal of Francia's period.

3444 Warren, Harris Gaylord. The Paraguayan Revolution of 1904 (AAFH/TAM, 36 : 3, Jan. 1980, p. 365–384)

First-class article by noted specialist ably leads one through the intricacies of 19th-century political factionalism. Describes preliminary phase and development of plot that ended Colorado rule and installed Liberal regime that lasted for next decades. Regards this revolution as marking the triumph of Argentina over Brazil for dominance of the country's domestic affairs: "The victor, in the Paraguayan revolution of 1904 was Argentina not the Paraguayan Liberals."

3445 Zarza, Idalia Flores de. El segundo consulado Mariano Roque Alonzo y Carlos Antonio López: su obra de gobierno (APH/HP, 18, 1981, p. 1–42)

Positive appraisal of diverse and constructive achievements of this administration, established after Francia's death. Covers 1840–43 period. Includes important information on foreign affairs and culture.

URUGUAY

3446 Acuña de Figueroa, Francisco Esteban. Diario histórico del sitio de Montevideo en los años 1812–13–14. Prólogo de Roger Basagoda. Preparación del texto y cuidado del mismo a cargo de José Pedro Barrán

y Benjamín Naham. Montevideo: Ministerio de Educación y Cultura, 1978. 2 v. (Biblioteca Artigas. Colección de clásicos uruguayos; v. 157/158)

Careful reprint of a classic versified chronicle.

3447 Assunção, Fernando O. El gaucho: estudio socio-cultural. Ilus. de Federico Reilly. Montevideo: Universidad Mayor de la Rep. Oriental del Uruguay, Dirección General de Extensión Universitaria, División Publicaciones y Ediciones, 1978/1979. 2 v.; bibl.; ill.

Outstanding contribution. Vol. 1 describes gaucho's environment, methods of warfare, *gauchería*'s development and notes impressions of travelers. Vol. 2 concerns gaucho's ethnography and thoroughly examines his attire. Also includes etimological analysis of term *gaucho.*

3448 Barrán, José Pedro and **Benjamín Nahum.** Batlle, los estancieros y el Imperio Británico. Montevideo: Ediciones de la Banda Oriental, 1979. 278 p.; bibl. (His El Uruguay del novecientos; t. 1)

Vol. 1 of major historiographical effort that will take four volumes. Consists of essential study of changing demographic structure and sociocultural dimensions in late 19th century. Examines reformist movement and its relation to conservatives such as big landowners as well as British capital. Brilliantly analyzes texture of society and political structures.

3449 Barrios Pintos, Aníbal. Paysandú en escorzo histórico. Paysandú, Uruguay: Intendencia Municipal de Paysandú, Dirección de Cultura, 1979. 399 p.; bibl.; ill.

Careful anecdotal account, full of information.

3450 Bresciano, Rubén H. La Junta Económico Administrativa de Montevideo. Montevideo: Intendencia Municipal de Montevideo, 1979. 61, 6 p.; 23 leaves of plates; bibl. ill.

Monographic study covers activities of municipal administration that replaced the Cabildo, between 1830–1919. Good description of its institutional character and organic structure.

3451 Claps, Manuel Arturo and **Mario Daniel Lamas.** José Batlle y Ordónez: estudio preliminar y selección documental.

Montevideo: Ediciones de la Casa del Estudiante, 1979. 166 p.; bibl. (Colección Los Americanos; t. 6)

Batlle's selected writings cover relevant institutional issues (e.g., state intervention in the economy, attitudes towards latifundia, landownership, foreign capital). Well written introductory study discusses this Colorado leader's ideology by placing him in the historical context of his times and tracing influences on his thoughts.

Comcord. Secretaría Técnica. Reflexiones sobre aspectos de la historia económica del Uruguay. See *HLAS 43:3611.*

3452 Ellis, Roberto J. G. Estampas del Cordón, Pocitos y Villa Colón. Montevideo: Impr. Mercur. 1980. 108 p.

Breezy account of everyday life in several popular neighborhoods.

3453 Finch, Martin Henry John. A political economy of Uruguay since 1870. New York: St. Martin's Press, 1982. 339 p.; bibl.; index; map.

Outstanding contribution examines crucial aspects of the country's economy over a century (1870–1970). Uses period's principal political phenomenon, *batllismo*, in order to analyze the nation's policies, goals, demographic and social realities, economic features, agrarian structure, foreign trade, and cyclical crisis. Uruguay's extremely vulnerable and stagnant economy is well depicted.

3454 Ganón, Isaac. El Uruguay en los años treinta (*in* América Latina en los años treinta. Luis Antezana E. *et al.* Coordinador, Pablo González Casanova. México: Instituto de Investigaciones Sociales, Universidad Nacional Autónoma de México, 1977, p. 451–511, tables)

Critical account of the 1930s in Uruguay by sociologist who regards period as prologue to country's later deterioration (for economist's comment, see *HLAS 43:3616*).

3455 Herrera, Luis Alberto de. Orígenes de la Guerra Grande. Montevideo: Editorial por la Patria, 1979. 2 v.; bibl.; indexes.

Reprints classic of revisionism. Vol. 2 has been enriched by including new French archival diplomatic and consular reports (1840–42).

Jacob, Raúl. El Frigorífico Nacional en el mercado de carnes: la crisis de 1929 en el Uruguay. See *HLAS 43:3618.*

3456 Martínez Díaz, Nelson. La immigración canaria en Uruguay durante la primera mitad del siglo XIX (IGFO/RI, 38: 151/152, enero/junio 1978, p. 349–402, tables)

Well researched demographic study sheds new light on explosive growth of Uruguay's population by mid 19th-century.

3457 Pivel Devoto, Juan E. La *Revista Histórica*: su aporte a la cultura nacional: índice analítico de autores y temas, 1907–1977. Montevideo: A. Monteverde, 1978. 271 p.; 3 leaves of plates; appendix; bibl.; ill.

Breezy account of this outstanding journal's life includes perceptive discussion of main historiographical trends. Also published in *Revista Histórica* (vol. 50, Nos. 148/150).

3458 Ponce de León, Luis. La Revolución del 97 [i.e. noventa y siete]: escenas y episodios de los combates, las marchas y los campamentos. Carátula, Emilio Cao Pochintesta. 2. ed. Montevideo: Arca, 1978. 156 p.

Second edition of beautifully written, vivid, day-by-day account of this seven-month uprising led by great Blanco caudillo Aparicio Saravia against Idiarte Borda's regime.

3459 Reyes Abadie, Washington. La visión geopolítica de Artigas (Geopolítica [Instituto de Estudios Geopolíticos, Buenos Aires] No. especial, 1981, p. 60–74)

Reprints remarkable earlier article showing how Artigas' goals for the creation of a Confederation were holistic in character.

3460 ———. and **Andrés Vázquez Romero.** Crónica general del Uruguay. Vol. 2, facs. 33, El estado cisplatino. Gráficas, Ruben Tracchia Racciati. Montevideo: Ediciones de la Banda Oriental, 1980? 1 v.

Well documented chronicle, part of popular monographic series, records historical, cultural, social, economic developments and institutional processes.

3461 Rial Roade, Juan. Estilos de desarrollo y primacia urbana en Uruguay, 1852–1933 (IGFO/RI, 40:159/162, enero/dic. 1980, p. 337–395, graph, tables)

Lucid, well informed and innovative attempt at understanding the historical process of Uruguay's urbanization. According to author, it was influenced by diverse "estilos de desarrollo," implemented by decisionmakers who favored overall urbanization.

3462 ———. Sources for studies of historical demography in Uruguay, 1728–1860 (LARR, 15:2, 1980, p. 180–200, bibl., maps, tables)

Describes these sources, particularly the existence of *padrones*, parish books, land grants registries, mostly in Montevideo. Notes important published surveys of colonial and independence periods.

3463 Rodríguez, Arturo. Biografía del Coronel Manuel M. Rodríguez. Montevideo: s.n., 1979. 133 p.; bibl.; port.

Life-and-deeds chronicle of prominent Colorado officer.

3464 Rossi, Rómulo F. Crónicas sabrosas del viejo Montevideo. Montevideo: Ediciones del Atlántico, 1980. 144 p. (Crónicas del pasado uruguayo; 1)

Accessible, anecdotical narrative recreates Montevideo's past.

3465 Sala de Touron, Lucía. El historiador uruguayo en la formación de una conciencia social y nacional latinoamericana (*in* Encuentro de Historiadores Latinoamericanos y del Caribe, 2d, Caracas, 1977. Los estudios históricos en América Latina; ponencias, acuerdos y resoluciones: Caracas, 20–26 de marzo de 1977. Caracas: Universidad Central de Venezuela, Facultad de Humanidades y Educación, Escuela de Historia, 1979, v. 1, t. 2, p. 748–759)

Scholarly appraisal examines leading historiographical trends in Uruguay from independence to present. Of special interest is section on more recent period in which historiography became politicized, polemical and tending towards socioeconomic interpretations.

3466 Suárez, José Benicio. Bonilla en la epopeya de la aviación heroica: el famoso aviador Francisco Eduardo Bonilla no ha muerto, ¡vive! Montevideo: Impr. Rosgal, 1979. 333 p.; 1 leaf of plates; ill.

Life-and-deeds sketch of Latin American aviation pioneer.

3467 Turcatti, Dante. El equilibrio difícil: política exterior del batllismo. Montevideo: Arca, Centro Latinoamericano de Economía Humana, 1981. 124 p.; bibl. (Colección El psadado inminente; 2)

Perceptive exploration of neglected topic notes significant issues such as ties with US, Panamericanism, and relations with Brazil and Argentina.

3468 El Uruguay y sus visitantes, 1926–1967. José María Firpo, comp. Montevideo: Fundación de Cultura Universitaria, 1978. 115 p.

Elementary travel vignettes written by foreign visitors (1928–67) nevertheless reveal slow process of deterioration undergone by Uruguay.

3469 Vanger, Milton I. The model country: José Batlle y Ordoñez of Uruguay, 1907–1915. Hanover, N.H.: Published for Brandeis University Press by University Press of New England, 1980. 436 p.; bibl.; ill.

Vol. 2 of life-and-deeds biography will be followed by third. Strong on politics, study provides accurate, dispassionate, and balanced account of social and political reforms.

3470 Viana, Javier de. Crónicas de la revolución del Quebracho. Carátula, Fernando Alvarez Cozzi. Montevideo: Arca, 1979. 140 p.; bibl. (Historia y testimonio)

Reprint of 1944 ed. Colorful narrative of 1886 rebellion, regarded as period's most popular movement. Includes short bio-bibliographical presentation by author.

3471 Villa, Oscar Jorge and **Gerardo Mendive.** La prensa y los constituyentes en el Uruguay de 1830: fundamentos técnicos, económicos y sociales. Montevideo: Biblioteca National, 1980 [i.e. 1981]. 258 p.; ill.

Important case-study makes good use of newspapers to analyze press response to particular issues and situations. Enhanced by wealth of information on personalities involved.

3472 Williman, José Claudio. Santos: la consolidación del Estado. Montevideo: Ediciones de la Banda Orienta, 1979. 196 p.; 4 leaves of plates; ill. (Historia uruguaya: Segunda serie, Los Hombres; 10)

Excellent political history ably reconstructs extent of this "populist" regime and rejects standard portrayal of it as militaristic. Sets record straight about Santos' origin, his wealth and repressive character of his administration (for other volumes in this popular series, see *HLAS 40:3928, HLAS 42:3483, HLAS 42:3491,* and *HLAS 42:3495*).

3473 Winter von Daack, Teresita. Los alemanes en el Uruguay. Montevideo: Universidad Mayor de la Rep. Oriental de Uruguay, Dirección General de Extensión Universitaria, División Publicaciones y Ediciones, 1979. 28 p.; bibl.

Short account of German participation in Uruguay's evolution.

3474 Zubillaga, Carlos. Las disidencias del tradicionalismo: el radicalismo blanco. Carátula, Ignacio González. Mon-

tevideo: ARCA/CLAEH, 1979. 167 p.; bibl. (Colección El Pasado inminente; 1)

Good monograph analyzes Nationalist Party's small splinter group, led by Lorenzo Carnelli (1920s–30s), in order to explain the failure of a progressive reformist movement.

BRAZIL

RODERICK J. BARMAN, *Associate Professor of History, University of British Columbia, Vancouver, Canada*
JEAN A. BARMAN, *University of British Columbia, Vancouver, Canada*
MICHAEL L. CONNIFF, *Associate Professor of History, University of New Mexico, Albuquerque*

FOR WHATEVER REASONS, HISTORICAL SCHOLARSHIP in Brazil has fallen into a serious slump, in virtually all areas and periods. Fewer books and articles appeared and many are reeditions. This is almost certainly a reflection of economic hard times rather than a diminution of interest on the part of researchers, but it is discouraging nonetheless.

Boris Fausto's vol. 3 in the republican *História geral* series (item **3588**) maintains a high quality of scholarship and coincides with the largest single interest among scholars: the Vargas Era. Of special note in this category are the publications of the Centro de Pesquisa e Documentação de História Contemporânea do Brasil (items **3575, 3592** and **3593**) and Conniff's study of populism (item **3566**). Camargo's thoughtful essays (items **3558** and **3559**) deepen our understanding of Vargas himself. Dulles' fine biography of Castello Branco (item **3572**) focuses on the first military president. However, McCann's work (items **3608** and **3609**) amazingly stands alone on the military history shelf. Diplomatic history too is slight, with only three entries (items **3587, 3601** and **3632**). But in general, the Vargas Era is well represented.

Among the new works on the 19th century, several stand out for excellence: Flory's monograph on the judiciary (item **3486**), Flores' on the Farroupilha (item **3577**), Holloway's on immigrants in São Paulo (item **3589**), Vieira's on the religious question (item **3640**) and Paiva's on Ceará politics (item **3621**). The colonial period, though much neglected, received some attention, notably from Novais (item **3526**), Ribeiro Júnior (item **3532**) and Costa (items **3484** and **3508**). In addition, two important studies by Kuznesof (items **3489** and **3490**) analyze São Paulo society in transition between the two eras.

Strong economic history contributions by Giroletti, Souza, Barman, Lima, Leme, Gordon-Ashworth and Costa (items **3578, 3633, 3478, 3551, 3600, 3602, 3579** and **3568**) were accompanied by a rising interest in agricultural history (items **3487, 3545–3546, 3571, 3603** and **3605**). Several intellectual histories and historiographical essays appeared during the biennium: Martinière, Matos, Queiroz, Manor, and Hall and Pinheiro (items **3493, 3494, 3500, 3611** and **3584**).

The wave of labor histories has subsided to a trickle (items **3606, 3612** and **3613**), as has the history of slavery (items **3483, 3497, 3520, 3537, 3629–3630** and **3634**) and the celebratory literature on immigrants (items **3582–3583, 3590, 3596** and **3620**).

GENERAL

3475 Andrade, Rômulo Garcia de. A real junta de comércio, agricultura, fábricas e navegação; o artesanato e a manufatura na cidade do Rio de Janeiro, 1808–50 (MAN, 10:12, 1979, p. 3–21, table)

Pioneering use of Junta records to study Real Companhia de Fábricas, training school set up in 1808 which closed in hopeless deficit in 1811, and two successor establishments which were equally unsuccessful. Concludes that development of manufacturing was not high on the government's priorities.

3476 Aufderheide, Patricia. Upright citizens in criminal investigations in Cachoeira and Geremoabo, Brazil (AAFH/TAM, 38:2, Oct. 1981, p. 173–184)

Quantification of characteristics of non-slave male court witnesses in two Bahian towns dominated by slaveholding. Pioneering use of court records is, unfortunately, not matched by depth of analysis or significance of conclusions.

Bahia, Brazil (state). **Universidade Federal. Centro de Estudos Baianos.** Catálogo da Biblioteca Frederico Edelweiss. v. 2. See item **91.**

3477 Barbosa, Waldemar de Almeida. História de Minas. v. 1/2. Belo Horizonte, Minas Gerais: Editora Comunicação, 1979. 2 v.; bibl.; ill.

First two volumes of new three-volume history of Minas Gerais concentrate on: 1) exploration and opening of the mines and 2) development of various aspects of the province, such as transportation, racial groups, economy. Although based on some archival research and critical of existing historiography, the study is not profound.

3478 Batista, Paulo Nogueira, Jr. Política tarifária britânica e evolução das exportações brasileiras na primeira metade do século XIX (IBE/RBE, 34:2, abril/junio 1980, p. 203–239, bibl., tables)

Well researched, well organized essay argues that British exclusion, up to the 1840s, of Brazilian sugar and coffee to protect its own colonial producers deprived Brazil of a natural market and distorted its economic development, already crippled by advantages given to British manufactured goods under 1810 and 1827 treaties.

3479 Burns, E. Bradford. A history of Brazil. 2d. ed. New York: Columbia University Press, 1980. 1 v.; bibl.; index.

Substantially unchanged from first edition, excepting larger print, some textual rephrasing, some reworking of post-colonial chapters and expansion of post-1964 years. Emphasis remains firmly on the national period.

3480 Campanhole, Adriano. Memória da cidade de Caconde: freguezia antiga de N.S. da Conseyção do Bom Sucesso do Rio Pardo. São Paulo: Editora Gráfica Latina, 1979. 554 p.; 2 p. of plates; bibl.; ill.; maps.

Heady, copious compilation of a lifetime of amateur research on a São Paulo coffee town founded in late 18th century. Useful for the archival material produced or summarized.

3481 Cardozo, Manoel da Silveira. Monarchy and republic: the Brazilian alternatives (RIB, 30:4, 1980, p. 355–374)

Possibly useful reiteration of views of leading Brazilianist on intellectual roots of Republicanism and their expression in late 18th and 19th-century Brazil. Well documented.

3482 Carvalho, Gilberto Vilar de. A liderança do clero nas revoluções republicanas: 1817 a 1824. Petrópolis: Vozes, 1980. 223 p.; bibl. (Historia; 9) (Publicações CID)

Study, based on published sources, of principal priests involved in the Pernambuco revolts of 1817 and 1824 and of what is known of their ideological outlook.

3483 Chiavenatto, Julio José. O negro no Brasil da senzala á Guerra do Paraguai. São Paulo: Brasiliense, 1980. 259 p.; bibl.

Despite its neutral title, a fiery denunciation of the treatment of blacks in Brazil up to 1889 mixed with a hot attack on British exploitation. For example, the Paraguayan War reduced blacks from 45 to 15 percent of Brazilian population due to policy of genocide. Based on good acquaintance with standard sources, but text is undocumented.

3484 Costa, Iraci del Nero da. Vila Rica, população (1719–1826). São Paulo: Instituto de Pesquisas Econômicas da Faculdade de Economia e Administração da Universidade de São Paulo, 1979. 268 p.; bibl.; ill. (Ensaios econômicos / IPE, USP; 01)

Careful study of sociodemographic structure of both the free and slave population based on the manuscript census of 1804 and on baptismal, marriage and death records, 1710–1856. Filled with well constructed graphs and tables. Originally master's thesis at University of São Paulo. Recommended.

3485 Delson, Roberta. Land and urban planning: aspects of modernization in early nineteenth-century Brazil (UW/LBR, 16:2, Winter 1979, p. 191–214, maps)

Innovative study of neglected aspect of 19th-century history. However, tends to outrun the evidence due to author's enthusiasm for her proposition that interest in planning urban centres began early in Brazil.

3486 Flory, Thomas. Judge and jury in imperial Brazil, 1808–1871: social control and political stability in the new State. Austin: University of Texas Press, 1981. 268 p.; bibl.; index (Latin American monographs; no. 53)

Thorough study of the rise and fall, between 1828–41, of the elective justice of the peace, a position whose strengths and weaknesses epitomized those of Liberalism in Brazil. Welcome, well researched addition to the history of Brazil during the Regency. Essential reading for both generalist and specialist.

3487 Freitas, Décio. O capitalismo pastoril. Porto Alegre, Brazil: Escola Superior de Teología São Lourenço de Brindes, 1980. 204 p.; tables (Coleção Temas gaúchos)

Analyzes ranching economy within framework of means of production, in 45-page essay, and then reprints four classic essays on the Rio Grande pampas.

3488 Jordão, Angelo. Povoamento, hegemonia e declínio de Goiana. Com pref. do goianense desembargador Luiz Marinho. Recife: s.n., 1977. 271 p.; 22 leaves of plates; bibl.; ill.; ports.

Contains some interesting information among tons of dross about a typical sugar town in the zona da mata of Pernambuco that went into decline at the end of 19th century.

3489 Kuznesof, Elizabeth Anne. Household composition and headship as related to changes in mode of production: São Paulo 1765 to 1836 (CSSH, 22:1, Jan. 1980, p. 78–108, tables)

Argues persuasively that change in mode of production from subsistence to export agriculture occasioned fundamental transition in *paulista* household composition similar to changes occurring elsewhere across Western society. Very impressive integration of census data, archival research, modern studies of São Paulo, analyses of family structure elsewhere, and theoretical literature. Required reading for the Brazilian historian.

3490 ———. The role of merchants in the economic development of São Paulo, 1765–1850 (HAHR, 60:4, Nov. 1980, p. 571–592)

Argues that São Paulo's transformation into an export economy was facilitated by mutually beneficial alliance forged between immigrant merchants and established land-biased elite. Stresses importance of intermarriage for creating permanent bonds.

3491 Leite, Aureliano and João de Scantimburgo. História da municipalidade de São Paulo. São Paulo: Câmara Municipal de São Paulo: Prefeitura do Município de São Paulo, 1977. 1 v.; bibl.; ill.; indexes.

Introductory description based on standard printed sources, lavishly produced.

3492 Loureiro, Antonio José Souto. Síntese da história do Amazonas. Manaus, Amazonas: Impr. Oficial do Estado do Amazonas, 1978. 299 p.; bibl.; ill.

Despite its lack of professionalism, this book serves as a reference for the nonspecialist. Virtually stops in early 20th century.

3493 Martinière, Guy. Nelson Werneck Sodré: l'historiographic marxiste et l'essor de la "brasilienité" (Nova Americana [Giulio Einaudi Editore, Torino, Italy] 3, 1980, p. 41–84)

Admiring essay, extracted from a University of Paris thesis, about Brazil's most prolific Marxist historian.

3494 Matos, Odilon Nogueira de. Afonso de Taunay, historiador de São Paulo e do Brasil: perfil biográfico e ensaio bibliográfico. São Paulo: Universidade de São Paulo, Fundo de Pesquisas do Museu Paulista, 1977. 267 p.; bibl.; index; port. (Série Ensaios - Fundo de Pesquisas do Museu Paulista; v. 1) (Coleção Museu Paulista)

Useful 40-page biography of famous Paulista historian, followed by annotated bibliography of Taunay's works.

3495 Mello, Alexandre and Nilva R. Mello. O Brasil e a Bacia do Prata. São Paulo: s.n., 1980. 364 p.; bibl.; facsims.

While text is standard, orthodox account of the formation of Brazil's southern frontier, introduction is a good example of how the military's "national security" doctrine has influenced Brazilians' perceptions of their neighbours.

3496 Moraes, Maria Augusta de Sant'Ana. Conjuntura económica, administrativa e política de Goiás nas primeiras décadas do Século XIX (Revista do Instituto Histórico e Geográfico de Goiás [Instituto Histórico e Geográfico de Goiás, Goiánia, Brazil] 6, dez. 1977, p. 27–37, bibl.)

Brief but welcome note on economic motives of independence movement in Goiás, where Crown policy of agricultural replacement of mining failed to bring recovery.

3497 Mott, Luiz R. B. Violencia e repressão em Sergipe: notícia sobre revoltas de escravos: século XIX (MAN, 11 : 5, maio 1980, p. 3–21)

Closely details some 17 cases of violence by slaves and free men of color against whites, 1808–37. Possibly useful to specialist.

3498 Osório, Ubaldo. A Ilha de Itaparica: história e tradição. 4. ed., rev. e ampliada. Salvador: Fundação Cultural do Estado da Bahia, 1979. 564 p.; 1 leaf of plates; bibl.; port.

Full chronology from 16th century to present of all aspects of life on an island off Salvador's coast, the fruit of a lifetime of devotion by local amateur historian.

3499 Parahym, Orlando da Cunha. Traços do Recife: ontem e hoje. Recife: Governo do Estado de Pernambuco, Secretaria de Educação e Cultura, 1978. 266 p.; 28 leaves of plates; bibl.; ill.

It is a pity that so much official money was expended on producing this compendium of trivia.

Queiroz, Maria Isaura Pereira de. Pecuária de vida pastoril: sus evolução em duas regiões brasileiras. See HLAS 43 : 8390.

3500 Queiroz, Suely Robles Reis de. Historiografia do Nordeste. São Paulo: Secretaria da Cultura, Coordenadoria de Atividades Culturais, Departamento de Artes e Ciências Humanas, Divisão de Arquivo do Estado, 1979. 73 p.; bibl. (Coleção Monografias - Divisão de Arquivo de Estado; 2)

This overview of writings on the Northeast is of special interest to historians.

3501 Rodrigues, José Honório. Varnhagen: o primeiro mestre da historiografia brasileira, 1816–1878 (PAIGH/H, 88, julio/dic. 1979, p. 93–122)

Praises Varnhagen for his ability to collect and present a mass of historical detail in a coherent form, while reproving his social conservatism, pro-Portuguese leanings and criticism of José Bonifácio.

3502 Santo Antônio dos Anjos da Laguna: seus valores históricos e humanos: publicação comemorativa da passagem do seu tricentenário de fundação. Florianópolis: Impr. Oficial do Estado de Santa Catarina, 1976. 326 p.; bibl.; ill.

Descriptive history combined with biographies of leading local figures. Possibly useful in conjunction with Alba's Laguna (see item **3597**).

3503 Vergueiro, Nicolau Pereira de Campos. História da Fábrica de Ipanema e Defesa perante o Senado. Brasília: Senado Federal, 1979. 153 p.; port. (Coleção Bernardo Pereira de Vasconcellos; v. no. 11: Série Estudos históricos)

Reprints: 1) rare account, published in 1822, of establishment of Brazil's first iron foundry in 1811; and 2) Vergueiro's rebuttal to the Senate of accusations that he was a leading figure behind the 1842 uprising in São Paulo.

COLONIAL

3504 Boschi, Caio César. Fontes primárias para a história de Minas Gerais em Portugal. Belo Horizonte: Conselho Estadual de Cultura de Minas Gerais, 1979. 193 p.; indexes (Mineirana; 3)

Checklist indexed by subject, person and place. Includes names and dates of ships (1710–1807) whose manifests included bullion and jewels. Extremely useful for colonial historians.

3505 Cardozo, Manoel da Silveira. António de Gouveia: adventurer and priest (in Struggle and survival in colonial America. Edited by David G. Sweet and Gary B. Nash.

Berkeley: University of California press, 1981, p. 142–164)

Graphic description of 16th-century deviant priest-adventurer who was, however, only briefly in Brazil.

3506 Chaim, Marivone Matos. A sociedade colonial goiana. Capa, Idéia de Neuder Mário Bonfocck: arte de Leonardo Lobo. Goiânia: Oriente, 1978. 114 p.; 1 fold. leaf of plates; bibl.; ill.

Unsophisticated presentation of information, much of it archival, on the cultural (particularly education) and economic structure of southern Goiás in late 18th and early 19th centuries.

3507 Cheyt, Stanley F. From a prison in Brazil, 1774 (AAFH/TAM, 35 : 4, April 1979, p. 573–580)

Letter from Yankee sperm whaling captain describing his fate on falling into the hands of Brazilian colonial authorities.

3508 Costa, Iraci del Nero da. As populações das Minas Gerais no século XVIII: um estudo de demografia histórica. São Paulo: Universidade de São Paulo, Faculdade de Economia e Administração, Departmento de Economia, 1978. 27 p.; bibl.; graphs (Série História econômica)

Population of Vila Rica set in larger socio-historical framework. A possible complement to item **3484.**

3509 Dias, Manuel Nunes. Ideia de capitania no Brasil (in Congreso Venezolano de Historia, 3rd, Caracas, 1977. Memoria. Caracas: Academia Nacional de la Historia, 1979, t. 2, p. 343–368)

Despite title, simply a resumé of author's published work on the development of Portuguese colonialism up to 1530s as part of "monarchical capitalism."

3510 Faraco, Sérgio. Tiradentes: a alguma verdade (ainda que tardia). Capa, Eugênio Hirsh. Rio de Janeiro: Civilização Brasileira, 1980. 81 p.; appendix; bibl. (Coleção Retratos do Brasil; v. 138)

Notable as a revisionist work on Tiradentes. Denounces him as a tool of self-seeking capitalist elements in Minas Gerais. Too overstated to be effective.

Ferreira, João da Costa. A Cidade do Rio de Janeiro e seu termo. See *HLAS 43 : 5331.*

3511 Galloway, J. H. Agricultural reform and the enlightenment in late colonial Brazil (UHS/AH, 53 : 2, April 1979, p. 763–779, map)

Brief analysis of proposals and actual projects for the reform of agriculture. Concludes that the Portuguese government was interested in "improvements" in the status quo that would increase the wealth of its American colonies, but not in any changes that might alter the structure of rural society. The Enlightenment in Brazil is seen as a conservative force.

3512 Galvão, Hélio. História da Fortaleza da Barra do Rio Grande. Rio de Janeiro: MEC, Conselho Federal de Cultura, 1979. 317 p.; bibl.; ill.; index.

Lavishly produced and well documented account of strategic fort in Rio Grande do Norte built between 1598–1628. Broadly focused, but mainly interesting to military historians.

3513 Gorenstein, Riva. Probidade, previdência, tranquilidade: as companhias de seguros do Rio de Janeiro no contexto da crise financeira, 1808–1822 (MP/AN, 29, 1979, p. 217–225)

Disappointing article that fails to make effective use of files of the Real Junta do Comercio to investigate role played by seven insurance companies established in Rio (1810–20) but does draw attention to the subject.

3514 Guerzoni Filho, Gilberto. Tributação das entradas na Capitania das Minas Gerais, 1776–1808 (Estudos Ibero-Americanos [Pontifícia Universidade Católica do Rio Grande do Sul, Instituto de Filosofia e Ciências Humanas, Departamento de História, Porto Alegre, Brazil] 5 : 2, dez. 1979, p. 219–250, bibl.; graphs, tables)

Archival research on taxes on commerce is subordinated to long exposition on development of colonial Minas Gerais as part of the process of "primitive accumulation."

3515 Karasch, Mary. Damiana da Cunha: catechist and *sertanista* (in Struggle and survival in colonial America. Edited by David G. Sweet and Gary B. Nash. Berkeley: University of California Press, 1981, p. 102–120, ill.)

From scanty evidence, recreates the life of a formidable Indian lady who in the early 19th century was the moving force in making the Cayapó tribe settle in villages and assimilate to Portuguese ways.

3516 Lavradio, Luis de Almeida Soares Portugal Alarcão Eça e Melo, *marquês de.* Cartas do Rio de Janeiro, 1769–1776. Rio de Janeiro: Secretaria de Estado de Educação e Cultura, Departamento de Cultura, Instituto Estadual de Livro, Divisão de Bibliotecas, Centro de Bibliografia e Documentação, 1978. 171 p. (Coleção Estado do Rio de Janeiro)

Transcript of the outletters of a top colonial administrator.

3517 Leite, Luís Philippe Pereira. Vilas e fronteiras coloniais. São Paulo: Editora Resenha Tributária, 1978/1980. 142 p.; ill.

This item is annotated only to warn the reader that, despite its title, the study contains nothing of value on the towns and frontiers of colonial Mato Grosso.

3518 Levy, Maria Bárbara. História financeira do Brasil colonial. Colaboração de Mercedes Gouvêa Curvello de Oliveira. Capa, F. Pardelhas, Sérgio Lima. Rio de Janeiro, IBMEC, 1979. 135 p.; bibl. (Coleção História financeira do Brasil; v. 1)

Fairly simple, if clearly written, account of the development of money and capital in colonial Brazil, drawing on printed sources.

3519 Lima, Ebion de. As missões oratorianos do Brasil (IHGB/R, 323, abril/junho 1979, p. 69–118)

Two articles on the Oratine order in Pernambuco: 1) the start of four missions in the interior, 1662–70; and 2) attempts to reform the order in Brazil, 1687–1701. Based on archival research in Brazil and Portugal.

3520 Luna, Francisco Vidal. Minas Gerais: escravos e senhores: análise da estrutura populacional e econômica de alguns centros mineratórios, 1718–1804. São Paulo: Instituto de Pesquisas Econômicas, Universidade de São Paulo, 1981. 1 v.; graphs, tables (Série ensaios econômicos; 8)

Using computer analysis of censuses and tax registers, author proves that slave ownership was not highly concentrated, that women rose in the ranks of slave owners, and that many former slaves themselves acquired slaves. Some 3400 owners and 15,000 slaves tabulated.

3521 ——— and **Iraci del Nero da Costa.** Algumas características do contingente de cativos em Minas Gerais (MP/AN, 29, 1979, p. 79–97, tables)

Quantitative study of origins of slaves in certain mining centres in 18th and early 19th centuries based on contemporary demographic data.

3522 ——— and ———. Contribuição ao estudo de um núcleo urbano colonial: Vila Rica, 1804 (IPE/EE, 8:3, set./dez. 1978, p. 41–68, tables)

Another variant of Costa's analyses of the population of Vila Rica, or Ouro Preto, in 1804, this one with an economic emphasis (see also items **3484, 3508** and *HLAS 42:3570*).

3523 ——— and ———. A presença do elemento forro no conjunto de proprietários de escravos (SBPC/CC, 32:7, julho 1980, p. 836–841, bibl., tables)

Quantitative survey of proportion of freed people among slave owners in 18th-century Minas Gerais.

Martinière, Guy. Frontières coloniales en Amérique du Sud: entre tierra firme et Maranhão, 1500–1800. See item **1769**.

———. Les stratégies frontalières du Brésil colonial et l'Amérique Espagnole. See item **1770**.

3524 Mendonça, Marcos Carneiro de. A rendição da Ilha de Santa Catarina (IHGB/R, 321, out./dez. 1978, p. 5–35, facsim., map, plates)

Attributes failure of Santa Catarina's governor to offer any defense against the Spanish attack of Feb. 1777 to obedience to secret orders from the wife of Dom José I, then Regent of Portugal and sister of King Charles III of Spain. These orders have disappeared without a trace!

Moraes, Rubens Borba de. Livros e bibliotecas no Brasil colonial. See *HLAS 42:82*.

3525 Mott, Luiz R. B. Os índios e a pecuária nas fazendas de gado do Piauí colonial (USP/RA, 22, 1979, p. 61–78)

Innovative analysis of racial and economic composition of Piauí's population (1697–1772) based on research in Portuguese archives. Concludes that original Indian tribes were, when not exterminated, not integrated but remained marginal to the cattle ranching economy of the captaincy, run by whites with black or mulatto slaves.

Nóbrega, Humberto Mello. História do Rio Tietê. See *HLAS 43:5389*.

3526 Novais, Fernando A. Portugal e Brasil na crise do antigo sistema colonial, 1777–1808. São Paulo: Editora HUCITEC, 1979. 420 p.; bibl.; graphs (Coleção Estudos históricos)

Belated appearance in book form of doctoral thesis which has been published in part (see *HLAS 38:3988*) and been influential (see item **3532**). Perceives development of Portuguese colonial Empire from 1640 to 1808 as part of the crisis and collapse of all European mercantilist colonial systems. Therefore, policies of Pombal and his successors were powerless to effect change, indeed irrelevant to the development of Portugal's American colonies. Not a work of archival research.

3527 Novinsky, Anita. Sistema de poder e repressão religiosa: para uma interpretação do fenômeno cristão novo no Brasil (MP/AN, 29, 1979, p. 5–12)

Sees the Inquisition as depriving Brazil in the 16th century of a large part of its "incipient national bourgeoisie" and as the means of eliminating "the men who might have upset the system."

3528 Oliveira, José Joaquim Machado d'. Quadro histórico da Província de São Paulo. Introd. e notas de Célio Débes. São Paulo: Governo do Estado de São Paulo, 1978. 343 p.; bibl.; index (Coleção paulística; v. 4)

First reprinting of 1864 ed. of classic chronology of São Paulo up to Independence.

3529 Oliveira, Tarquinio José Barbosa de. Secretismo e inconfidência (IHGB/R, 324, julho/set. 1979, p. 336–356)

Brief but well argued and rational attempt to show that the conspirators in the Inconfidência of 1788 did form a Masonic lodge.

3530 Registro de atos oficiais no Presídio do Rio Grande, 1737–1753. Porto Alegre: Arquivo Histórico do Rio Grande do Sul, 1977. 350 p. (Anais do Arquivo Histórico do Rio Grande do Sul; 1)

Transcription indexed by subject, person and place.

3531 Rendon, José Arouche de Toledo. Obras. Introd. e notas de Paulo Pereira dos Reis. São Paulo: Governo do Estado de São Paulo, 1978. 76 p.; bibl.; index; port. (Coleção paulística; v. 3)

Reprint, with good introduction, of es-says on agriculture and Indians of São Paulo at end of colonial period. Perhaps most useful as example of the effect of Enlightenment thought on the colonial elite.

3532 Ribeiro Júnior, José. Colonização e monopólio no nordeste brasileiro: a Companhia Geral de Pernambuco e Paraíba, 1759–1780. São Paulo: HUCITEC, 1976. 210 p.; bibl. (Estudos brasileiros; 3)

Within the conceptual framework provided by Fernando Novais (see item **3526**), author analyzes formation, activities and demise of a project authored by Pombal. Perceives the company as intrinsically unsound and exploitative. Based on thorough research in Portuguese archives.

3533 Rodrigues, José Wasth. Tropas paulistas de outrora. Introd. de José de Barros Martins. Ilustráções do autor e de Wladimir Douchkine. São Paulo: Governo do Estado de São Paulo, 1978. 83 p.; 11 leaves of plates; bibl.; ill. (some col.) (Coleção paulística; v. 10)

First appearance in book form of short account of the military forces maintained in São Paulo up to 1822. Most useful perhaps for its illustrations.

3534 Roteiros e notícias de São Paulo colonial, 1751–1804. Marcelino Pereira Cleto *et al.* Introd. e notas de Ernani Silva Bruno. São Paulo: Governo do Estado de São Paulo, 1977. 192 p.; index (Coleção paulística; v. 1)

Reprints five descriptions of São Paulo province between 1750–1810. Mainly of interest to São Paulo historians.

3535 Rubert, Arlindo. O missionário do Brazil: Padre Angelo de Sequeira, 1707–1776 (IHGB/R, 320, julho/set. 1978, p. 136–157, plates)

Study of secular priest whose energy and charisma were expressed in the foundation of churches and seminaries in Brazil, Portugal and Galicia, including 23 dedicated to Our Lady of Lapa.

3536 Seminário sobre a Cultura Mineira no Período Colonial, *Fundação Clóvis Salgado, 1978.* Seminário sobre a cultura mineira no período colonial. Belo Horizonte: Conselho Estadual de Cultura de Minas Gerais, 1979. 194 p.; bibl.

Essays on fine arts in 18th-century Minas Gerais.

3537 Silva, Maria Beatriz Nizza da. Casamentos de escravos na Capitania de São Paulo (SBPC/CC, 32:7, julho 1980, p. 816–821)

Despite Catholic Church's official admonitions that slaves marry, practical bureaucratic impediments made it virtually impossible for them to do so.

3538 ———. Cultura no Brasil colônia. Petrópolis: Vozes, 1981. 172 p. (História brasileira; 6)

Fine collection of essays on marriage, commerce, education and publishing in colonial Brazil, partly based on primary sources.

3539 Simpósio Comemorativo do Bicentenário da Restauração do Rio Grande, *Rio de Janeiro, 1976.* Anais do Simpósio Comemorativo do Bicentenário da Restauração do Rio Grande, 1776–1976. Rio de Janeiro: Instituto Histórico e Geográfico Brasileiro: Instituto de Geografia e História Militar do Brasil, 1979. 4 v.; bibl.; ill. (some fold.)

Compilation of: 1) modern essays in vols. 1/2; 2) genealogy of families who left Colônia do Sacramento in 1777, in vol. 2; 3) transcription of memoir by Lt. Gen. Boehm (1774–79) including much correspondence, in vol. 3; 4) account of life in Rio Grande do Sul, 1777, by military surgeon, in vol. 3; and 5) reprint of Jônathas da Costa Rego Monteiro's "Dominação Espanhola no Rio Grande do Sul," originally published 1935–37, in vol. 4.

3540 Soeiro, Susan A. Catarina de Monte Sinay: nun and entrepreneur (*in* Struggle and survival in colonial America. Edited by David G. Sweet and Gary B. Nash. Berkeley: University of California Press, 1981, p. 257–273)

Fairly static description of 18th-century Salvador viewed from a nunnery.

3541 Sousa, Maria Cecília Guerreiro de. Inventário de documentos históricos sobre o centro-oeste. Cuiabá: Fundação Universidade Federal de Mato Grosso, Núcleo de Documentação e Informação Histórica Regional, between 1977 and 1980. 4 v.; facsims. (Arquivo histórico ultramarino. Avulsos; 1/4) (Coleção Documentos ibéricos. Serie Inventários; v. 1/4)

Checklist of documents on Mato Grosso in the colonial period in Portuguese archives. Indexed by subject, person, place and date. Some sample facsimiles.

3542 Souza, José Antonio Soares de. Uma questão diplomática em seu início: Oiapoque (IHGB/R, 320, julho/set. 1978, p. 18–48, tables)

Using documents from French archives, discusses the first negotiations in 1680s and 1690s over possession of Amapa region, a question not settled until 1900.

3543 Souza, Washington Peluso Albino de. Ensaios sobre o ciclo de ouro. Belo Horizonte: The Author, 1978. 205 p.; bibl. (Publicação - Universidade Federal de Minas Gerais; no. 660)

Composed of two different studies: 1) evolving urban structure of Minas Gerais; and 2) treatment of the Methuen Treaty of 1703 by Adam Smith, Silva Lisboa and other writers on political economy. Recommended to specialists.

3544 Sweet, David G. Francisca: Indian slave (*in* Struggle and survival in colonial America. Edited by David G. Sweet and Gary B. Nash. Berkeley: University of California Press, 1981, p. 274–291, ill.)

Uses figure of an Indian slave to discuss social context of Indian slavery in Amazon region in the 18th century. Based on secondary sources.

Wiederspahn, Henrique Oscar. Bento Gonçalves e as guerras de Artigas. See item **2844.**

NATIONAL

3545 Abreu, Dióres Santos. Os Medeiros: uma família pioneira na ocupação do sertão do Paranapanema (SBPC/CC, 31:8, agosto 1979, p. 860–867, map)

Through the study of a migrant family, author analyzes first stages of Brazilian occupation of what is now the south of the Far West of São Paulo. Emphasizes that original settlers were more concerned to occupy land than to develop it and so depended on limited cattle raising for their cash needs.

Aguiar, Durval Vieira de. Descrições práticas da Província da Bahia: com declaração de todas as distâncias intermediárias das cidades, vilas e povoações. See *HLAS 43:5309.*

Alincourt, Luiz d'. Memória sobre a viagem do porto de Santos á cidade de Ciuabá. See *HLAS* 43:5310.

3546 Almeida, María da Glória Santana de. Estrutura de produção: a crise de alimentos na província de Sergipe, 1855–1860 (IGHS/R, 27, 1965/1978, p. 15–39, table) Description of the structure of agriculture in Sergipe based on local archival sources. Shows how the end of the slave trade and cholera epidemic created a labor shortage preventing the production of foodstuffs which then intensified inflation. Recommended.

3547 Anderson, Robin L. A government-directed frontier in the humid tropics: Pará, Brazil, 1870–1920 (AHS/AH, 55:4, Oct. 1981, p. 392–406) Short study of a colonization project which, by building railroad, opened up the Bragantina hinterland to Belém for foodstuff production by immigrant farmers.

3548 Andrade, Ana Isabel de Souza Leão and Carmen Lúcia de Souza Leão Rego. Catálogo da correspondência de Joaquim Nabuco. v. 1, 1865–1884. Capa e planejamento gráfico, Moisés Cruz. Recife: Ministério da Educação e Cultura, Instituto Joaquim Nabuco de Pesquisas Sociais, 1978. 1 v.; indexes (Série Documentos - Instituto Joaquim Nabuco de Pesquisas Sociais; 8) Checklist of correspondence in Arquivo Joaquim Nabuco, Recife, organized chronologically with subject and person indexes. For bibliographer's comment, see item 86.

Arquivo "Odilon Braga:" manifesto dos mineiros e revolução de 1930, v. 1. See item 90.

Augel, Moema Parente. Ludwig Riedel, viajante alemão no Brasil. See *HLAS 43:5315.*

3549 Autos dos inquéritos da Revolução de 1842 em Minas Gerais. Capa, Gaetano Ré/Cícero. Brasília: Senado Federal, 1979. 1 v. (Coleção Bernardo Pereira de Vasconcelos; v. no. 20–: Série Estudos históricos) These transcripts of prosecutions against men involved in the 1842 rebellion in southwest Minas Gerais are mainly useful for their information on police procedures and social structure.

3550 Bandeira, Dulcina. Antes que seja tarde: biografia de Alípio Bandeira. Rio de Janeiro: s.n., 1979. 198 p. The subject of this work of filial piety well illustrates an important historical type of the 1889–1930 period: men born into families in social decline who entered the army to gain an education, made a bureaucratic career, and were fervent converts to positivism. Unfortunately, poorly written.

3551 Barman, Roderick J. Business and government in Imperial Brazil: the experience of Viscount Mauá (JLAS, 13:2, Nov. 1981, p. 239–264) Close look at Mauá's banking ventures not only disproves accepted wisdom that the government undermined them, but demonstrates potential for better understanding of Brazil's financial and industrial problems of mid-19th century. Good antidote to pro-Mauá biographies. [M. L. Conniff]

3552 Barreira, Lauro. A Imperatriz desterrada. Rio de Janeiro: Editora Cia Brasileira de Artes Gráficas, 1979. 275 p.; bibl. Short account, using standard printed sources, of marriage and life of Dom Pedro I's second wife.

Barro, Máximo. Nosso Senhora do Ó. See *HLAS* 43:5316.

Bezerra, Gregório. Memórias. See *HLAS 43:6683.*

3553 Borges, Vavy Pacheco. Getúlio Vargas e a oligarquia paulista: história de uma esperança e de muitos desenganos através dos jornais da oligarquia, 1926–1932. Capa, Yvonne Saruê. São Paulo: Editora Brasiliense, 1979. 206 p.; bibl.; ill. Useful monograph which emphasizes the unity of the São Paulo oligarchy, especially after Vargas' rise to power in 1930. Based on newspaper research.

3554 Brandão, Berenice Cavalcante; Ilmar Rohloff de Mattos; and Maria Alice Rezende de Carvalho. A polícia e a força policial no Rio de Janeiro. Rio de Janeiro: Pontifícia Universidade Católica do Rio de Janeiro, 1981. 277 p.; tables (Série estudos; 4) Excellent and timely study of the police in Brazil's capital, during 1831–1930, with stress on their role in preserving "internal security and public tranquility."

3555 Brasiliense de Almeida e Melo, Américo. Os programmas dos partidos e o Segundo Império. Introdução de Washington Luis Neto. Brasília: Senado Federal; Rio de Janeiro: Fundação Casa de Rui Barbosa MEC, 1979. 231 p.; bibl.; index (Coleção Bernardo Pereira de Vasconcelos; 23)

Welcome reprint of classic work published in 1878 on the political ideologies of the Empire as expressed in party manifestos.

3556 Brazil. Congresso. O Parlamento e a evolução nacional, 1871–1889 (3a série). v. 1, Processo político. Questão servil. v. 2, Questão religiosa. Questão militar. v. 3, Economia e finanças. v. 4, Política externa. Poder judiciário. Instrução pública. v. 5, Legislação civil e comercial. Direitos civis. Forças armadas. v. 6, Problemas institucionais. Assuntos gerais. Organização e seleção de textos de Fábio Vieira Bruno. Capa, Gaetano Ré/Cícero. Brasília: Senado Federal, 1979, 6 v. Continuation of *HLAS 36:3562,* which began with 1826. Excellent précis of debates in Chamber and Senate obviating specialists from boring task of wading through the *Anais.*

3557 Brito, Raimundo Soares de. Estudos de história do oeste Potiguar. Mossoró, Brazil: Centro de Divulgação e Impressão Tércio Rosado, 1979. 170 p.; bibl. (Coleção mossoroense; v. 94)

Miscellany of information, mainly about individuals, on western Rio Grande do Norte in 19th and 20th centuries. Of use to specialists as raw material.

Buescu, Mircea. Brasil, disparidades de renda no passado: subsídios para o estudo dos problemas brasileiros. See *HLAS 43:3715.*

———. O café na história do Brasil. See *HLAS 43:3716.*

———. Inegalités regionales au Brésil dans la seconde moitié du XIX siècle. See *HLAS 43:3717.*

3558 Camargo, Aspásia Alcântara de. Authoritarianism and populism: bipolarity in the Brazilian political system (*in* The Structure of Brazilian development. Edited by Neuma Aguiar. New Brunswick, N.J.: Transaction Books, 1979, p. 99–126, bibl.)

Fresh treatment of two overarching tendencies in 20th-century Brazilian politics, with stress on the post-1955 period and especially on events in Pernambuco between 1955–64.

3559 ———. Carisma e personalidade política: Vargas, da conciliação ao maquiavelismo. Rio de Janeiro: Centro de Pesquisa e Documentação de História Contemporânea do Brasil, Fundação Getúlio Vargas, 1979 or 1980. 31 leaves; bibl.

Another fine revisionist look at Vargas, with the added benefit of recently available documents from the later Vargas papers (1945–54).

Cardoso, Eliana A. Incentivos as exportações de manufaturas: série histórica. See *HLAS 43:3719.*

3560 Carone, Edgard. Movimento operário no Brasil, 1877–1944. São Paulo: DIFEL, 1979. 578 p.; bibl. (Corpo e alma do Brasil; 56)

This hefty anthology loads more material on a field still begging for analysis and synthesis. Author tries to represent the totality of labor experience, not just strikes and militancy. Mostly pre-1919 material.

3561 ———. A Quarta República, 1945–1964. v. 1, Documentação. São Paulo: DIFEL, 1980. 1 v. (Corpo e alma do Brasil; 58)

Collection of documents which kicks off the author's treatment of the last phase of republican government. As in earlier sets, he begins with a collection of documents virtually all from published sources. While consistent with earlier volumes, this approach seems unusually elementary in a period already well-delineated in the secondary literature.

Carvalho, Laerte Ramos de. As reformas pombalinas da instrução pública. See *HLAS 43:4588.*

Castro, Ana Célia. As empresas estrangeiras no Brasil, 1860–1913. See *HLAS 43:3723.*

3562 Cervo, Amado Luis. Fontes parlamentares brasileiras e os estudos históricos (LARR, 16:2, 1981, p. 172–181)

Summary of historical materials available in congressional archives in Brasília, particularly for study of foreign relations.

3563 Cezimbra Jacques, João. Ensaio sobre os costumes do Rio Grande do Sul: precedido de uma ligeira descrição física e de uma noção histórica. Apresentação do autor pelo Coronel Helio Moro Mariante. Porto Alegre: ERUS, 1979. 123 p.; bibl.; port. Reprint of an 1883 work describing rural culture of Rio Grande do Sul. Suitable for anthropologist or social historian.

3564 Coleção Alfredo Varela. v. 1/2. Porto Alegre: Arquivo Histórico do Rio Grande do Sul, 1978/1979. 2 v. (487, 798 p.) (Anais do Arquivo Histórico do Rio Grande do Sul; 2/3)

Transcription of prime archival source on the Farroupilha uprising (1835–45). These second and third annual volumes of an ongoing series (for vol. 1, see item **3530**) reach correspondence of Domingos José de Almeida. Indexed by subject, place and name.

3565 Colson, Frank. On expectations: perspectives on the crisis of 1889 in Brazil (JLAS, 13:2, Nov. 1981, p. 265–292)

Examines coup's antecedents in great detail, using newspapers, PRO files, and memoirs, and concludes that powerful economic groups played dominant role in the events.

3566 Conniff, Michael L. Urban politics in Brazil: the rise of populism, 1925–1945. Pittsburgh, Pa.: University of Pittsburgh Press, 1981. 227 p.; bibl.; index; plates; tables (Pitt Latin American series)

Tightly written, well researched study of structural changes in politics in Rio de Janeiro's federal district from 1920s to 1937, centering on Pedro Ernesto's administration (1931–36). Presents Pedro Ernesto both as pioneer of populist politics in Brazil and as exemplar for Getúlio Vargas who, author argues, did not use populist techniques until *after* the 1937 coup. Well worth reading and recommended to expert and student. [R. J. Barman]

3567 Contier, Arnaldo Daraya. Imprensa e ideologia em São Paulo, 1822–1842: matizes do vocabulário político e social. Petrópolis, Brasil: Editora Vozes: Campinas, Brasil: Universidade Estadual de Campinas, 1979. 313 p.; bibl.; ill (Coleção História brasileira; 4)

Pioneer and important study of ideology during the first Empire and Regency, based upon São Paulo's press. Made unnecessarily difficult by preoccupation with methods, especially that of content analysis,

it nonetheless deserves the attention of specialists.

Corrêa da Costa, Sérgio. A diplomacia do Marechal: intervenção estrangeira na revolta da Armada. See *HLAS 43:7430.*

3568 Costa, Fernando N. Os antigos bancos mineiros (RBMC, 5:13, jan./abril 1979, p. 71–87, bibl.)

Extracted from author's MA thesis, article provides a fine overview of Minas' banking system and shows how it became incorporated into a national system in recent times (for economist's comment, see *HLAS 43:3729*).

3569 Coutinho, Edilberto. Rondon, o civilizador da última fronteira. Rio de Janeiro: Civilização Brasileira, 1975. 127 p.; bibl.; map (Coleção Retratos do Brasil; v. 94)

Admiring biography keeps alive the memory of the great pathfinder and founder of the Indian service. Based partly on interviews with author, book lacks scholarly apparatus but is trustworthy.

3570 Dantas, Antônio Arruda. Memória do patrimônio do Assis: história. 2. ed., rev., comemorativa ao centenário da Escritura de Avaré. São Paulo: Editora Pannartz, 1980. 228 p.; bibl.; ill.

Gives basic details about the development of one of the communities of São Paulo's far west brought into existence by railroads and advancing coffee frontier in the first decade of this century.

3571 Diniz, Diana Maria de Faro Leal. Nota sobre a história do algodão em Sergipe (IHGS/R, 27, 1965/1978, p. 41–54)

Discussion of state policy toward cotton in 19th and 20th centuries is the most useful contribution of this article. Author utilized state archives.

3572 Dulles, John W. F. President Castello Branco, Brazilian reformer. College Station: Texas A&M University Press, 1980. 557 p.; 12 leaves of plates; bibl.; ill.

Second of two-volume political biography. Richly documented and favorable, study looks deeply into first military administration following the 1964 coup. While the Castello years will remain controversial, this biography provides information essential to a revised and balanced judgment.

Economia brasileira: uma visão histórica. See *HLAS 43:3735.*

3573 Elias, Maria José. O problema da mão de obra numa perspectiva histórica: uma reflexão de a "transumância amazônica" (MP/AN, 29, 1979, p. 183–192)

Simplistic discussion of why the surplus of labor in the Northeast was directed into the rubber area of the Amazon rather than to the coffee lands of the South, which therefore turned to European immigrants.

3574 Evangelista, José Geraldo. Lorena no século XIX [i.e. dezenove]. Pref. de Nice Lecocq Müller. São Paulo: Governo do Estado de São Paulo, 1978. 223 p.; 16 leaves of plates; bibl.; ill.; index (Coleção paulística; v. 7)

Fairly thorough analysis of the development of a coffee town in 19th-century Paraíba Valley. Useful as a case study.

3575 Farias, Osvaldo Cordeiro de. Meio século de combate: diálogo com Cordeiro de Farias, Aspásia Camargo, Walder de Góes. Rio de Janeiro: Nova Fonteira, 1981. 757 p.; ill. (Coleção Brasil; século 20)

Text consists of lengthy interviews with one of Brazil's most colorful and influential military figures, a fascinating product of the CPDOC oral history project.

3576 Farina, Duílio Crispim. Tempo de vida, doença e morte na Casa de Bragança: ramo do Brasil. São Paulo: HUCITEC, 1979. 140 p.; bibl.

Collection of facts, taken from standard sources, about medical histories of members of Bragança family, and on doctors who attended them.

Federici, Hilton. História de cruzeiro. see *HLAS 43:5343.*

3577 Flores, Moacyr. Modelo político dos Farrapos: as idéias políticas da Revolução Farroupilha. Capa, ilustrações e diagramação, Marco Cena. Porto Alegre: Editora Mercado Aberto, 1978. 208 p.; bibl.; ill. (Série Documenta; 1: História)

This study, based on original research, particularly in newspapers, investigates several ideological aspects of the 1835–45 uprising in Rio Grande do Sul. In particular, analyzes influence of the American and Platine models, while discounting that of the Italian Risorgimento. Shows that the quarrel between executive and legislature that started the revolt persisted and prevented the adoption of a constitution. Recommended reading.

3578 Giroletti, Domingos. O processo de industrialização de Juiz de Fora: 1850 a 1930 (Fundação JP [Fundação João Pinheiro, Belo Horizonte, Brazil] 10:3, março 1980, p. 144–202, bibl., tables)

Sophisticated analysis argues that Juiz de Fora's industrial development was aided by the entrepreneurship of European immigrants introduced for road construction, by mobilization of local capital for banking and infrastructure, and by availability of markets for products. Principal drawback was that, in contrast to São Paulo city, the profits of coffee production in the region did not benefit its leading city. Also analyzes role of labour sector. Recommended.

Godoy, Joaquim Floriano de. A província de S. Paulo: trabalho estatístico, histórico e noticioso. See *HLAS 43:5350.*

3579 Gordon-Ashworth, Fiona. Agricultural commodity control under Vargas in Brazil, 1930–1945 (JLAS, 12:1, May 1980, p. 87–105, tables)

This timely study adds another dimension to the changing interpretation of the first Vargas administration, showing increased federal intervention into markets.

3580 Graham, Richard. The conservatism of Joaquim Nabuco, historian of the Empire (SBPC/CC, 31:2, Nov. 1979, p. 1233–1242, table)

By analyzing Nabuco's biography of his father, shows that Brazilian Liberalism, as epitomized by father and son, was in no way radical in its social goals. Useful overview.

3581 ———. Escravidão, reforma e imperialismo. São Paulo: Editora Perspectiva, 1979. 195 p.; tables (Coleção Debates; 146)

Compilation of articles published separately in English on slavery and diplomacy during the Empire. Useful for Portuguese reader.

3582 Groniowski, Krzysztof. As fontes de história da emigração para o Brasil situadas nos arquivos da Polonia (PAN/ES, 4, 1978, p. 301–312)

One of the more serious contributions in the wave of celebratory studies of the centenary of Polish immigration (see also item **3596**).

Guimarães, Lais de Barros Monteiro. Luz. See *HLAS 43 : 5355.*

3583 Hall, Michael M. Italianos em São Paulo, 1880–1920 (MP/AN, 29, 1979, p. 201–215)

Synthetic treatment of Italian immigrants in São Paulo during the period 1880–1920, focusing on their employment in coffee plantations and in factories.

3584 ——— and Paulo Sérgio Pinheiro. The Clarté Group in Brazil (Mouvement Social [Paris] 11, avril/juin 1980, p. 217–234)

Welcome contribution to the scant literature on intellectual trends in the 20th century, this article recounts the rise and decline of a small group of writers and politicians during and just after the First World War. Concludes that far from serving as a precursor of the Brazilian Communist Party, the Clarté movement actually had its biggest impact in the Vargas Labor Ministry after 1930.

3585 Hasenbalg, Carlos A. Discriminação e desigualdades raciais no Brasil. Translated by Patrick Burglin. Rio de Janeiro: Edições Graal, 1979. 302 p.; tables (Biblioteca de Ciências Sociais. Sociologia; 10)

Provides fine synthesis of race relations studies and then persuasively presents his findings, which show the existence of discrimination despite the myth of racial democracy. Based on Ph.D. dissertation in sociology, it is the best recent work on the subject, especially for the post-1950 period.

3586 Hendricks, Craig and Robert M. Levine. Pernambuco's political elite and the Recife Law School (AAFH/TAM, 37:3, Jan. 1981, p. 291–313, tables)

Rambling discussion of some of the social and political characteristics of the rulers of Pernambuco, 1889–1937, almost all of whom had attended the Recife Law School.

3587 Hilton, Stanley E. Brazil and the post-Versailles world: elite images and foreign policy strategy, 1919–1929 (JLAS, 12:2, Nov. 1980, p. 341–364)

This competent and heavily documented article examines military and diplomatic rivalry with Argentina and discusses relations with the US and the European powers in a decade without major upheavals.

3588 História geral da civilização brasileira. t. 3, v. 3, O Brasil republicano, sociedade e política, 1930–1964. Edited by Boris Fausto. São Paulo: DIFEL, 1981. 604 p.; ill.; tables.

Penultimate volume in this long and ambitious series begun by Sérgio Buarque in 1960. This collection of monographs represents some of the finest new scholarship being conducted today and is required reading for students of modern Brazil.

3589 Holloway, Thomas H. Immigrants on the land: coffee and society in São Paulo, 1886–1934. Chapel Hill: University of North Carolina Press, 1980. 218 p.; bibl.; ill.; index.

Through careful analysis of the coffee sector and migration patterns, author convincingly shows that immigrants fared relatively well in São Paulo, often becoming owners of medium-sized farms themselves. However, they never challenged the elite's political control which diversified into commerce and light industry.

3590 Hutter, Lucy Maffei. Saúde e imigração, 1902–1914: dados históricos (SBPC/CC, 31:6, junho 1979, p. 621–631, bibl., tables)

Shows how immigrants (largely Italian) received medical care in São Paulo. Useful information on little-studied subject.

3591 Iconografia de Joaquim Nabuco. Ministério da Educação e Cultura, Instituto Joaquim Nabuco de Pesquisas Sociais. Pref. de Gilberto Freyre. Recife: IJNPS, 1975. 81 p.; chiefly ill. (Série Documentos—Instituto Joaquim Nabuco de Pesquisas Sociais; 2)

Compilation of photographs of Nabuco from childhood to old·age.

Ilg, Karl. Das Deutschtum in Brasilien. See *HLAS 43 : 5357.*

3592 Instituto de Direito Público e Ciencia Política, Rio de Janeiro, Brasil. **Centro de Pesquisa e Documentação de Historia Contemporânea do Brasil** (CPDOC). Programa de história oral: catálogo de depoimentos. Rio de Janeiro: Fundação Getúlio Vargas, Instituto de Documentação, 1981. 207 p.; ill.; index.

First inventory of oral history tapes

(not all transcribed or open to researchers) shows that the CPDOC has emerged as the leading center of its type in Brazil today (for bibliographer's comment, see item **149**).

3593 ———, ———. ———. *Rio de Janeiro, Brasil.* A revolução de 1930 e seus antecedentes. Rio de Janeiro: Editora Nova Fronteira, 1980. 213 p.; ill.

Fine compilation of photos from the CPDOC archives, featuring events preceding and following the revolution. Editors provide informative captions for most plates.

3594 Jarnagin, Laura. The role and structure of the Brazilian imperial nobility in society and politics (MP/AN, 29, 1979, p. 99–157, tables)

Master's thesis uses much labour and data to demonstrate that acquisition of a title depended on various factors and in itself was not an independent variable determining subsequent career. Includes some useful data on early Instituto Histórico e Geográfico Brasileiro.

3595 Joffily, José. Revolta e revolução: cinqüenta anos depois. Capa, Mario Roberto Corrêa da Silva. Rio de Janeiro: Paz e Terra, 1979. 437 p.; bibl.; ill.; index (Coleção Estudos brasileiros; v. 43)

Author, third echelon politician from the Northeast, recounts sincerely and with considerable documentation events in his region accompanying the 1930 revolution. Flawed but useful source material.

Kubitschek, Juscelino. Meu caminho para Brasília: memórias. See *HLAS 43:6687.*

3596 Kula, Marcin. Polonia brazylijska (Poles established in Brazil). Warszawa: Ludowa Spódzielnia Wydawnicza, 1981. 232 p.; bibl.

Describes plight of Polish immigrants to Brazil (1900–30) and examines their contribution to Brazilian life; reasons for their low social status in comparison to other immigrant groups (e.g., Czechs, Germans, Italians); problems acculturation; and fate under Vargas dictatorship. Study dispels several misconceptions. Based on primary and archival research. [K. Complak]

3597 Laguna antes de 1880 [i.e. mil oitocentos e oitenta]: documentário. João Leonir dall'Alba, comp. Capa, Estúdio Lunardelli. Florianópolis, Brazil: Editora Lunardelli: UDESC/Editora, 1979. 715 p.; bibl.; ill.

Contains detailed description written in 1880; details of slave sales (1877–85); and letters of an Italian exile written in 1839.

3598 Lauderdale Graham, Sandra. The Vintem riot and political culture: Rio de Janeiro, 1880 (HAHR, 60:3, Aug. 1980, p. 431–449)

Pioneering analysis of 1880 Rio city riots well based in archival sources. More data is, however, needed to substantiate author's broader claim of their unique significance in altering Brazilian political culture.

3599 Leitão, Deusdedit. Bacharéis paraibanos pela Faculdade de Olinda, 1832–1853. João Pessoa: A União, 1978? 125 p.; bibl.

Individual biographies based on printed sources, including local newspapers.

3600 Leme, Marisa Saenz. A ideologia dos industriais, 1919–1945. Petrópolis: Vozes, 1978. 187 p.; bibl. (Coleção História brasileira; 2)

Solid, balanced survey of industrialists' associations between the wars, based on a University of São Paulo MA thesis. Special attention given to tariff, labor and macroeconomic policies. Essential for economic historians.

3601 Levine, Robert M. Perspectives on the mid-Vargas years, 1934–1937 (UM/ JIAS, 22:1, Feb. 1980, p. 57–80, bibl.)

New perspectives on mid-1930s, gleaned from US and British diplomatic files and from a review of recent secondary works. Helps correct many misconceptions about the early Vargas regime.

3602 Lima, João Heraldo. Café e indústria em Minas Gerais no início do século: algumas observações (IPE/EE, 8:2, maio/ agosto 1978, p. 191–246, tables)

Using methods of the new economic historians, author shows that the coffee sector, suffering from ecological limits and low productivity, could not contribute significantly to the overall development of the state.

3603 Linhares, Maria Yedda and **Francisco Carlos Teixeira Silva.** História da agricultura brasileira: combates e controvérsias. São Paulo: Brasiliense, 1981. 170 p.; graph; table.

Opening volume, of uneven quality, for much larger project on agricultural history. Of special interest are chapters that compare agrarian policies in the 1850s and 1950s and discuss quantitative sources for agricultural history.

3604 Lisanti, Luis. Urbanisation et folie, São Paulo, 1852–1929 (JGSWGL, 17, 1980, p. 297–315, tables)

Asserts but does not prove that growth in admissions to São Paulo's mental hospital was the consequence of: 1) violence inherent in slaveholding; 2) disorientation suffered by immigrants; and 3) dislocation caused by urbanization. Simplistic treatment of important topic.

3605 Lobo, Eulália Maria Lahmeyer. História político-adminstrativa da agricultura brasileira, 1808–1889. s.l.: s.n., 1980? 213 p.; tables.

Financed by the Ministry of Agriculture and part of a larger history of agriculture, this first installment provides an exciting new view of the economy during the Empire. Much of the text is devoted to tables.

3606 Loyola, Maria Andréa. Os sindicatos e o PTB: estudo de um caso em Minas Gerais. Petrópolis, Brazil: Editora Vozes and CEBRAP, 1980. 143 p.; ill.; tables (Cadernos CEBRAP; 35)

First-rate study of textile workers in Juiz de Fora traces rise of unionism in 1920s and 1930s and its subsequent ties with Vargas' labor party. Concludes that the personalism of politics merged easily with that of working class culture. Based on 1973 Paris Ph.D. dissertation.

3607 Lyra, Augusto Tavares de. Instituições políticas do Império. Intro. de Carlos Tavares de Lyra. Capa, Gaetano Ré/Cícero, foto de Tavares de Lyra, Quadro de Dimitri Ismailovitch. Brasília: Senado Federal, 1979. 349 p.; bibl.; index; port. (Coleção Bernardo Pereira de Vasconcelos; v. no. 16)

Useful compilation of articles on political structure of Empire which originally appeared in *Revista do Instituto Histórico e Geográfico Brasileiro*. Includes author's seminal biographies of all ministers, senators, members of the Council of State and Supreme Court justices. Name index.

3608 McCann, Frank D., Jr. The Brazilian army and the problem of mission, 1939–1964 (JLAS, 12:1, May 1980, p. 107–126, table)

This article focuses on the role of the Brazilian army in World War II and on the changes induced in army officer philosophy. Valuable analysis of the army's confused orientation before 1939.

3609 ———. Origins of the "new professionalism" of the Brazilian military (UM/JIAS, 21:4, Nov. 1979, p. 505–522, table)

Nice corrective to political analysis of the "new professionalism," shows that professional mission goes back to the 19th century and that origins of the present military posture predate World War II.

3610 Maciel, Frederico Bezerra. Lampião, seu tempo e seu reinado: um capítulo da evolução social do Nordeste. v. 1, As origens: por que Virgulino se tornou Lampião? Capas idealizadas pelo autor e desenhadas pelo pintor Borys. Recife: Editora Universitária, 1979. 1 v.; bibl.; ill. (His Série Lampião)

Vol. 1 of five dedicated to the famous bandit king. While inferior in scholarship, it attempts to portray the backlands in detail. Author is a priest who traveled and worked extensively in the *sertão*.

3611 Manor, Paul. The Liga Nacionalista de São Paulo: a political reformist group in paulista academic of yore, 1917–1924 (JGSWGL, 17, 1980, p. 317–353)

Thoughtful and valuable study of the rise of nationalist sentiment in the country's most dynamic city at the time. Reflects the generally preservative reform aspirations of university youth.

3612 Maram, Sheldon L. Urban labor and social change in the 1920s (UW/LBR, 16:2, Winter 1979, p. 215–223)

Compared with the "classic" period of 1906–20, the urban labor movement of the 1920s was moribund, and labor's weakness facilitated Vargas' cooptation of the sector in the 1930s. Author overlooks rich social and mutual aid activities of unions.

3613 Maranhão, Ricardo. Sindicatos e democratização, Brasil 1945–1950. São Paulo: Editora Brasiliense, 1979. 123 p.; tables.

Brief look at labor during the Dutra adminstration, based largely on newspaper research. Especially useful on the role of the Communist Party.

3614 Marchiori, Maria Emilia Prado. Engenhos centrais e usinas no norte fluminense, 1875–1909: algumas considerações (MAN, 11 : 128, 8 agôsto 1980, p. 3–12, bibl.)

Survey of sugar factories set up in the Campos sugar zone after passage of the 5 Nov. 1875 law that granted state subsidies, including some specific information on the Quissamã usina. Based on printed materials.

3615 Marinho, José Antônio. História da Revolução de 1842. Capa, Gaetano Ré/Cicero. Foto, Célio Alves de Azevedo. Edição do texto, Geraldo Sobral Rocha et al. Brasília: Senado Federal, 1978. 405 p.; ill. (Coleção Bernardo Pereira de Vasconcelos; v. 12)

Welcome reprint of classic Liberal account of 1842 revolt. Especially valuable for inclusion of many original documents.

3616 Martins, Eduardo. Primeiro jornal paraibano: apontamentos históricos. Ed. ilustrada. João Pessoa: A União, 1976. 107 p.; ill.

Slight account of printing of *Gazeta do Governo da Paraíba do Norte* (1826) does contain some data of use of the history of typography and journalism in Brazil.

3617 Matos, Odilon Nogueira de. Saint-Hilaire e o Brasil. São Paulo: Governo do Estado de São Paulo, Secretaria da Cultura, Divisão de Arquivo do Estado, 1980. 34 p.

Includes useful bibliography of Saint-Hilaire's published works on Brazil and of their translations into Portuguese.

3618 Moehlecke, Germano Oscar. O Vale do Sinos era assim. São Leopoldo, Brasil: s.n., 1978. 360 p.; ill. (Coleção de artigos de jornal)

Compilation of highly readable, intelligent newspaper articles on aspects of German settlement at São Leopoldo from 1824 to present. Generally undocumented but clearly researched in primary sources.

3619 Monteiro, Rolando. Hipólito da Costa e a Independência: documentário e apreciação. Capa, Stúdio Cátedra. Rio de Janeiro: Livraria Editora Cátedra, 1979. 351 p.; bibl.

Title is misleading: very little on Costa himself. Includes: 1) parts of debates in Lisbon Cortes (1821–22) concerning Brazil and Brazilian deputies; and 2) letters of Brant

Pontes while he served as Brazilian envoy in London (1822–23). Useful for specialists.

Montenegro, João Alfredo de Sousa. O liberalismo radical de Frei Caneca. See *HLAS 43:6706.*

Moura, Clóvis. Sacco e Vanzetti: o protesto brasileira. See *HLAS 43:6673.*

3620 Nogueira, Arlinda Rocha. Companhias interessadas na introdução de asiáticos em São Paulo nos primeiros anos de República. São Paulo: Centro de Estudos Nipo-Brasileiros, 1979. 40 p.; bibl. (Série A - Centro de Estudos Nipo-Brasileiros; no. 2)

Interesting study of unsuccessful efforts to bring Japanese immigrants into São Paulo in early 1800s.

Ottoni, Theóphilo Benedicto. Discursos parlamentares. See *HLAS 43:6698.*

3621 Paiva, Maria Arair Pinto. A elite política do Ceará provincial. Rio de Janeiro: Tempo Brasileiro, 1979. 219 p.; ill.

Detailed quantitative study of socioeconomic characteristics of provincial and national legislators during Empire. Stresses influence of droughts and large-scale landholding on political process, which was limited in any case to small number of individuals. Master's thesis at Rio's Pontificia Universidade Católica.

3622 Pereira, Nilo. D. [i.e. Dom] Pedro II, o trono e o altar. Recife: Universidade Federal de Pernambuco, Editora Universitária, 1976. 158 p.

Collection of rambling essays on Pedro II's character, historical reputation and life as seen from the perspective of Pernambuco.

3623 Poder legislativo e autoritarismo no Rio Grande do Sul, 1891–1937. Hélgio Trindade, comp. Porto Alegre, RS: Editora Sulina, 1980. 369 p.; 10 p. of plates; bibl.; ill.

Revealing selection of assembly debates in Rio Grande do Sul from the first state constitution until assembly's extinction in 1937. Supplemented with notes, rosters and governors' messages. Essential raw material for gaúcho history.

Reis, Antônio Carlos Konder. Encurtando distâncias. See *HLAS 43:6699.*

3624 Revolução de 30: partidos e imprensa partidária no RS, 1928–37. Organizador, Hélgio Trindade. Colaboradores, Aline

Luzardo Winter *et al.* Porto Alegre: Núcleo de Pesquisa e Documentação da Política Rio-Grandense, UFRGS: L&PM Editores, 1980. 552 p.; bibl.; ill.

Growing maturity of gaúcho history is attested by this and other volumes published recently. Although this is raw newspaper and archival material, it is intelligently selected and organized by the most active of the gaúcho historians.

3625 Rivière d'Arc, Hélène. La formation du lieu amazonie au XIXe siècle (CDAL, 18, 2. semestre, 1978, p. 183–213, bibl., maps)

Very superficial discussion of the development of frontiers of Brazilian Amazonia, to explain the success of the Brazilian government in settlement of frontier disputes during the Old Republic (for geographer's comment, see *HLAS: 5403*).

3626 Rodrigues, Edgar. Alvorada operária: os congressos operários no Brasil. Rio de Janeiro: Edições Mundo Livre, 1979. 357 p.; ill.

Useful collection of programs from national and state labor congresses (1906–20) without adequate sources or explication. Followed by cut-and-paste section of labor writings from the era. Raw data only.

3627 Rodrigues, José Honorio. Centenário da morte de José Tomás Nabuco de Araújo, 1813–1878 (PAIGH/H, 88, julio/dic. 1979, p. 75–92, bibl.)

Slight recounting of Senator Nabuco's life, based on his son's biography. Not in the class of item **3580**.

3628 Salles, Francisco José Monteiro. Joaquim Corrêa de Mello, sua vida e sua obra. Campinas, Brazil: Academia Campinense de Letras, 1978. 94 p.; bibl. (Publicações da Academia Campinense de Letras; no. 38)

Slight study of Campinas botanist and man of letters (1816–77). Reprints his articles.

3629 Santos, Carlos Roberto Atunes dos. L'économie et la société esclavagistes au Paraná, Brésil, de 1854 a 1887 (CDAL, 19, 1979, p. 101–111, table)

Short study shows that by the end of the 1850s, the capital invested annually in the purchase of slaves in Paraná equalled the province's revenues. Also sketches changing

role of slave labor in the province up to abolition.

3630 Santos, Ronaldo Marcos dos. Resistência e superação do escravismo na província de São Paulo, 1885–1888. São Paulo: Instituto de Pesquisas Econômicas, Universidade de São Paulo, 1980. 142 p.; tables (Ensaios econômicos; 5)

In-depth study at the município level of slave resistance, fomented by abolitionists, which forced planters to begin shifting to wage labor even before May 1888. Good statistics and coverage of local press.

Semana Nacional de Filosofia no Brasil, 1978. Anais. See item **7614.**

Silva, Sergio. Expansão cafeeira e origins da indústria no Brasil. See *HLAS 43:3786.*

3631 Silveira, Hemetério José Velloso da. As missões orientais e seus antigos domínios. Nota sobre ERUS por Lauro P. Guimarães. Apresentação de Barbosa Lessa. Porto Alegre, RG: ERUS, 1979. 548 p.; 1 fold. leaf of plates; bibl.; ill.

History and contemporary description of the Mission district of Rio Grande do Sul first published in 1909. Largely based on author's investigations while resident in the province's northwest between 1855–67. Therefore useful as primary source for the study of former Jesuit missions.

3632 Souza, Carlos Alves de. Um embaixador em tempos de crise. Capa, Teresa Corção. Rio de Janeiro: Livraria F. Alves Editora, 1979. 361 p.; ill.

Memoir, covering period from 1920s until mid-1960s, is well written and informative. Provides fresh material for diplomatic history.

3633 Souza, José Antonio Soares de. A estrada da serra da Estrela e os colonos alamães (IHGB/R, 322, jan./março 1979, p. 5–180, plates)

Well researched, intelligent study on the creation of infrastructure (roads, bridges, immigration) to foster economic development in central Rio province (1836–45). Recommended to specialists as a case study.

3634 ———. O final do tráfico de escravos (IHGB/R, 323, abril/junho 1979, p. 5–23, plates)

Short analysis of the train of events that led to the abolition of the African slave trade in 1851–52, intended to show that Viscount Mauá, despite his later claims, played no role in ending the trade.

3635 ———. A Província do Rio de Janeiro, nas vésperas da abolição (IHGB/R, 324, julho/set. 1979, p. 3–92, plates, tables)

Synopsis of a *Guide to Rio Province for emigrants* published in 1888, reproducing 14 fine woodcuts from the book.

Tobler, Hans Werner and **Peter Waldmann.** German colonies in South America: a new Germany in the Cono Sur? See item **1835**.

3636 Toledo, Francisco de Paula. História do Município de Taubaté. 2. ed., anotada. Taubaté, Brasil: Prefeitura Municipal de Taubaté, 1976. 73 p.; 8 leaves of plates; ill. (1 fold). (Serie Ruas e logradouros públicos de Taubaté) (Taubateana; no. 6)

Model re-edition with modern annotations of an 1877 description of a São Paulo coffee town. Excellent as case study of the sociopolitical structure of an urban centre. Includes rare photographs of street scenes (1856–65).

3637 Toplin, Robert Brent. Freedom and prejudice: the legacy of slavery in the United States and Brazil. Westport, Conn: Greenwood Press, 1981. 1 v.; bibl.; index (Contributions in Afro-American and African studies; no. 56 0069–9624)

Four of six essays are reprints and all are variations of the Carl Degler view of race relations in the US and Brazil.

3638 Uricoechea, Fernando. The patrimonial foundations of the Brazilian bureaucratic state. Berkeley: University of California Press, 1980. 233 p.; bibl.; index.

Political scientist's study of the National Guard of Imperial Brazil sees it as exemplifying the development of the Brazilian state in terms of Max Weber's theories. Not easy to read and uneven in its utilization of historical method and data, but does offer a fresh perspective different from most work on 19th-century Brazil (for political scientist's comment, see *HLAS 43:6681*).

3639 I veneti in Brasile: nel centenario dell'emigrazione, 1876–1976. A cura di Mario Sabbatini e Emilio Franzina. Vicenza: Edizioni dell'Accademia Olimpica, 1977. 157 p.; 60 leaves of plates (3 fold.); ill.

Collection of articles and documents on immigration from the hinterland of Venice to southern Brazil. Excellent series of photographs derived from an exhibition held in Caxias do Sul, 1975, and in Vicenza, Italy, 1976.

Versiani, Flávio Rabelo. Industrialização: a experiência brasileira antes de 1914. See *HLAS 43:3796*.

3640 Vieira, David Gueiros. O protestantismo, a maçonaria e a questão religiosa no Brasil. Preface, Gilberto Freyre. Brasília: Editora Universidade de Brasília, 1980. 409 p. (Coleção Temas brasileiros)

Exhaustive study, originally Ph.D. dissertation, based on archival sources in three continents. Shows that the religious question was far more complex than usually portrayed and that rising Protestant influence played an important role in the 1872 crisis.

3641 Wachowicz, Ruy Christovam. O "Uti possidetis" brasileiro na questão de palmas (Boletin [Instituto Historico, Geográfico e Etnográfico Paranaense, Curitiba, Brazil] 35, 1979, p. 193–217)

Short study of frontier question between Brazil and Argentina from the viewpoint of the state of Paraná. Brazilians entered the contested area to raise cattle while Argentines gathered maté, a difference which gave the former a greater claim to effective occupation in the arbitration proceedings of 1895.

3642 Weimer, Günter. Engenheiros alemães no Rio Grande do Sul, na década 1848–1858 (Estudos Ibero-Americanos [Pontifícia Universidade Católica do Rio Grande do Sul, Instituto de Filosofia e Ciências Humanas, Departamento de História, Porto Alegre, Brazil] 5:2, dez. 1979, p. 151–205, bibl., tables)

Thorough use of extensive archival material vividly demonstrates how difficult and thankless was the task of civil engineers in the mid-19th century, especially if they were foreigners. Much detail, poorly organized, on individual careers including works undertaken.

Xavier, Maria Elizabete Sampaio. Poder político e educação e elite. See *HLAS 43:4645*.

JOURNAL ABBREVIATIONS HISTORY

AAA/AE American Ethnologist. American Anthropological Association. Washington.

AAFH/TAM The Americas. A quarterly publication of inter-American cultural history. Academy of American Franciscan History. Washington.

ACH/B Boletín de la Academia Chilena de la Historia. Santiago.

ACH/BHA Boletín de Historia y Antigüedades. Academia Colombiana de Historia. Bogotá

ACHA/CHR Catholic Historical Review. American Catholic Historical Association. The Catholic Univ. of America Press. Washington.

AEJ/JQ Journalism Quarterly. Association for Education in Journalism *with the cooperation of the* American Association of Schools, Depts. of Journalism [and] Kappa Tau Alpha Society. Univ. of Minnesota. Minneapolis.

AESC Annales: Economies, Sociétés, Civilisations. Centre National de la Recherche Scientifique *avec la concours de la* VIe Section de l'Ecole Pratique des Hautes Etudes. Paris.

AFH Archivum Franciscanum Historicum. Firenze, Italy.

AGH/BHA *See* ACH/BHA.

AHA/R American Historical Review. American Historial Association. Washington.

AHG/R Revista del Archivo Histórico del Guayas. Guayaquil, Ecuador.

AHS/AH Agricultural History. Agricultural History Society. Univ. of California Press. Berkeley.

AHSI Archivum Historicum Societatis Iesu. Rome.

AI/A Antropos. Anthropos-Institut. Psoieux, Switzerland.

AN/AN American Neptune. The American Neptune, Inc. Salem, Mass.

ANA Análisis. Cuadernos de investigación. Apartado 11093. Correo Santa Beatriz. Lima.

ANH/B Boletín de la Academia Nacional de Historia. Buenos Aires.

ANH/E *See* ANH/IE.

ANH/IE Investigaciones y Ensayos. Academia Nacional de la Historia. Buenos Aires.

ANLE/B Boletín de la Academia Norteamericana de la Lengua Española. New York.

APH/H *See* APH/HP.

APH/HP Historia Paraguaya. Anuario de la Academia Paraguaya de la Historia. Asunción.

APHA/J American Journal of Public Health and the Nation's Health. The American Public Health Association. Albany, N.Y.

APS/P Proceedings of the American Philosophical Society. Philadelphia, Pa.

ARBOR Arbor. Madrid.

ASCH/CH Church History. American Society of Church History, Univ. of Chicago. Chicago, Ill.

ASE/E Ethnohistory. Journal of the American Society for Ethnohistory. Buffalo, N.Y.

ASNLH/J The Journal of Negro History. Association for the Study of Negro Life and History. Washington.

AVA Avances. Revista boliviana de estudios históricos y sociales. La Paz.

BBAA B.B.A.A. Boletín Bibliográfico de Antropología Americana. Instituto Panamericano de Geografía e Historia, Comisión de Historia. México.

BCE/C Cultura. Revista del Banco Central del Ecuador. Quito.

BCV/REL Revista de Economía Latinoamericana. Banco Central de Venezuela. Caracas.

BEPB Bulletin des Études Portugaises et Bresiliennes. Institut Français de Lisbonne *avec la collaboration de* Establissements Français d'Enseignment Supérieur, Instituto de Alta Cultura, et du Departamento Cultural do Itamarati. Lisbon.

BESPL Berichte zur Entwicklung in Spanien, Portugal, Lateinamerika. München, FRG.

BISRA/BS Belizean Studies. Belizean Institute of Social Research and Action [and] St. John's College. Belize City.

BMA/BB Boletim Bibliográfico. Biblioteca Mário de Andrade. São Paulo.

BNBD Boletín Nicaragüense de Bibliografía y Documentación. Banco Central de Nicaragua, Biblioteca. Managua.

BNJM/R   Revista de la Biblioteca Nacional José Martí. La Habana.

BU/JCH   *See* BU/JCS.

BU/JCS   A Journal of Church and State. Baylor Univ., J. M. Dawson Studies in Church and State. Waco, Tex.

CAAAP/AP   Amazonía Peruana. Centro Amazónico de Antropología y Aplicación Práctica, Depto. de Documentación y Publicaciones. Lima.

CAM   Cuadernos Americanos. México.

CCE/CHA   Cuadernos de Historia y Arqueología. Casa de la Cultura Ecuatoriana, Núcleo del Guayas. Guayaquil.

CDAL   Cahiers des Amériques Latines. Paris.

CDLA   Casa de las Américas. Instituto Cubano del Libro. La Habana.

CEDE/DS   Desarrollo y Sociedad. Univ. de los Andes, Facultad de Economía, Centro de Estudios sobre el Desarrollo Económico. Bogotá.

CEDLA/B   Boletín de Estudios Latinoamericanos. Centro de Estudios y Documentación Latinoamericanos. Amsterdam.

CEHA/NH   Nuestra Historia. Centro de Estudios de Historia Argentina. Buenos Aires.

CEHSMO   Historia Obrera. Centro de Estudios Históricos del Movimiento Obrero Mexicano. México.

CEM/ECM   Estudios de Cultura Maya. Univ. Nacional Autónoma de México, Centro de Estudios Mayas. México.

CH   Cuadernos Hispanoamericanos. Instituto de Cultura Hispánica. Madrid.

CHE/PE   Pensamiento Económico. Organo oficial de divulgación. Colegio Hondureño de Economistas. Tegucigalpa.

CLACSO/ERL   Estudios Rurales Latinoamericanos. Consejo Latinoamericano de Ciencias Sociales, Secretaría Ejecutiva y de la Comisión de Estudios Rurales. Bogotá.

CLAEH   Centro Latinoamericano de Economía Humana. Montevideo.

CLAPCS/AL   América Latina. Centro Latino-Americano de Pesquisas em Ciências Sociais. Rio de Janeiro.

CM/FI   Foro Internacional. El Colegio de México. México.

CM/HM   Historia Mexicana. El Colegio de México. México.

CM/RE   Relaciones. Estudios de historia y sociedad. El Colegio de Michoacán. Zamora, México.

CNC/RMA   Revista del México Agrario. Confederación Nacional Campesina. México.

CP   Cuadernos Políticos. Revista trimestral. Ediciones Era. México.

CPES/RPS   Revista Paraguaya de Sociología. Centro Paraguayo de Estudios Sociológicos. Asunción.

CPS   Comparative Political Studies. Northwestern Univ., Evanston, Ill. [and] Sage Publications. Beverly Hills, Calif.

CRAN/R   Revista del Archivo Nacional. San José.

CRIT   Criterio. Editorial Criterio. Buenos Aires.

CSIC/RIS   Revista Internacional de Sociología. Consejo Superior de Investigaciones Científicas. Instituto Balmes de Sociología. Madrid.

CSSH   Comparative Studies in Society and History. An international quarterly. Society for the Comparative Study of Society and History. The Hague.

CUH   Current History. A monthly magazine of world affairs. Philadelphia, Pa.

DADOS   Dados. Instituto Universitário de Pesquisas. Rio de Janeiro.

DEF/F   Folk. Dansk Etnografisk Forening. København.

DESCO/Q   Quehacer. Realidad nacional: problemas y alternativas. Revista del Centro de Estudios y Promoción del Desarrollo (DESCO). Lima.

DGV/ZE   Zeitschrift für Völkerkunde. Braunschweig, FRG.

EANH/B   Boletín de la Academia Nacional de Historia. Quito.

EAZ   Ethnographisch-Archäologische Zeitschrift. Deutscher Verlag Wissenschaften. East Berlin.

EEHA/AEA   Anuario de Estudios Americanos. Consejo Superior de Investigaciones Científicas [and] Univ. de Sevilla, Escuela de Estudios Hispano-Americanos. Sevilla.

EEHA/HBA Historiografía y Bibliografía Americanista. Escuela de Estudios Hispano-Americanos de Sevilla. Sevilla.

EHA *See* EHA/J.

EHA/J Journal of Economic History. New York Univ., Graduate School of Business Administration *for the* Economic History Association. Rensselaer.

EHESS/C Communications. École des Hautes Études en Sciences Sociales, Centre d'Études Transdisciplinaires. Paris.

EHR English Historical Review. Longman Group Ltd. Essex, England.

EME Revista Eme-Eme. Estudios dominicanos. Univ. Católica Madre y Maestra. Santiago de los Caballeros, Dominican Republic.

EPHE/H L'Homme. Revue française d'anthropologie. La Sorbonne, l'Ecole Pratique des Hautes Études. Paris.

FAIC/CPPT Comunicaciones Proyecto Puebla-Tlaxcala. Fundación Alemana para la Investigación Científica. Puebla, México.

FCE/TE El Trimestre Económico. Fondo de Cultura Económica. México.

FDD/NED Notes et Études Documentaires. France - Direction de la Documentation. Paris.

FEPA/EI F.E.P.A. Estudios e Investigaciones. Fundación para el Estudio de los Problemas Argentinos. Buenos Aires.

FFCLM/EH Estudos Históricos. Faculdade de Filosofia, Ciências e Letras, Depto. de História. Marília, Brazil.

FH Folia Humanistica. Ciencias, artes, letras. Editorial Glarma. Barcelona.

FHS/FHQ The Florida Historical Quarterly. The Florida Historical Society. Jacksonville.

FIU/CR The Florida Historical Quarterly. The Florida Historical Society. Jacksonville.

FIU/CR Caribbean Review. Florida International Univ., Office of Academic Affairs. Miami.

FJB/BH Boletín Histórico. Fundación John Boulton. Caracas.

FPRI/O Orbis. A journal of world affairs. Foreign Policy Research Institute, Philadelphia, Pa. *in association with the* Fletcher School of Law and Diplomacy, Tufts Univ., Medford, Mass.

FSCN/A Antropológica. Fundación La Salle de Ciencias Naturales, Instituto Caribe de Antropología y Sociología. Caracas.

GM The Geographical Magazine. London.

HAHR Hispanic American Historical Review. Duke Univ. Press *for the* Conference on Latin American History of the American Historical Association. Durham, N.C.

HSSC/SCQ Southern California Quarterly. Historical Society of Southern California. Los Angeles.

HU/BHR Business History Review. Harvard Univ., Graduate School of Business Administration. Boston, Mass.

IAA Ibero-Amerikanisches Archiv. Ibero-Amerikanisches Institut. Berlin, FRG.

IAEERI/E Estrategia. Instituto Argentino de Estudios Estratégicos y de las Relaciones Internacionales. Buenos Aires.

IAHG/AHG Antropología e Historia de Guatemala. Instituto de Antropología e Historia de Guatemala. Guatemala.

IAI/I Indiana. Beiträge zur Volker- und Sprachenkunde, Archäologie und Anthropologie des Indianischen Amerika. Ibero-Amerikanisches Institut. Berlin, FRG.

IAMEA Inter-American Economic Affairs. Washington.

IAS/ÑP Ñawpa Pacha. Institute of Andean Studies. Berkeley, Calif.

IBE/RBE Revista Brasileira de Economia. Fundação Getulio Vargas, Instituto Brasileiro de Economia. Rio de Janeiro.

ICA/RCA Revista Colombiana de Antropología. Ministerio de Educación Nacional, Instituto Colombiano de Antropología. Bogotá.

ICS/JCCP Journal of Commonwealth & Comparative Politics. Univ. of London, Institute of Commonwealth Studies. London.

IDES/DE The Developing Economies. Institute of Developing Economies. Tokyo.

IEP/RPI Revista de Política Internacional. Instituto de Estudios Políticos. Madrid.

IFEA/B   Bulletin de l'Institut Français d'Études Andines. Lima.

IGFO/RI   Revista de Indias. Instituto Gonzalo Fernández de Oviedo [and] Consejo Superior de Investigaciones Científicas. Madrid.

IGHS/R   *See* IHGS/R.

IHADER/B   Boletín del Instituto de Historia Argentina Doctor Emilio Ravignani. Buenos Aires.

IHGB/R   Revista do Instituto Histórico e Geográfico Brasileiro. Rio de Janeiro.

IHGGB/R   Revista do Instituto Histórico e Geográfico Guarujá/Bertioga. São Paulo.

IHGS/R   Revista do Instituto Histórico e Geográfico de Sergipe. Aracajú, Brazil.

IHGSP/R   Revista do Instituto Histórico e Geográfico de São Paulo. São Paulo.

IIEA/A   Anales del Instituto de Investigaciones Estéticas. Univ. Nacional Autónoma de México. México.

III/AI   América Indígena. Instituto Indigenista Interamericano. México.

IJ/JJ   Jamaica Journal. Institute of Jamaica. Kingston.

INAH/A   Anales del Instituto Nacional de Antropología e Historia. Secretaría de Educación Pública. México.

INEJ/AHD   Anuario de Historia del Derecho Español. Instituto Nacional de Estudios Jurídicos. Madrid.

IPA/A   Allpanchis. Instituto de Pastoral Andina. Cuzco, Peru.

IPA/AP   *See* IPA/A.

IPE/EE   Estudos Econômicos. Univ. de São Paulo, Instituto de Pesquisas Econômicas. São Paulo.

IPGH/FA   Folklore Americano. Instituto Panamericano de Geografía e Historia, Comisión de Historia, Comité de Folklore. México.

IRA/B   Boletín del Instituto Riva-Agüero. Pontificia Univ. Católica del Perú. Lima.

ISA/CUR   Comparative Urban Research. International Sociological Association, Committee for Community Research. College Park, Md.

ISTM/MH   Missionalia Hispanica. Instituto Santo Toribio de Mogrovejo [and] Consejo Superior de Investigaciones Científicas. Madrid.

JBA   Journal of Belizean Affairs. Belize City.

JDA   The Journal of Developing Areas. Western Illinois Univ. Press. Macomb.

JGSWGL   Jahrbuch für Geschichte von Staat, Wirtschaft und Gesellschaft Lateinamerikas. Köln, FRG.

JHI   Journal of the History of Ideas. City College. New York.

JHS/R   The Jamaican Historical Review. The Jamaican Historical Society. Kingston.

JIAS   *See* SAGE/JIAS.

JIH   The Journal of Interdisciplinary History. The MIT Press. Cambridge, Mass.

JLAS   Journal of Latin American Studies. Centers or institutes of Latin American studies at the university of Cambridge, Glasgow, Liverpool, London and Oxford. Cambridge Univ. Press. London.

JPHC/R   Revista de la Junta Provincial de Historia de Córdoba. Archivo Histórico Monseñor P. Cabrera. Córdoba, Argentina.

JPS   The Journal of Peasant Studies. Frank Cass & Co. London.

JW   Journal of the West. Los Angeles, Calif.

LAP   Latin American Perspectives. Univ. of California. Riverside.

LARR   Latin American Research Review. Univ. of North Carolina Press *for the* Latin American Studies Association. Chapel Hill.

LNB/L   Lotería. Lotería Nacional de Beneficencia. Panamá.

MAGN/B   Boletín del Archivo General de la Nación. Secretaría de Gobernación. México.

MAN   Mensário do Arquivo Nacional. Ministério da Justiça. Arquivo Nacional. Editoração e Expediente. Divisão de Publicaçoes. Rio de Janeiro.

MHS/J   The Journal of Mississippi History. Mississippi Historical Society *in cooperation with the* Mississippi Dept. of Archives and History. Jackson.

MN   Mundo Nuevo. Instituto Latinoamericano de Relaciones Internacionales. Paris.

MNDJG/A Anales del Museo Nacional David J. Guzmán. San Salvador.

MP/AN Anais do Museu Paulista. São Paulo.

MP/R Revista do Museu Paulista. São Paulo.

MVW/AV Archiv für Völkerkunde. Museum für Völkerkunde in Wien und von Verein Freunde der Völkerkunde. Wien.

NCFR/JFH Journal of Family History. Studies in family, kinship and demography. National Council on Family Relations. Minneapolis, Minn.

NGS/NGM National Geographic Magazine. National Geographic Society. Washington.

NS NS NorthSouth NordSud NorteSur NorteSul. Canadian journal of Latin American studies. Canadian Association of Latin American Studies. Univ. of Ottawa. Ottawa.

NSO Nueva Sociedad. Revista política y cultural. San José.

OAS/A Annals. Organization of American States. Washington.

OAS/AM Américas. Organization of American States. Washington.

PAIGH/H Revista de Historia de América. Instituto Panamericano de Geografía e Historia, Comisión de Historia. México.

PAIGH/R *See* PAIGH/H.

PAIGH/RHA *See* PAIGH/H.

PAN/ES Estudios Latinoamericanos. Polska Akademia Nauk [Academia de Ciencias de Polonia], Instytut Historii [Instituto de Historia]. Warszawa.

PAT/TH The Historian. A journal of history. Phi Alpha Theta, National Honor Society in History. Univ. of Pennsylvania. University Park.

PCCLAS/P Proceedings of the Pacific Coast Council on Latin American Studies. Univ. of California. Los Angeles.

PCE/TE *See* FCE/TE.

PEAGN/R Revista del Archivo General de la Nación. Instituto Nacional de Cultura. Lima.

PEBN/B Boletín de la Biblioteca Nacional. Lima.

PEIH/RH Revista Histórica. Instituto Histórico del Perú. Lima.

PEMN/R Revista del Museo Nacional. Casa de la Cultura del Perú, Museo Nacional de la Cultura Peruana. Lima.

PF/AIA Archivo Ibero-Americano. Los Padres Franciscanos. Madrid.

PJHC/R *See* JPHC/R.

PMNH/C *See* PMNH/HC.

PMNH/HC Historia y Cultura. Museo Nacional de Historia. Lima.

PP Past and Present. London.

PUCP/CSH Cuadernos del Seminario de Historia. Pontificia Univ. Católica del Perú. Instituto Riva-Agüero. Lima.

PUCP/DA Debates en Antropología. Pontificia Univ. Católica del Perú, Depto. de Ciencias Sociales. Lima.

PUCP/H Histórica. Pontificia Univ. Católica del Perú, Depto. de Humanidades. Lima.

PUF/RH Revue Historique. Presses Universitaires de France. Paris.

PUJ/UH Universitas Humanistica. Pontificia Univ. Javeriana, Facultad de Filosofía y Letras. Bogotá.

RAI/M Man. A monthly record of anthropological science. The Royal Anthropological Institute. London.

RCPC Revista del Pensamiento Centroamericano. Centro de Investigaciones y Actividades Culturales. Managua.

RIB Revista Interamericana de Bibliografía [Inter-American Review of Bibliography]. Organization of American States. Washington.

RSG/B Boletín de la Real Sociedad Geográfica. Madrid.

RU/MP Marxist Perspectives. Transaction Periodicals Consortium. Rutgers Univ. New Brunswick, N.J.

RU/SCID Studies in Comparative International Development. Rutgers Univ. New Brunswick, N.J.

RUC Revista de la Universidad Complutense. Madrid.

SA Scientific American. Scientific American, Inc. New York.

SA/J Journal de la Société des Américanistes. Paris.

SAA/AA American Antiquity. The Society for American Archaeology. Menasha, Wis.

SAA/R Relaciones de la Sociedad Argentina de Antropología. Buenos Aires.

SAGE/JIAS Journal of Inter-American Studies and World Affairs. Sage Publication *for the* Center for Advanced International Studies, Univ. of Miami. Coral Gables, Fla.

SBPC/CC Ciência e Cultura. Sociedade Brasileira para o Progresso da Ciência. São Paulo.

SBV/R Revista de la Sociedad Bolivariana de Venezuela. Caracas.

SCHG/R Revista Chilena de Historia y Geografía. Sociedad Chilena de Historia y Geografía. Santiago.

SDHS/J The Journal of San Diego History. The San Diego Historical Society. San Diego, Calif.

SECOLAS/A Annals of the Southeastern Conference on Latin American Studies. West Georgia College. Carrollton.

SECOLAS/SELA South Eastern Latin Americanist. Quarterly bulletin of the Southeastern Conference on Latin American Studies. Clemson Univ. Clemson, S.C.

SGHG/A Anales de la Sociedad de Geografía e Historia de Guatemala. Guatemala.

SHM/RHM Revista de Historia Militar. Servicio Histórico Militar. Madrid.

SPSA/JP The Journal of Politics. The Southern Political Science Association *in cooperation with the* Univ. of Florida. Gainesville.

SRA/A Anales de la Sociedad Rural Argentina. Revista pastoril y Agrícola. Buenos Aires.

SS Science and Society. New York.

SSA/B Bulletin. Société Suisse des Américanistes. Geneva.

TSHA/SHQ Southwestern Historical Quarterly. Texas State Historical Association. Austin.

UA Urban Anthropology. State Univ. of New York, Dept. of Anthropology. Brockport.

UA/AW Arizona and the West. Univ. of Arizona. Tucson.

UAEM/H Histórica. Univ. Autónoma del Estado de México, Instituto de Investigaciones Históricas. México.

UB/BA Boletín Americanista. Univ. de Barcelona, Facultad de Geografía e Historia, Depto. de Historia de América. Barcelona.

UB/GG Geschichte und Gesellschaft. Zeitschrift für Historische Sozialwissenschaft. Univ. Bielefeld, Fakultät für Geschichtswissenschaft. Bielefeld, FRG.

UBA/RIHD Revista del Instituto de Historia del Derecho. Univ. de Buenos Aires, Facultad de Derecho y Ciencias Sociales. Buenos Aires.

UBGI/E Erdkunde. Archiv für Wissenschaftliche Geographie. Univ. Bonn, Geographisches Institut. Bonn.

UBN/R Revista de la Biblioteca Nacional. Ministerio de Educación y Cultura. Montevideo.

UC/AT Atenea. Revista de ciencias, letras y artes. Univ. de Concepción. Concepción, Chile.

UC/CA Current Anthropology. Univ. of Chicago. Chicago, Ill.

UC/HR History of Religions. International journal for comparative historical studies. Univ. of Chicago. Chicago, Ill.

UC/PHR The Pacific Historical Review. Univ. of California Press. Los Angeles.

UC/S Signs. Journal of women in culture and society. The Univ. of Chicago Press. Chicago.

UCAB/M Montalbán. Univ. Católica Andrés Bello, Facultad de Humanidades y educación, Institutos Humanísticos de Investigación. Caracas.

UCC/NG Norte Grande. Revista de estudios integrados referentes a comunidades humanas del Norte Grande de Chile, en una perspectiva geográfica e histórico-cultural. Univ. Católica de Chile, Instituto de Geografía, Depto. de Geografía de Chile, Taller Norte Grande. Santiago.

UCCIH/H Historia. Univ. Católica de Chile, Instituto de Historia. Santiago.

UCEIA/H Humanitas. Boletín ecuatoriano de antropología. Univ. Central del Ecuador, Instituto de Antropología. Quito.

UCLA/JLAL Journal of Latin American Lore. Univ. of California, Latin American Center. Los Angeles.

UCLV/I Islas. Univ. Central de las Villas. Santa Clara, Cuba.

UCNSA/EP Estudios Paraguayos. Univ. Católica Nuestra Señora de la Asunción. Asunción.

UCNSA/SA Suplemento Antropológico. Univ. Católica de Nuestra Señora de la Asunción, Centro de Estudios Antropológicos. Asunción.

UCP/IAP Ibero-Americana Pragensia. Univ. Carolina de Praga, Centro de Estudios Ibero-Americanos. Prague.

UCP/JSH Journal of Social History. Univ. of California Press. Berkeley.

UCR/AEC Anuario de Estudios Centro-americanos. Univ. de Costa Rica. Ciudad Universitaria "Rodrigo Facio." San Jose.

UCSD/ND *See* UCSD/NS.

UCSD/NS The New Scholar. Univ. of California, Center for Iberian and Latin American Studies [and] Institute of Chicano Urban Affairs. San Diego.

UCV/E Escritura. Teoría y crítica literaria. Univ. Central de Venezuela, Escuela de Letras. Caracas.

UFMG/DCP Cadernos DCP. Univ. Federal de Minas Gerais, Faculdade de Filosofia e Ciências Humanas, Depto. de Ciência Política. Belo Horizonte, Brazil.

UH/U Universidad de La Habana. La Habana.

UHS/AH *See* AHS/AH.

UI/R *See* UY/R.

UM/JIAS *See* SAGE/JIAS.

UM/R Revista Universidad de Medellín. Centro de Estudios de Posgrado. Medellín, Colombia.

UM/REAA Revista Española de Antropología Americana (Trabajos y Conferencias). Univ. de Madrid, Facultad de Filosofía y Letras, Depto. de Antropología y Etnología de América. Madrid.

UMG/RBEP Revista Brasileira de Estudos Políticos. Univ. de Minas Gerais. Belo Horizonte, Brazil.

UMHN/RH Revista Histórica. Museo Histórico Nacional. Montevideo.

UNAM/AA Anales de Antropología. Univ. Nacional Autónoma de México, Instituto de Investigaciones Históricas. México.

UNAM/E Estudios de Historia Moderna y Contemporánea de México. Univ. Nacional Autónoma de México. México.

UNAM/ECN Estudios de Cultura Náhuatl. Univ. Nacional Autónoma de México, Instituto de Historia, Seminario de Cultura Náhuatl. México.

UNAM/EHN Estudios de Historia Novo-hispana. Univ. Nacional Autónoma de México, Instituto de Investigaciones Históricas. México.

UNAM/NMHR *See* UNM/NMHR.

UNAM/RFD Revista de la Facultad de Derecho. Univ. Nacional Autónoma de México. México.

UNAM/RMCPS Revista Mexicana de Ciencias Políticas y Sociales. Univ. Nacional Autónoma de México, Facultad de Ciencias Políticas y Sociales. México.

UNAM/RMS Revista Mexicana de Sociología. Univ. Nacional Autónoma de México, Instituto de Investigaciones Sociales. México.

UNAM/T Tlalocan. Revista de fuentes para el conocimiento de las culturas indígenas de México. Univ. Nacional Autónoma de México, Instituto de Investigaciones Antropológicas, Instituto de Investigaciones Históricas. México.

UNC/ACHSC Anuario Colombiano de Historia Social y de la Cultura. Univ. Nacional de Colombia, Facultad de Ciencias Humanas, Depto. de Historia. Bogotá.

UNC/K Katunob. Univ. of Northern Colorado, Museum of Anthropology. Greeley, Colo.

UNC/R Revista de la Universidad Nacional de Córdoba. Córdoba, Argentina.

UNC/RHAA Revista de Historia Americana y Argentina. Univ. Nacional de Cuyo, Facultad de Filosofía y Letras, Instituto de Historia. Mendoza, Argentina.

UNCR/R Revista de Historia. Univ. Nacional de Costa Rica, Escuela de Historia. Heredia.

UNESCO/CU Cultures. United Nations Educational, Scientific and Cultural Organization. Paris.

UNL/H Humanitas. Univ. de Nuevo León, Centro de Estudios Humanísticos. Monterrey, México.

UNL/U Universidad. Univ. Nacional del Litoral. Santa Fe, Argentina.

UNLP/TC Trabajos y Comunicaciones. Univ. Nacional de La Plata, Depto. de Historia. La Plata, Argentina.

UNM/NMHR New Mexico Historical Review. Univ. of New Mexico [and] Historical Society of New Mexico. Albuquerque.

UNS/CS Cuadernos del Sur. Univ. Nacional del Sur, Instituto de Humanidades. Bahia Blanca, Argentina.

UNV/ED *See* UNC/ED.

UP/A Apuntes. Univ. del Pacífico, Centro de Investigación. Lima.

UP/EA Estudios Andinos. Univ. of Pittsburgh, Latin American Studies Center. Pittsburgh, Pa.

UP/TM Tiers Monde. Problémes des pays sous-développés. Univ. de Paris, Institut d'Étude du Développement Économique et Social. Paris.

UPN/RCE Revista Colombiana de Educación. Univ. Pedagógica Nacional, Centro de Investigaciones, Bogotá.

UPR/RO Revista de Oriente. Univ. de Puerto Rico, Colegio Universitario de Humacao. Humacao.

URSS/AL América Latina. Academia de Ciencias de la URSS [Unión de Repúblicas Soviéticas Socialistas]. Moscú.

USMLA/LA La Antigua. Univ. de Santa María La Antigua, Oficina de Humanidades. Panamá.

USNSA/EP *See* UCNSA/EP.

USP/RA Revista de Antropologia. Univ. de São Paulo, Faculdade de Filosofia, Letras e Ciências Humanas and Associação Brasileira de Antropologia. São Paulo.

USP/RH Revista de História. Univ. de São Paulo, Faculdade de Filosofia, Ciências e Letras, Depto. de História [and] Sociedade de Estudos Históricos. São Paulo.

USP/RIEB Revista do Instituto de Estudos Brasileiros. Univ. de São Paulo, Instituto de Estudos Brasileiros. São Paulo.

UT/SSQ Social Science Quarterly. Univ. of Texas, Dept. of Government. Austin.

UTIEH/C Caravelle. Cahiers du monde hispanique et luso-brésilien. Univ. de Toulouse, Institut d'Études Hispaniques, Hispano-Americaines et Luso-Brésiliennes. Toulouse, France.

UUAL/U Universidades. Unión de Universidades de América Latina. Buenos Aires.

UV/PH La Palabra y el Hombre. Univ. Veracruzana. Xalapa, Mexico.

UW/LBR Luso-Brazilian Review. Univ. of Wisconsin Press. Madison.

UWI/CQ Caribbean Quarterly. Univ. of West Indies. Mona, Jamaica.

UWI/JCH The Journal of Caribbean History. Univ. of the West Indies, Dept. of History [and] Caribbean Universities Press. St. Lawrence, Barbados.

UWI/SES Social and Economic Studies. Univ. of the West Indies, Institute of Social and Economic Research. Mona, Jamaica.

UY/R Revista de la Universidad de Yucatán. Mérida, Mexico.

UZ/R Revista de la Universidad del Zulia. Maracaibo, Venezuela.

VAGN/B Boletín del Archivo General de la Nación. Ministerio de Justicia. Caracas.

VANH/B Boletín de la Academia Nacional de la Historia. Caracas.

VMJ/BIV Boletín Indigenista Venezolano. Comisión Indigenista. Ministerio de Justicia. Caracas.

WHQ The Western Historical Quarterly. Western History Association, Utah State Univ. Logan.

YAXKIN YaxKin. Instituto Hondureño de Antropología e Historia. Tegucigalpa.

ZMR Zeitschrift für Missionswissenschaft und Religionswissenschaft. Lucerne, Switzerland.

LANGUAGE

D. LINCOLN CANFIELD, *Professor Emeritus of Spanish, Southern Illinois University*

THE TRENDS IN STUDIES OF LATIN AMERICAN language phenomena continue to shift toward the realm of sociolinguistics, with several analyses of code-switching, especially among Chicanos and Puerto Ricans; languages in contact, notably Spanish-English and Spanish-Quechua; counter-prestige jargons; and youth-talk as a manifestation of language change (item **4523**).

In the realm of geographically-designated language differences, "new" data comes to light on Argentina (items **4540** and **4550**), Bolivia (item **4557**), Costa Rica (item **4553**), Cuba (items **4536** and **4552**), the Dominican Republic (item **4538**), Mexico (items **4567–4568** and **4590**), Paraguay (items **4558** and **4559**), Puerto Rico (item **4580**), and Venezuela (item **4585**). In Brazilian Portuguese, special lexicon seems to be of interest (items **4620** and **4622**), and in Creole languages, the "lingo" of Belize and the English called Gullah (items **4636** and **4638**).

There have been collections of articles published as Festschrifts: *Festschrift for Jacob Ornstein* (item **4546**) and *Homenaje a Fernando Antonio Martínez* (item **4508**); and the proceedings of conferences: *Actas del Sexto Congreso Internacional de Hispanistas*; National Conference on Chicano and Latino Discourse Behavior's *Latino Language and Communicative Behavior* (item **4565**), and the *Proceedings* of the Colloquium on Spanish and Luso-Brazilian Linguistics (item **4503**), as well as the *Estudios lingüísticos y dialectológicos* (item **4544**) that constitute a part of the project to study the Spanish of principal Hispanic cities (see *HLAS 42:4537*).

There were at least three diachronic studies that treated in some way the development of Andalusian Spanish in America (items **4513**, **4530** and **4539**).

It is a pleasure to report that the work in languages and linguistics that goes on in the Western Hemisphere is becoming increasingly objective and shows ever more research beyond the local scene. This is especially true in Argentina; Chile; Mexico; Brazil; Colombia; the US; and to an extent, Cuba; the Dominican Republic; and Puerto Rico.

Among significant PhD dissertations for the period covered in this bibliography, are the following: María Bernadette Marqués Abaurre-Gnerre's *Phono-stylistic aspects of Brazilian Portuguese dialect: implications for syllable structure constraints* (SUNY, Buffalo, J. Bybee); Silvia Anadón's *Contemporary usage of Spanish subjunctive tenses in Latin America* (University of Michigan, D. Wolfe); Timothy William Hagerty's *A phonological analysis of Spanish in Belize* (UCLA, S. L. Robe); Robert James Blake's *The acquisition of mood selection among Spanish-speaking children: ages 4 to 12* (University of Texas, Y. R. Solé); and Reynaldo F. Macías' *Mexicano/Chicano sociolinguistic behaviour and language policy in the United States* (Georgetown University, Roger Shuy).

Finally, it is heartwarming to this ancient reviewer to be able to report important contributions by Egea and Resnick (items **4513** and **4612**), two of his former students, along with his own work (item **4530**).

SPANISH
GENERAL AND BIBLIOGRAPHY

4501 Brakel, Arthur. The provenience and present status of Spanish *selo* (LING, 17:7/8, 1979, p. 659–670, bibl., tables)

Rejecting generative explanations and the suggestions of form-analysts that *lelo* sequences are semantically too close, Brakel says that *selo* can best be interpreted as a lexical item. It seems to the present reviewer that the best explanation is that the Old Spanish *gelo* from Latin *ille-illum* follows the fairly general trend of an evolution of [ž] to [š] to [s], because of the special nature of Spanish apico-alveolar /s/ in the phonological system!

4502 Cartagena, Nelson. Los estudios lingüísticos en Chile durante la década 1964–1974 (IAA, 6:1, 1980, p. 53–78, bibl.)

A panorama of the development of linguistic studies in Chile during the decade noted as well as an analysis of the teaching activities and research in the field, an account of the agenda of meetings, conventions, and the work of the Sociedad Chilena de Lingüística, founded in 1971. A good bibliography of the period.

4503 Colloquium on Hispanic and Luso-Brazilian Linguistics, State University of New York at Oswego, 1976. Colloquium on Spanish and Luso-Brazilian Linguistics. James P. Lantolf, Francine Wattman Frank, Jorge M. Guitart, editors. Washington: Georgetown University Press, 1979. 159 p.; bibl.

A 1976 colloquium on Hispanic and Luso-Brazilian linguistics, held at State University of New York, Oswego, third in series of annual conferences begun in 1974 at the University of Massachusetts. The Special Interest Group was chaired by Melvyn C. Resnick, with nine of 21 papers on phonology, syntax, and semantics, and Spanish in the US. See items **4510, 4517, 4519, 4562, 4614** and **4632.**

4504 Conceptos básicos de la lingüística: una antología. Ursula Kühl de Mones. Montevideo: Universidad de la República, División Publicaciones y Ediciones, 1978. 213 p.; bibl.

Mimeographed anthology of linguistic theories and statements from Saussure and Sapir to Chomsky. Designed as a text, with definitions and exercises.

4505 Epistolario de Miguel Antonio Caro, Rufino José Cuervo y otros colombianos con Joaquín García Icazbalceta. Edición, presentación y notas de Mario Germán Romero. Introducción de Ignacio Bernal. Bogotá: Instituto Caro y Cuervo, 1980. 485 p.; bibl.; ill.; plates (Archivo epistolar colombiano; 14)

As far as language is concerned, there are a certain number of items scattered throughout the correspondence: discussions of *renta* vs. *alquila*; *obsequiar con*; *reclamo*; *su madre*; *Andalucismos*, including *amarrar, arrancar*; and the *leísta* as opposed to the *loísta*.

4506 García González, José. Para una bibliografía de los estudios sobre el español de Cuba (UCLV/I, 64, set./dic. 1979, p. 185–202, bibl.)

Speaking of improved conditions for research after the *triunfo de la Revolución* compared to those during the *neocolonia yanqui*, author presents a fairly good bibliography of 193 items, alphabetically arranged, but omits one of the best of recent studies: Haden and Matluck's *El habla culta de La Habana* (see *HLAS 38:6087*).

4507 Hartman, Steven Lee. A universal alphabet for experiments in comparative phonology (Computers for the Humanities [Amsterdam, The Netherlands] 15, 1981, p. 75–82)

Although this article is not specifically related to American Spanish, it introduces the concept of computer use for the comparative study of the phonology of different languages (in this case the history of sound change in the evolution of modern Spanish from Latin). The program is written in PL/I, and it has a format based in binary distinctive features and proposes an alphabet-numeral approach to depict a sound system that is more numerous than the computer's character set. Program suggests new possibilities.

4508 Homenaje a Fernando Antonio Martínez: estudios de lingüística, filología, literatura e historia cultural. Bogotá: Instituto Caro y Cuervo, 1979. 769 p.; 14 leaves of plates; bibl.; ill. (Publicaciones del Instituto Caro y Cuervo; 48)

Volume dedicated to the memory of the indefatigable Colombian linguist and lexicographer who died in 1972. A large segment of Martínez's professional effort was dedicated to the continuation of the famous *Diccionario de construcción y régimen de la lengua castellana* of Rufino José Cuervo, quite unfinished at the time of the latter's death in 1911. The Instituto Caro y Cuervo, where Dr. Martínez worked, is trying to carry on this same project today (see item **4607**). The *homenaje* contains several articles by hispanic and non-hispanic writers divided into three groups: 1) Lingüística y Filología; 2) Literatura; and 3) Historia Cultural. Several of the contributions of the first section do not deal with the Spanish of Latin America, but those of Canfield (see *HLAS 42: 4523*), Fontanella, Arrom, López Morales, Montes Giraldo do. The last four of these are reviewed in this volume, items **4569**, **4576**, **4601** and **4613**.

4509 Montes Giraldo, José Joaquín. Lengua, dialecto y norma (ICC/T, 35, 1980, p. 237–255)

Speaks of the language-dialect problem as a hardy perennial. What is standard? He maintains that nobody speaks a language. He speaks in a language, and everybody has his subsystem, with many influences. Believes that criteria should be sociopolitical for classifications.

4510 Ornstein, Jacob and Guadalupe Valdés-Fallis. On defining and describing United States varieties of Spanish: implications of dialect contact (*in* Colloquium on Spanish and Luso-Brazilian Linguistics [see item **4503**] p. 141–159)

Noting that Spanish-speaking US citizens now constitute the only group of people who speak a foreign language that is not losing ground, authors advocate a much-needed coordinated investigation of the varieties of US Spanish to observe synchronic changes in process as a result of internal modifications and of language contact interference. The hope is expressed by these two, who know the situation about as well as any, that Hispanists will join social scientists in mounting research.

4511 Parodi, Claudia. La investigación lingüística en México, 1970–1980. México: UNAM, 1981. 181 p.; indexes.

Good description of current work in the field, by way of an annotated bibliography. Includes books and articles on Indian languages, and divides Spanish items by language levels: phonology, grammar, lexicon and semantics, history of the language.

4512 Pluto, Joseph A. Contribución a una bibliografía anotada de los estudios sobre el español de Colombia, 1965–1975 (ICC/T, 35, 1980, p. 288–358)

This well-annotated bibliography covers the decade following that of José Joaquín Montes Giraldo in *Thesaurus* (Instituto Caro y Cuervo, 20, 1965, p. 425–465). Writer expresses disagreement with what he calls the prescriptive intentions of Solé's critiques (*Bibliografía sobre el español de América, 1920–1967.* Washington: 1970) and thanks the faculty of Southern Illinois University for their help in preparing materials. Work contains two main sections: Estudios Generales and Estudios Especiales. Subsections of the latter are: Gramática; Fonología; Lexicografía; Historia de la Lengua; Estilística; Etnografía; Onomástica; Kinésica. Well indexed.

4513 Resnick, Melvyn C. Introducción a la historia de la lengua española. Washington, D.C.: Georgetown University Press, 1981. 203 p.; appendix.

Consists of an *introducción mínima* to the internal and external history of Spanish in terms of its Latin origins and the foreign influences that have contributed to its formation. The latter include lexical expansion in America involving several Indian languages as well as American English. Dialectal developments on the American scene include changes that have become part of American Spanish. Text describes in considerable detail the phonological, grammatical and lexical evolution of Spanish from Latin, and focuses on modern Spanish. The rules are clearly delineated, and the *expansión léxica* is much more up-to-date than similar treatises, and the processes of borrowing in the languages-in-contact situation are cleverly drawn. Includes very helpful appendix of *textos antiguos*, two from 16th-century Mexico. The notes and explanations on ontology, dialectology, are much more explicit and teachable than are those of most manuals.

4514 Rosenblat, Angel. Sentido mágico de la palabra y otros estudios. Caracas: Universidad Central de Venezuela, Ediciones de la Biblioteca, 1977. 311 p. (Colección Arte y literatura; 6)

Collection of articles published in periodicals between 1933–69, which might be termed "The Essence of Rosenblat in One Volume." Chief among his contributions have been "El Castellano de España y el Castellano de América" (a good picture of unity and of differences); "El Criterio de Corrección Lingüística;" "La Gramática y el Idioma;" and "El Futuro de Nuestra Lengua."

4515 Serrón, Sergio. Aporte para una ficha bibliográfica de la dialectología venezolana hasta 1975. Caracas: Centro de Investigaciones Lingüísticas y Literarias Andrés Bello, Departamento de Castellano, Literatura y Latin, Instituto Universitario Pedagógico de Caracas, 1978. 1 v.; index.

Includes items first of all Spanish American (phonology, morphosyntax, lexicon), then Venezuelan, and finally Papiamento. Several omissions in the general Spanish American section.

4516 Torres Quintero, Rafael. Caro, defensor de la integridad del idioma. Bogotá: Instituto Caro y Cuervo, 1979. 92 p. (Filólogos colombianos; 9)

Miguel Antonio Caro is presented as a "defender" of the language but in the context of his time. Torres explains that mistakes were due to the state of the science at that time.

SPANISH
PHONOLOGY AND GRAMMAR

4517 Elman, Jeffrey. Spanish noun and adjective stress assignment: a nonphonological account (*in* Colloquium on Spanish and Luso-Brazilian Linguistics [see item **4503**] p. 1–18)

In early Spanish stress assignment was a phonological rule. Since then other levels which interact with stress have entered the language, among them the influx of foreign words which have stress patterns atypical of Spanish. Morphological and semantic information also plays a role in determining the assignment in modern Spanish, as does analogical hypercorrection.

4518 Fernández-Sevilla, Julio. Los fonemas implosivos en español (ICC/T, 35, 1980, p. 456–505)

Suggests that linguists should give as much attention to the syntagmatic as to the paradigmatic, because operative efficacy depends on the place of the element in the *cadena fónica* and the dynamics of the system. Spanish does not tolerate final clusters, and only dentals, alveolars and liquids can be absolute finals. The tendency toward the weakening and loss of implosives is part of the history of the language, author says, and it began in Latin.

4519 Kvavik, Karen H. An interpretation of cadences in Mexican Spanish (*in* Colloquium on Spanish and Luso-Brazilian Linguistics [see item **4503**] p. 37–47)

Part of an acoustic project on Spanish dialect intonations, study uses the Melodic Analyzer of the University of Toronto. This probably is the first time that complex intonations have been treated in detail with regard to function. Article shows that no particular cadence type is peculiar to any particular sentence position. Writer believes that one might expect certain types of cadences to mark some styles more than others, and that "focus" is an aspect that must be considered. Kvavik would seem to be at the vanguard of work on Spanish intonation.

Polo Figueroa, Nicolás. Elementos de lingüística generativa. See item **4618**.

4520 Torreblanca, Máximo. Factores condicionadores de la distribución de los alófonos consonánticos españoles (AATSP/H, 63, 1980, p. 730–736)

Reviewing the findings of James W. Harris (Spanish Phonology), that allophone distribution depends to a degree on speed styles: *largo, andante, allegretto, presto,* with assimilation a big factor, writer maintains that articulatory tension of the speaker may vary considerably within one "style." One might add that dialectal variants and diachronic considerations complicate the picture even more!

4521 ——. La sílaba española y su evolución fonética (ICC/T, 35, 1980, p. 506–515)

Counters Bertil Malmberg's theory in *La estructura silábica del español* that Spanish evolves toward the open syllable, and points to Old Spanish *cibdat, noch, achac* and the Mexican tendency toward "apunts" (*apuntes*), "cochs" (*coches*). See article of Fernández-Sevilla (item **4518**).

SPANISH DIALECTOLOGY AND SOCIOLINGUISTICS

4522 Aguirre, Julio M. Influencia de la inmigración en el idioma de los argentinos (*in* La inmigración en la Argentina. San Miguel de Tucumán, Argentina: Universidad Nacional de Tucumán, Facultad de Filosofía y Letras, Centro de Historia y Pensamiento Argentinos, 1979, p. 207–231 [Publicación— Universidad Nacional de Tucumán; 1255])

Referring to Américo Castro's *Peculiaridad lingüística rioplatense* and the works of Rosenblat, Malmberg and Malaret, writer traces waves of 19th-century immigration, especially to Buenos Aires and nearby population centers, pointing out that between 1869–95, four foreigners entered the city for every three *criollos*. In Córdoba there was one for every 10 natives. The pronoun *vos* with its corresponding verb forms came into Buenos Aires after Independence and chiefly after 1852, he maintains. He ascribes to Italian influence some of the *lunfardo* jargon and many phonological traits of Argentine Spanish. It would seem that the author over-subscribes to the Italian influence. Many of the cases described are to be found in other parts of America where there is no Italian influence. They are more likely a part of the Castilian continuum!

4523 Alarcón, Alejandro. El habla popular de los jóvenes en la Ciudad de México. 2. ed. México: B. Costa-Amic, 1978. 158 p.; bibl.

An excellent picture of youth-talk in Mexico City in the late 1970s. Writer says that 50 percent of the terms have been invented by the young people, many are *pochismos*, involving border English, some are picardías. He presents in dialogue form what he claims is typical, and then lists hundreds of terms with definitions. This is a dialogue. Note how often the term *madre* occurs: "Tú sí eres a toda *madre*, mano, no como el Daniel que ya se le subió. Ya no quiere ni hablar. ¿Se le subió? pues, ¿en qué la gira? Está de jefe de personal en una fábrica y ya se cree la *mamá* de Tarzán, ya ni saluda. ¡Qué poca *madre*! ¿te acuerdas cuando andaba bien fregado y no tenía ni *madre* para comer? Pues, sí mano y todos le ayudábamos, pero pura *madre* que se acuerda.

4524 Amaro Gamboa, Jesús. El uayeismo en la cultura de Yucatán (UY/R, 21, nov./dic. 1979, p. 88–143)

Noting that the Maya word *uayé* means "here, in this place," author describes in the March/April number of this same journal how the independent spirit of Yucatán vis-à-vis the rest of Mexico can be referred to as *uayeísmo* and how anything typically Yucatec is *uayé*: *No puede estar más uayé ese traje que vistes.* Writer also shows a strong tendency in the Peninsula to use *apodos* for everyone.

4525 Amastae, Jon. On markedness and sociolinguistic variation (*in* Festschrift for Jacob Ornstein [see item **4546**] p. 10–17)

Amastae poses the intriguing query concerning the intersection of three aspects of language evolution in a bilingual community: language acquisition, sociolinguistic variation, and diachronic language change. A set of data may be interpreted in several ways according to the point of view of the linguist. Supposedly synchronic information may be of importance in what it reveals about both language acquisition and abstract structure.

4526 Anzadro C., Jorge. Influencia de la lengua rusa en el léxico del español en Cuba: 1959–1963 (UCLV/I, 64, set./dic. 1979, p. 65–109, tables)

Informative piece on the first real Slavic lexical incursion in the Hispanic world. Vocabulary collected from Cuban written sources, mainly daily papers. Examples: *camarada* (originally Spanish), *druzhba* (amistad), *cosmodromo*, *dacha* (finca de recreo), *sovnarjos* (consejo de economía). Spelling changes are interesting: *jruschov*.

4527 Bahamonde Silva, Mario. Diccionario de voces del norte de Chile. Santiago, Chile: Editorial Nascimento, 1978. 400 p.; bibl.

Terminology of the region that was once famous for its nitrate: geographic terms and toponyms, folkloric expressions and mining terminology. Many words are of indigenous origin, especially Quechua.

4528 Barrenechea, Ana María and **Mabel M. de Rosetti.** La voz pasiva en el español hablado en Buenos Aires (*in* Estudios lingüísticos y dialectológicos: temas hispánicos [see item **4544**] p. 61–72)

Based on 10 interviews of people 25

and older. Research tends to indicate in the first place that natives of Buenos Aires try to avoid the passive voice. Secondly, there was a marked preference for the *pasiva segura*: "se dictaron clases" and the *impersonal segura*: "se utiliza las visitas," and even ambiguous forms were popular: "En la calle se veía poca gente."

4529 Buffa, Josefa Luisa. Lo dialectal en Martiniano Leguizamón: a traves de *Montaraz* (UNL/U, 92, enero/abril 1979, p. 41–66, tables)

The author finds two main sources for the dialectal variants in *Montaraz*: gaucho, guaraní. The so-called *gaucho* influence is actually Spanish-colonial-rural and turns up in phonology (/h/ as ḥ), in syntax (*voseo*), and in vocabulary (*su mercé, vide, ansina* and a refined horse-color chart). Guaraní terms are chiefly nouns: *yaguareté, morajú*.

4530 Canfield, D. Lincoln. Spanish pronunciation in the Americas. Chicago: The University of Chicago Press, 1981. 118 p.; bibl.; index.

This compact volume puts the basics of American Spanish dialectology at the reader's fingertips. The introduction takes a historical viewpoint on the subject, pointing out the predominantly Andalusian origin of Spanish settlers in the New World, tracing the major developments in the phonology of Andalusian Spanish during the colonial period (1500–1800), and explaining the major American regional variations in terms of relative accessibility to trade with Spain—hence the basic *costeño*/highland dichotomy in American Spanish pronunciation. The main body of the book is a country-by-country survey, presenting in greater detail the phonological variations within each of the 18 Spanish-speaking republics, as well as Puerto Rico and the Spanish-speaking parts of the US. Information for each country is also displayed at a glance in a complete set of maps. Although the approach is primarily historical/geographical, additional factors such as the socioeconomic and "attitudinal" are cited where relevant. Author draws on a vast literature (the up-to-date bibliography cites over 300 items), as well as his own extensive field experience in most of the countries treated. Although the text is concise and to-the-point, it is often made more vivid by examples from the author's personal expe-

rience. [Steven Lee Hartman, Southern Illinois University]

4531 El Castellano hablado en Puno. Liliana Minaya Portella *et al.* Lima: Inide, 1975. 153 p.; ill. (Investigación El Lenguaje del niño peruano hispanohablante: Informe; no. 2)

Although rather poorly reproduced in mimeographed form, this is another in the series of studies of the Spanish of the Peruvian child. At the same time, it is one of the few on the phonology of the pronunciation of Spanish in Peru. The rare apico-alveolar /s/ is heard, the distinction between /y/ and /ḷ/ is maintained, and there is the tendency marked in so many places to assibilate /r̄/. In syntax several things are noted, among them the redundant object pronoun: "se lo han llevado los vientos al bote;" inversion is common: "Hay veces chocolate tomamos;" extra propositions seem to be popular "en ahí," "en allá."

4532 Chamberlain, Bobby J. Lexical similarities of lunfardo and giria (AATSP/H, 64, 1981, p. 417–423)

Describes the similarity between these counter-prestige jargons, which are spoken of as "specialized lexicons superimposed parasitically on their respective national dialects" (Argentine Spanish and Brazilian Portuguese). These modes of speech are used, it is said, to conceal, to render inaccessible, and to distinguish members of their community.

4533 Chiossone, Tulio. El lenguaje erudito, popular y folklórico de los Andes venezolanos. Caracas, Venezuela: Oficina Central de Información, 1977. 299 p.; bibl.; index (Biblioteca de autores y temas tachirenses; 69)

Based on the usage of Táchira, this examination of Andean vocabulary of Venezuela categorizes the lexicon into general Andean terms; classical Spanish words that survive, *andalucismos, germanía*; and terms that are like those of Santander, Colombia, nearby. Presents good list of proverbs and sayings and index of all words examined.

4534 Coluccio, Félix. Diccionario de voces y expresiones argentinas. Buenos Aires: Editorial Plus Ultra, 1979. 223 p.; bibl.

One of several recent vocabularies of popular Argentine speech (see items **4561** and **4593**). Sources of this author's terms are written: 10 *obras gauchescas*, six daily papers, four from Buenos Aires. He tends to classify terms as *vulgar, popular*, and *lunfardo*, and most seem to be of rural origins.

4535 Corzo Espinosa, César. Palabras de origen indígena en el español de Chiapas. Portada, Fidel Corzo Rivera. México, D.F.: Costa-Amic Editores, 1978. 326 p.; bibl.; index.

Follow-up of author's *Toponimia chiapaneca*, 1976. Good collection of words of Indian origin, with informative but somewhat rambling discussions of sources and usage. Interestingly enough, although the area is Maya territory, most of the words are of Náhuatl origin, testimony to the Spanish movements into Central America shortly after the conquest of Mexico. Some of the writer's best sources are 16th-century missionaries and chroniclers: Molina, Sahagún, de las Casas, Díaz del Castillo.

4536 Costa Sánchez, Manuel and **Susana Carreras Gómez.** Algunas características acústico-articulatorias de la vibrante múltiple en el español de Cuba (UCLV/I, 65, enero/abril 1980, p. 99–114, bibl., ill., photographs, tables)

Rather important confirmation of the impression that one has had of the /r̄/ of Cuban Spanish: 1) it has generally less articulatory tension than the standard; 2) it tends to have two vibrations instead of three or four; and 3) it tends to lose voiced quality.

4537 Cotton, Eleanor Greet and **John M. Sharp.** Neologistic palatal *ar* verbs in Mexican-American Spanish (*in* Festschrift for Jacob Ornstein [see item **4546**] p. 38–60)

Mexican-American Spanish has many more neologisms in *ear* than Mexican Spanish, and they are formed on both Spanish and English roots. They compare the process of adaptation to the one that took place when the Spaniards absorbed Indian terms in the early colonial period. Some extreme cases are cited: *bompear, güeldear, mopear, blofear*.

4538 Cruz Brache, José Antonio. 5600 [i.e. Cinco mil seiscientos] refranes y frases de uso común entre los dominicanos. Portada, Nicolás Pichardo. Santo Domingo: Editorial Galaxia: distribuidores exclusivos, Difusora Nacional, 1978. 311 p.; bibl.

Good account of vocabulary of the Dominican Republic, alphabetically arranged.

As is commonly the case, it includes hundreds of terms heard in other Hispanophone populations.

4539 Dalbor, John B. Observations on present-day *seseo* and *ceceo* in Spain (AATSP/H, 63, 1980, p. 5–19)

Although the data for this article came from a relatively short visit to sections of Southern Spain, principally Sevilla and Granada, the recorded perceptions of the author are very important links in the long history of the development of the Spanish sibilants through the centuries and hence help explain the status of American Spanish sibilants vis-à-vis those of Spain. Most descriptions of Andalusian Spanish pronunciation have been written by Spaniards, who hear and think in terms of their own apico-alveolar /s/ and interdental /Θ/. The sibilants of most of America are those of Andalusia: predorsal and coronal, unlike either of the "Castilian" sounds.

4540 Donni de Mirande, Nélida Esther. El estudio del español hablado en la Argentina: marco teórico y metodológico (UNL/U, 91, sept./dic. 1978, p. 25–39)

In spite of the fact that Argentina has a good natural background and very sound precepts for language research and teaching, not enough is being done today because of lack of *instrumentos* and *recursos*. The writer, one of a group of distinguished women linguists of the area, reviews the fine history of linguistic studies, with Buenos Aires and Montevideo as centers for the work of Amado Alonso, Rosenblat, Rona, and Vidal de Battini, and in recent years, Fontanella, Donni and others. The area offers, she believes, good examples of sociolinguistic phenomena. In fact, she and Fontanella have contributed much to this type of analysis.

4541 ———. Fonología del español en Rosario, Argentina (ICC/T, 33:3, sept./dic. 1978, p. 407–421, diagrams)

Excellent description of the pronunciation of what could be termed the *lengua nacional*, since it follows the Buenos Aires model. The writer and her colleague, María Beatriz Fontanella de Weinberg, have produced some of the best studies of Spanish sociolinguistic phenomena and have opened the door to research in "attitudinal" variants in Spanish. Her sound descriptions of Rosario Spanish are based on interviews with people of three age groups: 25–35; 36–55; 55 and older. She points out that the area has become one of high social mobility. A further division is made on the basis of education: *culto, popular, vulgar.* Her findings made a good depiction of a language in the course of change. The /y/ of the area which has been thought of as [ž], is gradually becoming [š]. The latter sound is practically universal among the young. It is also becoming popular among women and among the well educated. The /f/ is often bilabial, especially among the *popular* and *vulgar* classes, and *sg* and *sb* (*rasgo, esbelto*) tend to be [p] also. The /s/ syllable final tends to be [h] in the *culto* group, but is often [ø] in the lower groups.

4542 Doviak, Martin J. and Allison Hudson-Edwards. Phonological variation in Chicano English: word-final (z)—devoicing (*in* Festschrift for Jacob Ornstein [see item 4546] p. 82–96)

Study of the English pronunciation of 28 fourth-grade Chicanos to determine reasons for the unvoicing of /z/ in such words as *tigers, washes.* Several factors were considered: phonological, morphological, content, style, social situation, sex, language dominance. In a tendency that is rather general, linguistic factors would seem to be most important, especially phonological constraints.

4543 Elerick, Charles. On the form of bilingual grammars: the phonological component (*in* Festschrift for Jacob Ornstein [see item 4546] p. 104–113)

In spite of the needs of ethnic minorities and at least a decade of interest in the problems of bilingualism, there has been no sustained effort to construct a model of bilingual competence to serve as a point of departure in the construction of a restricted demonstration that might represent certain aspects of the competence of a Spanish/English bilingual.

4544 Estudios lingüísticos y dialectológicos: temas hispánicos. Ana Marí Barrenechea *et al.* s.l.: Hachette, 1979. 147 p.; bibl.; graphs (Colección Hachette universidad)

All but one of the articles of this volume were the result of investigations undertaken as a part of the *Proyecto de estudio coordinado de la norma lingüística culta de las principales ciudades de Iberoamérica y de la Península Ibérica* (see *HLAS 42:4537*) whose overall director has been Juan M.

Lope Blanch of Mexico. The director for the Buenos Aires area is Ana María Barrenechea, several of whose contributions appear in this volume, and two of which are reviewed in this section (see items **4528** and **4610**). The research of the Argentine linguists shows much background reading in the phenomena discussed, an acquaintance with European and North American linguistic research of recent years, and an objective approach to problems.

4545 Ferreccio Podestá, Mario. Las fuentes de la filología chilena; pt. 1, El Catálogo anónimo de 1843 (UC/AT, 440, 2. semestre, 1979, p. 39–59)

The anonymous *catálogo* is examined as one source in what will be an effort to publish sources of knowledge of the evolution of Spanish in Chile. Items that are among those found are: *arbañil, auja, Butiérrez, durarno, la idioma, naide, salí, zarza* (salsa).

4546 A Festschrift for Jacob Ornstein: studies in general linguistics and sociolinguistics. Edited by Edward L. Blansitt, Jr. and Richard V. Teschner. Rowley, MA: Newbury House Publishers, 1980. 331 p.; bibl.

Includes a biography of this authority on Spanish of the Southwestern US, a list of his contributions in the form of books, articles, in scholarly journals and anthologies, reviews and monographs. The articles that make up the volume are generally very good and represent the efforts of several American and Hispanic investigators who have been interested especially in Spanish in contact with English. Some of the chapters are reviewed herewith (see items **4525, 4537, 4542–4543, 4563, 4571–4572, 4584, 4588–4589, 4592, 4595** and **4598**).

4547 Flórez, Luis. Apuntes de español: pronunciación, ortografía, gramática, léxico, extranjerismos, el habla en la radio y la televisión, enseñanza del idioma y de la gramática en Colombia. Bogotá: Instituto Caro y Cuervo, 1977. 229 p. (Publicaciones del Instituto Caro y Cuervo: Series minor; 21)

Collection of "columns" written for the Bogotá daily *El Tiempo* with interesting popular usage heard in Colombia. Among several cases of hypercorrection is the use of *séktima* for *séptima* when speaking of

Bogotá's famous Carrera Séptima. One rather surprising case is the occurrence of the word *hasta* used as it is in Mexico with negative connotation: *hasta mañana llega.*

4548 ———. Datos de morfología y habla culta informal bogotana (ICC/T, 35, 1980, p. 1–79)

Compilation that author refers to as a *microinventario* of materials collected during the surveys for the *Atlas lingüístico* (see *HLAS 38:6063*) between 1950–79. Interesting cases of gender deviation: *tipa, marchanta, culebro, sodomisto;* of number, *papases, políticas, hace tiempos;* the expected *su merced* in Cundinamarca and Boyacá. Good collection of speech informalities in the possessives, the demonstratives, the relatives, and even in the numerals.

4549 ———. Muestra de formas nominales en uso (ICC/T, 34, 1979, p. 1–50)

Survey was done as part of the work on the *Atlas lingüístico* (see *HLAS 38:6063*) in 1975, 1976, 1977, in many places in Colombia but especially in Bogotá. Although this is simply a sample, it shows the rich and varied system of prefixes and suffixes of Spanish, diminutives, verbal derivatives, *gentilicios*, adjective-noun combinations. The study is as much a semantic one as morphological. Contains alphabetical list.

4550 Fontanella de Weinberg, María Beatriz. La oposición "cantes/cantés" en el español de Buenos Aires (ICC/T, 34, 1979, p. 72–83, bibl.)

Although the alternation of *cantes* and *cantés* is common in the Spanish of Ecuador and perhaps of Santiago del Estero, Argentina, Buenos Aires is not thought of as a community that uses any "tú" form. Fontanella indicates that in the latter city the unaccented form is thought of as present subjunctive and the accented, negative imperative, a case of semantic nuances reflected in grammatical forms.

4551 Gamero Idiáquez, Ibrahím. Mamíferos de mi tierra (AHL/B, 21:21, febrero 1978, p. 15–55)

Good example of regional lexicon, replete with popular etymology and indigenous terms. Large part of the vocabulary is common to El Salvador and some to all of Central America.

4552 García González, José. Acerca de la pronunciación de "R" and "L" implosivas en el español de Cuba: variantes e influencias (UCLV/I, 65, enero/abril 1980, p. 115–127, bibl.)

Writer shows that there may be as many as six different manifestations of the implosive /l/ or /r/: *porque* may be [porke], [polke], [poɫke], [poike], [pokke], [poɽke]. Popular misconceptions have ascribed these deviations to African influence. The writer correctly attributes them to the Andalusian origins of American Spanish.

4553 Garro, Joaquín. Habla que el tiempo se lleva? Diseño de la portada, Osvaldo Salas. San José, Costa Rica: Editorial Costa Rica, 1978. 129 p.

Exceptionally good depiction of language change, especially in the realm of vocabulary, during some 50 years. Writer says that in youth-talk hundreds of expressions of the 1920s and 1930s are forgotten. No young man today has the opportunity to "tomarse un trinquis en una taquilla con un pato hablantín, mucho menos si es de ñapa de choya o de gorra." Today he goes to a "centro licorero, jardín cervecero o a un bar, con un maicero o un chavalo pura vida." The *conductor* of the bus has become a *cobrador.* Even *ocho reales* sounds out of date.

4554 Geoffroy Rivas, Pedro. El español que hablamos en El Salvador. 3. ed. San Salvador: Ministerio de Educación, Dirección de Publicaciones, 1976. 117 p.

Although the writer does give a fairly good list of *nahuatlismos* that form a part of the lexicon of modern El Salvador, his explanations of regional pronunciations indicate that he has not steeped himself in the literature on the subject. The tendency that he exhibits is only too common among Spanish Americans who may not have read "beyond their borders," a tendency to attribute to the Indians the dialectal features of their own languages.

4555 ———. La lengua salvadoreña. San Salvador: Ministerio de Educación, Dirección de Publicaciones, 1978. 131 p.

Writer insists on calling the language *salvadoreño* rather than *español*, and to justify this designation, he seems to attribute even the phonology to influence of the local *nahuat* dialect of Uto-Aztecan language family. Unfortunately, practically all of the traits of Salvadorean phonology are to be found in other Spanish dialects where there is no *Nahuat* influence: [bwir] for *voy a ir* or [iβír] for *iba a ir*; [díya] for *día* are to be found in other Spanish-speaking areas. His vocabulary of *salvadoreñismos*, is quite good.

4556 Godínez, Manuel, Jr. An acoustic study of Mexican and Brazilian Portuguese vowels (AATSP/H, 64, 1981, p. 594–600)

Using recorded data from six informants from Tijuana, Mexico, for the Spanish, and four Brazilians from São Paulo, two from Rio and two from Espírito Santo for the Portuguese, writer shows that the traditional tongue-arching explanation of vowel quality is misleading. Spectrographic analyses indicate that vocal tract length, position of the tongue, and lip configuration are all involved, and quality is achieved in different ways by different speakers. One is reminded that this theory was first advanced in 1928 by Oscar Russell.

4557 Gordon, Alan M. Notas sobre la fonética del castellano en Bolivia (*in* Actas del Sexto Congreso Internacional de Hispanistas, Toronto, 1977. Toronto: University of Toronto, Department of Spanish and Portuguese, 1980, p. 349–352)

Although rather limited in scope by the circumstances of a *congreso*, this paper constitutes the first good description of the phonology of Bolivian Spanish, concerning which there have been many misconceptions. The writer links the origins of the settlers with the modern dichotomy in pronunciation, on the one side the speech of the *cordillera* and the *yungas* and on the other the vast *llanos*. He also convinces us that all Bolivians make the distinction between /y/ and /ʎ/. Apico-alveolar /s/ is common in the highlands as it is in Antioquia, Colombia. The *llanos* generally have *costeño* tendencies.

4558 Granda, Germán de. Algunos rasgos fonéticos del español paraguayo atribuibles a interferencia guaraní (Revista Española de Lingüística [Editorial Gredos, Madrid] 10, 1980, p. 339–349)

Testing the belief that languages in contact tend to amplify their systems, Granda finds that the Spanish of Paraguay has developed new allophones, new phonetic traits and an extension of the paradigmatic distribution. He refers to the event as multiple causation.

4559 ———. Calcos sintácticos del guaraní en el español del Paraguay (CM/NRFH, 28:2, 1979, p. 267–286)

This prolific contributor to languages-in-contact knowledge looks at the effects of Guaraní syntax and semantics on the Spanish of Paraguay. The sense loans he describes are in a population which is perhaps 48 percent bilingual, he says, 45 percent monolingual (Guaraní) and 4.4 percent monolingual Spanish: "Ya trabajé todo ya;" "no miré todo a ese muchacha," where *todo* would have a meaning similar to English *all*; "vení un poco, que te llama el patrón," where *un poco* is a phrase of courtesy; "nos dijo para venir hoy," sounds like a translation of an English-speaking student of Spanish.

4560 ———. Italianismos léxicos en el español paraguayo (ICC/T, 35, 1980, p. 258–287)

Indicating that Italian influences in Paraguay go back to the Renaissance, as one might expect, then there is the great stream of immigrants by way of Buenos Aires in the late 19th century and in the 20th. His long list and indicated scope of usage within the country include many items that are very common to the US and Europe: *mafia, lasaña, salami, brócoli, ricota.*

4561 Guarnieri, Juan Carlos. Diccionario del lenguaje rioplatense. Montevideo: Ediciones de la Banda Oriental, 1979. 199 p.

Author describes well the history of the two popular speeches of Argentina, gauchesco and lunfardo. Many elements of the first of these were in the vocabulary of the Spanish conquistadores, supplemented by sojourns in the Caribbean, Mexico, Peru, before getting to the Río de la Plata area. It is essentially country language. Lunfardo is a city dialect or jargon, an anti-prestige speech of *delincuentes porteños*, of rather obscure origins, but laced with Italianisms beginning in the late 19th century. His descriptions of typical phonology of the dialects are not too accurate in terms of descriptive phonetics, and the long vocabulary has a great many terms that are heard in several other parts of Latin America and are not simply *argentinismos*.

4562 Hammond, Robert M. The velar nasal in rapid Cuban Spanish (*in* Colloquium on Spanish and Luso-Brazilian Linguistics [see item **4503**] p. 19–36)

Several dialectal variants of American Spanish as well as Andalusian have been characterized by a velar allophone of /n/ in word final position or final before a pause. Using five hours of recorded tape of 21 native Cubans now living in Miami, and representing all Cuban provinces except Pinar del Río, Hammond finds that the tendency goes far beyond the usual, and Cubans are apt to velarize the nasal in almost any environment: absolute final, word final within a breath group, syllable final within a word, and even syllable initial position. Furthermore, in place of velarization of the nasal, about 33 percent simply nasalize the vowel before the /n/.

4563 Hudson-Edwards, Alan and **Garland D. Bills.** Intergenerational language shift in an Albuquerque barrio (*in* Festschrift for Jacob Ornstein [see item **4546**] p. 139–158)

In a state that has the highest retention of Spanish in the general population, a study was made in the Martineztown-Santa Barbara section of Albuquerque. A vast difference was shown between the young and the old in the retention of Spanish (44 percent compared with 87 percent). The encroachment of English on the scene would seem to indicate that Spanish will not survive forever.

4564 Jonz, Joh G. Language and la academia, if English works, ¿por qué se emplea español? (The Journal of Ethnic Studies [Western Washington State College, College of Ethnic Studies, Bellingham] 5:4, Winter 1978, p. 65–79, bibl.)

Examination of Chicano nationalism through a look at the ethnocentric and egocentric expression of Mexican-Americans, who, although they have been educated in English in US public schools, write and speak of themselves as *la Nueva Raza, el pueblo*, and of each other as *carnal, vate, manito*; and of those who may be turning to Anglo as *regalados, agringados, vendidos*. All of this is recognized, he says, as attempts to survive the social pressures, but the irony is that it is usually expressed in English with interjections of Spanish.

4565 Latino language and communicative behavior. Edited by Richard P. Durán. Norwood, N.J.: Ablex Pub. Corp., 1981. 363 p.; ill. (Advances in discourse processes; v. 6)

Uses psychological approach to examine Spanish-English bilingual situation. Pt. 1 looks into Hispanic trends in code switching and the possible sociolinguistic reasons for this speech behavior. Pt. 2 takes up communication and cognition in home, community and school settings. Contributors include several authorities in the field. Editor expresses need for sensitivity to sociocultural and language background factors which mediate the Chicano's proficiency in Spanish and English and in general communicative behavior. Ornstein and Peñalosa demonstrate the extreme heterogeneity of the Spanish-English contact situations of the Southwest. Reyes and Lavandera bring forth evidence that the Spanish of bilingual informants interviewed shows an essential mastery of Spanish rules for word formation and grammar and at the same time shows English influence. Valdés believes that code switching can be used as a strategy either to mitigate or aggravate. Zentella and Genishi think that code switching may be related to relative proficiency in the languages, to the teacher's proficiency and to social prestige. Huerta and Macías maintain that the switching has the function of signaling change from casual to formal. In a study of Puerto Ricans of Harlem, Poplack finds that code switching may indicate syntactic constraints in intersentential and intrasentential utterances. Marcos and Trujillo, psychiatrists, write of the quality of communication in diagnostic and therapeutic mental health settings. Lindholm and Padilla write of communication in mother-child discourses among 12 Mexican-American families in a home setting and reveal an elaborate coordination between good knowledge of the topic discussed and the grammatical form of the utterances. Both Durán's chapter and that of De Avila and Duncan stress the fact that high proficiency in two languages is coupled with stimulation of cognitive abilities to solve verbal deductive reasoning problems in either language.

4566 Lawton, David. Code-shifting in Puerto Rican Spanish/English (LING, 17:3/4, 1979, p. 257–265, bibl., table)

Spanish and English are contact languages in Puerto Rico and both languages function under social and cultural constraints, alternating at times. Writer suggests that there may be incipient creolization and he examines the phonological, lexical, and syntactic conditions of contact that can provide insights into the nature of linguistic change and the role of social constraints. Such examples as "Lo compro cash," "Jim está upstairs" and "María don't assist classes" may suggest that not only static situations but perhaps cases of dynamic change can help in the study of the process of creolization. He refers to those who do this type of code-switching as *Neorricans*.

4567 Lope Blanch, Juan M. La interferencia lingüística: un ejemplo del español yucateco (ICC/T, 35, 1980, p. 80–97)

Writer cites many cases of final /n/ as [m] in Yucatán Spanish. This had not been noted by Suárez (item **4590**). In the *encuestas* of Manuel Alvar, who worked with the Mexican project, final /n/ was [m] in about 20 percent of the cases: *jamóm, tacóm, sacristám*. Also reported, as one might anticipate, [ŋ] and in many cases just a nasalized vowel.

4568 ———. Investigaciones sobre dialectología mexicana. México: Universidad Nacional Autónoma de México, Instituto de Investigaciones Filológicas, 1979. 197 p.; bibl.; maps (Publicaciones del Centro de Lingüística Hispánica; 8)

In 1967 Lope Blanch initiated the project that has been designed to indicate the various dialect zones of Mexico. Many investigators have been working with him and under his direction in this project, and one of the concerns of all involved has been the frequency of polymorphism in the phonology and in the lexicon of that country, and to an extent in morphosyntactic phenomena. As a consequence, he insists on interviewing several people in each locale that is studied linguistically. The present volume has as its chief purpose the description of varieties of articulation and expression that exist in Mexico. Using Yucatán as a point of reference, the writer presents some of the cases of polymorphism that he and his researchers have found: /f/ as [f] and as [p]; /č/ as [č] and as [š]; /y/ as [y] as [ž]; /r̄/ as [r̄] and as [ř]; final /e/ as [e] and as [i]; indicative for subjunctive, and interesting cases of variety in

lexicon. As an example of vocabulary variation, he cites the term *Benjamín, hijo menor*, which turns up as *socoyote, šocoyote, jocoyote* and *babi, šunco, chunco, cóyotl*. Other words that vary a great deal geographically are: *pavo (guajolote, chompipe, cócono); monedas (suelto, feria); adehala (pilón, ñapa, encima)*. Maps show distribution of variants. In this same volume, Lope Blanch writes of Indian influence in the linguistic norm of Mexico and of English terms that have become part of the language of that country, dividing them by categories of general, moderate and little usage. These last two articles appeared in the *Proyecto de estudio de la norma lingüística culta* (see *HLAS 42:4537*).

4569 López Morales, Humberto. Velarización de /r̄/ en el español de Puerto Rico: índices de actitud y creencias (*in* Homenaje a Fernando Antonio Martínez [see item **4508**] p. 193–214)

Using Tomás Navarro's *El español en Puerto Rico* (1948, see *HLAS 14:2595*) as a point of departure, the Cuban linguist conducts a survey among students and faculty of the Facultad de Humanidades of the University of Puerto Rico on the merits of velar /r̄/ (It can't be accepted because . . . ; it shouldn't be rejected because . . .). Only those from the South of the Island were solidly behind acceptance. Those from the off-shore islands were all negative for acceptance, and most Puerto Ricans were negative. In fact, the pronunciation is very common today and may be gaining ground.

4570 Lozano, Anthony Gerard. Aztec traces in modern Spanish (AATSP/H, 64, 1981, p. 410–417)

An explanation of how the Náhuatl language became the *lingua franca* of Central Mexico and beyond, and a demonstration of how often the Mexican calls on this language background to express himself in Spanish.

4571 ———. English tense development in a Spanish-dominant child (*in* Festschrift for Jacob Ornstein [see item **4546**] p. 174–181)

An interesting study of pidginization in the acquisition of English by a 14 month-old child during the period Oct. 1977–Nov. 1978. Difficulty with the past and future tenses especially. Example: "One day this school snow."

4572 Matluck, Joseph H. Bilingualism of Mexican-American children: language characteristics (*in* Festschrift for Jacob Ornstein [see item **4546**] p. 211–228)

In a dialect that is essentially that of Northern Mexico, English-caused errors are common in Spanish tenses, gender, agreement, negation, case, interrogation.

4573 Mendoza Cuba, Aida. Sistema fonológico del castellano y variantes regionales. Con la colaboración de María del Carmen Cuba. Lima: Inide, Ministerio de Educación, Instituto Nacional de Investigación y Desarrollo de la Educación Augusto Salazar Bondy, Subdirección de Investigaciones Educacionales, 1976. 152 p.; bibl.; ill. (Investigación El Lenguaje del niño peruano hispanohablante; Informe parcial; no. 3 [pt. 2])

Very good study of regional pronunciation in Peru: Cuzco, Trujillo, Ica, Piura, Tacna, Huancayo, Cajamarca, Iquitos, Ayacucho. Lima is evidently considered a city of transients. The study shows more variants than had been realized, e.g., four different articulations of /s/: dorso-alveolar, coronal, apico-dental, apico-alveolar, the latter in the area near Bolivia, where this type of "Castilian" sound is heard in highland cities.

4574 Mesa Alonso, Milvia and **Nancy Porrero Marín.** La preposición de: algunas particularidades sobre su uso en el habla culta cubana (UCLV/I, 63, mayo/agosto 1979, p. 151–175, bibl.)

Study undertaken at the Universidad de las Villas, Las Villas, Cuba, in which the writers used 101 informants: 44 women and 57 men, most of whom were between the ages of 18 and 30. Records were kept of the instability of the preposition *de*, situations in which it was added where not needed, cases of loss, and cases of substitution of something else for *de*. Typical phrases were: "Ella dice de que vendrá; "Estamos convencidos que;" "Además que llegó tarde;" "Independientemente a eso;" "Hay situaciones de que no asiste."

4575 Minaya Portella, Liliana. Descripción sintáctica, la frase nominal en doce ciudades del país. Con la colaboración de Angélica Kameya Kamiya. Lima: Inide, 1976. 168 p.; bibl.; maps (Investigación El Lenguaje del niño peruano hispanohablante: Informe parcial; no. 3 [pt. 11])

Special study of the noun phrase in Peru, with maps of the country to indicate occurrence of phenomena. Principal places Huancayo, Ayacucho, Huaraz, Puno, Iquitos, Arequipa, Trujillo, Tacna.

4576 Montes Giraldo, José Joaquín. Un rasgo dialectal del occidente de Colombia: -n -m (*in* Homenaje a Fernando Antonio Martínez [see item **4508**] p. 215–220)

Good substudy based on the surveys made for the *Atlas lingüístico y etnográfico de Colombia* or *ALEC* (see *HLAS 38:6063*). In the territory from Quibdó in the Chocó to Bolívar in Cauca, there is a tendency to pronounce final /n/ as [m]: *pantalom, copetom, pam, corazom, cajom* in orthographic terms. The tendency is most marked in Cali, Palmira and Morales. The origin of the trait is not known, but Montes believes it must be of Peninsular origin.

4577 Mora Monroy, Siervo Custodio. Algunos zoónimos aplicados al hombre en el español coloquial de Colombia (ICC/T, 35, 1980, p. 143–151)

Collection made in 1979, mostly in Bogotá and environs and mostly among people of middle and lower sociocultural levels. Although many are common to general Spanish and even to other languages, such as *avispa, burro, águila, vaca sagrada*, there are some apparently limited to Colombia.

4578 Murray, Stephen O. Lexical and institutional elaboration: the species homosexual in Guatemala (IU/AL, 22:4, April 1980, p. 177–185, bibl.)

Using the institutionally complete situation of the homosexual in San Francisco as a point of departure, Murray states that separate specialized institutions for homosexuals generally have not developed in the large cities of the Hispanic American countries, including the largest city in the Western Hemisphere, Mexico, D.F. His study is lexically based and was done in Guatemala City, using 10 informants who might have homosexual tendencies and who would talk about the terms *de ambiente*. Although he gathered what represents a proliferation of vocabulary, there was not the institutional and cultural importance that one might expect. One might think, without some investigation, that the species doesn't exist in Mesoamerica.

4579 Ortiz Arellano, Carlos. Ecuador, sociedad y lenguaje. Cuenca, Ecuador: Departamento de Difusión Cultural, Universidad de Cuenca, 1979. 163 p. (Ensayo; 8)

Author laments what he perceives as an attitude of submission nurtured over 300 years of being a colony. He uses the language to show that the next bilingualism may be Spanish-English rather than Spanish-Quechua, because everybody wants to have what the English-speaking people have.

4580 Poplack, Shana. Deletion and disambiguation in Puerto Rican Spanish (LSA/L, 56:2, June 1980, p. 371–385, bibl.)

Writer demonstrates how functional factors come into play to offset consonant deletion in the Spanish of Puerto Rico and subsequent ambiguity, especially in plural situations and in verb forms. In a sentence such as "Bailaban unas nenas bien bonitas" there are several elements that may be deleted or modified by dialect traits or assimilation. Morphemic changes tend to grow to inhibit syntactic deviations and ambiguities.

4581 Porral, José Enrique. La palatalización española y sus implicaciones sociolingüísticas (ICC/T, 33, 1978, p. 515–522)

Article deals with language acquisition and change during the age period 18–36 months and the synchronic palatalization in infant speech that often leads to the formation of nicknames among adults. Sounds that are especially common to this age of growth are [č], [t'], [y], [š], [ñ]: *sucio* becomes [čučo]; *Julio* becomes [yuyo]; *Patricia* [t'iša], hence such nicknames as *Pancho, Tacho, Chenca, Gayo, Toño*, etc.

4582 Prudencio Claure, Alfonso. Diccionario del cholo ilustrado. Portada, Carmen Baptista. La Paz: Ojo Publicaciones, 1978. 295 p.

As the author indicates, this is a vocabulary of the *mestizaje indo-español* of Bolivia. It contains many quechismos, as one might expect, and has been composed with a good sense of humor. Author notes that the *cholos* of Bolivia call all Chileans *rotos*, regardless of class, because they are still longing for that ocean that Chile took from them. The wife is often spoken of as *la gorda*, a *taco* is a person "de mucha cultura alcohólica," men must have their *viernes de soltero* (a night with the boys). If they aren't allowed to, they are *muñequeados*. A *jodido*

is not a victim, as is usually the case, but one who bothers or criticizes.

4583 Ramírez Fajardo, César A. Lengua madre. Managua, Nicaragua: El Pez y la Serpiente, 1975. 109 p.

An interesting approach to the task of forming a lexical corpus. The writer, a Nicaraguan pediatrician, collects terms used by mothers who bring their children to be treated or diagnosed, and the result is one of the richest and most up-to-date records of the speech of that Central American country. It is especially rich in similes and metaphors, as well as onomatopoeia. Words of the Nahuat dialect of Uto-Aztecan are still heard, although the language is practically extinct.

4584 Resnick, Melvyn C. El lenguaje de la publicidad en Puerto Rico: usos y efectos del inglés (*in* Festschrift for Jacob Ornstein [see item **4546**] p. 249–264)

The very extensive use of English in advertising, especially on signs and shop names, makes one wonder how many Puerto Ricans understand what is indicated. Interviews with three generations seem to show that among young people well over half understand the advertisements, fewer than half of the old people know what is meant and the average would be about half.

4585 Rivas Torres, José E. Voces populares del sur merideño. Mérida, Venezuela: Universidad de los Andes, Consejo de Publicaciones, 1980. 78 p.

The classical conservatism and *hidalguización* of Venezuela's Andes is depicted lexically in an alphabetical list of terms, many of which are to be found in other parts of Latin America. The aspiration indicated by Old Spanish orthographic *h* is preserved in *jeder, joyo, joder, jalar*, and the typical Venezuelan *aguaite* reminds us of the Gothic origin of so many *arcaísmos*.

4586 Rodríguez, Oralia and **Rodney Williamson.** Diferencias sociales en el lenguaje: el caso de narraciones de niños mexicanos de seis años (*in* Actas del Sexto Congreso Internacional de Hispanistas, Toronto, 1977. Toronto: University of Toronto, Department of Spanish and Portuguese, 1980, p. 606–609)

In an effort to contribute to the studies of child speech, the writers had carried on a project in the Mexico City area involving children of six–seven years of age and of classes: *media* (sub-professional), *obrera* and *marginal*. Several interaction discourse experiments were performed involving narration, discussion, instructions one to another, *plática libre*, etc. The many variables notèd attest to the strong influence of the child's home background, and the *marginales* weren't the worst in everything!

4587 Ross, L. Ronald. La supresión de /y/ en el español chicano (AATSP/H, 63, 1980, p. 552–560)

Writer refers to the tendency heard among Mexican-Americans to vocalize or eliminate /y/ in certain intervocalic situations. He reviews the findings of Oroz concerning Chiloé, Toscano on coastal Ecuador, and Bowen on points in New Mexico. In several sections of the Spanish-speaking world *capilla* becomes *capía; billete, biete,* etc. Believing that definitions of occurrence have been inadequate, Ross writes: "Depende principalmente de la presencia en el contexto de una vocal que tenga el rasgo posterior."

4588 Solé, Carlos A. Language usage patterns among a young generation of Cuban-Americans (*in* Festschrift for Jacob Ornstein [see item **4546**] p. 274–281)

Results of a 1975 survey of Cuban-Americans in Miami. Informants were between the ages of 15 and 18, 67 percent born in Havana, 12 percent in US. 75 percent considered Spanish their first language in preschool days, now 26 percent to 78 percent still claim Spanish proficiency. Author links shift to upward social mobility, which he says is greater than among Mexicans and Puerto Ricans, and this is accompanied by a high degree of acculturation.

4589 Solé, Yolanda Russinovich. The Spanish/English contact situation in the Southwest (*in* Festschrift for Jacob Ornstein [see item **4546**] p. 282–291)

The writer says that language is a behavioral manifestation bound to the sociocultural sphere in which it takes place, and the psychological matrix from which it emanates. Mexican-American English and Southwestern Spanish vary from community to community according to the interpersonal influences whereby reality is mediated to the individual. They are not stable and cohesive systems.

4590 Suárez, Víctor Manuel. El español que se habla en Yucatán: apuntamientos filológicos. 2. ed. corr. y aumentada. Mérida, Yucatán, México: Ediciones de la Universidad de Yucatán, 1979. 194 p.; bibl.; maps.

Although this second edition of the 1945 book is announced as "corregida y aumentada," and although the author admits in the prologue that movies, radio, television and many *forasteros,* principally from Mexico City, have modified the language in certain ways since the first edition, few changes are noted, and his original sources seem to be about the same. Like many dialectal treatises on the Latin American scene, this study emanates from the *Cuestionario lingüístico* of Tomás Navarro, as far as approach is concerned. Maya influence in the Spanish of Yucatán is noted, even in Phonology, and it is interesting to note certain usages that are to be found in other countries: *saludes* (Colombia); [diya] for *día* (Central America).

4591 Terrell, Tracy D. Final /s/ in Cuban Spanish (AATSP/H, 62, 1979, p. 599–612)

Noting that most writers have maintained that aspiration and deletion of /s/ syllable final is socially and stylistically motivated, Terrell makes a case for several other factors: phonological environment, word length, grammatical function, position within the word. Using IBM cards and a coding system, he shows that while the overall situation is sibilant, 18 percent; aspiration, 61 percent; deletion, 21 percent; in the internal cases it is: sibilant; three percent; aspiration, 97 percent; deletion, zero percent. The work to date is "just a beginning," he says.

4592 ———. The problem of comparing variable rules across dialects: some examples from Spanish (*in* Festschrift for Jacob Ornstein [see item **4546**] p. 303–313)

To characterize the phonology of dialects it is necessary to determine the complex system of constraints which may operate on a single variable phonological rule. Aspiration and deletion of word final /s/ may involve both linguistic and extralinguistic factors: phonological context as well as sociolinguistic forces. Author gives data on deletion in Cuba, Puerto Rico, Panama, Caracas, Buenos Aires. In Caracas the trait would seem to be far more advanced than in Buenos Aires.

4593 Teruggi, Mario E. Panorama del lunfardo: génesis y esencia de las hablas coloquiales urbanas. 2. ed. ampliada y corr. Buenos Aires: Editorial Sudamericana, 1978. 383 p.; bibl.; index.

The second edition of a careful examination of Lunfardo, with new definitions, restrictions, generalizations, morphological changes, and loan words. Origins of this antiprestige social dialect are, according to Teruggi, Spanish *germanía*, Italian, French, English, Indian languages, and occupational jargon. See items **4534** and **4561**.

4594 Tumler, Tilman. La complejidad sintáctica en el castellano andino (Iberoromania [Max Niemeyer Verlag, Tübingen, FRG] 8, 1978, p. 90–102, diagram, table)

Using compositions written by students of the Andean region, a study of syntactic complexity was made, not with relation to the "standard" but on a differential basis. Three of the compositions are shown, one written by a person of the upper class, one by a student of the "popular" class and one by a *marginal*. The Quechua and Aymará influence is hard to find except in spelling and an occasional gerundive, but on the basis of prepositions, conjunctions, relatives, the *marginal* turns out to be the most complicated, although it took the student three times as long to write a shorter composition than the "élite."

4595 Valdés-Fallis, Guadalupe. Is codeswitching interference, integration, or neither? (*in* Festschrift for Jacob Ornstein [see item **4546**] p. 314–325)

Writer, who is eminently qualified to write on the topic, shows the difficulties of attempting a strict classification of codeswitching, given the varying interpretations of both of the concepts of interference and integration. In some cases bits of one language actually become a part of the other, and the person who says "Tengo que reduce" exhibits no morphological or phonological overlap. Analyses have been simplistic heretofore, and a definition will not be established in the near future.

4596 Venezuela. Universidad Central, Caracas. Instituto de Filología Andrés Bello. El habla culta de Caracas: materiales para su estudio. Carátula, Eduardo Orozco. Caracas: Ediciones de la Facultad de Humanidades y Educación, Instituto de Filología Andrés Bello, Universidad Central de Venezuela, 1979. 666 p.

One of the studies being conducted under the general direction of Juan M. Lope Blanch of the *habla culta* of the principal cities of the Spanish-speaking world. This one was directed by Angel Rosenblat. The recordings were made of people between the ages of 25 and 77. There were four types of interviews: 1) With a single informant; 2) Dialogues between two informants; 3) Lectures; and 4) Secret recordings of an individual. *Temas* included "Crisis de la Juventud Actual," "Recuerdos de Familia," "Educación Preescolar," and "Lengua y Literatura."

4597 Villafuerte, Carlos. Diccionario de topónimos indígenas de Catamarca. Buenos Aires: Editorial Plus Ultra, 1979. 93 p. (Temas argentinos; 3)

The remote mountainous province of Northwestern Argentina has numerous toponyms from both the Diaguitas inhabitants and the more common lingua franca of early days, Quechua.

4598 Webb, John T. Pidgins—and Creoles?—on the U.S.-Mexican border (*in* Festschrift for Jacob Ornstein [see item **4546**] p. 326–331)

Writer stresses the difference between the pochismo type of Spanglish that one hears along the border and the *caló* of the *tirilones* and former *pachucos* (the term *cholos* is becoming fashionable in places like Albuquerque). Caló (*replana* in Peru, *lunfardo* in Argentina) is "counter-prestige" language of rather old and obscure origins.

4599 Wolf, Clara and **Elena Jiménez.** El ensordecimiento del yeísmo porteño: un cambio fonológico en marcha (*in* Estudios lingüísticos y dialectológicos: temas hispánicos [see item **4544**] p. 115–135)

Similar study to another by these authors published in *Proyecto de estudio coordinado de la norma lingüística culta de las principales ciudades de Iberoamérica y de la Península Ibérica* (see HLAS 42:4537). A very good examination of a language change in process: the well-known *žeísmo* is turning to *šeísmo*, and although other investigators have not noted it, they find the presence of affricates as well. Wolf and Jiménez, using 36 informants with university education, find that the shift from [ž] to [š] is almost complete in the young, it is more common in women than in men, and it is more common in the upper economic class than in the lower.

4600 Zúñiga-Tristán, Virginia. El anglicismo en el habla costarricense. San José: Editorial Costa Rica, 1976. 166 p.; 3 leaves of plates; appendices; bibl.; ill.

Well-written account of English terms in the speech of Costa Rica, with a good documentation of the sources of the influences over the years: the *negro jamaicano*, the British and North American immigrants, the pressures in economics, education and industry. Each entry is rather thoroughly researched, including etymology, scientific name in the cases of flora and fauna, definition of variants, examples of usage. One finds such extreme examples as *japy berdi, beibi shauer, ay tenkiu, very güel, nai clob, mopa, doncar* (dump car).

SPANISH LEXICON

4601 Arrom, José Juan. Manatí: el testimonio de los cronistas y la cuestión de su etimología (*in* Homenaje a Fernando Antonio Martínez [see item **4508**] p. 186–192).

An interesting history of the sea lion of the Caribbean, which because it was a mammal and had breasts, was referred to by seamen as a mermaid!

4602 Bernal Jaramillo, Pedro. Terminología de negocios. Bogotá, Colombia: Ediciones Omicron, 1979. 410 p.

Basic vocabulary of business, technical and economic terms. Is not up-to-date in such things as the computer, and in some cases Colombian meanings are assigned the label *americanismo*, when actually the entry may mean something else in another country.

4603 Fabbri, Maurizio. A bibliography of Hispanic dictionaries: Catalan, Galician, Spanish, Spanish in Latin America and the Philippines. Appendix, A bibliography of Basque dictionaries. Imola: Galeati, 1979. 381 p.; index (Collana bibliografica; 1. Biblioteca di Spicilegio moderno)

Handy manual of dictionaries which includes monolingual, bilingual and multilingual. It lists those on dialectal variants such as Judeo-Spanish, and it has special categories of proverbs, slang, etymology, as well as those of specialized terminology: art, archaeology, music, food, meteorology, philology, physics, sociology, education, etc. It is revealing to see the variety of bilingual manuals there are that involve Spanish, all the way from Arabic to Russian. There are however, several rather serious inaccuracies and omissions. Indexes include authors, subjects, languages.

4604 Investigaciones lingüísticas en lexicografía. Luis Fernando Lara, Roberto Ham Chande, María Isabel García Hidalgo. México, D.F.: Colegio de México, Centro de Estudios Lingüísticos y Literarios, 1979. 266 p.; bibl.; ill. (Jornadas—El Colegio de México; 89)

Work first published in the *Nueva Revista de Filología Hispánica* (No. 23, 1974, p. 245–267). It is an excellent Spanish account of the problems that confront the lexicographer in "building" a dictionary, based on experience gained in the composition of the *Diccionario del español de México* (DEM). The problems are chiefly those associated with the ultimate goal of complete objectivity, and they are described as: a) the documents at the disposal of the lexicographer when the task is begun; b) the scientific value of these documents; c) the use that they can be put to for the task at hand; d) the collection of new data that will complement or take the place of that at hand. Using simple vocabulary items the writers show how complicated the matter of order and selection is. They use several pages, for instance, to illustrate how the lexeme *cabeza* would have to be accommodated.

4605 Lenz, Rudolf. Diccionario etimológico: de las voces chilenas derivadas de lenguas indígenas americanas. Ed. dirigida por Mario Ferreccio Podestá. Santiago de Chile: Universidad de Chile, Seminario de Filología Hispánica, 1980? 987 p.; bibl.; index (Theses et studia scholastica; 3)

Reprint of German scholar's famous dictionary first issued between 1905–10. Many studies of American Spanish have been made since then, so that although the vocabulary is extensive and a great deal of research went into the composition of this giant of lexicography, much that Lenz attributes to Indian influences has been shown to be internal to Spanish. The assibilation of /r/, for instance. The spelling changes that he sought to continue did not "take" in the Spanish-speaking world.

4606 Ordóñez Sabido, Raúl. Reflexiones de un lingüísta inconforme. México: B. Costa-Amic, 1977. 107 p.

Although the writer's attitude is normative and he decries the vast influence of English on modern Spanish, his examples are very good and reveal the extremes of sense loans in languages in contact. As examples of "contaminación ambiental" he offers such Spanish phrases as "en las rocas," "cruceros por el Caribe," *firmas* (firms), *retirarse* (to retire), and even *hijo de perra*.

4607 Porta Dapena, José Alvaro. Elementos de lexicografía: el diccionario de construcción y régimen de R. J. Cuervo. Prólogo de Rafael Torres Quintero. Bogotá: Publicaciones del Instituto Caro y Cuervo, LV, 1980. 449 p.; facs., ill.; plates; tables.

Good description of the famous Cuervo *Diccionario* and an outline of the lexicographic efforts that have been made since 1896 when Cuervo, failing in health, abandoned the project. There have been three phases to the continuation: 1942–49; 1949–72; and when it was abandoned at the death of Fernando Antonio Martínez (see item **4508**), and now work is progressing anew. Porto Dapena gives insights into the ways in which lexicographical materials have been treated in the project, how entries are selected and aligned, and how editors have changed plans with the march of time.

4608 Restrepo S., Carlos E. Términos económicos: diccionario inglés-español. Revisión de estilo del Dr. Jesús Villamizar Herrera. Bogotá, Colombia: Editorial Boss: distribuidores exclusivos, Red Informativa, 1979. 293 p.

Very good and up-to-date dictionary of economic and business terms which even lists some of the slang expressions of American English. One finds definitions of "acid test," "scab" (*esquirol, rompehuelgas*); "peak-hour traffic" (*hora de tráfico máximo*); "recoup" (*reintegro*); "payroll" (*nómina, lista de jornales*—Colombia, Argentina and Uruguay: *planilla de sueldos*; Ecuador: *rol de pago*; Mexico: *lista de raya*). Book has a long list of abbreviations used in the business world.

4609 Rodríguez Castelo, Hernán. Léxico sexual ecuatoriano y latinoamericano.

Portada, Kurt Muller, Peter Mussfeldt. Quito: Ediciones Libri Mundi; Otavalo: Instituto Otavaleño de Antropología, 1979. 399 p.; bibl.; ill.; index.

Well-researched comparative study of sexual terms used in Spanish America, including léxico gestual. Chapters: "Pene," "Testículos," "Sexo Femenino," "Pechos," "Trasero," "Coito," "Masturbación," "Prostituta," "Homosexual," and the various terms for each are given with definitions and origins in alphabetical order. At the end of each chapter is a list of words used for the entry in most of the countries of Spanish America. The wealth of terminology is noteworthy as is the sense of humor based on hyperbolic images.

SPANISH
SYNTAX

4610 Barrenechea, Ana María. Operadores pragmáticos de actitud oracional: los adverbios en -mente y otros signos (*in* Estudios lingüísticos y dialectológicos: temas hispánicos [see item **4544**] p. 39–59]

The director of the *Proyecto* in Buenos Aires is not satisfied with previous syntactic and semantic explanations, and in making her own analysis, finds that only a few of the cases show modal circumstances, and what seems to prevail is gradations of: "actitud oracional, suspensión motivada, refuerzo de la aserción, opinión meditada y enfatizadora, juicio no basado en la realidad."

4611 Cartagena, Nelson. Acerca de las categorías de tiempo y aspectos en el sistema verbal del español (Revista Española de Lingüística [Editorial Gredos, Madrid] 8:2, julio/dic. 1978, p. 373–408, bibl.)

The concern of this professor/writer is the presentation of the complicated temporal-aspectual system of Spanish in a concise way to the foreign student of Spanish. Recently he has been doing just this in Germany. Cartagena says that from a strictly morphological point of view, Spanish verbs are either finite (Vf), *am-á-ba-mos*, or infinite (Vif), *am-a-r, am-a-do, am-a-ndo*. His is an interesting picture of tense and aspect of the Spanish verb.

4612 Egea, Esteban Rafael. Los adverbios terminados en -*mente* en el español contemporáneo. Bogotá: Instituto Caro y Cuervo, 1979. 432 p.; bibl.; tables (Publicaciones del Instituto Caro y Cuervo; 49)

The corpus for this extensive investigation was a random sampling of contemporary Spanish American literature. The terms in -*mente* were analyzed as to semantic content, syntactic configuration, morphological structure, and frequency of occurrence, using for the latter classification Juilland and Chang-Rodríguez's *Frequency Dictionary of Spanish Words* (1964). IBM cards helped in the matter of order and category. The work has an excellent bibliography, an index and several appendices. Dwight Bolinger of Harvard University has said of the book: "The work of Egea is an important contribution to the study of Spanish syntax in an area not much researched up to this point, mainly because of lack of statistical evidence. He shows that the adverb, being the freest in position can best reveal the mechanics of syntactic order."

4613 Fontanella de Weinberg, María Beatriz. Algunos aspectos del voseo hispanoamericano (*in* Homenaje a Fernando Antonio Martínez [see item **4508**] p. 175–185)

Although strange to Spain, the *voseo* is an important aspect of American Spanish. While reviewing the up-to-date data of writers like Lapesa and Rona, Fontanella indicates that the situation is more complicated than many realize. The forms of the verbs vary (*hablás, habláis, hablai*), there are places where *tú* is used with *vos* verb forms and vice versa (highland Ecuador), it also varies socially and stylistically. Author indicates more data is needed.

4614 García, Maryellen. Spanish preverbal clitics: the affected entity construction (*in* Colloquium on Spanish and Luso-Brazilian Linguistics [see item **4503**] p. 48–58)

Proposes a deep abstract verb of affect to account for surface proclitics, with encoding of meaning by speaker even though such a verb may never explicitly surface. The clitic meaning is the result of the hearer's active processing and participation.

4615 Klein-Andreu, Flora. Distintos sistemas de empleo de "le," , "la," "lo" (ICC/T, 36, 1981, p. 284–304)

Although the tapes for this study were made in the Spanish provinces of Valladolid,

Burgos, Soria, Logroño and Toledo, the findings may be relevant to Spanish American situations which do not correspond to "general" usage. In certain zones of the region studied, usage corresponds not to case but is "referencial."

4616 Lope Blanch, Juan M. El concepto de oración en la lingüística española. México, D.F.: Universidad Nacional Autónoma de México, 1979. 112 p.; bibl. (Cuadernos de lingüística; 1)

There has been a distinction in recent years among linguists between *oración* and *proposición*, the latter a subject-predicate construction that may form part of a more complete statement, the *oración*. This concept, supported by Roca Pons and Martinet, and traced to Bloomfield, in which "estoy enfermo" is a *proposición* in the *oración*: "Aunque estoy enfermo, iré al trabajo." Lope Blanch goes back in history to find that the idea is not new and was put forth by Andrés Bello and Rodolfo Lenz and others.

4617 Parodi, Claudia. Orden de los pronombres átonos durante el primer cuarto del siglo XVI en el español novohispano (CM/NRFH, 28:2, 1979, p. 312–317)

Spanish American documents of the 16th and 17th centuries indicate that the position of the object pronouns in Old Spanish depended on place within the utterance. In Modern Spanish the position depends on the form of the verb. Documents seem to point to a gradual change during the 16th century, the same period that saw major changes in the Spanish sound system.

4618 Polo Figueroa, Nicolás. Elementos de lingüística generativa. Bogotá: Universidad Santo Tomás, Centro de Enseñanza Desescolarizada, 1980. 247 p.; bibl.; ill.

Good basic guide to generative linguistics in Spanish: language characteristics, functions, concepts, languages in contact, semantic, syntactic, and phonological components.

4619 Velleman, Barry L. Norma y sincronía en la gramática latinoamericana (ICC/T, 36, 1981, p. 1:13)

Using by way of comparison the writings of Bello and Cuervo, writer describes differences between grammars of the 19th century and those of the 20th. Those of the 19th were definitely normative, practical, cultural, and their mission was to teach. Bellow feared fragmentation and he describes gallicisms and neologisms as enemies of the "pureza del idioma." His examples were largely from the 17th century, especially Cervantes. Cuervo works from a corpus of more modern data and puts the normative and the descriptive into competition.

PORTUGUESE GRAMMAR

4620 Kono, Akira. A tratamento "Tu" no português do Brasil (*in* Colóquio de Estudos Luso-Brasileiros, XII, Tóquio, 1979. Anais. Tóquio, Brazil: Associação Japonesa de Estudos Luso-Brasileiros, 1979, p. 50–60, bibl.)

Contrary to popular misconceptions, *tu* has not been entirely replaced by *você* in Brazilian Portuguese. Writer indicates that the singular form is still used extensively in Rio Grande do Sul and certain sections of the North. Some grammars that are used for the teaching of Portuguese assume that *tu* is not heard, he says.

4621 Tláskal, Jaromí, Jr. Morphémes mono-phonématiques (vocaliques) en portugais du Brésil (ASB/PP, 24:1, 1981, p. 22–32, tables)

Interesting view of the peculiar morphemic situation of Brazilian Portuguese. The loss of certain consonants in the evolution from Latin has created many monophonematic morphemes in the form of vowels: /a/, /o/, /e/, etc. It is especially noticeable among the articles and pronouns, and even the verbs.

PORTUGUESE DIALECTOLOGY

4622 Almeida, Horácio de. Dicionário popular paraibano. João Pessoa, Brazil: Editora Universitária, UFPb, 1979. 179 p.

Another in the regional vocabularies of popular usage in Brazil. Rio Grande do Sul has produced six; Ceará, in the Northeast, three; Pernambuco, two. The Almeida dictionary has terms that could be called localisms, usually quite conservative in the history of the language, but also idioms and

slang of the area. On the root *galo*, for example, we have *galo cego*—indivíduo pretensioso; *galhudo*—homem chifrudo, cornudo.

Godínez, Manuel, Jr. An acoustic study of Mexican and Brazilian Portuguese vowels. See item **4556.**

4623 Gomes, José Maria Barbosa. Mário de Andrade e a revolução da linguagem: a gramatiquinha da fala brasileira. João Pessoa, Brazil: Editora Universitária/UFPb, 1979. 230 p.; bibl.; ill. (Coleção Estudos universitários: Série Língua e literatura; 2)

A good record of written usage, using as corpus Mário de Andrade's Macunaíma, 1928: *fazem anos* for *faz anos*; *entrar dentro* for *entrar em*; both *topar* and *topar com*.

PORTUGUESE LEXICON

4624 Azevedo, Milton M. Sobre o emprego de *você* no portugues brasileiro actual (AATSP/H, 64, 1981, p. 273–278)

Comparison of usage of 10 years ago with that of today seems to indicate that *você* is replacing *o senhor* in many situations where the latter would have been called for. The writer in attempting to explain the change expresses the belief that the shift corresponds to a growing feeling of "solidarity."

4625 Banco Pinto & Sotto Mayor, Lisbon. Direcção de Estudos Económicos. Dicionário comercial e bancário. 2. ed. Lisboa: Banco Pinto & Sotto Mayor, Direcção de Estudos Económicos, 1980? 94 p.

Another in a long series of special dictionaries in Brazilian Portuguese. Quite up-to-date, and as is to be expected today, replete with English terms and abbreviations.

4626 Cavalcante, José Cândido Marques. Dicionário inglês-português de termos econômicos & comerciais. Fortaleza: Banco do Nordeste do Brasil; Petrópolis: Editora Vozes, 1979. 408 p.

Rather good economics-commercial bilingual manual, made more practical and usable by copious examples of usage along with definitions.

4627 Cunha, Antônio Geraldo da. Dicionário histórico das palavras portuguesas de origem Tupí. Prefácio-estudo de Antônio Houaiss. São Paulo: Edições Melhoramentos com a colaboração da Editora da Universidade de São Paulo, 1978. 357 p.; indexes.

Excellent source of information on the Tupí elements in Brazilian Portuguese, with extensive quotations of terms as used and going back to 1500. The entry is followed by grammatical category, chronological variants, etymology phonetically indicated, definitions, encyclopedic interests.

4628 Santos, Fernando Nogueira dos. Dicionário inglês-português de economia. Mem Martins, Portugal: Publicações Europa-América, 1979? 212 p. (Dicionários Europa-América; 3)

Up-to-date useful instrument, made principally to aid in the translation of English texts into Portuguese. The device of using synonyms to distinguish definitions helps in making accurate choices among terms. Among the fields covered are public financing, statistics, agrarian economy, bookkeeping, banking, insurance, customs.

4629 Souza, Cilene Cunha de. Um método quantitativo para a análise lexical: aplicação a três poetas simbolistas, Alphonsus de Guimaraens, Cruz e Sousa e Edgard Mata. Capa de Maurício José Marchevsky. Rio de Janeiro: Edições Tempo Brasileiro em convênio com a Instituto Nacional do Livro, Ministério da Educação e Cultura, 1979. 190 p.; bibl.

An attempt to establish a system for lexical study, using statistics as an instrument. Goal is to quantify in terms of types, tokens, and frequency, using a random sample approach (*aleatoria*). Results are presented in informative *quadros*.

4630 Viégas, A. P. Dicionário de fitopatologia e micologia. Campinas, Brasil: Instituto Agronômico, 1979. 882 p.

Dictionary contains the common names of plants cultivated in South America with their respective families; a list of researchers in fungi; the names of institutions where fungi have been studied in the Southern Hemisphere of America; the names of diseases of cultivated and wild plants of South America. Appendices: "A Key to Fungi Families" by G. M. Martin, of the State University of Iowa; a minimum grammar of Latin; botanical journals and abbreviations.

PORTUGUESE
SYNTAX

4631 Borba, Francisco da Silva. Teoria sintática. São Paulo: T. A. Queiroz: Editora da Universidade de São Paulo, 1979. 310 p.; bibl.; diagrs.; index (Biblioteca universitária de língua de lingüística; v. 1)

Study in transformational terms of the syntax of Brazilian Portuguese in which author begins by indicating the advantages of the transformational approach over the structural. Chapters are dedicated to psychological syntax, structural syntax, constants and variants in syntax. Book has a good up-to-date bibliography of mostly North American sources.

4632 Pimenta-Bueno, Mariza. A proposal for a unified treatment of reflexive, reciprocal, intrinsic, and impersonal *se* in Portuguese (*in* Colloquium on Spanish and Luso-Brazilian Linguistics [see item **4503**] p. 92 : 123)

Advocates lexical redundancy rules distinct from transformational rules by exploring interaction of some syntactic, stylistic, and morphological phenomena which are related to uses of pronominal clitic *se* forms in Portuguese. Author says all Portuguese pronominal *se*-forms play the role of logical operators which form sentences by bleeding terms.

CREOLE

4633 Amastae, Jon. Dominican English Creole phonology: an initial sketch (IU/AL, 21 : 4, April 1979, p. 182–203, bibl.)

In an area known for its French Creole, the official language is English, and the *patois* is not just an interference but a Creole of its own. It occupies a fairly unique place in the Caribbean Creoles, with a seven-vowel system, [f] for [θ], elimination of /r/ final and a simplification of consonantal clusters.

4634 Cave, Roderick. Four slave songs from St. Bartholomew (UWI/CQ, 25 : 1/2, p. 85–90)

Linguistically-interesting collection of songs found in the Report of St. Bartholomew (1805). Few realize that the island of St. Bartholomew was a Swedish possession from

1784–1878, and that the Creole of the area shows both Swedish and English influences. Writer was supplied with microfilm through the courtesy of the Royal Library, Stockholm.

4635 Dejean, Yves. Dilemme en Haïti: français en péril ou péril français? Port-au-Prince: Editions Connaissance d'Haïti; New York: distribué par Connaissance Diffusion, 1975. 57 p.; bibl. (Collection Aujour'hui)

The situation of French in Haiti today is compared with that of a century ago. At that time there were only a few Francophones and a small circle of intellectuals, perhaps 10,000 students. Today there are 100,000 Francophones, 30 theaters that show French films, and it is heard constantly on the radio. Writer says that the Creole is not in danger, but there is the ever-present danger of obligatory French for instruction.

4636 Hancock, Ian F. Gullah and Barbadian: origins and relationships (AMS, 55:1, Spring 1980, p. 17:35, bibl.)

Maintaining that Gullah and Afro-Seminole are the only English-based Creoles that have survived in continental US, writer does not agree with claim that there was an English Creole in West Africa by 1550. The English dealt with slaves in Spanish, Dutch, or Portuguese, he says, until 1636. After this there grew up an English Creole on the Senegal coast. Further, he writes, there is no evidence that Gullah was brought from the Barbados.

4637 Jardel, J. P. De quelques usages des concepts de "bilinguisme" et de "diglossie" (ASHSH/B, 32:7, 1979, p. 4–20, bibl.)

Perceptive view of what is meant by *bilingualism* as opposed to *diglossia*. Jardel says that the former is essentially behavior and lies in the realm of psychology and pedagogy and may also be examined sociologically. *Diglossia* dates from Ferguson (1959) and as applied to Creole/standard language dichotomies, such as the Creole/French of Haiti, it becomes more a part of the discipline of political sociology.

4638 McKesey, George. Manuscript of the Belizean lingo. Belize: National Printers, 1974? 106 p.

Very interesting vocabulary of the Creole of Belize written by a Belizean who is fond of dialect study and once had a radio program there called "Dialect Rambling." Although much of the dialect would not be understood by one whose English is limited to so-called standard, there are elements in the Creole that remind one a lot of Charleston, South Carolina, and the Gullah of the offshore islands. There is a "Br'er Rabbit" flavor to some of it.

4639 Mirville, Ernst. La phrase Creole dans une perspective de grammaire structurale comparée (ASHSH/B, 32:7, 1979, p. 21–29, tables)

Examination of the parts of speech of Haitian Creole which shows that in the process of creolization there has been a leveling of morphemes to the extent that today the same word may have several functions.

4640 Naro, Anthony J. Pidgin and Creole linguistics (LSA/L, 55:4, Dec. 1979, p. 886–893)

In this article, which also reviews *Pidgin and Creole linguistics* edited by Albert Valdman (Bloomington: Indiana University Press, 1977. 399 p.), the reviewer considers briefly the works of authorities in the field: Reinecke, De Camp, Bickerton, Ferguson, and others and wonders if the problem of Pidgin/Creole origins is any closer to solution now than before the appearance of Valdman's book. His main criticism of those involved is that so many conclusions have been based on data-free theories, which are not likely to provide much understanding of the fundamental issues.

4641 Oliveira, Vera Lúcia Maia de. Considerações sobre pressupostos na controvérsia "crioulista:" resenha crítica (Construtura [Universidade Católica do Paraná, Curitiba, Brazil] 7:17, 1979, p. 54–74, bibl.)

Two great theoretical controversies prevail in the field of Creole studies: 1) The genetic controversy—on the origin of Creole languages; and 2) The typological controversy—over their structural characteristics. The writer reviews the points of view of several Creolists, including Hall, De Camp, Whinnom, Naro, Taylor, Dillard, and others. She finds that there are several general attitudes, among them disqualification, a negation of African or European roots; qualification, through an affirmation of its African origins; introduction of a new component, universality.

4642 Owens, Jonathan. Monogenesis, the universal and the particular in Creole studies (IU/AL, 22:3, March 1980, p. 97–117, bibl.)

Examination of the sequence, form, tense, aspect and mode of the noun phrase in several Creoles to determine whether there is commonality, which would support the theory of a Portuguese-based *lingua franca* as the structural "mother" of Creoles. Writer finds that Haitian and Hawaiian Creoles have the same pre-verbal tense-aspect system, for instance, but there are several that resemble their source language (French, English, Arabic, etc.) and are dissimilar.

JOURNAL ABBREVIATIONS
LANGUAGE

AATSP/H Hispania. American Association of Teachers of Spanish and Portuguese. Univ. of Cincinnati, Ohio.

ACO/B Boletín de la Academia Colombiana. Bogotá.

AHL/B Boletín de la Academia Hondureña de la Lengua. Tegucigalpa.

AMS American Speech. Columbia Univ. Press. New York.

ANLE/B Boletín de la Academia Norteamericana de la Lengua Española. New York.

ASB/PP Philologica Pragensia. Academia Scientiarum Bohemoslovenica. Praha.

ASHSH/B Bulletin de l'Académie des Sciences Humaines et Sociales d'Haiti. Port-au-Prince.

BNBD Boletín Nicaragüense de Bibliografía y Documentación. Banco Central de Nicaragua, Biblioteca. Managua.

BRP Beiträge zur Romanischen Philologie. Rütten & Loening. Berlin.

CIDG/O Orbis. Bulletin international de documentation linguistique. Centre International de Dialectologie Générale. Louvain, Belgium.

CM/NRFH Nueva Revista de Filología Hispánica. El Colegio de México [and] the University of Texas. México.

FFCLM/A Alfa. Univ. de São Paulo, Faculdade de Filosofia, Ciências e Letras. Marília, Brazil.

HR Hispanic Review. A quarterly devoted to research in the Hispanic languages and literatures. Univ. of Pennsylvania, Dept. of Romance Languages. Philadelphia.

HUN/RU Revista de la Universidad. Univ. Nacional Autónoma de Honduras. Tegucigalpa.

IAA Ibero-Amerikanisches Archiv. Ibero-Amerikanisches Institut. Berlin, FRG.

ICC/T Thesaurus. Boletín del Instituto Caro y Cuervo. Bogotá.

IGFO/RI Revista de Indias. Instituto Gonzalo Fernández de Oviedo [and] Consejo Superior de Investigaciones Científicas. Madrid.

IU/AL Anthropological Linguistics. A publication of the Archives of the Languages of the World. Indiana Univ., Anthropology Dept. Bloomington, Ind.

LINGUA Lingua. North-Holland Publishing Co. Amsterdam.

LSA/L Language. Journal of the Linguistic Society of America. Waverly Press, Inc. Baltimore, Md.

MLTA/MLJ Modern Language Journal. The National Federation of Modern Language Teachers Associations [and] Univ. of Pittsburgh. Pittsburgh, Pa.

PUC/L Lexis. Revista de lingüística y literatura. Pontificia Univ. Católica del Perú. Lima.

SBPC/CC Ciência e Cultura. Sociedade Brasileira para o Progresso da Ciência. São Paulo.

SBPL/RBL Revista Brasileira de Linguística. Sociedade Brasileira para Professores de Linguística. São Paulo.

UBN/R Revista de la Biblioteca Nacional. Ministerio de Educación y Cultura. Montevideo.

UC/AT Atenea. Revista de ciencias, letras y artes. Univ. de Concepción. Concepción, Chile.

UCLV/I Islas. Univ. Central de las Villas. Santa Clara, Cuba.

UCR/RF Revista de Filosofía de la Universidad de Costa Rica. San José.

UNAM/AL Anuario de Letras. Univ. Nacional Autónoma de México, Facultad de Filosofía y Letras. México.

UNL/U Universidad. Univ. Nacional del Litoral. Santa Fe, Argentina.

UNPHU/A Aula. Univ. Nacional Pedro Henríquez Ureña. Santo Domingo.

UPRM/RL Revista de Letras. Univ. de Puerto Rico en Mayagüez, Facultad de Artes y Ciencias. Mayagüez.

USP/LL Língua e Literatura. Univ. de São Paulo, Depto. de Letras, Faculdade de Filosofia, Letras e Ciências Humanas. São Paulo.

UWI/CQ Caribbean Quarterly. Univ. of the West Indies. Mona, Jamaica.

UWI/CS Caribbean Studies. Univ. of the West Indies. Mona, Jamaica.

UY/R Revista de la Universidad de Yucatán. Mérida, Mexico.

LITERATURE

SPANISH AMERICA: General

ROBERTO GONZALEZ ECHEVARRIA, *Professor of Spanish, Yale University*

RECENT LATIN AMERICAN LITERATURE continues to attract the attention of critics and historians who, seeking a reassessment and explanation of current trends, are projected toward the past. This trend has yielded a host of new anthologies, book-length studies of colonial and 19th-century figures, and radical revisions of the canon of Latin American literature, the latter being the most exciting new development in criticism. Ediciones Ayacucho renewed but did not fulfill the hope of producing a series of Latin American classics. Overall, these editions did not provide the faithful texts nor the scholarly apparatus that are determined by rigorous research. Moreover, these books are far too luxurious and expensive to serve as popular editions. That they should fall short both of scholarship and popular access at a time of rising interest in Latin American literature is unfortunate. Indeed, such a series would have been extremely useful for academic curricula. Still, there exists a number of new editions that partially fill this need for scholarly versions of classics such as those produced in Cuba which do not circulate for obvious reasons.

Exile, a recurring phenomenon among Latin American writers, has reached epidemic proportions in the past two or three years. Augusto Roa Bastos and Juan Carlos Onetti are in Spain, while a host of Chilean writers live scattered throughout the world. A notable number of significant writers have also left Cuba in the recent past, e.g.: Antonio Benítez Rojo, César Leante, Heberto Padilla, Belkis Cuza Malé, Reinaldo Arenas, José Triana and Edmundo Desnoes. The latter produced a controversial anthology of Cuban literature dealing with the Revolution that provoked much discussion (item **5314**). A significant trend in Latin American criticism is the easing of Cuba's ideological hold over most sectors of the left, a change that can be attributed partly to the exile of these prestigious writers who, together with Guillermo Cabrera Infante and Severo Sarduy, form a powerful dissidence abroad. In addition, exile is no longer, as in the past, merely a theme of Latin American literature but has become a mode of self-conscious interpretation in itself. A recent issue of *Review* focuses on this topic as do the Cuban exiled writers in their new journal, *Linden Lane Magazine* at Princeton (see item **5325**).

Octavio Paz received the Cervantes Prize as well as the Neustadt Prize, while Nicolás Guillén turned 80 and was fêted in Cuba and abroad. Although Borges continues to publish, his influence, as well as that of Paz, is on the wane. Younger masters like García Márquez, Vargas Llosa, Sarduy, Cabrera Infante, Puig, Cardenal and Luis Rafael Sánchez have moved decisively to center stage. Among older writers, the works of the deceased Lezama Lima continue to command attention and respect. His influence eventually may exceed that of Paz, Borges, Carpentier and Guillén. An international symposium on Lezama held at the Université Paul Valéry in Poitiers was attended by many writers and critics from all over the world.

Another writer whose influence is being felt somewhat belatedly is the Paraguayan Augusto Roa Bastos, whose *Yo el Supremo* is hailed as one of the masterpieces of the century. The University of Maryland held a symposium on his works. Another writer whose influence is being felt somewhat belatedly is the Paraguayan Augusto Roa Bastos, whose *Yo el Supremo* is hailed as one of the masterpieces of the century. The University of Maryland held a symposium on his works. Another important symposium took place at Barnard College (New York) focusing on the works of Juan Rulfo, while at Yale, a symposium on the Baroque and the Neo-Baroque centered for the most part on Sarduy.

To summarize, the most important trends in the biennial period are: 1) continued attention devoted to earlier literature, including that of the colonial period; 2) the apparent decline of interest in the works of influential older masters such as Borges, Paz, Guillén and the delayed recognition extended to two of them, Lezama Lima and Roa Bastos; 3) the overtaking of these older writers by those in their late 40s and 50s; 4) the shift away from Cuba as a focus of ideological support; and 5) the perception of exile less as historical trend and more as self-conscious interpretation of literature itself.

In criticism there continues to be a vague division between practitioners of Marxist criticism and those influenced by recent Structuralist and post-Structuralist criticism.

5001 Achúgar, Hugo. Notas para un debate sobre la crítica literaria latinoamericana (CDLA, 19:110, sept./oct. 1978, p. 3–18)

Scrupulous analysis of major issues facing Latin American criticism today: relationship between methodology and specific Latin American reality, problem of defining Latin America, differentiating the Latin American from the European tradition. Believes that autochthonous methods ought to be developed to deal with Latin American literature. Thinks that social reality conditions not only literary but critical production as well, so that as one works from and for Latin American reality inevitably a Latin American criticism will emerge. Useful point of departure.

5002 American Center of P.E.N. Freedom to Write Committee. Latin America, the freedom to write: a report. New York: The Center, 1980. 48 p.; bibl.

Balanced and well-informed, this pamphlet should be read by all interested in Latin American literature. Besides information regarding freedom of the press in each country, authors list all writers and journalists jailed or disappeared.

5003 Anderson Imbert, Enrique. La crítica literaria y sus métodos. 3. ed. México: Alianza Editorial Mexicana, 1979. 253 p.; bibl.; index (Biblioteca iberoamericana; 3)

Third ed. of Anderson Imbert's *La crítica literaria contemporánea* (1957), which appeared as *Métodos de crítica literaria* (1969). Continues to be useful for its clarity and elegance. In this version author takes into account—not too sympathetically—structuralist criticism. Good teaching aid.

5004 Arenas, Reinaldo. La cultura popular en la narrativa latinoamericana (Linden Lane Magazine [Princeton, N.J.] 1:1, enero/marzo 1982, p. 3–5)

Overview of the presence and relevance of popular culture in contemporary Latin American narrative, with special attention devoted to works of Luis Rafael Sánchez, Severo Sarduy, Guillermo Cabrera Infante, José Agustín and Manuel Puig. Important because of Arenas' own relevance as a writer rather than because of its novelty or insight.

5005 Arizpe, Lourdes. Interview with Carmen Naranjo: women and Latin American literature (UC/S, 5:1, Autumn 1979, p. 98–110)

Illuminating interview with the Costa Rican novelist and poet with insightful observations about Latin American literature written by women.

5006 Benedetti, Mario. El recurso del supremo patriarca. México: Editorial

Nueva Imagen, 1979. 175 p.; bibl. (Serie
Literatura)

Collection of minor critical pieces by
the Uruguayan writer, most ambitious of
which is on the dictator-novel. Important for
those interested in Benedetti's fiction.

5007 Bente, Thomas O. El lector frente a la·
obra: una nueva estética para la nueva
novela hispanoamericana (CAM, 221:6,
nov./dic. 1978, p. 70–79)

Superficial gloss of characteristics of
the new Latin American novel as set out by
Fuentes in his essay *La nueva novela hispanoamericana.* Useful for non-specialists.

5008 Carpentier, Alejo. La novela latinoamericana en vísperas de un nuevo
siglo y otros ensayos. México: Siglo Veintiuno Editores, 1981. 253 p.; 2 p. of plates; facsim.; port. (La Creación literaria)

Posthumous collection of essays, selected by Carpentier's Siglo XXI publishers,
takes its title from 1979 Yale lecture by Carpentier. Opening essay purports to be that
lecture but consists of notes Carpentier
wrote but did not read at Yale. Pieces range
from 1920s to present, most important ones
appear under "Visión de América," fragments
of book that became *Los pasos perdidos,* and
"Martí y Francia," Carpentier's best essay.
Also important Carpentier's Cervantes lecture delivered in Alcalá de Henares upon re-
ceiving Cervantes Prize from Spanish Kings.
Book lacks unity in terms of essays' quality
and themes but is useful for general reader to
have some pieces only found in journals.

5009 Casas de Faunce, María. La novela picaresca latinoamericana. Madrid:
Cupsa Editorial, 1977. 242 p.; bibl. (Pla-
neta/universidad; 9)

Thorough and comprehensive study
but author appears unaware of current polemics on the picaresque, and fails to establish links with non-Hispanic literatures.
Still, book is a good introduction to the
topic.

5010 The City in the Latin American novel.
Edited by Bobby J. Chamberlain. East
Lansing: Latin American Studies Center,
Michigan State University, 1980. 100 p.; bibl.
(Latin American Studies Center monograph
series; no. 19)

Interesting collection of papers dealing
with topic that will command future atten-

tion. Curiously, authors do not consider that
there is, from the picaresque on, a clear relationship between origins and development of
novel and city. Yates is most bold in asserting
that there is a relationship between Buenos
Aires as epitome of great metropolis and
boom of the Latin American novel.

5011 Coll, Edna. Indice informativo de la
novela hispanoamericana. t. 1, Las
Antillas. t. 2, Centroamérica. t. 3, Venezuela.
t. 4, Colombia. Río Piedras: Editorial Universitaria, Universidad de Puerto Rico, 1974. 4
v. (418, 343, 346, 587 p.); bibl.; index.

Useful reference work that contains
basic bibliography of each writer and in some
cases a general overview of his works, plus
some plot summaries. Nevertheless, there
are some errors and specialists should double
check the information contained (e.g., Lisandro Otero's novel *Pasión de Urbino* is attributed to Severo Sarduy).

**5012 El Cuento hispanoamericano contem-
poráneo.** José de la Cuadra *et al.* Selección y notas, Susana Zanetti. Buenos Aires:
Centro Editor de América Latina, 1977. 174
p. (Panoramas de la literatura; 13. Biblioteca
total; 51)

Good selection of short stories, with
reliable, if all too brief, introductions to various authors. Susana Zanetti's introduction
argues in favor of the short story as Latin
America's predominant narrative form.

5013 Detrás de la reja: antología crítica de
narradoras latinoamericanas del siglo
XX. Editores: Celia Correas de Zapata and
Lygia Johnson. Caracas, Venezuela: Monte
Avila Editores, 1980. 400 p. (Colección
Continentes)

Unconvincing introduction and whimsical selection mar this worthy effort. One is
startled to discover that writers as important
as Lydia Cabrera have been left out.

5014 Fernández Moreno, César. Latin America in its literature. General editor, César Fernández Moreno. Assistant editor, Julio
Ortega. Editor of the English edition, Iván A.
Schulman. Translated from the Spanish by
Mary G. Berg. New York: Holmes & Meier,
1980. 356 p.; bibl.; index (Latin America in
its culture; 1)

Originally published as *América Latina en su literatura,* volume was translated
and abridged for English-speaking reader in

order to provide background in social and literary history that would ease his understanding of current literature. Translations are not good but book does accomplish purpose, particularly through fine contributions by Haroldo de Campos, Severo Sarduy, Antonio Cândido, and a splendid essay by Lezama Lima. Pieces range in subject matter from colonial period to present and deal with broad issues such as modernity, dependence, underdevelopment and relationship between Latin American literature and European literary tradition.

5014a Foster, David William. Studies in the contemporary Spanish-American short story. Columbia: University of Missouri Press, 1979. 126 p.; bibl.; index.

Close readings of stories by Borges, Cortázar, García Márquez, Rulfo, Benedetti and Guillermo Cabrera Infante designed to uncover what author calls *écriture* of the modern Latin American short story. Analyses have several insights but they are quite independent from author's conventional and tenacious structural terminology.

5015 Franco, Jean. Narrador, autor, superestrella: la narrativa latinoamericana en la época de cultura de masas (IILI/RI, 47:114/115, enero/junio 1981, p. 129–148)

Interesting observations about relationship between traditional knowledge as handed down by narrator's voice and modern (pop-inspired) world-view which is the author's own; the former relies on voice, the latter on print. Though perhaps a bit hasty and overly general, the formulations in this article are worthy of consideration and debate.

5016 Gass, William H. A fiesta for the form (NER, 183:17[3433] 25 Oct. 1980, p. 33–39)

Brilliant and amusing essay celebrating the Latin American novel. Valuable insights from a North American's perspective on Cabrera Infante, Vargas Llosa, Lezama Lima, Cortázar and Goytisolo (whom Gass seems to think is Latin American). For Gass, of course, the new novel is a miracle, that is to say, it emerges suddenly, as if there were no previous narrative tradition of any distinction in Latin America. Worth reading despite this condescending assumption.

5017 Jozef, Bella. O jogo mágico. Rio de Janeiro: Livraria J. Olympio Editora,

1980. 197 p.; bibl.; index.

Collection of essays by noted Brazilian professor and critic. Ones on Gallegos and Vargas Llosa are more persuasive, though there are penetrating comments in many others. Given book's title and orientation, one misses a discussion of Carpentier's theories of "lo real maravilloso americano."

5018 Losada, Alejandro. Bases para un proyecto de una historia social de la literatura en América Latina, 1780–1970 (IILI/RI, 47:114/115, enero/junio 1981, p. 167–168)

Of all critics working from a Marxist perspective, Losada is the most lucid, though he also succumbs to jargon and name dropping. His project is ambitious: to rewrite the history of Latin American literature from a more systematic point of view, taking into account the sociohistorical bases of its production and reception. Though intention is commendable and need obvious, Losada is too vague and abstract in his formulations and winds up inveighing against contemporary authors (e.g., Donoso, Sarduy) with whom he disagrees for political reasons (his reasons, not theirs). One hopes that as the project develops these weaknesses will disappear.

5019 Marco, Joaquín. Latin American literature in Spain: three historical periods (UNESCO/CU, 7:1, 1980, p. 94–112)

Useful, well-informed overview, focuses on 1920s, early 1930s and 1960s. Background on presence of Spanish writers in Latin America in 1940s would have enhanced picture. Still, a good introductory piece, particularly for the non-specialist.

5020 Orjuela, Héctor H. Literatura hispanoamericana: ensayos de interpretación y de crítica. Bogotá: Instituto Caro y Cuervo, 1980. 148 p.

Orjuela's most ambitious piece concerns a new generational scheme to be applied to Latin American literary history. His generations last 40 years and, though linked to sociopolitical history do not pretend to cover entire evolution of culture. Other essays deal with Carrasquilla's *modernismo*; somewhat descriptive analysis of *El Carnero*; Martí's image of America; translation into English of an Heredia poem; and US image in recent Latin American poetry. Includes occasional facts and insights of interest to specialists.

5021 Perus, Françoise. Literatura y sociedad en América Latina. 2. ed. México: Siglo Veintiuno Editores, 1978. 139 p.; bibl. (Sociología y política)

New edition of Perus' controversial book is more suggestive than penetrating as criticism. Unfortunately, she has not corrected some obvious errors from first edition, nor added anything fresh to this one.

5022 Poniatowska, Elena. La literatura de las mujeres en América Latina (Revista de la Educación Superior [ANUIES, Asociación Nacional de Universidades e Institutos de Enseñanza Superior, México] 10:2[38], abril/junio 1981, p. 23–25)

Compelling essay on Latin American women writers written by an accomplished one herself. Argues that they write on larger issues rather than intimate matters because Latin America is face to face with urgent political, social and existential questions.

5023 Rincón, Carlos. Mitología y novela entre el Viejo y el Nuevo Mundo (ECO, 35[6]:216, oct. 1979, p. 561–568)

Readers should not be deceived by the promising title of this essay, which goes over well-known territory, while reaching new levels of stylistic turgidity. The inclusion of *Ulysses* in the discussion is invaluable, as a reminder that myth as a component of the modern novel is not necessarily a Latin American phenomenon. Essay does not take into account copious bibliography on subject, nor analyze in detail any specific text.

5024 ———. Sobre la actualidad de la vanguardia (Fragmentos [Centro de Estudios Latinoamericanos Rómulo Gallegos, Departamento de Investigaciones, Caracas, Venezuela] 3, 1978, p. 60–73)

As in previous cases, Rincón confuses the issue with his turgid style, name-dropping habit and incorrigible tendency to vapid generalization. To readers interested in the current debate on the *vanguardia*, this piece will exemplify how little the polemic has contributed to our knowledge of the topic. Article was reprinted in *Revista Iberoamericana*.

5025 Robb, James Willis. Estudios sobre Alfonso Reyes. Bogotá: Ediciones El Dorado, 1976. 167 p.; bibl. (Biblioteca hispanoamericana: Serie Crítica y ensayo; v. 1)

Seven important essays on Reyes, by one of his most authoritative critics, the best one being on Borges and Reyes. Important collection for students of the essay.

5026 Rojas-Mix, Miguel. El dictador si tiene quien le escriba (RCLL, 6:11, 1. semestre, 1980, p. 123–126)

Author reminds us that dictators have always had Latin American writers willing to sing their praises. Though journalistic, this piece contains some curious facts about the relationship between writers and political power in Latin America.

5027 Schwartz, Ronald. Nomads, exiles & emigrés: the rebirth of the Latin American narrative, 1960–80. Metuchen, N.J.: Scarecrow Press, 1980. 153 p.; bibl.; index.

Introduction for non-Spanish-speaking readers. Contains general commentary and plot summaries, plus useful bibliography for non-specialist.

5028 Shaw, D. L. Modern trends in Spanish American fiction (ATSP/VH, 28:2, Spring 1980, p. 19–25)

Interesting overview of Latin American novel was "author's inaugural lecture as Professor of Latin American Studies in the University of Edinburgh." Shaw divides history of Latin American novel into three periods: 1) beginning of century to publication *Doña Bárbara* (1929); 2) influence of Borges up to boom; and 3) the boom, dominated by García Márquez. Shaw notes increasing humor in recent novel as well as presence of the erotic. Pleasant introduction for non-specialists.

5029 Stabb, Martin S. Utopia and anti-utopia: the theme in selected essayistic writings of Spanish America (UA/REH, 15:3, oct. 1981, p. 377–393)

Overview of theme of utopia including current authors. Reinforces idea that in Latin America while there have been creators of utopias at conceptual level, utopia has been a major theme in its literature and thought. Utopia is a major, unifying trope in Latin American fiction beginning in colonial period. Carpentier and García Márquez not only write about utopia, but their fictions avail themselves of tropological structure of utopian writing. Well-informed article with many good insights.

5030 Wheelock, Carter. Fantastic symbolism in the Spanish American short story (HR, 48:4, Autumn 1980, p. 415–434)

Using Todorov's well-known (if hardly accepted) theories of fantastic literature, Wheelock proposes his own category: somewhat slippery "primal fantastic," to survey the Latin American short story (e.g., 19th-century writers and Quiroga, Murena, Fuentes, Novas, Calvo, Cortázar). More attention is due a Latin American fantastic tra-dition reaching back to prehispanic/African roots, and forward to a "literaturized" world (Borges) without distinction between fantastic and non-fantastic.

Colonial Period

DANIEL R. REEDY, *Professor of Spanish, University of Kentucky*

FOR MORE THAN A DECADE, THE AMOUNT of scholarly activity associated with Spanish American literature of the colonial period has been equaled in the main by a continuing rise in quality and innovation in approach. In part, the quality of today's scholarship is enhanced by the increasing availability of editions of many primary writers. Noteworthy editions of works by several major authors are included in this *HLAS* section. The edition of Ercilla y Zúñiga's *La Araucana* (item **5081**), prepared by Morínigo and Lerner, is a splendid two-volume presentation of the epic poem, and should be regarded as the most reliable version since that of José Toribio Medina in 1910–18. Other texts of poetry include Juan de Miramontes y Zuázola's lengthy *Armas antárticas* (item **5088**), the first complete edition since 1921, and Emilio Carilla's anthology of *Poesía de la Independencia* (item **5091**). There are also important editions of several prose works: the Inca Garcilaso de la Vega's *Comentarios reales* (item **5083**), prepared by the noted Peruvian scholar Aurelio Miró Quesada; Fray Servando Teresa de Mier's *Ideario político* (item **5087**); and the chronicle *El Carnero* (item **5093**) by Juan Rodríguez Freyle. Perhaps the most significant contribution in this group is the excellent edition of Guamán Poma (Waman Puma) de Ayala's *Primer nueva corónica y buen gobierno* (item **5092**).

The availability of standard editions of several major writers will serve to stimulate interest in their writings during the coming years. Such will certainly be the case with Guamán Poma's *Primer nueva corónica . . .* which has already attracted students and scholars from the social sciences as well as the humanities. Several entries on this subject are included herein, and we draw particular attention to the seminal articles by Rolena Adorno (items **5032–5035**), who with John Murra prepared the most recent edition of the chronicle.

Other writers of the colonial period continue to be subjects of significant research. Ercilla y Zúñiga's epic poem, the poetry of Tejeda y Guzmán and Pedro de Oña, as well as the works of Sigüenza y Góngora and Bernal Díaz, among others, continue to draw critical interest. The prose, verse and dramatic works of Sor Juana Inés de la Cruz continue to stimulate new research as, for example, her *Respuesta a Sor Filotea de la Cruz*, the object of recent serious analysis (item **5085**) and a worthwhile article by Montross (item **5055**) which compares Sor Juana's ideas to those of St. Thomas Aquinas, going beyond the usual superficial observations of Sor Juana as feminist. The essay by Octavio Paz on "Juana Ramírez" (item **5059**) is a fascinating psycho-literary study of Juana the woman. And the book-length study by Georgina Sabat de Rivers (item **5067**) is one of the most comprehensive examinations of Sor Juana's *Primero Sueño* in recent years. It builds well on the earlier study and edition by Alfonso Méndez Plancarte in 1951 and is a solid piece of scholarship.

Other items deserve special mention. The three volume *Teatro barroco hispanoamericano* (item **5075**) by Suárez Radillo is a valuable source of knowledge relating to the colonial theater in the Viceroyalties of New Spain and Peru between 1600 and 1750. Also, we draw attention to W. L. Siemens' imaginative article on an aspect of the *Comentarios reales* (item **5071**), relating to cycles of time and ideas of the cosmos in the story of Viracocha, the god/hero. Finally, we mention the articles of Browning (item **5094**) and Wilhite (items **5097** and **5098**) because they deal with one of the least researched periods of colonial Spanish American literature, the Enlightenment.

INDIVIDUAL FIGURES

5031 Achury Valenzuela, Dario. Luis José de Tejeda y Guzmán: espejo de peregrinos penitentes (CBR/BCB, 16:3, marzo 1979, p. 143–160)

General comments on the various works of Argentina's first poet, Tejeda y Guzmán (1604–80). Best known is his autobiographical poem *El peregrino en Babilonia*, begun around 1663. A modest contribution to our knowledge of Tejeda and his works.

5032 Adorno, Rolena. El arte de la persuasión: el padre de las Casas y Fray Luis de Granada en la obra de Waman Puma de Ayala (Escritura, Teoría y Críticas Literarias [Caracas] 4:8, julio/dic. 1979, p. 167–189)

Waman Puma's *Nueva corónica* shows the chronicler's familiarity with a number of Spanish writers, particularly Las Casas and Luis de Granada, and including Agustín de Zárate, Diego Fernández el Palentino and Luis Jerónimo de Oré. Article details the influence of these writers on the Peruvian chronicler.

5033 ———. Current research on Waman Puma and his *Nueva corónica* (UP/LAIL, 5:1, Spring 1981, p. 9–15)

Brief but valuable note which details the significant research on the *Nueva corónica*. Important for the bibliographical data supplied in the ample annotation.

5034 ———. The *Nueva corónica y buen gobierno*: a new look at the Royal Library's Peruvian treasure (Fund og Forskning [Copenhagen, Denmark] 24, 1979/1980, p. 7–28, bibl.)

Comprehensive report on Guamán Poma's chronicle of ancient and modern events in the Andes, which is seen as a literary work conceived both as history and as utopian treatise. Article contains a detailed,

first-hand description of the manuscript found in the Copenhagen Royal Library. Also details the history of the ms. from Lima to Copenhagen. Excellent bibliography.

5035 ———. Las otras fuentes de Guamán Poma: sus lecturas castellanas (PUCP/H, 2:2, dic. 1978, p. 137–158, bibl., ill.)

Provides considerable detail on points of contact between the *Primer nueva corónica* and the major works of Las Casas, Acosta and Oré. Of interest to both the literary critic and historian.

5036 Arróniz, Othón. Teatro de evangelización en Nueva España. México: Universidad Nacional Autónoma de México, 1979. 255 p.; bibl.; index (Textos y estudios—Instituto de Investigaciones Filológicas, Centro de Estudios Literarios: Letras mexicanas del XVI al XVIII)

Comprehensive study of the religious theater in New Spain. Chapters deal primarily with the contributions of the Franciscans, with comments on the Dominican and Jesuit theater. Extensive bibliography and an appendix which contains the text of "Egloga Pastoril al Nacimiento del Niño Jesús" by Juan de Cigorondo. Enlarges our knowledge of the early theater.

5037 Castro-Klarén, Sara. Huamán Poma y el espacio de la pureza (IILI/RI, 47:114/115, enero/junio 1981, p. 45–67)

Analyzes historical concepts in Poma de Ayala's *Primera nueva corónica* relating to the restauration of a racially homogeneous native reign and the expulsion of the Spanish intruders. Well-developed study.

5038 Chang-Rodríguez, Raquel. A forgotten Indian chronicle: Titu Cusi Yupanqui's *Relación de la conquista del Perú* (UP/LAIL, 4:2, Fall 1980, p. 87–95)

Examines the contemporary relevance

of the *Relación* (1570), written by the penultimate king of the Inca dynasty, which describes Inca resistance to the *conquistadores*. Author sees the *Relación* as a revolutionary and subversive work; well-documented and innovative approach to a little-known work.

5039 Colombí-Monguió, Alicia de. El poema del Padre Matías de Bocanegra: trayectoria de una imitación (ICC/T, 31:1, enero/abril 1981, p. 23–43)

Padre Bocanegra, S. J. (1612–68, Puebla) is best remembered for his "Canción a un Desengaño." Bocanegra's poem is directly related to "Canción Real a una Mudanza" by Fray Luis de León. Article offers an interesting, detailed comparison of the two texts. Worthwhile study of a little-known author and poem.

5040 Corominas, Juan María. Castiglione y La Araucana: estudio de una influencia. Madrid: J. Porrúa Turanzas; Potomac, Md.: distributor for U.S.A., Studia Humanitatis, 1980. 144 p.; bibl.; index (Studia humanitatis)

Through an analysis of the *Araucana*, author studies the person of Ercilla y Zúñiga as a prototype of the Renaissance Spanish courtier and humanist. The figure of Ercilla is judged against the model of the perfect courtier as delineated by Baltasar de Castiglione in his *El cortesano*.

5041 Durán-Cerda, Julio. Los empeños de una casa: comedia barroca (Explicación de Textos Literarios [California State University, Department of Spanish and Portuguese, Sacramento] 1979/1980, p. 45–50)

Compares Sor Juana's play with representative works by major dramatists of the Baroque in Spain, particularly Calderón, Moreto and Rojas Zorrilla, finding that her work is a typical Baroque *comedia*. Of moderate interest.

5042 Felker, William L. Some unpublished verse from colonial Guatemala: commentary and texts (HISP, 73, sept. 1981, p. 69–78)

Description of 12 anonymous poems found in the Archivo de Centro América, Guatemala City. Manuscripts are undated but appear to be from late 17th through early 19th centuries. Texts of five of the poems are reproduced. Of interest to bibliophiles.

5043 Flores, Félix Gabriel. El primer poeta del Río de la Plata (CH, 125:374, agosto 1981, p. 412–421)

General observations on Argentina's first poet, Luis José de Tejeda (b. Córdoba, 1604–1680) and author of *Coronas líricas* and *El peregrino en Babilonia*, first published in 1916 by Ricardo Rojas.

5044 García Barrón, Carlos. Algunos datos desconocidos sobre José Joaquín de Olmedo (ICC/T, 35:2, mayo/agosto 1980, p. 387–393)

In 1861 Manuel Nicholás Corpancho published five poems by Olmedo in the *Revista de Lima*. One of these, an untitled sonnet, has not been published subsequently in the *Obras*. Another shows significant variants. Of interest to the Olmedo specialist.

5045 Gimbernat de González, Ester. Mapas y texto: para una estrategia del poder (MLN, 95:2, March 1980, p. 388–399)

Studies Sigüenza y Góngora's *Los infortunios de don Alonso Ramírez*, offering an important analysis of the novel as a retold autobiography. Well-documented and persuasive.

5046 ———. Los romances filosóficos de Sor Juana Inés de la Cruz (Explicación de Textos Literarios [California State University, Department of Spanish and Portuguese, Sacramento] 9:1, 1980/1981, p. 47–53)

Analysis of three philosophical *romances* by Sor Juana and two by Lope de Vega, from *La Dorotea*, which are antecedents of the Monja's works. A thorough study with pertinent comments.

5047 Grunberg, Bernard. El universo de los conquistadores en la *Historia verdadera* de Bernal Díaz del Castillo (IGFO/RI, 39:155/158, enero/dic. 1979, p. 105–122)

Circumstances surrounding the heroic figure of the conquistador are examined in terms of stark reality and of imaginative, mythic dimensions. Important contribution for purposes of comparison with recent literary studies of the hero construct.

5048 International Congress of Hispanists, 6th, 1977, Toronto, Ontario. Actas del Sexto Congreso Internacional del Hispanistas, celebrado en Toronto del 22 al 26 de agosto de 1977. Publicadas bajo la dirección de Alan M. Gòrdon y Evelyn Rugg. Toronto,

Canada: Por la Asociación International de Hispanistas, Department of Spanish and Portuguese, University of Toronto, 1980. 830 p.; bibl.

Volume contains the following articles of interest: Peter Boyd-Bowman's "Sobre el Léxico-Hispanoamericano del Siglo XVII" (p. 123–125) reports on the preparation and orientation of a book-length study of the Hispano-American lexicon in the 17th century. Pedro R. León's "El Gesto Heróico: La Muerte de Francisco Pizarro en la Narración de Cieza de León" (p. 446–450) examines the imaginative recreation by Cieza de León of Pizarro's assassination, as presented in the "Guerra de Chupas" (Book II, Pt. IV of *Crónica del Perú*). Raimundo Lida's "Sor Juana y el Regateo de Abraham" (p. 455–458) discusses a Biblical reference in the *Respuesta* and shows its relationship to works by Pedro Cerone (*Melopeo*, 1613) and to Pietro del Bongo (*Numerorum Mysteria*, 1599) and Ruperto de Deutz (*De Operibus Sanctae Trinitatis*, 1117).

5049 Johnson, Julie Greer. The art of characterization in the *Quinquenarios* (UK/KRQ, 27:2, 1980, p. 189–203)

The *Quinquenarios*, an historical account of the Peruvian civil wars by Pedro Gutiérrez de Santa Cruz (1518?–1603?), is also a creative work of literary merit with elements of structure, setting and character portrayal common to the pre-novel. The portrayal of Francisco de Carvajal, Pizarro's commander in chief, is singled out for particular examination as an historical personage and literary figure in the chronicle.

5050 ———. A caricature of Spanish women in the New World by the Inca Garcilaso de la Vega (LALR, 9:18, Spring/Summer 1981, p. 47–51)

Treats an incident in the Inca's *Historia general del Perú* relating to Pedro de Alvarado and the bringing of Spanish women, as wives, to the New World. Spanish women are characterized in a negative light in this brief episode of considerable literary value.

5051 Lagos, Ramona. El incumplimiento de la programación épica en *La araucana* (CAM, 238:5, sept./oct. 1981, p. 157–191)

Attempt to reintegrate Ercilla's epic poem to the dynamics of the 16th century through a study of the problematics posed by its structural options. Careful study of considerable value which sees two possible structural developments within the text.

5052 Listerman, R. W. Sobre el arte dramático de Fernán González de Eslava y Sor Juana Inés de la Cruz a través de sus autos sacramentales (University of South Florida Language Quarterly [Tampa] 17:3/4, 1979, p. 12–18)

Comparison, with extensive textual quotations, of the *autos sacramentales* by Mexico's González de Eslava (1534–1601) and Sor Juana (1648–95). Of general interest.

5053 A Literary document: *Letter to a King* (REVIEW, 28, Jan./April 1981, p. 12–24)

Four items appear under the above heading: Rolena Adorno's "Waman Puma de Ayala: Author and Prince" provides a general introduction to the author and his work; George Urioste's "The Spanish and Quechua Voices of Waman Puma" finds that Waman Puma's use of Quechua demonstrates a verbal virtuosity in manipulating its expressive capacities, and explains his inconsistencies in Spanish; Regina Harrison's "The Quechua Oral Tradition: From Waman Puma to Contemporary Ecuador" compares Waman Puma's different styles in Quechua to the modern oral tradition of the language, particularly in Ecuadorian songs; Felipe Waman Puma de Ayala's "The Author's Travels" contains a brief excerpt from the *Letter to a King* translated by C. Dilke.

5054 Merrim, Stephanie. Historia y escritura en las crónicas de Indias: ensayo de un método (Explicación de Textos Literarios [California State University, Department of Spanish and Portuguese, Sacramento] 9:2, 1981, p. 193–200)

Treats the Renaissance concept of history as a sub-genre of literature. Ideas are applied to several texts, principally the *Verdadera historia* (Bernal Díaz), *Naufragios* (Cabeza de Vaca) and the *Comentarios reales* (Inca Garcilaso). A worthy contribution.

5055 Montross, Constance M. Virtue or vice?: the *Respuesta a Sor Filotea* and Thomistic thought (LALR, 9:17, Fall/Winter 1980, p. 17–27)

In the *Respuesta* Sor Juana defends her rights and those of all women through the use of Thomistic thought and logic. Comparisons of technique and ideas from the *Respuesta* and St. Thomas Aquinas' *Summa Theologica* are convincing evidence of the latter's contribution to Sor Juana's intellectual development. Excellent article.

5056 Ortega, Julio. Guamán Poma de Ayala y la producción del texto (CH, 120: 360, junio 1980, p. 600–611)

The *Primer nueva corónica y buen gobierno* is seen as a kind of encyclopedic text or American Bible which reproduces the books of the Origins, Mythic Ages, and native cultural and social models, and Christian world, while projecting a new political and utopian order. Excellent observations.

5057 ———. El Inca Garcilaso y el discurso de la cultura (CH, 357, marzo 1980, p. 670–676)

Observations based on the *Comentarios reales* and *Historia general del Perú* show the Inca Garcilaso's works to be the New World's first formalization of an *escritura crítica*. In his contemplation of the past, the Inca projects through his writings an alternate model of a more utopian system in the future.

5058 Pascual Buxó, José. Muerte y desengaño en la poesía novohispana, siglos XVI y XVII. México: Universidad Nacional Autónoma de México, 1975. 164 p.; bibl.; ill. (Textos y estudios—Instituto de Investigaciones Filológicas, Centro de Estudios Literarios; 2: Letras del XVI al XVIII)

From a thematic perspective, relating to the topics of *muerte* and *desengaño*, the author studies the productivity of poets (primarily minor figures) in the 16th and 17th centuries. Volume also contains an interesting section of "documentos" and the texts of several previously unpublished poems of the period. A valuable tome of interest to the specialist.

5059 Paz, Octavio. Juana Ramírez (UC/S, 5:1, Autumn 1979, p. 80–97)

Fascinating essay on Juana Inés, the woman, which speculates on her pre-convent life and motivations for taking the veil. Particularly intriguing are the statements by Paz on the *galanteos de Palacio*. A kind of psycho-literary analysis, translated into English from an essay published in 1978.

5060 Pease, Franklin. Felipe Guamán Poma de Ayala: mitos andinos e historia occidental (UTIEH/C, 37, 1981, p. 19–36)

Author deals with selected themes in the *Nueva corónica* relating to the mythology coming from European sources and their Andean counterparts. Focuses primarily on religious symbols. Well-documented and valuable source.

5061 Pozuelo Yvancos, José María. López de Velasco en la teoría gramatical del siglo XVI (Anales de la Universal de Murcia [Murcia, Spain] 38, 1979/1980, p. 3–93)

Buen estudio sobre el famoso cronista de Indias, pero se limita a su papel como gramático. [Lino Gómez Canedo]

5062 Presencia de Sor Juana. Toluca: Gobierno del Estado de México, Patrimonio Cultural y Artístico del Estado de México, 1978. 164 p. (Serie José Antonio Alzate y Ramírez; 12)

Collection of newspaper articles, biographical notes, and scholarly studies on the life and personality of Sor Juana. Authors include O. Paz, Castro Leal, L. G. Urbina, A. Yáñez, F. Monterde, De la Maza and a dozen more. Some essays contain worthwhile materials.

5063 Rodríguez, Ileana. Imagen de Nicaragua en la literatura imperial: exploración, conquista, colonización (IILI/RI, 47:114/115, enero/junio 1981, p. 277–291)

Details the characteristic narrative and classic peculiarities of the "imperial literature" written about Nicaragua by individuals involved in the exploration, conquest and colonization of the area between 1503–35. Thought-provoking essay which contends that these writings subsequently influenced the development of Latin-American literature.

5064 Román-Lagunas, Jorge. Obras de Pedro de Oña y bibliografía sobre él (RIB, 31:3, 1981, p. 345–365)

The 145 items listed include entries on works by Oña, bibliographies, books and articles of a critical nature. In the main, entries are annotated, providing some idea of their relative worth. Indispensable tool.

5065 Romero, Mario Germán. Aspectos literarios de la obra de Don Juan de Castellanos. Palabras preliminares de Isaac J. Pardo. Bogotá: Editorial Kelly, 1978. 399 p.; 3 leaves of plates; bibl.; ill.; index.

Materials in this volume were first

published between 1965–68 in the *Boletín Cultural y Bibliográfico* (Bogotá). This is primarily a stylistic study of diverse aspects of Castellanos' *Elegías de Varones Ilustres de Indias* (1589).

5066 Rublúo, Luis. Sor Juana ante la crítica española (CAM, 231:4, julio/agosto 1980, p. 183–204)

Examination of critical commentaries by several Spanish critics on the poetry of Sor Juana. Among others, author cites opinions of Menéndez Pelayo, Unamuno, José María Pemán and Gerardo Diego. Comments are anti-feminist and generally biased.

5067 Sabat de Rivers, Georgina. El "Sueño" de Sor Juana Inés de la Cruz: tradiciones literarias y originalidad. London: Tamesis, 1976. 160 p.; bibl. (Colección Támesis: Serie A, Monografías; 40)

Splendid study of Sor Juana's "Primero Sueño" and the most comprehensive examination of this work in some two decades or more. Pt. 1 treats the literary traditions on which the Décima Musa developed her work, and pt. 2 with the poem's originality. Bibliography is extensive and up-to-date.

5068 Salazar Mallén, Rubén. Apuntes para una biografía de Sor Juana Inés de la Cruz. 2. ed. México: Universidad Nacional Autónoma de México, Coordinación de Humanidades, 1978. 134 p.

Second edition of a study first published in 1952 (limited edition of 200 copies). Appendix has been added which contains the "Carta de Sor Filotea," the "Respuesta" and the Testaments of Sor Juana and of her mother, Isabel Ramírez.

5069 Salstad, Louise M. El símbolo de la fuente en *El divino Narciso* de Sor Juana Inés de la Cruz (Explicación de Textos Literarios [California State University, Department of Spanish and Portuguese, Sacramento] 9:1, 1980/1981, p. 41–46)

Article of interest to the specialist on the symbolic value of the fountain in Sor Juana's *El divino Narciso*. It represents a fusion of Biblical, liturgical and dogmatic motifs. Worthwhile contribution to the bibliography on the Décima Musa.

5070 Santa, Eduardo. Jiménez de Quesada y la literatura colombiana (CBR/BCB, 16:3, marzo 1979, p. 40–52)

Gonzalo Jiménez de Quesada, as explorer and conqueror of Nueva Granada, is ranked alongside Pizarro and Cortés as one of the three major figures of the Conquest. His monumental work, *El Antijovio* (written about 1567), initiates the history of Colombian literature. General but informative.

5071 Siemens, William L. Viracocha as god and hero in the *Comentarios reales* (HR, 47:3, 1979, p. 327–338)

Excellent article which considers the relationship of cycles of time to ideas of the cosmos in Indian religions, as seen in the story of the young prince (later called Viracocha) who is rejected by his father, Yáhuar Huácac. Innovative and imaginative approach.

5072 Smith, Octavio. Para una vida de Santiago Pita. La Habana, Cuba: Editorial Letras Cubanas, 1978. 145 p.; bibl.; 1 leaf of plates; maps (Colección Crítica)

Thorough study of known facts about the life and works of Santiago Pita de Figueroa, author of *El príncipe jardinero y fingido Cloridano*, the first work of Cuban theater. Two appendixes reproduce Church and legal documents related to the dramatist.

5073 Soons, Alan. An idearium and its literary presentation in *El lazarillo de ciegos caminantes* (Romanische Forschungen [Frankfurt, FRG] 92, 1979, p. 92–95)

Examination of Alonso Carrió de la Vandera's novel *El lazarillo de ciegos caminantes* (1775 or 1776) which finds that as a work of the imagination, the novel is grounded in a notion of dynamism and movement. A thought-provoking essay.

5074 Sor Juana Inés de la Cruz ante la historia: biografías antiguas: la Fama de 1700: noticias de 1667 a 1892. Recopilación de Francisco de la Maza. Revisión de Elías Trabulse. México: Universidad Nacional Autónoma de México, 1980. 612 p.; 17 p. of plates; bibl.; ill. (some col.) (Estudios de literatura; 4)

Fascinating compilation of commentaries on Sor Juana and her works from 1667 by Diego de Ribera to the comments by Menéndez y Pelayo in 1892. Published after F. de la Maza's death, this is a most worthwhile contribution to scholarship on Sor Juana. Extensive bibliography adds to the volume's importance.

5075 Suárez Radillo, Carlos Miguel. El teatro barroco hispanoamericano: ensayo de una historia crítico-antológica. Madrid: Ediciones J. Porrúa Turanzas, 1981. 3 v. (700 p.); bibl.; ill.; index (Ensayos)

Critical history together with anthologized selections of plays by major dramatists of the theater in Colonial Spanish America, 1600–1750. Vol. 1 covers the Viceroyalty of New Spain including Caribbean and Central American seats of culture; vol. 2, the Viceroyalty of Peru, primarily Lima; vol. 3, other centers of the Peruvian Viceroyalty—Bogotá, Quito, Caracas, Buenos Aires, etc. Extensive annotations. A most valuable addition to our knowledge of the colonial theater.

5076 Tamayo Vargas, Augusto. El mundo de las ideas precolombinas en el mito de Pacaritampu (CH, 121:363, sept. 1980, p. 569–579)

Examines the myth of Pacaritampu, the legendary and literary explanation of the advance of the Quechua tribes into the valley of Cuzco and the establishing of Tahuantinsuyo. Myth is mentioned by the Inca Garcilaso and in variant forms by Cieza de León, Betanzos, Santa Cruz and other chroniclers.

5077 Treviño, Gilberto. Bernardo del Carpio desencantado por Bernardo de Balbuena (CAM, 236:3, mayo/junio 1981, p. 79–102)

Author sees El Bernardo as a text of noteworthy unity of intent, style and design in which the exhaltation of the greatness of Spain becomes a predominant function of the poem. A well-written and convincing re-evaluation of Balbuena's epic.

TEXTS

5078 Anadón, José. Prosistas coloniales del siglo XVII, Rosales y Pineda Bascuñán: textos complementarios. Santiago de Chile: Seminario de Filología Hispánica, 1978. 140 p.; appendices (Theses et studia scholastica; 6)

Volume contains three chapters from Fray Diego de Rosales' Conquista espiritual, a work as yet unpublished in its entirety, and from Núñez de Pineda y Bascuñán's Recopilación, consisting of several folios of unpublished materials containing biographical

information on the author. Introduction provides background information.

5079 Casas, Bartolomé de las. Brevíssima relación. Breve resúmen del descubrimiento y destruición de las Indias. Madrid: Emiliano Escolar, D.L. 1979. 291 p.; 2 leaves (Historia) (Cultura clásica)

Edition of Las Casas' Breve resúmen del descubrimiento . . . in a modernized text without benefit of notes or bibliography. Valuable as a student text, but of scant worth to the scholar.

5080 Cronistas de Indias: antología. Introducción, notas y propuestas de trabajo, Silvia Calero y Evangelina Folino. Buenos Aires: Ediciones Colihue: distribución exclusiva, Librería Hachette, 1980. 172 p.; bibl.; ill. (Colección Literaria LYC [leer y crear])

Anthologized selections from writings of Columbus, Las Casas, Díaz del Castillo, Núñez Cabeza de Vaca and several others. Texts are prefaced by a chronology of major chroniclers and an introduction treating history and literature in the chronicles, problems relating to genre definition, themes, myths, etc. Primarily intended for classroom use.

5081 Ercilla y Zúñiga, Alonso de. La Araucana. Edición, introducción y notas de Marcos A. Morínigo e Isaías Lerner. Madrid: Castalia, 1979. 2 v. (440, 486 p.); bibl.; index (Clásicos Castalia; 91/92)

First accessible, scholarly edition of La araucana in more than 20 years and perhaps the most reliable one since Medina's (1910–18). Text is based on the Madrid edition of 1589–90 with punctuation, accentuation and spelling modernized. Introduction provides biographical, critical and bibliographical data. Notes explain lexical peculiarities and historical, geographic and mythological references. Textual variants from editions between (1569–97) are also recorded. An outstanding edition.

5082 Los Fundadores. M. del Barco Centenera, L. de Tejeda y otros. Antología por Bernardo Canal Feijóo. Prólogo y notas por Ricardo Figueira. Buenos Aires: Centro Editor de América Latina, 1979. 101 p. (Capítulo; 6)

Prose and verse selections from six writers associated with the River Plate region in the 16th and 17th centuries are included in this volume. Best known are Martín del Barco Centenera and Tejeda y Guzmán. Intended primarily for students.

5083 Garcilaso de la Vega. Comentarios reales de los incas. Prólogo, edición y cronología, Aurelio Miró Quesada. Caracas: Biblioteca Ayacucho, 1976. 2 v.; bibl. (Biblioteca Ayacucho; 5/6)

Excellent edition of the *Comentarios* prepared by an eminent scholar in the field of Garcilaso studies. Edition reproduces the Lisbon "princeps" of 1609. Texts have been modernized for the contemporary reader. Valuable, scholarly contribution.

5084 Iturriaga, José Mariano de. La californiada. Transcripción paleográfica, introducción, versión y notas de Alfonso Castro Pallares. México: Universidad Nacional Autónoma de México, 1979. 93 p.; bibl. (Cuadernos del Centro de Estudios clásicos; 7)

Bilingual edition of a Latin poem (810 hexameters) which shows Renaissance/Baroque influences. Authored by José Mariano de Iturriaga, about mid-18th century, it recounts the deeds of the heroes of the Society of Jesus in New Spain, especially of Fray Juan María Salvatierra, a missionary in California. An interesting curiosity.

5085 Juana Inés de la Cruz, Sister. Respuesta a Sor Filotea de la Cruz. Prólogo por el Grupo Feminista de Cultura. Barcelona: Laertes, D.L. 1979. 81 p.; 1 leaf.

Modernized edition of Sor Juana's *Respuesta a Sor Filotea* for general public consumption. Prologue by the Grupo Feminista de Cultura is in praise of the Monja as the Primera Feminista de América. Of general rather than scholarly interest.

5086 La Literatura virreinal: antología. J. B. Maciel, D. de Azcuénaga y otros. Selección, prólogo y notas por Bernardo Canal Feijóo. Buenos Aires: Centro Editor de América Latina, 1979. 122 p. (Capítulo; 7)

Brief anthology of viceregal writers from the Río de la Plata region containing selections from Carrió de la Vandera's *Lazarillo de ciegos caminantes* and from six little-known poets. Bio-bibliographical introductions to each writer are provided.

5087 Mier Noriega y Guerra, José Servando Teresa de. Ideario político. Prólogo,

notas y cronología, Edmundo O'Gorman. Caracas, Venezuela: Biblioteca Ayacucho, 1978. 443 p.; bibl. (Biblioteca Ayacucho; 43)

Volume offers a panoramic view of the political thoughts of Fray Servando Teresa de Mier. Pieces are selected from throughout his works, particularly the *Historia de la revolución de Nueva España* (1813) and *Las memorias* (1818-19). Texts are well annotated and accompanied by an introductory essay and up-to-date bibliography by and about Mier.

5088 Miramontes Zuázola, Juan. Armas antárticas. Prólogo y cronología, Rodrigo Miró. Caracas; Biblioteca Ayacucho, 1979. 403 p.; bibl. (Biblioteca Ayacucho; 35)

First edition of this lengthy poem (1704 octaves) since 1921. Poem was written between 1608-15. Edition is based on the 1921 publication compared to manuscript sources in Madrid and Lima. A most welcome addition to our list of colonial works available in modern editions.

5089 Oña, Pedro de. Arauco domado. Selección, prólogo y notas de Hugo Montes. Santiago de Chile: Editorial Universitaria, 1979. 161 p.; bibl. (Colección Escritores coloniales de Chile; no. 11)

Anthologized selections from Oña's *Arauco domado* based on the first edition of 1596. Brief introduction to author and works provides very general information. Primarily intended for student use.

5090 Orígenes de la poesía colonial venezolana. Recopilación de Mauro Páez Pumar. Con un estudio del Dr. Juan Ernesto Montenegro. Ordenada por la Presidencia del Concejo Municipal del Distrito Federal. Caracas: Concejo Municipal del Distrito Federal, 1979 [i.e. 1980]. 352 p.; bibl.

Preliminary study of precolumbian and colonial poets by J. E. Montenegro is general but informative (p. 11-71). Anthology compiled by M. Páez-Pumar contains selections from more than 35 colonial poets. Valuable source for the specialist and bio-bibliographical information enhances its worth.

5091 Poesía de la Independencia. Compilación, prólogo, notas y cronología, Emilio Carilla. Traducciones, Ida Vitale. Caracas, Venezuela: Biblioteca Ayacucho, 1979. 401 p.; bibl. (Biblioteca Ayacucho; 59)

In addition to a general introductory

section containing an historical panorama, each section of this anthology is headed by comments and a basic bibliography on the poet. Writers include Olmedo, Bello, Heredia, Hidalgo, Melgar and more than 20 other lesser-known poets from throughout Latin America. An excellent anthology.

5092 Poma de Ayala, Felipe Huamán. El primer *Nueva corónica y buen gobierno.* Edición crítica de John V. Murra y Rolena Adorno. Traducciones y análisis textual del quechua por Jorge L. Urioste. México, D.F.: Siglo Veintiuno, 1980. 3 v. (1175 p.); ill. (Colección América nuestra; 31. América antigua)

Guamán Poma completed his history of Peru between 1612–15 although it remained undiscovered until 1908 and unpublished until 1936. This critical edition, based on the original manuscript, is intended for the specialist. Punctuation and accentuation are modernized. Introductory essays by Murra, Adorno and Urioste, extensive notes, and a glossary-index add to the value of this edition. An outstanding contribution.

5093 Rodríguez Freyle, Juan. El carnero. Prólogo, notas y cronología, Darío Achury Valenzuela. Caracas: Biblioteca Ayacucho, 1979. 592 p.; bibl. (Biblioteca Ayacucho, 66)

Important edition of Rodríguez Freyle's historical/literary narrative, presented in à modernized text based on a comparison of the nine previous editions since the first in 1859 (Bogotá). Extensive Prologue (p. ix–lxxxv) gives ample information on the writer and comments about salient features of his work. This should be considered the standard edition for years to come.

MISCELLANEOUS

5094 Browning, John D. The periodical press: voice of the Enlightenment in Spanish America (Dieciocho [New York] 3:1, 1980, p. 5–16)

Author contends that the periodical press offers important insights into the nature of the Enlightenment in the Spanish New World. Periodicals treated: *Diario Literario* (1768); *Mercurio Volante* (1772) from Mexico; *Mercurio Peruano* (1791) from Peru; and the *Gazeta de Guatemala* (1796). Includes comments on Terralla y Landa's *Lima por dentro y fuera* (1797). Valuable article.

5095 García Sáiz, María Concepción. Nuevos aspectos de la pintura colonial del siglo XVIII (IFGO/RI, 39:155/158, enero/dic. 1979, p. 337–347)

Interesting article whose content has some applicability to literary currents of the colonial period. Comments on colonial painting, particularly of the 18th century are enhanced by 12 plates of paintings from Peru and the Quito area.

5096 Simmons, Merle E. Spanish and Spanish American writer politicians in Philadelphia, 1790–1830 (Dieciocho [New York] 3:1, 1980, p. 27–39)

Essay of limited scope which directs attention to an aspect of the intellectual and political history of the Hispanic world at the close of the colonial period. Of primary interest to the specialist.

5097 Wilhite, John F. The Enlightenment in Latin America: tradition versus change (Dieciocho [New York] 3:1, 1980, p. 18–26)

Valuable observations on the interests and activities of the Enlightenment in Latin America, in educational reform, scientific expeditions, economic societies, literary circles and the publication of periodicals.

5098 ———. The Inter-American Enlightenment (RIB, 30:3, 1980, p. 254–261)

Succinct, capsule view of the various concerns of the Enlightenment in education, science, philosophy, literature, political science and economics in both Americas. A most worthwhile article with valuable documentation.

Prose Fiction and Other Prose Writings: 19th Century

NICOLAS SHUMWAY, *Assistant Professor of Spanish, Yale University*

THE BIENNIUM SAW A NUMBER OF IMPORTANT publications, particularly in reinterpreting Spanish American Romanticism. Especially interesting is a fine article by Alejandro Losada, "¿Cultura nacional o literatura revolucionaria?" (item **5139**) in which he indulges in some illuminating revisionism on the role of Argentine writers during the turbulent years leading from Rosas to Roca. Also noteworthy are two excellent collections of essays on Bello and his times prior to his Chilean years, which usually receive most of the attention: *Bello y Caracas* and *Bello y Londres* (items **5121** and **5122**).

Two important biographies, one new and another republished, became available. The first is Luis Alberto Sánchez's extraordinary study of Manuel González Prada and his family: *Nuestras vidas son los ríos . . .* (item **5115**). This is clearly the best book available on González Prada and is written with a clarity and charm worthy of imitation. The second is Juan Bosch's *Hostos, el sembrador* (item **5123**). Both works reveal the author's reactions and involvement with their subjects to such a degree that one wonders if we are witnessing a new genre: biography as autobiography.

There were also a couple of surprises. The nicest came in the form of Antonio López Matoso's (I had never heard of him either) previously unpublished diary, *Viaje de Perico Ligero al país de los moros* (item **5108**) which gives a delightful account of one man's tribulations during the Mexican wars of independence. Cuba, however, again led the way in republishing forgotten or overlooked writers of the past century: for example, a collection of Esteban Borrero Echeverría's short fiction under the title of *Narraciones* (item **5100**).

Unfortunately, not all publications were equally successful. Without question the most disappointing affair is the much trumpeted Biblioteca Ayacucho's editions of 19th-century *clásicos*. Perhaps sitting for too long in cold libraries accounts for the hunger for "events" characteristic of literary scholars. At any rate, the event of several years ago was the announcement that the Biblioteca Ayacucho, under the direction of Angel Rama, would publish a hardcover series of essential works of Spanish American literature, many of them from the past century. Several of these are now out and described below, with varying degrees of enthusiasm. The failure of these editions can be attributed to the editorial decision to produce "popular editions" for the general public. Although such sentiment warms our democratic souls, it ignores the fact that popular editions of *Facundo, María* and so forth are available in inexpensive editions at every bookstore in Spanish America, frequently in the same prologue-plus-text format adopted by the Biblioteca Ayacucho. What is really needed are rigorous, scholarly editions—something like the Norton Critical Editions that have contributed so much to the study of English and North American literature. As it is, we are left with expensive books (occasionally with many misprints) that look pretty on the shelf without going beyond what has always been available. There are of course notable exceptions, as witnessed by José Miguel Oviedo's excellent new anthology of *Cien tradiciones peruanas* (item **5110**). At the same time, one regrets that a fine opportunity to create definitive, critical editions appears to have been lost.

PROSE FICTION

5099 Betancourt, José Ramón de. Una feria de la caridad en 183 . . . Prólogo de Raúl González de Cascorro. La Habana: Editorial Letras Cubanas, 1978. 231 p. (Biblioteca básica de literatura cubana)

Short prologue to this edition of Betancourt's youthful novel offers little more than a thumbnail biography of the author. The appendix, however, includes essays by Cirilo Villaverde and Javier Franch which provide an interesting glimpse of how Betancourt's contemporaries reacted to his work.

5100 Borrero Echeverría, Esteban. Narraciones. Selección, prólogo y notas de Manuel Cofiño. La Habana: Editorial Letras Cubanas, 1979. 182 p. (Biblioteca básica de literatura cubana)

Little known outside of Cuba, Borrero Echeverría's short fiction should gain a wider public through this short, inexpensive book. Worthwhile in its own right, his work also reflects the author's profound pessimism after seeing Cuba's aspirations for independence frustrated by North American expansionism—a fact ably satirized in "El Ciervo Encantado," included in this collection. Aside from a largely biographical prologue, this edition includes letters from Borrero to Luis Montané and Enrique José Varona, plus a reply from the latter, Borrero's short autobiography and articles on Borrero by Julián del Casal and Manuel de la Cruz.

5101 Cambacérès, Eugenio. En la sangre. Introducción, notas y propuestas de trabajo, Noemí Susana García y Jorge Panesi. Buenos Aires: Colihue/Hachette, 1980. 169, 7 p.; bibl. (Colección literaria LYC [leer y crear])

This inexpensive edition from the Colección Literaria LYC (Leer y Crear) is primarily aimed at beginning students of literature, and in that context is exceptionally well done. The prologue carefully lays out the major literary, social and political currents of the 1880s and their relationship to the novel. Moreover, the prologue includes a more than competent analysis of the novel and its place in Argentine naturalism.

5102 Isaacs, Jorge. María. Prólogo, notas, y cronología, Gustavo Mejía. Caracas,

Venezuela: Biblioteca Ayacucho, 1978. 292 p.; bibl. (Biblioteca Ayacucho; 34)

Another in the Biblioteca Ayacucho series, this edition of María offers little not available in dozens of cheaper editions. Mejía's prologue warms over Anderson Imbert's and Seymour Menton's well-known essays on the novel's structure, and ends up with an underdeveloped and unsubstantiated thesis which supposes María to be a nostalgic farewell to a colonial socioeconomic system soon to be overrun by bourgeois capitalism. Notes in the text are occasionally informative.

5103 López-Portillo y Rojas, José. Los precursores. v. 1, Crisálidas. v. 2, Mariposas. v. 3, La llama. 2. ed. Guadalajara, México: Ayuntamiento de Guadalajara, 1976–1978. 3 v.

This new edition of López Portillo's second novel is published in a large, three-volume format by the municipality of Guadalajara. The edition itself offers little in the way of scholarship, but may be of interest to libraries not owning a copy.

5104 Meza y Suárez Inclán, Ramón. Novelas breves. El duelo de mi vecino. Don Aniceto el tendero. Ultimas páginas. La Habana: Editorial Arte y Literatura, 1975. 310 p. (Biblioteca básica de literatura cubana)

Although Ramón Meza's youthful novels were first published during the early stirrings of Modernism (between 1886–91), they share much more with the sentimental realism of Isaacs and Villaverde than with the vigorous prose of Martí. This edition includes a competent prologue plus an appendix containing a short autobiography of Meza and a final note by Manuel de la Cruz which is almost a second prologue.

5105 Zeno Gandía, Manuel. La charca. Prólogo y cronología, Enrique Laguerre. Caracas: Biblioteca Ayacucho, 1978. 282 p.; bibl. (Biblioteca Ayacucho; 55)

This new edition makes available to a broad audience a fine Puerto Rican novel which is largely unknown outside of the Caribbean. The novel itself is one of the best of Spanish American naturalism and shows considerable inventiveness in applying Zola's theories to a rural situation in Puerto Rico. Laguerre's prologue provides an excellent introduction to Zeno Gandía and his place in Hispanic letters.

MISCELLANEOUS PROSE (ESSAYS, MEMOIRS, CORRESPONDENCE, ETC.)

5106 Acevedo Díaz, Eduardo. Correspondencia familiar e íntima de Eduardo Acevedo Díaz: 1880–1898. Presentación y notas por Héctor Galmés. Montevideo: Biblioteca Nacional, 1979. 66 p.; ill.

As one of Uruguay's and Spanish America's best 19th-century novelists, Eduardo Acevedo Díaz certainly does not deserve the critical silence that today surrounds much of his work. This short sampling of letters taken from a much larger collection kept at the Biblioteca Nacional de Montevideo reminds us of how much remains to be done on this activist-writer who both in his writings, particularly the historical novels, and in his life reflected many of the major intellectual concerns of his age.

5107 Bello, Andrés. Anthology. Compiled by Pedro Grases. Foreword by Rafael Caldera. Translated by Barbara D. Huntley and Pilar Liria. Washington, D.C.: Organization of American States, General Secretariat, 1981. 259 p.; bibl.

This anthology of Bello in translation not only fills a great need, but does so splendidly, offering a selection representative of the considerable breadth of Bello's work, from poetry to linguistic theory, from law to philosophy. Highly recommended.

5108 López Matoso, Antonio. *Viaje de Perico Ligero al país de los moros:* a critical edition of Antonio López Matoso's unpublished diary, 1816–1820. Edited by James T. Tatum. New Orleans: Middle American Research Institute, Tulane University, 1972. 114 p.; 6 leaves of plates; bibl.; 21 ill.; index (Publication—Middle American Research Institute, Tulane University; 36)

Antonio López Matoso did not make it into most political and literary histories, not because historians are any harder of heart than the rest of us, but because López Matoso was not a particularly important person. And therein lies the considerable charm of his diary, here published for the first time. Written while the author was travelling under custody as an accused insurgent, the diary itself is a collage of observations, satirical verse and personal experiences, written with the freshness and candor of a man not trying

to impress anyone; as such, it is a fascinating, personal view of Mexico during the final years of the Wars of Independence (1816–20). Tatum's introduction is extremely helpful, although the bibliography and illustrations alone would justify the book. Highly recommended.

5109 Martí, José. Thoughts on liberty, government, art and morality: a bilingual anthology (Pensamientos sobre la libertad, la política, el arte y la moral: antología bilingüe). Edited by Carlos Ripoll. New York: Las Américas Publishing Co., 1980. 123 p.

This bilingual book of quotations from José Martí on a variety of subjects shows him to be an able, if unintentional, aphorist, although one is usually left wondering at the larger context. The translations are adequate although occasionally Elizabethan in style—a fact that sometimes makes Martí sound like a creole Kahlil Gibran.

5110 Palma, Ricardo. Cien tradiciones peruanas. Prólogo, selección y cronología, José Miguel Oviedo. Caracas: Biblioteca Ayacucho, 1977. 532 p.; bibl. (Biblioteca Ayacucho; 7)

Another in the Biblioteca Ayacucho series, this anthology of *Tradiciones* is a welcome companion to the several collections already in print. Oviedo's informative prologue carefully traces development of the *tradiciones* in the twin contexts of Spanish American Romanticism and Palma's own artistic development. Selections follow order of eight series published by Palma (although Oviedo points out that this order is not necessarily chronological) and thus avoids some of the confusion in *Tradiciones peruanas completas* (Aguilar, 1964) where the selections are arranged according to theme. Although some selections appear in other readily available collections, there are enough surprises in this anthology, plus Oviedo's fine prologue, to make it worth the trouble.

5111 *Papel Periódico Ilustrado.* v. 3, 1883–1884. Edición facsimilar ilustrada. Edited by Alberto Urdaneta. Cali, Colombia: Carvajal & Cia., 1977. 400 p.

Vol. 3 of five large and sumptuous ones that will eventually include a complete set of the *Papel Periódico Ilustrado*, a biweekly magazine issued in Bogotá during the early 1880s. Magazine is a wonderful reflection of literary and artistic activities of the period, complete with articles, creative writing, reviews and sheet music. Particularly interesting are the numerous high-quality engravings.

5112 Rodó, José Enrique. Ariel. Motivos de Proteo. Prólogos, Carlos Real de Azúa. Edición y cronología, Angel Arma. Caracas: Biblioteca Ayacucho, 1976. 373 p.; bibl. (Biblioteca Ayacucho; 3)

Another in the sumptuous series published by the Biblioteca Ayacucho, this book is a good step towards a definitive, critical edition of the works in question. Carlos Real de Azúa in two separate prologues admirably describes and documents the social and intellectual environments surrounding the works and their creation, as well as the critical reaction both books, particularly *Ariel*, provoked throughout Spanish America. The texts themselves, however, are little more than copies of previous editions the editors considered reliable—as Angel Rama explains in his "Criterio de esta edición." Although much work has gone into this edition, and there is a lot to recommend it, it contributes little to our understanding of Rodó or the reliability of this particular text than was already available in other editions, particularly Aguilar's *Obras completas*.

5113 ———. Cartas de José Enrique Rodó a Juan Francisco Piquet: primera serie. Introducción y notas por Wilfredo Penco. Montevideo: Biblioteca Nacional, 1979 [i.e. 1980]. 86 p.; bibl.; ill.

Importance of Rodó's correspondence kept at the Biblioteca Nacional in Montevideo has long been recognized, yet, except for short quotations and references in other studies, the letters have never been available to the general public. This short selection of letters written to a close, life-long friend reveals what a treasure the entire collection must be, and leads us to hope that eventually Rodó's entire correspondence will be edited and published. The collection is particularly useful since the editor, Wilfredo Penco, has taken great pains to describe the context of each letter.

5114 Rojas, Arístides. Crónicas y leyendas. Selección y prólogo de Manuel Bermúdez. Caracas: Monte Avila Editores, 1979. 280 p.; bibl.; ill. (Colección Eldorado)

Arístides Rojas has met an unfortunate fate: although essentially a popular writer, his work has seen print only in limited or "official" editions, thus denying him access to the greater public. With this inexpensive edition, Monte Avila publishes selections from the breadth of his work, including historical and scientific treatises (clearly written with a general audience in mind) and gossipy anecdotes. Useful prologue and notes.

5115 Sánchez, Luis Alberto. Nuestras vidas son los ríos . . . : historia y leyenda de los González Prada. Lima: Universidad Nacional Mayor de San Marcos, Dirección Universitaria de Biblioteca y Publicaciones, 1977. 405 p.; bibl.

Important book about an important subject: Manuel González Prada (and his family), who is without question one of the most interesting and original thinkers of the last century. Written with charm and occasional authorial intrusion (forgiveable since González Prada more than any contemporary demands a personal response), the book does an exceptionally fine job of illuminating a period and a person. Good documentation. Highly recommended.

5116 Sarmiento, Domingo Faustino. Facundo: o, Civilización, y barbarie. Prólogo, Noé Jitrik. Notas y cronología, Nora Dottori, Silvia Zanetti. Caracas: Biblioteca Ayacucho, 1977. 371 p.; (Biblioteca Ayacucho; 12)

In his prologue to this edition of *Facundo* from the Biblioteca Ayacucho, Noé Jitrik inaugurates what could become an unfortunate new genre: the self-conscious prologue. After discoursing at length on how difficult, if not heroic, is his task, he supplies a very personal, highly theoretical, usually informed, often provocative and frequently frustrating *reading* (I emphasize the word since I am sure he would) of Sarmiento's seminal work. Fortunately, the text's extensive notes and appendixes by Nora Dottori and Silvia Zanetti make this the most useful edition of *Facundo* to date.

5117 Zorrilla de San Martín, Juan. Ensayos. Selección y prólogo de Arturo Sergio Visca. Montevideo: Ministerio de Educación, Biblioteca Artigas, 1978. 3 v. (Colección de clásicos uruguayos; 154)

Although all of the essays in these three volumes were written since 1900, in a sense they belong to the last century. Zorrilla de San Martín was one of our greatest romantic poets, and his attempts to reconcile the crises of our century with his basically optimistic, romantic and Catholic view of the world make for interesting reading. Particularly interesting is vol. 1, *El sermón de la paz*, in which he tries to reconcile a romantic view of peoplehood and patriotism with the destructive nationalism of Europe's declining nobility. Vol. 1's prologue provides a useful introduction to all of the essays.

LITERARY CRITICISM AND HISTORY

5118 Acutis, Cesare; Erica Gay di Carlo; and **Angelo Morino.** Fabulaciones de identidad: Argentina entre historia y mito (Nova Americana [Giulio Einaudi Editore, Torino, Italy] 3, 1980, p. 355–370)

Commentary on the image of the pampa and its inhabitants from the conquest through successive works of literature (*La cautiva, Amalia, Una excursión a los indios ranqueles*, etc.). Offers some interesting observations which could lead to a more substantial work. Much too vast a topic for a short piece.

5119 Altamirano, Carlos and **Beatriz Sarlo.** Una vida ejemplar: la estrategia de *Recuerdos de provincia* (UCV/E, 5 : 9, enero/junio 1980, p. 3–48)

Análisis lúcido del texto de Sarmiento. Sin distanciarse demasiado de algunos de los argumentos usados en *Facundo*, el recuento de su herencia otorga validez a sus excentricidades y a la particularidad de su talento. Si bien la familia no le otorgó propiedad y rango, obtuvo por ambos lados "los instrumentos morales e intelectuales con los que el periodista y el político aspiran al ascenso y la fama" (p. 48). [S. Sosnowski]

5120 Bastos, María Luisa. José Enrique Rodó: la parábola como paradigma dinámico (HR, Summer 1981, p. 261–269)

Excellent, close reading of one of Rodó's parables in *Motivos de Proteo*, article examines levels of rhetorical discourse in the parable, motives behind its composition, and possibilities of reading it in several ways. Highly recommended.

5121 Bello y Caracas: primer congreso del bicentenario. Caracas: Fundación La

Casa de Bello, 1979. 473 p.; bibl.; index.

Given the state of our knowledge concerning Bello's experiences prior to the important years he spent in Chile, this book and its companion, *Bello y Londres* (see item **5122**), deserve attention and appreciation. Although somewhat uneven in quality, some essays are very worthwhile, and others are outstanding. Particularly worthy of mention are Elías Pino Iturrieta's "1750–1810: un Período de Cambios en la Mentalidad Venezolana" and Arturo Ardao's "La Iniciación Filosófica de Bello." Highly recommended.

5122 Bello y Londres: segundo congreso del bicentenario. Caracas: Fundación la Casa de Bello, 1980. 1 v.; ill.

Similar to its companion volume, *Bello y Caracas* (item **5121**), this collection of essays studies Bello's years in London, perhaps with even greater success. Articles are uniformly of high quality and explore a variety of subjects with rigor and imagination. Particularly interesting are extensive studies on English contacts with the Hispanic world, and especially Jeremy Bentham's influence on Bello and other prominent Spanish Americans. Highly recommended.

5123 Bosch, Juan. Hostos, el sembrador. Río Piedras, P.R.: Ediciones Huracán, 1976. 207 p.; port. (Colección Norte)

New edition of Juan Bosch's 1934 biography of Eugenio María de Hostos is not a modern, scholarly biography, but an eloquent testimony of the personal encounter between an important modern writer and a major essayist, educator and libertarian of the last century. As a confrontation of two idealists of different generations, the book makes fascinating reading.

5124 Bouilly, Victor. Le mot *romantique* au Rio de la Plata vers 1830 (UCL/LR, 35 : 4, nov. 1981, p. 301–318)

This well-documented article carefully traces the use of the terms *romántico* and *romanticismo* in Argentina during the 1830s, both by its critics and its adherents. Although he offers no surprises, the author convincingly demonstrates that Argentina, like a distant mirror, reflected to a high degree much of the European romantic experience with all its vitality and confusion.

5125 Brieba, Liborio E. Episodios nacionales. v. 1, Los talaveras. El enviado. Entre las nieves. v. 2, La San Bartólome de los patriotas. El capitán San Bruno. Las prisiones de Juan Fernández. v. 3, Manuel Rodríguez. Los favoritos de Marco del Pont. Los guerrilleros insurgentes. Chacabuco y la libertad de Chile. Ilustrado por Julio Palazuelas. Santiago, Chile: Editorial Andrés Bello, 1975? 3 v.; ill.

New three-volume edition of Brieba's historical dramatizations of the Chilean independence movement. These works mark an important step in the development of Chilean narrative, but unfortunately, this edition contains no prologue, notes or bibliography.

5126 Bueno, Salvador. El negro en la novela romántica sentimental *María* (ICC/T, 35:3, sept./dic. 1980, p. 550–564)

Off to a bad start, Bueno insists on a rigid and pale caricature of European Romanticism which he then—not surprisingly—finds inapplicable to Spanish America. The rest of the article concerning blacks and social relationships in *María* is interesting and well thought out. In his analysis of the black presence, Bueno finds the much debated interpolated tale of Nay and Sinar not as out of place as often supposed.

5127 Cano, Vicente. Larra y Alberdi: paralelos y divergencias (Revista de Artes y Letras de la Universidad de Costa Rica [San José] 4:1, enero/junio 1980, p. 41–47)

Larra's influence on the Generation of 1837, particularly Sarmiento and Alberdi, has long been recognized. Through a detailed comparison of ideas, style and precursors, Cano shows the extent of the influence in Alberdi's case.

5128 Caparroso, Carlos Arturo. Clásicos colombianos. Bogotá: Instituto Caro y Cuervo, 1980. 226 p. (Serie "La Granada entreabierta;" 25)

Collection of essays on 19th-century Colombian writers provides an overview of and good introduction to the period. Although essays are informative, one wishes Caparroso had included more documentation and a bibliography. Footnotes with titles, publication data and page numbers would greatly increase the usefulness of this book.

5129 Fishburn, Evelyn. The concept of "civilization and barbarism" in Sarmiento's *Facundo*: a reappraisal (IAA, 5:4, 1979, p. 301–308, bibl.)

Article emphasizes two major aspects of the *Facundo* phenomenon: 1) the critical reaction (Unamuno, Palcos, Bunkley, Jitrik) to Sarmiento's famous dichotomy of civilization vs. barbarism; Fishburn shows that critics in this century emphasize Sarmiento's fundamental ambivalence towards both categories as well as individuals (Facundo, Rosas, Paz) and places (La Roija, Córdoba and Buenos Aires) that supposedly symbolize those categories; and 2) author's conclusion that, despite Sarmiento's evident ambivalence, there is no question that his overriding, ideological goal was "civilizing" Argentina.

5130 García, Germán. El ciudadano Payró (UNL/U, 91, sept./dic. 1978, p. 57–80)

Useful introduction to Payró the man as well as to Payró the writer, this article outlines his literary career in terms of his considerable journalistic effort and his notable political activism, first in the Radical movement, and later as a socialist under Juan B. Justo. Very informative although a little light on documentation.

5131 Gerling, David Ross. El parentesco literario entre la novela *Sin rumbo* de Cambaceres y una novela contemporánea de Amorim (RIB, 30:3, 1980, p. 238–245)

Detailed and convincing discussion of the commonality shared by *Sin rumbo* and *El paisano Aguilar*, demonstrates that Cambaceres and Amorim, despite nearly 50 years separating their works, selected similar themes, techniques and situations. Gerling does not explain the similarity in terms of influence but rather as response to similar stimuli (e.g., subject matter, personal disillusion, etc.).

5132 Giron, Nicole. La idea de "cultura nacional" en el siglo XIX: Altamirano y Ramírez (*in* Seminario de Historia de la Cultura Nacional, 1976. En torno a la cultura nacional. Héctor Aguilar Camín and others. México: Instituto Nacional Indigenista, Secretaría de Educación Pública, Instituto Nacional de Antropología e Historia, 1976, p. 51–83 [Colección SEP-INI, 51])

Rather than a study of the notion of national culture in 19th-century Mexico, article is a severe and largely unjustified criticism of Altamirano's and Ramírez's alleged failure to understand their country, especially the indigenous communities. Although Giron documents her observations extensively (therein lies article's value) quotations used do not always support author's thesis and occasionally contradict it. Particularly bothersome is Giron's tendency to criticize "contradictions and ambivalences" of 19th-century Mexican liberalism according to 20th-century criteria. Altamirano and Ramírez are notable because they tried to understand a complex society that did not fit established models. That they failed to arrive at 20th-century conclusions should not surprise anyone. That they repeatedly tried to transcend the ideological molds of their time should make us—and Giron—less complacent in repeating the commonplaces of our own time.

5133 Gómez, Argenis José. Juan Vicente González y los clásicos. Carátula, Nelly T. de Bruzual. Caracas: Facultad de Humanidades y Educación, Instituto de Filología Clásica, Universidad Central de Venezuela, 1979. 90 p.; bibl.

Along with Sarmiento of Argentina and Alemán of Mexico, Juan Vicente González distinguished himself as one of the early historians of the Independence period. Author goes beyond modest goal suggested by his title (i.e., to document González's debt to classical writers), and provides us with an excellent portrait of this conflicted and conflictive writer/historian.

5134 Hahn, Oscar. El cuento fantástico hispanoamericano en el siglo XIX. México: Premia Editora, 1978. 183 p. (La Red de Jonás)

This is an important book. The attention given to contemporary fantastic literature often overlooks the fact that fantastic literature in Spanish America dates back to the first documents of the conquest. Hahn, in a lengthy introductory essay, surveys current theory on the fantastic, with special reference to Todorov and Bessière, followed by detailed analysis of the fantastic in 19th-century authors, many of whom are represented in the anthology. Good basic bibliography.

5135 Isaza Calderón, Baltasar. El prólogo de La gramática de Bello (ACO/B, 31:131, 1981, p. 5–27)

Useful, well-organized commentary on the prologue to Bello's Gramática, this article locates Bello's ideas on language in the context of his times, in terms of both his audience and the grammatical tradition he either accepted, ignored or rebelled against.

5136 Juliá, Francisco. La generación del 80 en su narrativa (in La inmigración en la Argentina. San Miguel de Tucumán, Argentina: Universidad Nacional de Tucumán, Facultad de Filosofía y Letras, Centro de Historia y Pensamiento Argentinos, 1979, p. 193–206 [Publicación—Universidad Nacional de Tucumán; 1255])

Juliá's article has kind words for "La generación del 80," which has been much maligned by nationalists of all stripes as "bourgeois," "parasitical," "Frenchified" and, of course, "anti-national." Juliá argues that, in confronting changes wrought by inmigration to Argentina, Julián Martel, Miguel Cané and Eugenio Cambaceres, reflect tensions and frustrations of their period. Moreover, they contributed greatly to the "nationalist" preoccupation of continual self-definition that dominates so much Argentine prose. Juliá raises interesting questions but his evidence is not as plentiful as his conclusions.

5137 Karras, Bill J. Alexander Everett and Domingo Delmonte: a literary friendship, 1840–1845 (UPR/CS, 18:1/2, April/July 1978, p. 137–148)

Superbly researched account of Alexander Everett's contacts with Domingo Delmonte, major figure of 19th-century Cuban letters, contains much information and some pathos; theirs was not the first personal friendship between North American Hispanists and Cuban literati to suffer the strain of national and political differences. Includes interesting depiction of New England Hispanists (e.g., Longfellow, Prescott) and their Cuban counterparts in 1840s. Highly recommended.

5138 Leeder, Ellen Lismore. Justo Sierra y el mar. Miami, Fla.: Ediciones Universal, 1979. 83 p.; bibl. (Colección Polymita)

Well-researched and documented study of Justo Sierra's use of the image of the sea in critical works, letters, short stories, and poetry. Reminds us of how little has been done on Sierra's imaginative literature. Good bibliography.

5139 Losada, Alejandro. ¿Cultura nacional o literatura revolucionaria? (Nova Americana [Giulio Einaudi Editore, Torino, Italy] 3, 1980, p. 287–329)

Histories of literature often characterize Argentina's 1837 generation as a continuation of the Rivadavian *unitarios* on the one hand and a poor reflection of European Romanticism on the other. In this careful, well-argued essay, Losada offers a thorough overview of the concerns of the period, with particular reference to Esteban Echeverría, and shows how those concerns gave Argentine Romanticism a political emphasis not found in most occidental literature of the same period. Highly recommended.

5140 Magnarelli, Sharon. *María* and history (HR, 49:2, Spring 1981, p. 209–217) Despite its title, this lucid and imaginative article deals primarily with theories of narration and their proximity to the telling of history, with *María* serving as chief example. Interesting piece with implications way beyond the scope of *María*.

5141 Piossek de Zucchi, Lucía. Ideas que preparan la gran inmigración en el *Facundo* de Sarmiento (*in* La inmigración en la Argentina. San Miguel de Tucumán, Argentina: Universidad Nacional de Tucumán, Facultad de Filosofía y Letras, Centro de Historia y Pensamiento Argentinos, 1979, p. 45–57 [Publicación—Universidad Nacional de Tucumán; 1255])

Contains little about Sarmiento's ideas on immigration not available elsewhere (e.g., Allison Williams Bunkley, Alberto Palcos, etc.). When the author is not repeating commonplaces about *Facundo*, she does discuss some interesting points, notably Sarmiento's ultimate disillusionment with the results of immigration, and the commonality of his historiographical assumptions with those of Alberdi.

5142 Ramos, Carmen. Ideología y mitos colectivos en la novela del Porfiriato (Nova Americana [Giulio Einaudi Editore, Torino, Italy] 3, 1980, p. 271–286) Good discussion of intellectuals' role in Porfirista program of nationalization and internal pacification. Writing was pro-government propaganda. Application of thesis to Emilio Rabasa and José López Portillo is, superficial in light of a promising introduction. Good companion piece to Monsivais' article on national culture (item **5230**). [B. Novoa]

5143 Rivas Dugarte, Rafael Angel. Fuentes para el estudio de Rufino Blanco Fombona, 1874–1944. Caracas: Centro de Estudios Latinoamericanos Rómulo Gallegos, 1979. 244 p.; index (Colección Manuel Landaeta Rosales)

Superb bibliography sets a new standard of rigor and usability. A necessary addition to every Latin American research facility.

5144 Rodríguez Monegal, Emir. La utopía modernista: el mito del Nuevo y el Viejo Mundo en Darío y Rodó (IILI/RI, 112/113, julio/dic. 1980, p. 427–442) In addition to studying the utopian myth in Darío and Rodó, as the title suggests, this informative article explores the similarities and differences between the two writers in terms of influences from abroad and different approaches to a similar problem: the definition of utopia. Particularly interesting is an analysis of Rodó's evaluation of Darío.

5145 Salomon, Noël. Cuatro estudios martianos. Ciudad de La Habana, Cuba: Casa de las Américas, 1980. 99 p.; port. (Cuadernos de estudios martianos)

Any prologue announcing the revelation of "el verdadero Martí" should give one pause. These four essays, however, translated from the French Marxist Noël Saloman may not have much to do with the "real" Martí (should he ever be found), but are lucid, well-argued and well-documented studies of his thought on Latin American awareness, idealism, humanism and nationalism in a Pan-American context. Recommended.

5146 Shaw, D. L. Concerning the structure of *Facundo* (IAA, 6:3, 1980, p. 239–250, bibl.)

Perhaps because Sarmiento himself once called *Facundo* "ese libro extraño, sin pies ni cabeza," some critics disparage the book's supposed lack of unity and structure. Not so, maintains D. L. Shaw in this detailed and well-argued article. Although Shaw admits that Sarmiento was courting trouble by trying to serve the rival gods of history and myth, he shows that despite conflicting goals and rhetoric, the work itself is a complex, artistic entity whose every part is necessary to the whole. Highly recommended.

5147 Skirius, John A. José Martí's youthful romanticism: 1875–1876 (UCLA/M, 8:1/2, mayo 1978, p. 53–59)

Short, informative article is an excellent introduction to Martí's ideas on a variety of topics (e.g., beauty, religion, social issues, Pan-Americanism) as reflected in what he wrote in Mexico at 22. Question as to whether the term "Romanticism" really covers all subjects considered does not detract from article's considerable usefulness.

5148 Sosnowski, Saúl. Esteban Echeverría: el intelectual ante la formación del Estado (IILI/RI, 47:114/115, enero/junio 1981, p. 293–300)

Since subject addressed is clearly too vast for the space allowed, author can best be commended for covering a lot of ground quickly while including enough documentation to guide interested readers into further study.

5149 Suárez-Murías, Marguerite C. Cuba painted by Cubans: the nineteenth century journalistic essay (RIB, 30:4, 1980, p. 375–386, bibl.)

As a brief survey of 19th-century Cuban *costumbrismo*, article provides good introduction to *artículo de costumbres* in Cuba, its best practitioners and their principal concerns. Discusses the importance of *costumbrismo* in the formation of national identity—an important question overlooked by many critics. All in all, a very readable and worthwhile article.

5150 Subercaseaux, Bernardo. Liberalismo positivista y naturalismo en Chile: 1865–1875 (RCLL, 61:11, 1. semestre, 1980, p. 7–27)

Overview of Chilean positivism, article examines in detail work of several important Chilean positivists, with particular emphasis given to J. V. Lastarría and his attempts to combine Comte's social physics with his own brand of Chilean liberalism. Subercaseaux also outlines literary importance of Chilean positivism as precursor of Naturalism. Also describes political importance of positivism in Chile, where, unlike in Mexico and Brazil, it became a rallying point against government rather than a doctrine of officialist justification. An important article.

5151 Vera, Catherine. Symbolism in Spanish American literary periodicals, 1896–1910 (*in* Waiting for Pegasus: studies of the presence of symbolism and decadence in Hispanic letters. Edited by Roland Grass and William R. Risley. Macomb: Western Illinois University, 1979, p. 143–153 [An Essays in literature book])

Short but extensively documented article examines several turn-of-the-century Modernist magazines taken from Argentina, Peru, Venezuela, Mexico and France, and shows not only the pervasiveness of Parisian influence but also the degree to which Spanish American modernists were aware of each other while sharing similar concerns. Nicely complements certain details of Max Henríquez Ureña's seminal *Breve historia del modernismo.*

Prose Fiction: 20th Century: Mexico

BRUCE NOVOA, *Associate Professor of Spanish, Yale University*

MEXICAN PUBLISHING CONTINUES TO EXPAND at a rapid rate. The proliferation of government supported literary workshops, both in Mexico City and the provinces, and the substantial increase in literary contests with lucrative prizes, mentioned in *HLAS 42* (p. 495) have produced a steady outpouring of works by young writers. Although some prestigious publishers have switched to sociological works, several new publishers and numerous new magazines have provided outlets for the increase in literary works. At the same time, some of the best established writers, several of whom had not published books recently, have broken their silence with outstanding works. On the critical front, there is an upsurge of interest and activity, with a marked difference in focus between US and Mexican critics.

The level of craftsmanship among young writers has been rising steadily and can be attributed to the intensive training provided by writing workshops as well as to the overall rise in the educational level of what is now a relatively stable country. Nevertheless, the works of these talented young authors so professional in their craft are somewhat banal in their choice of themes and lack the passion and daring of the old existentialist writers. The vogue for proletarian topics that emerged a few years ago now dominates the production of a generation. One suspects, however, that the writers' depiction of social class is less the result of first-hand experience than an exercise in nostalgia for a vanished "common-man." Perhaps the popularity of this subject matter is another consequence of those above-mentioned workshops most of which are officially sponsored and committed to an obligatory proletarian rhetoric. However, one should not underestimate the profound disillusionment among the young caused by and since the 1968 crisis.

Hector Aguilar Camín—an exception to what is noted above—has written an outstanding and timely story on lower-class life: "Con el Filtro Azul" (item **5153**). Other young writers of notable promise are: Marco Antonio Campos, Samuel Walter Medina, Luis Arturo Ramos, Juan Villoro.

Although no longer newcomers, the following writers deserve mention: María Luisa Puga, whose *Las posibilidades del odio* (see *HLAS 42 : 5208*) was the most promising first novel reviewed in that volume of *HLAS*, unfortunately delivers less in her second one (item **5192**). Jorge Aguilar Mora's second novel, the monumental *Si muero lejos de tí* (item **5154**) is one of the most ambitious and admirable treatments of the Tlatelolco massacre but fails to achieve a convincing totality. Gerardo de la Torre's more modest approach to the same theme (item **5200**) also lacks cohesion. Perhaps the 1968 crisis was too traumatic to be encapsulated in *complete* texts. Yet both of these novels expand the literary interpretation of Tlatelolco by including segments of the society not previously discussed. Carlos Montemayor surpasses his prize-winning stories with a tightly constructed, short novel (item **5186**) in which a variety of narrative voices are expertly controlled in a stylistically interesting narrative. The reason this book about the oppressive conditions of working-class life is one of the best socially committed novels of recent years is largely due to the fact that the author never allows his opinions to intrude into the narrative with the sort of preaching that tends to vitiate political novels of this sort. René Avilés Fabila, another young old hand, has published four of his best stories (item **5157**).

The real discovery of this period is Jesús Gardea (item **5171**), a writer of consummate skill and talent, and the maturity of his 40 years. There is an echo of Rulfo, with whom he shares a sense of life's futility, in his stories of provincial life but Gardea's northern roots—he hails from Juárez—probably account for his less laconic, less hermetic characters. Gardea has published two more books, but they arrived too late for inclusion in this *HLAS*.

Significant texts have been produced by older, more established authors. Works published by Elena Poniatowska, Elena Garro, José Emilio Pacheco, and Carlos Fuentes are important more because of their authors' significance than because of the works themselves. Sergio Pitol's *Nocturno de Bujara* (item **5189**) reveals a mature author in his prime; his sophisticated stories of near perfect construction and elegant prose are literary masterworks. Esther Seligson's *Diálogos con el cuerpo* (item **5198**) is a beautiful, erotic prose-poem, in which she distills the best features of her prize-winning earlier prose. Jorge Ibargüengoitia reworks one and adds another installment to his hilarious satire of provincial society. Vicente Leñero proves again that he is one of his generation's most versatile and accomplished writers with two vastly different books: *Los periodistas* (item **5181**), a documentary on Mexican censorship, is a literary achievement thanks to Leñero's expert technique. His Mexicanization of the Gospel According to St. Luke (item **5180**) is a marvelous parody. Together they form a devastating indictment of Mexican society.

Finally, Juan García Ponce, after several years of uncharacteristic silence, has published two books that are by far the best of this biennium: *Erancia sin fin: Musil, Borges, Klossowski* (item **5170**) is a superb essay, an obsessive, intuitive exploration of how the texts of these authors deal with the question of identity. The work exemplifies what a master artist can do with criticism that never succumbs to the dull rhetoric of contemporary theory or to the facile reductionism into easily understandable concepts that would falsify the essence of the masterpieces he discusses. *Crónica de la intervención* (item **5168**), a massive two-volume novel, lives up to the expectations raised by preceding rumors. Although the varieties of techniques make this novel a stylistic tour de force, what predominates is the author's clear, yet elusive and evocative, prose. By exploring the extreme possibilities of eroticism the novel defies not merely social norms but individual identity itself. Like *Palinuro de México, Paradiso,* or *Terra Nostra,* this novel is not meant for the lazy or the prudish.

There is steady progress in Mexican criticism. Well trained essayists have emerged from workshops dedicted to literary analysis. During the past few years, Mexican critics have taken stock of the impact of a generation of writers about to reach 50 years of age. For better or worse, Carlos Fuentes is considered as belonging to another category, since his concerns are radically different from those of Mexican writers of his age. In contrast to their Mexican counterparts, US critics still focus almost exclusively on Fuentes and Rulfo, although Elizondo and Pacheco have attracted a following. There is also a welcome renewal of interest in classics of this century, such as Azuela and Guzmán.

The Fondo de Cultura Económica began publishing a highly significant series of research materials, *Revistas literarias mexicanas modernas,* of which the first 11 volumes are annotated below. The plan is to reprint in their entirety facsimiles of all of the major, and some minor, literary and cultural periodicals of this century. For the first time, readers will be able to follow the development of Mexican literary journalism without actually traveling to Mexico in order to search for the materials, or trying to tap the shrinking pool of inter-library loan resources in this country. We hope that, having covered the 1930s, Fondo de Cultura Económica will continue as projected to reprint journals up to the 1960s. No major library proud of its Latin American holdings should be without this collection, the most important series in Mexican literary history. Its availability should stimulate much significant future research.

PROSE FICTION

5152 A ustedes les consta. Antología de la crónica en México. Edited by Carlos Monsiváis. México: Ediciones Era, 1980. 366 p.; ill. (Biblioteca Era: Serie Crónicas)

Although usually ignored by contemporary readers, the chronicle genre always has been one of the most active in Latin America. Monsiváis provides a good selection from mid 1800s to today. His long introduction (57 p.) is most helpful.

5153 Aguilar Camín, Héctor. Con el filtro azul. México: Premiá Editora, 1979. 94 p. (La Red de Jonás)

Author's first book of fiction is a mature compilation of five stories that meet all demands of the genre. Material is carefully structured so that an element of suspected but unknown influences effect the story being told. Multiplicity of choices lead characters to a crisis that will change theirs and others' lives. Violence emerges without warning; nothing is secure. Treats themes fashionable among young authors but without boring or disappointing. Great promise.

5154 Aguilar Mora, Jorge. Si muero lejos de ti. México: J. Mortiz, 1979. 527 p. (Nueva narrativa hispánica)

Set in 1968, ambitious narrative comments on Mexican self-alienation, political unrest and frustration. Owner of illegal hospital and collector of stolen masterpieces employs young people who end up in Europe during Tlatelolco massacre. Distance (geographical, psychological, ideological, even plastic-surgical) does not spare them from destruction. Interesting and occasionally excellent novel suffers from lack of cohesion, loose ends, indecision and striving after symbols.

5155 Alvarez Acosta, Miguel. La frontera plural. México: J. Mortiz, 1979. 278 p. (Nueva narrativa hispánica)

Relates case of Mexican immigrant framed for mass murder in US. Denounces racial/class prejudice, civil rights abuses suffered by Mexicans in US. Plurality of borders in title reflects multiple barriers isolating Chicanos in US. Poorly written.

5156 Arreola, Juan José. La palabra educación. Texto ordenado y dispuesto para su publicación por Jorge Arturo Ojeda. México: Editorial Grijalbo, 1977. 173 p.; ill. (Best sellers)

What ever happened to Arreola? Alive and well and spinning off monologues on every subject proposed by TV sponsors. Presented as a philosophical musing by a declared irrationalist—a Mexican media parody of Nietzsche. An unfortunate example of what a respected writer of the 1950s and 1960s is generating now.

5157 Avilés Fabila, René. Lejos del Eden la tierra. Xalapa, México: Universidad Veracruzana, 1980. 143 p.

Author's light touch and irony are evident in four short stories. Three of them focus on female protagonists and frustrated love. "Miriam" is one of the best stories written by this author. "Dentro de la Piel del Lobo" shows how a cliché theme such as the vampire story can be given a fresh new twist.

5158 Blanco, José Joaquín. La vida es larga y además no importa. México: Premiá Editora, 1979. 93 p. (La Red de Jonás)

If the vogue among young Mexican writers is to express middle-class boredom in equally uninteresting prose, Blanco must be a leading exponent. Such works lack the existential angst or transcending mystery of the novels by the Generation of the 1930s or Onda's playful language. Still, students of the Mexican novel should be aware of this trend.

5159 Cabada, Juan de la. Un secreto en el paisaje. México: Terra Nova, 1980. 151 p. (Colección Letras)

Ten stories about childhood, in traditional realistic style, by one of the last representatives of the 19th-century generation.

5160 Campbell, Federico. Pretexta. México: Fondo de Cultura Económica, 1979. 132 p.

Nouveau roman style novel concerns slandered professor who defends himself. Multiple perspectives offered through different texts include medical and police or detective reports. Content, however, is not as interesting as style in that a banal subject is presented with superior technical skill, possibly to emphasize its reading as a work of art.

5161 Campos, Marco Antonio. La desaparición de Fabricio Montesco. México: Editorial J. Mortiz, 1977. 100 p. (Nueva narrativa hispánica)

Better known for criticism and poetry, Campos is a skillful prose writer. Not fantasy, his stories border on the incredible or concern psychological disturbances. A highly promising stylist in search of a worthy subject, Campos could become a brilliant novelist.

5162 Casa Velasco, Luis. Death show. México: Editorial J. Mortiz, 1981. 145 p. (Nueva narrativa hispánica)

Supposedly written after year 2032, this is the fictional biography of Mr. Death, a Mexican immigrant in US who built up a multimillion dollar business of death foods and shows. Format uses apocryphal sources such as autobiographies of Mr. Death and his partner. Funny, satirical view of US commercialism.

5163 Castañeda, Salvador. ¿Por qué no dijiste todo? México: Editorial Grijalbo, 1980. 182 p. (Escritores mexicanos)

Collection of short stories that becomes a novel through the common setting (prison) and the common moment (prisoners about to be released). Despite many clichés and stylistically awkward passages, this interesting first novel by ex-guerrilla fighter and political prisoner is written with the convincing power of firsthand experience.

5164 Delgado, Antonio. Figuraciones en el fuego. México: J. Mortiz, 1980. 161 p. (Nueva narrativa hispánica)

Another novel about a Mexican pueblo and its enigmatic inhabitants, one of whom wanders in search of the rest and himself. So many literary echoes reverberate through the text, the town sounds like *MexiLit*. Still, the evocative and poetic prose conveys the sense of difficult but unmistakable reality.

5165 Espejo, Beatriz. Muros de azogue. México: Editorial Diógenes, 1979. 161 p.

Series of interrelated stories gives schematic history of disintegration of a 20th-century provincial family. Espejo displays great skill at quick characterization, maximum utilization of few details, use of direct discourse being a better short story writer than novelist.

5166 Fuentes, Carlos. Agua quemada, cuarteto narrativo. México: Fondo de Cultura Económica, 1981. 139 p. (Tierra firme)

Four independent short stories linked through characters and settings form a loosely held unit. Fuentes returns to stock themes: Revolution betrayed, persistence of old customs, holidays as times of crisis, machismo, juxtaposition of classes; the ubiquitous city beyond hope and everyone being doomed. One feels little changed in 20 years for Fuentes, a great story writer and at his best when he treats themes and settings of urban folklore and familiar clichés.

5167 ——. Una familia lejana. México: Biblioteca Era, 1980. 214 p.

Mexican family plays international game in search of other possible existences. Aging narrator imposes poorly developed, unlikely story on a French Carlos Fuentes, burdening him with writer's destiny, and the reader a listener's responsibility. One of Fuentes' minor works, this novel is neither a good story nor convincing narrative and even lacks Fuentes' usual memorable characters or brilliant short scenes.

5168 García Ponce, Juan. Crónica de la intervención. Barcelona: Editorial Bruguera, 1982. 2 v. (573, 544 p.) (Narradores de hoy)

Two identical women come to know and love each other, causing havoc among the men involved in their multiple relationships. Author's obsessive themes are orchestrated into a total text. As eroticism permeates all levels of life, individual identities are undermined and alternatives open up for those used to the alienation and waste of socially defined existence. By exploring many writing techniques, García Ponce reveals his artistic maturity. A landmark text like *Paradiso*, this novel is a demanding, and intense experience for dedicated readers.

5169 ——. Cuentos: antología personal. México: Liberta-Sumaria, 1980. 109 p. (Colección Antología personal; no. 2)

Six short stories, drawn from three previous collections, allow the reader to follow author's evolution over a decade of writing.

5170 ——. La errancia sin fin: Musil, Borges, Klossowski. Barcelona: Editorial Anagrama, 1981. 85 p.

This long essay was awarded the ninth annual Premio Anagrama de Ensayo. García Ponce shows how three divergent authors created a literature beyond the false security of personal identity sought by other writers. Author's highly personal text on the writing of his three subjects creates an expository fiction in which identities blur and fuse. Yet one emerges from the reading with a new, if not better, understanding of each writer. Excellent example of why García Ponce is one of the most respected essayists in Latin America.

5171 Gardea, Jesús. Los viernes de Lautaro. Portada de Anhelo Hernández. México: Siglo XXI, 1979. 165 p. (La Creación literaria)

In his first short story collection, Gardea proves himself a highly accomplished stylist, whose mastery of detail and memorable characters overshadow his rather weak plots. Set in provincial Mexico, the stories are imbued with Juan Rulfo's sense of futility.

5172 Garrido, Felipe. Con canto no aprendido. México: Fondo de Cultura Económica, 1978. 117 p. (Letras mexicanas)

Another case of a worthy stylist selecting banal subjects. Only the title story rises above the commonplace. In it the dynamics of a family are conveyed through various time levels and thoughts, more through implication than exposition.

5173 Garro, Elena. Andamos huyendo Lola. México: J. Mortiz, 1980. 263 p. (Nueva narrativa hispánica)

The pervasive theme of this collection of 10 narratives is a sense of persecution, the fear of an alien reality awaiting at each turn. Although the book has been perceived as a radical departure from Garro's previous works, paranoia, for lack of a better word, was always present in them. What has changed is the focus on social reality and absence of fantasy or proustian aesthetics of previous fiction. A disappointing work.

5174 Gerardo, María. Fábrica de conciencias descompuestas. México: J. Mortiz, 1980. 159 p. (Serie del volador)

Fifteen short narratives form a loose *Bildungsroman* in which one follows the narrator from kindergarten to his expulsion from school for drug addiction at age 18. Relies on clichés of schoolboy experience. Reminds one of José Agustín's first *Onda* works, but lacks Agustín's ability to reveal the significance of banal experience. Superficial but technically skillful collection was awarded the 1979 National Prize for short story.

5175 Hernández, Luisa Josefina. Apostasía. México: Universidad Nacional Autónoma de México, Dirección General de Publicaciones, 1978. 269 p. (Cuento y relato)

Parable of two men in the desert, one sent by his people to hear God's message, the other for unknown reasons. Former lies claiming to have heard the message—that a temple must be built in which he will await some great event. Latter discovers that he is the real prophet and travels announcing the coming of God. In the end, one kills the other; but the temple remains sacred to the people. Traditional narrative parodies the traditional genre. Hernández is a superb stylist, even when writing something as forgettable as this.

5176 Hernández H., Esteban. El tesoro de la Malinche. México: B. Costa-Amic Editor, 1976. 231 p.

Well written, traditional novel hardly innovative but a delightful reading experience. Hilarious misadventures of a group of modern day treasure hunters.

5177 Hiriart, Hugo. Disertación sobre las telarañas y otros escritos. México: Martín Casillas Editores, 1981. 230 p.

Collection of brief essays, on the most common objects or themes, concerned with the development of language. Hiriart's destruction of the world through logical analysis reminds one of Wittgenstein, or of García Ponce's *Desconsideraciones*. Delightful reading.

5178 Ibargüengoitia, Jorge. Dos crímenes. México: J. Mortiz, 1979. 203 p.

Wrongly accused of one crime, Marcos flees Mexico City to seek refuge with a rich uncle. The story he invents and his sudden reappearance as a competitor for his uncle's fortune lead to murders and intrigue. Ibargüengoitia is an excellent humorist and his sociopolitical satire is subtle but acute. Entertaining reading.

5179 Jaula de palabras. Una antología de la nueva narrativa mexicana. Edited by Gustavo Sainz. México: Grijalbo, 1980. 478 p.

Widely promoted anthology marred by so many weaknesses one wonders what criteria guided the selection. Neither all stories nor all authors are that "new" (e.g., Fuentes, García Ponce, Pacheco, Dallal). Other authors are excluded as "too well known," as if the above were not (?). Authors appear alphabetically, without any attempt to identify them historically or critically. Introductions read like in-group gossip items; bibliographies are incomplete and often incorrect. Indeed, many of the authors anthologized never gave permission to reproduce their works, making this book a partly pirated edition. Not recommended.

5180 Leñero, Vicente. El evangelio de Lucas Gavilán. Barcelona: Seix Barral, 1979. 317 p.; ill. (Nueva narrativa hispánica)

Faithful parody of Saint Luke's gospel, set in contemporary Mexico, becomes scathing social satire. Leñero returns to the poor, the subject of his first novel, *Los albañiles* (1964). He handles their dialogue better than most of the new proletarian novelists. A brilliant novel by one of Mexico's best fiction writers.

5181 ———. Los periodistas. 3. ed. México: J. Mortiz, 1978. 412 p.; index (Nueva narrativa hispánica)

Factual account of the infamous *Excelsior* case in 1976 when President Echeverría silenced the newspaper's editors. Told from an insider's perspective by Leñero who worked for *Excelsior*. Expert use of dialogue, narrative techniques, and film/drama/script writing make it a fascinating text and its historical value a must for student of contemporary Mexico.

5182 López Páez, Jorge. La costa. Portada de Luis Miguel Quezada. Fotografía de Ricardo Salazar. México: J Mortiz, 1980. 260 p. (Nueva narrativa hispánica)

Young boy discovers sex, only to find out that the woman is his father's mistress. In spite of predictable plot, traditional, chronological treatment, and omniscient point of view, novel is well written and enjoyable.

5183 López Portillo y Pacheco, José. Quetzalcóatl. Barcelona: Salvat, D. L., 1976. 5 leaves, 173 p.

Prose version of the Quetzalcóatl myth draws from established academic sources. Author's style is clear but uninnovative. Of interest chiefly because its author was president of Mexico.

5184 Mancisidor, José. Obras completas de José Mancisidor. t. 1, A. Berrios, Vida y obras de José Mancisidor. M. Bustos Cerecedo, José Mancisidor, el hombre. G. Lizt Arzubide, La vida militar de José Mancisidor. t. 2. Novelas: *La asonada, La ciudad roja, Nueva York revolucionario, De una madre español, Se llamaba catalina.* t. 3, Novelas: *En la rosa de los vientos, Frontera junto al mar, El alba en las simas.* t. 4, La primera piedra, Como cayeron los héroes, Ciento veinte días, Me lo dijo Maria Kaimlova, El mundo de la infancia y la adolescencia de Juárez, La espalda mojada, Tierras de don Quijote. Xalapa, México: Gobierno del Estado de Veracruz, 1979/1980. 4 v. (344, 606, 872, 618 p.) bibl.

Mancisidor is considered the prototypical Mexican socialist realist. Vol. 1 of his complete works contains three essays about him that offer no critical analysis. The other vols. leave the impression of wasted talent, perhaps, but more strongly, of not that much talent to start with. Ironically, instead of communism undermining him as a writer, it is probably his political commitment that has saved him from oblivion.

5185 Medina, Samuel Walter. Sastrerías: textos. México: Ediciones Era, 1979. 109 p.; ill. (Biblioteca Era: Serie Claves)

Consists of highly experimental short fiction (longest five p.) and some concrete poems reminiscent of Italo Calvino's fantasies. Best pieces, stories of escape, are grouped under title "Fugas." Science-fiction motifs are unusual in Mexican letters. Medina is a writer of skill and imagination but ultimately lacking in power and depth.

5186 Montemayor, Carlos. Mal de piedra. México: Premiá Editora, 1981. 99 p. (La Red de Jonás)

Extremely well written Faulknerian novel about the miserable life of miners in northern Mexico, and by extension of the Latin American poor. Text focuses on death, the defining event in their lives, ironically juxtaposing religious funeral prayers and hopes of transcendence against the people's futile efforts to transcend their oppressive lives.

5187 Pacheco, José Emilio. Las batallas en el desierto. México: Ediciones Era, 1981. 70 p. (Biblioteca Era)

In a bourgeois voice nostalgically recalling Mexico City of the 1940s, Pacheco tells of a boy falling in love with his friend's mother, who later commits suicide. This intentional voice may disturb readers accustomed to Pacheco's usual fiction compared to which this work may appear as trivial and banal.

5188 Pettersson, Aline. Casi en silencio. México: Premiá Editora, 1980. 84 p. (La Red de Jonas)

Technically interesting attempt to write Virginia Woolf style prose (*Orlando*'s influence in particular) but a trite plot: a love triangle among a professor and two students. Also reminiscent of Juan García Ponce's much more successful *El libro*.

5189 Pitol, Sergio. Nocturno de Bujara. México, Siglo XXI Editores, 1981. 150 p.

Four stories by an experienced, talented writer at the peak of his creative production. Prototypical Pitol fiction, the tales are sophisticated; highly rational and intellectual; exotic in setting; and including precise, detailed description. However, Pitol deliberately undermines all of the above by a sort of mimetic, deceiving process whereby the text creates an apparently solid reality, that eventually dissolves into words.

5190 Ponce, Bernardo. Rapsodia española: una crónica del siglo XX. México: Editorial Porrúa, 1979. 246 p.; index.

One anticipates the anachronistic text from the title. Ponce recalls his student days in 1935–36 Madrid, the literary circle of the 1927 Generation, evenings with Lorca, Salinas, Neruda, Aleixandre, etc., a pre-Civil War, pre-World War II society of young artists. Not fictionalized, the memoirs are imbued with the romantic aura of a world about to disappear.

5191 Poniatowska, Elena. De noche vienes. 3. ed. México: Editorial Grijalbo, 1979. 231 p.

Stories confirm Poniatowska's wide range of themes over 25 years. Collection's unevenness, however, is due to the fact that almost half of the stories were written in early 1950s when author was virtually another person.

5192 Puga, María Luisa. Cuando el aire es azul. México: Siglo XXI, 1980. 338 p. (La creación literaria)

After the great promise of her first book, *Las posibilidades del odio* (see *HLAS 42:5028*), Puga's second novel is disappointing. Utopian fable about town, that won independence and complete isolation but outgrew its ability to survive autonomously. After reopening relations with the outside world, the town is recolonized but continues to hold on to its cultural identity. Characters often discuss the nature of history in brief essays or dialogue. Although the novel displays promising technical skill, the allegory is vague; the plot predictable; and the message about cultural identity trite.

5193 Ramos, Luis Arturo. Del tiempo y otros lugares. Xalapa, México: Editorial Amate, 1979. 99 p.

In contrast to most new Mexican writers who favor realism and the banal anecdote, Ramos' fantastic stories are in Cortázar's tradition. The latter's influence is especially noticeable in "El Sueño de los Corazones" and "Foto Click." And although Carlos Fuentes is another influence, Ramos is no one's imitator.

5194 ———. Violeta-Perú. Xalapa, México: Universidad Veracruzana, 1979. 127 p.

Another novel of proletarian frustration by a promising writer in which a young man, after being turned down for a chauffeur's job, takes a drunken ride on a Mexico City bus—its destinations making up the novel's title. The trip, however, is not through a city, but through imagination and memory. A sort of low-life *Under the volcano*, the novel reveals the protagonist's hopelessness as well as the writer's ability to integrate such diverse elements into a compact unit.

5195 Ruiz, Bernardo. La otra orilla. México: Premiá Editora, 1980. 84 p. (La Red de Jonás)

Short narratives that are not fully developed and do not have enough in common to justify a unitary reading. Their importance lies in Ruiz's control of language and his exploration of unusual themes. Much can be expected of this promising writer.

5196 Rulfo, Juan. Obra completa: *El llano en llamas, Pedro Páramo*, otros textos. Prólogo y cronología, Jorge Ruffinelli. Diseño, Juan Fresán. Caracas: Biblioteca Ayacucho, 1977. 299 p.; bibl. (Biblioteca Ayacucho; 13)

Since Rulfo's works are easily available and their distribution has never been a problem, the value of this volume must lie in what it offers besides the works themselves: large format; inclusion of "Paso del Norte," a story no longer found in the Fondo de Cultura edition of *El llano en llamas*; and some unavailable if uninteresting texts. Regrettably, the introduction is not outstanding, the chronological table close to meaningless, and the bibliography shockingly incomplete. Rulfo deserves better.

5197 Sánchez Cámara, Florencio. El notata y las mujeres mágicas. México: J. Mortiz, 1980. 178 p. (Nueva narrativa hispánica)

Collection of short narratives, few of which can be called stories, in which women are the central focus. *Notata* means the oldest member of a pueblo and the one who receives and transmits the oral tradition. Like oral memories, the text recalls characters, events, and information about regional inhabitants. Interesting fragments that lack any convincing centralizing agent.

5198 Seligson, Esther. Diálogos con el cuerpo. México: Artífice Ediciones, 1981. 47 p.

Poem/narrative/essay in the form of dialogue in which the bodies are the actors, both subject and object. A highly erotic depersonalized game of attraction, fusion, and distancing in which poetry and prose interact much as the bodies' own seductive game. The result is a hybrid text of unusual beauty.

5199 Spota, Luis. El rostro del sueño. México: Editorial Grijalbo, 1979. 407 p.

Expansion of Spota's series *La costumbre del poder* consists of a fifth convoluted tale of terrorist plot to steal the Shroud of Turin and hold it for ransom. Terrorists fail because they don't listen to television news! Least interesting of the five thrillers.

5200 Torre, Gerardo de la. Muertes de aurora. Cuidado de la edición, Miguel Angel Guzmán. México: Ediciones de Cultura Popular, 1980. 126 p. (Arte y literatura)

Another novel on the theme of Tlatelolco but lacking the intensity of previous works on the subject. Chronicles activities of few petroleum workers who participated in the 1968 protests but without a real focus or developed characters (e.g., protagonist's motivation is unclear).

5201 Torre, Joaquín de la. Anticipación de un burgués a la muerte. México: Premiá Editora, 1978. 78 p. (La Red de Jonás)

Middle-class man who believes in the inevitability of class struggle and favors victory of proletariat, while unable to relinquish his comfortable life, ends by anticipating his own death and that of his class. Author uses expository prose to convey thoughts of over-rationalizing bourgeois-narrator. Novel exemplifies self-flagellating propensities and "objective" thinking characteristic of some Mexican leftists.

5202 Usigli, Rodolfo. Ensayo de un crimen. México: V. Siglos, 1980. 300 p. (Terra nostra; 1)

New edition of Usigli's only novel, a psychological crime thriller. It will disappoint readers of Usigli's better works.

5203 Valadés, Edmundo. Sólo los sueños y los deseos son inmortales, Palomita. México: Editorial Diana, 1980. 127 p.

Consists of 13 tales, by one of Mexico's most respected short-story writers, many of which appeared in magazines and books. Eroticism is the collection's unifying theme and Valadés handles its various manifestations with freshness and stylistic variety.

5204 Villoro, Juan. La noche navegable. México: Editorial Joaquín Mortiz, 1980. 129 p. (Serie del volador)

Realistic stories about the hip adolescent scene familiar from Onda literature, some of which occasionally turn into fantasies reminiscent of Cortázar and one of which "El Mariscal de Campo," explores a proletarian theme. Like other Onda writers, Villoro creates characters through speech. A promising writer whose test will come when he turns to themes and characters beyond his immediate experience.

LITERARY CRITICISM AND HISTORY

5205 *Antena*, 1924; *Monterrey*, 1930–1937; *Examen*, 1932; *Número*, 1933–1935. México: Fondo de Cultura Económica, 1980. 478 p.; ill. (Revistas literarias mexicanas modernas)

Monterrey consists of Reyes' correspondence about literature with a wide spectrum of friends and collaborators and includes fascinating bibliographies of books received from world-wide sources. *Examen*, begun by Jorge Cuesta when *Contemporáneos* folded, lasted only three issues before being closed on obscenity charges. Of fleeting interest are *Número* and *Antena*.

5206 *Arte*, 1907–1909; *Argos*, 1912. México: Fondo de Cultura Económica, 1980. 558 p.; ill. (Revistas literarias mexicanas modernas)

Directed by Enrique González Martínez, *Arte* (julio 1907–mayo 1909) became his provincial refuge after initial failure in Mexico City. A strictly literary, modernist publication, it included works by stars such as Casal, Asunción Silva, etc. and served as a showcase for Ateneo de la Juventud members. He also published *Argos* (six issues, Jan.–Feb. 1912).

5207 Bautista, Miguel. Enseñar lo que significa la vida; entrevista con Sergio Fernández, Premio Villaurrutia (Semana de Bellas Artes [México] 169, 25 feb. 1981, p. 8–9)

Fernández discusses his novel *Segundo sueño* (see *HLAS 40:6571*) and his novelistic search for "immobility," inspired by José Gorostiza's poem *Muerte sin fin*.

5208 Beer, Gabriella de. La revolución en la narrativa de Campobello, Castellanos y Poniatowska (Semana de Bellas Artes

[México] 165, 28 enero 1981, p. 2–5)

Three women writers' different approaches to theme of Mexican Revolution: Campobello, a child during the war, sees it as chaos and suffering—a personal testimony. Castellanos, born afterwards, sees it as part of long historical process. For Poniatowska, it is a woman's oral history.

5209 Bruce-Novoa, Juan. Martín Luis Guzmán: un retrato de Diego Rivera (Casa del Tiempo [Universidad Autónoma Metropolitana, Dirección de Difusión Cultural, México] 2:16, dic. 1981, p. 4–8)

Textual analysis of Guzmán's essay on Rivera shows author's command of Cubist rhetoric.

5210 Brushwood, John S. La realidad de la fantasía, las novelas de Ignacio Solares (Semana de Bellas Artes [México] 143, 27, agosto 1980, p. 10–12)

Analyzes elements of mysticism and fantasy in Solares' narratives, admires his accessible style, but regards his themes as too eccentric to be representative of Mexican writing.

5211 Daydí, Santiago. Drinking: a narrative structural pattern in Mariano Azuela's Los de abajo (UK/KRQ, 27:1, 1980, p. 57–67)

Traces drinking motif to illustrate Azuela's technique of permutating leitmotifs to develop a plot.

5212 Duncan, J. Ann. The novel as poem and document: José Emilio Pacheco's Morirás lejos (IAA, 6:4, neue folge, 1980, p. 277–292)

Despite the erroneous claim that Morirás lejos is the first Latin American novel to combine "committed" and aesthetic purposes, Duncan offers a perceptive reading of the novel's reduction of all texts—eyewitness, documentary, or fictional—to the dubious. However, "the novel as poem" is not explored as much.

5213 Durán, Gloria. The archetypes of Carlos Fuentes: from witch to androgyne. Hamden, Conn.: Archon Books, 1980. 240 p.; bibl.

Much expanded and improved version of La magia y las brujas en la obra de Carlos Fuentes (see HLAS 42:5224), provides better application of Jung. Highly recommended.

5214 La Falange, 1922–1923. México: Fondo de Cultura Económica, 1980. 491 p.; ill. (Revistas literarias mexicanas modernas)

La Falange (Dec. 1922–Oct. 1923) was strictly literary in contrast to México Moderno (see item 5227), the other major contemporary journal. Though published by Torres Bodet, Ortiz de Montellano, Novo, and Xavier Villaurrutia, their best writing appeared in Mexico Moderno. Of special interest are Diego Rivera's essay on the origins of the muralist movement and a selection of North American poetry in translation.

5215 Five essays on Martín Luis Guzmán. Edited and with a foreword by William W. Megenney. Riverside: Latin American Studies Program, University of California, 1978. 121 p.; ill. (Commemorative series; no. 2)

Five essays on El águila y la serpiente by D. L. Shaw, Alberto Blasi, Hugo Rodríguez-Alcalá, Luis Leal, and Megenney. These stylistic studies are a refreshing change from customary historical interpretations of this book. Shaw's intertextual comparison with Rodó's Ariel is enlightening.

5216 Gerdes, Dick. Point of view in Los de abajo (AATSP/H, 64:4, Dec. 1981, p. 557–563)

Azuela uses omniscient narration but also variations (i.e., Neutral Omniscience, Selective Omniscience, and Dramatic Mode). Through these shifts, Azuela emphasizes certain passages, dramatizes others, and creates irony.

5217 Hoffman, Herbert H. Cuento mexicano: index. Newport Beach: Headway Publications, 1978. 600 p.

Consists of useful indexes of Mexican short stories by author, story title, and book title. Also provides addresses of publishers and periodicals.

5218 Icaza, Francisco A. de. Obras. Edición y estudio preliminar de Rafael Castillo. México: Fondo de Cultura Económica, 1980. 2 v.; bibl. (Letras mexicanas)

Collection of poetry and essays by this prolific critic. The criticism is dedicated mostly to Spanish peninsular literature of the Golden Age.

5219 Incledon, John. Salvador Elizondo's Farabeuf: the reader as victim (in

Latin American fiction today: a symposium. Edited by Rose S. Minc. Takoma Park, Md.: Hispamérica, 1980, p. 71–74)

Incledon posits that the novel shifts from *he* and *she* to *you* and *I*, with the last *I* being the reader. Thus, it is the reader who is subject to the violence at the end.

5220 Juan García Ponce. Edited by Roberto Vallarino (Semana de Bellas Artes [México] 182, 27 mayo 1981, p. 1–16, ill.)

Issue in tribute to this multifarious writer contains essays by Carlos Monsivais, Sergio Pitol, José de la Colina, Elena Poniatowska; and interview with and examples of García Ponce's writing in drama, novel, and essay.

5221 Labastida, Jaime. Para desmitificar a Revueltas (Plural [Excelsior, México] 10[3]: 111, dic. 1980, p. 26–31)

Glorified since his death for reasons other than literary, Revueltas has been made into a saint by the Mexican left and the US pseudo-left. Labastida's refreshing essay humanizes him, revealing the contradictions of a man of the left who being an intellectual elitist, a dogmatist and an undemocratic Stalinist, eventually became a petit-bourgeois. Controversial, but informative piece.

5222 Leal, Luis. Panorama de la literatura mexicana actual. Washington: Unión Panamericana, Secretaría General de la Organización de los Estados Americanos, 1968 [1975 printing]. 203 p.; bibl.; index.

New edition of schematic overview of Mexican literature (all genres) from Modernism to 1965 which has not been updated. Nevertheless, a useful book for quick consultations.

5223 *El Maestro.* Revista de cultura nacional. México: Fondo de Cultura Económica, 1979. 3 v. (642, 650, 512 p.); ill. (Revistas literarias mexicanas modernas)

Serial publication of Secretaría de Educación, *El Maestro* constituted best example of Vasconcelos' program of popular education. Included all major writers, Mexican and foreign, with translations of classical and contemporary writing from universal sources. Covered everything in installments, from farming advice to political speeches and literature. Distribution of 75,000 copies was world wide and influential. Organized into tomos, not years, with 14 issues, 18 numbers, April 1921–April 1922. Reprint, with introduction. A must for researchers of the Mexican Revolution.

5224 Maldonado, Ignacio. García Ponce: el aprendizaje de la perversión, el loco de los mundos subalternos. Narrativa de los sesentas / 6 (La Cultura en México [Comisión Mexicana de Cooperación, Intelectual, México] suplemento de *Siempre*, 1006, 8 julio 1981, p. 2–4)

States García Ponce's purpose is to pervert readers by turning them into voyeurs of life's alternative possibilities, mostly erotic. By resisting normal reading and eschewing accepted logic, his fiction does not tell a story but creates a code of allusions to another reality.

5225 Mansour, Mónica. Rulfo y el realismo mágico (Plural [Excelsior, México] 10[3]: 111, dic. 1980, p. 19–25)

After emphasizing certain techniques (e.g., ironic use of names, metaphor and simile, colors, indefinite or multiple pronouns and adverbs), Mansour analyzes the story "Es que somos muy pobres."

5226 Mercado, Enrique. Elena Garro: los fantasmas de la realidad, de la imaginación alegórica a la cotidianiedad de la prosa (La Cultura en México [Suplemento de Siempre, Comisión Mexicana de Cooperación Intelectual, México] 1004, 24 junio 1981, p. 2–7)

Mercado thinks that the novel *Los recuerdos del porvenir* has lost verisimilitude with age but that Garro's last novel, *Andamos huyendo, Lola,* marks a change of thematic interest with regard to problems of women alone.

5227 *México Moderno.* México: Fondo de Cultura Económica, 1971. 3 v. (408, 332, 281 p.) (Revistas literarias mexicanas modernas)

At the height of his literary influence, Enrique González Martínez founded *México Moderno,* the first successful literary magazine after the Revolution whose collaborators were all important writers of the time such as members of the Ateneo de la Juventud (see also item **5206**). Reprints all issues (1 Aug. 1920–1 June 1923) including important one dedicated to López Velarde upon his death.

5228 Miller, Beth Kurti. Rosario Castellanos' *Guests in August*: critical realism and the provincial middle class

(UK/LATR, 7:14, Spring/Summer 1979, p. 5–19)

Although Castellanos did not believe in fiction as a medium for conveying ideology, the four stories in *Los convidados de agosto* constitute ideological statements. By focusing on middle-class characters, Miller states Castellanos exposes their values and expresses her sympathies for characters who are victimized while ridiculing and condemning their exploiters.

5229 —— and **Alfonso González.** 26 [i.e. Veintiseis] autoras del México actual. México: B. Costa-Amic Editor, 1978. 463 p.; index.

Most of these women writers, unknown to US readers, will also be a surprise to Mexicans. This is an important contribution to the field even if the interviews are too short to allow for a full portrait of each author.

5230 Monsiváis, Carlos. La nación de unos cuantos y las esperanzas románticas: notas sobre la historia del término cultura nacional en México (*in* Seminario de Historia de la Cultura Nacional, Instituto Nacional de Antropología e Historia, 1976. En torno a la cultura nacional. Héctor Aguilar Camín et al. México: Instituto Nacional Indigenista, Secretaría de Educación Pública, 1976, p. 159–221, bibl. [Colección SEP-INI, 51])

Since mid 1800s, the notion of "national culture" in Mexico has been part of an intellectual program in which literature served as propaganda. Ideals adopted from Europe by an educated minority were "national culture" at first. The Revolution promised changes through a focus on popular culture. Post-revolutionary regimes imbued "national culture" with superficial folklorism for political and commercial ends. Includes interesting review of Octavio Paz' interpretation and, despite Monsiváis' bias, the article is informative and useful.

5231 ——. Las palabras cruzadas de Elena Poniatowska; "Mira, para que no comas olvido . . ." Las precisiones de Elena Poniatowska (La Cultura en México [Suplemento de *Siempre*, Comisión Méxicana de Cooperación Intelectual, México] 1007, 15 julio 1981, p. 2–5)

Monsiváis traces Poniatowska's development from naive story writer, and journalist to a socially committed chronicler of México's marginal people.

5232 Murad, Timothy. Foreshadowing, duplication, and structural unity in Mariano Azuela's *Los de abajo* (AATSP/H, 64:4, 1981, p. 550–556)

The structural unity underlying the apparently loose, episodic surface of *Los de abajo* is based on the repetition of events in separate scenes.

5233 Paley Francescato, Martha. Un desafío a la crítica literaria: *Tiene los cabellos rojizos y se llama Sabina* de Julieta Campos (RCLL, 7:13, 1. semestre 1981, p. 120–125)

Article accurately posits problem of critics who try to read a novel without plot or story line and one in which poetic language plays misleading game.

5234 *Pegaso.* México: Fondo de Cultura Económica, 1979. 365 p.; ill. (Revistas literarias mexicanas modernas)

Weekly cultural magazine included a short story-page, poetry-page, occasional literary essay, and authors such as Pellicer, López Velarde, Alfonso Reyes, and González Martínez. World War I is the dominant topic. Of special interest to students of history and popular culture. Reprints issues Año 1, No. 1–15 (8 March–21 June 1917). After these first 15 issues were reprinted, two additional ones were found: Año 1, No. 16 (29 June 1917) and No. 20 (27 July 1917) and published separately by Fondo de Cultura Económica.

5235 Pérez Gay, Rafael. Melo: la confesión y la máscara; la voluntad radical (La Cultura en México [Suplemento de *Siempre*, Comisión Mexicana de Cooperación Intelectual, México] 1002, 10 junio 1981, p. 2–5)

Melo's main themes are isolation; boredom; and existence at the edge of society.

5236 Picón Garfield, Evelyn and **Iván A. Schulman.** La estética extraVASANTE de la InNegAusencia o la modernidad de Arqueles Vela (UCV/E, 4:8, julio/dic. 1989, p. 259–267)

Analysis of *El intransferible* (written 1927, published 1977) shows that Vela, a leading Estridentista, anticipated many present-day techniques and concerns. His systematic destruction/construction, at multiple levels of content and form, is surprisingly contemporary. Inclusion of Vela's other works would have strengthened the argument. A good start at a necessary reevaluation of avant-garde Latin American fiction.

5237 Ramírez, Arthur. Spatial form and cinema techniques in Rulfo's *Pedro Páramo* (UA/REH, 15:2, mayo 1981, p. 233–249)

Insightful study applies Joseph Frank's theory of spatial form in literature as well as film montage techniques in order to examine how Rulfo uses juxtaposition to destroy the concept of temporal sequence in *Pedro Páramo.*

5238 Rendón Hernández, José Angel. Alfonso Reyes, instrumentos para su estudio. Monterrey: Universidad Autónoma de Nuevo León, Biblioteca Central, 1980. 173 p.; ill. (Serie Capilla Alfonsina; no. 1)

Useful bibliography of Reyes' works and studies on Reyes includes trivial introductory notes.

5239 Revueltas, José. Cartas a María Teresa. México: Premiá Editora, 1979. 197 p.; 4 leaves of plates; ill. (La Nava de los locos; 77)

Although Revueltas' letters rarely discuss subjects of more than passing interest (e.g., his dislike for Sartre, Neruda, and José Mancisidor, supposedly committed writers), the book is a must for Revueltas' scholars.

5240 Rivadeneira Prada, Raúl. Rulfo en llamas. Ilus. de la cubierta, Edgar Arandia. La Paz: Escuela de Artes Gráficas del Colegio Don Bosco, 1980. 136 p.; bibl.

Study of Rulfo's writings through communication theory uses much jargon and reveals little of interest.

5241 Robe, Stanley L. Azuela and the *Mexican Underdogs.* Los Angeles: University of California Press in cooperation with the University of California, Latin American Center, 1979. 223 p.; bibl.; facsims.; ill.; maps; table.

Invaluable addition to criticism on Azuela and novel of the Mexican Revolution. Makes available *Los de abajo*'s original version as well as new English translation. Enlightening introduction.

5242 Román, Alberto. Elizondo: una escritura en el agua, la tentación del signo (La Cultura en México [Suplemento de *Siempre,* Comisión Mexicana de Cooperación Intelectual, México] 1005, 1 julio 1981, p. 2–5)

Insightful, though biased and scathing, evaluation of Elizondo's fiction, that traces his narrow obsession with French eroticism and aestheticism.

5243 Rosas, Patricia. Destiempo y nostalgia, Elena Garro y *Los recuerdos del porvenir* (Semana de Bellas Artes [México] 152, 29 oct. 1980, p. 10–12)

Garro's novel portrays Mexican nostalgia for catastrophic violence as the people's answer to their insoluble problems.

5244 ———. *Farabeuf* o una alucinación ardiente (Semana de Bellas Artes [México] 173, 25 marzo 1981, p. 3–9)

Traces French influence in Elizondo's novel *Farabeuf,* specifically Robbe-Grillet and Bataille.

5245 Ruiz Abreu, Alvaro. Galindo: la provincia y sus personajes; lecturas en familia (La Cultura en México [Suplemento de *Siempre,* Comisión Mexicana de Cooperación Intelectual, México] 1008, 22 julio 1981, p. 2–4)

In Galindo's provincial middle class, the main themes are love, the family, and mediocrity. Ruiz Abreu believes his best work is yet to come.

5246 *San-ev-ank,* 1918; *Revista Nueva,* 1919. México: Fondo de Cultura Económica, 1979. 433 p.; ill. (Revistas literarias mexicanas modernas)

After losing their funding, *Gladios'* editors established *San-ev-ank* on a no-budget scale. Contributors: poets Pellicer, Ortiz de Montellano, Torres Bodet, González Rojo. Satirical and iconoclastic, *San-ev-ank* was first young people's underground magazine published in Mexico. Many of same Contemporáneos organized *Revista Nueva* whose purpose was to unite young people. *San-ev-ank*'s issues: tomo 1, nos. 1–14 (11 July–31 Oct. 1918) and tomo 2, no. 1 (15 Nov. 1918). *Revista Nueva*: tomo 1, nos. 1–2 (9 and 25 June 1919).

5247 *Savia Moderna,* 1906; *Nosotros,* 1912–1914. México: Fondo de Cultura Económica, 1980. 679 p.; ill. (Revistas literarias mexicanos modernas)

Savia Moderna (Año 1, Nos. 1–5, March–July 1906) was offshoot of *Revista Moderna*. Contributors: Max and Pedro Henríquez Ureña, Alfonso Reyes. Illustrations: Diego Rivera, Roberto Montenegro. "Revista de Revistas Section" briefly summarized major cultural publications of the day in Mexico. Translations of Oscar Wilde, Modernist in orientation. *Nosotros* (Año 1, Nos. 1–10, Dec. –June 1914) began as teachers' publication evolving into cultural magazine. Influenced by Ateneo de la Juventud (e.g., essays by Reyes, Pedro Henríquez Ureña's landmark essay on Ruiz de Alarcón, prose by Julio Torri).

5248 Schaffer, Susan. The development of the double in selected works of Carlos Fuentes (UCLA/M, 6:2, mayo 1977, p. 81–86)

Useful overview but obvious analysis of the Doppelganger in Fuentes' *Aura, Zona sagrada,* and *Cumpleaños.*

5249 Sefchovich, Sara. Luis Spota, la costumbre del poder (UNAM/RMS, 41[41]:3, julio/sept. 1979, p. 839–862)

Best article to date on Spota. Though restricted to only four novels—the tetralogy *La costumbre del poder*—observations and conclusions apply to his work in general. Spota produces novels for bourgeois readers that, in spite of social criticism, support and vindicate the sociopolitical *status quo.*

5250 Sergio Pitol: veinte años después. Edited by Roberto Vallarino (Semana de Bellas Artes [México] 195, 26 agosto 1981, p. 1–16, ill.)

Issue dedicated to the novelist and short story writer consists of essays by Monsiváis, García Ponce, Elena Urrutia, Elena Poniatowska, and Margo Glantz, among others; two texts by Pitol himself. Good introduction to a writer who deserves more critical attention.

5251 Sosnowski, Saúl. Entrevista a Carlos Fuentes (HISP, 9:27, dic. 1980, p. 69–67)

Fuentes rehashes familiar material, mixing it with current interests (e.g., model for a character in *Una familia lejana,* project for book on political power in Mexico, etc.)

5252 Sotomayor, Aurea M. *El hipogeo secreto:* la escritura como palíndromo y

cópula (IILI/RI, 112/113, julio/dic. 1980, p. 499–513)

Perceptive study of Elizondo's difficult novel claims that in this open, anti-realist fiction reader becomes author, and author a liar, player of games.

5253 Tatum, Chuck and **Harold Hinds.** Eduardo del Río (Rius): an interview and introductory essay (Chasqui [Revista de literatura latinoamericana, Brigham Young University, Provo, Utah] 1, Nov. 1979, p. 3–23)

Rius has wider readership than most Mexican novelists. As creator of *Los supermachos, Los agachados,* satirical comic books, and illustrated books such as *Cuba para principiantes,* this socially committed author is an influential force in contemporary Mexico. Any student of Mexican literature and culture should know of his work, contents and significance. This essay and interview make a good introduction.

5254 Titiev, Janice Geasler. Witchcraft in Carlos Fuentes' *Aura* (UA/REH, 15:3, oct. 1981, p. 395–405)

Excellent tracing of source material from Jules Michelet's *La sorcière* in Fuentes' *Aura.* Finds explanations for females' characteristics and direct quotes from Michelet.

5255 Torri, Julio. Diálogo de los libros. México: Fondo de Cultura Económica, 1980. 282 p.

Collection of Torri's non-fiction prose includes correspondence with Alfonso Reyes, unavailable early essays, introduction, and excellent bibliography.

5256 Trejo Fuentes, Ignacio. El que despalinurice a palinuro será un buen despalinurizador: entrevista con Fernando del Paso (Semana de Bellas Artes [México] 138, 23 julio 1980, p. 6–11)

Extensive, very informative interview with author of *José Trigo* (1966) and *Palinuro de México* (1977). Of particular interest is the discussion of intertextuality and encyclopedism so characteristic of del Paso's novels.

5257 ———. La vejez en la obra de Sergio Galindo (CM/D, 16:4[94], julio/agosto 1980, p. 32–38, bibl.)

Most valuable point raised is that Galindo is alone among Mexican writers in his extensive treatment of old age.

5258 *Ulises*, 1927–28; *Escala*, 1930. México: Fondo de Cultura Económica, 1980. 317 p.; ill. (Revistas literarias mexicanas modernas)

Ulises (Tomo 1, No. 1, May 1924, to Tomo 1, No. 6, Feb. 1928, irregular) directed by Novo and Xavier Villaurrutia was Contemporaneos' first mature collaboration. They admired and identified with European and North American avant-garde. Of interest: Novo's series *Return Ticket*, and Cuesta's refutation of Ortega y Gasset's *Deshumanización del arte* which anticipated aesthetic that predominated in 1960s Mexico. *Escala* (Tomo 1, No. 1, Oct. 1930 to Tomo 1, No. 2, Nov. 1930) was an ephemeral publication.

5259 Vela, Arqueles. Sincrónicas. v. 1. México: Liberta-Sumaria, 1980. 191 p.

Compilation of journalistic essays by *Estridentismo*'s leading protagonist selected and prologued by his widow, Lénica Puyhol. Valuable contribution to the study of this neglected Mexican novelist and Mexican avant-garde.

Prose Fiction: 20th Century: Central America

LISA E. DAVIS, *Assistant Professor of Foreign Languages, York College of the City University of New York*

IN THE STUDY OF CENTRAL AMERICA, we are most often obliged by historical circumstances to view each country as a separate entity, but on occasion certain tendencies emerge which argue for a more unified vision of the area. Certainly, in the last few years political and social upheavals, economic readjustments and rising nationalism have touched all the republics from Guatemala to the Isthmus of Panama, and these difficult moments translate themselves into literary production in the guise of several perceptible trends. First, most remarkable in this sense seems to us a determined re-examination of the national history, and particularly recent history, through fiction and literary analysis in such diverse countries as Guatemala and Costa Rica. In the former, the young Guatemalan writer Arturo Arias seeks a key to his country's present ills in the fall of Arbenz after the liberal reforms of 1944–54, in the novels *Después de las bombas* (item **5260**), and also, in a detailed analysis entitled *Ideologías, literatura y sociedad durante la revolución guatemalteca, 1944–1954* (item **5274**), about the fiction of that era. On the other hand, Argentina Díaz Lozano's novel *Y tenemos que vivir* (item **5263**) traces the misfortunes of the country under Ubico, and closes on an optimistic note with the dictator's overthrow (Oct. 1944). In Costa Rica, Quince Duncan's new novel *Final de calle* (item **5265**) and Fabián Dobles' *Los leños vivientes* (item **5264**) re-evaluate the civil war of 1948, while a brilliant essay by Manuel Picado Gómez, "Literatura, Ideología, Crítica: Notas para un Estudio de la Literatura Costarricense," (item **5285**) calls for a critical review of the decade 1940–50, one which contributed several exceptional authors and fine works to the national literature. In a lighter vein, Rogelio Sinán's *La isla mágica* (item **5272**) re-creates moments in the history of Panama during this century, emphasizing the role of the Canal.

As regards literary criticism, it is worthwhile to point out here the superior quality of many studies issued in Central America or about Central American fiction. Works like that of Picado Gómez and Arturo Arias, cited above, display a scientific rigor that will eventually change the history of literature in the area, while the essays chosen to accompany the *Obras completas* edition of *El Señor Presidente* (item **5275**) provide a variety of readings drawn from the latest advances in literary analysis. Mario Vargas Llosa remarks, in "Una Nueva Lectura de *Hom-*

bres de maíz" (item **5292**), the excellence of Gerald Martin's study of that novel for the *Obras completas* series, and from Mexico, "Apuntes para una Lectura Social de dos Novelas de Miguel Angel Asturias," by Jorge Fernández Font (item **5281**), offers a semiotic reading of *El Señor Presidente* and *Hombres de maíz* for structural and ideological parallels. More conventional studies of the literary process in Central America cannot easily stand comparison with these dynamic and provocative essays.

Another critical problem, significant for developing countries, has arisen out of recent political and social events. In Nicaragua, in the wake of the Sandinista victory, the role of the artist in society has become a topic of concern. Sergio Ramírez, in "Los Intelectuales en el Futuro Revolucionario" (item **5286**), and Lizandro Chávez Alfaro, in "Nación y Narrativa Nicaragüense" (item **5277**), envision the makers of culture as a force united with collective popular interests and the historical process of the nation. On the other hand, the elitism of a hierarchical society plagues the literature of the past, from which literary history derives. While a new reality forges different critical attitudes, books from Nicaragua continue to be difficult to obtain. The situation probably will not change until the Sandinista government sets aside funds for a national press. In the meantime, the publication of José Román's chronicle of Sandino's campaigns *Maldito país* (item **5288**), some 40 years after its completion, speaks well for the future, as do new works by the octogenarian Adolfo Calero Orozco (items **5261** and **5262**).

Unfortunately, we have seen little from Honduras and El Salvador, both of which suffer a lack of publishing facilities and, in the case of the latter, the trauma of total war. Nevertheless, Julio Escoto's essays (item **5279**) and José María Méndez's short stories (item **5269**), several of which illustrate well the conditions behind the Salvadoran conflict, represent valuable contributions to the literature of the area.

PROSE FICTION

5260 Arias, Arturo. Después de las bombas. México: J. Mortiz, 1979. 195 p. (Serie del volador: novela)

Imaginative novel by young Guatemalan reflects his preoccupation with the history of his country, particularly 1944–54: what possibilities were lost, and what disasters followed Arbenz' fall. Within a framework deliberately fantastic and unreal, the protagonist Máximo, who is five years old in 1954, when the novel begins, grows to political consciousness in the midst of a succession of brutal dictatorships.

5261 Calero Orozco, Adolfo. El cuento de un loco, más una historia de amor. Managua, Nicaragua: Editorial Tiposa, 1979. 97 p. (Narraciones pinoleras)

Collection of 18 short narratives by one of Nicaragua's finest storytellers. Some of the stories are of folk origin, others have become local classics (e.g., "La Maestrita y el Boticario") and others were written in the light of recent events (e.g., "Navidades Richter 6.5," about the 1972 earthquake).

5262 ———. Eramos cuatro: novela nicaragüense. 2. ed., rev. y ligeramente ampliada. Managua, Nicaragua: s.n., 1978. 126 p.

By author of *Sangre santa* (1940), this latest novel explores through the lives of four young men, the Nicaragua of 50 years ago, and especially Managua before its destruction by earthquake. Told by a masterful stylist with the freshness and charm of the era it portrays.

5263 Díaz Lozano, Argentina. Y tenemos que vivir: novela. 4. ed. Guatemala: Editorial José de Pineda Ibarra, 1978. 186 p.

Re-edition of distinguished writer's early novel (1959) which explores the development of a young man of the Guatemalan *petite bourgeoisie*, the simplicity and harshness of his existence, and his initiation into an awareness of collective issues that touch his life. Novel closes significantly with the overthrow of Ubico (1944).

5264 Dobles, Fabián. Los leños vivientes. 2. ed. San José: Editorial Costa Rica, 1979. 208 p.

As editor explains, the original (1962) edition of this novel did not have the diffusion and publicity it deserved, and a second edition seems appropriate. Here, the eminènt Costa Rican writer has woven several subplots and numerous characters into the national crisis of 1948, with excellent scenes of political demonstrations by workers on the banana plantations, of the difficult life of the poor of San José, and of the incarceration of leftists at the outset of the uprising.

5265 Duncan, Quince. Final de calle: novela. San José: Editorial Costa Rica, 1979. 112 p.

Author describes novel as a reflection on events of Costa Rica's 1948 civil war. For this purpose, traces family history of three generations, concluding that much remains to be realized of the patriotic ambitions that inspired Figueres' uprising. Youngest protagonist represents the discontent of the present generation as it re-evalutes the nation's history.

5266 García Monge, Joaquín. Abnegación: novela. 3. ed. San José, Costa Rica: Ministerio de Cultura, Juventud y Deportes, Departamento de Publicaciones, 1977. 157 p. (Serie del rescate; no. 5)

By no means great novels, García Monge's sentimental tales are nonetheless important in the development of Costa Rican narrative, particularly during its realist stages. This particular novel is interesting for its portrayal of an innocent woman wounded by an unjust society. [N. Shumway]

5267 Gutiérrez, Joaquín. Puerto Limón. La Habana: Casa de las Américas, 1977. 264 p. (Colección La Honda)

Re-edition by Casa de las Américas of the classic novel (1950) about Costa Rica's Atlantic Coast province in the throes of a massive strike by banana plantation workers against the United Fruit Co., machinations of local government and threat of foreign intervention are seen through the eyes of a youthful idealistic protagonist.

5268 Jaramillo Levi, Enrique. Duplicaciones. México: J. Mortiz, 1973. 179 p. (Nueva narrativa hispánica)

Unusual collection of 40 short stories by young Panamanian, which explores a multitude of fantastic possibilities beyond the limits of reality. Title and sub-titles ("Simultaneidades," "Metamorfosis," "Incidencias," etc.) indicate author's concern with coincidental, absurd and hallucinating aspects of an apparently banal existence.

5269 Méndez, José María. Tiempo irredimible. San Salvador, El Salvador: Ministerio de Educación, Dirección de Publicaciones, 1977. 80 p.

Recipient of First Prize in *Juegos Florales Centroamericanos* (Quetzaltenango, 1970), this collection of 14 short stories by the well-known Salvadoran writer shows again his capacity to deal artistically with the difficult reality of El Salvador, both directly, in tales where harsh poverty and desperation set the tone, and also metaphorically, in a deliberate evasion of time and space limitations.

5270 Payeras, Mario. Los días de la selva. La Habana: Casa de las Américas, 1981. 115 p.

Recipient of Casa de las Américas award for testimonial literature for 1980, this first-person narrative recalls recent activities of one guerrilla band in jungles and mountains of Quiché in northern Guatemala. Valuable descriptions of difficult terrain and political education of native population.

5271 Pitty, Dimas Lidio. El centro de la noche. San José, Costa Rica: Editorial Universitaria Centroamericana, 1977. 127 p. (Colección Séptimo día)

Excellent collection of 11 short stories by gifted Panamanian writer, also poet and novelist. His themes here range from political persecution and exile to erotic fantasies, always returning to the essential solitude of his characters ("el centro de la noche"), the tragedy of their lives, and their close proximity to sudden death.

5272 Sinán, Rogelio. La isla mágica. Panamá: Instituto Nacional de Cultura, 1979. 658 p. (Colección Premio Ricardo Miró. Novela; 1977)

Recipient of the Ricardo Miró prize for 1977, this lengthy but delightful novel relates the extraordinary history of an island which has its model in the famous author's native Taboga off the Pacific coast of Panama. Its inhabitants, and chief among them the prodigious lover and loafer Juan Felipe Dungel, pursue their lusty, vibrant and often violent lives over several generations.

LITERARY CRITICISM AND HISTORY

5273 Arellano, Jorge Eduardo. Panorama de la literatura nicaragüense. 3. ed., resumida e aumentada. Managua: Ediciones Nacionales, 1977. 195 p.; bibl.

Updated edition of a history of Nicaraguan literature by one of her foremost critics explores authors and works in question both chronologically and, in second series of essays, by genre. Very helpful supplementary materials include general bibliography and bibliographical sketches of Nicaragua's most prominent literary personalities.

5274 Arias, Arturo. Ideologías, literatura y sociedad durante la revolución guatemalteca, 1944–1954. La Habana, Cuba: Casa de las Américas, 1979. 304 p.; bibl.

Recipient of the Casa de las Américas Essay Prize in 1979, this volume analyzes with precision and rigor the Guatemalan novel *Entre la piedra y la cruz* (1948) by Mario Monteforte Toledo. After considering the novel's internal structure, Arias links the fictional creation to its historical milieu and to author's ideological stand within Guatemala's revolutionary government.

Arizpe, Lourdes. Interview with Carmen Naranjo: women and Latin American literature. See item **5005.**

5275 Asturias, Miguel Angel. *El señor presidente*: edición crítica. Testimonio, Arturo Uslar Pietri. Estudios, Ricardo Navas Ruiz . . . et al. Texto establecido por Ricardo Navas Ruiz, Jean-Marie Saint-Lu. Paris: Editions Klincksieck, 1978. 306 p.; bibl. (Edición crítica de las obras completas de Miguel Angel Asturias; 3)

Obviously a key volume in the critical edition of the *Obras completas*, this one includes a number of excellent essays. Several possible "lecturas" (semantic, contextual, structuralist) by such international experts as Jean-Marie Saint-Lu, Gerald Martin and Iber Verdugo, complement Uslar Pietri's warm opening statement, while Ricardo Navas Ruiz discusses present text and variants.

5276 ———. *Viernes de Dolores*: edición crítica. Prefacio, Marcel Brion. Estudios, Claude Couffon, Iber H. Verdugo. Texto establecido por Iber H. Verdugo. Paris: Editions Klincksieck, 1978. 266 p.; bibl. (Edición crítica de las obras completas de Miguel Angel Asturias; 13)

Critical edition of Asturias' last novel which recalls events he lived as a university student, strikes and early publications. Iber Verdugo places the work aesthetically within the corpus of author's writings and Claude Couffon provides information about historical context. Marcel Brion's brief introduction addresses the magical powers of language.

5277 Chávez Alfaro, Lizandro. Nación y narrativa nicaragüense (CDLA, 20: 120, mayo/junio 1980, p. 69–73)

Distinguished Nicaraguan novelist and short story writer discusses supposed predominance of poetry over prose in his country. Attributes rise of prose narrative to Sandino's campaigns and a growth of nationalism and concludes by outlining the artist's role in the new Nicaragua.

5278 Cuadra, Pablo Antonio. Relaciones entre la literatura nicaragüense y literatura francesa (UTIEH/C, 36, 1981, p. 75–86)

Speaking as a poet concerned with the history of his national literature and the future of letters in his country, Cuadra makes a case here for the Nicaraguan ability to borrow from the French without sacrificing originality and authenticity, exemplified by Darío and several lesser known writers.

5279 Escoto, Julio. Casa del agua: artículos, ensayos. Tegucigalpa: Banco Central de Honduras, 1975. 152 p.; bibl.

These 16 polished essays by distinguished Honduran novelist and short story writer treat a variety of literary issues, from Latin American cultural unity to his country's rural vocabulary. Nevertheless, his most valuable pieces deal with problems little known outside Honduras, such as early novels and the difficulties of publishing fiction locally.

5280 Felker, William. Flavio Herrera: a bibliography (RIB, 28:3, 1978, p. 291–304)

Based on extensive knowledge of Herrera who was Felker's subject for his doctoral thesis, critic provides details of the life and works of the Guatemalan (1894–1968), active in several genres represented in the bibliography. The background of Herrera's career was contemporary Guatemalan politics and literary practice.

5281 Fernández Font, Jorge. Apuntes para una lectura social de dos novelas de Miguel Angel Asturias (UNAM/RMS, 41[41]:3, julio/sept. 1979, p. 863–878)

Through a semiotic reading of *El Señor Presidente* and *Hombres de maíz*, critic explores certain parallels and contrasts in both novels as regards historical context, ideological content, conflicts presented and resolved. Concludes that on an individual moral plane the good are saved and the bad punished while the social order does not change.

5282 Fonseca, Virginia S. de. Resumen de literatura costarricense. San José: Editorial Costa Rica, 1978. 190 p.

Recent study by one of the country's best scholars brings history of Costa Rican letters—chronologically and by genre—almost to present day. There is little analysis of authors though preferences are made clear, but major tendencies are traced and welcome information is provided on many minor figures.

5283 Juárez Gutiérrez, Luisa Amanda. Adolfo Calero-Orozco en la narrativa nicaragüense: monografía. Managua: Universidad Nacional Autónoma de Nicaragua, Facultad de Humanidades, Escuela de Ciencias de la Educación, 1978. 173 p.; 7 leaves of plates; ports (Colección de estudios lingüísticos y literarios)

Very helpful monograph includes extensive bibliography by young Nicaraguan scholar on Calero-Orozco's career, with particular attention to *Sangre santa*. Interviews with the writer (b. 1899) provide information about his early publications and personal impressions which would have been lost otherwise.

5284 Monterroso. Compilador, Jorge Ruffinelli. Xalapa, México: Centro de Investigaciones Lingüístico-Literarias, Universidad Veracruzana, 1976. 75 p.; bibl. (Cuadernos de Texto crítico; 1)

Collection of 15 short essays, most of them reproduced from periodical publications, comments on Monterroso's three books: *Obras completas y otros cuentos, La*

oveja negra y demás fábulas, and *Movimiento perpetuo*. While all essays are rather general, of notable quality are those by Jorge Ruffinelli, José Durand, Angel Rama, Carlos Monsiváis, and José Miguel Oviedo. Certainly this series of "Cuadernos de Texto Crítico" could be helpful reference, including as this volume does, an extensive bibliography of the Guatemalan author, long-time resident in Mexico.

Pérez Venero, Mirna. La novela *canalera* de Panamá: antecedents literarios y sociales. See *HLAS 43:7202.*

5285 Picado Gómez, Manuel. Literatura, ideología, crítica: notas para un estudio de la literatura costarricense (Repertorio Americano [Universidad Nacional, Instituto de Estudios Latinoamericanos, Heredia, Costa Rica] 5:4, julio/set. 1979, p. 1–27)

Lengthy study addresses lack of rigor in analysis of the national literature, referring particularly to the production of 1940–50, which includes figures such as Fallas, F. Dobles, J. Gutiérrez and Y. Oreamuno. Suggests techniques of semiotic analysis to eliminate prejudices and shallow interpretations, and a partial model reading is put forth for Fallas' *Marco Ramírez*.

5286 Ramírez M., Sergio. Los intelectuales en el futuro revolucionario (NMC/N, 1, mayo/junio 1980, p. 158–162)

In a controversial analysis, author describes historical split in Nicaragua between an elitist culture, the one taken as a national model until now, and a collective popular culture which should be the first concern of Nicaraguan writers and artists today.

5287 ———. La narrativa centroamericana (BNBD, 29 mayo/junio 1979, p. 46–61)

In an unusual and commendable attempt to see Central American writing as a whole, author follows its development from precolumbian manuscripts through the sterility of the colonial period into its maturation after independence. For the modern period, down to 1971 (when article was written) Ramírez comments on many authors and their works.

5288 Román, José, Maldito país. Managua: Ediciones El Pez y la Serpiente, 1979. 202 p.

Author of novel *Cosmapa* completed in 1933 this excellent historical narrative based on personal interviews with Sandino in the field. Unpublished until 1979, it is essential to an understanding of contemporary Nicaragua and of Sandino's war against North American troops stationed in what was for them a "maldito país."

5289 Salinas Paguada, Manuel. Breve reseña del cuento moderno hondureño (UTIEH/C, 36, 1981, p. 63–74)

For this descriptive study, author takes us back to the beginning of this century and forward to the present day with an analysis of figures like Eduardo Bahr and Julio Escoto, together with younger contemporary writers. Critic also relates Honduras' economic and political history to its literary production.

5290 Smart, Ian I. Big rage and big romance: discovering a new Panamanian writer (FIU/CR, 8:3, Summer 1979, p. 34–39)

Consists of brief description of career and publications of Carlos Guillermo Wilson, black Panamanian living presently in the US. In both poetry and prose, this new author expresses the bitterness and anger of the black experience, and his tender vital attachment to life and hope.

5291 Soto de Cáceres, Alicia. Breve viaje a *La isla mágica* de Rogelio Sinán (LNB/L, 293/294, agosto/sept. 1980, p. 20–30, bibl.)

In recognition of difficulties inherent in Sinán's *La isla mágica*, offers guides to the interpretation of time in the novel, in which several historical periods blend imperceptibly in conformity with the general anti-realistic and often magical atmosphere of the book.

5292 Vargas Llosa, Mario. Una nueva lectura de *Hombres de maíz* (ECO, 34[6]:210, abril 1979, p. 637–644)

The occasion for this article was author's reading, in manuscript, of Gerald Martin's introductory essay to the new *Obras completas* edition of the novel. Recent research in anthropology and linguistics conforms Asturias' extraordinary accomplishments in depicting, as though from within, the transition from a tribal culture to a class society.

Prose Fiction: 20th Century: Hispanic Caribbean

CARLOS R. HORTAS, *Associate Professor of Spanish, Hunter College*
WILLIAM LUIS, *Assistant Professor of Spanish, Dartmouth College*

THE DEFECTION OF SIX OF CUBA'S most important writers is the most significant event in recent years. Heberto Padilla (March 1980), Reinaldo Arenas (May 1980) and José Triana (Dec. 1980) were granted exit visas by Cuban authorities. Antonio Benítez Rojo (May 1980) and César Leante (Sept. 1981) sought political asylum while en route to conferences in Europe. That Leante and Benítez Rojo sought exile was most startling since they had no known political problems and held high level positions in the Ministry of Culture and Casa de las Américas respectively. To this group, one must add Edmundo Desnoes, who has been in the US since Sept. 1979. Unlike the others, however, Desnoes retains permission to stay from the Cuban Ministry of Culture. That dissatisfied writers are allowed to leave marks a significant departure from Cuban policy. The desperation of those who have left without permission has also become evident.

All left seeking literary freedom. Some like Arenas (item **5368**), Padilla (items **5330** and **5363**) and Leante (item **5359**) are already relating their experiences in Cuba. Most have begun to publish their own works. This is the case with Desnoes' *Los dispositivos en la flor* (item **5314**); Padilla's *En mi jardín pastan los héroes* (item **5330**) and *Legacies*, a collection of poems and Arenas' *Termina el desfile* (item **5295**) and *El central*, a prose poem. Benítez Rojo has announced his *El paso de los vientos* and Arenas is completing his *Otra vez el mar*, initially written in

Cuba. Triana staged the premiere of his *Revolico en el campo de marte* (written in 1971), while a Visiting Professor at Dartmouth College in the fall of 1981. All live in the US except for Triana and Leante who have made Paris and Madrid their respective homes.

These events have overshadowed works by and about Alejo Carpentier and José Lezama Lima, the masters of Cuban literature. Recently published was Carpentier's posthumous *La novela latinoamericana en vísperas de un nuevo siglo y otros ensayos* (item **5307**) and what appears to be a pirated edition of his articles entitled *El adjetivo y sus arrugas* (item **5300**). In Lezama's case, Eloísa Lezama published her brother's *Cartas* (item **5322**) and an annotated edition of his *Paradiso* (item **5324**). The deaths of Carpentier and Lezama will lead to more comprehensive studies of their works as well as to their literary reappropriation by both island and exiled Cubans. These rival claims are already evident in the case of Lezama as presented by Emilio Bejel's "Entrevista a Cintio Vitier" (item **5340**) which stands in contrast to Padilla's "Lezama Lima Frente a su Discurso," (item **5363**) concerning his role in the events that led to the 1971 Padilla Affair.

Of particular interest is a new literary magazine, *Linden Lane* (item **5325**) edited by Heberto Padilla, Belkis Cuza Malé and Reinaldo Arenas. The first issue appeared in early 1982 and is dedicated to Cuban authors in exile. The magazine has a broad perspective encompassing a variety of literary and cultural themes in fiction, poetry, theatre, essay, testimonial, criticism and reviews. *Linden Lane* is a welcome addition to a field that needs new approaches to literature.

In Puerto Rico, José Luis González is once again proving that he is among the top two or three writers actively contributing to Puerto Rican letters. His *Balada de otro tiempo* and *La llegada* (item **5318**) are well crafted novels that explore different aspects of the island's history and culture. His volume of essays, *El país de cuatro pisos* (item **5319**) is an excellent publication, particularly the essay from which the book derives its title. This essay, along with Pedreira's *Insularismo* and René Marqués' "El Puertorriqueño Dócil" must be considered the basis for any future discussion of Puerto Rican identity and national character. Another important book that offers insights into González's ideas is *Conversaciones con José Luis González*.

As has been true in recent years, Puerto Rican narrative is healthy and in continued ferment. Authors like E. Laguerre and Pedro Juan Soto continue to add to their oeuvre and younger and very promising writers such as Juan A. Ramos are coming into their own.

Perhaps the most important publication in recent years is *Memorias de Bernardo Vega* (item **5335**) an impressive account of Vega's years in New York during the first half of this century. What Bernardo Vega reveals about the life of Puerto Ricans in New York, cigar makers, political events at the time, immigrant communities in the city and the role of Vito Marcantonio and Fiorello La Guardia in protecting the rights of ethnic minorities in New York City, constitutes a truly outstanding account. Well written and eminently readable, this remarkable autobiography was edited by César Andreu Iglesias who also writes the introduction.

Mention should be made here of Editorial Huracán, whose publishing record in the last few years has been exceptionally good. Editorial Huracán has chosen authors wisely and is possibly the quality publisher on the island today.

The Dominican Republic continues to be overshadowed by Cuba and Puerto Rico. We have received a number of anthologies like *Nueva narrativa dominicana* (item **5328**) and the complete works of well-known writers like Fabio Fiallo's *Obras completas* (item **5315**). It appears that Dominican publishers are taking stock of their established writers by publishing collective works.

PROSE FICTION

**5293 Antología de la literatura puertorri-
queña.** Madrid: Playor, 1980. 378 p.;
bibl.; ill.

Representative poets, essayists and
short-story writers. Two plays by Francisco
Arriví and one chapter from *La Charca* by
Zeno Gandía and another from *La Resaca* by
Laguerre. No introduction or notes. Useful
but limited bibliography which includes
largely general works of reference.

5294 Arenas, Reinaldo. El palacio de las
blanquísimas mofetas. Caracas: Monte
Avila Editores, 1980. 397 p.

Arenas' latest novel is a continuation
of his *Celestino antes del alba.* Narrates economic, political, cultural and psychological
traumas of family in Cuban countryside.
Written in 1972, it first appeared in French in
1975.

5295 ———. Termina el desfile. Barcelona:
Seix Barral, 1981. 174 p.

Same as his previous collection of
short stories, *Con los ojos cerrados* (published 1972), with the addition of "Termina
el Desfile," which narrates events of 1980
Peruvian Embassy takeover. Latter story at
end of collection challenges his opening
story, "Comienza el Desfile."

5296 ———. La Vieja Rosa. Sabana Grande,
Caracas: Librería Cruz del Sur, 1980.
114 p.; appendix (Cuadernos del Caribe)

Brief but powerful novel (written 1967)
about Rosa, an unyielding landowner in the
Revolution. Attractive but poorly-bound edition includes Christina Guzmán's uninformative interview with Arenas while still in
Cuba. Novel is also included in his *Termina
el desfile* (item **5295**).

5297 Cabrera, Lydia. Tres cuentos (Escanda-
lar [Escandalar, Inc., Elmhurst, N.Y.]
3:2, abril/junio 1980, p. 60–63)

Three brief stories by one of the best
Cuban folklore writers.

5298 Cabrera Infante, Guillermo. La Habana para un infante difunto. Barcelona: Seix Barral, 1979, 711 p.

Autobiographical novel of Cabrera Infante's sexual development. His childhood as
well as Havana are seen with nostalgia. Although similar to *Tres tristes tigres* in style,
the latter continues to be his best work.

5299 ———. Meta-End. Translated and annotated by Roberto González Echevarría (LALR, 8:16, 1980, p. 88–95)

Published as "Meta-final" in *El Ala-
crán Azul* (1:1, 1970, p. 18–22), this story
was the original ending of *Tres tristes tigres*
later eliminated by its author "because there
was already too much symmetry to add this
parody." Story narrates Estrella's accidental
burial at sea. González Echevarría's excellent
translation retains the humor of the original
text which is perhaps Cabrera Infante's most
important work.

5300 Carpentier, Alejo. El adjetivo y sus
arrugas. Buenos Aires: Editorial
Galerna, 1980. 127 p.

Pirated edition of selected writings
published by Carpentier in *Letra y Solfa* between 1950–60. Collection lacks introduction, dates of articles and editor's note. It can
be roughly divided into literature, music,
painting and general cultural interest.

5301 ———. El arpa y la sombra. La Habana: Editorial Letras Cubanas, 1979.
159 p.

In his last novel, Carpentier returns to
"origin" of American civilization. With same
stylistic rigor of previous works, he demys-
tifies effort to canonize Christopher Columbus and reveals the man, his intentions and
search for money and power (also published
Mexico: Siglo Veintiuno, 1979).

5302 ———. La consagración de la primavera. Novela. Madrid: Siglo Veintiuno de España, 1979. 576 p. (La Creación
literaria)

Carpentier's epic novel develops from
struggle against fascism in Spanish Civil War
to battle against imperialism in Bay of Pigs
Invasion.

5303 ———. La consagración de la primavera: capítulo inédito (RYC, 70,
junio 1978, p. 50–54)

Should not be mistaken for unknown
chapter of Carpentier's novel. This is first
chapter of *La consagración* which appeared
about same time as novel in 1978. Contains
some stylistic variations.

5304 ———. La cultura de los pueblos que
habitan en las tierras del mar Caribe
(CDLA, 20:18, enero/feb. 1980, p. 2–8)

Cuban television talk in celebration of
Carifesta '79, stresses themes common to

Caribbean countries and is included in *La novela latinoamericana en vísperas de un nuevo siglo y otros ensayos* (item **5307**).

5305 ———. ¡Ecue-Yamba-O! Barcelona: Bruguera, 1978. 215 p. (Libro amigo; 1502/634)

Reedition of Carpentier's first novel (published 1933). Unlike previous pirated editions, this one was approved by the author and contains his brief introduction.

5306 ———. Una fiesta de muchísimos personajes y un premio (UNEAC/GC, 167, mayo 1978, p. 2–3)

Acceptance speech of Miguel de Cervantes Saavedra prize for literature, received in 1978.

5307 ———. La novela latinoamericana en vísperas de un nuevo siglo y otros ensayos. México: Siglo Veintiuno, 1981. 252 p.

Siglo Veintiuno's posthumous homage to Carpentier is an anthology of articles, conferences, talks and prologues, revealing Carpentier's vast knowledge of literature, culture, music, painting, sociology, politics and history. Unfortunately, collection lacks organization and an introduction analyzing this important aspect of Carpentier's work.

5308 Corretjer, Juan Antonio. El cumplido: narraciones arbitrarias. Prólogo por Ramón Felipe Medina. Río Piedras, P.R.: Editorial Antillana, 1979. 135 p.; bibl.

Collection of stories first published in Puerto Rican newspapers and magazines. Interesting and carefully written narratives reveal another side of well-known Puerto Rican poet. Preceded by excellent introduction and bibliography by Ramón Felipe Medina. Includes glossary.

5309 Cuentos del Caribe. Compilados por Leonardo Fernández-Marcané. Madrid: Playor, D.L., 1978. 280 p.; bibl.

One of few anthologies of 20th-century Hispanic Caribbean short stories contains good selection, none new. Includes little-known writers of genre and excludes more important ones.

5310 Delgado, Emilio. Antología, en recuerdo de su vida y su obra. San Juan, P.R.: Instituto de Cultura Puertorriqueña, 1976. 216 p.; port.

Primarily a journalist whose articles regularly appeared in Puerto Rican newspapers, Delgado's anthology includes some of his poetry and a good sampling of interesting articles on various aspects of Puerto Rican life. Also includes articles on Puerto Rican writers and sampling of correspondence. Concludes with some appreciations of Delgado by writers who knew him well.

5311 Díaz Montero, Aníbal. Andy's bar: relatos. San Juan de Puerto Rico: Díaz Montero, 1978. 94 p.

All stories take place in Andy's bar but seldom become more than simple anecdotes. Indeed, even as anecdotes they are curiously flat and insipid reminding one of people who get together regularly but have nothing to say to one another.

5312 ———. Mocho y azada: cuentos jíbaros. Santurce, P.R.: Editorial Díaz Mont, 1979. 122 p.

Short stories about the Puerto Rican countryside, very much in the *costumbrista* style. Interesting glimpses of customs, habits and daily life in the country. Best stories are those in which animals are protagonists.

5313 Díaz Rodríguez, Jesús. De la patria y el exilio. La Habana: Unión de Escritores y Artistas de Cuba, 1979. 247 p.

Winner of 1978 UNEAC prize for testimony, Díaz' book is based on his film "55 Hermanos," documentary on first Antonio Maceo Brigade's visit to Cuba (Dec. 1977–Jan. 1978). Book is a revealing account of experiences of sons and daughters of Cuban refugees. Also contains selection from *Areito*.

5314 Los Dispositivos en la flor, Cuba: literatura desde la revolución. Edited by Edmundo Desnoes and William Luis. Hanover, N.H.: Ediciones del Norte, 1981. 557 p.

Most complete anthology to date on Cuban literature in the Revolution. Work covers last 20 years and includes writers of different generations and genres, not all living in Cuba. Contains useful bio-bibliography preceding each writer. All selections are from previous publications. A necessary classroom manual. Desnoes' epilogue is a testament of his difficult middle position regarding cultural policy in Cuba.

5315 Fiallo, Fabio. Obras completas. v. 1, La canción de una vida. v. 2, Cuentos frágiles. v. 3, Nacionalismo auténtico. v. 4, Estudios acerca de su vida y sus obras. Santo Domingo: Editora de Santo Domingo, 1980. 4 v.; bibl.; ill. (Colección de cultura dominicana; 33)

Much needed collection of Dominican poet-patriot's work. Vols. 1/3 include his poetry, short stories and essays; vol. 4 is dedicated to criticism of the man and his work.

5316 Franqui, Carlos. Retrato de familia con Fidel. Barcelona: Seix Barral, 1981. 536 p.

Journalistic, personal and even poetic account of years when Franqui directed the official Cuban newspaper *Revolución* (1959–63). Franqui's daring testimony offers an insider's view of political and historical aspects of the Cuban Revolution and is an important document for Cuban scholars. Also contains information on Cuban cultural policy and controversial literary supplement *Lunes de Revolución*.

5317 González, José Luis. En Nueva York y otras desgracias. Introducción de Andrés Avellaneda. 3a. ed., rev. y aum. Río Piedras, P.R.: Ediciones Huracán, 1981. 169 p.

Anthology of previously published short stories written 1943–54 but reworked and stylistically polished. Excellent examples of González's narrative prose, stories are preceded by very good introduction by Andrés Avellaneda.

5318 ———. La llegada: crónica con "ficción." Río Piedras, P.R.: Ediciones Huracán, 1980. 138 p.; 2 p. of plates; ill.

Fictional account of invasion of Puerto Rico by US military forces in Aug. 1898. Includes reactions of characters to events and political debates generated by U.S. military invasion. Novel's time frame is one day and one night and locale and characters represent different Puerto Rican social strata and political philosophies. Somewhat didactic historical novel but, as with all of González's works, well-written and eminently readable.

5319 ———. El país de cuatro pisos. Río Piedras, P.R.: Ediciones Huracán, 1980. 119 p.

Excellent group of essays, particularly the essay from which the book derives its title. Draws analogy between successive floors of a house, superimposed on each other, and imposition of different sovereignties and forms of government in Puerto Rico. Essay ranks alongside *Insularismo* and "El Puertorriqueño Dócil" as major contribution to interpretation of Puerto Rican character and island's historical development.

5320 Hernández Sánchez, Roberto. Yo soy el otro: cuentos. Prólogo por Washington Lloréns. San Juan, P.R.: Editorial Yaurel, 1979. 60 p.

Short short stories reflect on man's condition with interesting philosophical, surreal meditations but mini-tales lack development or plot. They are more essays than short stories, expressing author's anguish about existence.

5321 Leante, César. Los guerrilleros negros. Mexico: Siglo Veintiuno, 1979. 265 p.

Reedition of his 1976 novel which received 1975 UNEAC Prize. Leante's latest is a rewriting of the antislavery novels and reveals life of runaway slave communities in the mountains.

5322 Lezama Lima, José. Cartas: 1939–1976. Introducción y edición de Eloísa Lezama Lima. Madrid: Orígenes, 1979. 291 p.; ill. (Colección Tratados de testimonio)

Selection of Lezama's correspondence to his sister Eloísa, relatives and friends (e.g., Juan Ramón Jiménez, Julián Orbón, Severo Sarduy). Letters provide insights into Lezama's daily life, *Orígenes* (1944–56) and controversies like Rodríguez Feo's and Lezama's over the publication of Juan Ramón Jiménez's text. Eloísa's introduction is a mixture of Lezama's biography, his works and her own recollections of the author.

5323 ———. Obras completas. t. 1, Novela. Poesía completa. t. 2, Ensayos. Cuentos. México: Aguilar, 1975/1977. 2 v.; ports (Biblioteca de autores modernos)

Lezama's incomplete *Obras completas*, published before he died on 9 Aug. 1976, do not contain his posthumous *Oppiano Licario* (1977) and *Fragmentos a su imán* (1977). *Obras completas* includes section of poems not previously collected and Cintio Vitier's informative, though incomplete, bibliographical introduction. Although dated July 1971, he admits finishing it before Lezama concluded his *Paradiso*.

5324 ———. Paradiso. Edición de Eloísa Lezama Lima. Madrid: Ediciones Cátera, 1980. 653 p.

First annotated edition of *Paradiso*. Eloísa Lezama's introduction contains useful information on author's life and works. As the author's sister, she attempts to provide a privileged reading of *Paradiso*. Edition is based on original Cuban version. Errors are an intentional part of Lezama's novel.

5325 *Linden Lane Magazine.* Vol. 1, No. 1, enero/marzo 1982– . Princeton, N.J.

New literary magazine, published four times a year, edited by Heberto Padilla, Belkis Cuza Malé and Reinaldo Arenas. First issue is dedicated to works of exiled Cuban writers: Antonio Benítez Rojo, César Leante, Enrique Labrador Ruiz, Guillermo Cabrera Infante, José Triana, Juan Arcocha, Carlos Franqui, Carlos Alberto Montaner and others.

5326 Lugo, Américo. Antología de Américo Lugo. Julio Jaime Julia, comp. Santo Domingo: Taller, 1976/1978. 3 v.

Collection of Lugo's works (1916–24) includes his political and literary essays, mostly unknown to general public.

5327 Mir, Pedro. Cuando amaban las tierras comuneras. Ilus. y portada de Anhelo Hernández. México: Siglo XXI Editores, 1978. 332 p.; ill. (Creación literaria)

Based on 1916 and 1965 US invasions of Dominican Republic, Mir's novel relies on techniques associated with contemporary novel.

5328 La Nueva narrativa dominicana. Virgilio Díaz Grullón *et al.* Santo Domingo: Casagrande, 1978. 256 p.

Lipe Collado's selection consists of little-known but accessible stories of 15 contemporary narrators—all but del Risco Bermúdez are living. Anthology provides introduction to works of these known authors.

5329 Otero, Lisandro. General a caballo. La Habana: Editorial Letras Cubanas, 1980. 91 p.

In this dictator novel, retired general assumes presidency of imaginary republic for one day. Country's violent history justifies present action but general's unrealistic willingness to please everyone makes ending predictable.

5330 Padilla, Heberto. En mi jardín pastan los héroes. Barcelona: Editorial Argos Vergara, 1981. 270 p.

Padilla's first novel, written in and smuggled out of Cuba, mixes fact and fiction in Havana during the Revolution (e.g., Marx and Engels have a rock fight). His "Prólogo con Novela" explains events which followed novel's writing (1970).

5331 Ramos, Juan Antonio. Démosle luz verde a la nostalgia. Río Piedras, P.R.: Editorial Cultural, 1978. 194 p.

Characters in these 14 stories, excellent examples of genre, are described with bold, unsparing strokes, masterfully revealing their psychological realities. Very effective use of language and accurate rendition of Puerto Rican usage and diction by a very talented writer.

5332 Ramos Otero, Manuel. El cuento de la mujer del mar. Diseño portada, John Anthes. Río Piedras, P.R.: Ediciones Huracán, 1979. 116 p.

Stylistically sophisticated short stories by one of Puerto Rico's more accomplished young writers are well-crafted and worth reading, especially "Romance de Clara Gardenia Otero." Includes stream of consciousness, surreal narrative techniques, and experiments with punctuation.

5333 Sarduy, Severo. De donde son los cantantes. Barcelona: Seix Barral, 1980. 153 p.; 2 leaves (Nueva narrativa hispánica)

Reedition of Sarduy's second novel (published 1967). Unlike Spanish editions and like the French one, contains Roland Barthes' "La Faz Barroca" which has appeared elsewhere in Spanish. Differences in translations are due to translator's style.

5334 Seda Bonilla, Eduardo. Lumpen. Río Piedras, P.R.: Ediciones Bayoan, 1980? 136 p.

Novel is proof that Eduardo Seda should stick to the social sciences and forego further attempts at fiction. Narrative is moralistic and sentimental, style is heavy-handed, puerile and cliché-ridden.

5335 Vega, Bernardo. Memorias de Bernardo Vega. Río Piedras, P.R.: Ediciones Huracán, 1977. 282 p.

Probably most important book published in Puerto Rico during past five years, these *Memorias . . .* are personal account of Puerto Rican immigrant's years in New York City during early part of century. A cigar maker with highly-developed political conscience, Bernardo Vega recounts his personal exploits and political activism in the New

York of Fiorello La Guardia and Vito Marcantonio. An absolutely indispensable book.

5336 Verges, Pedro. Solo cenizas hallarás: bolero. Valencia: Editorial Prometeo, 1980. 414 p. (Colección sinople; 8)

Most significant Dominican novel to be published in recent years and winner of the Blasco Ibáñez Prize. Successfully mixes political, psychological and cultural elements and offers many perspectives of life immediately after the Trujillo dictatorship.

5337 Zavala, Iris M. Kiliagonía. México: Premia Editora, 1980. 75 p.; ill. (La Red de Jonás)

Author's baroque prose style is dense with symbols and mythological references. Heavy-handed, pretentious writing fails to evoke meaning or communicate message.

LITERARY CRITICISM AND HISTORY

5338 Alvarez García, Imeldo. La obra narrativa de César Leante (CDLA, 20:118, enero/feb. 1980, p. 108–113)

Good introductory article on life and works of important Cuban writer.

Arenas, Reinaldo. La cultura popular en la narrativa latinoamericana. See item **5004**.

5339 Barnet, Miguel. The documentary novel (UP/CSEC, 11:1, Jan. 1981, p. 49–64)

Explains Barnet's concept of "documentary novel" and describes characteristics and methodology used in his *Biografía de un cimarrón* and *Canción de Rachel*. Some of his ideas, expressed elsewhere, provide groundwork for new Latin American novel.

5340 Bejel, Emilio. Entrevista a Cintio Vitier (AR, 7:27, p. 30–34)

Candid interview outlines Vitier's position from within Revolution. Of primary importance is his reaction to Lezama's *Cartas* and Revolution's reevaluation of Lezama.

5341 Casanova Sánchez, Olga. La crítica social en la obra novelística de Enrique A. Laguerre. Río Piedras, P.R.: Editorial Cultural, 1975. 190 p.

Examination of Laguerre's novels, designed to identify their themes, reveals his preoccupation with Puerto Rican social issues. Chapters on major Puerto Rican writers who share Laguerre's social concerns precede study on him.

5342 Díaz Quiñones, Arcadio. Conversación con José Luis González. 2. ed. Santa Rita, Río Piedras, P.R.: Ediciones Huracán, 1977. 159 p. (Colección Norte)

Indispensable, revealing book on González's literary and philosophical opinions. Interview reveals his profound knowledge of Puerto Rico's history, commitment to a socialist alternative but, above all, his intellectual honesty. In a society where independence is a desired political goal for some but a state of mind for others, it is important to give due attention to an advocate of independence who is also an independent thinker.

5343 Diccionario de la literatura cubana. v. 1, A-LL. La Habana: Editorial Letras Cubanas, 1980. 537 p.

Excellent and much needed bibliographic tool compiled by the Instituto de Literatura y Lingüística de la Academia de Ciencias de Cuba. Vol. 1 of two corresponds to letters A to LL and includes themes, biographies of authors and a passive and active bibliography of and about their works. Unfortunately, controversial figures living outside of Cuba (e.g., Carlos Franqui, Guillermo Cabrera Infante) have been omitted.

5344 Escritores contemporáneos de Puerto Rico. San Juan de Puerto Rico: Sociedad de Autores Puertorriqueños, 1978. 224 p. (Biblioteca de autores puertorriqueños)

Consists of 20 essays about contemporary but mature Puerto Rican writers (age 60–80) by different critics. Transcriptions of after-dinner talks given to honor particular authors. Book lacks footnotes, bibliographies and critical apparatus.

5345 Fernández Retamar, Roberto. Calibán y otros ensayos: nuestra América y el mundo. La Habana, Cuba: Editorial Arte y Literatura, 1979. 294 p.; bibl. (Cuadernos de arte y sociedad)

Collection of previously published essays (1966–77) includes reedition of "Calibán." Of interest is follow-up note to "Calibán" written for, but excluded from, Italian version.

5346 García Cabrera, Manuel. Laguerre y sus polos de la cultura iberoamericana.

San Juan, P.R.: Biblioteca de Autores Puerto-rriqueños, 1978. 75 p.

Paean to Laguerre, in the form of an extended book-length review of his work *Polos de la cultura iberoamericana*, rehashes his ideas, quotes him and praises him.

5347 González, José Luis. Literatura y sociedad en Puerto Rico: de los cronistas de Indias a la generación del 98. México: Fondo de Cultura Económica, 1976. 246 p. (Colección Tierra firme)

Attempt to interpret Puerto Rican literature through island's historical, social, political, and economic development. Although interplay between the latter and literary production yields some interesting insights, González subscribes to a certain determinism by ignoring the creative process and fitting works of literature into preconceived cubbyholes.

5348 González Echevarría, Roberto. *Biografía de un cimarrón* and the novel of the Cuban Revolution (Novel [Providence, Rhode Island] 13 : 3, 1980, p. 249–263)

Insightful essay places Miguel Barnet's *Biografía de un cimarrón* and the Cuban documentary novel at the foreground of Cuban and Latin American literature. Shows how, in Barnet's work, writing addresses the problem of conversion and mediates between past and the present.

5349 ———. Carpentier, crítico de la literatura hispanoamericana: Asturias y Borges (SN, 12 : 2, julio/sept. 1981, p. 7–27)

Well researched article which uncovers Carpentier's chronicles on Borges and Asturias in *Letra y Solfa*. Influenced by their works, Carpentier developed a style that made him the transmitter of literary ideas in Spanish America.

5350 ———. Criticism and literature in Revolutionary Cuba (UP/CSEC, 11 : 1, Jan. 1981, p. 1–17)

Divides literary criticism in contemporary Cuba into journalistic and academic. Latter, which includes publication of texts, has improved; former, which concerns ongoing criticism, has not. However, González Echevarría sees encouraging signs.

5351 ———. Modernidad, modernismo y nueva narrativa: *El recurso del método* (RIB, 30 : 2, 1980, p. 157–163)

Brief but concise essay relating Modernity and Modernism to Carpentier's *El recurso del método*. Concepts help to understand novel and novel helps reveal their importance.

5352 Guinness, Gerald. Contemporary Puerto Rican fiction: an outsider's view. San Juan, P.R.: Department of Education, Commonwealth of Puerto Rico, 1979. 11 p.

Interesting pamphlet classifies Puerto Rican novels into: 1) nativist; 2) social protestant; and 3) experimental. Author prefers No. 2 but is disappointed by most noting obsessive concern with island's social and political burdens. Believes detachment would allow a more "magisterial view" of Puerto Rican reality.

5353 Janney, Frank. Alejo Carpentier and his early works. London: Tamesis Books Limited, 1981. 141 p.

Places five of Carpentier's early works (prior to *The kingdom of this world*) within Expressionist and Cubist currents. Provides useful summaries while pointing to theme and style. Appendix contains texts of "Histoire de Lune" and "Oficio de Tinieblas." Latter is not part of study. Active and passive bibliography does not include recent works.

5354 Junco Fazzolari, Margarita. Paradiso y el sistema poético de Lezama Lima. Buenos Aires: F. García Gambeiro, 1979. 180 p.; bibl. (Colección Estudios latinoamericanos; 26)

Good introductory text on Lezama's work.

5355 *Latin American Literary Review.* Carnegie-Mellon University, Department of Modern Languages. Vol. 8, No. 16, Spring/Summer 1980– . Pittsburgh, Pa.

Valuable issue devoted to literature of Cuba, Puerto Rico and Dominican Republic edited by González Echevarría. Insightful introduction on Caribbean literature describes issue as "reflection of current interests and a sample of literary production." Contains fiction, poetry, criticism; first time in translation works by Carpentier, Barnet, Sarduy, Cabrera Infante, Díaz Valcárcel, etc.; articles by José Arróm, Aníbal González, Stephanie Merrim, Emir Rodríguez Monegal, Enrico Mario Santí, Carlos Hortas, Rubén Ríos, William Luis, etc. As editor admits, major literary figures are missing and Cuba is emphasized.

5356 Lucyga, C. Zur Darstellung von Geschichte und Gegenwart im neuen kubanischen Roman (UR/L, 31:12, Herbstsemester 1978, p. 5–24)

Summary of Cuban literature since the Revolution up to the mid-1970s. In this last stage, man is viewed in relation to his social condition. Little new information.

5357 Luis, William. The antislavery novel and the concept of modernity (UP/CSEC, 11:1, Jan. 1981, p. 33–47)

Divides antislavery novel into three stages: 1) slavery; 2) post-slavery; and 3) Cuban revolutionary period. Periodization allows history and modernity to be seen as complementary instead of antagonistic forces.

5358 ———. Autopsia de *Lunes de Revolución:* entrevista a Pablo Armando Fernández (Plural [Excelsior, México] 17:126, marzo 1982, p. 52–62)

Pablo Armando Fernández discloses important information on polemical literary supplement *Lunes de Revolución* (1959–61, magazine of then official newspaper *Revolución,* now *Granma*). Views with nostalgia those important years of his life.

5359 ———. Con César Leante (BJCC, 70:48, 1 dic. 1978, p. 10–13)

Interview covers both Leante's life and works. Exemplifies writer who developed as a result of Cuban Revolution. Now lives outside of Cuba.

5360 ———. La novela antiesclavista: texto, contexto y escritura (CAM, 236:3, mayo/junio 1981, p. 103–116)

Attempt to redefine the antislavery novel by dialoguing with both history and contemporary critics and criticism.

5361 Márquez, Roberto. Racismo, cultura y revolución: ideología y política en la prosa de Nicolás Guillén (UCV/E, 4:8, julio/dic. 1979, p. 213–239)

Historical development of Guillén's little publicized but important essays. Racism, politics and culture are dominant and complement his poetic concerns.

5362 Méndez, Adriana. Carpentier en la actual generación de escritores cubanos (Plural [Excelsior, México] 16:114, marzo 1981, p. 20–25)

Useful analysis of Carpentier's influence on first and second generation writers of Cuban Revolution. Examines younger writers' reactions to his literary concerns in works of Edmundo Desnoes, César Leante, Guillermo Cabrera Infante, Severo Sarduy, and Reinaldo Arenas.

5363 Padilla, Heberto. Lezama Lima frente su discurso (Linden Lane Magazine [Princeton, N.J.] 1:1, enero/marzo 1982, p. 16–18, ill.)

Addendum to Padilla's staged confession of April 27, 1971 reveals how important yet polemical a figure Lezama was for Cuban authorities.

5364 Prieto, Abel E. Trayectoria de una ensayística (CDLA, 20:120, mayo/junio 1980, p. 45–55)

Prieto traces Retamar's essays from pre-revolutionary bourgeois days to his involvement with Cuban Revolution. Retamar's ideas are linked to Martí's. Article is prologue to Retamar's forthcoming book *Para el perfil definitivo del hombre.*

5365 Ripoll, Carlos. Censors and dissenters (Partisan Review [Boston University, Boston, Mass.] 48:4, Fall 1981, p. 3–16)

Seesawing of Cuban cultural policy is tied to historical events. Ripoll's intention is to publicize poets in Cuban jails but his analysis is not balanced.

5366 Rodríguez H., Luis. Cronología de la vida y la obra de Félix Pita Rodríguez (UCLV/I, 62, enero/abril 1979, p. 3–74, bibl., plates)

Very useful, almost yearly account of life and works of important Cuban short story writer and poet. Includes extensive active and passive bibliography, pictures and newspapers and magazine clippings.

5367 Santí, Enrico Mario. Edmundo Desnoes: the novel from under (UP/CSEC, 11:1, Jan. 1981, p. 49–64)

Santí comes to terms with four versions of *Memorias del subdesarrollo.* His analysis takes into consideration Desnoes' essays and segments of the film absent in the novel. Most comprehensive article on Desnoes to date.

5368 ———. Entrevista con Reinaldo Arenas (Vuelta [Revista mensual, México] 4:47, oct. 1980, p. 18–25, ill.)

Informative and polemical biographical interview. Arenas talks openly about his works, his difficult life as a writer under the

Castro government, his imprisonment and events surrounding his recent exit from Cuba.

5369 Sass, U. and C. Holtz. Die kubanische Revolution in den Werken von José Soler Puig (UR/L, 31:12, Herbstsemester 1978, p. 25–34)

Perceives three stages of José Soler Puig's works as representative of latest trend in literature of the Cuban Revolution.

5370 Schwartz, Kessel. *Ciclón* and Cuban culture (UPR/CS, 14:4, Jan. 1975, p. 151–161)

Overview of contributions of Cuban journal *Ciclón* (1955–59) to Cuban literature. Believes that although journal did not attempt to demystify Cuban culture, it served as bridge that led towards revolutionary changes that began in 1959. [N. Valdés]

Prose Fiction: 20th Century: Andean Countries (Bolivia, Colombia, Ecuador, Peru and Venezuela)

JOSE MIGUEL OVIEDO, *Professor of Spanish, University of California, Los Angeles*
DJELAL KADIR, *Associate Professor of Spanish and Comparative Literature, Purdue University*

AUNQUE EL INTERES CRITICO sigue concentrándose en dos de los grandes nombres de la narrativa de esta región (Vargas Llosa en el Perú, García Márquez en Colombia), es notorio que otros nuevos intereses han empezado a surgir, con nuevas propuestas teóricas y revalorizaciones estéticas, aparte de aquellos. Por un lado, han surgido variados juicios sobre el indigenismo literario en el Perú y Bolivia, varios de ellos realizados desde la perspectiva de la antropología y la crítica cultural (items **5404** y **5406**). Las figuras de José María Arguedas y de Alcides Arguedas han cobrado, así, nueva actualidad y presencia definitoria dentro de los respectivos procesos literarios de sus países. En el caso del segundo, ese interés ha sido activado por el reciente centenario de su nacimiento (1879). Las mismas razones explican el notable acopio de materiales documentales y algunos esfuerzos críticos dedicados a Rómulo Gallegos en Venezuela (items **5419–5420, 5422–5423, 5425** y **5427**), al cumplirse 50 años de la edición de *Doña Bárbara* y 10 de su muerte. Motivos semejantes dieron como resultado un libro crítico de homenaje consagrado a *Cumandá* en Ecuador, para celebrar el centenario de su publicación (item **5397**).

Buena parte del trabajo de los estudiosos de la literatura ha estado en el area de las recopilaciones de fuentes y materiales documentales: Valdelomar (item **5415**), José Eustasio Rivera (item **5372**), García Márquez (items **5388–5389**), entre otros, son ejemplo de ese tipo de interés. Varios aportes críticos han sido hechos desde el ángulo de la crítica cultural y ciencias sociales; un ejemplo notable de eso es el trabajo de Jonathan C. Brown sobre la cultura colombiana en el siglo XIX (item **5381**). Dos revaluaciones o recopilaciones de autores un tanto olvidados pero de interés, como el ecuatoriano Pablo Palacio (items **5401** y **5402**) y el boliviano Franz Tamayo (item **5379**), merecen también destacarse.

Pero al margen de centenarios y celebraciones, las figuras pivotales de la región siguen siendo Vargas Llosa y García Márquez, como viene ocurriendo desde hace ya un buen tiempo; en calidad y cantidad, superan las contribuciones críticas dedicadas a J. M. Arguedas y a Gallegos. Es curioso que el propio Vargas Llosa sea el autor de dos de los mejores trabajos críticos sobre Arguedas producidos en este período (items **5416** y **5417**), aunque no puede dejar de mencionarse el aporte, más integral y abarcador, de William Rowe sobre el mismo novelista andino (item **5413**).

Entre los libros y artículos dedicados a García Márquez, hay varios que tratan de fijar la cuestión del influjo faulkneriano en su obra; entre ellos, el de mayor importancia es el de Harley D. Oberhelman (item **5396**).

En cuanto a métodos cíticos, podría decirse que ha cedido un tanto, al menos en el conjunto de trabajos aquí anotados, el predominio de los diversos estructuralismos—aunque los trabajos de Forgues (item **5407**), Tarquini (item **5415**) y algunos de los consagrados a *Cumandá* (item **5397**) los siguen con distintas inflexiones—que, en años anteriores, era más fuerte y notorio. Los enfoques comparatista y sociológico perecen ahora más abundantes, especialmente cuando los críticos quieren escapar de los marcos del inmanentismo textual y de las limitaciones de la pura interpretación literaria para ofrecer los grandes cuadros que conectan una obra con la historia de su tiempo y los esfuerzos colectivos de elaboración cultural. La historia inmediata y los movimientos de la sociedad hispanoamericana empiezan a ser el trasfondo común de muchos estudios que ahora reclaman nuestra atención. [JMO]

HARSH ECONOMIC REALITIES are making themselves felt in the industry that publishes the region's fiction, just as the hemisphere's sociopolitics seem to exert an even greater measure of influence on the thematic concerns of what is being written and published. The two countries which command the greatest economic resources in the area—Venezuela and Colombia—dominate the production and publication of fiction. Monte Avila in Venezuela and Plaza y Janés in Colombia are by far the predominant commercial publishing houses, in quality as well as volume. Colombia's C. Valencia Editores is making inroads into a good segment of the industry, while in Venezuela the Biblioteca Ayacucho has been engaged in some high quality projects (items **5466** and **5469**). Peru, on the other hand, has suffered a reversal in the biennium of 1979–81, to the point that of the works annotated for the present volume of *HLAS*, not one has been commercially published in Peru itself. The three works from this selection to have appeared in Peru are privately financed. Obviously the publishing industry in Lima, as far as prose fiction is concerned, at any rate, is in less than optimum circumstances. Ecuador still depends heavily on the state-financed Casa de Cultura Ecuatoriana and the various regional university presses, also government financed. Bolivia is more diversified, albeit more limited in output, with Editorial los Amigos del Libro and Difusión doing most of the publishing of quality prose fiction.

Violence is by far the predominant theme that runs, overtly or surreptitiously, in all guises and modulations, through an overwhelming number of the works published in the last two years. Gabriel García Márquez (item **5439**), the best known and most popular narrator of the region, excels once again. He displays the greatest accomplishment in the literary depiction of violence. Given his mastery of the genre and the fact that he comes from a country where violence is written with a definite article and a capital letter, perhaps this achievement should not surprise anyone. Violence—political, social, economic—being no longer an isolated phenomenon restricted in intensity to geographical pockets but a most generalized, hemispheric plight that plagues all corners of the Americas, finds a broad range of esthetic nuances in its treatment as theme, subject, or symptom. Violence in these works of fiction becomes a variegated ritual, an ubiquitous and inevitable ceremony with varied and refined rites: a hemispheric rite of baptism. Its forms range from the "sacralized," collective murder in García Márquez to officially sanctioned mass murder in the Peruvian Osvaldo Salazar (item **5456**). Physical and psychological violence in the Peruvian Carlos Meneses (item **5455**) finds its psycho-sexual exacerbations in the Bolivian Nisttahuz—from the Manuel Vargas short story anthology (item **5434**)—and the Colombian Bastidas Padilla (item **5436**).

The twisted grimaces of violence peer through the drug-crazed mental states in the novel of the Bolivian Recacoechea (item **5432**) and through the ironic grotesques of the Colombian Celso Román (item **5443**). A more woeful countenance of violence's symptoms stares at us in the gallery of dementia populated by the imagination of the Venezuelan Julio Jáuregui (item **5463**). A more subtle and insipid form of violence inexorably dehumanizes its victims in the prison chronicles of the Venezuelan Carlos Ramírez Faría (item **5465**) as well as in the short stories of the Ecuadorian Pérez Torres (item **5447**) and those of the Colombian Flórez Brum (item **5438**).

The problem of madness is artfully portrayed by Amparo María Suárez Antturi (item **5444**), a young writer who makes her debut with this work. It is by far the most accomplished first novel of this biennium and she one of the most promising of the young novelists in the region.

Feminism and sexual politics begin to figure prominently in the area. The best fictionalization of these issues figures in two novels, one by the Ecuadorian Alicia Yáñez Cossío (item **5451**), the other by the Colombian Carlos Bastidas Padilla (item **5436**). The first of these is by far the most complete and most programmatic. It reads like a handbook/manifesto for the feminist movement in Latin America.

The most notable literary prize to be garnered by works of this region is the Cuban Casa de las Américas prize won by the Peruvian Osvaldo Salazar for his novel in 1980 (item **5456**) and by the Ecuadorian Pérez Torres in the same year for his collection of short stories (item **5447**). Such accolades notwithstanding, the most innovative and truly experimental prose is, oddly enough, the earliest to have been written. I am referring to the re-issued work of Venezuela's Ramos Sucre (item **5466**) which dates from the first part of the century. Equally of note in the category of re-editions or belated first printings, noteworthy more for their vintage and historical significance than the experimental innovations of Ramos Sucre, are the short stories of Ciro Alegría (item **5453**) as well as his 1954 novel (item **5452**). Just as significantly in this regard is Rómulo Gallegos' *El forastero* (item **5461**) whose original, 1942 version finally comes to light. Other notable re-editions include Biblioteca Ayacucho's Uslar Pietri (item **5469**) and Aguilar's selected works of Mario Vargas Llosa (item **5459**).

Among outstanding anthologies I should mention two Colombian collections, the first for its breadth—E. Pachón Padilla's *El cuento colombiano* (item **5437**); the second for its imaginative quality and selective inclusion—*El hombre y la máquina*, edited by David Sánchez Juliao (item **5442**). Worthy of mention, too, is the Bolivian collection of Aymara and Quechua tales by Frederico Aguiló and the multi-volume *Cuentos venezolanos* compiled by Castellanos (item **5460**). [DjK]

GENERAL

5371 González Echevarría, Roberto. The dictatorship of rhetoric/the rhetoric of dictatorship: Carpentier, García Márquez, and Roa Bastos (LARR, 15 : 3, 1980, p. 205–228)

Aunque es básicamente una reseña sobre *El recurso del método* de Carpentier, *El otoño del patriarca* de García Márquez y *Yo el Supremo* de Roa Bastos, este texto es mucho más que eso: constituye una lectura polémica de las estructuras filosófico-históricas y textuales de las tres novelas, y un intento por relacionarlas y verlas como una manifestación crucial de un momento determinado de la nueva novelística hispanoamericana. El trabajo utiliza ampliamente el concepto de "de-construcción" y presenta extensas notas (ver item **5380**). [JMO]

5372 Pérez Silva, Vicente. Del libro de las polémicas: José Eustasio Rivera y Eduardo Castillo (CBR/BCB, 16:11/12, 1979, p. 71–130)

Transcripción (sin referencias bibliográficas completas) de la polémica cruzada entre los dos escritores (1921–22), a propósito de *Tierra de promisión*. La presentación de Pérez Silva no ayuda en nada a situar esa polémica en el contexto de su tiempo ni en el actual. [JMO]

BOLIVIA

5373 Albarracín Millán, Juan. Armando Chirveches. La Paz, Bolivia: Ediciones Réplica, 1979. 295 p.; 6 leaves of plates; bibl.; ill.; index (Serie Clásicos bolivianos)

Aunque escrito a partir de una admiración ilimitada por Chirveches, este libro ofrece una útil visión de conjunto de su vida y su obra, y de la importancia de ésta en la literatura boliviana del siglo XX. El trabajo se complementa con varios índices y apéndices, que facilitan la consulta de fuentes y documentos relativos al autor. [JMO]

5374 Alcides Arguedas: juicios bolivianos sobre el autor de *Pueblo enfermo*. Mariano Baptista Gumucio, comp. Carátula de Gustavo Lara. La Paz; Cochabamba: Distribuidores, Editorial los Amigos del Libro, 1979. 282 p.; bibl.

Recopilación de textos (sin prácticamente ningún aparato crítico) realizada por Baptista Gumucio (ver items **5375**, **5377** y **5378**) con ocasión de cumplirse el centenario del nacimiento del narrador boliviano. El interés del libro es simplemente documental. [JMO]

5375 Baptista Gumucio, Mariano. Atrevámonos a ser bolivianos: vida y epistolario de Carlos Medinaceli. La Paz, Bolivia: Ultima Hora, 1979. 486 p.; bibl.; ill. (Biblioteca popular boliviana de Ultima Hora)

El subtítulo de este libro es inexacto: no se trata de una biografía del escritor boliviano, sino meramente de una recopilación, demasiado hinchada y heterogénea, de "materiales para una biografía," como señala el compilador en su prólogo. Aparte de los nu-

merosos testimonios sobre Medinaceli, el volumen incluye en epistolario y una sección iconográfica. [JMO]

5376 Castañón Barrientos, Carlos. La poesía de Wallparrimachi: y otros páginas de ensayo y evocación. La Paz, Bolivia: C. Castañón Barrientos, 1979. 131 p.

Este librito contiene varios trabajos breves sobre diversos temas bolivianos. Los únicos que tienen relativo interés son el que da título al libro—sobre la desgarrada lírica de ese poeta indígena no muy bien conocido—y el dedicado a examinar las "Primeras Críticas al Modernismo" en Bolivia. [JMO]

5377 Epistolario de Alcides Arguedas: la generación de la amargura. La Paz, Bolivia: Fundación Manuel Vicente Ballivián, 1979. 338 p.; ill.

Un esfuerzo más por recoger fuentes documentales que registran la vida de Alcides Arguedas (ver item **5374**). En este caso, se recopilan cartas de sus corresponsales nacionales (como Chirveches) o extranjeros (como Blanco Fombona, Darío, los García Calderón, Gabriela Mistral, Unamuno, etc.), más algunas cartas dirigidas por Arguedas a estos. [JMO]

5378 Mitre, Antonio F. Alcides Arguedas y la conciencia nacional (Nova Americana [Giulio Einaudi Editore, Torino, Italy] 3, 1980, p. 85–99)

A pesar de rarezas de exposición e incorrecciones expresivas, este trabajo examina un tema polémico—la relación estrecha entre la cuestión racial del indio y el mestizo y la ideología de los grupos que han detentado el poder en Bolivia—y ofrece de él una interpretación esclarecedora sobre la verdadera naturaleza de *Pueblo enfermo* y otras novelas. Salvando las posturas pro-arguediana y anti-arguediana que lo acusan de sostener concepciones opuestas a sus respectivos intereses, el autor señala que la importancia de las novelas del boliviano reside en demostrar "la imposibilidad de actualizar la idea de Nación sobre la vieja convicción de la superioridad racial" (p. 92), mito sostenido por la oligarquía. [JMO]

5379 Tamayo, Franz. Obra escogida. Selección, prólogo y cronología, Mariano Baptista Gumucio. Caracas, Venezuela: Biblioteca Ayacucho, 1979. 369 p.; bibl. (Biblioteca Ayacucho; 62)

Esta es la más amplia e importante selección de la obra poética y ensayística del escritor boliviano (1879–1956), cuya vida, pensamiento y actividad pública cubre toda una época de la historia de su país. En su prólogo, Gumucio traza sus orígenes, sus inicios literarios, la reacción de los críticos nacionales y extranjeros frente a su obra, su ardiente autodefensa y su ideología política. Como todos los libros de esta colección, la edición está impecablemente presentada y complementada con una minuciosa cronología y una bibliografía selecta. [JMO]

COLOMBIA

5380 Bedoya M., Luis Iván and **Augusto Escobar M.** Elementos para una lectura de *El otoño del patriarca.* Medellín, Colombia: Ediciones Pepe, between 1978 and 1980. 101 p.; bibl.; indexes.

Los únicos "elementos" válidos de esta lectura son los recuentos o listas de ciertas caracterizaciones, personajes, alusiones a etapas históricas, etc. El resto es totalmente prescindible como esfuerzo crítico (ver item **5371**). [JMO]

5381 Brown, Jonathan C. The genteel tradition of nineteenth century Colombian culture (AAFH/TAM, 36:4, April 1980, p. 445–464)

Excelente artículo que, en pocas páginas, ofrece una visión de conjunto de las actitudes sociales de la élite intelectual colombiana en el siglo pasado. Es esa época el país "witnessed a proliferation of cultural affectation which, because it was so divorced from reality, may be described as 'the genteel tradition'" (p. 445), expresión que Santayana aplicó a la realidad cultural de EE. UU. a fines de siglo. El autor no sólo demuestra cabalmente sus tesis de que los intelectuales colombianos formaron una especie de aristocracia alienada, sino que transmite con un lenguaje preciso e irónico, el clima literario dominante de la época. [JMO]

5382 Caballero Calderón, Eduardo. Hablamientos y pensadurías. Carátula, fragmento tomado de dibujo de Luis Caballero. Bogotá, Colombia: Tall. Gráf. de PROGRAFF, 1979. 362 p.

Menos que diario o libro de memorias, éste es, según su autor, "el registro ocasional

de lo que recuerdo, o sueño, o pienso, o imagino, y se me ocurre de pronto sin hilación y sin plan preconcebido." El carácter rapsódico de estas páginas no hace fácil su lectura continua, lo que se agrava por el hecho de que los cuadernos o capítulos no tienen sumillas que orienten al lector, y ni siquiera existe un índice general. [JMO]

5383 Corvalán, Octavio *et al.* Hacia las fuentes de García Márquez. Salta, Argentina: Univ. Nacional de Salta, Departamento de Humanidades, 1979. 169 p.; bibl. (Cuadernos de letras)

Cuaderno mimeografiado que reúne seis trabajos comparatistas de investigaciones de seminario. Los cuatro primeros estudian diversas relaciones entre las obras de García Márquez y las de Faulkner (ver item **5396**); los dos últimos señalan coincidencias entre *Cien años de soledad*, Rabelais y *Las historias de Jacob* de Thomas Mann. Algunos trabajos tienen apreciable valor, pero resulta discutible el hecho de que los autores hayan trabajado básicamente a partir de traducciones de los autores extranjeros, y no de las versiones originales. [JMO]

5385 *Estravagario:* revista cultural de El Pueblo. Selección de María Mercedes Carranza. Bogotá: Instituto Colombiano de Cultura, Subdirección de Comunicaciones Culturales, División de Publicaciones, 1976. 409 p.; bibl. (Biblioteca colombiana de cultura: Colección popular)

Selección del variado material literario, cultural y político aparecido en esta publicación cultural de Cali, que tiene el mérito de ofrecer una alternativa dinámica y renovadora a las revistas culturales de la capital. Su director, Fernando Garavito, presenta esta antología de lo difundido en sus páginas en 1975, con un tono un poco beligerante. [JMO]

5386 Farías, Víctor. Los manuscritos de Melquíades: *Cien años de soledad,* burguesía latinoamericana y dialéctica de la reproducción ampliada de negación. Frankfurt, FRG: Verlag Klaus Dieter Vervuert, 1981. 404 p.; bibl. (Editionene der Iberoamericana Reihe; 3. Monographien und Aufsätze; 5)

Este libro es más extenso que la novela misma, pero esa desmesura no parece ser suficiente para que el autor logre su propósito: demostrar que la obra de García Márquez es un alegato contra la burguesía. La estructura del libro, que comenta el texto capítulo por capítulo, contribuye a su densidad casi impenetrable. [JMO]

5387 Fau, Margaret Eustella. Gabriel Marcía Márquez: an annotated bibliography 1947–1979. Westport, Conn: Greenwood Press, 1980. 198 p.; index.

Este es el trabajo más completo de su tipo hasta el momento. Incluye las obras narrativas, artículos, guiones cinematográficos, cuentos recogidos en antologías y traducciones, entre las fuentes primarias; entre las secundarias, compila las bibliografías, libros y tesis, referencias en libros de crítica, artículos, reportajes y reseñas. En la primera parte, se ha usado el orden alfabético para ordenar los títulos del autor, lo que es menos recomendable para la consulta que el cronológico [JMO]

5388 García Márquez, Gabriel. Ceremonia inicial (ECO, 38[3]:231, enero 1981, p. 328–331)

Otro más de los numerosos hallazgos de Gilard en la época formativa del escritor, este texto de 1949 es el primer adelanto de sus ideas sobre el oficio del escritor y puede ofrecer una interesante lectura comparativa con textos más conocidos y tardíos, como *Dos o tres cosas sobre la novela de la violencia* y *Literatura colombiana: un fraude a la nación.* Util para documentar esa época juvenil del escritor. Véase en este mismo número de *Eco,* el artículo de Jacques Gilard "García Márquez y el Oficio de Escritor," (p. 327–328).

5389 ———. De viaje por los países socialistas: 90 días en la "Cortina de hierro." Cali, Colombia: Ediciones Macondo, 1978. 208 p.

Edición popular, sin ningún aparato crítico, de la serie periodística escrita por García Márquez tras su viaje de 1957 a los países de Europa Oriental, y que fue originalmente publicada en revistas de Colombia y Venezuela. La serie confirma lo que ya se sabía: las dotes de periodista del autor (ver item **5390**). [JMO]

5390 ———. Mucho de lo que he contado es la primera vez que lo digo (URSS/AL, 1, 1980, p. 79–105, plate)

Extensa e interesante entrevista hecha al autor en la Unión Soviética, con ocasión de haber aparecido la versión rusa de *Cien años de soledad,* en la que habla, mezclando siempre la ironía con la fantasía y los hechos reales, de su trabajo literario, de su vida personal y un poco de política. Las preguntas suelen ser obvias; las respuestas, brillantes (ver item **5389**). [JMO]

5391 Gyurko, Lanin A. The phantasmagoric world of Gardeazábal (IUP/HJ, 2:1, Fall 1980, p. 27–40)

El autor se concentra en los cuentos reunidos en *La boba y el Buda* (especialmente en el relato que da el título a la colección) y expone suficientemente lo que considera los rasgos esenciales de la narrativa del joven escritor colombiano: la violencia cataclísmica, lo extraño y lo grotesco, lo alucinatorio y la identidad degenerada. [JMO]

5393 Janes, Regina. Gabriel García Márquez: revolutions in wonderland. Columbia: University of Missouri Press, 1981. 115 p.; bibl. (A Literary frontiers edition)

Esfuerzo por examinar la obra de García Márquez desde sus cuentos de juventud hasta *El otoño del patriarca* (1975); en un centenar de páginas, cumple con presentar una imagen cautivante y a veces apasionada del escritor colombiano, válida sobre todo como introducción para el lector norteamericano. Destaca en su enfoque la relación entre el universo imaginario de García Márquez y sus ideas políticas. Quizá queriendo agregarle más interés a su libro y hacerlo más "popular," la autora incurre en aportar datos triviales, como el de observar que, según su signo zodiacal, el novelista es "a Piscis" (p. 9). [JMO]

5394 Levy, Kurt L. Tomás Carrasquilla. Boston: Twayne Publishers, 1980. 150 p.; bibl.; port. (Twayne's world authors series: TWAS 546: Colombia)

Este es el estudio más extenso, en inglés o en español, sobre la figura y obra de Carrasquilla. Es, por eso, una lástima que el aspecto valorativo del libro refleje un entusiasmo desmedido por el tema, y que el tono característico de la tesis doctoral (publicada 1958) se note demasiado. Más inexplicable es que el autor no haya actualizado suficientemente el libro; por ejemplo, para probar que "after a period of neglect Carrasquilla is coming into his own," cita obras críticas de los años 40 y 50. [JMO]

5395 Mena, Lucila Inés. La función de la historia en *Cien años de soledad.* Barcelona: Plaza & Janés, 1979. 222 p.; 1 leaf; bibl.

Analiza e interpreta el contexto histórico de la novela y sus contenidos sociopolíticos, a través de referencias objetivas y de los mismos símbolos míticos. Propone leer el libro como visión total de la historia de Colombia y, por extensión, de América Latina y la cultura humana. Aunque sus afirmaciones parecen razonables, la densidad expositiva y la extensión del libro no resultan del todo justificables: podía haber dicho lo mismo de modo más ameno y sucinto. [JMO]

5396 Oberhelman, Harley D. The presence of Faulkner in the writings of García Márquez. Lubbock: Texas Tech Press, 1980. 43 p.; col. ill. (Graduate studies, Texas Tech University; no. 22)

Aunque este trabajo no es el primero sobre el tema (cita y aprovecha aportes de por lo menos cuatro investigaciones anteriores), lo trata de manera muy completa y rigurosa. Dos primeras secciones que exponen el impacto de Faulkner en las letras hispánicas y los primeros contactos de García Márquez con el autor norteamericano, son un modelo impecable de documentación y ordenada argumentación crítica. Oberhelman afirma que es la presencia de lo mítico, como un elemento capaz de conectar lo local con lo universal, y algunos motivos como la decadencia y el temor al incesto, lo que constituye la parte más importante de la deuda del colombiano con el americano (ver item **5383**). [JMO]

ECUADOR

5397 Cumandá, 1879–1979: contribución a un centenario. Manuel Corrales Pascual, editor. Con la colaboración de Francisco E. Aguirre V. *et al.* Quito: Ediciones de la Universidad Católica, 1979. 285 p.

Repertorio crítico (12 trabajos) que intenta ser una contribución crítica sobre este clásico ecuatoriano al centenario de su publicación. Se tratan aspectos sociopolíticos de la novela, sus rasgos románticos, sus vínculos con *Atala*, sus raíces indigenistas, su estructura narrativa y estructura verbal, el estilo, personajes, ideología, intertextualidad y significación literaria. Los métodos tienden a ser variados y modernos. [JMO]

5398 Handelsman, Michael H. *Bruna, soroche y los tíos*: an Ecuadorian woman writer's contribution to contemporary feminist fiction (UA/REH, 15:1, enero 1981, p. 35–42)

Nota crítica sobre la novela de Alicia Yáñez Cossío, "the most important novel written by an Ecuadorian woman" (p. 35). Según el autor, el mérito de esta obra feminista reside en mostrar las restricciones e injusticias que sufre una mujer, su abierto desafío a los prejuicios sociales y las posibilidades de realización de las mujeres "as complete human beings" (p. 42). [JMO]

5399 Pareja Diezcanseco, Alfredo. El mayor de los cinco (UTIEH/C, 34, 1980, p. 117–139)

Semblanza de la vida y la obra de José de la Cuadra. Su mayor y casi único valor es el testimonial, pues Pareja Diezcanseco es uno del grupo de escritores guayaquileños al que pertenecía Cuadra, muerto en 1941. [JMO]

5400 Rabassa, Clementine Christos. Demetrio Aguilera-Malta and social justice: the tertiary phase of epic tradition in Latin American literature. Rutherford, N.J.: Fairleigh Dickinson University Press, 1980. 301 p.; bibl.; index.

Enfoque singular del narrador ecuatoriano, hecho desde el ángulo de la crítica comparatista para probar que en sus obras hay un predominante elemento épico. Entroncándolo con la tradición épica que arranca de Homero y llega hasta Milton, señala que Aguilera Malta representa una "tertiary phase" en esa tradición, en cuanto es "a return to the spirit of the great examples of epic literature which reveal the essential concern for man's destiny while he stands in the midst of death and misery" (p. 31). El trabajo, reelaborado a partir de una tesis doctoral, muestra al amplio conocimiento del mundo clásico por la autora, aunque no siempre sus aplicaciones a la obra de Aguilera-Malta resultant convincentes. [JMO]

5401 Robles, Humberto E. Pablo Palacio: el anhelo insatisfecho (UTIEH/C, 34, 1980, p. 141–156)

Revisión general de la obra literaria de Palacio (incluyendo poco conocidos relatos primerizos), en la que se destaca su percepción de la existencia como una realidad "abierta y absurda" (p. 144); el sentido de contradicción y desorden de la experiencia humana; la tendencia a describir psicologías anormales para estudiar su conducta y oponerlas críticamente a los patrones "normales;" el gusto por la parodia y la exageración formal, etc. El trabajo es una contribución más a la tarea de revaloración de este escritor ecuatoriano [ver item **5402**]. [JMO]

5402 Ruffinelli, Jorge. Pablo Palacio: literatura, locura y sociedad (RCLL, 5 : 10, 1979, p. 47–60)

Apartándose de las consabidas interpretaciones sobre la pretendida ausencia de preocupación social en la obra de Palacio, el autor prueba que, estando su creación dominada por las notas de singularidad, excentricidad y extrañeza, está bien lejos de haber sido indiferente a la situación sociopolítica de su país. Al contrario: Ruffinelli postula que, literariamente, Palacio tiene una estética más "progresista" que los escritores indigenistas ecuatorianos, cuyo sistema literario está ligado a un canon de origen burgués tradicional [ver item **5401**]. [JMO]

PERU

Arguedas, José María. Dos estudios sobre Huancayo. See *HLAS 43 : 1332.*

5403 Between fire and love: contemporary Peruvian writing. Edited by Lynn A. Darroch. Translators, Maureen Ahern *et al.* s.l.: Mississippi Mud, 1980. 117 p.; ill.

Material literario (poético y narrativo) recogido en esta antología tiene interés para el lector norteamericano, pues incluye una amplia selección de escritores que van desde Blanca Varela hasta los novísimos de hoy. La introducción es más un testimonio personal que un texto informativo sobre la literatura peruana; el material está distribuido en siete distintas secciones con un criterio vagamente temático o de tono, que no funciona del todo. [JMO]

5404 Cornejo Polar, Antonio. Literatura y sociedad en el Perú: la novela indigenista. Carátula y diagramación, JERM. Lima: Lasontay, 1980. 91 p.; bibl. (Biblioteca de cultura andina; 1)

Intento de revalorización de la novela indigenista peruana, desde el punto de vista sociológico, con algunos toques marxistas.

Examina: 1) ideología indigenista y base social, destacando el aporte de J. C. Mariátegui; 2) manifestaciones literarias, desde crónica de la conquista hasta López Albújar; y 3) proceso de maduración y profundización histórica, con Ciro Alegría y J. M. Arguedas. Dentro de su tono de exposición elemental y sobre todo didáctica, el esfuerzo es meritorio, aunque no todas sus bases teóricas sean compatibles. [JMO]

5404a Dauster, Frank N. Pantaleón and Tirant: points of contact (HR, 48 : 3, Summer 1980, p. 269–285)

Aunque señalado al pasar por muchos críticos, éste es el primer trabajo que trata en extenso el tema de la relación entre las novelas de caballerías y la narrativa de Vargas Llosa, usando como modelo *Pantaleón . . .* Los elementos comunes entre Martorell y Vargas Llosa son la "fascination with superimposed codes" (p. 274), el recurso—hasta entonces insólito en el novelista peruano—del humor, y sobre todo las respectivas "conceptions of the relations between fiction and reality" (p. 276). Dauster va un poco más allá y estudia también similaridades que podrían parecer sorprendentes, como las que observa entre la Princesa Carmesina y la Brasileña. Un trabajo importante y bien documentado. [JMO]

5405 Delgado, Wáshington. Historia de la literatura republicana: nuevo carácter de la literatura en el Perú independiente. Lima: Ediciones Rikchay Perú, 1980. 173 p. (Ediciones Rikchay Perú; no. 11)

Compendio en menos de 200 p. de un proceso literario que Luis Alberto Sánchez y otros han examinado en varios volúmenes. En vez de enciclopédica revisión histórica ofrece un compendio manuable y útil para el lector universitario y el público en general, llenando así una visible carencia. Prólogo señala diferencias de enfoque con los de Riva-Agüero, Sánchez y Mariátegui, y explica sus bases teóricas e historiográficas. El trabajo se amerita por su tono equilibrado y su buena prosa. [JMO]

5406 Escobar, Alberto. José María Arguedas, el desmitificador del indio y del rito indigenista (Nova Americana [Giulio Einaudi Editore, Torino, Italy] 3, 1980, p. 141–196, bibl.)

Título no indica bien el contenido del artículo que toma tres direcciones principales: señalar 1) la relación de Arguedas con el pensamiento social indigenista peruano, especialmente con el de José Carlos Mariátegui; 2) su visión personal de la cultura mestiza; y 3) la problemática de escritor culturalmente indígena que escribe en español. Las observaciones más válidas están en esta última sección, aunque el trabajo resulta innecesariamente literal y denso. [JMO]

5407 Forgues, Roland. La sangre en llamas: ensayos sobre literatura peruana. Lima, Perú: Librería Studium, 1979. 123 p.; bibl.

Aunque el autor proclame su "falta de respeto aparente por las grandes teorías de la crítica literaria," sus análisis tienden a seguir pautas generales de la *nouvelle critique*. Reúne seis trabajos sobre cinco narradores peruanos (Arguedas, Vargas Llosa, Vallejo, César Falcón y Ciro Alegría), con cierta preferencia por el género cuentístico. El más extenso, dedicado a Arguedas, describe en detalle el proceso de cambio social en el mundo andino. "Lectura de *Los cachorros* de Mario Vargas Llosa" es el más logrado. Su interés por textos poco recordados o estudiados es digno de mencionarse. [JMO]

5408 Gerdes, Dick. *Crónica de San Gabriel* y el rito de la iniciación en la novela de costumbres peruanas (JSSTC, 8:3, 1980, p. 233–247)

Visión de conjunto de esta primera novela que se examina como un caso de *Bildungsroman*, insistiendo en la forma como se presentan el rito de iniciación y conflicto entre ciudad y campo. La compara con otras novelas peruanas, como *Los Ingar* de Zavaleta y *El retoño* de Huanay. El texto debió ser sometido a una revisión más atenta, para evitar deslices como "la fuerza de sus pasiones son demasiado fuertes" (p. 238). [JMO]

5408a Haraszti, Zsuzsa. A megalázás problematikája Mario Vargas Llosa regényeiben. Budapest: Akadémiai Kiadó, 1977. 111 p.; bibl.

There is great interest in the works of Mario Vargas Llosa in Hungary, all of whose novels have been translated into Hungarian. Haraszti examines here the themes of oppression and humiliation and maintains that they accurately portray underdeveloped South American societies. Special emphasis is placed on *La ciudad y los perros*, *La casa verde, Conservaciones en la catedral*, and *Los cachorros.* Appended is a complete list of Vargas Llosa's works in Hungarian. [G. M. Dorn]

5409 Olivares, Jorge. El narrador en *La casa verde* (HISP, 70, sept. 1980, p. 29–44)

Intenta tipificar diferentes narradores de la novela según: "1) su capacidad de interpretación y grado de elaboración del mundo, 2) el punto de vista espacial, 3) el punto de vista temporal y 4) las restricciones que el narrador se impone a sí mismo" (p. 29). Detallado análisis ilumina algunas facetas del arte narrativo de Vargas Llosa aunque a veces repita lo ya estudiado por otros o incurra en lecturas dudosas. Pero es un estudio meritorio. [JMO]

5410 Ortega, Julio. Crisis, identidad y cultura en el Perú (*in* Perú, identidad nacional. César Arróspide de la Flor et al. Lima: Centro de Estudios para el Desarrollo y la Participación, 1979, p. 191–208, table [Serie Realidad nacional])

En parte cuestionamiento de formas "tradicionales" en que la cultura peruana ha sido entendida; y, en parte, manifiesto político, intenta ofrecer una nueva visión de la cultura nacional y una estrategia práctica para animadores culturales y políticos que compartan sus ideas. Trabajo polémico, no sólo por sus propuestas específicas, sino por los postulados teóricos en que se basa, que provienen del marxismo althusseriano, la semiótica cultural y las ideas de Benjamin. [JMO]

5411 Rodríguez-Peralta, Phyllis. Liberal undercurrents in Palma's *Tradiciones peruanas* (UA/REH, 15:2, mayo 1981, p. 283–297)

Repaso algo general de ciertos rasgos propios del autor en el tratamiento de la sociedad colonial y la de su tiempo. Se señala "the combination of conservative and liberal attitudes and perspectives" (p. 294) en sus *Tradiciones*, lo que es correcto, pero también se afirma que "Palma's historic past is without idealism" (p. 286), lo que es extremadamente discutible. [JMO]

5412 Rouillón, José. Arguedas y la idea del Perú (*in* Perú, identidad nacional. César Arróspide de la Flor et al. Lima: Centro de Estudios para el Desarrollo y la Participación, 1979, p. 379–402 [Serie Realidad nacional])

Síntesis casi totalmente descriptiva de la personalidad, el pensamiento y la actitud creadora de Arguedas. En el repaso se consideran las instancias de su niñez en el medio andino, su experiencia vital de "la patria dispersa," la cuestión del bilingüismo y el mestizaje, las etapas de su evolución política y su responsabilidad personal, etc., pero el artículo no desarrolla críticamente ninguna de ellas. [JMO]

5413 Rowe, William. Mito e ideología en la obra de José María Arguedas. Lima: Instituto Nacional de Cultura, 1979. 220 p.; bibl. (Cuadernos del INC; 3)

Estudio integral de la obra narrativa arguediana, centrado en el análisis e interpretación de cómo se presentan y funcionan los aspectos míticos y sociológicos en el autor. Los problemas de lenguaje literario, cultura, visión mítica y sustrato antropológico están observados en detalle y precisión. El mayor mérito del libro es que se acerca a los textos sin preconceptos ni prejuicios ideológicos y muestra los altibajos y diversas maneras en que "la historia se hace presente en Arguedas" (p. 14). [JMO]

5414 Tarquini, Francisco. La selva dallo stupore al riso: *Pantaleón y las visitadoras di Vargas Llosa* (Ispanoamericana [Università di Roma, Facoltà di Lettere e Filosofia [and] Facoltà di Magistero, Rome, Italy] 1 : 1, invero 1980, p. 83–107)

Apoyándose en ideas de Bachtin y Genette, el presente trabajo destaca los valores paródicos en *Pantaleón . . .*, y la función del "*pastiche*" lingüístico como una forma que reproduce, exagerado, el "lenguaggio autoritario e impoverito" (p. 89) del poder. El enfoque estructuralista usado por Tarquini le permite ubicar muy precisamente la obra de Vargas Llosa en el lugar que le corresponde, entre la tradición de "la novela de la selva" y la superación de esa línea narrativa. [JMO]

5415 Valdelomar, Abraham. Obras, textos y dibujos. Reunidos por Willy Pinto Gamboa. Prólogo de Luis Alberto Sánchez. Portada, óleo de Raúl María Pereyra. Lima: Editorial Pizarro, 1979. 913 p.; bibl.; ill.

Contiene toda la obra literaria, periodística, gráfica y epistolar del escritor peruano, en gran parte desconocida o inhallable. El considerable esfuerzo está en parte echado a perder por razones editoriales: incluir todo en un tomo de más de 900 p., lo hace inmanejable; el papel (salvo ilustraciones) es humildísimo e inadecuado, igual que las páginas publicitarias de los auspiciadores del proyecto. [JMO]

5416 Vargas Llosa, Mario. José María Arguedas, entre sapos y halcones. Madrid: Ediciones Cultura Hispánica del Centro Iberoamericano de Cooperación, 1978. 46 p.; bibl. (Colección Plural)

Texto leído al incorporarse a la Academia Peruana de la Lengua Correspondiente de la Española (agosto 1977). Examina tres temas de Arguedas: la violencia, lo ritual y el animismo natural. Examina estas cuestiones brevemente, pero con claridad y pasión, echando luz, como de costumbre, sobre sus propias convicciones de novelista. [JMO]

5417 ———. Literatura y suicidio: El caso Arguedas, *El zorro de arriba y el zorro de abajo* (IILI/RI, 110/111, enero/junio, 1980, p. 3–28)

Entre los numerosos trabajos que Vargas Llosa ha dedicado a J. M. Arguedas, éste es uno de los más lúcidos y cautivantes. No sólo ofrece una visión integral y en profundidad de la obra como un universo narrativo formado por muy complejos hilos y relaciones, sino que incluye una poética del arte de novelar y una lección crítica muy pertinente: aunque reconoce, como tantos otros, que en la estructura y el estilo de la novela póstuma de Arguedas hay abundantes imperfecciones, que el lector tiende sentimentalmente a llenar con los datos trágicos de su suicidio, el relato es más que "un documento clínico;" en verdad, una obra que "por su ambición y su forma, por el modo como se acerca y aleja de la realidad" puede considerarse de vanguardia (p. 7). [JMO]

VENEZUELA

5418 Azzario, Esther A. La prosa autobiográfica de Mariano Picón-Salas. Portada, Víctor Viano. Caracas: Equinoccio, 1980. 171 p.; bibl. (Colección Rescate)

El tono excesivamente académico y didáctico de este ensayo no hace muy grata su lectura, pero hay que reconocer que es un trabajo minucioso y paciente, cuyos mayores méritos de análisis están en la segunda parte, dedicada a los aspectos de contenido, estructura y estilo de dos libros de Picón Salas: *Viaje al amanecer* (1943) y *Regreso de tres mundos* (1959). La primera parte traza una biografía del autor que no era estrictamente necesaria para entender lo que sigue. [JMO]

5419 50 [i.e. Cincuenta] **años de Doña Bárbara:** número monográfico dedicado a Rómulo Gallegos. Caracas: Centro de Estudios Latinoamericanos "Romulo Gallegos," 1979. 163 p. (Actualidades; no. 5)

Una manifestación más del renovado aprecio por Gallegos, que contiene cinco trabajos de revisión crítica o de recopilación bibliográfica (que se superponen a los incluidos en los items **5420, 5422** y **5425**), más algunos homenajes y testimonios de escritores de su tiempo y de hoy. [JMO]

5420 Congreso Internacional de Literatura Iberoamericana, *19th, 1979, Caracas, Venezuela.* XIX [i.e. Décimo Noveno] Congreso Internacional de Literatura Iberoamericana. v. 1, Relectura de Rómulo Gallegos. Caracas: Ediciones del Centro de Estudios Latinoamericanos Rómulo Gallegos, 1980. 1 v.; bibl.; index.

Otra celebración crítica (50 textos) dedicada al autor de *Doña Bárbara,* que contiene textos de intención meramente laudatoria, semblanzas, testimonios, y enfoques que intentan revalorizar al autor y leerlo en un contexto más contemporáneo. Aportes son tan variados como los métodos críticos, lo que es también una forma de probar que el interés por el autor venezolano no ha decaído con el tiempo (ver item **5422**). [JMO]

5421 ——, ——, ——. v. 2, Narradores latinoamericanos: 1929–1979. Caracas: Ediciones del Centro de Estudios Latinoamericanos Rómulo Gallegos, 1980. 327 p.; bibl.; index.

Veintiséis críticos de Hispanoamérica, Europa y EE.UU. reúnen aquí trabajos dedicados a autores tan disímiles como Vargas Llosa y Lafourcade, y temas como "El Folletín en Venezuela" o los contactos entre Dylan Thomas y Julio Cortázar. Unicos criterios que los vinculan son el cronológico (la literatura producida entre 1929–79) y el temático ("Texto y contexto"), que por cierto permiten el máximo de flexibilidad. [JMO]

5422 Gallegos, materiales para el estudio de su vida y de su obra. Efraín Subero, compilador. Caracas: Ediciones del Congreso

de la República, 1980– . 4 v.; index.

Este es, sin duda, el mayor esfuerzo realizado por documentar la vida y la obra del escritor venezolano, en homenaje al cumplirse 50 años de la edición de *Doña Bárbara* y 10 de su muerte. Plan completo de la obra: cronología vital, histórica y literaria del autor y de su tiempo (versión reducida de la misma en items **5423** y **5425**); y una compilación de referencias bibliográficas sobre el autor, sus obras mayores, miscelánea, obra dispersa, y publicaciones y referencias críticas o biográficas. La falta de un índice general y de una mayor claridad en el plan general, la hacen menos fácil de consultar. [JMO]

5423 Gallegos, Rómulo. Cercanía de Rómulo Gallegas: homenaje en el cincuentenario de la primera edición de *Doña Bárbara.* Efraín Subero, editor. s.1.: Departamento de Relaciones Públicas de Lagoven, 1979. 81 p.; bibl.; 12 leaves of plates; ill. (Cuadernos Lagoven: Documentos)

Todo el valor de esta publicación de homenaje a Gallegos se reduce a la cronología (la misma que se encuentra en item **5422**) y al "ideario" entresacado de textos no literarios del autor y, por la tanto, poco conocidos fuera de Venezuela. [JMO]

5424 Garmendia, Salvador. Conversación formal con un escritor informal. Amaya Llebot, editora. Carátula, Víctor Suárez. Caracas: Facultad de Humanidades y Educación, Universidad Central de Venezuela, 1978. 42 p. (Colección Encuentros)

Este es el resultado de una larga charla con el autor realizada en 1975, al término de un seminario sobre su obra novelística, en cuya discusión participó el mismo. Aunque el título señale lo contrario, el tono es informal, pero alcanza a iluminar algunos aspectos interesantes de su narrativa. [JMO]

5425 Iconografía Rómulo Gallegos. Testimonios, Gonzalo Barrios *et al.* Textos de las gráficas, Efraín Subero. Caracas: Biblioteca Ayacucho, 1980. 34 p.; 66 p. of plates; ill.; ports. (Biblioteca Ayacucho)

Aparte de la interesante sección iconográfica que ocupa la mayor parte de este album, se publican testimonios de cuatro escritores ligados a su vida y su obra; una entrevista sobre la incursión de Gallegos en el campo cinematográfico; y la cronología de Efraín Subero (ver item **5422**). La publicación tiene solo interés documental. [JMO]

5426 Navarro, Armando. Narradores venezolanos de la nueva generación: ensayo. Portada, Víctor Viano. Caracas: Monte Avila Editores, 1970. 175 p.; bibl. (Colección Donaire)

Examina narradores venezolanos de la década del 50 hasta el presente (e.g., Adriano González León, Salvador Garmendia, Laura Antillano, Mary Guerrero). Aunque el conjunto de escritores bajo estudio es interesante, la imprecisión del lenguaje crítico del autor le resta valor; el tono es liviano y periodístico. Al publicar estos trabajos en forma de libro, no ha tenido cuidado de actualizarlos debidamente; de Garmendia, por ejemplo, no menciona sus libros posteriores a 1969 y habla como si fuese inédita, de una novela publicada hace mucho tiempo (p. 47). [JMO]

5427 Schärer-Nussberger, Maya. Rómulo Gallegos, el mundo inconcluso. Caracas: Monte Avila Editores, 1979. 246 p.; bibl. (Colección Estudios)

Considerable intento por revisar la obra novelística de Gallegos (su trilogía *Doña Bárbara, Cantaclaro y Canaima*), desde la perspectiva del mito y símbolos, generalmente olvidados por lecturas críticas que destacan lo más obvio: el realismo, el criollismo y la descripción del paisaje natural. Siguiendo intuiciones de Mariano Picón Salas pero sobre todo, la interpretación simbólica de mitos y arquetipos inconscientes realizada por Bachelard, Eliade y Jung, la autora analiza en detalle la trilogía y ofrece una visión sustancialmente nueva. Escrito en español (la autora es suiza), el libro es de lectura ardua y quizá demasiado pormenorizado, pero el enfoque es siempre coherente. [JMO]

5428 Uslar Pietri, Arturo. El globo de colores. Caracas: Monte Avila Editores, 1975. 313 p. (Colección Letra viva)

Impresiones de viajero por los más variados países, ciudades y regiones del mundo (New York, el Lejano Oriente, Israel, Holanda, Marruecos, Rusia, etc.), en las que el autor prueba su "inagotable curiosidad por la tierra y la gente" (p. 7). Aunque la prosa es elegante y plástica, el interés de estos textos no pasa de ser anecdótico. [JMO]

5429 Vestrini, Miyó. Isaac Chocrón frente al espejo. Caracas: Editorial Ateneo de Caracas, 1980. 224 p. (Colección Testimonios)

Esta entrevista hecha al dramaturgo y narrador venezolano por una conocida periodista, debe ser la más extensa que él jamás haya concedido y es el fruto de varias semanas de diálogo y charlas. Ofrece una buena incursión en la vida personal del escritor y en sus motivaciones creadoras, casi siempre en tono animado y confesional. [JMO]

PROSE FICTION
BOLIVIA

5430 Díez de Medina, Fernando. Copakawana: mirador de la piedra preciosa. La Paz: Librería Editorial Juventud, 1980. 143 p.

Mythological novel in three parts corresponding to three time frames—Incaic primordial time, colonial era, and contemporary period. Lyrical, spiritual exploration of mythopoeic constants, archetypes, and timeless yearning for the transcendent. The shrine of Copacabana on Lake Titicaca serves as spacial focus for each time frame. [DjK]

5431 Poppe, René. El paraje del tío y otros relatos mineros. La Paz: Ediciones Piedra Libre, 1979. 148 p. (Colección Narrativa)

Fourteen short pieces on plight of Bolivian Indian in mining industry. Effective and at times moving depiction of conditions in subterranean mines. In fact author points out that his is first collection of stories to focus entirely on theme of underground mining conditions. Stories are of uneven quality, some no more than sketches. [DjK]

5432 Recacoechea S., Juan. La mala sombra. La Paz: Editorial Los Amigos del Libro, 1980. 293 p.

Suspense novel on drug traffic and drug scene in Latin America. Explores psychic states and social circumstances of addiction. Interesting exposé, though author succumbs to moralizing. Narrative is fluid, characterization credible, depiction of narcotic effects convincing. [DjK]

5433 Saavedra, Rafael. Los inimitables: novela. La Paz: Editorial Los Amigos del Libro, 1980. 142 p.

Well-done political novel. Superimposed sociohistorical circumstances and characters from varying time frames into cinematic montage. Tragic plots are pretty predictable, of course, but language and manner of depiction show Saavedra's originality. Author has crisp narrative style, fast pace, direct language. Lacks ponderous declamations so characteristic of the region's political novel. [DjK]

5434 6 [i.e. Seis] nuevos narradores bolivianos. Manuel Vargas *et al.* La Paz, Bolivia: Universidad Mayor de San Andrés, 1979. 139 p. (Colección Literatura; no. 1)

Uneven anthology. Of six authors René Bascopé Aspiazu (see *HLAS 42:5335*) and Jaime Nisttahuz are by far the most convincing. Except for latter, all are in their early 30s with their first books having appeared in the last three or four years. Future of Bolivian short story may well be dominated by these young writers. [DjK]

COLOMBIA

5435 Aguilera Garramuño, Marco Tulio. Alquimia popular; El ritmo del corazón; Clemenica ojos de cierva; Biografía parcial de un frenáptero; Rostro con máscara: novela. Bogotá: Plaza y Janes Editores-Colombia, 1979. 138 p. (Rotativa)

Consists of four short stories and a long short story referred to as a short novel. They share an obsession with mythomania and an irrepressible urge to invent. While title story is the most accomplished, a fine story about the rich and inventive imagination of the down-and-out, the short novel falls prey to the lyricism of its solipsistic language. Second story won prize for best of the genre (Mexico 1978) and represents interesting sociological statement on poetic innocence vs. progress of economic modernization. [DjK]

5436 Bastidas Padilla, Carlos. Hasta que el odio nos separe: novela. Carátula, Manuel Estrada. Bogotá: Plaza y Janés, 1979. 131 p.

Unabashed exploration of eroticism, sexuality, and sexual politics. At times violence is overwhelming, ideological statement rhetorically declamatory, sexual obsession too cloying. Interesting and timely novel, nonetheless. Its feminist perspective, coming from a male writer, takes on special significance. Author is a young writer who won Casa de las Américas prize for his short stories (*Las raíces de la ira*) in 1975. This is his first novel. [DjK]

5437 El Cuento colombiano: antología, estudio histórico y analítico. t. 1, Estudio histórico y analítico, por generaciones, de los autores más representativos de la narrativa colombiana, desde 1820 hasta Manuel Mejía Vallejo. t. 2, Estudio histórico y analítico de los más modernos narradores colombianos, desde Gabriel García Márquez hasta Germán Santamaría. Compilado por Eduardo Pachón Padilla. Bogotá: Plaza y Janés Editores, 1980. 2 v.; bibl. (Narrativa colombiana) (Crítica literaria)

Useful, two-volume anthology begins with national independence, extends to modern writers, includes 52 authors, each represented by one story. Scheme is generational and chronological. Brief commentary on genre may be of interest to general reader. Short commentary on each generation and on each author could also benefit nonspecialist but includes little for the initiated. Some information (e.g., birth dates) is inaccurate. Bibliographies on anthologies, writers, and theory of genre at end are useful. Selections are representative. Good panoramic view of development of Colombian short story. Useful reference for libraries and individual readers. [DjK]

5438 Flórez Brum, Andrés Elías. Los perseguidos: cuentos. Dibujo carátula, Eliécer Camargo Osorio. Bogotá: Ediciones Puesto de Combate, 1980. 133 p. (Colección Línea de fuego)

Sixteen "realistic" short stories focus on people's dehumanization and institutionalization. The reality of human beings in these stories is hounded into inexistence by poverty, officialdom, indifference and necessity. Chronicle of the dispossessed narrated in the desperate language and by the impersonal voice of matter-of-factness. Well-executed collection, this is author's first book. [DjK]

5439 García Márquez, Gabriel. Crónica de una muerte anunciada. Buenos Aires: Editorial Sudamericana, 1981. 192 p.

In his latest novel (as of this writing), the Colombian master proves himself a virtuoso of controlled violence, deadly mystery, collective murder. It could be called a thriller if outcome was not known from outset. Instead, it is a compelling and nerve-wracking chronicle which unfolds slowly and with exquisite pain for the trapped reader. Language is characteristically García Márquez's, as is the inversion of the mystery play: what hovers mysteriously is not the outcome but the incomprehensible contingencies that make the outcome inevitable. The ultimate violence is not for the faint-hearted. [DjK]

5440 Hilarión Sánchez, Alfonso. Contrabando. Bogotá: Ediciones Tercer Mundo, 1979. 270 p.

Picaresque detective thriller which serves as exposé of Colombia's National Customs Office. Insiders' documentary, its revelations are stinging to the official world it exposes. A Customs official, author was relieved of his position when chapter from this novel was published in 1979. The novel comes off effectively on literary as well as documentary grounds. [DjK]

5441 ———. Los esmeralderos. Diseño de la portada, Ligia Córdoba. Bogotá: C. Valencia Editores, 1980. 177 p.

International intrigue story based on emerald traffic. Plot, as documentary of mineral exploitation and illicit trafficking, is more accomplished than character development or stylistic refinement. Exciting novel nonetheless, it captures the mentality of people obsessed with mineral wealth for its own sake. [DjK]

5442 El Hombre y la máquina: narraciones de Oscar Collazos et al. Selección y notas de David Sánchez Juliao, con la colaboración de Eduardo Marceles Daconte. Bogotá: Caja de Crédito Agrario Industrial y Minero, 1978. 155 p. (Colección Biblioteca Caja Agraria; no. 8)

Thematic anthology, representing 12 contemporary Colombian writers and their treatment of man in his relationship to machine and machine age. Each author is represented with one selection. Editor's "Prologue" is useful and convincingly justifies significance of theme. Includes very brief bibliographical note on each author. Selections are good, chosen authors significant, stories of high quality. [DjK]

5443 Román, Celso. Cuentos para tiempos poco divertidos. Diseño de la portada, Ligia Córdoba. Bogotá: Valencia Editores, 1981? 107 p.

Twenty-nine very short pieces border on the macabre. Some are truly grotesque, others are given to black humor or incisive social satire. Language and images are haunting, full of wry humor, bitter grimaces, and desperate laughter. Promising young author emerges as a strange combination of Poe, Horacio Quiroga, and Kurt Vonnegut. [DjK]

5444 Suárez Antturi, Amparo María. Santificar al diablo. Portada de M. Combariza. Bogotá: Plaza y Janés, 1980. 178 p. (Narrativa colombiana. Novelistas del día)

First and most promising novel by young writer. Explores limits of sanity and all-too-contagious realm of madness. In original manner which combines hyperbole of her countryman García Márquez and insane beatitude of saintly old ladies from novelistic world of Chilean José Donoso, author deftly manipulates religious credulity of simple people and steadfastness of conviction, especially when it is self-generating and self-justifying. She is an exciting novelist who promises great things for Colombian literature. [DjK]

5445 Suescún, Nicolás. El retorno a casa: relatos. Bogotá: Instituto Colombiano de Cultura, Subdirección de Comunicaciones Culturales, División de Publicaciones, 1978. 165 p. (Biblioteca colombiana de cultura: Colección popular; 24)

Collection of 10 pieces is author's second book of short stories. Unifying thread consists of cataleptic states which overtake all human activity and ultimately lead to varying forms of death. Style of narration, in first person, confessional voice, remains consistent and unnervingly successful in the sense that author achieves effects of psychological involution and paralysis he seems to seek for world of his fiction. [DjK]

ECUADOR

5446 Carrión, Carlos. Ella sigue moviendo las caderas. Loja, Ecuador: Editorial Universitaria, 1979. 207 p.

Witty, acerbic, articulate collection of eight short stories. No institution or quartet of Ecuadorian society escapes irreverence and iconoclasm of Carrión's irony and linguistic subterfuge. Deftly executed, lucid social commentary without compromising literary value. This is author's second collection of stories. [DjK]

5447 Pérez Torres, Raúl. En la noche y en la niebla. La Habana: Casa de las Américas, 1980. 69 p.

Eight powerful short stories. Author is most convincing when narrating through adolescent characters. Dominant theme is human alienation and/dehumanization which is wrought by social programs (planned parenthood), institutions (the work place), and pre-established expectations in human relationships. Collection won Casa de las Américas Short Story Prize 1980. Previously (1977), author won National Literary Prize of Ecuador for two earlier collections. [DjK]

5448 Selección del nuevo cuento cuencano. Prólogo de María R. Crespo. Cuenca, Ecuador: Casa de la Cultura Ecuatoriana, Núcleo del Azuay, 1979. 186 p.

Useful volume which anthologizes seven regional Ecuadorian writers, each represented with from two to four stories—20 in all. Brief biobibliographical note precedes each author's selections. Editor supplies a "Prologue" dedicated for the most part to summarizing each story and to few general comments on genre in Ecuador. [DjK]

5449 Vera, Pedro Jorge. El pueblo soy yo. Barcelona: Seix Barral, 1979. 289 p.; 2 leaves (Nueva narrativa hispánica)

Well-executed novel in best tradition of Ecuador's socially committed literature. Focus is on last 40 years of Ecuadorian history. Narrative shifts from national events to individual circumstances of people who, knowingly or not, endure consequences of historical contingencies they may or may not understand. It is a lyrical novel whose strongest artistic accomplishment is in dialogue and dramatic encounters. [DjK]

5450 Villasís Endara, Carlos. Las cometas se enredan en el verano. Guayaquil: Casa de la Cultura Ecuatoriana, Núcleo del Guayas, 1980. 132 p. (Colección Letras del Ecuador; 96)

Five short stories held together by common theme of coming of age. While some are more accomplished than others, all share tone and style of a language of fantasy—adolescent fantasies which transform one into hero and object of hero worship. [DjK]

5451 Yáñez Cossío, Alicia. Yo vendo unos ojos negros. Quito: Editorial Casa de la Cultura Ecuatoriana, 1979. 32 p.

Programmatic novel is well done, articulate, intense, polemical, and declamatory.

Its program is feminist consciousness raising. Those engaged in sexual politics, feminist and otherwise, will find this novel to be one of the most expressive, informed, and informing pieces of literature on the subject to come out of Latin America. [DjK]

PERU

5452 Alegría, Ciro. El dilema de Krause: Penitenciaría de Lima: novela póstuma. Lima: Ediciones Varona, 1979. 154 p.; ill.

Another admirable effort of Alegría's widow to make available the author's unpublished and uncompleted works. Present novel, nearly completed and dating from 1954, is a largely biographical work based on Alegría's internment in Lima's penitentiary. Useful work for students of author's oeuvre. Shows the other face, the philosophical and meditative face, of an author identified primarily with indigenismo. [DjK]

5453 ———. 7 [i.e. Siete] cuentos quirománticos. Lima: Ediciones Varona, 1978. 189 p.; port.

Very valuable collection, both as literature and document for Alegría scholars. These seven stories were written in New York and Puerto Rico in the early 1940s. Author shows another facet of his commitment to human rights and social justice—the racial struggle in the Americas. Stories were composed at a time when Alegría travelled to New York to accept Farrar and Rinehart's first prize for his novel *El mundo es ancho y ajeno*, only to be stranded with no means for a return ticket or self-support. An ironic twist which finds its way into the stories. [DjK]

5454 Hinostroza, Rodolfo. Aprendizaje de la limpieza. Barcelona: Tusquets, 1978. 163 p. (Cuadernos ínfimos; 84)

Cathartic confessions of psychiatric patient (narrator). In themselves these exhibitionist free-associations and self-conscious posturings can only remind reader of psychiatry's basic principles, from Freud to Lacan. What transforms these impostures into literature are projections unto reader and inescapable complicity they exact from reader. This turn in itself posits basic question on the nature of literature and narrative. [DjK]

5455 Meneses, Carlos. Seis y seis. México: Premia Editora, 1979. 116 p.; 1 leaf of plates; ill. (Red de Jonás)

Collection of 12 stories, six each from author's two earlier books written 1960s and early 1970s. Meneses is exasperatingly good as narrator of desperate human circumstances, brutality, psychological torture, and insurmountable situations. While first six stories are more graphic and predictable, later six are more subtle though no less mitigated in their desperation. There is also a shift from impoverished Lima neighborhoods in first set, to more diversified settings in second. Accomplished collection. [DjK]

5456 Salazar, Osvaldo. La ópera de los fantasmas. La Habana: Casa de las Américas, 1980. 173 p.; 24 p. of plates; ill.

Novelization of another of Peru's modern tragedies—Stadium massacre of May 1964. Scathing indictment of country's police, army, and judicial system. Well-documented work, complete with news clips and photographs. Narrative flows well, language is crisp and tinged with wry understatement. Timely work, tragically enough, as always for contemporary Latin America. Novel was winner of 1980 Casa de las Américas Prize. [DjK]

5457 Scorza, Manuel. La tumba del relámpago (quinto cantar). Portada de Anhelo Hernández. México: Siglo Veintiuno Editores, 1979. 267 p. (La Creación literaria)

Scorza has been one of strident voices decrying abuse and exploitation in Latin America. Present novel forms part of cycle of five works, collectively called *Cantatas*, which document struggle for human rights and dignity against overwhelming odds. In best tradition of region's socially committed literature, novel portrays drama of yet another resurgence of revolution which flashes like lightning only to be consumed once again by the quagmire. [DjK]

5458 Valdivia Ponce, Oscar. El andarín. Lima: s.n., 1980. 153 p.

Odyssey into psyche by psychiatrist turned novelist. Quest for identity and authenticity whose search founders on realization that our most inner reality and most intimate authenticity are apocryphal postures. Well-written novel. Perpetual self-unmasking of realities' fictions. [DjK]

5459 Vargas Llosa, Mario. Conversación en la catedral; la orgía perpetua; Pantaleón y las visitadoras. Madrid: Aguilar, 1978. 1290 p. (His Obras escogidas; t. 2. Biblioteca de autores modernos)

Vol. 2 of Vargas Llosa's collected works being prepared by Aguilar of Spain. Includes two very different novels and author's critical study of Flaubert and *Madame Bovary (La orgía perpetua)*. Well-produced as was vol. 1. Valuable acquisition for private and public libraries of work by Peru's most important writer today. [DjK]

VENEZUELA

5460 Castellanos V., Rafael Ramón. Cuentos venezolanos: antología. 3. ed. Caracas: Publicaciones Españolas, 1978. 3 v.; bibl.

Vols. 3/5 of five volume anthology (for vols. 1/2, see *HLAS 40:6788*) cover period from Modernism to end of 1970s and include 68 authors in generational, chronological scheme. Each is represented by one to three or four stories, last dating from 1977. Editor traces development of genre in Venezuela and impact of key periodicals on that development. Brief bio-bibliographical note introduces each author. Very valuable collection. [DjK]

5461 Gallegos, Rómulo. La primera versión de El forastero: novela inédita. Caracas: Equinoccio, 1980. 318 p.; bibl. (Colección Rescate)

Original version of *El Forastero* (1942) written by Gallegos in 1921–22 but not published then because of political climate. A more strident critique of Venezuela's social realities, it includes more transparent portrayal of strongman J. V. Gómez. Publication of this version is a significant event for Gallegos scholars and textualists. Original is different enough from 1942 published version to make for interesting comparison in terms of author's development, his impact on historical scene, and this early work's influence on author's better known works. [DjK]

5462 Garmendia, Salvador. Enmiendas y atropellos: cuentos. Prólogo de Oscar Rodríguez Ortíz. Caracas: Monte Avila, 1979. 215 p. (Colección Eldorado)

Garmendia is younger member of imposing trinity (other two being Uslar Pietri and Otero Silva) which dominates contemporary Venezuelan letters. Collection gathers short stories from author's previous anthologies which have appeared since 1965. Nine of 23 stories are collected into book form for first time here. They evince same attention to realistic detail, crude and anguished day-to-day reality of contemporary urban Latin America. Garmendia is a powerful narrator who succumbs neither to cynicism nor to sentimentality. Rodríguez Ortíz's prologue is helpful to uninitiated reader of Garmendia and offers valuable biographical and critical insight. [DjK]

5463 Jáuregui, Julio. Tercera sangre: cuentos. Caracas: Monte Avila Editores, 1980. 140. p. (Colección Donaire)

Tightly-woven collection of 18 short pieces. Stylistically held together by language of compulsive confession, stream of consciousness ravings of character voices that range from inmates in mental institutions, to political prisoners, obsessed artists, demented parents in search of children and lost children in search of childhood memories. Language is powerful. Monologue and soliloquies punctuated by occasional detail from outside that illumine circumstances of these ravings and free associations. [DjK]

5464 Noguera, Carlos. Inventando los días: novela. Portada, Juan Fresán. Caracas: Monte Avila Editores, 1979. 306 p. (Colección Continentes)

Intense novel which explores dialectical and at times embattled relationship between aesthetic experience and sociopolitical commitment. Well-structured, narrative opens with evocation of languages of art, all arts, and funnels progressively to entrap various protagonists in conflictive impasse where social commitment and artistic authenticity converge. Conflict is not resolved. Work ends with positing insurmountable questions. Structure dramatizes conflict rather than resolves it but dramatization is well-done, its stylistic means varied. [DjK]

5465 Ramírez Faría, Carlos. Cárcel del tiempo. Portada, Juan Fresán. Caracas: Monte Avila Editores, 1978. 239 p.; ill. (Colección Continentes)

Prison novel, narrated from point of view of inmate. Prison life becomes microcosm of the "outside" world. Fascinating exploration of prison psychology and human relationships viewed under magnifying glass of confinement. Especially interesting is relationship between prisoners and guards. Perturbingly lucid world of darkness and cruelty, resignation and philosophical acceptance, hope and desperate acts become highlighted. Well-executed novel, stylistically deft, penetrates man's potential for idealism and bestiality, solidarity and individual survival. [DjK]

5466 Ramos Sucre, José Antonio. Obra completa. Prólogo, José Ramón Medina. Cronología, Sonia García. Caracas: Biblioteca Ayacucho, 1980 printing. 589 p. (Biblioteca Ayacucho; 73)

Welcome revindication of one of the most neglected but also most influential literary figures of Venezuela. Ramos Sucre (1890–1930) and his work—a generic mixture of prose poetry—have long been recognized as a formative influence not only on poetic generations of 1940s and 1950s in Venezuela, but also on writers such as Jorge Luis Borges. Volume collects author's four books, his translations from German and Latin, works not published in book form, and letters. "Introduction" by Ramón Medina highlights significance of author to Venezuelan letters and Latin American literature in general. Historico-biographical chronology is helpful, as is bibliography. Excellent, indispensable volume. [DjK]

5467 Rodríguez, Argenis. El viento y la lluvia. Portada, Raúl Díaz L. Caracas: Monte Avila Editores, 1979. 124 p. (Colección Donaire)

Closely-knit collection of 16 pieces, narrated in direct, confessional, conversational tone. Language is reminiscent of Hemingway's simplicity and Thomas Wolfe's earthy lyricism. Confessional style lies somewhere between diary and journalistic reportage. Rodríguez derives his style from his three novels which appeared previously and which relate his personal experiences as a guerrillero. This collection is most captivating in its character studies—characters which range from children to prostitutes to overbearing, middle-class wives. Interesting social document. [DjK]

5468 Romero, Denzil. Infundios. Carátula, Eduardo Orozco. Ilus., carátula e interiores, Alirio Rodríguez. Caracas: Síntesis Dosmil, 1978. 186 p.; ill. (Colección Los Vasos comunicantes)

Erudite and entertaining collection of seven short stories. Based on broad range of readings in history, plots explore through fiction minute detail of *infra-historia*, tracing imaginary lives and extravagant events. Settings range from medieval Europe to contemporary Venezuela, and to futuristic 21st century. Evocative collection reminiscent of J. L. Borges' biographies of infamy and H. G. Wells' futuristic nightmares. Author's first book of stories. [DjK]

5469 Uslar Pietri, Arturo. Las lanzas coloradas y cuentos selectos. Prólogo y cronología, Domingo Miliani. Caracas: Biblio-

teca Ayacucho, 1979. 447 p.; bibl. (Biblioteca Ayacucho; 60)

Very useful volume from an admirable series. Miliani's introduction to author and his work is excellent, chronology which juxtaposes historical events within and outside of Venezuela with author's biography is concise and helpful. Volume includes, in addition to *Las lanzas coloradas*, a selection of Uslar Pietri's 18 best short stories. Bibliography of author's works is fairly complete and selected bibliography of studies on him is helpful, even though it is limited to studies done in Spanish. [DjK]

Prose Fiction: 20th Century: Chile

CEDOMIL GOIC, *Professor of Spanish American Literature, The University of Michigan, Ann Arbor*

LOS AÑOS 1979 Y 1980 SIGUEN MOSTRANDO la actividad particularmente productiva del novelista José Donoso (items **5472** y **5473**) quien experimenta con nuevos géneros y escribe después de sus obras más trascendentes, otras de más limitadas ambiciones. En la narrativa chilena la figura de Donoso llena la década que termina y comienza a sobrepasarla con nuevas experiencias. Al lado de él puede destacarse al poeta y narrador Enrique Lihn. Lihn define de una manera muy especial el desarrollo de una "nueva escritura," como última o más reciente modalidad que extiende tanto a su obra narrativa como a la obra poética. En su obra más reciente *El arte de la palabra* (item **5478**) parece haber tocado un límite de las posibilidades de una escritura autodestructiva que ataca no sólo modalidades parodiadas del discurso, sino fatiga y aniquila al lector con la eliminación de toda sustancia narrativa en favor del comentario y la descripción. En una línea próxima a Lihn desarrolla su narrativa más reciente Cristián Hunneus (item **5477**). Entre los escritores más jóvenes destaca el Premio Gabriela Mistral, José Luis Rosasco (item **5481**) quien muestra un recobrado interés por una historia bien contada con énfasis biográfico. Volodia Teitelboim (item **5483**), entre los representantes de la vieja generación, publica la más ambiciosa novela sobre el proceso chileno, antecedentes y consecuentes del golpe militar. El antiguo narrador del realismo social de los años 40, aparece ahora contagiado por la vigencia irrealista en la modalidad literaria de su novela, que en su caso significa una recuperación de su pasado creacionista, en la cercanía de Vicente Huidobro.

Otro aspecto en que continua la productividad de los años recientes es el determinado por la publicación de prosas de Pablo Neruda (item **5823**) y Gabriela Mistral (item **5820**). Ambos grandes poetas han mostrado las virtudes excepcionales de su prosa: más intelectual y razonada la de la Mistral, más intuitiva y sensible la de Neruda. La correspondencia con Héctor Eandi, de éste último (item **5822**) ha puesto a disposición del estudioso un material inapreciable para el conocimiento del poeta en su estancia oriental.

Finalmente, la crítica, como ha acontecido en los últimos años, sigue prestando atención preferente a la obra de José Donoso (items **5485, 5488, 5493, 5496–5497** y

5502), de María Luisa Bombal (items **5486–5487, 5490–5491** y **5498**), de Enrique Lihn (item **5494**), entre los autores contemporáneos. Mientras el interés por la obrà de Alberto Blest Gana (item **5499**) se sigue manteniendo por encima de otros escritores del pasado. Una monografía sobre José Victorino Lastarria, de Bernardo Subercaseaux (item **5503**), Premio Gabriela Mistral, renueva el interés por esta importante figura del pasado político y literario de Chile.

PROSE FICTION

5470 Blest Gana, Alberto. Martín Rivas: novela de costumbres político-sociales. Prólogo, notas, y cronología, Jaime Concha. Caracas: Biblioteca Ayacucho, 1977. 459 p.; bibl. (Biblioteca Ayacucho; 17)

Excelente edición de esta obra fundamental de la novelística chilena del siglo XIX. Prólogo de Jaime Concha constituye una lectura ideológica que desarrolla principalmente las implicaciones políticas y sociales de la representación de la sociedad chilena de 1850. La bibliografía merecía una elaboración más completa.

5471 Donoso, José. El jardín de al lado. Barcelona: Editorial Seix Barral, 1981. 264 p. (Biblioteca breve; 472. Novela)

Esta novela narra el mundo de exilados hispanoamericanos en España. Sitges y Madrid son escenarios más importantes. La novela es narrada en sus primeras cinco partes por Julio Méndez, novelista frustrado que intenta escribir la gran novela del golpe militar en su país, sin conseguir la aprobación de su agente literario. La sexta parte y final está narrada por Gloria, mujer del escritor, en diálogo con su agente literaria. Este capítulo resuelve acontecimientos suspendidos, en la quinta parte y sorpresivamente cambia la autoría del relato, atribuyendo a Gloria la redacción de la obra que leemos. Se establece así una duplicación de la situación narrativa y se modifica de un modo reflejo el carácter total de la novela. Ambigüedad, feminismo, destrucción del machismo, proponen los motivos modificadores de esta transformación narrativa. Donoso domina con absoluta maestría estos novedosos juegos de la imaginación.

5472 ———. La misteriosa desaparición de la marquesita de Loria. Barcelona: Editorial Seix Barral, 1980. 198 p. (Biblioteca breve; 459. Novela)

Séptima novela de Donoso es un divertimento. Parodia de novela erótica, galante y pornográfica con motivos alusivos a El Caballero Audaz, Felipe Trigo y Ruben Darío. Más en la órbita elegante y afrancesada del modernismo que del anarquismo español de los años 20. Pero tal, vez con la misma agresividad social de antaño y del "destape" de hoy. Un principio de misterio—encarnado en un perro sobrenatural, motivo conocido de Donoso—destrucción y violencia, se contrapone a la elegancia, refinamiento y erotismo del mundo narrado para minar su entereza real. Un juego de duplicaciones y contradicciones pone los signos actuales a esta novela paródica.

5473 ———. El obsceno pájaro de la noche. Barcelona: Argos Vergara, 1979. 476 p. (Libros DB; 9)

Reimpresión de esta magnífica novela bajo un nuevo sello editorial.

5474 Edwards, Jorge. El museo de cera. Barcelona: Bruguera, 1981. 189 p. (Narradores de hoy; 55)

La característica dominante de esta novela está dictada por la modalidad contradictoria de determinarse tanto la situación narrativa, comenzando por la discontinuidad del narrador, como el mundo narrado. En éste se confunden varios tiempos históricos superpuestos que hacen inevitablemente contradictoria la caracterización del protagonista y personajes restantes. Otro tanto ocurre con escenarios y acontecimientos mismos. Otro divertimento literario (item **5473**) intrascendente y satírico. Autoreferencias textuales sobre la índole de la narración aparecen duplicadas con variantes contradictorias que se renuevan con la mención final de la ineficacia de la literatura y del consentimiento que el orden establecido concede a su inocua agresividad verbal.

5475 Frías, Gustavo. Julio comienza en Julio. Novela. Santiago: Impreso en Talleres Gráficos Corporación Ltda., 1979. 251 p.

Novela de iniciación de un joven adolescente narrada en forma autobiográfica.

Representa un mundo tradicional, marcado por algunos indicios de descomposición, pero principalmente de choque brutal con la sensibilidad del protagonista herido por la crudeza de la supuesta realidad. La novela fue llevada al cine con el mismo título.

5476 Hamel, Teresa. Las causas ocultas: cuentos. Santiago: s.n., 1980. 80, 3 p.
Cuentos de contenido rural y énfasis feminista, escritos en una prosa debil. La autora abandona la tendencia fantástica de sus primeros libros.

5477 Hunneus, Cristian. El rincón de los niños. Novela. Nota final de Adriana Valdés. Santiago: Editorial Nascimento, 1980. 209 p.
Segunda novela del autor, despues de *Las dos caras de Jano* (Santiago: Editorial del Pacífico, 1962), trata de un antinovelístico juego de textos que miran a un pasado infantil, adolescente y adulto. Primeros textos, fechados en 1956, quedan enmarcados en el texto de 1975. Aquellos se citan en forma dispersa y esporádica. Los segundos se ordenan como un diario de rigurosas fechas. Lo distintivo de esta "neoescritura" es que unos textos son el comentario de los otros. La discontinuidad, la contradicción, la decepción afectan por igual a lo narrado y a la situación narrativa. El humor y la ironía dictan el tono dominante de los comentarios y manipulaciones del narrador en primera persona.

5478 Lihn, Enrique. El arte de la palabra. Barcelona: Editorial Pomaire, 1980. 358 p.
El arte de la palabra es el asunto de esta novela que la hace una obra de destinación limitada. La parodia de diversas modalidades de discurso: literario, poético, periodístico, político referidos a diversos aspectos fragmentarios de la imaginaria República de Miranda, constituye el nivel de mayor relieve. Multiples voces articulan estos discursos para construir al fin la imagen de un narrador básico quien como un Fregoli del lenguaje muda de identidades y discurso. Dentro del juego más descriptivo y digresivo, lleno de evaluaciones irónicas, humorísticas y desatinadas, saltan alegóricas visiones que aluden o resultan alusivas al contexto a la manera de una sátira quevedesca. Su nota salvadora es la autoridad con que se destruye a sí misma.

5479 Marchant Lazcano, Jorge. La Beatriz Ovalle, o como mató usted en mí toda aspiración arribista. Santiago: Editorial Renacimiento, 1980. 158 p. (Nueva narrativa)
Primera edición chilena de esta novela editada originalmente en Buenos Aires, Argentina, en 1977 (ver *HLAS 42:5466*).

5480 Panorama del cuento chileno. Selección y prólogo de Heber Raviolo. Montevideo: Ediciones de la Banda Oriental, 1981. 127 p.; bibl. (Lectores de Banda Oriental; 32) (Literatura universal)
Esta selección ofrece un panorama del cuento chileno destinada al público uruguayo. El prólogo está plagado de inexactitudes y revela una falta de comprensión de la historia del género narrativo en Chile.

5481 Rosasco, José Luis. Dónde estás, Constanza. Santiago: Editorial Andrés Bello, 1980. 112 p.
Esta es la primera novela de José Luis Rosasco (n. Santiago, 1935). Narrada en tercera persona por el protagonista Alex Corsiglia, de 13 años. El relato desarrolla una ventura pueril y alocada que adquiere signos desusados debido a la extraña personalidad de Constanza. El mundo evoca un barrio pintoresco del Santiago de los años 1940. Otros signos culturales—canciones, bailes populares, cine—fijan las vivencias infantiles. Rosasco muestra en esta obra habilidad para contar una historia y crear un tono de humor mezclada con tierna puericia. El autor ha conquistado un lenguaje que supera las limitaciones de su obra cuentística precedente.

5482 Sepúlveda, Ximena. El cuarto reino. Cubierta, Enrique Palma sobre un tapiz de la autora. Santiago: Nueva Novela, 1979. 138 p.
Novela de exploración psiquiátrica escrita en una alternancia de dos series narrativas. Una es autobiográfica, la otra, una serie de entrevistas con el psiquiatra que culmina en una revelación del ser de la protagonista merced a una experiencia con mezcalina. Novela de iniciación a la madurez.

5483 Teitelboim, Volodia. La guerra interna. México: J. Mortiz, 1979. 445 p. (Nueva narrativa hispánica)
Desde el exilio, Teitelboim (n. 1916) publica esta agresiva novela enciclopédica sobre el proceso chileno. A diferencia del neo-

rrealismo de las anteriores, en *La guerra interna*, mezcla efectos de realidad con las de irrealidad y deformación grotesca. Unos y otros funcionan en pasos narrativos de ópera cómica, cámara de terror cinematográfico o fantasmagoría angélica y popular. La cita y sus variaciones despliegan un juego paródico extensamente practicado, junto a otros juegos verbales y textuales. El tono narrativo es cómico-satírico, de lo blanco a lo negro. Claves denominativas que inducen el juego alegórico son de fácil solución. Signos positivos de la visión narrativa los da un personaje de nombre Esperanza a Pesar de Todo—que no puede disimular su lexicalización quevedesca—que dialoga secretamente con el fantasma del poeta. El Poeta es un personaje cuya caracterización reconstruye con fidelidad y detallada información los días finales de Pablo Neruda.

5484 Vila, Cristián. Procreaciones: relatos. Santiago: Editorial Nascimento, 1979. 139 p.

Primer libro de uno de los más jóvenes narradores chilenos (n. 1955). Hay en sus cuentos una fantasía atrevida y desenfadada que promete logros más maduros.

LITERARY CRITICISM AND HISTORY

5485 Achúgar Ferrari, Hugo. Algunos problemas en torno a *Este domingo* de José Donoso (Fragmentos [Centro de Estudios Latinoamericanos Romulo Gallegos, Departamento de Investigaciones, Caracas] 2, p. 78–102)

Anticipación del estudio más extenso del mismo autor *Ideología y estructuras narrativas en José Donoso* (see *HLAS 42:5469*).

5486 Agosin, Marjorie. Un recuerdo de María Luisa Bombal (RIB, 30:4, 1980, p. 402–405)

Artículo necrológico con motivo del fallecimiento de la autora chilena (n. Viña del Mar 8 junio 1910; m. Santiago 6 mayo 1980).

5487 Cárdenas, Daniel N. María Luisa Bombal: *"El Arbol"* (Revista de Artes y Letras de la Universidad de Costa Rica [Ciudad Universitaria Rodrigo Facio] 4:1, enero/junio 1980, p. 55–59)

Análisis del cuento "El Arbol," una de las magistrales narraciones de la Bombal,

hecho con método precario y poca adecuación al texto.

5488 Castillo-Feliú, Guillermo I. Reflexiones sobre el perspectivismo en *Coronación* de José Donoso (AATSP/H, 63:4, dic. 1980, p. 699–705)

Revisión de la crítica de la obra y análisis del perspectivismo. La comprensión de la omnisciencia selectiva múltiple aplicable a una obra de Virginia Woolf parece inadecuada a la comprensión del punto de vista de esta obra de Donoso.

5489 Cluff, Russell M. Eduardo Barrios y la novela de iniciación (UK/KRQ, 28:1, 1981, p. 37–51)

Análisis de *El niño que enloqueció de amor* (1915) y de *Páginas de un pobre diablo* (1923) desde el punto de vista de la novela de iniciación a la vida. Aplicación sin relieve de conceptos del crítico norteamericano Mordecai Marcus sobre tal tipo de novela.

5490 Cortés, Darío A. Bibliografía de y sobre María Luisa Bombal (IUP/HJ, 1:2, Spring 1980, p. 125–142)

La más completa bibliografía de y sobre María Luisa Bombal. Contiene sin embargo algunas omisiones y más de un error tipográfico (e.g., su año de nacimiento es 1910 y no 1920).

5491 Guerra-Cunningham, Lucía. La narrativa de María Luisa Bombal: una visión de la existencia femenina. Madrid: Playor, 1980. 205 p.; bibl. (Colección Nova-Scholar)

Ambicioso estudio de la obra narrativa de la Bombal hecho desde un punto de vista feminista y de interpretación arquetípica.

5492 Hunneus, Pablo. Lo comido y lo bailado: ensayos libres sobre la vida misma. Santiago: Editorial Renacimiento, 1980. 235 p. (Ensayo)

Colección de artículos de humor y sátira de las costumbres contemporáneas. Escenas, situaciones, tipos, modas innovadoras despiertan la vena humorística del autor. El autor, sociólogo en funciones de periodismo satírico, cultiva un género de larga tradición.

5493 Iñigo Madrigal, Luis. Alegoría, historia, novela, a propósito de *Casa de campo*, de José Donoso (HISPA, 9:25/26, 1980, p. 5–31)

Excelente análisis de la novela con especial atención en el enfoque ideológico que considera las posibilidades de interpretación alegórica del lector y la interpretación histórica conforme al contexto reciente del proceso chileno relacionado con el golpe militar.

5494 Lastra, Pedro. Conversaciones con Enrique Lihn. Xalapa, México: Centro de Investigaciones Lingüístico-Literarias, Instituto de Investigaciones Humanísticas, Universidad Veracruzana, 1980. 153 p. (Cuadernos de texto crítico; 10)

Excelente diálogo en el que se abordan varias cuestiones relacionadas con la poesía, la narrativa y la concepción de la literatura de Enrique Lihn. Se discuten también temas de la literatura hispanoamericana y sus más destacadas autores. Extraordinariamente útil para la comprensión de la obra de Lihn y en general para la posición del poeta y narrador chileno en la literatura de hoy. Incluye información biográfico o autobiográfica, generacional, y específicamente literaria, que iluminan variadamente la compleja figura del autor. Una completa bibliografía razonada, de y sobre el escritor cierra del volumen. Parte del contenido de estas conversaciones se ha publicado separadamente (ver *HLAS 42: 5475*).

5495 Lihn, Enrique and **Pedro Lastra.** Contrapunto de sobrelibro (UC/AT, 441, mayo 1981, p. 131–138)

Subproducto o coda de las *Conversaciones* (ver item **5494**) y como prólogo de otro libro, este diálogo trata de esclarecer la noción de un nuevo género de libro "el libro-ekeko," errátil, azaroso, torrencial, regido por el dios indígena de la abundancia.

5496 Morell, Hortensia R. El doble en *Gaspard de la Nuit*: José Donoso à la manière de Ravel, en imitación de Bertrand (UA/REH, 15:2, mayo 1981, p. 211–220)

Excelente artículo sobre una de las *Tres novelitas burguesas* de Donoso. Analiza la estructura del doble y aproxima las obras de Cortázar, Aloysius Bertrand y Maurice Ravel.

5497 Neghme Echevarría, Lidia. Tres novelitas burguesas y lo aleatorio de los eventos (Revista Lingua e Literatura [São Paulo] 7, 1978, p. 157–174)

Análisis del nivel de los acontecimientos en las tres novelitas, con ampliaciones sobre el contexto literario de la obra de Donoso y sus dimensiones redundantes. Un sobrio análisis semántico estructural esclarece

las oposiciones fundamentales puestas en juego en cada relato.

5498 Rodríguez-Peralta, Phyllis. María Luisa Bombal's poetic novels of female estrangement (UA/REH, 14:1, enero 1980, p. 139–155)

Comparación entre las características de las protagonistas de *La última niebla* y de *La Amortajada*. El artículo establece con claridad la distinción de estos caracteres frente a la novela tradicional y frente a la nueva novela hispanoamericana, así como frente a la visión de la mujer y del hombre en la literatura hispanoamericana.

5499 Román-Lagunas, Jorge. Bibliografía anotada de y sobre Alberto Blest Gana (IILI/RI, 46:112/113, julio/dic. 1980, p. 605–647)

La más completa bibliografía sobre el novelista más importante del siglo XIX. Aunque no se indica expresamente, la bibliografía se cierra hacia 1977 (ver item **5470**).

5500 Schopf, Federico. Dos novelas chilenas (ECO, 35[6]:216, oct. 1979, p. 653–668)

Excelente artículo sobre *Los convidados de piedra*, de Jorge Edwards (ver *HLAS 42: 5463* y *HLAS 42: 5491*) y *Casa de campo*, de José Donoso (*HLAS 42: 5462*) y su significación de acuerdo al contexto ideológico.

5501 Skármeta, Antonio. La reformulación del status del escritor en el exilio (ECO, 36[3]:219, enero 1980, p. 297–308)

Tentativa de definición de la crisis del escritor en el exilio y de la situación en que escribe, sus limitaciones y sus posibilidades. Tentativa también de redefinir la aspiración personal de una creación entre el compromiso y la libertad creadora.

5502 Solotorovsky, Myrna. Configuraciones espaciales en *El obsceno pájaro de la noche* de José Donoso (UB/BH, 1302:1/2, jan./juin 1980, p. 150–189)

Artículo extenso que elabora la variedad de espacios—en sentido literal o material y como ámbitos de organización o estructura determinadas—y sus funciones en una serie variada de oposiciones. Presta escasa atención o lo avanzado en este aspecto por la crítica de Donoso.

5503 Subercaseaux S., Bernardo. Cultura y sociedad liberal en el siglo XIX: Lastarria, ideología y literatura. Santiago: Editorial Aconcagua, 1981. 325 p. (Colección Bello)

Excelente monografía sobre la significación ideológica y política de José Victorino Lastarria. Análisis cuidadoso de su actuación pública: literaria, política y diplomática. El enfoque de la obra literaria es el más elaborado y forma la mejor parte del libro.

PROSE FICTION: 20th Century: River Plate Countries (Argentina, Paraguay and Uruguay)

EARL M. ALDRICH, JR., *Professor of Spanish, University of Wisconsin, Madison*
SAUL SOSNOWSKI, *Professor and Chairman, Department of Spanish and Portuguese, University of Maryland*

THE MAJORITY OF THE SHORT NARRATIVES and novels reviewed in this section were published between 1978–81. Fictional trends which were apparent in the early 1970s continue unabated: in some works authors have achieved a high level of abstraction through a relentless obscuring of logic and familiar points of reference; others have expanded the limits of the novel form by including a variety of narrative artifacts ranging from newspaper clippings to public documents. The concept of history as invention rather than objective accumulation of static facts adds a fascinating dimension to some novels.

Fantasy continues to attract Argentine writers in particular. The short story is a favorite genre for exploration of the bizarre and mysterious. A sort of existential anguish regarding the moral and political state of modern society deeply influences the literary production of Argentine and Uruguayan writers alike. Another trend is the persistence of limited but steady publication of conventional, regionalistic fiction in both countries.

During the period in question, established Argentine writers produced some notable works of fiction. In his fifth novel, *Pubis angelical* (item **5540**), Manuel Puig continues the successful use of narrative strategies developed in his previous works. Marta Lynch makes a compelling presentation of feminist concerns in her novel *La penúltima versión de la Colorada Villanueva* (item **5533**), and *La invitación* (item **5525**), a novel by Beatriz Guido, is rich in psychological insight. The short story is well-represented by Julio Cortázar's *Queremos tanto a Glenda* (item **5516**). Cortázar's unique ability to conceive realities which transcend the common sense world and his delightful sense of whimsy are again on display. Among the younger writers, Marcos Aguinis deserves special mention for his *La conspiración de los idiotas* (item **5504**), a provocative and controversial novel reminiscent of *Sobre héroes y tumbas*.

Given the current political and economic realities of Uruguay, it should not be surprising that the quantity and quality of its fiction remains at a low ebb. Carlos Martínez Moreno, who is proving to be both a gifted and productive author, is a notable exception. His latest novel, *El color que el infierno me escondiera* (item **5560**), gives a stark and disturbing presentation of life in contemporary Uruguay.

LITERARY CRITICISM: New introductions and studies of Borges continue to reflect the pervasive fascination with his work and with "the other Borges" that permits himself to be interviewed, analyzed, and provoked into situations where erudition cannot save him from animosity. His presence, like that of the "hrönir," alters the perception of literature (and, for some, of the world) and invariably tilts the balance of critical study of Argentine literature in his favor. Two valuable works in Italian (items **5569** and **5605**); two very different approaches and guides in English (items **5568** and **5593**), a Spanish version of one of Rodríguez Monegal's earlier works (item **5601**), Massuh's study (item **5595**) and Braceli's challenge (item **5574**), lead the notable number of works that have yet to cover the territory encompassed by Borges' writing. Victoria Ocampo's personal and cultural legacy—especially *Sur*—and occasional readings of Bioy Casares and Mallea exemplify one segment of a broad ideological spectrum (to which one could add a flawed version of Martínez Estrada).

It is encouraging to note in this volume of *HLAS* that there has been an increase in studies of 19th- and early 20th-century Argentine literature. Worthy of mention are Altamirano's and Sarlo's continuing and important research projects (item **5119**); other analyses include works on Sarmiento; the impact of immigration on literature (items **5570** and **5580**); Cambaceres; the magazine *Martín Fierro*; and Arlt (item **5599**). It is likely that Macedonio Fernández will be the subject of further study as well. A special issue of *Cuadernos Hispanoamericanos* (Madrid, Nos. 364/366, 741 p.; bibl.) constitutes this biennium's most voluminous contribution to Cortázar scholarship. *INTI* also published a special issue (Nos. 10/11) that gathers the papers read at the Barnard College Symposium on Cortázar in April 1980. Boldy's study of Cortázar's novels (item **5571**) and the conversations of Cortázar with González Bermejo (item **5584**) are welcome additions. As in previous years, Puig continues to earn critical attention. Of particular importance for offering a readable and generally reliable guide to the subject is the Centro Editor de América Latina's publication *Historia de la literatura argentina* (item **5585**), a much revised version following the format of the earlier series Capítulo. However, few scholars to date have attempted to outline existing modes of literary production or to single out promising authors that have yet to appear in reading lists.

Several articles on Roa Bastos attest to continuing interest in his work; scattered pages point to other Paraguayan writers.

Texto crítico's special double issue on Onetti (another issue is in press) offers analyses by his best critics. Readers will find Verani's thorough book a very useful study of Onetti's motifs (item **5619**). Quiroga continues to generate bibliographic interest and the customary curiosity.

The bibliography that follows constitutes a sampling of current materials reflecting a broad spectrum of critical readings and methodologies. Although there are no dominant theoretical lines or ideological tenets one notes a decline in "purely structural" works and a rise in the level of "contextual" preoccupations.

PROSE FICTION
ARGENTINA

5504 Aguinis, Marcos. La conspiración de los idiotas. Buenos Aires: Emecé Editores, 1979. 248 p. (Novelistas contemporáneos)

Narrator and protagonist of this extraordinary and controversial novel, Natalio Conte is obsessed with idea that he has discovered secret means by which a powerful, occult organization controls the world: By working through people who suffer from mental retardation, this *cenáculo* relentlessly carries out its evil designs. Deeply troubled, brilliant cynic, strongly reminiscent of hero of *Sobre héroes y tumbas*, Conte also seeks to objectivize mysterious forces of life. Black humor, irony, paranoia are developed effectively.

5505 Arlt, Roberto. Obra completa. Prefacio de Julio Cortázar. Buenos Aires: Carlos Lohlé, 1981. 2 v.

Vol. 1 of *Obra completa* contains Arlt's novels and short stories; vol. 2, essays and theater. Reader will be struck by Arlt's extraordinary sensitivity to major concerns of 20th-century man. Cortázar provides brief, impressionistic introduction.

5506 Bertero, Gloria de. Atrevimiento. Buenos Aires: Ediciones Crisol, 1979. 159 p.; ill.

Collection of 16 short stories in which creation of atmosphere and tone takes precedence over development of plot or concept. Love, loneliness, death, and friendship are concepts which are more hinted at than analyzed in these works.

5507 Bertolé de Cané, Cora María. La obsesión y otros cuentos. Tapa, Carlos Pérez Villamil. Buenos Aires: Plus Ultra, 1979. 116 p. (Nuestros cuentistas)

Major concern in this collection of 15 stories is vulnerability of old age. Explores with special sensitivity and skill physical weakness and isolation, loneliness, rejection, and fear.

5508 Bird, Poldy Lichtschein de. Reflejos. Tapa, Cristina Busca. Buenos Aires: Ediciones Orión, 1979. 205 p. (Narrativa contemporánea) (Colección Alfa de Orión)

Novelette divided into a number of brief, fragmentary sections in which narrative point-of-view fluctuates between first and third person. In each section narrator presents an intensely personal reponse to life. Fear, hope, love, betrayal, and pain are captured vividly.

5509 Boixadós, Alberto. Siembra de silencio. Diseño de tapa, Carlos Muleiro. Buenos Aires: Emecé Editores, 1979. 298 p. (Escritores argentinos)

La argentinidad (i.e., the essence of national identity) is examined in this novel which raises questions regarding traditions and influences of both rural Argentina and Europe.

5510 Bosco, María Angélica. Muerte en la costa del río. Buenos Aires: Emecé Editores, 1979. 214 p. (Escritores argentinos)

Vicious murder which takes place in Argentine resort city is the focal point of this novel of intrigue and mystery.

5511 Calcagno, Celia. Memorias de Almamía. Tapa de Mario Blanco. Fotografía de contratapa de Sylvina Ruiz Panelo. Buenos Aires: Editorial Sudamericana, 1980. 202 p.

Novel written from a child's perspective is convincing and consistent throughout. Achieves delicate irony through narrator's guileless interpretation of differences between the world of the adult and of the child.

5512 Casnati, Luis Ricardo. Historias de mi sangre. Diseño de la tapa, Luis Quesada. Buenos Aires: Emecé Editores, 1980. 228 p. (Escritores argentinos)

Death is the pervasive theme in this collection of 24 stories rich in symbolism and mystery.

5513 Ceppi Gambin, Estela. Los que viajan. Diseño de tapa, Oscar Díaz. Buenos Aires: Macondo Ediciones, 1979. 140 p. (Los que viven)

Collection of very short fiction works written in simple and direct language. Author succeeds in conveying the inner life of characters who are in physical or emotional pain and is especially effective in use of first-person narration.

5514 Cicco, Juan. Irene, la última vez. Portada, Lolo Villantime. Buenos Aires: Corregidor, 1979. 94 p. (Serie popular; P-1269)

Alienation is the recurring theme of these 14 stories. With restraint and subtlety, author explores indifference, hypocrisy, guilt, and unavoidable circumstances that contribute to the loneliness and isolation.

5515 Cócaro, Nicolás. Las sombras se alargan en la tierra. Fotografía de tapa, "El Hijo pródigo (detalle) de Hieronymus Bosch. Buenos Aires: Emecé Editores, 1979. 177 p.

Collection of 16 extraordinary short stories which could be characterized as works of mystery and fantasy. Title story presents apocalyptic vision in which vague fear of the unknown is conveyed with unusual effectiveness.

5516 Cortázar, Julio. Queremos tanto a Glenda. México: Nueva Imagen, 1980. 139 p.

Readers who have followed Cortázar's short story production through the years will find much that is familiar in these nine narratives. The fertile imagination which allows him to conceive realities that transcend the common sense world, the humor and whimsy that lurk delightfully beneath the surface of his fiction, and the inimitable use of language are again manifest in these works.

5517 Costantini, Humberto. De dioses, hombrecitos y policías. La Habana: Ediciones Casa de las Américas, 1979. 221 p.

Extraordinary novel examines with irony and compassion fate of people caught in conflicting currents of violent political struggles. Rival forces and victims are presented in a highly stylized, exaggerated, mythical manner—a literary strategy which is not meant to disguise the intent but to underscore the tragedy of people cornered and stripped of personal identity and dignity by arbitrary powers.

5518 ———. Háblenme de Funes. México: Nueva Imagen, 1980. 234 p.

Collection of 10 short stories, some of which were published in previous volumes. *Porteño* life is main inspiration for these works which go beyond anecdotal and costumbristic to capture popular spirit of that culture.

5519 El Cuento argentino: Quiroga, Borges, Cortázar y otros: antología. Antología y prólogo por Beatriz Sarlo. Notas, Sergio Visconti. Buenos Aires: Centro Editor de América Latina, 1979. 275 p. (Capítulo; 2)

Anthology of stories from 28 authors. Well represented are Quiroga and Borges and other established contemporary writers. Brief bio-bibliographies for each author.

5520 Cuentos argentinos del siglo xx [i.e. veinte]. Selección, estudio preliminar, notas y vocabulario, Susana Inés Rovere. Tapa, Hugo Campos. 2. ed. Buenos Aires: Editorial Huemul, 1978. 352 p.; bibl. (Colección Clásicos Huemul; 66)

Anthology of stories by 23 mostly well-known authors. Selections are preceded by useful observations regarding nature of short story genre and brief history of Argentine narrative. Bio-bibliographical section is provided for each author.

5521 Gambaro, Griselda. Dios no nos quiere contentos. Barcelona: Lumen, 1979. 254 p.

Perfectability of man, concept of progress toward moral enlightenment, and goal of a better life ahead are mercilessly attacked in this disturbing and extraordinary novel in which the protagonist finds the journey through life to be senseless and ultimately degrading. Chaotic, confused, and contradictory narrative style challenges the reader's comprehension and reinforces the harsh and cynical thesis to be inferred from the work.

5522 Gasulla, Luis. Enésimo. Diseño de tapa, Baldassari. Buenos Aires: S. Rueda, 1979. 199 p.

This novel deals with the ultimate alienation of modern civilization—man becoming a slave to the highly advanced technology of his own making.

5523 Gómez, Carlos María. Veneno de cachiporra. Buenos Aires: Nemont Ediciones, 1979. 171 p.

Detective fiction, which has a long tradition in Argentina, is the genre *par excellence* for involving the reader in the creative process. This novel, like that of Bosco (see item **5510**), is an excellent example of the serious side of that tradition.

5524 Grasso, Jorge. Casi Bocary. Portada del Departamento de Arte de Ediciones Corregidor. Buenos Aires: Corregidor, 1978. 223 p. (Serie popular; no. 1233)

Novel examines foibles of the privileged, well-to-do, provincial society of Argentina.

5525 Guido, Beatriz. La invitación. Cubierta de Silvio Baldessari. Buenos Aires: Editorial Losada, 1979. 197 p. (Novelistas de nuestra época)

Fascinating novel set in an *estancia* in Patagonia. Through carefully sustained ambiguity of action and dialogue and by subtle distortion of the setting, Guido skillfully creates an atmosphere of stifling oppression and terror in which character conflict mounts inexorably until the final, tragic outcome. This novel, rich in symbolism, is open to a variety of interpretations, including a national, political one.

5526 ———. Todos los cuentos, el cuento. Buenos Aires: Editorial Planeta Argentina, 1979. 189 p. (Biblioteca universal Planeta)

Guido's mature mastery of the short story genre is revealed in these 16 tales. Each offers an ideal blend of plot, idea, and emotional impact. With carefully developed irony, sometimes shocking violence, and subtly conveyed mystery, author presents unusual perceptions of reality. The style is sophisticated without being pretentious or self-conscious. Two selections—"Usurpación" and "Chocolates Uberallen" are scheduled for film production.

5527 Lacroix, Irma. Galope de un caballo muerto: cuentos y notas de una periodista. Prólogo, Roberto Tálice. Ilustración, Hermenegildo Sabat. Buenos Aires: Editorial Stilcograf, 1980. 128 p.

Rural characters and settings are the inspiration for the 21 short narratives in this collection.

5528 Lancelotti, Mario A. El hombre de un solo lado. Buenos Aires: Editorial Fraterna, 1978. 128 p.

Collection of author's very brief narratives, ranging in length from one paragraph to a couple of pages. Each selection is designed to raise subtle questions about the meaning of the universe, the meaning of our interpersonal relationships.

5529 Lichy, Victorio. Ramón y Romina. Ilus. de tapa, Francisco Ferrer. Buenos Aires: Editorial Stilcograf, 1979. 109 p.

In this self-consciously obscure novelette, author creates an atmosphere of obfuscation by stringing together a series of dialogues and monologues which have no comprehensible context.

5530 López de Gomara, Susana. Un ángel no es noticia. Buenos Aires: Casa Pardo, 1979. 60 p.

Collection of 15 stories that could best be described as allegories. Each one, whether humorous or mysterious, conveys a subtle lesson about life.

5531 Loyácono, Hugo. Imaginomagia. Diseño de tapa, Carlos Alfredo Ara Monti. Buenos Aires: Editorial Kyrios, 1978. 128 p. (Narradores latinoamericanos contemporáneos; 1)

Author introduces us to the world of childhood fantasy in 31 stories.

5532 Lynch, Marta. Los cuentos tristes. Tapa, Carlos Boccardo. Buenos Aires: Editorial Planeta-Argentina, 1979. 163 p. (Biblioteca universal Planeta)

Collection of 15 stories which, as the title indicates, range from melancholy to bitter disillusionment in their tone. Written and published earlier in Lynch's career, the stories are notable for sharp insights and emotional impact.

5533 ——. La penúltima versión de la Colorada Villanueva. Buenos Aires: Editorial Sudamericana, 1979. 365 p.

Lynch's most recent novel deals effectively and convincingly with many feminist concerns. Plight of the contemporary Argentine woman, within an essentially sexist society, is presented forcefully yet with restraint and objectivity. Narrative technique is sophisticated without being pretentious.

5534 Manauta, Juan José. Los degolladores. Portada de Fernando Almirón. Buenos Aires: Ediciones Corregidor, 1980. 189 p. (Serie popular; P-1298)

Death and the evocations of childhood predominate in these 18 stories. Plot is an important element in these selections; at the same time, author develops several levels of meaning in each work.

5535 Mastrángelo, Carlos. 21862 [i.e. Veintiún mil ochocientos sesenta y dos]: cuentos para releer y polemizar. Buenos Aires: Plus Ultra, 1978. 140 p. (Nuestros cuentistas)

Collection of short stories selected from Mastrángelo's previously published works. Includes some of his more traditional narratives as well as a few experimental, controversial pieces.

5536 Musacchio, Juan Carlos. Siete escarabajos. Buenos Aires: Ediciones Marymar, 1980. 118 p. (Colección Narrativa y novela)

Collection contains nine stories of mystery and fantasy. From a place of common sense reality, they phase into the realm of the bizarre and the inexplicable.

5537 Nos, Marta. A solas o casi. Diseño de la tapa, Carlos Alfredo Ara Monti. Buenos Aires: Editorial Kyrios, 1978. 129 p. (Narradores latinoamericanos contemporáneos; 2)

Collection of 14 stories by a promising writer which range in theme from alienation to initiation into the reality of the adult world.

5538 Orgambide, Pedro G. Aventuras de Edmund Ziller en tierras del nuevo mundo. Barcelona: Grijalbo, 1977. 317 p. (Best sellers)

In this pretentious but ingenious "renaissance" novel, author brings together variety of literary forms ranging from poetry to drama to correspondence. Madcap adventures of non-conformist protagonist, Ziller, his letters and apocryphal documents contribute to the unusual, whimsically humorous vein which runs through the work.

5539 Ossorio, Susana. Espejos. En portada, dibujo original de Heriberto Zorrilla. Buenos Aires: Ediciones Corregidor, 1979. 103 p. (Serie popular; P-1284)

Through use of the double, allegory, mythical allusions, and subjective concepts of time, author provides unusual interpretations of reality in these nine short stories. Style is free of affectation.

5540 Puig, Manuel. Pubis angelical. Barcelona: Seix Barral, 1979. 270 p.

Ana, Argentine protagonist of Puig's fifth novel, suffers profoundly from the sociopolitical influences of her native country. Using narrative strategies developed in his previous works, Puig records protagonist's discussions with other characters about her past, her very personal evocations and fantasies, and her diary. Immediate setting is Mexico City where Ana is confined to a hospital; however, the narrative ranges widely in time and space, even projecting into a highly speculative 21st century. Author's basic concerns and procedures will be familiar to readers of his earlier works.

5541 Robles Díez, María Dolores. Hurgando en la obscuridad. Ilus. de Miguel Gulizia. Buenos Aires: Editorial Crisol, 1979. 125 p.

Collection of 17 stories in which author explores a variety of emotions ranging from frustrations to fear. Plot is secondary to creation of an emotional climate. Most effective stories present the torment of fear.

5542 Schóo, Ernesto. El baile de los guerreros. Buenos Aires: Corregidor, 1979. 174 p. (Serie mayor; M. 1289)

In the vein of Mujica Láinez, but with considerable originality, Schóo has written a fascinating novel which covers a 100-year span of Argentine history. But it is history mixed ingeniously with fantasy; tragedy is blended with humor; the comic and the grotesque are fused.

5543 Shua, Ana María. Soy paciente. Buenos Aires: Editorial Losada, 1980. 138 p. (Novelistas de nuestra época)

Sensitive, delicately ironic novel in which first-person narrator interprets and reacts to his experience as a hospital patient. His sense of uncertainty, vague fears of the unknown, anger and frustration at his loss of dignity and lack of control of circumstances can be interpreted not only on a personal level but more generally as man's response to the human condition. Winner of the Concurso International de Narrativa Losada 1980.

5544 Siete para contar un cuento. Susana Boéchat *et al.* Buenos Aires: Ediciones Crisol, 1979. 127 p.

Anthology of uneven stories which range from enigmatic and fantastic to humorous by seven lesser known writers. Bio-bibliography for each contributor.

5545 Sorrentino, Fernando. Sanitarios centenarios. Tapa, Carlos Pérez Villamil. Buenos Aires: Plus Ultra, 1979. 142 p.

Outrageous mixture of satire, the absurd, and ribald humor characterize this novel.

5546 Tarnopolsky, Samuel. La rastrillada de Salinas Grandes. Diseño de tapa, Eduardo Súarez. Buenos Aires: Macondo Ediciones, 1979. 230 p. (Los Narradores)

Costumbristic-historical novel which depicts life in rural Argentina in first decade of 19th century.

5547 Velazco, Ana de. No es un juego del amor: canción de Eladia Blázquez. Tapa ilustrada por Isabel Merellano. Buenos Aires: Ediciones Crisol, 1980. 95 p.

Collection of 12 stories in which author has developed a subtly erotic atmosphere. Basically the same formula—a surprise ending—is used in all selections.

5548 Verbitsky, Bernardo. A pesar de todo. Caracas: Monte Avila Editores, 1978. 172 p. (Colección Continentes)

Characters in 12 stories of this collection experience loneliness, insecurity, and failure. Verbitsky presents his fictional creations with considerable sympathy.

5549 Walsh, Rodolfo J. Obra literaria completa. México: Siglo XXI Editores, 1981. 483 p. (La Creación literaria)

Collection of Walsh's literary production includes his fiction and two theatrical works. Brief but useful introduction by Pacheco.

5550 Wasserzug, Guillermo. Malas artes. Diseño la portada, Carlos Boccardo. Buenos Aires: Editorial R. Alonso, 1980. 93 p.

Death, the problem of suffering, and alienation are major themes in these nine stories.

5551 Yarade, Héctor Reinaldo. Los que no alcanzan. Salta?, Argentina: Ediciones Plutón, 1979. 147 p.; ill.

Novel explores themes of alienation, fear, and love.

URUGUAY

5552 Arregui, Mario. La escoba de la bruja. Montevideo: Acali Editorial, 1979. 139 p. (Colección ABC del lector; 9)

Very welcome collection contains six previously published but somewhat revised short stories and five that have not appeared before. Arregui is intimately acquainted with the rural world, and his best stories reflect that environment—but in a way that totally transcends local color. Ironic, tragic, violently primitive aspects of that world are conveyed with subtle insights.

5553 ———. Veinte cuentos. Cubierta, Enrique Lucio González. La Habana: Editorial Arte y Literatura, 1978. 192 p. (Ediciones Huracán)

Collection of 20 stories selected from author's four published books.

Benedetti, Mario. El recurso del supremo patriarca. See item **5006.**

5554 Bocage, Alberto C. Los tiempos del fin: cuentos. Prólogo de Alejandro Paternain. Montevideo: Ediciones de la Banda Oriental, 1979. 95 p. (Lectores de Banda Oriental; 11)

Collection of 14 local color stories depicting provincial Uruguay.

5555 Breve antología del cuento humorístico uruguayo. Mario Arregui et al. Montevideo: Acali Editorial, 1979. 63 p. (Colección ABC del lector; 8)

Anthology of stories selected from works of nine well-known Uruguayan authors such as Viana, Morosoli, and Arregui. As title indicates, humor—though mainly in the ironic, wry vein—is the prime ingredient of these stories.

5556 Butazzoni, Fernando. Los días de nuestra sangre. La Habana: Casa de las Américas, 1979. 99 p.

Collection of stories that have in common the theme of revolutionary struggle.

5557 Diez relatos y un epílogo. Campodónico et al. Postfacio de Armonía Somers. Montevideo: Fundación de Cultura Universitaria, 1979. 154 p.; bibl.

Contains stories by 10 Uruguayan writers. In post script, Somers provides serious and useful study of the selections.

5558 Ferrari, Hugo. Personas. San José?, Uruguay: Asociación de Escritores del Interior, 1979? 135 p.

Collection of four stories written in a traditionally realistic mode. Some costumbristic elements and heavy reliance on dialogue to portray the psychology of characters.

5559 Galeano, Eduardo H. Días y noches de amor y de guerra. La Habana: Casa de las Américas, 1978. 219 p. (Testimonio)

In this rambling, trivial novel, which evokes fragments of past experiences, narrator talks about life in exile and the struggle against dictatorships. A trite, unconvincing denunciation of political repression. Winner of Casa de las Américas prize, 1978.

5560 Martínez Moreno, Carlos. El color que el infierno me escondiera. México: Nueva Imagen, 1981. 260 p.

One of the most gifted and productive writers of the River Plate region, Martínez Moreno presents a stark portrayal of life in contemporary Uruguay. Dictatorial repression, violence, climate of uncertainty and fear are captured with a mature, skillful use of modern narrative techniques. With all its positive features, novel's shortcomings should be mentioned: unfair caricaturing of US government and ridiculously inaccurate depictions of life in North America.

5561 Mendive, Carlos L. Los globos. Montevideo: Acali Editorial, 1979. 133 p. (ABC del lector; 11)

Collection of 44 very brief narratives in which humor is the main ingredient. Of primary interest are colorful, witty, ironic dialogues which provide sharp insights into character and environment.

5562 Ricci, Julio. Ocho modelos de felicidad. Buenos Aires: Macondo, 1980. 127 p.

A competent short story writer, Ricci has produced some notable fiction in the past. This most recent book of narratives is no exception. Collection develops the familiar theme of unhappiness, life in the midst of problems without solutions and in an atmosphere of irony and melancholy.

5563 Rosa, Julio C. da. Rumbo sur: novela. Montevideo: Ediciones de la Banda Oriental, 1980. 127 p.

Costumbristic type novel which portrays life in an Uruguayan city of the interior during the 1930s through 1950s.

5564 20 [i.e. Veinte] **cuentos uruguayos magistrales.** Selección y notas bio-bibliográficas por Walter Rela. Buenos Aires: Plus Ultra, 1980. 237 p.; bibl.

Anthology contains selections by 20 well-known Uruguayan writers. Bio-bibliographical information is provided for each.

5565 Viana, Javier de. Con divisa blanca. Palabras iniciales, Enrique Beltrán. Carátula, José Mariño. 2. ed. Montevideo: Ediciones de la Plaza, 1979. 118 p. (Colección Periodismo y testimonio)

New edition of Viana's fascinating chronicle of civil war in Uruguay in 1904. Narrative, which depicts historical events, provides, at the same time, an intensely personal perspective. Beltrán's prologue to the work is useful.

LITERARY CRITICISM
AND HISTORY
ARGENTINA

5566 Alegría, Fernando. *Libro de Manuel*: un libro de preguntas (INTI, 10/11, otoño 1979/primavera 1980, p. 101–107)

Considera que esta novela es "fundamentalmente una poderosa y sombría historia de amor, un discurso romántico en términos que niegan validez a todo romanticismo, un ejercicio abierto de quienes desean explicar una derrota negándose a ver en ella la pasión que ha de convertirla en triunfo" (p. 106). Lectura en la que se intercalan motivos reconocibles en la ficción de Alegría, particularmente en optimismos denunciatorios más recientes.

5567 Barrenechea, Ana María. La génesis del texto: *Rayuela* y su *Cuaderno de bitácora* (INTI, 10/11, otoño 1979/primavera 1980, p. 78–92)

Afortunada posesión del "log book" de *Rayuela*, permite rastrear algunas líneas y las metas del autor. Al margen de fascinantes datos de construcción (dudas, vacilaciones, intentos), Barrenechea concluye: "Se trata de una busca que es siempre la busca de una escritura que alcance el milagro de la revelación—siempre inminente y siempre diferida, si hemos de creer a Borges—la revelación de una figura" (p. 88).

5568 Bell-Villada, Gene H. Borges and his fiction: a guide to his mind and art. Chapel Hill: University of North Carolina Press, 1981. 292 p.; bibl.; index; port.

Acertada presentación de Borges para los que aun no han fatigado los innumerables (no infinitos) catálogos de su bibliografía. Se atiene al recorte declarado en las palabras preliminares definiendo algunas de las preocupaciones centrales de su prosa y ubicándolo en un contexto histórico para delinear parámetros de su ideología. Tono irónico de Bell pone de relieve la distancia que lo separa de otros estudios sobre Borges.

5569 Bernardi Guardi, Mario. Lío plurale: Borges et Borges. Appendice scritti e testimonianze di Fausto Gianfranceschi *et al.* Milano: Il Falco, 1979. 170 p.; bibl.; ill. (Collana Il Ponte; n. 4)

Acertado título se disemina en varias direcciones que intentan singularizar la lectura de Borges. Puede resultar de especial interés el tercer capítulo, "Vortici e Frantumi del Cosmo: il Centro Segreto della Storia." El uso (¿acceso?) parcial a la bibliografía ha restringido el estudio de otros núcleos centrales de la obra. Los apéndices parecen cumplir una función de apoyatura y reconocimiento de la presencia de Borges en Italia más que de identificación de "Lío plurale."

5570 Blengino, Vanni. Immigrazione italiana, letteratura e identità nazionale argentina (Novo Americana [Giulio Einaudi Editore, Torino, Italy] 3, 1980, p. 331–353)

Revisión de actitudes poco alentadoras hacia inmigrantes italianos a partir de Sarmiento en *Facundo* con énfasis especial en obras de la Generación del 80. De parodia del gringo en *Martín Fierro* se pasa al escarnio de naturalistas xenofóbicos, a incorporación de nueva lengua en sainetes y el grotesco de Discépolo, y a otro signo en el teatro de Florencio Sánchez.

5571 Boldy, Steven. The novels of Julio Cortázar. Cambridge, UK: Cambridge University Press, 1980. 220 p.

Análisis metódico de *Los premios, Rayuela, 62. Modelo para armar* y *Libro de Manuel.* Estudia desplazamientos de un texto a otro; necesidad de recobrar la "presencia" perdida, lograr reconciliación del hombre con el monstruo que lo habita. Desde su lenguaje, y a través de fuerzas que pugnan entre sí en el *doppelgänger*, en noción de "figuras" y en "discursos dobles" (crítico y racional frente al más simbólico e irracional), la apuesta de Cortázar se da categóricamente en un futuro histórico.

5572 Borello, Rodolfo A. Charlie Parker: 'El perseguidor' (CH, 364/366, oct./dic. 1980, p. 573−594)

Estudia exhaustivamente la filiación de este texto con "la realidad preexistente." Narra detalles y crónicas de Charlie Parker como cotejo inicial con texto de Cortázar. Primera parte de estudio que se anuncia sobre el sentido que propone el texto de Cortázar a partir de la información primaria.

5573 Borges, Jorge Luis and María Esther Vázquez. Borges—imágenes, memorias, diálogos. 2a. ed., corr. y aum. Caracas: Monte Avila Editores, 1980. 298 p.; bibl. (Colección Estudios)

Más que otros escritores argentinos, Borges se ha sometido a charlas, entrevistas, interrogatorios, sobre su vida, obra, literatura. Conocimientos, el atrevimiento de unas frases, obsesiones que lo definen, páginas que lo justifican, surgen de entrevistas que Vázquez reproduce grabadas a partir de 1963. Incluye diálogos con Gudiño Kieffer (1972; muy marcados por esos tiempos) Francisco Luis Bernárdez (1974), Raimundo Lida (1977), y Manuel Mujica Láinez (1977).

5574 Braceli, Rodolfo Eduardo. Don Borges, saque su cuchillo porque he venido a matarlo. Foto de tapa, Juan Mestichelli. Tapa, Douglas Wright. Buenos Aires: Editorial Galerna, 1979. 189 p.; bibl.

Los Borges que se agitan en "Borges y Yo" y "El Centinela" se repliegan ante los cuestionamientos de Braceli de ese "tercer Borges," figura pública que no siempre responde acogedoramente a la imagen venerada que surge de sus escritos. De los tradicionales catálogos borgianos surge un marco que define más al que traza las preguntas (con humor, angustia, infinito y amistoso "cariño") que al sometido a este nuevo escrutiño.

5575 Carilla, Emilio. Autores, libros y lectores en la literatura argentina. Tucumán, Argentina: Universidad Nacional de Tucumán, Facultad de Filosofía y Letras, 1979. 106 p.; bibl.; ill. (Cuadernos de humanitas; no. 51)

Pocas y esquemáticas páginas describen lo anunciado en el título que, a falta de mayores méritos, denuncian la necesidad de estudios rigurosos sobre la difusión de la literatura en la Argentina. Los testimonios, que van de Sarmiento a Cortázar, de Gálvez a Silvina Bullrich proclaman oscilaciones que no siempre marcan el transcurso de la historia.

5576 Cohen, Howard. Critical approaches to Eduardo Mallea (UA/REH, 14:3, oct. 1980, p. 129−144)

Autor de bibliografía completa de Mallea, pasa revista a diversas actitudes críticas (término generoso en muchos casos) ante sus novelas. Resalta la importancia del autor de *Historia de una pasión argentina* y otras obras que han merecido la atención de cierto círculo de lectores.

5577 Cortázar, Julio. La literatura latinoamericana a la luz de la historia contemporánea (INTI, 10/11, otoño 1979/primavera 1980, p. 11−20)

Discurso pronunciado durante las sesiones del simposio sobre su obra en Barnard College (abril 1980). Revisa las pulsiones que animan su producción literaria; esos cruces de literatura y acción cotidiana que se traducen en algunos de sus textos como responsabilidad cultural. Elabora la situación actual en algunos sectores de América Latina y su relación dinámica con la literatura que signa otros despertares y apuestas hacia el futuro.

5578 Epple, Juan. Eugenio Cambaceres y el naturalismo en Argentina (IL, 3:14, Sept./Nov. 1980, p. 16−50)

Luego de breve presentación del contexto de la Generación del 80, analiza novela *Sin rumbo*, texto fundamental que obliga a la aristocracia bonaerense a mirarse a sí misma en momentos de crisis y así refleja, desde su propia ideología, los alcances y límites de esa élite. Subraya la "actitud alerta" de la novela ante problemas de período frente a actitudes disímiles de otros autores del 80.

5579 Fernández Latour, Enrique. Macedonio Fernández, candidato a presidente, y otros escritos de Enrique Fernández Latour. Con una carta-prólogo de Jorge Luis Borges. Buenos Aires: Ediciones Agon, 1980. 64 p.; port.

Muestrario de escritos de Fernández Latour (1898–1972), "señor argentino" y "caballero francés," según Borges, entre los que cabe destacar sus textos sobre Macedonio y Santiago Dabove. Poemas y comentarios críticos denotan ecos de sus días de martin-fierrista y momentos en que el diálogo importaba más que la urgencia de la página impresa.

5580 Fishburn, Evelyn. The portrayal of immigration in nineteenth century Argentine fiction: 1845–1902. Berlin, FRG: Colloquium Verlag, Bibliotheca Ibero-Americana, 1981. 262 p.; bibl.; index.

Ateniéndose a una organización temática (la presencia gráfica del inmigrante en la novela), divide el análisis en tres períodos: 1) 1845–80 (pre-immigration period); *Facundo*, de Sarmiento; *Peregrinación de luz del día*, de Alberdi; 2) 1880–90 (immigration period: anti-immigrant novels); *Inocentes o culpables*, de Argerich; *En la sangre*, de Cambaceres; *La bolsa*, de Martel; 3) 1890–1902 (immigration period: pro-immigrant novels); *Bianchetto: la patria del trabajo*, de Saldías; *Teodoro Foronda*, de Grandmontagne; las novelas de Sicardi. Concluye que "the portrayal of immigration in the literature reviewed is narrow, selective, and prescriptive" y que más que una representación de la inmigración delinea actitudes ante ella en momentos de transformaciones socioeconómicas. Hubiera resultado provechosa la integración del apéndice histórico al análisis mismo de las novelas. Una lectura ajustada de las propuestas del liberalismo desde la "selección natural" de Sarmiento ya apunta a la futura legislación de las leyes de residencia con que se cierra este análisis. Estudio metódico que responde adecuadamente a lo anunciado.

5581 Franco, Jean. Julio Cortázar: utopia and everyday life (INTI, 10/11, otoño 1979/primavera 1980, p. 108–118)

Relaciones lector-autor propuestas, con variaciones, en múltiples textos de Cortázar apuntan a la incorporación de lo literario—lo utópico que se inscribe en el Arte—en el contexto cotidiano. La utopía rela-

cionada con una visión privilegiada (elitista?) a través de su obra. *Fantomas* revela que solidaridad democrática no puede basarse en estética vanguardista, que lo utópico requiere de "alta cultura" para su transmisión, que el pueblo no necesita autores que creen por ellos. Esto, dice Franco, debería llevar a Cortázar a la noción de Benjamin y a aceptar "the democratizing and collective potential of art. His contradiction is that he has never quite been able to do so." (p. 117).

5582 ——. La máquina rota (Texto Crítico [Universidad Veracruzana, Centro de Investigaciones Lingüístico-Literarias, Xalapa, México] 6:18/19, julio/dic. 1980, p. 33–46)

Epígrafe de Wilson Harris sobre mundo fragmentado (ni capitalista ni comunista) y lectura de *Los Buddenbrook* de Thomas Mann, sirven de marco a esta importante lectura de *El astillero*. La trama denuncia el caos, la decadencia, el vacío de formas carentes de toda sustancia, origen y futuro. Larsen habita en cementerio de máquinas distanciado de todo poder redentor del hombre. El fracaso del orden social es consecuencia del derrumbe de un sistema de producción, la clausura de toda una historia, en que el hombre es ente superfluo. Como máquinas rotas, es parte del circuito comercial de la degeneración cuyo único refugio endeble son sus valores individuales.

5583 Glantz, Margo. Bioy Casares y la percepción privilegiada del amor: *La invención de Morel* y la Arcadia pastoril (Revista de Artes y Letras de la Universidad de Costa Rica [Ciudad Universitaria Rodrigo Facio] 4:1, enero/junio 1980, p. 19–31)

Conjunción de una cita de Paz sobre Bioy (de *La máscara y la transparencia*) y varios epígrafes de Jorge de Montemayor, organizan un contrapunto en que se hila *La invención de Morel* como metáfora que intenta nombrar otra forma acuñada del amor. Buen ejemplo de las líneas retóricas/eróticas de múltiples lecturas practicadas por Glantz.

5584 González Bermejo, Ernesto. Conversaciones con Cortázar. Barcelona: EDHASA, 1978? 190 p.; bibl. (Colección Perspectivas; 3)

Una charla con Cortázar siempre es una invitación a los placeres de la lucidez, del rigor y el respeto por la literatura y por el contexto que lo enmarca. Si bien no adelanta elementos inéditos, este ensamblaje de múltiples charlas a través de los años corrobora, una vez más, el lugar predominante que Cortázar ocupa (con justicia) en las letras latinoamericanas.

5585 Historia de la literatura argentina. v. 1, Desde la colonia hasta el romanticismo. v. 2, Del romanticismo al naturalismo. Buenos Aires: Centro Editor de América Latina, 1980. 2 v.; bibl.; ill.

Edición basada en la excelente serie "Capítulo de Literatura Argentina." Si bien ha mantenido el mismo formato, ampliamente ilustrado y con bibliografías básicas, y algunos de los textos originales de la serie, incluye ensayos panorámicos del proceso de producción siguiendo un orden genérico. La amplia gama ideológica y metodológica de algunos de los colaboradores (e.g., B. Sarlo, J. Rest, B. Canal Feijóo, Raúl H. Castagnino, F. Weinberg, N. Jitrik, J. Lafforgue, A. Prieto, L. Ordaz) asegura una solidez y amplitud de enfoques de gran utilidad. Es, a estas alturas, obra de consulta obligatoria.

5586 Ibañez Molto, María Amparo. Galería de arte en la obra de Julio Cortázar" (CH, 364/366, oct./dic. 1980, p. 624–639)

Describe y analiza presencia y función de imágenes artísticas que aportan otra dimensión a su vasta galería metafórica, otra exigencia al lector que solo desea *contemplar* lo ajeno a sí mismo. Es fascinante la organización de cuadros siguiendo la elemental división del arte para leer la "imagen," su "sentido" y "función" dentro del texto.

5587 Incledon, John. La "ejecución silenciosa" en *Libro de Manuel* (CH, 364/366, oct./dic. 1980, p. 510–517)

Aprovecha "ejecuciones bisémicas" para señalar que las novelas de Cortázar constituyen "una de las adaptaciones más complejas, interesantes y exitosas del estructuralismo a la literatura" (p. 517). Si bien Cortázar comparte algunas de las preocupaciones textuales de ciertos estructuralistas, cabe preguntar si la relación que se sugiere no debiera ser invertida en torno a algunos de sus lectores.

5588 Jurado, Alicia. Genio y figura de Jorge Luis Borges. 3a. ed., actualizada. Buenos Aires: Editorial Universitaria de Buenos Aires, 1980. 198 p.; bibl.; ill.; ports. (Genio y figura; 2)

Las citas y las fotografías de Borges

(ampliamente difundidas ambas) escasamente justifican esta presentación que ni siquiera se redime por la amistad.

5589 Katra, William. Psychological aspects of underdevelopment in the contemporary Argentine narrative (UA/REH, 14:3, Oct. 1980, p. 13–28)

Título excesivamente ambicioso para unas páginas que intentan "shed new light on the psychological factors underlying the recent social and political discord" (p. 13). Basándose en *Literatura y subdesarrollo* (1968), de Adolfo Prieto, Katra lee algunos elementos de Verbitsky, Sábato, Cortázar, Bullrich, Viñas y otros.

5590 King, John. Towards a reading of the Argentine literary magazine *Sur* (LARR, 16:2, 1981, p. 57–78)

Traza los orígenes y desarrollo de *Sur*, sus perspectivas ideológicas (inscripción de lo familiar como la historia nacional; énfasis en valores espirituales desprovistos del cuerpo contextual; declaraciones ante la guerra europea y el surgimiento y derrocamiento del peronismo, etc.), el lugar que ocupó en cuanto revista y editorial dentro de la cultura argentina, frente a la decadencia del liberalismo y figuras, como Victoria Ocampo, su hermana Silvina, Borges, Bioy Casares, José Bianco y otros. Sugiere que la historia que *Sur* quiso obviar es la que precisamente declaró su clausura dentro de su definición original.

5591 Lindstrom, Naomi. Macedonio Fernández. Lincoln, Neb.: Society of Spanish and Spanish-American Studies, 1981. 139 p.; bibl.

Estudio introductorio en que N.L. también recupera algunas de las nociones adelantadas en su *Literary expressionism in Argentina: the presentation of incoherence* (Arizona State University, 1977). Los capítulos "The Reform of Reading and Writing" y "Literary Creation as Play" serán de utilidad para incorporar a Macedonio Fernández a una lectura actualizada de la literatura contemporánea, siguiendo las pautas de ciertos lineamientos críticos formales.

5592 Literatura testimonial de los años 30. Introd. y compilación por Susana Pereira. Tapa, Cristina Brusca. Buenos Aires: Peña Lillo Editor, 1979. 157 p.; bibl.

Fatigada de tantos estudios no-literarios de los años 1930–43, la compiladora desea que nuevas generaciones reconozcan el testimonio literario, particularmente popular (no-académico), como manifestación del "estado espiritual propio" de ese período. Arlt, Santos Discépolo, Scalabrini Ortiz, E. González Tuñón, Cádicamo, Castelnuovo, Ugarte(!) son algunos de los que se ven alineados por unidades anuales sin que las fechas en sí provean otra clave que la de su publicación ni otro testimonio (suficiente quizá) que su reimpresión.

5593 McMurray, George R. Jorge Luis Borges. New York: Ungar, 1980. 255 p.; bibl.; index (Modern literature monographs)

Cataloga los cuentos según las siguientes categorías: 1) The Negation of Reason; 2) Idealism; 3) Pantheism; 4) The Treatment of Time; 5) The Double and the Mirror Image; and 6) The Machismo Cult. Ofrece finalmente unas páginas sobre la "estética de Borges." Responde a las normas de esta serie dedicada a presentaciones ante públicos no especializados de algunas figuras centrales de la literatura universal.

5594 Martínez Estrada, Ezequiel. Ezequiel Martínez Estrada. Selección de Oscar Bietti. Buenos Aires: Ediciones Culturales Argentinas, Ministerio de Cultura y Educación, Secretaría de Cultura y Educación, 1978. 333 p.; 2 leaves of plates; ill. (Colección Antologías)

Si Martínez Estrada es una "inteligencia con abismo" (p. 57), cabrá comprender la ausencia de una antología real del autor que articule el pensamiento de quien intentó despegar del liberalismo hacia una visión más abarcadora y un análisis menos esquemático de las fuerzas que organizan al país. Toda selección es parcial y la publicada aquí no es la peor; es muy lamentable la omisión (nada casual) de la producción de sus últimos años.

5595 Massuh, Gabriela. Borges: una estética del silencio. Buenos Aires: Editorial de Belgrano, 1980. 269 p.

Lectura mesurada que trasluce el ocultamiento en el lenguaje de Borges como su estética fundamental. Elaboraciones en torno a la relación del "lenguaje perfecto" con la paradójica destrucción de la obra de arte. Economía verbal que debe recabar en el silencio para subrayar su poder: ejercicio imposible ya que su propia denuncia exige la eliminación del pacto con el silencio inédito. Es

particularmente útil la ilación de los textos en el capítulo "Límites y superación del lenguaje."

5596 Morello-Frosch, Marta. Usos y abusos de la cultura popular: Pubis angelical de Manuel Puig (in Literature and Popular Culture in the Hispanic World, 4th, Montclair, New Jersey, 1981. Literature and popular culture in the Hispanic world: a symposium. Edited by Rose S. Minc. Gaithersburg, Md.: Hispamérica; Montclair, N.J.: Montclair State College, 1982, p. 31–42)

Las transformaciones del uso de la cultura popular a través de las novelas de Puig y los cambios de su función que propone Pubis . . . Frente a la Argentina de los años 1970, el juego entre la deserotización como acceso a una posible paz se da en un espacio ideológicamente neutro y deshistorificado. La lucha acaba en el sueño, gracias a la presencia angelical. Happy ending propio del género que ya no se somete a otras parodias.

5597 Omil, Alba. Frente y perfil de Victoria Ocampo. Buenos Aires: SUR, 1980. 242 p.; bibl.

La admiración y el tono elegíaco no están ausentes de la crónica de episodios fundamentales de la vida de la "patricia." La admiración, que omite el análisis riguroso y distanciado, no impide, sin embargo, el aporte de trazos que perfilan a la fundadora de Sur.

5598 Oviedo, José Miguel. El rostro en el espejo: para identificar a Un tal Lucas (INTI, 10/11, otoño 1979/primavera 1980, p. 179–187)

Considera Un tal Lucas como el cuarto de esos "libros raros, juguetones e indefinibles" que Cortázar publica desde los años 1960. Examina algunos de los planteos sucitados por esta miscelánea: 1) la cuestión u obsesión de la edad; 2) condición de argentino trasplantado a Europa; 3) libertad y responsabilidad del ejercicio de la imaginación literaria; 4) identidad y significado del personaje Lucas. El texto elabora la zona favorita de Cortázar: "hacer que el arte se parezca a la vida" (p. 187).

5599 Pastor, Beatriz. Roberto Arlt o la rebelión alienada. Gaithersburg, Md.: Ediciones Hispamérica, 1980. 126 p.; bibl.

Analiza el personaje arltiano en torno al problema de alienación en relación con el padre y la mujer. Estudia la relación dialéctica entre modo de conciencia y acción y las posibles opciones del personaje desde su percepción alienada: 1) intento de refugio en las relaciones personales y afectivas; 2) en el *lumpen* (se da la ruptura simbólica con los valores de clase); 3) proyecto de transformación de la realidad social. Analiza los personajes de Arlt desde una perspectiva marxista, la cual también es aplicada para evaluar la relación del autor con su práctica literaria.

Queiroz, Maria José de. Perón e o peronismo: uma visão literária. See *HLAS 43 : 8326.*

5600 Rama, Angel. Argentina: crisis de una cultura sistemática (INTI, 10/11, otoño 1979/primavera 1980, p. 49–60)

Características de la cultura argentina a partir de la crisis de 1930. De particular interés son las versiones culturales y los modelos impuestos por las elites nacionales. Mientras la clase obrera no logre expresar directamente su concepción social, "no se habrá producido la necesaria catarsis y renovación de la cultura argentina, para que vuelva a ser la pujante cultura del modernismo vanguardista que fue y le aseguró un puesto privilegiado en el continente." (p. 60)

5601 Rodríguez Monegal, Emir. Borges por él mismo. Caracas: Monte Avila Editores, 1980. 247 p.; bibl.; filmography (Colección Estudios)

Versión corregida y ampliada de *Borges par lui même* (1970; 1978). Los capítulos de este breviario por uno de sus mejores conocedores han sido ampliamente superados por la propia biografía literaria de Rodríguez Monegal. De gran valor son textos de Borges no incluidos en sus *Obras completas* y la famosa entrevista con César Fernández Moreno en 1966.

5602 Sarlo, Beatriz. Vanguardia y criollismo: la aventura de *Martín Fierro* (RCLL, 8 : 15, 1. semestre, 1982, p. 39–69)

Excelente análisis de revista fundada en 1924 que instaura la ruptura estética que es la vanguardia argentina. Estudia contextos y transformaciones de la concepción de literatura y debates entre colaboradores de la revista. Heterogeneidad martinfierrista contribuye a organizar tensiones "populismo/modernidad" o "nacionalismo/cosmopolitismo" que informan al discurso literario argentino del siglo XX.

5603 Sosnowski, Saúl. Imágenes del deseo: el testigo ante su mutación (INTI, 10/11, otoño 1979/primavera 1980, p. 93–97)

Lectura de "Las Babas del Diablo" (*Las armas secretas,* 1964) y "Apocalipsis de Solentiname" (*Alguien que anda por ahí,* 1977). Entre estos textos se da "el paso desde el pretendido engaño de lo ficticio al encuentro preciso de este lado de toda textura literaria" (p. 97).

5604 Tyler, Joseph. Borges y las literaturas germánicas medievales en *El libro de Arena* (IUP/HJ, 2 : 1, Fall 1980, p. 79–85)

Sugiere que más que en otros textos, la lectura de *Antiguas literaturas germánicas* o *Literaturas germánicas medievales* (que Tyler ha traducido al inglés; versión aun inédita), confirma la presencia de sus motivos en todos los cuentos de este libro, con excepción de "Avelino Arredondo."

5605 Vian, Cesco. Invito alla lettura di Jorge Luis Borges. Milano: Mursia, 1980. 222 p.; bibl.; indexes (Invito alla lettura: Sezione straniera; 28/29)

Sólida presentación para el público italiano: cuadro contextual de la vida de Borges, capítulo biográfico y lectura crítica de su obra hasta 1977. Capítulo "Temi e Motivi" y revisión comentada de la bibliografía demuestran la competencia del autor.

5606 Vidal, Hernán. En torno a Julio Cortázar: problemática sobre la vigencia histórica de las formas culturales (INTI, 10/11, otoño 1979/primavera 1980, 69–77)

Considera que el quiebre de Cortázar con una "definición tecnocrático-liberal" del escritor le ha permitido formular un "modelo de conducta constructivo que supera la obsesión por meditar nostálgicamente sobre un pasado convertido en utopía" (p. 76). Util ejemplo de lectura crítica que articula los textos dentro del panorama más amplio de la práctica social.

5607 Wyers, Frances. Manuel Puig at the movies (HR, 49 : 2, Spring 1981, p. 163–181)

Uso del cine como representación y creación narrativas en *El beso de la mujer araña.* Relación entre lenguaje visual y gráfico y el mundo narrado. Desacralización de versiones privilegiadas del arte promueve noción de que la fuerza inventiva del arte reside en que todo ser humano (aun Molina, aun el narrador Puig) puede ser Arte.

5608 Yúdice, George. *El beso de la mujer araña* y *Pubis angelical*: entre el placer y el saber (*in* Literature and Popular Culture in the Hispanic World, 4th, Montclair, New Jersey, 1981. Literature and popular culture in the Hispanic world: a symposium. Edited by Rose S. Minc. Gaithersburg, Md.: Hispamérica; Montclair, N.J. Montclair State College, 1982, p. 43–57)

Considera ambas novelas "alegorías de cómo se manifiesta el deseo." *El beso* representa la voluntad del placer y *Pubis . . .* del saber con lo cual esta última "elabora una rica alegoría de la resistencia." Cabe analizar la posición ideológica y las implicaciones de esas actitudes que aparentan acercar al autor al "activista político."

PARAGUAY

5609 Battilana, Carlos. Reflexiones sobre *Hijo de hombre* de Augusto Roa Bastos. Frankfurt am Main; Bern; Las Vegas: Lang, 1979. 81 p. (Publicaciones universitarias europeas: Serie 24, Lenguas y literaturas iberorrománicas; t. 10)

Analiza los nueve "cuentos" de la novela. Intenta elaborar la dialéctica que rige los estratos mágico-mítico y social de cada uno de ellos incorporando datos de la visión guaraní y cristiana del mundo a una tipología de los personajes. Estudio un tanto primerizo y esquemático que merece el desarrollo de sus propuestas.

5610 Ugalde, Sharon. The mythical origins of *El Supremo* (JSSTC, 8 : 3, Winter 1980, p. 293–304)

La presencia de mitos guaraníes intercalados/entretejidos con la documentación histórica difuminan los límites de sus respectivos discursos y producen la conjunción de una figura histórica arraigada en el mito popular. Se subrayan los orígenes del Dr. Francia para demostrar esta interacción. Algunos de estos elementos son retomados en "Binarisms in *Yo el Supremo*" (*Hispanic Journal*, 2 : 1, Fall 1980, p. 69–77).

URUGUAY

5611 Corral, Wilfrido H. Modos de representación del humor en los artículos de Graucho Marx (Texto Crítico [Universidad Veracruzana, Centro de Investigaciones Lingüístico-Literarias, Xalapa, México] 6 : 18/19, julio/dic. 1980, p. 171–177)

Revisa artículos de Onetti en *Marcha* (29 nov. 1940–25 abril 1941), postula que su humor presenta una sociedad tan conflictiva como la de las otras obras que distan de toda asociación con lo humorístico, ya que ambos registros se inscriben dentro del uso social de la literatura.

5612 Espinoza, Enrique. Trayectoria de Horacio Quiroga. Buenos Aires: Babel, 1980. 74 p.

Comentarios de Espinoza (seudónimo de Samuel Glusberg) sobre su relación personal con Quiroga; glosas de su obra y cartas de Quiroga (1934–35). Páginas, surgidas de una charla de conmemoración del centenario del nacimiento de Quiroga (1878), son más provechosas para conocimiento del autor de *Heine, Spinoza, La levita gris*, etc. que para análisis del autor de *Cuentos de amor, de locura y de muerte*.

5613 Gambarini, Elsa K. El discurso y su transgresión: *El almohadón de pluma*, de Horacio Quiroga (IILI/Ri, 112/113, julio/dic. 1980, p. 443–457)

Apoyándose terminología de Wayne C. Booth y lecturas de Barthes, Roussel y Bessière, Gambarini recorta aspectos planteados en su tesis doctoral (*La narratología en los cuentos fantásticos de Horacio Quiroga*, 1979). Apuesta al efecto que puede producir este cuento de 1917: "el deseo de transgredir las fronteras verbales que le corresponden, para violar el mundo de los objetos reales y lectores concretos" (p. 457).

5614 Gertel, Zunilda. *Para una tumba sin nombre*, ficción y teoría de la ficción (Texto Crítico [Universidad Veracruzana, Centro de Investigaciones Lingüístico-Literarias, Xalapa, México] 6 : 18/19, julio/dic. 1980, p. 178–194)

Esta obra de Onetti es la que más muestra que "la literatura es por excelencia función verbal." Su escritura "anticipa y prescribe la teoría creadora y crítica de producción textual" de la nueva novela de los años 1960 hasta comienzos del 1970 en la que se reconocen "entrecruzamiento, sustitución y transformación de textos-relatos." Demuestra que ésta es ficción dentro de la ficción y una teoría crítica de la creación literaria.

5615 Lewald, H. Ernest and **Doris Stephens.** Trends in the Uruguayan short story in the 1970s (RIB, 30:4, 1980, p. 387–401) Resume cuentos de Benedetti, Tarik Carson, Martínez Moreno, Ricci, Estrázulas y Campodónico para mostrar su conciencia de lo transitorio de la sociedad (e.g., representaciones realistas, psicológicas, simbólicas y alegóricas). Análisis detallado del contexto y transformaciones en la crucial década del 70 contribuiría a una mayor elucidación de estos autores (y de otros ausentes: Cristina Peri Rossi, entre ellos).

5616 Ludmer, Josefina. Figuras del género policial en Onetti (Texto Crítico [Universidad Veracruzana, Centro de Investigaciones Lingüístico-Literarias, Xalapa, México] 6:18/19, julio/dic. 1980, p. 47–50) A partir de *La vida breve* se impone a la ficción de Onetti el relato policial. La instauración de Santa María "coincide con la apertura del juego de las leyes policiales." Las leyes se ajustan ante la marginación de los que están fuera de la racionalidad pequeño burguesa. *Dejemos hablar al viento* "declara el fin del corpus" y afirma que "no hay orden sino cargado de desorden, no hay verdad ni ley sino penetradas de falsedad."

5617 Monsiváis, Carlos. Onetti: los monstruos engendran los sueños de la razón (Texto Crítico [Universidad Veracruzana, Centro de Investigaciones Lingüístico-Literarias, Xalapa, México] 6:18/19, julio/dic. 1980, p. 12–41) Resume impecablemente motivos centrales de la obra de Onetti y las propuestas que adelanta: el "rechazo frontal de una moral de buenos deseos y nobles declaraciones;" lo inexorable como punto de partida

y no como meta; la "libertad para elegir las consecuencias fatales;" los seres destruidos por "el tedio, el envejecimiento, la miseria económica, el fastidio de ser como los demás, la mezquindad de la rutina;" la congoja y el pesar como bagaje cómplice del hombre.

5618 Prada Oropeza, Renato. Las relaciones toponímicas en *El astillero* (Texto Crítico [Universidad Veracruzana, Centro de Investigaciones Lingüístico-Literarias, Xalapa, México] 6:18/19, julio/dic. 1980, p. 147–164) Este riguroso análisis parte de la noción que "un lugar geográfico en una narración literaria es un elemento de la modelización total del sentido que esa narración entraña y debe ser tomado en relación con el tejido semiótico que es un discurso" (p. 149). La oposición toponímica excluyente se establece entre Santa María y el astillero; la no excluyente, pero contraria entre los lugares que abarca el astillero, entre casilla, oficina/galpón, glorieta y casa.

5619 Verani, Hugo. Onetti: el ritual de la impostura. Caracas: Monte Avila, 1981. 331 p. Analiza cambios en la narrativa contemporánea y aísla elementos que definen la obra de Onetti (la invención de un mundo singular propio, la liquidación del héroe de tonalidades épicas, el pesimismo que condena todo desarrollo social en máscara de fracasos finales, la decrepitud de ese mundo— ya planteada por A. Rama—la desintegración de un mundo que irremediablemente se desmorona . . .) sin menoscabar la merecida atención que exigen los recursos formales que marcan a Onetti como figura fundamental de este siglo.

POETRY

HUMBERTO M. RASI, *Chief Editor, Inter-American Publications, Pacific Press*
RUBEN A. GAMBOA, *Assistant Professor of Spanish, Mills College*
OSCAR HAHN, *Associate Professor of Spanish, University of Iowa*
PEDRO LASTRA, *Professor of Spanish, State University of New York at Stony Brook*
CAROLYN MORROW, *Associate Professor of Spanish, University of Utah*
BETTY TYREE OSIEK, *Professor of Spanish, Southern Illinois University at Edwardsville*
ELIANA RIVERO, *Professor of Spanish, The University of Arizona*

ANTOLOGIAS Y TENDENCIAS

Tres colecciones se destacan entre los trabajos generales reseñados: una atractiva compilación de la poesía iberoamericana de la independencia (item **5635**); la selección de textos que presentan una matizada visión del modernismo desde la perspectiva de sus protagonistas (item **5770**); y una antología de la última poesía iberoamericana (item **5632**).

Los trabajos críticos de enfoque internacional reflejan, por un lado, un renovado interés en la vanguardia literaria y, por otro, una clara inclinación a evaluar los escritores y los movimientos literarios desde una perspectiva ideológica. A pesar del marcado aumento de los estudios críticos particulares, se echan de menos los trabajos destinados a ofrecer nuevas síntesis—abarcantes y esclarecedoras—de corrientes y períodos literarios.

Al cumplir con el presente volumen doce años de aportes a la sección de poesía, este colaborador se siente inclinado a realizar un somero balance:

La poesía hispanoamericana reciente avanza en tres direcciones principales, que ocasionalmente se entrecruzan: 1) la poesía comprometida y de protesta; 2) la poesía de reflexión existencial y metafísica; y 3) la poesía surrealista y experimental. Tres peligros la acosan, respectivamente: el prosaísmo chabacano, la incomunicación y el jugueteo intrascendente.

El número creciente de profesores e investigadores—especialmente en los Estados Unidos—está publicando un volumen cada vez mayor de estudios, monografías y disertaciones. Este fenómeno, en buena medida positivo, puede llegar a desequilibrar el balance necesario entre la obra creativa y su contorno crítico.

Los altibajos de la política y la economía siguen afectando el destino personal de los poetas y las tendencias editoriales de cada país. Pero ni la censura, el exilio, la existencia precaria de las revistas literarias, ni la circulación limitada de muchas ediciones poéticas han logrado marchitar esa flor, a la vez sensible y resistente, que es la poesía hispanoamericana. [HMR]

CHILE

En Chile, la crisis de la industria editorial se vio acompañada por un fuerte descenso en el número de librerías. De alrededor de 500 en los años 60, bajó a 120 en 1981. El permiso previo de circulación de libros—es decir, la censura—fue señalada como una de las causas principales. En relación con este fenómeno, el punto culminante fue la prohibición de *Mal de Amor*, de Oscar Hahn, hecho que alarmó a la intelectualidad chilena, pero que fue prácticamente ocultado por la prensa, con la sola excepción de la revista católica *Mensaje* (Vol. 12, No. 35, p. 81), cuyo colaborador, el novelista Jorge Edwards, escribió: "Si *Mal de Amor* tiene problemas, toda la poesía chilena tiene problemas. Mejor y mucho más claro sería prohibirla por decreto." La labor más destacada en la lucha contra la muerte de las publicaciones de poesía, correspondió a la pequeña y valerosa editorial Ganymedes, dirigida por el poeta David Turkeltaub, que contra viento y marea consiguió salir adelante, incorporando a su catálogo a la plana mayor de la literatura chilena actual: Nicanor Parra, Enrique Lihn, Jorge Edwards, José Donoso y Gonzalo Rojas, entre otros. A diferencia de años anteriores en los que se lamentaron las desapariciones de poetas de edad avanzada, los años 80 y 81 golpearon con la muerte de dos promisorios poetas jóvenes: Armando Rubio, en un extraño accidente, y Rodrigo Lira, por su propia mano. En el plano de los eventos culturales, cabe destacar las Jornadas de Poesía, bajo la dirección del poeta Jaime Quezada, con lecturas públicas individuales de Nicanor Parra, Gonzalo Rojas, Miguel Arteche y Floridor Pérez, bajo el auspicio de la Sociedad de Escritores de Chile. Por su parte, el poeta Eduardo Anguita obtuvo el Premio "María Luisa Bombal" de literatura, creado en Valparaíso para honrar la memoria de la gran escritora chilena. En el plano editorial, las publicaciones más destacadas fueron: *Conversaciones con Enrique Lihn*, de Pedro Lastra (item **5819**); las poesías completas de Gonzalo Rojas impresas por el Fondo de Cultura Económica, de México, con el título de *Del relámpago*; y *Purgatorio* de Raúl Zurita (item **5759**) notable primer libro de este poeta, que lo consagró de manera inmediata. [OH]

PERU, BOLIVIA Y ECUADOR

La actividad literaria de la región se ha mantenido en los apreciables niveles conocidos, en cuanto a la frecuencia de publicaciones y a la respuesta crítica que origina, especialmente en el Perú. En el plazo reseñado aparecieron en este país obras de César Moro y Martín Adán, notables por la cuidadosa presentación y por el propósito totalizador o por la posibilidad que abren para llegar a ese punto (items **5643** y **5712**). En el extranjero se editaron—además de una valiosa antología de César Moro (item **5713**)—otros tres libros fundamentales: la poesía de J. M. Arguedas, en Cuba; una nueva colección de C. G. Belli, en México, y la poesía completa de C. Vallejo, en Venezuela (items **5649, 5654** y **5754**). Estos aportes mayores suscitan variados y atendibles comentarios.

Las editoriales privadas siguen siendo las vías de expresión de los nuevos poetas peruanos: Ruray y Arybalo—empresas creadas por los propios autores—han intensificado su trabajo, como se advierte en el caso de la primera, que en 1981 publicó incluso a O. Hahn y a E. Lihn. Uno de sus títulos más novedosos fue *Desde Melibea* de E. O'Hara (item **5771**).

Una joven figura emergente en este panorama es Abelardo Sánchez León (item **5744**).

Nota aparte, y muy destacada, merece la revista *Hueso Húmero*, dirigida por Abelardo Oquendo y Mirko Lauer: en los 10 números entregados hasta la fecha registra aspectos relevantes del movimiento poético nacional, a través de análisis (items **5783** y **5785–5786**), entrevistas (item **5798**) y encuestas (item **5824**).

En Bolivia se editó la obra poética de Jaime Sáenz (item **5742**), el autor más significativo en esa literatura, pero escasamente difundido en Hispanoamérica. El libro trae también la tesis de Blanca Wiethüchter, presentada en la Universidad de París VIII en 1975, ensayo que sin duda invitará a otras revisiones.

En Ecuador se publicó un volumen de homenaje a Benjamín Carrión (1897–1979) con motivo del primer aniversario de su muerte: reúne algunos de sus trabajos y textos de escritores coetáneos suyos y de promociones posteriores (item **5789**). [PL]

COLOMBIA Y VENEZUELA

Se advierte en la poesía de Colombia y Venezuela la profundización de una actitud crítica y reflexiva, que busca objetivar y situar en los textos las percepciones de una realidad fuertemente conflictiva. El pesimismo que proyecta esta escritura suele resolverse por las vías de la ironía y del sarcasmo, o atenuarse en la recurrencia a los motivos propios de la poesía amorosa, como posibilidad compensatoria, aunque a menudo precaria. Las obras de Juan Gustavo Cobo Borda (item **5667**), Juan Liscano (item **5698**), Juan Manuel Roca (item **5736**), Ludovico Silva (item **5748**) y Enriqueta Arvelo Larriva (items **5651** y **5652**) muestran las variadas concreciones poéticas de esa actitud.

Entre los aportes críticos y eruditos aparecidos en Colombia deben destacarse la concienzuda edición de la poesía de José Asunción Silva preparada por Héctor H. Orjuela (item **5747**) y las sugerentes indagaciones de J. G. Cobo Borda sobre el proceso de la poesía en su país (item **5765**). Cobo Borda—que también ha editado en el período dos antologías importantes (items **5620** y **5621**)—es el animador de la revista *Eco*, establecida ya como un espacio de confluencia de la crítica hispanoamericana (items **5762** y **5806**). Otra contribución significativa al estudio de la poesía colombiana entre 1890 y 1978 es la de Jaime Mejía Duque (item **5769**). La antología de Fernando Garavito (item **5784**), aunque susceptible de reparos, se suma meritoriamente a los trabajos señalados.

La actividad crítica en Venezuela no ha sido tan intensa como en Colombia; sobresalen dos compilaciones bibliográficas, que merecen especial atención: el registro general de la producción poética venezolana de Oscar Sambrano Urdaneta (item **5774**) y el trabajo dedicado a la poesía de Miguel Otero Silva por Efraín Subero (item **5813**). [BTO]

CENTROAMERICA Y PANAMA

La poesía centroamericana no pierde vigencia. La actividad editorial es constante y vigorosa, en tanto que la producción dada a conocer sigue evidenciando el interés por el género así como el talento de aquellos escritores que se inician en el oficio poético. Entre éstos, cabe apuntar a los que aparecen en *La margarita emocionante* (item **5702**), seis poetas salvadoreños que le hacen frente a una experiencia vital marcada por el caos político con estilos muy individuales, sí, pero teñidos por el desafecto y la angustia ante una amarga circunstancia histórica.

En El Salvador, asimismo, se destaca la figura de David Escobar Galindo (items **5677** y **5678**). El indiscutible valor de su poesía, que va marcando hitos de excelencia en el panorama de la poesía salvadoreña, así como su continuo estímulo y apoyo a los más jóvenes, contribuyen para identificarlo desde ya como eje y promotor del quehacer poético en su país.

En el plano crítico, continúa revalorizándose la historia e importancia del movimiento modernista, sobre todo en Nicaragua. La publicación de antologías y de colecciones individuales (items **5640, 5650** y **5671**) y el estudio de José Varela-Ibarra sobre Cortés (item **5815**), dan razón de un continuado interés en la necesidad de establecer y fomentar una mejor comprensión del período dentro de los contornos de la literatura nicaragüense y centroamericana.

Para el conocimiento de la obra de Ernesto Cardenal, son importantes la publicación de *Poesía de uso* (item **5664**) y de la bibliografía compilada por Janet Lynn Smith (item **5812**). La primera da una visión orgánica de la poesía de Cardenal, en tanto que la segunda recoge y evalúa todo el material relacionado con obra y crítica hasta 1979. [RG]

CARIBE HISPANO

El desarrollo de la poesía antillana en lengua española sigue destacando figuras y textos nuevos, de prolífica producción en Cuba y en la República Dominicana. Es un momento en el cual se afianzan talentos maduros y se reconoce en detalle la obra de los jóvenes (items **5625, 5636** y **5773**). Por lo demás, continúa el rescate de obras clásicas a la evolución de una lírica nacional en los tres países: aparecen ediciones completas de Evaristo Ribera Chevremont en Puerto Rico, Luisa Pérez de Zambrana en Cuba, Fabio Fiallo en Santo Domingo. En Cuba ven la luz poemarios significativos de autores consagrados: Eliseo Diego, Cintio Vitier y Roberto Fernández Retamar (items **5674, 5679** y **5756**). La crítica enmienda silencios y reitera visiones (*Flor oculta de poesía cubana, Estudios heredianos*), mientras reelabora perspectivas analíticas de clásicos del XIX y el XX: Casal, Lezama Lima. Estudios dominicanos y puertorriqueños dan coherencia a la obra de poetas nacidos en los últimos 40 años, y las recopilaciones antológicas ofrecen variedad notable: Barradas, Marzán, Mateo, Santos Moray (items **5623, 5628–5630** y **5636**). La obra de poetas esenciales a una visión antillana general, como Nicolás Guillén, se disemina aun más en nuevas antologías publicadas en México y Argentina; el mayor número de estudios especiales se dedica a Lezama Lima, fallecido en 1976 (*HLAS 40*).

La expresión poética contemporánea, en rasgos generales, florece en un lenguaje escueto y cotidiano, aunque de palpable lirismo, que se evidencia en textos de figuras jóvenes como Eliseo Alberto (Cuba), Olga Nolla (Puerto Rico) y René del Risco Bermúdez (República Dominicana).

Muere en 1979 el dominicano Héctor Incháustegui Cabral, dejando obra poética notable además de su producción ensayística y crítica.

Sería de desear que la crítica considerara, en un estudio extensivo e intensivo, una obra poética madura como la de Roberto Fernández Retamar, recipiente del Premio Rubén Darío de Poesía 1980 (Nicaragua) de entre más de 300 poetas latinoamericanos concursantes (item **5679**). Dicho galardón acaba de corresponder en 1982 a otro poeta cubano, Víctor Casaus, por su libro *Los ojos sobre el pañuelo*. [ER]

MEXICO

La producción poética mexicana, abundante y diversa, innovadora y cambiante, se resume con propiedad en el lema sugerido por el título de la famosa antología de 1966: *Poesía en movimiento*. Su dirección lírica fundamental (soledad, desesperanza, erotismo) acoge e incorpora también las incitaciones de la vida cotidiana en el tráfago vertiginoso del espacio urbano o las intertextualidades históricas, en este caso provenientes de la cultura prehispánica, ampliando de este modo su espectro temático y expresivo. La poesía abiertamente social y política tiene escasos cultivadores de interés.

Antologías: Merecen mención la útil antología de la poesía joven, de Gabriel Zaid (item **5622**), y la colección de textos de poetisas mexicanas del siglo XX, de Héctor Valdés (item **5641**).

Libros de poesía: Entre los libros que reunen una parte sustancial de la producción de un autor se destacan los de Rubén Bonifaz Nuño (item **5659**), José Emilio Pacheco (item **5723**) y Gabriel Zaid (item **5758**). Otras obras importantes son las de Jaime García Terrés (item **5682**), Tomás Segovia (item **5746**) y Efraín Huerta (item **5694**). La muerte de Huerta—ocurrida en febrero de 1982—significa una gran pérdida para la cultura mexicana e hispanoamericana.

Son meritorios los trabajos críticos publicados en este último tiempo por Peter J. Roster (item **5809**), George Melnykovich (item **5797**) y Pedro Gimferrer (item **5790**). [CM]

ANTHOLOGIES

5620 Album de la nueva poesía colombiana: 1970–1980. Edición de Juan Gustavo Cobo Borda. Caracas: Fundación para la Cultura y las Artes del Distrito Federal (FUNDARTE), 1980. 224 p. (Colección Latinoamericana; 2)

Es una prolongación cronológica, de item **5621**. Aquí Cobo Borda selecciona a 37 poetas que exteriorizan un sentimiento de destierro en la década de 1970. Los poemas patentizan su opinión de "la tradición de pobreza" en la poesía de su país. El volumen contiene una corta e incisiva introducción e información bibliográfica sobre los poetas incluidos. [BTO]

5621 Album de poesía colombiana. Selección y prólogo, J. G. Cobo Borda. Bogotá: Instituto Colombiano de Cultura, Subdirección de Comunicaciones Culturales, 1980. 172, 7 p.; bibl. (Biblioteca básica colombiana; 41)

Cobo Borda, penetrante crítico de la poesía colombiana nos hace ver la utilidad de otra antología. Su prólogo enfatiza la pobreza de la poesía colombiana y usa criterios de discriminación selectiva para escoger a unos pocos autores que considera sobresalientes. Elige poemas de 25 poetas presentados cronológicamente desde José Eusebio Caro a Eduardo Escobar (ver item **5620**). [BTO]

5622 Asamblea de poetas jóvenes de México. Presentación de Gabriel Zaíd. México: Siglo Veintiuno Editores, 1980. 290 p.; (La Creación literaria)

Valuable anthology with one poem each from 164 authors who in 1980 were between ages of 18 and 30. Includes unknown to well-established (e.g., Alberto Blanco, Verónica Volkow, the late Joaquín Xirau Icaza, José de Jesús Sampedro and Rafael Segovia Albán). Contains brief biography and bibliography of each writer and excellent section on literary scene of young Mexican poets: major and minor poetry journals, publishing houses and census of other literary activities. [CM]

5623 Barradas, Efraín. Palabras asediadas: situación actual de la poesía puertorriqueña (CONAC/RNC, 39:235, marzo/abril 1978, p. 168–192, bibl., ill.)

Estudio precede muestra de 10 poetas actuales, y como parte de número especial dedicado a "Poesía del Caribe" (i.e., Trinidad, Tobago, Grenada, Jamaica, y poesía antillana de expresión francesa, así como textos representativos del área). Selección puertorriqueña comprende Juan Antonio Corretjer, Francisco Matos Paoli, Juan Martínez Capó, Laura Gallego, Olga Nolla, Marcos Rodríguez Frese, Andrés Castro Ríos, Iván Silén, Víctor Fragoso y José Luis Vega. Ensayo introductorio presenta una incisiva visión de la cultura y literatura puertorriqueñas en su ambiguo—y desgarrado—contexto (ver item **5628**). [ER]

5624 Breaking the silences: 20th century poetry by Cuban women. Edited and translated with historical introduction by Margaret Randall. Vancouver, B.C.: Pulp Press Book Publishers, 1982. 293 p.

Buena antología de la mujer cubana dentro y fuera del país. Introducción traza orígenes de poesía cubana escrita por mujeres; textos paralelos español inglés; notas biográficas interesantes provenientes de declaraciones propias de las poetas. Divididas en tres grupos generacionales: 1) *Our Living Mothers*: Dulce María Loynaz, Mirta Aguirre, Digdora Alonso, Fina García Marruz,

Carilda Oliver Labra, Rafaela Chacón Nardi, Cleva Solís, Teresita Fernández; 2) *Our Time Has Come*: Georgina Herrera, Lourdes Casal, Magaly Sánchez, Nancy Morejón, Minerva Salado, Milagros González, Lina de Feria, Excilia Saldaña; and 3) *We Speak Another Language:* Albis Torres, Mirta Yáñez, Yolanda Ulloa, Enid Vián, Soleida Ríos, Reina María Rodríguez, Zaida del Río, Marilyn Bobes, Chelly Lima. Texto diseñado para público anglo-americano, pero provechoso e interesante para un número más extenso de lectores. [ER]

5625 Codina, Norberto *et al.* Poesía joven. La Habana: Editorial Letras Cubanas, 1978. 237 p. (Colección Pluma en Ristre)

Muestrario de 33 poetas jóvenes. Se distinguen principalmente por su tono coloquial, y por enfrentarse a su experiencia vital con agudeza y amor: Carlos Aldana, Luis Beiro Alvarez, Víctor Casaus, Norberto Codina, Antonio Conde, Jesús Cos Causse, Héctor de Arturo, Luis Díaz, Roberto Díaz Muñoz, Eliseo Alberto Diego, Alex Fleites, Jorge Fuentes, Osvaldo Fundora, Francisco Garzón Céspedes, Waldo González López, Rafael Hernández Rodríguez, Nelson Herrera Ysla, Ariel James, Waldo Leyva Portal, Luis Lorente, Carlos Martí Brenes, Nancy Morejón, Osvaldo Navarro, Luis Rogelio Nogueras, Raúl Rivero, Roberto Rodríguez Menéndez, Reina María Rodríguez, Guillermo Rodríguez Rivera, Esbértido Roscendi, Minerva Salado, Emilio Surí Quesada, Yolanda Ulloa y Mirta Yáñez. [ER]

5626 Flor oculta de poesía cubana: siglos XVIII y XIX. Escogida y presentada por Cintio Vitier y Fina García Marruz. Viñetas de Samuel Feijóo. La Habana: Editorial Arte y Literatura, 1978. 350 p.; ill.; index (Biblioteca básica de literatura cubana)

Colección evidencia increíble trabajo de investigación, dedicado a una lírica en sus períodos nativista e independentista y presenta textos casi desconocidos de 115 poetas destacados como Luaces y "caseros" como Catalina Rodríguez, m. 1894. Valiosas notas histórico-literarias, biográficas y bibliográficas. Excelente ensayo introductorio de García Marruz. [ER]

5627 Ganymedes/6. Santiago: Ediciones Ganymedes, 1980. 62 p.

Selección panorámica de poesía chilena de años 1970 destinada a llenar el vacío dejado por el estancamiento de la actividad editorial en el género lírico. Incluye prólogo del editor, poemas recientes—muchos de ellos inéditos—de Gonzalo Rojas, Enrique Lihn, Cecilia Casanova, Pedro Lastra, David Turkeltaub, Oscar Hahn, Manuel Silva, Claudio Bertoni, Gonzalo Millán, Rodrigo Lira, Raúl Zurita, Paulo Jolly, Leonora Vicuña, Armando Rubio y Mauricio Electorat, además de notas sobre los poetas y dibujos de Nemesio Antúnez. [OH]

5628 Herejes y mitificadores: muestra de poesía puertorriqueña en los Estados Unidos. Introducción de Efraín Barradas. Selección, notas y bibliografía de Efraín Barradas y Rafael Rodríguez. Traducción de Carmen Lilianne Marín. Río Piedras, P.R.: Ediciones Huracán, 1980. 166 p.

Antología de 20 poetas nace de "una doble necesidad, estética y moral: dar a conocer, especialmente entre los puertorriqueños insulares, la labor poética de sus compatriotas que residen en los EE.UU., para de esa forma romper el aislamiento que domina las relaciones entre estas dos ramas de nuestro pueblo." [ER]

5629 Inventing a word: an anthology of twentieth-century Puerto Rican poetry. Edited by Julio Marzán. New York: Columbia University Press in association with the Center for Inter-American Relations, 1980. 181 p.

Util muestrario de 26 poetas cuya obra proviene de dos tradiciones: hispana lírica de fuertes lazos europeos; y puertorriqueña criolla, de evidente trasfondo separatista y visión antipoética del presente y futuro isleño. [ER]

5630 Meridiano 70: poesía social dominicana, siglo XX. Selección de Mercedes Santos Moray. La Habana: Casa de las Américas, 1978. 280 p. (Colección La honda)

Muestra de 27 poetas, que comprende la década 1920 (de los humildes y el postumismo), 1940 y 1950 (neopostumistas y "sorprendidos") y la década de 1960 (jornadas de abril y sus continuadores). Util compilación, ya reseñada en 1979 por la poeta Soledad Alvarez (ver *HLAS 42:5844*), que contiene principales manifiestos y documentos teóricos sobre poesía dominicana del presente siglo. [ER]

5631 Muchachos desnudos bajo el arcoiris de fuego: 11 jóvenes poetas latino-

americanos. Antologados por Roberto Bolaño. Presentación de Efraín Huerta. Prólogo de Miguel Donoso Pareja. México: Editorial Extemporáneos, 1979. 189 p. (Poesía Extemporáneos; 20)

Once representantes de la poesía hispanoamericana reciente se abocan a los temas tradicionales—amor, dolor, protesta y muerte—, experimentando con nuevas formas y buscando acentos nuevos. En el prólogo, Donoso Pareja (*Poesía rebelde de América*, 1971) los sitúa en la vertiente de tres movimientos renovadores: el "nadaísmo" colombiano, los "tzántzicos" ecuatorianos, y el movimiento "Hora Zero" peruano. [HMR]

5632 La novísima poesía latinoamericana. Compilado por Jorge Boccanera. 2. ed. México: Editores Mexicanos Unidos, 1980. 310 p.; bibl.

Boccanera, que ya ha colaborado en otras selecciones poéticas (ver *HLAS 42: 5657* y *HLAS 42:5667*), recoge en esta antología breves muestras de 118 poetas iberoamericanos nacidos después de 1940 y cuya obra se difunde en el período 1965–80. Introducción bosqueja actividad y tendencias poéticas de cada país, incluyendo Brasil y Puerto Rico. [HMR]

5633 O'Hara, Edgar. Siete poetas chilenos. Lima: Ruray, 1979. 46 p. (Poesía)

Libro dirigido a lectores peruanos, sobre poetas chilenos "reunidos más que nada por el simple gusto del compilador, sumado al azar de los viajes y a la amistad surgida en los encuentros fortuitos," según el poeta limeño O'Hara, que prologa la selección explicando y celebrando su vínculo personal con los autores incluidos: Pablo de Rokha, Gonzalo Rojas, Enrique Lihn, Pedro Lastra, Hernán Valdés, Oscar Hahn y Manuel Silva. Se cierra con un diálogo entre Lastra y Hahn sobre poesía y lenguaje coloquial, y con un estudio de O'Hara sobre la obra de Lihn. [OH]

5634 Poesía contemporánea: 11 poetas hondureños. v. 1, Clementina Suárez. v. 2, Jorge Federico Travieso. v. 3, Jaime Fontana. v. 4, Antonio José Rivas. v. 5, Pompeyo del Valle. v. 6, Roberto Sosa. v. 7, Oscar Acosta. v. 8, José Adán Castelar. v. 9, Edilberto Cardona Bulnes. v. 10, Rigoberto Paredes. v. 11, José Luis Quesada. Tegucigalpa: Consejo Metropolitano del Distrito Federal, 1978. 1 portfolio; 11 v.; ill.

Antología mínima de poesía hondureña contemporánea. Incluye autores nacidos 1903–48 y, dado el escaso número de poetas y poemas, funciona como somera introducción al quehacer poético en Honduras. [RG]

5635 Poesía de la Independencia. Compilación, prólogo, notas y cronología, Emilio Carilla. Traducciones, Ida Vitale. Caracas: Biblioteca Ayacucho, 1979. 401 p.; bibls. (Biblioteca Ayacucho; 59)

Pulcra antología de poesías compuestas por autores iberoamericanos entre 1800–30. Incluye muestras de 19 hispanoamericanos y siete brasileños (con texto en traducción paralela), precedidas de notas biobibliográficas. En el prólogo, Carilla reseña el marco histórico del período, el panorama literario, géneros y temas preferidos. Una cronología de acontecimientos coetáneos completa el atractivo volumen. [HMR]

5636 Poesía de post guerra/joven poesía dominicana. Prólogo y edición, Andrés L. Mateo. Santo Domingo, R.D.: Editora Alfa y Omega, 1981. 119 p.; ports.

Antología "de postguerra" incluye poetas que publican después de la guerra civil de 1965 y la invasión estadounidense. Voces nuevas surgidas de grupos literarios como El Puño, La Isla, La Máscara y La Antorcha integrados por figuras de la promoción de 1960 (ver items **5761** y **5773**). Los 11 poetas nuevos de calidad varia son: Norberto James Rawlings, Enriquillo Sánchez, Mateo Morrison, Cayo Claudio Espinal, Alexis Gómez, Tony Raful, Enrique Eusebio, Andrés L. Mateo, José Enrique García, Soledad Alvarez, Federico Jovine Bermúdez y José Molinaza. Edición tiene defectos de composición, pero presenta textos notables. [ER]

5637 Poesía panameña contemporánea, 1929–1979. Selección, prólogo y notas de Enrique Jaramillo Levi. México: Liberta-Sumaria, 1980. 339 p.; bibl. (Colección Continente; no. 4)

Dividida en poesía de vanguardia (dos etapas) y poesía contemporánea (dos etapas), la obra comprende una larga nómina de poetas. La selección poemática, exigua en cada caso, no permite formarse una idea concreta de la trayectoria o estilo de los autores incluidos. La antología presenta, no obstante, un ensayo introductorio que delinea el desarrollo del quehacer poético en Panamá, 1929–79. [RG]

5638 Poesía social cubana. Edición de Mirta Aguirre, Salvador Arias, David Chericián, Denia García Ronda, Virgilio López Lemus, Alberto Rocasolano. La Habana: Editorial Letras Cubanas, 1980. 574 p.

Tomo completísimo incluye poemas de 155 autores. Traza trayectoria de una poesía de tema social desde el romanticismo decimonónico, a través de la Guerra de Independencia y décadas republicanas hasta el presente. Junta obra de clásicos como Martí, Heredia y "Plácido," a la de "novísimos," como Soleida Ríos y Alex Fleites. Una de las pocas antologías de poesía cubana que incluye un número bastante representativo de mujeres, desde la Avellaneda a Reina María Rodríguez (ver item **5624**). [ER]

5639 Poesía y vida: antología de poesía cristiana contemporánea. Elsie Romanenghi de Powell et al. Buenos Aires: Ediciones Certeza, 1979. 106 p.

Selección de seis poetas hispanoamericanos contemporáneos—Argentina, El Salvador, Puerto Rico—que contemplan las experiencias de la vida desde una perspectiva cristiana. [HMR]

5640 Poetas modernistas de Nicaragua, 1880–1927. Introducción, selección y notas de Julio Valle-Castillo. Managua: Fondo de Promoción Cultural Banco de América, 1978. 370 p.; bibl. (Serie Literaria; no. 9) (Colección Cultural Banco de América)

Copiosa muestra de la obra de 13 modernistas nicaragüenses entre los que se destacan, claro está, Rubén Darío, Azarías H. Pallais y Alfonso Cortés. Incluye un importante ensayo crítico que amplía el panorama histórico-literario de la poesía nicaragüense, así como detalles bio-bibliográficos sobre cada poeta. Valiosa contribución al estudio de la poesía centroamericana. [RG]

5641 Poetisas mexicanas: siglo XX. Antología, introd. y notas, Héctor Valdés. México: Universidad Nacional Autónoma de México, Dirección General de Publicaciones, 1976. 227 p.; bibl.; index (Nueva biblioteca mexicana; 44)

Reasonably priced and well-done selection of two to 13 poems from: María Enriqueta Camarillo y Roa de Pereyra, Aurora Reyes, Concha Urquiza, Margarita Michelena, Emma Godoy, Griselda Alvarez, Guadalupe Amor, Margarita Paz Paredes, Dolores

Castro, Rosario Castellanos, Enriqueta Ochoa, Thelma Nava, Carmen Alardín, Isabel Fraire, Elva Macías, Elsa Cross, Germaine Calderón. Includes brief biographical and critical introduction to each writer and bibliography of books of verse of all at end of collection. [CM]

5642 Sensemayá: la poesía negra en el mundo hispanohablante: antología. Selección de textos, introducción crítica, vocabulario y bibliografía por Aurora de Albornoz y Julio Rodríguez-Luis. Madrid: Orígenes, 1980. 326 p.; bibl. (Colección Asomante de antología)

Compilación de poesía negra, con división temática y no simplemente geográfica. Incluye resumen completo de orígenes y evolución del género, junto a revisión de la crítica sobre el negrismo, un corto glosario y bibliografía de fuentes primarias y secundarias. De interés especial son la sección sobre precursores y la última. "Permanencia y Transformación de un Viejo Tema." De obligada consulta. [ER]

BOOKS OF VERSE

5643 Adán, Martín [*pseud. for* **Rafael de la Fuente Benavides**]. Obra poética. Edición, prólogo y notas de Ricardo Silva-Santisteban. Fotografía carátula, José Bracamonte. Lima: Fundación del Banco Continental para el Fomento de la Educación y la Cultura, Ediciones Edubanco, 1980. 499 p.; 20 leaves of plates; ill.; ports.

Avance notable en recopilación de poesía de Martín Adán (ver *HLAS 38:6913* y *HLAS 40:7230*), debido esta vez al fervor de Silva-Santisteban. Contiene informaciones detalladas acerca de los numerosos textos inéditos incorporados y distintas versiones de otros, cuyas variantes registra: "Canto a Machu Picchu," *La mano desasida* (p. 153–339), del cual sólo se conocían algunos fragmentos desde 1961. Considerables ampliaciones de sonetos *Mi Darío* (p. 363–381) y *Diario de poeta* (p. 387–469). No indica selección de este título publicada en 1975 (ver *HLAS 40:7110*). Buen aporte para el mejor conocimiento de una obra central en la literatura hispanoamericana contemporánea [PL]

5644 Alberto, Eliseo. Las cosas que yo amo. La Habana: Ediciones Unión, 1977. 57 p.

Segundo libro de un joven autor, prometedor en su lirismo preciso, de notable destello poético, y que ya había publicado *Importará el trueno* en 1975 (ver *HLAS 40:7036*). [ER]

5645 ————. Un instante en cada cosa. La Habana: Ediciones Unión, 1979. 83 p.

En este su tercer libro, el poeta (hijo de Eliseo Diego, ver items **5674** y **5802**) ha ganado ya un timbre seguro de voz y una profundidad delicada, que afirma el amor a la vida en sencillos gestos. [ER]

5646 Alvarez, Griselda. Antología: obras. México: Consorcio Minero Benito Juárez, Peña Colorada, 1976. 137 p.; 6 leaves of plates; ill. (Colección Peña Colorada)

Includes books of verse *Cementerio de pájaros* (1959); *Desierta compañía* (1961); *Letanía erótica para la paz* (1963); *Anatomía superficial* (1967); and *Estación sin nombre* (1972); and prose work *La sombra niña* (1965). Alvarez' sonnets show her admiration for Sor Juana and Salvador Novo. To a powerful erotic vein she joins an exuberance and enthusiasm that one does not often encounter in contemporary literature. [CM]

5647 Amighetti, Francisco. Poesías. Dibujos de Raúl Soldi. San José: Editorial Costa Rica, 1974. 119 p.; ill.

Poesía y pintura se amalgaman en la lírica de Amighetti, uno de los poetas postmodernistas más destacados de Costa Rica. La selección, que recoge lo mejor de su obra, pone de manifiesto el localismo y universalismo de su poesía. [RG]

5648 Arango E., Luis Alfredo. Archivador de pueblos. Guatemala: Editorial Universitaria, 1977. 210 p. (Colección Creación literaria; v. 9)

Arango traza contornos de una geografía poética de Guatemala, en un libro denso, rebosante de vivencia, de búsqueda, de honda palpitación afectiva. [RG]

5649 Arguedas, José María. Temblar; El sueño del pongo. La Habana: Casa de las Américas, 1976. 63, 64 p. (Colección La honda Casa de las Américas Cuba)

Edición bilingüe—quechua-español—de textos poéticos y cuento "El Sueño del Pongo" de J. M. Arguedas, prologada por Alberto Escobar. Volumen tiene el mérito de difundir internacionalmente la importante obra arguediana escrita en quechua. Nota de

Escobar orienta hacia una justa estimativa del ceñido quehacer poético del escritor, que adquiere personería "por la calidad y rango de sus significaciones" e ilumina todo su trabajo literario (ver *HLAS 38:7064*). [PL]

5650 Argüello, Lino. Obras en verso. Introd. y notas de Franco Cerutti. Managua: Fondo de Promoción Cultural, Banco de América, 1976. 178 p.; bibl.; indexes; port. (Serie literario; no. 6) (Colección cultural Banco de América)

Valiosa recopilación que pone al alcance del estudioso la obra en verso de uno de los modernistas nicaragüenses más importantes. [RG]

5651 Arvelo Larriva, Enriqueta. Antología poética. Selección y prefacio de Alfredo Silva Estrada. Caracas: Monte Avila Editores, 1977. 187 p.

Selecciones de poemas de la hermana del conocido poeta Alfredo Arvelo Larriva de la segunda generación de los modernistas de su país. Una de las voces femeninas más auténticas de la literatura venezolana de 1900–50. Prólogo señala la rigorosa y objetiva búsqueda de su propio mundo espiritual (ver item **5652**). [BTO]

5652 ———. Poesías. Selección, prólogo y notas de Carmen Mannarino. Caracas: Dirección de Cultura, Universidad Central de Venezuela, 1979. 214 p.; bibl. (Colección Letras de Venezuela: Serie Poesía; 64)

Prólogo presenta una concisa visión de la poetisa y su obra. Se incluyen los dos volúmenes *Poemas de una pena* y *Canto de recuento*; selecciones de *El cristal nervioso*, *Voz aislada*, *Mandato del canto* y *Poemas perseverantes*; y 15 composiciones publicadas en periódicos. Poesía a veces hermética sobre la búsqueda del ser humano en su esencia, manifiesta una angustia sublimada libre de sentimentalismo (ver item **5651**). [BTO]

5653 Avilés, Alejandro. Don del viento. Presentación, Raúl Navarrete, Joaquín Antonio Peñalosa. México: Editorial Club Primera Plana, between 1977 and 1980. 99 p.; ill.

Simple, direct poems on human emotions, the dignity of peasants, faith and the beauties of nature. Avilés' earlier books of poetry are *Madura soledad* (1948), *Libro de Eva* (1959) and *Los claros días* (1975). [CM]

5654 Belli, Carlos Germán. En alabanza del bolo alimenticio. México: Premia Editora, 1979. 80 p. (Libros del bicho; 2)

Además de la serie titulada "El Libro de los Nones" primera sección de este volumen adelantada en ¡*Oh Hada Cibernética!* (Caracas: 1971)—aparecen aquí poemas de los últimos 10 años. Se confirma la excepcional maestría y originalidad con que Belli realiza una compleja experiencia intertextual de fusiones de lenguajes y modalidades expresivas provenientes de distantes espacios literarios: una alianza del rigor constructivo de la poesía tradicional y de la audacia y libertad imaginativas propiciadas por la vanguardia. En este fascinante territorio verbal, Belli profundiza una indagación iluminadora de la naturaleza misma de la poesía. [PL]

5655 Bello, Andrés. Silvas americanas y otros poemas. Barcelona: Ramón Sopena, 1978. 204 p. (Biblioteca Sopena; 731)

Otra edición popular cuyo criterio de selección se basa en gustos personales que ni alude a notas y revisiones del propio Bello a sus "Silvas." Incluye cuadro sinóptico sobre la vida de Bello y acontecimientos literarios e históricos más importantes. [BTO]

5656 Blanco, Alberto. Giros de faros. México: Fondo de Cultura Económica, 1979. 124 p. (Colección Letras mexicanas)

Young Mexican writes moving and sensitive verse on a number of topics. In deceptively simple language and imagery, Blanco links scenes from the world of nature to meditations on the most serious issues of man (e.g., death and loneliness in "Un Escéptico Noé"). [CM]

5657 ———. El largo camino hacia ti. México: Universidad Nacional Autónoma de México, 1980. 60 p. (Colección Cuadernos de poesía)

Consists of 52 poems in prose describing a journey that is both outward and inward, movement toward another and illumination of the self. At moments, such as the last poem, the work is suggestive of a spiritual voyage as well. Blanco shows a wealth of talent as he creates a book quite different from his earlier *Giros de faros* (see item **5656**). [CM]

5658 Bobes León, Marilyn. La aguja en el pajar. Diseño y cubierta, Darío Mora.

La Habana: Unión de Escritores y Artistas de Cuba, 1979. 49 p. (Colección David)

Colección que reúne los mejores poemas de una joven autora, premiada desde 1977 por su contribución al Concurso "13 de marzo" (ver *HLAS 42:5650*). Libro distinguido con el Premio David de la Unión de Escritores y Artistas de Cuba en 1979 contiene textos de palabra lúcida y sensible, algunos decididamente feministas (ver item 5624). [ER]

5659 Bonifaz Nuño, Rubén. De otro modo lo mismo. México: Fondo de Cultura Económica, 1979. 471 p. (Letras mexicanas)

Well-done anthology of works of this important contemporary of Jaime García Terrés, Rosario Castellanos and Jaime Sabines. Includes published poetry from early *La muerte del ángel* (1945) to mature verse of *Fuego de pobres* (1961), *Algunos poemas no coleccionados* (1962–65), *Siete de espadas* (1966), *El ala del tigre* (1969) and *La flama en el espejo* (1971). Contains previously unpublished poems written between 1945–65. Valuable edition. [CM]

5660 Borrero, Juana. Poesías y cartas. Ordenación, prólogo y notas a cargo de Fina García Marruz y Cintio Vitier. La Habana: Editorial Arte y Literatura, 1978. 304 p.; bibl.; ill.

Nueva edición de la obra de una de las más complejas y trágicas figuras de la lírica cubana, que añade 16 cartas inéditas el *Epistolario* y reúne sus *Rimas* en un volumen completo y coherente (ver *HLAS 40:7192*). Inspirado ensayo introductorio de García Marruz. [ER]

5661 Boullosa, Carmen. Ingobernable. México: Universidad Nacional Autónoma de México, 1979. 77 p. (Colección Cuadernos de poesía)

Poetry of many tones. Sometimes the strange and fantastic dominates, as in "Ingle de Piedra;" elsewhere passion, silence and isolation are her principal themes, with death always hovering in the background. This is Boullosa's third book; others are *El hilo olvida* (1978) and *La memoria vacía* (1978), second of which is reprinted as final section of this volume. [CM]

5662 Brannon de Samayoa, Carmen. Claudia Lars, sus mejores poemas. Selección y nota preliminar de David Escobar Galindo.

San Salvador: Ministerio de Educación, Dirección de Publicaciones, 1976. 266 p. (Colección Poesía; v. 33)

Excelente antología que hace asequible el verso de una de las más grandes cantoras de América. Selección incluye poemas de cada uno de sus libros, dando así una visión clara de su desarrollo poético. [RG]

5663 Campos, Marco Antonio. Una seña en la sepultura, 1974–1977. México: Coordinación de Humanidades, Universidad Nacional Autónoma de México, 1978. 36 p.

Collection of poems in verse and in prose, concerns of which are many: sadness, exile, frustration at loss of the past, anger at the present. Inspiration for much of the book comes from France, Italy and Greece. [CM]

5664 Cardenal, Ernesto. Poesía de uso: antología 1949–1978. Introd. de Joaquín Marta Sosa. Selección de Ernesto Cardenal y Joaquín Marta Sosa. Buenos Aires: El Cid Editor, 1979. 387 p. (Colección Poesía mayor)

Recopilación más completa de la poesía de Cardenal publicada hasta el momento. El volumen, organizado con criterio estrictamente cronológico, presenta la obra escrita 1949–78, dando buena muestra del contenido de los libros publicados entre esas fechas. Recoge, además, poemas inéditos o no publicados en libro. [RG]

5665 Casal, Lourdes. Palabras juntan revolución. La Habana: Ediciones Casa de las Américas, 1981. 112 p.

Libro sorprendente y conmovedor, de una autora cubana emigrada fallecida en 1981, quien se distinguió por su vigorosa actividad intelectual y política. Su poesía se nutre de distancia y de nostalgia, y se crece en la reflexión desde y sobre el destierro. [ER]

5666 Cobo Borda, Juan Gustavo. Ofrenda en el altar del bolero. Caracas: Monte Avila Editores, 1981. 59 p. (Colección Altazor)

Selección para lectores venezolanos de los mejores poemas del ensayista, antólogo y crítico colombiano. Cobo Borda manifiesta gran claridad idiomática así como imágenes e ideas originales. La madurez y profundidad del arte poético de este joven escritor son deslumbrantes. [BTO]

5667 ———. Salón de té. Bogotá: Subdirección de Comunicaciones Culturales,

División de Publicaciones, Biblioteca Colombiana de Cultura, 1979. 77 p. (Colección Autores nacionales; 43)

Poesía de tono irónico y sarcástico presenta imágenes tiernas pero pesimistas que expresan las profundas contradicciones de la vida. El volumen contiene 32 poemas, algunos ya editados. [BTO]

5668 Contreras, Raúl. Niebla. Lydia Nogales [*pseud.*] 2. ed. San Salvador: Ministerio de Educación, Dirección de Publicaciones, 1977. 133 p. (Colección Poesía/Dirección de Publicaciones del Ministerio de Educación; v. 38)

Contreras se desdobla en Nogales y, a través de la creación de un cuerpo poemático, consigue configurar los contornos de un yo lírico y de una expresión poética. Publicado originalmente en 1947. [RG]

5669 Coronil Hartmann, Alfredo. Trabajos del amor y de la muerte: poemas. Caracas: Editorial Atenco de Caracas, 1979. 68 p. (Colección Poesía venezolana contemporánea)

Poeta cuya producción se hallaba hasta ahora esparcida, se adueña con esta colección de poemas de su voz más madura y profunda. Consciente búsqueda del significado de los temas del amor, odio, y del olvido. Para el poeta venezolano, el amor, y el arte hacen soportable la soledad de la vida. [BTO]

5670 Cortazar, Enrique. Otras cosas y el otoño. México: Editorial Diana, 1979. 148 p.

Cortázar explores epistemological matters, the nature of time, solitude and sadness, friendship and love in a sensitive and thoughtful series of poems written 1976–77. His language, at some moments prosaic ("Hay Días"), is at others one of striking imagery. Experimentation with verse patterns is reminiscent of later works of Octavio Paz. Several poems have sociopolitical themes: need for revolution, Allende and Chile, Che Guevara. [CM]

5671 Cortés, Alfonso. Poemas. Selección e introd. de Ernesto Cardenal. Ciudad Universitaria, San José: Editorial Universitaria Centroamericana, 1970. 139 p. (Colección Séptimo día)

Ernesto Cardenal selecciona 30 de los mejores poemas de Cortés, estableciendo claramente el alto valor literario de este modernista nicaragüense. [RG]

5672 Crespo, Luis Alberto. Resolana. Portada, Victor Viano. Caracas: Monte Avila Editores, 1980. 60 p. (Colección Altazor)

Esotéricos y difíciles, poemas sobre el significado de un país fantasmagórico y espectral donde se sufre privación y ausencia. Voz hermética deslumbra y ciega al lector en cuanto al sentido asignado a ideas e imágenes. [BTO]

5673 Dauajare Torres, Félix. Contraataque. Portada, Ariel Hernández. México: Ediciones Tierra Adentro, 1979. 58 p. (Serie Taller)

Previously published works: *De tu mar y de tu sueño* (1952), *Definiciones* (1960), *Cuarta dimensión* (1963), *El que domina en la aurora* (1964) and *La razón de la noche* (1965). First pages of *Contraataque* meditate on modern life (Marx, astronauts, Vietnam) and then reassert the value of the past (music of the spheres, man's relation to the earth). In later pages focus shifts to human isolation and ruptures that modern existence imposes on all. While poetry is admirable, edition's quality is poor, with several blank pages and some poems appearing twice. [CM]

5674 Diego, Eliseo. La casa del pan. La Habana: Editorial Letras Cubanas, 1978. 37 p. (Colección Mínima poesía; no. 17)

Breviario poético incluye una muestra acertada del poeta del grupo de *Orígenes* y lo perfila en su nítida visión cotidiana de objetos y percepciones, mostrando su forma fluida, a veces entre verso y prosa. Continúa su extensa obra poética posterior a *Nombrar las cosas* (1977) (ver HLAS 40:7066). [ER]

5675 Dorfman, Ariel. Pruebas al canto. México: Editorial Nueva Imagen, 1980. 155 p. (Serie Literatura)

Serie de poemas organizados en cinco partes, dos prólogos y un epílogo, centrados en situaciones derivadas del golpe militar chileno de 1973. Si bien es loable el propósito del autor de no permanecer indiferente ante las dimensiones de esa tragedia, no lo son los textos, en cambio, como logros poéticos. [OH]

5676 Echeverri Mejía, Oscar. Las cuatro estaciones: poemas, 1963–1964. Las ocho ilustraciones son originales de Alberto Soto. Bogotá: Instituto Caro y Cuervo, 1980.

105 p.; 8 leaves of plates; ill. (Serie La Granada entreabierta; 26)

Delicada poesía de los sentimientos cotidianos. Cuidadosa presentación con un prólogo de Lino Gil Jaramillo que cita la opinión de Ortega y Gasset sobre Azorín y "los primores de lo vulgar." Algunos poemas carecen de originalidad. [BTO]

5677 Escobar Galindo, David. El corazón de cuatro espejos. San Salvador: Ministerio de Educación, Dirección de Publicaciones, 1976. 334 p.; port. (Colección Poesía; v. 34)

Recoge poemas escritos 1971–73, algunos publicados con anterioridad en *Destino manifiesto* (1972), *Vigilia memorable* (1972) y *El despertar del viento* (1972). Registran una multiplicidad de voces con mezcla de formas libres y tradicionales, marcado todo por una robusta voluntad de estilo. [RG]

5678 ———. Primera antología: poemas. Barcelona: Rondas, 1977. 141 p.; ill.

Primera selección de poemas que incorpora material escrito y publicado 1968–75. Exterioriza no sólo la trayectoria que ha venido siguiendo el poeta, sino la alta calidad de producción de cada etapa creadora. [RG]

5679 Fernández Retamar, Roberto. Juana y otros poemas personales. Managua: Ministerio de Cultura, 1981. 66 p. (Colección Premio Latinoamericano Rubén Darío; 1)

Poemario último de un sobresaliente escritor, quizás más reconocido como ensayista, pero de sólida y continuada obra poética, en la cual se distingue por su sutil emotividad, su lirismo de lenguaje llano y preciso, su fina percepción de las cosas y las figuras. El jurado del premio (formado por Efraín Huerta, Ernesto Mejía Sánchez y Thelma Nava) distingue esta colección del poeta cubano por su madurez y originalidad. El libro está encabezado por un luminoso texto dedicado a Sor Juana. [ER]

5680 Ferrari, Américo. Tierra desterrada. Lima: Ediciones Arybalo, 1981. 55 p. (Las Musas inquietantes; 6)

El autor—mejor conocido por su actividad crítica y especialmente por su importante libro sobre Vallejo (1974)—es poeta de trayectoria muy sostenida aunque algo secreta, por las limitaciones que impone una publicación minoritaria. *Tierra desterrada* permitirá ahora valorar diversas exploraciones de Ferrari, tanto en el plano del

lenguaje como en el aspecto formal. Los sonetos de la primera parte del libro y los poemas de temple elegíaco o reflexivo de la segunda, alcanzan una intensidad considerable. [PL]

5681 Fiallo, Fabio. Obras completas. v. 1, La canción de una vida. v. 2, Cuentos frágiles. v. 3, Nacionalismo auténtico. v. 4, Estudios acerca de su vida y de sus obras. Santo Domingo: Editora de Santo Domingo, 1980. 4 v.; bibl.; ill. (Colección de cultura dominicana; 33)

Interesantísima edición que recopila la obra del modernista dominicano, su libro *Cantaba el ruiseñor*, con comentario de Rubén Darío aparecido originalmente en *El Fígaro* (La Habana, 1911). Obra reminiscente de Martí (*Versos sencillos*) y de Gutiérrez Nájera. Incluye tres estudios sobre Fiallo: Manuel Díaz Rodríguez "Cantaba el Ruiseñor;" Ana María Garasino "La Canción de una Vida;" Camila Henríquez Ureña "Fabio Fiallo: el Poeta del Amor." Edición de lujo rinde homenaje a la repatriación de los restos del poeta desde La Habana (m. 1942). De interés a los estudiosos del modernismo en las Antillas. [ER]

5682 García Terrés, Jaime. Corre la voz. México: J. Mortiz, 1980. 131 p. (Las Dos orillas)

Elegant poetry ranges over centuries and cultures, moving from Giordano Bruno to Robert Lowell. Prefacing the text are verses from the *Paradiso*, and Dante is a constant presence. Continuing concerns are epistemological and existential; elsewhere García Terrés meditates as well on human ethics, history of man and nature of art. He has been a significant figure in the Mexican literary world since his first book of verse, *El hermano menor* (1953). [CM]

5683 Garnier, Leonor. Los sueños recobrados. San José: Editorial Costa Rica, 1976. 88 p.

Al definir su posición ante el individuo y ante la sociedad, Garnier va definiendo asimismo su yo lírico, en un lenguaje cincelado y sencillo en el que se transparentan auténticas vivencias y angustias. [RG]

5684 Gatón Arce, Freddy. Son guerras y amores. Prólogo de Ramón Francisco. Ilustraciones de José Vela Zanetti. Santo Domingo: Editora Taller, 1980. 107 p.; ill.

Obra culminante de un miembro de la

"poesía sorprendida," quien se inició como surrealista en *Vlía* (1944), y publicó después *La leyenda de la muchacha* (1962) y *Magino Quezada* (1966). Aquí se adentra en la historia dominicana, y entrega visiones concretas de una tierra, un pasado y un futuro. Ecos de Cardenal y de Neruda, con fuertes matices intermitentes del discurso bíblico. [ER]

5685 Geoffroy Rivas, Pedro. Versos. San Salvador: Ministerio de Educación, Dirección de Publicaciones, 1978. 50 leaves.

Elaboración de un agregado poéticomitológico a imitación de los patrones de la poesía nahua. El libro fue publicado originalmente en 1965 bajo el título de *Yulcuicat*. [RG]

5686 Gerbasi, Vicente. Antología poética, 1943–1978. 2. ed. aum. Caracas: Monte Avila Editores, 1980. 366 p. (Colección Altazor)

Segunda edición (la. 1970) aumentada de antología de poemas intensos y de excelente técnica. Añade poemas de *Retumba como un sótano del cielo* (1977) y otros inéditos. Apéndice incluye "Una Posición Frente a la Poesía de Vicente Gerbasi" (p. 353–366) por el poeta venezolano Francisco Pérez Perdomo, que caracteriza el verso de Gerbasi como derivativo hasta 1940, momento, en que llega a la madurez poética. [BTO]

5687 Giordano, Jaime. Eres leyenda. New York: Editorial El Maitén, 1981. 1 v. (Cuadernos de poesía y prosa de América y España)

Libro constituido por un solo y extenso poema de amor articulado en varias secuencias, que oscilan entre los recuerdos de un pasado recurrente, rememorado como tal, y la actualización de ese pasado. Como la mujer amada y el país nativo del hablante se confunden en el poema, la separación amorosa es vivida como doble exilio. A diferencia de otros poemas largos recientes, que se caracterizan por la monotonía resultante de la adición mecánica de versos, Giordano maneja con habilidad los juegos de clímax y anticlímax, y crea una atmósfera emocional que consigue envolver eficazmente al lector. [OH]

5688 Gómez, Ana Ilce. Las ceremonias del silencio. Managua: Ediciones El Pez y la Serpiente, 1975. 113 p. (Colección Ahora; no. 2)

Ana Ilce elabora imágenes finas, depuradas, de engañosa sencillez: su lirismo, especial dentro de la poesía nicaragüense, se adentra en los recodos del alma femenina y descubre esencias primigenias. [RG]

5689 González Cosío Díaz, Arturo. Poemas. México: Coordinación de Humanidades, Dirección General de Publicaciones, Universidad Nacional Autónoma de México, 1978. 51 p. (Colección Poemas y ensayos)

In the 1950s González Cosío was a member of the same group as Marco Antonio Montes de Oca and Eduardo Lizalde. This book, however, with its simple vocabulary and imagery is very different from recent works of the other two poets. One finds as major topics a diaphanous praise of nature and gentle expressions of love. [CM]

5690 González de León, Ulalume. Plagio II. México: Joaquín Mortiz, 1980. 151 p. (Colección Las dos orillas)

Eclectic nature of work immediately captures reader's attention. One finds influences of many other poets (Robert Graves, Ronsard, Schlegel, Swinburne, Mariano Brull, Charles Tomlinson): González de León mentions in the epilogue that she has translated more than 50 poets in four languages. Her subjects are sometimes serious—our emotions, purposes, identity—and sometimes playful, as in "Nonsense, Canciones, Juegos," the second part of the collection. The use of language is striking, with brilliant and memorable images. Highly recommended. [CM]

5691 González Prada, Manuel. Cantos del otro siglo. Prólogo y notas de Luis Alberto Sánchez. Lima: Universidad Nacional Mayor de San Marcos, Dirección Universitaria de Biblioteca y Publicaciones, 1979. 200 p.

Poemas de los dos últimos cuadernos manuscritos de González Prada, recibidos por L. A. Sánchez junto con otros materiales inéditos: *Letrillas* (ver *HLAS 40:7079*) y *Ortometría*. El compilador data la escritura de estos poemas 1867–1900, considerando que éste fue un período de ensayo y experimentación con distintos tipos de versos, de formas y combinaciones métricas (redondillas, sonetos, rondeles, estornelos, trioletes, letrillas, epigramas). Es en este aspecto donde reside la importancia de la colección, presentada sin embargo con una ligereza crítica que reduce sensiblemente su interés. [PL]

5692 Hahn, Oscar. Mal de amor. Ilustraciones de Mario Toral. Santiago: Ediciones Ganymedes, 1981. 94 p.; ill.

Nuevo hito en la importante obra de Hahn, poeta que no deja de inquietar con su decidida vocación por lo que podría describirse como voluntad de cambio dentro de la permanencia: cuando parecía establecido en la región imaginaria que logró delimitar con singular maestría en *Arte de morir* (1977, ver *HLAS 40:7088* y *HLAS 42:5763*), en *Mal de amor* se desplaza hacia zonas que en el libro anterior se vislumbraban. Ambos manifiestan la esencialidad de la empresa de Hahn, experiencia de conciliación (conflictiva) de los contrarios: Tánatos y Eros, presencias fundantes de un universo verbal, unido por las peculiaridades de un fraseo sui generis—pródigo en sorpresas y felicidades para el lector—y por la destreza con que se enmascara, se distancia o se corporiza la voz poética. En *Mal de amor* es un fantasma que ocupa los desolados espacios de su propia escritura, gestualizando el lamento, la reflexión y la transgresión con una intensidad pocas veces conseguida en la poesía amorosa hispanoamericana. [PL]

5693 Herrera, Georgina. Granos de sol y luna. La Habana: Ediciones Unión, 1978. 54 p.

Obra recia y delicada a la vez, de una poeta de mérito que merece ser reconocida (ver item **5624**). Había publicado antes los poemarios *G.H.* (1962) y *Gentes y cosas* (1974). Este pequeño volumen contiene textos notables en su manejo del lenguaje y en su certera expresión de vivencias. Los dos primeros premios "Julián del Casal" en 1977 correspondieron así a dos excelentes poetas; la otra ganadora fue Minerva Salado (ver *HLAS 42:5825*). [ER]

5694 Huerta, Efraín. Transa poética. México: Ediciones Era, 1980. 132 p. (Biblioteca Era)

Huerta (1914–82), one of the most important poets of *Taller*, returns to many favorite themes: friendship, political issues, the nature of poetry, love and passion, urban life. The tone is either witty and cynical or gentle. Typical of the former is "Manifesto Nalgaísta / Aleluya Cocodrilos Sexuales Aleluya" and of the latter "Río San Lorenzo" and "Siempre Mía." Dominant in "El Tajín," a remarkable poem, is the mythical past that lives on in the present. While Huerta's *poesía comprometida* influenced many of Mexico's younger writers, this work is a lively example of the breadth of his subject matter. [CM]

5695 Jaramillo, Carlos Eduardo. Tralfamadore. Quito: Casa de la Cultura Ecuatoriana Núcleo del Guayas, 1977. 107 p. (Colección Letras del Ecuador; 51)

Breve nota inicial advierte que Jaramillo se orienta hacia una "filosofía del vivir más bien optimista, que busca o ha encontrado la vertiente secreta del júbilo" (p. 5). En relación con el escepticismo de sus primeros textos, el cambio es perceptible en la tonalidad cordial de esta poesía, que practica en esa dirección un ensayo con las posibilidades objetivadoras del habla cotidiana (ver *HLAS 40:7097–7098* y *HLAS 42:5664*). [PL]

5696 Jobet, Jorge. Sonetos de afecto y pensamiento. Santiago: Editorial Nascimento, 1979. 2 v.

Un buen soneto trasciende siempre su estructura formal, para instalarse en los abiertos dominios de la poesía. Los de Jorge Jobet permanecen enclaustrados en sus frágiles arquitecturas vacías, evidenciando sus limitaciones: rima ripiosa, ritmo de metrónomo, retórica fosilizada. [OH]

5697 Lerín, Manuel. Contra reloj. México: B. Costa-Amic Editor, 1978. 124 p.; bibl.

One finds echoes of Carlos Pellicer and the early works of Octavio Paz in the poetry of Manuel Lerín. His subjects are the beauties of the world, nature, love, art, certain figures of Mexican history. Poems, in which Lerín experiments with a variety of verse forms, were written between 1940–late 70s. [CM]

5698 Liscano Velutini, Juan. Rayo que al alcanzarme: 1974–1976. Caracas: Monte Avila Editores, 1978. 95 p. (Colección Altazor)

Poemas de profunda sensibilidad y disciplina rigurosa. Poeta reservado en su expresión de la vida aprisionada por el tiempo. Indica con brillante economía que sólo en el amor puede uno escapar de la caducidad y la muerte. [BTO]

5699 López Acuña, Daniel. Tú llegarás a mi ciudad vacía. México: Premia Editora, 1979. 90 p. (Libros del bicho; 7)

López Acuña achieves a fine blend of the personal and present with the mythical and past in poems such as "Viaje a Oaxaca." Other concerns are loneliness, love and passion, time and history. In "Edén Perdido," on Chapultepec, he takes up a theme common to many contemporary Mexican writers (Paz, Fuentes, Castellanos, Fernando del Paso). Of book's seven sections best are "Rudimentos" and "Día de Muertos," a sustained meditation on death. [CM]

5700 López Vallecillos, Italo. Inventario de soledad. San Salvador: Ministerio de Educación, Dirección de Publicaciones, 1977. 77 p. (Colección Poesía; v. 35)

Con sencillez aparente, López Vallecillos se adentra en el misterio de lo cotidiano y de lo eterno, abocetando, en el itinerario, los contornos de la incertidumbre. Es una entrega más de uno de los valores de la lírica salvadoreña. [RG]

5701 Manzano, Sonia. La semana que no tiene jueves. Guayaquil: Casa de la Cultura Ecuatoriana, Núcleo del Guayas, 1978. 106 p. (Colección Letras del Ecuador; 66)

Libro en cierto modo antológico, que agrega a los nuevos poemas una muestra de publicaciones anteriores: *El nudo y el trino* (1972), *Casi siempre las tardes* (1974) y *La gota en el cráneo* (1976). La actitud lúdica y el despliegue irónico de las situaciones imaginadas encubren una dimensión corrosiva; pero la eficacia de este discurso desenfadado, a veces tributario de la antipoesía, suele diluirse cuando se desliza hacia la mera ingeniosidad. [PL]

5702 La Margarita emocionante (seis poetas). Compilación y prólogo, Horacio Castellanos Moya. San Salvador: Editorial Universitaria, 1979. 103 p.; bibl. (Colección Contemporáneos)

Importante muestra de la poesía más joven de El Salvador. Seis poetas (nacidos 1954–57) dan buen indicio de oficio poético, en selecciones en que se transparenta ya una visión poética de la realidad así como una toma de conciencia, y de postura, ante la coyuntura histórica [RG]

5703 Marrufo, F. En la mula del rey David. Mérida, Yucatán, México: Universidad de Yucatán, 1979. 87 p.

Although Marrufo's experiments with language and form produce uneven results,

he is always of interest with his wit and wide choice of topics. Book's final section on folksongs is less successful. [CM]

5704 Mejía Sánchez, Ernesto. Recolección a mediodía. Portada, Ricardo Martínez de Hoyos. Dibujo, Alvaro Gutiérrez. México: J. Mortiz, 1980. 254 p.; ill. (Biblioteca paralela)

Mejía Sánchez hace entrega, en ordenación personal, de su obra poética escrita entre 1947–80. Recopilación valiosa para el conocimiento de uno de los mayores exponentes de la generación del 1940 en Nicaragua. [RG]

5705 Mendoza, Rafael. Los derechos humanos. Ilustraciones de Aleph. 2a ed. corr. San Salvador: Editorial Universitaria de El Salvador, 1980. 141 p.; ill. (Colección Literatura / EU)

Denuncia abierta, sistemática del quebrantamiento de los derechos humanos en El Salvador, en poemas de sátira acre y directa. [RG]

5706 Molina, Juan Ramón. Tierras, mares y cielos. Selección, introd. y notas de Julio Escoto. Ciudad Universitaria Rodrigo Facio, Costa Rica: Editorial Universitaria Centroamericana, 1977. 238 p.; bibl. (Colección Aula)

Con la publicación de este volumen se da a conocer la obra de uno de las más destacados poetas modernistas centroamericanos. El estudio de la poesía de Molina se hace esencial para establecer una valorización justa del modernismo en la región. [RG]

5707 Montalbetti Solari, Mario. Perro negro. 31 poemas. Lima: Ediciones Arybalo, 1978. 56 p.

Notable tratamiento del tema del desamor realizado por Montalbetti (n. 1953). Las singulares variaciones que constituyen sus textos se despliegan en una dimensión lúdica, casi siempre bien controlada. El recurso a la intertextualidad es otra vía productiva: lecturas diversas—literatura latina, budismo Zen—son procesadas irónicamente en ciertas zonas de este primer libro algo más que promisorio. [PL]

5708 Montejo, Eugenio. Terredad. Portada, Víctor Viano. Caracas: Monte Avila Editores, 1978. 70 p. (Colección Altazor)

Intensos poemas espirituales en los que el poeta acepta las limitaciones de la vida. En otros, cree ser su propio enemigo y vislumbra la angustia. [BTO]

5709 Montemayor, Carlos. Abril, y otros poemas. México: Fondo de Cultura Económica, 1979. 95 p. (Letras mexicanas)

Book divided into five sections, first and last of which develop same personal themes as *Las armas del viento* (see item **5710**) while limiting social comments. Result is more successful verse expressed in an elegant style—intimate poems on the small joys of life, Mexico City, love, sharing of the community, cycles of existence. Middle sections, one of which is an elegy to Tlatelolco (1968), are uneven. [CM]

5710 ———. Las armas del viento. México: Hiperión, 1977. 69 p.

Nine long poems that treat personal and sociopolitical concerns. [CM]

5711 Morejón, Nancy. Parajes de una época. La Habana: Editorial Letras Cubanas, 1979. 27 p. (Colección Mínima poesía; 22)

Otro ejemplo de la popular colección de breviarios poéticos, que compendian y popularizan la obra tanto de consagrados como de noveles. Este tomito entrega una muestra de la reconocida poeta, cuyo poema "Mujer Negra" ha dado la vuelta al mundo; se continúa así una obra de conciencia y belleza, comenzada desde 1962 con *Mutismo*, y continuada por *Amor, ciudad atribuida* (1964) y *Richard trajo su flauta* (1967, ver *HLAS 42: 5869*) [ER]

5712 Moro, César [pseud. for **Alfredo Quispez Asín**]. Obra poética. Prefacio de André Coyné. Edición, prólogo y notas de Ricardo Silva-Santisteban. Lima: Instituto Nacional de Cultura, 1980. 1 v.

Recopila textos que el poeta organizó en: *La tortuga ecuestre, Le château de grisou, Lettre d'amour, Pierre des soleils, Amour à mort, Trafalgar Square*, más algunas *Cartas* y una sección de "Ultimos Poemas." El trabajo de Silva-Santisteban permite un acceso más amplio a la poesía de Moro, gracias a la publicación bilingüe de su obra escrita en francés, y dispone el camino para una edición totalizadora, que habrá de recoger sus muchas páginas todavía inéditas. Util bibliografía de y sobre Moro, preparada por M. A. Rodríguez Rea (ver items **5713** y **5783**, y *HLAS 42: 6642*). [PL]

5713 ———. La tortuga ecuestre y otros textos. Edición de Julio Ortega. Caracas:

Monte Avila Editores, 1976. 194 p. (Colección Altazor)

Muestra antológica de prosa y poesía (ver item **5712** y *HLAS 42: 6642*) que pone al alcance de un público mayor la singular producción de César Moro (1903–56). Junto a los esfuerzos tempranos de André Coyné (ver item **5783**)—a quien se debe el conocimiento de numerosos textos inéditos, desde 1957—este trabajo de Ortega es pieza fundamental en una tarea de rescate. Además de poesía escrita en español, Ortega proporciona representativas selecciones de la prosa ("Biografía Peruana" e "Imagen de Proust") y de los poemas franceses, traducidos. En un apartado final se reproducen artículos de A. Coyné, E. A. Westphalen y M. Vargas Llosa, y un poema inédito de E. Molina [PL]

5714 Nandino, Elías. Nocturna palabra. México: Universidad Nacional Autónoma de México, 1976. 134 p. (Colección Poemas y ensayos)

Contains selections from the books *Nocturna suma* (1955), *Nocturno amor* (1958), *Nocturno día* (1959) and *Nocturna palabra* (1960). Contemporary of Gorostiza, Torres Bodet, Villaurrutia and Salvador Novo, Nandino writes a reflective poetry with death, solitude, love, existential anguish and the community of man as his major concerns. Verse forms he uses are largely traditional. [CM]

5715 Negrón Muñoz, Mercedes. Obra poética. Clara Lair [pseud.]. Ordenación, notas y prólogo de Vicente Géigel Polanco. San Juan: Instituto de Cultura Puertorriqueña, 1979. 110 p.

Obra completa de poeta y ensayista conocida como "la Alfonsina Storni de Puerto Rico." Premiada por el Instituto de Cultura Puertorriqueña, su obra gira alrededor de temas de amor, vida y muerte, y revela una visión neorromántica y sentimental expresada en estructuras tradicionales. Recoge su poemario *Arras de cristal* (1937) y el volumen triple *Trópico amargo. Arras de cristal. Mas allá del poniente* (1950), así como varios homenajes a raíz de su muerte en 1973. [ER]

5716 Nogueras, Luis Rogelio. Las quince mil vidas del caminante. La Habana: Ediciones Unión, 1977. 113 p. (Colección Manjuarí/poesía)

Colección recoge poemas de importante autor joven, reconocido desde su primer libro, *Cabeza de zanahoria* (Premio David, 1967), hasta el último, *Imitación de la vida* (Premio Casa de las Américas/poesía, 1981). Los textos presentes, escritos entre 1967–73, evidencian una rica visión, original en su poesía de circunstancia y fuertemente dulce en sus versos de amor. [ER]

5717 O'Hara, Edgar. Contaminado por la sombra del sol. Conciencia 1973–1978. Portada y diagramación de Luis Rebaza S. Lima: Ruray Editores, 1980. 96 p. (Ruray/poesía)

O'Hara actualiza la operación selectiva realizada en *Mientras una tórtola canta en el techo de enfrente* (1979, ver *HLAS 42:5798*), ahora con respecto a ese libro, a *Huevo en el nogal* (1979) y a los poemas inéditos de su "Cuaderno de Viaje." El conjunto no es sin embargo una antología sino una síntesis, que diseña un itinerario escrito como tentativa de autorreconocimiento. Logrado testimonio de ese empeño son los textos de las series finales, particularmente "El Oficio de Persistir." [PL]

5718 Olmedo, José Joaquín de. Obra poética. Quito: Editorial Casa de la Cultura Ecuatoriana, 1977. 275 p. (Colección básica de escritores ecuatorianos; 19)

Edición popular de la poesía de Olmedo, que sigue el texto establecido por el Padre Aurelio Espinosa Pólit en las *Obras completas* publicadas en 1945. Volumen útil para un público general de estudiantes y lectores no especializados, que apreciará la nota informativa de Galo René Pérez (p. 5–14). [PL]

5719 Oraá, Francisco de. Ciudad, ciudad. Diseño y cubierta, Héctor Villaverde. La Habana: Unión de Escritores y Artistas de Cuba, 1979. 60 p.

Este libro premiado, de poesía clara y hermosa, con temas testimoniales o íntimos, constituye una realización poética de madurez. Oraá ya había publicado *Es necesario* (1964), *Por nefas* (1966), *Con figura de gente y en uso de razón* (1968) y *Bodegón de las llamas* (1978, ver *HLAS 42:5799*). [ER]

5720 Orellana, Carlos. Aguas. Lima: Dedalus, 1980. 1 v. (Colección Poesía nueva; 5)

Los 13 poemas de *Aguas* confirman la fidelidad de Orellana a la conducta observada desde su primer libro (ver item **5721**). La exi-

gencia de control es aun más intensa en esta escritura imaginativa e irónica, uno de cuyos méritos principales es el de evitar celosamente las facilidades del artificio. La sobria producción del autor es ya un aporte a la poesía peruana. [PL]

5721 ———. La ciudad va a estallar. Lima: Dedalus, 1979. 1 v. (Colección Poesía nueva; 3)

En este pequeño volumen, como en *Aguas* (ver item **5720**), Orellana (n. 1950) elabora un discurso expresivo novedoso, que revela sus atentas lecturas de los poetas italianos contemporáneos y un buen acercamiento a esas lecciones del rigor. La inquietud metafísica y las preocupaciones que suscita un "paisaje social" e histórico en crisis se manifiestan de manera convincente en esta poesía. Una primera aproximación valorativa, en p. 76–79 del libro de E. O'Hara, *Desde Melibea* (ver item **5771**). [PL]

5722 Othón, Manuel José. Poemas rústicos. Presentación de José Joaquín Blanco. México: Premia Editora, 1979. 152 p.; port. (Libros del bicho; 8)

Inexpensive facsimile reproduction of what many consider the best work of Manuel José Othón (1858–1906). Celebrates an idyllic nature in the well-known "Himno de los Bosques" and "Noche Rústica de Walpurgis." Continuing motif throughout is his strong religious faith. [CM]

5723 Pacheco, José Emilio. Tarde o temprano. México: Fondo de Cultura Económica, 1980. 332 p. (Colección Letras mexicanas)

Selected poems from *Los elementos de la noche* (1958–62); *El reposo del fuego* (1963–64); *No me preguntes cómo pasa el tiempo* (1964–68); *Irás y no volverás* (1969–72); *Islas a la deriva* (1973–75); *Desde entonces* (1975–78); and *Aproximaciones* (1958–78). *Ayer es nunca jamás* (Caracas: Monte Avila Editores, 1978) is another recent anthology of Pacheco's first five books. Poet has reworked here some poems from *Los elementos de la noche* and *El reposo del fuego*, giving them the same conceptual brilliance and forcefulness of later verse. Last section, *Aproximaciones*, is composed of translations from other poets. Together with Marco Antonio Montes de Oca and Gabriel Zaid, also born in the 1930s, Pacheco writes lyrics that dazzle and convince. [CM]

5724 Pardo García, Germán. Himnos de la noche: poemas. México: Editorial Libros de México, 1975. 53 p.

Volumen de 12 sonetos impecables añade otro título a obras (escritas durante 53 años) esmeradamente editadas bajo la propia dirección del poeta. [BTO]

5725 Patán, Federico. Fuego lleno de semillas: poemas de un itinerario. México: Universidad Nacional Autónoma de México, 1980. 58 p. (Colección Cuadernos de poesía)

Gentle history of lost and regained love. Patán offers enough variety of tone and verse forms so that the result is memorable. [CM]

5726 Patiño, Maricruz. La circunstancia pesa. México: Universidad Nacional Autónoma de México, 1979. 97 p. (Colección Cuadernos de poesía)

Patiño writes movingly of the anguish and tedium of life and of the world of neon and bars and even more sensitively of the joys of love and passion. The tone, mood and attitudes are occasionally reminiscent of *onda* literature of the late 1960s. [CM]

5727 Paz Castillo, Fernando. Encuentros. Caracas: Equinoccio, Editorial de la Universidad Simón Bolívar, 1980. 61 p.; port. (Colección Garúa)

Libro póstumo, de un poeta de la generación de 1919, contiene profundas meditaciones sobre la vida y la muerte al acercarse al fin de su existencia. [BTO]

5728 Pellicer, Carlos. Reincidencias. México: Fondo de Cultura Económica, 1978. 157 p. (Letras mexicanas; 117)

Left unfinished at the time of poet's death, volume was organized by others in order to bring together verse of Pellicer's last years. Poems, dated 1966–76, show continuation of temporal and aesthetic concerns of earlier works. Nature, solitude, absent and idealized lover and author's profound Christian faith are other important subjects. Moving self-portraits appear in "Esto Soy" and "Estoy Todo lo Iguana que se Puede." Apparent is Pellicer's gift for striking metaphors, an aspect of his work that has left its mark on many later poets. [CM]

5729 Peralta, Bertalicia. Libro de las fábulas. Panamá: INAC, 1976. 127 p. (Colección múltiple; no. 9. Poesía)

Peralta desnuda el lenguaje y lo reduce a sus elementos esenciales para calar con él la realidad y para hacer reseña de la opresión e injusticia. [RG]

5730 Pérez de Zambrana, Luisa. Antología poética. Selección y prólogo de Sergio Chaple. La Habana: Editorial Arte y Literatura, 1977. 150 p.; bibl. (Biblioteca básica de literatura cubana)

Recopilación que otorga debido lugar a la única mujer, y la más joven, de las cuatro figuras líricas representativas en la segunda generación romántica cubana (los otros poetas son Rafael M. Mendive, José Joaquín Luaces y Clemente Zenea). Obra que rescata a una poeta notable de su época, y que incluye un prólogo esclarecedor, una bibliografía y una cronología. [ER]

5731 Ponce, Manuel. Antología poética. Selección y prólogo de Gabriel Zaid. México: Fondo de Cultura Económica, 1980. 114 p. (Letras mexicanas)

Selections from the works of a poet (b. 1913) who attempts to combine his love of artistic creation and his profound Catholic faith. Included are poems from *Ciclo de vírgenes* (1940); *Misterios para cantar bajo los álamos* (1947); *El jardín increíble*; *Cristo, María* (1962); and *Elegías y teofanías* (1968). [CM]

5732 Rebaza Soraluz, Luis. Hipervivientes (1975–1979). Lima: Ruray Editores, 1981. 70 p. (Poesía/Ruray)

Rebaza profundiza el trabajo poético iniciado con *Población activa* (1978, ver *HLAS 42:5817*), algunas de cuyas piezas integran también este volumen. El autor se propone extender ciertas líneas experimentales del libro anterior, buscando el pasaje de la condensación a la expansión imaginativa. El resultado de su tarea es desigual (los poemas en prosa, por ejemplo, no logran ordenarse en torno a un núcleo intensificador), pero revela una decidida vocación expresiva. [PL]

5733 Ribera Chevremont, Evaristo. Obra poética. Río Piedras: Editorial Universitaria, Universidad de Puerto Rico, 1980. 1 v.; bibl.

Recopilación de uno de los más distinguidos "poetas puros" de Puerto Rico, de obra con trazos vanguardistas. Orden e inclusión de los poemarios fue establecido por el mismo poeta, antes de su muerte. Se reproducen aquí dos útiles apéndices que había preparado Federico de Onís para la *Antología poética (1924–50)* del mismo autor y que apareció en 1957. También se añade una introducción crítica de José Emilio González; "La Poesía de Evaristo Ribera Chevremont," con mínima bibliografía que continúa la de Onís. [ER]

5734 Ríos, Soleida. De pronto abril. La Habana: Ediciones Unión, 1979. 47 p. (Colección David)

Conciso poemario de una autora reconocida ya entre los jóvenes talentos (ver item **5638**). Poesía que tiñe de fina nostalgia la objetividad. [ER]

5735 Riveros, Juan Pablo. Nimia. Poemas en prosa. Santiago: Alfabeta Impresores, 1980. 121 p.

Colección de prosas poéticas impregnadas de ese misterio que proviene del romanticismo alemán y de la *Aurelia* de Gerard de Nerval. Los mundos fundados por los textos se mueven en esa zona que separa la vigilia y el sueño, lo real y lo irreal, gracias al impulso de ciertas frases felices: "Las cosas del mundo están intensamente penetradas por el cielo." *Nimia* representa un sólido aporte al desigual desarrollo del poema en prosa en la literatura chilena. [OH]

5736 Roca, Juan Manuel. Señal de cuervos. Medellín, Colombia: Universidad de Antioquia, 1980. 115 p.; ill.

Poeta joven (n. 1946) y rebelde denuncia la violencia de su país con imágenes gráficas de sordidez y crueldad. Señala la incapacidad de Colombia de comprender su pasado y aprender de él. Otras composiciones son de franca sensualidad. [BTO]

5737 Rojas, Jorge. Obras completas. Madrid: Cultura Hispánica, 1978. 430 p.; 5 leaves (La Encina y el mar; no. 57)

Edición española atractiva pero carente de introducción, referencias bibliográficas, o indicación de criterios de selección. No explica el por qué de muchos cambios (e.g., títulos de poemas y de volúmenes, etc.). Rojas se merece una edición más cuidadosa, fiel a sus originales y crítica (ver item **5738**). [BTO]

5738 ———. Suma poética, 1939–1976. Bogotá: Instituto Colombiano de Cultura, Subdirección de Comunicaciones Culturales, División de Publicaciones, 1977. 511

p.; bibl. (Colección Autores nacionales; 20)

Recopila obra anterior a 1975, inclusive algunas poemas inéditos de Rojas, líder de los piedracielistas. Contiene: *La doncella del agua,* tragedia en dos actos en prosa poética y obra preferida del escritor; ensayos; traducciones de Paul Valéry; testimonios literarios sobre Rojas por amigos, poetas y críticos; y traducciones de sus poemas al italiano, euzkadi, francés e inglés (ver item **5737**). [BTO]

5739 Rosas, Rolando. En alguna parte ojos de mundo. Para decir buen provecho por Carlos Santibáñez. México: Liberta-Sumaria, 1980. 114 p. (Colección Taller; no. 2)

The tone of Rosas' three long poems is reminiscent of Baudelaire's "Spleen" as he writes of death, bitterness and the destructive force of religion. Santibáñez's works are mostly short, similar in tone, concerned with the absurdity of life. Influence of Nicanor Parra's *Antipoemas* is felt throughout. Both writers were born in 1954 and collaborated previously on another volume of poetry, *19 bajo cero* (1979). [CM]

5740 Rose, Juan Gonzalo. Camino real. Lima: Voz de Orden, 1980. 144 p.

Antología parcial, constituída por los libros *Cantos desde lejos* (1957), *Simple canción* (1960) y *Hallazgos y extravíos* (1968), más seis textos poco conocidos que no aparecen en su *Obra poética* (1974, ver *HLAS 40:7147* y *HLAS 42:5921*). Prólogo testimonial y temático de César Lévano. [PL]

5741 Ruiz Dueñas, J. Tierra final. La Paz, B.C.S.: Gobierno del Estado de Baja California Sur; México, D.F.: Federación Editorial Mexicana, 1980. 53 p. (Biblioteca selecta ALFEM; 11)

In his poetry of love and friendship, the sea and the seashore, author shows great promise. [CM]

5742 Saenz, Jaime. Obra poética. Estructuras de lo imaginario en la obra poética de Jaime Saenz, por Blanca Weithüchter. La Paz, Bolivia: Biblioteca del Sesquicentenario de la República, 1975. 436 p. (Biblioteca del Sesquicentenario de la República; 14)

Reúne la totalidad del trabajo poético de Jaime Saenz (n. 1921): *El escalpelo* (1955); *Muerte por el tacto* (1957); *Aniversario de una visión* (1960); *Visitante profundo* (1964);

El frío (1967) y *Recorrer esta distancia* (1973). Aunque esta obra es una de las más significativas y novedosas de la literatura boliviana del siglo XX, su difusión en Hispanoamérica ha sido escasa y ha estado limitada a un círculo de estudiosos de la poesía vinculada al discurso surrealista. Esa y otras lecturas sugiere la tesis de Blanca Wiethüchter (p. 267–425): un examen centrado en las instancias místicas del universo simbólico de Saenz y en su búsqueda de la trascendencia. [PL]

5743 Sánchez Hernani, Enrique. Violencia de sol. Dibujos interiores, Luis Rebaza. Lima: Ruray, 1980. 98 p.; ill. (Poesía/Ruray)

En la última parte del variado libro de Sánchez Hernani (ver *HLAS 42:5826*) se lee una reflexión que entrega la clave de esta escritura: ". . . oír y exigir ser oídos hacia arriba y hacia abajo las direcciones convenientes donde siempre hallaremos al sol como una hoguera" (p. 91); propósito de plenitud en una poesía abierta al acontecer político e histórico. Sobresale la sección "Tratado General de Escultura," como práctica intertextual sobre aspectos significativos de la vida y obra de Miguel Angel, Brancusi, Hans Arp, Calder y Giacometti, entre otros. [PL]

5744 Sánchez León, Abelardo. Oficio de sobreviviente. Lima: Mosca Azul Editores, 1980. 66 p.

Notoria ganancia en el trabajo expresivo con respecto a su interesante libro anterior *Rastro de caracol* (1977, ver *HLAS 42:5827*). Contribuye a la eficacia de esta escritura el distanciamiento irónico con que el sujeto se observa a sí mismo, a la vez que registra las precariedades de su contorno. Los poemas configuran a menudo situaciones problematizadoras de gran intensidad, y esa conquista es uno de sus valores sustanciales (ver item **5785**). [PL]

5745 Segovia, Francisco. El error. México: Universidad Nacional Autónoma de México, 1981. 102 p. (Colección Cuadernos de poesía)

"Dos Extremos," first section of this book, shows great imagination and flair for striking imagery. Among many writers whose influence is noted in second part are Nietzsche, Rimbaud, Poe; Mircea Eliade and the Bible are also significant. Last sections of work, in prose, seem to be fragments of essays rather than prose poems. Interesting but undisciplined. [CM]

5746 Segovia, Tomás. Figura y secuencias. México: Premia Editora, 1979. 102 p. (Libros del bicho; 4)

Important work from one of Mexico's leading poets. Segovia continues to explore some of the same themes as in his earlier books *Anagnórisis* (1967) and *Terceto* (1972). Divided into two parts, collection opens with poems on passion and sensuality, dedicated to Eros, and with great variety of form: free verse, poems in prose and, lastly, a number of finely wrought sonnets. Second section, "Palabras al Tiempo," continues experimentation in form while combining the personal and philosophical such as mediations on identity, art, time and love. A rewarding book. [CM]

5747 Silva, José Asunción. Poesías. Ed. crítica de Héctor H. Orjuela. Bogotá: Instituto Caro y Cuervo, 1979. 352 p.; bibl.; ill. (Biblioteca colombiana; 18)

Excelente edición crítica de la poesía de Silva preparada con el conocido rigor del erudito colombiano quien presenta en forma impecable todo el poemario de Silva encontrado hasta hoy (i.e., 130 poemas, inclusive versiones dobles, traducciones y fragmentos de poemas). Contiene además fecha de primera publicación de casi todos los poemas y, dentro de lo posible, fecha de composición. [BTO]

5748 Silva, Ludovico. Piedras y campanas. Carátula, Ligia Córdoba. Caracas: Editorial Rayuela; Bogotá: Editorial Pluma, 1979. 99 p.

Temas de la poesía: la muerte, el pasar del tiempo, la soledad. La simplicidad de su sintaxis contrasta con imágenes inusitadas. [BTO]

5749 Soto Vélez, Clemente. La tierra prometida. Ilustraciones de Antonio Martorell. San Juan, P.R.: Instituto de Cultura Puertorriqueña, 1979. 142 p.; ill.

Hermosísima edición de un poemalibro, debido a la pluma del reconocido nacionalista puertorriqueño de la generación de los Atalayistas. Antes tenía publicados *Abrazo interno* (1954), *Arboles* (1955), y *Caballo de palo* (1959 y 1976). Texto de versos encabalgados en sucesión, de fuerza y originalidad, y de novedosa tipografía, donde la imagen central se constituye en una poesía que recorre la tierra y descubre el futuro del hombre. Sutil transfiguración de una "búsqueda" del territorio nacional propio. [ER]

5750 Suárez del Real, Eduardo. Menos mi vientre. Dibujos, María Luisa Vázquez Martín. México: Ediciones de Cultura Popular, 1980. 95 p.; ill. (Arte y literatura)

Uneven collection that combines the sociopolitical and personal. Writer expresses his solidarity with movements of liberation in Basque country, Cuba, Nicaragua and El Salvador. In the personal moments he reflects on loss of love, human anguish and death. [CM]

5751 Trujillo, Carlos A. Escrito sobre un balancín. Castro, Chile: Ediciones Aumen, 1979. 77 p.; ill.

Colección de poemas epigramáticos sobre los reveses de la existencia, que cuando dan en el blanco—y esto ocurre ocasionalmente—desatan toda la concentración de su energía poética. Aunque falta un mayor rigor en la selección de los textos, el libro es una clara muestra de las potencialidades de este nuevo poeta. [OH]

5752 Turkeltaub, David. Códices. Santiago: Ediciones Ganymedes, 1981. 82 p.

Aquí está Turkeltaub en su labor primordial: la de poeta (la otra, significativa aunque de distinto modo, es la de fundador de las ya célebres Ediciones Ganymedes). Los poemas de *Códices*, corrosivos, irónicos, pero nunca asépticos, son una prueba de que el rigor de la forma no está necesariamente reñido con las potencialidades del lenguaje coloquial. A diferencia de otros poetas que ejercen su crítica del mundo de manera demasiado explícita, la poesía de Turkeltaub es contestataria en las zonas subliminales de la lectura. [OH]

5753 Uslar Pietri, Arturo. Escritura. Ilus. de Jesús Rafael Soto. Caracas: Ediciones Macanao, 1979. 81 p.; ill.

Contiene 13 poemas de interés que presentan una faceta menos conocida del ilustre escritor venezolano. La obra, publicada en Italia, contiene dibujos geométricos de Jesús Rafael Soto y versiones francesas de los poemas traducidos por Julián Garavito. [BTO]

5754 Vallejo, César Abraham. Obra poética completa. Ed., prólogo y cronología,

Enrique Ballón Aguirre. Caracas: Biblioteca Ayacucho, 1979. 329 p.; bibl. (Biblioteca Ayacucho; 58)

Excelente trabajo editorial de Ballón Aguirre de la poesía completa de Vallejo. La presente publicación supera intentos anteriores o paralelos, como el de Juan Larrea (ver item **5786** y *HLAS 42:5839*), por el rigor y claridad con que Ballón ha manejado y dispuesto el corpus poético vallejiano. Su extenso estudio preliminar—"Para una Definición de la Escritura de Vallejo"—y los apartados finales dedicados a la "Cronología" y a la "Bibliografía" del autor, son contribuciones considerables, fundadas en prácticas teóricas y documentales igualmente eficaces. [PL]

5755 Vera, Juan Dal. Poemas de blanco. Panamá: Ediciones INAC, 1977. 61 p. (Colección Premio Ricardo Miró)

Poemas eslabonados por la conformidad de ideación, tono, lenguaje y materia lírica. El libro da testimonio de una relación amorosa, a la vez que presenta una postura ante la época actual. [RG]

5756 Vitier, Cintio. La fecha al pie. La Habana: Ediciones Unión, 1981. 120 p. (Colección Contemporáneos)

Valiosa colección, por lo que ilustra de la evolución de un poeta y ensayista mayor, cuyo poemario último había aparecido en 1968 (*Testimonios*). En estas páginas se detectan el humanismo cristiano y la visión "trascendental" característica de la generación de Vitier; pero asimismo se palpa el recuento de una vida tocada por la historia nacional y por la Revolución, plasmado en un lenguaje de sencillez conversacional (ver item **5775**). [ER]

5757 Volkow, Verónica. Litoral de tinta. México: Universidad Nacional Autónoma de México, 1979. 50 p. (Colección Cuadernos de poesía)

Volkow (b. 1955) fulfills the promise of her first work, *La sibilia de Cumas* (1977). Prominent among her subjects are meditations on love and time, Mexico before the conquest, ancient and modern Greece. [CM]

5758 Zaid, Gabriel. Cuestionario: poemas 1951–1976. México: Fondo de Cultura Económica, 1976. 277 p. (Colección Letras mexicanas)

Anthology includes previously unpublished poems, some *publicaciones sueltas* not printed in any of his verse collections and his well-known books *Seguimiento* (1964), *Campo nudista* (1969) and *Práctica mortal* (1973). One has the opportunity here to study the evolution of the poet and his craft since various poems from *Seguimiento* and *Campo nudista* were rewritten before being included in *Práctica mortal,* an earlier selection of the writer's verse. Zaid is one of Mexico's leading poets and an important critic as well. [CM]

5759 Zurita, Raúl. Purgatorio de Raúl Zurita. Santiago: Editorial Universitaria, 1979. 61 p.

El libro no se llama *Purgatorio,* sino *Purgatorio de Raúl Zurita.* Esta puntualización no es ociosa; pone en evidencia un aspecto capital de esta obra: la voluntad de identificación absoluta del hablante de los poemas con el autor real. Mientras la poesía hispanoamericana inmediatamente anterior—el exteriorismo de Cardenal o el objetivismo de Gonzalo Millán—, busca la objetividad máxima, Zurita va tan lejos en su "subjetivismo" que termina por hacer estallar el sistema poético, inaugurando una nueva dimensión. Al mismo tiempo, resacraliza el lenguaje coloquial, rompiendo con los intentos desacralizadores de la antipoesía. Por lo menos dos de los textos incluidos en el libro—"El Desierto de Atacama" y "Areas Verdes"—pueden contarse desde ya entre las obras maestras de la poesía chilena. [OH]

GENERAL STUDIES

5760 Achugar, Hugo. Modernización, europeización, cuestionamiento: el lirismo social en Uruguay entre 1895 y 1911 (IILI/RI, 47:114/115, enero/junio 1981, p. 7–32)

Análisis de la poesía de Alvaro Armando Vasseur y Angel Falco, como ejemplos de la lírica social uruguaya, en el contexto hispanoamericano. [HMR]

5761 Alcántara Almánzar, José. Estudios de poesía dominicana. Ilus., Jorge Severino. Fotografías, Roberto Ricart. Santo Domingo: Editora Alfa y Omega, 1979. 435 p.; bibl.; ill.; index.

Ensayos recogen perspectiva amplia de la poesía dominicana, no a base de generaciones y grupos literarios (ver *HLAS 40:*

7166), sino de sus figuras más relevantes. Estudios dedicados a 15 poetas mayores del XIX y XX elaboran un enfoque histórico y sociológico, pero no soslayan la especificidad literaria. Replantean la búsqueda de la esencia de lo dominicano, universalismo de la década de 1940, tendencias vanguardistas y neorrealistas ante los regímenes políticos, pluralismo (experimentación aleatoria de música y lenguaje) en los 1970 (ver *HLAS 40:7149*). Los 15 poetas son: José Joaquín Pérez (1845–1900), Salomé Ureña (1850–1897), Gastón F. Deligne (1861–1913), Domingo Moreno Jiménes (1894–), Tomás Hernández Franco (1904–1952), Franklin Mieses Burgos (1907–1976), Aída Cartagena Portalatín, Freddy Gatón Arce (1920–), Manuel Rueda (1921–), Antonio Fernández Spencer (1922–), Lupo Hernández Rueda (1930–) y Máximo Avilés Blonda (1931–). Libro concebido para difundir la literatura dominicana, que en los 1980 evidencia un auge de su narrativa por encima de sus logros poéticos de décadas anteriores. Lectura recomendada. [ER]

5762 Araujo, Helena. Tres líricos colombianos (ECO, 36[5]:221, marzo 1980, p. 513–519)

Se analizan tres poetas: Giovani Quessep, Jaime García Maffla y Anabel Torres, de los años 1970, que han preferido evitar los elementos realistas e ideológicos para revelar lo imaginativo del lenguaje, reflejando una visión de su propia experiencia en lo inventado y lo vivido. [BTO]

5763 Baeza Flores, Alberto. Evolución en la poesía costarricense. San José: Editorial Costa Rica, 1978. 412 p.; bibl.

El estudio hace recuento de la poesía costarricense desde el período colonial hasta el presente. Carece, desafortunadamente, de sentido crítico definido y, en algunos casos, de concisión: el detalle anecdótico entorpece el discurso y hace difícil discernir los momentos significativos. La obra presenta, no obstante, una visión coherente de la poesía en el siglo XX. [RG]

5764 Canciones y poesías de la Guerra del Pacífico, 1879. Juan Uribe Echevarría. Ilus. de Lukas. s.i.: Editorial Renacimiento, 1979. 321 p.; ill.

Valioso trabajo de investigación sobre textos literarios relacionados con la guerra de 1879 entre Chile y la Confederación Perú-

Bolivia, publicado al cumplirse el primer centenario de la conflagración. Incluye selecciones de poesía popular, poesía culta, teatro y narrativa, precedidas por documentadas notas introductorias. Cabe destacar la amplitud de criterio del investigador chileno, que no vacila en incorporar textos de autores peruanos y bolivianos ofensivos para la nacionalidad del propio recopilador. [OH]

5765 Cobo Borda, Juan Gustavo. La nueva poesía colombiana: una década, 1970–1980 (CBR/BCB, 16:9/10, 1979, p. 75–122)

En base a un fichero de la nueva poesía colombiana de la década de 1970 que más tarde amplió e incorporó a una antología (ver item **5620**), Cobo Borda incluye breves notas bibliográficas y un poema representativo de cada poeta. Su criterio de selección es arbitrario y escoge poetas de desigual talento. [BTO]

5766 Jensen, Theodore W. *Modernista* pythagorean literature: the symbolist inspiration (*in* Waiting for Pegasus: studies of the presence of symbolism and decadence in Hispanic letters. Edited by Roland Grass and William R. Risley. Macomb: Western Illinois University, 1979, p. 169–179)

El ensayo explora las relaciones entre el pitagorismo modernista—Darío, Nervo, Lugones—y el simbolismo francés, a través del concepto de las "correspondencias" y las especulaciones del ocultismo. [HMR]

5767 Jrade, Cathy L. Tópicos románticos como contexto del modernismo (*in* Congreso de Literatura Iberoamericana, 19th, Pittsburgh, Pa., 1979. Memoria. Texto/contexto en la literatura iberoamericana. Edited by Keith McDuffie and Alfredo Roggiano. Pittsburgh, Pa.: Instituto Internacional de Literatura Iberoamericana, 1979, p. 173–180)

El pitagorismo esotérico—que busca la reconciliación con la naturaleza primigenia y cree en la existencia de individuos capaces de comunicar las verdades ocultas del universo—sería el nexo que conecta el romanticismo con el modernismo a través del simbolismo. [HMR]

5768 Martínez Masdeu, Edgar. La crítica puertorriqueña y el modernismo en Puerto Rico. San Juan: Instituto de Cultura Puertorriqueña, 1977. 302 p.; bibl.

Parte de la tesis doctoral del autor ("Desarrollo del Movimiento Modernista en Puerto Rico," Universidad Complutense de Madrid). De enfoque histórico positivista, ofrece sin embargo una plétora de datos y juicios que le hacen útil para una lectura especializada, sobre todo en el caso de un área como ésta, prácticamente desconocida al *scholar* hispanoamericanista que estudia el modernismo en otros países. [ER]

5769 Mejía Duque, Jaime. Momentos y opciones de la poesía en Colombia, 1890–1978. Carátula diseñada por Hugo Zapata. Bogotá: Inéditos, 1979. 200 p. (Colección La Carreta)

El poeta-crítico se propone ofrecer un esquema teórico sobre la poesía colombiana de 1890–1978, confrontándola como proceso social. De acuerdo con Cobo Borda (ver item **5620**) los colombianos han escrito poemas "por kilómetro." Analiza ciertos poetas como portavoces de su época y según criterio personal (e.g., ciertas configuraciones estéticas o ideológicas como la de los piedracielistas, etc.). Concluye que existe en Colombia una tradición nacional sobre la cual los jóvenes pueden edificar su arte. Juzga que el lirismo femenino, a pesar de aciertos individuales, ha sido de poca importancia, pero admite la necesidad de un estudio sobre el tema. Loable historia parcial de la lírica colombiana. [BTO]

5770 El Modernismo visto por los modernistas. Introducción y selección de Ricardo Gullón. Barcelona: Guadarrama, 1980. 507 p.; bibl. (Teoría y crítica literaria) (Colección Punto omega; 257)

Util selección de textos en prosa que se propone presentar el modernismo tal como lo pensaron y lo practicaron sus protagonistas. En el extenso ensayo introductorio, Gullón señala tendencias y matices de este amplio movimiento internacional. Dentro de su abarcante visión, adelantada en *Direcciones del modernismo* (Madrid: Gredos, 1963), el antólogo recoge testimonios de los españoles—Pío Baroja, Jacinto Benavente, Antonio y Manuel Machado, Ramiro de Maeztu, Salvador Rueda, Miguel de Unamuno—junto a los de los hispanoamericanos: Darío, Gómez Carrillo, Lugones, Gutiérrez Nájera, Martí, Mistral, Amado Nervo, José Enrique Rodó y otros. [HMR]

5771 O'Hara, Edgar. Desde Melibea. Lima: Ruray Editores, 1980. 168 p. (Ruray/Prosa)

Extractos de diario que registran el recorrido de una búsqueda reflexiva, o "Poética de la Conciencia" (ver *HLAS 42:5798*). O'Hara examina la obra de varios autores peruanos e hispanoamericanos de su cercanía: los poetas de su generación; algunos libros de escritores aparecidos en la década del 1960, como A. Cisneros (ver *HLAS 40:7059* y *HLAS 42:5712*) y A. Sánchez León (ver *HLAS 42:5827*), y publicaciones recientes de E. Lihn (ver *HLAS 42:6640* y *HLAS 42:5775*) y J. Gelman (ver *HLAS 40:7073*), entre otros. El capítulo final es un detenido análisis de la poesía de J. Heraud (ver *HLAS 40:7089–7090*). Trabajo muy importante, y no sólo por sus valores testimoniales sino también por las informaciones y las perspicaces, atendibles sugerencias críticas que contiene. [PL]

5772 Osorio T., Nelson. Para una caracterización histórica del vanguardismo literario hispanoamericano (IILI/RI, 47:114/115, enero/junio 1981, p. 227–254)

Claro replanteo de los factores socioculturales que condicionaron el surgimiento de la vanguardia literaria en Hispanoamérica (1918–30). Osorio admite concomitancias de este movimiento con tendencias europeas, pero destaca la importancia de condiciones propias de América Latina y la unidad continental de los diversos impulsos renovadores. [HMR]

5773 Perdomo J., Miguel Aníbal. La poesía joven dominicana, a través de sus textos fundamentales: pts. 1/2 (EME, 8:43, julio/agosto 1979, p. 109–169; 8:44, sept./dic. 1979, p. 29–82, bibl.)

Largo estudio publicado en dos partes analiza obra de 14 jóvenes poetas nacidos 1937–51, autores que escriben durante los últimos años del trujillato, grupo de 1960, y publican después de la revolución de 1965. Su obra se enmarca dentro de la búsqueda de lo nacional, el surrealismo simbólico de la "poesía sorprendida," y la poesía social de los más conocidos como Manuel del Cabral y Pedro Mir. Los 14 son: René del Risco Bermúdez, Juan José Ayuso, Miguel Alfonseca, Jeannette Miller, Norberto James, Apolinar Núñez, Enriquillo Sánchez, Andrés L. Mateo, Mateo Morrison, Enrique Eusebio, Luis Manuel Ledesma, Soledad Alvarez, Alexis Gómez y Tony Raful. Enfoque crítico ingenuamente ecléctico, pero valioso, resume: historia literaria, textos, perspectivas. [ER]

5774 Sambrano Urdaneta, Oscar. Contribución a una bibliografía general de la poesía venezolana en el siglo XX. Carátula, Eduardo Orozco. Caracas: Ediciones de la Facultad de Humanidades y Educación, Escuela de Letras, Universidad Central de Venezuela, 1979. 367 p.; indexes.

Bibliografía no selectiva pero tampoco exhaustiva de 2,321 fichas que abarcan 1900–75: libros de verso de diferentes autores (2,008); antologías y selecciones (126); y estudios críticos publicados en forma de libro o folleto (125). Provee notas sobre contenido en la última categoría. Incluye índices de autor, de título, de orden cronológica, y al final, de los autores que han recibido varios premios nacionales en poesía. Digno de elogio por ser uno de los primeros intentos hacia un registro de la bibliografía poética del siglo XX en Venezuela. [BTO]

SPECIAL STUDIES

5775 Barradas, Efraín. Premonición y esperanza: un momento de transición en la poesía de Cinto Vitier (UNION, 4; oct./dic. 1981, p. 52–63)

Sensitivo estudio donde se plantea la definición de una poética evolutiva en Vitier, como paradigma de la generación de *Orígenes* y su transformación. Crear poesía sobre objetos, sirve de puente a la inclusión de lo sociohistórico en la obra. Esta revela una visión religioso-materialista de la realidad, característica de la lírica última de Vitier (ver item 5756). [ER]

5776 Calderón, Germaine. El universo poético de Rosario Castellanos. México: Universidad Nacional Autónoma de México, 1979. 131 p.; bibl.; ill. (Cuadernos del Centro de Estudios Literarios)

While occasionally more eulogy than detailed examination, this study by poet-critic presents many insights into sources of Castellanos' poetry and into its relationship with her novels and short stories. Also offers valuable biobibliographical data and 16 poems that Castellanos did not include in *Poesía no eres tú* (1972), her collected poetry of 1948–72. [CM]

5777 Campos Cornejo, Francisco Javier. Enrique González Martínez: ensayo psicológico. México: Editorial Jus, 1978. 82

p.; 2 leaves of plates; bibl.; ports. (Colección Crítica literaria; 5)

After examining the poet's family life and works, concludes, among other things, that González Martínez suffered oral frustration and that this was the fundamental impulse for his artistic creation. While interesting points are made through analysis of the writer's poems and short stories, Campos Cornejo would have benefitted from contact with more recent research such as that of Jacques Lacan. [CM]

Castañón Barrientos, Carlos. La poesía de Wallparrimachi: y otros páginas de ensayo y evocación. See item **5376.**

5778 Cerón Portilla, Víctor. Lingüística y literatura en la obra poética (PUJ/UH, 11, dic. 1979, p. 189–202, bibl., ill.)

Contraste entre la comunicación lingüística y la poética a propósito de tres poemas sobre el mar, de Gabriela Mistral, Jorge Carrera Andrade y Pablo Neruda. [HMR]

5779 Chacón y Calvo, José María. Estudios heredianos. Selección y prólogo de Salvador Arias. La Habana: Editorial Letras Cubanas, 1980. 185 p.; bibl. (Colección Crítica)

Rescata y pone al día la obra del erudito herediano (la. ed. 1939): "Las Etapas Formativas de la Poesía de Heredia" (1915); "La Vida y la Poesía de Heredia" (1922); "Nueva Vida de Heredia" (1930); "El Horacianismo en la Poesía de Heredia" (1940); "Heredia Considerado como Crítico" (1947) y "Heredia y su Influjo en Nuestros Orígenes Nacionales" (1952). Suprime "Heredia Considerado como Jurista" y un testimonio del padre "Criticismo y Libertad: Evocación de José Francisco de Heredia, Regente de Caracas." Prólogo dibuja la trayectoria crítica de Chacón y Calvo e indaga sus nexos intelectuales con Heredia. [ER]

5780 Clay Méndez, Luis Felipe. Julián del Casal and the cult of artificiality: roots and functions (in Waiting for Pegasus: studies of the presence of symbolism and decadence in Hispanic letters. Edited by Roland Grass and William R. Risley. Macomb: Western Illinois University, 1979, p. 155–168)

Corto estudio de relativo interés, en cuanto a que desarrolla (comparando la prosa y el verso) criterios socioculturales para explicar lo que tradicionalmente se ha consi-

derado la pose alienada de Casal y su estética de lo artificial. [ER]

5781 Conde Abellán, Carmen. Gabriela Mistral. Madrid: E.P.E.S.A., 1970. 200 p.; bibl. (Grandes escritores contemporáneos)

Encabeza este libro una extensa introducción sobre la vida de la poetisa chilena, basada en gran parte en el estudio de Margot Arce sobre Gabriela Mistral, y en otras fuentes secundarias anticuadas, que por cierto ignoran los aportes de investigaciones más recientes. Incluye además algunas notas fragmentarias sobre libros específicos. El único aporte personal de este trabajo son las informaciones relativas a la amistad entre Gabriela Mistral y la poetisa española. El volumen se cierra con una antología de la ganadora del Premio Nobel. [OH]

5782 Cornejo Polar, Antonio. Sobre la literatura de la emancipación en el Perú (IILI/RI, 47:114/115, enero/junio 1981, p. 83–93)

En estas páginas se proponen algunos criterios para una reinterpretación de la literatura del período indicado. Con buenas razones, Cornejo Polar concluye que sólo en los yaravíes de Mariano Melgar se manifiesta una voluntad expresiva genuinamente emancipadora, que valoriza y asume la tradición poética indígena y popular, en contraste muy marcado con el canon entonces vigente (ver *HLAS 40:7116*). [PL]

5783 Coyné, André. Moro: una edición y varias discrepancias (Hueso Húmero [Lima] 10, julio/oct. 1981, p. 148–170)

Se refiere a la edición de la poesía de César Moro preparada por Ricardo Silva-Santisteban (ver item **5712**). Objeta algunos aspectos del criterio adoptado para seleccionar y disponer los textos de ese volumen, y discute ciertas interpretaciones adelantadas por Silva-Santisteban en su prólogo. El comentario suministra información importante sobre el poeta y su obra. [PL]

5784 Diez poetas colombianos. Selección y nota de Fernando Garavito. Bogotá: Corporación de Ahorro y Vivienda, COLMENA, 1976. 111 p.; bibl.

En un sucinto prólogo original e iconoclasta, el editor indica que ha seleccionado sólo jóvenes poetas (publicados 1966–75) que han logrado lo que proclamaron los nadaístas. Los siguientes poetas han reflejado las contradicciones que existen en Colombia al destruir sus falsos mitos de libertad, igualdad y fraternidad: Mario Rivera, Jaime Jaramillo Escobar, María Mercedes Carranza, Raúl Henao, Juan Manuel Roca, Juan Gustavo Cobo Borda, Darío Rúiz Gómez, Aníbal Manuel Venegas, Nicolás Suescún y Aníbal Arias. [BTO]

5785 Elmore, Peter. Sánchez León: la madurez alcanza al poeta (Hueso Húmero [Lima] 10, julio/oct. 1981, p. 177–183)

Comenta el último libro de Sánchez León *Oficio de sobreviviente* (ver item **5744**) a partir de un examen de la obra anterior del autor. Notas de interés sobre esta poesía "del desaliento y del disgusto," cuyo desarrollo debe medirse "no tanto por la evolución formal . . . sino por las distintas estancias a las que arriba en el proceso de maduración personal" (p. 178–179). Aporte crítico necesario (ver también item **5771**). [PL]

5786 Escobar, Alberto. Una discutible edición de Vallejo (Hueso Húmero [Lima] 5/6, abril/set. 1980, p. 134–140)

Convincente examen del volumen *Poesía completa* de César Vallejo en la "edición crítica y exegética" de Juan Larrea (1978, ver *HLAS 42:5839* y *HLAS 42:5879*). Escobar comprueba la carencia de aparato filológico, las ligerezas y el voluntarismo frecuentes en las interpretaciones y la arbitrariedad del reordenamiento cronológico de los textos. En un análisis notable por su rigor y por su elegancia expositiva, demuestra que el empeño de Larrea no da como resultado "una edición crítica," sino "una debatible edición comentada." [PL]

5787 Feustle, Joseph A., Jr. Poesía y mística: Rubén Darío, Juan Ramón Jiménez y Octavio Paz. Portada, Pepe Maya. Xalapa, México: Centro de Investigaciones Lingüístico-Literarias, Instituto de Investigaciones Humanísticas, Universidad Veracruzana, 1978. 100 p.; bibl. (Cuadernos de texto crítico; 6)

Feustle define el misticismo como "la tendencia por parte del ser humano hacia la unión con el Orden trascendental." Y luego de analizar aspectos de la obra de Darío, Jiménez y Paz concluye que los tres comparten estos rasgos: 1) una conciencia de escisión; 2) un empleo de símbolos característicos; 3) un mismo concepto de lo divino; 4) un progreso por vías poético-místicas; y 5) el empleo de la poesía y la mujer como mediadores en su búsqueda de lo trascendente. [HMR]

5788 Francovich, Guillermo. Tito Yupanqui; escultor indio. La Paz: Librería Editorial Juventud, 1978. 144 p. (Colección ayer y hoy)

Se incluyen en este libro dos artículos sobre poetas bolivianos actuales: un comentario de *Estrella segregada*, de Oscar Cerruto (p. 67–74, ver *HLAS 38:6931*), y una descripción de las diversas fases que se advierten en la obra de Yolanda Bedregal (p. 75–86). Notas algo generales, pero cuidadosas, de un lector atento a las sugerencias de una poesía que considera entre las manifestaciones más logradas en la literatura de su país (ver *HLAS 42:5380*). [PL]

5789 Geografía humana de Benjamín Carrión. Jorge Aravena, editor. Fotografías originales y reproducciones, Jorge Aravena. Quito: Música, Palabra e Imagen del Ecuador, 1980. 86 p.; ill.; disc (45 rpm. stereo. 7 in.)

Homenaje a Benjamín Carrión (1897–1979) en el primer aniversario de su muerte. Se reproducen sus poemas juveniles, una pequeña muestra de trabajos críticos (uno de ellos es el prólogo al *Indice de la poesía ecuatoriana contemporánea*, 1937), cartas y fotografías. Se incluye también un disco grabado por el grupo "Pueblo Nuevo." Los textos de A. Pareja Díez-Canseco, R. Andrade, J. E. Adoum y P. J. Vera destacan el magisterio y las generosas realizaciones culturales del escritor. [PL]

5790 Gimferrer, Pedro. Lecturas de Octavio Paz. Barcelona: Editorial Anagrama, 1980. 118 p. (Colección Argumentos; 59)

Thoughtful study that analyzes "Piedra de sol," *Blanco*, *Pasado en claro*, "La Arboleda" and the "Nocturno de San Ildefonso." While brief and impressionistic rather than detailed, it gives important insights into each of the poems. [CM]

5791 Gonzales, Norma and **Luis Zelkowics.** Breves notas en torno a la funcionalidad de la décima en la poesía venezolana (IPGH/FA, 25, junio 1978, p. 119–124)

Breve análisis de la funcionalidad estética de la décima folklórica en la poesía venezolana y su codificación idiolectal morfológica, sintática y semántica. [BTO]

5792 Larrea, Juan. Al amor de Vallejo. Valencia: Pre-Textos, 1980. 307 p.; 16 leaves of plates; bibl.; ill. (Pre-textos; 29)

Recopilación de 11 trabajos, algunos antiguos como "Inminencia de América" (1937), que muestran la devoción de toda una vida que el autor dedicó a la obra vallejiana. Su conocimiento (sobre todo documental) de esa obra es indudable y valioso, pues Larrea fue testigo de etapas cruciales del proceso creador de Vallejo; la impresión que estos trabajos producen es, sin embargo, confusa y desigual, especialmente por las vagas teorías filosóficas y mesiánicas a las que el crítico quiere adscribir la obra del poeta. [J. M. Oviedo]

5793 Llambías de Azevedo, Alfonso. El modernismo literario y otros estudios. Montevideo: Comisión Nacional de Homenaje del Sesquicentenario de los Hechos Históricos de 1825, 1976. 195 p.

Colección de conferencias y ensayos sobre autores hispanoamericanos. Se destacan los que analizan aspectos de la obra de algunos escritores y poetas uruguayos: Carlos Reyles, Julio Herrera y Reissig, Emilio Oribe y Eduardo Acevedo. [HMR]

5794 López Rueda, José. Sentido y sonido en *Oscuro* de Gonzalo Rojas (Tiempo Real [Universidad Simón Bolivar, Caracas] 7, marzo 1978, p. 95–101)

Nota de carácter general, en la que López Rueda examina los rasgos estilísticos, la visión del mundo y los temas conductores—el amor, la estirpe, la sociedad—en *Oscuro*, de Gonzalo Rojas. [OH]

5795 Lutz, Robyn R. The tribute to everyday reality in José Lezama Lima's *Fragmentos a su imán* (JSSTC, 8:3, Winter 1980, p. 249–266)

Coherente lectura en la que se analizan relaciones entre el mundo concreto y lo abstracto poético en Lezama, con lúcidos ejemplos de su último poemario (ver *HLAS 42:5774*). [ER]

5796 Martino, Florentino. La criba y el hisopo: estudios sobre poesía española e hispanoamericana. Caracas: Ediciones La Gran Papelería del Mundo, 1979. 247 p.; bibl.

Colección de 13 estudios, varios de los cuales analizan—a veces polémicamente—aspectos de la obra de poetas hispanoamericanos: Rubén Darío (innovador pero superficial); César Vallejo (poeta del sufrimiento); Pablo Neruda (contradicciones entre el poeta y el político); Ramón Palomares y Luis Alberto Crespo (poetas del mundo rural venezolano). [HMR]

5797 Melnykovich, George. Reality and expression in the poetry of Carlos Pellicer. Chapel Hill: University of North Carolina, Department of Romance Languages, 1979. 150 p.; bibl. (North Carolina studies in the Romance languages and literatures; no. 211)

Valuable study which situates Pellicer historically and considers those trends, poets and works which had a pronounced influence on the Mexican writer. Melnykovich finds that major difference between avant garde and Pellicer lies not in language or technique, but rather in their vision of the modern era. Particularly informative is author's chapter on the Bergsonian aesthetic and Pellicer, in which poetic devices of duration in the Mexican's works are discussed. [CM]

5798 Oquendo, Abelardo. Eielson: remontando la poesía de papel: una entrevista (Hueso Húmero [Lima] 10, julio/oct. 1981, p. 3–10)

Un diálogo sugerente, en el que Jorge Eduardo Eielson revisa con gran lucidez el itinerario de su poética, desde "el lujo verbal e imaginativo" de *Reinos* (ver *HLAS 40: 7067*) hasta el pasaje a una práctica más amplia, que en su última fase se empeña en reconocer la poesía fuera o más allá de las palabras (ver *HLAS 42:5734*). [PL]

5799 Porras Collantes, Ernesto. Estructura del *Nocturno* de José Asunción Silva (ICC/T, 33:3, sept./dic. 1978, p. 462–494)

Uso competente de un método hjelmsleviano lingüístico para analizar las estructuras paradigmáticas del "Nocturno" de José Asunción Silva. [BTO]

5800 Prats Sariol, José. Estudios sobre poesía cubana. La Habana: Ediciones Unión, 1980. 112 p. (Cuadernos de la revista *Unión*; 12)

Selección de ensayos críticos de intérprete de textos poéticos, tanto cubanos como latinoamericanos (Mención Honorífica Concurso Pellicer 1979, México, por "Aguas de Carlos Pellicer," ver item **5801**). Reúne textos de revistas cubanas y extranjeras 1973–78: "Martí, Rilke y la Bailarina Española;" "Nota a *Liberación* de Juan Marinello;" "Novedad y Sugerencia en el *Diario*" (sobre *El diario que a diario*, de Guillén); "Los Dientes de la Rueda" (sobre *La rueda dentada*, de Guillén;) "Guillén en un Barco de Papel" (sobre *Por el mar de las Antillas anda un barco de papel*, de Guillén); "La Joven Luz de Eliseo Diego;" "Del Polvo a la Tierra en la Poesía de Fayad Jamís;" "Retamar; Lucidez e Insuficiencia;" "La Poesía de Raúl Rivero;" "Nogueras el Caminante" (ver item **5716**) y "La Más Reciente Poesía Cubana" (ver *HLAS 42:5867*). Libro interesante y provechoso. [ER]

5801 El poema-abánico: lectura de José Lezama Lima (CM/D, 17:1[97], enero/feb. 1981, p. 35–40, ill.)

Comentario poético, más descriptivo y creativo que crítico, sobre el poema "Oda a Julián del Casal." Establece paralelos interesantes entre los dos autores cubanos; ofrece datos y testimonios biográficos. [ER]

5802 Quintero, Aramís. El tiempo y el grabado en la poesía de Eliseo Diego (UNION, 19:2, abril/junio 1980, p. 16–42)

Define la poética de Diego como la constancia en una mirada fija, "en una imagen instantánea, algo cuya esencia es fluir" (ver item **5674**), y se rastrea textualmente desde *En las oscuras manos del olvido* (1942) hasta el *Muestrario del mundo o Libro de las maravillas de Boloña* (1969), pero sobre todo por medio del análisis del poemario *En la Calzada de Jesús del Monte* (1949), memoria e historia a la vez, hecho de "cuadros" de objetos y figuras detenidos en el tiempo (ver *HLAS 40:7066*). [ER]

5803 Rama, Angel. Indagación de la ideología en la poesía: los dípticos seriados de *Versos sencillos* (IILI/RI, 112/113, julio/dic. 1980, p. 353–400)

Pormenorizada exploración del contenido ideológico de *Versos* sencillos, en los que Rama detecta la experiencia íntima y social de José Martí en Nueva York. [HMR]

5804 Ricardo Jaimes Freyre, estudios. La Paz: Academia Nacional de Ciencias de Bolivia: Instituto de Estudios Bolivianos, Universidad Boliviana, Universidad Mayor de San Andrés, 1978, i.e. 1979. 205 p.; bibl.

Trabajos biográficos y críticos sobre una figura principal y desatendida del modernismo hispanoamericano. Textos de valor desigual, reunidos sin ningún criterio de co-

herencia, pero algunos renovarán el interés por el autor, por sus adelantos teóricos en el campo de estudios sobre versificación española y por sus cuentos (ver *HLAS 40: 6750*). Aspectos novedosos: cartas y poemas inéditos presentados por Raquel M. de Von Vacano, Gunnar Mendoza L. y Oscar Rivera Rodas. Colaboraciones estimables son: Teresa Gisbert "Aproximación a Ricardo Jaimes Freyre;" Walter Navia Romero "Estilística de 'El hermano pintor' y 'Siempre' de Ricardo Jaimes Freyre;" Guillermo Francovich "Ricardo Jaimes Freyre;" y las páginas polémicas de Carlos Castañón Barrientos y Oscar Cerruto a propósito del libro *Leyes de la versificación castellana*. [PL]

5805 Rivas Dugarte, Rafael Angel. Fuentes para el estudio de Rufino Blanco Fombona, 1874–1944. Caracas: Centro de Estudios Latinoamericanos Rómulo Gallegos, 1979. 244 p.; bibl.; index (Colección Manuel Landaeta Rosales)

Admirable esfuerzo para ampliar, corregir y mejorar la bibliografía existente sobre el conocido escritor venezolano. Consulta, entre otras, la de Castellanos (ver *HLAS 42:5143*), distintos periódicos caraqueños, etc. Contiene 1,623 fichas, algunas comentadas, y una cronología bio-bibliográfica. [BTO]

5806 Rivera, Francisco. Mínima teoría del bolero (ECO, 36[2]:218, dic. 1979, p. 207–212)

Señala que los poemas llamados "boleros" de Juan Gustavo Cobo Borda no se prestan para tratamiento musical por su estilo conversacional, aun antimusical. Las características del bolero y de los poemas son, según Rivera, ternura, sensualidad simple, sentido de humor, tono paradójico, protesta contra lo cotidiano y el esfuerzo de conseguir el mayor público posible. Concluye que la forma literaria del bolero tiene origen en los modernistas y ciertos poetas cursis pero populares como el mexicano Juan de Dios Peza. [BTO]

5807 Rodríguez, Manuel Alfredo. La voz perenne de Andrés Eloy Blanco. Caracas: Ediciones Centauro, 1980. 70 p.; ill.

Contiene cuatro discursos y un prólogo sobre la vida y obra del escritor postmodernista venezolano. De interés por algunos detalles personales sobre el poeta. [BTO]

5808 Rojas Guzmán, Eusebio. Reinvención de la palabra: la obra poética de Octavio Paz. Portada, dibujo de Alvaro Rivera Medina. México: Costa-Amic, 1979. 57 p.; 16 leaves of plates; ill.

While biographical and eulogistic rather than analytical, Rojas Guzmán's brief volume is nevertheless a useful introduction to Paz's life and verse. Contains information on circumstances of composition of various works—largely biographical details—not found in extended studies of Rachel Phillips (see *HLAS 36:6672*), Jason Wilson (see *HLAS 42:5924*), Carlos H. Magis (see *HLAS 42:5898*) or Pere Gimferrer (see item **5790**). [CM]

5809 Roster, Peter J., Jr. La ironía como método de análisis literario: la poesía de Salvador Novo. Madrid: Gredos, 1978. 226 p.; bibl.

After an examination of types of irony and basic ironic techniques, Roster analyzes poetry from various periods of Novo's life. He finds that the poet employs metaphysical irony and that its major thematic manifestation could be characterized as a conflict between Ariel and Caliban, the spiritual and the material. A clear and convincing study. [CM]

5810 Russell Lamadrid, Enrique. La poesía de Antonio Cisneros: dialéctica de creación y tradición (RCLL, 6:11, 1er. semestre, 1980, p. 85–106)

Excelente ensayo introductorio (primer capítulo de una tesis doctoral), muy informado y perspicaz, que diseña con claridad el contexto literario y las relaciones intertextuales de la poesía de A. Cisneros (ver *HLAS 40:7159*, *HLAS 40:7860* y *HLAS 42:5712*). [PL]

5811 Salcedo Pizani, Ernestina. Manuel Felipe Rugeles, poeta de la montaña y de los niños venezolanos. Madrid: La Muralla, 1978. 102 p.; bibl.; port.

Versión condensada de tesis doctoral (Universidad de Madrid, 1971). Trabajo claro y bien organizado sobre una figura menor en la lírica venezolana, poeta de temas infantiles y de la naturaleza. [BTO]

5812 Smith, Janet Lynn. An annotated bibliography of and about Ernesto Cardenal. Tempe: Center for Latin American Studies, Arizona State University, 1979. 61 p.; index (Special studies—Arizona State University, Center for Latin American Studies; 21)

Valiosa e indispensable contribución al estudio de la obra de Cardenal. Extensa bibliografía presenta todos los aspectos de la obra en prosa y verso, y recopila la crítica existente, con anotaciones descriptivas y valorativas. [RG]

5813 Subero, Efraín. Cercanía de Miguel Otero Silva. Caracas: Oficina Central de Información, 1975. 85 p.; bibl.; index.

Cuidadosa bibliografía de 1,000 fichas, algunas comentadas, en homenaje a los 70 años del escritor. Corta introducción de Subero esboza ideas para un estudio cabal de la poesía de Otero Silva. Volumen incluye entrevista sobre obras de prosa, cronología de fechas importantes, la propia bibliografía, índice alfabético, y comentarios por varios escritores, en verso y prosa (25 p.). [BTO]

5814 Tello, Marco. Olmedo, magia y fulguración de la palabra. Cuenca, Ecuador: Departamento de Difusión Cultural de la Universidad de Cuenca: Casa de la Cultura Ecuatoriana, Núcleo del Azuay, 1980. 178 p.; bibl.

Examen de procedimientos y recursos barrocos en la poesía de J. J. Olmedo. El registro del hipérbaton en las odas "La Victoria de Junín" y "Al General Flores" tiende a probar que esa forma de desviación, teóricamente extraña a las costumbres literarias de la época, es de marcada estirpe gongorina y revela un cruce de preferencias inadvertido por la crítica. Formulación y verificaciones interesantes, aunque estas últimas suelen ser más adjetivales que iluminadoras. [PL]

5815 Varela-Ibarra, José. La poesía de Alfonso Cortés. León: Universidad Nacional Autónoma de Nicaragua, 1976 [i.e. 1977]. 173 p.; bibl. (Colección Ensayo—Universidad Nacional Autónoma de Nicaragua; no. 5)

Primera aproximación sistemática a la obra de Alfonso Cortés plantea un análisis estilístico de su poesía sin intentar situarlo dentro de los movimientos literarios en Nicaragua ni de relacionarlo con los otros miembros de su generación. Es un punto de partida para el estudio más amplio de esta difícil figura del parnaso nicaragüense. [RG]

5816 Villegas, Juan. La dimensión apocalíptica de la poesía de Miguel Arteche (UC/AT, 439, 1979, p. 87–100)

Aunque el título de esta nota anuncia un trabajo de índole más vasta, lo cierto es que está centrada en un solo poema de Arteche: "El Ojo." Villegas documenta bien la presencia en el texto de lo que él denomina la "dimensión apocalíptica," pero la suspensión de su sentido crítico lo lleva a pasar por alto el hecho de que el establecimiento de dicha "dimensión" es mero producto de una manipulación retórica y no el resultado de una conciencia poética auténticamente visionaria. [OH]

5817 Xirau, Ramón. Poesía y conocimiento: Borges, Lezama Lima, Octavio Paz. México: Editorial J. Mortiz, 1978. 141 p.; bibl. (Cuadernos de Joaquín Mortiz)

Tres densos ensayos que exploran la posibilidad del conocimiento mediante la poesía, a propósito de tres poetas hispanoamericanos de nuestro tiempo. Xirau ve en Borges, Lezama Lima y Paz tres actitudes diversas ante la realidad, pero a la vez una sugestiva confluencia de poesía y metafísica. [HMR]

MISCELLANEOUS

5818 Cabel, Jesús. Bibliografía de la poesía peruana: 1965/1979. Lima: Amaru Editores, 1980. 142 p.

Acucioso registro de la producción poética peruana aparecida en el país y en el extranjero durante el plazo indicado. Cabel dispone el repertorio—constituído por más de 1,200 entradas—en tres secciones: Libros, Antologías (incluidas las publicadas por autores no peruanos) y Plaquetas, y lo cierra con dos ilustrativas estadísticas: "Número de Títulos por Departamentos y Países" y "Número de Títulos por Años." Una contribución documental de gran utilidad para los estudiosos del proceso de la poesía peruana, resultado de "la constancia y la pasión" que el autor encarece justamente en su prólogo. [PL]

Jackson, Richard L. The Afro-Spanish American author: an annotated bibliography of criticism. See *HLAS 42:46.*

5819 Lastra, Pedro. Conversaciones con Enrique Lihn. Xalapa, México: Centro de Investigaciones Lingüístico-Literarias, Universidad Veracruzana, 1980. 153 p. (Cuadernos de texto crítico; 10)

Para los que disfrutan del diálogo intelectual de alto nivel, exento de pedanterías, este libro es un festín. Aunque siempre el punto de partida es la vasta obra literaria de Lihn—su poesía, sus cuentos, sus ensayos, sus novelas—tanto Lastra como su interlocutor despegan desde allí, para examinar diversos problemas relacionados con la escritura y la creación artística. En un intercambio rico y enriquecedor, se examina la prehistoria del Lihn poeta, *La pieza oscura*, los "Monólogos" y su vinculación con los cuentos, el establecimiento de una escritura *in situ*, las venturas y desventuras de la forma soneto, la figura de Borges, la palabra productiva de Gabriela Mistral, la estrategia de las novelas, la función de la crítica literaria en Chile y la biografía de don Gerardo de Pompier. El volumen se cierra con un completísima bibliografía de y sobre Enrique Lihn, con anotaciones en las entradas significativas. Obra infaltable en la más exigente de las bibliotecas. [OH]

5820 Mistral, Gabriela. Grandeza de los oficios. Selección de prosas y prólogo de Roque Esteban Scarpa. Portada, Alvaro Donoso. Santiago: Editorial Andrés Bello, 1979. 226 p.

Unos 40 artículos selccionados en función del concepto mistraliano de la profesión, los oficios y, en general, de la actividad creadora. Páginas notables de la gran escritora. [C. Goić]

5821 Neruda, Pablo. Cartas a Laura. Estudio preliminar de Hugo Montes. Madrid: Ediciones Cultura Hispánica del Centro Iberoamericano de Cooperación, 1978. 87 p.; bibl.; facsims. (inserted in pocket)

Contiene 28 cartas y 17 tarjetas postales de Pablo Neruda, dirigidas a su hermana Laura desde distintos países, entre los años 1920–60. Correspondencia, escrita sin propósitos literarios, muestra una interesante dimensión de Neruda: "el hombre común y corriente apremiado por la pobreza, pendiente del empleo esquivo, urgido por una inmensa necesidad de comunicación humana," según Hugo Montes. Hermoso volumen, que incorpora excelentes reproducciones facsimilares de las cartas, es un significativo aporte al conocimiento de la figura humana y literaria del poeta chileno. [OH]

5822 ———. Pablo Neruda, Héctor Eandi: correspondencia durante *Residencia* *en la tierra* por Margarita Aguirre. Buenos Aires: Editorial Sudamericana, 1980. 180 p.; 12 p. of plates; bibl.; ill.; ports.

Correspondencia completa entre Neruda y el escritor argentino Héctor Eandi corresponde a la estada del poeta en Oriente entre 1927–31, pero se extiende hasta 1966. Es importante para establecer el contexto biográfico y literario de parte de *Residencia en la tierra*, especialmente por la autointerpretación del poeta y sus ideas poéticas. La compiladora, Margarita Aguirre, completa aquí la difusión de estas cartas comenzada en sus ensayos biográficos sobre Neruda. La presentación y las notas que acompañan la presente edición no son siempre felices ni adecuadas. [C. Goić]

5823 ———. El río invisible: poesía y prosa de juventud. Recopilación de Matilde Neruda. Edición y notas, Jorge Edwards. Barcelona: Seix Barral, 1980. 212 p.; 2 leaves of plates; bibl.; ill. (Biblioteca breve; 457: Poesía)

Los textos en prosa se encierran en la última parte del libro: "El Dolor de los Otros" (p. 135–194) y forman un variado conjunto. Se trata de pequeños artículos publicados en el diario *La Mañana* de Temuco; en el periódico *Claridad*, de la Federación de Estudiantes; y el diario *El Mercurio*, de Santiago. También se recogen algunas páginas del "Album Terusa" y otras publicadas en la revista *Zig-Zag*. Páginas interesantes para la biografía literaria e ideológica de Neruda. [C. Goić]

5824 **Preferencias literarias I:** poetas, encuesta (Hueso Húmero [Lima] 2, julio/ set. 1979, p. 110–117)

Valioso aporte de datos para un "estudio del gusto" en los medios literarios de una época determinada. Sesenta y cuatro intelectuales respondieron a esta encuesta, indicando 10 nombres en cada caso. El orden de las preferencias según el número de menciones fue el siguiente: C. Vallejo (60); M. Adán (53); J. M. Eguren (52); C. Oquendo de Amat (36); J. E. Eielson (35); A. Cisneros y A. Romualdo (29); E. A. Westphalen (28); C. Moro (26); C. G. Belli y J. Sologuren (22); W. Delgado (20). [PL]

5825 **Vallejo, Georgette.** Vallejo, allá ellos, allá ellos, allá ellos! Lima?: Editorial Zalvac, 1978. 170 p.; ill.

Versión ampliada y actualizada de los mismos "Apuntes Biográficos sobre César Vallejo" que la viuda del poeta preparó para la edición facsimilar de la *Obra poética completa* (Lima, 1968), reproducidos también en la edición no facsimilar (Lima, 1974) de la misma obra. Aunque hay datos de importancia, el beligerante tono polémico de la autora y el confuso estilo autojustificatorio, complican su lectura y limitan su valor. [J. M. Oviedo]

5826 **Zamora Saldaño, Raquel.** Poetisas chilenas: dos palabras (EC/M, 27, 1979, p. 87–96)

Especie de pequeño diccionario incluye alrededor de 300 nombres de poetisas chilenas, ordenados alfabéticamente. Las entradas son desiguales; en algunos casos se incorporan datos biográficos y bibliográficos; en otros, se omiten las referencias a la vida de las autoras. Las menciones de libros publicados contienen solamente el título y el año de impresión. [OH]

Drama

GEORGE WOODYARD, *Professor of Spanish, University of Kansas*

SOCIOPOLITICAL CONSIDERATIONS continue to be a major preoccupation of the theatre during this biennium, as the theatre throughout Latin America struggles against political and social repression, censorship and other vitiating conditions. *Conjunto* focuses on ideological theatre and reports of new plays and activities that embrace "el nuevo teatro," as the *engagé* theatre of the left is known. In quantity of publication, Cuba dominates with new editions of plays and now an additional journal, *Tablas* (item **5968**) new in 1982, published by the Ministry of Culture. *Tramoya* and *La Cabra* in Mexico and the *Latin American Theatre Re-*

view in the US contribute to the dissemination of plays and critical material.

The cycle of festivals, *encuentros* and symposia begun several years ago has continued, with the felicitous result of interchanging ideas on acting styles, performance standards and critical methods on a regular basis (items **5934** and **5965**). The Centro Latinoamericano de Creación e Investigación Teatral (CELCIT) located in Caracas promotes theatre through its subsidiaries in Latin America with festivals and publications. In conjunction with CERTAL (an equivalent organization in Spain), it has already launched one major trans-Atlantic theatrical event.

One of the most exciting recent phenomena is the Teatro Abierto of Argentina (item **5939**) which has brought renewed vigor to the Argentine theatre. Familiar names still appear with regularity: Buenaventura, Cabrujas, Chalbaud, Chocrón, Franklin Domínguez, Carlos Gorostiza, Vicente Leñero, Eduardo Pavlovsky, and others. The prolific Emilio Carballido works to promote an entire new generation of young playwrights in Mexico, and everywhere a new wave of writers has begun to capture serious critical attention, such as Oscar Villegas (Mexico) and Mariela Romero (Venezuela). Even established novelists Severo Sarduy and Marco Denevi have turned their hand to the stage, as has Mario Vargas Llosa (item **5908**) with surprising results.

Theatre histories are still in short supply, although Bolivia has two (!) in this period (items **5959** and **5972**). Carballido (item **5961**) and Luisa Josefina Hernández (item **5942**) rate individual monographs, and good articles appear on Gambaro (item **5937**) and others. Several new bibliographies are available (items **5913, 5916** and **5940**), but the field still suffers from a lack of adequate bibliographical control as well as from the wider application of recent critical methods.

PLAYS

5827 Agostini de del Río, Amelia. 6 [i.e. Seis] voces y dos sainetes más. Direcciones escénicas de Andrés Quiñones Vizcarrondo. San Juan: s.n., 1978. 88 p.

Inspired by a gravediggers' strike in New York, six voices with dubious quality bring the dead to life to discuss their frustrations and shattered dreams. The other two sainetes are no more promising.

5828 Alfonso, Paco. Teatro. Prólogo de Nicolás Dorr. La Habana: Editorial Letras Cubanas, 1981. 388 p.

Collection of 11 plays with typical Cuban dialect and didactic tone, verging on the melodramatic. In *El caso del día* (1941), the poor people overcome the judicial system; *Cañaveral* (1950) deals with the eviction of rural people from their lands; *Sangre negra* (1942) departs from the social posture to explore the black man's world through myths.

5829 El Amor de la estanciera. El detalle de la acción de Maipú. Anónimo. Arío revuelto ganancia de pescadores por Juan Cruz Varela. El gigante Amapolas por Juan Bautista Alberdi. Selección, prólogo y notas por Luis Ordaz. Buenos Aires: Centro Editor de América Latina, 1979. 117 p. (El Teatro argentino; 1) (Capítulo; 15)

Useful collection of early plays ranging from two early anonymous works to *El gigante Amapolas* (1841), Alberdi's famous Romantic play which prefigures some 20th-century techniques.

5830 Antezana Claure, Rosa. La joya de Chuquiabo: comedia histórica en tres actos. La Paz, Bolivia: Mundi Graf Impresores, 1980. 47 p.; 6 leaves of plates; ill.

Historical play celebrating founding of city of La Paz in 1548 by Captain Alonso de Mendoza. Little dramatic value.

5831 Antología del género chico criollo. Alejandro Berrutti et al. Selección de Susana Marcó et al. Buenos Aires: Editorial Universitaria de Buenos Aires, 1976. 215 p. (Colección Argentina: Teatro)

Includes works of eight dramatists most representative of popular national theatre from 1890–1930, from early *sainetes* (*Los óleos del chico*) to Pirandellian characters in *Tres personajes a la pesca de un autor.*

5832 Armagno Cosentino, José. 67 [i.e. Sesenta y siete] personajes reclaman un escenario. Prólogo de José Marial. Buenos Aires: S.E.P.A., 1979. 180 p.; ill. (Colección Dionisios)

Six short poetic/symbolic pieces that have, unfortunately, a distracting separation from reality. Language is stilted; situations artificial.

5833 Armijo, Roberto. Los rapaces (CDLA/CO, 47, oct./dic. 1980, p. 40–54)

Two friends lament the misery of life under the *cacique*, but their plan to get even turns against them.

5834 Baldrich, Alberto. Manuelita Rosas, la Reina del Plata: guión para cinematografía. La Plata, Argentina: Ramos Americana, 1980. 191 p. (Autores argentinos; 021)

This attempt to capture the spirit of sweetness and grace of Manuelita Rosas, the dictator's daughter, during a disturbing period of Argentine history (1834–50), fails because of the fragmentation (more than 70 brief scenes) and the intervention of great numbers of historical figures who hinder the development of character.

5835 Bolt, Alan. *Adelaida* (CDLA/CO, 45, julio/sept. 1980, p. 21–32)

Bolt's *Adelaida*, an Antigone in Nicaraguan dress, is principal play in issue devoted to post-Somoza Nicaragua. Also contains four other very short sketches: *La justicia, En el hospital, Las mercaderas,* and *Visión social,* all of them brief scenes of an emerging society.

5836 Buenaventura, Enrique. *Historia de una bala de plata:* creación colectiva del Teatro Experimental de Cali. La Habana: Casa de las Américas, 1980. 70 p.

TEC's inimitable style of historical-documentary collective creation concerns efforts to exploit Christophe Jones (alias Louis Poitié) in the black liberation of a Caribbean island (Haiti) which fails, but sets the stage for later revolutionary efforts. Excellent.

5837 Cabrujas, José Ignacio. El día que me quieras: pieza en dos tiempos. Portada, John Lange. Caracas: Monte Avila Editores, 1979. 77 p. (Colección Teatro)

Another successful play by this talented writer, director and author. Cabrujas captures the sentiments of a romanticized group in Caracas looking to join the idealized communist state in Russia during a documented visit to Caracas by the famous Carlos Gardel. Excellent contrasts.

5838 Carballido, Emilio. Carpintería dramática. Antología de un taller. México: Universidad Autónoma Metropolitana, 1979. 112 p.

Consists of 14 brief plays and vignettes plus some mere conversations by 11 authors, resulting from Carballido's UAM workshop in the spring of 1979. In his introduction, Carballido explains the creative and instructive process.

5839 ———. Teatro joven de México. México: Editores Mexicanos Unidos, 1979. 352 p.

Collection of 16 plays by new young Mexican playwrights, some of whose earlier works have been collected in an early edition with the same title. Some have proved their talent (e.g., Villegas, Liera, Willebaldo López, Agustín, etc.), others have great potential.

5840 ———. Tres comedias. Mexico: Editorial Extemporáneos, 1980. 240 p.

La danza and *Felicidad* are here reprinted with *Un vals sin fin por el planeta* which shows influence and effect two strangers have on a large family with different interests; a study in relativism and perspectives.

5841 ———. 26 [i.e. Veintiséis] obras en un acto. 2. ed. México: Editorial Grijalbo, 1978. 375 p.; 9 p. of music.

Yet another version, with some additions and deletions, of Carballido's now-famous, mostly delightful, always genuine vignettes about characters, life and reality in his beloved Mexican capital.

5842 Castillo, Ernesto. Costumbres (CDLA/CO, 49, julio/sept. 1981, p. 39–84)

Repression characteristic of modern-day Uruguay is depicted metaphorically in this work set in a bourgeois household in the epochs of Battle and William (early 20th century).

5843 Cea, José Roberto. Escenas cumbres. San Salvador: Canoa Editores, 1967? 98 p.

Three-act play loosely based on *Wait-*

ing for Godot in which various characters question man's existence in a hostile environment. Heavy symbolism damages an otherwise well-made play.

5844 Chalbaud, Román. Teatro. Ratón en ferretería. Caracas: Monte Avila Editores, 1977. 94. (Colección Teatro)

Well-written play that presents a balanced view between the flamboyant behavior of an artist and the depressing truths of a life starved for love. The protagonist half-reflects/half-hallucinates about his life style after an auto accident leaves him hospitalized and anguished.

5845 Chocrón, Isaac E. Mónica y el florentino: pieza en dos actos y cuatro escenas. Caracas: Monte Avila Editores, 1980. 94 p. (Colección Teatro)

Reprint of Chocrón's first play, occasioned by a 20th-anniversary production (1979) by El Nuevo Grupo. A clear technique and a theme of solitude prefigures Chocrón's development as a major Venezuelan playwright.

5846 Comedias cubanas siglo XIX. t. 1, Una aventura, o, El camino más corto por José Agustín Millán. La hija de las flores por Gertrudis Gómez de Avellaneda. Los montes de oro por Francisco Javier Balmaseda. t. 2, Ojo a la finca por José Jacinto Milanés. Cuatro a una! por Rafael Otero Marín. A tigre, zorra y bull-dog por Joaquín Lorenzo Luaces. Una sesión de hipnotismo por Ramón Meza y Suárez Inclán. Selección y prólogo de Rine Leal. La Habana: Editorial Letras Cubanas, 1979. 2 v.: bibl. (Biblioteca básica de literatura cubana)

Vol. 1: Flowers and money function as metaphors in these three 19th-century Cuban plays. Millán's play is filled with confusions but true love wins out; Avellaneda's play destroys common family conventions of choosing a bride; Balmaseda's play creates a fictitious society to criticize the artificiality of the stock exchange. Vol. 2: A collection of four plays including *sainetes*, comedy of manners and farces by leading 19th-century Cuban writers.

5847 Corleto, Manuel. Teatro. v. 2., ¿Quién va a morderse los codos? Lluvia de vincapervincas. Vade retro. El día que a mí me maten. Guatemala: Editorial Piedra Santa, 1979. 1 v.

Four plays that attempt to be van-

guardist in presenting relationships with fear, underdevelopment, oppression and hunger. They do not succeed.

5848 Cossier, Darío. *Bajo el alero* y otras comedias: repertorio del teatro obrero del Ministerio de Trabajo y Previsión Social. A manera de prólogo, Cesar Tiempo. San Salvador: Impr. Nacional, Ministerio del Interior, 1979? 73 p.

Melodramatic play in rural setting where peasants affected by drought discover an underground river which solves their problems. No transcendental value.

5849 Cruz Rodríguez, Pedro. Teatro de expresión popular. Guayaquil: Casa de la Cultura Ecuatoriana, Núcleo del Guayas, 1980. 133 p. (Colección Letras del Ecuador, 105)

Collection of two short plays, *Rumipata* (1974) and *Los cargadores* (1975), one full-length play, *Historia nuevamente a contar* (1977), and two children's plays. Strong social messages of exploitation and rebellion by colonists, Indians and workers in the plays of this young guayaquileño (b. 1953).

5850 Denevi, Marco. *Los expedientes*: nueva versión. Buenos Aires: Talía, 1978. 66 p. (Colección Argentina de teatro; 95)

Humorous full-length play dealing with paper shuffling and intricate office relationships with mild satire about bureaucracy.

5851 Díaz Machicao, Porfirio. Antología del teatro boliviano. La Paz: Editorial Don Bosco, 1979. 285 p.; 16 leaves of plates; ill.

Collection of scenes from 50 Bolivian plays from 19th and 20th centuries. Excessive fragmentation destroys anthology's goal of preserving the theatre. A few complete plays chosen for their quality would have served the purpose.

5852 Domínguez, Franklin. Lisístrata odia la política. Obra teatral en 3 actos inspirada en un tema de Aristófanes. Santo Domingo: Editorial Duarte, 1981. 127 p.

Entertaining work in which the women unite to prevent their men from spending so much time with politics and so little time with them. Predictable comedy ending gives women the upper hand.

5853 ———. Omar y los demás. Santo Domingo: Secretaría de Estado de Educación, Bellas Artes y Cultos, 1976. 92 p.

Fantasy about a man of good intentions who dreams of being the new Buddha, Christ, Shakespeare *et al.* throughout history. Good use of traditional theatrical conventions coupled with Brechtian audience confrontation to support basic philosophical premise.

5854 Dorr, Nicolás. Cinco farsas y dos comedias. La Habana: Ediciones Unión, 1978. 388 p.

Five short pieces, including Dorr's well-known *Las pericas,* plus two full-length plays, of which the best is *La chacota* for its lucid presentation of economic and cultural degradation during a political campaign in the 1950s.

5855 Duarte, Augusto. La cruz del Chaco: comedia en tres actos. Asunción: s.n., 1980. 69 p.

A 1980 printing of a 1949 play focusing on three brothers involved in the Chaco War. Bombastic and patriotic, simplistic in construction, but with considerable human interest.

5856 Enríquez, José Ramón. Héctor y Aquiles. Editores, Carlos Isla y Ernesto Trejo. Viñeta, Basia Batorska. México: Editorial Latitudes, 1979. 61 p. (Colección El Pozo y el péndulo; 15)

Metatheatrical reconstruction of Hector's and Achilles' relationship, the great heroes of the Trojan War, who search in vision and history for motivations and objectives before dying. Poetic language but little dramatic tension.

5857 Fernández, Gerardo. A nivel de cuadra: comedia musical en tres actos. Ed., Nancy Morejón. La Habana: Unión de Escritores y Artistas de Cuba, 1979. 131 p.

Musical comedy that draws on different points of view about the utility of the vegetation around an apartment complex. Objective is to resolve these differences within the context of a Revolutionary spirit through the local CDR (Committee for Defense of the Revolution). Better than most.

5858 Flores Magón, Ricardo. Obras de teatro: Tierra y libertad; Verdugos y víctimas. México: Ediciones Antorcha, 1977. 139 p.

Reprints two plays written 1916–17 that capture the essence of Mexico's proletarian revolution but are merely of historical interest because of their simplistic technique and exaggerated language.

5859 Fox, Lucía. Ayer es nunca jamás. Colección de dramas. Introducción de Flora Werner. Lima: Editorial del Colegio Salesiano, 1980. 255 p.

Collection of eight short plays, most dealing with problems of Latin American women from various social classes facing changing attitudes in themselves and a male-oriented society. Superficial treatment of the encroaching identity crises for each character.

5860 Gorostiza, Carlos. Los hermanos queridos. La nona por Roberto M. Cossa. Buenos Aires: Sociedad General de Autores de la Argentina, 1980. 182 p. (Colección teatral de Argentores)

Los hermanos queridos is another Gorostiza tour-de-force between two discrete and non-interactive groups of characters who plan the reunion of two brothers. Frustration is the dominant emotion in both works.

5861 Hernández Espinosa, Eugenio. La Simona. Teatro. La Habana: Casa de las Américas, 1977. 169 p. (Premio Casa de las Américas 1977)

Poetic play about a people's revolt in a small Chilean town. A story of deceit, treachery and venality in which La Simona, a colorful and dominant figure, leads the popular resistance against the "invaders" of Don Diego Almagro by tricking them with misleading sexual advances. The message is clear: a people united and disposed to defend itself can withstand any invasion.

5862 Laferrère, Gregorio de. Jettatore!; Las de Barranco. Selección, prólogo y notas por Luis Ordaz. Buenos Aires: Centro Editor de América Latina, 1980. 187 p. (El Teatro argentino; 5)

New edition of Laferrère's two principal works with good introduction and notes by Luis Ordaz. *Jettatore* and *Las de Barranco* epitomize the psychological dexterity and farcical tone of these turn-of-the-century pieces.

5863 Larco, Juan. Ubú Presidente (CDLA/CO, 48, abril/junio 1981, p. 91–109)

Selected scenes from Larco's farcical and Jarry-esque vision of a Central American republic dominated by the ubiquitous fruit company, in which the Captain of the Guard

Ubú tests his loyalty. Better than most plays of this type.

5864 Leguizamón, Martiano. Calandria. Ensalada criolla por E. De. María. Selección, prólogo y notas por Luis Ordaz. Ilus. de tapa, Leónidas Gambartes. Buenos Aires: Centro Editor de América Latina, 1980. 1 v. (El teatro argentino; 2)

Two plays from the 1890s and the Podestá tradition that reflect the so-called "género chico" and the "zarzuelismo criollo" that led to the creation of an Argentine national theatre.

5865 Leis, Raúl. María Picana. Panamá: Ediciones Aspan Pipigua, 1980. 80 p.

Tension-filled play deals with horrors of torture and possible awakening of love and hope for mankind in the protagonist. Potential impact in epilogue is lost when actors discard roles to address audience directly.

5866 Leñero, Vicente. Martirio de Morelos. México: Editorial Ariel y Seix Barral, 1981. 135 p.

Another Leñero documentary-drama that captures the last days of the Mexican patriot (5 Nov.–22 Dec. 1815). A "lector" serves as the narrative voice to recreate dramatically the historical account of judicial and religious sanctions against Morelos that justified his martyrdom.

5867 ———. La mudanza. Fotografías de Rogelio Cuéllar. México: J. Mortiz, 1980. 123 p.; 8 p. of plates; ill. (Teatro del volador)

Leñero's prize-winning play about a couple moving into a different residence. The simple action becomes increasingly more tense in proportion to their personal problems and the enigmatic features of the colonial house. A gripping, chilling work.

5868 Maldonado, Patricia et al. Así ocurrió cuando los blancos no fueron malos (Taller de Teatro [Grupo Texco, Bogotá] 1, abril/junio 1979, p. 35–88, photographs)

Collective creation based on the Cuiba Indians—their discovery by the Spanish, the process of catechization and colonization, the ubiquitous Summer Linguistics Institute, and their eventual annihilation. Simplistic but probably true account.

5869 Marechal, Leopoldo. Antígona Vélez. Introducción, notas y propuestas de trabajo, Hebe Monges. Buenos Aires: Ediciones Colihue: Distribución, Librería Hachette, 1981. 93 p.; bibl.; ill.; ports. (Colección Literaria LYC (leer y crear)

New printing of Marechal's gauchesque version of Antigone, with substantial critical introduction and chronology.

5870 Montes Huidobro, Matías. Ojos para no ver. Miami, Fla.: Ediciones Universal, 1979. 59 p.

Heavy symbolism mars this play which attempts to be an allegory about terror and genocide.

5871 Morales, Jacobo. Muchas gracias por las flores: cinco alegres tragedias. Río Piedras: Editorial Antillana, 1978. 107 p.; ill.

Five brief male monologues (with occasional voices off-stage) with poignant to bitter interpretations of life and death in varied settings. All incorporate flowers as the leitmotif. Entertaining but not great theatre.

5872 Nari, Fortunato E. El habitante. Santa Fe, Argentina: Librería y Editorial Colmegna, 1973. 72 p.

Four main characters question man's reason for being in a powerful allegory of life and death. Dynamic, convincing one-act play.

5873 ———. La tierra está. Santa Fe, Argentina: Librería y Editorial Colmegna, 1975. 79 p.

Couple fights ravages of drought and husband finds solace with his sister-in-law. Slow-moving, with underdeveloped characters and stilted dialogue.

5874 Núñez, José Gabriel. La visita del extraño señor. Los pájaros se van con la muerte por Edilio Peña. Un desayuno cualquiera por José Manuel Peláez. Caracas: Taller de Creación Literaria, Centro de Estudios Latinoamericanos Rómulo Gallegos, 1978. 173 p. (Teatro; 1) (Colección Voces nuevas)

La visita del extraño señor has God and St. Peter return to earth in the midst of political upheaval to try to renew man's hope in salvation: Peña's play portrays a mother and daughter reenacting their guilt and suffering through a series of games and rituals; Peláez's work is the best of the collection: a couple (reminiscent of Cepillo de dientes) play-acts through moments of their lives only to find that everything is a game.

5875 Orihuela, Roberto. Los novios. La Habana: Editorial Letras Cubanas, 1980. 88 p. (Colección Mínima; no. 10)

Developed on the basis of over 400 personal interviews, this popular recent play deals with the questions of morality and responsibility in a revolutionary society. A pregnant teenager provokes a crisis for her militant communist father. Good views of a changing society.

5876 Oteiza, Alberto M. La loca del puerto: pieza teatral en un acto de larga duración. La Plata, Argentina: Ediciones Olimpo, 1979. 91 p.; port.

Excessively sentimental portrait of a bereaved mother who transposes her son, unexpectedly home for a visit, for another son who was drowned. Has limited dramatic value.

5877 Panorama del teatro en El Salvador. Selección, prólogo y notas de Edmundo Barbero. San Salvador: Editorial Universitaria, 1972. 1 v.; bibl.

Trilogy by Francisco Gavidia and three separate plays by Joaquín Emilio Aragón. Both dramatists from the mid-19th century reflect the romantic nationalistic views prevalent at the time. Excellent introduction promises more volumes up to the present.

5878 Pavlovsky, Eduardo A. La mueca. Buenos Aires: Talía, between 1971 and 1980. 37 p. (Colección argentina de teatro; 14) 14)

This bitter 1971 play about a film crew that invades a private home to capture on film the decadence of bourgeois values turns into a realistic commentary on violence and sociopolitical actions in present times. One of the best plays of the decade.

5879 ———. Teatro. Introducción de George O. Schanzer. Madrid: Editorial Fundamentos, 1980. 196 p.

Collection of three plays within the framework of Artaud's theatre of cruelty meant to jolt the public with violence and non-conformist ideology. In addition to *La mueca* and *El Señor Galíndez*, the volume contains *Telarañas*, a series of 18 vignettes exploring memories of the past, rites of puberty, and generation gaps—all centered around soccer as a metaphor for patriotism, religiosity, and ideology.

5880 Pizarro Castro, Pablo. A pesar de la lluvia: drama en tres actos. San Juan: Instituto de Cultura Puertorriqueña, 1980. 92 p. (Serie Literature hoy; 1980)

Effort to be *engagé* in a Puerto Rican political and cultural sense without developing a line of dramatic conflict and action. Normal, everyday conversation cannot be the norm for the theatre.

5881 Ramos, José A. Teatro. Selección y prólogo de Francisco Garzón Céspedes. La Habana: Editorial Arte y Literature, 1976. 420 p.

Collection of four plays by Ramos purported to follow the trajectory from growing social awareness in *Calibán Rex* (1914) to total political commitment in *FU-3001* (1944). All four are idealistic, political and social commentaries using traditional theatrical techniques Ramos developed in comedies.

5882 Rascón Banda, Víctor Hugo. Los ilegales. México: Dirección de Difusión Cultural, Departamento Editorial, 1980. 83 p. (Serie Molinos de viento)

Emotional play that combines effectively human interest element with documentary evidence of Mexican "wetbacks" entering the US. Gripping and convincing portrayal of a difficult problem.

5883 Rela, Walter. Florencio Sánchez, persona y teatro: *Barranca abajo* y *En familia*. Montevideo: Editorial Ciencias, 1981. 223 p.

New and corrected versions of two of Sánchez's major plays with introductory material previously published by the indefatigable Rela in another edition of Sánchez.

5884 Rengifo, César. Teatro breve: cinco obras en un acto. Diseño de portada, Santiago Pol. Caracas: Editorial Ateneo de Caracas, 1979. 158 p. (Colección Teatro venezolano contemporáneo)

Promised vol. 1 of Rengifo's short plays (1948–1976), previously difficult or impossible to locate. Themes range from personal frustration (*Los canarios*, 1948) to the historical (*Manuelote*, 1950), to domestic reaction to political disturbances (*El caso de Beltrán Santos*, 1976). Interesting pieces by a major, recently deceased Venezuelan playwright.

5885 Riera S., Pedro. Obras de teatro para jóvenes y niños. Ciudad capital por Carlos Sánchez. Caracas: Taller de Creación Literaria, Centro de Estudios Latinoamericanos Rómulo Gallegos, 1978. 176 p. (Teatro; 2) (Colección Voces nuevas)

Riera's five plays are a valuable addition to the repertory of children's theatre; Sánchez's two-act play couches protest in an elevated style that is not effective.

5886 Romero, Mariela. El inevitable destino de Rosa de la Noche: obra en tres escenas. Caracas: Dirección General de Cultura de la Gobernación del Distrito Federal y Fundarte, 1980. 112 p. (Cuadernos de difusión. Series "Breves)

Another very promising play by the author of El juego and El vendedor. This one focuses on the intimate relationships of two derelicts and a prostitute. An intriguing vision of companionship, presentiments and death.

5887 Rossell, Levy. Lo mío me lo dejan en la olla. Caracas: Monte Avila Editores, 1979. 79 p. (Colección Teatro)

Musical history of Venezuela from its beginnings to the present day in a series of delightful vignettes that are simultaneously costumbristic and piquant. Rossell's best to date.

5888 Salazar Tamariz, Hugo. En tiempos de la colonia: teatro. Babahoyo, Ecuador: Ediciones Uso de la Palabra, 1977/1978 i.e. 1979. 99 p. (Colección de literatura; 1)

Curious and moderately effective mixture of contemporary social protest with historical figures of colonial times (e.g., the Gobernador Barros de San Millán, episode of the Revolution of the Alcabalas). Fragmented sequencing of dialogue to achieve group participation is tiresome and affected.

5889 Sánchez, Luis Rafael. La pasión según Antígona Pérez. 6. ed. Río Piedras, P.R.: Editorial Cultural, 1978. 122 p.

Reprints Sánchez's very successful docudrama of 1968, modeled on Antigone in an imaginary Latin American dictatorship. Excellent play.

5890 ———. Teatro de Luis Rafael Sánchez. t. 1, Farsa del amor compradito. La hiel nuestra de cada día. Los ángeles se han fatigado. Río Piedras, P.R.: Editorial Antillana, 1976. 1 v.

Contains the two parts of Sol 13, Interior plus La farsa del amor compradito, a three-act farce which borrows from Brecht and the commedia dell'arte to present multiple love triangles.

5891 Santander, Felipe. El extensionista. La Habana: Casa de las Américas, 1980. 112 p.

Tremendously popular play (over 1500 performances) about a young country extension agent in Mexico who struggles to gain the respect of his clientele. Moving and very effective.

5892 Sarduy, Severo. Para la voz. La playa. La caída. Relato. Los matadores de hormigas. Madrid: Editorial Fundamentos, 1978. 138 p.; ill. (Teatro) (Colección Espiral; 41)

La playa is an erotic, multilingual completely fluid collage about a beach fantasy, without any specific reality other than the language itself. La caída is an equally poetic vision of degradation and death. Fascinating pieces by a celebrated novelist.

5893 Schmidhuber de la Mora, Guillermo. Los herederos de Segismundo. Monterrey, México: Fonapas, 1982. 282 p. (Colección Taller)

La vida es sueño, 20–50 years later, with Segismundo as king facing a rebellious son, Américo, in an ubiquitous cycle of treason and hatred between father and son. The other leitmotif is the life-is-a-dream current, handled with originality by this young Mexican playwright.

5894 ———. Nuestro Señor Quetzalcóatl. Monterrey, México: Ediciones Sierra Madre, 1979. 77 p.

Idealized historical play in two acts plus epilogue recounting the changing religions through Quetzalcóatl to conquest. Too romanticized for good effect.

5895 Solórzano, Carlos. Teatro breve. México: J. Mortiz, 1977. 118 p.; 2 leaves of plates; ill. (Teatro del volador)

Collection of six one-acts with a general scheme of relationships between people, from lack of communication to allegorical messages to family love-hate relationships in Zapato, the new item in this grouping.

5896 Suárez Radillo, Carlos Miguel. El teatro barroco hispanoamericano. Ensayo de una historia crítico-antológica. Madrid:

José Porrúa Turanzas, 1980/1981. 3 v.
(700 p.)

First comprehensive effort to capture the essence and spirit of the Spanish American theatre during the baroque period. Imbedded in the critical text, which relies heavily on previous critics, are fragments of representative works by the playwrights presented. Useful for its panoramic view, careful composition and documentation; less useful for critical insights and sample texts.

5897 Teatro Alhambra: antología. Selección, prólogo y notas de Eduardo Robreño. Estudio complementario Alvaro López. La Habana: Editorial Letras Cubanas, 1979. 706 p.; bibl. (Biblioteca básica de literatura cubana)

Selection of 11 vaudeville and Cuban operettas, 1898–1930. Notes and complementary study attempt to force this diversionary theatre into a Marxist framework.

5898 Teatro bufo, siglo XIX. t. 2, Antología. Selección y prólogo de Rine Leal. La Habana: Editorial Arte y Literatura, 1975. 346 p.

Seven bufo-style comedies by six writers. Ramón Morales Alvarez's *El proceso del oso* typifies the musical review in which the effects of French can-can are compared to other typical Cuban rhythms of the era; others focus on Cuban historical figures, black influences on Cuban society, and especially the Cuban songs, dances and rhythms employed for nationalistic goals.

5899 Teatro centroamericano contemporáneo. San Salvador, El Salvador: Ediciones del Pulgarcito, 1977. 163 p.

Cheap reprinting of two earlier plays, Daniel Gallegos' *Los profanos* (1959) and Carlos Solórzano's now-classic *Las manos de Dios* (1956) that, interestingly, have similarities in both theme and structure.

5900 Teatro en Honduras. v. 2. Selección y notas, Alma Caballero y Francisco Salvador. Tegucigalpa: Departamento de Producción Intelectual de la Secretaría de Cultura, Turismo e Información, 1977. 1 v.; ill. (Colección Docencia)

Three Honduran plays, a rare sight. *Los chapetones*, by Medardo Mejía, is a family feud over inherited land; *Timoteo se divierte* by Daniel Laínez, is a "juguete cómico" in popular language; *La peste negra* by Ramón Amaya Amador, protests the injustices of the foreign pharmaceutical industry. All three suffer from a lamentable dramatic naiveté.

5901 Teatro 4, New York. Gimme five. Con libreto de Alberto Adellach (CDLA/CO, 44, abril/junio 1980, p. 16–73)

Collective creation of Teatro 4 and Alberto Adellach, this mordant play penetrates the Hispanic district of Manhattan. The particular combination of Spanish and English, the drugs and judicial problems, the brutality and tenderness of interpersonal relationships—all characterize the realities of life on the Lower East Side.

5901a Teatro peruano. v. 2 and 4. Lima: Ediciones Homero Teatro de Grillos, 1974?/1978. 2 v. (137, 54 p.)

Vol. 2 consists of four short plays by the very young César de María (b. 1960), who shows promise in dealing with the rough-and-tumble problems of his age group. Sara Joffre's four plays show dedication to political and social problems. For vol. 1, see *HLAS 38:7204*.

5902 Tovar, Juan. La madrugada. México: Editorial Latitudes, 1979. 44 p.

A maudlin tribute to General Francisco Villa, dealing with his assassination. Unsatisfying and untheatrical.

5903 *Tramoya.* Cuaderno de teatro. Universidad Veracruzana. No. 17, oct./dic. 1979– . Xalapa, México.

In addition to Carballido's commentary on the 10th Festival of Chicano Theatre in Santa Barbara, this issue contains two plays: Luisa Josefina Hernández's *La fiesta del mulato* (1966), which examines the racial consciousness of Mexico during the early years of independence; and *Los hijos de Bato y Bras* (1859) by the obscure Mariano Osorno (1821–1900), a *pastorela* with a surprising freshness and light verse.

5904 ——. ——. ——. No. 18, enero/feb. 1980– . Xalapa, México.

An editorial decision to publish no criticism in this issue results in 11 plays by as many authors. Among the best: Luisa Josefina Hernández's *Ciertas cosas*, a servant girl's monologue asking Zeus for pardon; Antonio Argudín's *Cypris*, about the transcendence of lust and passion; Alejandro Licona's

Cuentas por cobrar, a male conquest with a surprise ending; and Reynaldo Carballido's *Sombras ajenas*, a bizarre lovers' quarrel which ends in Russian roulette.

5905 ——. ——. ——. No. 20, julio/ sept. 1980– . Xalapa, México.

Carballido's comments about collective creation, Susana Castillo's analysis of Romero's *El juego* and Dean Zayas' observations about the formation of the actor in Puerto Rico intersect the three plays in this issue: Tomás Espinoza's *Santísima la nauyaca*, a farcial illusion of power and importance through identification with a celebrity; Felipe Galván's *La historia de Miguel* (1980), a spine-chilling military kidnap of a grocer suspected of illicit arms traffic; and *Superocho* by Pilar Campesino (formerly Pilar Retes), in which a filming confuses reality and fantasy regarding terrorist activities in 1968.

5906 Trejo, Nemesio. Los políticos. Canillita por Florencio Sánchez. Los disfrazados por Carlos M. Pacheco. Babilonia por Armando Discépolo. Los de la mesa diez por Osvaldo Dragún. Selección, prólogo y notas por Jorge Lafforgue. Buenos Aires: Centro Editor de América Latina, 1979. 189 p.; bibl. (Capítulo; 3)

Five River Plate plays spanning 60 years (1897–1957) and reflecting the transition from the *criollo* to the contemporary theatre. Prepared as a school text with notes and vocabulary.

5907 Valcárcel, Carlos Daniel. Teatro popular Túpac Amaru: drama. Lima: Comisión Universitaria del Bicentenario de Túpac Amaru, Universidad Nacional Mayor de San Marcos: SAIS Túpac Amaru Ltda. No. 1, 1979/1980 [i.e. 1980]. 77 p.; 3 leaves of plates; col. ill. (Serie Kilcacamáyoc; 2)

Reprints one of the many theatrical versions of the history of this famous Incan revolutionary hero. Carlos Daniel Valcárcel knows the history as well as anyone, but the work is melodramatic and deficient.

5908 Vargas Llosa, Mario. La señorita de Tacna, pieza en dos actos. Mexico: Editorial Seix Barral, 1981, 146 p.

Interweaves themes of love, hate, pride, jealousy with individual destiny and family disintegration through writer's onstage presence who recaptures age-old

Chilean-Peruvian conflicts in 1950s setting. Skillful, original novelistic techniques applied to theatre that works.

5909 Vega Herrera, César. Qué sucedió en Pasos? Madrid: Ediciones Cultura Hispánica del Centro Iberoamericano de Cooperación, 1978. 57 p. (Colección de teatro)

Allegory of life and death, living and existing, two puppet artists arrive in a remote Indian village to perform, only to find the town chillingly strange, oddly unreal.

5910 Villabella, Manuel. Jucaral. Cubierta, Roberto Artemio. La Habana: Unión de Escritores y Artistas de Cuba, 1979. 109 p. (Manjuarí: Teatro)

Historical play inspired by legendary figure Joaquín de Agüero y Agüero, who struck for anti-slavery and Cuban independence as early as 1851. Agile dialogue and construction avoid usual pitfalls of historical patriotism.

5911 Villasis Endara, Carlos. Los caminos oscuros de la gloria y otras piezas de teatro. Quito: Editorial Casa de la Cultura Ecuatoriana, 1978. 157 p.; ill.

Five plays of uneven quality by this Ecuadorian writer (b. 1930). Common denominators are sociopolitical protest and metatheatrical quality of playing with actor/public relations. *La ciudad es una trampa* is the best of the collection.

5912 Villegas, Oscar. La pira (Tramoya [Cuaderno de teatro. Universidad Veracruzana, Xalapa, México] 9, oct./dic. 1977, p. 5–21)

Devastating view of the consequences of the double standard governing male/female sexual relationships among a group of Mexican adolescents. *La pira* ("gang bang") is a good play by one of the best of the younger generation of Mexican playwrights.

CRITICISM

5913 Acuña, René. El teatro popular en Hispanoamérica: una bibliografía anotada. México: Universidad Nacional Autónoma de México, Instituto de Investigaciones Filológicas, Centro de Estudios Literarios, 1979. 114 p.; index.

Unique and sometimes annotated bibliography of popular theatre which includes valuable entries on Spanish precedents, then focuses primarily on popular theatre from the US Southwest to Guatemalan border, with a bird's-eye view of the rest of Spanish America. Very useful.

5914 Arróniz, Othón. Teatro de evangelización en Nueva España. México: Universidad Nacional Autónoma de México, 1979. 255 p.; bibl.; index (Textos y estudios—Instituto de Investigaciones Filológicas, Centro de Estudios Literarios; Letras mexicanas del XVI al XVIII).

Carefully documented study traces contributions of Franciscans, Dominicans and Jesuits to religious theatre in the New World. Concludes that catechetical theatre is an instrument of spiritual conquest that can be defined more easily by its Christian doctrines than by its formal structure. Includes bibliography and one *égloga*.

5915 Azor Hernández, Ileana. Entrevista con Rogelio Sinán: anécdotas y fábulas de un cuentista dramaturgo (UEAC/GC, 184, dic. 1979, p. 14–16)

Author of several children's plays, Sinán explains background and circumstances, including some bizarre events, that led to his creative expression as a committed playwright.

5916 Becco, Horacio Jorge. Bibliografía general de las artes del espectáculo en América Latina. Paris: UNESCO, 1977. 188 p.; index (América Latina en su cultura)

A long-term UNESCO project, this bibliography of the "artes del espectáculo" includes 1797 entries organized geographically. Includes a few items not reported in the 1976 bibliography of Lyday and Woodyard (see *HLAS 40:7353*).

5917 Bixler, Jacqueline Eyring. Freedom and fantasy: a structural approach to the fantastic in Carballido's *Las cartas de Mozart* (UK/LATR, 14:1, Fall 1980, p. 15–23)

Todorov's theories of the fantastic prove the merit of Carballido's play as an aesthetic work in which conventional reality is transformed according to the free will of participants. An excellent play and study.

5918 Boal, Augusto. Teatro del oprimido y otras poéticas políticas. Buenos Aires: Ediciones de la Flor, 1974. 238 p.

Boal contends that *all* theatre is politi-

cal, a theory that he applies from Aristotle through Shakespeare to the present. The "practice" includes his Teatro Arena in Brazil and later experiments with journalistic theatre, invisible theatre and others. A primer on revolutionary theatre.

5919 Burgess, Ronald D. Willebaldo López: Mexico on stage (UK/LATR, 14:2, Spring 1981, p. 27–39)

First thorough examination of one of Mexico's most promising younger playwrights, author of *Cosas de muchachos* and other plays that criticize Mexican socioeconomic problems, especially those of the young and the lower class.

5920 *La Cabra.* Revista de teatro. Universidad Nacional Autónoma de México. Epoca 3, Nos. 30/32, marzo/mayo 1981– México.

Issue is devoted exclusively to activities of UNAM'S Teatro Universitario in 1980. Also includes: Guillermo Schmidhuber de la Mora's *Los héroes inútiles*; article on José Revueltas' theatre by Ignacio Hernández; and interview with Hugo Argüelles by Agustín García.

5921 Callan, Richard J. El misterio femenino en *Los perros* de Elena Garro (IILI/RI, 110/111, enero/junio 1980, p. 231–235)

Penetrating myth analysis of Garro's play relates characters to classical figures Demeter and Persephone and Aztec goddesses Xilonen and Chicomecoatl. Also comments on masculine/feminine roles in Mexico, à-la-Octavio Paz.

5922 Castillo, Susana D. El desarraigo en el teatro venezolano: marco histórico y manifestaciones modernas. Caracas: Editorial Ateneo de Caracas, 1980. 189 p.

Explores theme of alienation within history of developing Venezuelan theatre and as philosophical concept. Textual analyses of works by eight contemporary Venezuelan writers uses thematic and expressionistic points of view. A solid study.

5923 ———. Un friso histórico: la obra de César Rengifo (CDLA/Co, 49, julio/sept. 1981, p. 26–38)

Literary tribute to recently departed muralist, painter, dramatist, professor, director, journalist and historian, this article focuses on Rengifo's *Las torres y el viento*, one of the works in the petroleum cycle.

5924 ———. *El juego*: texto dramático y montaje (UK/LATR, 14:1, Fall 1980, p. 25–33)

Young Venezuelan Mariela Romero uses Artaudian techniques to portray and denounce violence in contemporary society. Insightful article compares two stage versions of this "open text" as well.

5925 ———. Ironía y ternura: el extraño teatro de Elisa Lerner (*in* Mujer y sociedad en América Latina. Selection and prologue by Lucía Guerra Cunningham. Santiago, Chile: Coedición Universidad de California-Irvine and Editorial del Pacífico, 1980, p. 223–232)

Overview of Venezuelan lawyer-playwright's works, ranging from existential monologue *La bella de inteligencia* (1949) to psychological-political *Vida con mamá* (1975). Useful introduction to one of the most important contemporary women writers.

5926 Chió, Evangelina. El Galpón de nuestra América (RYC, 66, feb. 1978, p. 30–35, ill., plates)

Quick look at background of one of the long-standing (since 1949) revolutionary theatre groups in Latin America, now in exile in Mexico, based on an interview with the director, César Campodónico.

5927 Collins, J. A. Contemporary theatre in Puerto Rico: the decade of the seventies. Río Piedras: Editorial Universitaria, Universidad de Puerto Rico, 1981. 1 v.; bibl.

Brief overview by *Star* critic Collins highlights historical development of Puerto Rican theatre, and attributes a lot of credit to Spaniard Luis Molina for promoting theatre activity in the 1970s. Illuminating, but much too brief.

5928 Colón Zayas, Eliseo R. René Marqués, 1919–1979 (IILI/RI, 110/111, enero/junio 1970, p. 237–240)

Concise eulogistic statement about Marqués' efforts and success in renovating Puerto Rican stage during his lifetime. Some focus on *Los soles truncos* and *Sacrificio en el Monte Moriah* as key plays in his technical development.

5929 *Conjunto*. Casa de las Américas. Nos. 45, 47/49, 1980/1981– . La Habana.

All four issues are devoted to Latin American theatre (for annotations of individual plays, see items **5833, 5835, 5842, 5863** and **5923**).

5930 Cypess, Sandra Messinger. Women dramatists of Puerto Rico (RRI, 9:1, Spring, 1979, p. 24–41)

Catalogue of 12 or so women playwrights of Puerto Rico from 19th century (three of them) to present. Absence of a thesis leads to vague conclusions, but intent seems to be to document extraordinary efforts of women to write effective drama under unusual hardships.

5931 Díaz Roque, José and **Francisco Rodríguez Alemán.** José Antonio Ramos: su teatro y su ideología (UCLV/I, 63, mayo/agosto 1979, p. 91–150, bibl., table)

Extensive review of Ramos' background, followed by discussion of his 15 extant plays, leads to conclusion that key elements in his ideological development are his individualism, patriotism and anti-imperialism.

5932 En el Parque Lenín. los juglares y la peña del amor de todos. Compilación, prólogo y entrevistas: Carlos Espinosa Domínguez. La Habana: Editorial Orbe, 1979. 265 p.

Collection of testimonials, interviews, photos, commentaries and selections from work of Teresita Fernández and Francisco Garzón Céspedes regarding their Sunday volunteer entertainment in Parque Lenín, Havana.

5933 Espinosa, Tomás. Teatro de la Nación (Tramoya [Cuaderno de teatro. Universidad Veracruzana, Xalapa, México] 9, oct./dic. 1977, p. 43–59, photographs)

Broad view of Mexican theatre program initiated by the López Portillos. Espinosa takes analytical and sometimes critical look at all five cycles, from motivation to selection to production. Good insights.

5934 Festival de Teatro de La Habana. La Habana: Editorial ORBE, 1982. 241 p.

Complete digest of First Festival de Teatro de La Habana (12–22 Jan. 1980) includes ample documentation and illustrations, position papers by Rine Leal, Francisco Garzón Céspedes, Graziella Pogolotti, Marcia Leiseca and others, plus commentaries on the importance of the festival and individual performances by authors, directors, and critics. A valuable document.

5935 Foster, David William. El lenguaje como vehículo espiritual en *Los siameses* de Griselda Gambaro (UCV/E, 4:8, julio/dic. 1979, p. 241–257)

Thorough and discerning analysis of language in *Los siameses*, using semiotics, speech art theory, common sense, and good knowledge of Argentine culture and sociolinguistic patterns. Valuable study.

5936 ———. Semantic relativity in Ricardo Monti's *La visita* (The American Hispanist [Clear Creek, Ind.] 4:34/35, March/April 1979, p. 17–20)

Foster uses semiological systems to analyze *La visita* and concludes that neither the grotesque nor the absurd are wholly accountable for the ill-defined meaning of the play.

5937 ———. The texture of dramatic action in the plays of Griselda Gambaro (IUP/HJ, 1:2, Spring 1980, p. 57–66)

Brilliant but limited analysis of how the final scenes of two Gambaro plays (*Los siameses* and *El campo*) reveal complex interaction of multiple sign system, à-la-Bernard Beckerman's "dramatic activity."

5938 García, Santiago. Ponencia sobre "la creación colectiva" como proceso de trabajo en "La Candelaria" (Taller de Teatro [Grupo Texco, Bogotá] 1, abril/junio 1979, p. 5–22, photographs)

One of Latin America's most respected directors explains the seven-step process of developing a new play by "collective creation:" 1) motivation, 2) investigation, 3) third step, 4) first structural hypothesis, 5) thematic lines, 6) plot lines, and 7) staging and text. Revealing and useful presentation.

5939 Giella, Miguel Angel. Teatro Abierto: fenómeno socioteatral argentino (UK/LATR, 15:1, Fall 1981, p. 89–93)

One of most ambitious theatre activities of recent years, the Teatro Abierto in its first stage (July–Aug. 1981) paired 20 authors and 20 directors to present as many new plays in Teatro del Picadero. Although the theatre itself burned under mysterious circumstances, program continued with renewed emphasis on dedication to principles of free expression.

5940 González, Nilda. Bibliografía de teatro puertorriqueño: siglos XIX y XX. Río Piedras: Editorial Universitaria, Universidad de Puerto Rico, 1977. 223 p.; bibl.; index.

Truly invaluable bibliography contains essentially a *curriculum vitae* of every Puerto Rican playwright of the 19th and 20th centuries (plays, publications, criticism, reviews). Various appendices fill in on theatre groups, prizes, festivals. Very useful.

5941 Kaiser-Lenoir, Claudia. El avión negro: de la realidad a la caricatura grotesca (UK/LATR, 15:1, Fall 1981, p. 5–11)

Author shows how this composite and anachronistic play about Perón's return to Argentina combines caricature and the grotesque to create a shocking, yet recognizable, reality. Perceptive interpretation.

5942 Knowles, John Kenneth. Luisa Josefina Hernández: teoría y práctica del drama. Translation by Antonio Argudín. Revised with introd. by Thomas Espinosa. México: Universidad Nacional Autónoma de México, 1980. 134 p.

The application of Hernández's dramatic theory to eight of her own plays leads Knowles to conclude that she learned well her early lessons from Tennessee Williams. After 1960, however, her plays show a marked preference for sociopolitical themes.

5943 Korn, Guillermo. Teatro en Caracas, febrero 1978/abril 1979. Miguel Gracia, fotos. Caracas: Ediciones Casuz, 1979. 141 p.; 19 leaves of plates; ill. (Colección Varia)

Up-date in Korn's series of postcard-style reviews of major hits on the Caracas stage during period indicated. Includes 50 reviews with photos ranging from Chocrón's *El acompañante* to Ibsen's *Doll House*. Anecdotal and interesting but limited critical value.

5944 *Latin American Theatre Review.* Center of Latin American Studies. Vol. 13, No. 2; Vol. 14, Nos. 1/2; Vol. 15, Nos. 1/2, 1980/1981– . Lawrence, Kansas.

In addition to articles annotated elsewhere in this section, these issues contain reports on theatre festivals, symposia and seasons in Buenos Aires, Bogotá, Lima, Caracas, Havana, San Juan, Rio, various US sites, etc. Major articles focus on plays (e.g., Wilberto Cantón, Florencio Sánchez, Armando

Discépolo, Rodolfo Usigli, Roberto Arlt, Osvaldo Dragún, Andrés Lizárraga, Ricardo Monti, Egon Wolff, Jorge Adrade, etc.) as well as on aspects of language, myth and ideology.

5945 ——. ——. Vol. 13, No. 2, Supplement, Summer 1980– . Lawrence, Kansas.

Special issue is devoted to proceedings of Symposium on Latin American Theatre, Florida International University, April 1979, directed by Maida Watson Espener. Contains 16 articles by noted Latin American authors and critics, plus keynote address by Frank Dauster.

5946 Lerner, Elisa. Una visita sin antesala (*in* Segal, Alicia Freilich de. Entrevistados en carne y hueso. Caracas: Librería Suma, 1976 or 1977, p. 91–102)

Interview with Elisa Lerner, Venezuela's foremost woman playwright, in which she talks about her background, her objectives, her political compromises, and especially about her prize-winning *Vida con mamá* (1975), based on Allende's death in Chile but which was really inspired by Rómulo Gallegos' fall in 1948.

5947 López, Ana Lucía. Teatro panameño contemporáneo (UCR/AEC, 1976, p. 369–373)

Misleading title to cursory review of five plays by José de Jesús Martínez (published under the title *Caifás y otras piezas*) with a common denominator, the exposure of social injustice.

5948 Luzuriaga, Gerardo. La generación del 60 y el teatro (UTIEH/C, 34, 1980, p. 157–170, bibl.)

Thorough and serious effort to document the generational patterns in Ecuadorian theatre, carried out with good historical and critical sense of dominant figures, groups, and plays.

5949 McNair, Nora de M. de. El sainete porteño y el teatro menor de Florencio Sánchez (*in* Estudios literarios sobre Hispanoamérica: homenaje a Carlos M. Raggi y Ageo. Troy, N.Y.: Círculo de Cultura Panamericano, 1976, p. 67–75)

Using Vaccarezza's definition of the Argentine *sainete*, McNair measures Sánchez's minor theatre and finds it both original and traditional. A brief but acute study.

5950 Martin, Eleanor Jean. *Dos viejos pánicos:* a political interpretation of the Cuban theater of the absurd (RRI, 9:1, Spring 1979, p. 50–55)

Martin sees the Piñera play, not as a European absurdism, but as a political work that embodies the optimism of the Revolution by parodying the bourgeois values which demand a new order for life.

5951 Mengod Gimeno, Rosa María. Presencias en el teatro chileno del siglo XX (UC/AT, 440, 2. semestre, 1979, p. 101–135, bibl.)

Very rapid overview of Chilean theatre from its origins to the present (Egon Wolff gets nine lines). Concludes that playwrights understand the two components of the Chilean character—the historical and the "projective" (future)—which allows the presentation of national themes with a universal vision.

5952 Montes Huidobro, Matías. Luis Rafael Sánchez: lenguaje e identidad en el teatro puertorriqueño (The American Hispanist [Cedar Creek, Ind.] 4:30/31, Nov./Dec. 1978, p. 22–25)

Montes studies ritual effects achieved through "verbal subtraction" and "numerical addition" in Sánchez's *La hiel nuestra de cada día*, and deduces that linguistic features of this early play (half of the diptych *Sol 13, Interior*) prefigured Sánchez's later successes.

5953 ——. *Vejigantes:* síntesis erótica de la historia puertorriqueña (ICP/R, 20:75, abril/junio 1977, p. 33–40, ill.)

Montes considers the active and passive erotic qualities of the Hispanic, Puerto Rican and North American cultures in order to explain the particular qualities of miscegenation and conquest. Intriguing and thoughtful analysis of *Vejigantes*. Bill's authenticity as a character, however, is overemphasized.

5954 ——. Zambullida en el *Orinoco* de Carballido (UK/LATR, 15:2, Spring 1982, p. 13–52)

Another Carballido work which plays with fantasy on a mysterious boat trip down the Orinoco River; Montes points out mythological parallels with the River Styx.

5955 Moreno, Norma. Reflexiones sobre el teatro cordobés (Andén para la Cultura

[Ediciones Candilejas, Córdoba, Argentina]
1 : 1, sept./oct. 1979, p. 56–58, plates]

Brief report on theatre in Córdoba where *San Vicente Super Star* was the hit of 1978. Interesting view of theatre efforts in a provincial city.

5956 Moretta, Eugene L. Spanish American theatre of the 50s and 60s: critical perspectives on role playing (UK/LATR, 13 : 2, Spring 1980, p. 5–30)

Examines principally *Los soles truncos, Medusa, ¿A qué jugamos?,* and *La noche de los asesinos* as characteristic plays dealing with game theory and role playing as a way of dealing with larger issues of life and reality. Provocative and sensitive study.

5957 Morfi, Angelina. Historia crítica de un siglo de teatro puertorriqueño. San Juan: Instituto de Cultura Puertorriqueña, 1980. 569 p.

Misleading title for study which covers virtually all Puerto Rican theatre, with special attention on the 19th and 20th centuries. Well-organized and well-documented, replete with quotations from the texts and from the critics; shy on critical analysis, however. A labor of great love whose major strengths are in the earlier periods.

5958 Munizaga, Giselle and **María de la Luz Hurtado.** Testimonios del teatro: 35 años de teatro en la Universidad Católica. Santiago: Ediciones Nueva Universidad, 1980. 186 p.

Sometimes uneven presentation of 35 years of history in Chile's Catholic University theatre. Directors, actors, writers and others comment on politics, theatrical concepts, teaching and administrative organization.

5959 Muñoz Cadima, W. Oscar. Teatro boliviano contemporáneo. La Paz: Biblioteca Paceña, 1981. 214 p.

History of largely unknown and ignored theatre divided into two parts: pre- and post-Chaco War. Pt. 1 establishes antecedents; pt. 2 gives close readings of better texts, such as Suárez Figueroa's *El hombre del sombrero de paja* and Calabi's *La nariz.* Best among recent efforts to write Bolivian theatre history.

5960 Neglia, Erminio G. El asedio a la casa: un estudio del decorado en *La noche de los asesinos* (IILI/RI, 110/111, enero/junio 1980, p. 139–149)

Neglia studies set of *La noche de los asesinos* in its broadest terms, including both imaginary space (police station, court) and dramatic objects (knife, ashtray, etc.). Using Kowzan's article as a semiotic base, concludes that space changes on the imaginative level throughout the play.

5961 Peden, Margaret Sayers. Emilio Carballido. Boston: Twayne Publishers, 1980. 192 p.; bibl.; index; port. (Twayne's world authors series; TWAS 561; Mexico)

Penetrating analysis of all of Carballido's plays and fiction up to press time. Peden groups by style and technique; the categories may be restrictive, but the analyses are impeccable. Selective bibliography.

5962 Pereira, Teresinka. La actual dramaturgia latinoamericana. Bogotá: Ediciones Tercer Mundo, 1979. 87 p.

Collection of 10 brief essays with personal recollections and subjective views of recent plays from Latin America that coheres around a central theme of social protest with a strident tone.

5963 Pilditch, Charles. Theatre in Puerto Rico: a brief history (RRI, 9 : 1, Spring 1979, p. 5–8)

Very brief history, indeed, but with some interesting observations about the stature of Puerto Rican theatre in its own environment.

5964 Quackenbush, L. Howard. The legacy of Albee's *Who afraid of Virginia Woolf?* in the Spanish American absurdist theatre (RRI, 9 : 1, Spring 1979, p. 58–71)

Quackenbush makes a good case for the parallelism in technique (influence?) between Albee's *Virginia Woolf* and four Spanish American plays: *El apartamiento* (Marqués), *Segundo asalto* (Martínez), *Dos viejo pánicos* (Piñera), and *Esta noche juntos, amándonos tanto* (Vilalta). Careful and convincing evidence of the "legacy."

5965 V [i.e. Quinto] Festival Internacional de Teatro. Caracas: Editorial Ateneo, 1981. 248 p.

Amply illustrated volume with commentary on the multiple entries in the lavish international theatre festival sponsored by the Venezuelan government and Ateneo de

Caracas. Various Latin American participants (Argentina, Brazil, Colombia, Cuba, Mexico, etc.).

5966 Rela, Walter. Teatro brasileño. Montevideo: Instituto de Cultura Uruguayo-Brasileño, 1980. 141 p.

Historical survey of 400 years of Brazilian theatre that is long on bibliographical data, short on critical interpretation. Includes ephemeral reviews of some performances difficult to locate other places.

5967 ———. Teatro uruguayo, 1907–1979. Montevideo: Alianza Cultural Uruguay-EE.UU., 1980. 149 p.; bibl.; index (Ediciones de la Alianza; 3)

Thorough study of Uruguayan theatre since its beginnings with a wealth of bibliographical-historical information, although short on critical perspective.

5968 *Revista Tablas.* Centro de Investigación y Desarrollo de las Artes Escénicas. No. 1, enero/mayo 1982– . La Habana.

New Cuban theatre journal published by the Ministry of Culture with Rosa Ileana Boudet as editor. Initial issue has good range of articles by *teatristas* Rine Leal, Vicente Revuelta, Carlos Espinosa, Francisco Garzón Céspedes *et al* on Cuban theatre and other politically committed theatre groups and activities.

5969 Royero, Maida. 20 [i.e. Veinte] años de Teatro Estudio (RYC, 66, feb. 1978, p. 60–67, plates)

Historical overview of Teatro Estudio—from its inception in Paris in 1954, its early efforts (e.g., *Juana de Lorena*, 1955), its official founding in 1958, through initial years of the Revolution, with hopes and aspirations and philosophy—all told in interview form by principal participants.

5970 Sánchez, Luis Alberto. El señor Segura, hombre de teatro: vida y obra con textos y documentos originales. 2. ed. Lima: Universidad Nacional Mayor de San Marcos, Dirección Universitaria de Biblioteca y Publicaciones, 1976. 236 p.; bibl.

Slightly revised version of the 1947 edition of Sánchez's thorough study on Manuel Ascencio Segura, the *costumbrista* writer whose delightful plays dominated the Peruvian theatre of the mid-19th century.

5971 Romero, Silvia. Aproximación a *Antígona Vélez* de Leopoldo Marechal (RIB, 31:2, 1981, p. 227–245)

Thorough study of the action, symbols, style and antecedents (Sophocles and Anouilh) of Marechal's tragedy of the pampa. Adds little to Alyce de Kuehne's work done in 1970.

5972 Soria, Mario T. Teatro boliviano en el siglo XX. La Paz: Editorial Casa Municipal de la Cultura Franz Tamayo, 1980. 217 p.; ill. (Biblioteca Paceña)

History of 20th century Bolivian theatre collects essential information about plays, authors, and dates. Author promises that critical analysis will appear in later study. Includes complete bibliography of 20th-century Bolivian theatre, plus bio-bibliographical sketches of six principal playwrights.

5973 Strout, Lilia Dapaz. Razón, mito e individualización en *La cola de la sirena* de Conrado Nalé Roxlo (UC/AT, 11:3/4, sept./dic. 1978, p. 37–56)

Detailed study of philosophy and myth (abundant references to Tao and the Bible) fails to prove its declared intention of showing that the play is the product of author's subconscious dream. Too much symbol hunting.

5974 El Teatro de participación popular y el teatro de la comunidad: un teatro de sus protagonistas. Francisco Garzón Céspedes, editor. Diseño y cubierta, Darío Mora. La Habana: Unión de Escritores y Artistas de Cuba, 1977. 146 p.; bibl.; ill.

Analysis and description of two dominant theatre styles in present-day Cuba: 1) theatre of "participación popular" which includes vast sectors of people and breaks with previous structures; and 2) theatre of "la comunidad" in which community residents represent themselves. Interviews and discussions by initiators and proponents of both styles accompany text.

5975 Teatro popular y cambio social en América Latina: panorama de una experiencia. Edited by Sonia Gutiérrez. Portada, Hugo Díaz. Ciudad Universitaria Rodrigo Facio, Costa Rica: Editorial Universitaria Centro Americana, 1979. 487 p.; bibl.; index (Colección DEI)

Collection of 13 essays on popular

(read: *engagé*) theatre in Latin America; some new material, some reprints by such notables as Augusto Boal, Domingo Piga, Enrique Buenaventura, Santiago García, Atahualpa del Cioppo, and others. Also includes eight recent plays of different degrees of technical difficulty. Comprehensive overview of the movement, but unfortunately, poorly printed (cheap paper) and bound.

5976 Unger, Roni. Poesía en Voz Alta in the theater of Mexico. Columbia: University of Missouri Press, 1981. 182 p.; bibl.; ill.; index.

Penetrating inside-view of one of Mexico's avant-garde theatre groups which existed 1956–63. Thoroughly researched and abundantly documented, this critical study examines company's history and influence, but more importantly, it discusses role of mainstream Mexican intellectuals and artists affiliated with theatre group's short existence. Important analysis.

Vestrini, Miyó. Isaac Chocrón frente al espejo. See item **5429.**

5977 Vidal, Hernán. *Deja que los perros ladren* de Sergio Vodanović: desarrollismo, democracia cristiana, dictadura (IILI/RI, 47:114/115, enero/junio 1981, p. 313–335)

Extraordinarily thorough study of the Chilean political and moral environment, dominated by Prebisch and the Consejo Económico para América Latina (CEPAL), in which Vodanović wrote *Deja que los perros ladren* (1958). Sees in the play the qualities inherent in the Christian Democratic Party, a fascinating revelation given Vodanović's current political stance.

5978 Villaverde, Luis G. Panorámica del teatro hispanoamericano contemporáneo (*in* Estudios literarios sobre Hispanoamérica: homenaje a Carlos M. Raggi y Ageo. Troy, N.Y.: Círculo de Cultura Panamericano, 1976, p. 77–83)

Reviews four plays, from Usigli to Carballido, but data base is too superficial to arrive at any valid conclusions.

5979 Woodyard, George W. Perspectives on Cuban theatre (RRI, 9:1, Spring 1979, p. 42–48)

Quick overview of major developments in Cuban theatre in post-Revolutionary days. Some attention to Triana, Piñera, Arrufat and the *creación colectiva.*

BRAZIL: Novels

ALEXANDRINO SEVERINO, *Professor, Department of Spanish and Portuguese, Vanderbilt University*

THE BEST NOVELS OF THE BIENNIEUM annotated in this volume are, in alphabetical order, Josué Guimarães *Camilo Mortágua* (item **5996**); Ricardo Hoffman's *A Superfície* (item **5997**); Josué Montello's *A Coroa de Areia* (item **6003**); and João Ubaldo Ribeiro's *Vila Real* (item **6007**). Other examples of the genre published during the period, written by such masters as Adonias Filho, Antonio Callado, Moacyr Scliar, and Autran Dourado, have not been received for review at this writing. Consequently, if the quality of the works here reviewed is not particularly noteworthy, the overall picture may be improved, once the output of these writers is considered. For a better idea of the present state of the Brazilian novel, it would be indispensable to take into account the work of writers who have not been active in the period but are of recognizable merit: Loyola Brandão (*Zero*), Nelida Piñon (*A Força do Destino*), Ivan Angelo (*Festa*), Lygia Fagundes Telles (*As Meninas*), Márcio de Souza (*Galves, Imperador do Acre*), and, of course, Jorge Amado, Brazil's greatest literary export, albeit not, in the opinion of many, its best novelist.

Nevertheless, there is no doubt that after a period of extraordinary literary brilliance, exemplified by the work of such novelists as Guimarães Rosa, Clarice Lispector, Osman Lins and Ariano Suassuna, the first three dead prematurely and the last renouncing creative prose fiction of his own free will, the Brazilian novel is at a standstill. It is too early to detect in the younger writers, either through the quality of their writings or the number of written works, the same level of excellence established by masters who transformed the regional into the universal by means of superior craftsmanship, nurtured in the best examples of world literature.

The four novelists identified above as the most distinguished of those reviewed all follow, with varying degrees of success, the above general trends as well as others peculiar to the times. Among these, the most obvious are an open discussion of political dissidence, arbitrary imprisonment, and senseless torture brought about by the *abertura* (items **5996** and **6003**). Sex and violence are other major themes exemplified by these two novels. Both of them are reflections of life in Brazil's crowded cities, where relationships are impersonal, the family is in the process of coming apart, and the struggle for survival, fierce and at times inhuman. A good example of disintegrating human relations may be found in *O ventre da baleia* (item **6005**) in which Brasília, the city of maximum impersonality, smothers its inhabitants. Still within the topic of sex and violence, a curious trend to note is the description of intimate relationships from the point of view of a woman narrator. Such descriptions, heretofore made only by men, are unique to Brazilian literature and reveal the extent of women's liberation, at least among the country's writers. A different kind of violence is portrayed in João Ubaldo Ribeiro's *Vila real* (item **6007**). It is the violence between two totally different worlds, that of the toilers of the land and that of the invading technocrats, locked in mythical conflict.

Craftsmanship in the Brazilian novel is especially noticeable in a group of writers, all Jewish, among whom are the excellent Ricardo Hoffman (item **5997**) and Judith Grossmann (item **5995**). Like their North American counterparts, these thought-provoking writers modify the established language in order to express a more complex existential reality by means of innovative structures and advanced craftsmanship. To the already distinguished list of Jewish Brazilian writers such as Clarice Lispector, Moacyr Scliar and Samuel Rawet one must add the names of Eliza Bandeira, Judith Grossman, and Ricardo Hoffman.

As mentioned above, the writers here reviewed, in spite of their superb analysis of Brazilian society and some structural ingenuity, are not, in the overall, particularly distinguished. On one side, the traditional novelists lack structural inventiveness while the structural innovators (i.e., Judith Grossman's *Outros trópicas*, item **5995**) allow the craft to smother content. The most distinguished Brázilian novel of the period was not written by a Brazilian, but by a Peruvian, Mario Vargas Llosa, and it was entitled *A guerra do fim do mundo*.

None of the novels here reviewed received literary prizes in the biennium. The Fernando Chinaglia Prize for 1981 was awarded to Ruth Bueno for *Asilo nas torres* and the coveted Jabuti Prize was awarded to Dyonélio Machado for the novel *Endiabrados*. In the US a new series of translations of Brazilian novels is being planned. Lygia Fagundes Telles' *As meninas* appeared in Aug. 1982 as *The girl in the photograph*, translated by Thomas Colchie, who has also translated Loyola Brandão's *Zero* and *The celebration* (Festa) by Ivan Angelo.

5980 Abbate, José Carlos. Eu também sinto medo, Patricia Neal: romance. Capa, Mari. São Paulo: Vertente Editora, 1979. 167 p.; ports.

For nearly 20 years, Brazilian literature has been eschewing social themes. Nevertheless, a writer still apologizes when writing a non-political novel, such as this one. A powerful, profound account of a man's painful road to physical recovery. The example of an American actress steadies him on the way. A minor novel that deserves to be read. Recommended.

5981 Almeida, José Américo de. A bagaceira, 1928–1978: romance. Com ilus. de Poty e trabalhos de Alceu Amoroso Lima *et al.* 15. ed. Rio de Janeiro: Livraria J. Olympio Editora; João Pessoa: Secretaria de Educação e Cultura do Governo do Estado da Paraíba, 1978. 267 p.; 4 leaves of plates; appendices; ill.

Anniversary edition of an old classic (1928). This novel was responsible for launching the Northeastern novel, a new prose movement in Brazil. It called attention to human conditions in backland areas through a style which included regional language and folk themes. Edition includes testimonials from Alceu Amoroso Lima, Gilberto Freyre, Rachel de Queiroz and others. Recommended.

5982 Bandeira, Elisa. A verdadeira história de Jacob Grinberg, o marido de Sarah. Rio de Janeiro: Bureau Editora, 1979. 304 p.; ill.

Novel follows the life of a Romanian Jew from his country of origin to Israel and Brazil, including sympathetic comments on the plight of Palestinians. Unimpressive as a literary achievement but interesting because it reflects an important trend in contemporary prose fiction: the concern with the process of acculturation in Brazil.

5983 Bilac, Olavo and Carlos Magalhães de Azeredo. Sanatorium. Recolhido, anotado e prefaciado por R. Magalhães Júnior. São Paulo: Clube do Livro, 1977. 136 p.; ill.

Little-known novel, never before published in book form, written by the renowned Parnassian poet in collaboration with a friend. First published in 1894 as a serial in a Rio newspaper, it portrays a group lodged at a hotel bearing the title name. Interesting for what it reveals of the period.

5984 Blanco, Armindo. A lei e o ordem. Capa e ilustrações, Mariza. Rio de Janeiro: Editora Codecri, 1979. 157 p.; ill. (Coleção Edições do Pasquim; v. 45)

Novel written with much humor about what happens to common folk when they confront the forces of law and order. Narrated in colloquial language which reflects the colorful idioms and slang of Rio de Janeiro. Much social criticism implicit in this delightful narrative. Recommended.

5985 Brasil, Assis. Os crocodilos: romance. Capa, Jane Maia. Rio de Janeiro: Nórdica, 1980. 124 p.

Five protagonists from different walks of life are brought together when they accidentally fall into a well. Like a crocodile devouring its own tail, the five humans are dehumanized by the struggle to survive. The novel is a naturalistic study of human behavior freed from social convention and confronting survival. The novel is structured like a play, and its five characters live intensely dramatic roles within the confines of time and space.

5986 ———. Deus, o sol, Shakespeare: romance. Rio de Janeiro: Nórdica, 1978. 135 p.; ill.

Chaotic world perceived through the equally disarrayed mind of the protagonist. The hallucinatory, fragmented narrative conveys the resulting vision. A study guide and explanation accompanies this complex novel, which includes a series of photographs depicting world violence. Tolerable.

5987 Caldas, José Alberto. Confissões de um mendigo. Ilustrações, Carlos Jorge. Belo Horizonte, Minas Gerais: Editora Comunicação, 1980. 78 p.; ill.

Novel deservedly won coveted Belo Horizonte City First Prize for the Novel. The new technological society is seen through the eyes of a street beggar who becomes its victim. A moving theme, told in direct plain language, and in diary form. Recommended.

5988 Cheuiche, Alcy José de Vargas. O mestiço de São Borja. Porto Alegre: Editora Sulina, 1980. 285 p.

Another panoramic novel which portrays political events in Rio Grande do Sul from the turbulent 1930s to the present as seen through the eyes of a Brazilian prototype. Born of a white mother and an Indian father, Oswald is reared by a German European, has a mulatto brother, and marries a French black, who embodies the two principal Brazilian strains: the black and the European. If the story is somewhat flimsy, the political ideas are vigorous, forceful and relevant to present events. Recommended.

5989 Donato, Hernâni. O caçador e esmeraldas. Capa, Jane Maia. Rio de Janeiro: Nórdica, 1980. 125 p.; ill.

One of several novels written to evoke the *bandeirante* (pathfinder) Fernão Dias Paes. This fictionalized account also served as the script of a well-known movie on the subject and describes the "emerald hunter's" last incursion into the backland, at age 66. Novel should appeal to those interested in Brazilian colonial history. Includes scenes from the film.

5990 Escorel, Silvia. Um telefone é muito pouco. Ilustrações, Hugo Rodas. Capa, Silvia Helena de Moraes Zelda e Wagner Hermuche. Brasília: s.n., 1979. 139 p.; 12 leaves of plates; ill.

Apart from an unusually graphic presentation and transcription of current Rio slang, this novel has little to recommend it. One of many works on the adventures of lost youth in search of the meaning of life.

5991 Ferrante, Miguel Jeronymo. O silêncio: romance. Capa, ilustração, Mário Cafiero. Gravura em madeira, René Etiene Ardanuy. Foto, José Góes. Arte final, Mara Patrícia Feixas. Revisão, Marina Appenzeller. São Paulo: Editora Atica, 1979. 127 p.; ill. (Coleção de Autores brasileiros; 42)

Novel opens with a man returning to a city in the Amazon, seeking revenge. From thereon the city itself becomes the protagonist: the power of the baron, the factions and rivalries manifested at Carnival time and, above all, love's sweet and bitter exigencies. A rapidly fading world is vividly portrayed through a harmonious blending of descriptions and dialogue. Recommended.

5992 Ferraz, Eneas. Adolescência tropical. Apresentação de Maria de Lourdes Teixeira. 2. ed. brasileira. São Paulo: Academia Paulista de Letras, 1978. 147 p. (Biblioteca Academia Paulista de Letras; v. 8)

First published in 1931, the novel provides a vivid, realistic description of middle class life intertwined with political events, in a manner reminiscent of Lima Barreto who was a good friend of the author's. The novel deserves a better reception than what it was accorded when first published, a period when Brazilian literature was dominated by the Northeastern novel. Recommended.

5993 Gattai, Zélia. Anarquistas, graças a Deus. Capa de Floriano Teixeira. Rio de Janeiro: Editora Record, 1979. 271 p.

In old São Paulo the Italian population was larger than Rome's. Mrs. Jorge Amado's

nostalgic reminiscences cover her adolescent years, spent within the close family circle, and little or no justification may be found for the political connotation implied in the title. Recommended.

5994 Gikovate, Ceci. O circo vem ai. Capa, MIRO. São Paulo: MG Editores Associados, 1979. 166 p.

Profound, psychological account of the predicament of two people in love who are finally brought together by a week's separation and a circus' troupe. Intelligent, well done.

5995 Grossmann, Judith. Outros trópicos. Rio de Janeiro: Livraria José Olympio Editora; Brasília: em convênio com o Instituto Nacional do Livro, Ministério da Educação e Cultura, 1980. 174 p.; port.

Innovative novel, written by one of Brazil's most distinguished practitioners of the art, has no plot but describes a metaphysical quest through language akin to music. The writer, who teaches literary theory at the University of Bahia, is part of a group of distinguished writers of Jewish ancestry, among whom are Clarice Lispector, Samuel Rawet, and Macyr Sinclair.

5996 Guimarães, Josué. Camilo Mortágua. Porto Alegre, Rio Grande do Sul: L&PM Editores, 1980. 454 p.

One of the best prose fiction accomplishments of the biennium. Beyond the indispensable elements of contemporary Brazilian fiction—politics and sex—this novel of a rural family's decadence and final disintegration comes to its inevitable conclusion in the days following the 1964 military coup. Political events give the novel credibility while the innovative technique (i.e., showing past events on a film screen the protagonist watches every evening) highlights its literary achievement. Excellent.

5997 Hoffmann, Ricardo L. A superfície. 2d. ed. Rio de Janeiro: Ediçoes Antares, 1978. 148 p.; bibl.; plates (Colección Diadorim)

Superficially, this novel is merely the story of a German family's acculturation to the Brazilian milieu (first ed. 1967). At a deeper level, however, it is the account of man's striving for metaphysical understanding through art. An unusually expressive language is used to convey the complexities of the protagonist's thoughts. Another example of the Jewish literary movement referred to in item **5995.** Highly recommended.

5998 Junqueira Smith, Lígia. O painel de gardênia. Capa de Carlos Cézar. São Paulo: IBRASA, 1979. 238 p. (Biblioteca Literatura moderna; 50)

Novel about an independent, resourceful woman, written by a well-known woman writer with several novels to her credit. Gardênia, the protagonist, accepts a triangular liaison but not confined by it, seeks fulfillment elsewhere. Provides refreshing female perspective of woman's sexual behavior, after so many accounts of seduction and lovemaking told by men. Recommended.

5999 Jurandir, Carlos. Morto Moreno: romance. Capa, Dounê. Sobre foto de Walter Quintino. Rio de Janeiro: Civilização Brasileira, 1979. 136 p. (Coleção Vera Cruz; v. 277)

Plot revolves around the death of a famous young singer and composer. Theme concerns passing fashions in the world of popular music, police violence and press corruption. Coarse and punchy style resembles a boxing match with words being thrown at the reader like rocks. Interesting.

6000 Lima, Geraldo França de. A pedra e a pluma. Rio de Janeiro: Livraria J. Olympio Editora, 1979. 140 p.

Mythical account of human conflict in an isolated community in the interior of Minas Gerais. Several generations are portrayed in a language replete with metaphors appropriate to the majestic theme. Recommended.

6001 Lyra, Sophia A. Vida íntima das moças de ontem: novela. Capa, Daniel de Almeida. Rio de Janeiro: Sophia Rosa Editora, 1980. 208 p.

This "intimate life" is not intimate at all, judging from other novels annotated in this section. Familial relationships, carnival, dances are some subjects portrayed, along with women's behavior patterns that greatly differ from today's. Interesting.

6002 Machado, Dyonelio. Prodígios. Capa, Antonio Hélio Cabral. São Paulo: Editora Moderna, 1980. 189 p.

This is the last of a trilogy (the others are Os deuses econômicos and O sol subterrâneo) by the venerable Rio Grandense author. Events in Nero's Rome reaffirm the value of freedom. The historical happenings are relevant to wherever and whenever the conditions of the novel exist. Recommended.

6003 Montello, Josué. A coroa de areia: romance. Rio de Janeiro: Livraria J. Olympio Editora, 1979. 319 p.

Fact and fiction combine to make this novel, the 14th in the author's Maranhão saga, a vivid account of revolutionary struggle and human forbearance against tyranny and oppression. Brazil's most important social struggles of this century—the Copacabana revolt, the Prestes' column, the Getulio Vargas' dictatorship—acquire a new meaning and a new reality seen through the eyes of the idealist João Mauricio and his wife, Agaia, and unforgettable women, whose indomitable courage is responsible for the novel's happy ending. The latter, and the surprising event which brings it about are the only flaws in an otherwise perfect blending of fact and fiction into an organic whole. Highly recommended.

6004 ———. O silêncio da confissão: romance. Rio de Janeiro: Editora Nova Fronteira, 1980. 307, 5 p.; bibl.

Novel represents a curious fictional departure for the author. Unlike the customary chronicles of his native state of Maranhão, this is an absorbingly suspenseful detective story, set amid Rio's upper-classes with a few political intimations. Another example of Montello's gift for story-telling. Recommended.

6005 Nascimento, Esdras do. O ventre da baleia: romance. Rio de Janeiro: Nórdica, 1980. 150 p.

Strange murder provides the action for his novel, which is really about Brasília (the whale of the title). The people who have come to inhabit this most recent world's metropolis, their background and painful acculturation to the new environment, are portrayed in traditional language, but through a modern novelistic structure. Recommended.

6006 Pompeu, Renato. A greve da rosa: romance. Capa, Vera Altenburg. Revisão, Ana Catarina M. F. Nogueira, Izilda de Oliveira. São Paulo: Editora Alfa-Omega, 1980. 171 p. (Biblioteca Alfa-Omega de literatura latino-americana; Série 2a., Nova ficção brasileira; v. 4)

Novel about paraplegic characters

written by a paraplegic narrator is actually about the multiple creative paths faced by an author in the act of creation. Not particularly effective.

6007 Ribeiro, João Ubaldo. Vila Real. Capa, Dulce Mary. Rio de Janeiro: Editora Nova Fronteira, 1979. 177 p.

The most impressive novel of the biennium. The struggle to the death of a band of backlanders being dispossessed by the arrival of the all-powerful company. The novel achieves archetypal dimensions as it is told in majestic, powerful language. Highly recommended.

Short Stories

MARIA ANGELICA GUIMARAES LOPES DEAN, *Lecturer in the Humanities, Carthage College*

THE 80 OR SO COLLECTIONS EXAMINED for this volume of *HLAS* in the last biennium reveal that good short stories continue to be written in Brazil and that three major trends dominate the genre: 1) first rate fiction by women; 2) the prevalence of fantastic themes; and 3) the expression of political and social protest.

The striking event of the last two years is the number of consistently good collections by women. Traditionally and because of their assignment to a domestic role by patriarchal society, *brasileiras* have participated in literature only indirectly, either as muses in the 18th century (e.g., Marília and Barbara Heliodora), or, in the 19th century, as readers (e.g., Machado's *leitoras*). Nevertheless, 30 years ago Clarice Lispector won recognition as one of Brazil's two greatest writers. Now, the short-story writer and novelist Nélida Piñón has attained equal status. The latest example of Piñón's astonishing imagination, syntactical magic and daring word play, is *O calor das coisas* (item **6037**) a collection of stories mostly about women in various stages of love. That short fiction by women is becoming the norm rather than the exception is exemplified not only by Piñón's latest collection but by preceding ones such as *O conto da mulher brasileira* (see *HLAS 42:6125*) and *Mulheres a mulheres* (see *HLAS 42:6152*) and more recent ones by Sonia Coutinho, Helena Parente Cunha, and Yêda Schmaltz. Coutinho's *Os venenos de Lucrécia* (item **6020**) resumes the theme of her previous *Uma certa felicidade* (see *HLAS 40:74330*), the plight of the provincial young woman searching for independence and happiness in the metropolis. Coutinho is a lucid observer and compassionate commentator of the process of severing patriarchal ties. A first collection, Cunha's *Os provisórios* (item **6021**), is not the work of a beginner and reveals literary skill, humor, and vision. Schmaltz's *Miserere* (item **6038**) is exuberant in the use of tropes, literary allusions, proverbs, and popular songs, a firework's display reminiscent of Piñón's own works.

The prevalence of the fantastic short story is the second trend noted in this biennium. Confined until recently to regional ghost stories, this subgenre was much favored by Machado de Assis in his 19th-century short fiction. The fantastic did not reemerge in Brazilian literature until the last three decades, a phenomenon that can be attributed to the impact of *Grande sertão: veredas*, the rediscovery of Murilo Rubião, and the international success of Spanish American magic realism. As a consequence, the fantastic short story is no longer merely accepted but almost *de rigueur* in any short story compilation. The nature of fantasy ranges from the merely exotic tale to the moral fable, and their ancestors include Poe, Kafka, the surrealists, and science fiction. Three collections annotated below by Brandão,

Giudice, and Gomes are entirely devoted to the fantastic. Brandão's *Cadeiras proibidas* (item **6011**) uses fantasy to decry the twin evils of contemporary Brazil: political repression and industrial society gone awry. In a postface to this second edition, the author makes an impassioned plea for the closing of his "open book," so that when political and social circumstances change, no more horror stories will have to be added. Giudice, translated abroad and famous for his brilliantly witty *Neocrológios* (see *HLAS 38:7364*) expands his repertoire in *Os banheiros* (item **6026**) by confining social criticism to longer, more sustained fables. Gomes' *O senhor dos porcos* (item **6027**), consisting of "extremely new cruel stories," is a tour de force that will shock more than move the reader.

Another interesting development is the contribution of ethnology to the fantastic as exemplified by Berthier Brasil's *O caríua* (item **6013**), a collection of marvelous Amazonian legends, and Raul Longo's *Filhos de Olorum* (item **6030**), described as "contos e cantos de candomblé," a literary skillful, warm and compassionate portrayal of the Afro-Brazilian lore of poor Bahians.

The third and last trend noted in the stories annotated for this biennium, is political and social protest presented in either a realistic or fantastic mode. Brandão's *Cadeiras proibidas* (item **6011**) succeeds on both counts as does Ivan Angelo's *A casa de vidro* (item **6010**), especially the title story. The collection is an exuberant concoction of diverse modes, styles and characters drawn from various social strata by the pen of a fictitious 19th-century writer. An acute, unrelenting moralist, Angelo is well-known for his novel *A festa*, another example of protest as allegory. Political and social condemnation are also at the heart of Edilberto Coutinho's remarkable collection. The relevance of *Maracanã, adeus* (item **6018**) to the Latin American plight was recognized by the Casa de las Américas Jury which awarded it the 1980 Short Story Prize. In Coutinho's fictional country the powerful exploit the weak and in soccer, the collection's main theme, the player is, invariably, the loser. By turning Brazil's national sport into a metaphor for the game of life, Coutinho transmutes the regional into the universal.

Another strong denunciation of social injustice appears in Chico Junior's borderline stories/crônicas, *Históricas de sexo, amor e porrada* (item **6017**) set in Rio and reminiscent of Nelson Rodrigues' famous 1960s newspaper *crônicas*. However, Chico's stories excel Rodrigues' *crônicas* in their skillful and perceptive portrayal of the miseries of rich and poor alike.

In conclusion, the three major trends detected in this biennium, superior fiction by women, the prevalence of the fantastic as theme, and effective social and political protest, augur well for the future of the Brazilian story.

6008 Almeida, Márcia de. Sob o signo da chuva: contos. Ilustrações de Lapí. Rio de Janeiro: Editora Codecri, 1979. 156 p.; ill. (Coleção Edições do Pasquim; v. 46)

Powerful, painful stories by angry young woman tell of lives amputated by despair of childhood memories and by political repression in dense, packed monologues. Preface denounces political situation in 60s and 70s, citing names of victims, many of which were Almeida's friends and acquaintances. Ironically, setting is Rio, "Cidade Maravilhosa."

6009 Andrade, Jeferson Ribeiro de. Senhoras e senhores, a Voz do Brasil: ficção-reportagem. Revisão, Armandina Venâncio. Foto da capa, Walter Firmo. Rio de Janeiro: Editora Record, 1980. 103 p.

Skillful stories have Odilon's Bar—featured in author's previous collection—as background. Author's marvelous ear captures radio announcers' style in dialogues that expose Odilon's cutomers, their individual sorrows, and social injustice. Informed by wit, and illumined by compassion, book deserves to be read.

6010 Angelo, Ivan. A casa de vidro: cinco histórias do Brasil. Capa de Luiz Gregório. Foto da contra-capa de Lamberto Scipioni. São Paulo: Livraria Cultura Editora, 1979. 258 p.

Strong, often brilliant, and always panoramic, "Brasil stories" show reality as seen by shrewd moralist and presented from all angles. Exuberant writer can also be terse when x-raying contemporary society. Novellas' thrust and length confirm that Angelo is more a novelist than a short story writer.

6011 Brandão, Ignácio de Loyola. Cadeiras proibidas: contos. Capa, Trimano. Foto, Madalena Schwartz. 2. ed. rev. e aumentada. Rio de Janeiro: Editora Codecri, 1979. 147 p.; ill. (Coleção Edições do Pasquim; v. 52)

Second edition of protest fables (first published 1976 after relaxation of censorship), include six new stories. To Brandão, this is "an open book" with narratives added until "absurd Brazilian conditions change." Not only sociopolitical protest but format makes of stories a harmonious whole. Classic in their sparseness, they echo Kafka, Wells, Orwell, and surrealists. Outstanding.

6012 Brant, Vera. A solidão dos outros. Capa, montagem sobre "Figura reclinada," 1938, escultura de Henry Moore depositada na Tate Gallery, Londres. São Paulo: Massao Ohno, 1980. 78 p.; ill.

Not all these stories are of the same caliber but the best—the majority—show a decided literary power. Language is notable: plastic, syntactically correct but sprinkled with slang. They are mostly interior monologues by humorous, self-deprecating narrator.

6013 Brasil, Altino Berthier. O Caríua e outros contos amazônicos. Ilustração e capa, Manoel Borges. Manaus: Impr. Oficial do Estado do Amazonas, 1978. 107 p.; 21 leaves of plates; bibl.; ill.

Valuable collection because of subject matter: Brazilian aboriginal legends, some of which were popularized as fine literature by Modernistas, such as the "muiraquitã" in Mário de Andrade's *Macunaíma*, and Cobra Norato in Raul Bopp's poem.

6014 Campos, Eduardo. Dia da caça: contos. Capa, Luiz Falcão. Rio de Janeiro: Livraria Editora Cátedra; Brasília: Instituto Nacional de Livro, Ministério da Educação e Cultura, 1980. 123 p.

Distinguished fiction by writer with 40 years' experience, these stories reveal not only his keen imagination and literary skill—limpid style, vivid dialogues, firm structure—but his insight and compassion in the depiction of proletarian lives: flower maker, laid-off bricklayer, grocery clerk, sailor. Recommended.

6015 Carone Netto, Modesto. Aos pés de Matilda. Capa de Sérgio Síster. São Paulo: Summus Editorial, 1980. 104 p.

Elegant stories that read like classics conjure mysterious world in which objects are animated, dreams take over characters' lives, and a double torments the narrator. Reminiscent of Kafka, Borges, and surrealists, these stories exemplify the current trend towards fantasy in Brazilian writing.

6016 Carvalho, Walden Camilo de. Cordiais saudações. Capa, Humberto Borém. Rio de Janeiro: Editora Codecri, 1979. 78 p. (Coleção Edição do Pasquim; v. 61)

First collection by very talented author whose literary ancestry includes the Bible, Poe, Lins do Rego, Graciliano, Bradbury, and cartoons. Narratives about corruption by either the government or money flow spontaneously although tone is controlled. Includes remarkable monologues and good use of irony.

6017 Chico, Júnior. Histórias de sexo, amor, e porrada. Capa, Rafael Siqueira. Rio de Janeiro: Editora Codecri, 1979. 78 p. (Coleção Edições do Pasquim; v. 56)

Bawdy title is appropriate for stories in the manner of Nelson Rodrigues, the Brazilian Tennessee Williams of the 1960s. The sensationalist themes of sexual polymorphism and/or aberrations, suicides, and murders, do not detract from author's perception, compassion, and literary skill.

6018 Coutinho, Edilberto. Maracanã, adeus. La Habana: Casa de las Américas, 1980. 136 p.; ill.

A craftsman, Coutinho succeeds in using soccer as theme. He builds dramatic stories without bathos in which protagonists, often soccer players, are the losers. Soccer serves admirably as a symbol not only of the Brazilian ethos but of the game of life elsewhere. Awarded the Cuban Casa de las Américas' 1980 Short Story Prize.

6019 ———. Sangue na praça. Posfácio de Jorge de Sá. Ilustrações de Urian. Capa, Humberto Borém. Rio de Janeiro: Editora Codecri, 1979. 125 p.; ill. (Coleção Edições do Pasquim; v. 34)

Collection stands out among others because of the "punch and poetry" of the human suffering conveyed. Acclaimed as one of Brazil's finest story writers, Coutinho was a precocious author, noted at 17. He attended the Iowa International Writing Program.

6020 Coutinho, Sônia. Os venenos de Lucrécia: contos. Capa e ilustrações, Jader Estevão. São Paulo: Editora Atica, 1978. 88 p.; ill. (Coleção de autores brasileiros; 33)

One of the ablest observers of the female psyche, Coutinho resumes the theme of her previous and equally impressive collection, *Uma certa felicidade* (see *HLAS* 40:7433): "the kind of happiness" which characters expect but do not necessarily achieve upon leaving provincial monotony for the glittering metropolis. Alas, bonds are neither easily severed nor formed. Admirable compilation.

6021 Cunha, Helena Parente. Os provisórios. Rio de Janeiro: Edições Antares, 1980. 113 p.; 2 p. of plates; ill. (Coleção Diadorim)

Essayist and poet makes auspicious beginning in new genre. Bold poetical devices, and juxtaposed time periods succeed in this "salto mortal" (for Assis Brasil). Parente is well versed in experimenting and developing literary techniques. Accomplished stories are dramatic, compassionate, humorous and include remarkable interior monologues.

6022 Curado, Roberto Fleury. Cemitério de gritos. Goiânia, Goiás: Oriente, 1978. 84 p. (Publicação / Editora Oriente; no. 258)

Versatile author from Goiás conveys the lyricism, pathos, farce, and fear of diverse characters. A worthwhile debut.

6023 Farias Júnior, Herculano. Força bruta: contos. Capa, Mário Röhnelt. Porto Alegre: Editora Movimento, 1979. 55 p. (Coleção Santa Catarina; v. 14)

Apt title for stylistically and thematically varied collection in which human beings attack one another: husband vs. wife; mob vs. pederast; master vs. servant, etc. Includes fine internal monologues, and use of taut language in dramatic situations. Some stories are fables in the fantastic vein.

6024 Fester, Ribeiro. O mar tem várias cores. São Paulo: Livraria Duas Cidades, 1979. 133 p.

Title conveys collection's variety and poetry. Epigraph from Mário de Andrade is pertinent since some of these "paulistas" stories resemble his: "Paulo e Virgínia" is reminiscent of "Vestida de Preto." Restrained in tone, flexible in dialogue and narration, this is a first-rate collection.

6025 Foseca, Rubem. O cobrador. Capa, Victor Burton. Rio de Janeiro: Editora Novo Fronteira, 1979. 182 p.

Major short story writer presents his customary dramatic, violent world (title story), as well as imaginative variations and Brazilian adaptations of the themes and techniques of others (e.g. Nabokov's *Lolita*, Capote's non-fiction novels, and Chandler's *The big sleep*). Includes noteworthy treatment of historical figures (Alvares de Azevedo and Gen. Osório).

6026 Giudice, Victor. Os banheiros: contos. Capa, Humberto Borém. Rio de Janeiro: Editora Codecri, 1979. 139 p. (Coleção Edições do Pasquim; v. 60)

Masterful stories, mostly "family chronicles" written in elegant, concise style, depict strange doings of eccentric members. The family is Giudice's framework as in his *Necrológios* (see*HLAS* 40:7364). Recommended.

6027 Gomes, Alvaro Cardoso. O senhor dos porcos: novíssimos contos cruéis. Capa, Maria Cristina Simi Carletti. São Paulo: Editora Moderna, 1979. 194 p.

"Cruel stories" about destruction and death, literally and figuratively, are set in a fantastic universe of lugubrious and vile scenarios lacking in either beauty or peace. The refined cruelty with which the gory themes are presented constitute a tour de force. Stories are symptomatic of the impressionistic, naturalistic trend in Brazilian literature, some of whose manifestations are unavoidably farcical.

6028 Imbassahy Filho, Eduardo. A noite dos impossíveis: contos. Capa, Aderbal Moura. São Paulo: Editora Atica, 1980. 79 p.; ports. (Coleção de autores brasileiros; 55)

"Enigma," the title of one of these evanescent prose poems / stories exemplifies a collection of tales in which strange characters perform mysterious actions, or lead inexplicable lives. Stories are printed to look like poems. A valid, interesting attempt by author of more traditional narratives (see *HLAS 38:7365*).

6029 Linhares, Erasmo do Amaral. O tocador de charamela. Manaus, Amazonas: Ediçoes Rádio Rio Mar, 1979. 110 p.

Linhares handles the short story, the Portuguese language, metaphysical topics, and irony with a sure hand although he presents his "Flute Player" modestly, as a collection of "poorly played" pieces. Excellent collection by Amazonas radio executive about human values which does not overemphasize local color.

6030 Longo, Raul. Filhos de Olorum. Curitiba: Coo Editora, 1980. 130 p.; ill.

Stories about Brazilian traditions, mostly candomblé, are varied in style and themes. Author skillfully blends ancient myths with lives of poor Bahian blacks today and conveys the locale through able use of vocabulary and description of setting. Includes useful glossary.

6031 Maciel, Laury. Corpo e sombra: contos. Porto Alegre: Editora Movimiento, 1977. 51 p. (Coleção Rio Grande; v. 31)

Well-crafted, varied stories by journalist/author present wide cast of characters in everyday as well as unusual and even fantastic situations. Collection exemplifies the fine art of the short story as practiced in Brazil today.

6032 Martins, Glória. Reencontro: contos. Pref., Pedro Paulo Montenegro. Fortaleza: s.n., 1978. 117 p.; ill.

Impressive compilation, some of whose stories received prizes, is varied in tone and style and ranges from well-sustained comedy of bourgeois idiosyncracies (e.g., "Sim, Doutor") to science fiction (e.g., "Fiction") to the fantastic ("Terror") and poetic ("Fantasia"). First and third-person monologues by women narrators are especially moving.

6033 Miguel, Salim. A morte do tenente e outras mortes. Capa, AG Comunicação Visual, Arquitetura Ltda. Rio de Janeiro: Edições Antares, 1979. 153 p. (Coleção Diadorim)

Fine collection by experienced author includes Proustian story of title: "A Aranha," and "O Gramofone." For Hélio Pólvora, Mi-

guel is "writer who remembers his life . . . and gives himself to the conceptual game that [marks] all good fiction . . . including Machado de Assis's . . . whom he resembles . . . in certain tone and phrase resonances."

6034 Noll, João Gilberto. O cego e a dançarina: contos. Capa, Eugênio Hirsch. Rio de Janeiro: Civilização Brasileira, 1980. 135 p. (Coleção Vera Cruz; v. 293)

Acclaimed first collection by imaginative young writer. Reveals enviable thematic and stylistic versatility in the use of monologue and narrative for developing dramatic situations many of which are erotic. Sustained monologues admirably depict numerous characters and their adventures. A dreamy, vague, though powerful atmosphere pervades the stories.

6035 Ortêncio, W. Bariani. Estórias de crimes e do detetive Waldir Lopes: contos policiais. São Paulo: Editora Atica, 1980. 223 p.; port. (Coleção de autores brasileiros; 59)

A rarity in Brazil where murder mysteries are mostly imported (e.g., Agatha Christie, Chandler, Ellery Queen, etc.), Ortêncio's stories are well-crafted, and humorous. Some present sophisticated situations in urban settings, others traditional mores in rural areas, but all are suspenseful with fine plots and characterization. Compilation far above the usual in this genre.

6036 Perez, Renard. Irmãos da noite: contos. Capa, Dounê. Rio de Janeiro: Civilização Brasileira, 1979. 138 p. (Coleção Vera Cruz; v. 276)

In these stories about the pleasures and perils of alcohol, some Rio characters are drawn together by drink and darkness. Author is very good at developing personality and suspense ("Hugo").

6037 Piñón, Nélida. O calor das coisas: contos. Capa, Victor Burton. Rio de Janeiro: Editora Novo Fronteira, 1980. 204 p.

Another successful collection by one of Brazil's most accomplished short story writers. Her tales, mostly concerned with physical love, are sensual, emotional and especially successful in the use of tropes and proverbs. Paradoxically, this author reminds of Lispector and Rosa, two opposite poles.

6038 Schmaltz, Iêda. Miserere. Painel, Luciano Figueiredo e Oscar Ramos. Rio

de Janeiro: Edições Antares, 1980. 153 p.;
1 leaf of plates; ill. (Coleção Diadorim)
    Stories by prize-winning author are
notable for breadth, narrative techniques,
rhetorical devices, fantasy, pathos, and humor. Multi-layered tales interweave popular
songs, myths, the Bible, Brazilian and other
literature. *Miserere* has been recognized by
eminent writers as major work. Title and epigraph taken from Guimarães Rosa.

6039 Trevisan, Dalton. Virgem louca,
    loucos beijos. Rio de Janeiro: Editora
Record, 1979. 101 p.
    Trevisan again and welcome again be-
cause of his unique virtuosity. Is he mellow-
ing? If hints of muted optimism can be
interpreted as such, perhaps. Required
reading.

Crônicas

GERALD M. MOSER, *Professor Emeritus of Spanish and Portuguese, The Pennsylvania State University*

THE SMALL DIMENSION of this year's section of Brazilian *crônicas* should not be interpreted to mean that the genre was on the decline between 1978–81. The smallness of the section is partly due to the elimination of almost half of the collections received as either inferior in literary quality or falling outside the category. A more serious reason is the fact that books by well known and talented writers were not received in time at the Library of Congress: *70 historinhas* (1979) and *O pipoqueiro da esquina* (1981) by Carlos Drummond de Andrade; *Crônicas escolhidas* (1981) by Paulo Mendes Campos; *Transistor* (1980) by Murilo Mendes; *O balé Quebra-Nós* (1979), *A cadeira do dragão* (1980) and *Democracia à vista* (1981) by Carlos Eduardo Novaes; *O jogador de sinuca* (1980) by Rachel de Queiroz; *A Praça dos Sem Poderes* (1980) by Flávio Rangel; *Dias îdos e vividos* (1981), a large anthology of José Lins do Rogo's *crônicas*; *A falta que ela me faz* (1980) by Fernando Sabino; *Ed Mort e outras histórias* (1979) and *Sexo na cabeça* (1980) by Luís Fernando Veríssimo—all of these writers remain to be evaluated in future volumes of *HLAS*.

    Further proof of the popularity of the genre and its acceptance as reading material for students is provided by the publication of many collective anthologies. The *Elenco de cronistas modernos*, published by the house of José Olympio, reached its seventh edition in 1979, and the same publisher launched a new series, *O Melhor da Crônica Brasileira*, in 1981. The Editora Atica of São Paulo published vols. 4/7 of its collection *Para Gostar de Ler*. Contests for the writing of *crônicas* were held and the best were published (e.g., *Prêmio Apesul 1979: Conto-Crônica*, item **6046**).

    The difficulty in defining the polymorphous *crônica* was recognized by members of the jury of the Apesul contest, who wrote: "It seemed to us that the greatest difficulty consisted in distinguishing between *crônica* and story, *crônica* and essay, *crônica* and a mere dissertation, even between *crônica* and poems. We were to give prizes to *crônicas*, that is, to accounts or sketches of exterior or interior day-by-day life that were concise, expressive, original" (item **6046,** p. 63)..

    For the two reasons cited above the section is not only shorter than in previous years but it cannot give a general idea of the development of the genre since 1979.

    Critical literature about *crônica* writers increased through articles on "João do Rio" (Paulo Barreto) on the occasion of the centenary of his birth (1981), evocations of Luís Martins, who died in 1981, and a textbook on the writer who has become a modern classic, Rubem Braga: Lygia Marina Moraes' *Conheça Rubem Braga* (Rio de Janeiro: 1979).

CRONICAS

6040 Andrade, Maria Julieta Drummond de. Un buquê de alcachofras. Rio de Janeiro: Livraria J. Olympio Editora, 1980. 165 p.; port.

Sketches of Maria Julieta, who lives and lectures in Buenos Aires, appeared in *O Globo* (Rio, 1977–80). They read like pages from a chatty diary, reporting on festivities, plants, animals, people—including literary celebrities (Borges, Lispector, Sábato), her son Pedro and her father Carlos. At her best, she plays word games.

6041 Campos, Paulo Mendes. Os bares morrem numa quarta-feira: crônicas. Capa, Wanduir Durant. São Paulo: Editora Atica, 1980. 173 p.; port. (Coleção de autores brasileiros; 58)

The poet, old hand at *crônicas*, tends to be ponderous, even pedantic, in what are essays, rather than sketches. Some have permanent value as personal memories of fellow writers. Title corresponds to main theme: anecdotal history of Rio bars frequented by artists and writers.

Castello Branco, Carlos. Os militares no poder. See *HLAS 43:6662.*

6042 Martínez, Altino. Crônicas tupãenses. São Paulo: Editora Soma, 1979. 333 p.

Written 1959–79 for *Jornal de Tupã* by teacher, articles present suggestions and criticisms intended to improve Tupã, a recent and growing town in western São Paulo. Without great literary merit, they nevertheless possess value for future regional historians, with their references to individuals, Japanese colony, and theater.

6043 Mello, Gustavo Bandeira de. Histórias de gente. Capa, Neusa d'Arcanchy. Brasília: Thesaurus Editora e Sistemas Audio-Visuais, 1979. 166 p.

The stress is on "simple" people, such as auto mechanics, joggers, office clerks, and not on scenery, in sketches of journeys to places ranging from Amazonas and Brasília to São Paulo and Rio. Observations on aging provide common psychological theme and produce a melancholy undertone.

6044 Oliveira, Emerson Rogério de. Pote de barro. Capa, Mauro Ruschel. União de Vitória: Departamento de Letras, Fundação Facultade Estadual de Filosofia, Ciências e Letras, 1979. 76 p. (Coleção Vale do Iguaçu; v. 32)

Almost all 16, carefully elaborated, sentimental articles could be expanded into short stories with a message of Christian charity. Few qualify as *crônicas* (e.g., "Siglas") dealing with day-to-day experiences, to justify inclusion in this section.

6045 Pinto, Aurea Netto. O preço da bandeira. Belo Horizonte: Rona Editora, 1979? 113 p.

Ending with a dozen well-meant poems, author addresses diseases of modern urban society, as experienced in Minas Gerais, in heartfelt, feminine appeals to her readers' consciences, to turn back from "our daily violence." She points to exemplary personalities, such as Eunice Weaver, who helped the lepers of Brazil.

6046 Prêmio Apesul revelação literária 79: conto-crônica. Capa de Ruben Herrmann. Porto Alegre: Instituto Estadual do Livro, Secretaria da Cultura, Desporto, e Turismo, 1979. 103 p.

Most of 20 articles written by as many fledgling authors and selected through contest disappoint by dealing with fantasies instead of reflecting on observed reality. Among few in latter category are good pieces on vagrant children, a children's birthday party, and a barrage of bad news from consumers.

6047 Rangel, Flávio. Seria cômico se não fosse trágico: crônicas. Capa, Eugênio Hirsch. Rio de Janeiro: Civilização Brasileira, 1979. 192 p. (Coleção Vera Cruz; v. 290)

One of the witty founders of *O Pasquim*, Rangel directs brilliant barbs at present Brazilian government in articles first published in *Folha de S. Paulo* (1978–79). There are tributes to artists, composers, dramatists and two highlights: impressions of Spain and impressions of a tragically "surrealistic" Brazil, attributed to a fictitious French visitor.

6048 Reverbel, Carlos. Barco de papel. Porto Alegre: Editora Globo, 1979. 186 p.

Good-humored nostalgia colors most of the *crônicas* which first appeared in *Folha da Tarde* or *Correio do Povo* (Porto Alegre, 1976–78), forming an archive of regional lore, including literature; for Reverbel loves books. Also breaks lances for good causes, especially the humanization of big cities.

6049 ———. Saudações aftosas. Porto Alegre: Martins Livreiro—Editor, 1980. 103 p.

Craftsmanlike evocations of regional interest, written for *Correio do Povo* and *Folha da Tarde* (Porto Alegre, 1977–79), by experienced journalist. Some are weighted down with historical documentation, but others delight as anecdotes of human interest. Title is a dreadful pun.

6050 Sousa, Henrique de. Henfil na China, antes da Coca-Cola. Capa, Hélio de Almeida. Rio de Janeiro: Codecri, 1980. 309 p.; ill. (Coleção Edições do Pasquim; v. 80)

First published as a series in satirical weekly *O Pasquim*, work does not consist of real *crônicas* but offers a reportage of quick trip to Red China in 1977. Ostensibly swallowing official propaganda, author cleverly insinuates second thoughts. Information is serious, only Henfil's own drawings are amusing.

6051 Tarquínio, Luiz Eugênio. Quinta Ilusão: crônicas. Salvador: Gráfica Econômico e Administração, 1979. 131 p.

Having started out as a sports writer in Bahia, Tarquínio offers collection of anecdotal articles written 1971–79. First part tells of travels (e.g., Greece and Morocco); second, better one, of persons, chiefly Brazilians, but including splendid *crônica* on Muhammad Ali's sportsmanship. Misprints mar text.

Poetry

RALPH E. DIMMICK, *General Secretariat, Organization of American States*

WHILE THE QUANTITY OF MATERIAL available for examination during this biennium fell well below the level of the late past, overall quality was higher than at any time within recent memory.

Two poets made debuts with works of exceptional merit, widely different in character: while Luís Augusto Cassas' *República dos becos* (item **6070**) takes its inspiration from daily life in provincial Maranhão, João Manuel Simões' *Suma poética* (item **6123**) draws upon the world of imagination. Notable too were the collections published by two other authors new to the reviewer: the nostalgic *Pastor de temporais* (item **6062**) of J. Antônio d'Avila and Walker Luna's *Companheiro* (item **6091**), which imparts an unusual direction to Brazilian amatory verse.

Publication of collected works by Zila Mamede (item **6096**), Alberto da Costa e Silva (item **6161**), and Hilda Hilst (item **6083**), permits an appreciation of the evolution of three significant contemporaries during the past quarter century. The Domingos Carvalho da Silva anthology (item **6122**), on the other hand, shows him to have been relatively static.

New works by Neide Archanjo (item **6059**), Wilson Alvarenga Borges (item **6065**), Astrid Cabral (item **6068**), Helena Parente Cunha (item **6076**), Ferreira Gullar (item **6082**), Nauro Machado (items **6093–6094**), Domingos Paoliello (items **6104–6105**), and Cyro Pimentel (item **6108**) well maintain established reputations.

Three deceased poets have found new life through first-time publication of their work in book form: Duque-Costa, a figure of great notoriety during the second decade of the century (item **6078**); Vito Pentagna, an urban recluse oriented toward the Symbolist past (item **6107**); and Sosígenes Costa, a provincial Modernist whose *Iararana* (item **6074**) might be termed a verse pendant to Mário de Andrade's *Macunaíma*. Attention should also be called to Sérgio Buarque de Hollanda's *Antologia dos poetas brasileiros da fase colonial* (item **6067**). Exhausted immediately upon publication, it has at long last reappeared in a much-needed reprint.

It is encouraging to note that, in this age of increasing urban concentration, poetry can still flourish in a provincial setting. São Luís do Maranhão seems to be rejustifying its nineteenth-century reputation as a Brazilian Athens: no fewer than six among the more six significant poets here listed have or had that city as their center of activity and, in many cases, their inspiration as well—Luís Augusto Cassas, José Chagas, Nauro Machado, Ademir dos Santos, José Sarney, and Bandeira Tribuzi.

6052 Abreu, Paulo Plínio. Poesia. Pref., notícias e notas de F. Paulo Mendes. Belém: Universidade Federal do Pará, 1978. 214 p.; port. (Coleção amazônica: Série Inglês de Souza)

The call of the beyond—ultimately death—fills delicately crafted verse of this admirer and translator of Rilke.

6053 Albuquerque, Terêza Tenório de. Mandala: poesia. Rio de Janeiro: Civilização Brasileira, 1980. 87 p. (Coleção Poesia hoje; v. 40)

The poet's declaration "Vivo numa dimensão ultra-real" is well supported by these dreamlike poems, rich in Jungian symbolism, on love, death, and man's relation to the world of legend and magic.

6054 Almeida, Carlos Fernando Fortes de. Raiz da dor: poesias. Rio de Janeiro: Gráfica Olímpica Editora, 1979. 72 p.

A sequence of 48 sonnets, thoroughly classical in expression and metrification, occasionally religious in inspiration, followed by more "modern" pieces, one of which ("Pássaro") is a real gem.

6055 Amaral, Edson C. O avesso de mim. Teresópolis, Brazil: Edições Cadernos da Serra, 1980. 64 p.

Amaral's celebrations of carnal love bear a note of conviction, but his apostrophes to liberty, brotherhood, and the like are at best sophomoric.

6056 Andrade, Andréa. Metamorfose: poemetos. Desenho da capa, Paulo Eduardo Queiroz Campos, Manoel Araujo. João Pessoa, Brazil: Gráfica Santa Marta, 1979. 103 p.

Harmonious verse, expressive of an ill-defined spiritual disquietude.

6057 Andrade, Carlos Drummond de. Carlos Drummond de Andrade. Seleção de textos, notas, estudos biográfico, histórico e crítico e exercícios por Rita de Cássia Barbosa. São Paulo: Abril Educação, 1980. 105 p.; bibl.; ill. (Literatura comentada)

Didactically useful selection of compositions by a major poet, emphasizing the autobiographical.

6058 Aragão, Caetano Ximenes. O pastoreio da nuvem e da morte: poemas. Ilustração, Estrigas. Fortaleza: Gráfica Editorial Cearense, 1975. 129 p.; 5 leaves of plates; ill.

A physician with a social conscience, Aragão suffers "a angústia . . . da bomba / da fome / da guerra / do homen / não existir / como homem."

6059 Archanjo, Neide. Escavações. Rio de Janeiro: Editora Nova Fronteira, 1980. 113 p. (Coleção Poiesis)

"Quem senão o poeta / para acordar o coração das coisas / e chamar os mortos?" asks Archanjo. Her response, couched in newly accessible language, is brilliantly successful in its evocations of the family home and the first experiences of love.

6060 Assumpção, Lucy. Estágios. Rio de Janeiro: Nórdica, 1979. 88 p.

Assumpção defines poetry as "Reduto final / que acolhe / sem pedir senha / do jeito que ali chegar / toda forma de sentir / e devolve / sublimada / na força do dizer / um todo que se repete / no sempre de cada um."

6061 Avelino, Gilberto. O moinho e o vento. Natal, Brazil: Fundação José Augusto, 1977. 70 p.

The best of this collection are simple lyrics inspired by the wind and the sea, which beg to be set to music.

6062 Avila, Jesuino Antonio d'. Pastor de temporais. Ilustrações de Clóvis Graciano e Aldemir Martins. São Paulo: Massao Ohno, 1979. 100 p.; ill.

Regret, both for what has ceased to be p.; ill.

Regret, both for what has ceased to be and for what never was, is the dominant note of these exceptionally fine lyrics.

6063 Barbeiro, Walter de Souza. Esquizoramas: evocação de Augusto dos Anjos. São Paulo: A Gazeta Maçônica, 1977. 56 p.

Inspired by a "scientific" poet of the turn of the century, Barbeiro has composed sonnets in which death and dissolution of the body are described in the language of pathology.

6064 Bilac, Olavo. Olavo Bilac. Seleção de textos, notas, estudos biográfico, histórico e crítico e exercícios por Norma Goldstein. São Paulo: Abril Educação, 1980. 107 p.; bibl.; ill. (Literatura comentada)

Didactically useful selection from works of a leading Parnassian.

6065 Borges, Wilson Alvarenga. Flor de extremos: poesia. Rio de Janeiro: Edições Porta de Livraria, 1981. 93 p.; port.

"O ser só vive / quando se estuda," "se alarga / com o que de si oferece . . . e se eterniza / no que de si projeta" declares the poet in sententious verse characterized by precision of thought, sobriety of language, and rigorous control of form.

6066 Brito, Mário da Silva. Jogral do frágil e do efêmero: poesia. Capa, Eduardo sobre pintura de Paul Klee. Rio de Janeiro: Civilização Brasileira, 1979. 165 p. (Coleção Vera Cruz; v. 284)

Commonplace thoughts and emotions, versified in a pleasing but commonplace manner.

6067 Buarque de Hollanda, Sergio. Antologia dos poetas brasileiros da fase colonial. São Paulo: Editora Perspectiva, 1979. 512 p. (Coleção Textos; 2)

Excellent anthology, first printed four decades ago but unavailable ever since.

6068 Cabral, Astrid. Ponto de cruz: poemas. Rio de Janeiro: Livraria Editora Cátedra, 1979. 107 p.; port.

An acute awareness of the transitory nature of human existence, an exceptional sense of the value of words, and skilled handling of tropes contribute to Cabral's transformation of everyday objects and actions into symbols of universal significance.

6069 Carvalho, Cid. Opus 78 [i.e. setenta e oito]. Rio de Janeiro: Editora Artenova, 1978. 76 p.

Though highly eclectic in choice of themes and techniques, at heart Carvalho remains a traditionalist.

6070 Cassas, Luís Augusto. República dos becos: poesia. Prefácio de Josué Montello. Rio de Janeiro: Civilização Brasileira, 1981. 107 p.; ill. (Coleção Vera Cruz; 329)

In simple but telling language, with touches of ironic humor and a brilliant use of metaphor, Cassas imparts universal significance to daily life in the provinces and poignancy to the social ills that stir his conscience.

6071 Chagas, José. Poesia reunida. Capa de Jomar Moraes. São Luís, Maranhão: Edições SIOGE, 1980. 597 p.; ill.

São Luís—its past, its politics, its poor—is the central theme of this prolific and generally rather pedestrian provincial poet.

6072 Coppieters, Percy. Tocaia: ou, Pelos caminhos alucinantes do grito. Capa, Rui Douglas Cattai. São Paulo: s.n., 1979. 52 p.

A call to arms against oppression and imperialism, in the name of liberty and human solidarity.

6073 Costa, Odylo. Boca da noite. Capa e diagramação, Pedro Costa. Rio de Janeiro: Salamandra, 1979. 150 p.; port.

A gently elegiac tone, perhaps premonitory of Costa's approaching death, pervades these poems, largely inspired by love, situated in the mainstream of the Portuguese lyric tradition.

6074 Costa, Sosígenes. Iararana. Introd., apuração do texto e glossário por José Paulo Paes. Apresentação de Jorge Amado. Ilustrações e capa de Aldemir Martins. São Paulo: Editora Cultrix, 1979. 115 p.; bibl.; ill.

Written about 1933 and previously unpublished, this Modernist saga of the cacao region of southern Bahia, composed in popular style and ultra-Brazilian language, mingles, delightfully, classic mythology with elements of native folklore.

6075 Couto, Carlos. Rosas e porradas: poesia com alças. Niterói: Edições Zagorá, 1979. 86 p.; ill.

The deceptively direct language of Couto's vibrant compositions disguises rather than emphasizes the irony of his views of the social hierarchy and accepted standards of sexual morality.

6076 Cunha, Helena Parente. Maramar. Rio de Janeiro: Edições Tempo Brasileiro; Brasília: em convênio com o Instituto Nacional do Livro, 1980. 118 p. (Coleção Tempoesia; no. 22)

Reflecting as it were the endless expanse of the sea, which is Cunha's constant motif, present fuses with past and future, and destination with point of departure in these vague but exceptionally musical compositions.

6077 Curvello, Aricy. Os dias selvagens te ensinam. Capa, Branca de Castro. Belo Horizonte: Editora Vega, 1979. 95 p.

Curvello's message is a simple one of social and political protest, but his typographical complications—words within words, passages to be read in two different senses, backward spellings—are such that its force is lost in the decipherment process.

6078 Duque-Costa, Hermínio. O livro poético de Duque-Costa. Pref. de Andrade Muricy. Rio de Janeiro: Editora Fon-Fon e Seleta, 1980. 148 p.; ill.

First publication in book form of the work of a post-Symbolist, much discussed in the second decade of the century, who placed great emphasis on sound values, seeking to write "poetic music."

6079 Fatal, Paulo [*pseud. for* Paulo Silva de Oliveira]. Vapor de mercúrio. Rio de Janeiro: Arquimedes Edições, 1979. 110 p.

Well characterized by Sérgio A. Cyrino da Costa as "Um retrato falado do inconsciente enorme de todos nós . . . sem as prisões da lógica, do começo e do fim."

6080 Ferreira, Climério. Alguns pensames. Brasília: Tao Livraria e Editora, 1979. 117 p.

A skillful application of sophisticated technique to popular motifs such as *saudade* and concern for the rural underclass gives Ferreira's verse a broad appeal.

6081 Garcia, Pedro. Trapézio & trapezista. Florianópolis: Universidade para o Desenvolvimento do Estado de Santa Catarina, 1978. 84 p.

Like the headlines which inspired some of his verse, Garcia's compositions are telegraphically concise, often suggestive of interpretations that go far beyond the literal meaning conveyed.

6082 Gullar, José Ribamar Ferreira. Na vertigem do dia: poemas. Capa, Eugênio Hirsch sobre foto de Paulo Bondar. Rio de Janeiro: Civilização Brasileira, 1980. 106 p. (Coleção Vera Cruz; v. 292)

The poet reflects on his own nature and achievement and on what time has taken away from him, in gracefully simple, sincere compositions, one of which, "Cantiga para não Morrer," is a masterpiece of nostalgic charm.

6083 Hilst, Hilda. Poesia (1959–1979). São Paulo: Edições Quíron, 1980. 325 p.; ill. (Coleção Sélesis; 19)

Largely a reprint of previous collections, in which this distinguished poet sought to define her own image and the relationship between man and divinity and man and earthly forces, plus a new section in which she seeks for the ultimate significance of death. Extensive study of author's work by Nelly Novaes Coelho (p. 275–325).

6084 Kellner, Alexandr. Dizeres. Rio de Janeiro: Edições Zagorá, 1979. 59 p.

"Tudo está escrito: mas o homem acrescenta" observes Kellner in closing this set of lyric reflections on introductory apothegms.

6085 Kempf, Roswitha. Reflexos, reflexões. Capa e ilustrações feitas por Margot. São Paulo: Massao Ohno Editor, 1979. 63 p.; ill.

Superior to the author's humdrum philosophizing are her simple but effective lyric expansions.

6086 Lages, Solange Bérard. Canto/ desencanto: poesia. Maceió: s.n., 1975. 125 leaves.

Life for the poet is an unending voyage, of unmarked destination.

6087 Leitão, Augusto Sergio. A coerência do medo: poemas & lutas. Porto Alegre: Pirâmides, 1979. 82 p.

Title composition of this collection should have been "Poema por um Hoje Melhor." Sincere but prosaic.

6088 Lima, Airton Garcia de. Sábado à noite na capital. Ilustrações de Max Trifler. Brasília: Senado Federal, 1979. 132 p.; ill. (Coleção Machado de Assis; v. 15)

The disorder of Lima's expression is such that he conveys little to the reader other than the sincerity of his affection for an old love.

6089 Lisboa, Henriqueta. Casa de pedra: poemas escolhidos. Capa, projeto gráfico, Antônio do Amaral Rocha, gravura de Conceição Piló; arte final, René Etiene Ardanuy e Mara Patrícia Feixas. São Paulo: Editora Atica, 1979. 95 p.; bibl.; port.

Brief selections from previous collections, plus four new compositions ("Celebração dos Elementos") which show the poet at her solemn neo-Symbolist best. Introduction by Fábio Lucas; bibliography of works by and about the author.

6090 Lucena, Antonio Carlos. Para latir na calçada. Ilustradora, Elvira Macri. Autor da capa, Flávio del Carlo. São Paulo: Lucena, 1978. 89 p.; ill. (Coleção Sanguinova; v. 1)

"Achei na poesia um caminho . . . que me leva a tentar entender meu tempo, minha vida, minha utopia," says Lucena. All is still tentative, but not without promise.

6091 Luna, Walker. Companheiro. Rio de Janeiro: Gráfica Olímpica Editora, 1979. 98 p.

Dealing with an aspect of human passion generally avoided since classic Greek times, Luna's verse conveys in a remarkably effective—and affective—manner the sentiment of the lover who exists solely as a function of his beloved.

6092 Macário, Pedro. Vida substantiva. Rio de Janeiro: Edições Porta de Livraria, 1980. 65 p. (Série Poesia; 21)

Macário's pessimistic view of the mechanization of human life is summed up in the verse "Ganhar a vida é ganhar a morte: sorte."

6093 Machado, Nauro. O calcanhar do humano: poemas. São Luís, Brazil: FUNC: SIOGE, 1981. 87 p.

Faced with a world in which "tudo é pó" and a heaven whose god "tem fome da angústia humana," Machado is consoled by the reflection that "o cérebro é maior que a extensão do céu em Deus" and that by the power of thought man can "ganhar a eternidade."

6094 ———. Masmorra didática. Montagem de capa, Eduardo. Sobre desenho de Thereza Miranda. Rio de Janeiro: Civilização Brasileira, 1979. 107 p. (Coleção Poesia hoje; v. 26)

"Meu único sonho é acabar-me . . . perdendo tudo que me faz consciente até que surja . . . o nada" declares Machado in gloomy but impressive verse that denies the value and meaning of existence.

6095 Maciel, José Paschoal Pires. Entre cantos: poemas. São Paulo: Editora Soma, 1980. 53 p.

The author's faith in humanity, love, and poetry is expressed in gentle lyrics notable for the hauntingly suggestive power of their imagery.

6096 Mamede, Zila. Navegos: poesia reunida, 1953–1978. Capa e ilustrações, Paul Bernardo F. Vaz. Belo Horizonte: Editora Vega, 1978. 200 p.; ill.

While in the course of 25 years Mamede's poetic horizon has constantly expanded, her verse has become increasingly terse and charged with meaning: an apparently simple composition such as "Retrato de Minha Mãe Costurando," for example, synthesizes the whole cycle of human existence.

6097 Meireles, Cecília. Flores e canções. Com ilustrações de Vieira da Silva. Rio de Janeiro: Confraria dos Amigos do Livro, 1979. 70 p.; 1 leaf of plates; ill.; ports.

Aesthetically a Symbolist, Meireles was nonetheless the outstanding feminine voice of the Modernist generation. Brief but good selection of her compositions, handsomely presented. Biographical notes on poet and illustrator.

6098 Mello, Gustavo Bandeira de. Saciara. Capa de Neusa d'Arcanchy. Bonecos do autor. Brasília: Gráfica e Editora Itamarati, 1978 or 1979. 86 p.; ill.

Mello recognized life's imperfections, but feels the most suitable course lies in acceptance.

6099 Mendes, Cleise Furtado. Agora, praça do tempo: poemas. Capa, Ernesto José

J. de Oliveira. Salvador, Brazil: Fundação Cultural do Estado da Bahia, 1979. 78 p. (Coleção Ilha de Maré; v. 3)

If "A Máquina de Escrever" poses the problem of poetic composition, "A Onda" resolves it brilliantly.

6100 Mendes, Murilo. O menino experimental: antologia. São Paulo: Summus Editorial, 1979. 164 p. (Coleção Palavra poética; 3)

Selection, didactic in intent, from the work of a poet whose development closely parallels the evolution of Brazilian verse from Modernist days till 1975, the year of his death.

6101 Moura Júnior, João. Chega de choro. Desenhos de Tunga. Capa, João Moura, Jr. Ilustrações de G. J. Xavery para um argumento de Commedia dell'arte, Amsterdam, século XVIII. Rio de Janeiro?: s.n., 1979. 97 p.; ill.

Classical motifs with a wryly modern twist.

6102 Oliveira, Eduardo de. Túnica de ébano: sonetos e trovas. Capa, Luiz Cláudio Barcellos. Piracicaba, Brazil: Tribuna Piracicabana, 1980. 122 p.; 2 p. of music.

Sonnets and quatrains in the 19th-century Romantic manner, distinguished occasionally by a note of protest at discrimination against blacks.

6103 Osório, Laci. Comício das canções: poesia. Capa, Mário Röhnelt. Porto Alegre: Movimento, 1978. 85 p. (Coleção Poesiasul; v. 19)

While social criticism lies at the heart of these compositions, it is most effective when conveyed by metaphor, heightened by the spareness of Osório's poetic language.

6104 Paoliello, Domingos. Poemas de sazão. São Paulo: Clube de Poesia de São Paulo, 1980. 77 p. (Tarefa imemorial; 4)

In stately, classic verse, solemn in tone and at times religious in inspiration, Paoliello pursues his "inexorável vocação de poeta, / de sentir pelos outros / o que os outros não ousam / sentir até o fim."

6105 ———. Secreto enxame: poemas. São Paulo: Clube de Poesia de São Paulo, 1979. 45 p.; ill. (Poemas da difícil madureza; 2)

Like Picasso in the paintings of his classical period, Paoliello here resorts to antique motifs and forms in capturing in words the world around him.

6106 Peliano, José Carlos Pereira. Passagem de nível. Capa, Itamar de Freitas Barros. Brasília: Livraria Galilei, 1979. 77 p.

A verbal alchemist, Peliano invests with spirituality the most commonplace of themes—an open door, a growing plant, a bird in flight.

6107 Pentagna, Vito. Poemas. Ilustrações, Paulo Bernardo Ferreira Vaz. Capa, layout de Paulo B. F. Vaz sobre vinheta de Aubrey Beardsley in Le morte d'Arthur. Belo Horizonte: Editora Vega, 1978. 142 p.; 6 leaves of plates; ill.

The nebulous thought, recherché vocabulary, and nocturnal-funeral atmosphere of Symbolism mark the well-wrought verse of this "leap-year" poet. Unpublished until 20 years after his death (1958), even in life he belonged to the past.

6108 Pimentel, Cyro. Poemas atonais. São Paulo: Clube de Poesia, 1979. 69 p.

Though possessed by the gods and the vision of beauty, the poet, a "prisioneiro no homem," is compelled to lament what man has brought into the world—atomic warfare, pollution, and death.

6109 Proença, Ivan Cavalcanti. Castro Alves falou: antologia (comentada) didática. Capa, Eugenio Hirsch. Rio de Janeiro: Livraria J. Olympio Editora, 1979. 119 p.; bibl.

Didactically useful selection of writings by major Romantic poet.

6110 Radtke, Eulália Maria. Espiral: poemas. Florianópolis, Santa Catarina: Secretaria de Cultura, Esporte e Turismo, Fundação Catarinense de Cultura, 1980. 87 p.; ill. (Coleção Cultura catarinense. Série Literatura, poesia)

"Ternura" is the keynote of these short, gentle lyrics.

6111 Rodrigues, José Roberto. Poliedro. Florianópolis, Santa Catarina: Fundação Catarinense de Cultura, 1980. 63 p.; ill. (Coleção Cultura catarinense. Série Literatura, poesia)

Love—treated sensuously, but with delicacy—human solitude, childhood memories, and the poet's calling constitute the thematic faces of Rodrigues' lyric polyhedron. A work of unusual promise.

6112 Roviralta, Raúl J. F. Idem, ibidem. Capa e ilustrações, Silvia Furmam. São Paulo, M. Ohno Editor, 1978. 95 p.; ill.

While poetry may reflect the world, their relation to one another is essentially one of confrontation.

6113 Salenses, Ludovicus. Eu sem pejo: poesias. Capa, Júlio Gonçalves. Recife: Governo do Estado de Pernambuco, Secretaria de Educação e Cultura, 1979. 110 p.

Parnassian sonnets, largely inspired by carnal—and frequently adulterous—love, of which the poet takes a singularly dispassionate, almost practical view.

6114 Sampaio, Carlos. Cavalaria: poemas. Capa, Edvaldo Gato. São Paulo: Editora Gráfica Cairú, 1976. 38 p.; ill.

Celebration of horses, in which ample use is made of alliteration.

6115 Sampaio, Renato. Lições de pedramor. Ilustrações, Chanina. Capa Chanina, Hélio Faria. Belo Horizonte, Brazil: Editora Comunicação, 1978. 79 p.; ill.

The cautious, questioning spirit of Minas pervades Sampaio's lyric reflections, the most successful of which are the reminiscences of childhood entitled "Solo."

6116 Sant'Anna, Affonso Romano de. Que país é este? e outros poemas. Capa, Victor Burton. Rio de Janeiro: Civilização Brasileira, 1980. 175 p. (Coleção Poesia hoje; v. 38)

Depth of the poet's concern for the state of his country and the dehumanization of life in general is clearly evident, but, given the wry mockery with which it is voiced, response comes more from the head than from the heart.

6117 Santos, Ademir dos. Os ratos do beco. São Luis: Edições SIOGE, 1979. 62 p.

"De uma Janela na Praça Gonçalves Dias" suggests that Santos' true talent lies in descriptive verse, rather than the cryptic utterances that constitute the majority of his compositions.

6118 Santos, Ronaldo. 14 [i.e. Quatorze] bis. Ilustrações são de Ovídio Villela *et al.* Capa, Claudio, Resende, Paulin. Rio de Janeiro: à venda na Livraria Muro, 1979. 52 p.; ill.

The devil-may-care verse of a young man for whom the simplest aspects of daily living constitute poetic inspiration.

6119 Sarney, José. Os maribondos de fogo. Capa, Studio Artenova. Ilustrações, Péricles Rocha. Rio de Janeiro: Editora Artenova, 1978. 99 p.; ill.

Sarney evokes the past by metaphor, rather than literal description, in language rich in terms peculiar to Brazil, most particularly Maranhão.

6120 Savary, Olga. Altaonda. Ilustrações de Calasans Neto. Pref. de Jorge Amado. Salvador: Edições Macunaíma; São Paulo: Massao Ohno, 1979. 47 p.; ill.

Birds, and above all the sea are the principal motifs of these poems characterized by "o rigor da ordem sobre o ardor da chama."

6121 Silva, Alberto da Costa e. As linhas da mão. Rio de Janeiro: DIFEL, 1978. 139 p.

Da Costa e Silva early proclaimed the realm of childhood to be "minha pátria" and its magic persists in his most recent compositions, in one of which he declares: "em nos o tempo / refaz de claridade o que perdemos / e repõe no universo o que foi sonho." A difficult but rewarding poet.

6122 Silva, Domingos Carvalho da. Múltipla escolha: selecão de poemas dos livros Bem-amada Ifigênia . . . Introdução, Diana Bernardes. Rio de Janeiro: Livraria José Olympio Editora; Brasília: Instituto Nacional do Livro, Ministério da Educação e Cultura, 1980. 160 p.; bibl.; port.

Bernardes acutely observes: "poeta da vida, do tempo, do amor e da morte, . . . [seu] compromisso único é com a palavra: . . . é . . . o 'fixador de instantes,' recriados na e pela linguagem." Biobibliographic material accompanying this selection by author makes it singularly useful to scholars.

6123 Simões, João Manuel. Suma poética. Capa do autor. Curitiba: Academia Paranaense de Letras, 1979. 159 p. (Coleção Academia Paranaense de Letras)

Dreams, evocations of the past, flights into the future constitute the material of Simões' verse; even soccer ("Ode a Pelé") takes on other-worldly beauty in the hands of this master of rhythm, form, and poetic language. Winner of the 1978 Fernando Chinaglia Prize. Outstanding.

6124 Sousa, Afonso Félix de. Chão básico & itinerário leste. Capa, Edison Braga.

São Paulo: Edições Quíron, 1978. 83 p.; port. (Coleção Sélesis; 18)

At 50, the poet is conscious how little his accomplishments correspond to his expectations, but continues "a extrair das palavras / a polpa e o sumo / e a devolvê-las / ao mundo / mexidas a meu modo."

6125 Souto, Jomar Morais. Fazenda de murmúrios. João Pessoa, Paraíba: Editora Universitária/UFPb, 1980. 115 p.

Poems of social protest, directed chiefly against conditions in the Northeast, and lyrics of a more personal nature, all handled with a good feeling for words and a keen ear for music.

6126 Souza, Tárik de. Autópsia em corpo vivo. Porto Alegre, Rio Grande do Sul: L & PM Editores, 1979. 78 p.; ill.

Remarkable, not for what they actually say, but for the variety of their suggestion, are these "palavras detonadas, cada qual, atômica por sua voz . . . vestida no rigor dos infinitos sentidos."

6127 Torres, Ulysses Lemos. Introspectiva. Capa e ilustrações, Capi, José Carlos Ramasini. São Paulo: Milesa Editora, 1979. 160 p.; ill.

A simple and charming lyric such as

6128 Trevisan, Armindo. O rumor do sangue. Capa, Mário Röhnelt. Porto Alegre, Brasil: Editora Movimento, 1979. 71 p. (Coleção Poesiasul; v. 23)

Though so brief as to appear but fragments, these poems inspired by childbirth and infancy are charged with a sense of the mystery of life.

6129 Tribuzi, Bandeira. Poesias completas. Pref. de Josué Montello. Capa, Studio Cátedra. Rio de Janeiro: Livraria Editora Cátedra, 1979. 285 p.; port.

"Sou filho do ruído das palavras," said Tribuzi, who also spoke of "meu estar entre diversas forças, neutro." True; despite a vast repertory of themes, rich vocabulary, and rhythmic versatility, Tribuzi remained conventional in thought and emotionally uninvolved at all times.

6130 Vianna, Fernando Mendes. Embarcado em seco: poemas. Capa, Eugênio Hirsch. Rio de Janeiro: Civilização Brasileira, 1978. 116 p. (Coleção Poesia hoje; v. 23)

In composing these celebrations of the sea, Vianna seems to have striven less for *le mot juste* than *le mot rare.*
"Colibrí" is all but lost amid compositions burdened with scientific terminology.

Drama

BENJAMIN M. WOODBRIDGE, JR., *Professor of Portuguese, Emeritus, University of California, Berkeley*

MANY OF THE PLAYS REVIEWED here won prizes, but none of the newer ones is particularly distinguished. By all odds the best is the late (1936–74) Oduvaldo Viana Filho's *Rasga Coração* (item **6144**). Banned by censors in 1975, the play, characterized by Yan Michalski (item **6155**, p. 53) as an "obra-prima definitiva da dramaturgia nacional," was finally liberated and performed in 1979. The topical nature of the setting requires, for full understanding, a detailed knowledge of recent Brazilian history, but the theme emerges clearly even for those only vaguely aware of the background. The pervasive slang further limits an outsider's enjoyment and may eventually date the play for future readers. Other playwrights also abuse of contemporary idiom; and beyond that, presumably in the name of a dourly-conceived realism, they indulge in vulgarity of both language and situation that contributes nothing essential to the drama and in reality damages the quality of the production. Most exploit the uglier aspects of the contemporary scene, but fail to achieve Viana Filho's fusion of the psychological and the ephemeral. The pervasive and one-sided somberness and heaviness of most contemporary drama give added charm to the contrasting lightness of such earlier playwrights as Macedo (item

6138) and Varejão (item **6143**). Unfortunately, there are no notes or dates for the Macedo plays, and the text, inadequately proofread, is not always reliable.

Related to the variety of dramatic practice, essays on theory of theater attest to lively interest and commitment. Soul-searching on what theater should be appears in Fernando Peixoto's work (item **6156**); Augusto Boal's vision and practice of a theater of the oppressed (item **6153**) stress an activist view, but unfortunately he gives no evidence of the source of economic support for his wide-ranging activity.

In the area of critical work, two essays on Nelson Rodrigues (items **6150** and **6152**) testify to the appeal of his theater. On the historical side the continuation of the Hessel-Raeders history of Brazilian theater (item **6147**) and Amaral's exhaustive monograph on São Paulo theaters (item **6145**) are particularly welcome.

ORIGINAL PLAYS

6131 Accioly, Marcus. Ixion. Rio de Janeiro: Edições Tempo Brasileiro, 1978. 147 p.; port. (Coleção Tempoesia; 16)
Verse play on themes from classical mythology, buttressed with elaborate notes for the unenlightened reader. Neither action nor meaning is clear (on earlier poems by Accioly, see *HLAS 38:7439*).

6132 Aguiar, Cláudio. Flor destruída: drama. São Paulo: Editora do Escritor, 1976. 83 p.; 1 leaf of plates; port. (Coleção de teatro; v. 3)
The flower, according to the author, is hope, ever reborn after temporary destruction. An improbable plot hardly illustrates the concept.

6133 Araújo, Alcione. Sob neblina use luz baixa. Capa, Glória Itabirano Gomide. Belo Horizonte: Edições Soma, 1978. 51 p.; ill. (Coleção Tempo de teatro)
Contemporary jargon mars this drama of a disintegrating family caught in a nightmare world.

6134 Assunção, Leilah. A kuka de Kamaiorá. Rio de Janeiro: Ministério da Educação e Cultura/DAC/FUNARTE/ Serviço Nacional de Teatro/Departamento de Documentação e Divulgação, 1978. 148 p. (Coleção Prêmios; v. 13)
The meaning of this play of ideas is not clear; prominent themes seem to be the folly of attempting to establish a uniform society and the exploitation of the ignorant by the powerful (for an earlier play by this author, see *HLAS 42:6353*).

6135 Fagundes, Antonio Augusto. Por telefone. Capa desenho, Ancheta. São Paulo: Global Editora, 1980. 53 p. (Teatro urgente; no. 4)
Use, misuse, and abuse of a telephone constitute the outward trappings of what is perhaps meant as a play of social protest. Dialogue is deliberately slangy.

6136 Fernandes, Millôr. É . . .: baseado num fato verídico que apenas ainda não aconteceu. Capa, Caulos. Fotos, Max Hanemberg. Porto Alegre: L&PM Editores, 1977. 174 p.; ill. (Coleção Teatro de Millôr Fernandes; v. 1)
The bitter irony of life works havoc with people who think of themselves as liberated from traditional values. Intellectualized monologues detract from fine dialogue (for earlier works of a different sort by Fernandes, see *HLAS 38:7537, HLAS 40:7520,* and *HLAS 42:6367–6369*).

6137 Gregori, Ana Elisa and **Mauro Chaves.** Barreado por Ana Elisa Gregori. Os executivos por Mauro Chaves. Brasília: Departamento de Documentação e Divulgação, 1977. 160 p. (Coleção Prêmios; 5)
Gregori: nature wins a contest with death in this slow-moving play; *caipira* dialogue. Chaves: a satire on the spiritual and moral bankruptcy of multinational corporation executives and their wives (for another play by Chaves, see *HLAS 42:6359*).

6138 Macedo, Joaquim Manuel de. Teatro completo. t. 2. Rio de Janeiro: Ministério da Educação e Cultura, Fundação Nacional de Arte, Serviço Nacional de Teatro, 1979. 268 p.; port (Clássicos do teatro brasileiro; v. 3:2)
Volume contains a historical drama in prosaic blank verse (*Cobé*); a Biblical drama in rhymed verse (*O sacrifício de Isaac*); an opera (*O fantasma branco*); a contemporary

drama (*Lusbela*); and a comedy (*O novo Otelo*, see *HLAS 40:7630*). Exacerbated Romantic passion, melodrama, sentimentality, slapstick, bourgeois morality are hallmarks of Macedo's theater.

6139 Muniz, Lauro Cesar. Sinal de vida. Capa, Carlos Clémen. São Paulo: Global Editora, 1979. 107 p. (Teatro urgente; no. 2)

Tight dramatic technique, but too long-drawn-out anguish of an ex-revolutionary obsessed with feelings of guilt at the violent death of a young woman who had put his teaching into action.

6140 Pinto, Benedito Rodrigues. Meia-sola. São Paulo: Departamento de Artes e Ciências Humanas, Comissão de Teatro, 1979. 67 p. (Coleção de textos de teatro; 1)

Underprivileged people driven to madness by their poverty work out their frustrations on one another. The characters are treated coldly, without sympathy.

6141 ———. Na fronteira. São Paulo: Departamento de Artes e Ciências Humanas, Comissão de Teatro, 1979. 92 p. (Coleção de textos de teatro; 3)

Hate maddens and destroys a once powerful and wealthy landowning family.

6142 Prata, Mário. Fábrica de chocolate: um ato. São Paulo: Editora Hucitec, 1979. 56 p. (Coleção Teatro)

Violence, cynicism, and hypocrisy in a security police office; self-conscious "realism."

6143 Varejão, Lucilo. Teatro . . . quase completo. Recife: Prefeitura Municipal do Recife, Secretaria de Educação e Cultura, Conselho Municipal de Cultura, 1979. 294 p.; 5 leaves of plates; ill. (Coleção Recife; 3)

Clever dialogue in three situation comedies (1921–39), heavy preaching in a bourgeois drama (1939) by a writer from Pernambuco (1892–1965). For a novel by Varejão, see *HLAS 23:5499*.

6144 Viana Filho, Oduvaldo. Rasga coração. Rio de Janeiro: Ministério da Educação e Cultura / SEAC, FUNARTE / Serviço Nacional de Teatro, 1980. 322 p.; 2 leaves of plates; ill. (Coleção Prêmios; v. 22)

Viana's image of the true revolutionary hero—an ordinary man who keeps up the struggle over the years through thick and thin—emerges from a play in which individual and generational views clash. Several decades are involved, especially the 1930s; scenes from past and present alternate in elaborate and illuminating counterpoint. Appendix (p. 79–322) comprises an unedited potpourri of linguistic and sociological notes on the period covered, some of them used in the play; only a part of the slang spoken by the characters is interpreted in the glossaries.

CRITICISM AND HISTORY

6145 Amaral, Antônio Barreto do. História dos velhos teatros de São Paulo: da Casa da Opera à inauguração do Teatro Municipal. Pref. de Miroel Silveira. São Paulo: Governo do Estado de São Paulo, 1979. 402, 59 p.; 80 leaves of plates; bibl.; ill.; indexes (Coleção paulística; v. 15)

Detailed, factual, amply-documented and generously-illustrated survey, theater by theater, covering period 1763–1911 and including opera as well as theater. Occasional picturesque anecdotes.

6146 Araújo, Nelson Correia de. Duas formas de teatro popular do Recôncavo baiano. Cidade da Bahia: Edições O ViceRey, 1979. 103 p.; 8 leaves of plates; bibl.; ill. (A Bahia e o Recôncavo; 5: Série Sociedade e cultura)

Based largely on field research, amply-documented essays concern circus plays and *reisados*, followed by texts (of no literary value) and by photographs (for earlier piece by author, see *HLAS 42:6352*).

Boal, Augusto. Milagre no Brasil. See *HLAS 43:6714*.

6147 Hessel, Lothar F. and Georges Raeders. O teatro no Brasil sob Dom Pedro II. Capa, Sônia Maria Mendonça Heinz. Porto Alegre: URGS: Instituto Estadual do Livro, Departamento de Cultura, Secretaria de Cultura, Desporto e Turismo, 1979. 1 v.; bibl.; indexes (Coleção Teatro; 3, 1. pt.)

Presentation, based on specialized studies, of actor João Caetano and of major dramatists is followed by detailed review of theatrical activity in various provinces, of opera, and of folkloric theater. Bibliographical footnotes, indexes of authors, titles, places. A continuation of authors' *O teatro jesuítico no Brasil* (see *HLAS 38:7616*) and *O teatro no Brasil da colônia à Regência* (1974).

6148 Khéde, Sônia Salomão. Discurso ideológico da censura teatral: séc. XIX (VOZES, 74:6, agosto 1980, p. 31–46)

Somewhat pretentious study of principles and practices of censorship in Rio de Janeiro (1830–60); offers eight examples of censors' judgments (1844–50).

6149 Lima, Mariángela Alves. Teatro brasileiro moderno: uma reflexão (Dionysos [Ministério da Educação e Cultura, Serviço Nacional de Teatro, São Paulo] 25, set. 1980, p. 21–29)

The role of various theatrical groups in the renovation of Brazilian theater since the 1940s.

6150 Lins, Ronaldo Lima. O teatro de Nelson Rodrigues: uma realidade em agonia. Rio de Janeiro: Livraria Francisco Alves Editora, 1979. 223 p.; bibl.

Objective study of five plays (1943–65), considered as literary reflections of sociological reality. Literary considerations, treated at much greater length, are by far the more convincing.

6151 Oliveira, Valdemar de. O capoeira, um teatro do passado por Valdemar de Oliveira. Da análise do texto teatral por Maria de Lourdes Rabetti Gianella, Tania Brandão Pereira das Neves. Brasília: Departamento de Documentação, 1977. 102 p.; bibl. (Coleção Prêmios; v. 9, no. 1)

Oliveira's notes on the role of a Recife theater (1772–1850) concern the social and cultural life of the city. Gianella and Neves provide a formalistic, compartmentalized student analysis of Roberto Freire's *Quarto de empregada* (see *HLAS 32:4870*). Practical value for actresses not clear.

6152 Sussekind, Maria Flora. Nelson Rodrigues e o fundo falso. Introdução ao teatro jesuítico no Brasil por Milton João Bacarelli. Brasília: Ministério da Educação e Cultura, Fundação Nacional de Arte, Serviço Nacional de Teatro, Departamento de Documentação e Divulgação, 1977. 131 p.; bibl.; ill. (Coleção Prêmios; v. 9, t. 2)

Discusses Nelson Rodrigues' critical disarticulation of accepted social norms in his plays. Bacarelli writes about the Jesuit theater in its historical background, with special attention to Anchieta and his plays.

MISCELLANEOUS

6153 Boal, Augusto. Stop, c'est magique! Rio de Janeiro: Civilização Brasileira, 1980. 163 p. (Coleção Teatro hoje; v. 34)

Techniques are illustrated with numerous experiments in several cities, for actors interested in awakening consciousness of oppression in various situations ("teatro do oprimido"): author advocates a theater that involves the spectator and thus helps him to liberate himself by changing his environment.

6154 Leite, Luiza Barreto. Teatro e criatividade. Rio de Janeiro: Serviço Nacional de Teatro, Ministério da Educação e Cultura, 1975. 219 p. (Coleção Ensaios; 2)

Delight and enthusiasm pervade this selection of articles by devoted and articulate teacher of dramatic art. Exercise and development of creativity are constant themes ("deixar de experimentar é estagnar," p. 114), whether she deals with her own innovative experiments or with criticism of authors, actors, and performances.

6155 Michalski, Yan. O palco amordaçado. Rio de Janeiro: Avenir Editora, 1979. 95 p. (Coleção Depoimentos; v. 13)

Reflections by mature and committed critic on the consequences of theatrical censorship (1964–79). Last chapter (p. 59–95) grimly catalogues salient events.

6156 Peixoto, Fernando. Teatro em pedaços: 1959–1977. São Paulo: Editora Hucitec, 1980. 361 p. (Coleção Teatro)

Collected articles on plays, actors, and playwrights by perceptive and sensitive actor, director, and critic torn between appreciation for expensive artistic production and belief in theater of and for the masses.

Literary Criticism and History

WILSON MARTINS, *Professor of Portuguese, New York University*

ALL QUIET ON THE WESTERN FRONT . . . One could take the famous title of Remarque's novel to describe the state of literary criticism and history for the period covered in this volume of *HLAS*. After multiplying like the proverbial mushrooms in the rain of the last 20 to 30 years, theories, doctrines and methodologies have come to a standstill, at least temporarily. As noted in *HLAS 42* (p. 656), the history of literary criticism consists of a continual process of shedding as well as of a state of permanent dissatisfaction. To further pursue our mycological metaphor, one could say that some of the methodological "mushrooms" harvested in recent years have proven hazardous to the health of literary criticism.

At present, the armies of theoreticians have abandoned war of movement in favor of trench warfare, each battalion fighting to retain its territory and consolidate its position. Hopes for additional conquests have been abandoned and, on the contrary, there is risk of losing ground. Evidence of the risk became apparent when, among the books examined in this biennium, so many had to be discarded as merely routine, so few retained as useful, and none found to be truly innovative.

Under the general subsection below, one notes critics who have retired, such as Sérgio Buarque de Hollanda (item **6160**) and Antônio Cândido (item **6169**), or the growing rebellion against Coutinho's personal "nova crítica" (item **6161**), or mere reprints such as Sílvio Romero's (item **6183**). Special mention should be made of José Veríssimo's *Ultimos estudos de literatura brasileira* (item **6186**), a collection of articles published in one volume for the first time and including pieces that were missing from the original series (see *HLAS 40:6455, HLAS 40:7700* and *HLAS 40:7742*).

There are a number of interesting critical studies of prose fiction, such as Del Fiorentino's *Utopia e realidade* (item **6189**), Fábio Freixieiro on Alencar (item **6194**), and, from a "modern" vantage point, the younger critic's round table *Ficção em debate* (item **6192**), plus Zilberman's *Do mito ao romance* (item **6206**).

With regard to poetry criticism, there are some useful books such as those in the Fortuna Crítica series, and a few truly capable works that clearly overshadow the current production on poetry criticism, Ramos' *Do barroco ao modernismo* (item **6212**), and Sayers' *The impact* . . . (item **6213**). But in poetry, as in all other genres, criticism eventually will be forced to prove that it can still move, by moving.

GENERAL

6157 Academia Paulista de Letras, *São Paulo, Brazil.* 70 [i.e. Setenta] anos da Academia Paulista de Letras. São Paulo: A Academia, 1979. 248 p.; ports.

Very useful, almost indispensable reference.

6158 Arrigucci Júnior, Davi. Achados e perdidos: ensaios de crítica. Capa de Léo Togashi. São Paulo, Polis, 1979. 171 p. (Coleção Estética; 3)

Compilation of short essays, first published in newspapers, with books and authors of Spanish America and a few Brazilian writers (e.g., Murilo Rubião, Antonio Callado, Guimarães Rosa, Antônio Cândido, and Rubem Braga).

6159 Athanázio, Enéas. Godofredo Rangel. Curitiba: Gráfica Editora 73, 1977. 106 p.; bibl.; ill.

Godofredo Rangel (1884–1951) is a minor writer who refuses to die. Athanázio revives him again.

6160 Buarque de Hollanda, Sérgio. Tentativas de mitologia. São Paulo: Editora Perspectiva, 1979. 284 p.; bibl. (Coleção Debates; 161 [i.e. 160]: Crítica)

Collection of literary criticism first published as newspaper articles (up to 1952, with three more recent ones). Introduction deserves special mention as a "testament" to Buarque de Hollanda as literary critic (see HLAS 42:6396).

6161 Campos, Marta. Questionamento sobre a crítica estética (Revista de Comunicação Social [Universidade Federal do Ceará, Centro de Humanidades, Departamento de Comunicação Social e Biblioteconomia, Fortaleza, Brasil] 10:1/2, jan./dez. 1980, p. 69–80, bibl.)

Solid, competent article questioning the validity of Afrânio Coutinho's "esthetic" methodology (see HLAS 42:6411).

6162 Cândido, Antônio. Teresina, etc. Capa, Lila Galvâo de Figueiro. Rio de Janeiro: Paz e Terra, 1980. 171 p.; bibl.; ill. (Coleção Literatura e teoria literária; v. 38)

Sundry chapters of personal memoirs, some of them of interest to literary history, as the one about the journal Clima.

6163 Carolo, Cassiana Lacerda. Do método crítico de Nestor Victor (UFP/EB, 4[4]:7, junho 1979, p. 7–69, bibl.)

Comprehensive and useful survey.

6164 Castro, Silvio. Teoria e política do modernismo brasileiro. Petrópolis: Editora Vozes, 1979. 146 p.; bibl.; index.

Good and competent study which sometimes interprets as "Modernism" what is simply "modern."

6165 Chamie, Mário. A linguagem virtual. São Paulo: Edições Quíron, 1976. 221 p.; bibl.; port. (Coleção Logos; 10)

According to the author, these essays (first published in periodicals), have in common the fact that they "discuss, explicitly or implicitly, the problem of language," in literature, the cinema and folk-music. Among specific works examined are Oswald de Andrade, Glauber Rocha, Carlos Drummond and A. J. Greimas. Competent and very up-to-date (see also HLAS 38:7598 and HLAS 42:6399).

6166 Colares, Otacílio. Lembrados e esquecidos: ensaios sobre literatura cearense. Fortaleza: Imprensa Universitária da Universidade Federal do Ceará, 1975. 204 p.; bibl.

Among the "forgotten," author exhumes Emília de Freitas (1855–1908), whose novel A raínha do ignoto he proposes as a "pioneer in the literature of the fantastic in Brazil." Another "forgotten" author worthy of his attention is Carlos de Vasconcelos (see also HLAS 40:7710 and HLAS 42:6400).

6167 Compitello, Malcolm A. Region's Brazilian backlands: the link between Volverás a Region and Euclides da Cunha's Os sertões (IUP/HJ, 1:2, Spring 1980, p. 25–45)

Important study in comparative literature shows that Euclides da Cunha's Os sertões was the model for some stylistic features of Juan Benet's novel, Volverás a Region (1967).

6168 Documentário do modernismo, Alagoas, 1922/31. Pesquisa e seleção de Moacir Medeiros de Sant'Ana. Maceió: Universidade Federal de Alagoas, 1978. 168 p.; index.

Invaluable compilation of 102 newspaper articles and related news about the impact of Modernismo in Alagoas, 1922–31. Indispensable for the movement's history, particularly in Northeastern Brazil.

6169 Esboço de figura: homenagem a Antonio Candido por Afonso Arinos et al. Projeto gráfico de Diana Mindlin. Revisão de Elisabete Oréfice. São Paulo: Livraria Duas Cidades, 1979. 391 p.; bibl.; ports.

Consists of a "Festschrift" in honor of the respected critic at the time of his retirement.

6170 Faria, João Roberto Gomes de. Mário de Andrade e a questão da língua brasileira (UFP/EB, 3[3]:6, 1978, p. 129–156, bibl.)

Excellent survey.

6171 Freixieiro, Fábio. Diversos/dispersos: literatura brasileira. Apresentação, Gilberto M. Teles. Rio de Janeiro: Edições Tempo Brasileiro, 1980. 202 p.; bibl.

Faithful to its title, this is a collection of impressionistic criticism.

6172 Gomes, Danilo. Escritores brasileiros ao vivo. Capa e ilustrações, José Roberto. Belo Horizonte: Editora Comunicação, 1979. 1 v.

Interviews of unequal interest with

major and lesser writers (e.g., Esdras do Nascimento, Dinah Silveira de Queirós, Ary Quintella, Josué Montello, Otávio de Faria).

6173 Guichard, Cláudia. Blaise Cendrars, 1887–1961: témoignages enregistrés au Brésil en 1974 (Centre de Recherches Latino-Américaines [Université Paris X-Nanterre, France] 11, mars 1976, p. 33–59, bibl.)

Interesting article on a marginal topic (see also *HLAS 42:6398* and *HLAS 42:6406*).

6174 Irmão, José Aleixo. Júlio Ribeiro: discurso de posse no Instituto Histórico e Geográfico de São Paulo. Sorocaba, Brazil: s.n., between 1976 and 1979. 227 p.; 2 leaves of plates; bibl.; ill.

This is the most comprehensive biography of Júlio Ribeiro, although digressive and not scholarly.

6175 Leitão da Cunha, José Maria Tristão. Obras de Tristão da Cunha. v. 1, Coisas do tempo. A beira do Styx. Histórias do bem e do mal. v. 2, Ouro das horas. Fábulas humanas. Caderno de versos. Torre de marfim. Hamleto (tradução). Capa de Isabel Sodré. Rio de Janeiro: Livraria AGIR Editora, 1979. 2 v.; port.

During 1910–28, the author wrote a column about Brazilian books for the *Mercure de France*. More of an old-fashioned humanist than a critic, he belongs to intellectual rather than to literary history. Thus, not everything in these volumes pertains to literary criticism.

6176 Litrento, Oliveiros Lessa. Apresentação da literatura brasileira. t. 1, História literária. t. 2, Antologia. Rio de Janeiro: Biblioteca do Exército-Editora, 1974. 2 v.; bibl.; index (Coleção General Benício; v. 116) (Biblioteca do Exército; publicação 439)

Textbook consists of vol. 1, a survey of Brazilian literature, and vol. 2, a comprehensive anthology.

6177 Lyra, Pedro. O real no poético: textos de jornalismo literário. Rio de Janeiro: Livraria Editora Cátedra; Brasília: Instituto Nacional do Livro, Ministério da Educação e Cultura, 1980. 244 p.; bibl.; index.

According to author's definition, these are "texts of literary journalism," meaning brief reviews, generally impressionist and cursory.

6178 Merquior, José Guilherme. O fantasma romântico e outros ensaios. Petrópolis: Vozes, 1980. 167 p.; bibl.; index (Coleção Theoremata; 1)

Varied essays range from psychoanalysis and literature to modernism (in the Anglo-Saxon sense of the term) to Brazilian Modernismo, and from Murilo Mendes to the latest Brazilian poetry.

6179 Monteiro, Mário Ypiranga. Fases da literatura amazonense. Manaus: Impr. Oficial, 1977. 1 v.; bibl.; ill.

For the record.

6180 Nunes, Benedito. Oswald Canibal. São Paulo: Editora Perspectiva, 1979. 77 p.; bibl. (Coleção Elos; 26)

Collected articles on Oswald de Andrade by a specialist in Oswaldian studies.

6181 A Polêmica de Tobias Barreto com os padres do Maranhão. Josué Montello, compilador. Rio de Janeiro: Livraria J. Olympio Editora, 1978. 124 p.; bibl. (Coleção Documentos brasileiros; v. no. 183)

Excellent research about one of the many anticlerical polemics which involved Tobias Barreto. Good contribution to the history of the Escola do Recife.

6182 Primeiras manifestações da ficção na Bahia. David Salles, compilador, organização, introd. e notas. Nova ed., rev. e ampliada. São Paulo: Editora Cultrix, 1979. 153 p.

Good survey of minor literature merely of historical interest.

6183 Romero, Sílvio. História da literatura brasileira: contribuições e estudos gerais para o exato conhecimento da literatura brasileira. 7. ed. organizada e prefaciada por Nelson Romero. Rio de Janeiro: Livraria J. Olympio Editora; Brasília: Instituto Nacional do Livro, Ministério da Educação e Cultura, 1980. 5 v. (1855 p.); bibl.; index; port.

Reprint of a classic (see *HLAS 9:4199*).

6184 Sant'Ana, Moacir Medeiros de. Angelo Rodrigues de Melo: Judas Isgorogota (IHGA/R, 35, 1979, p. 57–66, bibl.)

Informative biobibliographical dictionary's entry about a minor writer.

6185 Sousa, José Galante de. Machado de Assis e outros estudos. Capa, Luis Carlos Dias. Rio de Janeiro: Livraria Editora Cátedra, 1979. 247 p.; bibl.; ill.

Good studies on different subjects of literary history by a masterful researcher.

6186 Veríssimo de Mattos. José. Ultimos estudos de literatura brasileira: 7. série. Introd. de Luis Carlos Alves. Belo Horizonte: Editora Itatiaia; São Paulo: Editora da Universidade de São Paulo, 1979. 252 p. (Biblioteca de estudos brasileiros; v. 17)

Important and indispensable volume prepared by the author, shortly before his death and only made available now.

PROSE FICTION

6187 Clark, Fred M. O romance brasileiro para os norte-americanos: pt. 1, Problemas: Alencar a Aluísio Azevedo &UFP/EU, 17:1/4, jan./dez. 1979, p. 5–17)

Informative, useful, but cursory study.

6188 Costa, Edison. Tipologia e procedimentos convencionais na ficção produzida no Brasil antes de *O filho do pescador* e *A Moreninha* (Construtura [Revista de lingüística, língua e literatura. Universidade Católica do Paraná, Curitiba, Brazil] 7:19, 1979, p. 5–51, bibl.)

Faithful to its title, article is more useful than provocative.

6189 Del Fiorentino, Teresinha Aparecida. Utopia e realidade: o Brasil no começo do século XX. Pref. de Maria Beatriz Nizza da Silva. São Paulo: Editora Cultrix em convênio com o Instituto Nacional do Livro, 1979. 153 p.; bibl.; ill. (Coleção Brasil através dos textos; v. 3)

First study of two "utopias" written by Brazilians at the beginning of the century, one of which is Rodolfo Teófilo's *O reino de Kiato.*

6190 Denis, Ferdinand. Os maxacalis. Ed. crítica com introd. Notas e apêndice de Jean-Paul Bruyas. Tradução de Maria Cecília de Moraes Pinto. São Paulo: Secretaria da Cultura, Ciência e Tecnologia, Conselho Estadual de Cultura, 1979. 97 p.; 1 fold. leaf of plates; bibl.; map (Coleção Ensaio; 92)

Denis' novel takes up 44 out of book's 157 p., or less than a third, the rest is devoted to the critical apparatus. Despite such critical overkill about a meager work, the

accomplishment must be recognized as a model of research.

6191 Epple, Juan Armando. Aluisio Azevedo y el naturalismo en Brasil (RCLL, 6:11, 1. semestre, 1980, p. 29–46, 129–136)

Despite a couple of factual mistakes and a somewhat blurred historical perspective, this is a good guide to Azevedo's works.

6192 Ficção em debate e outros temas por Davi Arrigucci Jr. *et al.* São Paulo: Livraria Duas Cidades; Campinas, Brazil: Universidade Estadual de Campinas, 1979. 172 p.; bibl. (Coleção Remate de males; 1)

Interesting round table discussion of young Brazilian critics about problems, authors and works of contemporary literature.

6193 Fonseca, Maria Augusta. Palhaço da burguesia: Serafim Ponte Grande de Oswald de Andrade, e suas relações com o universo do circo. Capa, Leo Togashi. São Paulo: Polis, 1979. 148 p.; bibl.; ports. (Coleção Estética; 5)

Taking literally Oswald de Andrade's deprecatory self-definition as a "clown of the bourgeoisie," Fonseca analyzes *Serafim Ponte Grande* within the context of the circus world.

6194 Freixieiro, Fábio. Alencar, os bastidores e a posteridade. Introd., bibliografia passiva, textos éditos e inéditos, notas, a cargo de Fábio Freixieiro. Pref. de Afrânio Coutinho. Rio de Janeiro: Museu Histórico Nacional, 1977. 237 p.; 5 leaves of plates; bibl.; facsims. (Coleção Estudos e documentos—Museu Histórico Nacional; v. 4, t. 1)

Rescues from oblivion a number of occasional texts by Alencar and offers additional material for Alencarian studies. Includes good introduction by Freixieiro about the novelist's posthumous "fortuna crítica."

6195 Hollanda, Heloísa Buarque de. *Macunaíma*, da literatura ao cinema. Apresentação, Leandro Tocantins. Depoimentos, Mário de Andrade, Joaquim Pedro de Andrade. Rio de Janeiro: Empresa Brasileira de Filmes, 1978. 127 p.; bibl.; ill. (Cinebiblioteca Embrafilme)

Tells *Macunaíma*'s story from text to film without adding much that is new and in a somewhat impressionistic, arbitrary manner.

6196 José Geraldo Vieira no quadragésimo ano da sua ficção: 5 conferências de Maria de Lourdes Teixeira, José Geraldo Nogueira Moutinho, Nelly Novaes Coelho, Luís Martins e Antônio Rangel Bandeira, precididas de uma nota de Fernando Góes, organizador da edição, e seguidas de 2 depoimentos do romancista. São Paulo: Secretaria da Cultura, Ciência e Tecnologia, Conselho Estadual de Artes e Ciências Humanas, 1979. 129 p.; bibl. (Coleção Ensaio; 93)

Useful contribution to a future biography of José Geraldo Vieira.

6197 Lara, Elizabeth Rizzato. O gaúcho a pé: um processo de desmitificação. Porto Alegre: Pontifícia Universidade Católica do Rio Grande do Sul, Instituto de Letras e Artes, Curso de Pós-graduação em Lingüística e Letras, 1979. 100 leaves.

One may refer only figuratively to the "myth" of the Brazilian gaúcho. Consequently, this is a sociological study rather than a contribution to "myth" criticism, as the author suggests. As such, it is an interesting examination of a minor novelist from Rio Grande do Sul (Ciro Martins).

6198 Lima Barreto, Afonso Henrique de. Lima Barreto, bibliography and translations. Compiled and edited by Maria Luisa Nunes. Boston: G. K. Hall, 1979. 227 p. (The Yale series of Afro-American reference publications)

Interested in Lima Barreto as a black writer, the author arranged for the English translation of *Vida e morte de M. J. Gonzaga de Sá* and of *Clara dos Anjos* for her Yale course on the subject. Includes texts, introduction to both works, and good bibliography of and about Lima Barreto.

6199 López Heredia, José. Matéria e forma narrativa de "O ateneu." São Paulo: Edições Quíron, 1979. 145 p.; bibl. (Coleção Logos; 12)

Good contribution to the revival of Raul Pompéia.

6200 Panorama do conto paranaense. Seleção de textos e introd., Andrade Muricy. Notas biobibliográficas, Leopoldo Scherner. Colaboradores, Maria Ignez O. Guimarães, José Borges Neto, Orlando Bogo. Capa, Guinski. Curitiba: Fundação Cultural de Curitiba, 1979. 317 p.; 1 leaf of plates; bibl.; port.

Provides useful biobibliographical information on several minor authors usually omitted from current dictionaries.

6201 Patai, Dephne. Clarice Lispector and the clamor of the ineffable (UK/KRQ, 27:2, 1980, p. 133–149)

Interesting essay about a boring book also serves to demystify readings of Clarice Lispector.

6202 Perrone-Moisés, Leyla. Lautréamont e Raul Pompéia (VOZES, 74:6, agosto 1980, p. 5–20)

Good study in comparative literature prompts question as to whether aspects shared by both writers prove their similarity, or are merely the consequence of background experiences common to boarding school students.

6203 Secco, Carmen Lúcia Tindó. Morte e prazer em João do Rio. Capa, Cecília Jucá. Rio de Janeiro: Livraria F. Alves Editora: SEEC, 1978. 81 p.; bibl.; ill. (Coleção Estado do Rio de Janeiro)

João do Rio (pseudonym for Paulo Barreto, 1881–1921) is being rediscovered as a writer and even celebrated as an early "radical" (e.g., Cândido's *Teresina, Etc.*, see item **6162**). Secco's book, annotated here for the record, is not only elementary and shallow but pretentious as well.

6204 Souza, Gilda de Mello e. O tupi e o alaúde: uma interpretação de *Macunaíma*. São Paulo: Livraria Duas Cidades, 1979. 105 p.; bibl.

Brief but perceptive study that rectifies certain excesses of recent criticism.

6205 Tavares, Paulo. O baiano Jorge Amado e sua obra. Rio de Janeiro: Editora Record, 1980. 196 p.; bibl.; port.

Includes a careful bibliography and interesting iconography but a useless synopsis of Amado's works.

6206 Zilberman, Regina. Do mito ao romance: tipologia da ficção brasileira contemporânea. Arte, Vera Gonzatto e Diva Guizzo. Caxias do Sul: Universidade de Caxias do Sul; Porto Alegre: Escola Superior de Teologia São Lourenço de Brindes, 1977. 196 p.; bibl.; diagrs. (Coleção Chronos; 15)

Systematic and comprehensive work of myth criticism is a first in Brazilian literature.

POETRY

6207 Cassiano Ricardo. Coletânea organizada por Sônia Brayner. Desenho de capa, Dounê. Rio de Janeiro: Civilização Brasileira, 1979. 364 p.; bibl. (Coleção Fortuna crítica; v. 3)

Another volume in the Fortuna Crítica series (see *HLAS 40:7734, HLAS 42:6410, HLAS 42:6492, HLAS 42:6501*, and in this volume, see also item **6210**).

6208 Castello Branco, Carlos Heitor. Salusse, o poeta dos cisnes. São Paulo: Editora Hucitec, 1979. 110 p.; ill.

A sentimental biography by a friend is not scholarly but valuable for its personal insights.

6209 Cruz, Diniz Ferreira da. Afonso Schmidt, o homem e o poeta. Santos: D. F. da Cruz, 1980. 125 p.; facsims.; port.

Includes biobibliographical information of interest.

6210 Cunha, Helena Parente. Jeremias, a palavra poética: leitura de Cassiano Ricardo. Capa, Eugenio Hirsch. Rio de Janeiro: J. Olympio, 1979. 91 p.; bibl.; port.

Textual analysis of Cassiano Ricardo's poetry.

6211 Magalhães Júnior, Raimundo. Poesia e vida de Casimiro de Abreu. Capa, Dounê. 3. ed. revista e aum. Rio de Janeiro: Editora Civilização Brasileira em convênio com o Instituto Nacional do Livro, Ministério da Educação e Cultura, 1980. 293 p. (Coleção Vera Cruz. Literatura brasileira; v. 298)

Another biography by a master biographer who as usual is stronger in research than in literary analysis (see also *HLAS 38:7626* and *HLAS 42:6419–6421*).

6212 Ramos, Péricles Eugênio da Silva. Do barroco ao modernismo: estudos de poesia brasileira. 2. ed., rev. e aumentada. Rio de Janeiro: Livros Técnicos e Científicos Editora; São Paulo: SC-S.P., 1979. 320 p.; bibl.; index (Biblioteca universitária de literatura brasileira: Série A, Ensaio, crítica, história literária; v. 7)

Indispensable for the study of Brazilian poetry.

6213 Sayers, Raymond S. The impact of symbolism in Portugal and Brazil (*in* Waiting for Pegasus: studies of the presence of symbolism and decadence in Hispanic letters. Edited by Roland Grass and William R. Risley. Macomb: Western Illinois University, 1979, p. 125–141 [An Essays in literature book])

This is criticism at its best and unparalleled in English on its subject.

6214 Val, Waldir Ribeiro do. Vida e obra de Raimundo Correia. Capa, Luiz Falcão. Rio de Janeiro: Livraria Editora Cátedra; Brasília: Instituto Nacional do Livro, Ministério da Educação e Cultura, 1980. 293 p.; 6 leaves of plates; bibl.; ill.; index.

Best work on the topic.

6215 Xavier, Raul. Vocabulário de poesia. Capa, Mauro Kleiman. Rio de Janeiro: Imago, 1979. 224 p.; bibl. (Série Poesia Imago)

Useful.

MISCELLANEOUS

6216 Almeida, Ipergnon Paulista de. Sociedade Kukomká. São Paulo: Oficinas Gráficas da Editora Cupolo, 1979. 104 p.

Wryly humorous apothegms focusing on relations between the sexes and the exercise of the legal profession. [R. E. Dimmick]

6217 Cassab, Phelippe João. Atrás do tempo seguro. Depoimento de Carlos Burlamáqui Köpke. Ilus., Antonio Luiz Lauriello Filho. São Paulo: Editora Boa Viagem, 1978. 101 p.; ill.

Sentimental, unpretentious verse on scenes and events of everyday life, followed by six short *crônicas* of similar character. [R. E. Dimmick]

6218 Dórea, Juraci. Eurico Alves, poeta baiano. Capa, Juraci Dórea. Feira de Santana, Brasil: Casa do Sertão, Lions Clube de Feira de Santana, 1978. 90 p.; ill.

Biographical data concerning the Modernist poet Eurico Alves Boaventura (1909–74), who published only in periodicals of the Bahia area, notably the magazine *Arco & Flexa*. [R. E. Dimmick]

6219 Franco, Afonso Arinos de Melo. Diário de bolso, seguido de Retrato da noiva. Pref. de Carlos Drummond de Andrade. Rio de Janeiro: Editora Nova Fronteira, 1979. 355 p.; ill.

Forming as it were parentheses around Franco's previously published memoirs (see *HLAS 42:6525–6526*) are these final reflections, dating from 1977–78, and the correspondence exchanged with his wife-to-be in 1927–28. The latter brings vividly to life both the writers and the long-dead society in which they lived. [R. E. Dimmick]

6220 João Antônio [Ferreira Filho]. Lambões de caçarola: trabalhadores do Brasil. Ilustrações de Edgar Vasques. Porto Alegre: L&PM Editores, 1977. 40 p.; ill. (Série ilustrada; v. 1)

In the savory language of the people, João Antônio brilliantly recaptures the spirit of the slum dwellers of the Vargas era to whom "Gegê" brought a spark of hope and a sense of "being someone." [R. E. Dimmick]

6221 Lisboa, Henriqueta. Vivência poética: ensaios. Belo Horizonte: Editora São Vicente, 1979. 129 p.; bibl.

In addition to critical appreciations of Vicente Huidobro, Guimarães Rosa, Severiano de Rezende, Alphonsus de Guimaraens, Mário Casassanta, Abgar Renault, Emílio Moura, Guilhermino César, and Jorge Guillén, contains author's view of the poetic art as she practices it. [R. E. Dimmick]

6222 Reis, Marcos Konder. O irmão da estrada. Capa, Estúdio Lunardelli. Florianópolis, Brazil: Editora Lunardelli em convênio com o Instituto Nacional do Livro, Ministério da Educação e Cultura, 1979. 91 p.

Stream-of-consciousness agglomeration of fleeting impressions and recollections of localities in Minas, Bahia, and above all Santa Catarina, partly in prose, partly in verse. [R. E. Dimmick]

6223 Teixeira, Maria de Lourdes. Gregório de Matos: estudo e antologia. São Paulo: Edições Melhoramentos, 1977. 195 p.; bibl. (Memória literária)

While the "biography" of Matos is based largely on reasonable conjecture, the known facts of his life being few, it provides a useful background for an understanding of his poetry, particularly in its amatory and satirical aspects. Standard selections in accompanying anthology. [R. E. Dimmick]

FRENCH AND ENGLISH WEST INDIES AND THE GUIANAS

ETHEL O. DAVIE, *West Virginia State College*
NAOMI M. GARRETT, *Professor Emeritus, West Virginia State College*

THE SIGNIFICANT GROWTH in the volume of literature from the French and English West Indies in this biennium allowed for greater selectivity in the choice of items annotated below. Although fewer creative works than usual are available from the English-speaking Caribbean, there is no dearth of critical studies. Derek Walcott and Edward Brathwaite are attracting increasing attention from critics in a number of significant articles (items **6269, 6277–6278** and **6280–6282**). Similarly, valuable studies on French language writers such as Léon Damas (item **6255**) and Jean Price-Mars (item **6252**) contribute to the growing body of scholarly criticism. Vol. 4 of the *Cahiers Césairiens* (item **6254**) adds more research material on this outstanding writer.

Haitian poetry remains very much alive. One of the more established poets is Anthony Phelps whose *La bélière caraïbe*, is reviewed below (item **6247**). Young Haitian poets are still trying to live up to their country's literary reputation and some of their efforts are promising. Christophe Charles lends encouragement to such aspiring writers in a second volume of poetry by students (item **6249**). Edward Brathwaite edited a similar collection of verse by new Jamaican poets, the majority of whom had not published before (item **6264**).

No dramas of apparent value in either language were received for review in this volume of *HLAS*.

A broad range of prose fiction from the French Antilles includes Frankétienne's *Les affres d'un défi* (item **6229**), René Delmas' *Le pont* (item **6227**) and Klen Kerguelen's *Contes des sept îles* (item **6233**). Marie-Thérèse Colimon Hall contributes two prose works; her *Fils de misère* (item **6231**) won the Prix France-Haiti for fiction.

A number of available works are not included in this article because of space limitation. Among these are new editions of Victor Hugo's *Bug-Jargal* and Pierre Faubert's *Ogé*, both 19th-century classics set in the Caribbean. Current attention to earlier works is indicated by the variety of reprints accessible.

The increased interest in literature from the West Indies and The Guianas is giving impetus to an impressive production, inspiring contemporary writers to greater efforts.

FRENCH WEST INDIES
PROSE FICTION

6224 Bervin, Antoine. La vie étourdissante de Jean Lucksa, le roi des veinards. Port-au-Prince: Presses Nationales d'Haïti, 1975. 226 p.

Naive young man from Haitian lower middle class is surprisingly successful in his undertakings. Prolonged detailing of protagonist's life is interspersed with author's commentary on social and political trends at turn of century. Omission of much of the author's opinions would have improved the work.

6225 Calbindage. Compilation de Wilhem Romeus. Port-au-Prince: Impr. Rodriguez, 197-? 50 p.; index.

Collection of maxims, proverbs, sayings, on a variety of subjects from works by Haitian writers. Majority refer to Haitian life, politics, and people. Well documented, clever work.

6226 Clitandre, Pierre. Cathédrale du mois d'août: roman. Port-au-Prince, Haïti: Editions Fardin, 1980. 178 p.; ill.

Uses magic realism to depict the poverty, suffering and abuse of the inhabitants of a Haitian shanty town. Injustices committed by local authorities and encroachment on their land by a giant factory push the masses to rebel. Descriptions of sights, sounds, odors and people are memorable.

6227 Delmas, René. Le pont: roman. Port-au-Prince, Haïti: Impr. H. Deschamps, 1980. 253 p. (Les Moeurs haïtiennes; 3)

Returnee, motivated by idealism, tries to organize the community in reconstructing

a bridge. Plan ends in disillusion and death, resulting from his failure to respect the social and political system. Entertaining tale.

6228 Dorval, Gerald. Ma terre en bleu: roman. Port-au-Prince: Ateliers Fardin, 1975. 136 p. (His Sur les chemins de l'action; 3)

Author's third novel in which protagonist wishes to improve the lot of his compatriots (see *HLAS 38:7672*). Young man travels throughout Haiti seeking to understand why an island formerly so peaceful is now so unfortunate. Sees unification of social classes and of geographical sections as means of changing Haiti from an "île damnée" to a "terre bénie."

6229 Frankétienne. Les affres d'un défi. Port-au-Prince: Impr. H. Deschamps, 1979. 240 p.

Graphic portrayal of extreme poverty and oppression of the inhabitants of a fictitious rural Haitian community. An unusual revolt liberates the people from their tormentors. In typical Frankétienne style, the story is similar to author's *Dézafi* (see *HLAS 42:6569*) in stressing the idea that *dezombification* of the populace will solve Haiti's problems.

6230 Hall, Marie Thérèse Colimon. Le chant des sirènes: nouvelles. Port-au-Prince: Editions du Doleil, 1979. 145 p.

Six well-told stories revealing the lure of travel to the North American continent for Haitians of all classes. An occasional wry sense of humor does not obscure author's sympathy for her characters. Volume reveals skill and talent formerly seen in the author's poetry (see *HLAS 40:7786*).

6231 ———. Fils de misère: roman. Port-au-Prince: Editions Caraíbes, 1974. 199 p.

Interesting novel about Haitian peasant woman who dedicates her life to her son's education to prepare him for a successful career. Author gives good picture of life and trials among underprivileged masses.

6232 Juminer, Bertène. Les bâtards. Paris: Présence Africaine, 1977. 206 p. (Ecrits)

Reprint of autobiographical first novel relating vicissitudes in the lives of Guyanese students at French provincial university. Talented author reflects on problems of acculturation and reintegration into a ruthlessly bureaucratic society.

6233 Kerguelen, Klen. Contes des sept isles. Paris: Editions Louis Soulanges, 1975. 222 p.

Tales, short stories and folk poems drawn from daily life and traditions of Guadeloupe and nearby islands. Author skillfully employs varied language patterns to convey island's atmosphere.

6234 Patient, Serge. Le Nègre du gouverneur: chronique coloniale. 2. éd. Paris: Editions L'Harmattan, 1978. 86 p. (Poésie/prose guyanaise; 26 0335-3311)

Narrative in uneven style, ostensibly based on an episode in La Guyane during the governorship of the strange historical figure, Victor Hugues. This period during which slavery was briefly reinstated inspires a plot which is not successfully developed.

6235 Philoctète, Raymond. Minichronique. Préf. de Popol Lamusique. Port-au-Prince: Editions Fardin, 1979. 189 p.

Variety of articles of social criticism comment with gentle humor on local customs, activities and human foibles.

6236 Tirolien, Guy. Feuilles vivantes au matin: nouvelles. Paris: Présence Africaine, 1977. 175 p. (Ecrits)

Consists of eight poems and 11 short stories or prose selections by an accomplished writer. Works have authentic ring of personal recollections. One memorable selection, "Mémoires d'un Nègre Blanc," evokes experiences of the 1930s Parisian literary scene.

POETRY

6237 Anthologie de la poésie haïtienne d'expression créole. Editeur, Christophe Charles. Port-au-Prince: Editions Choucoune, 1979. 1 v.; ill.

Consists of 45 poems in Haitian Creole by 21 poets. Two were written during colonial period; Oswald Durand's "Choucoune" represents late 19th century. Outstanding contemporary writers Emile Roumer, Félix Morisseau-Leroy and Jean Brierre contributed to the collection. Of special interest to scholars of folk languages.

6238 Antoine, Yves. Alliage. Hull, Québec: Impr. Gasparo Ltée, 1978. 103 p.

Very sensitive verse by author of *Les sabots de la nuit* (see *HLAS 40: 7782*). In exile, the poet writes nostalgically of Haiti and hopes for a better day for her people. An artistic expression of universal love.

6239 Charles, Christophe. Cicatrices: poèmes. Port-au-Prince: Editions Choucoune, 1979. 20 p. (Collection Poésie; 4)

Plaquette of nine poems, each bearing the name of the young woman who inspired it.

6240 Doret, Michel. Isolement: recueil de poèmes. New York: Editions Francophones, 1979. 23 p.

Maurice Lubin wrote preface for this small volume of nostalgic verse. Isolated from his native land, the poet sees a destiny of grandeur for Haiti.

6241 Janvier, Gérard Pricorne. Miroir. Port-au-Prince: Presses Nationales d'Haiti, 1979 or 1980. 65 p.; port.

Includes 23 short poems of varied inspiration. Promising young poet occasionally employs surrealist techniques.

6242 Jean Casimir, Bérard. Chaque doigt de ton étoile. Port-au-Prince: s.n., 1979. 40 p.

Forty poems in which the poet muses upon his misfortune, the suffering of Haitian masses and indifference of upper classes. An occasional well chosen allusion adds to quality of his verse.

6243 Laraque, Paul. Poésie quotidienne. La Habana: Casa de las Américas, 1979. 77 p.

Memories of Haiti, protest against oppression and a hope for a brighter future for Haitians pervade most of the verse of this double collection. Several poems in first volume were written prior to poet's exile and previously appeared in Haiti.

6244 Large, Josaphat. Nerfs du vent: poèmes. Préf. de Gérard Campfort. Paris: P. J. Oswald, 1975. 136 p. (Collection J'exige la parole; 39)

Collection of nine long poems; inspired imagery (see *HLAS 42:6551*).

6245 Mégalos, Hérodote. Voix pour la fraternité humaine, suivi de Daniella. Port-au-Prince: Editions Fardin, 1976. 89 p.

Small volume of verse, majority of which pleads for universal understanding and brotherhood. One section of the poetry won fourth prize in Arts et Poésie de Touraine competition, 1972.

6246 Patient, Serge. Guyane pour tout dire. Suivi de Le mal du pays. Paris: Editions Caribéennes, 1980. 91 p. (Collection Texte poétique)

First part of this double collection contains nostalgic poems recalling poet's youth and that of his race. In "Le mal du Pays" writer suffers a double exile from his native Cayenne and from the land of his ancestors. Rhythmic, melodic verse is often enhanced by alliteration and well chosen allusions.

6247 Phelps, Anthony. La bélière caraïbe. La Habana: Casa de las Américas, 1980. 131 p.

Identifying himself as a son of the Caribbean rather than of Africa or Europe, the poet, in exile, longs for his country and region. Praising Haiti and the Caribbean, he dreams of the day when he can return there. Another elegant, artistic production by the gifted poet (see *HLAS 34:4336*).

6248 Pierre-Louis, Frantz. A l'encre noire. Préf. de Joseph Désir. Port-au-Prince: Ateliers Fardin, 1976. 67 p.; port.

Consists of 51 short poems of personal observations and reflections. Young poet presents his impressions in artistic terms.

6249 Rêves d'or: 50 poèmes-naïfs de 27 poètes-écoliers. Selectionnés par Christophe Charles. Port-au-Prince: Collection Revue des Ecoliers, 1977. 48 p.

Love and death are main sources of inspiration for poems in this second collection

of verse by Haitian students (see *HLAS 40:7793*). Some selections appeared previously in student publications. While a few young writers show preference for Creole, majority write in French.

6250 St. Vil, Jean Claude. Régalade et sanglots. Port-au-Prince?" s.n., 1978 or 1979. 61 p.

Over half of these 30 poems lament the suffering of the Haitian indigent and indifference of the bourgeoise. Smaller group of poems expresses young writer's longing for his absent beloved.

SPECIAL STUDIES

6251 Alexis, Jacques Stéphen. Le Romancero aux étoiles et l'oeuvre romanesque. Extraits présentés par Maximilien Laroche. Ouvrage réalisé sous la direction de Michel Tetu. Paris: F. Nathan, 1978. 77 p.; bibl. (Classiques du monde: Littérature antillaise)

Excellent study of Jacques-Stéphen Alexis with special emphasis on his *Romancero aux étoiles*, a collection of tales based on Haitian folk beliefs and legends. Critic notes skillful use of indigenous metaphors by talented young writer whose literary life was cut short by an untimely death.

6252 Antoine, Jacques Carmeleau. Jean Price-Mars and Haiti. Preface by Jean F. Brierre. Washington, D.C.: Three Continents Press, 1981. 224 p.; bibl.; ill.

Study of the life of Jean Price-Mars and his role in Haiti's history. The outstanding ethnologist and anthropologist inspired young writers, awakening them to the reservoir of Haitian folklore from which to draw material for their works. Price-Mars pleaded for racial pride and solidarity to force the world to recognize the black man as an equal.

6253 Auguste, Yves L. Littérature noire des Etats-Unis et d'Haiti; la couleur: appât ou barrière? (IFH/C, 141/142, fév. 1979, p. 84–92)

In the past, literature by black Americans and Haitians revealed great interest in the color question and miscegenation. Author perceives the ending, or at least, subsiding of this obsession, as race relations improve.

6254 *Cahiers Césairiens.* Pennsylvania State University, French Department. No. 4, Automne 1980– . University Park, Pennsylvania.

Nine scholars contributed articles, essays, interviews and reviews to this vol. 4 in series of *Cahiers* devoted to the study of Aimé Césaire (see *HLAS 42:6560*). Abstracts of theses and dissertations on the Martinican poet, dramatist, essayist and scholar show the continuing interest in his works and thought. Of great value to researchers.

Fouché, Franck. Voudou et théâtre. See *HLAS 43:982*.

6255 **Hommage posthume à Léon-Gontran Damas, 1912–1979.** Paris: Présence Africaine, 1979. 430 p.; 2 leaves of plates; ill.

Over 60 international writers, artists and colleagues pay homage to the memory of the French Guyanese poet, Léon-G. Damas, one of the founders of Négritude and author of the first work of that movement. Divided into "Témoignage," "Discours," and "Etudes," the collection presents a valuable study of the poet and his works, including his last public address (see also *HLAS 42:6572*).

6256 **Lafontant, Julien J.** De l'imitation à l'authenticité dans la poésie haïtienne. (French Review [American Association of Teachers of French, Chapel Hill, North Carolina] 54:4, March 1981, p. 551–557)

Discusses progression of Haitian poetry from servile imitation of French models to an authentic indigenous form. Though the means of expression are generally French, the verse has become truly Haitian in thought and outlook since 1925.

6257 **Laroche, Maximilien.** Le rôle des traditions orales et populaires dans la littérature en haitien (IFH/C, 145/146, 1979, p. 49–68)

Author stresses the difference in perspective of Haitians who write in French and those who use Creole. Credits second group with representing the true personality and characteristics of the people.

6258 **Roget, Wilbert J.** Littérature, conscience nationale, écriture aux Antilles: entretien avec Edouard Glissant (CLA/J, 24:3, March 1981, p. 304–320)

Enlightening interview with Martinican writer (see *HLAS 34:4229*) who dis-

cusses his ideas on literature, politics and education. Glissant stresses his quest for the Antillean personality and identity.

Steins, Martin. La négritude: un second souffle? See *HLAS 43:1052*.

ENGLISH WEST INDIES
PROSE FICTION

6259 **Clarke, Austin Chesterfield.** The Prime Minister: a novel. Don Mills, Ont. General Pub. Co., 1977. 191 p.

Novel of political intrigue. Reputedly a "roman à clef," it is a tale of exile and alienation. Prodigal returns only to become the scapegoat for unscrupulous politicians and an outsider in his native land.

6260 **Ellis, Hall Anthony.** The silence of Barabomo. Cover by Errol Moo Young. s.1.: Ellis, 1979. 54 p.

Novelette condemning indifference and malevolence of human beings towards one another. Though action is universal, locale is a composite Caribbean nation.

6261 **Keane, Shake.** One a week with water: rhymes and notes. Habana: Casa de las Américas, 1979. 74 p. (Premio Casa de las Américas poetry)

Author's native St. Vincent furnished inspiration and flavor for this interesting collection of personal musings interspersed with rhymes, prose selections and popular songs. Standard English and local patois are used interchangeably. Premio Casa de las Américas, 1979.

POETRY

6262 **Escoffery, Gloria.** Landscape in the making: poems. s.1.: The Herald, 1976. 8 p.

Small volume takes its name from title of first poem. Poet draws inspiration from climate, soil and nature of her native Jamaica.

6263 **McNeill, Anthony.** Credences at the Alter of Cloud. Kingston: Institute of Jamaica, 1979. 142 p.; 2 leaves of plates; ill. (A Hummingbird publication)

Significant volume by a talented young poet. His verse, which often reveals a dream-like quality, veers between jesting and a seriousness. Author is generally considered one of the best poets of the younger generation in Jamaica.

6264 **New poets from Jamaica:** an anthology. Edited with an introd. by Edward Kamau Brathwaite. Kingston, Jamaica: Savacou Publications, 1979. 134 p. (Poets series; 5) (Savacou; 14/15)

Brathwaite wrote the introduction and edited this collection of verse by 13 young Jamaican poets of varied literary experience. Seven are women; all write of their society from different perspectives. Standard English is used for most of the poems but some are in nation-language. Includes biographical sketches.

6265 **Salkey, Andrew.** In the hills where her dreams live: poems for Chile, 1973–1978. Habana: Casa de las Américas, 1979. 46 p. (Premio Casa de las Américas poetry)

Small volume of verse devoted to the cause of civil liberties in Chile by well-known Jamaican writer and anthologist.

SPECIAL STUDIES

6266 **Austin, Harry T.** Paradise in the mind (FIU/CR, 8:4, Fall 1979, p. 38–39)

Dominant theme of Clarke's partially autobiographical novel (*The Prime Minister*) is the nature of evil and the Edenic myth.

6267 **Babin, Maria Teresa.** Trends in Caribbean English fiction (UPR/CS, 20:1, March 1980, p. 70–74)

English writers of fiction in the Caribbean, like their French and Spanish counterparts, are finding subjects, language patterns and structures in their native cultures. Critic seems more knowledgeable about Spanish than English speaking writers.

6268 **Brathwaite, Edward.** Barbados poetry, ?1661–1979: a checklist: books, pamphlets, broadsheets. Mona, Jamaica; Savacou Publications, 1979. 16 p.

Partially annotated list of poetry mainly by Barbadians is divided into: 1) Settlement and Slavery; 2) Colonial Period; and 3) Initiation into Nationhood. Good research source for Barbadian poetry. Lists works by 75 writers.

6269 **Breiner, Laurence.** Tradition, society, the figure of the poet (UWI/CQ, 26: 1/2, March/June 1980, p. 1–12)

Contrasts opposing concepts of the West Indian poet's mission. Author views Edward Brathwaite as proposing an alternative to an imposed inherited condition while Derek Walcott is seen as believing that the poet is beneficiary of a complex history.

6270 **Campbell, Elaine.** Oroonoko's heir: the West Indies in late eighteenth-century novels by women (UWI/CQ, 25:1/2, March/June 1979, p. 80–84)

Discusses works of five female novelists whose anti-slavery views contributed to abolitionist sentiment of the period.

6271 **Carew, Jan.** The Caribbean writer and exile (UPR/CS, 19:1/2, April/July 1979, p. 111–132)

Caribbean writers often suffer from a sense of exile at home as well as abroad. To overcome the former, a writer must know thoroughly the past of his people and be fully aware of his cultural roots. He must feel himself a part of the majority population of his native land.

6272 **Carr, Bill.** In memoriam: Gabriel Coulthard, friendship and scholarship (UPR/CS, 12:2, July 1975, p. 157–162)

Tribute to the memory of a gifted writer and scholar followed by a partial list of his works.

6273 **Cooke, John.** "A vision of the land:" V. S. Naipaul's later novels (UWI/CQ, 25:4, Dec. 1979, p. 31–47)

Naipaul's novels after 1960 reveal that an emphasis on history embedded in the landscape is crucial for developing a sense of order and stable identity.

6274 **Cudjoe, Selwyn Reginald.** Resistance and Caribbean literature. Athens: Ohio University Press, 1980. 319 p.; bibl.; index.

Marxist oriented study examines literature from the point of view of economic inequities and class struggle. History is viewed as an activity of the oppressor class preventing social and cultural development while the masses safeguard their culture and identity. Perceives resistance and revolt as central to novelistic production.

6275 Greenberg, Robert. Idealism and realism in the fiction of Claude McKay (CLA/J, 24:3, March 1981, p. 237–261)

Examines McKay's three novels and concludes that *Banana bottom* is the most realistic because the locale is a small community of his native Jamaica.

6276 Hoffman, León-François. An eighteenth century exponent of black power: Moses Bon Sa'am (UPR/CS, 15:3, Oct. 1975, p. 149–161)

Reproduces and analyzes historic text published 1735 in London and attributed to Maroon leader. Since runaways spoke a form of Creole and were illiterate, critic concludes that text was written by an Englishman. However, it shows the influence of expressions typical of black orators involved in the struggle for freedom.

6277 Izevbaye, D. S. The exile and the prodigal: Derek Walcott as West Indian poet (UWI/CQ, 26:1/2, March/June 1980, p. 70–82)

Discusses Walcott's position as one of two divergent attitudes to the theme of identity. Solutions for discovery are not in the past but in the experience of exile and homecoming. Poet's task is to create a new language and culture.

6278 Lyn, Diana. The concept of the mulatto in some works of Derek Walcott (UWI/CQ, 26:1/2, March/June 1980, p. 49–68, bibl.)

Long and somewhat repetitive discussion of symbols found principally in *Dream on Monkey Mountain.*

6279 Mohr, Eugene V. The other Caribbean: concerns of West Indian writing. San Juan: Department of Education, Commonwealth of Puerto Rico, 1979. 12 p.

Asserts that for the West Indian writer, an historical awareness of his area and a thorough knowledge of its cultural, socioeconomic and political life are essential in reaching self-understanding and developing a sense of identity.

6280 Pollard, Velma. "The Dust:" a tribute to the folk (UWI/CQ, 26:1/2, March/June 1980, p. 41–48)

Comments on Brathwaite's well-known poem as an exemplary expression of the folk tradition.

6281 Rohlehr, Gordon. Bridges of sound: an approach to Edward Brathwaite's "Jah" (UWI/CQ, 26:1/2, March/June 1980, p. 13–31, bibl.)

Perceptive discussion of Brathwaite's metaphorical treatment of myth and music showing the poetic correlation between black social experience and musical form.

6282 ———. Notes on background music to *Rights of Passage* (UWI/CQ, 26:1/2, March/June 1980, p. 32–41)

Explication of 32 recordings identified with E. K. Brathwaite's 1961 volume of poetry.

6283 Winford, Donald. Creole culture and language in Trinidad: a sociohistorical sketch (UPR/CS, 15:3, Oct. 1975, p. 31–56)

Presents the history of the emergence of English as Trinidad's preponderant language from the mid 19th century to the present. Explains dominance of English as consequence of immigration patterns.

TRANSLATIONS INTO ENGLISH

MARGARET SAYERS PEDEN, *Professor of Spanish, University of Missouri, Columbia*

FIGURES CITED BY *PUBLISHERS WEEKLY* in 1982 concerning English-language publication of foreign works, indicate that Latin American literature, supposedly in the vanguard of translations published in this country, in fact, lags well behind European literatures—amazingly so when one considers that the category "Spanish" includes Spain and all Latin American countries. The magazine cited lists for 1980 only 40 translations from Spanish as compared to 220 titles from both French and German literatures. Russian translations numbered 106. Italian, 62. Works translated from the German will soon increase significantly: Continuim Books, beginning in 1982, plans to publish 100 volumes of newly-translated German works in the series *The German Library*. Latin American literature has never benefitted from such a massive organized program of translation, and considering these statistics, one feels even more keenly the loss of a pioneer program like that sponsored a number of years ago by the University of Texas Press. There are, however, indications that paperback publishers may be moving toward a leadership role in translation of Latin American literature—Avon has been particularly active, bypassing hardcover publication to offer first publication in English in paper.

Among the most important translations of the period 1980–82 are Osman Lins' *Avalovara* (item **6330**) translated by Gregory Rabassa (recipient of the Calouste Gulbenkian-PEN Translation Prize awarded every other year for the best translation from Portuguese); Alastair Reid and Emir Rodríguez Monegal's *Borges: a reader* (item **6284** surely the ultimate Borges anthology); Helen Lane's translation of Ernest Sábato's *On heroes and tombs* (item **6316**, a translation delayed for many years by the economic problems that beset commercial publication of translations); and Thomas Colchie's rendition of the bright comic Brazilian novel by Márcio Souza, *The emperor of the Amazon* (item **6334**).

But the most important recent book in the field is John Felstiner's *Translating Neruda: the way to Macchu Picchu* (item **6336**), a translation and critical study of Neruda's master poem. In the *New York Review of Books*, Alastair Reid describes its uniqueness: "Felstiner has managed to write a number of books in one: a discussion of translating poetry, a critical study of *Macchu Picchu*, and a quite unique demonstration of translation as criticism. While it would be too much to say that his book creates a genre . . . it sets such a sensible precedent that I would not be surprised to see other translators write similar books."

In late Oct. 1982, Frank Manheim, the great translator of German literature, came from Paris to address the meetings of the American Literary Translators Association held at the University of Indiana. In April 1982, the University of Kansas sponsored an important symposium on translation with Frank MacShane as principal speaker. The fact that these two events were held on university campuses underscores—whether for good or for ill—the increasing visibility of the university-based translator. Felstiner's book is an example of the natural affinity between the roles of scholar and creative writer in the act of translation. While a few of the best practice their skills independent of any affiliation, the university translator / teacher, following the analogous model of writer / teacher, is an increasingly visible phenomenon in the field.

TRANSLATIONS INTO ENGLISH
FROM SPANISH
ANTHOLOGIES

6284 Borges, Jorge Luis. Borges, a reader: a selection from the writings of Jorge Luis Borges. Edited by Emir Rodríguez Monegal and Alastair Reid. New York: Dutton, 1981. 369 p.; bibl.

Most comprehensive Borges anthology to date. Arranged chronologically from "a young poet's voice" to "old poet's voice" and "brief return to realism." Title heading of pt.

2, "The Dictator," somewhat misleadingly refers not to a neo-Peron, but to one-who-dictates. Editors have tried to select major texts as well as little-known ones in compiling an anthology which covers virtually Borges' "entire production." Omissions, due to permissions difficulties, are compensated by some previously uncollected pieces. Balance is excellent. Reference system somewhat confusing; brief introductions to sections strike bizarre, semi-condescending tone. It is impossible to address quality of the many translations other than to accept the editor's opinion—who commissioned many new ones—that these are the best available.

Breaking the silence: 20th century poetry by Cuban women. See item **5624.**

6285 Echad: an anthology of Latin American Jewish writings. General editors: Robert and Roberta Kalechofsky. Marblehead, Mass.: Micah Publications, 1980. 282 p.

Gathers 24 writers from 12 countries in first anthology of Latin American Jewish writing intended to illustrate that "Differences are real. The particular is real . . . People everywhere must learn that about other people." Includes poems, a play, newspaper articles, fiction, and essays by: Clarice Lispector, Isaac Goldemberg, and Isaac Chocrón. Of less familiar names, Esther Seligson is probably one to watch. David Unger appears as writer and translator, though he is best known as translator. Benno Weiser Varon contributes single most interesting non-literary essay, a personal account of the Mengele presence in Paraguay; best literary essay is Jaime Alazraki's study of the influence of the Kabbala in Borges writing. These above average translations were collective effort. Most disappointing translations are of César Tiempo, considered by editors the Dean of Argentinian Jewish poetry.

6286 Inventing a word: an anthology of twentieth-century Puerto Rican poetry. Edited by Julio Marzán. New York: Published by Columbia University Press, in association with the Center for Inter-American Relations, 1980. 184 p.

Traces modern history of poetry in Puerto Rico, noting two dominant and persistent currents: 1) Hispanist-reformist tradition, tending toward "the purely poetic, the lyrical, the metaphorical sublimation of social reality; and 2) Puerto Rican-separatist tradition, tending toward "anti-poetic," a stark representation of reality that "identifies with Latin America's American heritage." Best collection of Puerto Rican poetry as long as one is aware that editor's cut-off date was 1950. Most successful translations are those of the editor in conjunction with Carmen Valle. *En face.*

6287 Open to the sun. A bilingual anthology of Latin American women poets. Edited by Nora Jacquez Wieser. Various translators. Van Nuys, Calif.: Perivale Press, 1979. 279 p.; bibl.

Since no such book exists, one would like to be enthusiastic about this one. Among good things: editor proves that Latin America has poets other than the hallowed four (e.g., Mistral, Agustini, Storni, Ibarbourou, also included). New, identifiable voices: Amanda Berenguer, Belkis Cuza Malé, Olga Orozco. But why so few strong voices from a culture so receptive to poetry? Translations are adequate, occasionally unfortunate (e.g., translation of "shrew" even in so iconoclastic a poem as "Mujer Brava que Casó con Dios"). Also, why is physical space—line length, number of lines—so consistently violated? One wishes for more fidelity along with, paradoxically, more bravado: most challenging poem in collection is declared "untranslatable." *En face.*

6288 Poetas norteamericanos traducidos por poetas venezolanos: una antología. Escogida por Jaime Tello. Caracas: Ministerio de Educación, Dirección de Apoyo Docente, División de Tecnología Educativa, Departamento de Publicaciones, 1976. 426 p.; index.

Among tributes offered by Venezuela for US bicentennial was this Spanish-language anthology of selected poems. Quality of translations varies and basis of selection seems arbitrary. Most obvious *omis*sion is Robert Frost, most obvious *comi*ssion is large number of poems by John Tagliabue.

PRECOLUMBIAN, CONQUEST, COLONIAL, AND 19TH-CENTURY WORKS

6289 Abreu Gómez, Ermilo. Canek: history and legend of a Maya hero. Translated, with an introduction by Marlo L. Dávila and Carter Wilson. Berkeley: University of California Press, 1979. 68 p.

Translated into several languages (this is second English translation). Volume had 34 Spanish editions. Difficult to classify—not narrative, not poetry—these impressionistic fragments are unforgettable. Two interrelated stories: first one portrays relationship between youngster identified as author's alter ego—and Canek; second recounts eruption of long-dormant Indian resentment against cruel Spanish lords. Translator-editors describe historical rebellion as "brief and terrible moment" later resurrected as rallying cry in 1848 "Caste War." Despite occasional stylistic flaws, the translation admirably captures the prose's poetic and mythic tone.

6290 Civrieux, Marc de. *Watunna*: an Orinoco creation cycle. Translated from the Spanish by David Guss. San Francisco, Calif.: North Point Press, 1980. 195 p.; glossary; ill.

Translation from 1790 Spanish version of oral history of "religious and social models" of peoples of the Upper Orinoco River, Venezuela. *Watunna* comprises "the sacred deeds and actions of the heroes in primordial times." Those who share in this long oral tradition, speak Watunna language, are true humans, the So'to. John Updike wrote that of oral narratives collected by anthropologists and folklorists, "little . . . is as readable, coherent, and thought-provoking" as this volume. Outstanding translator spent three years among the Makiritare in order to capture directly the flavor of the original "telling." Translation is breezy, colloquial, staccato. Includes excellent glossary.

6291 Durán, Diego. Book of the gods and rites and The ancient calendar. Translated and edited by Fernando Horcasitas and Doris Heyden. Foreword by Miguel León-Portilla. Norman: University of Oklahoma Press, 1971. 502 p.; bibl.; col. plates; ill.; maps (The Civilization of the American Indian series; 102)

Dominican friar Diego Durán wrote two valuable accounts of Aztec ethnography and calendar. After centuries of oblivion, manuscripts have been translated from 19th-century version of Mexican scholar, José Fernando Ramírez but corrected against microfilm of original (see *HLAS 34:1036*). Also provided useful bibliography of works relevant to Durán accounts, as well as study of author's life and works.

6292 Juana Inés de la Cruz, *Sor*. A woman of genius, an intellectual autobiography. Translation of "La respuesta a Sor Filotea." Translated and with an introduction by Margaret Sayers Peden. Photographs by Gabriel North Seymour. Salisbury, Conn.: Lime Rock Press, 1982. 190 p.

6293 Manzano, Juan Francisco. The life and poems of a Cuban slave. Edited by Edward J. Mullen. Translated from the Spanish by Richard Robert Madden. Hamden, Conn.: Archon Books, 1981. 237 p.; bibl.

Reproduces rare 1840 British edition of only document on 19th-century Cuban slavery written by a slave. All other major works on slave problem notes Mullen's excellent introduction, "were written by white Creole intellectuals and were developed within the narrative traditions of nineteenth-century Hispanic literature." Includes poems written by Manzano and translated by Madden; appendix of items on background of slavery; conditions suffered by slaves; laws regarding slaves and their emancipation; and glossary of Cuban terms. Of most interest, is relation itself. "Life of the Negro Poet, Written by Himself," fascinating account that appeared in Madden's translation before it did in Spanish. Translator's life is also interesting. Translations vary: prose seems timeless, poetry dated. Valuable addition to studies of black literature, sociology, ethnography, and history.

6294 Mugaburu, Josephe de. Chronicle of colonial Lima; the diary of Josephe and Francisco Mugaburu, 1640–1694. Translated and edited by Robert Ryal Miller. Norman: University of Oklahoma Press, 1975. 324 p.; ill.

This translation of diary kept in Lima by 17th-century Spanish soldier is another in excellent series on colonial and precolumbian Latin America published by University of Oklahoma Press (see *HLAS 40:3227*). Diary spans 57 years (1640–97) of daily activities of Lima's Spanish community.

6295 Poma de Ayala, Felipe Huamán. Letter to a king: a picture-history of the Inca civilisation. Arranged and edited with an introduction by Christopher Dilke and translated from the Spanish. London: Allen and Unwin, 1978. 248 p.; ill.; facsims.; index; map.

Adventure of this translation approaches epic proportions of original, including "five and a half years of continuous effort on the manuscript" and long peregrination beginning with quest for genuine source-book for information about the Incas, which led translator from La Paz to Buenos Aires to British Museum to Royal Library, Christiansborg Castle, Copenhagen. In deciphering original Spanish Dilke relied upon a version in modern Spanish (that translator devoted

10 years to the project), though he continued to adapt directly from original manuscript. For more on this work, see *HLAS 42 : 1707*.

POETRY

6296 Aridjis, Homero. Exaltation of light.
Edited and translated from the Spanish by Eliot Weinberger. Brockport, N.Y.: Boa Editions, 1981. 157 p.

Poems by major Mexican poet reflect inspirations as diverse as the Flemish mystic Ruystroeck and ancient Aztec ceremonials though they are synthesized in an affirmation of the mystery of renewal. One hears echoes of the "blue" metaphor of *Blue Spaces*, an earlier collection in English, but here the dominant figure (predictably, given the title) is light. Translation of long title poem (indebted to St. John, Ruysbroeck, Holderlin, Dante, Plotinus) does not express well its mystical transport. There are inexplicable shifts in line numbers, line length, omissions of key words, questionable interpretations, strange aversion to connecting words, so that the English sounds more choppy, less flowing, than the Spanish. *En face.*

6297 Borges, Jorge Luis. Selected poems 1923–1967. Edited with an introduction and notes, Norman Thomas di Giovanni. New York: Delacorte, 1972. 328 p.; appendices; index.

Fascinating book for translator, scholar, reader. Di Giovanni, who had most unusual relationship ever granted translator—a live-in, working collaboration—considers Borges first and foremost a poet (Borges considers himself a reader, a poet, then a short story writer). In active cooperation with many translators—the best in the field, too numerous to list here—di Giovanni offered literal, annotated versions derived from conferences with Borges. Result is previously unavailable commentary *from* Borges *on* Borges and some remarkable translations. Not satisfied with addressing problems in English, di Giovanni gives corrections for Spanish text. For translator, introduction offers informative model of ideal working process. Superior compilation. *En face.*

6298 Cardenal, Ernesto. Apocalypse and other poems. Edited by Robert Pring-Mill and Donald D. Walsh. Translated from the Spanish by Thomas Merton, Kenneth Rexroth and Mireya Jaimes-Freyre, and the editors. New York: New Directions, 1977. 78 p.

Contains more than 78 p. would indicate: all Epigrams, sections from "Homage to the American Indians," "Prayer for Marilyn Monroe," and many others. Except for omission of "Hora O," this is a very representative selection from the poet Eliot Weinberger called "last Beat poet on earth." What emerges is the discernible framework of now-familiar touchstones: Merton, Gethsemani, anti-Yankee, social injustice, Solentiname. Translations are good, Walsh's best. Pring-Mill's translations tend to be elevated in tone for the conscious anti-poetry of Cardenal, though this is also a reflection of British and American usage. The "identifications" are largely unnecessary.

6299 ———. Zero hour and other documentary poems. Selected and edited by Donald D. Walsh. With an introductory essay by Robert Pring-Mill. Translations by Paul W. Borgeson, Jr. *et al.* New York: New Directions, 1980. 106 p.

As Pring-Mill points out in good introduction, these poems, more than Cardenal's previous collection, "set out to 'document' reality (and so redeem it) in a more dialectically visual way: picturing things, peoples and events in the light of a clear-cut sociopolitical commitment." Poems are so political, so didactic, so "flat" in their narrative reporting that though one is accustomed to political poetry in Spanish America, this group nearly fails as poetry. Even Cardenal says "This is almost not a poem." They *are* savage and memorable. Translations strike appropriate tone. Donald Walsh died as he was completing his translation.

6300 Contemporary Argentine poetry.
Edited and translated by William Shand. Introduction by Aldo Pellegrini. Buenos Aires: Fundación Argentina para la Poesía, 1969. 275 p.

Pellegrini's introduction states that anthologies like this one (never annotated in *HLAS*) may include inferior poets but at least avoid risk of excluding "poets of real value." Unfortunately, few poets of value are *in*-cluded. Translator is of English origin, but spelling and printing errors, even non-words ("extasis"), are probably result of Buenos Aires publication. It is difficult to judge many translations since Spanish original is not reproduced. Volume confirms long-standing conviction that Borges is difficult to translate badly, his poems do read like poems.

6301 Gorostiza, José. Death without end. Translated from the Spanish by Laura Villaseñor. Introduction by Salvador Novo. Illustrated by Elvira Gascon. Austin: University of Texas Press, 1969. 39 p.; bibl.; ill.

One admires dedication devoted to translation of this most Mexican of Mexican poems (never annotated in *HLAS*). Translation has moments of real poetry. Generally accurate, it has its lapses (why "blisters" for *llagas*?). Weakness of translations lies in tone and in English form. Translator hasn't taken enough chances. This great poem, whose principal metaphor revolves around the paradox of form in formlessness, needs a more daring, less literal translation, but one which strictly adheres to its "shape." Notes are largely superfluous. Handsome bookmaking. *En face.*

6302 Mistral, Gabriela. Selected poems of Gabriela Mistral. Edited by Doris Dana. Translated from the Spanish by the editor. Baltimore, Md.: Johns Hopkins Press, 1971. 235 p.; ill.

Physically handsome book (never annotated in *HLAS*) features Antonio Frasconi's woodcuts. Translations are almost uniformly accurate, but there is no spark of poetry (e.g., "The Disburdened" for "La Desasida"). Also, why are her most famous poems (e.g., "Sonnets of Death") not included? Without them, any anthology—which suggests a representative selection—seems incomplete. *En face.*

6303 Neruda, Pablo. A call for the destruction of Nixon and praise for the Chilean revolution. Translated from the Spanish by Teresa Anderson. Cambridge, Mass.: West End Press, 1980. 1 v.

Earnestness of publisher, translator, Neruda himself cannot be placed in question just as the tragic plight of Chile can never be forgotten. But translator is in error when she claims this is a *difficult* book. Reminiscent of ringing passion of "Yo Acuso," Neruda's prose denunciation of González Videla, and, like it, "A Call for Destruction . . . ," book will survive as political, patriotic document,

not as poetry. Rare pieces, in the vein of Neruda's more polemical writing but rich in rhyme, a feature translation does not address. *En face.* For another translation, see item **6304.**

6304 ———. Incitación al Nixonicide y alabanza de la Revolución Chilena—Incitement to Nixonicide and praise for the Chilean Revolution. Translated by Steve Kowit. Houston, Tex.: Quixote Press, 1979. 81 p.; 1 leaf of plates; ill.

Like item **6303**, translation cannot be blamed in intent, but result is unfortunate. Reveals haste in preparation—pages are reversed in order, entire stanzas omitted—and in translation (e.g., in "Victoria" Neruda writes, "Cuando la Braden les movió la cola," translated as "Braden swished his picket tail," although Braden refers to la Compañía Braden. Similarly, in same brief poem, Nixon's name is deleted and Jesus added in translation. Allusions are in order—both having to do with 30 pieces of silver—but such leaps need not be made in translation. Unlike Anderson (item **6303**), Kowit does approach satirical "Doña Cacerolina Lagañín" with rhyme, and rather well, except for some startling introductions, such as "a street of turtles" apparently for sake of an (unsatisfactory) rhyme with "purple" (which is not in the text). *En face.*

6305 ———. Isla Negra a notebook. Translated from the Spanish by Alastair Reid. Afterword by Enrico Mario Santí. New York: Farrar, Straus & Giroux, 1981. 414 p.

Santí's afterword identifies this collection as Neruda's "third excursion into autobiography." Here, however, Neruda was "less involved with history than with his previous selves, and becomes the ever-changing poet bringing the past into the present for review." Reid, who has translated "mostly the poetry Neruda wrote after he came to rest in Isla Negra in the fifties," the poetry with which he feels greatest affinity, has captured in English the deep humanity of these widely ranging poems. It would be difficult to find a better translation. *En face.*

6306 Pacheco, José Emilio. Signals from the flames. Translated from the Spanish by Thomas Hoeksema. Pittsburgh, Pa.: Latin American Literary Review Press, 1980. 97 p.

Title of fine collection by major poet derives from translator/critic's appraisal of

Pacheco as "the poet signalling through the flames." Selections span 13 years and show development of his poetic voice. Translator has respected the physical space of the poetry, as well as meaning and sound. Pacheco does not present great difficulties to a translator, but when necessary, the opening lines of "Becerrillo" are a good example, Hoeksema is willing to take the changes and make the adjustments necessary to create poetry in English. *En face.*

6307 Padilla, Heberto. Legacies, selected poems. Translated from the Spanish by Alastair Reid and Andrew Hurley. New York: Farrar, Straus & Giroux, 1982. 179 p.

First collection of Padilla's poems in English since 1971 British translation of *Fuera de Juego* (1968 Cuban writer's Union Prize). Padilla, who now lives in New York following 1980 exile from Cuba, confesses his debt to English poetry: "my first love is English literature—especially English poetry." Eliot's "April is the cruelest month" is transmuted as title "Between March and April is my Cruelest Month," poems marking his imprisonment in Castro's Cuba. Lacks mention of how translators worked, separately? together? on all or part? Translations are deft, but line numbers and length are not observed, and some strange word choices.

6308 Paz, Octavio. A draft of shadows and other poems. Edited and translated from the Spanish by Eliot Weinberger. With translations by Elizabeth Bishop and Mark Strand. New York: New Directions Publishing Corp., 1979. 186 p. (A New Directions book)

Reflects 16 years of Paz's writing. Poems range far in space and time, from brief Borgesian "Homage to Claudius Ptolemy" to gods of Mother India to constructs of Joseph Cornell to Mixcoac, "the return," and to Mexico, where "We have dug up rage." But his synthesis, cyclical time, fuses disparities. Paz moves through time and space without moving (e.g., "I walk and do not move forward," a doomed, blasted city repeats its ruin "in its circular fever"). Most interesting poem is long autobiographical title poem. Note explains English title for *pasado en claro* as "collaborative invention." Why the autonomous choice of "shadows" in the invention? Generally, however, translations are good. *En face.*

6309 Teresa, Saint. De repente / All of a sudden. Translated from the Spanish by Maria A. Proser, Arlene Scully, and James Schully. Willimantic, Conn.: Curbstone Press, 1979. 91 p.

Teresa de Jesús is pseudonym for Chilean poet whose caustic criticism of Pinochet government was smuggled out and published in US. Translations are accurate (despite mistranslating something like "15 días") but fail to convey original's force (e.g., "me da una rabia," excoriating denunciation of poverty as repeated line "it makes me furious" is not strong enough in English to convey original's outrage). Still translators and press deserve credit to make this strong new voice available to English- and Spanish-language audiences.

6310 Zaldívar, Gladys. Fabulación de Eneas—The keeper of the flame. With translation by Elias L. Rivers. Miami, Fla.: Ediciones Universal, 1979. 67 p. (Colección Vortex)

Beautifully produced *en face* edition of 12 poems (plus three in an appendix) evolving from lines from the *Aeneid*. Poems are overpraised on back cover as "most intense, innovative, and profound written in Spanish . . ." Style actually is "informed by a certain metaphoric *culteranismo*," as said of an earlier book. Considering originals' opaqueness, translations are appropriate and accurate.

6311 Zeller, Ludwig. In the country of the antipodes: poems 1964–1979. Oakville, Ont.: Mosaic Press, 1979. 170 p.; ill.; ports.

Mortiz's introduction situates Zeller's poetry in streams of "uniquely Spanish" Baroque and dream of reality of surrealism. Anna Balakian, however, points out that Zeller's "mystic horrors" are essentially different from Bréton's "exalting dream" and that Zeller pursued the dynamism of surrealism rather than its "conventionalized imagery." Translators acknowledge series of debts to prior translators, advisers, commentators: one longs to judge those debts but lamentably Spanish originals are missing.

NOVELS

6312 Aguilera-Malta, Demetrio. Don Goyo. Translated by John and Carolyn Brushwood. Clifton, N.J.: The Humana Press, 1980. 200 p.; ill.

John Brushwood describes this novel elsewhere as counterpoint between character of title (both legend and man) and realistic character, Cusumbo, who demonstrates the *cholo*'s unhappy plight, forced by "progress" to abandon old ways of his people. In addition to *Seven moons and seven serpents*, book confirms Aguilera-Malta's primacy in genre of magical realism. Published in Spanish in 1933, novel offers very interesting evidence of the emergence of a "Latin American Novel," an authentic and original voice, prior to the "Boom." Brushwoods are to be credited for bringing this significant work into English.

6313 Díaz Valcárcel, Emilio. Schemes in the month of March. Translated from the Spanish by Nancy A. Sebastiani. New York: Bilingual Press/Editorial Bilingüe, 1979. 285 p.

Interesting novel in *"novela álbum"* style. Julio Marzán's perceptive review calls it a collage novel, a kind of "postal picaresque." *Schemes . . .* is a comic, yet brutal attack on negative influences of North American capitalist consumerism on a society whose economy does not afford the majority of its people a decent living, let alone the joys of conspicuous consumption. Protagonist is also victim of very problems he attacks—too cosmopolitan to revert to provincialism, and yet too aware of evils of his sophistication to profit from it. Novel's language is difficult, laced with puns and satire, often bilingual. Translation—though conceded to be difficult—does not do justice to the original, especially in dialogue. Exaggerated adherence to Spanish structure and rhetorical level, creates English effect not representative of Spanish text. Great sense of linguistic play is necessary for such a translation; unfortunately this difficult task is not achieved.

6314 Fuentes, Carlos. Distant relations. Translated from the Spanish by Margaret Sayers Peden. New York: Farrar, Straus & Giroux, 1982. 225 p.

6315 Puig, Manuel. Kiss of the spider woman. Translated from the Spanish by Thomas Colchie. New York: Alfred A. Knopf, 1979. 281 p.

Puig's fourth novel continues to explore possibilities of narrating without traditional novelistic narrative: dialogue, movie plots, essayistic footnotes, police blotters, are some narrative devices. Relies heavily on *signs* of various typefaces, so it is essential that they be carried over into the translation. This is effectively accomplished in the English version. Some footnotes have a different spatial arrangement, which is somewhat disorienting, but they are there. Colchie has a good ear for this very oral prose, and produces necessary contrast in official and semi-official reports. It is—I guess one must finally accept it—impossible to convey the *voseo* of Puig's Argentine voices.

6316 Sábato, Ernesto. On heroes and tombs. Translated from the Spanish by Helen R. Lane. Boston: David R. Godine, 1981. 479 p.

Sábato enjoys a much greater vogue in Europe than in US. Translation brings him attention long overdue, as in Robert Coover's review: "he stands apart from most of the writers of the 'Boom'—and for good reason;" Jim Miller's review: "a master of 'magical realism';" Michael Wood's: "shows us another face of Latin American writing." Book is an expansion of *El tunél*'s obsessions. Helen Lane offers another impeccable translation (inexplicably ignored in reviews). Sábato's text does not offer difficulties of other writers but his rhetorical level could easily sound false notes if not intelligently translated.

6317 Sánchez, Luis Rafael. Macho Camacho's beat. Translated from the Spanish by Gregory Rabassa. New York: Pantheon Books, 1980. 211 p.

Jerome Charyn describes this novel as funny, mordant, an extended raucous song. Sánchez's stretching, warping, twisting, funny-house manipulation of language, depiction of a reality whose principal metaphor is found in the dance, music, and song of the *guaracha*, his outrageous puns, his down-and-out, on-the-way-up, never-were-or-will-be characters, all blend together to create a portrait of a city (San Juan) that inevitably recalls the Havana of Cabrera Infante's *Tres tristes tigres*. Rabassa—among few translators who would attempt such a translation, an expert at invention—has done wonders with novel's silly-putty prose, closely approximating original Spanish-not-Spanish in an analogous English-not-English.

BRIEF FICTION

6318 Borges, Jorge Luis and **Adolfo Bioy-Casares.** Six problems for don Isidro Parodi. Translated from the Spanish by Norman Thomas di Giovani. New York: E. P. Dutton, 1981. 160 p.

John Spurling's review: "it is the predominance of these other voices, these extra, deliberately ridiculous and reliable narrators, which makes the book both laborious and extravagant." Strange foreword (by "Gervasio Montenegro") refers to H. Bustos Domecq—the pseudonym used by Bioy and Borges for this book—but the name is omitted from book's English title page. Lack of explanation adds falsely Borgesian obscurity to English publication. Period tone of pieces comes through very well in the translation.

6319 Cabrera Infante, Guillermo. View of dawn in the tropics. Translated from the Spanish by Suzanne Jill Levine. New York: Harper & Row, 1978. 145 p.

Cabrera Infante calls book first version of *Three trapped tigers* although it was published 10 years after TTT. Whether old or new, *View of dawn* could not be more remote from puns and play, steamy, smoky night life of Havana that characterize his best-known novel. Terse and crisp, unremittingly political—though Cabrera has denounced political writing—these well translated prose poems trace history of a struggle against oppression that is as old as Cuba's discovery by the Spanish. Interesting modulation in a well-known voice.

6320 Cortázar, Julio. A change of light and other stories. Translated from the Spanish by Gregory Rabassa. New York: Knopf, 1980. 275 p.

It is seven years since a collection of Cortázar stories has appeared in English, gathered from two Spanish publications, *Octaedro* and *Alguien anda por ahí*. David Press sees logical progression in stories from "frightened and desperate characters" to those "who try and usually fail to bridge the gap between dream and words." One hears self-conscious echoes (e.g., character in "apocalypse at Solentiname" undergoes a *Blow up* experience and refers to that film). One wonders why editors chose "A Change of Light" for title story since is far from the best. The usual dependable translation from Rabassa.

6321 Fuentes, Carlos. Burnt water. Translated from the Spanish by Margaret Sayers Peden. New York: Farrar, Straus & Giroux, 1980. 231 p.

Eleven short stories by a prolific and respected Mexican author.

6322 Valenzuela, Luisa. Strange things happen here. Translated from the Spanish by Helen Lane. New York: Harcourt, Brace & Jovanovich, 1979. 220 p.

Subtitle *Twenty-six short stories and a novel* should be questioned: "stories" in no way fit form's classical definition and novel is closer to novella by US standards. Cortázar called these pieces "brilliant" praising writing's "true freedom and liberty." Valenzuela is reminiscent of Cortázar himself (e.g., "cronopio" who wants to manufacture horizontal ladders). Valenzuela's escape into metaphor may be partly motivated by need to outwit censors. Some puns are brilliantly translated by Helen Lane but this is not one of her most successful translations probably because of difficult slang and colloquialisms.

ESSAYS, REPORTAGE AND LITERARY CRITICISM

6323 Boal, Augusto. Theater of the oppressed. Translated from the Spanish by Charles A. and Maria-Odilia Leal McBride. New York: Urizen Books, 1979. 197 p.

Important essays on theater (Aristotle to experimental People's Theater in Peru). Basic premise: theater is, was, must be, political. Argues that theater has been removed from the people—who originated it. Present distance among spectator, protagonist, and chorus must be eliminated to arrive at poetics of the oppressed. Highly intellectual, theoretical argument promotes genre's popularization. One of the most literate voices to emerge from Latin American theater. Excellent translation.

6324 Cardenal, Ernesto. In Cuba. Translated from the Spanish by Donald D. Walsh. New York: New Directions Publications Corp., 1974. 340 p.; appendix (A New directions book)

Miscellaneous collage records Cuba 11 years after Revolution. Interesting in view of Cardenal's later commitment to Nicaraguan revolution, book reflects honest curiosity, unbiased probing of Marxist priest exploring reconciliation of contradictory extremes: communism and the Church. No explicit conclusions drawn but there is implicit approval of the Revolution. Excellent insights into lives of Cubans in early 1970s from Fidel to factory workers. Good prose translation with an ear for ordinary speech. Less effective on the poetry.

6325 Donoso, José. The boom in Spanish American literature, a personal history. Translated from the Spanish by Gregory Kolovakos. Introduction by Ronald Christ. New York: Columbia University Press, 1977. 122 p.; index (A Center for Inter-American Relations book)

Author proposes interesting division of Latin American novelists into the *gratin*, a mafia-like core of writers, a second group of the almost-"in," and cluster of late-comers compromising a kind of "proto-Boom." Suggests that principal reason that most major Boom novels were written outside authors' countries and that so many live in exile, is due to fact that only abroad can traditional Spanish envy be minimized and literary friendships made possible. Translation occasionally reveals underlying Spanish structure, but successfully recreates book's informal, almost chatty, tone.

6326 Paz, Octavio. Children of the mire. Modern poetry from romanticism to the avant-garde. Translated from the Spanish by Rachel Phillips. Cambridge, Mass.: Harvard University Press, 1974. 176 p.; index.

States that study's purpose is to describe from perspective of Spanish American poet, the modern poetic movement and its contradictory relationships with what we call "the modern." Book becomes social and intellectual portrait of Spanish America. Paz insists on contradiction between linear time of the modern age as opposed to the rhythmic, cyclical time of the poem. Brilliant study from one whose arguments always sound irrefutable. Rachel Phillips has made another fine translation of dense and difficult prose.

6327 ———. Marcel Duchamp: appearance stripped bare. Translated from the Spanish by Rachel Phillips and Donald Gardner. New York: The Viking Press, 1973. 211 p.; chronology (A Richard Seaver book)

Paz argues that Duchamp ranks as one of the two greatest painters of the century

(the other, Picasso), by virtue of one work, *Large glass*, "that is nothing less than the negation of work in the modern sense of the word." Paz marks 1923 as year *Large glass* was "definitively unfinished." Hinging on questions of transparency, illumination, vision, and knowledge, study seems strangely opaque. Translation is occasionally inconsistent, perhaps due to the work of two translators.

6328 ———. The other Mexico: critique of the pyramid. Translated by Lysander Kemp. New York: Grove Press, 1972. 148 p.; bibl. (An Evergreen black cat book; B-359)

Continuation and development of *The labyrinth of solitude*, study addresses 20 critical years following its publication (see *HLAS 35:7529*). Includes section in English translation not contained in original Spanish publication, a letter to Adolfo Gilly in which Paz responds—agreeing and disagreeing—to arguments in Gilly's book *La revolución interrumpida*, a history of the Mexican Revolution. *The other Mexico* (Posdata in Spanish) is translated by Kemp. The "Post Script" (really, then, a post-post script) is translated by Helen Lane. Paz is fortunate in both translators.

TRANSLATIONS INTO ENGLISH FROM BRAZILIAN LITERATURE FICTION AND POETRY

6329 Amado, Jorge. Tereza Batista, home from the wars. Translated from the Portuguese by Barbara Shelby. New York: Avon, 1975. 558 p.; glossary.

Barbara Shelby, whose translation is not credited on title page, is an outstanding translator of Portuguese novels. This is another fine translation of a complex yet humorous and tender work that interweaves two strands of popular Brazilian culture: the African thread and the ballad tradition known as *literatura de cordel*.

6330 Lins, Osman. Avalovara. Translated from the Portuguese by Gregory Rabassa. New York: distributed by Random House, 1980. 331 p.; index.

Extremely complex book is rigorously plotted yet also surreal, elusive, chaotic. Book did not receive critical attention it deserves. Translation was awarded Calouste

Gulbenkian-Pen Translation Prize given every two years for best translation from Portuguese. Rabassa was cited for "bringing a masterpiece of modern Brazilian and Latin American narrative to the attention of the English reader . . . without sacrificing its intense lyricism."

6331 Love stories, a Brazilian collection. Edited and annotated by Edla van Steen. Translated from the Portuguese by Elizabeth Lowe. Drawings by Italo Cencini. Introd. by Fabio Lucas. São Paulo?: Gráfica Editora Hamburg, 1978. 198 p.; ill.

Brazilian industry occasionally sponsors publication of worthy books (see *HLAS 42:6672*). This thematic anthology contains work of best contemporary Brazilian writers. Attractively bound edition printed and illustrated with special paper, large pages and type, is collector's item. High quality translations, not without infelicity, but one hears individual voices of 15 contributors. It is regrettable book will not have audience it deserves.

6332 Poesía brasileira moderna. A bilingual anthology. Edited, and with introduction and notes by José Neistein. Translated from the Portuguese by Manoel Cardozo. Washington: Brazilian-American Cultural Institute, Inc., 1972. 207 p.; bibl.

Editor explains volume's purpose: "to survey the poetic output of the various generations of poets between 1922 and 1972 . . . having a specifically Brazilian quality and at the same time an undeniable universality" (see *HLAS 34:7104*). Translations are, usually, good literal renditions of Portuguese. However, translation lacks cohesive approach, or method adopted to convey *poetry* of lines. Often English version illustrates that translation is inevitably augmentation. One is grateful for information conveyed by volume, and with aid of *en face* publication even non-specialists can approximate originals.

6333 Queiroz, Dinah Silveira de. The women of Brazil. Translated from the Portuguese by Roberta King. New York: Vantage Press, 1980. 289 p.

Novel of great sweeping scene, exuberant nature, war, pestilence, love, death, jealousy, hate, reconciliation. Might find a popular audience, but it is difficult from the translation to understand basis of author's reputation.

6334 Souza, Márcio. The emperor of the Amazon. Translated from the Portuguese by Thomas Colchie. New York: Avon, 1977. 190 p.

Michael Wood called this novel "a trip through a world of allusions, spiced with knock-about adventures." One wonders why Brazilian writers are so much more humorous than Spanish ones. Souza burlesques the picaresque, 19th-century *feuilleton*, the epigram, theater, opera, while slyly slipping in acerbic social commentary. Book is probably most closely related to comic opera, extravagant, entertaining, exhuberant. Thomas Colchie has produced an excellent translation of this lively narrative.

TRANSLATION THEORY, CRITICISM, JOURNALS, BIBLIOGRAPHIES

6335 Bagby Júnior, Alberto. Machado de Assis traduzido (PUC/V, 25:97, março 1980, p. 89–102)

Admittedly incomplete as Machado de Assis' bibliography in English, article's purposes: 1) to provide interested reader and specialist the languages in which Machado's works may be read; and 2) to suggest names of other Brazilian and Portuguese authors who have become known through translation (e.g., Jorge Amado, Enrico Verissimo, Cecilia Meirelles, Eça de Queiros). Bibliography (difficult to read in terms of organization) lists translations and their reviews, and provides brief annotations as to the quality of translations.

6336 Felstiner, John. Translating Neruda: the way to Macchu Picchu. Stanford: University of California Press, 1980. 273 p.; bibl.; index.

Breakthrough work is first book-length study in new sub-genre of literary criticism: Translator as critic. Before discussing translation of *Alturas de Macchu Picchu*, Felstiner studies evolution of events and emotions leading to masterwork. Chaps. 2/4 demonstrate thorough knowledge of Neruda bibliography and biography. Chaps. 1 and 5 concern translation process. Chap. 1 examines previous translators, and ease or difficulty with which Spanish moves into other languages (some good generalizations here). Chap. 3 is heart of study: close reading of the poem illuminated by translation, explicit evidence of author's interpretation. How well has translator "comprehended and made actual the original?" Very well.

6337 Kalicki, Rajmund. Algunos aspectos sobre la recepción de la literatura iberoamericana en Polonia (CH, 358, abril 1980, p. 172–178)

Very interesting brief history of Polish appreciation and receptivity to Spanish American literature which is significantly higher, proportionately, than in US. Cites founding of "Series of Spanish American Prose" publications as instrumental in introducing contemporary Spanish American novelists. Although fewer poets are translated, author believes Spanish American writers have influenced young Polish novelists *and* poets. To underscore dramatic nature of author's statistics: in Poland, 1974, 17 titles were translated from Spanish; in 1976, 32. By comparison, in US, 1980: only 40.

6338 Marrodan Casas, Carlos. ¿Narrativa o cultura? Apuntes sobre las traducciones de narrativa latinoamericana en Polonia (PAN/ES, 4, 1978, p. 232–236)

Careful examination of central aspect of Polish receptivity to Spanish American literature (see item **6337**), whether the "Spanish American Prose series" were guided by "commercial rather than cultural motivation." Argues that purpose of such publications is to help Polish reader to "form a more complete image of the societies and cultures of Latin America." Author would prefer publication of *Popul Vuh* over mythic interpretations of Asturias, or essays of Paz and Zea over novelization of their themes. Questions continuing emphasis on the novel when poetry, drama, essay, and social thought of Latin American countries are so little known in Poland.

6339 *Mundus Artium.* Ohio University, Department of English. Vol. 3, No. 1, Winter 1969– . Athens, Ohio.

Special issue on Latin American poetry (edited by Rainer Schulte with Sergio Mondragon as guest editor) is like *Tri-Quarterly*'s special issue (see *HLAS 40: 7848*), a classic. Except for one essay on Latin American art, volume is devoted to Spanish American poetry (e.g., Huidobro, Guillén, Lezama Lima, Paz, Parra, Cardenal, Sabines, Pacheco, and Aridjis). Excludes Borges, Ne-

ruda and Vallejo because "practically all the poems they have written have been translated." Includes: foreword by Mondragón, a brief meditation on poetry by Octavio Paz, and informative overview of contemporary (1920–60) Spanish American poetry by Ramón Xirau. Translations by many are uniformly good. *En face.*

6340 *Poetics Today.* Porter Institute for Poetics and Semiotics. Vol. 2, Summer/Autumn 1981– . Tel Aviv, Israel.

Special issue on translation theory and intercultural relations, edited by Itamar Even-Sohar and Gideon Toury, and divided into: 1) Translation Theory and Methodology; 2) Translation Theory and Contrastive Linguistics; 3) Texts and Textual Options; 4) Literary polysystem and Translation Processes; and 5) Translation Models and Literary History. Editors explain how awareness of features laid bare in translation process have encouraged theorists "to take more interest in using translation as a method for a more sustainable procedure for detection of textual laws." Also, translation has proved fruitful source for understanding interference between cultural systems, as well as in code switching and merging.

6341 Teoría y práctica de la traducción. Primer encuentro internacional de traductores. Santiago: Ediciones Universidad Católica de Chile, 1981. 99 p.

Distinguished group of translators (e.g., Georges Mounin, France; Eugene Nida, US; René Chapero, US; Hugo Montes, Chile) met Oct. 1980 to discuss translation problems. Objectives: review of present state of translation; problems concerning training specialists in translation; exchange of experiences and research among Chilean and other specialists. Papers tend slightly—not exclusively—toward scientific and linguistic approach. Most valuable to literary translator is Luis Enrique Jara's "Lo Etnolingüístico: un Problema de Traducción."

6342 *Translation Review.* University of Texas at Dallas. Vol. 1, Spring 1978– . Richardson, Tex.

First issue of official journal of American Literary Translators Association (ALTA) was edited by Rainer Schulte and James P. White. Goals are: "evaluation of translations into English, discussion of books on the theory of translation, portraits of individual translators." Journal also will address many technical problems confronting translators, including those of copyright, translation programs, and clearinghouse activities. Issue's highlight is interview with premier translator Gregory Rabassa.

6343 ——. ——. Vol. 2, Fall 1978–
Richardson, Tex.
In addition to articles on translating Greek and German, includes Elain de Rosa's well-deserved commendation for activities of Center for Inter-American Relations. Reviews of translations by *translators* is feature of first importance in this journal.

6344 ——. ——. Vol. 3, Summer
1979– . Richardson, Tex.
Major commentary, Octavio Paz's "Translation: Literature and Literality," is excerpted here in translation by Lynn Tuttle. Great poet's comments on influence of translation on poetry are of deep interest: "Translation and creation are twin operations . . . On the other hand, there is an incessant flow between the two, a continuous and mutual fertilization. The great creative periods of Western poetry . . . have been preceded or accompanied by the interweaving of different poetic traditions . . ." Most of issue consists of reviews, and interview with Christopher Middleton.

6345 ——. ——. Vol. 4, Spring
1979– . Richardson, Tex.
Interview with Richard and Clara Winston reveals working habits of most famous contemporary team of translators (Richard Winston died recently). Thea Hoekzema surveys potential of "publishing translations with University Presses." Skip Acuff and Claudia Johnson offer a most practical guide to publication of translations and list ca. 75 journals that responded to questionnaire about policy of accepting translations: whether journal will accept xerox of original, what languages they feature, whether they have special thematic issues, whether they prefer period or contemporary pieces, and contractual arrangements. A must for the working translator.

6346 ——. ——. Vol. 5, Summer
1980– . Richardson, Tex.
Ronald Christ interviews Helen Lane, whose translations are aimed at giving "the English-speaking reader a good idea of what the original would have 'been like' if it had

been written in English, yet at the same time retain enough of a flavor of the original . . . to give the reader a hint of an area that writers in his own language had not yet explored." Interview is particularly valuable as learning tool for both experienced and beginning translators. Issue also contains listing of courses and programs in translations offered in North American colleges and universities.

6347 ——. ——. Vol. 6, Winter
1980– . Richardson, Texas.
Carol Meier discusses dialogue with professor-critic who contends that translation is a "task that does not occur in the realms of thought but between the pages of a dictionary." Her argument is that "having seen its [the work's] formation from within, the translator is . . . not less, and perhaps even more able to respond critically than the professor-critic." Jonathan Cohen interviews H. R. Hays on his translations of South American poets, and Thomas Hoeksema interviews Willis Barnstone.

6348 ——. ——. Vol. 7, Winter
1981– . Richardson, Tex.
Thomas Hoeksema examines renewed interest in Esperanto with Humphrey Tonkin, including overview of world authors translated into it. Burton Raffel discusses manner of choosing author or specific work to translate, period of the translation, and kind of translation: 1) formal; 2) interpretive; 3) expansive or "free"; and 4) imitation ("which in plain truth I must call no translation at all"). Margaret Sayers Peden reviews John Felstiner's breakthrough study *Translating Neruda*, and Elizabeth Gamble Miller discusses problems encountered in translating Hugo Lindo's poetry: "maintaining the multiple levels of the poetic, the human and the divine throughout the poem."

6349 **Translation spectrum.** Essays in theory and practice. Edited by Marilyn Gaddis Rose. Albany: State University of New York Press, 1981. 172 p.
Broad variety of approaches. Of most interest to practicing translator are: 1) Rose's accurate analysis of steps in translation process; 2) Straight's essay on three dimensions of translation (i.e., knowledge, purpose, and intuition—both Rose and Straight concede indispensable role of intuition); 3) Jasenas' helpful list of sources for all languages; 4) Rose and Doron's discussion of matters of

professionalism; and 5) Sticca and Well-warth's comments on specific translation problems, medieval and dramatic texts. All avoid the esoteric and offer valuable insights.

6350 Zierer, Ernesto. Algunos conceptos básicos de la ciencia de la traducción. Trujillo, Perú: Universidad Nacional de Tru-jillo, Departamento de Idiomas y Lingüística, 1979. 212 p.; bibl.; diagrs.

Reviews translation as a science or dis-cipline encompassing translation theory, translation practice, translation critique, and translation didactics. Diligent reader will find isolated headings of use but book's over-all organization is chaotic (e.g., one finds "general rules" on p. 121). Quality of type and paper make reading extremely difficult.

JOURNAL ABBREVIATIONS LITERATURE

A Abside. Revista de cultura mexicana. México.

AAFH/TAM The Americas. A quarterly publication of inter-American cultural his-tory. Academy of American Franciscan His-tory. Washington.

AATSP/H Hispania. American Association of Teachers of Spanish and Portuguese. Univ. of Cincinnati. Cincinnati, Ohio.

ACO/B Boletín de la Academia Colom-biana. Bogotá.

AFH Archivum Franciscanum Historicum. Firenze, Italy.

ANLE/B Boletín de la Academia Norte-americana de la Lengua Española. New York.

AR Areito. Areíto, Inc. New York.

ARBOR Arbor. Madrid.

ASB/PP Philologica Pragensia. Academia Scientiarum Bohemoslovenica. Praha.

ATSP/VH Vida Hispánica. Journal of the Association of the Teachers of Spanish and Portuguese. Wolverhampton, U.K.

AU/P Phylon. Atlanta Univ. Atlanta, Ga.

BEPB Bulletin des Études Portugaises et Bresiliennes. Institut Français de Lisbonne *avec la collaboration de* Etablissements Français d'Enseignement Supérieur, Instituto de Alta Cultura, et du Departamento Cul-tural do Itamarati. Lisbon.

BJCC Bohemia. Jahrbuch des Collegium Carolinum. Munich, FRG.

BNBD Boletín Nicaragüense de Bibliografía y Documentación. Banco Centra de Nica-ragua. Managua.

BNJM/R Revista de la Biblioteca Nacional José Martí. La Habana.

BRP Beitrâge zur Romanischen Philologie. Rütten & Loening. Berlin.

CAM Cuadernos Americanos. México.

CBR/BCB Boletín Cultural y Bibliográfico. Banco de la República, Biblioteca Luis-Angel Arango. Bogotá.

CDLA Casa de las Américas. Instituto Cubano del Libro. La Habana.

CDLA/CO Conjunto. Revista de teatro latinoamericano. Casa de las Américas *for the* Comité Permanente de Festivales. La Habana.

CH Cuadernos Hispanoamericanos. Insti-tuto de Cultura Hispánica. Madrid.

CLA/J CLA Journal. A quarterly official publication of The College Language Associ-ation. Morgan State College. Baltimore, Md.

CM/D Diálogos. Artes/Letras/Ciencias Humanas. El Colegio de México. México.

CM/NRFH Nueva Revista de Filología His-pánica. El Colegio de México [and] the Univ. of Texas. México.

CONAC/RNC Revista Nacional de Cul-tura. Consejo Nacional de Cultura. Caracas.

CU/D Diacritics. A review of contempo-rary criticism. Cornell Univ., Dept. of Ro-mance Studies. Ithaca, N.Y.

EC/M Mapocho. Biblioteca Nacional, Ex-tensión Cultural. Santiago.

ECO Eco. Librería Bucholz. Bogotá.

EME Revista Eme-Eme. Estudios domini-canos. Univ. Católica Madre y Maestra. San-tiago de los Caballeros, Dominican Republic.

FENIX Fénix. Biblioteca Nacional. Lima.

FIU/CR Caribbean Review. Florida Interna-tional Univ., Office of Academic Affairs. Miami.

HISP Hispanófila. Univ. of North Carolina. Chapel Hill.

HISPA Hispamérica. Revista de literatura. Takoma Park, Md.

HIUS/R Revista Hispánica Moderna. Columbia Univ., Hispanic Institute in the United States. New York.

HR Hispanic Review. A quarterly devoted to research in the Hispanic languages and literatures. Univ. of Pennsylvania, Dept. of Romance Languages. Philadelphia.

HU Hojas Universitarias. Revista de la Fundación Univ. Central. Bogotá.

IA/ZK Zeitschrift für Kulturaustausch. Institut für Auslandsbeziehungen. Berlin, FRG.

IAA Ibero-Amerikanisches Archiv. Ibero-Amerikanisches Institut. Berlin, FRG.

ICC/T Thesaurus. Boletín del Instituto Caro y Cuervo. Bogotá.

ICP/R Revista del Instituto de Cultura Puertorriqueña. San Juan.

IFH/C Conjonction. Institut Français d'Haïti. Port-au-Prince.

IGFO/RI Revista de Indias. Instituto Gonzalo Fernández de Oviedo [and] Consejo Superior de Investigaciones Científicas. Madrid.

IHGA/R Revista do Instituto Histórico e Geográfico de Alagoas. Maceió, Brazil.

IILI/RI Revista Iberoamericana. Instituto Internacional de Literatura Iberoamericana. *Patrocinada por la* Univ. de Pittsburgh. Pittsburgh, Pa.

IJZ/H Hispania. Revista española de historia. Instituto Jerónimo Zurita, Consejo Superior de Investigaciones Científicas. Madrid.

IL Ideologies & Literature. A journal of Hispanic and Luso-Brazilian literatures. Univ. of Minnesota, Institute for the Study of Ideologies and Literature. Minneapolis.

INDEX Index on Censorship. Writers & Scholars International. London.

INSULA Insula. Madrid.

INTI Inti. Univ. of Connecticut, Dept. of Romance Languages. Storrs.

IPGH/FA Folklore Americano. Instituto Panamericano de Geografía e Historia, Comi-

sión de Historia, Comité de Folklore. México.

IUP/HJ Hispanic Journal. Indiana Univ. of Pennsylvania, Dept. of Foreign Languages. Indiana.

JSSTC Journal of Spanish Studies: Twentieth Century. Kansas State Univ., Dept. of Modern Languages. Manhattan.

LALR Latin American Literary Review. Carnegie-Mellon Univ., Dept. of Modern Languages. Pittsburgh, Pa.

LAP Latin American Perspectives. Univ. of California. Riverside.

LARR Latin American Research Review. Univ. of North Carolina Press *for the* Latin American Studies Association. Chapel Hill.

LNB/L Lotería. Lotería Nacional de Beneficencia. Panamá.

MLN Modern Language Notes. Johns Hopkins Press. Baltimore, Md.

NER The New Republic. Washington.

NMC/N Nicaráuac. Revista bimestral del Ministerio de Cultura. Managua.

NR Die Neue Rundschau. S. Fischer Verlag. Frankfurt.

NS NS NorthSouth NordSud NorteSur NorteSul. Canadian journal of Latin American studies. Canadian Association of Latin American Studies. Univ. of Ottawa.

PAN/ES Estudios Latinoamericanos. Polska Akademia Nauk (Academia de Ciencias de Polonia), Instytut Historii (Instituto de Historia). Warszawa.

PMLA Publications of the Modern Language Association of America. New York.

PUC/V Veritas. Revista. Pontifícia Univ. Católica do Rio Grande do Sul. Porto Alegre, Brazil.

PUCP/H Histórica. Pontificia Univ. Católica del Perú, Depto. de Humanidades. Lima.

PUJ/UH Universitas Humanistica. Pontificia Univ. Javeriana, Facultad de Filosofía y Letras. Bogotá.

QIA Quaderni Ibero-Americani. Associazione per i Rapporti Culturali con la Spagna, il Portogallo e l'America Latina. Torino, Italy.

RCLL Revista de Crítica Literaria Latinoamericana. Latinoamericana Editores. Lima.

REVIEW Review. Center for Inter-American Relations. New York.

RIB Revista Interamericana de Bibliografía (Inter-American Review of Bibliography). Organization of American States. Washington.

RRI Revista/Review Interamericana. Univ. Interamericana. San Germán, Puerto Rico.

RYC Revolución y Cultura. Publicación mensual. Ministerio de Cultura. La Habana.

SN Sin Nombre. Revista trimestral literaria. Ediciones Sin Nombre, Inc. San Juan.

UA/REH Revista de Estudios Hispánicos. Univ. of Alabama, Dept. of Romance Languages, Office of International Studies and Programs. University.

UA/U Universidad. Univ. de Antioquia. Medellín, Colombia.

UAEM/H Histórica. Univ. Autónoma del Estado de México, Instituto de Investigaciones Históricas. México.

UB/BH Bulletin Hispanique. Univ. de Bordeaux *avec le concours du* Centre National de la Recherche Scientifique. Bordeaux, France.

UBN/R Revista de la Biblioteca Nacional. Ministerio de Educación y Cultura. Montevideo.

UC/A Anales de la Universidad de Cuenca. Cuenca, Ecuador.

UC/AT Atenea. Revista de ciencias, letras y artes. Univ. de Concepción. Concepción, Chile.

UC/S Signs. Journal of women in culture and society. The Univ. of Chicago Press. Chicago.

UCL/LR Les Lettres Romanes. Univ. Catholique de Louvain, Fondation Universitaire de Belgique. Louvain, Belgium.

UCLA/JLAL Journal of Latin American Lore. Univ. of California, Latin American Center. Los Angeles.

UCLA/M Mester. Univ. of California, Dept. of Spanish and Portuguese. Los Angeles.

UCLV/I Islas. Univ. Central de las Villas. Santa Clara, Cuba.

UCNSA/EP Estudios Paraguayos. Univ. Católica Nuestra Señora de la Asunción. Asunción.

UCR/AEC Anuario de Estudios Centroamericanos. Univ. de Costa Rica. Ciudad Universitaria "Rodrigo Facio." San José.

UCV/E Escritura. Teoría y crítica literaria. Univ. Central de Venezuela, Escuela de Letras. Caracas.

UEAC/GC Gaceta de Cuba. Unión de Escritores y Artistas de Cuba. La Habana.

UFP/EB Estudos Brasileiros. Univ. Federal do Paraná, Setor de Ciências Humanas, Centro de Estudos Brasileiros. Curitiba, Brazil.

UH/RJ Romanistisches Jahrbuch. Univ. Hamburg, Romanisches Seminar, Ibero-Amerikanisches Forschungsinstitut. Hamburg, FRG.

UH/U Universidad de La Habana. La Habana.

UIA/C Comunidad. Revista de la U.I.A. Cuadernos de difusión cultural. Univ. Iberoamericana. México.

UK/KRQ Kentucky Romance Quarterly. Univ. of Kentucky. Lexington.

UK/LATR Latin American Theatre Review. A journal devoted to the theatre and drama of Spanish and Portuguese America. Univ. of Kansas, Center of Latin American Studies. Lawrence.

UNAM/AL Anuario de Letras. Univ. Nacional Autónoma de México, Facultad de Filosofía y Letras. México.

UNAM/RMS Revista Mexicana de Sociología. Univ. Nacional Autónoma de México, Instituto de Investigaciones Sociales. México.

UNAM/RUM Revista de la Universidad de México. México.

UNESCO/CU Cultures. United Nations Educational, Scientific and Cultural Organization. Paris.

UNION Unión. Unión de Escritores y Artistas de Cuba. La Habana.

UNL/U Universidad. Univ. Nacional del Litoral. Santa Fe, Argentina.

UNMSM/L Letras. Univ. Nacional Mayor de San Marcos. Lima.

UP/CSEC Cuban Studies/Estudios Cubanos. Univ. of Pittsburgh, Univ. Center for International Studies, Center for Latin American Studies. Pittsburgh, Pa.

UP/LAIL Latin American Indian Literatures. A new review of American Indian texts and studies. Univ. of Pittsburgh, Dept. of Hispanic Languages and Literatures. Pittsburgh, Pa.

UPR/CS Caribbean Studies. Univ. of Puerto Rico, Institute of Caribbean Studies. Río Piedras.

UR/L Lateinamerika. Univ. Rostock. Rostock, GDR.

URSS/AL América Latina. Academia de Ciencias de la URSS (Unión de Repúblicas Soviéticas Socialistas). Moscú.

USP/LL Língua e Literatura. Univ. de São Paulo, Depto. de Letras, Faculdade de Filosofia, Letras e Ciências Humanas. São Paulo.

USP/RH Revista de História. Univ. de São Paulo, Faculdade de Filosofia, Ciências e Letras, Depto. de História [and] Sociedade de Estudos Históricos. São Paulo.

UTIEH/C Caravelle. Cahiers du monde hispanique et luso-brésilien. Univ. de Toulouse, Institut d'Études Hispaniques, Hispano-Americaines et Luso-Brésiliennes. Toulouse, France.

UV/PH La Palabra y el Hombre. Univ. Veracruzana. Xalapa, Mexico.

UW/LBR Lus-Brazilian Review. Univ. of Wisconsin Press. Madison.

UWI/CQ Caribbean Quarterly. Univ. of the West Indies. Mona, Jamaica.

VIA Via. A new literary magazine. Univ. of California, Office of Student Activities. Berkeley.

VOZES Vozes. Revista de cultura. Editora Vozes. Petrópolis, Brazil.

MUSIC

ROBERT STEVENSON, *Professor of Music, University of California, Los Angeles*

AMONG LITERARY MASTERS, only George Bernard Shaw and Alejo Carpentier doubled as musical journalists. The publication at Havana in 1980 [1981] of an indexed three-volume sampling of Carpentier's profuse musical journalism (item **7002**) adds much to his critical stature. In contrast with Shaw who wielded the pen like a machete and who never stopped to consider blighted careers, Carpentier encouraged vines not yet in full flower. His gracious deference to local musicians in Caracas (where he published far more musical information in his long running column *Letras y Solfa* than could be contained in the present three volumes compiled exclusively from his saved clippings) may have been mere prudence. In his nest at Caracas, common sense forbade his angering Venezuelans powerful enough to destroy his eyrie. But it is more likely he was considerate of Caracas' local musicians because he had already grown into the habit of encouraging young American talent wherever he found it—Havana, studying at Paris, or visiting Spain.

The openness and generosity about Latin American music that distinguished Carpentier's journalism also pervades a November 1980 publication venture on a far more grandiose scale—the 20-volume "musicological marvel" long awaited from Macmillan (London, selling for approximately $1900), *The New Grove Dictionary of Music and Musicians*. Ten years in active preparation, this monumental encyclopedia was immediately hailed in *Latin American Music Review* (edited by Gerard Béhague, item **7001**) as the all-sufficient authority on Latin American music for the remainder of the century. Unfortunately, however, *New Grove* contributors on Latin American topics often failed to take account of important scholarly findings divulged during the several years that their articles awaited publication.

Among new periodicals, *Revista Musical de Venezuela*, handsomely directed by José Vicente Torres with Miguel Castillo Didier as coordinator, began publication in 1980 with two thick issues containing historical studies, data on contemporary events and composers, chronicles of Venezuelan activities, and reviews. Sponsored by the Venezuelan Consejo Nacional de la Cultura (CONAC) of which Torres is *secretario*, this new journal is a great credit to its Venezuelan backers and participants. *Revista Inidef* continued in the forefront of ethnomusicological studies during the biennium, thanks to the outstanding direction of Isabel Aretz and her eminent husband Luis Felipe Ramón y Rivera. The universal recognition accorded *Revista Musical Chilena*, directed by Samuel Claro Valdés and Luis Merino with the invaluable cooperation of Magdalena Vicuña Lyon is well deserved, especially its publication during a period fraught with financial difficulties for the sponsoring Universidad de Chile, Facultad de Ciencias y Artes Musicales y de la Representación. *Heterofonía*, directed by Esperanza Pulido, entered a second epoch with an enlarged format in 1981, when the Mexican Conservatorio Nacional de Música headed by Armando Montiel Olvera took over this leading Mexican musical magazine and added a section (printed in red type) devoted to conservatory history and current events.

Despite valiant efforts such as the above at printing archival materials, time lags between publication and distribution—extended by exorbitant prices charged for unreviewed material by a few US distributors—seriously damaged inter-American musical relations during the biennium. As an example of time lags: in late Nov. 1981 there arrived hand-carried from Buenos Aires, the long-awaited first two installments of Vicente Gesualdo's *Historia de la música en la Argentina* (second ed., see item **7016**, first ed. 1961). Considerably revised and updated, these installments covering 1536–1809 and 1810–29 reveal crucial new information such as the successful production at Buenos Aires on four consecutive nights in Nov. 1760 of an opera by Bartolomé Massa (1721–96, resident in Argentina 1752–61) and the birth at Murcia in 1776 and death at Mataró (near Barcelona) 7 Jan. 1840 of Blas Parera, composer of the Argentine national anthem.

The continuing problem of time lag that delayed until Nov. 1981 receipt of these installments published in Buenos Aires in April and Aug. 1978, accounts for the omission from this *HLAS 44* of four fascicles announced as published in 1981 by Brazilian Pro-Memus, of 19 works published about 1980 by the Liga de Compositores de México, and of recently announced histories of music in colonial Cuba and Peru.

GENERAL

7001 Béhague, Gerard. Latin American music and *The New Grove dictionary of music and musicians* (LAMR, 2:1, Spring/Summer 1981, p. 168)

The 16,000-page *New Grove* published in Nov. 1980, took 10 years to prepare, and its 20 volumes provide "the most comprehensive and up-to-date coverage of Latin American music and musicians." For comprehensive review of North and South American coverage in this dictionary, see *Inter-American Music Review* (3:2, Spring/Summer 1981).

7002 Carpentier, Alejo. Ese músico que llevo dentro. Selection, prologue, and name indexes by Zoila Gómez García. Havana: Editorial Letras Cubanas, 1980 [1981]. 3 v. (479, 589, 354 p.)

Unable to organize Carpentier musical journalism (1923–77) chronologically because of the number of undated clippings, the editor of these volumes arranged them according to subject matter. Vol. 1 covers Latin American composers, other composers, orchestra directors, and other interpreters. Vol. 2 includes critiques of specific works as well as articles on jazz, festivals and competitions, recordings sent to Caracas for review, ensembles, methods of notation, musical editions, film music, and a wide variety of other miscellaneous topics. Vol. 3 treats of stage music, followed by philosophical discourses related to music. The divisions are not watertight. For a full review of all three volumes, see *Inter-American Music Review* (4:2, Spring/Summer 1982, p. 88–90).

7003 Davis, Peter G. Grabaciones de música latinoamericana (UCIEM/R, 34:152, oct./dic. 1980, p. 81–84)

Article translated from *The New York Times* (20 July 1980) lists discs issued up to then by the OAS in a projected series of Inter-American Musical Editions directed by Efraín Paesky. The first (OAS-001) contains orchestral works by Villa-Lobos, Marlos Nobre, and Cláudio Santoro.

7004 Entrevistas con Christine Walewska, Martha Argerich, Alicia Alonso, José Rodríguez Frausto, Fernando Lozano (HET, 13:3, julio/sept. 1980, p. 20–30)

During the VIII Festival Cervantino held May 1980, at Guanajuato, five orchestras played concerts at the Teatro Juárez: 1) Filarmónica de la Ciudad de México (Lozano, conductor); 2) Sinfónica de Guanajuato (Frausto); 3) Gewandhaus of Leipzig (Masur); 4) Sinfónica de Xalapa (Herrera de la Fuente); and 5) Sinfónica Nacional (Sergio Cárdenas). The soloists with these orchestras included the first two interviewees (Dvořák *Cello Concerto* and Prokofieff *Piano Concerto No. 3*). Lozano's interlocutors strongly resisted the preponderance of foreigners in the Philharmonic of Mexico City which played in

Guanajuato only a day after returning from a triumphal tour of Japan. The 70-year-old Cuban dancer Alicia Alonso complimented the Mexican ballet and spoke of mounting two Cuban ballets at Havana—by Amadeo Roldán and Caturla (the latter's *El Drama de Olvido*). The Argentine pianist Martha Argerich (b. Buenos Aires, 5 June 1941), echoed by her mother Juanita Argerich, voiced an interest in conducting. Due to depart after playing with Lozano, she listed recent ovations in Israel (Rachmaninoff, op. 30), and bespoke her record of 80 concerts annually, plus assorted chamber music performances. Despite the glamor of the VIII Festival Cervantino that also included performances by Arrau, Cherkassky, Weissenberg, and Angélica Morales, only two music critics covered the entire festival, Esperanza Pulido and José Antonio Alcaraz.

7005 Kuss, Malena. Charles Seeger and Latin America: themes and contributions (RIB, 30:3, 1980, p. 231–237)

Memorial tribute. The last paragraph begins: "Seeger's colossal perception of the field of music, its boundaries, problems and relationships, can only be matched by the perception of other outstanding individuals who raised fundamental questions in their disciplines and conceived—as did Einstein—of the possibility of unity in nature."

7006 ———. Leitmotive de Charles Seeger sobre Latinoamérica (UCIEM/R, 34:151, julio/sept. 1980, p. 29–37)

Translation of a heartfelt tribute previously published in *Inter-American Review of Bibliography*.

7007 Lindstrom, Fred B. and **Naomi Lindstrom.** A little-known Latin American cultural territory: aspects of U.S. jazz (ASU/LAD, 15:1, 1980, p. 1–3, 20, ill.)

Father-daughter pair urge fresh attention to Latin American music influences rampant in New Orleans at the turn of the century. Mexican musicians sent to the Cotton Exposition by Porfirio Díaz, publication of scores of Latin compositions, and a constant inflow of Caribbean musicians made New Orleans a leading entrepôt for Latin American rhythms, which already before arrival were African-tinctured.

7008 Nobre, Marlos. La problemática de la música latinoamericana (UCIEM/R,

32:142/144, abril/dic. 1978, p. 125–130)

Delivered at the Festival Latinoamericana de Música Contemporánea "Ciudad Maracaibo" 22 Nov. 1977, and transmitted by Francisco Curt Lange, this gloomy lecture bemoans the minimal interest that Latin Americans take in their own achievements, past and present. Only foreign music and musicians get attention in conservatories.

7009 Olsen, Oscar. Antepasados de la guitarra en América Latina (UCC/RU, 3, abril 1980, p. 77–86, bibl., facsim., ill.)

In Chile and Argentina *vihuela* and *vigüela* are still used as synonyms for *guitarra*. At Quito the relics of Santa Mariana de Jesús (d. 1645) kept at the Jesuit church include a "guitarra" that is in reality a 16th-century vihuela comparable to the one at the Jacquemart-André Museum in Paris. The Quito vihuela measures 100 cm in total length; strings measure 66 cm; pegbox and bridge accommodate 12 strings (two to a course). The guitar of four single strings is pictured by Felipe Guamán Poma de Ayala. In his drawing of a Creole couple, the man plays while the woman snaps her fingers at a fiesta. The *cuatro* that is the Venezuelan national favorite is a small guitar tuned variously (g, d^1, b$^\flat$, f; a^1, e^1, c^1, g). The Venezuelan *cinco* (known·in the state of Lara as *quinto* or *tiple*) can be tuned e^1, b, g, d, a. The Latin American *bandola* or *mandola* is ovoidally shaped but with flat back; strings are of metal.

7010 Stevenson, Robert. The last musicological frontier: cathedral music in the colonial Americas (IAMR, 3:1, Fall 1980, p. 49–54)

Whereas European musical treasures of the 16th through 18th centuries have been so exhaustively mined that important new discoveries are rarely made, the riches of Latin American colonial cathedrals remain still largely untranscribed and therefore unassessed.

7011 ———. The Latin American music educator's best ally: the Latin American musicologist (IAMR, 2:2, Spring/Summer 1980, p. 117–122)

Paper read at V Conferencia Interamericana Internacional de Educación Musical, Mexico City, Oct. 1979.

7012 ———. The Latin tinge: 1800–1900 (IAMR, 2:2, Spring/Summer 1980, p. 73–101)

Sheet music published in the US before 1900 attests to the impact of Latin America. Near the close of the century, expositions at New Orleans and Chicago highlighted Mexican and Brazilian achievements.

7013 ——. National Library publications in Brazil, Peru, and Venezuela (IAMR, 3:1, Fall 1980, p. 39–48)

Revised, amplified version of article "South American National Library Publications" in *Notes* (35:1, Sept. 1978, p. 31–41).

7014 Valencia López, Raymond. Panorama de la música virreinal en Latinoamérica: conferencias y conciertos (HET, 14:1[72], 2. época, enero/marzo 1981, p. 43–48)

During the week of 3–7 Nov. 1980, CENIDIM (Centro Nacional de Investigación, Documentación e Información Músical, Liverpool 16, México 6, D.F.) sponsored a week of lectures and concerts exposing the Latin American colonial music heritage. With rare knowledge of the repertory and its makers, López records the composers, works performed, performers' names, and sites where the week's music was heard.

ARGENTINA

7015 Edelstein, Oscar. Mariano Etkin: música contemporánea argentina (Andén para la Cultura [Ediciones Candilejas, Córdoba, Argentina] 1:1, set./oct. 1979, p. 69–74)

Etkin (b. Buenos Aires, 1943) studied with Ernesto Epstein and Guilhermo Graetzer before enrolling in the Rockefeller Foundation-sponsored Centro Latinoamericano de Altos Estudios Musicales of the Instituto Di Tella. In 1979 he taught music analysis at the Universidad Nacional del Litoral. Despite the title of this interview, he mentions no present-day Argentine composer, focusing instead on such questions as the relative merits of electronic versus conventional instruments playing Bach, dicta of Edgard Varèse and Morton Feldman, the value of teaching non-Western musics to conservatory and university music students, and the Zen parabola. According to him, composers unknown by present-day audiences may tomorrow be hailed as masters. But he names no living candidates for such future distinction.

7016 Gesualdo, Vicente. Historia de la música en la Argentina: t. 1, La época colonial, 1536–1809; t. 2, La independencia y la época de la Rivadavia, 1810–1829. Buenos Aires: Libros de Hispanoamérica, 1978. 2 v. (107, 124 p.)

Revision of author's history (published 1961). Vol. 1: first four chapters include valuable new data (p. 28, 38, 47, 51–52, 57–60, 62–65, 87–88, 103–107). The revelation that Bartolomé Massa (1721–96) produced his own opera *Las Variedades de Proteo* in Buenos Aires between 4–21 Nov. 1760 is especially important. Vol. 2: among new data, Blas Parera's dates and places of birth and death (Murcia, 1776; Mataró near Barcelona, 7 Jan. 1840) will be early adopted by encyclopedias. His music for the Argentine National Anthem was decreed official 11 May 1813 by the Buenos Aires cabildo (López y Planes' text was printed 14 May 1813 by Niños Espósitos).

7017 Hodge, John E. The construction of the Teatro Colón (AAFH/TAM, 36:2, Oct. 1979, p. 235–255)

Entertaining and well-researched history of the planning and building of Latin America's greatest opera house. From 1884 to the long delayed opening with *Aida* 25 May 1908, author traces the social, financial, and legislative roadblocks that had to be overcome.

7018 Lemmon, Alfred E. Domenico Zipoli: algunos aspectos de su relación con la Argentina (HET, 14:1[72], 2. época, enero/marzo 1981, p. 35–38)

To anyone acquainted with present-day conditions in inter South America it may seem strange that Zipoli would have abandoned a promising career in Rome for Córdoba, where he emigrated in 1717. But at the time, the musical ambiance throughout the Paraguay reductions fully justified such a move. Although he was not the only outstanding musician assigned to Jesuit missions in colonial America, he enjoys today fame greater than any other because his music was published in 1716, before he left Europe.

7019 McLellan, Joseph. Bruno Gelber and the loneliness of the long-distance pianist (OAS/AM, 32:9, Sept. 1980, p. 28–30, plates)

Reprinted from the *Washington Post*, this article draws together Gelber and Argerich as the two best Argentine pianists. A victim of polio in 1948, Gelber recovered to win at age 18, Third Prize in the Long-Thibaud Competition at Paris. Unfortunately, article lacks precise details useful for encyclopedists (e.g., exact dates, titles of pieces played, etc.).

7020 Moreno Chá, Ercilia. El *término*: aportes musicológicos para su estudio (IPGH/FA, 27, junio 1979, p. 195–209, bibl., music)

Examination of an almost extinct milonga-type dance of Buenos Aires province. Carlos Vega registered an example taken at Chivilcoy 9 July 1954. At present, only San Antonio de Areco preserves the *término*. E Major is the preferred key of the guitar-accompanied *término*—whether sung or purely instrumental dance music.

7021 Pickenhayn, Jorge O. Alberto Williams. Buenos Aires: Ministerio de Cultura y Educación, Secretaría de Estado de Cultura, Ediciones Culturales Argentinas, 1979. 150 p.; 12 p. of plates; ill.; ports.; music.

Valuable study divided into three sections: Biography, Analysis of Williams' works, Catalog and Bibliography. Williams (b. 23 Nov. 1862, Buenos Aires; died there 17 June 1952) was much resented by younger composers and critics who considered his nine symphonies scattered among 136 opus numbers hopelessly *derrière garde*. Author avoids polemics but does not provide the wealth of detail that would make this a definitive book (e.g., dates of symphony premieres, exact quotations from Buenos Aires press, historical facts concerning the Williams conservatory chain and the press that published his works, La Quena, etc.). C. G. Röder and Breitkopf und Härtel printed his Opp. 18 and 55.

7022 Sizonenko, Alexandr. Fiodor Chaliapin en América del Sur (URSS/AL, 4, 1979, p. 167–175)

Chaliapin visited South America twice, 1908 and 1930. During his first visit he played the title role of Boito's *Mefistofele* during the opening season of the new Teatro Colón. During the second, he sang the title role of *Boris Godunov* in Russian at the Colón. On both visits he sang Don Basilio in Rossini's *Il Barbiere di Siviglia*, in Italian. He extended his second South American visit to include Montevideo, Santiago de Chile, and Rio de Janeiro. Quotations from Argentine newspapers attest to Chaliapin's

rapturous reception both times at the Teatro Colón. Chaliapin praised the Colón as an eighth wonder of the world in 1908. In 1930 he lamented that standard repertory routinely performed suffocated opera at Buenos Aires.

BRAZIL

7023 Alcántara, Edson Mario de. Desvios de linguagem na música popular brasileira: pesquisa disco-bibliográfica (Educação Hoje [Faculdade de Filosofia, Ciência e Letras de Palmas, Brazil] 6 : 1, julho 1980, p. 47–69)

Pt. 1 of a diffuse study devoted to "deformations" of Portuguese in selected Brazilian popular songs. The songs chosen for analysis were broadcast Feb. through June 1977 at 5:30 pm over Radio Difusora of Alagoas (state official radio).

7024 Appleby, David P. Trends in recent Brazilian piano music (LAMR, 2 : 1, Spring/Summer 1981, p. 91–102)

Knowledgeable, sympathetic analysis of works by Gilberto Mendes, Ernst Widmer, Willy Corrêa de Oliveira, Marlos Nobre, Jorge Antunes, and José António de Almeida Prado, by an Eastern Illinois University piano professor who wrote his Indiana doctoral dissertation on 20th-century Brazilian piano music.

7025 Aytai, Desidério. A música instrumental Xavante (LAMR, 2 : 1, Spring/Summer 1981, p. 103–129)

Penetrating study of purely instrumental music of the Xavante, based on contact at Salesian mission stations in Mato Grosso going back to 1960. Music transcriptions, photographs, diagrams enhance this well-documented analysis by a professor of anthropology at the Catholic University of Campinas, São Paulo. Author dismisses as unacceptable Castelnau's supposition that the Xavante in 1949 frequently danced to the sound of *trompas*.

Bastos, Rafael José de Menezes. A musicológica Kamayurá: para uma antropologia da comunicação no Alto Xingú. See *HLAS* 43 : 1074.

7026 Bispo, Antonio Alexandre. O século XIX na pesquisa histórico-musical brasileira: necessidade de sua reconsideração (LAMR,2:1, Spring/Summer 1981, p. 130–142)

After taking a Cologne University Ph.D. in 1979 with a dissertation entitled "Die katholische Kirchenmusik in der Provinz São Paulo zur Zeit des brasilianischen Kaiserreiches" (Regensburg: Gustave Bosse, 1981), author joined the staff of Institut für Hymnologische und Musikethnologische Studien E.V. in Maria Laach. In this article he summons musicologists to join him, Lange, Cleofe Person de Mattos, Moura Reis, and Ayres de Andrade, in reevaluating Brazilian empire music. Brazilian sacred music in the present century has reached respectable levels only with foreigners such as Furio Franceschini and Pedro Sinzig.

7026a Garcia, José Maurício Nunes. Matinas do Natal para coro, solistas, orquestra e orgão. Rio de Janeiro: FUNARTE-MEC, Associação de Canto Coral, 1978. xiv p. of text in Portuguese and English, 69 p. of music; portrait.

Composed for performance Dec. 25, 1799, the year after Garcia became music director of Rio de Janeiro cathedral, these eight orchestrally accompanied Christmas responsories for four-pt. chorus (soprano, alto, tenor, bass) and soloists, are of highest value. They show how accomplished a composer Garcia had already become a decade before the court moved from Lisbon to Rio de Janeiro. They also prove how capable were both singers and instrumentalists in Rio de Janeiro cathedral in 1799 (date of organ accompanied version) and in 1801 (orchestral version). On their evidence, Rio de Janeiro did not lag notably behind contemporary Lisbon. In conformity with classic era key preferences, every responsory is in major (B flat, F, G, D, G, C, E flat, C [starting in c minor]). Where key shifts occur, they are always to the dominant (responsories 1, 2, 5–8). For variety, Garcia relies on meter, tempo, and texture changes. In her valuable bilingual introduction, Cleofe Person de Mattos—maximum authority on Garcia—ascribes the manuscripts used as sources for the present edition to the chapter library of Rio de Janeiro cathedral. Of Garcia's seven *matinas* surviving in whole or part, this set is both earliest and the only set for Christmas. René Brighenti realized the figured bass, and in 1967 Ernelinda do Couto prepared the exquisite hand-copied score.

Hill, Jonathan. Kamayurá flute music; a study of music as meta-communication. See *HLAS 43:1128.*

7027 Lange, Francisco Curt. Certidão de batismo de Victória Maria de Cruz, mae do Padre José Maurício Nunes Garcia; 16 de novembre de 1738 (Barroco [Minas Gerais] 11, 1981, p. 91–94)

The black mother of the "father of Brazilian music" was baptized at São Gonçalo do Monte chapel near Cachoeira do Campo, Minas Gerais. The famous composer born when she was 29 was her son by a second marriage after she left Minas.

7028 ———. História da música na Capitania Geral das Minas Gerais. v. 2, A Irmandade de São José dos Homens Pardos ou Bem Casados. Ouro Preto, Brazil: Museo da Inconfidência, 1979. 231 p.; facs.; ill.; tables (Anuário; 6)

Vol. 2 in Lange's projected 12-volume *História da música na Capitania Geral das Minas Gerais.* In admirable detail he rescues names, biographies to the extent possible, and functions of 228 musicians belonging to St. Joseph's Brotherhood of Colored Men in Vila Rica between 1752–1821. Lange's impartiality enables him to surround the more famous mulatto musicians such as Inácio Pareiras Neves (director of St. Joseph festivities in 1759, 1760, 1762, 1776, 1778, 1784, 1786, 1788); Francisco Gomes da Rocha (1791, 1795, 1798, 1799, 1801); and Marcos Coelho Netto Senior (1781, 1782, 1783); and Júnior (1808–1813) with a galaxy of singers and of instrumentalists who played rabeca, rabecão, trompa, clarim, flauta, clarineta, fagote, and organ.

7029 ———. Passaportes de passageiros, alunos do Real Seminário Patriarcal de Música e famílias de músicos que partiram para o Brasil (Barroco [Minas Gerais] 11, 1981, p. 83–91)

Theodore Cyro de Souza, born at Caldas da Raynha in late 1761 entered the Patriarcal 14 May 1768. He left Lisbon 26 Nov. 1781 for Bahia, where he was royally appointed to be cathedral chapelmaster. The article contains biographical data concerning other emigrating musicians copied from passports and concludes with a list of Brazilian composers' music in the palace music collection at Vila Viçosa that includes

Raphael Coelho Machado's orchestral *Te Deum* (1855), an Adolph Maersch's *Marcha* dedicated to Pedro V (7 Aug. 1855), and Francisco Xavier Bomtempo's *Doze Valsas* published at Rio by Heaton e Rensburg (1847).

7030 ———. Rio de Janeiro Ordem Terceira de Nossa Senhora do Carmo Livros de Despesas e Ternos: 1753–1805 (Barroco [Minas Gerais] 11, 1981, p. 94–114)

Lists of Rio musicians and their payments compiled from Third Order of Our Lady of Mount Carmel account books. Names include six mestres de capela active 1766–1805 and six organists.

7031 Maciel, Argentina. Valsas para piano. Prefácio: Dados biográficos de autora, por Jaime C. Diniz. Recife, Brazil: Edição do Coro Guararapes do Recife, 1980. 14 p.; facsims.; music; plate.

Welcome addition to the slim body of published compositions by women of Northeastern Brazil. Argentina Barbosa Vianna Maciel (b. Recife, 7 March 1888), studied piano there with Tereza Diniz before marrying in 1910 José do Rego Araújo Maciel, businessman in Pesqueira, Pernambuco. Settled there, she dedicated her maiden published composition *Meu Amor* (*Gazeta de Pesqueira*, 26 Nov. 1915) to her husband. The first music teacher of the author of the preface (who now ranks among principal Brazilian musicologists), she remained a central figure in Pesqueira music life until her husband's death in 1936. Her numerous compositions ranged from Te Deums to tangos. Of the six exquisite valsas in the present edition, all were composed at Pesqueira except *Dolores* (at Olinda). All except the last (*Alma de Elite*, dedicated to her father who died in 1920) are in minor (one, two, or three flats) with a tonic major trio.

7032 Mariz, Vasco. Heitor Villa-Lobos compositor brasileiro. 5. ed. Rio de Janeiro: MEC/DAC/Museu Villa-Lobos, 1977. 173 p.; bibl.; facsims.; plates.

First published in 1949, twice translated into English (1963 and 1970), and once into French (1965), this discriminating life-and-works account has been notably enriched during the 28 intervening years with new data and criticism generously utilized by the illustrious author in this "final" and definitive edition.

7033 Martínez, Mayra A. Solo canto cuando vengo a Cuba (RYC, 90, feb. 1980, p. 58–61, plates)

According to Chico Buarque de Hollanda, the record industry and TV do much less for young Brazilian composers and interpreters of would-be popular music now than in 1970. Foreign chains presently control what limited Brazilian entertainment product gets exposure. Rio attracts any entertainment talent that sprouts up. Regional opportunities for emerging entertainment talent do not exist.

7034 Peppercorn, Lisa M. The fifteen-year-periods in Villa-Lobos' life (IAA, 5:2, 1979, p. 179–197)

In this valuable essay—replete with complete names, exact dates and places, the author groups events in the composer's life into 15-year-spans (except for 1887–1900; his father Raúl died in 1899). Among enticing features, she gives thumbnail biographies of Brazilians who influenced Villa-Lobos' life. During maturity, the least productive period (creatively) elapsed 1930–45. Immersed in well-paid duties as Superintendente da Educação Musical e Artística do Departamento de Educação da Prefeitura do Distrito Federal, he composed little of consequence during this period except the *Bachianas Brasileiras* series.

Seeger, Anthony. Por que os indios suyá cantam para as suas irmãs? See *HLAS 43:1194.*

———. What can we learn when they sing? Vocal genres of the Suyá Indians of Central Brazil. See *HLAS 43:1195.*

7035 Stevenson, Robert. El Obispo benedictino brasileño a quien se debe la primera publicación pianística, 1732 (HET, 13:2, abril/junio 1980, p. 9–13)

Translation of article that appeared in *Inter-American Music Review* (1:2, Spring/Summer 1979, p. 211–215).

CARIBBEAN (except Cuba)

Cave, Roderick. Four slave songs from St. Bartholomew. See item **4634**.

Daniel, Yvonne. The potency of dance: a Haitian examination. See *HLAS 43:971.*

7036 Dower, Catherine A. They kept a tradition going (Dateline [Puerto Rico] 2 : 1, July/Aug. 1980, p. 23–25, ill.)

Survey article assessing the careers of four Puerto Rican women: Amalia Paoli Marcano (1861–1942), dramatic soprano; Elisa Tavárez de Storen (1879–1960), pianist; Monsita Ferrer Orero (1882–1966), pianist and composer; and Genoveva De Arteaga (1898–), pianist, composer, and pedagogue.

7037 Golden, Kathleen. Justino Díaz: more than good enough (Dateline [Puerto Rico] 2 : 1, July/Aug. 1980, p. 4–7, ill.)

Tribute to the operatic basso (b. Santurce, P.R. 29 Jan. 1940) creator of the role of Antony at the opening of the Lincoln Center Metropolitan Opera house (15 Sept. 1966), Mahomet in the 1969 revival of Rossini's *L'Assedio di Corinto* at La Scala. Mistakes mar the article (e.g., *Don Juan* and *Don Giovanni* are not two different operas; wrong race assigned to Marilyn Horne, b. Bradford, Pa., 16 Jan. 1934, married Henry Lewis 2 July 1960, separated 1976).

7038 Hopkin, John Barton. Music in the Jamaican Pentecostal churches (IJ/JJ, Sept. 1978, p. 23–40, music)

In preparation for his undergraduate thesis at Harvard University, author visited 16 Pentecostal services in Kingston between mid-June and Sept. of 1973. He taped an evening service (16 Sept. 1973) at the Pentecostal Gospel Temple, 111 Windward Road, Kingston 2. The transcriptions (not published with this paper) are at the Institute of Jamaica's West India Reference Library. Author's account describes and illustrates clapping patterns, tambourine, drum, and other percussion interventions, organ, electric guitar, and piano accompaniments, congregational alterations of printed gospel hymns, differences between texts favored by Pentecostals and Baptists, roles of preacher and choirs. Author clearly delineates limitations of his study, which nonetheless goes far toward capturing the ambiance, style, and function of the music here discussed.

7039 LaBrew, Arthur R. George Augustus Polgreen Bridgetower (Afro-American Music Review [Detroit] 1 : 1, July/Dec. 1981, p. 127–164)

Famous as first violinist to play the *Kreutzer Sonata* with Beethoven, Bridgetower (b. 11 Oct. 1778) was the son of a Jamaican black who upon emigrating to Europe was taken into the service of Prince Nikolaus Esterházy ("The Magnificent"), Haydn's patron. Bridgetower studied with Haydn sometime before 1789 and in the summer of that year was exhibited as a 10-year-old prodigy in England. Article contains data not hitherto used in editions of *Grove* or any other encyclopedia on the London sojourn Sept. (not Dec.) 1789 to June 1790 of Saint Georges, the mulatto violinist born on Guadeloupe (French West Indies) in 1739.

Laguerre, Michel S. Bizango: a voodoo secret society in Haiti. See *HLAS 43 : 1010.*

7040 Lalla, Barbara. Quaco Sam: a relic of archaic Jamaican speech (IJ/JJ, 45, 1981, p. 20–29, ill., music)

Author dates the song extolling plantation singer Quaco Sam 1812–1823. Text of quatrain verse and chorus published in this article need fitting to the separately published melody. However fitted, the melody recalls the gospel hymn beginning "From all the dark places of earth's heathen races"— not anything distinctively African.

7041 Lizardo, Fradique. El baile del Caimán (MHD/B, 6 : 10, May 1978, p. 62–75, bibl., ill., music)

Essay combines discussion of the bamboula with material published in *Revista/Review Interamericana* (9 : 1, Spring 1979). Enhanced with better drawn musical examples, diagrams of the steps, and photos of dancers.

7042 ———. Dos bailes dominicanos: el *Caimán* y el *Bamboulá* (RRI, 9 : 1, Spring 1979, p. 72–94, bibl., ill., map, plates)

Now preserved only at the northern coastal Puerto Plata, the "alligator dance" was brought to the Dominican Republic (presumably in the latter third of the last century) by expatriated Cubans. The dance originated in Venezuela, where Isabel Aretz has reported its continued existence. Ten incises in the "alligator dance" song collected by Ramón Díaz (transcribed in C Major, 2/4) end with a syncopated bump on a 16th-note tied to a quarter. Accompanying instruments include accordion, maracas, claves, and tambora. The *bamboulá*, now known only in Samaná province, belongs to the cult of San Rafael, and is danced the night of Oct. 23 until daybreak. Formerly danced to the sound of hourglass drums 70–80 cm high by 23 cm in diameter, the *bamboulá* was brought to the Dominican Republic around 1825 by blacks who had escaped from Louisiana. Author (who at the time of writing directed the Ballet Folklórico Dominicano) includes diagrams of dance steps, costume details, texts of the dance songs, and literary references (both dances).

7043 López Cruz, Francisco. El cabayo (ICP/R, 14:72, julio/set. 1976, p. 32–37, bibl., ill., music)

Between 1750–90, the *caballo* (or *cabayo*) was "the estribillo of such songs as tiranas, gallardas, villanescas" sung in the Spanish *tonadilla escénica*. The caballo emigrated to Puerto Rico where in the 1840s it was danced slower than the seis. However, six decades later it counted among the fastest and most repetitious sung and danced coplas. Includes six musical examples.

7044 ———. La marumba (ICP/R, 20:74, enero/marzo 1977, p. 36–39, scores)

The *marumba* (*marunga*) is a fast rural Puerto Rican couples dance. In some regions it is a subtype of the seis. The five music examples involve alternating tonic/dominant-7th major harmonies. Melodies constantly fit either the cinquillo pattern or the 3+3+2 pattern (16th-note values) in a 2/4 frame.

Macdonald, Annette C. The big drum dance of Carriacou. See *HLAS 43:1020.*

Pearse, Andrew. Music in Caribbean popular culture. See *HLAS 43:1030.*

7045 Ríos Colón, Nydia A. Bailes de Puerto Rico: apuntes para un estudio (RRI, 9:1, Spring 1979, p. 96–112, ill., plates)

Observations on the origin, provenience, and choreography of the seis, its regional variants, the *plena*, the African *bomba*, and *danza*. Musical characteristics receive scant attention.

7046 Ryman, Cheryl. The Jamaican heritage in dance (IJ/JJ, 44, 1980?, p. 2–14, map, photos)

Alphabetical glossary of dance types known in specified Jamaican localities during the last half century. Types range from quadrille and maypole to *kongo* and *kumina*. The *gere* is a funeral jump dance (western end of Jamaica). Sankey-type hymns "continue the after-burial nine-night observances."

7047 Schwartz, Francis. The bureaucracy of music in Puerto Rico (FIU/CR, 9:3, Summer 1980, p. 19–21, ill., plates)

Former music editor of the *San Juan Star* and head of the University of Puerto Rico Music Department knowingly discusses the coming role of ADAC (Administration for the Development of Art and Culture) vis-à-vis other musical entities in the island—the moribund Casals Festival, Puerto Rico Symphony Orchestra, University of Puerto Rico Music Department, Conservatory of Music, Inter-American University Music Department, and Institute of Puerto Rican Culture.

CENTRAL AMERICA

7048 Borg, Paul. The Jacaltenango miscellany: a revised catalogue (IAMR, 3:1, Fall 1980, p. 55–64)

Working from a microfilm, Borg identified works by Loyset Compère, Rodrigo de Ceballos, and provided concordances of anonymous works with numerous other manuscript sources.

7049 Flores, Bernal. La música en Costa Rica. San José: Editorial Costa Rica, 1978. 141 p.; bibl.; ill.; index.

A distinguished composer with a Ph.D. (Eastman School of Music, University of Rochester, 1964), author urges his compatriots to interest themselves in Costa Rican composers who made international reputations. Alejandro Monestel (1865–1950) after studying in the Brussels National Conservatory, returned to become organist of San José Cathedral. Later in New York, he published numerous compositions (mostly choral works) with Theodore Presser, G. Schirmer, Carl Fischer and other important firms. Julio Fonseca (1885–1950), subject of a biography in *Die Musik in Geschichte und Gegenwart*, excelled as a composer of chamber and piano works, and as song writer. Among other composers, Flores profiles Julio Mata (1899–1969), Rocío Sanz, and Benjamín Gutiérrez. Flores studies both the 19th and 20th centuries under four headings: 1) Bands, Orchestras, and Choral Groups; 2) Opera, Operetta, and Zarzuela; 3) Music Education; and 4) Musical Creation. Costa Rica's population of only 17,000 inhabitants in 1569 and slow growth during the two succeeding centuries, inhibited any spectacular developments before independence in the impoverished province of which Cartago was colonial capital.

7050 Guevara, Concepción Clara de. Los bailes de historiantes e historias de moros y cristianos (Anales [Administración del Patrimonio Cultural, San Salvador] 50, 1977, p. 33–89, bibl., maps, plates)

Moros y cristianos dance dramas reached the New World no later than 1524 or 1525 during Cortés' expedition to Honduras. Bernal Díaz del Castillo specified Coatzcoalcos in southern Mexico as the place where the indigenes' entertainment included "ciertas emboscadas de cristianos y moros." In El Salvador the Departamento de Etnografía del Patrimonio Cultural in 1975–76 registered 28 librettos for variants of the dance drama as executed in 23 different localities scattered through 10 departments of the republic.

7051 Meléndez Chaverri, Carlos. Don Manuel María Gutiérrez. San José, Costa Rica: Ministerio de Cultura, Juventud y Deportes, Departamento de Publicaciones, 1979. 194 p.; 19 leaves of plates; ill. (Serie quién fue y qué hizo?; no. 26)

This biography of the composer (1829–87) of the Costa Rican national anthem (1852) counts as one of the best thus far published of any Latin American anthem composer. Amply documented, free of cant and legend, devoid of chauvinistic zeal, the biography is notably rich in data on military band history, music education, and civic celebrations in Costa Rica, that represent hard won archival gleanings. Especially welcome are the data on José Martínez, native of St. Augustine, Florida, who after conducting the Band of the Regimiento de León at Havana, arrived in San Miguel, El Salvador in 1841, where he organized the first military band in Central America. In Oct. 1843 he was transferred to Guatemala, and in Oct. 1845 to Costa Rica, organizing and directing national bands in each country. Gutiérrez, who succeeded Martínez at his death in 1852, rose to the rank of captain in 1858—in that same year studying briefly with Espadero at Havana. In 1864 and 1882 he visited Europe to buy band instruments. In 1883 he rose to the rank of colonel.

7052 Sarmientos, Jorge. Raíces y futuro de la música en Guatemala y Latino América (Alero [Universidad de San Carlos, Guatemala] 4:1, mayo/junio 1979, p. 29–36, plates)

Sarmientos deals chiefly with the milestones in his own career as composer. While valuable as autobiography, the lecture delves no deeper into Guatemala's musical past than the Castillo brothers, Jesús (1877–1946) and Ricardo (1894–1966). Lecture was delivered in Mexico City, 4–8 Dec. 1978, at the Seminario Internacional de Creación Musical y Futura, organized by UNAM's Departamento de Investigaciones Estéticas, Facultad de Humanidades.

7053 Stevenson, Robert. Guatemala Cathedral to 1803 (IAMR, 2:2, Spring/Summer 1980, p. 27–71)

Founded in 1534, the see of Guatemala witnessed spectacular musical developments during the colonial epoch.

7054 Vela, David. Música tradicional y folklórica en América Central (SGHG/A, 47:1/4, enero/dic. 1974, p. 250–256)

Veteran author makes no new discoveries, but instead uses excerpts from the *Popol Vuh*, Bernal Díaz del Castillo, Sahagún, and Fuentes y Guzmán to define the ambience and character of indigenous music in Guatemala. Among recent writers he uncritically quotes Jesús Castillo, Segundo Luis Moreno, and Samuel Martí.

CHILE

7055 Bastos, Raquel. Ida Vivado Orsini (UCIEM/R, 32:142/144, abril/dic. 1978, p. 106–112)

The composer (b. Tacna, Peru, 1913, but brought up in Chile from age five) became a piano teacher in the Chilean National Conservatory in 1941, studied composition with Domingo Santa Cruz (1944–48) and with Free Focke in 1954. Her *Picaresca* for voice and orchestra (her own text) was premiered at Santiago by the Orquesta Sinfónica of the Universidad de Chile in Aug. 1978.

Böning, Edwald F. Das *kultrún*, die *machi*-Trommel der Mapuche. See *HLAS 43:1297*.

7056 Claro-Valdés, Samuel. Eugenio Pereira Salas, 1904–1979: in memoriam (IAMR, 2 : 2, Spring/Summer 1980, p. 146–147)

Tribute to the preeminent Chilean historian of his generation.

7057 ——. José Zapiola, músico de la Catedral de Santiago (ACH/B, 88 : 1974, 1978, p. 221–235, bibl.)

Exemplary account of the cathedral associations of Chile's "first republican musician," José Zapiola Cortés (1802–85). Documents reproduced include Zapiola's petition (9 Nov. 1827) for the post of first clarinetist in the cathedral orchestra, chapelmaster José Antonio González's report on the drunken derelictions of William Carter, deserter from the English warship *Phoebe* (1814, dated 23 Nov. 1827), and González's exaggerated report on Zapiola's "misconduct" (20 Nov. 1828). Claro Valdés adds an extremely convenient chronology of Zapiola's life. The *Himno de Yungay* of 1839 and *Himno a la Bandera* of 1848 landmarked Zapiola's composing career. In 1864 he succeeded Alzedo as cathedral chapelmaster, holding the post 10 years. His contributions to Chile's first musical periodical, *El Semanario Musical* (1852), his teaching activities in the Conservatorio Nacional beginning in 1853, and his autobiography serialized in *La Estrella de Chile* beginning in 1872, distinguish him as one of Chile's outstanding 19th-century musicians.

7058 ——. Música catedralicia en Santiago durante el siglo pasado (UCIEM/R, 33 : 148, oct./ dic. 1979, p. 7–36)

With his accustomed authority and mastery of detail derived from primary documents, Claro Valdés traces the history of cathedral music from the period of José de Campderrós (1793–1812) to the close of the 19th century. Claro Valdés' knowledge of the cathedral music archive and of all documentation having to do with musical life inside and outside the cathedral is unsurpassed and his essay ought to serve as a model of what is needed for other South American cathedrals. One example of detail hitherto ignored is the following: the London contact with B. Flight organ-makers was Alexander Caldcleugh. Having spent 1819–21 in Chile, he returned with Henry Flight and the 2,500-pound-sterling three-manual organ to Valparaíso and Santiago in 1849.

7059 ——. Recuerdos de Eugenio Pereira Salas (El Mercurio [Santiago de Chile] 80 : 28691, 2 dic. 1979, p. E4)

Recollections of the polymath who was the first to write fully documented histories of music in a South American nation.

7060 Garrido, Pablo. Historial de la cueca. Valparaíso, Chile: Ediciones Universitarias de Valparaíso, 1979. 245 p.

Luxurious history of the Chilean national dance by the prolific author of *Biografía de la Cueca* (2. ed., 1976). For a review by Daniel Quiroga, see *Revista Musical Chilena* (34 : 151, julio/sept. 1980, p. 69–70)

7061 Lémann Cazabon, Juan. Catálogo de la obra musical de Juan Lémann (UCIEM/R, 34 : 152, oct./dic. 1980, p. 28–36)

Preceded by an analysis of Lémann's three-part ballet, *Leyenda del Mar* (first part premiered 30 Nov. 1979; premiered complete Teatro Victoria, Santiago, 4 Sept. 1980), this chronological catalogue of his works composed between 1952–79 includes all desirable data. Lémann (b. Vendôme, France, 7 Aug. 1928) studied at the Chilean National Conservatory and in 1970–71 at the Juilliard School of Music, New York City (piano).

7062 Merino, Luis. Andrés Bello y la música (UCIEM/R, 35 : 153/155, enero/sept. 1981, p. 5–51)

Magisterial article embraces not only all aspects of Andrés Bello's musical interests (including translations and reviews) but also illuminates his world with great authority. This article is a triumph of Latin American musicology. The 97-item bibliography includes 24 Bello citations plus a listing of 16 periodicals published 1826–82 used in footnoting.

7063 ——. Catálogo de la obra musical de Alfonso Letelier (UCIEM/R, 35 : 153/155, enero/sept. 1981, p. 97–116)

Compiled with author's usual meticulousness, this beautiful catalogue includes every desirable information: origin of texts; length; medium; publisher and recorded versions (if any); date of premiere; and observations (including when, why, and where works were conceived).

7064 ——. Los festivales de música chilena: génesis, propósitos y trascendencia (UCIEM/R, 34 : 149/150, enero/junio 1980, p. 80–105, bibl.)

Between 1948–66, 10 biennial festivals were held, followed by the 11th in 1969. Afterwards none followed until the 12th in 1979. In this splendid history of the festivals, the editor tabulates works premiered, composers represented, genres included, and explains the mechanics of the festivals that brought unique glory to Chile during the Santa Cruz era.

7065 ———. Victor Tevah, Premio Nacional de Arte en Música, 1980 (UCIEM/R, 34 : 152, oct./dic. 1980, p. 5–22)

With his usual authority, the editor of the leading Latin American musical journal traces the career of the Chilean conductor (b. Smyrna, Greece, 26 April 1912), who was also the first interpreter to receive the National Prize of Music. Prefacing his article with a history of the National Prize, Merino concludes it with a catalogue of works by Chileans and by foreigners premiered under Tevah's baton.

7066 Pérez-Freire, Lily. Osmán Pérez Freire: 1880–1930 (EC/M, 27, 1979, p. 75–77, score)

Pérez Freire (b. Santiago, Chile, 22 Jan. 1880) was taken to Buenos Aires in 1891. He gained international fame through popular songs, including *Ay, ay, ay,* still sung by Engelbert Humperdinck, Julio Iglesias, and Antonio Zabaleta. In 1925 his *Gloria, Victoria* and *Canción Tacneña* aroused fervor during the territorial dispute between Chile and Peru. Honored in Spain where his *Himno al Soldado Español* became an official song of the royal guard by order of King Alfonso XIII, Pérez Freire died in Madrid (2 April 1930).

7067 Quiroga, Daniel. Rosita Renard en el recuerdo (UCIEM/R, 32 : 142/144, abril/dic. 1978, p. 131–136)

The eminent pianist (b. Santiago, 8 Feb. 1894) also died therein (24 May 1949) shortly after an acclaimed Carnegie Hall, New York, recital (Jan. 1949). She studied with Martin Krause at Berlin in 1910, and taught at Rochester (New York, 1917) but spent her later years teaching Bach, Mozart, Beethoven, Chopin, and Debussy at the Santiago conservatory on San Diego St.

7068 Torres, Rodrigo. Andrés Alcalde: un nuevo compositor chileno (UCIEM/R, 32 : 142/144, abril/dic. 1978, p. 113–124)

Alcalde (b. Santiago, 14 Sept. 1952)

studied composition with Alfonso Letelier Llona. His catalogue began in 1973–74 with piano works; in 1976–77 he wrote his first orchestral pieces premiered in July 1978 at the Teatro Astor by the Orquesta Sinfónica of the Universidad de Chile.

7069 Vicuña Lyon, Magdalena. Claudio Arrau a los 75 años (UCIEM/R, 32 : 142/144, abril/dic. 1978, p. 137–139)

In 1911 the Chilean government sent Arrau to Berlin for two years with Martin Krause. To make Arrau's 75th birthday, Phillips issued his version of the complete works of Chopin, and with orchestra, Brahms' Concerto, op. 15, and Liszt's 12 transcendental études. Arrau's gargantuan programs have at one time or another encompassed the entire classic repertory.

COLOMBIA

7070 Guzmán Esponda, E. Monseñor José Ignacio Perdomo Escobar (IAMR, 3 : 1, Fall 1980, p. 117–118)

Necrology reprinted from *El Tiempo* (Bogotá, 13 mayo 1980).

7071 Perdomo Escobar, José Ignacio. La ópera en Colombia. Bogotá: Litografía Arco, 1979. 107 p.; 17 leaves of plates; bibl.; ill.

Reviewed in *Inter-American Music Review* (3 : 2, Spring/Summer 1981), this handsome volume worthily closes the career of Colombia's outstanding musical historian. Valuable facsimiles of programs, arguments, advertisements, reproductions in color of scenic designs, and photographs of operatic personalities enhance the volume. A list of all operas mounted in Colombia, with precise dates (when known) follows the 75 end-notes. The text is enriched with numerous quotations from 19th-century Bogotá newspapers.

7072 Robledo de Correa, Edelmira. Olvidé tu risa: bambuco (Revista Aleph [Manizales, Colombia] 34, julio/sept. 1980, p. 17–19, musical score)

Characteristic accompaniment rhythm of this *bambuco* in 3/4 involves vigorous eighth-notes throughout the bar except on the first eighth of second beat (rest). *Bambuco* is followed by biography of the female singer-composer (b. Manizales, July

1931) who has recorded 3 LPs conjointly with tenor Gustavo Gómez Calle (a physician).

7073 Textos sobre música y folklore: Boletín de programas de la Radiodifusora Nacional de Colombia. t. 1, La música en Colombia. t. 2, La música en Latinoamérica. La música en Europa. Selección, Hjalmar de Greiff, David Feferbaum. Bogotá: Instituto Colombiano de Cultura, Subdirección de Comunicaciones Culturales, División de Publicaciones, 1978. 2 v.; bibl. (Serie Las revistas. Colección Autores nacionales; 29–30. Biblioteca colombiana de cultura)

This basic pair belongs in every prominent college and university library: vol. 1, the more valuable for the foreigner, contains 31 reprints of articles and monographs on Colombian music and folklore originally published in periodicals ranging from *Repertorio Colombiano* (15 sept. 1879) and *El Correo Musical Sudamericano* (Buenos Aires, 22 sept. 1915) to the *Boletín de Historia y Antigüedades* (22:254/255, sept. 1935). Most of these reprinted articles are nowadays inaccessible except in this volume. The most fully represented recent author in vol. 1 (p. 104–221) is Andrés Pardo Tovar (1911–72), dynamic director of Radiodifusora Nacional (1963–72). Vol. 2 begins with 21 reprinted articles dealing with music of other Latin American countries. Translated articles discuss European music and musicians (p. 285–672). Vol. 2 concludes with a useful index of all articles published in the *Boletín de Programas*, except those included in the present two-volume set.

CUBA

7074 Acosta, Leonardo. Eterna juventud de nuestra música popular (RYC, 66, fev. 1978, p. 52–59, plates)

In this survey of popular music currents since the Cuban Revolution, author concedes that bureaucracy hampered developments until the advent of the Revé orchestra in 1968. Juan Fornell, electric bassist who was Revé's arranger, formed his own band in 1969, the Van Van—with the expert in Afro-Cuban rhythms José L. Quintana (Changuito) as lead percussionist. In 1969 Leo Brouwer organized the Grupo de Experimentación Sonora, which used the most up-to-date recording techniques and electronic

aids to produce Cuban film music. New dance vogues emanated during the early 1970s from the Salón Mambí in Havana. Irakere, a 1970s offshoot of the Orquesta Cubana de Música Moderna, incorporated Cuba's best black jazz players. Directed by Chucho Valdés, this group played not only his compositions but arrangements of contradanzas by Saumell and Cervantes. Algo Nuevo, a group organized by trombonist and arranger Juan Pablo Torres, is another ensemble that used electronic instruments and synthesizers to re-create Cuban classics.

7075 Arozarena, Marcelino. Encuentro con el joven Egües (UEAC/GC, 167, mayo 1978, p. 5–6, plate)

According to the interviewer, Rémbert Egües who is of African descent occupied the highest posts in the Cuban musical hierarchy before he was 30 (President of the Ministry of Culture, Popular Music Section; Director of the TV "Youth, Dance, and Music Program;" Musical Director of the Cuban National Ballet; Vice-President of the Music Section of the Cuban League of Writers and Artists). Awarded the Order of Merit "Rubén Márquez Villena," the highest Cuban prize for artists (given by the Union of Young Communists in which he had long been an activist). Egües became a member of the Cuban Communist Party shortly before the interview.

7076 Benmayor, Rina. La *nueva trova*: new Cuban song (LAMR, 2:1, Spring/Summer 1981, p. 11–44)

Author states that "over the years, the presence of new Cuban song in the United States has consisted of less than five albums, with limited distribution, and four small concert tours—by Silvio Rodríguez, Pablo Milanés, Grupo Manguaré, and Grupo Moncada—primarily on the East Coast and only since the easing of travel restrictions in 1977. In order to hear the *nueva trova* you have to go to Cuba, acquire records somewhere outside the United States (Mexico, Venezuela, Puerto Rico, Spain, Italy, Finland, or Sweden), or plug into a network of Cubaphiles." She adds as a "complement to the essentially historical overview" a discography, and publishes 16 representative texts.

7077 Carpentier, Alejo. La música en Cuba. La Habana: Editorial Letras Cubanas, 1979. 290 p.; music; ports.

Second edition, published 26 years

after the first, corrects misprints listed in errata sheet pasted in the 1946 Mexico City edition, but leaves untouched the wrong clef in the musical example at the bottom of p. 67 (= p. 69 in 1946). The present edition adds photographs of Saumell, Cervantes, Jiménez, White, Fuentes Matons, Villate, Sánchez de Fuentes, Mauri, García Caturla, and Roldán. The musical examples at p. 121, 123, 125, not in the Mexico City edition, come without acknowledgement from Serafín Ramírez. Nine other examples are new. The major difference in the present edition is the exclusion of the last chapter "Estado Actual de la Música Cubana." As a result, the 1979 edition is less up to date than the 1946 one. For example, the 1979 one never mentions Hilario González, Argeliers León, Edgardo Martín, or so popular a composer as Ernesto Lecuona, all of whom appeared in the last chapter of the 1946 edition. The 1979 bibliography, although copy edited, still misspells the name of Mexico's leading music historian, Gabriel Saldívar y Silva. Carpentier's prejudices against Espadero, Villate, and Sánchez de Fuentes are evident as well. His greatest service to Cuban music history remains the rediscovery of Esteban Salas y Castro.

7078 Cuza Malé, Belkis. Jorge Luis Prats habla de Beethoven, Mozart y del festival (UEAC/GC, 167, mayo 1978, p. 4–5, plate)

Jorge Luis Prats (b. Camagüey, 3 July 1956) studied piano at the Conservatorio Fernández Vilar in Havana with Bárbara Díaz Alea from age six to 10. While an altar boy in an Episcopal church he learned English. In 1971 playing Beethoven's Opus 57 and Liszt studies he entered Cubanacán, where he studied four years. Cuban pedagogues highly esteemed by him include Ninoska Fernández Brito, Silvio Rodríguez Cárdenas, Harold Gramatges, and Frank Fernández. In 1977 he won the Marguerite Long-Jacques Thibaud international contest at Paris. At the time of this interview with Belkis Cuza Malé, he was preparing to record two discs in Paris (Pattern Marconi and Vogue) and to perform with three French orchestras playing Rachmaninoff's Opus 18 (May 1978).

7079 Entrevista a José María Vitier (AR, 5 : 19/20, 1979, p. 52–54, plates)
"Heart songs" sung during the 1930s

in night clubs were self-accompanied on the guitar and were often influenced by jazz. The best singers (*trovadores*) of these heart songs included Rosando Ruiz, Manuel Corona, Sindo Garay, and Alberto Villalón. The organizers of the post-Revolutionary *nueva trova* still sing their sentimental songs to the inevitable guitar with no other accompaniment.

7080 LaBrew, Arthur R. The Brindis de Salas family (Afro-American Music Review [Detroit] 1 : 1, July/Dec. 1981, p. 15–57)

The black violinist Claudio Brindis de Salas (b. Havana, 4 Aug. 1852) studied with Dancla at the Paris Conservatoire 1872–74. Beginning in 1875 he toured the Antilles. He triumphed at Mexico City in April and May of 1878. In Jan. 1882 he performed the Mendelssohn Concerto at Hannover; in Sept. 1882 he earned a sensational success at Vienna; in Oct. he played at Stuttgart; in Dec. at Dresden. Further European victories followed. He reappeared at the Teatro de Tacón 13 May 1886. On 2 Jan. 1887 he made his New York début, on 4 Jan. he played the *Kreutzer Sonata* with William Sherwood at Chickering Hall, New York, and in Feb. he played at Boston. He gave his first public concert at Buenos Aires (27 Aug. 1889), followed by four others. He gave three concerts at Santo Domingo (beginning 10 Nov. 1895) earning extravagant praise for his octaves and portamenti, but reproof for his limited repertory. In early 1911 after a concert at Ronda, Spain, he embarked for Buenos Aires where his fame had faded; he died there in obscurity (2 June 1911). Claudio's brother José Rosario Brindis de Salas, like him a violinist, toured the US as a minstrel attraction during the 1880s.

7081 ———. Doña María Martínez (Afro-American Music Review [Detroit] 1 : 1, July/Dec. 1981, p. 89–98)

María Martínez (b. Havana ca. 1827) was orphaned and thereafter adopted by a Spanish military couple at age two. The black contralto (or mezzo-soprano) accompanied her adoptive parents to Spain upon Lieutenant Aguilar y Conde's recall to the peninsula. She studied voice at Seville, won the protection of Queen Cristina of Spain and made her Parisian début (1 June 1850) in an afternoon concert at which she sang *El Tango Americano* and two other Spanish songs to her own guitar accompaniment. Gorin played Gottschalk's *Le Bananier* at the same concert. She returned to Paris in May 1852 to sing Spanish folk songs to her own guitar accompaniment at a wedding party covered by the press.

7082 Rivero, Angel. La reina cantadora (RYC, 90, feb. 1980, p. 26–28)
Interview with a black singer of Santiago de Cuba (b. 3 Sept. 1895). Interviewer eulogizes her but denies her claim of being a descendant of "French singers." Her children, grandchildren, and great-grandchildren follow her example in being "all dancers, singers, or players of catá."

7083 Struiski, Pavel. Hacia las cumbres de la maestría musical (URSS/AL, 1, 1979, p. 188–194, plate)
Jorge López Marín (b. Havana, 8 May 1949) studied with Amadeo Roldán at the National Conservatory and with José Ardévol (composition) and Federico Smith (theory) at the Escuela Nacional de Artes. In 1968 the Soviet orchestra director Daniil Tiulin, then in Cuba, recommended him for study in the Soviet Union. From 1969–75 he was enrolled in composition with Lev Kolodub and in orchestra conducting with Mikail Kaperstein at Kiev Conservatory. Graduating with honors, he next studied with Aram Khatchaturian at Moscow Conservatory. In the summer of 1978 he returned to Cuba. His numerous compositions include *Symphony No. 1*; *Concerto for Flute and Orchestra*; *Concerto for Trumpet and Orchestra*; *Concerto for Viola and Strings* (the latter two composed at Moscow); an *Obertura Cubana for Orchestra*; *Sonata for Violin and Organ*; and *Variations on Cuban Rhythms for String Quartet* (composed at Kiev). Since article lacks any musical examples, author fails to show what is peculiarly Cuban about López Marín's output.

ECUADOR

7084 Coba Andrade, Carlos A. Estudio sobre el *tumank o tsayantur*: arco musical del Ecuador (IPGH/FA, 25, junio 1978, p. 79–100, bibl., ill., map)
Contrary to other investigators who have wished to class the New World mouthbow as an importation from Africa, the author (director of Ethnomusicology, Instituto Otavaleño de Antropología) considers the *tumank* or *tsayantur* of the Shuar culture (eastern Ecuador) to be an autochthonous instrument. Author cites Izikowitz, Moreno, Bianchi, Aretz, and others in support of his thesis that the South American mouth-bow may have preceded European penetration. He adds five pages of useful diagrams showing elements of the *tumank* as presently played.

7085 Stevenson, Robert. Quito Cathedral: four centuries (IAMR, 3 : 1, Fall 1980, p. 18–38)
Describes musical life, from Diego Lobato to mid-18th-century, with synopsis of later conditions.

MEXICO

7086 Adomian, Lan. Carta abierta a mis amigos mexicanos (HET, 13 : 2, abril/junio 1980, p. 22–26)
Adomian (b. near Mogiliov-Podolsk, Ukraine, 29 April 1904) lived in Mexico from age 47 to death at 75 (9 May 1979). In 1975 he won the Premio Silvestre Revueltas. Works composed after becoming a Mexican citizen include eight symphonies, one opera, four cantatas, and a plethora of chamber works. But like most of his contemporaries, he seldom heard his works competently performed.

7087 Alcázar, Miguel. Suite para guitarra. México: Liga de Compositores, 1979. 8 p.; music.
Alcázar (b. Mexico City, 26 April 1942) organized in 1979 a Composers' Cooperative that published the following works (in 1979 unless otherwise specified): Salvador Contreras (10 Nov. 1912, Cuerámaro, Guanajuato), *Sonatina No. 1 para Piano* [Allegro Moderato-Andante Comodo e Cantabile-Allegro], 1980, 11 p.; Juan Helguera (14 Feb. 1932, Mérida, Yucatán), *Homenaje a Silvestre Revueltas para Guitarra*, 7 p.; Mario Kuri-Aldana (3 Aug. 1931, Tampico, Tamaulipas), *Tres Preludios para Piano*, 7 p.; Raúl Ladrón de Guevara (20 Oct. 1934, Naolinco, Veracruz), *Preludio y Minuetto para Guitarra*, 7 p.; Sergio Ortiz (6 June 1947, Jalapa, Veracruz), *Trio para Oboe, Clarinete y Fagot*, 14 p.; Luis Sandi (22 Feb. 1905, México), *Sinfonía Mínima para Orquesta de Arcos* [four

metronomically titled brief episodes for five strings], 15 p.; Enrique Santos (2 April 1930, México), *Fantasía para Piano*, 12 p.; Mario Stern (12 May 1936, México), *Pequeño Ostinato para Soprano, Clarinete, Viola y Violoncello*, 1979, 4 p.; Leonardo Velázquez (6 Nov. 1935, Oaxaca), *Siete Piezas Breves para Piano*, 9 p.; Jesús Villaseñor (1936, Uruapán, Michoacán), *Tripartita para Piano* [Preludio-Fuga-Toccata] (composed 1973), 11 p. All these works are handsomely printed, brief, performable, and (with the exception of Stern) not avant-garde. Address of the Liga de Compositores: Dolores 2–3° piso, México 1, D.F.; Apartado Postal M-2904; (teléfono 5-85-60-32).

7088 Bellinghausen Zinser, Karl. Jorge González Avila (HET, 14:72, enero/marzo 1981, p. 49–50)

Profiled in *Baker's Biographical Dictionary* (6. ed., 1978, p. 625) González Avila (b. Mérida, Yucatán, 10 Dec. 1925) here reveals his background before moving to Mexico City in June 1949. After studying piano eight years with Emilio Puerto Molina at his private academy and at the Conservatorio del Estado in Mérida, he won a scholarship offered by the Sociedad Amigos del Arte to study at the Conservatorio Nacional in Mexico City. Up to then he wrote neo-romantic music. In Mexico City Rodolfo Halffter converted him to serialism.

7089 Crossley-Holland, Peter. Musical artifacts of pre-hispanic Mexico: towards an interdisciplinary approach. Los Angeles: Program in Ethnomusicology, Department of Music, University of California, Los Angeles, 1980. 45 p.; bibl.; diagrams; ill.; music (Monograph Series in Ethnomusicology; no. 1)

Prefaced by J. H. Kwabena Nketia, Chairman of UCLA's Council on Ethnomusicology, this very valuable essay combines material presented 6 March 1977, San Diego, and 18 Nov. 1978, Los Angeles. The distinguished author promises "a larger work on the musical artifacts of pre-hispanic West Mexico," of which the present essay is an earnest. Deploring Curt Sachs' decree that Mesoamerica "remained astonishingly behind in music, at least in instrumental music," Crossley-Holland offers the present paper as an antidote. The eight photographs, all taken of instruments in his own personal collection, show a vessel rattle in form of gourd, tubular duct flute (stylized dog), and vessel duct flute (dog), all from Colima, preclassic; plus an annular duct flute from Nayarit, preclassic. Ten observations in the present monograph that are likely to be repeated: a tubular duct flute may well have been fitted with framed aperture not to produce beat tone, as José Luis Franco thought in Oct. 1968, but instead to lower the pitch; "it may well be that deep sounds were especially sought after in West Mexican antiquity;" Colima preclassic tubular and vessel flutes "are noticeably richer in their tonal spectra than those from other parts of West Mexico: (19 partials for lowest pitch, 11–14 for "open-fingered" positions discovered in a summer of 1977 test); when pitch series are used to diagnose cultural identity, Colima preclassic (200 BC–AD 500) tubular flutes (four holes) yield approximately a semitone series within a minor-3rd ambit, Michoacán late postclassic (AD 900–1500) tubular flutes (four holes) yield a series approximating the black keys of the piano within a major-6th, minor-6th, or minor-7th ambit; in clay group scenes, musicians never play together two different-type melody instruments (*ocarinas* and tubular flutes together, for instance); an *ocarina* and a tubular flute together do not enter Colima gravesites; rattles predominated in ensembles, suggesting "rhythm as probably the element most in evidence;" among geometric motifs delineated on music instruments, the "St. Andrew's Cross" refers plausibly to the four cardinal directions; biomorphism does not occur haphazardly in musical instruments, but rather the preferred shapes were those of living beings that were prominent in ritual; distinctively "Indian" physiognomies were not too dominant until relatively late, "say AD 300–900."

7090 Ergood, Bruce. Enfoque al corrido mexicano, tejano y gringo folk (UY/R, 21:122, marzo/abril 1979, p. 17–26)

M. E. Simmons' catalogue of Mexican corridos extended only to 1950. Contemporary corridos, which along the border harp on themes of discrimination, derive from specified individuals, and are not group compositions. While both rock and country and western outdistance ballads in border popularity, ballads persist because they fulfill group social needs.

7091 Halffter, Rodolfo. *Capricho para Violín Solo.* México: Ediciones Mexicanas de Música *in cooperation with* Ediciones de Plural, 1980. 11 p.; music.

Finished 28 June 1978, this one-movement *capriccio* runs the gamut of Paganini devices, but daubed with dissonances. Formally tooled with the composer's usual meticulous craftsmanship, the *capriccio* divides into sections. Subject B begins p. 2, line 5. Recapitulation begins p. 7, Tempo I.

7092 Lavista, Mario. Canto del alba para flauta amplificada. México: Ediciones Mexicanas de Música, 1980. 6 p.; music.

This dawnsong, prefaced by lines from Wang Wei (Tang dynasty), exploits sounds obtained by non-traditional fingering taken from Robert Dick, *The other flute* (Oxford University Press, 1975). "Excellent amplifying equipment is needed."

7093 Lemmon, Alfred E. El Archivo General de la Nación Mexicana: un fundo musical (HET, 13:2, abril/junio 1980, p. 13–18)

With maximum effect in his history of music in Mexico (1934) Gabriel Saldívar used the Ramo Inquisición of the Mexican National Archive for obtaining intriguing data on African influence, corrido, son, jarabe, huapango, and introduction of the valse. Later scholars who effectively exploited the same ramo included Gonzalo Aguirre (1970) and Noemí Quezada (1975). In *Boletín del Archivo General de la Nación* (No. 16, supplement) Vicente T. Mendoza published *tonos* by Manuel de Villaflor and Antonio Literes. Lemmon invites musical historians to exploit other ramos. He illustrates from *Colegios* (No. 33, dated 1781–82); *Temporalidades* (dated 1775); *Bienes Nacionales* (1768).

7094 Montiel Olvera, Armando. El nacionalismo musical mexicano (HET, 14:72, enero/marzo 1981, p. 17–20)

Lecture delivered by the director of the Mexican Conservatorio Nacional de Música in the conservatory auditorium "Silvestre Revueltas" (7 Nov. 1980) on the occasion of his reception as a *miembro de número* of the Ateneo Mexicano de Ciencias de la Educación. The distinguished author reviews attempts to generate a Mexican nationalist music exemplified in works by Julio Ituarte (1845–1905), Felipe Villanueva (1862–

93), Aniceto Ortega (1823–75), Gustavo E. Campa (1863–1934), Ricardo Castro (1866–1907), Manuel M. Ponce (1882–1948), José Rolón (1883–1945), Candelario Huízar (1883–1970), and others of more recent vintage. In contrast to his predecessors, Revueltas wrote nationalistic music that has been widely diffused so that Mexico is in an enviable position vis-à-vis other Spanish-speaking countries of the Americas.

7095 Pulido, Esperanza. Un corto viaje a Los Angeles (HET, 13:71, oct./dic. 1980, p. 34–36)

Summary of Latin American music instructional activities at UCLA and at East Los Angeles College (where Raymond Valencia López teaches Mexican music courses).

7096 ———. Homenaje a Lan Adomian (HET, 14:72, enero/marzo 1981, p. 67)

On 3 Nov. 1980 a concert at the Pinacoteca Virreinal was dedicated to the memory of the naturalized Mexican Lan Adomian and was sponsored by the Mexican Branch of Friends of the Hebrew University, Jerusalem. The world premiere of Adomian's *Soledades* for violin and orchestra and a performance of his flute *Balada de Terezin* revealed the composer's exceptional merits that rank him among the best creators of his time in Mexico.

7097 ———. La Universidad de California honra a Robert Stevenson (HET, 13:71, oct./dic. 1980, p. 30–32)

Biographical article.

7098 Narváez, Peter. Afro-American and Mexican street singers: an ethnohistorical hypothesis (UF/SFQ, 42:1, 1978, p. 73–84)

In a closely reasoned attempt to redress the balance tipped always toward Africa by the Herskovits school of analysis, author seeks to link blues and other Afro-American expressions with Mexican street singers' music heard along the Texas border. While not disputing the *habanera* rhythms that infected Handy's blues, author says too little concerning other recognizable Afro-Cuban infusions.

7099 Romero, Jesús C. Historia del Conservatorio Nacional de Música (HET, 14:74/75, 1981, p. 91–100)

Reprinted from *Carnet Musical* (mayo 1957, p. 206–208). Pt. 1 of this article traces the history of a foiled attempt to found a national conservatory in 1854. Giovanni Bottesini, Antonio Barilli, and Tomás León were the three-member jury deputized to examine the four candidates 9 May 1854 at 5 pm in the Teatro Principal. After considerable political maneuvering, José Antonio Gómez and Santa Anna's favorite Jaime Nunó were on 27 May declared co-winners—one to serve as director during the odd months, the other during the even. Pt. 2 of the present installment describes intrigues that preceded the premiere of Melesio Morales' opera *Ildegonda* by a traveling Italian opera troupe at the Teatro Imperial (27 Jan. 1866). Emperor Maximilian guaranteed the impresario $6000 to cover any deficits. The Conservatorio Nacional came to birth in 1866 as a project of the Sociedad Filarmónica Mexicana (founded 24 Dec. 1865). First public reunion of this society took place 18 Feb. 1866 in the Salón de Actos of the School of Medicine. Angela Peralta sang and received a diploma. Melesio Morales received a prize for the triumph of *Ildegonda*.

7100 Saldívar y Silva, Gabriel. Música y danzas en las obras de Cervantes y algunas de sus presencias en México (HET, 13:3, julio/sept. 1980, p. 3–12; 13:4, oct./dic. 1980, p. 13–20)

With his usual acuteness, Saldívar spears William Barclay Squire (1855–1927) who in his article on the "saraband" for *Grove's Dictionary*, 1908 (reprinted 1918), decreed that "New Spain is Castile." To make matters worse, A. Hyatt King in *The New Grove* (1980) labeled Squire "a competent geographer." As early as 1567 New Spain—more specifically Pátzcuaro—knew the saraband, not mentioned until 1583 in peninsular literature. Saldívar's lecture delivered 12 May 1980 during the 8th Festival Cervantino at Guanajuato concluded with a program of 19 musical numbers related to Cervantes in one way or another. Saldívar's program notes itemize Mexican counterparts or relatives of the *folía, jácara, villano, chacona,* and romances included in the program.

7101 Stevenson, Robert. Jaime Nunó after the Mexican National Anthem (IAMR, 2:2, Spring/Summer 1980, p. 103–116)

Composer's trajectory from 1854 to his death in 1908.

7102 ———. Mexican musicology, 1980 (IAMR, 3:1, Fall 1980, p. 65–87)

Aperçu of recent scholarly research by veterans Jesús Estrada (d. Mexico City, 22 Nov. 1980), Gabriel Saldívar y Silva (d. 18 Dec. 1980), and others.

7103 ———. Musicología mexicana, 1980 (HET, 13:4, oct./dic. 1980, p. 2–12)

Editor's translation of article published in *Inter-American Music Review* (3:1, Fall 1980, p. 65–87). See item **7102.**

7104 ———. Santiago de Murcia (HET, 14:72, enero/marzo 1981, p. 5–16)

Translation of article in *Inter-American Music Review* (3:1, Fall 1980, p. 89–101). See item **7105.**

7105 ———. Santiago de Murcia: a review article (IAMR, 3:1, Fall 1980, p. 89–101)

Biographical details and analysis of published and unpublished works by Murcia, whose Mexican name and fame after 1730 are thoroughly documented here.

7106 Summers, William J. Orígenes hispanos de la música misional de California (UCIEM/R, 34:149/150, enero/junio 1980, p. 34–48, ill., 5 music notations)

Owen da Silva's *Mission music of California* (Los Angeles, 1941) oversimplified California's early music history. Not only the famous Narciso Durán but also Juan Sancho, Estevan Tapis, Felipe Arroyo de la Cuesta, José Viader, and Ignacio Ibáñez came well prepared to promote instrumental and vocal performances before secularization in 1833. Santa Clara's musical library and collection of instruments excelled. Mission Indians performed works as difficult as an orchestral mass by Ignacio Jerusalem, Mexico City Cathedral Chapelmaster (1749–69).

7107 Velazco, Jorge. La música (*in* Las Humanidades en México 1950–1975. México: Universidad Nacional Autónoma de México, 1978, p. 143–164, bibl.)

Authoritative panorama by the best informed Mexican conductor-musicologist. Critical reviews of the established creators and of the emerging generation (e.g., Manuel Enríquez, Héctor Quintanar, Mario Lavista, Eduardo Mata, Jesús Villaseñor, José Luis González, Fernando Guadarrama, Jorge González Avila). Author pays Rodolfo Halffter deserved tribute. "The admirable unique

Esperanza Pulido, whose unaided titanic labors surpass all praise, has maintained continuously alive from its founding in 1968 the only Mexican music periodical, *Heterofonía.*" With rare insight Velazco touches numerous other topics, such as radio, television, opera, orchestras, music education.

7108 Warkentin, Larry. The rise and fall of Indian music in the California missions (LAMR, 2:1, Spring/Summer 1981, p. 45–65)

General survey, including a nine-page bibliography of "books, manuscripts, and articles relating to cultural life in California before 1846." Most recent publication mentioned in author's footnotes is dated 1967. Neither footnotes nor bibliography include any of the writings of William John Summers who wrote the article on "California Mission Music" for *The New Grove.* Nor does his bibliography include items by Cudworth, Göllner, Geiger, Crouch, and Higgins appended to the *New Grove* article.

PERU

7109 Claro Valdés, Samuel. Contribución musical del Obispo Martínez Compañón en Trujillo, Perú, hacia fines del siglo XVIII (UCIEM/R, 34:149/150, enero/junio 1980, p. 18–33, bibl., music)

Definitive study of music and musical information collected (1782–85) during tours of Trujillo diocese by Baltasar Martínez Compañón (1738–97). When he was transferred to Bogotá, the nine volumes of his compilations were dispatched to the Royal Library of Madrid where they have been studied often. The musical data in vol. 2, however, was never codified as well as in this essay. Includes four music notations.

7110 Mastrogiovanni, Antonio. Alejandro Núñez Allauca (Revista Musical de Venezuela [Caracas] 1:2, sept./dic. 1980, p. 101–108)

Excellent as is the intent of this first installment in an anticipated series on young Latin Americans, the information is less useful than it should be for lack of precise dates. For example, the following statements are incomplete in that they lack the specifications of exact days necessary for use in an encyclopedia: that the composer was born at Mo-

quega, Peru, "in 1943;" that "in 1969 he presented in public his *Variables para seis y Cinto Magnética* acting as conductor;" and that "in 1979 his orchestral suite in six movements *Koribeni* was premiered by the Peruvian Orquesta Sinfónica Nacional conducted by Leopoldo La Rosa."

7110a Pinilla, Enrique. Informe sobre la música en el Perú (*in* Historia del Perú. v. 9, Procesos e instituciones. Lima: Editorial Juan Mejía Baca, 1980, p. 363–671, bibl., ill., music)

First general survey of his country's music by native-born Peruvian usefully compiles information from Sas, Barbacci, Holzmann, Claro Valdés and others. Author, having long studied music composition in Spain, France, Germany and the US, fully comprehends the importance of the Peruvian past as well as present and treats diverse epochs and classes of music with a sympathy rarely found among vanguard composers. Unfortunately, numerous imprecisions, errors and irrelevancies plague otherwise authoritative *informe.*

7111 Schechter, John. El cantar histórico incaico (UCIEM/R, 34:151, julio/sept. 1980, p. 38–60)

Valuable study of Quechua terms. The *cantar histórico* persisted until 1551 (Betanzos) and 1553 (Cieza de León) but subsequently died out. *Araui* during Inca times meant love song or festive song, but by 1600 had taken on additional meanings, thanks to Christian influences.

7112 Stevenson, Robert. Cuzco Cathedral: 1546–1750 (IAMR, 2:2, Spring/Summer 1980, p. 1–25)

History of music in the South American cathedral which has the oldest book of capitular acts.

Stocks, Anthony. Tendiendo un puente entre el cielo y la tierra en alas de la canción: el uso de la música en un ritual alucinógeno de curación en el bajo Huallaga, Loreto, Perú. See *HLAS 43:1203.*

URUGUAY

7113 Pulido, Esperanza. Entrevista con Francisco Curt Lange (HET, 13:1, enero/ marzo 1980, p. 17–23)

Curt Lange (b. Eilenburg, Germany, 12 Dec. 1903) outlined his career during the 5th Conferencia sobre Educación Musical (held Mexico City, Oct. 1979) to which he and his wife María Luisa were invited by the OAS. His father, who was a piano manufacturer at Koblenz interested in pianos made especially for the tropics, played seven instruments. During study for his doctorate at Bonn in 1929, F. C. Lange simultaneously studied piano making and acoustics at the nearby Ibach factory. Lange continues with reflections on his activities after emigrating to Uruguay that effectively complement his biography in *The New Grove* (1980), 10, p. 446–447.

VENEZUELA

7114 Guido, Walter. Ficha biográfica y catálogo de la obra musical de Juan Vicente Lecuna (Revista Musical de Venezuela [Caracas] 2:3, enero/abril 1981, p. 13–25)

Lecuna (b. Valencia, Venezuela, 20 Nov. 1891), died in Rome, 15 April 1954. The present catalogue excludes works now lost, but does include unfinished works and also mentions five popular pieces signed with the pseudonym of Vincent Lander. The catalogue lists place and date of composition, instrumentation, authors of texts, language of texts, dedicatees, data on premieres, copyists, and other valuable observations.

7115 ———. Síntesis de la historia de la música en Venezuela: pt. 2 (Revista Musical de Venezuela [Caracas] 1:2, sept./dic. 1980, p. 61–73)

Excellent succinct summary of Venezuelan art music history from the Romantic epoch to the 1970s.

7116 Olsen, Dale A. Magical protection songs of the Warao Indians: pt. 2, Spirits (LAMR, 2:1, Spring/Summer 1981, p. 1–10)

Valuable study by a major authority.

7117 Peñín, José. Los estudios musicológicos en Venezuela (Revista Musical de Venezuela [Caracas] 1:2, sept./dic. 1980, p. 75–87)

Among the many virtues of this listing, the locations of newspaper articles by Manuel Landaeta Rosales and of magazine contributions by Juan Bautista Plaza are spec-

ified. However, page numbers are usually omitted and when given are not always accurately specified.

7118 Plaza, Juan Bautista. José Angel Lamas (Revista Musical de Venezuela [Caracas] 2:3, enero/abril 1981, p. 76–95)

Fundamental essay on Venezuela's premier composer (1775–1814), revised from an article published in *Revista Nacional de la Cultura* (Caracas, 14:100, sept./oct. 1953).

7119 ———. Juan Manuel Olivares: el más antiguo compositor venezolano (Revista Musical de Venezuela [Caracas] 1:1, mayo/agosto 1980, p. 57–71)

Reprinted from *Revista Nacional de Cultura* (Caracas, 8:63, julio/agosto 1947).

7120 Stevenson, Robert. José Antonio Calcaño: 1900–1978 (IAMR, 2:2, Spring/Summer 1980, p. 141–145)

Life and works of the leading Venezuelan music historian.

7121 ———. La música en la Catedral de Caracas hasta 1836: pt. 2 (Revista Musical de Venezuela [Caracas] 1:2, sept./dic. 1980, p. 15–60)

This installment, covering years 1774–1836, is enriched with four pages of musical examples by José Angel Lamas not included in article that appeared in *Revista Musical Chilena* (see *HLAS 42:7164*).

7122 Velásquez, Ronny. Notas sobre Rafael María Avila: cantor popular del Zulia, Venezuela (IPGH/FA, 29, junio 1980, p. 5–30, bibl., music, photos)

Gravedigger was the chief occupation of Rafael María Avila ("Titán"), a popular verse maker of Zulia state who died in 1945. The article, though chiefly concerned with his poetry circulating orally, concluded with the transcribed guitar-accompanied A Minor Music for Décimas glossing an Avila *cuarteta*. Ezequiel Sangroni (d. ca. 1956), who like Avila was a native of Puertos de Altagracia, wrote the décimas.

JOURNAL ABBREVIATIONS
MUSIC

AAFH/TAM The Americas. A quarterly publication of inter-American cultural history. Academy of American Franciscan History. Washington.

ACH/B Boletín de la Academia Chilena de la Historia. Santiago.

AR Areito. Areito, Inc. New York.

ASU/LAD Latin American Digest. Arizona State Univ., Center for Latin American Studies. Tempe.

BNBD Boletín Nicaragüense de Bibliografía y Documentación. Banco Central de Nicaragua, Biblioteca. Managua.

BNJM/R Revista de la Biblioteca Nacional José Martí. La Habana.

CH Cuadernos Hispanoamericanos. Instituto de Cultura Hispánica. Madrid.

EC/M Mapocho. Biblioteca Nacional, Extensión Cultural. Santiago.

FIU/CR Caribbean Review. Florida International Univ., Office of Academic Affairs. Miami.

HET Heterofonía. Revista musical bimestral. México.

IAA Ibero-Amerikanisches Archiv. Ibero-Amerikanisches Institut. Berlin, FRG.

IAMR Inter-American Music Review. R. Stevenson. Los Angeles, Calif.

ICP/R Revista del Instituto de Cultura Puertorriqueña. San Juan.

IHS/SJ Staden-Jahrbuch. Beiträge zur Brasilkunde. Instituto Hans Staden. São Paulo.

IJ/JJ Jamaica Journal. Institute of Jamaica. Kingston.

IPGH/FA Folklore Americano. Instituto Panamericano de Geografía e Historia, Comisión de Historia, Comité de Folklore. México.

LAMR Latin American Music Review. Univ. of Texas. Austin.

LARR Latin American Research Review. Univ. of North Carolina Press *for the* Latin American Studies Association. Chapel Hill.

MGG Die Musik in Geschichte und Gegenwart. Kassel. Wilhelmshöhe, FRG.

MHD/B Boletín del Museo del Hombre Dominicano. Santo Domingo.

MVW/AV Archiv für Völkerkunde. Museum für Völkerkunde in Wien und von Verein Freunde der Völkerkunde. Wien.

OAS/AM Américas. Organization of American States. Washington.

RIB Revista Interamericana de Bibliografía (Inter-American Review of Bibliography). Organization of American States. Washington.

RRI Revista/Review Interamericana. Univ. Interamericana. San Germán, Puerto Rico.

RYC Revolución y Cultura. Publicación mensual. Ministerio de Cultura. La Habana.

SGHG/A Anales de la Sociedad de Geografía e Historia de Guatemala. Guatemala.

UCC/RU Revista Universitaria. Anales de la Academia Chilena de Ciencias Naturales. Univ. Católica de Chile. Santiago.

UEAC/GC Gaceta de Cuba. Unión de Escritores y Artistas de Cuba. La Habana.

UF/SFQ Southern Folklore Quarterly. Univ. of Florida *in cooperation with the* South Atlantic Language Association. Gainesville.

UCIEM/R Revista Musical Chilena. Univ. de Chile, Instituto de Extensión Musical. Santiago.

UFP/EB Estudos Brasileiros. Univ. Federal do Paraná, Setor de Ciências Humanas, Centro de Estudos Brasileiros. Curitiba, Brazil.

UNM/JAR Journal of Anthropological Research. Univ. of New Mexico, Dept. of Anthropology. Albuquerque.

URSS/AL América Latina. Academia de Ciencias de la Unión de Repúblicas Soviéticas Socialistas. Moscú.

USP/LL Língua e Literatura. Univ. de São Paulo, Depto. de Letras, Faculdade de Filosofia, Letras e Ciências Humanas. São Paulo.

UY/R Revista de la Universidad de Yucatán. Mérida, México.

PHILOSOPHY

JUAN CARLOS TORCHIA ESTRADA, *General Secretariat, Organization of American States*

EL MATERIAL CONTENIDO EN ESTA ENTREGA—con todas sus limitaciones en cuanto a exhaustividad—no autoriza a hablar de cambios considerables en el pensamiento latinoamericano. El espectro de sus tendencias sigue siendo amplio, tal como lo indicamos en números anteriores de este *Handbook*. Lo que en ese pensamiento puede considerarse propio, en el sentido de característico o distintivo, se manifiesta en dos formas: por las filosofías que tienen por tema la realidad latinoamericana (la llamada "filosofía de la liberación," por ejemplo), y por las demás expresiones filosóficas cuando alcanzan, dentro de una temática compartida con el pensamiento europeo, rasgos originales.

La relativa estabilidad se debe también a que la filosofía occidental de estos años no muestra grandes o revolucionarias variantes. Por su parte, el estilo de trabajo filosófico actual, proveniente casi exclusivamente de fuente académica y caracterizado por una combinación del rigor metodológico con la prudente limitación del alcance temático, no se presta al trazado de grandes doctrinas.

En esta entrega, y en lo que corresponde a la interpretación de América Latina en general, deben destacarse dos obras: una de Arturo Ardao (item **7501**), valiosa y que va mucho más allá del problema que enuncia el título, y otra de Leopoldo Zea (item **7526**), que continúa el afinamiento de las tesis del autor sobre la filosofía de la historia de América Latina.

Con motivo del bicentenario del nacimiento de Andrés Bello han sido numerosas las publicaciones que se le han dedicado. De los trabajos que se refieren a su obra filosófica y recogidos en este volumen destacamos los de Arturo Ardao (item **7528**) by Olivier Baulny (item **7530**).

Vamireh Chacon ha hecho una útil contribución al editar el original alemán y la versión portuguesa de tres textos de Tobias Barreto, representante de la Escuela de Recife (item **7529**). Como presentación de textos clásicos es también de gran valor la antología del pensamiento positivista latinoamericano que Leopoldo Zea preparó para la Biblioteca Ayacucho (item **7558**). No existe dentro de ese tema, que sepamos, nada semejante.

Registramos dos obras de enfoque global sobre el pensamiento filosófico latinoamericano: la útil reedición ampliada de una obra anterior de Larroyo, ahora titulada *La filosofía iberoamericana* (item **7547**), y una nueva *Historia de la filosofía latinoamericana*, de Jaime Rubio Angulo, de la cual conocemos solamente el primer volumen (item **7566**).

Panoramas nacionales encontramos varios: un nuevo número del anuario *Cuyo*, dedicado al pensamiento argentino (item **7535**); un tercer *Cuaderno* de la Historia del Pensamiento Filosófico Argentino, que anima Diego F. Pro (item **7559**); y los *Esquemas para una historia de la filosofía ecuatoriana*, de Arturo A. Roig (item **7536**), que comporta una verdadera novedad y abre camino en un terreno prácticamente sin desbrozar.

Trabajos destacables sobre períodos o autores son: el dedicado a Djacir Menezes (item **7537**); el de Tiago Lara sobre Antonio Pedro de Figueiredo (item **7546**); el de Jorge Liberati sobre Vaz Ferreira (item **7549**); el de Solomon Lipp sobre Leopoldo Zea (item **7550**); el de Borges de Macedo sobre *A liberdade no Império* (item **7551**); el de Javier Sasso sobre Salazar Bondy (item **7567**); y el de Vera y Cuspinera sobre Vasconcelos (item **7576**). En conjunto es una contribución apreciable, a la que habría que agregar algunos buenos artículos.

El Banco Central del Ecuador ha comenzado una serie de gran valor: la Biblioteca Básica del Pensamiento Ecuatoriano, de la cual conocemos ocho volúmenes. Sabemos sin embargo que se han publicado otros, algunos de los cuales incluiremos en el próximo número de este *Handbook*. En esta sección hemos recogido las antologías de Julio Enrique Moreno (item **7554**), Alfredo Espinoza Tamayo (item **7585**), Federico González Suárez (item **7588**), Jacinto Jijón y Caamaño (item **7592**), Angel Modesto Paredes (item **7602**), y los correspondientes al *Pensamiento idealista ecuatoriano* (item **7604**) y al *Pensamiento romántico ecuatoriano* (item **7605**). Es una iniciativa realmente encomiable.

En materia de historia de las ideas, continúa la profusión de publicaciones sobre Mariátegui. La Biblioteca Ayacucho ha reeditado los *Siete ensayos* en una cuidada edición (item **7599**), y los 50 años de la aparición de ese libro se han celebrado con una publicación especial (item **7615**). Otros escritos políticos de Mariátegui se han recogido en una edición mexicana (item **7598**). La bibliografía sobre al autor peruano ha trascendido la lengua española, como puede verse en varios trabajos (items **7582, 7616, 7626 y 7627**). Un útil ensayo bibliográfico es el de Harry E. Vanden en la *Latin American Research Review* (item **7621**).

Una de las obras más útiles que se han publicado recientemente en el campo de la historia de las ideas es la preparada por el eminente historiador argentino José Luis Romero en colaboración con Luis Alberto Romero: *El pensamiento conservador: 1815–1898* (item **7603**).

Destacables obras de conjunto son también la de Boleslao Lewin sobre Rousseau en la independencia de Latinoamérica (item **7593**), la de Juan Marichal sobre la historia intelectual latinoamericana (item **7600**) y la de Abelardo Villegas sobre *Transformismo y revolución en el pensamiento latinoamericano* (item **7622**). En cuanto a estudios dedicados a figuras individuales se destacan la escrita sobre José Bonifácio de Andrade e Silva por Vicente Barreto (item **7579**), y la de García Salvatecci sobre Haya de la Torre (item **7591**).

Dos trabajos sobre la relación de Bentham con América Latina resultan muy oportunos: el de Pedro Schwartz (item **7514**) y el de Miriam Williford (item **7625**).

Otros estudios dignos de mención—siempre en el campo más amplio de la historia de las ideas—son el de Hugo Biagini sobre la generación argentina del 80 (item **7580**); el de Nick Mills sobre el liberalismo en Ecuador (item **7601**); el de Arturo A. Roig sobre Deodoro Roca (item **7610**); el de Bernardo Subercaseaux sobre positivismo y liberalismo en Chile (item **7618**); y el de Caio Navarro de Toledo sobre el Instituto Superior de Estudios Brasileiros (ISEB, item **7619**).

Las obras de crítica sobre historia de la filosofía y filosofía contemporánea revisten las características que hemos señalado en otras oportunidades. En esta entrega, las de contenido más ambicioso son: la de Rodolfo Agoglia sobre la filosofía moderna (item **7637**); la de Carla Cordua sobre Hegel (item **7644**); la de Dino Garber sobre Leibniz (item **7646**); la dedicada a diversas corrientes contemporáneas bajo la coordinación de Abelardo Villegas (item **7671**); la de Francovich sobre los "nuevos filósofos" franceses (item **7672**); la de Eduardo Rabossi sobre la filosofía analítica (item **7685**); y la de Javier Sasso sobre Althusser (item **7688**). La calidad de muchos artículos hace imposible mencionarlos sin hacer la lista muy extensa o caer en injustas omisiones.

Entre las obras de mayor contenido técnico recordamos la de Miró Quesada (item 7705), a pesar de su carácter introductorio; los libros de Eduardo Rabossi sobre ética desde el ángulo analítico (items 7711 y 7712) y la de Rodolfo Agoglia sobre filosofía de la historia (item 7714).

Un grupo de destacados autores ha rendido justiciero homenaje a la labor filosófica—aún en pleno desarrollo—del Profesor Risieri Frondizi (item 7719). Jorge Gracia ha sido el editor de ese valioso volumen.

Del 18 al 23 de octubre de 1981 tuvo lugar en Florida State University (Tallahassee, Florida), el Décimo Congreso Interamericano de Filosofía, auspiciado por la Sociedad Interamericana de Filosofía y la American Philosophical Association. El tema central del Congreso fue: "Los Derechos Humanos." No se ha tenido noticia aún sobre la publicación de sus actas.

A partir de la próxima entrega (*HLAS 46*), se modificará la estructura de esta Sección. El material anotado se limitará a la literatura crítica sobre el pensamiento latinoamericano y a los trabajos actualmente recogidos en la Subsección Historia de las Ideas. Podrán incluirse también escritos que se refieran a la interpretación de América Latina en general, desde un punto de vista filosófico muy amplio. La producción filosófica propiamente dicha (trabajos críticos sobre historia de la filosofía e investigación en los campos de las distintas disciplinas filosóficas) se recogerá en la Introducción, pero sólo en sus aspectos más salientes o que impliquen mayor novedad. No se pretenderá, como hasta ahora, que esa producción se refleje en el cuerpo de la Sección, con una anotación para cada trabajo.

Ello obedece a dos principales razones. La primera es la tendencia del *Handbook* a limitarse a materiales referentes a América Latina, excluyendo los propios de disciplinas académicas. La segunda razón es la imposibilidad de abarcar hoy la totalidad de la producción filosófica latinoamericana sin excederse de un espacio razonable dentro de la economía total del volumen.

En lo que respecta al segundo motivo, puede observarse que entre el *HLAS 20* (1958) y *HLAS 42* (1980) la Sección de Filosofía acrecentó tres veces su extensión, proporción que es aplicable tanto al número de páginas como al número de trabajos recogidos.

No obstante la intensa selectividad que producirá el reducirse a la Introducción— aun ampliando sus dimensiones—para recoger la producción filosófica propiamente dicha, trataremos de darle el carácter más representativo posible. Si bien el criterio de calidad será por fuerza predominante, este criterio deberá aplicarse a *todas* las manifestaciones y corrientes filosóficas, con independencia de las preferencias personales del responsable de la Sección. Esta práctica de la máxima amplitud es una regla de oro para todo instrumento bibliográfico que pretende ser un servicio al investigador, pero conviene reiterarla a pesar de su carácter obvio.

En esta bibliografía se incluyen libros y artículos filosóficos de autores latinoamericanos, y trabajos de autores no latinoamericanos que se ocupen del pensamiento de América Latina.

Bastante más de la mitad de las publicaciones recogidas corresponden a los años 1979 y 1980, en tanto más de la cuarta parte de ellas son del año 1978 y anteriores. El número más pequeño corresponde a 1981 y 1982. Hemos continuado la práctica de incorporar publicaciones anteriormente no incluidas, aunque no fueran recientes.

En la Subsección "Obras Generales y Didácticas" se agrupan los trabajos que corresponden a ese título, pero también otros que, por su número, no justificarían una subsección independiente. También se incluyen en ella libros y artículos que se refieren a Latinoamérica en general, como tema o problema. Las demás divisiones son las habituales en esta Sección.

OBRAS GENERALES Y DIDACTICAS

7501 Ardao, Arturo. Génesis de la idea y el nombre de América Latina. Caracas, Venezuela: Centro de Estudios Latinoamericanos Rómulo Gallegos, 1980. 254 p. (Colección Enrique Bernardo Nuñez; 3)

Investiga: 1) el origen del nombre "América Latina;" 2) las ideas de unión de las Repúblicas hispanoamericanas antes de 1890; y 3) la participación de José M. Torres Caicedo (crítico colombiano que vivió casi toda su vida en Europa) en los dos primeros temas. (Torres Caicedo habría sido el primero en emplear la expresión 'América Latina'.) En varios sentidos es una investigación valiosa y original.

7502 Arroyave Calle, Julio César. La filosofía en América: fenomenología del conocimiento, filosofía del ser y los valores, teoría de la ciencia. Medellín, Colombia: Editorial Etcétera, 1979. 355 p.; bibl.

Se trata, en realidad, de un intento de introducción a la filosofía.

7503 Bobbio Rosas, Fernando. El concepto de realidad (UNMSM/L, 48:84/85, 2. semestre, 1976, p. 49–70)

Se buscan precisiones sobre conceptos como "realidad," "cosa," "objeto," etc., a la luz de numerosas citas de filósofos contemporáneos.

7504 Briceño Guerrero, José M. La identificación americana con la Europa segunda. Mérida, Venezuela: Universidad de los Andes, Ediciones del Rectorado, 1977. 106 p.; bibl.

Reflexiones sobre las relaciones entre Europa y América. Distingue entre una "razón primera" (mítica) y una "razón segunda" (científica y racionalista), de donde su aplicación al título. Trabajo de naturaleza ensayística.

7505 Casas, Miguel Gonzalo. Introducción al pensamiento real. Edición al cuidado de Delia Ruiz y Armando Martínez; portada, Carlos Duguech. Buenos Aires, Argentina: Editorial Hypatia, 1979. 114 p.

Reproduce seis "encuentros" o charlas que el autor diera en Mendoza (Argentina) en 1976. Expresa libremente el pensamiento personal de Casas, de base cristiana y enraizado en clásicos como San Agustín, Platón y Aristóteles, pero matizado también por la influencia de autores modernos y contemporáneos como Hegel, Husserl, Sciacca y Buber, entre otros.

7506 Castro H., Guillermo. El proceso de la cultura latinoamericana, 1898–1930: José Carlos Mariátegui (CDLA, 20:118, enero/feb. 1980, p. 9–34)

Capítulo de una tesis de maestría. El enfoque es marxista.

7507 Chong, Moisés M. Panorama de la filosofía en España (LNB/L, 291, junio 1981, p. 29–67)

Visión panorámica desde el siglo XIII al XIX.

7508 Coloquio Latinoamericano sobre Pluralismo Cultural, 2d, *Buenos Aires, 1978.* Pluralismo cultural. Segundo Coloquio Latinoamericano, organizado por el Congreso Judío Latinoamericano, rama del Congreso Judío Mundial, Centro Cultural Gral. San Martín de la Municipalidad de la Ciudad de Bs.As., 4, 5 y 6 de diciembre de 1978. Consejo asesor del coloquio, Natalio Botana *et al.* Coordinación del coloquio, Elena Saidman. Desgrabación del coloquio, Emilia Pepa. Buenos Aires: Congreso Judío Latinoamericano, 1980. 252 p.; ill.

Los tres grandes temas de este coloquio fueron: "Pluralismo en Ciencia y Filosofía;" "Pluralismo en Ciencias Sociales;" e "Inmigración, Integración y Pluralismo en América Latina." El más directamente relacionado con esta Sección es el trabajo de Eugenio Pucciarelli, "El Pluralismo en Filosofía."

7509 El Compromiso del intelectual: ensayos. José Martí *et al.* Introd. y selección, María Guerra y Ezequiel Maldonado. México, D.F.: Editorial Nuestro Tiempo, 1979. 244 p.; bibl. (Colección Pensamiento latinoamericano)

Libro antológico, alineado claramente en favor de la Revolución cubana y posiciones afines. Recoge textos de Martí, Juan Marinello, Fidel Castro, Raúl Roa, Ernesto Che Guevara, Mariátegui, Martínez Estrada, Aníbal Ponce, etc.

7510 Cortés del Moral, Rodolfo. Dialéctica. Diseño de la portada, Arturo Silva. México: Editorial Edicol, 1978. 239 p.; bibl. (Sociológica, conceptos; 22)

Introducción que expone el concepto de dialéctica históricamente, en casos salientes desde los presocráticos hasta Marx, y luego en varios sectores del pensamiento contemporáneo. Siguen luego consideraciones del autor sobre el tema y una breve antología.

7511 Encontro Nacional de Professores de Filosofia, *São Paulo, Brazil, 1978.* A filosofia e o ensino da filosofia: teses e debates apresentados no Encontro Nacional de Professores de Filosofia, São Paulo, 26 a 29 de outubro de 1978. Capa, Francisco Amêndola. São Paulo: Editora Convívio, 1979. 315 p.; bibl.

Recoge las exposiciones de los ponentes y los comentarios realizados. La primera parte se refiere a la enseñanza de la filosofía en todos los niveles, abierta por una presentación del filósofo francés Georges Gusdorf sobre "Filosofía y Universidad." La segunda se dedica al tema "Filosofía y Sociedad," y en ella destacamos las exposiciones de Miguel Reale, "A Filosofia e a Cultura Brasileira;" de Ubiratan de Macedo, "A Filosofia e a Ideologia;" y de Adolpho Crippa, "A Filosofia e o Desenvolvimento Brasileiro."

7512 *Escritos de Filosofía.* Academia Nacional de Ciencias, Centro de Estudios Filosóficos. Vol. 2, No. 3, enero/junio 1979– . Buenos Aires.

Siguiendo con la característica de esta revista, de tratar un tema especial en cada número. El presente está dedicado al mito, con el siguiente contenido: L. Noussan Lettry, "Mito y Pregunta;" M. Riani, "Proximidad y Distancia en la Interpretación Contemporánea de los Mitos;" F. García Bazán, "La Estructura de la Conciencia Mítica;" E. J. Cordeu, "Reflexiones sobre la Hermenéutica del Mito en la Etnología;" A. Pérez Diez, "La Aproximación Etnográfica al Mito en el Contexto Cultural;" E. Albizu, "Un Aporte a la Concepción Simbológica del Mito: G. F. Creuzer;" N. L. Cordero, "El Mito Hesiódico de las Edades del Hombre;" C. M. Herrán, "Los Mitos y la Filosofía de Platón;" E. La Croce, "El Mito de la Caverna;" A. Camarero Benito, "El 'Mythos' de la Poética Aristotélica: Estructura Literaria;" H. F. Bauzá,

"Roma: Síntesis entre Mito e Historia;" G. Maturo, "El Mito, Fundamento y Clave de la Cultura;" A. Castellán, "Persistencia de un Mito: las Formas Históricas del Laberinto;" E. Tabernig, "La Degradación del Mito;" E. Pucciarelli, "La Ambigüedad del Tiempo en el Mito."

7513 Gallardo, Helio. Comunicación filosófica y coloquios de filosofía (UCR/RF, 16:44, julio/dic. 1978, p. 203–210)

Se compone de dos partes, ambas presentadas al Coloquio Centroamericano de Profesores Universitarios de Filosofía (1978). La primera es una reflexión sobre el valor y la oportunidad del Coloquio, que concluye, parafraseando una expresión de Ernesto Che Guevara, con esta frase: "el filósofo debe ser, también, una fría máquina de matar." La segunda parte es un breve trabajo sobre Althusser.

7514 García Bacca, Juan David. Lecciones de historia de la filosofía. v. 2. Caracas: Universidad Central de Venezuela, Ediciones de la Biblioteca, 1973– 1 v. (842 p.) (Colección Filosofía; 2. Ediciones de la Biblioteca; 44)

Los autores tratados en este tomo son Kant, Hegel y Marx. A pesar de su título no es un manual. El estilo de exposición está tan alejado de lo convencional como es dable esperar de este autor, que en general requiere un particular esfuerzo de comprensión.

7515 Hualde de Pérez Guilhou, Margarita and **Marta Bronislawa Duda.** Las dos visitas de Ortega y Gasset a Mendoza (UNC/RHAA, 9:17/18, 1972/1979, p. 99–107)

Se reconstruye el efecto de las visitas (1916, 1928 y durante la Guerra Civil española), más bien en sus manifestaciones externas, a través de las crónicas periodísticas de la época.

7516 Lértora Mendoza, Celina A. Análisis de las proposiciones filosóficas (UI/RF, 11:32, mayo/agosto 1978, p. 307–317)

Intento beneficamente afectado por las exigencias del método científico, pero que encuentra una justificación razonable para la función de las proposiciones filosóficas.

7517 Marquinez A., Germán. Fernando González: filósofo de la autoexpresión latinoamericana (USB/F, 22:64, enero/abril 1980, p. 105–115)

El objetivo es reivindicar el título de

"filósofo" para un escritor colombiano habitualmente no reconocido como tal.

7518 Miró Quesada, Francisco. Los nuevos valores de la cultura contemporánea y su proyección en el futuro de la humanidad (PAIGH/H, 89, enero/junio 1980, p. 75–90)

Es un interesante trabajo sobre el racionalismo como característica de la cultura occidental, su valor para la plena realización humana, sus consecuencias inconvenientes y la necesidad de continuarlo críticamente en función de lo que puede avizorarse del futuro de la humanidad. Tema de filosofía de la historia por un autor que quizá sea quien con más propiedad científica se ha ocupado en América Latina del problema de la razón.

7519 Pensamento parcial e total. Idealizador e coordenador da coleção, Stanislavs Ladusāns. São Paulo: Edições Loyola, 1977. 294 p.; bibl. (Série Investigações filosóficas de atualidade; v. 1)

El título no da idea del contenido. Las tres primeras partes se ocupan, respectivamente, de algunas ideologías actuales; del pensamiento de Husserl y Heidegger en relación con las ideologías; y de ideología, religión y metafísica. La cuarta parte contiene un conjunto de trabajos sobre la filosofía cristiana. La que más interesa para nuestro propósito es la quinta y última, sobre filosofía e ideologías y universidad en el país. Sus autores son: C. Lopes de Mattos, M. Reale, J. A. Tobias, M. R. y R. C. Covian, I. Brandão y S. Ladusāns. Los artículos de las otras partes están escritos en su mayor parte por autores europeos, pero además de dos brasileños hay dos hispanoamericanos: Alberto Caturelli, de Argentina, y Agustín Basave, de México.

7520 Perdomo de González, Mireya. Bibliografía de Juan D. García Bacca. Presentación, Ermila Elíes de Pérez Perazzo. Caracas: Universidad Central de Venezuela, Dirección de Bibliotecas, Información, Documentación y Publicaciones, Departamento de Orientación, Información y Documentación, 1981. 77 p.; index.

García Bacca, uno de los principales "transterrados" españoles, enseña en Venezuela desde 1946. Esta bibliografía contiene 500 títulos. La precede un sintético *curriculum vitae*.

7521 Pino Iturrieta, Elías. Latinoamérica en el positivismo venezolano (*in* Encuentro de Historiadores Latinoamericanos y del Caribe, 2d, Caracas, 1977. Los estudios históricos en América Latina: ponencias, acuerdos y resoluciones: Caracas, 20–26 de marzo de 1977. Caracas: Universidad Central de Venezuela, Facultad de Humanidades y Educación, Escuela de Historia, 1979, v. 1, t. 2, p. 715–722)

Los autores considerados (Arcaya, Gil Fortoul, Vallenilla Lanz, Zumeta) se ocuparon sólo lateralmente de América Latina en su conjunto. El artículo, breve pero útil, trata de las categorías positivistas con que lo hicieron.

7522 Roig, Arturo Andrés. La experiencia iberoamericana de lo utópico y las primeras formulaciones de una "utopía para sí" (IPGH/RHI, 3, 2. época, 1971, p. 53–67)

La utopía es entendida en un sentido amplio, que permite al autor hablar de una "función utópica," presente de un modo u otro en todas las sociedades. Señala luego el elemento utópico en varias manifestaciones de la historia latinoamericana, culminando con la "utopía" de la unidad regional en Bolívar.

7523 Salmerón, Fernando. El Instituto de Investigaciones Filosóficas: informe de doce años (UV/PH, 26, nueva época, abril/junio 1978, p. 3–19)

Importante documento para seguir la marcha de un sector muy relevante de la filosofía en México desde mediados de la década del 60 hasta la actualidad. Ilustra sobre aspectos institucionales pero también sobre la orientación filosófica (filosofía "científica" o "analítica"). El Instituto a que se refiere es el de la Universidad Nacional de México.

7524 Sánchez Vázquez, Adolfo. Filosofía, ideología y sociedad (CAM, 220:5, sept./oct. 1979, p. 149–169)

El tema es estudiado en función del análisis crítico, desde el punto de vista marxista del autor, de un grupo de trabajos del filósofo español José Ferrater Mora (del mismo autor, véase *HLAS 42:7537*).

7525 Torchia Estrada, Juan Carlos. América Latina: origen de un nombre y una idea (RIB, 32:1, 1982, p. 47–53)

Ensayo bibliográfico sobre el libro de Arturo Ardao, *Génesis de la idea y el nombre de América Latina* (1980, véase item **7501**).

7526 Zea, Leopoldo. Latinoamérica en la encrucijada de la historia. México: Universidad Nacional Autónoma de México, Coordinación de Humanidades, Centro Coordinador y Difusor de Estudios Latinoamericanos, 1981. 205 p.; bibl. (Nuestra América; 1)

Reúne 12 trabajos, de los cuales tres son inéditos y el resto publicados recientemente. Se reiteran las principales tesis expuestas en obras básicas del autor, como *América en la historia* (1957) y *Filosofía de la historia americana* (1978), además de numerosos otros escritos; pero ello se hace como es frecuente en Zea: viendo los mismos problemas desde diferentes ángulos, perfilando las tesis en función de nuevos enfoques, propios o ajenos, y poniendo dichas tesis a la prueba de nuevos hechos y nuevas opiniones.

PENSAMIENTO LATINOAMERICANO: FILOSOFIA LATINOAMERICANA

7527 Ardao, Arturo. Bello y el concepto de "fundadores" de la filosofía latinoamericana (IPGH/RHI, 3, 2. época, 1981, p. 21–28)

Destaca con justicia la posición de Andrés Bello en el grupo de los filósofos latinoamericanos que Francisco Romero denominó de "los fundadores."

7528 ———. La etapa filosófica de Bello en Londres (*in* Bello y Londres: segundo congreso del bicentenario. Caracas: Fundación La Casa de Bello, 1981, t. 2, p. 145–169)

Excelente trabajo que analiza las relaciones de Bello, durante su estadía en Londres, con los ideólogos franceses, con la escuela utilitarista y con la escuela escocesa. Concluye que la influencia predominante fue la de la filosofía francesa.

7529 Barreto de Menezes, Tobias. Monografias em alemão. Prefácio, tradução e notas do Vamireh Chacon, em colaboração com Theodor Huckelmann e Heinrich Konig. Brasília, D.F.: Editora Gráfica Alvorada, 1978. 74 p.; bibl.; facsims.

Interessante publicación que pone a mano tres textos de Tobias Barreto, escritos y publicados en alemán. El más extenso, *El Brasil tal como es, desde el punto de vista literario*, apareció en Escada (Pernambuco), en 1876. Los textos se presentan en el original alemán y una traducción al portugués y son precedidos de una breve introducción a

cargo de Vamireh Chacon: "O Germanismo da Escola do Recife."

7530 Baulny, Olivier. Andrés Bello et la philosophie anglaise (*in* Bello y Londres: segundo congreso del bicentenario. Caracas: Fundación La Casa de Bello, 1981, t. 2, p. 191–209)

Exposición muy completa de las lecturas filosóficas de Bello (6 no sólo inglesas), destacando el interés de Bello por la filosofía del lenguaje.

7531 Cerutti-Guldberg, Horacio. Concepto y modalidades de la filosofía de la liberación latinoamericana (BCE/C, 2:5, sept./dic. 1979, p. 128–138)

Partidario y estudioso de la filosofía de la liberación, el autor distingue y expone cuatro corrientes dentro de ella. Util como esta caracterización es, se limita por el hecho de que no se señalan autores y obras dentro de cada corriente estudiada.

7532 Cesar, Constança Marcondes. Vicente Ferreira da Silva e o pensamento sulamericano (Reflexão [Pontifícia Universidade Católica de Campinas, Instituto de Filosofia e Teologia, São Paulo, Brasil] 5:17, maio/agosto 1980, p. 19–24)

Este breve trabajo se refiere a lo que Vicente Ferreira da Silva, destacado pensador brasileño, pensó sobre la filosofía en América, por comparación con los temas y la modalidad de la filosofía europea.

7533 Chile. Congreso. Biblioteca. Bibliografía chilena de filosofía: desde fines del siglo XVI hasta el presente. Ilus. de la portada, Lucca de la Robbia, Duomo de Florencia. Santiago de Chile: La Biblioteca, 1979. 315 p.; indexes.

Se trata de la primera bibliografía de esta índole que se publica en Chile. Contiene 1.819 fichas, divididas en: 1) Libros y Publicaciones Periódicas; 2) Memorias, Tesis y Seminarios; y 3) Traducciones. Contiene índice de autores y de revistas.

7534 Costa Leiva, Miguel da. La contribución filosófica de Enrique Molina Garmendia a la cultura chilena (UC/AT, 438, 1978, p. 77–96)

Síntesis de la acción intelectual y el pensamiento de Molina.

7535 *Cuyo*. Anuario de historia del pensamiento argentino. Instituto de Filosofía, Universidad Nacional de Cuyo. Vol. 12,

1979– . Mendoza, Argentina.
Este número está dedicado, como es usual, al pensamiento argentino. Diego Pro, en "Juan Dalma: el Psicólogo y las Interciencias" estudia la obra psicológica de dicho autor, "adicto de la filosofía científica de Reichenbach y de la epistemología de Piaget." Celina Lértora Mendoza agrega una más de sus provechosas contribuciones al estudio de las manifestaciones filosóficas coloniales con "Las Fuentes Utilizadas en la Enseñanza de la Filosofía en el Período Hispano." Otros artículos son: A. M. Introna de Barraquero, "El Pensamiento Filosófico del Dr. Sisto Terán;" T. Sallenave de Sagui, "Las Ideas Estéticas en José León Pagano" y "Las Ideas Estéticas en Leopoldo Lugones;" Ignacio T. Lucero, "La Filosofía del Derecho del Dr. Tomás D. Casares;" y M. I. García Losada, "Carlos Alberto Erro y la Filosofía Existencial." El volumen contiene una bibliografía de y sobre Nimio de Anquín.

7536 Díaz Araujo, Enrique. José Ingenieros y la evolución de las ideas alberdianas (CEHA/NH, 11:21, 1978, p. 158–179)
Violento ataque, desde un ángulo tradicionalista y nacionalista, a *La evolución de las ideas argentinas*, obra de José Ingenieros.

7537 Djacir Menezes e as perspectivas do pensamento contemporâneo. A. Machado Paupério, Oliveiros Litrento, coordenadores *et al.* Rio de Janeiro: Editora Rio, 1979. 213 p.; bibl.
Volume de homenaje. Antonio Paim sitúa a Menezes en la corriente culturalista en Brasil. Otros autores examinan la filosofía del derecho de Menezes o escriben sobre temas afines. Contiene un *curriculum vitae* y una bibliografía de Djacir Menezes.

7538 Don Pedro León Loyola. Santiago: Instituto de Chile, Academia de Ciencias Sociales Políticas y Morales; Editorial Universitaria, 1979. 28 p.
Loyola (1889–1978) fue un maestro de gran influencia en la primera época postpositivista en Chile. Este folleto recoge tres intervenciones de homenaje con motivo de su fallecimiento.

7539 Encuentro Ecuatoriano de Filosofía, 3d, Quito, 1978. Problemas actuales de la filosofía en el ámbito latinoamericano: III Encuentro Ecuatoriano de Filosofía. Quito: Universidad Católica, 1979. 450 p.; bibl.
La actividad filosófica se ha incrementado recientemente en Ecuador, y especialmente el estudio del pensamiento latinoamericano en general y el nacional de ese país. El Tercer Encuentro Ecuatoriano de Filosofía tuvo lugar en junio de 1978, y este volumen reproduce la mayoría de los trabajos presentados. Los referidos al pensamiento latinoamericano y ecuatoriano son los siguientes: H. Cerutti Guldberg, "Series y Utópicas en el Pensamiento Cuencano;" S. Guerra Bravo, "La Dimensión Filosófica en el Pensamiento de Eugenio Espejo;" E. Terzaga, "Hegel y el Pensamiento Hispánico;" C. Paladines E., "Notas sobre Metodología e Investigación del Pensamiento Ecuatoriano;" H. Cerutti Guldberg, "Implicaciones Filosóficas Latinoamericanas en el Teatro Popular;" F. Olmedo Llorente, "La Dialéctica de Complementaridad en Miguel Reale;" P. Escobar, "Bolívar: Pensador Político Hispanoamericano;" A. A. Roig, "Problemática de la Filosofía Latinoamericana;" E. Pucciarelli, "Integridad y Diversidad Cultural en América Latina;" F. Tijanero, "Del Discurso Ideológico al Conocimiento: Notas para el Estudio de la Cultura Ecuatoriana;" H. Rodríguez Castelo, "La Expresión Plástica Ecuatoriana del Siglo XX como Forma de Reflexión Filosófica;" F. Miró Quesada, "Filosofía Científica y Filosofía de la Ciencia en América Latina." Otros trabajos de filosofía en general son: J. Terán D., "Cristianismo y Filosofía Hoy;" R. M. Agoglia, "El Nexo Epistemológico entre Lógica Formal y Lógica Dialéctica en la Investigación Contemporánea" y "La Relación Sistemática de Antropología Filosófica y Filosofía de la Historia como Fundamento de las Ciencias Humanas;" A. A. Roig "La Filosofía de la Historia desde el Punto de Vista del Discurso Filosófico-Político;" L. Zea, "Crisis del Sentido de la Historia Occidental;" H. Malo González, "Pensamiento Mítico y Pensamiento Lógico."

7540 Estrada, José María de. El pensamiento filosófico de Octavio Nicolás Derisi (UCA/S, 35:137/138, julio/dic. 1980, p. 183–188)
Trata de captar el núcleo básico de la posición filosófica de Octavio N. Derisi, dentro del espíritu tomista que—"sin claudicaciones y desviaciones"—lo anima.

7541 Gaos, José. En torno a la filosofía mexicana. México, D.F.: Alianza Editorial Mexicana, 1980. 187 p. (Biblioteca Iberoamericana; 4)

Oportuna reedición de este libro de José Gaos sobre temas de filosofía mexicana. A esta edición se agrega un apéndice de escritos de Gaos de su primera época en México. Leopoldo Zea le pone un emotivo y justiciero prólogo.

7542 Gomes, Roberto. Para colocar as idéias no lugar (Reflexão [Pontifícia Universidade Católica de Campinas, Instituto de Filosofia e Teologia, São Paulo, Brasil] 15, set./dez. 1979, p. 40–68)

Incisiva respuesta a la crítica de C. A. Ramos al libro del autor (véase item **7560** en esta sección). Uno de los principales puntos es la discusión sobre la dependencia.

7543 Guadarrama González, Pablo. El papel de Enrique Piñeiro en la introducción del positivismo en Cuba (UCLV/I, 65, enero/abril 1980, p. 157–170)

Piñeiro (1839–1911) fue crítico literario que por la vía de Taine habría comenzado la introducción de ideas positivistas en Cuba. El autor de este trabajo ha estudiado, desde una perspectiva marxista, al principal representante del positivismo en Cuba: Enrique José Varona (véase *HLAS 42*, p. 729–731).

7544 ———. El positivismo en Manuel Sanguily (UCLV/I, 64, sept./dic. 1979, p. 155–184)

Sanguily (1848–1925) expresó el clima positivista en sus escritos, aunque éstos no compusieron un pensamiento filosófico sistemático. Los comentarios del autor resultan de su posición marxista-leninista, pero no impiden aprovechar el material que presenta.

7545 Guerra Bravo, Samuel. El pensamiento ecuatoriano en los siglos XVI, XVII y XVIII (BCE/C, 2:4, mayo/agosto 1979, p. 65–94)

Descontadas afirmaciones tales como que la escolástica fue en América la filosofía de la dominación, que dan un tono combativo al comienzo del artículo, su parte informativa constituye uno de los pocos trabajos con noticias de conjunto sobre la filosofía colonial en Ecuador.

7546 Lara, Tiago Adão. As raízes cristãs do pensamento de Antônio Pedro de Figueiredo. São João del-Rei, Brasil: Faculdade Dom Bosco de Filosofia, Ciências e Letras, 1977. 345 p.; bibl.

Obra monográfica, muy útil. Figueiredo (1814–59) tiene su lugar en la historia de las ideas políticas en Brasil, dentro de la adhesión al eclecticismo filosófico. Prologa la obra situando a Figueiredo y a la presente investigación Antonio Paim. La obra estudia escritos periodísticos poco frecuentados de Figueiredo. Contiene también una valiosa antología de sus escritos, con buena bibliografía.

7547 Larroyo, Francisco. La filosofía iberoamericana: historia, formas, temas, polémica, realizaciones. 2. ed. México: Editorial Porrúa, 1978. 304 p.; bibl.; index (Colección Sepan cuantos . . . ; no. 333)

Es ampliación de una obra aparecida por primera vez en 1958. En cuanto al contenido, es la obra más completa sobre el tema, pues comprende exposiciones de: las distintas opiniones sobre el problema de la filosofía iberoamericana; la historia del pensamiento filosófico en Iberoamérica; la historiografía americana; y la filosofía de la historia de América.

7548 Lértora Mendoza, Celina Ana. La enseñanza de la filosofía en tiempos de la colonia: análisis de cursos manuscritos. Buenos Aires: Fundación para la Educación, la Ciencia y la Cultura, 1979. 381 p.; bibl.

Aunque no lo indica el título, se trata de filosofía colonial en la Argentina. Se toman 10 autores y el total de cursos analizados es de 15: cuatro de Lógica, siete de Física y cuatro de Metafísica. Los cursos son descritos y comentados por la autora, y de cada uno se reproduce el índice completo. Es una contribución de indudable utilidad, que representa un considerable progreso en la historiografía sobre el tema, no sólo por el material, sino también por el conocimiento de primera mano y el juicio equilibrado.

7549 Liberati, Jorge. Vaz Ferreira, filósofo del lenguaje. Montevideo: Arca, 1980. 122 p.; bibl.

La obra de Vaz Ferreira—especialmente la *Lógica viva*—es interpretada según los temas y categorías de la filosofía contemporánea del lenguaje.

7550 Lipp, Solomon. Leopoldo Zea: from *Mexicanidad* to a philosophy of history. Waterloo, Ontario: Wilfrid Laurier University Press, 1980. 146 p.; bibl.; index.

Trata los dos principales aspectos de la obra de Zea (si se excluyen sus trabajos historiográficos): el análisis del "ser" del mexicano, correspondiente a la primera etapa de dicho autor, y el posterior y más valioso intento de una "filosofía de la historia" de América Latina. Para el primero de esos dos aspectos, Lipp recurre también a ciertos resultados de las ciencias sociales. Zea es el mayor latinoamericanista en el campo filosófico y es autor de una vasta obra, centrada en una constante meditación sobre la realidad latinoamericana. Lipp la expone y comenta con criterio amplio, y esa amplitud no es comprometida ni siquiera cuando se atiene a parámetros culturales diferentes, propios de la investigación en Estados Unidos. El autor ha llevado a cabo un trabajo arduo y la sola dedicación de una obra especial sobre Leopoldo Zea, escrita en inglés, es de por sí encomiable.

7551 Macedo, Ubiratan Borges de. A liberdade no Império. São Paulo: Editora Convivio, 1977. 214 p; bibl.

Obra importante en la historiografía del pensamiento brasileño. Sigue la línea de un problema, el de la libertad, en su sentido filosófico y en su sentido político, que el autor no considera correcto separar. Se detiene specialmente en tres corrientes: el espiritualismo, el pensamiento católico en el Segundo Reinado y la Escuela de Recife. La intención es realizar una historia "interna" del pensamiento local en relación con el pensamiento europeo, como primer paso de establecimiento del tema. Antonio Paim destaca en la Presentación el valor de la obra como parte de un movimiento de renovación en el estudio del pensamiento filosófico brasileño.

7552 Machado, Geraldo Pinheiro. Um aspecto da filosofia brasileira e portuguesa no século XIX (Reflexão [Pontifícia Universidade Católica de Campinas, São Paulo, Brasil] 15, set./dez. 1979, p. 90–95)

Llama la atención sobre la conveniencia de enfocar conjuntamente los problemas de la filosofía en Brasil y en Portugal, y lo ilustra con el caso de dos estudios: Sílvio Romero, A filosofia no Brasil (1878) y J. J. Lopes Praça, História da filosofia en Portugal (1868).

7553 Mons. Dr. Octavio Nicolás Derisi (UCA/S, 35 : 137/138, julio/dic. 1980, p. 169–[181])

Contiene la bibliografía completa (hasta 1980) de Derisi (n. 1907), uno de los

más destacados pensadores tomistas de América Latina, actualmente Rector de la Pontificia Universidad Católica de Buenos Aires.

7554 Moreno, Julio Enrique. Pensamiento filosófico-social. Estudio y selección de textos de Hernán Malo González. Quito: Banco Central del Ecuador; Corporación Editora Nacional, 1979. 326 p. (Biblioteca básica del pensamiento ecuatoriano; 1)

Julio E. Moreno (1879–1952) actuó en la política ecuatoriana y es autor de trabajos muy poco conocidos por la historiografía de las ideas en América Latina. Aquí se reproducen: "El Problema de Nuestra Política Educacional" (1935); *Humanidad y espiritualidad: bosquejo de una antropología sociológica* (1939); *El sentido histórico y la cultura* (1940); y *Filosofía de la existencia: notas sobre Ortega y Gasset* (1940). El estudio preliminar de Malo González plantea la cuestión de si se puede decir que hubo filosofía en Ecuador (lo que de hecho es una contribución al debatido tema del sentido de la filosofía latinoamericana), y expone el pensamiento de Moreno. La edición, como otras similares del Banco del Ecuador, es una útil contribución a la historia de las ideas en Latinoamérica.

7555 Olarte, Láscaris y la filosofía latinoamericana. Introducción y recopilación de Guillermo Malavassi V. San José: Editorial Universidad de Costa, 1980. 247 p.; bibl.

A pesar de su heterogeneidad y de no responder exactamente a su título, esta antología tiene cierta utilidad. Constantino Láscaris (1923–79) y Teodoro Olarte (1908–80) fueron españoles que se radicaron en Costa Rica y allí se dedicaron a la enseñanza y la producción filosóficas. Hay útiles datos sobre ambos y textos sobre temas de filosofía en América de que son autores. Sobre esos mismos temas hay también escritos de muchos otros autores, la mayoría costarricenses, y algunos muy representativos del pensamiento latinoamericano, como Francisco Romero, José Luis Romero y Leopoldo Zea.

7556 Osandon, Carlos A. Concepción de una filosofía americana en Alberdi (RFL, 3 : 5/6, enero/dic. 1977, p. 95–109)

El reiterado tema de la filosofía americana en Alberdi es expuesto con cierto detalle para extraer luego conclusiones sobre el problema desde el punto de vista actual. En tal sentido, el aporte de Alberdi se considera "de extraordinaria significación."

7557 Paim, Antonio. Indicadores do término do ciclo positivista (IBF/RBF, 30:120, out./dez. 1980, p. 335–349)

Muestra el debilitamiento del positivismo en el Brasil, hacia la segunda década del siglo XX, en el campo de la ciencia, en el de la educación y con el libro de João Arruda, *Do regime democrático* (1927).

7558 Pensamiento positivista latinoamericano. v. 1. Compilación, prólogo y cronología, Leopoldo Zea. Traducciones, Marta de la Vega, Margara Russotto y Carlos Jacques. Caracas, Venezuela: Biblioteca Ayacucho, 1980– . 1 v.; bibl. (Biblioteca Ayacucho; 71)

Esta valiosa antología, de la cual el presente es vol. 1, va precedida de un trabajo de Leopoldo Zea que trasciende las expresiones filosóficas para ser un capítulo de historia de las ideas y una interpretación de América Latina en la época estudiada. Contribución muy importante al estudio del positivismo en Latinoamérica.

7559 Pro, Diego F.; Clara A. Jalif de Bertranon; and Gloria I. Prada de Pardo. Historia del pensamiento filosófico argentino. Mendoza: Facultad de Filosofía y Letras, Instituto de Filosofía, Universidad Nacional de Cuyo, 1980. 382 p. (Colección de historia de la filosofía argentina. Serie Expositiva. Cuaderno; 3)

Este tercer *Cuaderno* examina las ideas epistemológicas de pensadores y científicos argentinos. Ha sido elaborado por Diego F. Pro, Clara A. J. de Bertranon y Gloria I. P. de Pardo. Los autores estudiados son: Alberto Rougès, H. Broggi, T. Ricaldoni, R. G. Loyarte, E. Butty, N. Laclau, F. Romero, E. Loedel Palumbo, M. Neuschlosz, J. Dalma, E. Gaviola, H. Catalano, A. Asti Vera y—desde las ciencias sociales—M. Herrera Figueroa. Además de otras colaboraciones, Diego Pro, bajo cuya dirección está el proyecto, cierra el volumen con un trabajo ("Para la Historia Epistemológica Argentina") que contribuye a darle unidad.

7560 Ramos, César Augusto. Crítica da crítica da razão tupiniquim (Reflexão [Pontificia Universidade Católica de Campinas, Instituto de Filosofia e Teologia, São

Paulo, Brasil] 15, set./dez. 1979, p. 5–29, bibl.)

Crítica, con herramentaje marxista, del libro de Roberto Gomes, *Crítica da razão tupiniquim* (1977, sobre este libro véase HLAS 42:7570).

7561 Redmond, Walter. Un ejemplo de la cuantificación múltiple en la lógica del siglo XVI (UI/RF, 14:40, enero/abril 1981, p. 27–37)

Se presenta en lenguaje formalizado un aspecto de la cuantificación en la lógica de Fray Alonso de la Veracruz (específicamente, en su *Recognitio Summularum*, México, 1554). Ilustra sobre la revisión que los especialistas en historia de la lógica están haciendo de la lógica escolástica, y correspondientemente lo que de ella as aplicable a la filosofía colonial en América.

7562 Rodríguez Castelo, Hernán. Historia general y crítica de la literatura ecuatoriana. v. 3, Literatura en la Audiencia de Quito: siglo XVII. Quito: Banco Central del Ecuador, 1980. 583 p.

Se trata, como indica el título, del vol. 3 de una extensa historia de la literatura ecuatoriana, en curso de publicación. Interesa para esta Sección el capítulo IX, "Filósofos y Teólogos, y otros prosistas," así como un "Indice de Obras de Filosofía y Teología, en Latín, Escritas por Autores de la Audiencia de Quito en el Siglo XVII."

7563 Roig, Arturo Andrés. Esquemas para una historia de la filosofía ecuatoriana. Quito: Centro de Publicaciones, Pontificia Universidad Católica del Ecuador, 1977. 145 p.; bibl.

La significación de esta obra va mucho más allá de su contenido. Representa una revaloración del pensamiento ecuatoriano que por su carácter puede dar lugar—y ya hay algunos signos de ello—a una serie de estudios en un campo anteriormente descuidado. Además de una Introducción que tiende a corregir ese descuido, contiene un proyecto de periodización del pensamiento ecuatoriano, y capítulos sobre José Peralta (1855–1935), el positivismo en Ecuador en general y el positivismo en Belisario Quevedo (1883–1921).

7564 ———. El manifiesto de una "filosofía americana" de 1840 y la problemática del "discurso propio" en la literatura rioplatense (BCE/C, 3:7, mayo/agosto 1980, p. 13–38)

Reflexiones dignas de consideración sobre el célebre texto de Alberdi, que es el punto de partida de una posible "filosofía americana."

7565 Rojo, Roberto. Ameghino y la inmigración de las ideas científicas (*in* La inmigración en la Argentina. San Miguel de Tucumán, Argentina: Universidad Nacional de Tucumán, Facultad de Filosofía y Letras, Centro de Historia y Pensamiento Argentinos, 1979, p. 173–178 [Publicación—Universidad Nacional de Tucumán; 1255])

Vida, obra científica y pensamiento de Ameghino, en el contexto de la influencia del positivismo y el evolucionismo y en el de la historia de la ciencia natural en la Argentina.

7566 Rubio Angulo, Jaime. Historia de la filosofía latinoamericana. v. 1. Bogotá: Universidad Santo Tomás, Centro de Ensenanza Desescolarizada, 1979. 308 p.; bibl.

Este vol. 1 se abre con una discusión sobre el concepto de "Historia de las Ideas" y con la exposición de las doctrinas "filosóficas" anteriores a la colonización (filosofía náhuatl). Luego examina: los problemas jurídico-filosóficos a que dio lugar la conquista; representantes salientes de la escolástica hispanoamericana; el eclecticismo en España y América; el pensamiento de la Ilustración en general y en particular en México, Ecuador y Cuba. Al final incluye algunas indicaciones bibliográficas. En el caso de algunos autores tratados se reproducen textos en forma antológica.

7567 Sasso, Javier. Salazar Bondy como teórico de la ética: reflexiones sobre *Para una filosofía del valor* (Fragmentos [Centro de Estudios Latinoamericanos Rómulo Gallegos, Departamento de Investigaciones, Caracas] 6, enero/abril 1980, p. 1–76)

La selección del tema es oportuna y el estudio está inteligentemente realizado. Muestra el paso de Salazar Bondy desde la fenomenología a la filosofía analítica y critica en detalle la obra en cuestión.

7568 Severino, Antônio Joaquim. O papel da filosofia no Brasil: compromissos e desafios atuais (Reflexão [Pontificia Universidade Católica de Campinas, Instituto de Filosofia e Teologia, Brasil] 5:17, maio/agosto 1980, p. 5–12, bibl.)

Artículo crítico de la situación actual, que tiende a identificar la tarea de la filosofía

con la problemática nacional y a concebirla como filosofía aplicada.

7569 Sutherland, Stewart R. La influencia de la filosofía escocesa en Andrés Bello (*in* Bello y Londres: segundo congreso del bicentenario. Caracas: Fundación La Casa de Bello, 1981, t. 2, p. 171–190)

El trabajo está dedicado a Reid, Steward y Brown, y a cómo influyeron sobre Bello.

7570 Torchia Estrada, Juan Carlos. Alejandro Korn: la primera profesión (UNLP/R, 26, 1973/1980, p. 73–94)

Síntesis de los escritos psiquiátricos de la primera época de Alejandro Korn y de su labor asistencial al frente del Hospital de Alienados de Melchor Romero.

7571 ———. En el centenario de Alberto Rougès (RIB, 30:4, 1980, p. 422–426)

Breve ensayo recordatorio, con motivo del centenario del nacimiento del destacado filósofo argentino.

7572 ———. La escolástica colonial en América Latina: algunas observaciones sobre criterios de interpretación (RFL, 5:9/10, enero/dic. 1979, p. 171–178)

Sostiene que el estudio de la escolástica colonial está necesitado de una visión sin prejuicios, ni a favor ni en contra, que se caracterice por un sano historicismo. Da algunos ejemplos y señala algunas pautas.

7573 ———. Francisco Romero: hacia la filosofía (RIB, 31:4, 1981, p. 483–506)

Estudio sobre la primera época de Francisco Romero (aproximadamente hasta 1924), con intención de biografía intelectual, incluyendo análisis de producciones literarias de ese período del autor estudiado.

7574 ———. *Locura y crimen* (1883): tesis de grado de Alejandro Korn (RIB, 26:3, julio/sept. 1976, p. 282–314)

Expone el contenido de la tesis con que Alejandro Korn se graduó en medicina y la pone en relación con la psiquiatría del siglo XIX, ilustrando sobre las primeras opiniones filosóficas del filósofo argentino.

7575 Vasconcelos Aguilar, Mario. José Vasconcelos, maestro de América. México: Jus, 1978. 171 p.; bibl.

Libro de tono ecomiástico, destinado a difundir el pensamiento de Vasconcelos, que se expone a través de un largo diálogo imaginario. Se recogen también opiniones sobre Vasconcelos y páginas antológicas.

7576   Vera y Cuspinera, Margarita. El pensamiento filosófico de Vasconcelos. México, D.F.: Extemporáneos, 1979. 246, [10] p.; bibl. (Colección Latinoamérican: Serie Ensayo; 8)

Se cuenta entre lo mejor que se ha escrito sobre Vasconcelos. El centro de la exposición y de las reflexiones críticas lo ocupa el pensamiento filosófico, pero también hay capítulos sobre la política y el americanismo en Vasconcelos. Buena bibliografía.

7577   Yepez Arboleda, Federico. Juan Bautista de Aguirre, filósofo (BCE/C, 2:4, mayo/agosto 1979, p. 95–113)

Trabajo de interés sobre un campo inexplorado. Se trata especialmente de un texto de Aguirre, parte de su Curso de Filosofía, de fines del siglo XVIII, del cual se reproducen párrafos.

PENSAMIENTO LATINOAMERICANO: HISTORIA DE LAS IDEAS

7578   Albarracín Millán, Juan. La sociedad opresora: la transición del positivismo al materialismo histórico. La Paz, Bolivia: Empresa Editora Universo, 1979. 333 p.; [6] leaves of plates; bibl.; index; ports (Sociología boliviana contemporánea; 3)

El vol. 1 de esta obra fue comentado de *HLAS 42:7616.* El presente volumen trata de la producción "sociológica" sobre la realidad boliviana entre 1920 y 1940. Algunas de las corrientes estudiadas son: las que se basan en estudios antropológicos y etnográficos; las que dan primacía al factor geográfico e económico; el irracionalismo de raíz spengleriana; el anarquismo; el populismo; y el materialismo dialéctico.

7579   Barreto, Vicente. Ideologia e política no pensamento de José Bonifácio de Andrada e Silva. Rio de Janeiro: Zahar Editores, 1977. 149 p.; bibl. (Atualidade)

Esta obra, bien elaborada, se inicia con consideraciones metodológicas sobre la historia de las ideas políticas. Luego examina el liberalismo en general, para finalmente ocuparse de José Bonifácio de Andrada e Silva, a quien considera "representante típico del liberalismo brasileño."

7580   Biagini, Hugo Edgardo. Cómo fue la generación del 80. Buenos Aires: Plus Ultra, 1980. 190 p.; bibl. (Colección Esquemas históricos; 32)

El título se refiere a la generación argentina de 1880. Se compone de tres trabajos. Los dos primeros, sobre las actitudes ante la idea y la realidad del progreso, y ante las razas indígenas, respectivamente, cuestionan afirmaciones tradicionales utilizando abundantes fuentes, especialmente el segundo, al cual conviene poner en relación con el mismo tema en otros países latinoamericanos. El tercer trabajo rescata una figura de la historia de las ideas escasamente conocida: Carlos Encina, de quien se dan también valiosas indicaciones bibliográficas. Concluye con un útil bibliografía.

7581   Caballero, Manuel. La Sección Venezolana de la Internacional Comunista: un tema para el estudio de las ideas en el siglo XX venezolano (*in* Encuentro de Historiadores Latinoamericanos y del Caribe, 2d, Caracas, 1977. Los estudios históricos en América Latina: ponencias, acuerdos y resoluciones: Caracas, 20–26 de marzo de 1977. Caracas: Universidad Central de Venezuela, Facultad de Humanidades y Educación, Escuela de Historia, 1979, v. 1, t. 2, p. 798–807)

Desbroza el tema, como contribución a la historia de las ideas.

7582   Casetta, Giovanni. Il problema indigeno dalla tradizione alla modernità: José Carlos Mariátegui (Nova Americana [Giulio Einaudi Editore, Torino, Italy] 3, 1980, p. 101–140)

Detenido examen de la cuestión indígena en Mariátegui. Lo elogia por haber sostenido que el problema del indio requiere una teoría y una práctica política de tipo socialista, y considera que la solución de Mariátegui es aplicable, en líneas generales, a otros países latinoamericanos de estructura social semejante a la del Perú.

7583   Caturelli, Alberto. La pedagogía, la política y la mística en José Antonio de San Alberto (UNL/H, 18, 1977, p. 183–214)

Se refiere principalmente a los escritos pastorales de J. A. de San Alberto (1727–1804), Obispo de Córdoba y Arzobispo de Charcas. Destaca el carácter anti-iluminista de sus ideas.

7584   Davis, Harold Eugene. Elements of traditionalism in Latin American thought

(UNL/H, 20, 1979, p. 83–92)

Se refiere a varias formas de tradicionalismo en América Latina en el siglo XIX, pero hay también alusiones al siglo XX.

7585 Espinosa Tamayo, Alfredo. Psicología y sociología del pueblo ecuatoriano. Estudio introductorio de Arturo Andrés Roig. Quito: Banco Central del Ecuador, Corporación Editora Nacional, 1979. 361 p. (Biblioteca básica del pensamiento ecuatoriano; 2)

Se reproduce el libro de Alfredo Espinosa Tamayo (fallecido en 1918), *Psicología y sociología del pueblo ecuatoriano,* cuya última redacción es de 1917. La extensa introducción de Arturo A. Roig, "Los Comienzos del Pensamiento Social y los Orígenes de la Sociología en el Ecuador," va mucha más allá de situar el libro que aquí se reedita y es un importante estudio de historia de las ideas en América Latina.

7586 Falcón, Jorge. Amauta, polémica y acción de Mariátegui. Lima: Empresa Editora Amauta, 1979. 246 p.

Acción de Mariátegui en torno a la fundación y edición de la revista *Amauta.* Escrito con simpatía y no sin cierto desaliño de forma, contiene información de interés. Una de las preocupaciones del autor es la polémica con Haya de la Torre y Luis Alberto Sánchez.

7587 ———. Anatomía de los 7 ensayos de Mariátegui. Lima: Empresa Editora Amauta, 1978. 150 p.

Aparentemente se trata del vol. 1 de un proyecto mayor del autor. Obra de redacción confusa.

7588 Federico González Suárez y la polémica sobre el Estado laico. Estudio introductorio y selección de Enrique Ayala Mora. Quito: Banco Central del Ecuador, Corporación Editora Nacional, 1980. 516 p. (Biblioteca básica del pensamiento ecuatoriana; 4)

Esta antología contiene escritos de Federico González Suárez, Obispo de Ibarra, que van de 1877 a 1911. (González Suárez falleció en 1917.) Además, incluye expresiones de otros autores que intervinieron en la polémica entre el liberalismo y el sector católica del Ecuador.

7589 Flores, Juan. Insularismo e ideología burguesa en Antonio Pedreira. La Habana: Casa de las Américas, 1979. 95 p.

Pedreira, destacado intelectual puertorriqueño (m. 1939) publicó *Insularismo: ensayos de interpretación puertorriqueña,* en 1934. El libro se dedica a la crítica de esta obra, que el autor estima debe hacerse "a la luz de la teoría revolucionaria contemporánea." Su lectura tiene aspectos aprovechables a pesar de su tono militante.

7590 Freile Granizo, Carlos E. Un milenarista ecuatoriano del siglo XVIII: José de Valdivieso, introducción a su estudio (IPHG/RHI, 3, 2. época, 1981, p. 83–92)

Se refiere a una "Carta Apologética" escrita por el Jesuita José de Valdivieso, en 1795. Valdivieso, antes de la expulsión, había pertenecido a la Orden en Quito. La "Carta" es una defensa del milenarismo sostenido por el P. Manuel Lacunza (jesuita chileno muerto en 1801) en su *Venida del Mesías en gloria y majestad.* Sin embargo, hay más consideraciones generales sobre milenarismo y escatología que sobre la "Carta" misma, lo cual es lamentable porque esta última es un documento prácticamente desconocido.

7591 García Salvattecci, Hugo. Haya de la Torre o el marxismo indoamericano. Lima, Peru: M. Ramírez V., 1980. 264 p.

Los dos capítulos centrales comparan el marxismo con la ideología aprista. Los precede una exposición de ideas y movimientos latinoamericanos precursores del APRA y una semblanza de Haya de la Torre. Escrito con simpatía pero sin estrechez partidista.

7592 Jijón y Caamaño, Jacinto. Política conservadora. Estudio introductorio y selección de Ricardo Muñoz Chávez. Quito: Banco Central del Ecuador, Corporación Editora Nacional, n.d. 303 p. (Biblioteca básica del pensamiento ecuatoriano; 7)

Reproduce antológicamente parte de la obra en dos volúmenes, *Política conservadora,* publicada en 1929 por el dirigente conservador Jacinto Jijón y Caamaño.

7593 Lewin, Boleslao. Rousseau en la independencia de Latinoamérica. Buenos Aires: Ediciones Depalma, 1980. 157 p.; bibl.

Contribución a la historia de las ideas, en el sentido de rastrear la influencia de las ideas sobre la acción. La mayor parte del libro se dedica a la influencia de Rousseau en el Río de la Plata, pero hay también capítulos sobre los otros países latinoamericanos.

7594 Lima, José Ignacio de Abreu e. O socialismo. 2. ed., com prefácio de Barbosa Lima Sobrinho. Rio de Janeiro: Paz e

Terra, 1979. 343 p.; bibl. (Coleção Pensamento crítico; v. 29)

Este libro apareció por primera vez en Recife, en 1855. Su autor (1794–1869), incluido en la corriente denominada "socialismo romántico," había sido anteriormente general en el ejército de Bolívar. El prefacio de Barbosa Lima Sobrinho es ilustrativo sobre la vida y el pensamiento de Abreu e Lima. Por lugar y época este autor puede ponerse en relación con Antonio Pedro de Figueiredo (véase item **7546**).

7595 Lovera, José Rafael. La conciencia del papel del conocimiento científico y de la tecnología en el desarrollo de la sociedad: el caso de Venezuela en la segunda mitad del siglo XIX (*in* Encuentro de Historiadores Latinoamericanos y del Caribe, 2d, Caracas, 1977. Los estudios históricos en América Latina: ponencias, acuerdos y resoluciones: Caracas, 20–26 de marzo de 1977. Caracas: Universidad Central de Venezuela, Facultad de Humanidades y Educación, Escuela de Historia, 1979, v. 1, t. 2, p. 723–727)

Util por algunos datos institucionales y bibliográficos.

7596 Maldonado Denis, Manuel. Breve esbozo de la historia de las ideas en Puerto Rico (*in* Encuentro de Historiadores Latinoamericanos y del Caribe, 2d, Caracas, 1977. Los estudios históricos en América Latina: ponencias, acuerdos y resoluciones: Caracas, 20–26 de marzo de 1977. Caracas: Universidad Central de Venezuela, Facultad de Humanidades y Educación, Escuela de Historia, 1979, v. 1, t. 2, p. 653–662, bibl.)

Visión de conjunto, menos interesada en el recuento histórico que en manifestar una posición política ("anti-imperialista" y proclive al marxismo). Quizá sea lo más rescatable lo que se expone sobre la "ideología nacionalista puertorriqueña."

7597 ———. Introducción al pensamiento social de Eugenio María de Hostos (CDLA, 21:124, enero/feb. 1981, p. 51–66)

Util trabajo panorámico sobre el pensamiento de Hostos. Aunque contradice las simpatías del autor el que Hostos no haya advertido el valor del marxismo, ese juicio no impide las bondades de este artículo.

7598 Mariátegui, José Carlos. Obra política. Prólogo, selección y notas de Rubén Jiménez Ricárdez. México: Ediciones Era, 1979. 327 p. (El Hombre y su tiempo)

Recoge conferencias y artículos de Mariátegui sobre temas políticos, en general de 1923 en adelante. Desde el punto de vista filosófico—tomada la expresión en sentido amplio—interesan los pocos escritos de la última sección, titulada por el compilador "La Filosofía Moderna y el Marxismo." El prólogo es de aquellos—pocos—en que la simpatía política que trasuntan no les impide ser esclarecedores. Es útil especialmente para situar a Mariátegui en su época.

7599 ———. 7 [i.e. Siete] ensayos de interpretación de la realidad peruana. Prólogo, Anibal Quijano. Notas y cronología, Elizabeth Gerrels. Caracas, Venezuela: Biblioteca Ayacucho, 1979. 335 p.; bibl. (Biblioteca Ayacucho; 69)

Precede al texto de Mariátegui en extenso prólogo de Aníbal Quijano, que interpreta a Mariátegui desde el punto de vista del "socialismo revolucionario," que se distingue sin embargo del trozkismo y el comunismo oficial (y naturalmente de toda forma de reformismo). Sigue al texto una útil cronología de la vida y obra de Mariátegui en el contexto de la vida peruana y mundial, y una bibliografía de y sobre Mariátegui.

7600 Marichal, Juan Augusto. Cuatro fases de la historia intelectual latinoamericana: 1810–1970. Madrid: Fundación Juan March, 1978. 102 p. (Crítica literaria)

Aunque se trata de una obra panorámica, su interés no reside tanto en el beneficio de una imagen de conjunto como en aciertos específicos de visión a lo largo del libro. Tras consideraciones sobre la historia intelectual como disciplina, aplicada a América Latina, la obra se estructura en base a rápidos enfoques de un grupo de figuras: Moreno y Bolívar; Echeverría, Sarmiento y Alberdi; Martí y Rodó; Martínez Estrada y Octavio Paz.

7601 Mills, Nick D. Liberalismo, ideología y tradición en la nacionalidad ecuatoriana: un ensayo interpretativo (UNC/RAHC, 7:4, junio 1978, p. 31–57, bibl.)

Además de la utilidad que el trabajo tiene para el caso particular de Ecuador, interesa por el enfoque de la discrepancia entre las ideas políticas en que se quisieron basar las nuevas repúblicas hispanoamericanas y su realidad social, económica y político-institucional. Estudio bien elaborado.

7602 Paredes, Angel Modesto. Pensamiento sociológico. Estudio introductorio y selección de Rafael Quintero. Quito: Banco Central del Ecuador, Corporación Editora Nacional, 1981. 454 p. (Biblioteca básica del pensamiento ecuatoriana; 6)

La obra de Paredes se desarrolló entre 1924–58 y esta extensa antología se destina a sus expresiones sociológicas, recogiendo textos de libros como *Sociología general* (1924), *La conciencia social* (1927), *Los resultados sociales de la herencia* (1935) y *Biología de las clases sociales* (1954). El estudio preliminar es posiblemente el único especialmente dedicado a tratar con cierta extensión el pensamiento sociológico de Paredes. La obra contiene además una bibliografía del autor estudiado y de algunos trabajos sobre la sociología en el Ecuador.

7603 Pensamiento conservador, 1815–1898. Prólogo, José Luis Romero. Compilación, notas y cronología, José Luis Romero y Luis Alberto Romero. Caracas: Biblioteca Ayacucho, 1978. 501 p.; bibl. (Biblioteca Ayacucho; 31)

La utilidad de esta selección para el investigador del pensamiento político latinoamericano es incuestionable. El lúcido estudio preliminar de José Luis Romero ilumina el pensamiento conservador tanto desde el punto de vista conceptual como desde el ángulo histórico. Una de las conclusiones que se desprenden de él es la dificultad de estudiar ese pensamiento con toda propiedad histórica, por la mezcla de lo doctrinario y lo práctico, y porque no siempre lo doctrinario—lo más fácilmente aprehensible—se hace completamente explícito. La cronología que sigue a los textos antológicos es un valioso instrumento, y se completa con una bibliografía básica.

7604 Pensamiento idealista ecuatoriano. Estudio introductorio y selección de Horacio Cerutti Guldberg. Quito: Banco Central del Ecuador, Corporación Editora Nacional, 1981. 533 p. (Biblioteca básica del pensamiento ecuatoriano; 8)

Los autores considerados y antológicamente presentados son: Gonzalo Zaldumbide, Nicolás Jiménez, José Rafael Bustamante, Fernando Chávez, Aurelio García Gallegos, Víctor Gabriel Garcés y Guillermo Bustamante, todos nacidos entre 1880–1905. La calificación de "idealistas" se les atribuye en el sentido en que se aplica al pensamiento de Rodó y dentro de la primera etapa de superación del positivismo. En un prólogo de

indudable utilidad, Cerutti Guldberg señala que el tema está en la etapa de la reunión sistemática de materiales, y a su avance contribuye sin duda la presente edición.

7605 Pensamiento y romántico ecuatoriano. Estudio introductorio y selección de Rodolfo Agoglia. Quito: Banco Central del Ecuador, Corporación Editora Nacional, 1980. 440 p. (Biblioteca básica del pensamiento ecuatoriano; 5)

Los autores representados en esta antología son Juan León Mera, Juan Montalvo, Elías Laso, Federico González Suárez, Remigio Crespo Toral y Luis A. Martínez. El provechoso estudio preliminar de Rodolfo Agoglia coloca a esos autores en el contexto del pensamiento romántico latinoamericano en general y en el de los antecedentes europeos de la misma corriente.

7606 Peralta Brito, Rafael and **José Chez Checo.** Religión, filosofía y política en Fernando A. de Meriño, 1857–1906: contribución a la historia de las ideas en la República Dominicana. Portada de Nicolás Pichardo. Santo Domingo, R.D.: s.n., 1979. 148 p.; bibl.; ports.

En el plano de las ideas, expone la oposición que desde el lado católica Meriño representó frente al liberalismo y el positivismo (concretamente y en especial, ante la prédica de Hostos). También expone la acción política del personaje estudiado.

7607 Prieto Castillo, Daniel. El arte y el anarquismo mexicano (IPGH/RHI, 3, 2. época, 1981, p. 93–124)

De interés para el estudio de las ideas anarquistas en México.

Rodó, José Enrique. La América nuestra. *Véase HLAS 36:5078.*

7608 Rodríguez-Peralta, Phyllis. González Prada's social and political thought (RIB, 30:2, 1980, p. 148–156)

Panorama de las ideas de González Prada y breve apreciación crítica.

7609 Roig, Arturo Andrés. Aurelio Espinosa Pólit: humanista y filósofo. Liminar de Marco V. Rueda. Quito: Ediciones de la Universidad Católica, 1980. 78 p.; bibl. (Cuadernos universitarios)

Fina semblanza de Espinosa Pólit, humanista ecuatoriano, de quien se destacan las raíces filosóficas de su posición espiritualista cristiana, especialmente en el campo de lo estético-religioso. Contiene bibliografía de y sobre Espinosa Pólit.

7610 ———. Deodoro Roca y el Manifiesto de la Reforma de 1918 (UUAL/U, 20: 79, 3. serie, enero/marzo 1980, p. 88–115)

Estudia la función de Deodoro Roca en la Reforma Universitaria de Córdoba (Argentina) en 1918, y cómo evolucionó su interpretación de ese fenómeno. Es un trabajo imprescindible para el conocimiento del tema, con muy útiles referencias a un amplio contexto de ideas en el que se situán las manifestaciones reformistas estudiadas.

7611 Salomon, Noël. Cosmopolitism and internationalism in the history of the ideas in Latin America (UNESCO/CU, 6:1, 1979, p. 83–108)

Interesante repaso de cómo las expresiones indicadas en el título han sido usadas y pensadas por numerosos intelectuales latinoamericanos, especialmente en el período 1880–1940.

7612 Sanguinetti, Horacio J. Historia de las ideas políticas, universales y argentinas. Prólogo de Jorge Xifra Heras. Buenos Aires: Cooperadora de Derecho y Ciencias Sociales, 1977. 308 p.; bibl.; index.

Se compone de dos partes: un resumen de la historia de las ideas políticas occidentales, y otra sobre la evolución institucional y las ideas políticas argentinas. Contiene bibliografía de obras en español.

7613 Schwartz, Pedro. La correspondencia ibérica de Jeremy Bentham (*in* Bello y Londres: segundo congreso del bicentenario. Caracas: Fundación La Casa de Bello, 1980, t. 1, p. 225–307)

Es un trabajo muy valioso, tanto por su exposición como por sus apéndices documentales.

7614 Semana Nacional de Filosofia no Brasil, *1978.* Anais. João Pessoa: Universidade Federal de Paraíba, Editora Universitária, 1979. 1 v. (Estudos universitários. Série filosofia)

Contiene varias contribuciones a la historia de las ideas en diferentes regiones de Brasil: Minas Gerais, Rio Grande do Sul y Bahía. Hay además trabajos sobre filosofía católica en el país, sobre Jackson de Figueiredo y Tristão de Athayde, sobre la influencia de Maritain y sobre la Escuela de Recife. Otros trabajos se refieren a la relación de la filosofía con las prioridades educacionales y con el desarrollo en Brasil, respectivamente.

7615 7 [i.e. Siete] **ensayos:** 50 años en la historia. Emilio Romero *et al.* Lima: Biblioteca Amauta, 1979. 295 p.; bibl.

Contiene 11 trabajos, debidos a diferentes autores, sobre los *Siete ensayos* de Mariátegui, de cuya aparición se cumplieron 50 años en 1978. Una nota editorial presenta la historia de las ediciones de los *Siete ensayos* en los diversos idiomas en que se publicó, que es de obvia utilidad bibliográfica.

7616 Skinner, Geraldine. José Carlos Mariátegui and the emergence of the Peruvian socialist movement (SS, 43:4, Winter 1979/1980, p. 447–471)

Niega a Mariátegui la condición de verdadero marxista y la reprocha haber preferido a Sorel en lugar de Lenin.

7617 Soler, Ricaurte. La idea nacional-hispanoamericana del liberalismo: Justo Arosemena (*in* Encuentro de Historiadores Latinoamericanos y del Caribe, 2d, Caracas, 1977. Los estudios históricos en América Latina: ponencias, acuerdos y resoluciones: Caracas, 20–26 de marzo de 1977. Caracas: Universidad Central de Venezuela, Facultad de Humanidades y Educación, Escuela de Historia, 1979, v. 1, t. 2, p. 707–714)

Sobre las ideas que animaron el proyecto de la nación panameña y de una "liga" hispanoamericana en el caso de Justo Arosemena. La línea de interpretación histórica es marxista.

7618 Subercaseaux, Bernardo. Liberalismo positivista y naturalismo en Chile: 1865–1875 (RCLL, 6:11, 1. semestre, 1980, p. 7–27)

Dedicado principalmente a Lastarria. Una parte está consagrada a aspectos estéticos y literarios. Trabajo útil.

7619 Toledo, Caio Navarro de. ISEB: fábrica de ideologias. São Paulo: Editora Atica, 1977. 194 p.; bibl. (Ensaios; 28)

Expone la ideología "nacional-desarrollista" del ISEB (Instituto Superior de Estudos Brasileiros), así como sus fuentes filosóficas y las diferencias entre los intelectuales que lo animaron. La acción del ISEB se extendió entre 1955/1964. Util para la reciente historia de las ideas en Brasil y para la comprensión del "desarrollo" en América Latina.

7620 Vallejo H., Hilario René. Ramón Rosa y el positivismo en Honduras. Tegucigalpa: Universidad Nacional Autónoma de Honduras, Departamento de Filosofía, 1978. 148 p.; bibl.

Aparentemente se trata de una tesis de Licenciatura. Su utilidad reside en los aspectos informativos del capítulo específicamente referido a Ramón Rosa.

7621 Vande, Harry E. Mariátegui: marxismo, comunismo, and other bibliographic notes (LARR, 14:3, 1979, p. 61–86, bibl.)

Llena con buen conocimiento del asunto la necesidad de contar con un análisis bibliográfico sobre la creciente literatura dedicada a Mariátegui. De obvia utilidad.

7622 Villegas, Abelardo. Reformismo y revolución en el pensamiento latinoamericano. 5. ed. México: Siglo Veintiuno Editores, 1980. 359 p. (Sociología y política)

Dada la amplia, compleja y difícil materia que trata, y la intención participatoria que la anima, es una obra que puede leerse con provecho. Los movimientos ideológicopolíticos que estudia son: la revolución mexicana, la revolución batllista en Uruguay, el "pensamiento revolucionario sin revolución" de Mariátegui y Haya de la Torre, el reformismo argentino de Irigoyen a Perón, el reformismo brasileño (Vargas), la Revolución cubana—sobre la cual debe destacarse la serenidad de juicio del autor—, y otros movimientos posteriores, reformistas o "revolucionarios," que se consideran "alternativas a la Revolución cubana." Sin inclinarse por una clara posición revolucionaria, el autor desconfía de la eficacia del reformismo. A lo largo de la obra se encuentran útiles consideraciones sobre el problema de la democracia en América Latina.

7623 Weinberg, Gregorio. Consideraciones sobre la historia de la tradición científica en el desarrollo de la conciencia social y su importancia en la formación de la conciencia nacional y latinoamericana (in Encuentro de Historiadores Latinoamericanos y del Caribe, 2d, Caracas, 1977. Los estudios históricos en América Latina: ponencias, acuerdos y resoluciones: Caracas, 20–26 de marzo de 1977. Caracas: Universidad Central de Venezuela, Facultad de Humanidades y Educación, Escuela de Historia, 1979, v. 1, t. 2, p. 688–699)

Con rápidos pero bien elegidos ejemplos que revelan dominio del tema, reivindica el valor de la historia de la tradición científica latinoamericana.

7624 Wilhite, John F. The inter-American enlightenment (RIB, 30:3, 1980, p. 254–261)

Semejanzas e interrelaciones entre el Norte y el Sur de América en relación con el iluminismo. Panorámico, pero con abundantes referencias bibliográficas.

7625 Williford, Miriam. Jeremy Bentham on Spanish America: an account of his letters and proposals to the New World. Baton Rouge: Louisiana State University Press, 1980. 150 p.; bibl.; index.

Se trata de un libro imprescindible para el conocimiento del tema, que es de gran interés para la historia de las ideas en Latinoamérica. No pretende estudiar el grado de influencia real de Bentham en América Latina, sino difundir e interpretar documentos y correspondencia que se encuentran en el University College y en el Museo Británico, de Londres.

7626 Wise, David O. Labor, Lima, 1928–1929: José Carlos Mariátegui's working class counterpart to Amauta (UA/REH, 14:3, oct. 1980, p. 117–128)

Breve pero útil nota sobre el periódico Labor, que Mariátegui fundara como una extensión más periodísticas de Amauta y con la intención de llegar a los trabajadores, por su naturaleza informativa y menos intelectual.

7627 Womack, John, Jr. Mariátegui, Marxism and nationalism (RU/MP, 3:2, Summer 1980, p. 170–175)

Sobre la obra de Jesús Chavarría, J. C. Mariátegui and the Rise of Modern Perú: 1890–1930 (1979).

HISTORIA DE LA FILOSOFIA: ANTIGUA Y MEDIEVAL

7628 Bolzán, J. E. Aristóteles y la lista de cualidades en Meteor: 385 a 10 (UNL/H, 18, 1977, p. 113–127)

Se ofrece una traducción castellana del pasaje indicado en el título y se justifica con comentario aparte cada uno de los vocablos básicos, comparando con otras cinco traducciónes del texto.

7629 Cappelletti, Angel J. Biología y antropología de Anaxágoras (USB/RVF, 13, 1980, p. 7–20)

Exposición bien fundamentada en textos de primera mano.

7630 Darós, W. R. Nota sobre el concepto de "ente" en Tomás de Aquino: Dios ¿ser o ente? (UCA/S, 33:130, 1978, p. 285–296)

Contrariamente a lo que han sostenido algunas autoridades tomistas, para Santo Tomás Dios es ser (subsistente) y ente (por esencia). La argumentación se origina en una afirmación de Heidegger.

7631 Derisi, Octavio N. El fundamento de la metafísica tomista: el *esse* e *intelligere* divino, fundamento y causa de todo ser y entender participados (UCA/S, 35:135, enero/marzo 1980, p. 9–26)

Sobre las relaciones entre la gnoseología y la metafísica tomistas.

7632 García Bazán, Francisco. Tres décadas de estudios plotinianos (UCA/S, 35: 137/138, julio/dic. 1980, p. 281–300)

Artículo bibliográfico que muestra un seguro dominio del tema.

7633 Lértora Mendoza, Celina A. Ciencia y método en Roberto Grosseteste (UNL/H, 18, 1977, p. 153–182)

Trabajo monográfico sobre el método científico en Grosseteste y su aplicación al comentario de la *Física* aristotélica. La conclusión más general es la adhesión a la opinión de que la ciencia moderna aparece más gradualmente de lo que se consideraba anteriormente.

7634 Morales, Cesáreo. Platón, la línea y la dialéctica (Thesis [Nueva Revista de Filosofía y Letras, Universidad Nacional Autónoma de México, México] 2:6, julio 1980, p. 19–27)

Especialmente sobre el libro VI de la *República*.

7635 Sánchez Sorondo, Marcelo. La querella antropológica del siglo XIII: Sigerio y Santo Tomás (UCA/S, 35:137/138, julio/dic. 1980, p. 325–358)

Extenso trabajo monográfico sobre la contraposición de Sigerio de Brabante y Santo Tomás en la exégesis aristotélica y sus consecuencias para la verdad cristiana.

7636 Vélez Correa, Jaime. Reflexión tomista sobre la verdad: cuestionamiento al "cientismo" (PUJ/UH, 11, dic. 1979, p. 111–122)

Traducción libre y comentario del art. 9, cuestión la. del *De Veritate* de Santo Tomás. Lo anterior sirve para cuestionar al "cientismo."

HISTORIA DE LA FILOSOFIA: FILOSOFIA MODERNA

7637 Agoglia, Rodolfo Mario. Sentido y trayectoria de la filosofía moderna: la filosofía moderna como desarrollo y consumación del humanismo renacentista. Quito: Ediciones de la Universidad Católica, 1978 [i.e. 1979]. 149 p.; bibl.

Contiene trabajos críticos sobre Leonardo, Kant, Herder, Fichte y Hegel, precedidos por un estudio de conjunto: "La Filosofía Moderna y el Nuevo Humanismo."

7638 Battro, Antonio M. Psicología, geometría y filosofía del espacio visual (CIF/RLF, 5:2, julio 1979, p. 19–31, abstract)

"El objeto de este trabajo consiste en presentar algunos resultados recientes de la psicofísica y de la geometría, que pueden ser útiles para discutir el problema filosófico del espacio, tal como lo planteara Kant." Una de las conclusiones es que, "a diferencia de lo que pensaba Kant, el espacio percibido no es una forma, sino que 'engendra formas'."

7639 Braun, Rafael. Hobbes y las causas de la guerra civil (CIF/RLF, 6:1, marzo 1980, p. 27–35)

La guerra civil o la inestabilidad del régimen político, que fue gran preocupación de Hobbes, es analizada en los capítulos correspondientes de las obras de este filósofo.

7640 Brunelli, Marilene Rodrigues de Mello. ¿Que é o saber? (UMGFF/K, 68, jan./ dez. 1975, p. 77–88)

Se trata de una comparación entre la analítica de los conceptos en la *Crítica de la razón pura* de Kant y el capítulo III de la *Fenomenología del espíritu*, de Hegel.

7641 Carrión, Rejane. Notas: Hume e as "causas ocultas" (CIF/RLF, 5:3, nov. 1979, p. 263–272)

En base a los textos de Hume establece la distinción entre causas (todavía) desconocidas y causas (para siempre) inaccesibles, intentando con ello aclarar el problema de las "causas ocultas" en el filósofo inglés.

7642 Casalla, Mario. La filosofía hegeliana de la historia: presentación y crítica (RFL, 3 : 5/6, enero/dic. 1977, p. 111–142)

Constituye el marco de referencia para tratar el tema: "América en el pensamiento de Hegel," que el autor desarrollará en un libro próximo a publicarse.

7643 Chaui, Marilena de Souza. Direito natural e direito civil em Hobbes e Espinosa (CIF/RLF, 6 : 1, marzo 1980, p. 57–71)

Semejanzas y diferencias entre ambos filósofos, siendo las segundas, para la autora, más numerosas y basándose en dos motivos: la concepción de la causalidad y la concepción del *conatus*.

7644 Cordua, Carla. Idea figura: el concepto hegeliano de arte. Río Piedras, P.R.: Editorial Universitaria, 1979. 293 p.; bibl.; index.

Obra monográfica realizada con toda seriedad técnica, la primera que se ocupa del tema, con tales características, en lengua castellana. Aunque por la naturaleza del pensamiento de Hegel el contexto total es ineludible, el propósito más restringido de la investigación es "sacar a luz de manera expresa y nítida el concepto hegeliano de arte, separando el problema del ser del arte de los otros muchos asuntos de que la estética del filósofo trata."

7645 Cruz Vélez, Danilo. Marx y el problema de la confusión de la filosofía con la política (CIF/RLF, 5 : 3, nov. 1979, p. 235–248)

Analizando los primeros escritos de Marx y su relación con Hegel, muestra cómo con Marx se produce por primera vez la confusión entre filosofía y política, confusión que el autor considera necesario despejar.

7646 Garber E., Dino. El espacio como relación en Leibniz. Caracas, Venezuela: Equinoccio, 1980. 285 p.; bibl. (Colección mayor)

Trabajo monográfico seriamente elaborado. La hipótesis que lo guía es que la concepción del espacio en Leibniz es compatible con su sistema y que sólo entendiendo el espacio como una relación se pueden resolver ciertas paradojas en sus ideas.

7647 Guariglia, Osvaldo N. Hobbes y la justificación de las normas (CIF/RLF, 6 : 1, marzo 1980, p. 47–55)

En torno al hecho de que Hobbes sería el primero en fundamentar la justificación "instrumental" de las normas.

7648 Jaguaribe, Helio. El pensamiento social y político de Marx (FCE/TE, 46[4] : 184, oct./dic. 1979, p. 805–830)

Presentación de las principales tesis y breve análisis crítico de las mismas. ". . . el Marx filósofo del humanismo y sociólogo e historiador del capitalismo [y su posible superación es] el que se reviste de una relevancia permanente para el pensamiento y la acción contemporáneos."

7649 Lafer, Celso. Hobbes e a filosofia do direito (CIF/RLF, 6 : 1, marzo 1980, p. 17–25)

Sobre el peso del Estado y el soberano en la interpretación hobbesiana del derecho. Hobbes habría sido antecedente del positivismo jurídico de los siglos XIX y XX.

7650 Lima, Rômulo de Araújo and Rubens Pinto Lyra. A visão rousseauniana: o estado como instrumento de igualidade e de liberdade (Horizonte [Universidade Federal de Paraíba, João Pessoa, Brasil] 3 : 7, abril/junho 1978, p. 146–161)

Contiene una parte expositiva y otra crítica. En la segunda se señala el carácter "idealista" de las principales tesis de Rousseau, desde una posición de cierta coloración marxista.

7651 Mantilla Pineda, Benigno. La filosofía del derecho de G.W.F. Hegel (UA/U, 52 : 200/201, enero/junio 1977, p. 5–11, bibl., ill., plate)

Visión general comentada de la filosofía del derecho de Hegel.

7652 Martins, Estevão de Rezende. O caminho para a autonomia (CIF/RLF, 6 : 2, julio 1980, p. 99–117)

Buen trabajo monográfico que estudia la influencia de Baumgarten en la formación de la ética kantiana, y en especial en la concepción de la libertad en el Kant pre-crítico.

7653 Monteiro, João Paulo. Estado e ideologia em Thomas Hobbes (CIF/RLF, 6 : 1, marzo 1980, p. 37–45)

Se desestima en la interpretación de Hobbes la "imagen" de una "neutralidad filosófica" y la de una representación de la ideología burguesa. El autor se inclina por una interpretación "ideológica," pero de rasgos diferentes.

7654 Olaso, Ezequiel de. La historia del escepticismo moderno y el problema de los escepticismos (CIF/RLF, 6:3, nov. 1980, p. 267–276)

El centro del análisis crítico es la obra de Popkin, *The history of scepticism from Erasmus to Spinoza* (1979), pero revisa también otros trabajos y hace reflexiones propias en un tema del cual el autor es buen conocedor.

7655 ———. Hobbes y la formación del análisis del discurso ideológico (CIF/RLF, 6:1, marzo 1980, p. 3–16)

Trabajo interesante que hace de Hobbes un antecedente de los materialistas franceses del siglo XVIII en lo que se refiere a percibir el carácter ideológico de ciertas doctrinas. El autor sostiene que la bibliografía sobre el asunto no ha reconocido esa posición de Hobbes en la historia del "discurso ideológico."

7656 Oliveira, Antonio Eunizé de. Jean-Jacques Rousseau: pedagogia da liberdade. João Pessoa: Editora Universitária UFPb, 1977. 100 p.; bibl. (Série Ciências sociais; 1. Estudos universitários)

Sobre el *Emilio* de Rousseau, con intención de contribuir a una filosofía de la educación.

7657 Oviedo, José. Génesis y desarrollo del problema metodológico en Marx: elementos introductorios. Santo Domingo?: Ediciones Poder Popular, 1980. 117 p.; bibl.; ill. (Colección Poder popular)

Se trata de una introducción a la obra de Marx. La intención es promover la acción marxista militante.

7658 *Revista de Filosofía de la Universidad de Costa Rica.* Número Extraordinario sobre Spinoza. Vol. 15, No. 42, dic. 1977– San José.

Este número especial contiene tres artículos sobre Spinoza: E. Venegas Villegas, "El Derecho en el Pensamiento de Baruch Spinoza;" F. Alvarez González, "Dos Ensayos Spinoza" ("Racionalidad y Libertad en Spinoza" y "Spinoza y el Pensamiento Alemán"); y A. Bernardini, "Spinoza: Dios como Substancia y *causa sui.*"

7659 Rodríguez Bustamante, Norberto. El concepto de libertad en John Stuart Mill (IDES/DE, 19:73, abril/junio 1979, p. 95–106, table)

Exposición de *On liberty*, con el fin de señalar "las principales tesis del autor con miras al examen de su validez actual."

7660 Rodríguez Larreta, Juan. Cuatro argumentos de Berkeley contra el realismo representativo (Análisis Filosófico [Sociedad Argentina de Análisis Filosófico (SADAF), Buenos Aires] 1:1, mayo 1981, p. 1–18)

Ilustra sobre la habilidad argumentativa de Berkeley. Trata de mostrar, en los mencionados argumentos, "su grado de vigencia y de fertilidad teóricas." Siguen al artículo discusiones de Alberto Moretti y Eduardo Rabossi.

7661 Rosales, Alberto. El problema de la unidad de la subjetividad en la *Crítica de la razón pura* de Kant (USB/RVF, 13, 1980, p. 81–93)

El tema es cuidadosamente examinado y, al final, puesto en relación con la interpretación heideggeriana de la *Crítica.*

7662 Vásquez, Eduardo. Algunas consideraciones sobre la relación entre Hegel y Marx (USB/RVF, 13, 1980, p. 95–121)

A pesar de tratarse de un tema sumamente transitado, las consideraciones del autor son aprovechables. Tienen utilidad también las aclaraciones terminológicas que hace sobre algunas versiones castellanas de conceptos hegelianos.

7663 Vaz, Henrique Cláudio de Lima. Uma nova edição da filosofia do direito de Hegel (UMGFF/K, 68, jan./dez. 1975, p. 1–12)

Informa sobre la edición de la *Filosofía del derecho* de Hegel realizada por Karl-Heinz Ilting y examina críticamente varias obras sobre la filosofía política de Hegel.

7664 Velloso, Arthur Versiani. Filosofia da história (UMGFF/K, 68, jan./dez. 1975, p. 13–29)

Sobre la filosofía de la historia de Kant y Herder.

7665 Xirau, Ramón. Vico: historia real, historia ideal, sabiduría y carencia de utopía (CM/D, 17:1[97], enero/feb. 1981, p. 31–34, bibl., ill.)

Uno de los temas principales es la posibilidad de distinguir rasgos utopistas en Vico. Artículo no muy ordenado de un autor que suele ser lúcido y poseer elegancia de expresión.

HISTORIA DE LA FILOSOFIA: FILOSOFIA CONTEMPORANEA

7666 Basave Fernández del Valle, Agustín. Pensamiento y trayectoria de Max Scheler (UNL/H, 18, 1977, p. 13–28) Apreciación general de Max Scheler, en la cual las críticas no impiden la simpatía.

7667 Beuchot, Mauricio. Filosofía analítica y conocimiento (UI/RF, 11:32, mayo/ agosto 1978, p. 289–305) Presentación sintética y general del movimiento analítico de habla inglesa.

7668 Casaubón, Juan A. Apéndice sobre intencionalidad (UCA/S, 34:131/132, enero/junio 1979, p. 47–54) Complemento a un trabajo inédito más extenso: *La intencionalidad del conocimiento en Husserl y Santo Tomás.*

7669 Cruz Vélez, Danilo. El porvenir de la fenomenología trascendental (UCR/ RF, 17:46, julio/dic. 1979, p. 161–164) Intenta, "en actitud estrictamente histórica," aclarar "la situación a que ha llegado la fenomenología trascendental a causa del hecho histórico de su superación, con el propósito de averiguar qué problemas vivos hay aún en ella." La "superación" (como "potenciación") proviene de la obra de Heidegger y el avance de la filosofía y las ciencias. Excelente por su claridad dentro de una extensión mínima para el tema.

7670 Derisi, Octavio N. Los aportes de M. Scheler a la ética (UCA/S, 34:131/ 132, enero/junio 1979, p. 61–66) Favorable y resumido juicio sobre el valor de la *Etica* de Scheler. Este, sin embargo, fue sólo un fenomenólogo y no llegó a alcanzar "la realidad del ser de la metafísica."

7671 La Filosofía. Coordinador, Abelardo Villegas. Colaboradores, Ramón Xirau *et al.* México: Universidad Nacional Autónoma de México, 1979. 280 p. (Las Humanidades en el siglo XX; 5) Obra colectiva. Cada autor expone una de las grandes corrientes filosóficas contemporáneas. El contenido es el siguiente: Ramón Xirau, "El Espiritualismo Contemporáneo;" Margarita Vera y Cuspinera, "Retorno al Idealismo: Neokantismo y Neohegelianismo;" María R. Palazón, "Historicismo o Historicidad;" Juliana González, "La Fenomenología;" Juan G. Bates, "El Existencia-lismo;" Abelardo Villegas, "El Marxismo del Siglo XX;" Wonfilio Trejo, "La Filosofía Analítica en Moore y Russell;" Eduardo A. Rabossi, "La Filosofía Analítica;" Jesús Vergara Aceves, "Filosofía Cristiana y Tomismo en el Siglo XX;" Gustavo Escobar V., "La Filosofía Latinoamericana en el Siglo XX."

7672 Francovich, Guillermo. El odio al pensamiento: los nuevos filósofos franceses. Buenos Aires: Editorial Depalma, 1982. 130 p. Visión de conjunto, creemos que la única en castellano, que ofrece una exposición clara de una materia de por sí poco sistemática y diversificada según los distintos autores. Se tratan con mayor detalle libros de Guy Lardreau y Christian Jambet; André Glucksman; Jean-Marie Benoist; Bernard-Henry Lévy; Jean Dollé; Françoise Lévy; y Michel Le Bris. Señala posibles influencias y recoge útiles materiales periodísticos. La obra se completó en 1978.

7673 Gaos, José. La profecía en Ortega (CAM, 220:5, sept./oct. 1978, p. 87–148) Aparentemente se trata de un antiguo artículo de Gaos que se vuelve a publicar como homenaje a ese autor. Es de un alto grado de detalle en el análisis de la obra de Ortega en lo que se refiere al tema indicado por el título.

7674 García Bazán, Francisco. Max Scheler y la fenomenología de la religión (RFL, 3:5/6, enero/dic. 1977, p. 171–179) Tras exponer las líneas principales de *De lo eterno en el hombre*, se agregan comentarios personales para "ampliar los horizontes de comprensión que sobre la realidad religiosa" proporcionara Max Scheler.

7675 González G., Ricardo. Libertad y ateísmo en Jean Paul Sartre (UPB, 35:123, abril 1979, p. 25–40) Trabajo de naturaleza primordialmente expositiva, en el cual sin embargo se rechazan las conclusiones ateístas de Sartre.

7676 Gutiérrez, Carlos B. La filosofía hermenéutica de Gadamer (ECO, 36:222, abril 1980, p. 588–596) Exposición muy general de la hermenética de Gadamer.

7677 Lanchas, J. Felipe. Heidegger desde la perspectiva de Agustín de Hipona (PUJ/ UH, 10, 1979, p. 117–126)

Intento de contribuir a la comprensión de Heidegger a través de San Agustín.

7678 Martínez Contreras, Jorge. Sartre: la autenticidad y la violencia (Nexos [Sociedad/ciencia/literatura, Centro de Investigación Cultura y Científica, México] 3 : 30, junio 1980, p. 27–32, ill.)

Artículo panorámico sobre ciertos aspectos de la filosofía de Sartre. Considera que en el problema de la autenticidad moral y en el del papel del individuo en los fenómenos sociales "Sartre ha dado más luces de las que se cree."

7679 Montemayor Salazar, Jorge. Apreciaciones de Nicolás Berdiaeff sobre el sentido de la historia (UNL/H, 20, 1979, p. 31–40, bibl.)

Expone *El sentido de la historia*, de Berdiaeff.

7680 Mora Rodríguez, Arnoldo. Existencialismo y epistemología (UCR/RF, 17 : 45, enero/junio 1979, p. 43–48)

Crítica al "idealismo" que estaría en la base de la posición existencialista.

7681 Moura, Carlos Alberto Riberio. A cera e o abelhudo (CIF/RLF, 6 : 3, nov. 1980, p. 235–253, tables)

El subtítulo es expresivo del contenido de esta exposición: "Expresión y percepción en Merleau-Ponty."

7682 Neves, Flávio. Brentano e psicologia do ponto de vista empírico (UMGFF/K, 68, jan./dez. 1975, p. 89–104)

Trabajo de índole expositiva sobre la mencionada obra de Brentano.

7683 Nunes, J. Paulo. Teilhard de Chardin, o Santo Tomás do século XX: paralelismo filosófico-teológico, convergências e divergências. São Paulo: Edições Loyola, 1977. 212 p.; bibl.

Paralelo entre Teilhard y Santo Tomás, tendiente a mostrar lo que hay de tomismo (letra o espíritu) en el primero, contrariamente a opiniones de Gilson y Maritain.

7684 Posse, Abel. Recuerdo de una visita a Martin Heidegger (ECO, 36/3 : 219, enero 1980, p. 230–235)

El acierto del autor hace que el breve testimonio trascienda lo anecdótico.

7685 Rabossi, Eduardo A. Análisis filosófico, lenguaje y metafísica: ensayos sobre la filosofía analítica y el análisis filosófico "clásico." Caracas: Monte Avila Editores, 1977. 244 p.

El concepto de "filosofía analítica" tiene la vigencia que le otorga designar un movimiento filosófico contemporáneo de gran magnitud, pero a la vez su elasticidad y falta de precisos límites semánticos es muy grande. De ahí la utilidad de esta exposición aclaratoria, basada en un buen conocimiento del tema y una simpatía que no obstaculiza la serenidad del enfoque. Básicamente, ofrece en la primera parte una aproximación al concepto de filosofía analítica, y en la segunda un análisis de su primera etapa, centrada en la exposición de Russell, Moore y Wittgenstein.

7686 Rufino, Antonio. O personalismo e o anti-humanismo: dois enfoques para se estudar a obra de Max Scheler (IBF/RBF, 30 : 120, out./dez. 1980, p. 375–383)

La antropología filosófica de Scheler tendría consecuencias "antihumanistas."

7687 Sánchez Puentes, Ricardo. La intencionalidad fenomenológica (UI/RF, 11 : 32, mayo/agosto 1978, p. 227–242)

Panorama de la fenomenología como modo de conocimiento.

7688 Sasso, Javier. La fundamentación de la ciencia según Althusser. 2. ed. Caracas, Monte Avila Editores, 1980. 92 p. (Colección Estudios)

Se expone el intento de Althusser de fundamentar el marxismo como ciencia y se concluye que la epistemología althusseriana no logra su objeto. No es, sin embargo, obra polémica, sino de argumentación.

7689 Silveira, Paulo. Do lado da história: uma leitura crítica da obra de Althusser. Prefácio de Marilena de Sousa Chauí. São Paulo: Livraria Editora Polis [distribuido por Editora Estrutura], 1978. 135 p.; bibl. (Coleção Teoria e história; 1)

Minuciosa crítica a varios aspectos del marxismo de Althusser desde una posición no ajena al marxismo.

7690 Stam, Juan. El ateísmo existencialista de J. P. Sartre (UCR/RF, 17 : 45, enero/junio 1979, p. 37–42)

Artículo de naturaleza expositiva, cuyo principal tema es Dios y la libertad en Sartre.

LOGICA, GNOSEOLOGIA Y TEORIA DE LA CIENCIA

7691 Angelelli, Ignacio. Abstracción y reduplicación (CIF/RLF, 6:3, nov. 1980, p. 255–256)

Breve nota que se propone "señalar una cierta coincidencia entre la abstracción moderna y la reduplicación en la lógica escolástica."

7692 Aquino, Marcelo F. de. Certeza sensível e percepção na esfera da consciência: duas experiências na Fenomenologia do Espírito (UMGFF/K, 68, jan./dez. 1975, p. 30–49)

Exposición del tema del título, con apoyo en las obras críticas de P. J. Labarrière y L. B. Puntel.

7693 Asenjo, F. G. La topología de la localización múltiple (CIF/RLF, 5:2, julio 1979, p. 41–50, bibl.)

En último análisis, el propósito del trabajo es contribuir a la construcción de "una geometría que incorpore . . . aspectos dinámicos de la realidad física tal como la conocemos por medio de la ciencia física y de la astronomía."

7694 Botero Uribe, Darío. Teoría y práctica (UN/IV, 55/56, agosto 1979, p. 43–58)

Reflexiones sobre el tema desde el punto de vista de un marxismo amplio.

7695 Bunge, Mario. El finalismo en biología, psicología y sociología (CIF/RLF, 5:2, julio 1979, p. 33–40, bibl.)

La tesis principal es que, en los campos seleccionados, la intención (como propensión teleológica) no existe, o si parece existir es susceptible de explicación científica.

7696 Camacho N., Luis A. Lógica del cambio-desarrollo y cálculo proposicional: análisis y comparaciones (UCR/RF, 17:45, enero/junio 1979, p. 49–56)

El propósito es exponer la sistematización de la "lógica del cambio y del desarrollo," realizada por B. V. Sesic, esperando que con ello se aclare la supuesta oposición de "lógica formal" y "lógica dialéctica."

7697 ———. "Lógica" dialéctica y lógica "formal:" hacia una precisión mayor en términos, conceptos y métodos (UCR/RF, 16:44, julio/dic. 1978, p. 153–157)

Crítica a lo que el autor considera indebida importancia concedida a la "lógica dialéctica" y en especial a la escasa consideración que sus defensores atribuyen a la "lógica formal." Tal vez lo más interesante de las muy razonables reflexiones del autor es que muestran la irreductible distancia que separa a los autores marxistas de los especialistas en lógica y filosofía de la ciencia. El breve artículo muestra asimismo que la cuestión va más allá del plano teórico.

7698 Castañeda, Héctor Neri. El espacio perceptual y la forma lógica básica de las proposiciones perceptuales (UCR/RF, 17:46, julio/dic. 1979, p. 165–172)

Atribuyendo menor importancia al problema clásico de la naturaleza de las cualidades secundarias en la filosofía de la percepción, ofrece "un punto de vista estructural" (no atomista), "en conexión con los hechos físicos elementales sobre percepción y con la estructura lógica de las oraciones que describen los contenidos de percepción."

7699 ———. El método filosófico y el conocimiento directo del yo (CIF/RLF, 6:2, julio 1980, p. 171–183)

La meditación del autor se hace de la mano del análisis crítico de un capítulo de la obra de Chisholm, *Person and object: a metaphysical study* (1976).

7700 ———. Negaciones, imperativos y colores (USB/RVF, 13, 1980, p. 21–69)

Extenso y complejo trabajo (caracterizado como "una contribución a la tipología semántica y ontológica") sobre el problema de la naturaleza y funciones de la negación, que se vincula a las tesis del autor de su obra *Thinking and doing*.

7701 Gianelli, Alicia E. Los enunciados analíticos en la epistemología actual (CIF/RLF, 6:1, marzo 1980, p. 73–84)

El tema de la analiticidad se examina en al ámbito de la filosofía de la ciencia y en el contexto de la bibliografía reciente de lengua inglesa.

7702 Klimovsky, Gregorio. Tipos de base empírica (Análisis Filosófico [Sociedad Argentina de Análisis Filosófico, Buenos Aires] 1:1, mayo 1981, p. 59–70)

Entendiendo la "base empírica" como lo que permite el control de las teorías científicas, muestra que la concepción de dicha base no es simple, sino que permite distinguir cinco tipos: filosófica, epistemológica, metodológica, relativa y ficticia.

7703 Lungarzo, Carlos. Lógica dialéctica y coherencia lógica (CIF/RLF, 5:3, nov. 1979, p. 249–262)

Sobre las condiciones en que sería posible una lógica dialéctica, desde las premisas de la lógica formal.

7704 Malo González, Hernán. Pensamiento lógico y pensamiento mítico (Cultura [Revista del Banco Central de Ecuador, Quito] 2:4, mayo/agosto 1979, p. 47–65)

Es en general una defensa del pensar mítico frente a lo que el autor estima incorrectas apreciaciones racionalistas de raíz occidental.

7705 Miró Quesada Cantuarias, Francisco. Filosofía de la matemáticas. Lima, Perú: Ignacio Prado Pastor, 1980. 1 v.; bibl.; indexes (Lógica; 1)

Este manual, único en castellano, que sepamos, intenta ser una introducción al "contenido teórico de la moderna filosofía de la lógica y de la matemática." El presente es sólo el primer volumen de los dos de que se compondrá la obra. Quiere ser autosuficiente desde el punto de vista didáctico y proporcionar todos los elementos necesarios para la comprensión del tema. El autor advierte que se trata en realidad de una obra filosófica, cuyo objetivo último es contribuir a una teoría de la razón. Sobre este último tema, véase, del autor, *HLAS 40:9657* y otros varios valiosos trabajos.

7706 Newman, Jaime García. Epistemología dialéctica (USB/F, 22:64, enero/abril 1980, p. 5–60)

Contrapone al "reduccionismo" (el neopositivismo, el funcionalismo, el estructuralismo, etc.) la epistemología dialéctica, que estima como la verdadera. La lógica formal es "el soporte lógico de las ciencias reduccionistas." Apoya lo anterior un cuadro histórico que naturalmente culmina en Marx.

7707 Prada de Moulière, Blanca I. Ciencia y epistemología (USB/F, 22:64, enero/abril 1980, p. 61–84)

Panorama de cuestiones y opiniones sobre la epistemología en el sentido amplio de teoría de la ciencia.

7708 Reig, Osvaldo A. Proposiciones para una solución al problema de la realidad de las especies biológicas (USB/RVF, 11, 1979, p. 79–106)

El tema es de metabiología o filosofía de la biología, y reproduce en ese campo la contraposición clásica de nominalismo y realismo. El autor adelanta una tesis personal, en un meritorio trabajo que combina la seriedad científica con el conocimiento filosófico.

7709 Sosa, Ernesto. Los fundamentos del fundacionismo (CIF/RLF, 5:2, julio 1979, p. 3–17, abstract)

El "fundacionismo" es la posición gnoseológica que sostiene que el conocimiento tiene un verdadero fundamento. A esta posición se opone el "coherentismo." La contraposición de ambos puntos de vista ha originado una discusión, a clarificar la cual este trabajo quiere contribuir.

7710 Trejo, Wonfilio. Fenomenalismo y realismo. México: Universidad Nacional Autónoma de México, 1977. 52 p.; bibl. (Colección Cuadernos. Centro de Investigaciones de Filosofía de la Ciencia y del Lenguaje)

El tema es la relación entre los datos sensibles y los objetos físicos. La discusión se realiza en torno a los opiniones de Moore y Ayer.

AXIOLOGIA Y ETICA

7711 Rabossi, Eduardo. Estudios éticos: cuestiones conceptuales y metodológicas. Valencia, Venezuela: Oficina Latinoamericana de Investigaciones Jurídicas y Sociales, Universidad de Carabobo, 1979. 179 p. (Colección Temas y problemas; 2)

Contiene los siguientes trabajos: "Notas sobre la Moral y sus Niveles Metodológicos de Estudio;" "Análisis Filosófico y Teorías Eticas" (véase *HLAS 40:9670*); "La Falacia Naturalista;" "Acerca de una Prueba Posible de los Primeros Príncipios Eticos" (véase *HLAS 42:7789*); "Emotivismo Etico, Positivismo Lógico e Irracionalismo;" "Relativismo y Ciencias Sociales." Orientado en la corriente analítica, el autor ha mostrado una persistencia en estos temas que ya va dando por resultado una obra significativa, no sólo vista desde Argentina sino en el plano latinoamericano en general.

7712 ——. La justificación moral del castigo. Buenos Aires: Editorial Astrea, 1976. 131 p. (Filosofía y derecho; 5)

Examen expositivo y crítico del tema

en algunos clásicos y especialmente en la bibliografía actual de habla inglesa. El eje de la obra es la exposición o "reconstrucción" de las dos posiciones que se han adoptado frente a la justificación moral del castigo: la "retribucionista" y la "utilitarista." Reconociendo que las dos producen un *impase*, el esfuerzo del autor se dirige a ampliar críticamente el campo mediante ciertas preguntas y a dar su aportación personal al tema. Complementa lo central de la obra una serie de comentarios sobre diversos textos y valiosas informaciones bibliográficas. Tiene el doble valor de ser una visión de conjunto y una contribución al tema.

7713 ———. Naturaleza humana y moralidad (CIF/RLF, 6:2, julio 1980, p. 119–136)

El tema lo constituyen las "cuestiones acerca de la naturaleza altruísta o egoísta del hombre." Lo estudia a través del análisis de los moralistas británicos del siglo XVIII. Los problemas que ellos se plantearon se consideran, con el consiguiente traslado, todavía vigentes.

ANTROPOLOGIA FILOSOFICA Y CIENCIAS HUMANAS

7714 **Casaubón, Juan.** Los problemas epistemológicos del hombre (UCA/S, 35:137/138, julio/dic. 1980, p. 251–272)

Visión tomista de las distintas ciencias y formas de saber que se ocupan del hombre, tendiente a la unificación de ciencia y filosofía en el campo antropológico.

7715 **Caturelli, Alberto.** Los "humanismos" y el humanismo cristiano (UCA/S, 35:137/138, julio/dic. 1980, p. 189–216)

El verdadero humanismo es el cristocéntrico y católico. Este se enfrenta a otros humanismos seculares e inclusive al de la teología de la liberación.

7716 ———. Reflexiones para una filosofía cristiana de la educación (Revista de la Universidad Nacional de Córdoba [Dirección General de Publicaciones, Córdoba, Argentina] 2:1/5, 3. serie, marzo/dic. 1978, p. 51–88)

Este extenso artículo responde plenamente a su título. Del "inmanentismo" contemporáneo se critica especialmente al marxismo y expresiones latinoamericanas como la de Paulo Freire.

7717 **Francovich, Guillermo.** El hombre, el mundo y los valores. La Paz: Librería Editorial Juventud, 1981. 141 p.

Este libro se originó en conferencias dadas en 1945. Con un agregado, fueron publicadas en forma de libro de La Paz, con el título actual, en 1950. El volumen se reeditó en México en 1967, con el título de *Restauración de la filosofía*. Vuelve a aparecer, sin cambios, con el título original.

7718 **González Salas, Carlos.** El concepto del hombre en la filosofía (UNL/H, 18, 1977, p. 29–44)

En esta exposición general se destacan las ideas de Pascal, Nietzsche y Jaspers.

7719 **El Hombre y su conducta:** ensayos filosóficos en honor de Risieri Frondizi / Man and his conduct: philosophical essays in honor of Risieri Frondizi. Jorge J. E. Gracia, editor. Río Piedras, P.R.: Editorial Universitaria, 1980. 346 p.

En la clásica manera del *Festschrift*, esta obra representa el merecido homenaje a una seria y persistente labor filosófica desarrollada en medios académicos de América Latina y Estados Unidos. Jorge Gracia hace una breve presentación biográfica de Frondizi y Leopoldo Montoya presenta su bibliografía. Francisco Miró Quesada, una de las principales figuras del pensamiento latinoamericano actual, destaca en un enjundioso artículo los valores del pensamiento filosófico de Frondizi. Los demás estudios tratan temas relacionados con "el hombre y su conducta" y están firmados por relevantes autores como J. Ferrater Mora, Eduardo Nicol, P. A. Schilpp, Marvin Farber, Arturo Ardao, A. Berendtson, M. Bunge, A. J. Cappelletti, H. N. Castañeda, Ch. Hartshorne, R. Maliandi, E. Mayz Vallenilla, E. Rabossi, Ernesto Sosa, y Alfred Stern, entre otros.

7720 **Kothe, Flávio René.** Caminhos e descaminhos da crítica: encontro marcado com Heidegger (Reflexão [Pontifícia Universidade Católica de Campinas, Instituto de Filosofia e Teologia, São Paulo, Brasil] 15, set./dez. 1979, p. 69–89, bibl.)

O trabalho está enfocado desde el punto de vista de la metodología de la crítica literaria.

7721 **Lira, Osvaldo.** Verdad y libertad. Santiago: Ediciones Nueva Universidad, Universidad Católica de Chile, 1977. 206 p.

Reflexiones de inspiración tomista sobre la verdad (como *adecuación*), la libertad (en el sentido de "libre albedrío") y la relación entre ambas.

7722 Palerm, Angel. Antropología y marxismo. México: Centro de Investigaciones Superiores del Instituto Nacional de Antropología e Historia; Editorial Nueva Imagen, 1980. 224 p.; ill.

Reúne un conjunto de trabajos histórico-antropológicos animados por la idea de la contribución que el marxismo (en sentido teórico, no ideológico ni partidario) puede dar a la antropología y a las ciencias sociales en general.

7723 Pescador Sarget, Augusto. ¿Qué es el hombre? (UC/AT, 438, 1978, p. 55–75)

Se repasan teorías del hombre de la filosofía alemana contemporánea; se propone una "descripción temporal del hombre;" y se reflexiona sobre las actitudes ante la muerte.

7724 Ponferrada, Gustavo E. Antropología filosófica y pedagogía (UCA/S, 34: 131/132, enero/junio 1979, p. 37–46)

La tesis básica es que toda concepción pedagógica depende de la correspondiente teoría del hombre (antropología filosófica).

7725 Strasser, Carlos. La razón científica en política y sociología. Buenos Aires: Amorrortu Editores, 1979. 226 p.; bibl. (Biblioteca de sociología)

Contribución a la epistemología de la ciencia política y de la sociología. El punto de partida es situar en su correcto valor y alcance "la orientación conductista microempírica y/o matematizante" (o "empirionaturalismo," o "empirismo conductista"), sin desconocer sus méritos ni caer en la politización sin valor científico alguno, como ha ocurrido y ocurre en ciertos sectores de América Latina. (Con acierto dice el autor que estos sectores "a una ciencia sin política la cambiaron por una política sin ciencia".) La obra se articula en torno a los grandes conceptos de ciencia, poder y saber. El capítulo de mayor interés epistemológico es el titulado: "De la naturaleza y la estructura del conocimiento en política y sociología."

7726 Trindade, Liana Salvia. As raízes ideológicas das teorias sociais. São Paulo: Editora Atica, 1978. 164 p.; bibl. (Ensaios; 40)

El tema central es el pensamiento de Joseph de Maistre. Este se pone en relación con la mentalidad conservadora en general y con la constitución de la sociología en Comte, Durkheim y Lévi-Strauss.

7727 Valdés, Margarita M. Funcionalismo y fisicalismo (CIF/RLF, 6:3, nov. 1980, p. 195–212)

Funcionalismo y fisicalismo se consideran aquí como soluciones al problema de la naturaleza de los estados mentales, según han sido considerados en reciente bibliografía de habla inglesa (Block, Fodor, Nelson, Putnam, etc.). Comentando esta literatura especializada la autora propone un refinamiento del funcionalismo que no sería incompatible con el fisicalismo y que de hecho vendría a resultar un funcionalismo fisicalista.

FILOSOFIA DEL DERECHO Y FILOSOFIA POLITICA

7728 Arnáiz Amigo, Aurora. Estructura del estado. Prólogo de Héctor González Uribe. México: M. A. Porrúa, 1979. 361 p.; bibl.

Texto de estudio (se reseñaron otros textos de la autora en *HLAS 42:7816–7817*). Analiza los elementos componentes del Estado y el problema más básico de la naturaleza y justificación del poder político.

7729 Basave Fernández del Valle, Agustín. Fundamento y esencia de la politosofía (UCA/S, 35:137/138, julio/dic. 1980, p. 519–540)

Distingue la *politología* de la *politosofía* (en grandes líneas, ciencia y filosofía de la política) y dibuja el campo de la segunda. Tal vez más importante que eso, el ensayo viene a ser una síntesis de filosofía política de inspiración cristiana.

7730 Cappelletti, Angel J. Génesis y desarrollo de la filosofía social de Kropotkin (UCR/RF, 16:44, julio/dic. 1978, p. 143–152)

Clara exposición de la filosofía social del pensador anarquista, que el autor considera poco estudiada.

7731 Cappelletti, Angel J. La teoría de la propiedad en Proudhon y otros momentos del pensamiento anarquista. Madrid: Las Ediciones de la Piqueta; Editores Mexicanos Unidos, n.d. 198 p.

El título proviene del primero de los ensayos recogidos en el libro. Hay otros sobre Bakunin, Kropotkin, Rudolf Rocker y Rafael

Barret, todos vinculados al pensamiento anarquista.

7732 Castagno, Antonio. Símbolos y mitos políticos. Buenos Aires: Editorial Universitaria de Buenos Aires, 1980. 93 p.; bibl. (Temas)

Se trata más bien de una exposición general de los conceptos de símbolo y mito, con aplicación a la realidad política. Aunque consulta una bibliografía considerable, carece de una tesis bien definida.

7733 Chaui, Marilena de Souza. O que é ideologia? Capa, Otávio Roth, Felipe Doctors. Caricaturas, Emílio Damiani. Ilustração, Joji Kussunoki. São Paulo: Editora Brasiliense, 1980. 125 p.; ill. (Coleção Primeiros passos)

Obra de iniciação. Se dedica principalmente al concepto marxista de ideologia.

7734 Democracia: una bibliografía selectiva sobre el tema; el concepto en Aristóteles, Rousseau y Max Weber, se discuten los trabajos de Prebisch, Muñoz, Germani, Faletto y otros acerca de las condiciones sociales de la democracia en América Latina. Buenos Aires: El Cid Editor, 1979. 234 p.; bibl. (Crítica y utopía; 1)

Contiene trabajos de Gino Germani, Raúl Prebisch, Oscar Muñoz, Enzo Faletto y otros, discutidos a su vez por otros autores. Incluye además una bibliografía sobre la democracia y notas históricas sobre Aristóteles, Rousseau, Burke y Max Weber.

7735 El Discurso político. Mario Monteforte Toledo, coordinador. México, D.F.: Universidad Nacional Autónoma de México: Editorial Nueva Imagen, 1980. 342 p.

Recoge los resultados de un encuentro entre especialistas franceses y latinoamericanos. Según se expresa en la introducción, se trataría de la primera reunión sobre el tema que se realiza en el mundo. Las aportaciones latinoamericanas en forma de ponencia fueron: Gilberto Giménez, "Teorías sobre las Ideologías: Estado Actual de la Cuestión;" Eliseo Verón, "La Semiosis Social;" y J. M. Bulnes Aldunate, "Determinaciones Retóricas del Discurso Político Latinoamericano." En la temática confluyen lingüística, semiótica, sociología, crítica de la ideología y variantes marxistas.

7736 Epistemología y política: crítica al positivismo de las ciencias sociales en América Latina desde la racionalidad dialéctica. Guillermo Hoyos Vásquez *et al.* Bogotá, Colombia: Fundación Friedrich Naumann: Centro de Investigación y Educación Popular, 1980. 345 p.; bibl.

Recoge trabajos (18 en total) de dos seminarios sobre "Epistemología y Política," llevados a cabo uno en Lima (1977) y el otro en Bogotá (1979). El título es correcto, pero el subtítulo puede conducir a error y no representa el punto de vista de algunos participantes, como por ejemplo el de Francisco Miró Quesada, cuyos trabajos—dicho sea de paso—posiblemente sean lo mejor del volumen.

7737 Farrell, Martín Diego. Acerca de las obligaciones *prima facie* (CIF/RLF, 6:2, julio 1980, p. 137–150)

Con excepción de la obligación que el juez tiene de escuchar al acusado, todas las obligaciones jurídicas son obligaciones *prima facie*, es decir, no son absolutas sino que pueden ser dejadas de lado por obligaciones posteriores. Se discuten opiniones de Ross, Rawls, Hart y Hare.

7738 ———. Las circunstancias de justicia (CIF/RLF, 5:2, julio 1979, p. 71–75, abstract)

Breve crítica a un aspecto de *A theory of justice,* de Rawls.

7739 García Huidobro, Juan E. El proyecto cultural gramsciano: la reforma intelectual y moral (UN/IV, 55/56, agosto 1979, p. 3–42, bibl., table)

Extensa exposición del tema. Muy brevemente, al final sugiere aplicaciones al caso de América Latina.

7740 Ghirardi, Olsen A. La sofística y el origen de la filosofía del derecho (Revista de la Universidad Nacional de Córdoba [Dirección General de Publicaciones, Córdoba, Argentina] 2:1/5, 3. serie, marzo/dic. 1978, p. 113–133)

Exposición de índole general. Entre otras cosas, señala cómo la filosofía del derecho habría nacido del relativismo, especialmente el de Protágoras.

7741 Hernández, Héctor H. Sobre la democracia en Kelsen (UNC/BCPS, 23, 1978, p. 145–173)

Crítica a Kelsen en *Esencia y valor de la democracia,* pero también a la democracia misma y al liberalismo. No extraña así que Maurras sea un autor elogiado en el artículo.

7742 Konder, Leandro. Introdução ao fascismo. Rio de Janeiro: Graal, 1977. 128 p.; bibl. (Série Teoria e realidade; no. 1. Biblioteca de estudos humanos)

Além de intentar la determinación de la naturaleza del fenómeno fascista, se examinan las interpretaciones que se dieron del fascismo durante su vigencia y posteriormente. Contiene una considerable bibliografía de fuentes y de obras secundarias en los principales idiomas europeos.

7743 Libertad y libertades. Percival Cowley V. et al. Santiago, Chile: Ediciones Aconcagua, 1977. 139 p.; bibl. (Colección Lautaro)

Unifica a estos ensayos un punto de vista cristiano y el apoyo a la democracia, el pluralismo y las libertades concretas (políticas, sociales, económicas, autonomía de lo cultural, etc.).

7744 Neira, Enrique. ¿Cristianos-marxistas?: algunos puntos de cuestionamiento. Caracas: Universidad Católica Andrés Bello, 1977. 116 p.; bibl. (Colección Manoa; 3)

Impugnación de la posibilidad de que puedan unirse el marxismo y el cristianismo, sin peligro de desnaturalización de ambos, pero especialmente del segundo. La argumentación es respetuosa.

7745 Nino, Carlos Santiago. Dworkin y la disolución de la controversia "positivismo vs. iusnaturalismo" (CIF/RLF, 6:3, nov. 1980, p. 213–234)

Se analiza la posición de Dworkin en Taking rights seriously como ataque al positivismo jurídico. Se considera que la crítica no es acertada. Finalmente se reelabora la tesis de Dworkin para hacerla eficaz, pero concluyendo que "la posición de Dworkin presupone la adopción de un concepto de derecho que, si bien es antagónico con el que los positivistas defienden, puede coexistir con éste en contextos diferentes y para fines diversos."

7746 Reale, Miguel. O legado de Hobbes a filosofia do direito e do estado (CIF/RLF, 6:2, julio 1980, p. 165–169)

Exposición sucinta sobre el tema.

7747 Soler, Sebastián. Temas antiliberales, marxistas y autoritarios. Buenos Aires: Sur, Editorial Sudamericana, 1977. 179 p.; bibl.

La base de la propaganda política consiste en que la repetición de ciertas palabras termina por generar un "pensamiento"—irracional—y la consiguiente adhesión a él. Este es el punto de partida para el trabajo aclaratorio que el autor lleva a cabo con expresiones como "clase trabajadora," "enajenación," "ideología," "superestructura ideológica," etc.

7748 Souza, Daniel Coelho de. Interpretação e democracia. 2. ed., refundida. São Paulo: Editora Revista dos Tribunais, 1979. 211 p.; bibl.

Con abundante apelación a fuentes, el tema de la obra es la interpretación de la ley, primero examinado en general y en las distintas posiciones que se han adoptado ante él, y luego en particular, dentro del regimen democrático.

7749 La Violencia y sus máscaras: dos ensayos de filosofía. Jorge Millas, Edison Otero Bello. Santiago, Chile: Ediciones Aconcagua, 1978. 109 p.; bibl. (Colección Lautaro)

Se compone de dos ensayos: Jorge Millas, "Las Máscaras Filosóficas de la Violencia," y Edison Otero Bello, "El Tema de la Violencia y sus Implicaciones para la Filosofía." El primero, además de criticar el pensamiento filosófico justificatorio de la violencia revolucionaria, enlaza la reflexión con el tema de la utopía. El segundo pone el tema en relación con recientes resultados de las ciencias humanas.

FILOSOFIA DE LA HISTORIA Y DE LA CULTURA

7750 Agoglia, Rodolfo Mario. Conciencia histórica y tiempo histórico. Quito: Ediciones de la Universidad Católica, 1980. 216 p.; bibl.

Contrariamente a la concepción más corriente, concibe la historia como una ciencia "contemporánea," lo que indica que debe versar" sobre nuestro propio presente" y que el historiador debe tener una visión "desde su propio presente." La historia real es "praxis social presentiva y consciente." El último capítulo trata de la "filosofía latinoamericana como filosofía del Tercer Mundo."

7751 ———. La cultura como facticidad y reclamo (Cultura [Revista del Banco Central del Ecuador, Quito] 2:5, sept./dic. 1979, p. 13–32)

Contiene amplias consideraciones sobre la cultura en la historia de la filosofía y en el trabajo de las ciencias sociales, que concluyen en el establecimiento y la defensa del concepto de "cultura nacional," entendido en general dentro de la línea de la filosofía de la liberación.

7752 Calderón Bouchet, Rubén. Esperanza, historia y utopía. Mendoza, Argentina: Universidad Nacional de Cuyo, Facultad de Ciencias Políticas y Sociales, Centro de Investigaciones, Instituto de Ciencias Políticas, 1978. 260 p.; bibl. (Serie Cuadernos. Universidad Nacional de Cuyo, Facultad de Ciencias Políticas y Sociales, Centro de Investigaciones; 48)

Se mezclan en esta obra temas de teoría de la ciencia histórica y de filosofía de la historia, tratados de la mano con un repaso de ciertos autores que a lo largo de la historia del pensamiento se han ocupado de dichos temas. La inspiración básica del escrito es cristiana, aunque no concentra la exposición en una tesis final y definida.

7753 Escobar, Carlos Henrique de. Ciência da história e ideologia. Rio de Janeiro: Graal, 1979. 168 p.; bibl. (Biblioteca de história; v. no. 3)

Después de un primer capítulo sobre "La Ciencia de la Historia," siguen otros sobre la ideología, las clases sociales, el Estado y sus "aparatos ideológicos," etc. La reflexión se mueve en el ámbito del marxismo francés contemporáneo.

7754 Gallo, Ezequiel. Lo inevitable y lo accidental en la historia (CIF/RLF, 6:3, nov. 1980, p. 257–266, bibl.)

Reflexiones sobre la naturaleza de la historia, desde el punto de vista del historiador y repasando variadas opiniones de la bibliografía sobre el tema.

7755 Giqueaux, Eduardo Julio. El mito y la cultura. Buenos Aires: Ediciones Castañeda, 1979. 178 p.; bibl. (Colección Estudios filosóficos; 7)

Segunda parte de la obra *Elementos para una filosofía de la cultura*, de la cual fue la primera, *Hacia una nueva definición esencial del mito*. El punto de partida es el mito como origen de la cultura (transición del mito al logos). Se analizan así, entre otras, las relaciones del mito con la ciencia, la filosofía, la religión y el arte.

7756 González Rojo, Enrique. Teoría científica de la historia. México: Editorial Diógenes, 1977. 403 p.; bibl.

Obra de intención introductoria. Su orientación está dada por el título del tercer capítulo, el más sistemático: "El Materialismo Histórico como Ciencia de la Historia."

7757 Guzmán Jorquera, Arsenio. Intervención en los procesos y modificación del futuro (UNMSM/L, 48:84/85, 2. semestre, 1976, p. 41–48, ill.)

El tema es la supuesta posibilidad de modificar el futuro. Fragmento de un próximo libro sobre el tiempo y la historia.

FILOSOFIA DEL LENGUAJE

7758 Amaral, Márico Tavares d'. Filosofia da comunicação da linguagem. Rio de Janeiro: Civilização Brasileira *em convênio com o* Instituto Nacional do Livro, Ministério da Educação e Cultura, 1977. 136 p.; bibl. (Coleção Perspectivas do homem; v. 108)

Conjunto de trabalhos que constituyen el inicio de una reflexión sistemática sobre los temas indicados en el título. El autor desea utilizar las tesis de Heidegger para tal propósito.

7759 García Cafarena, Judith. Improntas filosóficas en la lingüística de Noam Chomsky y su concepción del uso creativo del lenguaje (UNL/H, 18, 1977, p. 227–241)

Apreciación general de Chomsky, especialmente desde el punto de vista filosófico.

METAFISICA

7760 Albizu, Edgardo. Esquemas de tiempo (UNMSM/L, 48:84/85, 2. semestre, 1976, p. 16–40, ill.)

Análisis de tres básicas concepciones del tiempo, que son caracterizadas por las experiencias básicas en que respectivamente se fundan.

7761 Argerami, Omar. Experiencia y metafísica (UCA/S, 34:131/132, enero/junio 1979, p. 55–60)

Sólo el conocimiento de lo que es absolutamente necesario es conocimiento metafísico. Se intenta mostrar el valor de la experiencia del propio ser para arribar al conocimiento metafísico.

7762 Ponferrada, Gustavo Eloy. La metafísica y las ciencias del hombre (UCA/S, 35:137/138, julio/dic. 1980, p. 627–635) Defensa de la posibilidad de la metafísica, desde un punto de vista tomista.

JOURNAL ABBREVIATIONS
PHILOSOPHY

AAFH/TAM The Americas. A quarterly publication of inter-American cultural history. Academy of American Franciscan History. Washington.

AI/I Interciencia. Asociación Interciencia. Caracas.

ANA Análisis. Cuadernos de investigación. Apartado 11093. Correo Santa Beatriz. Lima.

ARBOR Arbor. Madrid.

BCE/C Cultura. Revista del Banco Central del Ecuador. Quito.

BMA/BB Boletim Bibliográfico. Biblioteca Mário de Andrade. São Paulo.

BRP Beiträge zur Romanischen Philologie. Rütten & Loening. Berlin.

CAM Cuadernos Americanos. México.

CBR/BCB Boletín Cultural y Bibliográfico. Banco de la República, Biblioteca Luis-Angel Arango. Bogotá.

CDLA Casa de las Américas. Instituto Cubano del Libro. La Habana.

CEHA/NH Nuestra Historia. Centro de Estudios de Historia Argentina. Buenos Aires.

CELRG/A Araisa. Anuario del Centro de Estudios Latinoamericanos Rómulo Gallegos. Caracas.

CH Cuadernos Hispanoamericanos. Instituto de Cultura Hispánica. Madrid.

CIF/RLF Revista Latinoamericana de Filosofía. Centro de Investigaciones Filosóficas. Buenos Aires.

CLAEH Centro Latinoamericano de Economía Humana. Montevideo.

CM/D Diálogos. Artes/Letras/Ciencias Humanas. El Colegio de México. México.

CM/HM Historia Mexicana. El Colegio de México. México.

CONAC/RNC Revista Nacional de Cultura. Consejo Nacional de Cultura. Caracas.

CPES/PE Política y Espíritu. Cuadernos de cultura política, económica y social. Santiago.

CPES/RPS Revista Paraguaya de Sociología. Centro Paraguayo de Estudios Sociológicos. Asunción.

CPU/ES Estudios Sociales. Corporación de Promoción Universitaria. Santiago.

EC/M Mapocho. Biblioteca Nacional, Extensión Cultural. Santiago.

ECO Eco. Librería Bucholz. Bogotá.

FCE/TE El Trimestre Económico. Fondo de Cultura Económica. México.

FFCLM/EH Estudos Históricos. Faculdade de Filosofia, Ciências e Letras, Depto. de História. Marília, Brazil.

FH Folia Humanistica. Ciencias, artes, letras. Editorial Glarma. Barcelona.

FJB/BH Boletín Histórico. Fundación John Boulton. Caracas.

HAHR Hispanic American Historical Review. Duke Univ. Press *for the* Conference on Latin American History of the American Historical Association. Durham, N.C.

HISP Hispanófila. Univ. of North Carolina. Chapel Hill.

IBF/RBF Revista Brasileira de Filosofia. Instituto Brasileiro de Filosofia. São Paulo.

IDES/DE Desarrollo Económico. Instituto de Desarrollo Económico y Social. Buenos Aires.

IEH/A Anuario. Univ. Central de Venezuela, Instituto de Estudios Hispanoamericanos. Caracas?

IEP/REP Revista de Estudios Políticos. Instituto de Estudios Políticos. Madrid.

IGFO/RI Revista de Indias. Instituto Gonzalo Fernández de Oviedo [and] Consejo Superior de Investigaciones Científicas. Madrid.

IPGH/RHI Revista de Historia de las Ideas. Instituto Panamericano de Geografía e Historia. Editorial Casa de la Cultura Ecuatoriana. Quito.

ISTMO Istmo. Revista del pensamiento actual. México.

LARR Latin American Research Review. Univ. of North Carolina Press *for the* Latin American Studies Association. Chapel Hill.

LNB/L Lotería. Lotería Nacional de Beneficencia. Panamá.

PAIGH/H Revista de Historia de América. Instituto Panamericano de Geografía e Historia, Comisión de Historia. México.

PUC/V Veritas. Revista. Pontifícia Univ. Católica do Rio Grande do Sul. Porto Alegre, Brazil.

PUJ/UH Universitas Humanistica. Pontificia Univ. Javeriana, Facultad de Filosofía y Letras. Bogotá.

RCLL Revista de Crítica Literaria Latinoamericana. Latinoamericana Editores. Lima.

RFL Revista de Filosofía Latinoamericana. Ediciones Castañeda. San Antonio de Padua, Arg.

RIB Revista Interamericana de Bibliografía [Inter-American Review of Bibliography]. Organization of American States. Washington.

RU/MP Marxist Perspectives. Transaction Periodicals Consortium. Rutgers Univ. New Brunswick, N.J.

SBPC/C Ciência e Cultura. Sociedade Brasileira para o Progresso da Ciência. São Paulo.

SECOLAS/A Annals of the Southeastern Conference on Latin American Studies. West Georgia College. Carrollton.

SHA/D Davar. Revista literaria. Sociedad Hebraica Argentina. Buenos Aires.

SS Science and Society. New York.

UA/REH Revista de Estudios Hispánicos. Univ. of Alabama, Dept. of Romance Languages, Office of International Studies and Programs. University.

UA/U Universidad. Univ. de Antioquia. Medellín, Colombia.

UBAFFL/C Cuadernos de Filosofía. Univ. de Buenos Aires, Facultad de Filosofía y Letras. Buenos Aires.

UBN/R Revista de la Biblioteca Nacional. Ministerio de Educación y Cultura. Montevideo.

UC/A Anales de la Universidad de Cuenca. Cuenca, Ecuador.

UC/AT Atenea. Revista de ciencias, letras y artes. Univ. de Concepción, Chile.

UCA/S Sapientia. Organo de la Facultad de Filosofía. Univ. Católica Argentina Santa María de los Buenos Aires. Buenos Aires.

UCAB/M Montalbán. Univ. Católica Andrés Bello, Facultad de Humanidades y Educación, Institutos Humanísticos de Investigación. Caracas.

UCE/A Anales de la Universidad Central del Ecuador. Quito.

UCLV/I Islas. Univ. Central de las Villas. Santa Clara, Cuba.

UCNSA/EP Estudios Paraguayos. Univ. Católica Nuestra Señora de la Asunción. Asunción.

UCP/IAP Ibero-Americana Pragensia. Univ. Carolina de Praga, Centro de Estudios Ibero-Americanos. Prague.

UCR/RCS Revista de Ciencias Sociales. Univ. de Costa Rica. San José.

UCR/RF Revista de Filosofía de la Universidad de Costa Rica. San José.

UHB/EHA Etudes Hispano-Américaines. Univ. de Haute Bretagne, Centre d'Etudes Hispaniques, Hispano-Américaines et Luso-Brésiliennes. Rennes, France.

UI/RF Revista de Filosofía. Univ. Iberoamericana, Depto. de Filosofía and Asociación Fray Alonso de la Veracruz. México.

UM/JIAS Journal of Inter-American Studies and World Affairs. Univ. of Miami Press *for the* Center for Advanced International Studies. Coral Gables, Fla.

UM/R Revista Universidad de Medellín. Centro de Estudios de Posgrado. Medellín, Colombia.

UMGFF/K Kriterion. Revista da Faculdade de Filosofia da Univ. de Minas Gerais. Belo Horizonte, Brazil.

UN/IV Ideas y Valores. Revista del Instituto de Filosofía y Letras. Univ. Nacional. Bogotá.

UNAM/D Diánoia. Univ. Nacional Autónoma de México, Centro de Estudios Filosóficos. México.

UNAM/RMCPS Revista Mexicana de Ciencias Políticas y Sociales. Univ. Nacional

Autónoma de Mexico, Facultad de Ciencias Políticas y Sociales. México.

UNC/BCPS Boletín de Ciencias Políticas y Sociales. Univ. Nacional de Cuyo, Facultad de Ciencias Políticas y Sociales. Mendoza, Argentina.

UNC/RAHC Revista del Archivo Histórico del Cuzco. Univ. Nacional del Cuzco, Peru.

UNC/RHAA Revista de Historia Americana y Argentina. Univ. Nacional de Cuyo, Facultad de Filosofía y Letras, Instituto de Historia. Mendoza.

UNESCO/CU Cultures. United Nations Educational, Scientific and Cultural Organization. Paris.

UNL/H Humanitas. Univ. de Nuevo León, Centro de Estudios Humanísticos. Monterrey, México.

UNLP/R Revista de la Universidad Nacional de La Plata, Argentina.

UNMSM/L Letras. Univ. Nacional Mayor de San Marcos. Lima.

INDEXES

ABBREVIATIONS AND ACRONYMS

Except for journal acronyms which are listed at a) the end of each major disciplinary section, (e.g., Art, Film, History, etc.); and b) after each serial title in the *Title List of Journals Indexed*.

a	annual
ABC	Argentina, Brazil, Chile
A.C.	antes de Cristo
ACAR	Associação de Crédito e Assistência Rural, Brazil
AD	Anno Domini
A.D.	Acción Democrática, Venezuela
ADESG	Associação dos Diplomados de Escola Superior de Guerra, Brazil
AGI	Archivo General de Indias, Sevilla
AGN	Archivo General de la Nación
AID	Agency for International Development
Ala.	Alabama
ALALC	Asociación Latinoamericana de Libre Comercio
ANAPO	Alianza Nacional Popular, Colombia
ANCARSE	Associação Nordestina de Crédito e Assistência Rural de Sergipe, Brazil
ANCOM	Andean Common Market
ANDI	Asociación Nacional de Industriales, Colombia
AP	Acción Popular
APRA	Alianza Popular Revolucionaria Americana
Ariz.	Arizona
Ark.	Arkansas
ASA	Association of Social Anthropologists of the Commonwealth, London
ASSEPLAN	Assessoria de Planejamente e Acompanhamento, Recife, Brazil
Assn.	Association
Aufl.	Auflage (edition, edición)
AUFS	American Universities Field Staff Reports, Hanover, N.H.
Aug.	August, Augustan
b.	born (nacido)
BBE	Bibliografia Brasileira de Educação
b.c.	indicates dates obtained by radio-carbon methods
BC	Before Christ
bibl(s).	bibliography(ies)
BID	Banco Interamericano de Desarrollo
BNDE	Banco Nacional de Desenvolvimento Econômico, Brazil
BNH	Banco Nacional de Habitação, Brazil
BP	before present
b/w	black-and-white
C14	Carbon 14
ca.	circa
CACM	Central American Common Market
CADE	Conferencia Anual de Ejecutivos de Empresas, Peru
CAEM	Centro de Altos Estudios Militares, Peru
Calif.	California
CARC	Centro de Arte y Comunicación
CARICOM	Caribbean Common Market

CARIFTA	Caribbean Free Trade Association
CBD	central business district
CD	Christian Democrats, Chile
CDI	Conselho de Desenvolvimento Industrial
CEBRAP	Centro Brasileiro de Análise e Planejamento, São Paulo
CECORA	Central de Cooperativas de la Reforma Agraria, Colombia
CEDAL	Centro de Estudios Democráticos de América Latina, Costa Rica
CEDE	Centro de Estudios sobre Desarrollo Económico, Univ. de los Andes, Bogotá
CEDEPLAR	Centro de Desenvolvimento e Planejamento Region, Belo Horizonte, Brazil
CEDES	Centro de Estudios de Estado y Sociedad, Buenos Aires
CEESTEM	Centro de Estudios Económicos y Sociales del Tercer Mundo, México
CELADE	Centro Latinoamericano de Demografía
CEMLA	Centro de Estudios Monetarios Latinoamericanos, Mexico
CENDES	Centro de Estudios del Desarrollo, Venezuela
CENIDIM	Centro Nacional de Información, Documentación e Investigación Musicales, Mexico
CENIET	Centro Nacional de Información y Estadísticas del Trabajo, México
CEPADE	Centro Paraguayo de Estudios de Desarrollo Económico y Social
CEPA-SE	Comissão Estadual de Planejamento Agrícola, Sergipe, Brazil
CEPAL	*See* ECLA.
CES	constant elasticity of substitution
cf.	compare
CFI	Consejo Federal de Inversiones, B.A.
CGE	Confederación General Económica, Argentina
CGTP	Confederación General de Trabajadores del Perú
ch., chap.	chapter
CHEAR	Council on Higher Education in the American Republics
Cía.	Compañía
CIA	Central Intelligence Agency
CIDA	Comité Interamericano de Desarrollo Agrícola
CIDE	Centro de Investigación y Desarrollo de la Educación, Chile
CIE	Centro de Investigaciones Económicas, Buenos Aires
CIP	Conselho Interministerial de Preços
CLACSO	Consejo Latinoamericano de Ciencias Sociales, Secretaria Ejecutiva, Buenos Aires
CLASC	Confederación Latinoamericana Sindical Cristiana
CLE	Comunidad Latinoamericana de Escritores, Mexico
cm	centimeter
CNI	Confederação Nacional da Industria, Brazil
Co.	company
COBAL	Companhia Brasileira de Alimentos
Col.	collection, colección, coleção
Colo.	Colorado
COMCORDE	Comisión Coordinadora para el Desarrollo Económico, Uruguay
comp.	compiler
CONDESE	Conselho de Desenvolvimento Econômico de Sergipe, Brazil
Conn.	Connecticut
COPEI	Comité Organizador Pro-Elecciones Independientes, Venezuela
CORFO	Corporación de Fomento de la Producción, Chile
CORP	Corporación para el Fomento de Investigaciones Económicas, Colombia
Corp.	Corporation
CPDOC	Centro de Pesquisa e Documentação de História Contemporânea do Brasil, Rio de Janeiro.
CRIC	Consejo Regional Indígena dek Cauca, Colombia
CUNY	City University of New York

CVG	Corporación Venezolana de Guayana
d.	died
DANE	Departamento Nacional de Estadística, Colombia
DC	developed country, Demócratas Cristianos, Chile
d.C	después de Cristo
déc.	décembre
Dec.	December
Del.	Delaware
dept.	department
depto.	departamento
dez.	dezembre
dic.	deciembre
DNOCS	Departamento Nacional de Obras Contra as Sécas, Brazil
Dr.	Doctor
Dra.	Doctora
ECLA	Economic Commission for Latin America
ECOSOC	UN Dept. of Economic and Social Affairs
ed(s).	edition(s), edición(es), editor(s), redactor(es)
EDEME	Editora Emprendimentos Educacionais, Florianópolis, Brazil
Edo.	Estado
EEC	European Economic Community
EFTA	European Free Trade Association
e.g.	exempio gratia (for example)
ELN	Ejército de Liberación Nacional, Colombia
ESG	Escola Superior de Guerra. Brazil
estr.	estrenado
et al	et alia (and others)
ETENE	Escritório Técnico de Estudos Econômicos do Nordeste, Brazil
ETEPE	Escritório Técnico de Planejamento, Brazil
EUDEBA	Editorial Universitaria de Buenos Aires
EWG	Europaische Wirtschaftsgemeinschaft. *See* EEC.
facsim(s).	facsimile(s)
FAO	Food and Agriculture Organization of the United Nations
FDR	Frente Democrático Revolucionario, El Salvador
feb.	February, febrero
FEDECAFE	Federación Nacional de Cafeteros, Colombia
fev.	fevreiro, février
ff.	following
FFMLN	Frente Farabundo Martí de Liberación Nacional, El Salvador
FGTS	Fundo do Garantia do Tempo de Serviç, Brazil
FGV	Fundação Getúlio Vargas
FIEL	Fundación de Investigaciones Económicas Latinoamericanos, ARgentina
film.	filmography
fl.	flourished, floresció
Fla.	Florida
FLACSO	Facultad Latinoamericano de Ciencias Sociales, Buenos Aires
fold.	folded
fol(s).	folio(s)
FRG	Federal Republic of Germany
ft.	foot, feet
FUAR	Frente Unido de Acción Revolucionaria, Colombia
Ga.	Georgia
GAO	General Accounting Office, Washington
GATT	General Agreement on Tariffs and Trade
GDP	gross domestic product

GDR	German Democratic Republic
GEIDA	Grupo Executivo de Irrigação para o Desenvolvimento Agrícola, Brazil
Gen.	General
GMT	Greenwich Meridian Time
GPA	grade point average
GPO	Government Printing Office
h.	hijo
ha.	hectares, hectáreas
HLAS	*Handbook of Latin American Studies*
HMAI	*Handbook of Middle American Studies*
Hnos.	Hermanos
IBBD	Instituto Brasileiro de Bibliografia e Documentação
IBRD	International Bank of Reconstruction and Development
ICA	Instituto Colombiano Agropecuario
ICAIC	Instituto Cubano de Arte e Industria Cinematográficas
ICCE	Instituto Colombiano de Construcción Escolar
ICSS	Instituto Colombiano de Seguridad Social
ICT	Instituto de Crédito Territorial, Colombia
IDB	Inter-American Development Bank
i.e.	id est (that is)
IEL	Instituto Euvaldo Lodi, Brazil
IEP	Instituto de Estudios Peruanos
IERAC	Instituto Ecuatoriano de Reforma Agraria y Colonización
III	Instituto Indigenista Interamericana, Mexico
IIN	Instituto Indigenista Nacional, Guatemala
ill.	illustrations(s)
Ill.	Illinois
ILO	International Labour Organization, Geneva
IMES	Instituto Mexicano de Estudios Sociales
in.	inches
INAH	Instituto Nacional de Antropología e Historia, Mexico
INBA	Instituto Nacional de Bellas Artes, Mexico
Inc.	incorporated
INCORA	Instituto Colombiano de Reforma Agraria
Ind.	Indiana
INEP	Instituto Nacional de Estudios Pedagógicos, Brazil
INI	Instituto Nacional Indigenista, Mexico
INIT	Instituto Nacional de Industria Turística, Cuba
INPES/IPEA	Instituto de Planejamento Econômico e Social, Instituto de Pesquisas, Brazil
IPA	Instituto de Pastoral Andina, Univ. de San Antonio de Abad, Seminario de Antropología, Cuzco, Peru
IPEA	Instituto de Pesquisa Econômico-Social Aplicada, Brazil
IPES/GB	Instituto de Pesquisas e Estudos Sociais, Guanabara, Brazil
IPHAN	Instituto de Patrimônio Histórico e Artístico Nacional, Brazil
ir.	irregular
ITT	International Telephone and Telegraph
jan.	janeiro, janvier
Jan.	Janaury
JLP	Jamaican Labour Party
JUCEPLAN	Junta Central de Planificación, Cuba
Kan.	Kansas
km	kilometers, kilómetres
Ky.	Kentucky
l.	leaves, hojas (páginas impresas por una sola cara)

La.	Louisiana
LASA	Latin American Studies Association
LCD	less developed countries
Ltda.	Limitada
m.	meters, metros, monthly, murió (died)
M	mille, mil, thousand
MAPU	Movimiento de Acción Popular Unitario, Chile
MARI	Middle American Research Institute, Tulane University, New Orleans
Mass.	Massachusetts
MCC	Mercado Común Centro-Americano
MCN	multinational corporation
Md.	Maryland
MDB	Movimiento Democrático Brasileiro
MDC	more developed countries
MEC	Ministério de Educação e Cultura, Brazil
Mich.	Michigan
mimeo	mimeographed, mimeografiado
min.	minutes, minutos
Minn.	Minnesota
MIR	Movimiento de Izquierda Revolucionaria, Chile
Miss.	Mississippi
MIT	Massachusetts Institute of Technology
MLN	Movimiento de Liberación Nacional
mm.	millimeter
MNR	Movimiento Nacionalista Revolucionario, Bolivia
Mo.	Missouri
MOIR	Movimiento Obrero Independence y Revolucionario, Colombia
Mont.	Montana
MRL	Movimiento Revolucionario Liberal, Colombia
ms.	manuscript
msl	mean sea level
n.	nacido (born)
N.C.	North Carolina
N.D.	North Dakota
Neb.	Nebraska
neubearb.	neubearbeitet (revised, corregida)
Nev.	Nevada
n.f.	neue Folge
N.H.	New Hampshire
NIEO	new international economic order
NIH	National Institutes of Health, Washington
N.J.	New Jersey
N.M.	New Mexico
no(s).	number(s), número(s)
NOSALF	Scandanavian Committee for Research in Latin America
nov.	noviembre, novembre, novembro
Nov.	November
NSF	National Science Foundation
N.Y.	New York
N.Y.C.	New York City
OAS	Organization of American States
oct.	octubre
Oct.	October
ODEPLAN	Oficina de Planificación Nacional, Chile
OEA	Organización de los Estados Americanos

OIT	*See* ILO.
Okla.	Oklahoma
Okt.	Oktober
op.	opus
OPANAL	Organismo para la Proscripción de las Armas Nucleares en América Latina
OPEC	Organization of Petroleum Exporting Countries
OPEP	Organización de Países Exportadores de Petróleo
OPIC	Overseas Investment Corporation
Or.	Oregon
ORIT	Organización Regional Interamericana del Trabajo
out.	outubre
p.	page(s)
Pa.	Pennsylvania
PAN	Partido Acción Nacional, Mexico
PC	partido comunista
PCR	Partido Comunista Revolucionario, Chile and Argentina
PCV	Partido Comunista de Venezuela
PDC	Partido Demócrata Cristiano, Chile
PEMEX	Petróleos Mexicanos
PETROBRAS	Petróleo Brasileiro
PIMES	Programa Integrado de Mestrado em Economia e Sociologia, Brazil
PIP	Partido Independiente de Puerto Rico
PLANAVE	Engenharia e Planejamento Limitada, Brazil
PLANO	Planejamento e Assesoria Limitada, Brazil
PLN	Partido Liberación Nacional, Costa Rica
PNM	People's National Movement, Trinidad and Tobago
PNP	People's National Party, Jamaica
pop.	population
port(s).	portrait(s)
PPP	purchasing power parities
PRD	Partido Revolucionario Dominicano
PRI	Partido Revolucionario Institucional, Mexico
PROABRIL	Centro de Projetos Industrias, Brazil
Prof.	Professor
PRONAPA	Programa Nacional de Pesquisas Arqueológicas, Brazil
prov.	province, provincia
PS	Partido Socialista, Chile
pseud.	pseudonym, pseudónimo
pt(s).	part(s), parte(s)
pub.	published
PUC	Pontificia Universidad Católica, Rio
PURSC	Partido Unido de la Revolución Socialista de Cuba
q.	quarterly
rev.	revisada, revised
R.I.	Rhode Island
s.a.	semiannual
SALALM	Seminar on the Acquisition of Latin American Library Materials
sd.	sound
S.D.	South Dakota
SDR	special drawing rights
SELA	Sistema Económico Latinoamericano
SENAC	Serviço Nacional de Aprendizagem Comercial, Rio de Janeiro
SENAI	Serviço Nacional de Aprendizagem Industrial, São Paulo
sept.	septiembre, septembre
Sept.	September

SES	socio-economic status
SESI	Serviço Social de Industria, Brazil
set.	setembre
SIECA	Secretaría Permanente del Tratado General de Integración Centroamericana
SIL	Summer Institute of Linguistics
SINAMOS	Sistema Nacional de Apoyo a la Movilización Social, Peru
S.J.	Society of Jesus
s.l.	sine loco (place of publication unknown)
s.n.	sine nomine (publisher unknown)
SNA	Sociedad Nacional de Agricultura, Chile
SPVEA	Superintendência do Plano de Valorização Econômica de Amazônia, Brazil
sq.	square
SUDAM	Superintendência de Desenvolvimento da Amazônia, Brazil
SUDENE	Superintendência de Desenvolvimento do Nordeste, Brazil
SUFRAME	Superintendência da Zona Franca de Manaus, Brazil
SUNY	State University of New York
t.	tomo(s), tome(s)
TAT	Thematic Apperception Test
TB	tuberculosis
Tenn.	Tennessee
Tex.	Texas
TG	transformational generative
TL	Thermoluminescent
TNP	Tratado de No Proliferación
trans.	translator
U.K.	United Kingdom
UN	United Nations
UNAM	Universidad Nacional Autónoma de México
UNCTAD	United Nations Conference on Trade and Development
UNDP	UN Development Programme
UNEAC	Unión de Escritores y Artistas de Cuba
UNESCO	UN Educational, Scientific and Cultural Organization
univ.	university, universidad, universidade, université, universität
uniw.	uniwersytet
UP	Unidad Popular, Chile
URD	Unidad Revolucionaria Democrática
URSS	Unión de Repúblicas Soviéticas Socialistas
US	United States
USIA	US Information Agency, Washington
USSR	Union of the Soviet Socialist Republics
UTM	Universal Transverse Mercator
v.	volume(s), volumen (volúmenes)
Va.	Virginia
viz.	videlicet, that is, namely
vol(s).	volume(s), volumene (volúmenes)
vs.	versus
Vt.	Vermont
W. Va.	West Virginia
Wash.	Washington
Wis.	Wisconsin
Wyo.	Wyoming

TITLE LIST OF JOURNALS INDEXED

Journals that have been included in the *Handbook* as individual items are listed alphabetically by title in the Author Index.

Abside. Revista de cultura mexicana. México. (A)

Actualidades. Centro de Estudios Latinoamericanos Rómulo Gallegos. Caracas.

Affari Esteri. Associazione Italiana per gli studi di politica estera. Roma.

Afro-American Music Review. Detroit, Mich.

Agricultural History. Agricultural History Society. Univ. of California Press. Berkeley. (AHS/AH)

Alero. Univ. de San Carlos, Guatemala.

Alfa. Univ. de São Paulo, Faculdade de Filosofia, Ciências e Letras. Marília, Brazil. (FFCLM/A)

Allpanchis. Instituto de Pastoral Andina. Cuzco, Perú. (IPA/A)

Amazonia Peruana. Centro Amazónica de Antropología y Aplicación Práctica. Lima.

América Indígena. Instituto Indigenista Interamericano. México. (III/AI)

América Latina. Academia de Ciencias de la URSS /Unión de Repúblicas Soviéticas Socialistas/. Moscú. (URSS/AL)

América Latina. Centro Latino-Americano de Pesquisas em Ciências Sociais. Rio de Janeiro. (CLAPCS/AL)

American Anthropologist. American Anthropological Association. Washington. (AAA/AA)

American Antiquity. The Society for American Archaeology. Menasha, Wis. (SAA/AA)

American Ethnologist. American Anthropological Association. Washington. (AAA/AE)

American Historical Review. American Historical Association. Washington. (AHA/R)

American Journal of Public Health and the Nation's Health. The American Public Health Association. Albany, N.Y. (APHA/J)

American Neptune. The American Neptune, Inc. Salem, Mass. (AN/AN)

American Speech. Columbia Univ. Press. New York. (AMS)

Américas. Organization of American States. Washington. (OAS/AM)

The Americas. A quarterly publication of inter-American cultural history. Academy of

American Franciscan History. Washington. (AAFH/TAM)

Anais. Arquivo Histórico do Rio Grande do Sul. Porto Alegre, Brazil.

Anais do Museu Paulista. São Paulo. (MP/AN)

Anales. Administración del Patrimonio Cultural. San Salvador.

Anales de Arqueología y Etnología. Univ. Nacional de Cuyo, Facultad de Filosofía y Letras. Mendoza, Argentina. (UNC/AAE)

Anales de la Sociedad de Geografía e Historia de Guatemala. Guatemala. (SGHG/A)

Anales de la Universidad Central del Ecuador. Quito. (UCE/A)

Anales de la Universidad Central del Ecuador. Quito. (UCE/A)

Anales de la Universidad de Cuenca. Cuenca, Ecuador. (UC/A)

Anales del Instituto de Investigaciones Estéticas. Univ. Nacional Autónoma de México. México. (IIE/A)

Anales del Instituto Nacional de Antropología e Historia. Secretaría de Educación Pública. México. (INAH/A)

Anales del Museo Nacional David J. Guzmán. San Salvador. (MNDJG/A)

Análisis. Cuadernos de investigación. Apartado 11093. Correo Santa Beatriz. Lima. (ANA)

Andén para la Cultura. Ediciones Candilejas. Córdoba, Argentina.

Annales: Économies, Sociétés, Civilisations. Centre National de la Recherche Scientifique *avec le concours de la* VIeme Section de la'École Pratique des Hautes Etudes. Paris. (AESC)

Annales de Démographie Historique. Société Demographie Historique. Paris.

Annals. Organization of American States. Washington. (OAS/A)

Annals of the Southeastern Conference on Latin American Studies. West Georgia College. Carrollton. (SECOLAS/A)

Anthropological Linguistics. A publication of the Archives of the Languages of the

World. Indiana Univ., Anthropology Dept. Bloomington. (IU/AL)

Anthropos. Anthropos-Institut. Psoieux, Switzerland. (AI/A)

La Antigua. Univ. de Santa María La Antigua, Oficina de Humanidades. Panamá. (USMLA/LA)

Antropología. La Paz.

Antropología Andina. Cuzco, Peru.

Antropología e Historia de Guatemala. Instituto de Antropología e Historia de Guatemala. Guatemala. (IAHG/AHG)

Antropológica. Fundación La Salle de Ciencias Naturales, Instituto Caribe de Antropología y Sociología. Caracas. (FSCN/A)

Anuario. Instituto de Investigaciones Históricos Dr. José Gaspar Rodríguez de Francia. Asunción.

Anuario. Univ. Central de Venezuela, Instituto de Estudios Hispanoamericanos. Caracas. (IEH/A)

Anuario. Univ. Michoacán de San Nicolás de Hidalgo, Escuela de Historia. Morelia, México.

Anuario Bibliográfico Ecuatoriano 1976 y 1977 y Bibliografía Ecuatoriana. Univ. Central del Ecuador, Biblioteca General, Editorial Universitaria. Quito.

Anuario Bibliográfico Uruguayo de 1978. Biblioteca Nacional. Montevideo.

Anuario Colombiano de Historia Social y de la Cultura. Univ. Nacional de Colombia, Facultad de Ciencias Humanas, Depto. de Historia. Bogotá. (UNC/ACHSC)

Anuario de Estudios Americanos. Consejo Superior de Investigaciones Científicas /and/ Univ. de Sevilla, Escuela de Estudios Hispano-Americanos. Sevilla. (EEHA/AEA)

Anuario de Estudios Centroamericanos. Univ. de Costa Rica. Ciudad Universitaria "Rodrigo Facio." San José. (UCR/AEC)

Anuario de Historia del Derecho Español. Instituto Nacional de Estudios Jurídicos. Madrid. (INEJ/AHD)

Anuario de Letras. Univ. Nacional Autónoma de México, Facultad de Filosofía y Letras. México. (UNAM/AL)

Anuario Musical. Barcelona.

Apollo. London.

Apuntes. Univ. del Pacífico, Centro de Investigación. Lima. (UP/A)

Araisa. Anuario del Centro de Estudios Latinoamericanos Rómulo Gallegos. Caracas. (CELRG/A)

Arbor. Madrid. (ARBOR)

Archiv für Völkerkunde. Museum für Völkerkunde in Wien und von Verein Freunde der Völkerkunde. Wien. (MVW/AV)

Archivo Artigas. Comisión Nacional Archivo Artigas. Montevideo.

Archivo Ibero-Americano. Los Padres Franciscanos. Madrid. (PF/AIA)

Archivos del Folklore Chileno. Santiago.

Archivum Franciscanum Historicum. Firenze, Italy. (AFH)

Archivum Historicum Societatis Iesu. Rome. (AHSI)

Areito. Areíto, Inc. New York. (AR)

Arizona and the West. Univ. of Arizona. Tucson. (UA/AW)

The Art Bulletin. College Art Association of America. New York.

Art Journal. College Art Association of America. New York.

Artes de México. Revista bimestral. México. (ARMEX)

Asclepio. Consejo Superior de Investigaciones Científicas, Instituto Arnau de Vilanova de Historia de la Medicina, Archivo Iberoamericano de Historia de la Medicina y Antropología Médica. Madrid. (CSIC/A)

Asien, Afrika, Lateinamerika. Deutscher Verlag der Wissenschaften. Berlin, GDR.

Atenea. Revista de ciencias, letras y artes. Univ. de Concepción, Chile. (UC/AT)

Aula. Univ. Nacional Pedro Henríquez Ureña. Santo Domingo. (UNPHU/A)

B.B.A.A. Boletín Bibliografico de Antropología Americana. Instituto Panamericano de Geografía e Historia, Comisión de Historia. México. (BBAA)

Barroco. Minas Gerais, Brazil.

Beiträge zur Romanischen Philologie. Rütten & Loening. Berlin. (BRP)

Belizean Studies. Belize Institute of Social Research and Action. Belize City.

Berichte zur Entwicklung in Spanien, Portugal, Lateinamerika. München, FRG. (BESPL)

Bibliografía Histórica Mexicana: 1976–1978. El Colegio de México, Centro de Estudios Históricos. México.

Bibliographie d'Articles des Revues: Novembre 1979–Juillet 1980. Institut des Hautes Études de l'Amérique Latine. Centre de Documentation. Paris.

Bibliography of the English-Speaking Caribbean. Books, articles and reviews in English from the arts, humanities, and social sciences. Iowa City, Iowa.

Boletim. Instituto Histórico, Geográfico e Etnográfico Paranaense. Curitiba. Brazil.

Boletim Bibliográfico. Biblioteca Mário de Andrade. São Paulo. (BMA/BB)

Boletim Bibliográfico da Biblioteca Nacional. Biblioteca Nacional. Rio de Janeiro.

Boletim da Cidade do Recife. Prefeitura Municipal do Recife, Conselho Municipal de Cultura. Recife, Brazil.

Boletim Informativo e Bibliográfico de Ciências Sociais. Associação Nacional de Pós-Graduação e Pesquisa em Ciências Sociais. Rio de Janeiro.

Boletim Informativo SIP: Anuário. Instituto Nacional do Cinema. Rio de Janeiro.

Boletín. Academia de Historia del Cauca. Popayán, Colombia.

Boletín. Museo Arqueológico de la Serena, Chile.

Boletín. Provincia de Santa Fe. Ministerio de Gobierno. Archivo General de la Provincia. Santa Fe, Argentina.

Boletin: Handbook of Latin American Art. New Haven, Conn.

Boletín Americanista. Univ. de Barcelona, Facultad de Geografía e Historia, Depto. de Historia de América. Barcelona. (UB/BA)

Boletín Bibliográfico. Banco Central de Nicaragua. Managua.

Boletín Bibliográfico. Biblioteca del Congreso Nacional. Sección Procesamiento. Santiago.

Boletín Cultural y Bibliográfico. Banco de la República, Biblioteca Luis-Angel Arango. Bogotá. (CBR/BCB)

Boletín de Antropología Americana. Instituto Panamericano de Geografía e Historia. México.

Boletín de Artes Visuales. Anuario. Organización de los Estados Americanos, Secretaría General. Washington.

Boletín de Ciencias Económicas y Sociales. Univ. Centroamericana José Simeón Cañas, Departamento de Economía. San Salvador.

Boletín de Ciencias Políticas y Sociales. Univ. Nacional de Cuyo, Facultad de Ciencias Políticas y Sociales. Mendoza, Argentina. (UNC/BCPS)

Boletín de Coyuntura Socioeconómica. Universidad del Valle, División de Ciencias Sociales y Económicas, Centro de Investigación, y Documentación Socioeconómica. Cali, Colombia.

Boletín de Estudios Latinoamericanos. Centro de Estudios y Documentación Latinoamerica- nos. Amsterdam. (CEDLA/B)

Boletín de Filología. Univ. de Chile, Instituto de Filología. Santiago. (UC/BF)

Boletín de Historia y Antigüedades. Academia Colombiana de Historia. Bogotá. (ACH/BHA)

Boletín de Información. Centro Interamericano de Artesanía y Artes Populares (CIDAP). Cuenca, Ecuador.

Boletín de la Academia Chilena de la Historia. Santiago. (ACH/B)

Boletín de la Academia Colombiana. Bogotá. (ACO/B)

Boletín de la Academia Hondureña de la Lengua. Tegucigalpa. (AHL/B)

Boletín de la Academia Nacional de Historia. Buenos Aires. (ANH/B)

Boletín de la Academia Nacional de la Historia. Caracas. (VANH/B)

Boletín de la Academia Norteamericana de la Lengua Española. New York. (ANLE/B)

Boletín de la Biblioteca Nacional. Lima. (PEBN/B)

Boletín de la Facultad de Derecho y Ciencias Sociales. Univ. Nacional de Córdoba, Argentina.

Boletín de la Real Sociedad Geográfica. Madrid. (RSG/B)

Boletín del Archivo General de la Nación. Managua.

Boletín del Archivo General de la Nación. Secretaría de Gobernación. México. (MAGN/B)

Boletín del Archivo Histórico. Congreso de la República. Caracas.

Boletín del Archivo Histórico de Jalisco. Guadalajara, México.

Boletín del Archivo Histórico de Miraflores. Caracas.

Boletín del Departamento de Investigación de las Tradiciones Populares. México.

Boletín del Instituto de Historia Argentina y Americana "Emilio Ravignani." Facultad de Filosofía y Letras, Universidad Nacional de Buenos Aires. (IHADER/B)

Boletín del Instituto Riva-Agüero. Pontifica Univ. Católica del Perú. Lima. (IRA/B)

Boletín del Museo del Hombre Dominicano. Santo Domingo. (MHD/B)

Boletín del Sistema Bibliotecario de la UNAH. Universidad Nacional Autónoma de Honduras. Tegucigalpa.

Boletín Histórico. Fundación John Boulton. Caracas. (FJB/BH)

Boletín Informativo para Asuntos Migratorios y Fronterizos. Comité de Servicio de Los Amigos, Centro de Información para Migración y Desarrollo. México.

Boletín Informativo Trotskysta. Tendencia Cuartainternacionalista. Organización Trotskysta Revolucionaria. Lima.

Boletín Nicaragüense de Bibliografía y Documentación. Banco Central de Nicaragua, Biblioteca. Managua. (BNBD)

Brasil Açucareiro. Instituto do Açucar e do Alcool. Rio de Janeiro. (IAA/BA)

Brasile: "Cinema Novo" e Dopo. Quaderni della Mostra Internazionale del Nuovo Cinema. Venezia.

Britain and Latin America. An annual review of British-Latin American relations. Latin American Bureau. London.

Bulletin. Société Suisse des Américanistes. Geneva. (SSA/B)

Bulletin de l'Académie des Sciences Humaines et Sociales d'Haiti. Port-au-Prince. (ASHSH/B)

Bulletin de l'Institut Français d'Études Andines. Lima. (IFEA/B)

Bulletin des Études Portugaises et Bresiliennes. Institut Français de Lisbonne avec la collaboration de Etablissements Français d'Enseignement Supérieur, Instituto de Alta Cultura, et du Depto. Cultural do Itamarati. Lisbon. (BEPB)

Bulletin d'Information. Association des Archivistes, Bibliothecaires, Documentalistes Francophones de la Caraïbe, Section Haiti. Port-au-Prince.

CCS Current Awareness Service. Caribbean Community Secretariat. Information and Documentation Section. Georgetown, Guyana.

CENIDIM. Boletín informativo. Centro Nacional de Investigación e Información Musical Carlos Chávez. México.

Cadernos DCP. Univ. Federal de Minas Gerais, Faculdade de Filosofia e Ciências Humanas, Depto. de Ciência Política. Belo Horizonte, Brazil. (UFMG/DCP)

Cahiers Césairiens. Pennsylvania State Univ., French Dept. University Park.

Cahiers des Amériques Latines. Paris. (CDAL)

Cahiers du Cinéma. Paris.

Canadian Journal of History/Annales Canadiennes d'Histoire. Journal of History Co., Ltd. Saskatoon, Canada.

Canadian Psychiatric Association Journal. Ottawa.

Canadian Review of Studies in Nationalism/ Revue Canadienne des Études sur le Nationalisme. Univ. of Prince Edward Island. Charlottetown.

Caravelle. Cahiers du monde hispanique et luso-brésilien. Université de Toulouse, Institut d'Études Hispaniques, Hispano-Americaines et Luso-Brésiliennes. Toulouse France. (UTIEH/C)

Caribbean Quarterly. Univ. of the West Indies. Mona, Jam. (UWI/CQ)

Caribbean Review. Florida International Univ., Office of Academic Affairs. Miami. (FIU/CR)

Caribbean Studies. Univ. of Puerto Rico, Institute of Caribbean Studies. Río Piedras. (UPR/CS)

Caribbean Studies. Univ. of the West Indies. Mona, Jamaica. (UWI/CS)

Caribe. Univ. of Hawaii, Dept. of European Languages and Literatures. Honolulu.

El Caribe Contemporáneo. Univ. Nacional Autónoma de México, Facultad de Ciencias Políticas y Sociales, Centro de Estudios Latinoamericanos. México.

Caricom Perspective. Caribbean Community Secretariat. Georgetown, Guyana.

Casa de las Américas. Instituto Cubano del Libro. La Habana. (CDLA)

Casa del Tiempo. Univ. Autónoma Metropolitana. Dirección de Difusión Cultural. México.

Casas Reales. Museo de las Casas Reales. Santo Domingo.

Centro Latinoamericano de Economía Humana. Montevideo. (CLAEH)

Church History. American Society of Church History, Univ. of Chicago. Chicago, Ill. (ASCH/CH)

Ciência e Cultura. Sociedade Brasileira para o Progresso da Ciência. São Paulo. (SBPC/CC)

Ciencia y Sociedad. Instituto Tecnológica. Santo Domingo.

Ciencia y Tecnología. Editorial Universidad de Costa Rica. San José.

Cine Cubano. La Habana.

Cine Olho. São Paulo.

Cinejornal. Embrafilme. Rio de Janeiro.

Cinema. Fundação Cinemateca Brasileira. São Paulo.

Cinéma. Paris.

Cinema BR. São Paulo.

Cladindex. Resúmen de documentos CEPAL/ ILPES. Organización de las Naciones Unidas. Comisión Económica para América Latina (CEPAL). Centro Latinoamericano de Documentación Económica y Social (CLADES). Santiago.

Clio. Academia Dominicana de la Historia. Santo Domingo. (ADH/C)

Colección Documental de la Independencia del Perú. Comisión Nacional del Sesquicentenario de la Independencia. Lima.

Colóquio. Fundação Calouste Gulbenkian. Lisboa.

Communications. École des Hautes Études en Sciences Sociales, Centre d'Études Trans- disciplinaires. Paris. (EHESS/C)

Comparative Political Studies. Northwestern Univ., Evanston, Ill. and Sage Publications, Beverly Hills, Calif. (CPS)

Computers for the Humanities. Amsterdam, The Netherlands.

Comunicações e Artes. Univ. de São Paulo, Escola de Comunicações e Artes. São Paulo.

Comunidad. Revista de la U.I.A. Cuadernos de difusión cultural. Univ. Iberoamericana. México. (UIA/C)

Conjonction. Institut Français d'Haïti. Port-au-Prince. (IFH/C)

Conjunto. Casa de las Américas. La Habana.

Construtura. Univ. Católica do Paraná. Curitiba, Brazil.

Controversia: Para el Exámen de la Realidad Argentina. México.

Convivium. Revista bimestral de investigação e cultura. Editora Convívio. São Paulo.

Creación & Crítica. Lima.

Criterio. Editorial Criterio. Buenos Aires. (CRIT)

Critica d'Arte. Studio Italiano di Storia dell'Arte. Vallecchi Editore. Firenze, Italy. (CA)

Cuaderno del Centro de Estudios Interdisciplinarios de Fronteras Argentinas. Buenos Aires?

Cuadernos Americanos. México. (CAM)

Cuadernos de Filosofía. Univ. de Buenos Aires, Facultad de Filosofía y Letras. Buenos Aires. (UBAFFL/C)

Cuadernos de Filosofía. Univ. de Buenos Aires, Facultad de Filosofía y Letras. Buenos Aires. (UBAFFL/C)

Cuadernos de Filosofía. Univ. de Concepción, Instituto Central de Filosofía. Concepción.

Cuadernos del Consejo Nacional de la Universidad Peruana. Lima.

Cuadernos del Seminario de Historia. Pontificia Univ. Católica del Perú, Instituto Riva-Agüero. Lima. (PUCP/CSH)

Cuadernos del Sur. Univ. Nacional del Sur, Instituto de Humanidades. Bahia Blanca, Argentina. (UNS/CS)

Cuadernos Hispanoamericanos. Instituto de Cultura Hispánica. Madrid. (CH)

Cuadernos Hispanoamericanos. Revista mensual de cultura hispánica. Centro Iberoamericano de Cooperación. Madrid.

Cuadrante. Centro de Estudios Regionales. Tucumán, Argentina. (CER/C)

Cuban Studies / Estudios Cubanos. Univ. of Pittsburgh, Univ. Center for International Studies, Center for Latin American Studies. Pittsburgh, Pa. (UP/CSEC)

Cultura. Ministério da Educação e Cultura, Diretoria de Documentação e Divulgação e Divulgação. Brasília. (MEC/C)

Cultura. Revista del Banco Central del Ecuador. Quito. (BCE/C)

Cultures. United Nations Educational, Scientific and Cultural Organization. Paris. (UNESCO/CU)

Current Anthropology. Univ. of Chicago, Ill. (UC/CA)

Dateline. San Juan, Puerto Rico?

Davar. Revista literaria. Sociedad Hebraica Argentina. Buenos Aires. (SHA/D)

Denver Quarterly. Univ. of Denver. Denver, Colo.

Desarrollo Económico. Instituto de Desarrollo Económico y Social. Buenos Aires. (IDES/DE)

The Developing Economies. Institute of Developing Economies. Tokyo. (IDE/DE)

Diacritics. A review of contemporary criticism. Cornell Univ., Dept. of Romance Studies. Ithaca, N.Y. (CU/D)

Diálogos. Artes/Letras/Ciencias Humanas. El Colegio de México. México. (CM/D)

Diánoia. Univ. Nacional Autónoma de México, Centro de Estudios Filosóficos. México. (UNAM/D)

Dispositio. Univ. of Michigan, Dept. of Romance Languages. Ann Arbor.

Documentos de Arquitectura Nacional y Americana. Univ. Nacional del Nordeste, Depto. de Historia de la Arquitectura. Resistencia, Argentina.

El Dorado. Univ. of Northern Colorado, Museum of Anthropology. Greeley. (UNC/ED)

Eco. Librería Bucholz. Bogotá. (ECO)

Económico. Ministerio de Economía y Finanzas. Montevideo.

Ecuador, Bibliografía Analítica. Banco Central del Ecuador. Centro de Investigación y Cultura. Cuenca.

Educação Hoje. Faculdade de Filosofia, Ciências e Letras de Palmas, Brazil.

La Educación. Organization of American States, Dept. of Educational Affairs. Washington. (OAS/LE)

Ele, Ela. Rio de Janeiro.

Encuentro: Selecciones para Latinoamérica. Centro de Proyección Cristiana. Lima.

English Journal. East Lansing, Mich.

Ensaios de Opinião. Rio de Janeiro.

Escritos de Filosofía. Academia Nacional de Ciencias, Centro de Estudios Filosóficos. Buenos Aires.

Escritura. Teoría y crítica literaria. Univ. Central de Venezuela, Escuela de Letras. Caracas. (UCV/E)

Esquire. New York.

Estrategia. Instituto Argentino de Estudios Estratégicos y de las Relaciones Internacionales. Buenos Aires. (IAEERI/E)

Estudios Andinos. Univ. of Pittsburg, Latin American Studies Center. Pittsburg, Pa. (UP/EA)

Estudios Atacameños. San Pedro de Atacama, Chile.

Estudios Contemporáneos. Univ. Autónoma de Puebla, Instituto de Ciencias, Centro de Estudios Contemporáneos. Puebla, México.

Estudios de Cultura Náhuatl. Univ. Nacional Autónoma de México, Instituto de Historia, Seminario de Cultura Náhuatl. México. (UNAM/ECN)

Estudios de Historia Moderna y Contemporánea de México. Univ. Nacional Autónoma de México. México. (UNAM/E)

Estudios de Historia Novohispana. Univ. Nacional Autónoma de México, Instituto de Investigaciones Históricas. México. (UNAM/EHN)

Estudios Fiscales. México.

Estudios Latinoamericanos. Polska Akademia Nauk /Academia de Ciencias de Polonia/, Instytut Historii / Instituto de Historia /. Warszawa. (PAN/ES)

Estudios Paraguayos. Univ. Católica Nuestra Señora de la Asunción. (UCNSA/EP)

Estudios Sociales. Corporación de Promoción Universitaria. Santiago. (CPU/ES)

Estudos Brasileiros. Univ. Federal do Paraná, Setor de Ciências Humanas, Centro de Estudos Brasileiros. Curitiba, Brazil. (UFP/EB)

Estudos e Pesquisas em Administração. Univ. Federal de Paraíba, Curso Mestrado em Administração. João Pessoa, Brazil.

Estudos Históricos. Faculdade de Filosofia, Ciências e Letras, Depto. de História. Marília, Brazil. (FFCLM/EH)

Estudos Ibero-Americanos. Depto. de Historia, Pontificia Univ. Católica do Rio Grande do Sul. Porto Alegre.

Ethnicity. New York.

Ethnohistory. Journal of the American Society for Ethnohistory. Buffalo, N.Y. (ASE/E)

Ethnology. Univ. of Pittsburgh, Pa. (UP/E)

Ethnomusicology. Ann Arbor, Mich.

Etnohistoria y Antropología Andina. Museo Nacional de Historia. Lima.

Etnologia Polona. Warsaw.

Études Hispano-Américaines. Univ. de Haute Bretagne, Centre d'Études Hispaniques, Hispano-Américaines et Luso-Brésiliennes. Rennes, France. (UHB/EHA)

Europe. Revue littéraire mensuelle. Paris.

Excelsior. Diorama de la cultura. México.

Explicación de Textos Literarios. California State Univ., Dept. of Spanish and Portuguese. Sacramento.

FEM. Publicación femenina. Nueva Cultura Feminista. México.

Fénix. Biblioteca Nacional. Lima. (FENIX)

Film Quarterly. Univ. of California. Berkeley.

Filme Cultura. Ministério de Educação Cultural, Embrafilme (Empresa Brasileira de Filmes). Rio de Janeiro. (MEC/FC)

The Florida Historical Quarterly. The Florida Historical Society. Jacksonville. (FHS/FHQ)

Folia Histórica del Nordeste. Instituto de Historia, Facultad de Humanidades, Univ. Nacional del Nordeste, Instituto de Investigaciones Geohistóricas. Resistencia, Argentina.

Folia Humanistica. Ciencias, artes, letras. Editorial Glarma. Barcelona. (FH)

Folklore Americano. Instituto Panamericano de Geografía e Historia, Comisión de Historia, Comité de Folklore. México. (IPGH/FA)

Folklore Annual. Austin, Tex.

Foreign Language Index. Public Affairs Information Service. New York.

Foro Internacional. El Colegio de México. México. (CM/FI)

Franciscanum. Revista de las ciencias del espíritu. Univ. de San Buenaventura. Bogotá. (USB/F)

Fund og Forskning i det kongelige samlinger. Copenhagen.

Futurable. Fundación Argentina Año 2000. Buenos Aires.

Gaceta de Cuba. Unión de Escritores y Artistas de Cuba. La Habana. (UEAC/GC)

The Geographical Magazine. London. (GM)

Geosur. Asociación Sudamericana de Estudios Geopolíticos e Internacionales. Montevideo.

Geschichte und Gesellschaft. Zeitschrift für Historische Sozialwissenschaft. Univ. Bielefeld, Fakultät für Geschichtswissenschaft. Bielefeld, FRG. (UB/GG)

Guatemala. Unión de Guatemaltecos. La Habana.

Guías y Catálogos. Archivo General de la Nación. México.

Hablemos de Cine. Lima

Handbook of Latin American Art. New Haven, Conn.

Heterofonía. Revista musical bimestral. México. (HET)

Hispamérica. Revista de literatura. Takoma Park, Md. (HISPA)

Hispania. American Association of Teachers of Spanish and Portuguese. Univ. of Cincinnati, Ohio. (AATSP/H)

Hispania. Revista española de historia. Instituto Jerónimo Zurita, Consejo Superior de Investigaciones Científicas. Madrid. (IJZ/H)

Hispanic American Historical Review. Duke Univ. Press *for the* Conference on Latin American History of the American Historical Association. Durham, N.C. (HAHR)

Hispanic Review. A quarterly devoted to research in the Hispanic languages and literatures. Univ. of Pennsylvania, Dept. of Romance Languages. Philadelphia. (HR)

Hispanófila. Univ. of North Carolina. Chapel Hill. (HISP)

Historia. Revista-Libro trimestral. Buenos Aires.

Historia. Univ. Católica de Chile, Instituto de Historia. Santiago. (UCCIH/H)

Historia Crítica. Revista de la Carrera de Historia. Univ. Nacional Autónoma de Honduras. Tegucigalpa.

Historia Mexicana. El Colegio de México. México. (CM/HM)

Historia Obrera. Centro de Estudios Históricos del Movimiento Obrero Mexicano. México. (CEHSMO)

Historia Paraguaya. Anuario de la Academia Paraguaya de la Historia. Asunción. (APH/HP)

Historia y Cultura. Museo Nacional de Historia. Lima. (PMNH/HC)

The Historian. A journal of history. Phi Alpha Theta, National Honor Society in History. Univ. of Pennsylvania. University Park. (PAT/TH)

Histórica. Pontificia Univ. Católica del Perú, Depto. de Humanidades. Lima. (PUCP/H)

Histórica. Univ. Autónoma del Estado de México, Instituto de Investigaciones Históricas. México. (UAEM/H)

Historical Reflections/Reflexions Historiques. Univ. of Waterloo, Dept. of History. Waterloo, Canada.

Históricas. Univ. Nacional Autónoma de México, Instituto de Investigaciones Históricas. México.

Historiografía Rioplatense. Instituto Bibliográfico Antonio Zinny. Buenos Aires.

History Today. Longman Group, Ltd., Periodicals and Directories Division. London

Hojas Universitarias. Revista de la Fundación Univ. Central. Bogotá. (HU)

L'Homme. Revue française d'anthropologie. La Sorbonne, l'École Pratique des Hautes Études. Paris. (EPHE/H)

Humanitas. Boletín ecuatoriano de antropología. Univ. Central del Ecuador, Instituto de Antropología. Quito. (UCEIA/H)

Humanitas. Univ. de Nuevo León, Centro de Estudios Humanísticos. Monterrey, México. (UNL/H)

Humboldt. Revista para o mundo ibérico. Ubersee-Verlag. Hamburg, FRG. (HUMB)

Ibero-Americana Pragensia. Univ. Carolina de Praga, Centro de Estudios Ibero-Americanos. Prague. (UCP/IAP)

Ibero-Amerikanisches Archiv. Ibero-Amerikanisches Institut. Berlin, FRG. (IAA)

Iberoromania. Max Niemeyer Verlag. Tübingen, FRG.

Ideas y Valores. Revista del Instituto de Filosofía y Letras. Univ. Nacional. Bogotá. (UN/IV)

Ideologies & Literature. A journal of Hispanic and Luso-Brazilian literatures. Univ. of Minnesota, Institute for the Study of Ideologies and Literature. Minneapolis. (IL)

Inca. Centro de Estudiantes de Arqueología. Lima.

Index on Censorship. Writers & Scholars International. London. (INDEX)

Index Translationum. UNESCO, International Institute of Intellectual Cooperation. Geneva.

The Indian Historian. American Indian Historical Society. San Francisco, Calif.

Indiana. Beiträge zur Volker-und Sprachenkunde, Archäologie und Anthropologie des Indianischen Amerika. Ibero-Amerikanisches Institut. Berlin, FRG. (IAI/I)

Indiana Folklore. Bloomington.

Indice de Artículos de Publicaciones Periódicas en el Area de Ciencias Sociales y Humanidades. Instituto Colombiano para el Fomento de la Educación Superior (ICFES). División de Documentación e Información. Bogotá.

Indice de Ciências Sociais. Instituto Universitário de Pesquisas do Rio de Janeiro (IUPERJ). Rio de Janeiro.

Información Documental Costarricense y Centroamericana. Univ. de Costa Rica. Instituto de Investigaciones Sociales. San José.

Informaciones. Univ. Nacional de Asunción, Escuela de Bibliotecología. Asunción.

Informações sobre a Indústria Cinematográfica Brasileira. Embrafilme. Rio de Janeiro.

Insula. Madrid. (INSULA)

Inter-American Economic Affairs. Washington. (IAMEA)

Inter-American Music Review. R. Stevenson. Los Angeles, Calif. (IAMR)

Interciencia. Asociación Interciencia. Caracas. (AI/I)

Interior. Revista bimestral. Ministério do Interior. Brasília.

International History Review. Univ. of Toronto Press. Toronto.

International Review. United States Department of Housing and Urban Development, Office of International Affairs. Washington.

Inti. Univ. of Connecticut, Dept. of Romance Languages. Storrs. (INTI)

Investigaciones y Ensayos. Academia Nacional de la Historia. Buenos Aires. (ANH/IE)

Islas. Univ. Central de las Villas. Santa Clara, Cuba. (UCLV/I)

Istmo. Revista del pensamiento actual. México. (ISTMO)

Jahrbuch für Geschichte von Staat, Wirtschaft und Gesellschaft Lateinamerikas. Köln, FRG. (JGSWGL)

Jamaica Journal. Institute of Jamaica. Kingston. (IJ/JJ)

Jamaican Historical Review. The Jamaican Historical Society. Kingston. (JHS/R)

Jeune Cinéma. Paris.

Journal de la Société des Américanistes. Paris. (SA/J)

Journal of American Folklore. American Folklore Society. Austin, Tex. (AFS/JAF)

Journal of Anthropological Research. Univ. of New Mexico, Dept. of Anthropology. Albuquerque. (UNM/JAR)

Journal of Belizean Affairs. Belize City. (JBA)

Journal of Caribbean History. Univ. of the West Indies, Dept. of History /and/ Caribbean Universities Press. St. Lawrence, Barbados. (UWI/JCH)

A Journal of Church and State. Baylor Univ., J.M. Dawson Studies in Church and State. Waco, Tex. (BU/JCS)

Journal of Commonwealth & Comparative Politics. Univ. of London, Institute of Commonwealth Studies. London. (ICS/JCCP)

Journal of Developing Areas. Western Illinois Univ. Press. Macomb. (JDA)

Journal of Economic History. New York Univ., Graduate School of Business Administration *for the* Economic History Association. Rensselaer. (EHA/J)

Journal of Ethnic Studies. Western Washington State College, College of Ethnic Studies. Bellingham.

Journal of European Economic History. Banco de Roma. Roma.

Journal of Family History. Studies in family, kinship and demography. National Council on Family Relations. Minneapolis, Minn. (NCFR/JFH)

Journal of Historical Geography. Academic Press. London.

Journal of Information Science, Librarianship and Archives Administration. United Nations Educational, Scientific and Cultural Organization. Paris. (UNESCO/JIS)

Journal of Inter-American Studies and World Affairs. Sage Publication *for the* Center for Advanced International Studies, Univ. of Miami. Coral Gables, Fla. (SAGE/JIAS. *See also* UM/JIAS)

Journal of Interdisciplinary History. The MIT Press. Cambridge, Mass. (JIH)

Journal of Latin American Lore. Univ. of California, Latin American Center. Los Angeles. (UCLA/JLAL)

Journal of Latin American Studies. Centers or institutes of Latin American studies at the universities of Cambridge, Glasgow, Liverpool, London and Oxford. Cambridge Univ. Press. London. (JLAS)

Journal of Negro History. Association for the Study of Negro Life and History. Washington. (ASNLH/J)

Journal of Peasant Studies. Frank Cass & Co. London. (JPS)

Journal of Popular Culture. Bowling Green, Ohio.

The Journal of San Diego History. San Diego Historical Society. San Diego, Calif. (SDHS/J)

Journal of Social and Political Studies. Council on American Affairs. Washington.

Journal of Social History. Univ. of California Press. Berkeley. (UCP/JSH)

Journal of Spanish Studies: Twentieth Century. Kansas State Univ., Dept. of Modern Languages. Manhattan. (JSSTC)

Journal of the Folklore Institute. Indiana Univ. Bloomington. (IU/JFI)

Journal of the History of Ideas. City College. New York. (JHI)

Journal of the West. Los Angeles, Calif. (JW)

Journalism Quarterly. Association for Education in Journalism *with the cooperation of the* American Association of Schools, Depts. of Journalism /and/ Kappa Tau Alpha Society. Univ. of Minnesota. Minneapolis. (AEJ/JQ)

Jump Cut. A review of contemporary cinema. Berkeley, Calif.

Kaie. National History and Arts Council of Guyana. Georgetown. (NHAC/K)

Karukinka. Instituto de Investigaciones Históricas de Tierra del Fuego. Buenos Aires.

Kentucky Romance Quarterly. Univ. of Kentucky. Lexington. (UK/KRQ)

Kriterion. Revista da Faculdade de Filosofia da Univ. de Minas Gerais. Belo Horizonte, Brazil. (UMGFF/K)

Labor Information Bulletin. Organization of American States. Inter-American Commission of Women. Washington.

Language. Journal of the Linguistic Society of America. Waverly Press, Inc. Baltimore, Md. (LSA/L)

Latin American Digest. Arizona State Univ., Center for Latin American Studies. Tempe. (ASU/LAD)

Latin American Literary Review. Carnegie-Mellon Univ., Dept. of Modern Languages. Pittsburgh, Pa. (LALR)

Latin American Perspectives. Univ. of California. Riverside. (LAP)

Latin American Research Review. Univ. of North Carolina Press *for the* Latin American Studies Association. Chapel Hill. (LARR)

Latin American Theatre Review. A journal devoted to the theatre and drama of Spanish and Portuguese America. Univ. of Kansas, Center of Latin American Studies. Lawrence. (UK/LATR)

Latinoamérica. Anuario de estudios latinoamericanos. Univ. Nacional Autónoma de México, Facultad de Filosofía y Letras, Centro de Estudios Latinoamericanos. México. (UNAM/L)

Latinamericanist. Center for Latin American Studies, Univ. of Florida. Gainesville.

Letras. Univ. Nacional Mayor de San Marcos. Lima. (UNMSM/L)

Letras de Hoje. Pontifícia Univ. Católica do Rio Grande do Sul, Centro de Estudos da Lingua Portuguesa. Porto Alegre, Brazil.

Les Lettres Romances. Univ. Catholique de Louvain, Fondation Universitaire de Belgique. Louvain, Belgium. (UCL/LR)

Lexis. Revista de lingüística y literatura. Pontificia Univ. Católica del Perú. Lima. (PUC/L)

Libros al Día. Caracas.

Lingua. North-Holland Publishing Co. Amsterdam. (LINGUA)

Língua e Literatura. Univ. de São Paulo, Depto. de Letras, Faculdade de Filosofia, Letras e Ciências Humanas. São Paulo. (USP/LL)

Logos. Revista de la Facultad de Filosofía y Letras, Univ. de Buenos Aires.

Lotería. Lotería Nacional de Beneficencia. Panamá. (LNB/L)

Louisiana History. Univ. of Southwestern Louisiana, Louisiana Historical Association. Lafayette.

Luso-Brazilian Review. Univ. of Wisconsin Press. Madison. (UW/LBR)

664 / Handbook of Latin American Studies

Man. A monthly record of anthropological science. The Royal Anthropological Institute. London. (RAI/M)

Mapocho. Biblioteca Nacional, Extensión Cultural. Santiago. (EC/M)

Mariner's Mirror. Society for Nautical Research. Sussex, United Kingdom.

Marxist Perspectives. Transaction Periodicals Consortium. Rutgers Univ. New Brunswick, N.J. (RU/MP)

Megafón. Centro de Estudios Latinoamericanos. Buenos Aires.

Mélanges de la Casa de Velázquez. Paris.

Mensário do Arquivo Nacional. Rio de Janeiro.

El Mercurio. Santiago de Chile.

México: Artículos Clasificados. Univ. Nacional Autónoma de México. Facultad de Ciencias Políticas y Sociales. Centro de Documentación. México.

Mexicon. Aktuelle Informationen und Studien zu Mesoamerika. Internationale Gesellschaft für Mesoamerika-Forschung (IGM). Berling, FRG.

Meyibó. Univ. Nacional Autónoma de México, Centro de Investigaciones Históricas /and/ Univ. Autónoma de Baja, Centro de Investigaciones Históricas. México.

Military History of Texas and the Southwest. Military History Press. Austin.

Millenium. London School of Economics. London.

Missionalia Hispanica. Instituto Santo Toribio de Mogrovejo /and/ Consejo Superior de Investigaciones Científicas. Madrid. (ISTH/MH)

Modern Language Journal. The National Federation of Modern Language Teachers Associations /and/ Univ. of Pittsburgh. Pittsburgh, Pa. (MLTA/MLJ)

Modern Language Notes. Johns Hopkins Univ. Press. Baltimore, Md. (MLN)

Modern Language Review. Univ. of Guyana, Dept. of Modern Languages. Georgetown.

Montalbán. Univ. Católica Andrés Bello, Facultad de Humanidades y Educación, Institutos Humanísticos de Investigación. Caracas. (UCAB/M)

Mundo Nuevo. Instituto Latinoamericano de Relaciones Internacionales. Paris. (MN)

Die Musik in Geschichte und Gegenwart. Kassel. Wilhelmshöhe, FRG. (MGG)

NS NorthSouth NordSud NorteSur NorteSul. Canadian journal of Latin American studies. Canadian Association of Latin American Studies. Univ. of Ottawa. (NS)

The National Bibliography of Barbados. Public Library. Bridgetown.

National Geographic Magazine. National Geographic Society. Washington. (NGS/NGM)

Natural History. American Museum of Natural History. New York. (AMNH/NH)

Ñawpa Pacha. Institute of Andean Studies. Berkeley, Calif. (IAS/ÑP)

Die Neue Rundschau. S. Fischer Verlag. Frankfurt. (NR)

New Mexico Historical Review. Univ. of New Mexico /and/ Historical Society of New Mexico. Albuquerque. (UNM/NMHR)

The New Scholar. Univ. of California, Center for Iberian and Latin American Studies / and/ Institute of Chicano Urban Affairs. San Diego (UCSD/NS)

New Scholasticism. Catholic Univ. of America, Catholic Philosophical Association. Washington.

Nexos. Sociedad de Ciencia y Literatura, Centro de Investigación Cultural y Científica. México.

Nicaráuac. Revista bimestral del Ministerio de Cultura. Managua.

Niterói. Revista brasiliense. Ciências, letras e artes. Academia Paulista de Letras. São Paulo.

Norte Grande. Revista de estudios integrados referentes a comunidades humanas del Norte Grande de Chile, en una perspectiva geográfica e histórico-cultural. Univ. Católica de Chile, Instituto de Goegrafía, Depto. de Geografía de Chile, Taller Norte Grande. Santiago. (UCC/NG)

North Dakota Quarterly. Univ. of North Dakota. Grand Forks.

Notes et Études Documentaires. France—Direction de la Documentation. Paris. (FDD/NED)

Nova Americana. Giulio Einaudi Editora. Torino, Italy.

Nuestra Historia. Centro de Estudios de Historia Argentina. Buenos Aires. (CEHA/NH)

Nueva Narrativa Hispanoamericana. Adelphi Univ., Latin American Studies Program. Garden City, N.Y.

Nueva Revista de Filología Hispánica. El Colegio de México /and/ the Univ. of Texas. México. (CM/NRFH)

L'Oeil. Revue d'art mensuelle. Nouvelle
Sedo. Lausanne, Switzerland. (OEIL)

Orbis. Bulletin international de documenta-
tion linguistique. Centre International de
Dialectologie Générale. Louvain, Belgium.
(CIDG/O)

Orbis. A journal of world affairs. Foreign Policy Research Institute, Philadelphia, Pa. *in
association with the* Fletcher School of
Law and Diplomacy, Tufts Univ., Medford,
Mass. (FPRI/O)

The Pacific Historical Review. Univ. of California Press. Los Angeles. (UC/PHR)

Pájaro de Fuego. Sequals Editora. Buenos
Aires.

La Palabra y el Hombre. Univ. Veracruzana.
Xalapa, México. (UV/PH)

El Palacio. School of American Research,
Museum of New Mexico /and/ Archae-
ological Society of New Mexico. Santa Fe.
(SAR/P)

Past and Present. London. (PP)

Patrimonio Histórico. Instituto Nacional de
Cultura, Dirección del Patrimonio Histórico. Panamá. (INC/PH)

Pensamiento Económico. Organo oficial de
divulgación. Colegio Hondureño de Economistas. Tegucigalpa. (CHE/PE)

Pesquisas: História. Univ. do Vale do Rio dos
Sinos, Instituto Anchietano de Pesquisas.
São Leopoldo, Brazil.

Philologica Pragensia. Academia Scientiarum
Bohemoslovenica. Praha. (ASB/PP)

Philosophica. Rijksuniversiteit. Gent, The
Netherlands.

Phylon. Atlanta Univ. Atlanta, Ga. (AU/P)

Planindex. Resúmen de documentos sobre
planificación. Organización de las Naciones Unidas. Comisión Económica para
América Latina (CEPAL). Centro Latinoamericano de Documentación Económica y Social (CLADES). Santiago.

Plantation Society. Univ. of New Orleans.
New Orleans, La.

Ploughshares. A journal of the arts. Massachusetts Council on the Arts. Cambridge.

Point of Contact. New York Univ., Ibero-
American Language and Area Center. New
York.

Polémica. Univ. de Carabobo, Dirección de
Cultura. Valencia, Venezuela.

Política y Espíritu. Cuadernos de cultura
política, económica y social. Santiago.
(CPES/PE)

Positif. Paris.

Presença Filosófica. Sociedade Brasileira de
Filósofos Católicos. São Paulo.

Proceedings of the American Philosophical
Society. Philadelphia, Pa. (APS/P)

Proceedings of the Pacific Coast Council on
Latin American Studies. Univ. of California. Los Angeles. (PCCLAS/P)

Proceso. Huancayo, Peru.

Publicaciones. Univ. de San Juan, Instituto de
Investigaciones Arqueológicas. San Juan,
Argentina.

Publications of the Modern Language Association of America. New York. (PMLA)

Pucará. Univ. de Cuenca, Facultad de Filosofía, Letras y Ciencias de la Educación.
Cuenca, Ecuador.

Quaderni Ibero-Americani. Associazione per
i Rapporti Culturali con la Spagna, il Portogallo e l'America Latina. Torino, Italy.
(QIA)

Quarterly Review of Film Studies. Redgrave
Publishing Co. Pleasantville, N.Y.

Red River Valley Historical Journal. Red
River Valley Historical Association. Durant, Okla.

Relaciones. Estudios de historia y sociedad.
El Colegio de Michoacán. Zamora, México.

Relaciones de la Sociedad Argentina de
Antropología. Buenos Aires. (SAA/R)

Res Gesta. Facultad de Derecho y Ciencias
Sociales, Instituto de Historia, Univ. Pontifícia Católica Argentina. Rosario.

Research Center for the Arts Review. University of Texas. San Antonio.

Research in African Literatures. Univ. of
Texas Press. Austin.

Review. Center for Inter-American Relations.
New York. (REVIEW)

Revista Aleph. Manizales, Colombia.

Revista Argentina de Administración Pública. Instituto Nacional de la Administración Pública. Buenos Aires.

Revista Brasileira de Biblioteconomia e
Documentação. Federação Brasileira de As-
sociações de Bibliotecários. São Paulo.

Revista Brasileira de Cultura. Ministério da
Educação e Cultura, Conselho Federal de
Cultura. Rio. (CFC/RBC)

Revista Brasileira de Estudos Políticos. Univ.
de Minas Gerais. Belo Horizonte, Brazil.
(UMG/RBEP)

Revista Brasileira de Folclore. Ministério da

Educação e Cultura, Campanha de Defesa do Folclore Brasileiro. Rio. (CDFB/RBF)

Revista Brasileira de Lingüística. Sociedade Brasileira para Professores de Lingüística. São Paulo. (SBPL/RBL)

Revista Canadiense de Estudios Hispánicos. Univ. of Toronto. Toronto.

Revista Centroamericana de Economía. Univ. Nacional Autónoma de Honduras, Programa de Postgrado Centroamericano en Economía y Planificación del Desarrollo. Tegucigalpa.

Revista Chicano-Riqueña. Gary, Ind.

Revista Chilena de Antropología. Santiago.

Revista Chilena de Historia y Geografía. Sociedad Chilena de Historia y Geografía. Santiago. (SCHG/R)

Revista Chilena de Literatura. Editorial Universitaria. Santiago.

Revista Civilização Brasileira. Editora Civilização Brasileira. Rio de Janeiro. (RCB)

Revista Coahuilense de Historia. Colegio Coahuilense de Investigaciones Históricas. Saltillo, México.

Revista Colombiana de Antropología. Ministerio de Educación Nacional, Instituto Colombiano de Antropología. Bogotá.

Revista de Atualidade Indígena. Mina Gráfica Editora. Brasília.

Revista de Biblioteconomia de Brasília. Univ. de Brasília, Associação dos Bibliotecários do Distrito Federal e Departamento Biblioteconomia. Brasília.

Revista de Ciencias Sociales. Univ. de Costa Rica. San José. (UCR/RCS)

Revista de Comunicação Social. Ceará, Brazil.

Revista de Crítica Literaria Latinoamericana. Latinoamericana Editores. Lima. (RCLL)

Revista de Cultura Brasileña. Embajada del Brasil en España. Madrid.

Revista de Dialectología y Tradiciones Populares. Centro de Estudios de Etnología Peninsular, Depto. de Dialectología y Tradiciones Populares, Consejo Superior de Investigaciones Científicas. Madrid. (CEEP/RD)

Revista de Economía Latinoamericana. Banco Central de Venezuela. Caracas. (BCV/REL)

Revista de Estadística y Geografía. Secretaría de Programación y Presupuesto, Coordinación General de los Servicios Nacionales de Estadística, Geografía e Informática, Dirección General de Estadística. México.

Revista de Estudios Hispánicos. Univ. of Alabama, Dept. of Romance Languages, Office of International Studies and Programs. University. (UA/REH)

Revista de Estudios Políticos. Instituto de Estudios Políticos. Madrid. (IEP/REP)

Revista de Filosofía de la Universidad de Costa Rica. San José. (UCR/RF)

Revista de Filosofía Latinoamericana. Ediciones Castañeda. San Antonio de Padua, Argentina. (RFL)

Revista de Historia. Univ. de Concepción, Instituto de Antropología, Historia y Geografía. Concepción, Chile.

Revista de História. Univ. de São Paulo, Faculdade de Filosofia, Ciências e Letras, Depto. de História /and/ Sociedade de Estudos Históricos. São Paulo. (USP/RH)

Revista de Historia. Univ. Nacional de Costa Rica, Escuela de Historia. Heredia. (UNCR/R)

Revista de Historia Americana y Argentina. Univ. Nacional de Cuyo, Facultad de Filosofía y Letras, Instituto de Historia. Mendoza. (UNC/RHAA)

Revista de Historia de América. Instituto Panamericano de Geografía e Historia, Comisión de Historia. México. (PAIGH/H)

Revista de Historia del Derecho. Buenos Aires.

Revista de Historia Militar. Servicio Histórico Militar. Madrid. (SHM/RHM)

Revista de Indias. Instituto Gonzalo Fernández de Oviedo /and/ Consejo Superior de Investigaciones Científicas. Madrid. (IGFO/RI)

Revista de Información Científica y Técnica Cubana. Academia de Ciencias de Cuba. Instituto de Documentación e Información Científica y Técnica. La Habana.

Revista de la Academia Boliviana de Ciencias Económicas. Cochabamba, Bolivia.

Revista de la Biblioteca Nacional. Ministerio de Educación y Cultura. Montevideo. (UBN/R)

Revista de la Biblioteca Nacional José Martí. La Habana. (BNJM/R)

Revista de la Escuela de Comando de la Fuerza Aérea Argentina. Buenos Aires.

Revista de la Facultad de Derecho. Univ. Autónoma de México. México. (UNAM/RFD)

Revista de la Historia del Derecho. Buenos Aires.

Revista de la Junta Provincial de Historia de Córdoba. Archivo Histórico Monseñor P. Cabrera. Córdoba, Argentina. (JPHC/R)

Revista de la Sociedad Bolivariana de Venezuela. Caracas. (SBV/R)

Revista de la Universidad. Univ. Nacional Autónoma de Honduras. Tegucigalpa. (HUN/RU)

Revista de la Universidad Complutense. Madrid. (RUC)

Revista de la Universidad de Costa Rica. San José. (UCR/R)

Revista de la Universidad de México. Univ. Nacional Autónoma de México. México. (UNAM/RUM)

Revista de la Universidad de Yucatán. Mérida, Mex. (UY/R)

Revista de la Universidad del Zulia. Maracaibo, Venezuela. (UZ/R)

Revista de la Universidad Nacional de Córdoba. Dirección General de Publicaciones. Córdoba, Argentina. (UNC/R)

Revista de Letras. Univ. de Puerto Rico en Mayagüez, Facultad de Artes y Ciencias. Mayagüez. (UPRM/RL)

Revista de Oriente. Univ. de Puerto Rico, Colegio Universitario de Humacao. Humacao. (UPR/RO)

Revista de Política Internacional. Instituto de Estudios Políticos. Madrid. (IEP/RPI)

Revista de SINASBI. Información Científica y Tecnológica de Archivos y de Estadística e Informática, Comisión Coordinador del Sistema Nacional de Servicios de Bibliotecas e Información. Caracas.

Revista del Archivo General de la Nación. Buenos Aires.

Revista del Archivo General de la Nación. Instituto Nacional de Cultura. Lima. (PEAGN/R)

Revista del Archivo Histórico del Guayas. Guayaquil, Ecuador. (AHG/R)

Revista del Instituto de Antropología. Univ. Nacional de Tucumán. San Miguel de Tucumán, Arg. (UNTIA/R)

Revista del Instituto de Cultura Puertorriqueña. San Juan. (ICP/R)

Revista del México Agrario. Confederación Nacional Campesina. México. (CNC/RMA)

Revista del Museo Nacional. Casa de la Cultura del Perú, Museo Nacional de la Cultura Peruana. Lima. (PEMN/R)

Revista del Pensamiento Centroamericano. Centro de Investigaciones y Actividades Culturales. Managua. (RCPC)

Revista do Arquivo Municipal. Prefeitura do Município de São Paulo, Depto. Municipal de Cultura. São Paulo. (AM/R)

Revista do Instituto de Estudos Brasileiros. Univ. de São Paulo, Instituto de Estudos Brasileiros. São Paulo. (USP/RIEB)

Revista do Instituto do Ceará. Fortaleza, Brazil.

Revista do Instituto Histórico e Geográfico Brasileiro. Rio. (IHGB/R)

Revista do Instituto Histórico e Geográfico de São Paulo. São Paulo. (IHGSP/R)

Revista do Instituto Histórico e Geográfico Guarujá/Bertioga. São Paulo. (IHGGB/R)

Revista do Museu Paulista. São Paulo. (MP/R)

Revista dos Tribunais. São Paulo.

Revista Eme-Eme. Estudios dominicanos. Univ. Católica Madre y Maestra. Santiago de los Caballeros, República Dominicana. (EME)

Revista Española de Lingüística. Editorial Gredos. Madrid.

Revista Geográfica. Instituto Panamericano de Geografía e Historia, Comisión de Geografía. México. (PAIGH/G)

Revista Hispánica Moderna. Columbia Univ., Hispanic Institute in the United States. New York. (HIUS/R)

Revista Histórica. Museo Histórico Nacional. Montevideo. (UMHN/RH)

Revista Iberoamericana. Instituto Internacional de Literatura Iberoamericana *patrocinada por la* Univ. de Pittsburgh, Pa. (IILI/RI)

Revista Interamericana de Bibliografía /Inter-American Review of Bibliography/. Organization of American States. Washington. (RIB)

Revista Latinoamericana de Filosofía. Centro de Investigaciones Filosóficas. Buenos Aires. (CIF/RLF)

Revista Letras. Univ. Federal do Paraná, Setor de Ciências Humanas, Letras e Artes. Curitiba, Brazil. (UFP/RL)

Revista Lotería. Lotería Nacional de Beneficencia. Panamá. (LNB/L)

Revista Mexicana de Ciencias Políticas y Sociales. Univ. Nacional Autónoma de México, Facultad de Ciencias Políticas y Sociales. México. (UNAM/RMCPS)

Revista Mexicana de Sociología. Univ. Nacional Autónoma de México, Instituto de Investigaciones Sociales. México. (UNAM/RMS)

Revista Musical Chilena. Univ. de Chile, Instituto de Extensión Musical. Santiago. (UCIEM/R)

Revista Musical de Venezuela. Caracas.

Revista Nacional de Cultura. Consejo Nacional de Cultura. Caracas. (CONAC/RNC)

Revista Nacional de Cultura. Ministerio de Cultura y Educación, Secretaría de Estado de Cultura. Buenos Aires.

Revista Paraguaya de Sociología. Centro Paraguayo de Estudios Sociológicos. Asunción. (CPES/RPS)

Revista/Review Interamericana. Univ. Interamericana. San Germán, Puerto Rico. (RRI)

Revista Universidad de Medellín. Centro de Estudios de Posgrado. Medellín, Colombia. (UM/R)

Revista Universitaria. Anales de la Academia Chilena de Ciencias Naturales. Univ. Católica de Chile. Santiago. (UCC/RU)

Revista Venezolana de Filosofía. Univ. Simón Bolívar /and/ Sociedad Venezolana de Filosofía. Caracas. (USB/RVF)

Revolución y Cultura. Publicación mensual. Ministerio de Cultura. La Habana. (RYC)

Revue d'Histoire Economique et Sociale. Editions Marcel Rivière *avec le concours du* Centre National de la Recherche Scientifique. Paris.

Revue Francaise d'Histoire d'Outre-Mer. Société de l'Histoire des Colonies Francaises. Société Francaise d'Histoire d'Outre-Mer. Paris.

Ritmo. La Plata, Argentina.

Ritmo. Revista del Conservatorio de Música Juan José Castro. México.

Romanistisches Jahrbuch. Univ. Hamburg, Romanisches Seminar, Ibero-Amerikanisches Forschungsinstitut. Hamburg, FRG. (UH/RJ)

SECOLAS Annals. Kennesaw College, Southeastern Conference on Latin American Studies. Marietta, Georgia.

SELA en Acción. Secretaría Permanente del Sistema Económico Latinoamericano, Oficina

San Marcos. Lima.

Santiago. Univ. de Oriente. Santiago de Cuba.

Sapientia. Organo de la Facultad de Filosofía. Univ. Católica Argentina Santa María de los Buenos Aires. Buenos Aires. (UCA/S)

Sarance. Instituto Otavaleño de Antropología. Otavalo, Ecuador.

Savacou. Caribbean Artists Movement. Kingston.

Science and Society. New York. (SS)

Scientific American. Scientific American,

Inc. New York. (SA) de Información. Caracas.

Screen. London.

La Semana de Bellas Artes. México.

Semestre de Filosofía. Univ. Central de Venezuela. Caracas.

Semiosis. Seminario de Semiótica, Teoría, Análisis. México.

Série de História. Coleçao Museu Paulista, Univ. de São Paulo, Brazil.

Signos. Estudios de lengua y literatura. Univ. Católica de Valparaíso, Instituto de Literatura y Ciencia del Lenguaje. Valparaío, Chile. (UCV/S)

Signs. Journal of women in culture and society. The Univ. of Chicago Press. Chicago, Ill. (UC/S)

Síntesis Informativa Iberoamericana. Instituto de Cultura Hispánica. Centro de Documentación Iberoamericana. Madrid.

Smithsonian. Smithsonian Institution. Washington.

Social and Economic Studies. Univ. of the West Indies, Institute of Social and Economic Research. Mona, Jamaica. (UWI/SES)

Social Science Quarterly. Univ. of Texas, Dept. of Government. Austin. (UT/SSQ)

South Atlantic Bulletin. South Atlantic Modern Language Association. Chapel Hill, N.C.

Southern California Quarterly. Historical Society of Southern California. Los Angeles. (HSSC/SCQ)

Southern Folklore Quarterly. Univ. of Florida *in cooperation with the* South Atlantic Language Association. Gainesville. (UF/SFQ)

Southwestern Historical Quarterly. Texas State Historical Association. Austin. (TSHA/SHQ)

Staden-Jahrbuch. Beiträge zur Brasilkunde. Instituto Hans Staden. São Paulo. (IHS/SJ)

Statistical Bulletin of the OAS. Organization of American States. General Secretariat. Washington.

Status. São Paulo.

Studi di Letteratura Ispanoamericana. Milano.

Studies in Comparative International Development. Rutgers Univ. New Brunswick, N.J. (RU/SCID)

Studies in Latin American Popular Culture. New Mexico State Univ., Dept. of Foreign Languages. Las Cruces.

Studies in the Anthropology of Visual Communication. Society for the Anthropology of Visual Communication. Washington.

Studies in the Social Sciences. West Georgia College. Carrollton.

Suplemento Antropológico. Univ. Católica de Nuestra Señora de la Asunción, Centro de Estudios Antropológicos. Asunción. (UCNSA/SA)

Sur. Revista semestral. Buenos Aires.

Temas Económicos. Univ. de Antioquia, Facultad de Ciencias Económicas, Dept. de Economía. Medellín, Colombia.

Texto Crítico. Univ. Veracruzana, Centro de Investigaciones Lingüístico-Literarias. Xalapa, México.

Thesaurus. Boletín del Instituto Caro y Cuervo. Bogotá. (ICC/T)

Thesis. Nueva revista de filosofía y letras. Univ. Nacional Autónoma de México, Facultad de Filosofía y Letras. México.

Tiemporeal. Simón Bolívar Univ. Caracas.

Tiers Monde. Problèmes des pays sous-développés. Univ. de Paris, Institut d'Étude du Dévellopement Économique et Social. Paris. (UP/TM)

Trabajos y Comunicaciones. Univ. Nacional de La Plata, Depto. de Historia. La Plata, Argentina. (UNLP/TC)

Tradición Popular. Univ. de San Carlos de Guatemala, Centro de Estudios Folklóricos. San Carlos. (USCG/TP)

Tradiciones de Guatemala. Guatemala.

Tramoya. Univ. Veracruzana. Xalapa, México.

Transactions of the Institute of British Geographers. London.

Trans/Form/Ação. Faculdade de Filosofia, Ciência e Letras de Assis. Assis, Brazil.

Translation Review. Richardson, Tex.

Trimestre Económico. Fondo de Cultura Económica. México. (FCE/TE)

Trinidad and Tobago National Bibliography. Central Library of Trinidad and Tobago /and/ The University of the West Indies Library. Port of Spain.

Unesco Journal of Information Science, Librarianship and Archives Administration. United Nations Educational, Scientific and Cultural Organization. Paris. (UNESCO/JIS)

Unión. Unión de Escritores y Artistas de Cuba. La Habana. (UNION)

Universidad. Univ. de Antioquia. Medellín, Colombia. (UA/U)

Universidad. Univ. Nacional del Litoral. Santa Fe, Argentina. (UNL/U)

Universidad de La Habana. La Habana. (UH/U)

Universidad Nacional de Colombia. Revista de extensión cultural. Medellín.

Universidad Pontificia Bolivariana. Medellín, Colombia. (UPB)

Universo. Univ. Autónoma de Santo Domingo, Facultad de Humanidades. Santo Domingo. (UASD/U)

Urban Anthropology. State Univ. of New York, Dept. of Anthropology. Brockport. (UA)

Veritas. Revista. Pontifícia Univ. Católica do Rio Grande do Sul. Porto Alegre, Brazil. (PUC/V)

Via. A new literary magazine. Univ. of California, Office of Student Activities. Berkeley. (VIA)

Vozes. Revista de cultura. Editora Vozes. Petrópolis, Brazil. (VOZES)

Vuelta. México.

Wari. Ayacucho, Peru.

Washington Review. Washington.

Western Folklore. Univ. of California Press for the California Folklore Society. Berkeley. (CFS/WF)

The Western Historical Quarterly. Western History Association, Utah State Univ. Logan. (WHQ)

YaxKin. Instituto Hondureño de Antropología e Historia. Tegucigalpa. (YAXKIN)

Yucatán: Historia y Economía. Revista de análisis socioeconómico regional. Univ. de Yucatán, Centro de Investigaciones Regionales, Depto. de Estudios Económicos y Sociales. Mérida, México.

Zacatecas. Anuario de historia. Univ. Autónoma de Zacatecas, Depto. de Investigaciones Históricas. Zacatecas, México.

Zeitschrift für Kulturaustausch. Institut für Auslandsbeziehungen. Berlin, FRG. (IA/ZK)

Zeitschrift für Missionswissenschaft und Religionswissenschaft. Lucerne, Switzerland. (ZMR)

SUBJECT INDEX

Abascal, José de, 2821.
Abela, Eduardo, 419.
Abolition of Slavery. *See also Slavery.* Brazil, 3634. Colombia, 2814, 2848. Cuba, 2541. in Literature, 6270. United States, 2108. Venezuela, 2875.
Abreu, Casimiro de, 6211.
Academia Paulista de Letras, São Paulo, Brazil, 6157.
Academic Degrees. *See also Dissertations and Theses; Education.* United States, 185.
Accounting. *See also Business.* Dominican Republic, 129.
Acculturation. *See also Anthropology; Assimilation; Culture; Ethnology; Race and Race Relations.* Latin America, 1728.
Acevedo Díaz, Eduardo, 5106.
Aconcagua, Chile (province). History, 3106.
Acre, Brazil (state). History, 3009.
Administrative Law. *See also Constitutional Law; Law; Local Government; Political Science.* Mexico, 2119.
Admirals. *See also Maritime History; Military.* Peru, 3004.
Adomian, Lan, 7086, 7096.
Advertising. *See also Business; Mass Media.* Puerto Rico, 4584.
Aeronautics. *See also Air Pilots; Transportation.* Argentina, 3296, 3407.
Aesthetics. *See also Art; Philosophy; Romanticism; Surrealism; Values.* Mexico, 380.
Aged. in Literature, 5257.
Agrarian Reform. *See also Agricultural Cooperatives; Agricultural Policy; Agriculture; Economic Policy; Land Tenure; Land Use; Social Policy.* Bolivia, 3012. Chile, 3073, 3085, 3130–3131. Dominican Republic, 2550a–2551. Law and Legislation, 2063, 3012. Mexico, 1996, 2063, 2092, 2152, 2180, 2188, 2193, 2255. Peru, 2948. Uruguay, 2839.
Agricultural Colonies. *See also Land Settlement; Land Tenure.* Mexico, 2055.
Agricultural Cooperatives. *See also Agrarian Reform; Agriculture; Ejidos; Land Tenure.* Mexico, 2229.
Agricultural Industries. *See also Agriculture; Cocoa Trade; Coffee Industry and Trade; Cotton Industry and Trade; Food Industry and Trade; Forests and Forest Industry; Fruit Trade; Pulque Trade; Rubber Industry and Trade; Sugar Industry and Trade; Tobacco Manufacture and Trade; Wheat Trade; Wool Industry and Trade.* Costa Rica, 2464.
Agricultural Laborers. *See also Agriculture; Internal Migration; Labor and Laboring Class; Peasants; Peonage; Rural-urban Migration.* Peru, 2914.
Agricultural Policy. *See also Agrarian Reform; Agriculture; Economic Policy; Rural Development.* Argentina, 3253, 3336. Brazil, 3571, 3579, 3603. Chile, 3073, 3130. Mexico, 2055, 2071, 2234.
Agriculture. *See also Agrarian Reform; Agricultural Cooperatives; Agricultural Industries; Agricultural Laborer; Agricultural Policy; Anil; Cacao; Ejidos; Henequen; Irrigation; Land Tenure; Land Use; Livestock; Maize; Produce Trade; Soils.* Alto Peru, 2717. Argentina, 3210, 3230, 3252–3254, 3402. Bibliography, 21, 32. Bolivia, 3049. Brazil, 3489, 3511, 3531, 3546, 3603, 3605. Dominican Republic, 129. Guatemala, 2360. Haiti, 2565. Honduras, 21. Latin America, 32. Mexico, 194, 1558, 1929, 1996, 2077. Peru, 2945, 2960. Venezuela, 2601. Viceroyalty of New Spain, 99, 1941. Viceroyalty of Peru, 2672, 2688.
Aguilera Malta, Demetrio, 5400.
Aguirre, Francisco de, 2580.
Aguirre, Juan Bautista de, 7577.
Aguirre, Juan Pedro, 2837.
Aguirre Benavides, Eugenio, 2187.
Air Pilots. *See also Aeronautics.* Argentina, 3286. Uruguay, 3466.
Alagoas, Brazil (state). *See also the region of Northeast Brazil.* Art, 6168. Prose Literature, 6168.

Alanís, Lázaro S., 2140.
Alberdi, Juan Bautista, 3226, 3297, 3340, 3389, 5127, 7536, 7556.
Albizu Campos, Pedro, 2493, 2559.
Albuquerque, New Mexico (city). History, 1972. Language, 4563.
Alcalde, Andrés, 7068.
Alcaldes. *See also Colonial Administrators.* Viceroyalty of New Spain, 1791, 1847. Viceroyalty of Peru, 1672, 1791.
Alcohol and Alcoholism. *See also Diseases; Drug Abuse; Pulque Trade; Wine and Wine Making.* Borderlands, 2260. in Literature, 5211. Mexico, 2022. Viceroyalty of New Spain, 1847, 1933.
Aleijandinho / *pseudonym for* Lisboa, Antônio Francisco /.
Aleman, Miguel, 2273.
Alencar, José Martiniano de, 6194.
Alessandri, Arturo, 3120.
Alexis, Jacques-Stéphen, 6251.
Alfaro, Eloy, 2898.
Allende Gossens, Salvador, 3075.
Almeida, José Américo de, 1088.
Almeida, José Ferraz de, 472.
Alonso de la Cruz, *Brother,* 7561.
Alotenango, Guatemala (city). Ethnohistory, 1553. History, 2350.
Altamiro, Ignacio Manuel, 5132.
Althusser, Louis, 7688–7689.
Alto Perú. *See also Audiencia of Charcas; Colonial History under Bolivia.* History, 2821, 2824.
    Ethnohistory, 1582–1583.
    Colonial Period, 2709–2725.
Alvarado, Alonso de, 1581.
Alvarado, Salvador, 2151.
Alvarado Bonilla, Pablo de, 2430.
Alvear, Carlos, 3231.
Alvear Family, 3223.
Alves Boaventura, Eurico, 6218.
Alvim, Fausto, 495.
Amado, Jorge, 6205.
Amapá, Brazil (territory). History, 3542.
Amaral, Olga de, 435.
Amazonas, Brazil (state). History, 3492. Prose Literature, 6179.
AMAZONIA. *See also the countries of Bolivia, Brazil, Colombia, Ecuador, French Guiana, Guyana, Peru, Surinam, Venezuela; the region of South America.*
Art, 502–503.
History, 3573, 3625.
    Ethnohistory, 1568, 1679.
    Colonial Period. *See Colonial History under Brazil; Viceroyalty of Peru.*

Literature.
    Poetry, 502.
Ambassadors. *See also Diplomats.* Argentina, 3229, 3272. Haitian, 2539. to Mexico, 2282. United States, 2107, 2473.
Ambato, Ecuador (city). History, 2642, 2897.
Ameghino, Florentino, 7565.
Amelia, Empress, Consort of Pedro I, 3552.
American Revolution (1776–1783). *See also Revolutions and Revolutionary Movements; Wars of Independence.* in Florida, 51. Influence on British West Florida, 2519. Influence on Spanish Colonies, 1816.
Amorim, Enrique, 5131.
Ampiés, Juan de, 1781, 2610.
Analysis (Philosophy). *See also Philosophy; Philosophy under Language and Languages.* 7685.
Anarchism and Anarchists. *See also Crime and Criminals; Liberty; Political Science; Socialism and Socialist Parties.* Argentina, 3326. Mexico, 7607. Peru, 2914, 2918, 2926, 2928, 2941.
Anaxagoras, 7629.
ANDEAN REGION. *See also the countries of Bolivia, Chile, Colombia, Ecuador, Peru, Venezuela; the region of South America.*
Art, 1604.
History.
    Ethnohistory. *See also the Viceroyalty of Peru.* 1586, 1603, 1606–1607, 1620, 1647, 1649, 1694.
    Colonial History. *See Viceroyalty of Peru.*
    19th Century, 3111.
    20th Century, 3286.
Language, 4533, 4594.
Literature.
    Prose Literature, 5371–5503.
Andrade, João Batista de, 995.
Andrade, Joaquim Pedro de, 985, 1030.
Andrade, Mário de, 478, 1009, 1025, 1030, 4623, 6170, 6195, 6204.
Andrade, Oswald de, 981, 6180, 6193.
Anil. *See also Agriculture; Indigo.* Guatemala, 2346. Viceroyalty of New Spain, 1930.
Animals. *See also Livestock.* in Art, 470–471, 474. Brazil, 470–471, 474.
Anonyms and Pseudonyms. *See also Authors; Bibliography.* Dominican Republic, 163.
Anquín, Nimio de, 7535.
Anthropological Linguistics. *See also Anthropology; Indigenous Languages;*

Linguistics. Andean Region, 1569. Meso-america, 1535. Methodology, 1535.
Anthropologists. *See also Anthropology.* Peru, 2963.
Anthropology. *See also Acculturation; Archaeology; Anthropological Linguistics; Anthropologists; Assimilation; Blacks; Cultural Development; Ethnology; Human Geography; Indigenous Languages; Indigenous Peoples; Language and Languages; National Characteristics; Paleoanthropology; Philosophical Anthropology; Race and Race Relations; Social Change; Social Sciences; Social Structure; Sociology; Women.* Bibliography, 54. Guatemala, 147. in Literature, 5292. Paraguay, 31. Venezuela, 54.
ANTIGUA. *See also Commonwealth Caribbean; Lesser Antilles.*
History.
19th Century, 2544.
Antigua, Guatemala (city). Art, 285, 317, 319. History, 2343.
Antilles. *See Greater Antilles; Lesser Antilles; West Indies.*
Antioquia, Colombia (city). History, 2814, 2865.
Antonio Maceo Brigade (1977). in Literature, 5313.
Apasa, Julián. *See Insurrection of Tupac Katari (1781).*
APRA. *See Alianza Popular Revolucionario Americana (APRA, Peru) under Political Parties.*
Apure, Venezuela (state). History, 2871.
Aragón, Rafael, 339.
Araucano (indigenous group), 1573, 3091, 3123, 3376, 5078, 5081, 5089.
Araújo, Maurino de, 482.
Araújo, Pedro Luiz Correira de, 525.
Archaeological Dating. *See also Archaeology.* Mesoamerica, 274.
Archaeologists. *See also Archaeology; Historians.* 2115.
Archaeology. *See also Anthropology; Archaeological Dating; Archaeologists; Artifacts; Astronomy; Calendrics; Codices; Cultural Development; Ethnohistory; Ethnology; Excavations; Historic Sites; History; Inscriptions; Mortuary Customs; Mythology; Paleoanthropology; Precolumbian Architecture; Precolumbian Art; Precolumbian Civilizations; Precolumbian Cultures; Precolombian Land Settlement Patterns; Precolumbian Pottery; Pre-*

columbian Trade; Religion; Rites and Ceremonies. Mexico, 1878. Peru, 1567.
Archbishops. *See also Catholic Church; Clergy.* Chile, 3104. Viceroyalty of Peru, 2670.
Architects. *See also Architecture.* Colombia, 438. Viceroyalty of New Spain, 1890.
Architecture. *See also Architects; Art; Churches; City Planning; Colonial Architecture; Engineering; Housing; Modern Architecture; Monuments; Precolumbian Architecture.* Brazil, 455, 460, 463. Caribbean Area, 368. Colombia, 328. Dominican Republic, 405. Guatemala, 403. Mexico, 298, 2034. Panama, 323. Periodicals, 253. Peru, 357. Venezuela, 363.
Archives. *See also Bibliography; Colonial History; History; Libraries and Library Services; Manuscripts.* Archivo de la Antigua Academia de San Carlos (Mexico), 376. Archivo Galtinara (Italy), 1855, 1857. Archivo General (Argentina), 120. Archivo General de Centroamérica (Guatemala), 89, 134. Archivo General de Indias (Spain), 2351, 2648. Archivo General de la Nación (Mexico), 87, 1917, 7093. Archivo General de la Orden Franciscana del Ecuador, 109. Archivo General del Estado de México, 1838, 1842. Archivo Histórico Ultramarino (Brazil), 3541. Archivo Municipal de Cuauhtinchán, Puebla, Mexico, 141. Archivo Nacional de Historia (Ecuador), 88. Arquivo Odilon Braga (Brazil), 90. Bolivia, 2577, 2720. Brazil, 114, 3562. Chile, 2577, 3119. Colombia, 2626. Cuba, 66, 106. Ecuador, 2577, 2635, 2647, 2906. Instituto Joaquim Nabuco de Pesquisas Sociais (Brazil), 86, 3543. Law and Legislation, 114. Mexico, 1847, 1851, 1900, 2050. Peru, 2577. Real Academia de la Historia (Spain), 99–100, 118. Rosenbach Museum Library (Pennsylvania), 1852. Stanford University, Hoover Institute on War, Revolution and Peace (California), 167. Venezuela, 2612. Viceroyalty of New Spain, 1855.
Arenas, Domingo, 2217.
Arenas, Reinaldo, 5296, 5368.
Arequipa, Peru (city). Art, 353. History, 2910, 2921, 2923, 2936–2937, 2977.
Arequipa, Peru (department). Ethnohistory, 1655. History, 2696.
Arévalo Cedeño, Emilio, 2868.
Arévalo González, Rafael, 2869.
ARGENTINA. *See also the cities of Bahía Blanca, Buenos Aires, Carmen de Pa-*

Cathedrals. *See Churches.*

Catholic Church. *See also Archbishops; Bishops; Cardinals; Church History; Churches; Clergy; Inquisition; Missions; Monasticism and Religious Orders; Popes; Religion.* Argentina, 3164, 3166, 3203, 3289. Bibliography, 27. Bolivia, 3034, 3036. Caribbean Area, 27. Chile, 3104. Colombia, 2854, 2863. El Salvador, 2388. Guatemala, 2295. Honduras, 2387. Mexico, 155, 2070, 2184. Paraguay, 30, 2832, 3426. Peru, 2952–2953, 2994, 2999. Spanish Colonies, 1734, 1756, 1774. Viceroyalty of New Spain, 1861.

The Catholic University of America, Washington. Oliveira Lima Library, 505.

Cattle Trade. *See also Meat Industry and Trade.* Argentina, 3206, 3251. Brazil, 3545. Peru, 2961, 2976.

Caudillismo. *See also Caudillos.* Bolivia, 3025. Mexico, 2231, 2268.

Caudillos. *See also Caudillismo; Dictators.* Argentina, 3244, 3330, 3401. Guatemala, 2418. Mexico, 2161. Peru, 2998.

Cavalcânti, Alberto, 988.

Cayambé (indigenous group), 1598.

Cayapó (indigenous group), 3515.

CAYMAN ISLANDS. *See also the Commonwealth Caribbean.*
History, 2488.

Cazal, José María, 3422.

Ceará, Brazil (state). *See also the region of Northeast Brazil.* History, 3621. Prose Literature, 6166.

Ceballos, Rodrigo de, 7048.

Cedillo, Saturnino, 2218, 2231.

Cendrars, Blaise, 6173.

Censorship. *See also Censorship under specific subjects; Civil Rights; Freedom of the Press; Journalism; Mass Media; Press; Publishers and Publishing Industry.* Argentina, 3261. Brazil, 977, 980, 985, 1057, 1086, 6148, 6155. Cuba, 5365. Latin America, 175, 5002. in Literature, 5181.

Censuses. *See also Demography; Population; Statistics.* Alto Peru, 2714. Mexico, 1847.

CENTRAL AMERICA. *See also the countries of Belize, Costa Rica, El Salvador, Guatemala, Honduras, Nicaragua, Panama; the region of Latin America.*
Art, 316–323, 402–404.
Bibliography, 4.
History, 2304, 2314.
   Ethnohistory. *See Mesoamerica.*
   Colonial Period. *See also Captaincy*
   General of Guatemala; Viceroyalty of New Spain. 2315–2363.
   Independence Period, 2299.
   19th Century. *See also Federation of Central America.* 2108, 2364–2475, 2946, 2949.
   20th Century, 2364–2475.
Language, 4551.
Literature.
   Drama, 5899.
   Prose Literature, 5011, 5260–5292.
Music, 7048–7054.

Centralized Government. *See also Federal Government; Federalism; Local Government; Political Science.* Latin America, 1725. Mexico, 1981, 2054, 2057, 2069, 2205, 2231.

Centro Interamericano de Artesanías y Artes (CIDAP). Periodicals, 252.

Cerra, Mirta, 423.

Cervecería Backus y Johnston. History, 2983.

Césaire, Aimé, 6254.

Céspedes y del Castillo, Carlos de, 2523.

Cevallos, Pedro, 2744.

Chachapoya (indigenous group), 2674.

Chaco, Argentina (province). History, 3395, 3397.

CHACO (region). *See also the countries of Argentina, Paraguay.*
History, 3164, 3398.

Chaco War (1932–1935). *See also names of specific battles.* 3013, 3017, 3028, 3030, 3059, 3061, 3415, 3422–3423, 3425, 3434, 3440. in Literature, 5609, 5855.

Chaliapin, Fiodor, 7022.

Chamula (indigenous group), 1522–1523.

Chancay Valley, Peru. History, 2917, 2924.

Charcas, Ecuador (city). History, 2927.

Chaves, Alonso de, 2326.

Chávez Morado, José, 382.

Chayanta, Bolivia (province). Ethnohistory, 1657.

Chiapas, Mexico (city). Ethnohistory, 1609.

Chiapas, Mexico (state). Art, 317. History, 2149, 2196. Language, 4535.

Chibcha (indigenous group), 2634.

Chicanos. *See Mexican Americans.*

Chichimec (indigenous group), 1515, 1537, 1556, 1863.

Chihuahua, Mexico (state). History, 1954, 2130.

Chilam Balam, 1517–1518.

Children. *See also Family and Family Relationships; Sociology; Youth.* in Art, 395,

munity Development; Housing; Land Use; Regional Planning. Bibliography, 18. Brazil, 460, 511, 516, 3485. Guatemala, 320. Latin America, 372. Mexico, 18, 332–333. Peru, 354. Precolumbian, 1509. South America, 370. Viceroyalty of Rio de la Plata, 2770.

Ciudad de Galeana, Mexico (city). History, 1950.

Civil Rights. See also Censorship; Constitutional Law; Freedom of the Press; Human Rights; Liberty; Political Science. 7743. Latin America, 5002.

Civil War. See also Revolutions and Revolutionary Movements. in Literature, 5049.

Civilian Governments. See also Federal Government; Military Governments; Political Science. Peru, 2986.

Clarté Group, Brazil, 3584.

Class Conflict. See Social Conflict.

Clergy. See also Archbishops; Bishops; Cardinals; Catholic Church; Church History; Military Chaplains; Monasticism and Religious Order; Popes. Argentina, 3135, 3203. Audiencia of Quito, 2807. Borderlands, 1953. Brazil, 3482, 3505. Central America, 2327. Cuba, 176. Mexico, 2065. Peru, 2821. Spanish Colonies, 1779. Viceroyalty of New Spain, 1870, 1892, 1949. Viceroyalty of Peru, 2676, 2681, 2692, 2697, 2705, 2821.

Climatology. Spanish Colonies, 1798. Viceroyalty of New Spain, 1876.

Coahuila, Mexico (state). History, 1967, 2017, 2021, 2248.

Coal Mines and Mining. See also Minerals and Mining Industry. Chile, 3103.

Coatlinchán, Mexico (city). History, 1504.

Cobo Borda, Juan Gustavo, 5806.

Coca Leaf. See also Drug Trade. Precolumbian, 1662.

Cochabamba, Bolivia (city). History, 2717–2719, 3032, 3057.

Coclé, Panama (province). History, 2397.

Cocoa Trade. See also Agricultural Industries. Ecuador, 2899.

Codallos, Juan José, 2011.

Codices. See also Archaeology; Manuscripts. Aubin, 1514. Bibliography, 1525. Botuini, 1550. Colombino-Becker, 1564. Florentine, 1559. Mendoza, 1509. Mesoamerica, 1525, 1555. Mexico, 1847. Mixtec, 1513. Nuttall, 251. Vergara, 1565.

Coffee Industry and Trade. See also Agricultural Industries. Bibliography, 104. Brazil, 3480, 3574, 3589, 3602, 3636. Colom-

bia, 104. Costa Rica, 2289, 2386, 2420, 2424. El Salvador, 2431. Guatemala, 2308. Puerto Rico, 2537, 2540.

Cofradías. See Confraternities.

Colegio de la Merced, Lima, Peru, 2700.

Colegio de Rosario, Bogotá, Colombia, 2624.

Colegio Jesuítico de Maracaibo, Venezuela, 2612–2613.

Colegio San Pablo de Alcalá, Spain, 1796.

COLOMBIA. See also the cities of Antioquia, Barranquilla, Bogotá, Cartagena, Pamplona, Popayán; the commissary of Putumayo; the intendancy of San Andrés y Providencia; the regions of Amazonia, Andean Region, South America.

Art, 326–328, 370, 374, 435–440.

Bibliography, 12, 46.

History, 2864, 5381.

Ethnohistory, 1637.

Colonial Period. See also Viceroyalty of New Granada; Viceroyalty of Peru. 2621–2622, 2629, 2633.

Independence Period. See also Gran Colombia. 2804, 2808.

19th Century, 2574, 2846, 2848–2850, 2855, 2858, 2861, 2862–2863, 2865–2867, 2889a–2890.

20th Century, 2574, 2845–2847, 2851, 2853–2854, 2856, 2859, 2862, 2865, 2867, 2889a–2890.

Language, 4505, 4512, 4547, 4576–4577.

Literature.

Drama, 5868.

Poetry, 5620–5621, 5667, 5676, 5736, 5738, 5747, 5765, 5769, 5784, 5799.

Prose Literature, 5011, 5111, 5128, 5371–5372, 5380–5396, 5435–5445.

Music, 7070–7073.

Philosophy, 7517.

Colombia and Venezuela Relations, 2873, 2890.

Colonial Administration. See also Colonial Administrators; Colonial History; Political Science; Visitas. Alto Peru, 2721. Spanish Colonies, 1752, 1759, 1762, 1774, 1797–1798, 1814, 1873, 2336. Venezuela, 2595, 2609, 2618–2619. Viceroyalty of New Spain, 1757, 1791, 1847, 1889, 1908, 1913, 1932, 1975, 1983, 2307, 2354, 2509, 2517. Viceroyalty of Peru, 1757, 1791, 1932, 2584, 2588, 2648, 2686, 2690, 2695, 2727, 2741, 2779. Viceroyalty of Rio de la Plata, 2779.

Colonial Administrators. See also Alcaldes; Colonial Administration; Corregidores;

2884, 2891. Partido Obrero Revolucionario (Bolivia), 3041. Peru, 2920, 7591. Venezuela, 7581.

Communists. *See also Communism and Communist Parties.* Mexico, 2246.

Community Development. *See also City Planning; Economic Development; Rural Development; Social Change.* Abstracts, 23. Venezuela, 23.

Companhia Geral de Pernambuco e Paraíba, Brazil, 3532.

Compañía de Salitres de Antofagasta, Chile, 3097.

Comparative Grammar. *See also Generative Grammar; Language and Languages; Linguistics; Phonology.* Brazil, 4631. Mexico, 4511.

Composers. *See also Music; Musicians.* Argentina, 7021. Brazil, 7027, 7031–7035. Central America, 7048, 7051. Chile, 7055, 7057, 7061, 7063, 7066, 7068–7069. Costa Rica, 7049, 7051. Cuba, 7077, 7083. Guatemala, 7052. Latin America, 7002. Mexico, 7086, 7087–7088, 7094, 7096, 7101, 7104–7105, 7107. Peru, 7110. Puerto Rico, 7036. Venezuela, 7114, 7118–7119.

Comuneros, Revolt of the (New Grenada). *See Insurrection of the Comuneros (Viceroyalty of New Granada, 1781).*

Concepción, Chile (city). History, 3071.

Conductors. *See Music Conductors.*

Confederación de Trabajadores Mexicanos, 393.

Confederación General del Trabajo de la República Argentina (CGT), 3398.

Confederación Regional Obrero Mexicana (CROM), 2169.

Confraternities. *See also Monasticism and Religious Orders; Religion.* Mexico, 1901. Viceroyalty of New Spain, 1911. Viceroyalty of Peru, 1579.

Conquest. *See Spanish Conquest.*

Conquest of the Desert (Argentina, 1878–1880), 3184, 3213, 3378.

Conquistadors. *See also Explorers; names of specific conquistadors; Spanish Conquest.* 5047, 5070. Central America, 2334. Costa Rica, 2335, 2348. Honduras, 2322. Nicaragua, 2335. Panama, 2293. Peru, 2335. Viceroyalty of New Spain, 1875. Viceroyalty of Peru, 2729, 2740.

Conservatism. *See also Authoritarianism; Political Philosophy; Political Science; Social Sciences; Sociology.* Latin America, 1703, 7584, 7603, 7726.

Conservatorio Nacional de Música, Mexico, 7099.

Constitutional History. *See also Constitutional Law; Democracy; History; Political Science.* Argentina, 3188. Bolivia, 3010. Central America, 2468. Colombia, 2864. Costa Rica, 2446. Latin America, 1816. Mexico, 1989–1990, 2017, 2046, 2067, 2088, 2178. Peru, 2909. Venezuela, 2883. Viceroyalty of New Spain, 1733.

Constitutional Law. *See also Administrative Law; Civil Rights; Constitutional History; Democracy; Expropriation; Federal Government; Human Rights; Law; Political Science.* Mexico, 1989.

Contract Labor. *See also Forced Labor; Labor and Laboring Classes; Peonage; Slavery.* Jamaica, 2545. Peru, 2915, 2945.

Convento Hospital de Nuestra Señora de Guadeloupe del Señor San José Recolección de Nuestro Padre San Juan de Dios de Toluca, Mexico, 345.

Cordero y Bustamante, Antonio, 1967.

Córdoba, Argentina (city). Drama, 5955. History, 2770, 3138, 3221, 3390.

Córdoba, Argentina (province). *See also the region of the Pampas.* History, 3140, 3230, 3293, 3307, 3352–3353, 3403.

Corn Islands. *See Great Corn Island.*

Coro, Venezuela (city). History, 2609–2610.

Coronel, Rafael, 395.

Corporation Law. *See also Corporations; Law; Monopolies; Multinational Corporations.* Colombia, 2858.

Corporations. *See also Business; Commerce; Corporation Law; Multinational Corporations; Private Enterprises.* Colombia, 2858.

Corral, Juan del, 2814.

Corral viuda de Villa, Luz, 2168.

Correa, José Celso Martinez, 997.

Corregidores. *See also Colonial Administrators.* Viceroyalty of New Spain, 1791. Viceroyalty of Peru, 1791, 2693.

Correia, Raymundo, 6214.

Corretjer, Juan Antonio, 5308.

Corridos. *See also Songs.* 7090.

Corrientes, Argentina (city). History, 3354.

Corrientes, Argentina (province). *See also the region of Northeast Argentina.* History, 3308.

Cortázar, Julio, 5567, 5571–5572, 5581, 5584, 5586–5587, 5598, 5606.

Cortes, Alfonso, 5815.

Cortes de Cádiz. *See Spain.*

Corwin, Thomas, 2107.

Diáz, Félix, 2195.

Diáz, Porfirio, 380, 393, 1984, 2055, 2059, 2125–2126, 2128, 5142.

Diáz Pimenta, José, 176.

Dictator Novels. *See also Dictators; Prose Literature.* 5006. Cuba, 5329. Latin America, 5371.

Dictators. *See also Authoritarianism; Caudillos; Dictator Novels; Heads of State; Military Governments; names of specific dictators; Presidents; Totalitarianism.* Argentina, 3300. in Literature, 1704, 5026. Paraguay, 3414, 3433, 3438. Venezuela, 2882.

Dictionaries. *See also Dictionaries under specific subjects; Language and Languages; Reference Books.* Business Dictionary in English/Spanish, 4608. Business Dictionary in Spanish, 4602. Commercial and Banking Dictionary in Portuguese, 4625. Historical Dictionary of Music and Musicians, 7001. Poetry Dictionary in Portuguese, 6215. Tupi Words in Portuguese, 4627. Popular Language Dictionary in Portuguese, 4622. Spanish Dialects, 4603.

Diego, Eliseo, 5802.

Diegues, Carlos, 958, 1003–1005, 1012, 1031, 1057, 1066, 1075, 1089.

Diglossia. *See Bilingualism.*

Diplomatic History. *See also Diplomats; Foreign Policy; History; International Relations.* Argentina, 2828a, 3250, 3376. Bolivia, 2955, 3017, 3108. Brazil, 3271, 3581, 3619, 3632. Chile, 2955, 3108. Costa Rica, 2310. France, 3436. Guatemala, 2287. Latin America, 3439. Mexico, 1999, 2018, 2057, 2107, 2259, 2282, 2287. Nicaragua, 2310. Paraguay, 3436, 3439. Peru, 2944, 2955. Union of the Soviet Socialist Republics, 2282. United Kingdom, 3439. United States, 1999, 2107, 2259, 2892, 2944. Venezuela, 2892.

Diplomats. *See also Ambassadors; Diplomatic History; Foreign Policy; International Relations; Statesmen.* Argentina, 3224, 3377. Nicaragua, 2449. Venezuela, 64.

Disaster Relief. Bolivia, 179. Caribbean Area, 182.

Discovery and Exploration. *See also Colonial History; Expeditions; Explorers; History; Spanish Conquest.* Congresses, 1723. Spanish, 1723, 1734, 1750, 1754, 1780, 1785, 1788, 2641, 2657, 2758. Viceroyalty of Peru, 2641, 2657. Viceroyalty of Rio de la Plata, 2758.

Diseases. *See also Alcohol and Alcoholism; Folk Medicine; Medical Care; Public Health.* Borderlands, 1973. Brazil, 3546. Cholera, 2465, 3546. Guatemala, 2465. Venezuela, 2872.

Dissertations and Theses. *See also Academic Degrees; Bibliography; Dissertations and Theses under specific subjects; Universities.* Bolivia, 142. Dominican Republic, 129. North American, 3, 126. Venezuela, 54.

Doll, Ramón, 3168.

DOMINICA. *See also Commonwealth Caribbean; Lesser Antilles.*
History.
　19th Century, 2544.
Language, 4633.

DOMINICAN REPUBLIC. *See also the cities of Jacagua, Santo Domingo; Greater Antilles; Hispaniola.*
Art, 309–310, 373, 405, 411–412, 414.
Bibliography, 15, 19, 25, 129.
History, 2497, 5327.
　Colonial Period, 2481.
　19th Century, 2481, 2522, 2529.
　20th Century, 2477, 2522, 2549, 2550a–2551, 2554.
Language, 4538.
Literature.
　Drama, 5852–5853.
　Poetry, 5315, 5630, 5636, 5681, 5684, 5761, 5773.
　Prose Literature, 5309, 5315, 5326–5328, 5336, 5355.
Music, 7042.

Dominican Republic and United States Relations, 2549.

Dominicans. *See also Monasticism and Religious Orders.* Guatemala, 2356.

Donoso, José, 5485, 5488, 5493, 5496–5497, 5500, 5502.

Drake, Francis, 1648, 1955.

DRAMA (items 5827–5979, 6131–6156). *See also Drama under specific countries and regions; Drama Criticism; Dramatists; Literature; Opera; Performing Arts; Theater.* Bibliography, 5940. Juvenile, 5885. Methodology, 5938.

Drama Criticism. *See also Drama; Theater.* Argentina, 5935–5937, 5941, 5949, 5971, 5973. Brazil, 6150, 6152. Chile, 5977. Cuba, 5931–5932, 5950. Latin America, 5913. Mexico, 5917, 5919–5921, 5942, 5954, 5961. Panama, 5915, 5947. Puerto Rico, 5928, 5952. Venezuela, 5922–5925, 5943.

Dramatists. *See also Drama.* Argentina, 173.

495–500. Congresses, 294, 461. Guatemala, 285. Latin America, 407. Mexico, 254, 347. Periodicals, 252. Peru, 288. Puerto Rico, 407. South America, 287. Venezuela, 286.

Folk Medicine. *See also Diseases; Folklore; Medical Care; Medicine; Shamanism; Witchcraft.* Bibliography, 48. Mexico, 48.

Folk Music. *See also Dancing; Folklore; Indigenous Music; Music; Popular Music; Songs.* Brazil, 6165. Central America, 7054. Dominican Republic, 7042. Peru, 7109.

Folklore. *See also Dancing; Ethnology; Festivals; Folk Art; Folk Medicine; Folk Music; Legends; Myth; Mythology; Witchcraft.* Borderlands, 2198. Brazil, 6146. Chile, 4527. Colombia, 7073. Venezuela, 6290.

Fondo Simón Bolívar, 32.

Fonseca Amador, Carlos, 2380.

Food Industry and Trade. *See also Agricultural Industries; Fish and Fishing Industry; names of specific commodities; Meat Industry and Trade; Produce Trade.* Brazil, 3546. Viceroyalty of New Spain, 1847, 1935. Viceroyalty of Peru, 2699.

Forced Labor. *See also Contract Labor; Labor and Laboring Classes; Peonage; Slavery.* Alto Peru, 2723.

Foreign Investments in. *See also Capital; Capitalism; Commerce; Economic History; External Debts; Foreign Trade; International Economic Relations; Multinational Corporations.* Argentina, 3284, 3346. Chile, 3096, 3128. Cuba, 2199. Latin America, 168. Mexico, 2087, 2145, 2199, 2208, 2240. Peru, 2938, 2983. Uruguay, 3448.

Foreign Policy. *See also Armaments; Boundary Disputes; Diplomatic History; Diplomats; Geopolitics; Good Neighbor Policy; International Economic Relations; International Relations; Monroe Doctrine; National Security; Nationalism; Refugees.* Argentina, 3215, 3217–3218, 3227–3228, 3234, 3318, 3377, 3411. Brazil, 3587. Mexico, 2164, 2177, 2209. Spain, 1831. United States, 1825, 2107–2108, 2548, 3411. Venezuela, 2886.

Foreign Relations. *See International Relations.*

Foreign Trade. *See also Commerce; Foreign Investments; International Economic Relations; Multinational Corporations; Trade Policy; Transportation.* Argentina,

3146, 3254, 3260, 3275–3276, 3343, 3350, 3352. Bolivia, 2916, 3276. Borderlands, 33, 47. Chile, 3276. Colombia, 2861. Ecuador, 2900, 2904. Latin America, 29, 168, 1721. Mexico, 2211. Peru, 2917, 3276. South America, 3275.

Forests and Forest Industry. *See also Agricultural Industries; Ecology; Natural Resources; Rubber Industry and Trade.* Chile, 3076.

Fort Nogales (present-day site of Vicksburg, Mississippi). History, 1961.

Forte dos Reis Magos (Natal, Brazil). History, 3512.

Fortifications. *See also Military History; Palenques.* Brazil, 3512. Viceroyalty of Peru, 2706, 2732. Viceroyalty of Rio de la Plata, 2749.

France and Mexico Relations, 2000, 2136.

France and Paraguay Relations, 3436.

France and Spanish Colonies Relations, 1765, 1811.

Francia, José Gaspar Rodríguez de, 2745, 3414, 3433, 3438, 3442.

Franciscans. *See also Monasticism and Religious Orders.* Argentina, 3164. Borderlands, 1951. Colombia, 2629. Ecuador, 109. Spain, 1796. Viceroyalty of New Granada, 2629. Viceroyalty of New Spain, 1867, 1921, 1954, 1959, 1977–1980.

Franco, Afonso Arinos de Melo, 6219.

Franqui, Carlos, 5316.

Free Trade and Protection. *See also Commerce; Economic Policy; Economics; Foreign Trade; Trade Policy.* Argentina, 3136. Brazil, 3478. Latin America, 1804. Peru, 2985. United Kingdom, 3478.

Free Will and Determinism. *See also Ethics; Philosophy; Philosophy under Law.* 7721.

Freedom of the Press. *See also Censorship; Civil Rights; Journalism; Newspapers; Periodicals; Press; Public Opinion.* Latin America, 175, 5002.

Freemasons, 3529.

Freire, Paulo, 7716.

Freire, Roberto, 6151.

French. in Argentina, 3278. in Mexico, 2078.

French Antilles. *See French West Indies.*

FRENCH GUIANA. *See also the regions of Amazonia, South America.*
History.
Colonial Period. *See Viceroyalty of Peru.*
19th Century, 2526.
20th Century, 2526.
Literature.

2780, 2828a, 3093, 3105, 3243, 3262, 3272, 3396. Bolivia, 3007, 5374. Brazil, 3493–3494, 3501. Central America, 2305, 2391. Chile, 3093, 3105, 3129, 3132. Haiti, 6252. Inca, 1671. Mexico, 2201, 2210, 2256, 2263. Paraguay, 2775. Peru, 1621, 1652, 1687, 2913, 2959. United States, 1652. Uruguay, 3465. Venezuela, 64, 3105, 5133.

Historic Sites. See also Archaeology; History; Monuments. Mexico, 400.

Historical Geography. See also Geography; History. Alto Peru, 2722. Central America, 2326. Colombia,2633. Ecuador, 2636, 2658. Venezuela, 2633. Viceroyalty of New Spain, 138.

Historical Materialism. See also Philosophy under History; Marxism. 1698, 7756.

Historiography. See also Historians; History; Methodology under History. 7756, 2236. Argentina, 3093, 3333, 3392, 3398. Belize, 2495. Bolivia, 3058, 3060. Brazil, 3500–3501. Chile, 2577, 3093, 3117, 3129, 3132. Commonwealth Caribbean, 2486. Dominican Republic, 2529. Latin America, 1701, 1707, 1712, 1722, 3105, 7547. Mexico, 1846, 1991, 1996, 2029, 2066, 2200–2201, 2256. Paraguay, 3421. Peru, 2577, 2663, 2959. Uruguay, 3465. Venezuela, 2889.

HISTORY (items 1501–3642). See also Archaeology; Archives; Biography; Church History; Colonial Period under names of specific countries and regions; Constitutional History; Coups d'Etat; Diplomatic History; Discovery and Exploration; Economic History; Enlightenment; Ethnohistory; Genealogy; Historians; Historic Sites; Historical Geography; Historiography; History under names of countries and regions; Human Geography; Independence Period under names of specific countries and regions; Intellectual History; International Relations; Maritime History; Military History; names of specific battles; Natural History; 19th Century under names of specific countries and regions; Oral History; Political Science; Revolutions and Revolutionary Movements; Riots; Social History; 20th Century under names of specific countries and regions. Abstracts, 164. Bibliography, 3159. Congresses, 2479, 3182–3185, 3250, 3539. Methodology, 1826, 5140. Periodicals 1900, 2873, 3148, 3398, 3457, 5234. Philosophy, 1698, 2221, 7539, 7550, 7664, 7679, 7750, 7752–7754, 7756–7757. Study and Teaching, 2236, 2932, 3250.

History, 19th and 20th Centuries. See History 19th and 20th Centuries under names of specific countries and regions.

Hitchcock, Ethan Allen, 2052.

Hobbes, Thomas, 7639, 7643, 7647, 7649, 7653, 7655, 7746.

HONDURAS. See also the city of Comayagua; the region of Central America.
Bibliography, 21.
History, 2471, 5289.
    Colonial Period. See also Viceroyalty of New Spain. 89, 2321–2322.
    19th Century, 2290, 2384, 2450–2451.
    20th Century, 2290, 2387.
Literature.
    Drama, 5900.
    Poetry, 5634.
    Prose Literature, 5279, 5289.
Philosophy, 7620.

Hopper, Edward, 373.

Hostos y Bonilla, Eugenio María de, 5123, 7597.

Households. See also Cost and Standard of Living; Family and Family Relationships; Housing; Population. Brazil, 3489.

Housing. See also Architecture; City Planning; Households. Latin America, 372. Mexico, 298. Viceroyalty of Rio de la Plata, 2767.

Houssay, Bernardo A., 3155.

Huamantla, Mexico (city). History, 2084, 2152.

Huancavélica, Peru (city). History, 2712.

Huancavélica, Peru (department). History, 2934.

Huaraz, Peru (city). History, 2703.

Huarochiri, Peru (province). Ethnohistory, 1646.

Huaura Valley, Peru. History, 2926.

Huerta, Epitacio, 1987.

Huerta, Victoriano, 2214.

Human Geography. See also Anthropology; Emigration and Immigration; Ethnology; Geography; Geopolitics; History; Land Settlement; Regionalism. Viceroyalty of New Spain, 1914.

Human Rights. See also Civil Rights; Constitutional Law; Political Science; Revolutions and Revolutionary Movements; Violence. Argentina, 3387. Bibliography, 36. Latin America, 36, 186. in Literature, 5705, 6265.

Humanism. See also Culture; Literature; Philosophy; Philosophical Anthropology. 1778, 5145, 7637, 7715. Mexico, 2285.

Humanities. *See also Art; Films; Language and Languages; Literature; Music; Philosophy.* Bibliography, 2–3.

Humberstone, J.T., 3086.

Hume, David, 7641.

Hunting. Precolumbian, 1631. Viceroyalty of Peru, 1635.

Husserl, Edmund, 7668.

Hydrology. Ecuador, 2658.

Ibarguren, Carlos, 3168.

Idealism. *See also Philosophy; Positivism; Realism.* 5145. Ecuador, 7604.

Ideology. *See also Epistemology; names of specific ideologies; Philosophy; Political Philosophy; Political Science; Psychology.* 7619, 7753. History, 7655, 7733.

Iglesias, Rafael, 2386.

Immigration. *See Emigration and Immigration.*

Imperialism. *See also International Relations; Militarism; Political Science.* in Literature, 5302.

Imports. *See Foreign Trade.*

Inca. *See also Precolumbian Civilizations.* 304, 352, 1569, 1576, 1580–1581, 1584, 1587, 1593, 1595, 1598, 1604–1608, 1611, 1614, 1617, 1621, 1627, 1630, 1639, 1646, 1648, 1653, 1671–1673, 1675–1677, 1686, 1688, 1693–1694, 2654, 2788, 5083, 5092, 7111.

Income. *See also Capital; Economics; Finance; National Income; Wages.* Argentina, 3269.

Independence Period History. *See also Independence Period under names of specific countries and regions; Revolutions and Revolutionary Movements; Wars of Independence.* Bibliography, 52. Congresses, 1803.

Indiana University, Lilly Library, Bloomington, Indiana, 52.

Indians. *See Indigenous Peoples.*

Indigenismo. *See also Indigenous Peoples.* Argentina, 2788. Peru, 2929, 2933, 2971, 2991, 5404, 5406.

Indigenous Languages. *See also Anthropological Linguistics; Anthropology; Ethnology; Indigenous Peoples; Language and Languages.* Argentina, 4597. Guaraní, 4558–4559. Influences on Portuguese Language, 4627. Influences on Spanish Language, 4529, 4535, 4554–4555, 4558–4559, 4570, 4582, 4590, 4605. Koli, 1619. Maya, 4590. Mesoamerica, 1532. Mexico, 4511. Náhuatl,

1532, 1534, 2217, 4554, 4570. Quechua, 1569, 1614. Tupi, 4627. Watunna, 6290.

Indigenous Music. *See also Folk Music; Indigenous Peoples; Music.* Brazil, 7025. Central America, 7054. Inca, 7111. Peru, 7111. United States, 7108. Warao, 7116.

Indigenous Peoples. *See also Anthropology; Caciques; Ethnohistory under names of specific countries and regions; Ethnology; Indigenismo; Indigenous Languages; Indigenous Music; Mestizos and Mestizaje; names of specific indigenous groups; Nativistic Movements; Peasants; Precolumbian Civilizations; Precolumbian Cultures; Race and Race Relations.* Alto Peru, 2721. Amazonia, 1568, 1600, 6013. Andean Region, 1578, 1656. Argentina, 3091, 3219, 3259, 3293, 4597, 7580. in Art, 467, 470, 472, 474, 994, 1045, 1094. Bibliography, 44, 48. Biographies, 1570. Bolivia, 98, 183, 2573, 3019–3020, 3029, 3048, 3050. Borderlands, 1964, 2111, 2123, 2131, 2516. Brazil, 452, 467, 470, 472, 474, 501, 1045, 1094, 1640–1641, 3525, 3531, 3544. Caribbean Area, 44. Chile, 1624, 3091. Colombia, 1638. Costa Rica, 2319. Ecuador, 1600, 1643, 2898, 2902. Guatemala, 2350. Latin America, 5079, 7582. Law and Legislation, 1801. Mexico, 48, 2063, 2111. Origin, 1650. Panama, 2329, 2333. Paraguay, 3421. Peru, 1568, 2573, 2819, 2823, 2915, 2929, 2933, 2957–2958, 2963, 2967, 2971, 2991. Policy, 1797, 1942, 2123, 2131. Spanish Colonies, 1728, 1743, 1774. Treatment of, 1728–1729, 1743, 1781, 1791, 1954, 1978, 2063, 2614, 2625, 2721, 2779, 2971, 5079. Uruguay, 2829. Venezuela, 1570, 1588, 2614, 2617. Viceroyalty of New Granada, 2625, 2902. Viceroyalty of New Spain, 192, 1847, 1861, 1869–1870, 1872, 1921, 1930, 1940, 1942–1943, 1954, 1966, 1971, 1978, 2340, 2342, 2358, 2516. Viceroyalty of Peru, 192, 2573, 2587, 2593, 2640, 2652–2654, 2656, 2660, 2686, 2691, 2693, 2697, 2743. Viceroyalty of Rio de la Plata, 2751, 2755–2756, 2779, 3425a.

Indigo. *See also Anil; Textiles and Textile Industry.* El Salvador, 2344. Viceroyalty of New Spain, 1930.

Industrial Relations. *See also Industry and Industrialization; Labor and Laboring Classses; Strikes and Lockouts; Trade Unions.* Brazil, 3600. Latin America, 1821.

Industry and Industrialization. *See also Business; Businessmen; Economic Devel-*

Literary Criticism. *See also Authors; Literary Critics; Literature; names of specific authors; Prose Literature; Structuralism (Literary Analysis).* Andean Region works, 5371–5429. Argentine works, 5118–5119, 5124, 5129–5131, 5136, 5141, 5146, 5566–5608, 5817. Barbadian works, 6266, 6280–6281. Bolivian works, 5373–5379, 5804. Brazilian works, 1025, 1082, 6109, 6157–6223. Caribbean Area works, 5338–5370. Central American works, 5273–5292. Chilean works, 5485–5503, 5794, 5816, 5819, 6336. Colombian works, 5128, 5380–5396, 5762, 5769, 5799. Congresses, 5010. Costa Rican works, 5763. Cuban works, 5350, 5338, 5340, 5343, 5348, 5350–5351, 5353–5370, 5775, 5780, 5795, 5800–5803, 5817. Dominican Republic works, 5773. Ecuadorian works, 5397–5402, 5814. French Guianese works, 6255. Haitian works, 6251, 6256–6257. Jamaican works, 6275. Latin American works, 5001, 5006, 5009–5010, 5013–5014, 5017, 5020–5021, 5048, 5349, 5770–5771, 5778, 5796. Martinican works, 6254, 6258. Methodology, 5001, 5003, 6161, 6163, 7720. Mexican works, 5132, 5205–5259, 5776, 5797, 5808–5809, 5817. Nicaraguan works, 5815. Paraguayan works, 5609–5610. Peruvian works, 5403–5417, 5771, 5783, 5785–5786, 5792, 5798, 5810. Puerto Rican works, 5341, 5344, 5346–5347, 5352, 5768. Saint Lucian works, 6278. Study and Teaching, 5003. Trinidadian works, 6273. Uruguayan works, 5120, 5131, 5611–5619. Venezuelan works, 5133, 5418–5429, 5779, 5805, 5811.

Literary Critics. *See also Literary Criticism.* Brazil, 6169.

LITERATURE (items 5001–6350). *See also Authors; Drama; Fantastic Literature; Humanism; Humanities; Journalism; Language and Languages; Legends; Literary Criticism; Literature under names of specific countries and regions; Magic Realism; Modernism; Picaresque Literature; Poetry; Popular Literature; Prose Literature; Revolutionary Literature; Romanticism; Translations of Latin American Literary Works into English; Vanguardism; Wit and Humor.* Congresses, 5420–5421. History, 5018, 5020, 5300, 7562. Methodology, 5015. Periodicals, 5205–5206, 5214, 5227, 5246–5247, 5258, 5355, 5370, 5385, 5590, 5602. Study and Teaching, 5019.

Livestock. *See also Agriculture; Animals.* Viceroyalty of New Spain, 1862, 1901, 1927.

Llanos y Nava, Eduardo, 3088.

Lloyd, Errol, 406.

Lobo Guerrero, Bartolomé, 2670.

Local Government. *See also Administrative Law; Ayuntamientos; Centralized Government; Cities and Towns; Federal Government; Governors; Mayors; Political Boundaries; Political Science.* Argentina, 3181, 3202, 3342. Brazil, 3530, 3586, 3623. Mexico, 2152. Uruguay, 3450.

Logic. *See also Epistemology; Philosophy; Psychology.* 5055, 7539, 7691, 7696–7698, 7700, 7703, 7705. History, 7561.

López, Carlos Antonio, 3426, 3445.

López, Francisco Solano, 3171, 3432.

López, Juan Pablo, 3198.

López, Vicente F., 3245.

López, Willebaldo, 5919.

López de Velasco, Juan, 5061.

López Marín, Jorge, 7083.

López Matoso, Antonio, 5108.

López Medel, Tomás, 2330.

López Méndez, Luis, 2801.

López Rega, José, 3328.

López Velarde, Ramón, 5227.

Lorena, Brazil (city). History, 3574.

Louisiana, United States (state). *See also the region of the Borderlands.* History, 2518.

Louverture, Toussaint, 2538.

Loyola, Pedro León, 7538.

Lufti, Dib, 1034.

Luis de Granada, *Brother,* 1566.

Lunfardo. *See also Spanish Language.* 4532, 4534, 4561, 4593.

Luque, Argentina (city). History, 3299.

Maceo, Antonio, 2535.

Machacha, Jesús de, 3020.

Machachi Valley, Ecuador. History, 2639.

Machado de Assis, Joaquim Maria, 6335.

Machismo. *See also Sex and Sexual Relations.* Latin America, 1709.

McKay, Claude, 6275.

Madero, Francisco Indalecio, 2139.

Maeso, Justo, 3349.

Magallanes, Chile (province). History, 3094.

Magic Realism. *See also Art; Literature; Prose Literature; Surrealism.* Mexico, 389, 5225.

Maistre, Joseph Marie, 7726.

Maize. *See also Agriculture.* Mesoamerica, 1543.

Makiritare (indigenous group), 6290.

Malespín, Francisco, 2366.
Mallea, Eduardo, 5576.
Malthus, Thomas Robert, 2267.
Malvinas. *See Falkland Islands.*
Mamulengo, 499.
Mancisidor, José, 5184.
Mannerism (Art). Latin America, 299.
Mansilla, Lucio Victorio, 3216.
Manuscripts. *See also Archives; Bibliography; Codices.* Captaincy General of Cuba, 1847. Guatemala, 105. Huarochirí, 1683. Mexico, 1838, 1852. Spain, 99–100. Spanish Colonies, 1759. Viceroyalty of New Spain, 1757, 1838, 1847, 1852, 1867. Viceroyalty of Peru, 1683, 1757.
Maps and Cartography. *See also Atlases; Geography.* Colombia, 2633. Mesoamerica, 1525. Mexico, 251. Venezuela, 2633. Viceroyalty of New Spain, 1525, 1890. Viceroyalty of Peru, 1657.
Marcoleta, José de, 2449.
Marcos Paz, Argentina (city). History, 3316.
Marechal, Leopoldo, 5971.
Maríategui, José Carlos, 2907, 2935, 2942–2943, 2951, 2957, 2971, 2992, 7506, 7582, 7586–7587, 7598–7599, 7615–7616, 7621, 7626–7627.
Maríategui, José Gabriel, 2940.
MARIE GALANTE. *See also French West Indies; Guadeloupe.*
History, 2508.
Marine Resources. *See also Biology; Fish and Fishing Industry; Minerals and Mining Industry; Natural Resources; Pearl Industry and Trade.* Bibliography, 19. Dominican Republic, 19.
Maritime History. *See also Admirals; History; Military History; Shipbuilding; Shipwrecks.* Argentina, 3146. Dominican Republic, 2497. Spanish Colonies, 2507.
Mark, Edward Walhouse, 437.
Marketing and Product Distribution. *See also Business; Commerce; Economic History; Markets; Produce Trade; Production (economic).* Mexico, 2060.
Markets. *See also Marketing and Product Distribution.* Mesoamerica, 1526. Mexico, 1853, 2034.
Maroons. *See also Blacks; Slavery.* Caribbean Area, 2511, 2541, 6276. Guadeloupe, 2515. Spanish Colonies, 1753. Viceroyalty of Peru, 2682.
Marqués, René, 5928.
Marriage. *See also Family and Family Relationships; Kinship; Sex and Sexual*

Relations. Brazil, 176, 3537–3538. Viceroyalty of New Spain, 1872, 1905.
Marroquín, Francisco, 2320.
Marroquín Rojas, Clemente, 2395.
Martel, Julián, 5136.
Martí, José, 177, 5109, 5145, 5147, 5803.
Martínez, Fernando Antonio, 4508.
Martínez, José, 7051.
Martínez, José de Jesús, 5947.
Martínez, María, 7081.
Martínez Campañón, Baltazar Jaime, 2684, 2702, 7109.
Martínez Sanabria, Fernando, 438.
MARTINIQUE. *See also French West Indies; Lesser Antilles.*
History.
    19th Century, 2524.
Literature.
    Prose Literature, 6254, 6258.
Martins, Cyro, 6197.
Marx, Karl, 2267, 7514, 7645, 7648, 7657, 7662.
Marxism. *See also Communism and Communist Parties; Historical Materialism; Political Philosophy; Socialism and Socialist Parties.* 7722, 7747. Peru, 2941–2942.
Masacali (indigenous group), 6190.
Masiel, Leonel, 389.
Masks. *See also Costume and Adornment.* Mexico, 293, 297.
Masons. *See Freemasons.*
Mass Media. *See also Advertising; Cartoons; Censorship; Comic Books and Strips; Communication; Education; Film; Newspapers; Periodicals; Popular Culture; Press; Television.* Brazil, 990, 7033. Latin America, 175.
Mata Machado, Edgar de Godoi da, 4629.
Mathematics. Inca, 1571–1572, 1626. Philosophy, 7705.
Matlatzinca (indigenous group), 1558, 1929.
Mato Grosso, Brazil (state). History, 3517, 3541.
Matta Echeaurren, Sebastian Antonio, 431.
Mattos Guerra, Gregório, 6223.
Mauá, Irineo Evangelista de Souza, 3551, 3634.
Mauro, Humberto, 1026.
Maximilian, 2009, 2032.
May, Morton D. Art collection, 260.
Maya. *See also Chontal-Maya; Precolumbian Civilizations.* 277, 291, 1518, 1529, 1542, 1552, 1897, 1943. Congresses, 266.
Mayors. *See also Local Government; Politicians.* Mexico, 2117.

Meat Industry and Trade. *See also Cattle Trade; Food and Food Industry.* Argentina, 3209, 3255.

Medical Care. *See also Diseases; Folk Medicine; Public Health; Physicians.* Bolivia, 3018. Brazil, 3590, 3604. Mexico, 2037, 2265. Spanish Colonies, 1740. Viceroyalty of New Spain, 1884.

Medicine. *See also Folk Medicine.* Latin America, 1700. Viceroyalty of New Spain, 99.

Medina, Anacleto, 3401.

Medina, José, 1085.

Medina Angarita, Isaías, 2877.

Medinaceli, Carlos, 5375.

Meinvielle, Julio, 3168.

Melgarejo, Mariano, 3062.

Mello, Joaquim Corrêa de, 3628.

Melo, Angelo Rodrigues de, 6184.

Mendoza, Argentina (city). History, 2771, 3134–3135.

Mendoza, Argentina (province). *See also the region of Cuyo.* History, 3181, 3236, 3273, 3310, 3335.

Mendoza, Pedro de, 2764.

Meneses, Djacir, 7537.

Mercedarians. *See also Monasticism and Religious Orders.* Viceroyalty of Peru, 2700.

Merchants. *See also Businessmen; Commerce.* Argentina, 3355. Brazil, 3490. Ecuador, 2899. Spanish Colonies, 1787, 1791. Viceroyalty of Peru, 2591. Viceroyalty of Rio de la Plata, 2781.

Mercury Mines and Mining. *See also Minerals and Mineral Industry.* Alto Peru, 2712. Bolivia, 3037.

Mérida, Venezuela (state). Language, 4585.

Meriño, Fernando Arturo de, 7606.

Merleau-Ponty, Maurice, 7681.

MESOAMERICA. *See also Caribbean Area; Central America.*
Art, 251, 254, 257, 263–278, 292, 378.
Bibliography, 259.
History, 2297.
  Ethnohistory, 266, 1501–1565, 1897, 2297, 2502.
Literature, 1541.
Music, 7089.

Mestizos and Mestizaje. *See also Indigenous Peoples; Race and Race Relations.* in Art, 472. Brazil, 472. Spanish Colonies, 1775.

Metallurgy. *See also Iron Industry and Trade; Minerals and Mining Industry; Silversmith.* Congresses, 261. Mexico, 2073. Periodicals, 174. South America, 261. Viceroyalty of New Spain, 2073.

Metaphysics. *See also Cosmology; Epistemology; Philosophy; Values.* 7631, 7699, 7760–7762.

Mexica. *See Aztec.*

Mexican Americans. *See also Hispanic Americans.* 2198, 4537, 4542, 4564–4565, 4572, 4587, 4589. Borderlands, 2104. in Literature, 5155.

Mexican Revolution (1910–1920). *See also Revolution and Revolutionary Movements.* 1847, 2031, 2045, 2085, 2130, 2138–2141, 2144, 2147–2149, 2159, 2161, 2166, 2175–2176, 2179, 2185, 2192, 2195–2196, 2204, 2206, 2209, 2211, 2220, 2225–2226, 2247, 2249, 2254, 2256–2257, 2259, 2264, 2268, 2270, 2272, 2276. in Literature, 2226, 5208, 5241, 5858. Periodicals, 5223.

Mexican War. *See United States War with Mexico.*

Mexicans. *See also Latin Americans.* in the United States, 2028, 2245.

MEXICO. *See also the cities of Campeche, Chiapas, Ciudad de Galeana, Coahuila, Coatlinchán, Cuauhtinchán, Guadalajara, Guanajuato, Huamantla, Ixcateopan, Ixmiquilpan, Ixtapalapa, La Barca, Mexico, Monterrey, Ocuilán, Pisaflores, Polotitlán, Puebla, Querétaro, Saltillo, San Francisco de Umán, San Francisco Javier de La Parada, San Luis Potosí, Tecali, Tenango, Tetla del Volcán, Texúpa, Toluca, Tonantzintla, Topolobampo, Veracruz, Veracruz Llave, Zacatecas, Zamora; the states of Baja California, Campeche, Chiapas, Chihuahua, Coahuila, Durango, Guadalajara, Guanajuato, Hidalgo, Jalisco, Mexico, Michoacán, Morelia, Morelos, Nuevo León, Oaxaca, Puebla, Querétaro, San Luis Potosí, Sinaloa, Sonora, Tabasco, Tamaulipas, Tlaxcala, Veracruz, Yucatán, Zacatecas; the valleys of Mexico, Toluca; the Rio Grande River; the regions of the Borderlands, Latin America, Sierra Gorda.* Art, 139, 251, 254, 292–293, 296–298, 329–349, 370, 374–401, 2243.
Bibliography, 4, 17–18, 22, 33, 39, 43, 47–48, 153.
Film, 199.
History, 39, 139, 1705, 1708, 1839, 1841–1844, 1854, 1912, 5181, 5234, 6328.
  Ethnohistory. *See Mesoamerica.*
  Colonial Period. *See the Viceroyalty of New Spain.*
  19th Century, 43, 87, 1838, 1840–1841,

Mines and Mining; Gold; Iron Industry and Trade; Marine Resources; Mercury Mines and Mining; Metallurgy; Natural Resources; Nitrate Industry; Salt Industry and Trade; Silver; Silver Mines and Mining Industry. Bolivia, 2575, 3037. Chile, 3076, 4527. Congresses, 2079. Law and Legislation, 2980. in Literature, 5431. Mexico, 2073, 2077, 2079, 2090. Periodicals, 174. Peru, 2575, 2954, 2960, 2980. Terminology, 4527. Viceroyalty of New Spain, 99, 1885, 1948, 2073, 2079, 2575.

Minifundios. *See also Land Tenure.* Dominican Republic, 2550a.

Miramón, Miguel, 2032.

Miranda, Francisco de, 2801.

Miret, Pedro, 2550.

Misiones, Argentina (province). *See also the region of Northeast Argentina.* History, 2785, 3250.

Missionaries. *See also Missions.* Argentina, 3166–3167. Brazil, 3535. Mexico, 5084. Tierra del Fuego, 3173.

Missions. *See also Catholic Church; Church History; Missionaries; Monasticism and Religious Orders; Protestant Churches.* Alto Peru, 2710. Argentina, 3164, 3219. Borderlands, 1951, 1953. Brazil, 3519, 3631. Colombia, 2629. Mexico, 1847. Spanish Colonies, 1729, 1745. United States, 7108. Viceroyalty of New Granada, 2629. Viceroyalty of New Spain, 1861, 1950, 1954, 1956, 1960, 1977, 5914. Viceroyalty of Peru, 2685. Viceroyalty of Rio de la Plata, 2755–2756, 2769, 3425a.

Mistral, Gabriela, 101, 5778, 5781.

Mitre, Bartolomé, 3093, 3172, 3186, 3245, 3258, 3340.

Mixtec (indigenous group). *See also Precolumbian Civilizations.* 251, 1513, 1927.

Modern Architecture. *See also Architecture; Modern Art.* Argentina, 370, 429, 3266. Bolivia, 370. Brazil, 511, 522. Chile, 370. Colombia, 370, 438. Cuba, 370, 372. Latin America, 367, 372. Mexico, 370. Panama, 402. Surinam, 415.

Modern Art. *See also Art; Modern Architecture; Photography.* Argentina, 424–427. Bibliography, 366. Brazil, 457, 472–494, 523. Colombia, 435. Haiti, 413. Latin America, 373. Mexico, 254, 374, 376, 383. Venezuela, 446.

Modern Philosophy. *See also Existentialism; Phenomenology; Philosophy; Positivism.* 7637, 7683.

Modernism (Literature). *See also Literature;*

Poetry; Prose Literature. 5766–5767. Brazil, 6164, 6168, 6178. Cuba, 5351. Latin America, 5021, 5770. Mexico, 396. Periodicals, 5151, 5247. Puerto Rico, 5768.

Molina, Juan Ignacio, 2735, 2738.

Molina, Pedro, 2385.

Molina Garmendia, Enrique, 7534.

Molinari, Diego Luis, 3396.

Monasterio de Ocuila, Ocuilán, Mexico, 1557.

Monasticism and Religious Orders. *See also Augustinians; Carmelites; Catholic Church; Church History; Clergy; Confraternities; Dominicans; Franciscans; Jesuits; Mercedarians; Missionaries; Nuns; Oratines; Salesians.* Mexico, 341. Paraguay, 2831. Vicroyalty of Peru, 2581.

Monetary Policy. *See also Banking and Financial Institutions; Economic Policy; Fiscal Policy; Public Finance.* Mexico, 2277. Paraguay, 3442. Viceroyalty of Peru, 2590.

Monopolies. *See also Business; Capital; Commerce; Corporation Law; Economics.* Mexico, 2265.

Monroe Doctrine. *See also Foreign Policy; International Relations; Pan-Americanism.* 1829, 2177, 2543.

Montalbán, Venezuela (city). History, 2604.

Montaño, José Manuel, 1981.

Monteforte Toledo, Mario, 5274.

Montenegro, Carlos, 3045.

Monterrey, Mexico (city). History, 1949, 1974, 2162.

Monterroso, Augusto, 5284.

Montevideo, Uruguay (city). History, 2749, 2776, 2843, 3446, 3450, 3452, 3464. Language, 4540. Poetry, 3446.

Montevideo. Junta Económico-Administrativa, 3450.

Monti, Ricardo, 5936.

MONTSERRAT. *See also Commonwealth Caribbean; Lesser Antilles.* History, 2483.

Monuments. *See also Architecture; Historic Sites; National Parks and Reserves; Precolumbian Architecture; Sculpture.* Mexico, 390. Peru, 353, 355.

Moore, George Edward, 7710.

Moquegua, Peru (department). Ethnohistory, 1655.

Moquegua Valley, Peru. Ethnohistory, 1619.

Moraes, Vinícius de, 987.

Moraña, José M., 428.

Morelia, Mexico (state). History, 2081.

Morelos, Mexico (state). History, 2071–2072, 2142, 2176.

Pluralism. *See also Ethnicity; Philosophy; Race and Race Relations; Reality; Social Sciences.* Congresses, 7508.

POETRY (items 5620–5826, 6052–6156, 6237–6250, 6262–6265, 6268, 6280). *See also Literature; Modernism; Poetry under specific countries and regions; Poets; Sonnets; Vanguardism.* Anthologies, 5620–5642. Bibliographies, 5774, 5818, 6268. Dictionaries, 6215. History, 6326. Periodicals, 5622. Public Opinion, 5824. Theory, 5806.

Poets. *See also Authors; Poetry.* Argentina, 5031, 5043. Bolivia, 5804. Brazil, 6208–6209, 6211, 6214, 6218, 6223. Caribbean Area, 6269. Chile, 56, 5781, 5821–5823, 5826. Colombia, 5762. Cuba, 5365, 5812. Jamaica, 6263–6264. Latin America, 5091, 5117, 6287. Mexico, 5622. Nicaragua, 2402. Puerto Rico, 5308. Saint Lucia, 6277–6278. Venezuela, 5090, 5807.

Pokomchi, 1563.

Poleo, Héctor, 447.

Poles in Brazil, 3582, 3596.

Police. *See also Crime and Criminals; Military.* Brazil, 3554. Mexico, 2125, 2187.

Political Boundaries. *See also Boundary Disputes; Federal Government; International Relations; Local Government; Political Science; Territorial Claims; Territorial Waters.* Costa Rica, 2310. Mexico, 1975. Nicaragua, 2310. Panama, 2298.

Political Cartoons. *See also Cartoons; Political Science.* Mexico, 393.

Political Participation. *See also Democracy.* Argentina, 3384. Mexico, 2146, 2179, 2264. Windward Islands, 2533.

Political Parties. *See also Communism and Communist Parties; Political Science; Socialism and Socialist Parties.* Acción Democrática (Venezuela), 2878, 2880–2881, 2886, 2891. Alianza Popular Revolucionaria Americana (APRA, Peru), 2908, 2920, 2942, 2947–2948, 2950, 2981–2982, 2988, 2995. Argentina, 3175, 3220, 3410. Brazil, 3555, 3624. Chile, 3069, 3113, 3133. Colombia, 2854. Frente Sandinista de Liberación Nacional (FSLN, Nicaragua), 2443, 2474. Mexico, 2237, 2251. Movimiento de Izquierda Revolucionaria (MIR, Venezuela), 2879. Movimiento Nacionalista Revolucionario (MNR, Bolivia), 3040. Paraguay, 3416, 3444. Partido Colorado (Paraguay), 3431. Partido Conservador (Argentina), 3195. Partido Conservador (Colombia),

2850, 2853. Partido Liberal (Colombia), 2850, 2853, 2862. Partido Liberal (Paraguay), 3430. Partido Liberal Mexicano (Mexico), 2113, 2191, 2250. Partido Nacional (Uruguay), 3474. Partido Nacional Revolucionario (PNR, Mexico), 2212–2213. Partido Radical (Argentina), 3175. Partido Revolucionario Cubano, 2534. Partido Revolucionario Institutional (PRI, Mexico), 393. Partido Socialcristiano (Venezuela), 2886, 2891. Partido Trabalhista Brasileiro (PTB, Brazil), 3606. Puerto Rico, 2493. Unidad Popular (UP, Chile), 3075. Venezuela, 2878–2879.

Political Philosophy. *See also Communism and Communist Parties; Conservatism; Ideology; Liberalism; Marxism; Philosophy; Philosophy of Liberation; Political Science; Socialism and Socialist Parties; The State.* 7639, 7694, 7729. Argentina, 3410, 7612. Brazil, 3481, 7546. Ecuador, 7592. Latin America, 7599, 7603, 7622. Mexico, 1936. Peru, 7608, 7615–7616, 7621.

Political Prisoners. *See also Crime and Criminals; Prisoners.* in Literature, 5163. Peru, 2788. Venezuela, 2869.

Political Refugees. *See also Exiles; Refugees.* United States, 2245.

Political Science. *See also Anarchism and Anarchists; Authoritarianism; Bureaucracy; Centralized Government; Civil Rights; Civilian Governments; Colonial Administration; Communism and Communist Parties; Conservatism; Constitutional History; Constitutional Law; Coups d'Etat; Democracy; Elections; Federal Government; Geopolitics; History; Human Rights; Imperialism; Liberalism; Liberty; Local Government; Military; Military Governments; Nationalism; Nationalization; Oligarchy; Political Boundaries; Political Cartoons; Political Parties; Political Philosophy; Politicians; Politics and Government; Populism; Public Opinion; Radicalism; Revolutions and Revolutionary Movements; Social Sciences; Socialism and Socialist Parties; The State; Taxation; Utopias; World Politics.* History, 3416, 7579, 7612, 7622, 3416. Philosophy, 7725. Study and Teaching, 139.

Politicians. *See also Legislators; Mayors; Political Science; Presidents; Statesmen.* Argentina, 3189, 3221, 3357, 3361, 3393, 3396. Brazil, 149, 3592, 3599. Colombia, 2847. Latin America, 5096. Mexico, 393,

Pozo, Castro, 2963.
Prada, González, 2979.
Prado, Carlos, 481.
Prado, Manuel, 2968.
Prats, Jorge Luis, 7078.
Precolumbian Architecture. *See also Archaeology; Architecture; Monuments; Precolumbian Civilizations.* Andean Region, 1607–1608. Aztec, 1509. Bolivia, 304. Inca, 304, 1639. Peru, 304, 1567.
Precolumbian Art. *See also Archaeology; Art; Artifacts; Precolumbian Civilizations; Precolumbian Pottery; Precolumbian Sculpture; Precolumbian Textile Industry and Fabrics.* Bolivia, 304. Congresses, 266. Inca, 304. Maya, 264–266. Mesoamerica, 251, 254, 257, 260, 263–265, 270, 296, 378. Moche, 281. Olmec, 264. Peru, 279, 282, 304. Study and Teaching, 263.
Precolumbian Civilizations. *See also Archaeology; Aztec; Chimú; Ethnohistory under names of specific countries and regions; Inca; Indigenous Peoples; Maya; Mixtec; Olmec; Precolumbian Architecture; Precolumbian Art; Precolumbian Cultures; Precolumbian Land Settlement Patterns; Precolumbian Trade.* Congresses, 262. Mexico, 1865–1866, 1878. Peru, 5092.
Precolumbian Cultures. *See also Archaeology; Ethnohistory under names of specific countries and regions; Indigenous Peoples; Precolumbian Civilizations.* Andean Region, 1615, 1662. Chachapoya, 1675. Chavín, 283. Classification, 1615. Costa Rica, 2345. Ecuador, 1673, 2659. Guarco, 1664. Honduras, 2317. Lunaguana, 1664. Mesoamerica, 1512, 1537–1538, 1548. Moche, 280–281. Peru, 1592, 1598, 1658, 1664. Venezuela, 1585.
Precolumbian Land Settlement Patterns. *See also Archaeology; Land Settlement; Precolumbian Civilizations.* 1607–1608. Bolivia, 1668–1669. Mesoamerica, 1519, 1560. Peru, 1658, 1666.
Precolumbian Pottery. *See also Archaeology; Artifacts; Pottery; Precolumbian Art.* Mesoamerica, 260. Moche, 280. Peru, 279–280. Venezuela, 256.
Precolumbian Sculpture. *See also Precolumbian Art; Sculpture.* Maya, 277. Mesoamerica, 268–269, 272, 274–275, 277. Olmec, 268–269, 274–275. Peru, 279.
Precolumbian Textile Industry and Fabrics. *See also Artifacts; Precolumbian Art; Textile Industry and Trade.* Congresses, 258. Peru, 258, 279, 282.
Precolumbian Trade. *See also Archaeology; Commerce; Precolumbian Civilizations.* Congresses, 262. Mesoamerica, 1947.
Presidents. *See also Dictators; Federal Government; Heads of State; names of specific presidents; Politicians; Statesmen.* Argentina, 3161, 3166, 3172, 3186, 3190–3191, 3194, 3258, 3302, 3364, 3368. Bolivia, 3014, 3047, 3062. Brazil, 3572. Chile, 3067, 3120. Colombia, 2846, 2849, 2855–2856. Costa Rica, 2374, 2381, 2386, 2422, 2440, 2453. Cuba, 2523. El Salvador, 2366, 2426, 2437. Guatemala, 2296, 2370, 2378, 2412–2413, 2418, 2425, 2459, 2466. Honduras, 2451. Mexico, 2139, 2148, 2155, 2174, 2177–2178, 2188, 2190, 2234, 2244, 2273. Office, 2188. Panama, 2398. Paraguay, 3432, 3445. Peru, 3005. Uruguay, 3472. Venezuela, 5422, 5425.
Press. *See also Censorship; Freedom of the Press; Journalism; Mass Media; Newspapers; Periodicals; Public Opinion; Publishers and Publishing Industry.* Argentina, 3261, 3342, 3409. Brazil, 3553, 3567, 3616. Chile, 3077. Latin America, 5094. Mexico, 292, 2096, 2252, 2261. South America, 2838. Uruguay, 3471. Venezuela, 2812.
Price-Mars, Jean, 6252.
Prim, Juan, 2008.
Primo de Rivera, José Antonio, 3231.
Printing. *See also Bibliography; Books; Publishers and Publishing Industry.* Brazil, 3616. Latin America, 50. Paraguay, 3441. Spain, 50.
Prints. *See also Art; Graphic Arts; Printmakers.* Brazil, 463, 465, 483, 488, 498. Colombia, 440. Cuba, 421, 423. Mexico, 377–378, 382, 401.
Prisoners. *See also Crime and Criminals; Political Prisoners; Prisons.* United States, 2944.
Prisons. *See also Crime and Criminals; Prisoners.* Argentina, 3247. Brazil, 3507. United States, 2944. Venezuela, 1795, 2616. Viceroyalty of New Spain, 1850.
Private Enterprises. *See also Business; Corporations; Multinational Corporations; Public Enterprises.* Argentina, 3351.
Produce Trade. *See also Agriculture; Commerce; Food Industry and Trade; Marketing and Product Distribution.* Viceroyalty of New Spain, 1941.

AUTHOR INDEX